Auditing Standards 2015

Standards examinable in 2015 ICAEW ACA examinations

Auditing Standards 2015

Standards examinable in 2015 ICAEW ACA examinations

Disclaimer

This publication is sold with the understanding that neither the publisher nor the authors, with regard to this publication, are engaged in rendering legal or professional services. The material contained in this publication neither purports, nor is intended to be, advice on any particular matter.

Although this publication incorporates a considerable degree of standardisation, subjective judgment by the user, based on individual circumstances, is indispensable. This publication is an 'aid' and cannot be expected to replace such judgment.

Neither the publisher nor the authors can accept any responsibility or liability to any person, whether a purchaser of this publication or not, in respect of anything done or omitted to be done by any such person in reliance, whether sole or partial, upon the whole or any part of the contents of this publication.

© 2014 Wolters Kluwer (UK) Ltd

Wolters Kluwer
145 London Road
Kingston upon Thames
KT2 6SR

ISBN 978-1-84798-948-2

Documents in Parts One, Eight, Ten and the Glossary of Terms reproduced with the permission of the Financial Reporting Council (FRC) and the International Federation of Accountants (IFAC)

Documents in Parts Two to Seven and Nine are copyright July 2014 by the International Federation of Accountants (IFAC). All rights reserved. Used with permission of IFAC. Contact permissions@ifac.org for permission to reproduce, store or transmit, or to make other similar uses of this document.

No responsibility for loss occasioned to any person acting or refraining from action as a result of any material in this publication can be accepted by the author or publisher.

Material is contained in this publication for which copyright is acknowledged. Permission to reproduce such material cannot be granted by the publisher and application must be made to the copyright holder.

Crown copyright is reproduced with the permission of the Controller of Her Majesty's Stationery Office.

British Library Cataloguing-in-Publication Data.

A catalogue record for this book is available from the British Library.

Typeset by YHT Ltd, London

Printed in Spain by Rotabook, S.L.

Auditing Standards 2015

Standards examinable in 2015 ICAEW ACA examinations

This publication is recommended for students sitting all Audit and Assurance exams in 2015.

The text may be annotated **ONLY** to the extent of underlining, sidelining and highlighting. Page tabs may be used, but must not be written on.

For more information on suggested texts and exam regulations, please visit icaew.com/exams

Preface

Welcome to ICAEW

ICAEW is a professional membership organisation, supporting over 142,000 chartered accountants around the world. Through our technical knowledge, skills and expertise, we provide insight and leadership to the global accountancy and finance profession.

Our members provide financial knowledge and guidance based on the highest professional, technical and ethical standards. We develop and support individuals, organisations and communities to help them achieve long-term sustainable economic value.

Because of us, people can do business with confidence.

The ICAEW faculties, which include the Audit and Assurance Faculty, provide additional specialised support to faculty members in key areas and invaluable networking opportunities. Support and first-hand knowledge has never been more valuable to the audit profession and the Audit and Assurance Faculty is at the cutting edge of all audit and assurance developments. The faculty provides a comprehensive and accessible package of essential and timely guidance and technical advice which enables its members to stay ahead of the rest.

What do you get from the faculty?

Adding value to your career – the faculty will give you access to expert, exclusive and unbiased information.

Providing a single, authoritative source of information on audit and assurance – via impeccable sources from leading technical experts, a team of dedicated technical managers as well as influential volunteers working in the profession.

Staying ahead of the rest – faculty publications will provide perspectives on wider issues affecting the profession and will give you competitive advantage in the workplace.

Your voice will be heard – the faculty is ICAEW's voice on all audit and assurance related matters. In addition to its proactive work, the faculty responds to consultations, giving you the opportunity to input into developments affecting the profession.

Networking opportunities – as well as providing timely and practical guidance, our regional events can also be a useful networking opportunity.

To find out more, visit www.icaew.com/aaf.

Contents

Part One

*International Standards on Auditing
(UK and Ireland)*

International Standard on Auditing (UK and Ireland) 200

Overall objectives of the independent auditor and the conduct of an audit in accordance with International Standards on Auditing (UK and Ireland)

(Effective for audits of financial statements for periods ending on or after 15 December 2010)[1a]

Contents

[1a] *Conforming amendments to this standard as a result of ISA (UK and Ireland) 610 (Revised June 2013), Using the Work of Internal Auditors, are included that are effective for audits of financial statements for periods ending on or after 15 June 2014. Details of the amendments are given in the Annexure to ISA (UK and Ireland) 610 (Revised June 2013).*

Introduction

Scope of this ISA (UK and Ireland)

1   This International Standard on Auditing (UK and Ireland) (ISA (UK and Ireland)) deals with the independent auditor's overall responsibilities when conducting an audit of financial statements in accordance with ISAs (UK and Ireland). Specifically, it sets out the overall objectives of the independent auditor, and explains the nature and scope of an audit designed to enable the independent auditor to meet those objectives. It also explains the scope, authority and structure of the ISAs (UK and Ireland), and includes requirements establishing the general responsibilities of the independent auditor applicable in all audits, including the obligation to comply with the ISAs (UK and Ireland). The independent auditor is referred to as "the auditor" hereafter.

2   ISAs (UK and Ireland) are written in the context of an audit of financial statements by an auditor. They are to be adapted as necessary in the circumstances when applied to audits of other historical financial information. ISAs (UK and Ireland) do not address the responsibilities of the auditor that may exist in legislation, regulation or otherwise in connection with, for example, the offering of securities to the public[1b]. Such responsibilities may differ from those established in the ISAs (UK and Ireland). Accordingly, while the auditor may find aspects of the ISAs (UK and Ireland) helpful in such circumstances, it is the responsibility of the auditor to ensure compliance with all relevant legal, regulatory or professional obligations.

An Audit of Financial Statements

3   The purpose of an audit is to enhance the degree of confidence of intended users in the financial statements. This is achieved by the expression of an opinion by the auditor on whether the financial statements are prepared, in all material respects, in accordance with an applicable financial reporting framework. In the case of most general purpose frameworks, that opinion is on whether the financial statements are presented fairly, in all material respects, or give a true and fair view in accordance with the framework. An audit conducted in accordance with ISAs (UK and Ireland) and relevant ethical requirements enables the auditor to form that opinion. (Ref: Para. A1)

4   The financial statements subject to audit are those of the entity, prepared by management of the entity with oversight from those charged with governance[1c]. ISAs (UK and Ireland) do not impose responsibilities on management or those charged with governance and do not override laws and regulations that govern their responsibilities. However, an audit in accordance with ISAs (UK and Ireland) is conducted on the premise that management and, where appropriate, those charged with governance have acknowledged certain responsibilities that are fundamental to the conduct of the audit. The audit of the financial statements does not relieve management or those charged with governance of their responsibilities. (Ref: Para. A2-A11)

[1b] *In the UK and Ireland, standards and guidance for accountants undertaking engagements in connection with an investment circular are set out in APB's Standards for Investment Reporting (SIRS).*

[1c] *In the UK and Ireland, those charged with governance are responsible for the preparation of the financial statements. For corporate entities, directors have a collective responsibility; those charged with governance of other types of entity may also have a collective responsibility established in applicable law or regulation or under the terms of their appointment.*

As the basis for the auditor's opinion, ISAs (UK and Ireland) require the auditor to   5
obtain reasonable assurance about whether the financial statements as a whole are
free from material misstatement, whether due to fraud or error. Reasonable assurance is a high level of assurance. It is obtained when the auditor has obtained
sufficient appropriate audit evidence to reduce audit risk (that is, the risk that the
auditor expresses an inappropriate opinion when the financial statements are
materially misstated) to an acceptably low level. However, reasonable assurance is
not an absolute level of assurance, because there are inherent limitations of an audit
which result in most of the audit evidence on which the auditor draws conclusions
and bases the auditor's opinion being persuasive rather than conclusive. (Ref: Para.
A28-A52)

The concept of materiality is applied by the auditor both in planning and performing   6
the audit, and in evaluating the effect of identified misstatements on the audit and of
uncorrected misstatements, if any, on the financial statements.[1] In general, misstatements, including omissions, are considered to be material if, individually or in
the aggregate, they could reasonably be expected to influence the economic decisions
of users taken on the basis of the financial statements. Judgments about materiality
are made in the light of surrounding circumstances, and are affected by the auditor's
perception of the financial information needs of users of the financial statements, and
by the size or nature of a misstatement, or a combination of both. The auditor's
opinion deals with the financial statements as a whole and therefore the auditor is not
responsible for the detection of misstatements that are not material to the financial
statements as a whole.

The ISAs (UK and Ireland) contain objectives, requirements and application and   7
other explanatory material that are designed to support the auditor in obtaining
reasonable assurance. The ISAs (UK and Ireland) require that the auditor exercise
professional judgment and maintain professional skepticism throughout the planning and performance of the audit and, among other things:

- Identify and assess risks of material misstatement, whether due to fraud or
  error, based on an understanding of the entity and its environment, including
  the entity's internal control.
- Obtain sufficient appropriate audit evidence about whether material misstatements exist, through designing and implementing appropriate responses to the
  assessed risks.
- Form an opinion on the financial statements based on conclusions drawn from
  the audit evidence obtained.

The form of opinion expressed by the auditor will depend upon the applicable   8
financial reporting framework and any applicable law or regulation. (Ref: Para. A12-
A13)

The auditor may also have certain other communication and reporting responsi-   9
bilities to users, management, those charged with governance, or parties outside the
entity, in relation to matters arising from the audit. These may be established by the
ISAs (UK and Ireland) or by applicable law or regulation.[2]

---

[1] ISA (UK and Ireland) 320, "Materiality in Planning and Performing an Audit" and ISA (UK and Ireland) 450, "Evaluation of Misstatements Identified during the Audit."

[2] See, for example, ISA (UK and Ireland) 260, "Communication with Those Charged with Governance;" and paragraph 43 of ISA (UK and Ireland) 240, "The Auditor's Responsibilities Relating to Fraud in an Audit of Financial Statements."

Effective Date

10   This ISA (UK and Ireland) is effective for audits of financial statements for periods ending on or after 15 December 2010.[1a]

Overall Objectives of the Auditor

11   In conducting an audit of financial statements, the overall objectives of the auditor are:

(a)   To obtain reasonable assurance about whether the financial statements as a whole are free from material misstatement, whether due to fraud or error, thereby enabling the auditor to express an opinion on whether the financial statements are prepared, in all material respects, in accordance with an applicable financial reporting framework; and

(b)   To report on the financial statements, and communicate as required by the ISAs (UK and Ireland), in accordance with the auditor's findings.

12   In all cases when reasonable assurance cannot be obtained and a qualified opinion in the auditor's report is insufficient in the circumstances for purposes of reporting to the intended users of the financial statements, the ISAs (UK and Ireland) require that the auditor disclaim an opinion or withdraw (or resign)[3] from the engagement, where withdrawal is possible under applicable law or regulation.

Definitions

13   For purposes of the ISAs (UK and Ireland), the following terms have the meanings attributed below:

(a)   Applicable financial reporting framework – The financial reporting framework adopted by management and, where appropriate, those charged with govern-ance in the preparation of the financial statements that is acceptable in view of the nature of the entity and the objective of the financial statements, or that is required by law or regulation.

The term "fair presentation framework" is used to refer to a financial reporting framework that requires compliance with the requirements of the framework and:

(i)   Acknowledges explicitly or implicitly that, to achieve fair presentation of the financial statements, it may be necessary for management to provide disclosures beyond those specifically required by the framework; or

(ii)   Acknowledges explicitly that it may be necessary for management to depart from a requirement of the framework to achieve fair presentation of the financial statements. Such departures are expected to be necessary only in extremely rare circumstances.

The term "compliance framework" is used to refer to a financial reporting framework that requires compliance with the requirements of the framework, but does not contain the acknowledgements in (i) or (ii) above.

(b)   Audit evidence – Information used by the auditor in arriving at the conclusions on which the auditor's opinion is based. Audit evidence includes both infor-mation contained in the accounting records underlying the financial statements and other information. For purposes of the ISAs (UK and Ireland):

---

[3] *In the ISAs (UK and Ireland), only the term "withdrawal" is used.*

(i) Sufficiency of audit evidence is the measure of the quantity of audit evidence. The quantity of the audit evidence needed is affected by the auditor's assessment of the risks of material misstatement and also by the quality of such audit evidence.

(ii) Appropriateness of audit evidence is the measure of the quality of audit evidence; that is, its relevance and its reliability in providing support for the conclusions on which the auditor's opinion is based.

(c) Audit risk – The risk that the auditor expresses an inappropriate audit opinion when the financial statements are materially misstated. Audit risk is a function of the risks of material misstatement and detection risk.

(d) Auditor – "Auditor" is used to refer to the person or persons conducting the audit, usually the engagement partner or other members of the engagement team, or, as applicable, the firm. Where an ISA (UK and Ireland) expressly intends that a requirement or responsibility be fulfilled by the engagement partner, the term "engagement partner" rather than "auditor" is used. "Engagement partner" and "firm" are to be read as referring to their public sector equivalents where relevant.

(e) Detection risk – The risk that the procedures performed by the auditor to reduce audit risk to an acceptably low level will not detect a misstatement that exists and that could be material, either individually or when aggregated with other misstatements.

(f) Financial statements – A structured representation of historical financial information, including related notes, intended to communicate an entity's economic resources or obligations at a point in time or the changes therein for a period of time in accordance with a financial reporting framework. The related notes ordinarily comprise a summary of significant accounting policies and other explanatory information. The term "financial statements" ordinarily refers to a complete set of financial statements as determined by the requirements of the applicable financial reporting framework, but can also refer to a single financial statement.

(g) Historical financial information – Information expressed in financial terms in relation to a particular entity, derived primarily from that entity's accounting system, about economic events occurring in past time periods or about economic conditions or circumstances at points in time in the past.

(h) Management – The person(s) with executive responsibility for the conduct of the entity's operations. For some entities in some jurisdictions, management includes some or all of those charged with governance, for example, executive members of a governance board, or an owner-manager.

In the UK and Ireland, management will not normally include non-executive directors.

(i) Misstatement – A difference between the amount, classification, presentation, or disclosure of a reported financial statement item and the amount, classification, presentation, or disclosure that is required for the item to be in accordance with the applicable financial reporting framework. Misstatements can arise from error or fraud.

Where the auditor expresses an opinion on whether the financial statements are presented fairly, in all material respects, or give a true and fair view, misstatements also include those adjustments of amounts, classifications, presentation, or disclosures that, in the auditor's judgment, are necessary for the financial statements to be presented fairly, in all material respects, or to give a true and fair view.

(j) Premise, relating to the responsibilities of management and, where appropriate, those charged with governance, on which an audit is conducted – That management and, where appropriate, those charged with governance have acknowledged and understand that they have the following responsibilities that are fundamental to the conduct of an audit in accordance with ISAs (UK and Ireland). That is, responsibility:

    (i) For the preparation of the financial statements in accordance with the applicable financial reporting framework, including where relevant their fair presentation;

    (ii) For such internal control as management and, where appropriate, those charged with governance determine is necessary to enable the preparation of financial statements that are free from material misstatement, whether due to fraud or error; and

    (iii) To provide the auditor with:

        a. Access to all information of which management and, where appropriate, those charged with governance are aware that is relevant to the preparation of the financial statements such as records, documentation and other matters;

        b. Additional information that the auditor may request from management and, where appropriate, those charged with governance for the purpose of the audit; and

        c. Unrestricted access to persons within the entity from whom the auditor determines it necessary to obtain audit evidence.

In the case of a fair presentation framework, (i) above may be restated as "for the preparation and *fair* presentation of the financial statements in accordance with the financial reporting framework," or "for the preparation of financial statements *that give a true and fair view* in accordance with the financial reporting framework."

The "premise, relating to the responsibilities of management and, where appropriate, those charged with governance, on which an audit is conducted" may also be referred to as the "premise."

(k) Professional judgment – The application of relevant training, knowledge and experience, within the context provided by auditing, accounting and ethical standards, in making informed decisions about the courses of action that are appropriate in the circumstances of the audit engagement.

(l) Professional skepticism – An attitude that includes a questioning mind, being alert to conditions which may indicate possible misstatement due to error or fraud, and a critical assessment of audit evidence.

(m) Reasonable assurance – In the context of an audit of financial statements, a high, but not absolute, level of assurance.

(n) Risk of material misstatement – The risk that the financial statements are materially misstated prior to audit. This consists of two components, described as follows at the assertion level:

    (i) Inherent risk – The susceptibility of an assertion about a class of transaction, account balance or disclosure to a misstatement that could be material, either individually or when aggregated with other misstatements, before consideration of any related controls.

    (ii) Control risk – The risk that a misstatement that could occur in an assertion about a class of transaction, account balance or disclosure and that could be material, either individually or when aggregated with other misstatements, will not be prevented, or detected and corrected, on a timely basis by the entity's internal control.

(o) Those charged with governance – The person(s) or organization(s) (for example, a corporate trustee) with responsibility for overseeing the strategic direction of the entity and obligations related to the accountability of the entity. This includes overseeing the financial reporting process. For some entities in some jurisdictions, those charged with governance may include management personnel, for example, executive members of a governance board of a private or public sector entity, or an owner-manager.

In the UK and Ireland, those charged with governance include the directors (executive and non-executive) of a company and the members of an audit committee where one exists. For other types of entity it usually includes equivalent persons such as the partners, proprietors, committee of management or trustees.

Requirements

Ethical Requirements Relating to an Audit of Financial Statements

The auditor shall comply with relevant ethical requirements, including those pertaining to independence, relating to financial statement audit engagements. (Ref: Para. A14-A17) **14**

Professional Skepticism

The auditor shall plan and perform an audit with professional skepticism recognizing that circumstances may exist that cause the financial statements to be materially misstated. (Ref: Para. A18-A22) **15**

Professional Judgment

The auditor shall exercise professional judgment in planning and performing an audit of financial statements. (Ref: Para. A23-A27) **16**

Sufficient Appropriate Audit Evidence and Audit Risk

To obtain reasonable assurance, the auditor shall obtain sufficient appropriate audit evidence to reduce audit risk to an acceptably low level and thereby enable the auditor to draw reasonable conclusions on which to base the auditor's opinion. (Ref: Para. A28-A52) **17**

Conduct of an Audit in Accordance with ISAs (UK and Ireland)

Complying with ISAs (UK and Ireland) Relevant to the Audit

The auditor shall comply with all ISAs (UK and Ireland) relevant to the audit. An ISA (UK and Ireland) is relevant to the audit when the ISA (UK and Ireland) is in effect and the circumstances addressed by the ISA (UK and Ireland) exist. (Ref: Para. A53-A57) **18**

The auditor shall have an understanding of the entire text of an ISA (UK and Ireland), including its application and other explanatory material, to understand its objectives and to apply its requirements properly. (Ref: Para. A58-A66) **19**

The auditor shall not represent compliance with ISAs (UK and Ireland) in the auditor's report unless the auditor has complied with the requirements of this ISA and all other ISAs (UK and Ireland) relevant to the audit. **20**

Objectives Stated in Individual ISAs (UK and Ireland)

21   To achieve the overall objectives of the auditor, the auditor shall use the objectives stated in relevant ISAs (UK and Ireland) in planning and performing the audit, having regard to the interrelationships among the ISAs (UK and Ireland), to: (Ref: Para. A67-A69)

(a)   Determine whether any audit procedures in addition to those required by the ISAs (UK and Ireland) are necessary in pursuance of the objectives stated in the ISAs (UK and Ireland); and (Ref: Para. A70)

(b)   Evaluate whether sufficient appropriate audit evidence has been obtained. (Ref: Para. A71)

Complying with Relevant Requirements

22   Subject to paragraph 23, the auditor shall comply with each requirement of an ISA (UK and Ireland) unless, in the circumstances of the audit:

(a)   The entire ISA (UK and Ireland) is not relevant; or

(b)   The requirement is not relevant because it is conditional and the condition does not exist. (Ref: Para. A72-A73)

23   In exceptional circumstances, the auditor may judge it necessary to depart from a relevant requirement in an ISA (UK and Ireland). In such circumstances, the auditor shall perform alternative audit procedures to achieve the aim of that requirement. The need for the auditor to depart from a relevant requirement is expected to arise only where the requirement is for a specific procedure to be performed and, in the specific circumstances of the audit, that procedure would be ineffective in achieving the aim of the requirement. (Ref: Para. A74)

Failure to Achieve an Objective

24   If an objective in a relevant ISA (UK and Ireland) cannot be achieved, the auditor shall evaluate whether this prevents the auditor from achieving the overall objectives of the auditor and thereby requires the auditor, in accordance with the ISAs (UK and Ireland), to modify the auditor's opinion or withdraw from the engagement (where withdrawal is possible under applicable law or regulation). Failure to achieve an objective represents a significant matter requiring documentation in accordance with ISA (UK and Ireland) 230.[4] (Ref: Para. A75-A76)

***

Application and Other Explanatory Material

An Audit of Financial Statements

Scope of the Audit (Ref: Para. 3)

A1   The auditor's opinion on the financial statements deals with whether the financial statements are prepared, in all material respects, in accordance with the applicable financial reporting framework. Such an opinion is common to all audits of financial statements. The auditor's opinion therefore does not assure, for example, the future

[4] *ISA (UK and Ireland) 230, "Audit Documentation," paragraph 8(c).*

viability of the entity nor the efficiency or effectiveness with which management has conducted the affairs of the entity. In some jurisdictions, however, applicable law or regulation may require auditors to provide opinions on other specific matters, such as the effectiveness of internal control, or the consistency of a separate management report with the financial statements. While the ISAs (UK and Ireland) include requirements and guidance in relation to such matters to the extent that they are relevant to forming an opinion on the financial statements, the auditor would be required to undertake further work if the auditor had additional responsibilities to provide such opinions.

Preparation of the Financial Statements (Ref: Para. 4)

Law or regulation may establish the responsibilities of management and, where **A2** appropriate, those charged with governance in relation to financial reporting. However, the extent of these responsibilities, or the way in which they are described, may differ across jurisdictions. Despite these differences, an audit in accordance with ISAs (UK and Ireland) is conducted on the premise that management and, where appropriate, those charged with governance have acknowledged and understand that they have responsibility:

(a) For the preparation of the financial statements in accordance with the applic-
    able financial reporting framework, including where relevant their fair
    presentation;
(b) For such internal control as management and, where appropriate, those charged
    with governance determine is necessary to enable the preparation of financial
    statements that are free from material misstatement, whether due to fraud or
    error; and
(c) To provide the auditor with:
    (i)   Access to all information of which management and, where appropriate,
          those charged with governance are aware that is relevant to the preparation
          of the financial statements such as records, documentation and other
          matters;
    (ii) Additional information that the auditor may request from management
          and, where appropriate, those charged with governance for the purpose of
          the audit; and
    (iii) Unrestricted access to persons within the entity from whom the auditor
          determines it necessary to obtain audit evidence.

The preparation of the financial statements by management and, where appropriate, **A3** those charged with governance requires:

- The identification of the applicable financial reporting framework, in the context of any relevant laws or regulations.
- The preparation of the financial statements in accordance with that framework.
- The inclusion of an adequate description of that framework in the financial
  statements.
  The preparation of the financial statements requires management to exercise
  judgment in making accounting estimates that are reasonable in the circumstances, as well as to select and apply appropriate accounting policies. These
  judgments are made in the context of the applicable financial reporting
  framework.

The financial statements may be prepared in accordance with a financial reporting **A4** framework designed to meet:

- The common financial information needs of a wide range of users (that is,
  "general purpose financial statements"); or

- The financial information needs of specific users (that is, "special purpose financial statements").

A5   The applicable financial reporting framework often encompasses financial reporting standards established by an authorized or recognized standards setting organization, or legislative or regulatory requirements. In some cases, the financial reporting framework may encompass both financial reporting standards established by an authorized or recognized standards setting organization and legislative or regulatory requirements. Other sources may provide direction on the application of the applicable financial reporting framework. In some cases, the applicable financial reporting framework may encompass such other sources, or may even consist only of such sources. Such other sources may include:

- The legal and ethical environment, including statutes, regulations, court decisions, and professional ethical obligations in relation to accounting matters;
- Published accounting interpretations of varying authority issued by standards setting, professional or regulatory organizations;
- Published views of varying authority on emerging accounting issues issued by standards setting, professional or regulatory organizations;
- General and industry practices widely recognized and prevalent; and
- Accounting literature.
  Where conflicts exist between the financial reporting framework and the sources from which direction on its application may be obtained, or among the sources that encompass the financial reporting framework, the source with the highest authority prevails.

A6   The requirements of the applicable financial reporting framework determine the form and content of the financial statements. Although the framework may not specify how to account for or disclose all transactions or events, it ordinarily embodies sufficient broad principles that can serve as a basis for developing and applying accounting policies that are consistent with the concepts underlying the requirements of the framework.

A7   Some financial reporting frameworks are fair presentation frameworks, while others are compliance frameworks. Financial reporting frameworks that encompass primarily the financial reporting standards established by an organization that is authorized or recognized to promulgate standards to be used by entities for preparing general purpose financial statements are often designed to achieve fair presentation, for example, International Financial Reporting Standards (IFRSs) issued by the International Accounting Standards Board (IASB).

A8   The requirements of the applicable financial reporting framework also determine what constitutes a complete set of financial statements. In the case of many frameworks, financial statements are intended to provide information about the financial position, financial performance and cash flows of an entity. For such frameworks, a complete set of financial statements would include a balance sheet; an income statement; a statement of changes in equity; a cash flow statement; and related notes. For some other financial reporting frameworks, a single financial statement and the related notes might constitute a complete set of financial statements:

- For example, the International Public Sector Accounting Standard (IPSAS), "Financial Reporting Under the Cash Basis of Accounting" issued by the International Public Sector Accounting Standards Board states that the primary financial statement is a statement of cash receipts and payments when a public sector entity prepares its financial statements in accordance with that IPSAS.
- Other examples of a single financial statement, each of which would include related notes, are:

○ Balance sheet.
○ Statement of income or statement of operations.
○ Statement of retained earnings.
○ Statement of cash flows.
○ Statement of assets and liabilities that does not include owner's equity.
○ Statement of changes in owners' equity.
○ Statement of revenue and expenses.
○ Statement of operations by product lines.

ISA (UK and Ireland) 210 establishes requirements and provides guidance on determining the acceptability of the applicable financial reporting framework.[5] ISA 800 deals with special considerations when financial statements are prepared in accordance with a special purpose framework.[6]   **A9**

Because of the significance of the premise to the conduct of an audit, the auditor is required to obtain the agreement of management and, where appropriate, those charged with governance that they acknowledge and understand that they have the responsibilities set out in paragraph A2 as a precondition for accepting the audit engagement.[7]   **A10**

Considerations Specific to Audits in the Public Sector

The mandates for audits of the financial statements of public sector entities may be broader than those of other entities. As a result, the premise, relating to management's responsibilities, on which an audit of the financial statements of a public sector entity is conducted may include additional responsibilities, such as the responsibility for the execution of transactions and events in accordance with law, regulation or other authority.[8]   **A11**

Form of the Auditor's Opinion (Ref: Para. 8)

The opinion expressed by the auditor is on whether the financial statements are prepared, in all material respects, in accordance with the applicable financial reporting framework. The form of the auditor's opinion, however, will depend upon the applicable financial reporting framework and any applicable law or regulation. Most financial reporting frameworks include requirements relating to the presentation of the financial statements; for such frameworks, *preparation* of the financial statements in accordance with the applicable financial reporting framework includes *presentation*.   **A12**

Where the financial reporting framework is a fair presentation framework, as is generally the case for general purpose financial statements, the opinion required by the ISAs (UK and Ireland) is on whether the financial statements are presented fairly, in all material respects, or give a true and fair view. Where the financial reporting framework is a compliance framework, the opinion required is on whether the financial statements are prepared, in all material respects, in accordance with the   **A13**

---

[5] *ISA (UK and Ireland) 210, "Agreeing the Terms of Audit Engagements," paragraph 6(a).*

[6] *ISA 800, "Special Considerations—Audits of Financial Statements Prepared in Accordance with Special Purpose Frameworks," paragraph 8.*
ISA 800 has not been promulgated by the APB for application in the UK and Ireland.

[7] *ISA (UK and Ireland) 210, paragraph 6(b).*

[8] *See paragraph A57.*

framework. Unless specifically stated otherwise, references in the ISAs (UK and Ireland) to the auditor's opinion cover both forms of opinion.

Ethical Requirements Relating to an Audit of Financial Statements (Ref: Para. 14)

A14   The auditor is subject to relevant ethical requirements, including those pertaining to independence, relating to financial statement audit engagements. Relevant ethical requirements ordinarily comprise Parts A and B of the International Ethics Standards Board for Accountants' *Code of Ethics for Professional Accountants* (IESBA Code) related to an audit of financial statements together with national requirements that are more restrictive.

A14-1   Auditors in the UK and Ireland are subject to ethical requirements from two sources: the APB Ethical Standards for Auditors concerning the integrity, objectivity and independence of the auditor, and the ethical pronouncements established by the auditor's relevant professional body. The APB is not aware of any significant instances where the relevant parts of the IESBA Code of Ethics are more restrictive than the APB Ethical Standards for Auditors.

A15   Part A of the IESBA Code establishes the fundamental principles of professional ethics relevant to the auditor when conducting an audit of financial statements and provides a conceptual framework for applying those principles. The fundamental principles with which the auditor is required to comply by the IESBA Code are:

(a)   Integrity;
(b)   Objectivity;
(c)   Professional competence and due care;
(d)   Confidentiality; and
(e)   Professional behavior.
(f)   Part B of the IESBA Code illustrates how the conceptual framework is to be applied in specific situations.

A16   In the case of an audit engagement it is in the public interest and, therefore, required by the IESBA Code, that the auditor be independent of the entity subject to the audit. The IESBA Code describes independence as comprising both independence of mind and independence in appearance. The auditor's independence from the entity safeguards the auditor's ability to form an audit opinion without being affected by influences that might compromise that opinion. Independence enhances the auditor's ability to act with integrity, to be objective and to maintain an attitude of professional skepticism.

A17   International Standard on Quality Control (ISQC) 1[9], or national requirements that are at least as demanding,[10] deal with the firm's responsibilities to establish and maintain its system of quality control for audit engagements. ISQC 1 sets out the responsibilities of the firm for establishing policies and procedures designed to provide it with reasonable assurance that the firm and its personnel comply with relevant ethical requirements, including those pertaining to independence.[11] ISA (UK

---

[9] *International Standard on Quality Control (ISQC) 1, "Quality Control for Firms that Perform Audits and Reviews of Financial Statements, and Other Assurance and Related Services Engagements."*

[10] *ISA (UK and Ireland) 220, "Quality Control for an Audit of Financial Statements," paragraph 2.*

[11] *ISQC (UK and Ireland) 1, paragraphs 20-25.*

and Ireland) 220 sets out the engagement partner's responsibilities with respect to relevant ethical requirements. These include remaining alert, through observation and making inquiries as necessary, for evidence of non-compliance with relevant ethical requirements by members of the engagement team, determining the appropriate action if matters come to the engagement partner's attention that indicate that members of the engagement team have not complied with relevant ethical requirements, and forming a conclusion on compliance with independence requirements that apply to the audit engagement.[12] ISA (UK and Ireland) 220 recognizes that the engagement team is entitled to rely on a firm's system of quality control in meeting its responsibilities with respect to quality control procedures applicable to the individual audit engagement, unless information provided by the firm or other parties suggests otherwise.

Professional Skepticism (Ref: Para. 15)

Professional skepticism includes being alert to, for example: **A18**

- Audit evidence that contradicts other audit evidence obtained.
- Information that brings into question the reliability of documents and responses to inquiries to be used as audit evidence.
- Conditions that may indicate possible fraud.
- Circumstances that suggest the need for audit procedures in addition to those required by the ISAs (UK and Ireland).

Maintaining professional skepticism throughout the audit is necessary if the auditor   **A19**
is, for example, to reduce the risks of:

- Overlooking unusual circumstances.
- Over generalizing when drawing conclusions from audit observations.
- Using inappropriate assumptions in determining the nature, timing, and extent of the audit procedures and evaluating the results thereof.

Professional skepticism is necessary to the critical assessment of audit evidence. This   **A20**
includes questioning contradictory audit evidence and the reliability of documents and responses to inquiries and other information obtained from management and those charged with governance. It also includes consideration of the sufficiency and appropriateness of audit evidence obtained in the light of the circumstances, for example in the case where fraud risk factors exist and a single document, of a nature that is susceptible to fraud, is the sole supporting evidence for a material financial statement amount.

The auditor may accept records and documents as genuine unless the auditor has   **A21**
reason to believe the contrary. Nevertheless, the auditor is required to consider the reliability of information to be used as audit evidence.[13] In cases of doubt about the reliability of information or indications of possible fraud (for example, if conditions identified during the audit cause the auditor to believe that a document may not be authentic or that terms in a document may have been falsified), the ISAs (UK and Ireland) require that the auditor investigate further and determine what modifications or additions to audit procedures are necessary to resolve the matter.[14]

---

[12] *ISA (UK and Ireland) 220, paragraphs 9-11.*

[13] *ISA (UK and Ireland) 500, "Audit Evidence," paragraphs 7-9.*

[14] *ISA (UK and Ireland) 240, paragraph 13; ISA (UK and Ireland) 500, paragraph 11; ISA (UK and Ireland) 505, "External Confirmations," paragraphs 10-11, and 16.*

A22   The auditor cannot be expected to disregard past experience of the honesty and integrity of the entity's management and those charged with governance. Nevertheless, a belief that management and those charged with governance are honest and have integrity does not relieve the auditor of the need to maintain professional skepticism or allow the auditor to be satisfied with less-than-persuasive audit evidence when obtaining reasonable assurance.

Professional Judgment (Ref: Para. 16)

A23   Professional judgment is essential to the proper conduct of an audit. This is because interpretation of relevant ethical requirements and the ISAs (UK and Ireland) and the informed decisions required throughout the audit cannot be made without the application of relevant knowledge and experience to the facts and circumstances. Professional judgment is necessary in particular regarding decisions about:

- Materiality and audit risk.
- The nature, timing, and extent of audit procedures used to meet the requirements of the ISAs (UK and Ireland) and gather audit evidence.
- Evaluating whether sufficient appropriate audit evidence has been obtained, and whether more needs to be done to achieve the objectives of the ISAs (UK and Ireland) and thereby, the overall objectives of the auditor.
- The evaluation of management's judgments in applying the entity's applicable financial reporting framework.
- The drawing of conclusions based on the audit evidence obtained, for example, assessing the reasonableness of the estimates made by management in preparing the financial statements.

A24   The distinguishing feature of the professional judgment expected of an auditor is that it is exercised by an auditor whose training, knowledge and experience have assisted in developing the necessary competencies to achieve reasonable judgments.

A25   The exercise of professional judgment in any particular case is based on the facts and circumstances that are known by the auditor. Consultation on difficult or contentious matters during the course of the audit, both within the engagement team and between the engagement team and others at the appropriate level within or outside the firm, such as that required by ISA (UK and Ireland) 220,[15] assist the auditor in making informed and reasonable judgments.

A26   Professional judgment can be evaluated based on whether the judgment reached reflects a competent application of auditing and accounting principles and is appropriate in the light of, and consistent with, the facts and circumstances that were known to the auditor up to the date of the auditor's report.

A27   Professional judgment needs to be exercised throughout the audit. It also needs to be appropriately documented. In this regard, the auditor is required to prepare audit documentation sufficient to enable an experienced auditor, having no previous connection with the audit, to understand the significant professional judgments made in reaching conclusions on significant matters arising during the audit.[16] Professional judgment is not to be used as the justification for decisions that are not otherwise supported by the facts and circumstances of the engagement or sufficient appropriate audit evidence.

[15] *ISA (UK and Ireland) 220, paragraph 18.*

[16] *ISA (UK and Ireland) 230, paragraph 8.*

Sufficient Appropriate Audit Evidence and Audit Risk (Ref: Para. 5 and 17)

Sufficiency and Appropriateness of Audit Evidence

Audit evidence is necessary to support the auditor's opinion and report. It is   **A28**
cumulative in nature and is primarily obtained from audit procedures performed
during the course of the audit. It may, however, also include information obtained
from other sources such as previous audits (provided the auditor has determined
whether changes have occurred since the previous audit that may affect its relevance
to the current audit[17]) or a firm's quality control procedures for client acceptance and
continuance. In addition to other sources inside and outside the entity, the entity's
accounting records are an important source of audit evidence. Also, information that
may be used as audit evidence may have been prepared by an expert employed or
engaged by the entity. Audit evidence comprises both information that supports and
corroborates management's assertions, and any information that contradicts such
assertions. In addition, in some cases, the absence of information (for example,
management's refusal to provide a requested representation) is used by the auditor,
and therefore, also constitutes audit evidence. Most of the auditor's work in forming
the auditor's opinion consists of obtaining and evaluating audit evidence.

The sufficiency and appropriateness of audit evidence are interrelated. Sufficiency is   **A29**
the measure of the quantity of audit evidence. The quantity of audit evidence needed
is affected by the auditor's assessment of the risks of misstatement (the higher the
assessed risks, the more audit evidence is likely to be required) and also by the quality
of such audit evidence (the higher the quality, the less may be required). Obtaining
more audit evidence, however, may not compensate for its poor quality.

Appropriateness is the measure of the quality of audit evidence; that is, its relevance   **A30**
and its reliability in providing support for the conclusions on which the auditor's
opinion is based. The reliability of evidence is influenced by its source and by its
nature, and is dependent on the individual circumstances under which it is obtained.

Whether sufficient appropriate audit evidence has been obtained to reduce audit risk   **A31**
to an acceptably low level, and thereby enable the auditor to draw reasonable
conclusions on which to base the auditor's opinion, is a matter of professional
judgment. ISA (UK and Ireland) 500 and other relevant ISAs (UK and Ireland)
establish additional requirements and provide further guidance applicable throughout the audit regarding the auditor's considerations in obtaining sufficient
appropriate audit evidence.

Audit Risk

Audit risk is a function of the risks of material misstatement and detection risk. The   **A32**
assessment of risks is based on audit procedures to obtain information necessary for
that purpose and evidence obtained throughout the audit. The assessment of risks is
a matter of professional judgment, rather than a matter capable of precise
measurement.

For purposes of the ISAs (UK and Ireland), audit risk does not include the risk that   **A33**
the auditor might express an opinion that the financial statements are materially
misstated when they are not. This risk is ordinarily insignificant. Further, audit risk
is a technical term related to the process of auditing; it does not refer to the auditor's

---

[17] *ISA (UK and Ireland) 315, "Identifying and Assessing the Risks of Material Misstatement through
Understanding the Entity and Its Environment," paragraph 9.*

business risks such as loss from litigation, adverse publicity, or other events arising in connection with the audit of financial statements.

Risks of Material Misstatement

A34   The risks of material misstatement may exist at two levels:

- The overall financial statement level; and
- The assertion level for classes of transactions, account balances, and disclosures.

A35   Risks of material misstatement at the overall financial statement level refer to risks of material misstatement that relate pervasively to the financial statements as a whole and potentially affect many assertions.

A36   Risks of material misstatement at the assertion level are assessed in order to determine the nature, timing, and extent of further audit procedures necessary to obtain sufficient appropriate audit evidence. This evidence enables the auditor to express an opinion on the financial statements at an acceptably low level of audit risk. Auditors use various approaches to accomplish the objective of assessing the risks of material misstatement. For example, the auditor may make use of a model that expresses the general relationship of the components of audit risk in mathematical terms to arrive at an acceptable level of detection risk. Some auditors find such a model to be useful when planning audit procedures.

A37   The risks of material misstatement at the assertion level consist of two components: inherent risk and control risk. Inherent risk and control risk are the entity's risks; they exist independently of the audit of the financial statements.

A38   Inherent risk is higher for some assertions and related classes of transactions, account balances, and disclosures than for others. For example, it may be higher for complex calculations or for accounts consisting of amounts derived from accounting estimates that are subject to significant estimation uncertainty. External circumstances giving rise to business risks may also influence inherent risk. For example, technological developments might make a particular product obsolete, thereby causing inventory to be more susceptible to overstatement. Factors in the entity and its environment that relate to several or all of the classes of transactions, account balances, or disclosures may also influence the inherent risk related to a specific assertion. Such factors may include, for example, a lack of sufficient working capital to continue operations or a declining industry characterized by a large number of business failures.

A39   Control risk is a function of the effectiveness of the design, implementation and maintenance of internal control by management to address identified risks that threaten the achievement of the entity's objectives relevant to preparation of the entity's financial statements. However, internal control, no matter how well designed and operated, can only reduce, but not eliminate, risks of material misstatement in the financial statements, because of the inherent limitations of internal control. These include, for example, the possibility of human errors or mistakes, or of controls being circumvented by collusion or inappropriate management override. Accordingly, some control risk will always exist. The ISAs (UK and Ireland) provide the conditions under which the auditor is required to, or may choose to, test the operating effectiveness of controls in determining the nature, timing and extent of substantive procedures to be performed.[18]

---

[18] ISA (UK and Ireland) 330, "The Auditor's Reponses to Assessed Risks," paragraphs 7-17.

The ISAs (UK and Ireland) do not ordinarily refer to inherent risk and control risk **A40** separately, but rather to a combined assessment of the "risks of material misstatement." However, the auditor may make separate or combined assessments of inherent and control risk depending on preferred audit techniques or methodologies and practical considerations. The assessment of the risks of material misstatement may be expressed in quantitative terms, such as in percentages, or in non-quantitative terms. In any case, the need for the auditor to make appropriate risk assessments is more important than the different approaches by which they may be made.

ISA (UK and Ireland) 315 establishes requirements and provides guidance on **A41** identifying and assessing the risks of material misstatement at the financial statement and assertion levels.

Detection Risk

For a given level of audit risk, the acceptable level of detection risk bears an inverse **A42** relationship to the assessed risks of material misstatement at the assertion level. For example, the greater the risks of material misstatement the auditor believes exists, the less the detection risk that can be accepted and, accordingly, the more persuasive the audit evidence required by the auditor.

Detection risk relates to the nature, timing, and extent of the auditor's procedures **A43** that are determined by the auditor to reduce audit risk to an acceptably low level. It is therefore a function of the effectiveness of an audit procedure and of its application by the auditor. Matters such as:

- adequate planning;
- proper assignment of personnel to the engagement team;
- the application of professional scepticism; and
- supervision and review of the audit work performed,

assist to enhance the effectiveness of an audit procedure and of its application and reduce the possibility that an auditor might select an inappropriate audit procedure, misapply an appropriate audit procedure, or misinterpret the audit results.

ISA (UK and Ireland) 300 [19] and ISA (UK and Ireland) 330 establish requirements **A44** and provide guidance on planning an audit of financial statements and the auditor's responses to assessed risks. Detection risk, however, can only be reduced, not eliminated, because of the inherent limitations of an audit. Accordingly, some detection risk will always exist.

Inherent Limitations of an Audit

The auditor is not expected to, and cannot, reduce audit risk to zero and cannot **A45** therefore obtain absolute assurance that the financial statements are free from material misstatement due to fraud or error. This is because there are inherent limitations of an audit, which result in most of the audit evidence on which the auditor draws conclusions and bases the auditor's opinion being persuasive rather than conclusive. The inherent limitations of an audit arise from:

- The nature of financial reporting;
- The nature of audit procedures; and

[19] *ISA (UK and Ireland) 300, "Planning an Audit of Financial Statements."*

- The need for the audit to be conducted within a reasonable period of time and at a reasonable cost.

The Nature of Financial Reporting

A46   The preparation of financial statements involves judgment by management in applying the requirements of the entity's applicable financial reporting framework to the facts and circumstances of the entity. In addition, many financial statement items involve subjective decisions or assessments or a degree of uncertainty, and there may be a range of acceptable interpretations or judgments that may be made. Consequently, some financial statement items are subject to an inherent level of variability which cannot be eliminated by the application of additional auditing procedures. For example, this is often the case with respect to certain accounting estimates. Nevertheless, the ISAs (UK and Ireland) require the auditor to give specific consideration to whether accounting estimates are reasonable in the context of the applicable financial reporting framework and related disclosures, and to the qualitative aspects of the entity's accounting practices, including indicators of possible bias in management's judgments.[20]

The Nature of Audit Procedures

A47   There are practical and legal limitations on the auditor's ability to obtain audit evidence. For example:

- There is the possibility that management or others may not provide, intentionally or unintentionally, the complete information that is relevant to the preparation of the financial statements or that has been requested by the auditor. Accordingly, the auditor cannot be certain of the completeness of information, even though the auditor has performed audit procedures to obtain assurance that all relevant information has been obtained.
- Fraud may involve sophisticated and carefully organized schemes designed to conceal it. Therefore, audit procedures used to gather audit evidence may be ineffective for detecting an intentional misstatement that involves, for example, collusion to falsify documentation which may cause the auditor to believe that audit evidence is valid when it is not. The auditor is neither trained as nor expected to be an expert in the authentication of documents.
- An audit is not an official investigation into alleged wrongdoing. Accordingly, the auditor is not given specific legal powers, such as the power of search, which may be necessary for such an investigation.

Timeliness of Financial Reporting and the Balance between Benefit and Cost

A48   The matter of difficulty, time, or cost involved is not in itself a valid basis for the auditor to omit an audit procedure for which there is no alternative or to be satisfied with audit evidence that is less than persuasive. Appropriate planning assists in making sufficient time and resources available for the conduct of the audit. Notwithstanding this, the relevance of information, and thereby its value, tends to

---

[20] *ISA (UK and Ireland) 540, "Auditing Accounting Estimates, Including Fair Value Accounting Estimates, and Related Disclosures," and ISA 700, "Forming an Opinion and Reporting on Financial Statements," paragraph 12.*

The APB has not promulgated ISA 700 as issued by the IAASB for application in the UK and Ireland. In the UK and Ireland the applicable auditing standard is ISA (UK and Ireland) 700, "The Auditor's Report on Financial Statements." Paragraph 8 of ISA (UK and Ireland) 700 includes requirements equivalent to those in paragraph 12 of ISA 700.

diminish over time, and there is a balance to be struck between the reliability of information and its cost. This is recognized in certain financial reporting frameworks (see, for example, the IASB's "Framework for the Preparation and Presentation of Financial Statements"). Therefore, there is an expectation by users of financial statements that the auditor will form an opinion on the financial statements within a reasonable period of time and at a reasonable cost, recognizing that it is impracticable to address all information that may exist or to pursue every matter exhaustively on the assumption that information is in error or fraudulent until proved otherwise.

Consequently, it is necessary for the auditor to: **A49**

- Plan the audit so that it will be performed in an effective manner;
- Direct audit effort to areas most expected to contain risks of material misstatement, whether due to fraud or error, with correspondingly less effort directed at other areas; and
- Use testing and other means of examining populations for misstatements.

In light of the approaches described in paragraph A49, the ISAs (UK and Ireland)   **A50** contain requirements for the planning and performance of the audit and require the auditor, among other things, to:

- Have a basis for the identification and assessment of risks of material misstatement at the financial statement and assertion levels by performing risk assessment procedures and related activities;[21] and
- Use testing and other means of examining populations in a manner that provides a reasonable basis for the auditor to draw conclusions about the population.[22]

Other Matters that Affect the Inherent Limitations of an Audit

In the case of certain assertions or subject matters, the potential effects of the   **A51** inherent limitations on the auditor's ability to detect material misstatements are particularly significant. Such assertions or subject matters include:

- Fraud, particularly fraud involving senior management or collusion. See ISA (UK and Ireland) 240 for further discussion.
- The existence and completeness of related party relationships and transactions. See ISA (UK and Ireland) 550[23] for further discussion.
- The occurrence of non-compliance with laws and regulations. See ISA (UK and Ireland) 250[24] for further discussion.
- Future events or conditions that may cause an entity to cease to continue as a going concern. See ISA (UK and Ireland) 570[25] for further discussion. Relevant ISAs (UK and Ireland) identify specific audit procedures to assist in mitigating the effect of the inherent limitations.

[21] *ISA (UK and Ireland) 315, paragraphs 5-10.*

[22] *ISA (UK and Ireland) 330; ISA (UK and Ireland) 500; ISA 520, "Analytical Procedures;" ISA (UK and Ireland) 530, "Audit Sampling."*

[23] *ISA (UK and Ireland) 550, "Related Parties."*

[24] *ISA (UK and Ireland) 250, "Consideration of Laws and Regulations in an Audit of Financial Statements."*

[25] *ISA (UK and Ireland) 570, "Going Concern."*

A52   Because of the inherent limitations of an audit, there is an unavoidable risk that some material misstatements of the financial statements may not be detected, even though the audit is properly planned and performed in accordance with ISAs (UK and Ireland). Accordingly, the subsequent discovery of a material misstatement of the financial statements resulting from fraud or error does not by itself indicate a failure to conduct an audit in accordance with ISAs (UK and Ireland). However, the inherent limitations of an audit are not a justification for the auditor to be satisfied with less-than-persuasive audit evidence. Whether the auditor has performed an audit in accordance with ISAs is determined by the audit procedures performed in the circumstances, the sufficiency and appropriateness of the audit evidence obtained as a result thereof and the suitability of the auditor's report based on an evaluation of that evidence in light of the overall objectives of the auditor.

Conduct of an Audit in Accordance with ISAs (UK and Ireland)

Nature of the ISAs (UK and Ireland) (Ref: Para. 18)

A53   The ISAs (UK and Ireland), taken together, provide the standards for the auditor's work in fulfilling the overall objectives of the auditor. The ISAs (UK and Ireland) deal with the general responsibilities of the auditor, as well as the auditor's further considerations relevant to the application of those responsibilities to specific topics.

A54   The scope, effective date and any specific limitation of the applicability of a specific ISA (UK and Ireland) is made clear in the ISA (UK and Ireland). Unless otherwise stated in the ISA (UK and Ireland), the auditor is permitted to apply an ISA (UK and Ireland) before the effective date specified therein.

A55   In performing an audit, the auditor may be required to comply with legal or regulatory requirements in addition to the ISAs (UK and Ireland). The ISAs (UK and Ireland) do not override law or regulation that governs an audit of financial statements. In the event that such law or regulation differs from the ISAs (UK and Ireland), an audit conducted only in accordance with law or regulation will not automatically comply with ISAs (UK and Ireland).

A56   The auditor may also conduct the audit in accordance with both ISAs (UK and Ireland) and auditing standards of a specific jurisdiction or country. In such cases, in addition to complying with each of the ISAs (UK and Ireland) relevant to the audit, it may be necessary for the auditor to perform additional audit procedures in order to comply with the relevant standards of that jurisdiction or country.

Considerations Specific to Audits in the Public Sector

A57   The ISAs (UK and Ireland) are relevant to engagements in the public sector. The public sector auditor's responsibilities, however, may be affected by the audit mandate, or by obligations on public sector entities arising from law, regulation or other authority (such as ministerial directives, government policy requirements, or resolutions of the legislature), which may encompass a broader scope than an audit of financial statements in accordance with the ISAs (UK and Ireland). These additional responsibilities are not dealt with in the ISAs (UK and Ireland). They may be dealt with in the pronouncements of the International Organization of Supreme Audit Institutions or national standard setters, or in guidance developed by government audit agencies.

Contents of the ISAs (UK and Ireland) (Ref: Para. 19)

In addition to objectives and requirements (requirements are expressed in the ISAs **A58** (UK and Ireland) using "shall"), an ISA (UK and Ireland) contains related guidance in the form of application and other explanatory material. It may also contain introductory material that provides context relevant to a proper understanding of the ISA (UK and Ireland), and definitions. The entire text of an ISA (UK and Ireland), therefore, is relevant to an understanding of the objectives stated in an ISA (UK and Ireland) and the proper application of the requirements of an ISA (UK and Ireland).

Where necessary, the application and other explanatory material provides further **A59** explanation of the requirements of an ISA (UK and Ireland) and guidance for carrying them out. In particular, it may:

- Explain more precisely what a requirement means or is intended to cover.
- Include examples of procedures that may be appropriate in the circumstances. While such guidance does not in itself impose a requirement, it is relevant to the proper application of the requirements of an ISA (UK and Ireland). The application and other explanatory material may also provide background information on matters addressed in an ISA (UK and Ireland).

Appendices form part of the application and other explanatory material. The pur- **A60** pose and intended use of an appendix are explained in the body of the related ISA (UK and Ireland) or within the title and introduction of the appendix itself.

Introductory material may include, as needed, such matters as explanation of: **A61**

- The purpose and scope of the ISA (UK and Ireland), including how the ISA (UK and Ireland) relates to other ISAs (UK and Ireland).
- The subject matter of the ISA (UK and Ireland).
- The respective responsibilities of the auditor and others in relation to the subject matter of the ISA (UK and Ireland).
- The context in which the ISA (UK and Ireland) is set.

An ISA (UK and Ireland) may include, in a separate section under the heading **A62** "Definitions," a description of the meanings attributed to certain terms for purposes of the ISAs (UK and Ireland). These are provided to assist in the consistent appli- cation and interpretation of the ISAs (UK and Ireland), and are not intended to override definitions that may be established for other purposes, whether in law, regulation or otherwise. Unless otherwise indicated, those terms will carry the same meanings throughout the ISAs (UK and Ireland). The Glossary of Terms relating to International Standards issued by the International Auditing and Assurance Stan- dards Board in the *Handbook of International Quality Control, Auditing, Review, Other Assurance, and Related Services Pronouncements* published by IFAC contains a complete listing of terms defined in the ISAs (UK and Ireland). It also includes descriptions of other terms found in ISAs (UK and Ireland) to assist in common and consistent interpretation and translation.

When appropriate, additional considerations specific to audits of smaller entities and **A63** public sector entities are included within the application and other explanatory material of an ISA (UK and Ireland). These additional considerations assist in the application of the requirements of the ISA (UK and Ireland) in the audit of such entities. They do not, however, limit or reduce the responsibility of the auditor to apply and comply with the requirements of the ISAs (UK and Ireland).

Considerations Specific to Smaller Entities

A64   For purposes of specifying additional considerations to audits of smaller entities, a "smaller entity" refers to an entity which typically possesses qualitative characteristics such as:

(a) Concentration of ownership and management in a small number of individuals (often a single individual – either a natural person or another enterprise that owns the entity provided the owner exhibits the relevant qualitative characteristics); and

(b) One or more of the following:
  (i) Straightforward or uncomplicated transactions;
  (ii) Simple record-keeping;
  (iii) Few lines of business and few products within business lines;
  (iv) Few internal controls;
  (v) Few levels of management with responsibility for a broad range of controls; or
  (vi) Few personnel, many having a wide range of duties.

These qualitative characteristics are not exhaustive, they are not exclusive to smaller entities, and smaller entities do not necessarily display all of these characteristics.

A65   The considerations specific to smaller entities included in the ISAs (UK and Ireland) have been developed primarily with unlisted entities in mind. Some of the considerations, however, may be helpful in audits of smaller listed entities.

A66   The ISAs (UK and Ireland) refer to the proprietor of a smaller entity who is involved in running the entity on a day-to-day basis as the "owner-manager."

Objectives Stated in Individual ISAs (UK and Ireland) (Ref: Para. 21)

A67   Each ISA (UK and Ireland) contains one or more objectives which provide a link between the requirements and the overall objectives of the auditor. The objectives in individual ISAs (UK and Ireland) serve to focus the auditor on the desired outcome of the ISA (UK and Ireland), while being specific enough to assist the auditor in:

- Understanding what needs to be accomplished and, where necessary, the appropriate means of doing so; and
- Deciding whether more needs to be done to achieve them in the particular circumstances of the audit.

A68   Objectives are to be understood in the context of the overall objectives of the auditor stated in paragraph 11 of this ISA (UK and Ireland). As with the overall objectives of the auditor, the ability to achieve an individual objective is equally subject to the inherent limitations of an audit.

A69   In using the objectives, the auditor is required to have regard to the interrelationships among the ISAs (UK and Ireland). This is because, as indicated in paragraph A53, the ISAs (UK and Ireland) deal in some cases with general responsibilities and in others with the application of those responsibilities to specific topics. For example, this ISA (UK and Ireland) requires the auditor to adopt an attitude of professional skepticism; this is necessary in all aspects of planning and performing an audit but is not repeated as a requirement of each ISA (UK and Ireland). At a more detailed level, ISA (UK and Ireland) 315 and ISA (UK and Ireland) 330 contain, among other things, objectives and requirements that deal with the auditor's responsibilities to identify and assess the risks of material misstatement and to design and perform further audit procedures to respond to those assessed risks, respectively; these objectives and requirements apply throughout the audit. An ISA (UK and Ireland) dealing with specific aspects of the audit (for example, ISA (UK and Ireland) 540) may expand on how the objectives and requirements of such ISAs (UK and Ireland) as ISA (UK and Ireland) 315 and ISA (UK and Ireland) 330 are to be applied in relation to the subject of the ISA (UK and Ireland) but does not repeat them. Thus, in achieving the objective stated in ISA (UK and Ireland) 540, the auditor has regard to the objectives and requirements of other relevant ISAs (UK and Ireland).

Use of Objectives to Determine Need for Additional Audit Procedures (Ref: Para. 21(a))

The requirements of the ISAs (UK and Ireland) are designed to enable the auditor to   **A70**
achieve the objectives specified in the ISAs (UK and Ireland), and thereby the overall objectives of the auditor. The proper application of the requirements of the ISAs (UK and Ireland) by the auditor is therefore expected to provide a sufficient basis for the auditor's achievement of the objectives. However, because the circumstances of audit engagements vary widely and all such circumstances cannot be anticipated in the ISAs (UK and Ireland), the auditor is responsible for determining the audit procedures necessary to fulfill the requirements of the ISAs (UK and Ireland) and to achieve the objectives. In the circumstances of an engagement, there may be particular matters that require the auditor to perform audit procedures in addition to those required by the ISAs (UK and Ireland) to meet the objectives specified in the ISAs (UK and Ireland).

Use of Objectives to Evaluate Whether Sufficient Appropriate Audit Evidence Has Been Obtained (Ref: Para. 21(b))

The auditor is required to use the objectives to evaluate whether sufficient appro-   **A71**
priate audit evidence has been obtained in the context of the overall objectives of the auditor. If as a result the auditor concludes that the audit evidence is not sufficient and appropriate, then the auditor may follow one or more of the following approaches to meeting the requirement of paragraph 21(b):

- Evaluate whether further relevant audit evidence has been, or will be, obtained as a result of complying with other ISAs (UK and Ireland);
- Extend the work performed in applying one or more requirements; or
- Perform other procedures judged by the auditor to be necessary in the circumstances.

Where none of the above is expected to be practical or possible in the circumstances, the auditor will not be able to obtain sufficient appropriate audit evidence and is required by the ISAs (UK and Ireland) to determine the effect on the auditor's report or on the auditor's ability to complete the engagement.

Complying with Relevant Requirements

Relevant Requirements (Ref: Para. 22)

In some cases, an ISA (UK and Ireland) (and therefore all of its requirements) may   **A72**
not be relevant in the circumstances. For example, if an entity does not have an internal audit function, nothing in ISA (UK and Ireland) 610 (Revised June 2013)[26] is relevant.

---

[26] *ISA UK and Ireland) 315 (Revised June 2013), paragraph A116.*

A73   Within a relevant ISA (UK and Ireland), there may be conditional requirements. Such a requirement is relevant when the circumstances envisioned in the requirement apply and the condition exists. In general, the conditionality of a requirement will either be explicit or implicit, for example:

- The requirement to modify the auditor's opinion if there is a limitation of scope[27] represents an explicit conditional requirement.
- The requirement to communicate significant deficiencies in internal control identified during the audit to those charged with governance,[28] which depends on the existence of such identified significant deficiencies; and the requirement to obtain sufficient appropriate audit evidence regarding the presentation and disclosure of segment information in accordance with the applicable financial reporting framework,[29] which depends on that framework requiring or permitting such disclosure, represent implicit conditional requirements.

In some cases, a requirement may be expressed as being conditional on applicable law or regulation. For example, the auditor may be required to withdraw from the audit engagement, *where withdrawal is possible under applicable law or regulation*, or the auditor may be required to do something, *unless prohibited by law or regulation*. Depending on the jurisdiction, the legal or regulatory permission or prohibition may be explicit or implicit.

Departure from a Requirement (Ref: Para. 23)

A74   ISA (UK and Ireland) 230 establishes documentation requirements in those exceptional circumstances where the auditor departs from a relevant requirement.[30] The ISAs (UK and Ireland) do not call for compliance with a requirement that is not relevant in the circumstances of the audit.

Failure to Achieve an Objective (Ref: Para. 24)

A75   Whether an objective has been achieved is a matter for the auditor's professional judgment. That judgment takes account of the results of audit procedures performed in complying with the requirements of the ISAs (UK and Ireland), and the auditor's evaluation of whether sufficient appropriate audit evidence has been obtained and whether more needs to be done in the particular circumstances of the audit to achieve the objectives stated in the ISAs (UK and Ireland). Accordingly, circumstances that may give rise to a failure to achieve an objective include those that:

- Prevent the auditor from complying with the relevant requirements of an ISA (UK and Ireland).
- Result in its not being practicable or possible for the auditor to carry out the additional audit procedures or obtain further audit evidence as determined necessary from the use of the objectives in accordance with paragraph 21, for example due to a limitation in the available audit evidence.

---

[27] *ISA (UK and Ireland) 705, "Modifications to the Opinion in the Independent Auditor's Report," paragraph 13.*

[28] *ISA (UK and Ireland) 265, "Communicating Deficiencies in Internal Control to Those Charged with Governance and Management," paragraph 9.*

[29] *ISA (UK and Ireland) 501, "Audit Evidence—Specific Considerations for Selected Items," paragraph 13.*

[30] *ISA (UK and Ireland) 230, paragraph 12.*

Audit documentation that meets the requirements of ISA (UK and Ireland) 230 and   **A76**
the specific documentation requirements of other relevant ISAs (UK and Ireland)
provides evidence of the auditor's basis for a conclusion about the achievement of
the overall objectives of the auditor. While it is unnecessary for the auditor to
document separately (as in a checklist, for example) that individual objectives have
been achieved, the documentation of a failure to achieve an objective assists the
auditor's evaluation of whether such a failure has prevented the auditor from
achieving the overall objectives of the auditor.

International Standard on Auditing (UK and Ireland) 210

Agreeing the terms of audit engagements

(Effective for audits of financial statements for periods ending on or after 15 December 2010)

Contents

International Standard on Auditing (UK and Ireland) (ISA (UK and Ireland)) 210, "Agreeing the Terms of Audit Engagements" should be read in conjunction with ISA (UK and Ireland) 200, "Overall Objectives of the Independent Auditor and the Conduct of an Audit in Accordance with International Standards on Auditing (UK and Ireland)."

Introduction

Scope of this ISA (UK and Ireland)

This International Standard on Auditing (UK and Ireland) (ISA (UK and Ireland)) **1**
deals with the auditor's responsibilities in agreeing the terms of the audit engagement
with management and, where appropriate, those charged with governance. This
includes establishing that certain preconditions for an audit, responsibility for which
rests with management and, where appropriate, those charged with governance, are
present. ISA (UK and Ireland) 220[1] deals with those aspects of engagement acceptance that are within the control of the auditor. (Ref: Para. A1)

Effective Date

This ISA (UK and Ireland) is effective for audits of financial statements for periods **2**
ending on or after 15 December 2010.

Objective

The objective of the auditor is to accept or continue an audit engagement only when **3**
the basis upon which it is to be performed has been agreed, through:

(a) Establishing whether the preconditions for an audit are present; and
(b) Confirming that there is a common understanding between the auditor and
     management and, where appropriate, those charged with governance of the
     terms of the audit engagement.

Definitions

For purposes of the ISAs (UK and Ireland), the following term has the meaning **4**
attributed below:

Preconditions for an audit – The use by management[1a] of an acceptable financial
reporting framework in the preparation of the financial statements and the agreement of management and, where appropriate, those charged with governance to the
premise[2] on which an audit is conducted.

For the purposes of this ISA (UK and Ireland), references to "management" should **5**
be read hereafter as "management and, where appropriate, those charged with
governance."

---

[1] *ISA (UK and Ireland) 220, "Quality Control for an Audit of Financial Statements."*

[1a] *In the UK and Ireland those charged with governance are responsible for the preparation of the financial
statements.*

[2] *ISA (UK and Ireland) 200, "Overall Objectives of the Independent Auditor and the Conduct of an Audit in
Accordance with International Standards on Auditing," paragraph 13.*

Requirements

Preconditions for an Audit

6   In order to establish whether the preconditions for an audit are present, the auditor shall:

(a) Determine whether the financial reporting framework to be applied in the preparation of the financial statements is acceptable; and (Ref: Para. A2-A10)

(b) Obtain the agreement of management that it acknowledges and understands its responsibility: (Ref: Para. A11-A14, A20)

  (i) For the preparation of the financial statements in accordance with the applicable financial reporting framework, including where relevant their fair presentation; (Ref: Para. A15)

  (ii) For such internal control as management determines is necessary to enable the preparation of financial statements that are free from material misstatement, whether due to fraud or error; and (Ref: Para. A16-A19)

  (iii) To provide the auditor with[2a]:

  a.   Access to all information of which management is aware that is relevant to the preparation of the financial statements such as records, documentation and other matters;

  b.   Additional information that the auditor may request from management for the purpose of the audit; and

  c.   Unrestricted access to persons within the entity from whom the auditor determines it necessary to obtain audit evidence.

Limitation on Scope Prior to Audit Engagement Acceptance

7   If management or those charged with governance impose a limitation on the scope of the auditor's work in the terms of a proposed audit engagement such that the auditor believes the limitation will result in the auditor disclaiming an opinion on the financial statements, the auditor shall not accept such a limited engagement as an audit engagement, unless required by law or regulation to do so.

Other Factors Affecting Audit Engagement Acceptance

8   If the preconditions for an audit are not present, the auditor shall discuss the matter with management. Unless required by law or regulation to do so, the auditor shall not accept the proposed audit engagement:

(a) If the auditor has determined that the financial reporting framework to be applied in the preparation of the financial statements is unacceptable, except as provided in paragraph 19; or

(b) If the agreement referred to in paragraph 6(b) has not been obtained.

Agreement on Audit Engagement Terms

9   The auditor shall agree the terms of the audit engagement with management or those charged with governance, as appropriate. (Ref: Para. A21)

[2a] *Sections 499 and 500 of the Companies Act 2006 set legal requirements in relation to the auditor's right to obtain information. For the Republic of Ireland, relevant requirements are set out in Section 193(3), Companies Act 1990.*

Subject to paragraph 11, the agreed terms of the audit engagement shall be recorded   **10**
in an audit engagement letter or other suitable form of written agreement and shall
include: (Ref: Para. A22-A25)

(a) The objective and scope of the audit of the financial statements;
(b) The responsibilities of the auditor;
(c) The responsibilities of management[2b];
(d) Identification of the applicable financial reporting framework for the prepara-
    tion of the financial statements; and
(e) Reference to the expected form and content of any reports to be issued by the
    auditor and a statement that there may be circumstances in which a report may
    differ from its expected form and content.

If law or regulation prescribes in sufficient detail the terms of the audit engagement   **11**
referred to in paragraph 10, the auditor need not record them in a written agreement,
except for the fact that such law or regulation applies and that management
acknowledges and understands its responsibilities as set out in paragraph 6(b). (Ref:
Para. A22, A26-A27)

If law or regulation prescribes responsibilities of management similar to those   **12**
described in paragraph 6(b), the auditor may determine that the law or regulation
includes responsibilities that, in the auditor's judgment, are equivalent in effect to
those set out in that paragraph. For such responsibilities that are equivalent, the
auditor may use the wording of the law or regulation to describe them in the written
agreement. For those responsibilities that are not prescribed by law or regulation
such that their effect is equivalent, the written agreement shall use the description in
paragraph 6(b). (Ref: Para. A26)

Recurring Audits

On recurring audits, the auditor shall assess whether circumstances require the terms   **13**
of the audit engagement to be revised and whether there is a need to remind the
entity of the existing terms of the audit engagement. (Ref: Para. A28)

Acceptance of a Change in the Terms of the Audit Engagement

The auditor shall not agree to a change in the terms of the audit engagement where   **14**
there is no reasonable justification for doing so. (Ref: Para. A29-A31)

If, prior to completing the audit engagement, the auditor is requested to change the   **15**
audit engagement to an engagement that conveys a lower level of assurance, the
auditor shall determine whether there is reasonable justification for doing so. (Ref:
Para. A32-A33)

If the terms of the audit engagement are changed, the auditor and management shall   **16**
agree on and record the new terms of the engagement in an engagement letter or
other suitable form of written agreement.

If the auditor is unable to agree to a change of the terms of the audit engagement and   **17**
is not permitted by management to continue the original audit engagement, the
auditor shall:

(a) Withdraw from the audit engagement where possible under applicable law or
    regulation; and

[2b] *In the UK and Ireland, the engagement letter sets out the responsibilities of those charged with governance.*

(b)   Determine whether there is any obligation, either contractual or otherwise, to report the circumstances to other parties, such as those charged with governance, owners or regulators. (Ref: Para. A33-1)

Additional Considerations in Engagement Acceptance

Financial Reporting Standards Supplemented by Law or Regulation

18   If financial reporting standards established by an authorized or recognized standards setting organization are supplemented by law or regulation, the auditor shall determine whether there are any conflicts between the financial reporting standards and the additional requirements. If such conflicts exist, the auditor shall discuss with management the nature of the additional requirements and shall agree whether:

(a)   The additional requirements can be met through additional disclosures in the financial statements; or

(b)   The description of the applicable financial reporting framework in the financial statements can be amended accordingly.

If neither of the above actions is possible, the auditor shall determine whether it will be necessary to modify the auditor's opinion in accordance with ISA (UK and Ireland) 705.[3] (Ref: Para. A34)

Financial Reporting Framework Prescribed by Law or Regulation—Other Matters Affecting Acceptance

19   If the auditor has determined that the financial reporting framework prescribed by law or regulation would be unacceptable but for the fact that it is prescribed by law or regulation, the auditor shall accept the audit engagement only if the following conditions are present: (Ref: Para. A35)

(a)   Management agrees to provide additional disclosures in the financial statements required to avoid the financial statements being misleading; and

(b)   It is recognized in the terms of the audit engagement that:

(i)   The auditor's report on the financial statements will incorporate an Emphasis of Matter paragraph, drawing users' attention to the additional disclosures, in accordance with ISA (UK and Ireland) 706;[4] and

(ii)   Unless the auditor is required by law or regulation to express the auditor's opinion on the financial statements by using the phrases "present fairly, in all material respects," or "give a true and fair view" in accordance with the applicable financial reporting framework, the auditor's opinion on the financial statements will not include such phrases.

20   If the conditions outlined in paragraph 19 are not present and the auditor is required by law or regulation to undertake the audit engagement, the auditor shall:

(a)   Evaluate the effect of the misleading nature of the financial statements on the auditor's report; and

(b)   Include appropriate reference to this matter in the terms of the audit engagement.

---

[3] ISA (UK and Ireland) 705, *"Modifications to the Opinion in the Independent Auditor's Report."*

[4] ISA (UK and Ireland) 706, *"Emphasis of Matter Paragraphs and Other Matter Paragraphs in the Independent Auditor's Report."*

Auditor's Report Prescribed by Law or Regulation

In some cases, law or regulation of the relevant jurisdiction prescribes the layout or **21** wording of the auditor's report in a form or in terms that are significantly different from the requirements of ISAs (UK and Ireland). In these circumstances, the auditor shall evaluate:

(a) Whether users might misunderstand the assurance obtained from the audit of the financial statements and, if so,

(b) Whether additional explanation in the auditor's report can mitigate possible misunderstanding.[5]

If the auditor concludes that additional explanation in the auditor's report cannot mitigate possible misunderstanding, the auditor shall not accept the audit engagement, unless required by law or regulation to do so. An audit conducted in accordance with such law or regulation does not comply with ISAs (UK and Ireland). Accordingly, the auditor shall not include any reference within the auditor's report to the audit having been conducted in accordance with ISAs (UK and Ireland).[6] (Ref: Para. A36-A37)

***

Application and Other Explanatory Material

Scope of this ISA (UK and Ireland) (Ref: Para. 1)

Assurance engagements, which include audit engagements, may only be accepted **A1** when the practitioner considers that relevant ethical requirements such as independence and professional competence will be satisfied, and when the engagement exhibits certain characteristics.[7] The auditor's responsibilities in respect of ethical requirements in the context of the acceptance of an audit engagement and in so far as they are within the control of the auditor are dealt with in ISA (UK and Ireland) 220.[8] This ISA (UK and Ireland) deals with those matters (or preconditions) that are within the control of the entity and upon which it is necessary for the auditor and the entity's management to agree.

Preconditions for an Audit

The Financial Reporting Framework (Ref: Para. 6(a))

A condition for acceptance of an assurance engagement is that the criteria referred to **A2** in the definition of an assurance engagement are suitable and available to intended

---

[5] *ISA (UK and Ireland) 706.*

[6] *See also ISA 700, "Forming an Opinion and Reporting on Financial Statements," paragraph 43.*
The APB has not promulgated ISA 700 as issued by the IAASB for application in the UK and Ireland. In the UK and Ireland the applicable auditing standard is ISA (UK and Ireland) 700, "The Auditor's Report on Financial Statements." Paragraph 5 of ISA (UK and Ireland) 700 explains that compliance with that ISA (UK and Ireland) does not preclude the auditor from being able to assert compliance with ISAs.

[7] *"International Framework for Assurance Engagements," paragraph 17.*
The "International Framework for Assurance Engagements" has not been promulgated by the APB for application in the UK and Ireland.

[8] *ISA (UK and Ireland) 220, paragraphs 9-11.*

users.[9] Criteria are the benchmarks used to evaluate or measure the subject matter including, where relevant, benchmarks for presentation and disclosure. Suitable criteria enable reasonably consistent evaluation or measurement of a subject matter within the context of professional judgment. For purposes of the ISAs (UK and Ireland), the applicable financial reporting framework provides the criteria the auditor uses to audit the financial statements, including where relevant their fair presentation.

A3   Without an acceptable financial reporting framework, management does not have an appropriate basis for the preparation of the financial statements and the auditor does not have suitable criteria for auditing the financial statements. In many cases the auditor may presume that the applicable financial reporting framework is acceptable, as described in paragraphs A8-A9.

Determining the Acceptability of the Financial Reporting Framework

A4   Factors that are relevant to the auditor's determination of the acceptability of the financial reporting framework to be applied in the preparation of the financial statements include:

- The nature of the entity (for example, whether it is a business enterprise, a public sector entity or a not for profit organization);
- The purpose of the financial statements (for example, whether they are prepared to meet the common financial information needs of a wide range of users or the financial information needs of specific users);
- The nature of the financial statements (for example, whether the financial statements are a complete set of financial statements or a single financial statement); and
- Whether law or regulation prescribes the applicable financial reporting framework.

A5   Many users of financial statements are not in a position to demand financial statements tailored to meet their specific information needs. While all the information needs of specific users cannot be met, there are financial information needs that are common to a wide range of users. Financial statements prepared in accordance with a financial reporting framework designed to meet the common financial information needs of a wide range of users are referred to as general purpose financial statements.

A6   In some cases, the financial statements will be prepared in accordance with a financial reporting framework designed to meet the financial information needs of specific users. Such financial statements are referred to as special purpose financial statements. The financial information needs of the intended users will determine the applicable financial reporting framework in these circumstances. ISA 800 discusses the acceptability of financial reporting frameworks designed to meet the financial information needs of specific users.[10]

A7   Deficiencies in the applicable financial reporting framework that indicate that the framework is not acceptable may be encountered after the audit engagement has

---

[9] *"International Framework for Assurance Engagements," paragraph 17(b)(ii).*
The "International Framework for Assurance Engagements" has not been promulgated by the APB for application in the UK and Ireland.

[10] *ISA 800, "Special Considerations—Audits of Financial Statements Prepared in Accordance with Special Purpose Frameworks," paragraph 8.*
ISA 800 has not been promulgated by the APB for application in the UK and Ireland.

been accepted. When use of that framework is prescribed by law or regulation, the requirements of paragraphs 19-20 apply. When use of that framework is not prescribed by law or regulation, management may decide to adopt another framework that is acceptable. When management does so, as required by paragraph 16, new terms of the audit engagement are agreed to reflect the change in the framework as the previously agreed terms will no longer be accurate.

General purpose frameworks

At present, there is no objective and authoritative basis that has been generally recognized globally for judging the acceptability of general purpose frameworks. In the absence of such a basis, financial reporting standards established by organizations that are authorized or recognized to promulgate standards to be used by certain types of entities are presumed to be acceptable for general purpose financial statements prepared by such entities, provided the organizations follow an established and transparent process involving deliberation and consideration of the views of a wide range of stakeholders. Examples of such financial reporting standards include: **A8**

- International Financial Reporting Standards (IFRSs) promulgated by the International Accounting Standards Board;
- International Public Sector Accounting Standards (IPSASs) promulgated by the International Public Sector Accounting Standards Board; and
- Accounting principles promulgated by an authorized or recognized standards setting organization in a particular jurisdiction, provided the organization follows an established and transparent process involving deliberation and consideration of the views of a wide range of stakeholders.

These financial reporting standards are often identified as the applicable financial reporting framework in law or regulation governing the preparation of general purpose financial statements.

Financial reporting frameworks prescribed by law or regulation

In accordance with paragraph 6(a), the auditor is required to determine whether the financial reporting framework, to be applied in the preparation of the financial statements, is acceptable. In some jurisdictions, law or regulation may prescribe the financial reporting framework to be used in the preparation of general purpose financial statements for certain types of entities. In the absence of indications to the contrary, such a financial reporting framework is presumed to be acceptable for general purpose financial statements prepared by such entities. In the event that the framework is not considered to be acceptable, paragraphs 19-20 apply. **A9**

Jurisdictions that do not have standards setting organizations or prescribed financial reporting frameworks

When an entity is registered or operating in a jurisdiction that does not have an authorized or recognized standards setting organization, or where use of the financial reporting framework is not prescribed by law or regulation, management identifies a financial reporting framework to be applied in the preparation of the financial statements. Appendix 2 contains guidance on determining the acceptability of financial reporting frameworks in such circumstances. **A10**

Agreement of the Responsibilities of Management (Ref: Para. 6(b))

A11   An audit in accordance with ISAs is conducted on the premise that management has acknowledged and understands that it has the responsibilities set out in paragraph 6(b).[11] In certain jurisdictions, such responsibilities may be specified in law or regulation. In others, there may be little or no legal or regulatory definition of such responsibilities. ISAs (UK and Ireland) do not override law or regulation in such matters. However, the concept of an independent audit requires that the auditor's role does not involve taking responsibility for the preparation of the financial statements or for the entity's related internal control, and that the auditor has a reasonable expectation of obtaining the information necessary for the audit in so far as management is able to provide or procure it. Accordingly, the premise is fundamental to the conduct of an independent audit. To avoid misunderstanding, agreement is reached with management that it acknowledges and understands that it has such responsibilities as part of agreeing and recording the terms of the audit engagement in paragraphs 9-12.

A12   The way in which the responsibilities for financial reporting are divided between management and those charged with governance will vary according to the resources and structure of the entity and any relevant law or regulation, and the respective roles of management and those charged with governance within the entity. In most cases, management is responsible for execution while those charged with governance have oversight of management. In some cases, those charged with governance will have, or will assume, responsibility for approving the financial statements or monitoring the entity's internal control related to financial reporting. In larger or public entities, a subgroup of those charged with governance, such as an audit committee, may be charged with certain oversight responsibilities.

A13   ISA (UK and Ireland) 580 requires the auditor to request management to provide written representations that it has fulfilled certain of its responsibilities.[12] It may therefore be appropriate to make management aware that receipt of such written representations will be expected, together with written representations required by other ISAs (UK and Ireland) and, where necessary, written representations to support other audit evidence relevant to the financial statements or one or more specific assertions in the financial statements.

A14   Where management will not acknowledge its responsibilities, or agree to provide the written representations, the auditor will be unable to obtain sufficient appropriate audit evidence.[13] In such circumstances, it would not be appropriate for the auditor to accept the audit engagement, unless law or regulation requires the auditor to do so. In cases where the auditor is required to accept the audit engagement, the auditor may need to explain to management the importance of these matters, and the implications for the auditor's report.

Preparation of the Financial Statements (Ref: Para. 6(b)(i))

A15   Most financial reporting frameworks include requirements relating to the presentation of the financial statements; for such frameworks, *preparation* of the financial statements in accordance with the financial reporting framework includes *presentation*. In the case of a fair presentation framework the importance of the reporting

---

[11] *ISA (UK and Ireland) 200, paragraph A2.*

[12] *ISA (UK and Ireland) 580, "Written Representations," paragraphs 10-11.*

[13] *ISA (UK and Ireland) 580, paragraph A26.*

objective of fair presentation is such that the premise agreed with management includes specific reference to fair presentation, or to the responsibility to ensure that the financial statements will "give a true and fair view" in accordance with the financial reporting framework.

Internal Control *(Ref: Para. 6(b)(ii))*

Management maintains such internal control as it determines is necessary to enable the preparation of financial statements that are free from material misstatement, whether due to fraud or error. Internal control, no matter how effective, can provide an entity with only reasonable assurance about achieving the entity's financial reporting objectives due to the inherent limitations of internal control.[14]   **A16**

An independent audit conducted in accordance with the ISAs (UK and Ireland) does not act as a substitute for the maintenance of internal control necessary for the preparation of financial statements by management. Accordingly, the auditor is required to obtain the agreement of management that it acknowledges and understands its responsibility for internal control. However, the agreement required by paragraph 6(b)(ii) does not imply that the auditor will find that internal control maintained by management has achieved its purpose or will be free of deficiencies.   **A17**

It is for management to determine what internal control is necessary to enable the preparation of the financial statements. The term "internal control" encompasses a wide range of activities within components that may be described as the control environment; the entity's risk assessment process; the information system, including the related business processes relevant to financial reporting, and communication; control activities; and monitoring of controls. This division, however, does not necessarily reflect how a particular entity may design, implement and maintain its internal control, or how it may classify any particular component.[15] An entity's internal control (in particular, its accounting books and records, or accounting systems) will reflect the needs of management, the complexity of the business, the nature of the risks to which the entity is subject, and relevant laws or regulation.   **A18**

In some jurisdictions, law or regulation may refer to the responsibility of management for the adequacy of accounting books and records, or accounting systems. In some cases, general practice may assume a distinction between accounting books and records or accounting systems on the one hand, and internal control or controls on the other. As accounting books and records, or accounting systems, are an integral part of internal control as referred to in paragraph A18, no specific reference is made to them in paragraph 6(b)(ii) for the description of the responsibility of management. To avoid misunderstanding, it may be appropriate for the auditor to explain to management the scope of this responsibility.   **A19**

Considerations Relevant to Smaller Entities *(Ref: Para. 6(b))*

One of the purposes of agreeing the terms of the audit engagement is to avoid misunderstanding about the respective responsibilities of management and the auditor. For example, when a third party has assisted with the preparation of the financial statements, it may be useful to remind management that the preparation of   **A20**

---

[14] *ISA (UK and Ireland) 315, "Identifying and Assessing the Risks of Material Misstatement through Understanding the Entity and Its Environment," paragraph A46.*

[15] *ISA (UK and Ireland) 315, paragraph A51 and Appendix 1.*

the financial statements in accordance with the applicable financial reporting framework remains its responsibility.

Agreement on Audit Engagement Terms

Agreeing the Terms of the Audit Engagement (Ref: Para. 9)

A21   The roles of management and those charged with governance in agreeing the terms of the audit engagement for the entity depend on the governance structure of the entity and relevant law or regulation.

Audit Engagement Letter or Other Form of Written Agreement[16] (Ref: Para. 10-11)

A22   It is in the interests of both the entity and the auditor that the auditor sends an audit engagement letter before the commencement of the audit to help avoid misunderstandings with respect to the audit. In some countries, however, the objective and scope of an audit and the responsibilities of management and of the auditor may be sufficiently established by law, that is, they prescribe the matters described in paragraph 10. Although in these circumstances paragraph 11 permits the auditor to include in the engagement letter only reference to the fact that relevant law or regulation applies and that management acknowledges and understands its responsibilities as set out in paragraph 6(b), the auditor may nevertheless consider it appropriate to include the matters described in paragraph 10 in an engagement letter for the information of management.

Form and Content of the Audit Engagement Letter

A23   The form and content of the audit engagement letter may vary for each entity. Information included in the audit engagement letter on the auditor's responsibilities may be based on ISA (UK and Ireland) 200.[17] Paragraphs 6(b) and 12 of this ISA (UK and Ireland) deal with the description of the responsibilities of management. In addition to including the matters required by paragraph 10, an audit engagement letter may make reference to, for example:

- Elaboration of the scope of the audit, including reference to applicable legislation, regulations, ISAs (UK and Ireland), and ethical and other pronouncements of professional bodies to which the auditor adheres.
- The form of any other communication of results of the audit engagement.
- The fact that because of the inherent limitations of an audit, together with the inherent limitations of internal control, there is an unavoidable risk that some material misstatements may not be detected, even though the audit is properly planned and performed in accordance with ISAs (UK and Ireland).
- Arrangements regarding the planning and performance of the audit, including the composition of the audit team.
- The expectation that management will provide written representations (see also paragraph A13).
- The agreement of management to make available to the auditor draft financial statements and any accompanying other information in time to allow the auditor to complete the audit in accordance with the proposed timetable.

---

[16] *In the paragraphs that follow, any reference to an audit engagement letter is to be taken as a reference to an audit engagement letter or other suitable form of written agreement.*

[17] *ISA (UK and Ireland) 200, paragraphs 3-9.*

- The agreement of management to inform the auditor of facts that may affect the financial statements, of which management may become aware during the period from the date of the auditor's report to the date the financial statements are issued.
- The basis on which fees are computed and any billing arrangements.
- A request for management to acknowledge receipt of the audit engagement letter and to agree to the terms of the engagement outlined therein.

When relevant, the following points could also be made in the audit engagement letter: **A24**

- Arrangements concerning the involvement of other auditors and experts in some aspects of the audit.
- Arrangements concerning the involvement of internal auditors and other staff of the entity.
- Arrangements to be made with the predecessor auditor, if any, in the case of an initial audit.
- Any restriction of the auditor's liability when such possibility exists.
- A reference to any further agreements between the auditor and the entity.
- Any obligations to provide audit working papers to other parties.

An example of an audit engagement letter is set out in Appendix 1.[17a]

Audits of Components

When the auditor of a parent entity is also the auditor of a component, the factors that may influence the decision whether to send a separate audit engagement letter to the component include the following: **A25**

- Who appoints the component auditor;
- Whether a separate auditor's report is to be issued on the component;
- Legal requirements in relation to audit appointments;
- Degree of ownership by parent; and
- Degree of independence of the component management from the parent entity.

Responsibilities of Management Prescribed by Law or Regulation (Ref: Para. 11-12)

If, in the circumstances described in paragraphs A22 and A27, the auditor concludes that it is not necessary to record certain terms of the audit engagement in an audit engagement letter, the auditor is still required by paragraph 11 to seek the written agreement from management that it acknowledges and understands that it has the responsibilities set out in paragraph 6(b). However, in accordance with paragraph 12, such written agreement may use the wording of the law or regulation if such law or regulation establishes responsibilities for management that are equivalent in effect to those described in paragraph 6(b). The accounting profession, audit standards setter, or audit regulator in a jurisdiction may have provided guidance as to whether the description in law or regulation is equivalent.   **A26**

Considerations specific to public sector entities

Law or regulation governing the operations of public sector audits generally mandate the appointment of a public sector auditor and commonly set out the public sector auditor's responsibilities and powers, including the power to access an entity's   **A27**

[17a] *The example letter in the Appendix has not been tailored for the UK and Ireland.*

records and other information. When law or regulation prescribes in sufficient detail the terms of the audit engagement, the public sector auditor may nonetheless consider that there are benefits in issuing a fuller audit engagement letter than permitted by paragraph 11.

Recurring Audits (Ref: Para. 13)

A28   The auditor may decide not to send a new audit engagement letter or other written agreement each period. However, the following factors may make it appropriate to revise the terms of the audit engagement or to remind the entity of existing terms:

- Any indication that the entity misunderstands the objective and scope of the audit.
- Any revised or special terms of the audit engagement.
- A recent change of senior management.
- A significant change in ownership.
- A significant change in nature or size of the entity's business.
- A change in legal or regulatory requirements.
- A change in the financial reporting framework adopted in the preparation of the financial statements.
- A change in other reporting requirements.

Acceptance of a Change in the Terms of the Audit Engagement

Request to Change the Terms of the Audit Engagement (Ref: Para. 14)

A29   A request from the entity for the auditor to change the terms of the audit engagement may result from a change in circumstances affecting the need for the service, a misunderstanding as to the nature of an audit as originally requested or a restriction on the scope of the audit engagement, whether imposed by management or caused by other circumstances. The auditor, as required by paragraph 14, considers the justification given for the request, particularly the implications of a restriction on the scope of the audit engagement.

A30   A change in circumstances that affects the entity's requirements or a misunderstanding concerning the nature of the service originally requested may be considered a reasonable basis for requesting a change in the audit engagement.

A31   In contrast, a change may not be considered reasonable if it appears that the change relates to information that is incorrect, incomplete or otherwise unsatisfactory. An example might be where the auditor is unable to obtain sufficient appropriate audit evidence regarding receivables and the entity asks for the audit engagement to be changed to a review engagement to avoid a qualified opinion or a disclaimer of opinion.

Request to Change to a Review or a Related Service (Ref: Para. 15)

A32   Before agreeing to change an audit engagement to a review or a related service, an auditor who was engaged to perform an audit in accordance with ISAs (UK and Ireland) may need to assess, in addition to the matters referred to in paragraphs A29-A31 above, any legal or contractual implications of the change.

A33   If the auditor concludes that there is reasonable justification to change the audit engagement to a review or a related service, the audit work performed to the date of change may be relevant to the changed engagement; however, the work required to be performed and the report to be issued would be those appropriate to the revised engagement. In order to avoid confusing the reader, the report on the related service would not include reference to:

(a) The original audit engagement; or
(b) Any procedures that may have been performed in the original audit engagement, except where the audit engagement is changed to an engagement to undertake agreed-upon procedures and thus reference to the procedures performed is a normal part of the report.

Statement by Auditor on Ceasing to Hold Office (Ref: Para. 17)

The auditor of a limited company in the UK who ceases to hold office as auditor   **A33-1**
is required to comply with the requirements of sections 519 and 521 of the Companies Act 2006 regarding the statement to be made by the auditor in relation to ceasing to hold office. For the Republic of Ireland, equivalent requirements are contained in section 185 of the Companies Act 1990. In addition, in the UK the auditor may need to notify the appropriate audit authority in accordance with section 522 of the Companies Act 2006.

Additional Considerations in Engagement Acceptance

Financial Reporting Standards Supplemented by Law or Regulation (Ref: Para. 18)

In some jurisdictions, law or regulation may supplement the financial reporting   **A34**
standards established by an authorized or recognized standards setting organization with additional requirements relating to the preparation of financial statements. In those jurisdictions, the applicable financial reporting framework for the purposes of applying the ISAs (UK and Ireland) encompasses both the identified financial reporting framework and such additional requirements provided they do not conflict with the identified financial reporting framework. This may, for example, be the case when law or regulation prescribes disclosures in addition to those required by the financial reporting standards or when they narrow the range of acceptable choices that can be made within the financial reporting standards.[18]

Financial Reporting Framework Prescribed by Law or Regulation—Other Matters Affecting Acceptance (Ref: Para. 19)

Law or regulation may prescribe that the wording of the auditor's opinion use the   **A35**
phrases "present fairly, in all material respects" or "give a true and fair view" in a case where the auditor concludes that the applicable financial reporting framework prescribed by law or regulation would otherwise have been unacceptable. In this case, the terms of the prescribed wording of the auditor's report are significantly different from the requirements of ISAs (UK and Ireland) (see paragraph 21).

---

[18] *ISA 700, paragraph 15, includes a requirement regarding the evaluation of whether the financial statements adequately refer to or describe the applicable financial reporting framework.*
The APB has not promulgated ISA 700 as issued by the IAASB for application in the UK and Ireland. In the UK and Ireland the applicable auditing standard is ISA (UK and Ireland) 700, "The Auditor's Report on Financial Statements." Paragraph 9(a) of ISA (UK and Ireland) 700 includes a requirement regarding evaluation of whether the financial statements adequately refer to or describe the relevant financial reporting framework.

Auditor's Report Prescribed by Law or Regulation (Ref: Para. 21)

A36   ISAs (UK and Ireland) require that the auditor shall not represent compliance with ISAs (UK and Ireland) unless the auditor has complied with all of the ISAs (UK and Ireland) relevant to the audit.[19] When law or regulation prescribes the layout or wording of the auditor's report in a form or in terms that are significantly different from the requirements of ISAs (UK and Ireland) and the auditor concludes that additional explanation in the auditor's report cannot mitigate possible mis-understanding, the auditor may consider including a statement in the auditor's report that the audit is not conducted in accordance with ISAs (UK and Ireland). The auditor is, however, encouraged to apply ISAs (UK and Ireland), including the ISAs (UK and Ireland) that address the auditor's report, to the extent practicable, notwithstanding that the auditor is not permitted to refer to the audit being conducted in accordance with ISAs (UK and Ireland).

Considerations Specific to Public Sector Entities

A37   In the public sector, specific requirements may exist within the legislation governing the audit mandate; for example, the auditor may be required to report directly to a minister, the legislature or the public if the entity attempts to limit the scope of the audit.

Appendix 1   (Ref: Paras. A23-24)

The example letter in this Appendix has not been tailored for the UK and Ireland.

Example of an Audit Engagement Letter

The following is an example of an audit engagement letter for an audit of general purpose financial statements prepared in accordance with International Financial Reporting Standards. This letter is not authoritative but is intended only to be a guide that may be used in conjunction with the considerations outlined in this ISA. It will need to be varied according to individual requirements and circumstances. It is drafted to refer to the audit of financial statements for a single reporting period and would require adaptation if intended or expected to apply to recurring audits (see paragraph 13 of this ISA). It may be appropriate to seek legal advice that any proposed letter is suitable.

***

To the appropriate representative of management or those charged with governance of ABC Company:[20]

[The objective and scope of the audit]

You[21] have requested that we audit the financial statements of ABC Company, which comprise the balance sheet as at December 31, 20X1, and the income statement,

---

[19] *ISA (UK and Ireland) 200, paragraph 20.*

[20] *The addressees and references in the letter would be those that are appropriate in the circumstances of the engagement, including the relevant jurisdiction. It is important to refer to the appropriate persons – see paragraph A21.*

[21] *Throughout this letter, references to "you," "we," "us," "management," "those charged with governance" and "auditor" would be used or amended as appropriate in the circumstances.*

statement of changes in equity and cash flow statement for the year then ended, and a summary of significant accounting policies and other explanatory information. We are pleased to confirm our acceptance and our understanding of this audit engagement by means of this letter. Our audit will be conducted with the objective of our expressing an opinion on the financial statements.

[*The responsibilities of the auditor*]

We will conduct our audit in accordance with International Standards on Auditing (ISAs). Those standards require that we comply with ethical requirements and plan and perform the audit to obtain reasonable assurance about whether the financial statements are free from material misstatement. An audit involves performing procedures to obtain audit evidence about the amounts and disclosures in the financial statements. The procedures selected depend on the auditor's judgment, including the assessment of the risks of material misstatement of the financial statements, whether due to fraud or error. An audit also includes evaluating the appropriateness of accounting policies used and the reasonableness of accounting estimates made by management, as well as evaluating the overall presentation of the financial statements.

Because of the inherent limitations of an audit, together with the inherent limitations of internal control, there is an unavoidable risk that some material misstatements may not be detected, even though the audit is properly planned and performed in accordance with ISAs.

In making our risk assessments, we consider internal control relevant to the entity's preparation of the financial statements in order to design audit procedures that are appropriate in the circumstances, but not for the purpose of expressing an opinion on the effectiveness of the entity's internal control. However, we will communicate to you in writing concerning any significant deficiencies in internal control relevant to the audit of the financial statements that we have identified during the audit.

[*The responsibilities of management and identification of the applicable financial reporting framework (for purposes of this example it is assumed that the auditor has not determined that the law or regulation prescribes those responsibilities in appropriate terms; the descriptions in paragraph 6(b) of this ISA are therefore used).*]

Our audit will be conducted on the basis that [management and, where appropriate, those charged with governance][22] acknowledge and understand that they have responsibility:

(a) For the preparation and fair presentation of the financial statements in accordance with International Financial Reporting Standards;[23]
(b) For such internal control as [management] determines is necessary to enable the preparation of financial statements that are free from material misstatement, whether due to fraud or error; and
(c) To provide us with:
  (i) Access to all information of which [management] is aware that is relevant to the preparation of the financial statements such as records, documentation and other matters;

[22] *Use terminology as appropriate in the circumstances.*

[23] *Or, if appropriate, "For the preparation of financial statements that give a true and fair view in accordance with International Financial Reporting Standards."*

(ii) Additional information that we may request from [management] for the purpose of the audit; and

(iii) Unrestricted access to persons within the entity from whom we determine it necessary to obtain audit evidence.

As part of our audit process, we will request from [management and, where appropriate, those charged with governance], written confirmation concerning representations made to us in connection with the audit.

We look forward to full cooperation from your staff during our audit.

[*Other relevant information*]

[*Insert other information, such as fee arrangements, billings and other specific terms, as appropriate.*]

[*Reporting*]

[*Insert appropriate reference to the expected form and content of the auditor's report.*]

The form and content of our report may need to be amended in the light of our audit findings.

Please sign and return the attached copy of this letter to indicate your acknowledgement of, and agreement with, the arrangements for our audit of the financial statements including our respective responsibilities.

XYZ & Co.

Acknowledged and agreed on behalf of ABC Company by

(signed)
....
Name and Title
Date

Appendix 2 (Ref: Para. A10)

Determining the Acceptability of General Purpose Frameworks

Jurisdictions that Do Not Have Authorized or Recognized Standards Setting Organizations or Financial Reporting Frameworks Prescribed by Law or Regulation

1 As explained in paragraph A10 of this ISA (UK and Ireland), when an entity is registered or operating in a jurisdiction that does not have an authorized or recognized standards setting organization, or where use of the financial reporting framework is not prescribed by law or regulation, management identifies an applicable financial reporting framework. Practice in such jurisdictions is often to use the financial reporting standards established by one of the organizations described in paragraph A8 of this ISA (UK and Ireland).

2 Alternatively, there may be established accounting conventions in a particular jurisdiction that are generally recognized as the financial reporting framework for

general purpose financial statements prepared by certain specified entities operating in that jurisdiction. When such a financial reporting framework is adopted, the auditor is required by paragraph 6(a) of this ISA (UK and Ireland) to determine whether the accounting conventions collectively can be considered to constitute an acceptable financial reporting framework for general purpose financial statements. When the accounting conventions are widely used in a particular jurisdiction, the accounting profession in that jurisdiction may have considered the acceptability of the financial reporting framework on behalf of the auditors. Alternatively, the auditor may make this determination by considering whether the accounting conventions exhibit attributes normally exhibited by acceptable financial reporting frameworks (see paragraph 3 below), or by comparing the accounting conventions to the requirements of an existing financial reporting framework considered to be acceptable (see paragraph 4 below).

Acceptable financial reporting frameworks normally exhibit the following attributes **3**
that result in information provided in financial statements that is useful to the intended users:

(a) Relevance, in that the information provided in the financial statements is relevant to the nature of the entity and the purpose of the financial statements. For example, in the case of a business enterprise that prepares general purpose financial statements, relevance is assessed in terms of the information necessary to meet the common financial information needs of a wide range of users in making economic decisions. These needs are ordinarily met by presenting the financial position, financial performance and cash flows of the business enterprise.

(b) Completeness, in that transactions and events, account balances and disclosures that could affect conclusions based on the financial statements are not omitted.

(c) Reliability, in that the information provided in the financial statements:
   (i) Where applicable, reflects the economic substance of events and transactions and not merely their legal form; and
   (ii) Results in reasonably consistent evaluation, measurement, presentation and disclosure, when used in similar circumstances.

(d) Neutrality, in that it contributes to information in the financial statements that is free from bias.

(e) Understandability, in that the information in the financial statements is clear and comprehensive and not subject to significantly different interpretation.

The auditor may decide to compare the accounting conventions to the requirements **4**
of an existing financial reporting framework considered to be acceptable. For example, the auditor may compare the accounting conventions to IFRSs. For an audit of a small entity, the auditor may decide to compare the accounting conventions to a financial reporting framework specifically developed for such entities by an authorized or recognized standards setting organization. When the auditor makes such a comparison and differences are identified, the decision as to whether the accounting conventions adopted in the preparation of the financial statements constitute an acceptable financial reporting framework includes considering the reasons for the differences and whether application of the accounting conventions, or the description of the financial reporting framework in the financial statements, could result in financial statements that are misleading.

A conglomeration of accounting conventions devised to suit individual preferences is **5**
not an acceptable financial reporting framework for general purpose financial statements. Similarly, a compliance framework will not be an acceptable financial reporting framework, unless it is generally accepted in the particular jurisdictions by preparers and users.

International Standard on Auditing (UK and Ireland) 220

Quality control for an audit of financial statements

*(Effective for audits of financial statements for periods
ending on or after 15 December 2010)*[1a]

Contents

International Standard on Auditing (UK and Ireland) (ISA (UK and Ireland)) 220, "Quality Control for an Audit of Financial Statements" should be read in conjunction with ISA (UK and Ireland) 200, "Overall Objectives of the Independent Auditor and the Conduct of an Audit in Accordance with International Standards on Auditing (UK and Ireland)."

[1a] *Conforming amendments to this standard as a result of ISA (UK and Ireland) 610 (Revised June 2013), Using the Work of Internal Auditors, are included that are effective for audits of financial statements for periods ending on or after 15 June 2014. Details of the amendments are given in the Annexure to ISA (UK and Ireland) 610 (Revised June 2013).*

Introduction

Scope of this ISA (UK and Ireland)

This International Standard on Auditing (UK and Ireland) (ISA (UK and Ireland)) **1**
deals with the specific responsibilities of the auditor regarding quality control procedures for an audit of financial statements. It also addresses, where applicable, the
responsibilities of the engagement quality control reviewer. This ISA (UK and Ireland) is to be read in conjunction with relevant ethical requirements.

System of Quality Control and Role of Engagement Teams

Quality control systems, policies and procedures are the responsibility of the audit   **2**
firm. Under ISQC (UK and Ireland) 1, the firm has an obligation to establish and
maintain a system of quality control to provide it with reasonable assurance that:

(a) The firm and its personnel comply with professional standards and applicable
    legal and regulatory requirements; and
(b) The reports issued by the firm or engagement partners are appropriate in the
    circumstances.[1]

This ISA (UK and Ireland) is premised on the basis that the firm is subject to ISQC
(UK and Ireland) 1 or to national requirements that are at least as demanding. (Ref:
Para. A1)

Within the context of the firm's system of quality control, engagement teams have a   **3**
responsibility to implement quality control procedures that are applicable to the
audit engagement and provide the firm with relevant information to enable the
functioning of that part of the firm's system of quality control relating to
independence.

Engagement teams are entitled to rely on the firm's system of quality control, unless   **4**
information provided by the firm or other parties suggests otherwise. (Ref: Para. A2)

Effective Date

This ISA (UK and Ireland) is effective for audits of financial statements for periods   **5**
ending on or after 15 December 2010.[1a]

Objective

The objective of the auditor is to implement quality control procedures at the   **6**
engagement level that provide the auditor with reasonable assurance that:

(a) The audit complies with professional standards and applicable legal and reg-
    ulatory requirements; and
(b) The auditor's report issued is appropriate in the circumstances.

---

[1] *ISQC (UK and Ireland) 1, "Quality Control for Firms that Perform Audits and Reviews of Financial
Statements, and Other Assurance and Related Services Engagements," paragraph 11.*

Definitions

7   For purposes of the ISAs (UK and Ireland), the following terms have the meanings attributed below:

(a) Engagement partner[2] – The partner or other person in the firm who is responsible for the audit engagement and its performance, and for the auditor's report that is issued on behalf of the firm, and who, where required, has the appropriate authority from a professional, legal or regulatory body.

(b) Engagement quality control review – A process designed to provide an objective evaluation, on or before the date of the auditor's report, of the significant judgments the engagement team made and the conclusions it reached in formulating the auditor's report. The engagement quality control review process is only for audits of financial statements of listed entities and those other audit engagements, if any, for which the firm has determined an engagement quality control review is required.

(c) Engagement quality control reviewer – A partner, other person in the firm, suitably qualified external person, or a team made up of such individuals, none of whom is part of the engagement team, with sufficient and appropriate experience and authority to objectively evaluate the significant judgments the engagement team made and the conclusions it reached in formulating the auditor's report.

(d) Engagement team – All partners and staff performing the engagement, and any individuals engaged by the firm or a network firm who perform audit procedures on the engagement. This excludes an auditor's external expert engaged by the firm or by a network firm.[3] The term "engagement team" also excludes individuals within the client's internal audit function who provide direct assistance on an audit engagement when the external auditor complies with the requirements of ISA (UK and Ireland) 610 (Revised June 2013).[4]

(e) Firm – A sole practitioner, partnership or corporation or other entity of professional accountants.

(f) Inspection – In relation to completed audit engagements, procedures designed to provide evidence of compliance by engagement teams with the firm's quality control policies and procedures.

(g) Listed entity – An entity whose shares, stock or debt are quoted or listed on a recognized stock exchange, or are marketed under the regulations of a recognized stock exchange or other equivalent body.

(h) Monitoring – A process comprising an ongoing consideration and evaluation of the firm's system of quality control, including a periodic inspection of a selection of completed engagements, designed to provide the firm with reasonable assurance that its system of quality control is operating effectively.

(i) Network firm – A firm or entity that belongs to a network.

(j) Network – A larger structure:

(i)   That is aimed at cooperation, and

---

[2] *"Engagement partner," "partner," and "firm" should be read as referring to their public sector equivalents where relevant.*

[3] *ISA (UK and Ireland) 620, "Using the Work of an Auditor's Expert," paragraph 6(a), defines the term "auditor's expert."*

[4] *ISA 610 (Revised June 2013),* Using the Work of Internal Auditors, *establishes limits on the use of direct assistance. It also acknowledges that the external auditor may be prohibited by law or regulation from obtaining direct assistance from internal auditors. Therefore, the use of direct assistance is restricted to situations where it is permitted. The use of internal auditors to provide direct assistance is prohibited in an audit conducted in accordance with ISAs (UK and Ireland) – see ISA (UK and Ireland) 610 (Revised June 2013), paragraph 5-1.*

(ii) That is clearly aimed at profit or cost-sharing or shares common ownership, control or management, common quality control policies and procedures, common business strategy, the use of a common brand name, or a significant part of professional resources.

(k) Partner – Any individual with authority to bind the firm with respect to the performance of a professional services engagement.

(l) Personnel – Partners and staff.

(m) Professional standards – International Standards on Auditing (UK and Ireland) (ISAs (UK and Ireland)) and relevant ethical requirements.

(n) Relevant ethical requirements – Ethical requirements to which the engagement team and engagement quality control reviewer are subject, which ordinarily comprise Parts A and B of the International Ethics Standards Board for Accountants' *Code of Ethics for Professional Accountants* (IESBA Code) related to an audit of financial statements together with national requirements that are more restrictive.

> Auditors in the UK and Ireland are subject to ethical requirements from two sources: the APB Ethical Standards for Auditors concerning the integrity, objectivity and independence of the auditor, and the ethical pronouncements established by the auditor's relevant professional body. The APB is not aware of any significant instances where the relevant parts of the IESBA Code of Ethics are more restrictive than the APB Ethical Standards for Auditors.

(o) Staff – Professionals, other than partners, including any experts the firm employs.

(p) Suitably qualified external person – An individual outside the firm with the competence and capabilities to act as an engagement partner, for example a partner of another firm, or an employee (with appropriate experience) of either a professional accountancy body whose members may perform audits of historical financial information or of an organization that provides relevant quality control services.

Requirements

Leadership Responsibilities for Quality on Audits

The engagement partner shall take responsibility for the overall quality on each audit engagement to which that partner is assigned. (Ref: Para. A3)   8

Relevant Ethical Requirements

Throughout the audit engagement, the engagement partner shall remain alert, through observation and making inquiries as necessary, for evidence of non-compliance with relevant ethical requirements by members of the engagement team. (Ref: Para. A4-A5)   9

If matters come to the engagement partner's attention through the firm's system of quality control or otherwise that indicate that members of the engagement team have not complied with relevant ethical requirements, the engagement partner, in consultation with others in the firm, shall determine the appropriate action. (Ref: Para. A5)   10

Independence

11   The engagement partner shall form a conclusion on compliance with independence requirements that apply to the audit engagement. In doing so, the engagement partner shall: (Ref: Para. A5)

(a) Obtain relevant information from the firm and, where applicable, network firms, to identify and evaluate circumstances and relationships that create threats to independence;

(b) Evaluate information on identified breaches, if any, of the firm's independence policies and procedures to determine whether they create a threat to independence for the audit engagement; and

(c) Take appropriate action to eliminate such threats or reduce them to an acceptable level by applying safeguards, or, if considered appropriate, to withdraw from the audit engagement, where withdrawal is possible under applicable law or regulation. The engagement partner shall promptly report to the firm any inability to resolve the matter for appropriate action. (Ref: Para. A6-A7)

Acceptance and Continuance of Client Relationships and Audit Engagements

12   The engagement partner shall be satisfied that appropriate procedures regarding the acceptance and continuance of client relationships and audit engagements have been followed, and shall determine that conclusions reached in this regard are appropriate. (Ref: Para. A8-A9)

13   If the engagement partner obtains information that would have caused the firm to decline the audit engagement had that information been available earlier, the engagement partner shall communicate that information promptly to the firm, so that the firm and the engagement partner can take the necessary action. (Ref: Para. A9)

Assignment of Engagement Teams

14   The engagement partner shall be satisfied that the engagement team, and any auditor's experts who are not part of the engagement team, collectively have the appropriate competence and capabilities to:

(a) Perform the audit engagement in accordance with professional standards and applicable legal and regulatory requirements; and

(b) Enable an auditor's report that is appropriate in the circumstances to be issued. (Ref: Para. A10-A12)

Engagement Performance

Direction, Supervision and Performance

15   The engagement partner shall take responsibility for:

(a) The direction, supervision and performance of the audit engagement in compliance with professional standards and applicable legal and regulatory requirements; and (Ref: Para. A13-A15, A20)

(b) The auditor's report being appropriate in the circumstances.

Reviews

The engagement partner shall take responsibility for reviews being performed in **16** accordance with the firm's review policies and procedures. (Ref: Para. A16-A17, A20)

On or before the date of the auditor's report, the engagement partner shall, through **17** a review of the audit documentation and discussion with the engagement team, be satisfied that sufficient appropriate audit evidence has been obtained to support the conclusions reached and for the auditor's report to be issued. (Ref: Para. A18-A20)

Consultation

The engagement partner shall: **18**

(a) Take responsibility for the engagement team undertaking appropriate consultation on difficult or contentious matters;
(b) Be satisfied that members of the engagement team have undertaken appropriate consultation during the course of the engagement, both within the engagement team and between the engagement team and others at the appropriate level within or outside the firm;
(c) Be satisfied that the nature and scope of, and conclusions resulting from, such consultations are agreed with the party consulted; and
(d) Determine that conclusions resulting from such consultations have been implemented. (Ref: Para. A21-A22)

Engagement Quality Control Review

For audits of financial statements of listed entities, and those other audit engage- **19** ments, if any, for which the firm has determined that an engagement quality control review is required, the engagement partner shall:

(a) Determine that an engagement quality control reviewer has been appointed;
(b) Discuss significant matters arising during the audit engagement, including those identified during the engagement quality control review, with the engagement quality control reviewer; and
(c) Not date the auditor's report until the completion of the engagement quality control review. (Ref: Para. A23-A25)

The engagement quality control reviewer shall perform an objective evaluation of the **20** significant judgments made by the engagement team, and the conclusions reached in formulating the auditor's report. This evaluation shall involve:

(a) Discussion of significant matters with the engagement partner;
(b) Review of the financial statements and the proposed auditor's report;
(c) Review of selected audit documentation relating to the significant judgments the engagement team made and the conclusions it reached; and
(d) Evaluation of the conclusions reached in formulating the auditor's report and consideration of whether the proposed auditor's report is appropriate. (Ref: Para. A26-A27, A29-A31)

For audits of financial statements of listed entities, the engagement quality control **21** reviewer, on performing an engagement quality control review, shall also consider the following:

(a) The engagement team's evaluation of the firm's independence in relation to the audit engagement;

(b)   Whether appropriate consultation has taken place on matters involving differences of opinion or other difficult or contentious matters, and the conclusions
arising from those consultations; and

(c)   Whether audit documentation selected for review reflects the work performed in
relation to the significant judgments and supports the conclusions reached. (Ref:
Para. A28-A31)

Differences of Opinion

22   If differences of opinion arise within the engagement team, with those consulted or,
where applicable, between the engagement partner and the engagement quality
control reviewer, the engagement team shall follow the firm's policies and procedures
for dealing with and resolving differences of opinion.

Monitoring

23   An effective system of quality control includes a monitoring process designed to
provide the firm with reasonable assurance that its policies and procedures relating
to the system of quality control are relevant, adequate, and operating effectively. The
engagement partner shall consider the results of the firm's monitoring process as
evidenced in the latest information circulated by the firm and, if applicable, other
network firms and whether deficiencies noted in that information may affect the
audit engagement. (Ref: Para A32-A34)

Documentation

24   The auditor shall include in the audit documentation:[5]

(a)   Issues identified with respect to compliance with relevant ethical requirements
and how they were resolved.

(b)   Conclusions on compliance with independence requirements that apply to the
audit engagement, and any relevant discussions with the firm that support these
conclusions.

(c)   Conclusions reached regarding the acceptance and continuance of client relationships and audit engagements.

(d)   The nature and scope of, and conclusions resulting from, consultations undertaken during the course of the audit engagement. (Ref: Para. A35)

25   The engagement quality control reviewer shall document, for the audit engagement
reviewed, that:

(a)   The procedures required by the firm's policies on engagement quality control
review have been performed;

(b)   The engagement quality control review has been completed on or before the
date of the auditor's report; and

(c)   The reviewer is not aware of any unresolved matters that would cause the
reviewer to believe that the significant judgments the engagement team made
and the conclusions it reached were not appropriate.

***

---

[5] *ISA (UK and Ireland) 230, "Audit Documentation," paragraphs 8-11, and paragraph A6.*

Application and Other Explanatory Material

System of Quality Control and Role of Engagement Teams (Ref: Para. 2)

ISQC (UK and Ireland) 1, or national requirements that are at least as demanding, **A1** deals with the firm's responsibilities to establish and maintain its system of quality control for audit engagements. The system of quality control includes policies and procedures that address each of the following elements:

- Leadership responsibilities for quality within the firm;
- Relevant ethical requirements;
- Acceptance and continuance of client relationships and specific engagements;
- Human resources;
- Engagement performance; and
- Monitoring.

National requirements that deal with the firm's responsibilities to establish and maintain a system of quality control are at least as demanding as ISQC (UK and Ireland) 1 when they address all the elements referred to in this paragraph and impose obligations on the firm that achieve the aims of the requirements set out in ISQC (UK and Ireland) 1.

Reliance on the Firm's System of Quality Control (Ref: Para. 4)

Unless information provided by the firm or other parties suggest otherwise, the **A2** engagement team may rely on the firm's system of quality control in relation to, for example:

- Competence of personnel through their recruitment and formal training.
- Independence through the accumulation and communication of relevant independence information.
- Maintenance of client relationships through acceptance and continuance systems.
- Adherence to applicable legal and regulatory requirements through the monitoring process.

Leadership Responsibilities for Quality on Audits (Ref: Para. 8)

The actions of the engagement partner and appropriate messages to the other **A3** members of the engagement team, in taking responsibility for the overall quality on each audit engagement, emphasize:

(a) The importance to audit quality of:
    (i) Performing work that complies with professional standards and applicable legal and regulatory requirements;
    (ii) Complying with the firm's quality control policies and procedures as applicable;
    (iii) Issuing auditor's reports that are appropriate in the circumstances; and
    (iv) The engagement team's ability to raise concerns without fear of reprisals; and
(b) The fact that quality is essential in performing audit engagements.

Relevant Ethical Requirements

Compliance with Relevant Ethical Requirements (Ref: Para. 9)

A4   The IESBA Code[5a] establishes the fundamental principles of professional ethics, which include:

(a) Integrity;
(b) Objectivity;
(c) Professional competence and due care;
(d) Confidentiality; and
(e) Professional behavior.

Definition of "Firm," "Network" and "Network Firm" (Ref: Para. 9-11)

A5   The definitions of "firm," "network" or "network firm" in relevant ethical require-ments may differ from those set out in this ISA (UK and Ireland). For example, the IESBA Code[5a] defines the "firm" as:

(a) A sole practitioner, partnership or corporation of professional accountants;
(b) An entity that controls such parties through ownership, management or other means; and
(c) An entity controlled by such parties through ownership, management or other means.

The IESBA Code also provides guidance in relation to the terms "network" and "network firm."

In complying with the requirements in paragraphs 9-11, the definitions used in the relevant ethical requirements apply in so far as is necessary to interpret those ethical requirements.

Threats to Independence (Ref: Para. 11(c))

A6   The engagement partner may identify a threat to independence regarding the audit engagement that safeguards may not be able to eliminate or reduce to an acceptable level. In that case, as required by paragraph 11(c), the engagement partner reports to the relevant person(s) within the firm to determine appropriate action, which may include eliminating the activity or interest that creates the threat, or withdrawing from the audit engagement, where withdrawal is possible under applicable law or regulation.

Considerations Specific to Public Sector Entities

A7   Statutory measures may provide safeguards for the independence of public sector auditors. However, public sector auditors or audit firms carrying out public sector audits on behalf of the statutory auditor may, depending on the terms of the man-date in a particular jurisdiction, need to adapt their approach in order to promote compliance with the spirit of paragraph 11. This may include, where the public sector auditor's mandate does not permit withdrawal from the engagement, disclosure

---

[5a] *Auditors in the UK and Ireland are subject to ethical requirements from two sources: the APB Ethical Standards for Auditors concerning the integrity, objectivity and independence of the auditor, and the ethical pronouncements established by the auditor's relevant professional body. The APB is not aware of any significant instances where the relevant parts of the IESBA Code of Ethics are more restrictive than the APB Ethical Standards for Auditors.*

through a public report, of circumstances that have arisen that would, if they were in the private sector, lead the auditor to withdraw.

Acceptance and Continuance of Client Relationships and Audit Engagements (Ref: Para. 12)

ISQC (UK and Ireland) 1 requires the firm to obtain information considered **A8** necessary in the circumstances before accepting an engagement with a new client, when deciding whether to continue an existing engagement, and when considering acceptance of a new engagement with an existing client.[6] Information such as the following assists the engagement partner in determining whether the conclusions reached regarding the acceptance and continuance of client relationships and audit engagements are appropriate:

- The integrity of the principal owners, key management and those charged with governance of the entity;
- Whether the engagement team is competent to perform the audit engagement and has the necessary capabilities, including time and resources;
- Whether the firm and the engagement team can comply with relevant ethical requirements; and
- Significant matters that have arisen during the current or previous audit engagement, and their implications for continuing the relationship.

Considerations Specific to Public Sector Entities (Ref: Para. 12-13)

In the public sector, auditors may be appointed in accordance with statutory pro- **A9** cedures. Accordingly, certain of the requirements and considerations regarding the acceptance and continuance of client relationships and audit engagements as set out in paragraphs 12, 13 and A8 may not be relevant. Nonetheless, information gathered as a result of the process described may be valuable to public sector auditors in performing risk assessments and in carrying out reporting responsibilities.

Assignment of Engagement Teams (Ref: Para. 14)

An engagement team includes a person using expertise in a specialized area of **A10** accounting or auditing, whether engaged or employed by the firm, if any, who performs audit procedures on the engagement. However, a person with such expertise is not a member of the engagement team if that person's involvement with the engagement is only consultation. Consultations are addressed in paragraph 18, and paragraph A21-A22.

When considering the appropriate competence and capabilities expected of the **A11** engagement team as a whole, the engagement partner may take into consideration such matters as the team's:

- Understanding of, and practical experience with, audit engagements of a similar nature and complexity through appropriate training and participation.
- Understanding of professional standards and applicable legal and regulatory requirements.
- Technical expertise, including expertise with relevant information technology and specialized areas of accounting or auditing.
- Knowledge of relevant industries in which the client operates.
- Ability to apply professional judgment.

---

[6] *ISQC (UK and Ireland) 1, paragraph 27(a).*

- Understanding of the firm's quality control policies and procedures.

Considerations Specific to Public Sector Entities

A12   In the public sector, additional appropriate competence may include skills that are necessary to discharge the terms of the audit mandate in a particular jurisdiction. Such competence may include an understanding of the applicable reporting arrangements, including reporting to the legislature or other governing body or in the public interest. The wider scope of a public sector audit may include, for example, some aspects of performance auditing or a comprehensive assessment of compliance with law, regulation or other authority and preventing and detecting fraud and corruption.

Engagement Performance

Direction, Supervision and Performance (Ref: Para. 15(a))

A13   Direction of the engagement team involves informing the members of the engagement team of matters such as:

- Their responsibilities, including the need to comply with relevant ethical requirements, and to plan and perform an audit with professional skepticism as required by ISA (UK and Ireland) 200.[7]
- Responsibilities of respective partners where more than one partner is involved in the conduct of an audit engagement.
- The objectives of the work to be performed.
- The nature of the entity's business.
- Risk-related issues.
- Problems that may arise.
- The detailed approach to the performance of the engagement.

Discussion among members of the engagement team allows less experienced team members to raise questions with more experienced team members so that appropriate communication can occur within the engagement team.

A14   Appropriate teamwork and training assist less experienced members of the engagement team to clearly understand the objectives of the assigned work.

A15   Supervision includes matters such as:

- Tracking the progress of the audit engagement.
- Considering the competence and capabilities of individual members of the engagement team, including whether they have sufficient time to carry out their work, whether they understand their instructions, and whether the work is being carried out in accordance with the planned approach to the audit engagement.
- Addressing significant matters arising during the audit engagement, considering their significance and modifying the planned approach appropriately.
- Identifying matters for consultation or consideration by more experienced engagement team members during the audit engagement.

---

[7] *ISA (UK and Ireland) 200, "Overall Objectives of the Independent Auditor and the Conduct of an Audit in Accordance with International Standards on Auditing (UK and Ireland)," paragraph 15.*

Reviews

Review Responsibilities (Ref: Para. 16)

Under ISQC (UK and Ireland) 1, the firm's review responsibility policies and procedures are determined on the basis that work of less experienced team members is reviewed by more experienced team members.[8]　**A16**

A review consists of consideration whether, for example:　**A17**

- The work has been performed in accordance with professional standards and applicable legal and regulatory requirements;
- Significant matters have been raised for further consideration;
- Appropriate consultations have taken place and the resulting conclusions have been documented and implemented;
- There is a need to revise the nature, timing and extent of work performed;
- The work performed supports the conclusions reached and is appropriately documented;
- The evidence obtained is sufficient and appropriate to support the auditor's report; and
- The objectives of the engagement procedures have been achieved.

The Engagement Partner's Review of Work Performed (Ref: Para. 17)

Timely reviews of the following by the engagement partner at appropriate stages during the engagement allow significant matters to be resolved on a timely basis to the engagement partner's satisfaction on or before the date of the auditor's report:　**A18**

- Critical areas of judgment, especially those relating to difficult or contentious matters identified during the course of the engagement;
- Significant risks; and
- Other areas the engagement partner considers important.

The engagement partner need not review all audit documentation, but may do so. However, as required by ISA (UK and Ireland) 230, the partner documents the extent and timing of the reviews.[9]

An engagement partner taking over an audit during the engagement may apply the review procedures as described in paragraphs A18 to review the work performed to the date of a change in order to assume the responsibilities of an engagement partner.　**A19**

Considerations Relevant Where a Member of the Engagement Team with Expertise in a Specialized Area of Accounting or Auditing Is Used (Ref: Para. 15-17)

Where a member of the engagement team with expertise in a specialized area of accounting or auditing is used, direction, supervision and review of that engagement team member's work may include matters such as:　**A20**

- Agreeing with that member the nature, scope and objectives of that member's work; and the respective roles of, and the nature, timing and extent of communication between that member and other members of the engagement team.

---

[8] *ISQC (UK and Ireland) 1, paragraph 33.*

[9] *ISA (UK and Ireland) 230, paragraph 9(c).*

- Evaluating the adequacy of that member's work including the relevance and reasonableness of that member's findings or conclusions and their consistency with other audit evidence.

Consultation (Ref: Para. 18)

A21   Effective consultation on significant technical, ethical, and other matters within the firm or, where applicable, outside the firm can be achieved when those consulted:

- Are given all the relevant facts that will enable them to provide informed advice; and
- Have appropriate knowledge, seniority and experience.

A22   It may be appropriate for the engagement team to consult outside the firm, for example, where the firm lacks appropriate internal resources. They may take advantage of advisory services provided by other firms, professional and regulatory bodies, or commercial organizations that provide relevant quality control services.

Engagement Quality Control Review

Completion of the Engagement Quality Control Review before Dating of the Auditor's Report (Ref: Para. 19(c))

A23   ISA (UK and Ireland) 700 requires the auditor's report to be dated no earlier than the date on which the auditor has obtained sufficient appropriate evidence on which to base the auditor's opinion on the financial statements.[10] In cases of an audit of financial statements of listed entities or when an engagement meets the criteria for an engagement quality control review, such a review assists the auditor in determining whether sufficient appropriate evidence has been obtained.

A24   Conducting the engagement quality control review in a timely manner at appropriate stages during the engagement allows significant matters to be promptly resolved to the engagement quality control reviewer's satisfaction on or before the date of the auditor's report.

A25   Completion of the engagement quality control review means the completion by the engagement quality control reviewer of the requirements in paragraphs 20-21, and where applicable, compliance with paragraph 22. Documentation of the engagement quality control review may be completed after the date of the auditor's report as part of the assembly of the final audit file. ISA (UK and Ireland) 230 establishes requirements and provides guidance in this regard.[11]

Nature, Extent and Timing of Engagement Quality Control Review (Ref: Para. 20)

A26   Remaining alert for changes in circumstances allows the engagement partner to identify situations in which an engagement quality control review is necessary, even though at the start of the engagement, such a review was not required.

---

[10] *ISA 700, "Forming an Opinion and Reporting on Financial Statements," paragraph 41.*

The APB has not promulgated ISA 700 as issued by the IAASB for application in the UK and Ireland. In the UK and Ireland the applicable auditing standard is ISA (UK and Ireland) 700, "The Auditor's Report on Financial Statements." Paragraphs 23 and 24 of ISA (UK and Ireland) 700 establish requirements regarding dating of the auditor's report.

[11] *ISA (UK and Ireland) 230, paragraphs 14-16.*

The extent of the engagement quality control review may depend, among other things, on the complexity of the audit engagement, whether the entity is a listed entity, and the risk that the auditor's report might not be appropriate in the circumstances. The performance of an engagement quality control review does not reduce the responsibilities of the engagement partner for the audit engagement and its performance. **A27**

Engagement Quality Control Review of Listed Entities (Ref: Para. 21)

Other matters relevant to evaluating the significant judgments made by the engagement team that may be considered in an engagement quality control review of a listed entity include: **A28**

- Significant risks identified during the engagement in accordance with ISA (UK and Ireland) 315,[12]and the responses to those risks in accordance with ISA (UK and Ireland) 330,[13] including the engagement team's assessment of, and response to, the risk of fraud in accordance with ISA (UK and Ireland) 240.[14]
- Judgments made, particularly with respect to materiality and significant risks.
- The significance and disposition of corrected and uncorrected misstatements identified during the audit.
- The matters to be communicated to management and those charged with governance and, where applicable, other parties such as regulatory bodies.

These other matters, depending on the circumstances, may also be applicable for engagement quality control reviews for audits of financial statements of other entities.

Considerations Specific to Smaller Entities (Ref: Para. 20-21)

In addition to the audits of financial statements of listed entities, an engagement quality control review is required for audit engagements that meet the criteria established by the firm that subjects engagements to an engagement quality control review. In some cases, none of the firm's audit engagements may meet the criteria that would subject them to such a review. **A29**

Considerations Specific to Public Sector Entities (Ref: Para. 20-21)

In the public sector, a statutorily appointed auditor (for example, an Auditor General, or other suitably qualified person appointed on behalf of the Auditor General), may act in a role equivalent to that of engagement partner with overall responsibility for public sector audits. In such circumstances, where applicable, the selection of the engagement quality control reviewer includes consideration of the need for independence from the audited entity and the ability of the engagement quality control reviewer to provide an objective evaluation. **A30**

Listed entities as referred to in paragraphs 21 and A28 are not common in the public sector. However, there may be other public sector entities that are significant due to **A31**

---

[12] *ISA (UK and Ireland) 315, "Identifying and Assessing the Risks of Material Misstatement through Understanding the Entity and Its Environment."*

[13] *ISA (UK and Ireland) 330, "The Auditor's Responses to Assessed Risks."*

[14] *ISA (UK and Ireland) 240, "The Auditor's Responsibilities Relating to Fraud in an Audit of Financial Statements."*

size, complexity or public interest aspects, and which consequently have a wide range of stakeholders. Examples include state owned corporations and public utilities. Ongoing transformations within the public sector may also give rise to new types of significant entities. There are no fixed objective criteria on which the determination of significance is based. Nonetheless, public sector auditors evaluate which entities may be of sufficient significance to warrant performance of an engagement quality control review.

Monitoring (Ref: Para. 23)

A32   ISQC (UK and Ireland) 1 requires the firm to establish a monitoring process designed to provide it with reasonable assurance that the policies and procedures relating to the system of quality control are relevant, adequate and operating effectively.[15]

A33   In considering deficiencies that may affect the audit engagement, the engagement partner may have regard to measures the firm took to rectify the situation that the engagement partner considers are sufficient in the context of that audit.

A34   A deficiency in the firm's system of quality control does not necessarily indicate that a particular audit engagement was not performed in accordance with professional standards and applicable legal and regulatory requirements, or that the auditor's report was not appropriate.

Documentation

Documentation of Consultations (Ref: Para. 24(d))

A35   Documentation of consultations with other professionals that involve difficult or contentious matters that is sufficiently complete and detailed contributes to an understanding of:

- The issue on which consultation was sought; and
- The results of the consultation, including any decisions taken, the basis for those decisions and how they were implemented.

[15] *ISQC (UK and Ireland) 1, paragraph 48.*

International Standard on Auditing (UK and Ireland) 230
Audit Documentation

*(Effective for audits of financial statements for periods
ending on or after 15 December 2010)*[1a]

Contents

International Standard on Auditing (UK and Ireland) (ISA (UK and Ireland)) 230, "Audit Documentation" should be read in conjunction with ISA (UK and Ireland) 200, "Overall Objectives of the Independent Auditor and the Conduct of an Audit in Accordance with International Standards on Auditing (UK and Ireland)."

[1a] *Conforming amendments to this standard as a result of ISA (UK and Ireland) 610 (Revised June 2013), Using the Work of Internal Auditors, are included that are effective for audits of financial statements for periods ending on or after 15 June 2014. Details of the amendments are given in the Annexure to ISA (UK and Ireland) 610 (Revised June 2013).*

Introduction

Scope of this ISA (UK and Ireland)

1   This International Standard on Auditing (UK and Ireland) (ISA (UK and Ireland)) deals with the auditor's responsibility to prepare audit documentation for an audit of financial statements. The Appendix lists other ISAs (UK and Ireland) that contain specific documentation requirements and guidance. The specific documentation requirements of other ISAs (UK and Ireland) do not limit the application of this ISA (UK and Ireland). Law or regulation may establish additional documentation requirements.

Nature and Purposes of Audit Documentation

2   Audit documentation that meets the requirements of this ISA (UK and Ireland) and the specific documentation requirements of other relevant ISAs (UK and Ireland) provides:

(a)   Evidence of the auditor's basis for a conclusion about the achievement of the overall objectives of the auditor;[1] and

(b)   Evidence that the audit was planned and performed in accordance with ISAs (UK and Ireland) and applicable legal and regulatory requirements.

3   Audit documentation serves a number of additional purposes, including the following:

●   Assisting the engagement team to plan and perform the audit.

●   Assisting members of the engagement team responsible for supervision to direct and supervise the audit work, and to discharge their review responsibilities in accordance with ISA (UK and Ireland) 220.[2]

●   Enabling the engagement team to be accountable for its work.

●   Retaining a record of matters of continuing significance to future audits.

●   Enabling the conduct of quality control reviews and inspections in accordance with ISQC (UK and Ireland) 1[3] or national requirements that are at least as demanding.[4]

●   Enabling the conduct of external inspections in accordance with applicable legal, regulatory or other requirements.

Effective Date

4   This ISA (UK and Ireland) is effective for audits of financial statements for periods ending on or after 15 December 2010.[a]

---

[1] ISA (UK and Ireland) 200, "Overall Objectives of the Independent Auditor and the Conduct of an Audit in Accordance with International Standards on Auditing (UK and Ireland)," paragraph 11.

[2] ISA (UK and Ireland) 220, "Quality Control for an Audit of Financial Statements," paragraphs 15-17.

[3] ISQC (UK and Ireland) 1, "Quality Control for Firms that Perform Audits and Reviews of Financial Statements, and Other Assurance and Related Services Engagements," paragraphs 32-33, 35-38, and 48].

[4] ISA (UK and Ireland) 220, paragraph 2.

Objective

The objective of the auditor is to prepare documentation that provides: 5

(a) A sufficient and appropriate record of the basis for the auditor's report; and
(b) Evidence that the audit was planned and performed in accordance with ISAs (UK and Ireland) and applicable legal and regulatory requirements.

Definitions

For purposes of the ISAs (UK and Ireland), the following terms have the meanings   6 attributed below:

(a) Audit documentation – The record of audit procedures performed, relevant audit evidence obtained, and conclusions the auditor reached (terms such as "working papers" or "workpapers" are also sometimes used).
(b) Audit file – One or more folders or other storage media, in physical or electronic form, containing the records that comprise the audit documentation for a specific engagement.
(c) Experienced auditor – An individual (whether internal or external to the firm) who has practical audit experience, and a reasonable understanding of:
   (i) Audit processes;
   (ii) ISAs and applicable legal and regulatory requirements;
   (iii) The business environment in which the entity operates; and
   (iv) Auditing and financial reporting issues relevant to the entity's industry.

Requirements

Timely Preparation of Audit Documentation

The auditor shall prepare audit documentation on a timely basis. (Ref: Para. A1)   7

Documentation of the Audit Procedures Performed and Audit Evidence Obtained

Form, Content and Extent of Audit Documentation

The auditor shall prepare audit documentation that is sufficient to enable an   8 experienced auditor, having no previous connection with the audit, to understand: (Ref: Para. A2-A5, A16-A17)

(a) The nature, timing and extent of the audit procedures performed to comply with the ISAs (UK and Ireland) and applicable legal and regulatory requirements; (Ref: Para. A6-A7)
(b) The results of the audit procedures performed, and the audit evidence obtained; and
(c) Significant matters arising during the audit, the conclusions reached thereon, and significant professional judgments made in reaching those conclusions. (Ref: Para. A8-A11)

In documenting the nature, timing and extent of audit procedures performed, the   9 auditor shall record:

(a) The identifying characteristics of the specific items or matters tested; (Ref: Para. A12)

(b) Who performed the audit work and the date such work was completed; and

(c) Who reviewed the audit work performed and the date and extent of such review. (Ref: Para. A13)

10   The auditor shall document discussions of significant matters with management, those charged with governance, and others, including the nature of the significant matters discussed and when and with whom the discussions took place. (Ref: Para. A14)

11   If the auditor identified information that is inconsistent with the auditor's final conclusion regarding a significant matter, the auditor shall document how the auditor addressed the inconsistency. (Ref: Para. A15)

Departure from a Relevant Requirement

12   If, in exceptional circumstances, the auditor judges it necessary to depart from a relevant requirement in an ISA (UK and Ireland), the auditor shall document how the alternative audit procedures performed achieve the aim of that requirement, and the reasons for the departure. (Ref: Para. A18-A19)

Matters Arising after the Date of the Auditor's Report

13   If, in exceptional circumstances, the auditor performs new or additional audit procedures or draws new conclusions after the date of the auditor's report, the auditor shall document: (Ref: Para. A20)

(a) The circumstances encountered;

(b) The new or additional audit procedures performed, audit evidence obtained, and conclusions reached, and their effect on the auditor's report; and

(c) When and by whom the resulting changes to audit documentation were made and reviewed.

Assembly of the Final Audit File

14   The auditor shall assemble the audit documentation in an audit file and complete the administrative process of assembling the final audit file on a timely basis after the date of the auditor's report. (Ref: Para. A21-A22)

15   After the assembly of the final audit file has been completed, the auditor shall not delete or discard audit documentation of any nature before the end of its retention period. (Ref: Para. A23)

16   In circumstances other than those envisaged in paragraph 13 where the auditor finds it necessary to modify existing audit documentation or add new audit documentation after the assembly of the final audit file has been completed, the auditor shall, regardless of the nature of the modifications or additions, document: (Ref: Para. A24)

(a) The specific reasons for making them; and

(b) When and by whom they were made and reviewed.

***

Application and Other Explanatory Material

Timely Preparation of Audit Documentation (Ref: Para. 7)

Preparing sufficient and appropriate audit documentation on a timely basis helps to **A1** enhance the quality of the audit and facilitates the effective review and evaluation of the audit evidence obtained and conclusions reached before the auditor's report is finalized. Documentation prepared after the audit work has been performed is likely to be less accurate than documentation prepared at the time such work is performed.

Documentation of the Audit Procedures Performed and Audit Evidence Obtained

Form, Content and Extent of Audit Documentation (Ref: Para. 8)

The form, content and extent of audit documentation depend on factors such as: **A2**

- The size and complexity of the entity.
- The nature of the audit procedures to be performed.
- The identified risks of material misstatement.
- The significance of the audit evidence obtained.
- The nature and extent of exceptions identified.
- The need to document a conclusion or the basis for a conclusion not readily determinable from the documentation of the work performed or audit evidence obtained.
- The audit methodology and tools used.

Audit documentation may be recorded on paper or on electronic or other media. **A3** Examples of audit documentation include:

- Audit programs.
- Analyses.
- Issues memoranda.
- Summaries of significant matters.
- Letters of confirmation and representation.
- Checklists.
- Correspondence (including e-mail) concerning significant matters.

The auditor may include abstracts or copies of the entity's records (for example, significant and specific contracts and agreements) as part of audit documentation. Audit documentation, however, is not a substitute for the entity's accounting records.

The auditor need not include in audit documentation superseded drafts of working **A4** papers and financial statements, notes that reflect incomplete or preliminary thinking, previous copies of documents corrected for typographical or other errors, and duplicates of documents.

Oral explanations by the auditor, on their own, do not represent adequate support **A5** for the work the auditor performed or conclusions the auditor reached, but may be used to explain or clarify information contained in the audit documentation.

Documentation of Compliance with ISAs (Ref: Para. 8(a))

A6   In principle, compliance with the requirements of this ISA (UK and Ireland) will result in the audit documentation being sufficient and appropriate in the circumstances. Other ISAs (UK and Ireland) contain specific documentation requirements that are intended to clarify the application of this ISA (UK and Ireland) in the particular circumstances of those other ISAs (UK and Ireland). The specific documentation requirements of other ISAs do not limit the application of this ISA (UK and Ireland). Furthermore, the absence of a documentation requirement in any particular ISA (UK and Ireland) is not intended to suggest that there is no documentation that will be prepared as a result of complying with that ISA (UK and Ireland).

A7   Audit documentation provides evidence that the audit complies with the ISAs (UK and Ireland). However, it is neither necessary nor practicable for the auditor to document every matter considered, or professional judgment made, in an audit. Further, it is unnecessary for the auditor to document separately (as in a checklist, for example) compliance with matters for which compliance is demonstrated by documents included within the audit file. For example:

- The existence of an adequately documented audit plan demonstrates that the auditor has planned the audit.
- The existence of a signed engagement letter in the audit file demonstrates that the auditor has agreed the terms of the audit engagement with management or, where appropriate, those charged with governance.
- An auditor's report containing an appropriately qualified opinion on the financial statements demonstrates that the auditor has complied with the requirement to express a qualified opinion under the circumstances specified in the ISAs (UK and Ireland).
- In relation to requirements that apply generally throughout the audit, there may be a number of ways in which compliance with them may be demonstrated within the audit file:
  o For example, there may be no single way in which the auditor's professional skepticism is documented. But the audit documentation may nevertheless provide evidence of the auditor's exercise of professional skepticism in accordance with the ISAs (UK and Ireland). Such evidence may include specific procedures performed to corroborate management's responses to the auditor's inquiries.
  o Similarly, that the engagement partner has taken responsibility for the direction, supervision and performance of the audit in compliance with the ISAs (UK and Ireland) may be evidenced in a number of ways within the audit documentation. This may include documentation of the engagement partner's timely involvement in aspects of the audit, such as participation in the team discussions required by ISA (UK and Ireland) 315.[5]

Documentation of Significant Matters and Related Significant Professional Judgments (Ref: Para. 8(c))

A8   Judging the significance of a matter requires an objective analysis of the facts and circumstances. Examples of significant matters include:

---

[5] *ISA (UK and Ireland) 315, "Identifying and Assessing the Risks of Material Misstatement through Understanding the Entity and Its Environment," paragraph 10.*

- Matters that give rise to significant risks (as defined in ISA (UK and Ireland) 315).[6]
- Results of audit procedures indicating (a) that the financial statements could be materially misstated, or (b) a need to revise the auditor's previous assessment of the risks of material misstatement and the auditor's responses to those risks.
- Circumstances that cause the auditor significant difficulty in applying necessary audit procedures.
- Findings that could result in a modification to the audit opinion or the inclusion of an Emphasis of Matter paragraph in the auditor's report.

- Concerns about the entity's ability to continue as a going concern.

An important factor in determining the form, content and extent of audit documentation of significant matters is the extent of professional judgment exercised in performing the work and evaluating the results. Documentation of the professional judgments made, where significant, serves to explain the auditor's conclusions and to reinforce the quality of the judgment. Such matters are of particular interest to those responsible for reviewing audit documentation, including those carrying out subsequent audits when reviewing matters of continuing significance (for example, when performing a retrospective review of accounting estimates). **A9**

Some examples of circumstances in which, in accordance with paragraph 8, it is appropriate to prepare audit documentation relating to the use of professional judgment include, where the matters and judgments are significant: **A10**

- The rationale for the auditor's conclusion when a requirement provides that the auditor "shall consider" certain information or factors, and that consideration is significant in the context of the particular engagement.
- The basis for the auditor's conclusion on the reasonableness of areas of subjective judgments (for example, the reasonableness of significant accounting estimates).
- The basis for the auditor's conclusions about the authenticity of a document when further investigation (such as making appropriate use of an expert or of confirmation procedures) is undertaken in response to conditions identified during the audit that caused the auditor to believe that the document may not be authentic.

The auditor may consider it helpful to prepare and retain as part of the audit documentation a summary (sometimes known as a completion memorandum) that describes the significant matters identified during the audit and how they were addressed, or that includes cross-references to other relevant supporting audit documentation that provides such information. Such a summary may facilitate effective and efficient reviews and inspections of the audit documentation, particularly for large and complex audits. Further, the preparation of such a summary may assist the auditor's consideration of the significant matters. It may also help the auditor to consider whether, in light of the audit procedures performed and conclusions reached, there is any individual relevant ISA (UK and Ireland) objective that the auditor cannot achieve that would prevent the auditor from achieving the overall objectives of the auditor. **A11**

---

[6] *ISA (UK and Ireland) 315, paragraph 4(e).*

Identification of Specific Items or Matters Tested, and of the Preparer and Reviewer
(Ref: Para. 9)

A12   Recording the identifying characteristics serves a number of purposes. For example, it enables the engagement team to be accountable for its work and facilitates the investigation of exceptions or inconsistencies. Identifying characteristics will vary with the nature of the audit procedure and the item or matter tested. For example:

- For a detailed test of entity-generated purchase orders, the auditor may identify the documents selected for testing by their dates and unique purchase order numbers.
- For a procedure requiring selection or review of all items over a specific amount from a given population, the auditor may record the scope of the procedure and identify the population (for example, all journal entries over a specified amount from the journal register).
- For a procedure requiring systematic sampling from a population of documents, the auditor may identify the documents selected by recording their source, the starting point and the sampling interval (for example, a systematic sample of shipping reports selected from the shipping log for the period from April 1 to September 30, starting with report number 12345 and selecting every 125th report).
- For a procedure requiring inquiries of specific entity personnel, the auditor may record the dates of the inquiries and the names and job designations of the entity personnel.
- For an observation procedure, the auditor may record the process or matter being observed, the relevant individuals, their respective responsibilities, and where and when the observation was carried out.

A13   ISA (UK and Ireland) 220 requires the auditor to review the audit work performed through review of the audit documentation.[7] The requirement to document who reviewed the audit work performed does not imply a need for each specific working paper to include evidence of review. The requirement, however, means documenting what audit work was reviewed, who reviewed such work, and when it was reviewed.

Documentation of Discussions of Significant Matters with Management, Those Charged with Governance, and Others (Ref: Para. 10)

A14   The documentation is not limited to records prepared by the auditor but may include other appropriate records such as minutes of meetings prepared by the entity's personnel and agreed by the auditor. Others with whom the auditor may discuss significant matters may include other personnel within the entity, and external parties, such as persons providing professional advice to the entity.

Documentation of How Inconsistencies have been Addressed (Ref: Para. 11)

A15   The requirement to document how the auditor addressed inconsistencies in information does not imply that the auditor needs to retain documentation that is incorrect or superseded.

Considerations Specific to Smaller Entities (Ref. Para. 8)

A16   The audit documentation for the audit of a smaller entity is generally less extensive than that for the audit of a larger entity. Further, in the case of an audit where the

---

[7] *ISA (UK and Ireland) 220, paragraph 17.*

engagement partner performs all the audit work, the documentation will not include matters that might have to be documented solely to inform or instruct members of an engagement team, or to provide evidence of review by other members of the team (for example, there will be no matters to document relating to team discussions or supervision). Nevertheless, the engagement partner complies with the overriding requirement in paragraph 8 to prepare audit documentation that can be understood by an experienced auditor, as the audit documentation may be subject to review by external parties for regulatory or other purposes.

When preparing audit documentation, the auditor of a smaller entity may also find it helpful and efficient to record various aspects of the audit together in a single document, with cross-references to supporting working papers as appropriate. Examples of matters that may be documented together in the audit of a smaller entity include the understanding of the entity and its internal control, the overall audit strategy and audit plan, materiality determined in accordance with ISA (UK and Ireland) 320,[8] assessed risks, significant matters noted during the audit, and conclusions reached. **A17**

Departure from a Relevant Requirement (Ref: Para. 12)

The requirements of the ISAs (UK and Ireland) are designed to enable the auditor to achieve the objectives specified in the ISAs (UK and Ireland), and thereby the overall objectives of the auditor. Accordingly, other than in exceptional circumstances, the ISAs (UK and Ireland) call for compliance with each requirement that is relevant in the circumstances of the audit. **A18**

The documentation requirement applies only to requirements that are relevant in the circumstances. A requirement is not relevant[9] only in the cases where: **A19**

(a) The entire ISA (UK and Ireland) is not relevant (for example, if an entity does not have an internal audit function, nothing in ISA (UK and Ireland) 610 (Revised June 2013)[10] is relevant); or
(b) The requirement is conditional and the condition does not exist (for example, the requirement to modify the auditor's opinion where there is an inability to obtain sufficient appropriate audit evidence, and there is no such inability).

Matters Arising after the Date of the Auditor's Report (Ref: Para. 13)

Examples of exceptional circumstances include facts which become known to the auditor after the date of the auditor's report but which existed at that date and which, if known at that date, might have caused the financial statements to be amended or the auditor to modify the opinion in the auditor's report.[11] The resulting changes to the audit documentation are reviewed in accordance with the review responsibilities set out in ISA (UK and Ireland) 220,[12] with the engagement partner taking final responsibility for the changes. **A20**

---

[8] *ISA (UK and Ireland) 320, "Materiality in Planning and Performing an Audit."*

[9] *ISA (UK and Ireland) 200, paragraph 22.*

[10] *ISA (UK and Ireland) 610 (Revised June 2013), "Using the Work of Internal Auditors," paragraph 2.*

[11] *ISA (UK and Ireland) 560, "Subsequent Events," paragraph 14.*

[12] *ISA (UK and Ireland) 220, paragraph 16.*

Assembly of the Final Audit File (Ref: Para. 14-16)

A21   ISQC (UK and Ireland) 1 (or national requirements that are at least as demanding) requires firms to establish policies and procedures for the timely completion of the assembly of audit files.[13] An appropriate time limit within which to complete the assembly of the final audit file is ordinarily not more than 60 days after the date of the auditor's report.[14]

A22   The completion of the assembly of the final audit file after the date of the auditor's report is an administrative process that does not involve the performance of new audit procedures or the drawing of new conclusions. Changes may, however, be made to the audit documentation during the final assembly process if they are administrative in nature. Examples of such changes include:

- Deleting or discarding superseded documentation.
- Sorting, collating and cross-referencing working papers.
- Signing off on completion checklists relating to the file assembly process.
- Documenting audit evidence that the auditor has obtained, discussed and agreed with the relevant members of the engagement team before the date of the auditor's report.

A23   ISQC (UK and Ireland) 1 (or national requirements that are at least as demanding) requires firms to establish policies and procedures for the retention of engagement documentation.[15] The retention period for audit engagements ordinarily is no shorter than five years from the date of the auditor's report, or, if later, the date of the group auditor's report.[16]

A24   An example of a circumstance in which the auditor may find it necessary to modify existing audit documentation or add new audit documentation after file assembly has been completed is the need to clarify existing audit documentation arising from comments received during monitoring inspections performed by internal or external parties.

Appendix   (Ref: Para. 1)

Specific Audit Documentation Requirements in Other ISAs

This appendix identifies paragraphs in other ISAs (UK and Ireland) in effect for audits of financial statements for periods ending on or after 15 December 2010 that contain specific documentation requirements. The list is not a substitute for considering the requirements and related application and other explanatory material in ISAs.

- ISA (UK and Ireland) 210, "Agreeing the Terms of Audit Engagements" – paragraphs 10-12
- ISA (UK and Ireland) 220, "Quality Control for an Audit of Financial Statements" – paragraphs 24-25

---

[13] *ISQC (UK and Ireland) 1, paragraph 45.*

[14] *ISQC (UK and Ireland) 1, paragraph A54.*

[15] *ISQC (UK and Ireland) 1, paragraph 47.*

[16] *ISQC (UK and Ireland) 1, paragraph A61.*

In the UK and Ireland the auditor has regard to specific requirements of the auditor's relevant professional body.

- ISA (UK and Ireland) 240, "The Auditor's Responsibilities Relating to Fraud in an Audit of Financial Statements" – paragraphs 44-47
- ISA (UK and Ireland) 250, Section A "Consideration of Laws and Regulations in an Audit of Financial Statements" – paragraph 29
- ISA (UK and Ireland) 260, "Communication with Those Charged with Governance" – paragraph 23
- ISA (UK and Ireland) 300, "Planning an Audit of Financial Statements" – paragraph 12
- ISA (UK and Ireland) 315, "Identifying and Assessing the Risks of Material Misstatement through Understanding the Entity and Its Environment" – paragraph 32
- ISA (UK and Ireland) 320, "Materiality in Planning and Performing an Audit" – paragraph 14
- ISA (UK and Ireland) 330, "The Auditor's Responses to Assessed Risks" – paragraphs 28-30
- ISA (UK and Ireland) 450, "Evaluation of Misstatements Identified During the Audit" – paragraph 15
- ISA (UK and Ireland) 540, "Auditing Accounting Estimates, Including Fair Value Accounting Estimates, and Related Disclosures" – paragraph 23
- ISA (UK and Ireland) 550, "Related Parties" – paragraph 28
- ISA (UK and Ireland) 600, "Special Considerations—Audits of Group Financial Statements (Including the Work of Component Auditors)" – paragraph 50
- ISA (UK and Ireland) 610, "Using the Work of Internal Auditors" – paragraph 13

- ISA (UK and Ireland) 720, Section B "The Auditor's Statutory Reporting Responsibility in Relation to Directors' reports" – paragraph 12

International Standard on Auditing (UK and Ireland) 240

The auditor's responsibilities relating to fraud in an audit of financial statements

(Effective for audits of financial statements for periods ending on or after 15 December 2010)[1a]

Contents

[1a] Conforming amendments to this standard as a result of ISA (UK and Ireland) 610 (Revised June 2013), Using the Work of Internal Auditors, are included that are effective for audits of financial statements for periods ending on or after 15 June 2014. Details of the amendments are given in the Annexure to ISA (UK and Ireland) 610 (Revised June 2013).

International Standard on Auditing (UK and Ireland) (ISA (UK and Ireland)) 240, "The Auditor's Responsibilities Relating to Fraud in an Audit of Financial Statements" should be read in conjunction with ISA (UK and Ireland) 200, "Overall Objectives of the Independent Auditor and the Conduct of an Audit in Accordance with International Standards on Auditing (UK and Ireland)."

Introduction

Scope of this ISA (UK and Ireland)

1   This International Standard on Auditing (UK and Ireland) (ISA (UK and Ireland)) deals with the auditor's responsibilities relating to fraud in an audit of financial statements. Specifically, it expands on how ISA (UK and Ireland) 315[1] and ISA (UK and Ireland) 330[2] are to be applied in relation to risks of material misstatement due to fraud.

Characteristics of Fraud

2   Misstatements in the financial statements can arise from either fraud or error. The distinguishing factor between fraud and error is whether the underlying action that results in the misstatement of the financial statements is intentional or unintentional.

3   Although fraud is a broad legal concept, for the purposes of the ISAs (UK and Ireland), the auditor is concerned with fraud that causes a material misstatement in the financial statements. Two types of intentional misstatements are relevant to the auditor – misstatements resulting from fraudulent financial reporting and misstatements resulting from misappropriation of assets. Although ... or, in rare cases, identify the occurrence of fraud, the auditor does not make legal determinations of whether fraud has actually occurred. (Ref: Para. A1-A6)

Responsibility for the Prevention and Detection of Fraud

4   The primary responsibility for the prevention and detection of fraud rests with both those charged with governance of the entity and management. It is important that management, with the oversight of those charged with governance, place a strong emphasis on fraud prevention, which may reduce opportunities for fraud to take place, and fraud deterrence, which could persuade individuals not to commit fraud because of the likelihood of detection and punishment. This involves a commitment to creating a culture of honesty and ethical behavior which can be reinforced by an active oversight by those charged with governance. Oversight by those charged with governance includes considering the potential for override of controls or other inappropriate influence over the financial reporting process, such as efforts by management to manage earnings in order to influence the perceptions of analysts as to the entity's performance and profitability.

Responsibilities of the Auditor

5   An auditor conducting an audit in accordance with ISAs (UK and Ireland) is responsible for obtaining reasonable assurance that the financial statements taken as a whole are free from material misstatement, whether caused by fraud or error. Owing to the inherent limitations of an audit, there is an unavoidable risk that some material misstatements of the financial statements may not be detected, even though

---

[1] *ISA (UK and Ireland) 315, "Identifying and Assessing the Risks of Material Misstatement through Understanding the Entity and Its Environment."*

[2] *ISA (UK and Ireland) 330, "The Auditor's Responses to Assessed Risks."*

the audit is properly planned and performed in accordance with the ISAs (UK and Ireland).[3]

As described in ISA (UK and Ireland) 200,[4] the potential effects of inherent lim- **6** itations are particularly significant in the case of misstatement resulting from fraud. The risk of not detecting a material misstatement resulting from fraud is higher than the risk of not detecting one resulting from error. This is because fraud may involve sophisticated and carefully organized schemes designed to conceal it, such as forgery, deliberate failure to record transactions, or intentional misrepresentations being made to the auditor. Such attempts at concealment may be even more difficult to detect when accompanied by collusion. Collusion may cause the auditor to believe that audit evidence is persuasive when it is, in fact, false. The auditor's ability to detect a fraud depends on factors such as the skillfulness of the perpetrator, the frequency and extent of manipulation, the degree of collusion involved, the relative size of individual amounts manipulated, and the seniority of those individuals involved. While the auditor may be able to identify potential opportunities for fraud to be perpetrated, it is difficult for the auditor to determine whether misstatements in judgment areas such as accounting estimates are caused by fraud or error.

Furthermore, the risk of the auditor not detecting a material misstatement resulting **7** from management fraud is greater than for employee fraud, because management is frequently in a position to directly or indirectly manipulate accounting records, present fraudulent financial information or override control procedures designed to prevent similar frauds by other employees.

When obtaining reasonable assurance, the auditor is responsible for maintaining **8** professional skepticism throughout the audit, considering the potential for management override of controls and recognizing the fact that audit procedures that are effective for detecting error may not be effective in detecting fraud. The requirements in this ISA (UK and Ireland) are designed to assist the auditor in identifying and assessing the risks of material misstatement due to fraud and in designing procedures to detect such misstatement.

Effective Date

This ISA (UK and Ireland) is effective for audits of financial statements for periods **9** ending on or after 15 December 2010.[1a]

Objectives

The objectives of the auditor are: **10**

(a) To identify and assess the risks of material misstatement of the financial statements due to fraud;
(b) To obtain sufficient appropriate audit evidence regarding the assessed risks of material misstatement due to fraud, through designing and implementing appropriate responses; and
(c) To respond appropriately to fraud or suspected fraud identified during the audit.

---

[3] *ISA (UK and Ireland) 200, "Overall Objectives of the Independent Auditor and the Conduct of an Audit in Accordance with International Standards on Auditing (UK and Ireland)," paragraphs A51-A52.*

[4] *ISA (UK and Ireland) 200, paragraph A51.*

Definitions

11 For purposes of the ISAs (UK and Ireland), the following terms have the meanings attributed below:

(a) Fraud – An intentional act by one or more individuals among management, those charged with governance, employees, or third parties, involving the use of deception to obtain an unjust or illegal advantage.

(b) Fraud risk factors – Events or conditions that indicate an incentive or pressure to commit fraud or provide an opportunity to commit fraud.

Requirements

Professional Skepticism

12 In accordance with ISA (UK and Ireland) 200, the auditor shall maintain professional skepticism throughout the audit, recognizing the possibility that a material misstatement due to fraud could exist, notwithstanding the auditor's past experience of the honesty and integrity of the entity's management and those charged with governance. (Ref: Para. A7- A8)

13 Unless the auditor has reason to believe the contrary, the auditor may accept records and documents as genuine. If conditions identified during the audit cause the auditor to believe that a document may not be authentic or that terms in a document have been modified but not disclosed to the auditor, the auditor shall investigate further. (Ref: Para. A9)

14 Where responses to inquiries of management or those charged with governance are inconsistent, the auditor shall investigate the inconsistencies.

Discussion among the Engagement Team

15 ISA (UK and Ireland) 315 requires a discussion among the engagement team members and a determination by the engagement partner of which matters are to be communicated to those team members not involved in the discussion.[5] This discussion shall place particular emphasis on how and where the entity's financial statements may be susceptible to material misstatement due to fraud, including how fraud might occur. The discussion shall occur setting aside beliefs that the engagement team members may have that management and those charged with governance are honest and have integrity. (Ref: Para. A10-A11)

Risk Assessment Procedures and Related Activities

16 When performing risk assessment procedures and related activities to obtain an understanding of the entity and its environment, including the entity's internal control, required by ISA (UK and Ireland) 315,[6] the auditor shall perform the procedures in paragraphs 17-24 to obtain information for use in identifying the risks of material misstatement due to fraud.

[5] *ISA (UK and Ireland) 315, paragraph 10.*

[6] *ISA (UK and Ireland) 315, paragraphs 5-24.*

Management and Others within the Entity

The auditor shall make inquiries of management regarding: **17**

(a) Management's assessment of the risk that the financial statements may be materially misstated due to fraud, including the nature, extent and frequency of such assessments; (Ref: Para. A12-A13)
(b) Management's process for identifying and responding to the risks of fraud in the entity, including any specific risks of fraud that management has identified or that have been brought to its attention, or classes of transactions, account balances, or disclosures for which a risk of fraud is likely to exist; (Ref: Para. A14)
(c) Management's communication, if any, to those charged with governance regarding its processes for identifying and responding to the risks of fraud in the entity; and
(d) Management's communication, if any, to employees regarding its views on business practices and ethical behavior.

The auditor shall make inquiries of management, and others within the entity as   **18**
appropriate, to determine whether they have knowledge of any actual, suspected or alleged fraud affecting the entity. (Ref: Para. A15-A17)

For those entities that have an internal audit function, the auditor shall make   **19**
inquiries of appropriate individuals within the function to determine whether they have knowledge of any actual, suspected or alleged fraud affecting the entity, and to obtain its views about the risks of fraud. (Ref: Para. A18)

Those Charged with Governance

Unless all of those charged with governance are involved in managing the entity,[7] the   **20**
auditor shall obtain an understanding of how those charged with governance exercise oversight of management's processes for identifying and responding to the risks of fraud in the entity and the internal control that management has established to mitigate these risks. (Ref: Para. A19-A21)

Unless all of those charged with governance are involved in managing the entity, the   **21**
auditor shall make inquiries of those charged with governance to determine whether they have knowledge of any actual, suspected or alleged fraud affecting the entity. These inquiries are made in part to corroborate the responses to the inquiries of management.

Unusual or Unexpected Relationships Identified

The auditor shall evaluate whether unusual or unexpected relationships that have   **22**
been identified in performing analytical procedures, including those related to revenue accounts, may indicate risks of material misstatement due to fraud.

Other Information

The auditor shall consider whether other information obtained by the auditor   **23**
indicates risks of material misstatement due to fraud. (Ref: Para. A22)

---

[7] *ISA (UK and Ireland) 260, "Communication with Those Charged with Governance," paragraph 13.*

Evaluation of Fraud Risk Factors

24   The auditor shall evaluate whether the information obtained from the other risk assessment procedures and related activities performed indicates that one or more fraud risk factors are present. While fraud risk factors may not necessarily indicate the existence of fraud, they have often been present in circumstances where frauds have occurred and therefore may indicate risks of material misstatement due to fraud. (Ref: Para. A23-A27)

Identification and Assessment of the Risks of Material Misstatement Due to Fraud

25   In accordance with ISA (UK and Ireland) 315, the auditor shall identify and assess the risks of material misstatement due to fraud at the financial statement level, and at the assertion level for classes of transactions, account balances and disclosures.[8]

26   When identifying and assessing the risks of material misstatement due to fraud, the auditor shall, based on a presumption that there are risks of fraud in revenue recognition, evaluate which types of revenue, revenue transactions or assertions give rise to such risks. Paragraph 47 specifies the documentation required where the auditor concludes that the presumption is not applicable in the circumstances of the engagement and, accordingly, has not identified revenue recognition as a risk of material misstatement due to fraud. (Ref: Para. A28-A30)

27   The auditor shall treat those assessed risks of material misstatement due to fraud as significant risks and accordingly, to the extent not already done so, the auditor shall obtain an understanding of the entity's related controls, including control activities, relevant to such risks. (Ref: Para. A31-A32)

Responses to the Assessed Risks of Material Misstatement Due to Fraud

Overall Responses

28   In accordance with ISA (UK and Ireland) 330, the auditor shall determine overall responses to address the assessed risks of material misstatement due to fraud at the financial statement level.[9] (Ref: Para. A33)

29   In determining overall responses to address the assessed risks of material misstatement due to fraud at the financial statement level, the auditor shall:

   (a) Assign and supervise personnel taking account of the knowledge, skill and ability of the individuals to be given significant engagement responsibilities and the auditor's assessment of the risks of material misstatement due to fraud for the engagement; (Ref: Para. A34-A35)

   (b) Evaluate whether the selection and application of accounting policies by the entity, particularly those related to subjective measurements and complex transactions, may be indicative of fraudulent financial reporting resulting from management's effort to manage earnings; and

   (c) Incorporate an element of unpredictability in the selection of the nature, timing and extent of audit procedures. (Ref: Para. A36)

[8] *ISA (UK and Ireland) 315, paragraph 25.*

[9] *ISA (UK and Ireland) 330, paragraph 5.*

Audit Procedures Responsive to Assessed Risks of Material Misstatement Due to Fraud at the Assertion Level

In accordance with ISA (UK and Ireland) 330, the auditor shall design and perform further audit procedures whose nature, timing and extent are responsive to the assessed risks of material misstatement due to fraud at the assertion level.[10] (Ref: Para. A37-A40)   **30**

Audit Procedures Responsive to Risks Related to Management Override of Controls

Management is in a unique position to perpetrate fraud because of management's ability to manipulate accounting records and prepare fraudulent financial statements by overriding controls that otherwise appear to be operating effectively. Although the level of risk of management override of controls will vary from entity to entity, the risk is nevertheless present in all entities. Due to the unpredictable way in which such override could occur, it is a risk of material misstatement due to fraud and thus a significant risk.   **31**

Irrespective of the auditor's assessment of the risks of management override of controls, the auditor shall design and perform audit procedures to: **32**

(a) Test the appropriateness of journal entries recorded in the general ledger and other adjustments made in the preparation of the financial statements. In designing and performing audit procedures for such tests, the auditor shall:
   (i) Make inquiries of individuals involved in the financial reporting process about inappropriate or unusual activity relating to the processing of journal entries and other adjustments;
   (ii) Select journal entries and other adjustments made at the end of a reporting period; and
   (iii) Consider the need to test journal entries and other adjustments throughout the period. (Ref: Para. A41-A44)
(b) Review accounting estimates for biases and evaluate whether the circumstances producing the bias, if any, represent a risk of material misstatement due to fraud. In performing this review, the auditor shall:
   (i) Evaluate whether the judgments and decisions made by management in making the accounting estimates included in the financial statements, even if they are individually reasonable, indicate a possible bias on the part of the entity's management that may represent a risk of material misstatement due to fraud. If so, the auditor shall reevaluate the accounting estimates taken as a whole; and
   (ii) Perform a retrospective review of management judgments and assumptions related to significant accounting estimates reflected in the financial statements of the prior year. (Ref: Para. A45-A47)
(c) For significant transactions that are outside the normal course of business for the entity, or that otherwise appear to be unusual given the auditor's understanding of the entity and its environment and other information obtained during the audit, the auditor shall evaluate whether the business rationale (or the lack thereof) of the transactions suggests that they may have been entered into to engage in fraudulent financial reporting or to conceal misappropriation of assets. (Ref: Para. A48)

The auditor shall determine whether, in order to respond to the identified risks of management override of controls, the auditor needs to perform other audit procedures in addition to those specifically referred to above (that is, where there are   **33**

---

[10] *ISA (UK and Ireland) 330, paragraph 6.*

specific additional risks of management override that are not covered as part of the procedures performed to address the requirements in paragraph 32).

Evaluation of Audit Evidence (Ref: Para. A49)

34   The auditor shall evaluate whether analytical procedures that are performed near the end of the audit, when forming an overall conclusion as to whether the financial statements are consistent with the auditor's understanding of the entity, indicate a previously unrecognized risk of material misstatement due to fraud. (Ref: Para. A50)

35   If the auditor identifies a misstatement, the auditor shall evaluate whether such a misstatement is indicative of fraud. If there is such an indication, the auditor shall evaluate the implications of the misstatement in relation to other aspects of the audit, particularly the reliability of management representations, recognizing that an instance of fraud is unlikely to be an isolated occurrence. (Ref: Para. A51)

36   If the auditor identifies a misstatement, whether material or not, and the auditor has reason to believe that it is or may be the result of fraud and that management (in particular, senior management) is involved, the auditor shall reevaluate the assessment of the risks of material misstatement due to fraud and its resulting impact on the nature, timing and extent of audit procedures to respond to the assessed risks. The auditor shall also consider whether circumstances or conditions indicate possible collusion involving employees, management or third parties when reconsidering the reliability of evidence previously obtained. (Ref: Para. A52)

37   If the auditor confirms that, or is unable to conclude whether, the financial statements are materially misstated as a result of fraud the auditor shall evaluate the implications for the audit. (Ref: Para. A53)

Auditor Unable to Continue the Engagement

38   If, as a result of a misstatement resulting from fraud or suspected fraud, the auditor encounters exceptional circumstances that bring into question the auditor's ability to continue performing the audit, the auditor shall:

   (a) Determine the professional and legal responsibilities applicable in the circumstances, including whether there is a requirement for the auditor to report to the person or persons who made the audit appointment or, in some cases, to regulatory authorities;
   (b) Consider whether it is appropriate to withdraw from the engagement, where withdrawal is possible under applicable law or regulation; and
   (c) If the auditor withdraws:
      (i)   Discuss with the appropriate level of management and those charged with governance the auditor's withdrawal from the engagement and the reasons for the withdrawal; and
      (ii) Determine whether there is a professional or legal requirement to report to the person or persons who made the audit appointment or, in some cases, to regulatory authorities, the auditor's withdrawal from the engagement and the reasons for the withdrawal. (Ref: Para. A54-A57)

Written Representations

39   The auditor shall obtain written representations from management and, where appropriate, those charged with governance that:

(a) They acknowledge their responsibility for the design, implementation and maintenance of internal control to prevent and detect fraud;

(b) They have disclosed to the auditor the results of management's assessment of the risk that the financial statements may be materially misstated as a result of fraud;

(c) They have disclosed to the auditor their knowledge of fraud or suspected fraud affecting the entity involving:
   (i) Management;
   (ii) Employees who have significant roles in internal control; or
   (iii) Others where the fraud could have a material effect on the financial statements; and

(d) They have disclosed to the auditor their knowledge of any allegations of fraud, or suspected fraud, affecting the entity's financial statements communicated by employees, former employees, analysts, regulators or others. (Ref: Para. A58-A59)

Communications to Management and with Those Charged with Governance

If the auditor has identified a fraud or has obtained information that indicates that a **40** fraud may exist, the auditor shall communicate these matters on a timely basis to the appropriate level of management in order to inform those with primary responsibility for the prevention and detection of fraud of matters relevant to their responsibilities. (Ref: Para. A60)

Unless all of those charged with governance are involved in managing the entity, if **41** the auditor has identified or suspects fraud involving:

(a) management;
(b) employees who have significant roles in internal control; or
(c) others where the fraud results in a material misstatement in the financial statements,

the auditor shall communicate these matters to those charged with governance on a timely basis. If the auditor suspects fraud involving management, the auditor shall communicate these suspicions to those charged with governance and discuss with them the nature, timing and extent of audit procedures necessary to complete the audit. (Ref: Para. A61-A63)

The auditor shall communicate with those charged with governance any other **42** matters related to fraud that are, in the auditor's judgment, relevant to their responsibilities. (Ref: Para. A64)

Communications to Regulatory and Enforcement Authorities

If the auditor has identified or suspects a fraud, the auditor shall determine whether **43** there is a responsibility to report the occurrence or suspicion to a party outside the entity. Although the auditor's professional duty to maintain the confidentiality of client information may preclude such reporting, the auditor's legal responsibilities may override the duty of confidentiality in some circumstances. (Ref: Para. A65-A67)

Documentation

44   The auditor shall include the following in the audit documentation[11] of the auditor's understanding of the entity and its environment and the assessment of the risks of material misstatement required by ISA (UK and Ireland) 315:[12]

    (a)   The significant decisions reached during the discussion among the engagement team regarding the susceptibility of the entity's financial statements to material misstatement due to fraud; and

    (b)   The identified and assessed risks of material misstatement due to fraud at the financial statement level and at the assertion level.

45   The auditor shall include the following in the audit documentation of the auditor's responses to the assessed risks of material misstatement required by ISA (UK and Ireland) 330:[13]

    (a)   The overall responses to the assessed risks of material misstatement due to fraud at the financial statement level and the nature, timing and extent of audit procedures, and the linkage of those procedures with the assessed risks of material misstatement due to fraud at the assertion level; and

    (b)   The results of the audit procedures, including those designed to address the risk of management override of controls.

46   The auditor shall include in the audit documentation communications about fraud made to management, those charged with governance, regulators and others.

47   If the auditor has concluded that the presumption that there is a risk of material misstatement due to fraud related to revenue recognition is not applicable in the circumstances of the engagement, the auditor shall include in the audit documentation the reasons for that conclusion.

***

Application and Other Explanatory Material

Characteristics of Fraud (Ref: Para. 3)

A1   Fraud, whether fraudulent financial reporting or misappropriation of assets, involves incentive or pressure to commit fraud, a perceived opportunity to do so and some rationalization of the act. For example:

    •   Incentive or pressure to commit fraudulent financial reporting may exist when management is under pressure, from sources outside or inside the entity, to achieve an expected (and perhaps unrealistic) earnings target or financial outcome – particularly since the consequences to management for failing to meet financial goals can be significant. Similarly, individuals may have an incentive to misappropriate assets, for example, because the individuals are living beyond their means.

---

[11] *ISA (UK and Ireland) 230, "Audit Documentation," paragraphs 8-11, and paragraph A6.*

[12] *ISA (UK and Ireland) 315, paragraph 32.*

[13] *ISA (UK and Ireland) 330, paragraph 28.*

- A perceived opportunity to commit fraud may exist when an individual believes internal control can be overridden, for example, because the individual is in a position of trust or has knowledge of specific deficiencies in internal control.
- Individuals may be able to rationalize committing a fraudulent act. Some individuals possess an attitude, character or set of ethical values that allow them knowingly and intentionally to commit a dishonest act. However, even otherwise honest individuals can commit fraud in an environment that imposes sufficient pressure on them.

Fraudulent financial reporting involves intentional misstatements including omissions of amounts or disclosures in financial statements to deceive financial statement users. It can be caused by the efforts of management to manage earnings in order to deceive financial statement users by influencing their perceptions as to the entity's performance and profitability. Such earnings management may start out with small actions or inappropriate adjustment of assumptions and changes in judgments by management. Pressures and incentives may lead these actions to increase to the extent that they result in fraudulent financial reporting. Such a situation could occur when, due to pressures to meet market expectations or a desire to maximize compensation based on performance, management intentionally takes positions that lead to fraudulent financial reporting by materially misstating the financial statements. In some entities, management may be motivated to reduce earnings by a material amount to minimize tax or to inflate earnings to secure bank financing. **A2**

Fraudulent financial reporting may be accomplished by the following: **A3**

- Manipulation, falsification (including forgery), or alteration of accounting records or supporting documentation from which the financial statements are prepared.
- Misrepresentation in, or intentional omission from, the financial statements of events, transactions or other significant information.
- Intentional misapplication of accounting principles relating to amounts, classification, manner of presentation, or disclosure.

Fraudulent financial reporting often involves management override of controls that otherwise may appear to be operating effectively. Fraud can be committed by management overriding controls using such techniques as: **A4**

- Recording fictitious journal entries, particularly close to the end of an accounting period, to manipulate operating results or achieve other objectives.
- Inappropriately adjusting assumptions and changing judgments used to estimate account balances.
- Omitting, advancing or delaying recognition in the financial statements of events and transactions that have occurred during the reporting period.
- Concealing, or not disclosing, facts that could affect the amounts recorded in the financial statements.
- Engaging in complex transactions that are structured to misrepresent the financial position or financial performance of the entity.
- Altering records and terms related to significant and unusual transactions.

Misappropriation of assets involves the theft of an entity's assets and is often perpetrated by employees in relatively small and immaterial amounts. However, it can also involve management who are usually more able to disguise or conceal misappropriations in ways that are difficult to detect. Misappropriation of assets can be accomplished in a variety of ways including: **A5**

- Embezzling receipts (for example, misappropriating collections on accounts receivable or diverting receipts in respect of written-off accounts to personal bank accounts).
- Stealing physical assets or intellectual property (for example, stealing inventory for personal use or for sale, stealing scrap for resale, colluding with a competitor by disclosing technological data in return for payment).
- Causing an entity to pay for goods and services not received (for example, payments to fictitious vendors, kickbacks paid by vendors to the entity's purchasing agents in return for inflating prices, payments to fictitious employees).
- Using an entity's assets for personal use (for example, using the entity's assets as collateral for a personal loan or a loan to a related party).

Misappropriation of assets is often accompanied by false or misleading records or documents in order to conceal the fact that the assets are missing or have been pledged without proper authorization.

Considerations Specific to Public Sector Entities

A6   The public sector auditor's responsibilities relating to fraud may be a result of law, regulation or other authority applicable to public sector entities or separately covered by the auditor's mandate. Consequently, the public sector auditor's responsibilities may not be limited to consideration of risks of material misstatement of the financial statements, but may also include a broader responsibility to consider risks of fraud.

Professional Skepticism (Ref: Para. 12-14)

A7   Maintaining professional skepticism requires an ongoing questioning of whether the information and audit evidence obtained suggests that a material misstatement due to fraud may exist. It includes considering the reliability of the information to be used as audit evidence and the controls over its preparation and maintenance where relevant. Due to the characteristics of fraud, the auditor's professional skepticism is particularly important when considering the risks of material misstatement due to fraud.

A8   Although the auditor cannot be expected to disregard past experience of the honesty and integrity of the entity's management and those charged with governance, the auditor's professional skepticism is particularly important in considering the risks of material misstatement due to fraud because there may have been changes in circumstances.

A9   An audit performed in accordance with ISAs (UK and Ireland) rarely involves the authentication of documents, nor is the auditor trained as or expected to be an expert in such authentication.[14] However, when the auditor identifies conditions that cause the auditor to believe that a document may not be authentic or that terms in a document have been modified but not disclosed to the auditor, possible procedures to investigate further may include:

- Confirming directly with the third party.
- Using the work of an expert to assess the document's authenticity.

---

[14] *ISA (UK and Ireland) 200, paragraph A47.*

Discussion among the Engagement Team (Ref: Para. 15)

Discussing the susceptibility of the entity's financial statements to material mis-   **A10**
statement due to fraud with the engagement team:

- Provides an opportunity for more experienced engagement team members to share their insights about how and where the financial statements may be susceptible to material misstatement due to fraud.
- Enables the auditor to consider an appropriate response to such susceptibility and to determine which members of the engagement team will conduct certain audit procedures.
- Permits the auditor to determine how the results of audit procedures will be shared among the engagement team and how to deal with any allegations of fraud that may come to the auditor's attention.

The discussion may include such matters as: **A11**

- An exchange of ideas among engagement team members about how and where they believe the entity's financial statements may be susceptible to material misstatement due to fraud, how management could perpetrate and conceal fraudulent financial reporting, and how assets of the entity could be misappropriated.
- A consideration of circumstances that might be indicative of earnings management and the practices that might be followed by management to manage earnings that could lead to fraudulent financial reporting.
- A consideration of the known external and internal factors affecting the entity that may create an incentive or pressure for management or others to commit fraud, provide the opportunity for fraud to be perpetrated, and indicate a culture or environment that enables management or others to rationalize committing fraud.
- A consideration of management's involvement in overseeing employees with access to cash or other assets susceptible to misappropriation.
- A consideration of any unusual or unexplained changes in behavior or lifestyle of management or employees which have come to the attention of the engagement team.
- An emphasis on the importance of maintaining a proper state of mind throughout the audit regarding the potential for material misstatement due to fraud.
- A consideration of the types of circumstances that, if encountered, might indicate the possibility of fraud.
- A consideration of how an element of unpredictability will be incorporated into the nature, timing and extent of the audit procedures to be performed.
- A consideration of the audit procedures that might be selected to respond to the susceptibility of the entity's financial statement to material misstatement due to fraud and whether certain types of audit procedures are more effective than others.
- A consideration of any allegations of fraud that have come to the auditor's attention.
- A consideration of the risk of management override of controls.

Risk Assessment Procedures and Related Activities

Inquiries of Management

Management's Assessment of the Risk of Material Misstatement Due to Fraud (Ref: Para. 17(a))

A12 Management[14a] accepts responsibility for the entity's internal control and for the preparation of the entity's financial statements. Accordingly, it is appropriate for the auditor to make inquiries of management regarding management's own assessment of the risk of fraud and the controls in place to prevent and detect it. The nature, extent and frequency of management's assessment of such risk and controls may vary from entity to entity. In some entities, management may make detailed assessments on an annual basis or as part of continuous monitoring. In other entities, management's assessment may be less structured and less frequent. The nature, extent and frequency of management's assessment are relevant to the auditor's understanding of the entity's control environment. For example, the fact that management has not made an assessment of the risk of fraud may in some circumstances be indicative of the lack of importance that management places on internal control.

Considerations specific to smaller entities

A13 In some entities, particularly smaller entities, the focus of management's assessment may be on the risks of employee fraud or misappropriation of assets.

Management's Process for Identifying and Responding to the Risks of Fraud (Ref: Para. 17(b))

A14 In the case of entities with multiple locations management's processes may include different levels of monitoring of operating locations, or business segments. Management may also have identified particular operating locations or business segments for which a risk of fraud may be more likely to exist.

Inquiry of Management and Others within the Entity (Ref: Para. 18)

A15 The auditor's inquiries of management may provide useful information concerning the risks of material misstatements in the financial statements resulting from employee fraud. However, such inquiries are unlikely to provide useful information regarding the risks of material misstatement in the financial statements resulting from management fraud. Making inquiries of others within the entity may provide individuals with an opportunity to convey information to the auditor that may not otherwise be communicated.

A16 Examples of others within the entity to whom the auditor may direct inquiries about the existence or suspicion of fraud include:

- Operating personnel not directly involved in the financial reporting process.
- Employees with different levels of authority.
- Employees involved in initiating, processing or recording complex or unusual transactions and those who supervise or monitor such employees.
- In-house legal counsel.
- Chief ethics officer or equivalent person.

[14a] *In the UK and Ireland those charged with governance are responsible for the preparation of the financial statements.*

- The person or persons charged with dealing with allegations of fraud.

Management is often in the best position to perpetrate fraud. Accordingly, when   **A17**
evaluating management's responses to inquiries with an attitude of professional
skepticism, the auditor may judge it necessary to corroborate responses to inquiries
with other information.

Inquiries of the Internal Audit Function (Ref: Para. 19)

ISA (UK and Ireland) 315 (Revised June 2013) and ISA (UK and Ireland) 610   **A18**
(Revised June 2013) establish requirements and provide guidance relevant to audits
of those entities that have an internal audit function.[15] In carrying out the requirements of those ISAs (UK and Ireland) in the context of fraud, the auditor may
inquire about specific activities of the function including, for example:

- The procedures performed, if any, by the internal audit function during the year
  to detect fraud.
- Whether management has satisfactorily responded to any findings resulting
  from those procedures.

Obtaining an Understanding of Oversight Exercised by Those Charged with
Governance (Ref: Para. 20)

Those charged with governance of an entity oversee the entity's systems for mon-   **A19**
itoring risk, financial control and compliance with the law. In many countries,
corporate governance practices are well developed and those charged with governance play an active role in oversight of the entity's assessment of the risks of fraud
and of the relevant internal control. Since the responsibilities of those charged with
governance and management may vary by entity and by country, it is important that
the auditor understands their respective responsibilities to enable the auditor to
obtain an understanding of the oversight exercised by the appropriate individuals.[16]

An understanding of the oversight exercised by those charged with governance may   **A20**
provide insights regarding the susceptibility of the entity to management fraud, the
adequacy of internal control over risks of fraud, and the competency and integrity of
management. The auditor may obtain this understanding in a number of ways, such
as by attending meetings where such discussions take place, reading the minutes from
such meetings or making inquiries of those charged with governance.

Considerations Specific to Smaller Entities

In some cases, all of those charged with governance are involved in managing the   **A21**
entity. This may be the case in a small entity where a single owner manages the entity
and no one else has a governance role. In these cases, there is ordinarily no action on
the part of the auditor because there is no oversight separate from management.

---

[15] *ISA (UK and Ireland) 315 (Revised June 2013), paragraphs 6(a) and 23, and ISA (UK and Ireland) 610*
(Revised June 2013), Using the Work of Internal Auditors.

[16] *ISA (UK and Ireland) 260, paragraphs A1-A8, discuss with whom the auditor communicates when the entity's*
governance structure is not well defined.

Consideration of Other Information (Ref: Para. 23)

A22   In addition to information obtained from applying analytical procedures, other information obtained about the entity and its environment may be helpful in identifying the risks of material misstatement due to fraud. The discussion among team members may provide information that is helpful in identifying such risks. In addition, information obtained from the auditor's client acceptance and retention processes, and experience gained on other engagements performed for the entity, for example engagements to review interim financial information, may be relevant in the identification of the risks of material misstatement due to fraud.

Evaluation of Fraud Risk Factors (Ref: Para. 24)

A23   The fact that fraud is usually concealed can make it very difficult to detect. Nevertheless, the auditor may identify events or conditions that indicate an incentive or pressure to commit fraud or provide an opportunity to commit fraud (fraud risk factors). For example:

- The need to meet expectations of third parties to obtain additional equity financing may create pressure to commit fraud;
- The granting of significant bonuses if unrealistic profit targets are met may create an incentive to commit fraud; and
- A control environment that is not effective may create an opportunity to commit fraud.

A24   Fraud risk factors cannot easily be ranked in order of importance. The significance of fraud risk factors varies widely. Some of these factors will be present in entities where the specific conditions do not present risks of material misstatement. Accordingly, the determination of whether a fraud risk factor is present and whether it is to be considered in assessing the risks of material misstatement of the financial statements due to fraud requires the exercise of professional judgment.

A25   Examples of fraud risk factors related to fraudulent financial reporting and misappropriation of assets are presented in Appendix 1. These illustrative risk factors are classified based on the three conditions that are generally present when fraud exists:

- An incentive or pressure to commit fraud;
- A perceived opportunity to commit fraud; and
- An ability to rationalize the fraudulent action.

Risk factors reflective of an attitude that permits rationalization of the fraudulent action may not be susceptible to observation by the auditor. Nevertheless, the auditor may become aware of the existence of such information. Although the fraud risk factors described in Appendix 1 cover a broad range of situations that may be faced by auditors, they are only examples and other risk factors may exist.

A26   The size, complexity, and ownership characteristics of the entity have a significant influence on the consideration of relevant fraud risk factors. For example, in the case of a large entity, there may be factors that generally constrain improper conduct by management, such as:

- Effective oversight by those charged with governance.
- An effective internal audit function.
- The existence and enforcement of a written code of conduct.

Furthermore, fraud risk factors considered at a business segment operating level may provide different insights when compared with those obtained when considered at an entity-wide level.

Considerations Specific to Smaller Entities

In the case of a small entity, some or all of these considerations may be inapplicable or less relevant. For example, a smaller entity may not have a written code of conduct but, instead, may have developed a culture that emphasizes the importance of integrity and ethical behavior through oral communication and by management example. Domination of management by a single individual in a small entity does not generally, in and of itself, indicate a failure by management to display and communicate an appropriate attitude regarding internal control and the financial reporting process. In some entities, the need for management authorization can compensate for otherwise deficient controls and reduce the risk of employee fraud. However, domination of management by a single individual can be a potential deficiency in internal control since there is an opportunity for management override of controls.

A27

Identification and Assessment of the Risks of Material Misstatement Due to Fraud

Risks of Fraud in Revenue Recognition (Ref: Para. 26)

Material misstatement due to fraudulent financial reporting relating to revenue recognition often results from an overstatement of revenues through, for example, premature revenue recognition or recording fictitious revenues. It may result also from an understatement of revenues through, for example, improperly shifting revenues to a later period.

A28

The risks of fraud in revenue recognition may be greater in some entities than others. For example, there may be pressures or incentives on management to commit fraudulent financial reporting through inappropriate revenue recognition in the case of listed entities when, for example, performance is measured in terms of year-over-year revenue growth or profit. Similarly, for example, there may be greater risks of fraud in revenue recognition in the case of entities that generate a substantial portion of revenues through cash sales.

A29

The presumption that there are risks of fraud in revenue recognition may be rebutted. For example, the auditor may conclude that there is no risk of material misstatement due to fraud relating to revenue recognition in the case where a there is a single type of simple revenue transaction, for example, leasehold revenue from a single unit rental property.

A30

Identifying and Assessing the Risks of Material Misstatement Due to Fraud and Understanding the Entity's Related Controls (Ref: Para. 27)

Management may make judgments on the nature and extent of the controls it chooses to implement, and the nature and extent of the risks it chooses to assume.[17] In determining which controls to implement to prevent and detect fraud, management considers the risks that the financial statements may be materially misstated as a result of fraud. As part of this consideration, management may conclude that it is

A31

---

[17] *ISA (UK and Ireland) 315, paragraph A48.*

not cost effective to implement and maintain a particular control in relation to the reduction in the risks of material misstatement due to fraud to be achieved.

A32   It is therefore important for the auditor to obtain an understanding of the controls that management has designed, implemented and maintained to prevent and detect fraud. In doing so, the auditor may learn, for example, that management has consciously chosen to accept the risks associated with a lack of segregation of duties. Information from obtaining this understanding may also be useful in identifying fraud risks factors that may affect the auditor's assessment of the risks that the financial statements may contain material misstatement due to fraud.

Responses to the Assessed Risks of Material Misstatement Due to Fraud

Overall Responses (Ref: Para. 28)

A33   Determining overall responses to address the assessed risks of material misstatement due to fraud generally includes the consideration of how the overall conduct of the audit can reflect increased professional skepticism, for example, through:

- Increased sensitivity in the selection of the nature and extent of documentation to be examined in support of material transactions.
- Increased recognition of the need to corroborate management explanations or representations concerning material matters.

It also involves more general considerations apart from the specific procedures otherwise planned; these considerations include the matters listed in paragraph 29, which are discussed below.

Assignment and Supervision of Personnel (Ref: Para. 29(a))

A34   The auditor may respond to identified risks of material misstatement due to fraud by, for example, assigning additional individuals with specialized skill and knowledge, such as forensic and IT experts, or by assigning more experienced individuals to the engagement.

A35   The extent of supervision reflects the auditor's assessment of risks of material misstatement due to fraud and the competencies of the engagement team members performing the work.

Unpredictability in the Selection of Audit Procedures (Ref: Para. 29(c))

A36   Incorporating an element of unpredictability in the selection of the nature, timing and extent of audit procedures to be performed is important as individuals within the entity who are familiar with the audit procedures normally performed on engagements may be more able to conceal fraudulent financial reporting. This can be achieved by, for example:

- Performing substantive procedures on selected account balances and assertions not otherwise tested due to their materiality or risk.
- Adjusting the timing of audit procedures from that otherwise expected.
- Using different sampling methods.
- Performing audit procedures at different locations or at locations on an unannounced basis.

Audit Procedures Responsive to Assessed Risks of Material Misstatement Due to Fraud at the Assertion Level (Ref: Para. 30)

The auditor's responses to address the assessed risks of material misstatement due to fraud at the assertion level may include changing the nature, timing and extent of audit procedures in the following ways: **A37**

- The nature of audit procedures to be performed may need to be changed to obtain audit evidence that is more reliable and relevant or to obtain additional corroborative information. This may affect both the type of audit procedures to be performed and their combination. For example:
  - Physical observation or inspection of certain assets may become more important or the auditor may choose to use computer-assisted audit techniques to gather more evidence about data contained in significant accounts or electronic transaction files.
  - The auditor may design procedures to obtain additional corroborative information. For example, if the auditor identifies that management is under pressure to meet earnings expectations, there may be a related risk that management is inflating sales by entering into sales agreements that include terms that preclude revenue recognition or by invoicing sales before delivery. In these circumstances, the auditor may, for example, design external confirmations not only to confirm outstanding amounts, but also to confirm the details of the sales agreements, including date, any rights of return and delivery terms. In addition, the auditor might find it effective to supplement such external confirmations with inquiries of non-financial personnel in the entity regarding any changes in sales agreements and delivery terms.
- The timing of substantive procedures may need to be modified. The auditor may conclude that performing substantive testing at or near the period end better addresses an assessed risk of material misstatement due to fraud. The auditor may conclude that, given the assessed risks of intentional misstatement or manipulation, audit procedures to extend audit conclusions from an interim date to the period end would not be effective. In contrast, because an intentional misstatement – for example, a misstatement involving improper revenue recognition – may have been initiated in an interim period, the auditor may elect to apply substantive procedures to transactions occurring earlier in or throughout the reporting period.
- The extent of the procedures applied reflects the assessment of the risks of material misstatement due to fraud. For example, increasing sample sizes or performing analytical procedures at a more detailed level may be appropriate. Also, computer-assisted audit techniques may enable more extensive testing of electronic transactions and account files. Such techniques can be used to select sample transactions from key electronic files, to sort transactions with specific characteristics, or to test an entire population instead of a sample.

If the auditor identifies a risk of material misstatement due to fraud that affects inventory quantities, examining the entity's inventory records may help to identify locations or items that require specific attention during or after the physical inventory count. Such a review may lead to a decision to observe inventory counts at certain locations on an unannounced basis or to conduct inventory counts at all locations on the same date. **A38**

The auditor may identify a risk of material misstatement due to fraud affecting a number of accounts and assertions. These may include asset valuation, estimates relating to specific transactions (such as acquisitions, restructurings, or disposals of a segment of the business), and other significant accrued liabilities (such as pension **A39** and other post-employment benefit obligations, or environmental remediation liabilities). The risk may also relate to significant changes in assumptions relating to recurring estimates. Information gathered through obtaining an understanding of the entity and its environment may assist the auditor in evaluating the reasonableness of such management estimates and underlying judgments and assumptions. A retrospective review of similar management judgments and assumptions applied in prior periods may also provide insight about the reasonableness of judgments and assumptions supporting management estimates.

A40   Examples of possible audit procedures to address the assessed risks of material misstatement due to fraud, including those that illustrate the incorporation of an element of unpredictability, are presented in Appendix 2. The appendix includes examples of responses to the auditor's assessment of the risks of material misstatement resulting from both fraudulent financial reporting, including fraudulent financial reporting resulting from revenue recognition, and misappropriation of assets.

Audit Procedures Responsive to Risks Related to Management Override of Controls

Journal Entries and Other Adjustments (Ref: Para. 32(a))

A41   Material misstatement of financial statements due to fraud often involve the manipulation of the financial reporting process by recording inappropriate or unauthorized journal entries. This may occur throughout the year or at period end, or by management making adjustments to amounts reported in the financial statements that are not reflected in journal entries, such as through consolidating adjustments and reclassifications.

A42   Further, the auditor's consideration of the risks of material misstatement associated with inappropriate override of controls over journal entries is important since automated processes and controls may reduce the risk of inadvertent error but do not overcome the risk that individuals may inappropriately override such automated processes, for example, by changing the amounts being automatically passed to the general ledger or to the financial reporting system. Furthermore, where IT is used to transfer information automatically, there may be little or no visible evidence of such intervention in the information systems.

A43   When identifying and selecting journal entries and other adjustments for testing and determining the appropriate method of examining the underlying support for the items selected, the following matters are of relevance:

- *The assessment of the risks of material misstatement due to fraud* – the presence of fraud risk factors and other information obtained during the auditor's assessment of the risks of material misstatement due to fraud may assist the auditor to identify specific classes of journal entries and other adjustments for testing.
- *Controls that have been implemented over journal entries and other adjustments* – effective controls over the preparation and posting of journal entries and other adjustments may reduce the extent of substantive testing necessary, provided that the auditor has tested the operating effectiveness of the controls.
- *The entity's financial reporting process and the nature of evidence that can be obtained* – for many entities routine processing of transactions involves a combination of manual and automated steps and procedures. Similarly, the processing of journal entries and other adjustments may involve both manual and automated procedures and controls. Where information technology is used

in the financial reporting process, journal entries and other adjustments may exist only in electronic form.

- *The characteristics of fraudulent journal entries or other adjustments* – inappropriate journal entries or other adjustments often have unique identifying characteristics. Such characteristics may include entries (a) made to unrelated, unusual, or seldom-used accounts, (b) made by individuals who typically do not make journal entries, (c) recorded at the end of the period or as post-closing entries that have little or no explanation or description, (d) made either before or during the preparation of the financial statements that do not have account numbers, or (e) containing round numbers or consistent ending numbers.
- *The nature and complexity of the accounts* – inappropriate journal entries or adjustments may be applied to accounts that (a) contain transactions that are complex or unusual in nature, (b) contain significant estimates and period-end adjustments, (c) have been prone to misstatements in the past, (d) have not been reconciled on a timely basis or contain unreconciled differences, (e) contain inter-company transactions, or (f) are otherwise associated with an identified risk of material misstatement due to fraud. In audits of entities that have several locations or components, consideration is given to the need to select journal entries from multiple locations.
- *Journal entries or other adjustments processed outside the normal course of business* – non standard journal entries may not be subject to the same level of internal control as those journal entries used on a recurring basis to record transactions such as monthly sales, purchases and cash disbursements.

The auditor uses professional judgment in determining the nature, timing and extent of testing of journal entries and other adjustments. However, because fraudulent journal entries and other adjustments are often made at the end of a reporting period, paragraph 32(a)(ii) requires the auditor to select the journal entries and other adjustments made at that time. Further, because material misstatements in financial statements due to fraud can occur throughout the period and may involve extensive efforts to conceal how the fraud is accomplished, paragraph 32(a)(iii) requires the auditor to consider whether there is also a need to test journal entries and other adjustments throughout the period.   **A44**

Accounting Estimates (Ref: Para. 32(b))

The preparation of the financial statements requires management[14a] to make a number of judgments or assumptions that affect significant accounting estimates and to monitor the reasonableness of such estimates on an ongoing basis. Fraudulent financial reporting is often accomplished through intentional misstatement of accounting estimates. This may be achieved by, for example, understating or overstating all provisions or reserves in the same fashion so as to be designed either to smooth earnings over two or more accounting periods, or to achieve a designated earnings level in order to deceive financial statement users by influencing their perceptions as to the entity's performance and profitability.   **A45**

The purpose of performing a retrospective review of management judgments and assumptions related to significant accounting estimates reflected in the financial statements of the prior year is to determine whether there is an indication of a possible bias on the part of management. It is not intended to call into question the auditor's professional judgments made in the prior year that were based on information available at the time.   **A46**

A47   A retrospective review is also required by ISA (UK and Ireland) 540.[18] That review is conducted as a risk assessment procedure to obtain information regarding the effectiveness of management's prior period estimation process, audit evidence about the outcome, or where applicable, the subsequent re-estimation of prior period accounting estimates that is pertinent to making current period accounting estimates, and audit evidence of matters, such as estimation uncertainty, that may be required to be disclosed in the financial statements. As a practical matter, the auditor's review of management judgments and assumptions for biases that could represent a risk of material misstatement due to fraud in accordance with this ISA (UK and Ireland) may be carried out in conjunction with the review required by ISA (UK and Ireland) 540.

Business Rationale for Significant Transactions (Ref: Para. 32(c))

A48   Indicators that may suggest that significant transactions that are outside the normal course of business for the entity, or that otherwise appear to be unusual, may have been entered into to engage in fraudulent financial reporting or to conceal misappropriation of assets include:

- The form of such transactions appears overly complex (for example, the transaction involves multiple entities within a consolidated group or multiple unrelated third parties).
- Management has not discussed the nature of and accounting for such transactions with those charged with governance of the entity, and there is inadequate documentation.
- Management is placing more emphasis on the need for a particular accounting treatment than on the underlying economics of the transaction.
- Transactions that involve non-consolidated related parties, including special purpose entities, have not been properly reviewed or approved by those charged with governance of the entity.
- The transactions involve previously unidentified related parties or parties that do not have the substance or the financial strength to support the transaction without assistance from the entity under audit.

Evaluation of Audit Evidence (Ref: Para. 34-37)

A49   ISA (UK and Ireland) 330 requires the auditor, based on the audit procedures performed and the audit evidence obtained, to evaluate whether the assessments of the risks of material misstatement at the assertion level remain appropriate.[19] This evaluation is primarily a qualitative matter based on the auditor's judgment. Such an evaluation may provide further insight about the risks of material misstatement due to fraud and whether there is a need to perform additional or different audit procedures. Appendix 3 contains examples of circumstances that may indicate the possibility of fraud.

Analytical Procedures Performed Near the End of the Audit in Forming an Overall Conclusion (Ref: Para. 34)

A50   Determining which particular trends and relationships may indicate a risk of material misstatement due to fraud requires professional judgment. Unusual

---

[18] *ISA (UK and Ireland) 540, "Auditing Accounting Estimates, Including Fair Value Accounting Estimates, and Related Disclosures," paragraph 9.*

[19] *ISA (UK and Ireland) 330, paragraph 25.*

relationships involving year-end revenue and income are particularly relevant. These might include, for example: uncharacteristically large amounts of income being reported in the last few weeks of the reporting period or unusual transactions; or income that is inconsistent with trends in cash flow from operations.

Consideration of Identified Misstatements (Ref: Para. 35-37)

Since fraud involves incentive or pressure to commit fraud, a perceived opportunity to do so or some rationalization of the act, an instance of fraud is unlikely to be an isolated occurrence. Accordingly, misstatements, such as numerous misstatements at a specific location even though the cumulative effect is not material, may be indicative of a risk of material misstatement due to fraud. **A51**

The implications of identified fraud depend on the circumstances. For example, an otherwise insignificant fraud may be significant if it involves senior management. In such circumstances, the reliability of evidence previously obtained may be called into question, since there may be doubts about the completeness and truthfulness of representations made and about the genuineness of accounting records and documentation. There may also be a possibility of collusion involving employees, management or third parties. **A52**

ISA (UK and Ireland) 450[20] and ISA (UK and Ireland) 700[21] establish requirements and provide guidance on the evaluation and disposition of misstatements and the effect on the auditor's opinion in the auditor's report. **A53**

Auditor Unable to Continue the Engagement (Ref: Para. 38)

Examples of exceptional circumstances that may arise and that may bring into question the auditor's ability to continue performing the audit include: **A54**

- The entity does not take the appropriate action regarding fraud that the auditor considers necessary in the circumstances, even where the fraud is not material to the financial statements;
- The auditor's consideration of the risks of material misstatement due to fraud and the results of audit tests indicate a significant risk of material and pervasive fraud; or
- The auditor has significant concern about the competence or integrity of management or those charged with governance.

Because of the variety of the circumstances that may arise, it is not possible to describe definitively when withdrawal from an engagement is appropriate. Factors that affect the auditor's conclusion include the implications of the involvement of a member of management or of those charged with governance (which may affect the reliability of management representations) and the effects on the auditor of a continuing association with the entity. **A55**

The auditor has professional and legal responsibilities in such circumstances and these responsibilities may vary by country. In some countries, for example, the **A56**

---

[20] *ISA (UK and Ireland) 450, "Evaluation of Misstatements Identified during the Audit."*

[21] *ISA 700, "Forming an Opinion and Reporting on Financial Statements."*
The APB has not promulgated ISA 700 as issued by the IAASB for application in the UK and Ireland. In the UK and Ireland the applicable auditing standard is ISA (UK and Ireland) 700, "The Auditor's Report on Financial Statements." Paragraph 8(b) of ISA (UK and Ireland) 700 requires evaluation of whether uncorrected misstatements are material, individually or in aggregate.

auditor may be entitled to, or required to, make a statement or report to the person or persons who made the audit appointment or, in some cases, to regulatory authorities. Given the exceptional nature of the circumstances and the need to consider the legal requirements, the auditor may consider it appropriate to seek legal advice when deciding whether to withdraw from an engagement and in determining an appropriate course of action, including the possibility of reporting to share-holders, regulators or others.[22]

Considerations Specific to Public Sector Entities

A57   In many cases in the public sector, the option of withdrawing from the engagement may not be available to the auditor due to the nature of the mandate or public interest considerations.

Written Representations (Ref: Para. 39)

A58   ISA (UK and Ireland) 580[23] establishes requirements and provides guidance on obtaining appropriate representations from management and, where appropriate, those charged with governance in the audit. In addition to acknowledging that they have fulfilled their responsibility for the preparation of the financial statements, it is important that, irrespective of the size of the entity, management and, where appropriate, those charged with governance acknowledge their responsibility for internal control designed, implemented and maintained to prevent and detect fraud.

A59   Because of the nature of fraud and the difficulties encountered by auditors in detecting material misstatements in the financial statements resulting from fraud, it is important that the auditor obtain a written representation from management and, where appropriate, those charged with governance confirming that they have dis-closed to the auditor:

(a)   The results of management's assessment of the risk that the financial statements may be materially misstated as a result of fraud; and

(b)   Their knowledge of actual, suspected or alleged fraud affecting the entity.

Communications to Management and with Those Charged with Governance

Communication to Management (Ref: Para. 40)

A60   When the auditor has obtained evidence that fraud exists or may exist, it is important that the matter be brought to the attention of the appropriate level of management as soon as practicable. This is so even if the matter might be considered inconsequential (for example, a minor defalcation by an employee at a low level in the entity's organization). The determination of which level of management is the appropriate one is a matter of professional judgment and is affected by such factors as the likelihood of collusion and the nature and magnitude of the suspected fraud. Ordinarily, the appropriate level of management is at least one level above the persons who appear to be involved with the suspected fraud.

---

[22] *The IESBA* Code of Ethics for Professional Accountants *provides guidance on communications with an auditor replacing the existing auditor*

In the UK and Ireland the relevant ethical guidance on proposed communications with a successor auditor is provided by the ethical pronouncements relating to the work of auditors issued by the auditor's relevant professional body.

[23] *ISA (UK and Ireland) 580, "Written Representations."*

Communication with Those Charged with Governance (Ref: Para. 41)

The auditor's communication with those charged with governance may be made **A61** orally or in writing. ISA (UK and Ireland) 260 identifies factors the auditor considers in determining whether to communicate orally or in writing.[24] Due to the nature and sensitivity of fraud involving senior management, or fraud that results in a material misstatement in the financial statements, the auditor reports such matters on a timely basis and may consider it necessary to also report such matters in writing.

In some cases, the auditor may consider it appropriate to communicate with those **A62** charged with governance when the auditor becomes aware of fraud involving employees other than management that does not result in a material misstatement. Similarly, those charged with governance may wish to be informed of such circumstances. The communication process is assisted if the auditor and those charged with governance agree at an early stage in the audit about the nature and extent of the auditor's communications in this regard.

In the exceptional circumstances where the auditor has doubts about the integrity or **A63** honesty of management or those charged with governance, the auditor may consider it appropriate to obtain legal advice to assist in determining the appropriate course of action.

Other Matters Related to Fraud (Ref: Para. 42)

Other matters related to fraud to be discussed with those charged with governance of **A64** the entity may include, for example:

- Concerns about the nature, extent and frequency of management's assessments of the controls in place to prevent and detect fraud and of the risk that the financial statements may be misstated.
- A failure by management to appropriately address identified significant deficiencies in internal control, or to appropriately respond to an identified fraud.
- The auditor's evaluation of the entity's control environment, including questions regarding the competence and integrity of management.
- Actions by management that may be indicative of fraudulent financial reporting, such as management's selection and application of accounting policies that may be indicative of management's effort to manage earnings in order to deceive financial statement users by influencing their perceptions as to the entity's performance and profitability.
- Concerns about the adequacy and completeness of the authorization of transactions that appear to be outside the normal course of business.

Communications to Regulatory and Enforcement Authorities (Ref: Para. 43)

The auditor's professional duty to maintain the confidentiality of client information **A65** may preclude reporting fraud to a party outside the client entity. However, the auditor's legal responsibilities vary by country[24a] and, in certain circumstances, the duty of confidentiality may be overridden by statute, the law or courts of law. In some countries, the auditor of a financial institution has a statutory duty to report

---

[24] *ISA (UK and Ireland) 260, paragraph A38.*

[24a] *In the UK and Ireland, anti-money laundering legislation imposes a duty on auditors to report suspected money laundering activity. Suspicions relating to fraud are likely to be required to be reported under this legislation (see paragraph A11-1 in ISA (UK and Ireland) 250 Section A, "Consideration of laws and regulations").*

the occurrence of fraud to supervisory authorities. Also, in some countries the auditor has a duty to report misstatements to authorities in those cases where management and those charged with governance fail to take corrective action.

A66   The auditor may consider it appropriate to obtain legal advice to determine the appropriate course of action in the circumstances, the purpose of which is to ascertain the steps necessary in considering the public interest aspects of identified fraud.

Considerations Specific to Public Sector Entities

A67   In the public sector, requirements for reporting fraud, whether or not discovered through the audit process, may be subject to specific provisions of the audit mandate or related law, regulation or other authority.

Appendix 1   (Ref: Para. A25)

Examples of Fraud Risk Factors

The fraud risk factors identified in this Appendix are examples of such factors that may be faced by auditors in a broad range of situations. Separately presented are examples relating to the two types of fraud relevant to the auditor's consideration – that is, fraudulent financial reporting and misappropriation of assets. For each of these types of fraud, the risk factors are further classified based on the three conditions generally present when material misstatements due to fraud occur: (a) incentives/pressures, (b) opportunities, and (c) attitudes/rationalizations. Although the risk factors cover a broad range of situations, they are only examples and, accordingly, the auditor may identify additional or different risk factors. Not all of these examples are relevant in all circumstances, and some may be of greater or lesser significance in entities of different size or with different ownership characteristics or circumstances. Also, the order of the examples of risk factors provided is not intended to reflect their relative importance or frequency of occurrence.

Risk Factors Relating to Misstatements Arising from Fraudulent Financial Reporting

The following are examples of risk factors relating to misstatements arising from fraudulent financial reporting.

Incentives/Pressures

Financial stability or profitability is threatened by economic, industry, or entity operating conditions, such as (or as indicated by):

- High degree of competition or market saturation, accompanied by declining margins.
- High vulnerability to rapid changes, such as changes in technology, product obsolescence, or interest rates.
- Significant declines in customer demand and increasing business failures in either the industry or overall economy.
- Operating losses making the threat of bankruptcy, foreclosure, or hostile takeover imminent.

- Recurring negative cash flows from operations or an inability to generate cash flows from operations while reporting earnings and earnings growth.
- Rapid growth or unusual profitability especially compared to that of other companies in the same industry.
- New accounting, statutory, or regulatory requirements.

Excessive pressure exists for management to meet the requirements or expectations of third parties due to the following:

- Profitability or trend level expectations of investment analysts, institutional investors, significant creditors, or other external parties (particularly expectations that are unduly aggressive or unrealistic), including expectations created by management in, for example, overly optimistic press releases or annual report messages.
- Need to obtain additional debt or equity financing to stay competitive – including financing of major research and development or capital expenditures.
- Marginal ability to meet exchange listing requirements or debt repayment or other debt covenant requirements.
- Perceived or real adverse effects of reporting poor financial results on significant pending transactions, such as business combinations or contract awards.

Information available indicates that the personal financial situation of management or those charged with governance is threatened by the entity's financial performance arising from the following:

- Significant financial interests in the entity.
- Significant portions of their compensation (for example, bonuses, stock options, and earn-out arrangements) being contingent upon achieving aggressive targets for stock price, operating results, financial position, or cash flow.[25]
- Personal guarantees of debts of the entity.

There is excessive pressure on management or operating personnel to meet financial targets established by those charged with governance, including sales or profitability incentive goals.

Opportunities

The nature of the industry or the entity's operations provides opportunities to engage in fraudulent financial reporting that can arise from the following:

- Significant related-party transactions not in the ordinary course of business or with related entities not audited or audited by another firm.
- A strong financial presence or ability to dominate a certain industry sector that allows the entity to dictate terms or conditions to suppliers or customers that may result in inappropriate or non-arm's-length transactions.
- Assets, liabilities, revenues, or expenses based on significant estimates that involve subjective judgments or uncertainties that are difficult to corroborate.
- Significant, unusual, or highly complex transactions, especially those close to period end that pose difficult "substance over form" questions.
- Significant operations located or conducted across international borders in jurisdictions where differing business environments and cultures exist.
- Use of business intermediaries for which there appears to be no clear business justification.

---

[25] *Management incentive plans may be contingent upon achieving targets relating only to certain accounts or selected activities of the entity, even though the related accounts or activities may not be material to the entity as a whole.*

- Significant bank accounts or subsidiary or branch operations in tax-haven jurisdictions for which there appears to be no clear business justification.

The monitoring of management is not effective as a result of the following:

- Domination of management by a single person or small group (in a non owner-managed business) without compensating controls.
- Oversight by those charged with governance over the financial reporting process and internal control is not effective.

There is a complex or unstable organizational structure, as evidenced by the following:

- Difficulty in determining the organization or individuals that have controlling interest in the entity.
- Overly complex organizational structure involving unusual legal entities or managerial lines of authority.
- High turnover of senior management, legal counsel, or those charged with governance.

Internal control components are deficient as a result of the following:

- Inadequate monitoring of controls, including automated controls and controls over interim financial reporting (where external reporting is required).
- High turnover rates or employment of staff in accounting, information technology, or the internal audit function that are not effective.
- Accounting and information systems that are not effective, including situations involving significant deficiencies in internal control.

Attitudes/Rationalizations

- Communication, implementation, support, or enforcement of the entity's values or ethical standards by management, or the communication of inappropriate values or ethical standards, that are not effective.
- Nonfinancial management's excessive participation in or preoccupation with the selection of accounting policies or the determination of significant estimates.
- Known history of violations of securities laws or other laws and regulations, or claims against the entity, its senior management, or those charged with governance alleging fraud or violations of laws and regulations.
- Excessive interest by management in maintaining or increasing the entity's stock price or earnings trend.
- The practice by management of committing to analysts, creditors, and other third parties to achieve aggressive or unrealistic forecasts.
- Management failing to remedy known significant deficiencies in internal control on a timely basis.
- An interest by management in employing inappropriate means to minimize reported earnings for tax-motivated reasons.
- Low morale among senior management.
- The owner-manager makes no distinction between personal and business transactions.
- Dispute between shareholders in a closely held entity.
- Recurring attempts by management to justify marginal or inappropriate accounting on the basis of materiality.
- The relationship between management and the current or predecessor auditor is strained, as exhibited by the following:
  - Frequent disputes with the current or predecessor auditor on accounting, auditing, or reporting matters.

- ○ Unreasonable demands on the auditor, such as unrealistic time constraints regarding the completion of the audit or the issuance of the auditor's report.
- ○ Restrictions on the auditor that inappropriately limit access to people or information or the ability to communicate effectively with those charged with governance.
- ○ Domineering management behavior in dealing with the auditor, especially involving attempts to influence the scope of the auditor's work or the selection or continuance of personnel assigned to or consulted on the audit engagement.

Risk Factors Arising from Misstatements Arising from Misappropriation of Assets

Risk factors that relate to misstatements arising from misappropriation of assets are also classified according to the three conditions generally present when fraud exists: incentives/pressures, opportunities, and attitudes/rationalization. Some of the risk factors related to misstatements arising from fraudulent financial reporting also may be present when misstatements arising from misappropriation of assets occur. For example, ineffective monitoring of management and other deficiencies in internal control may be present when misstatements due to either fraudulent financial reporting or misappropriation of assets exist. The following are examples of risk factors related to misstatements arising from misappropriation of assets.

Incentives/Pressures

Personal financial obligations may create pressure on management or employees with access to cash or other assets susceptible to theft to misappropriate those assets.

Adverse relationships between the entity and employees with access to cash or other assets susceptible to theft may motivate those employees to misappropriate those assets. For example, adverse relationships may be created by the following:

- Known or anticipated future employee layoffs.
- Recent or anticipated changes to employee compensation or benefit plans.
- Promotions, compensation, or other rewards inconsistent with expectations.

Opportunities

Certain characteristics or circumstances may increase the susceptibility of assets to misappropriation. For example, opportunities to misappropriate assets increase when there are the following:

- Large amounts of cash on hand or processed.
- Inventory items that are small in size, of high value, or in high demand.
- Easily convertible assets, such as bearer bonds, diamonds, or computer chips.
- Fixed assets which are small in size, marketable, or lacking observable identification of ownership.

Inadequate internal control over assets may increase the susceptibility of misappropriation of those assets. For example, misappropriation of assets may occur because there is the following:

- Inadequate segregation of duties or independent checks.
- Inadequate oversight of senior management expenditures, such as travel and other re-imbursements.

- Inadequate management oversight of employees responsible for assets, for example, inadequate supervision or monitoring of remote locations.
- Inadequate job applicant screening of employees with access to assets.
- Inadequate record keeping with respect to assets.
- Inadequate system of authorization and approval of transactions (for example, in purchasing).
- Inadequate physical safeguards over cash, investments, inventory, or fixed assets.
- Lack of complete and timely reconciliations of assets.
- Lack of timely and appropriate documentation of transactions, for example, credits for merchandise returns.
- Lack of mandatory vacations for employees performing key control functions.
- Inadequate management understanding of information technology, which enables information technology employees to perpetrate a misappropriation.
- Inadequate access controls over automated records, including controls over and review of computer systems event logs.

Attitudes/Rationalizations

- Disregard for the need for monitoring or reducing risks related to misappropriations of assets.
- Disregard for internal control over misappropriation of assets by overriding existing controls or by failing to take appropriate remedial action on known deficiencies in internal control.
- Behavior indicating displeasure or dissatisfaction with the entity or its treatment of the employee.
- Changes in behavior or lifestyle that may indicate assets have been misappropriated.
- Tolerance of petty theft.

Appendix 2 (Ref: Para. A40)

Examples of Possible Audit Procedures to Address the Assessed Risks of Material Misstatement Due to Fraud

The following are examples of possible audit procedures to address the assessed risks of material misstatement due to fraud resulting from both fraudulent financial reporting and misappropriation of assets. Although these procedures cover a broad range of situations, they are only examples and, accordingly they may not be the most appropriate nor necessary in each circumstance. Also the order of the procedures provided is not intended to reflect their relative importance.

Consideration at the Assertion Level

Specific responses to the auditor's assessment of the risks of material misstatement due to fraud will vary depending upon the types or combinations of fraud risk factors or conditions identified, and the classes of transactions, account balances, disclosures and assertions they may affect.

The following are specific examples of responses:

- Visiting locations or performing certain tests on a surprise or unannounced basis. For example, observing inventory at locations where auditor attendance has not been previously announced or counting cash at a particular date on a surprise basis.

- Requesting that inventories be counted at the end of the reporting period or on a date closer to period end to minimize the risk of manipulation of balances in the period between the date of completion of the count and the end of the reporting period.
- Altering the audit approach in the current year. For example, contacting major customers and suppliers orally in addition to sending written confirmation, sending confirmation requests to a specific party within an organization, or seeking more or different information.
- Performing a detailed review of the entity's quarter-end or year-end adjusting entries and investigating any that appear unusual as to nature or amount.
- For significant and unusual transactions, particularly those occurring at or near year-end, investigating the possibility of related parties and the sources of financial resources supporting the transactions.
- Performing substantive analytical procedures using disaggregated data. For example, comparing sales and cost of sales by location, line of business or month to expectations developed by the auditor.
- Conducting interviews of personnel involved in areas where a risk of material misstatement due to fraud has been identified, to obtain their insights about the risk and whether, or how, controls address the risk.
- When other independent auditors are auditing the financial statements of one or more subsidiaries, divisions or branches, discussing with them the extent of work necessary to be performed to address the assessed risk of material misstatement due to fraud resulting from transactions and activities among these components.
- If the work of an expert becomes particularly significant with respect to a financial statement item for which the assessed risk of misstatement due to fraud is high, performing additional procedures relating to some or all of the expert's assumptions, methods or findings to determine that the findings are not unreasonable, or engaging another expert for that purpose.
- Performing audit procedures to analyze selected opening balance sheet accounts of previously audited financial statements to assess how certain issues involving accounting estimates and judgments, for example, an allowance for sales returns, were resolved with the benefit of hindsight.
- Performing procedures on account or other reconciliations prepared by the entity, including considering reconciliations performed at interim periods.
- Performing computer-assisted techniques, such as data mining to test for anomalies in a population.
- Testing the integrity of computer-produced records and transactions.
- Seeking additional audit evidence from sources outside of the entity being audited.

Specific Responses—Misstatement Resulting from Fraudulent Financial Reporting

Examples of responses to the auditor's assessment of the risks of material misstatement due to fraudulent financial reporting are as follows:

Revenue Recognition

- Performing substantive analytical procedures relating to revenue using disaggregated data, for example, comparing revenue reported by month and by product line or business segment during the current reporting period with comparable prior periods. Computer-assisted audit techniques may be useful in identifying unusual or unexpected revenue relationships or transactions.

- Confirming with customers certain relevant contract terms and the absence of side agreements, because the appropriate accounting often is influenced by such terms or agreements and basis for rebates or the period to which they relate are often poorly documented. For example, acceptance criteria, delivery and payment terms, the absence of future or continuing vendor obligations, the right to return the product, guaranteed resale amounts, and cancellation or refund provisions often are relevant in such circumstances.
- Inquiring of the entity's sales and marketing personnel or in-house legal counsel regarding sales or shipments near the end of the period and their knowledge of any unusual terms or conditions associated with these transactions.
- Being physically present at one or more locations at period end to observe goods being shipped or being readied for shipment (or returns awaiting processing) and performing other appropriate sales and inventory cutoff procedures.
- For those situations for which revenue transactions are electronically initiated, processed, and recorded, testing controls to determine whether they provide assurance that recorded revenue transactions occurred and are properly recorded.

Inventory Quantities

- Examining the entity's inventory records to identify locations or items that require specific attention during or after the physical inventory count.
- Observing inventory counts at certain locations on an unannounced basis or conducting inventory counts at all locations on the same date.
- Conducting inventory counts at or near the end of the reporting period to minimize the risk of inappropriate manipulation during the period between the count and the end of the reporting period.
- Performing additional procedures during the observation of the count, for example, more rigorously examining the contents of boxed items, the manner in which the goods are stacked (for example, hollow squares) or labeled, and the quality (that is, purity, grade, or concentration) of liquid substances such as perfumes or specialty chemicals. Using the work of an expert may be helpful in this regard.
- Comparing the quantities for the current period with prior periods by class or category of inventory, location or other criteria, or comparison of quantities counted with perpetual records.
- Using computer-assisted audit techniques to further test the compilation of the physical inventory counts – for example, sorting by tag number to test tag controls or by item serial number to test the possibility of item omission or duplication.

Management Estimates

- Using an expert to develop an independent estimate for comparison to management's estimate.
- Extending inquiries to individuals outside of management and the accounting department to corroborate management's ability and intent to carry out plans that are relevant to developing the estimate.

Specific Responses—Misstatements Due to Misappropriation of Assets

Differing circumstances would necessarily dictate different responses. Ordinarily, the audit response to an assessed risk of material misstatement due to fraud relating to misappropriation of assets will be directed toward certain account balances and classes of transactions. Although some of the audit responses noted in the two categories above may apply in such circumstances, the scope of the work is to be linked to the specific information about the misappropriation risk that has been identified.

Examples of responses to the auditor's assessment of the risk of material misstatements due to misappropriation of assets are as follows:

- Counting cash or securities at or near year-end.
- Confirming directly with customers the account activity (including credit memo and sales return activity as well as dates payments were made) for the period under audit.
- Analyzing recoveries of written-off accounts.
- Analyzing inventory shortages by location or product type.
- Comparing key inventory ratios to industry norm.
- Reviewing supporting documentation for reductions to the perpetual inventory records.
- Performing a computerized match of the vendor list with a list of employees to identify matches of addresses or phone numbers.
- Performing a computerized search of payroll records to identify duplicate addresses, employee identification or taxing authority numbers or bank accounts
- Reviewing personnel files for those that contain little or no evidence of activity, for example, lack of performance evaluations.
- Analyzing sales discounts and returns for unusual patterns or trends.
- Confirming specific terms of contracts with third parties.
- Obtaining evidence that contracts are being carried out in accordance with their terms.
- Reviewing the propriety of large and unusual expenses.
- Reviewing the authorization and carrying value of senior management and related party loans.
- Reviewing the level and propriety of expense reports submitted by senior management.

Appendix 3 (Ref: Para. A49)

Examples of Circumstances that Indicate the Possibility of Fraud

The following are examples of circumstances that may indicate the possibility that the financial statements may contain a material misstatement resulting from fraud.

Discrepancies in the accounting records, including:

- Transactions that are not recorded in a complete or timely manner or are improperly recorded as to amount, accounting period, classification, or entity policy.
- Unsupported or unauthorized balances or transactions.
- Last-minute adjustments that significantly affect financial results.
- Evidence of employees' access to systems and records inconsistent with that necessary to perform their authorized duties.

- Tips or complaints to the auditor about alleged fraud.

Conflicting or missing evidence, including:

- Missing documents.
- Documents that appear to have been altered.
- Unavailability of other than photocopied or electronically transmitted documents when documents in original form are expected to exist.
- Significant unexplained items on reconciliations.
- Unusual balance sheet changes, or changes in trends or important financial statement ratios or relationships – for example, receivables growing faster than revenues.
- Inconsistent, vague, or implausible responses from management or employees arising from inquiries or analytical procedures.
- Unusual discrepancies between the entity's records and confirmation replies.
- Large numbers of credit entries and other adjustments made to accounts receivable records.
- Unexplained or inadequately explained differences between the accounts receivable sub-ledger and the control account, or between the customer statements and the accounts receivable sub-ledger.
- Missing or non-existent cancelled checks in circumstances where cancelled checks are ordinarily returned to the entity with the bank statement.
- Missing inventory or physical assets of significant magnitude.
- Unavailable or missing electronic evidence, inconsistent with the entity's record retention practices or policies.
- Fewer responses to confirmations than anticipated or a greater number of responses than anticipated.
- Inability to produce evidence of key systems development and program change testing and implementation activities for current-year system changes and deployments.

Problematic or unusual relationships between the auditor and management, including:

- Denial of access to records, facilities, certain employees, customers, vendors, or others from whom audit evidence might be sought.
- Undue time pressures imposed by management to resolve complex or contentious issues.
- Complaints by management about the conduct of the audit or management intimidation of engagement team members, particularly in connection with the auditor's critical assessment of audit evidence or in the resolution of potential disagreements with management.
- Unusual delays by the entity in providing requested information.
- Unwillingness to facilitate auditor access to key electronic files for testing through the use of computer-assisted audit techniques.
- Denial of access to key IT operations staff and facilities, including security, operations, and systems development personnel.
- An unwillingness to add or revise disclosures in the financial statements to make them more complete and understandable.
- An unwillingness to address identified deficiencies in internal control on a timely basis.

Other

- Unwillingness by management to permit the auditor to meet privately with those charged with governance.
- Accounting policies that appear to be at variance with industry norms.

- Frequent changes in accounting estimates that do not appear to result from changed circumstances.
- Tolerance of violations of the entity's code of conduct.

International Standard on Auditing (UK and Ireland) 250

Section A – Consideration of laws and regulations in an audit of financial statements

*(Effective for audits of financial statements for periods
ending on or after 15 December 2010)*

Contents

International Standard on Auditing (UK and Ireland) (ISA (UK and Ireland)) 250, "Consideration of Laws and Regulations in an Audit of Financial Statements" should be read in conjunction with ISA (UK and Ireland) 200, "Overall Objectives of the Independent Auditor and the Conduct of an Audit in Accordance with International Standards on Auditing (UK and Ireland)."

Introduction

Scope of this ISA (UK and Ireland)

This International Standard on Auditing (UK and Ireland) (ISA (UK and Ireland)) deals with the auditor's responsibility to consider laws and regulations in an audit of financial statements. This ISA (UK and Ireland) does not apply to other assurance engagements in which the auditor is specifically engaged to test and report separately on compliance with specific laws or regulations.   **1**

Guidance on the auditor's responsibility to report direct to regulators in the financial sector is provided in Section B of this ISA (UK and Ireland).   **1-1**

Effect of Laws and Regulations

The effect on financial statements of laws and regulations varies considerably. Those laws and regulations to which an entity is subject constitute the legal and regulatory framework. The provisions of some laws or regulations have a direct effect on the financial statements in that they determine the reported amounts and disclosures in an entity's financial statements. Other laws or regulations are to be complied with by management or set the provisions under which the entity is allowed to conduct its business but do not have a direct effect on an entity's financial statements. Some entities operate in heavily regulated industries (such as banks and chemical companies). Others are subject only to the many laws and regulations that relate generally to the operating aspects of the business (such as those related to occupational safety and health, and equal employment opportunity). Non-compliance with laws and regulations may result in fines, litigation or other consequences for the entity that may have a material effect on the financial statements.   **2**

Responsibility for Compliance with Laws and Regulations (Ref: Para. A1-A6)

It is the responsibility of management, with the oversight of those charged with governance, to ensure that the entity's operations are conducted in accordance with the provisions of laws and regulations, including compliance with the provisions of laws and regulations that determine the reported amounts and disclosures in an entity's financial statements.[1a]   **3**

Responsibility of the Auditor

The requirements in this ISA (UK and Ireland) are designed to assist the auditor in identifying material misstatement of the financial statements due to non-compliance with laws and regulations. However, the auditor is not responsible for preventing non-compliance and cannot be expected to detect non-compliance with all laws and regulations.   **4**

The auditor is responsible for obtaining reasonable assurance that the financial statements, taken as a whole, are free from material misstatement, whether caused by   **5**

[1a] *In the UK and Ireland those charged with governance are responsible for the preparation of the financial statements.*

fraud or error.[1] In conducting an audit of financial statements, the auditor takes into account the applicable legal and regulatory framework. Owing to the inherent limitations of an audit, there is an unavoidable risk that some material misstatements in the financial statements may not be detected, even though the audit is properly planned and performed in accordance with the ISAs (UK and Ireland).[2] In the context of laws and regulations, the potential effects of inherent limitations on the auditor's ability to detect material misstatements are greater for such reasons as the following:

- There are many laws and regulations, relating principally to the operating aspects of an entity, that typically do not affect the financial statements and are not captured by the entity's information systems relevant to financial reporting.
- Non-compliance may involve conduct designed to conceal it, such as collusion, forgery, deliberate failure to record transactions, management override of controls or intentional misrepresentations being made to the auditor.
- Whether an act constitutes non-compliance is ultimately a matter for legal determination by a court of law.

Ordinarily, the further removed non-compliance is from the events and transactions reflected in the financial statements, the less likely the auditor is to become aware of it or to recognize the non-compliance.

6   This ISA (UK and Ireland) distinguishes the auditor's responsibilities in relation to compliance with two different categories of laws and regulations as follows:

   (a) The provisions of those laws and regulations generally recognized to have a direct effect on the determination of material amounts and disclosures in the financial statements such as tax and pension laws and regulations (see paragraph 13); and

   (b) Other laws and regulations that do not have a direct effect on the determination of the amounts and disclosures in the financial statements, but compliance with which may be fundamental to the operating aspects of the business, to an entity's ability to continue its business, or to avoid material penalties (for example, compliance with the terms of an operating license, compliance with regulatory solvency requirements, or compliance with environmental regulations); non-compliance with such laws and regulations may therefore have a material effect on the financial statements (see paragraph 14).

7   In this ISA (UK and Ireland), differing requirements are specified for each of the above categories of laws and regulations. For the category referred to in paragraph 6(a), the auditor's responsibility is to obtain sufficient appropriate audit evidence regarding compliance with the provisions of those laws and regulations. For the category referred to in paragraph 6(b), the auditor's responsibility is limited to undertaking specified audit procedures to help identify non-compliance with those laws and regulations that may have a material effect on the financial statements.

8   The auditor is required by this ISA (UK and Ireland) to remain alert to the possibility that other audit procedures applied for the purpose of forming an opinion on financial statements may bring instances of identified or suspected non-compliance to the auditor's attention. Maintaining professional skepticism throughout the audit, as

---

[1] ISA (UK and Ireland) 200, "Overall Objectives of the Independent Auditor and the Conduct of an Audit in Accordance with International Standards on Auditing," paragraph 5.

[2] ISA (UK and Ireland) 200, paragraph A51.

required by ISA (UK and Ireland) 200,[3] is important in this context, given the extent of laws and regulations that affect the entity.

Effective Date

This ISA (UK and Ireland) is effective for audits of financial statements for periods ending on or after 15 December 2010.   9

Objectives

The objectives of the auditor are: 10

(a) To obtain sufficient appropriate audit evidence regarding compliance with the provisions of those laws and regulations generally recognized to have a direct effect on the determination of material amounts and disclosures in the financial statements;

(b) To perform specified audit procedures to help identify instances of non-compliance with other laws and regulations that may have a material effect on the financial statements; and

(c) To respond appropriately to non-compliance or suspected non-compliance with laws and regulations identified during the audit.

Definition

For the purposes of this ISA (UK and Ireland), the following term has the meaning attributed below: 11

Non-compliance – Acts of omission or commission by the entity, either intentional or unintentional, which are contrary to the prevailing laws or regulations. Such acts include transactions entered into by, or in the name of, the entity, or on its behalf, by those charged with governance, management or employees. Non-compliance does not include personal misconduct (unrelated to the business activities of the entity) by those charged with governance, management or employees of the entity.

This ISA (UK and Ireland) also refers to 'money laundering'. 'Money laundering' is defined in legislation[3a] and in general terms involves an act which conceals, disguises, converts, transfers, removes, uses, acquires or possesses property resulting from criminal conduct.   11-1

---

[3] *ISA (UK and Ireland) 200, paragraph 15.*

[3a] *In the UK, the Money Laundering Regulations 2007 and the requirements of the Proceeds of Crime Act 2002 (POCA) bring auditors within the regulated sector, requiring them to report suspected money laundering activity and adopt rigorous client identification procedures and appropriate anti-money laundering procedures. In Ireland, the Criminal Justice Act 1994 (Section 32) Regulations 2003 designate accountants, auditors, and tax advisors and others for the purposes of the anti-money laundering provisions of the Criminal Justice Act, 1994, as amended.*

Requirements

The Auditor's Consideration of Compliance with Laws and Regulations

12   As part of obtaining an understanding of the entity and its environment in accordance with ISA (UK and Ireland) 315,[4] the auditor shall obtain a general understanding of:

   (a) The legal and regulatory framework applicable to the entity and the industry or sector in which the entity operates; and

   (b) How the entity is complying with that framework. (Ref: Para. A7)

13   The auditor shall obtain sufficient appropriate audit evidence regarding compliance with the provisions of those laws and regulations generally recognized to have a direct effect on the determination of material amounts and disclosures in the financial statements. (Ref: Para. A8 – A8-1)

14   The auditor shall perform the following audit procedures to help identify instances of non-compliance with other laws and regulations that may have a material effect on the financial statements: (Ref: Para. A9 – A10-1)

   (a) Inquiring of management and, where appropriate, those charged with governance, as to whether the entity is in compliance with such laws and regulations; and

   (b) Inspecting correspondence, if any, with the relevant licensing or regulatory authorities.

15   During the audit, the auditor shall remain alert to the possibility that other audit procedures applied may bring instances of non-compliance or suspected non-compliance with laws and regulations to the auditor's attention. (Ref: Para. A11 – A11-2)

16   The auditor shall request management and, where appropriate, those charged with governance to provide written representations that all known instances of non-compliance or suspected non-compliance with laws and regulations whose effects should be considered when preparing financial statements have been disclosed to the auditor. (Ref: Para. A12)

17   In the absence of identified or suspected non-compliance, the auditor is not required to perform audit procedures regarding the entity's compliance with laws and regulations, other than those set out in paragraphs 12-16.

Audit Procedures When Non-Compliance Is Identified or Suspected

18   If the auditor becomes aware of information concerning an instance of non-compliance or suspected non-compliance with laws and regulations, the auditor shall obtain: (Ref: Para. A13)

   (a) An understanding of the nature of the act and the circumstances in which it has occurred; and

   (b) Further information to evaluate the possible effect on the financial statements. (Ref: Para. A14)

---

[4] *ISA (UK and Ireland) 315, "Identifying and Assessing the Risks of Material Misstatement through Understanding the Entity and Its Environment," paragraph 11.*

If the auditor suspects there may be non-compliance, the auditor shall[4a] discuss the   **19**
matter with management and, where appropriate, those charged with governance. If
management or, as appropriate, those charged with governance do not provide
sufficient information that supports that the entity is in compliance with laws and
regulations and, in the auditor's judgment, the effect of the suspected non-compliance may be material to the financial statements, the auditor shall consider the
need to obtain legal advice. (Ref: Para. A15-A16)

If sufficient information about suspected non-compliance cannot be obtained, the   **20**
auditor shall evaluate the effect of the lack of sufficient appropriate audit evidence on
the auditor's opinion.

The auditor shall evaluate the implications of non-compliance in relation to other   **21**
aspects of the audit, including the auditor's risk assessment and the reliability of
written representations, and take appropriate action. (Ref: Para. A17- A18-1)

Reporting of Identified or Suspected Non-Compliance

Reporting Non-Compliance to Those Charged with Governance

Unless all of those charged with governance are involved in management of the   **22**
entity, and therefore are aware of matters involving identified or suspected non-
compliance already communicated by the auditor,[5] the auditor shall[4a] communicate
with those charged with governance matters involving non-compliance with laws and
regulations that come to the auditor's attention during the course of the audit, other
than when the matters are clearly inconsequential.

If, in the auditor's judgment, the non-compliance referred to in paragraph 22 is   **23**
believed to be intentional and material, the auditor shall[4a] communicate the matter to
those charged with governance as soon as practicable. (Ref: Para. A18-2)

If the auditor suspects that management or those charged with governance are   **24**
involved in non-compliance, the auditor shall[4a] communicate the matter to the next
higher level of authority at the entity, if it exists, such as an audit committee or
supervisory board. Where no higher authority exists, or if the auditor believes that
the communication may not be acted upon or is unsure as to the person to whom to
report, the auditor shall consider the need to obtain legal advice. (Ref: Para. A18-3)

[4a] *Subject to compliance with legislation relating to 'tipping off' or "prejudicing an investigation".*
In the UK, 'tipping off' is an offence under POCA section 333A. It arises when an individual discloses:
*(a) that a report (internal or external) has already been made where the disclosure by the individual is likely to
    prejudice an investigation which might be conducted following the internal or external report that has been
    made; or*
*(b) that an investigation is being contemplated or is being carried out into allegations that a money laundering
    offence has been committed and the disclosure by the individual is likely to prejudice that investigation.*
*Whilst 'tipping off' requires a person to have knowledge or suspicion that a report has been or will be made, a
further offence of prejudicing an investigation is included in POCA section 342. Under this provision, it is an
offence to make any disclosure which may prejudice an investigation of which a person has knowledge or
suspicion, or to falsify, conceal, destroy or otherwise dispose of, or cause or permit the falsification, concealment,
destruction or disposal of, documents relevant to such an investigation.*
*The disclosure offences under sections 333A and 342 are not committed if the person disclosing does not know or
suspect that it is likely to prejudice an investigation.*
*In Ireland Section 58 of the Criminal Justice Act, 1994, as amended, establishes the offence of "prejudicing an
investigation". This relates both to when a person, knowing or suspecting that an investigation is taking place,
makes any disclosure likely to prejudice the investigation or when a person, knowing that a report has been made,
makes any disclosure likely to prejudice any investigation arising from the report.*

[5] *ISA (UK and Ireland) 260, "Communication with Those Charged with Governance," paragraph 13.*

Reporting Non-Compliance in the Auditor's Report on the Financial Statements

25   If the auditor concludes that the non-compliance has a material effect on the financial statements, and has not been adequately reflected in the financial statements, the auditor shall,[4a] in accordance with ISA (UK and Ireland) 705, express a qualified opinion or an adverse opinion on the financial statements.[6]

26   If the auditor is precluded by management or those charged with governance from obtaining sufficient appropriate audit evidence to evaluate whether non-compliance that may be material to the financial statements has, or is likely to have, occurred, the auditor shall[4a] express a qualified opinion or disclaim an opinion on the financial statements on the basis of a limitation on the scope of the audit in accordance with ISA (UK and Ireland) 705.

27   If the auditor is unable to determine whether non-compliance has occurred because of limitations imposed by the circumstances rather than by management or those charged with governance, the auditor shall evaluate the effect on the auditor's opinion in accordance with ISA (UK and Ireland) 705. (Ref: Para. A18-4)

Reporting Non-Compliance to Regulatory and Enforcement Authorities

28   If the auditor has identified or suspects non-compliance with laws and regulations, the auditor shall determine whether the auditor has a responsibility to report the identified or suspected non-compliance to parties outside the entity. (Ref: Para. A19-A20)

Documentation

29   The auditor shall include in the audit documentation identified or suspected non-compliance with laws and regulations and the results of discussion with management and, where applicable, those charged with governance and other parties outside the entity.[7] (Ref: Para. A21)

***

Application and Other Explanatory Material

Responsibility for Compliance with Laws and Regulations (Ref: Para. 3-8)

A1   It is the responsibility of management, with the oversight of those charged with governance, to ensure that the entity's operations are conducted in accordance with laws and regulations. Laws and regulations may affect an entity's financial statements in different ways: for example, most directly, they may affect specific disclosures required of the entity in the financial statements or they may prescribe the applicable financial reporting framework. They may also establish certain legal rights and obligations of the entity, some of which will be recognized in the entity's financial statements. In addition, laws and regulations may impose penalties in cases of non-compliance.

---

[6] *ISA (UK and Ireland) 705, "Modifications to the Opinion in the Independent Auditor's Report," paragraphs 7-8.*

[7] *ISA (UK and Ireland) 230, "Audit Documentation," paragraphs 8-11, and paragraph A6.*

The following are examples of the types of policies and procedures an entity may   **A2**
implement to assist in the prevention and detection of non-compliance with laws and
regulations:

- Monitoring legal requirements and ensuring that operating procedures are designed to meet these requirements.
- Instituting and operating appropriate systems of internal control.
- Developing, publicizing and following a code of conduct.
- Ensuring employees are properly trained and understand the code of conduct.
- Monitoring compliance with the code of conduct and acting appropriately to discipline employees who fail to comply with it.
- Engaging legal advisors to assist in monitoring legal requirements.
- Maintaining a register of significant laws and regulations with which the entity has to comply within its particular industry and a record of complaints.

In larger entities, these policies and procedures may be supplemented by assigning
appropriate responsibilities to the following:

- An internal audit function.
- An audit committee.
- A compliance function.

In the UK and Ireland, in certain sectors or activities (for example financial   **A2-1**
services), there are detailed laws and regulations that specifically require directors
to have systems to ensure compliance. Breaches of these laws and regulations
could have a material effect on the financial statements.

In the UK and Ireland, it is the directors' responsibility to prepare financial   **A2-2**
statements that give a true and fair view of the state of affairs of a company or
group and of its profit or loss for the financial year. Accordingly it is necessary,
where possible non-compliance with law or regulations has occurred which may
result in a material misstatement in the financial statements, for them to ensure
that the matter is appropriately reflected and/or disclosed in the financial
statements.

In the UK and Ireland directors and officers of companies have responsibility to   **A2-3**
provide information required by the auditor, to which they have a legal right of
access[7a]. Such legislation also provides that it is a criminal offence to give to the
auditor information or explanations which are misleading, false or deceptive.

Responsibility of the Auditor

Non-compliance by the entity with laws and regulations may result in a material   **A3**
misstatement of the financial statements. Detection of non-compliance, regardless of
materiality, may affect other aspects of the audit including, for example, the auditor's consideration of the integrity of management or employees.

Whether an act constitutes non-compliance with laws and regulations is a matter for   **A4**
legal determination, which is ordinarily beyond the auditor's professional competence to determine. Nevertheless, the auditor's training, experience and
understanding of the entity and its industry or sector may provide a basis to

---

[7a] *In the UK under Section 499 of the Companies Act 2006 or Sections 193(3) and 197 of the Companies Act 1990 in Ireland.*

recognize that some acts, coming to the auditor's attention, may constitute non-compliance with laws and regulations.

A5   In accordance with specific statutory requirements, the auditor may be specifically required to report, as part of the audit of the financial statements, on whether the entity complies with certain provisions of laws or regulations. In these circumstances, ISA (UK and Ireland) 700[8] or ISA 800[9] deal with how these audit responsibilities are addressed in the auditor's report. Furthermore, where there are specific statutory reporting requirements, it may be necessary for the audit plan to include appropriate tests for compliance with these provisions of the laws and regulations.

Considerations Specific to Public Sector Entities

A6   In the public sector, there may be additional audit responsibilities with respect to the consideration of laws and regulations which may relate to the audit of financial statements or may extend to other aspects of the entity's operations.

The Auditor's Consideration of Compliance with Laws and Regulations

Obtaining an Understanding of the Legal and Regulatory Framework (Ref: Para. 12)

A7   To obtain a general understanding of the legal and regulatory framework, and how the entity complies with that framework, the auditor may, for example:

- Use the auditor's existing understanding of the entity's industry, regulatory and other external factors;
- Update the understanding of those laws and regulations that directly determine the reported amounts and disclosures in the financial statements;
- Inquire of management as to other laws or regulations that may be expected to have a fundamental effect on the operations of the entity;
- Inquire of management concerning the entity's policies and procedures regarding compliance with laws and regulations; and
- Inquire of management regarding the policies or procedures adopted for identifying, evaluating and accounting for litigation claims.

Laws and Regulations Generally Recognized to Have a Direct Effect on the Determination of Material Amounts and Disclosures in the Financial Statements (Ref: Para. 13)

A8   Certain laws and regulations are well-established, known to the entity and within the entity's industry or sector, and relevant to the entity's financial statements (as described in paragraph 6(a)). They could include those that relate to, for example:

- The form and content of financial statements[9a];

---

[8] *ISA (UK and Ireland) 700, "Forming an Opinion and Reporting on Financial Statements," paragraph 38. The APB has not promulgated ISA 700 as issued by the IAASB for application in the UK and Ireland. In the UK and Ireland the applicable auditing standard is ISA (UK and Ireland) 700, "The Auditor's Report on Financial Statements." Paragraph 21 of ISA (UK and Ireland) 700 is the equivalent to paragraph 38 of ISA 700.*

[9] *ISA 800 "Special Considerations—Audits of Financial Statements Prepared in Accordance with Special Purpose Frameworks," paragraph 11. ISA 800 has not been promulgated by the APB for application in the UK and Ireland.*

[9a] *In the UK under The Small Companies and Groups (Accounts and Directors' Report) Regulations 2008 (SI 2008-409) and The Large and Medium-sized Companies and Groups (Accounts and Reports) Regulations 2008 (SI 2008-410) or The Companies (Amendment) Act, 1986 in Ireland.*

- Industry-specific financial reporting issues;
- Accounting for transactions under government contracts; or
- The accrual or recognition of expenses for income tax or pension costs.

> In the UK and Ireland, these laws and regulations include:
>
> - Those which determine the circumstances under which a company is pro-hibited from making a distribution except out of profits available for the purpose[9b].
> - Those laws which require auditors expressly to report non-compliance, such as the requirements relating to the maintenance of adequate accounting records[9c] or the disclosure of particulars of directors' remuneration in a company's financial statements[9d].

Some provisions in those laws and regulations may be directly relevant to specific assertions in the financial statements (for example, the completeness of income tax provisions), while others may be directly relevant to the financial statements as a whole (for example, the required statements constituting a complete set of financial statements). The aim of the requirement in paragraph 13 is for the auditor to obtain sufficient appropriate audit evidence regarding the determination of amounts and disclosures in the financial statements in compliance with the relevant provisions of those laws and regulations.

Non-compliance with other provisions of such laws and regulations and other laws and regulations may result in fines, litigation or other consequences for the entity, the costs of which may need to be provided for in the financial statements, but are not considered to have a direct effect on the financial statements as described in para-graph 6(a).

> In the UK and Ireland, the auditor's responsibility to express an opinion on an entity's financial statements does not extend to determining whether the entity has complied in every respect with applicable tax legislation. The auditor needs to obtain sufficient appropriate evidence to give reasonable assurance that the amounts included in the financial statements in respect of taxation are not materially misstated. This will usually include making appropriate enquiries of those advising the entity on taxation matters (whether within the audit firm or elsewhere). If the auditor becomes aware that the entity has failed to comply with the requirements of tax legislation, the auditor considers whether to report the matter to parties outside the entity.

A8-1

Procedures to Identify Instances of Non-Compliance – Other Laws and Regulations
(Ref: Para. 14)

Certain other laws and regulations may need particular attention by the auditor because they have a fundamental effect on the operations of the entity (as described in paragraph 6(b)). Non-compliance with laws and regulations that have a

A9

[9b] *In the UK under Section 830 of the Companies Act 2006 or Section 45 of the Companies (Amendment) Act, 1983 in Ireland.*

[9c] *In the UK under Section 498 of the Companies Act 2006 and, in Ireland, under Section 193 and 194 of the Companies Act 1990.*

[9d] *In the UK under Section 497 of the Companies Act 2006. There is no equivalent in Ireland.*

fundamental effect on the operations of the entity may cause the entity to cease operations, or call into question the entity's continuance as a going concern. For example, non-compliance with the requirements of the entity's license or other entitlement to perform its operations could have such an impact (for example, for a bank, non-compliance with capital or investment requirements)[9e]. There are also many laws and regulations relating principally to the operating aspects of the entity that typically do not affect the financial statements and are not captured by the entity's information systems relevant to financial reporting.

A10   As the financial reporting consequences of other laws and regulations can vary depending on the entity's operations, the audit procedures required by paragraph 14 are directed to bringing to the auditor's attention instances of non-compliance with laws and regulations that may have a material effect on the financial statements.

A10-1   When determining the type of procedures necessary in a particular instance the auditor takes account of the particular entity concerned and the complexity of the regulations with which it is required to comply. In general, a small company which does not operate in a regulated area will require few specific procedures compared with a large multinational corporation carrying on complex, regulated business.

Non-Compliance Brought to the Auditor's Attention by Other Audit Procedures (Ref: Para. 15)

A11   Audit procedures applied to form an opinion on the financial statements may bring instances of non-compliance or suspected non-compliance with laws and regulations to the auditor's attention. For example, such audit procedures may include:

- Reading minutes;
- Inquiring of the entity's management and in-house legal counsel or external legal counsel concerning litigation, claims and assessments; and
- Performing substantive tests of details of classes of transactions, account balances or disclosures.

A11-1   In the UK and Ireland, the auditor is alert for instances of possible or actual non-compliance with laws and regulations including those that might incur obligations for partners and staff in audit firms to report to a regulatory or other enforcement authority. See paragraphs A11-2 and A19-1 – A19-12.

Money Laundering Offences

A11-2   Anti-money laundering legislation in the UK and Ireland imposes a duty on the auditor to report suspected money laundering activity. There are similar laws and regulations relating to financing terrorist offences[9f]. The detailed legislation in both countries differs but the impact on the auditor can broadly be summarised as follows:

[9e] *Such requirements exist in the UK under the Financial Services and Markets Act 2000 and in Ireland under the Investment Intermediaries Act 1995, the Central Bank Acts 1942 to 1989 and the Credit Union Act, 1997.*

[9f] *In the UK, the Terrorism Act 2000 contains reporting requirements for the laundering of terrorist funds which include any funds that are likely to be used for the financing of terrorism.*
In Ireland, the Criminal Justice Act 1994 (as amended) requires reporting suspicions of terrorist financing to the appropriate authorities.

- Partners and staff in audit firms are required to report suspicions of conduct which would constitute a criminal offence which gives rise to direct or indirect benefit.
- Partners and staff in audit firms need to be alert to the dangers of 'tipping-off' (in the UK) or 'prejudicing an investigation' (in Ireland), as this will constitute a criminal offence under the anti-money laundering legislation.[4a]

For the UK further detail is set out in Practice Note 12 (Revised): Money Laundering – Guidance for auditors on UK legislation.

Written Representations (Ref: Para. 16)

Because the effect on financial statements of laws and regulations can vary considerably, written representations provide necessary audit evidence about management's knowledge of identified or suspected non-compliance with laws and regulations, whose effects may have a material effect on the financial statements. However, written representations do not provide sufficient appropriate audit evidence on their own and, accordingly, do not affect the nature and extent of other audit evidence that is to be obtained by the auditor.[10] **A12**

Audit Procedures When Non-Compliance Is Identified or Suspected

Indications of Non-Compliance with Laws and Regulations (Ref: Para. 18)

If the auditor becomes aware of the existence of, or information about, the following matters, it may be an indication of non-compliance with laws and regulations: **A13**

- Investigations by regulatory organizations and government departments or payment of fines or penalties.
- Payments for unspecified services or loans to consultants, related parties, employees or government employees.
- Sales commissions or agent's fees that appear excessive in relation to those ordinarily paid by the entity or in its industry or to the services actually received.
- Purchasing at prices significantly above or below market price.
- Unusual payments in cash, purchases in the form of cashiers' cheques payable to bearer or transfers to numbered bank accounts.
- Unusual transactions with companies registered in tax havens.
- Payments for goods or services made other than to the country from which the goods or services originated.
- Payments without proper exchange control documentation.
- Existence of an information system which fails, whether by design or by accident, to provide an adequate audit trail or sufficient evidence.
- Unauthorized transactions or improperly recorded transactions.
- Adverse media comment.

[10] *ISA (UK and Ireland) 580, "Written Representations," paragraph 4.*

Matters Relevant to the Auditor's Evaluation (Ref: Para. 18(b))

A14   Matters relevant to the auditor's evaluation[10a] of the possible effect on the financial statements include:

- The potential financial consequences of non-compliance with laws and regulations on the financial statements including, for example, the imposition of fines, penalties, damages, threat of expropriation of assets[10b], enforced discontinuation of operations, and litigation.
- Whether the potential financial consequences require disclosure.
- Whether the potential financial consequences are so serious as to call into question the fair presentation of the financial statements, or otherwise make the financial statements misleading.

Audit Procedures (Ref: Para. 19)

A15   The auditor may discuss the findings with those charged with governance where they may be able to provide additional audit evidence. For example, the auditor may confirm that those charged with governance have the same understanding of the facts and circumstances relevant to transactions or events that have led to the possibility of non-compliance with laws and regulations.

A16   If management or, as appropriate, those charged with governance do not provide sufficient information to the auditor that the entity is in fact in compliance with laws and regulations, the auditor may consider it appropriate to consult with the entity's in-house legal counsel or external legal counsel about the application of the laws and regulations to the circumstances, including the possibility of fraud, and the possible effects on the financial statements. If it is not considered appropriate to consult with the entity's legal counsel or if the auditor is not satisfied with the legal counsel's opinion, the auditor may consider it appropriate to consult the auditor's own legal counsel as to whether a contravention of a law or regulation is involved, the possible legal consequences, including the possibility of fraud, and what further action, if any, the auditor would take.

Evaluating the Implications of Non-Compliance (Ref: Para. 21)

A17   As required by paragraph 21, the auditor evaluates the implications of non-compliance in relation to other aspects of the audit, including the auditor's risk assessment and the reliability of written representations. The implications of particular instances of non-compliance identified by the auditor will depend on the relationship of the perpetration and concealment, if any, of the act to specific control activities and the level of management or employees involved, especially implications arising from the involvement of the highest authority within the entity.

A18   In exceptional cases, the auditor may consider whether withdrawal from the engagement, where withdrawal is possible under applicable law or regulation, is

---

[10a] *ISA (UK and Ireland) 620, "Using the Work of an Auditor's Expert" applies if the auditor judges it necessary to obtain appropriate expert advice in connection with the evaluation of the possible effect of legal matters on the financial statements.*

[10b] *The Proceeds of Crime Act 2002 ("POCA") provides procedures to enable the authorities to confiscate in criminal proceedings or bring an action for civil recovery of assets which represent the benefits of criminal conduct.*
In Ireland, the Criminal Assets Bureau, an agency responsible for the confiscation of assets, was established by the Criminal Assets Bureau Act 1996.

necessary when management or those charged with governance do not take the remedial action that the auditor considers appropriate in the circumstances, even when the non-compliance is not material to the financial statements. When deciding whether withdrawal from the engagement is necessary, the auditor may consider seeking legal advice. If withdrawal from the engagement is not possible, the auditor may consider alternative actions, including describing the non-compliance in an Other Matter(s) paragraph in the auditor's report.[11]

Withdrawal from the engagement by the auditor is a step of last resort. It is normally preferable for the auditor to remain in office to fulfil the auditor's statutory duties, particularly where minority interests are involved. However, there are circumstances where there may be no alternative to withdrawal, for example where the directors of a company refuse to issue its financial statements or the auditor wishes to inform the shareholders or creditors of the company of the auditor's concerns and there is no immediate occasion to do so.   **A18-1**

Reporting of Identified or Suspected Non-Compliance

Reporting Non-Compliance to Those Charged with Governance (Ref: Para. 23)

If a non-compliance is intentional but not material the auditor considers whether the nature and circumstances make it appropriate to communicate to those charged with governance as soon as practicable.   **A18-2**

Suspicion that Management or Those Charged with Governance are Involved in Non-Compliance (Ref: Para. 24)

In the case of suspected Money Laundering it may be appropriate to report the matter direct to the appropriate authority.   **A18-3**

Reporting Non-Compliance in the Auditor's Report on the Financial Statements (Ref: Para. 27)

In the UK and Ireland, when considering whether the financial statements reflect the possible consequences of any suspected or actual non-compliance, the auditor has regard to the requirements of applicable accounting standards. Suspected or actual non-compliance with laws or regulations may require disclosure in the financial statements because, although the immediate financial effect on the entity may not be material[11a], there could be future material consequences such as fines or litigation. For example, an illegal payment may not itself be material but may result in criminal proceedings against the entity or loss of business which could have a material effect on the true and fair view given by the financial statements.   **A18-4**

---

[11] *ISA (UK and Ireland) 706, "Emphasis of Matter Paragraphs and Other Matter Paragraphs in the Independent Auditor's Report," paragraph 8.*
In the UK and Ireland, if the auditor concludes that the view given by the financial statements could be affected by a level of uncertainty concerning the consequences of a suspected or actual non-compliance which, in the auditor's opinion, is significant, the auditor, subject to a consideration of 'tipping off' or 'prejudicing an investigation' (see footnote 4a), includes an explanatory paragraph referring to the matter in the auditor's report.

[11a] *As discussed in ISA (UK and Ireland) 320, "Materiality in Planning and Performing an Audit," judgments about materiality are made in light of surrounding circumstances and are affected by the size or nature of a matter or a combination of both.*

Reporting Non-Compliance to Regulatory and Enforcement Authorities (Ref: Para. 28)

A19   The auditor's professional duty to maintain the confidentiality of client information may preclude reporting identified or suspected non-compliance with laws and regulations to a party outside the entity. However, the auditor's legal responsibilities vary by jurisdiction and, in certain circumstances, the duty of confidentiality may be overridden by statute, the law or courts of law. In some jurisdictions, the auditor of a financial institution has a statutory duty to report the occurrence, or suspected occurrence, of non-compliance with laws and regulations to supervisory authorities. Also, in some jurisdictions, the auditor has a duty to report misstatements to authorities in those cases where management and, where applicable, those charged with governance fail to take corrective action. The auditor may consider it appropriate to obtain legal advice to determine the appropriate course of action.

A19-1   Legislation in the UK and Ireland establishes specific responsibilities for the auditor to report suspicions regarding certain criminal offences (for example, in relation to money laundering offences (see paragraph A11-2) and, in the Republic of Ireland, indictable offences under company law and the Criminal Justice (Theft and Fraud Offences) Act 2001). In addition, the auditor of entities subject to statutory regulation[11b], has separate responsibilities to report certain information direct to the relevant regulator. Standards and guidance on these responsibilities is given in Section B of this ISA (UK and Ireland) and relevant APB Practice Notes.

A19-2   The procedures and guidance in Section B of this ISA (UK and Ireland) can be adapted to circumstances in which the auditor of other types of entity becomes aware of a suspected instance of non-compliance with laws or regulations which the auditor is under a statutory duty to report.

Timing of Reports

A19-3   Some laws and regulations stipulate a period within which reports are to be made. If the auditor becomes aware of a suspected or actual non-compliance with law and regulations which gives rise to a statutory duty to report, the auditor complies with any such stipulated periods for reporting. Ordinarily the auditor makes a report to the appropriate authority as soon as practicable.

Reporting in the Public Interest

A19-4   Where the auditor becomes aware of a suspected or actual instance of non-compliance with law or regulations which does not give rise to a statutory duty to report to an appropriate authority the auditor considers whether the matter may be one that ought to be reported to a proper authority in the public interest and, where this is the case, except in the circumstances covered in paragraph A19-6 below, discusses the matter with those charged with governance, including any audit committee[11c].

[11b] *Auditors of financial service entities, pension schemes and, in the UK, charities have a statutory responsibility, subject to compliance with legislation relating to 'tipping off' or 'prejudicing an investigation' (see footnote 4a), to report matters that are likely to be of material significance to the regulator.*

[11c] *In rare circumstances, according to common law, disclosure might also be justified in the public interest where there is no instance of non-compliance with law or regulations, e.g. where the public is being misled or their financial interests are being damaged; where a miscarriage of justice has occurred; where the health and safety of members of the public or the environment is being endangered – although such events may well constitute breaches of law or regulation.*

If, having considered any views expressed on behalf of the entity and in the light of any legal advice obtained, the auditor concludes that the matter ought to be reported to an appropriate authority in the public interest, the auditor notifies those charged with governance in writing of the view and, if the entity does not voluntarily do so itself or is unable to provide evidence that the matter has been reported, the auditor reports it.

A19-5

The auditor reports a matter direct to a proper authority in the public interest and without discussing the matter with the entity if the auditor concludes that the suspected or actual instance of non-compliance has caused the auditor no longer to have confidence in the integrity of those charged with governance.

A19-6

Examples of circumstances which may cause the auditor no longer to have confidence in the integrity of those charged with governance include situations:

A19-7

- Where the auditor suspects or has evidence of the involvement or intended involvement of those charged with governance in possible non-compliance with law or regulations which could have a material effect on the financial statements; or
- Where the auditor is aware that those charged with governance are aware of such non-compliance and, contrary to regulatory requirements or the public interest, have not reported it to a proper authority within a reasonable period. In such a case, if the auditor determines that continued holding of office is untenable or the auditor is removed from office by the client, the auditor will be mindful of the auditor's reporting duties[11d].

Determination of where the balance of public interest lies requires careful consideration. An auditor whose suspicions have been aroused uses professional judgment to determine whether the auditor's misgivings justify the auditor in carrying the matter further or are too insubstantial to deserve reporting. The auditor is protected from the risk of liability for breach of confidence or defamation provided that:

A19-8

- In the case of breach of confidence, disclosure is made in the public interest, and such disclosure is made to an appropriate body or person[11e], and there is no malice motivating the disclosure; and
- In the case of defamation disclosure is made in the auditor's capacity as auditor of the entity concerned, and there is no malice motivating the disclosure.

[11d] *In the UK, under Part 16 of the Companies Act 2006.*

[11e] *In the UK, proper authorities could include the Serious Fraud Office, the Crown Prosecution Service, police forces, the Financial Services Authority the Panel on Takeovers and Mergers, the Society of Lloyd's, local authorities, the Charity Commissioners for England and Wales, the Scottish Office For Scottish Charities, HM Revenue and Customs, the Department of Business Innovation and Skills and the Health and Safety Executive. In Ireland, comparable bodies could include the Garda Bureau of Fraud Investigation, the Revenue Commissioners, the Irish Stock Exchange, the Irish Financial Services Regulatory Authority, the Pensions Board, the Director of Corporate Enforcement, the Health and Safety Authority, The Charities Regulatory Authority and the Department of Enterprise Trade and Employment.*

In addition, the auditor is protected from such risks where the auditor is expressly permitted or required by legislation to disclose information[11f].

A19-9   'Public interest' is a concept that is not capable of general definition. Each situation must be considered individually. In the UK, legal precedent indicates that matters to be taken into account when considering whether disclosure is justified in the public interest may include:

- The extent to which the suspected or actual non-compliance with law or regulations is likely to affect members of the public;
- Whether those charged with governance have rectified the matter or are taking, or are likely to take, effective corrective action;
- The extent to which non-disclosure is likely to enable the suspected or actual non-compliance with law or regulations to recur with impunity;
- The gravity of the matter;
- Whether there is a general ethos within the entity of disregarding law or regulations; and
- The weight of evidence and the degree of the auditor's suspicion that there has been an instance of non-compliance with law or regulations.

A19-10   An auditor who can demonstrate having acted reasonably and in good faith in informing an authority of a breach of law or regulations which the auditor thinks has been committed would not be held by the court to be in breach of duty to the client even if, an investigation or prosecution having occurred, it were found that there had been no offence.

A19-11   The auditor needs to remember that the auditor's decision as to whether to report, and if so to whom, may be called into question at a future date, for example on the basis of:

- What the auditor knew at the time;
- What the auditor ought to have known in the course of the audit;
- What the auditor ought to have concluded; and
- What the auditor ought to have done.

The auditor may also wish to consider the possible consequences if financial loss is occasioned by non-compliance with law or regulations which the auditor suspects (or ought to suspect) has occurred but decided not to report.

A19-12   The auditor may need to take legal advice before making a decision on whether the matter needs to be reported to a proper authority in the public interest.

Considerations Specific to Public Sector Entities

A20   A public sector auditor may be obliged to report on instances of non-compliance to the legislature or other governing body or to report them in the auditor's report.

[11f] *In the UK, the Employments Rights Act 1996 would give similar protection to an individual member of the audit engagement team who made an appropriate report in the public interest. However, ordinarily a member of the engagement team who believed there was a reportable matter would follow the audit firm's policies and procedures to address such matters. ISA (UK and Ireland) 220, "Quality Control for an Audit of Financial Statements," paragraph 18(a), requires that the engagement partner shall take responsibility for the engagement team undertaking appropriate consultation on difficult or contentious matters. If differences of opinion arise within the engagement team, ISA (UK and Ireland) 220, paragraph 22, requires that the engagement team shall follow the firm's policies and procedures for dealing with and resolving differences of opinion.*

Documentation (Ref: Para. 29)

The auditor's documentation of findings regarding identified or suspected non- **A21**
compliance with laws and regulations may include, for example:

- Copies of records or documents.
- Minutes of discussions held with management, those charged with governance or parties outside the entity.

International Standard on Auditing (UK and Ireland) 250

Section B – The auditor's right and duty to report to regulators in the financial sector

*(Effective for audits of financial statements for periods
ending on or after 15 December 2010)*

Contents

International Standard on Auditing (UK and Ireland) (ISA (UK and Ireland))
250, "Consideration of Laws and Regulations in an Audit of Financial
Statements" should be read in conjunction with ISA (UK and Ireland) 200,
"Overall Objectives of the Independent Auditor and the Conduct of an Audit
in Accordance with International Standards on Auditing (UK and Ireland)."

Introduction

Scope of this Section

This Section of ISA (UK and Ireland) 250 deals with the circumstances in which the auditor of a financial institution subject to statutory regulation (a 'regulated entity') is required to report direct to a regulator information which comes to the auditor's attention in the course of the work undertaken in the auditor's capacity as auditor of the regulated entity. This may include work undertaken to express an opinion on the entity's financial statements, other financial information or on other matters specified by legislation or by a regulator.

1

The Auditor's Responsibilities (Ref: Para. A1-A8)

The auditor of a regulated entity generally has special reporting responsibilities in addition to the responsibility to report on financial statements. These special reporting responsibilities take two forms:

2

(a) *A responsibility to provide a report on matters specified in legislation or by a regulator.* This form of report is often made on an annual or other routine basis and does not derive from another set of reporting responsibilities. The auditor is required to carry out appropriate procedures sufficient to form an opinion on the matters concerned. These procedures may be in addition to those carried out to form an opinion on the financial statements; and

(b) *A statutory duty to report certain information, relevant to the regulators' functions, that come to the auditor's attention in the course of the audit work.* The auditor has no responsibility to carry out procedures to search out the information relevant to the regulator. This form of report is derivative in nature, arising only in the context of another set of reporting responsibilities, and is initiated by the auditor on discovery of a reportable matter.

This section of this ISA (UK and Ireland) deals with both forms of direct reports. Guidance on the auditor's responsibility to provide special reports on a routine basis on other matters specified in legislation or by a regulator is given in the Practice Notes dealing with regulated business, for example banks, building societies, investment businesses and insurers.

3

The statutory duty to report to a regulator applies to information which comes to the attention of the auditor in the auditor's capacity as auditor. In determining whether information is obtained in that capacity, two criteria in particular need to be considered: first, whether the person who obtained the information also undertook the audit work; and if so, whether it was obtained in the course of or as a result of undertaking the audit work. Appendix 2 to this Section of this ISA (UK and Ireland) sets out guidance on the application of these criteria.

4

The auditor may have a statutory right to bring information to the attention of the regulator in particular circumstances which lie outside those giving rise to a statutory duty to initiate a direct report. Where this is so, the auditor may use that right to make a direct report relevant to the regulator on a specific matter which comes to the auditor's attention when the auditor concludes that doing so is necessary to protect the interests of those for whose benefit the regulator is required to act.

5

6   The requirements and explanatory material in this section of this ISA (UK and Ireland) complement but do not replace the legal and regulatory requirements applicable to each regulated entity. Where the application of those legal and regulatory requirements, taking into account any published interpretations, is insufficiently clear for the auditor to determine whether a particular circumstance results in a legal duty to make a report to a regulator, or a right to make such a report, it may be appropriate to take legal advice.

Effective Date

7   This Section of ISA (UK and Ireland) 250 is effective for audits of financial statements for periods ending on or after 15 December 2010.

Objective

8   The objective of the auditor of a regulated entity is to bring information of which the auditor has become aware in the ordinary course of performing work undertaken to fulfil the auditor's audit responsibilities to the attention of the appropriate regulator as soon as practicable when:

(a)   The auditor concludes that it is relevant to the regulator's functions having regard to such matters as may be specified in statute or any related regulations; and

(b)   In the auditor's opinion there is reasonable cause to believe it is or may be of material significance to the regulator.

Definitions

9   For purposes of this Section of this ISA (UK and Ireland), the following terms have the meanings attributed below:

(a)   **The Act(s)**: means those Acts that give rise to a duty to report to a regulator. For example:
In the United Kingdom, this includes the Financial Services and Markets Act 2000 and regulations made under that Act, and any future legislation including provisions relating to the duties of auditors similar to those contained in that statute.
In the Republic of Ireland, this includes the Central Bank Acts 1942 to 1989, the Building Societies Act 1989, The Central Bank and Financial Services Authority of Ireland Act, 2003, the Trustees Savings Bank Act 1989, the Insurance Act 1989, the European Communities (Undertakings for Collective Investment in Transferable Securities) Regulations 1989, the Unit Trusts Act 1990 and, in the case of investment companies, the Companies Act 1990 and any future legislation including provisions relating to the duties of auditors similar to those contained in those Acts, together with other regulations made under them.

(b)   **Audit**: for the purpose of this Section of this ISA (UK and Ireland), the term *audit* refers both to an engagement to report on the financial statements of a regulated entity and to an engagement to provide a report on other matters specified by statute or by a regulator undertaken in the capacity of auditor.

(c)   **Auditor**: the term 'auditor' should be interpreted in accordance with the requirements of the Acts. Guidance on its interpretation is contained in

Practice Notes relating to each area of the financial sector to which the duty applies.

(d) **Material significance**: the term 'material significance' requires interpretation in the context of the specific legislation applicable to the regulated entity. A matter or group of matters is normally of material significance to a regulator's functions when, due either to its nature or its potential financial impact, it is likely of itself to require investigation by the regulator. Further guidance on the interpretation of the term in the context of specific legislation is contained in Practice Notes dealing with the rights and duties of auditors of regulated entities to report direct to regulators.

(e) **Regulated entity**: an individual, company or other type of entity authorised to carry on business in the financial sector which is subject to statutory regulation.

(f) **Regulator**: such persons as are empowered by the Act to regulate business in the financial sector. The term includes the Financial Services Authority (FSA), Irish Financial Services Regulatory Authority (IFSRA) and such other bodies as may be so empowered in future legislation.

(g) **'Tipping off'** involves a disclosure that is likely to prejudice any investigation into suspected money laundering which might arise from a report being made to a regulatory authority[1]. Money laundering involves an act which conceals, disguises, converts, transfers, removes, uses, acquires or possesses property which constitutes or represents a benefit from criminal conduct.

Requirements

Conduct of the Audit

Planning

When obtaining an understanding of the business for the purpose of the audit, the auditor of a regulated entity shall obtain an understanding of its current activities, the scope of its authorisation and the effectiveness of its control environment. (Ref: Para. A9-A16)

10

Supervision and Control

The auditor shall ensure that all staff involved in the audit of a regulated entity have an understanding of:

11

(a) The provisions of applicable legislation;
(b) The regulator's rules and any guidance issued by the regulator; and
(c) Any specific requirements which apply to the particular regulated entity,

appropriate to their role in the audit and sufficient (in the context of that role) to enable them to identify situations which may give reasonable cause to believe that a matter should be reported to the regulator. (Ref: Para. A17-A23)

---

[1] *More detail is provided in the definition contained in Section A of ISA (UK and Ireland) 250.*

Identifying Matters Requiring a Report Direct to Regulators

12   Where an apparent breach of statutory or regulatory requirements comes to the auditor's attention, the auditor shall:

(a) Obtain such evidence as is available to assess its implications for the auditor's reporting responsibilities;

(b) Determine whether, in the auditor's opinion, there is reasonable cause to believe that the breach is of material significance to the regulator; and

(c) Consider whether the apparent breach is criminal conduct that gives rise to criminal property and, as such, should be reported to the specified authorities. (Ref: Para. A24-A30)

Reporting (Ref: Para. A31-A46)

The Auditor's Statutory Duty to Report Direct to Regulators

13   When the auditor concludes, after appropriate discussion and investigations, that a matter which has come to the auditor's attention gives rise to a statutory duty to make a report the auditor shall[2] bring the matter to the attention of the regulator as soon as practicable in a form and manner which will facilitate appropriate action by the regulator. When the initial report is made orally, the auditor shall make a contemporaneous written record of the oral report and shall confirm the matter in writing to the regulator. (Ref: Para. A31-A35)

14   When the matter giving rise to a statutory duty to make a report direct to a regulator casts doubt on the integrity of those charged with governance or their competence to conduct the business of the regulated entity, the auditor shall[2] make the report to the regulator as soon as practicable and without informing those charged with governance in advance. (Ref: Para. A35)

The Auditor's Right to Report Direct to Regulators

15   When a matter comes to the auditor's attention which the auditor concludes does not give rise to a statutory duty to report but nevertheless may be relevant to the regulator's exercise of its functions, the auditor shall[2]:

(a) Consider whether the matter should be brought to the attention of the regulator under the terms of the appropriate legal provisions enabling the auditor to report direct to the regulator; and, if so

(b) Advise those charged with governance that in the auditor's opinion the matter should be drawn to the regulators' attention.

Where the auditor is unable to obtain, within a reasonable period, adequate evidence that those charged with governance have properly informed the regulator of the matter, the auditor shall[2] make a report direct to the regulator as soon as practicable. (Ref: Para. A36-A37)

---

[2] *In the UK, subject to compliance with legislation relating to 'tipping off'.*

Contents of a Report Initiated by the Auditor

When making or confirming in writing a report direct to a regulator, the auditor shall: **16**

(a) State the name of the regulated entity concerned;
(b) State the statutory power under which the report is made;
(c) State that the report has been prepared in accordance with ISA (UK and Ireland) 250, Section B 'The Auditor's Right and Duty to Report to Regulators in the Financial Sector';
(d) Describe the context in which the report is given;
(e) Describe the matter giving rise to the report;
(f) Request the regulator to confirm that the report has been received; and
(g) State the name of the auditor, the date of the written report and, where appropriate, the date on which an oral report was made to the regulator and the name and title of the individual to whom the oral report was made. (Ref: Para. A38-A39)

Relationship With Other Reporting Responsibilities

When issuing a report expressing an opinion on a regulated entity's financial statements or on other matters specified by legislation or a regulator, the auditor: **17**

(a) Shall consider whether there are consequential reporting issues affecting the auditor's opinion which arise from any report previously made direct to the regulator in the course of the auditor's appointment; and
(b) Shall assess whether any matters encountered in the course of the audit indicate a need for a further direct report. (Ref: Para. A40-A43)

***

Application and Other Explanatory Material

The Auditor's Responsibilities (Ref: Para. 2-6)

Before accepting appointment, the auditor follows the procedures identified in the APB's Ethical Standards for Auditors and the ethical pronouncements and Audit Regulations issued by the auditor's relevant professional body.   **A1**

In the case of regulated entities, the auditor would in particular obtain an understanding of the appropriate statutory and regulatory requirements and a preliminary knowledge of the management and operations of the entity, so as to enable the auditor to determine whether a level of knowledge of the business adequate to perform the audit can be obtained. The procedures carried out by the auditor in seeking to obtain this preliminary understanding may include discussion with the previous auditor and, in some circumstances, with the regulator.   **A2**

On ceasing to hold office, the auditor may be required by statute or by regulation to make specific reports concerning the circumstances relating to that event, and would also follow the procedures identified in the ethical guidance issued by the relevant professional body.   **A3**

In addition, the auditor of a regulated entity would assess whether it is appropriate to bring any matters of which the auditor is then aware to the notice of the   **A4** regulator. Under legislation in the UK, this may be done either before or after ceasing to hold office, as the auditor's statutory right to disclose to a regulator information obtained in the course of the auditor's appointment is not affected by the auditor's removal, resignation or otherwise ceasing to hold office.

A5   The duty to make a report direct to a regulator does not impose upon the auditor a duty to carry out specific work: it arises solely in the context of work carried out to fulfil other reporting responsibilities. Accordingly, no auditing procedures in addition to those carried out in the normal course of auditing the financial statements, or for the purpose of making any other specified report, are necessary for the fulfilment of the auditor's responsibilities.

A6   It will, however, be necessary for the auditor to take additional time in carrying out a financial statement audit or other engagement to assess whether matters which come to the auditor's attention should be included in a direct report and, where appropriate, to prepare and submit the report. These additional planning and follow-up procedures do not constitute an extension of the scope of the financial statement audit or of other work undertaken to provide a specified report relating to a regulated entity. They are necessary solely in order to understand and clarify the reporting responsibility and, where appropriate, to make a report.

A7   The circumstances in which the auditor is required by statute to make a report direct to a regulator include matters which are not considered as part of the audit of financial statements or of work undertaken to discharge other routine responsibilities. For example, the duty to report would apply to information of which the auditor became aware in the course of the auditor's work which is relevant to the FSA's criteria for approved persons, although the auditor is not otherwise required to express an opinion on such matters. However, the legislation imposing a duty to make reports direct to regulators does not require the auditor to change the scope of the audit work, nor does it place on the auditor an obligation to conduct the audit work in such a way that there is reasonable certainty that the auditor will discover all matters which regulators might consider as being of material significance. Therefore, whilst the auditor of a regulated entity is required to be alert to matters which may require a report, the auditor is not expected to be aware of all circumstances which, had the auditor known of them, would have led the auditor to make such a report. It is only when the auditor becomes aware of such a matter during the conduct of the normal audit work that the auditor has an obligation to determine whether a report to the regulator is required by statute or appropriate for other reasons.

A8   Similarly, the auditor is not responsible for reporting on a regulated entity's overall compliance with rules with which it is required to comply nor is the auditor required to conduct the audit work in such a way that there is reasonable certainty that the auditor will discover breaches. Nevertheless, breaches of rules with which a regulated entity is required to comply may have implications for the financial statements and, accordingly, the auditor of a regulated entity needs to consider whether any actual or contingent liabilities may have arisen from breaches of regulatory requirements. Breaches of a regulator's requirements may also have consequences for other matters on which the auditor of a regulated entity is required to express an opinion and, if such breaches represent criminal conduct, could give rise to the need to report to specified authorities.

Conduct of the Audit

Planning (Ref: Para. 10)

ISAs (UK and Ireland) require the auditor to obtain an understanding of the entity and its environment[3].

A9

In the context of a regulated entity, the auditor's understanding of its business needs to extend to the applicable statutory provisions, the rules of the regulator concerned and any guidance issued by the regulator on the interpretation of those rules, together with other guidance issued by the APB.

A10

The auditor is also required to identify and assess the risks of material misstatements to provide a basis for designing and performing further audit procedures[4]. In making such an assessment the auditor takes into account the control environment, including the entity's higher level procedures for complying with the requirements of its regulator. Such a review gives an indication of the extent to which the general atmosphere and controls in the regulated entity are conducive to compliance, for example through consideration of *inter alia:*

A11

- The adequacy of procedures and training to inform staff of the requirements of relevant legislation and the rules or other regulations of the regulator;
- The adequacy of procedures for authorisation of transactions;
- Procedures for internal review of the entity's compliance with regulatory or other requirements;
- The authority of, and any resources available to, the compliance officer/ Money Laundering Reporting Officer ('MLRO'); and
- Procedures to ensure that possible breaches of requirements are investigated by an appropriate person and are brought to the attention of senior management.

In some areas of the financial sector, conducting business outside the scope of the entity's authorisation is a serious regulatory breach, and therefore of material significance to the regulator. In addition, it may result in fines, suspension or loss of authorisation.

A12

Where the auditor's review of the reporting entity's activities indicates that published guidance by the regulator may not be sufficiently precise to enable the auditor to identify circumstances in which it is necessary to initiate a report, the auditor would consider whether it is necessary to discuss the matters specified in legislation with the appropriate regulator with a view to reaching agreement on its interpretation.

A13

Similarly, where a group includes two or more companies separately regulated by different regulators, there may be a need to clarify the regulators' requirements in any overlapping areas of activity. However, the statutory duty to make a report as presently defined arises only in respect of the legal entity subject to regulation. Therefore the auditor of an unregulated company in a group that includes one or more other companies which are authorised by regulators would not have a duty to report matters to the regulators of those companies.

A14

---

[3] *ISA (UK and Ireland) 315, "Identifying and Assessing the Risks of Material Misstatement through Understanding the Entity and Its Environment," paragraph 11.*

[4] *ISA (UK and Ireland) 315, paragraph 25.*

A15   When a regulated entity is subject to provisions of two or more regulators, the auditor needs to take account of the separate reporting requirements in planning and conducting the audit work. Arrangements may exist for one regulatory body to rely on financial monitoring being carried out by another body (the 'lead regulator') and where this is the case, routine reports by the regulated entity's auditor may be made to the lead regulator alone.

A16   However, the auditor's statutory duty to report cannot be discharged by reliance on the lead regulator informing others. Therefore, where the auditor concludes that a matter is of material significance to one regulator, the auditor needs to assess the need for separate reports informing each regulator of matters which the auditor concludes are or may be of material significance to it.

Supervision and Control (Ref: Para. 11)

A17   ISAs (UK and Ireland) require the engagement partner to take responsibility for the direction, supervision and performance of the audit engagement in compliance with professional standards and applicable legal and regulatory requirements[5]. Consequently, in planning and conducting the audit of a regulated entity the auditor needs to ensure that staff are alert to the possibility that a report to its regulator may be required.

A18   Auditing firms also need to establish adequate procedures to ensure that any matters which are discovered in the course of or as a result of audit work and may give rise to a duty to report are brought to the attention of the partner responsible for the audit on a timely basis.

A19   The right and duty to report to a regulator applies to information of which the auditor becomes aware in the auditor's capacity as such. They do not extend automatically to any information obtained by an accounting firm regardless of its source. Consequently partners and staff undertaking work in another capacity are not required to have detailed knowledge of the regulator's requirements (unless necessary for that other work) nor to bring information to the attention of the partner responsible for the audit on a routine basis.

A20   However, as discussed further in Appendix 2, firms need to establish lines of communications, commensurate with their size and complexity, sufficient to ensure that non-audit work undertaken for a regulated entity which is likely to have an effect on the audit is brought to the attention of the partner responsible for the audit, who will need to determine whether the results of non-audit work undertaken for a regulated entity ought to be assessed as part of the audit process.

Reliance on Other Auditors

A21   An auditor with responsibilities for reporting on financial statements including financial information of one or more components audited by other auditors is required to obtain sufficient appropriate audit evidence that the work of the other auditors is adequate for the purposes of the audit. The same principle applies to reliance on another auditor in a different type of engagement. The auditor of a regulated entity who relies on work undertaken by other auditors needs to establish reporting arrangements such that the other auditors bring to the

---

[5] *ISA (UK and Ireland) 220, "Quality Control for an Audit of Financial Statements," paragraph 15.*

attention of the auditor of the regulated entity matters arising from their work which may give rise to a duty to report to a regulator.

The nature of the reporting arrangements will depend on the nature of the work undertaken by the other auditors. For example, the statutory duty to make a report relates to the legal entity subject to regulation rather than to the entire group to which that entity may belong. Consequently, the auditor of a holding company authorised by one regulator would not be expected to have knowledge of all matters which come to the attention of a subsidiary's auditor. The auditor of the regulated entity would, however, have a duty to report, where appropriate, matters which arise from the audit of the regulated entity's own financial statements and of the consolidated group figures.

A22

Where the audit of a regulated entity is undertaken by joint auditors, knowledge obtained by one auditing firm is likely to be deemed to be known by the other. Care will therefore be needed in agreeing and implementing arrangements to exchange information relating to matters which may give rise to a duty to report to a regulator.

A23

Identifying Matters Requiring a Report Direct to Regulators (Ref: Para. 12)

The precise matters which give rise to a statutory duty on auditors to make a report to a regulator derive from the relevant Acts. Broadly, such matters fall into three general categories:

A24

(a) The financial position of the regulated entity;
(b) Its compliance with requirements for the management of its business; and
(c) The status of those charged with governance as fit and proper persons.

Further detailed guidance on the interpretation of these matters in the context of specific legislation applicable to each type of regulated entity is contained in Practice Notes dealing with the rights and duties of auditors of regulated entities to report direct to regulators.

In assessing the effect of an apparent breach, the auditor takes into account the quantity and type of evidence concerning such a matter which may reasonably be expected to be available. If the auditor concludes that the auditor has been prevented from obtaining all such evidence concerning a matter which may give rise to a duty to report, the auditor would normally make a report direct to the regulator as soon as practicable.

A25

An apparent breach of statutory or regulatory requirements may not of itself give rise to a statutory duty to make a report to a regulator. There will normally be a need for some further investigation and discussion of the circumstances surrounding the apparent breach with the directors in order to obtain sufficient information to determine whether it points to a matter which is or may be of material significance to the regulator. For example, a minor breach which has been corrected by the regulated entity and reported (if appropriate) to the regulator, and which from the evidence available to the auditor appears to be an isolated occurrence, would not normally give the auditor reasonable cause to believe that it is or may be of material significance to the regulator. However a minor breach that results in a criminal offence that gave rise to the criminal property would be reportable to the specified authorities under the anti-money laundering legislation.

A26

A27   When determining whether a breach of statutory or regulatory requirements gives rise to a statutory duty to make a report direct to a regulator, the auditor considers factors such as:

- Whether the breach, though minor, is indicative of a general lack of compliance with the regulator's requirements or otherwise casts doubt on the status of those charged with governance as fit and proper persons;
- Whether a breach which occurred before the auditor's visit to the regulated entity was reported by the entity itself and has since been corrected, such that, at the date of the auditor's discovery, no breach exists;
- Whether the circumstances giving rise to a breach which occurred before the auditors visit to the regulated entity continue to exist, or those charged with governance have not taken corrective action, or the breach has re-occurred; and
- Whether the circumstances suggest that an immediate report to the regulator is necessary in order to protect the interests of depositors, investors, policyholders, clients of the entity or others in whose interests the regulator is required to act.

A28   The auditor would normally seek evidence to assess the implications of a suspected breach before reporting a matter to the regulator. However, the auditor's responsibility to make a report does not require the auditor to determine the full implications of a matter before reporting: the auditor is required to exercise professional judgment as to whether or not there is reasonable cause to believe that a matter is or may be of material significance to the regulator. In forming that judgment, the auditor undertakes appropriate investigations to determine the circumstances but does not require the degree of evidence which would be a normal part of forming an opinion on financial statements. Such investigations would normally include:

- Enquiry of appropriate level of staff;
- Review of correspondence and documents relating to the transaction or event concerned; and
- Discussion with those charged with governance, or other senior management where appropriate.

In the case of a life company, it would also be appropriate to consult with the appointed actuary, who also has various statutory duties under insurance companies legislation.

A29   The potential gravity of some apparent breaches may be such that an immediate report to the regulator is essential in order to enable the regulator to take appropriate action: in particular, prompt reporting of a loss of client assets may be necessary to avoid further loss to investors or others in whose interests the regulator is required to act. The auditor is therefore required to balance the need for further investigation of the matter with the need for prompt reporting.

A30   On completion of the auditor's investigations, the auditor needs to ensure that the facts and the basis for the auditor's decision (whether to report or not) is adequately documented such that the reasons for that decision may be clearly demonstrated should the need to do so arise in future.

Reporting

The Auditor's Statutory Duty to Report Direct to Regulators (Ref: Para. 13-14)

Except in the circumstances referred to in paragraph 14 the auditor seeks to reach   **A31**
agreement with those charged with governance on the circumstances giving rise to
a report direct to the regulator. However, where a statutory duty to report arises,
the auditor is required to make such a report regardless of:

(a) Whether the matter has been referred to the regulator by other parties
(including the company, whether by those charged with governance or
otherwise); and

(b) Any duty owed to other parties, including those charged with governance of
the regulated entity and its shareholders (or equivalent persons).

Except in the circumstances set out in paragraph 14, the auditor sends a copy of   **A32**
the auditor's written report to those charged with governance and (where
appropriate) audit committee of the regulated entity.

In normal circumstances, the auditor would wish to communicate with the reg-   **A33**
ulator with the knowledge and agreement of those charged with governance of the
regulated entity. However, in some circumstances immediate notification of the
discovery of a matter giving reasonable grounds to believe that a reportable
matter exists will be necessary – for example, a phone call to alert the regulator
followed by a meeting to discuss the circumstances.

Speed of reporting is essential where the circumstances cause the auditor no   **A34**
longer to have confidence in the integrity of those charged with governance. In
such circumstances, there may be a serious and immediate threat to the interests
of depositors or other persons for whose protection the regulator is required to
act; for example where the auditor believes that a fraud or other irregularity may
have been committed by, or with the knowledge of, those charged with governance, or have evidence of the intention of those charged with governance to
commit or condone a suspected fraud or other irregularity.

In circumstances where the auditor no longer has confidence in the integrity of   **A35**
those charged with governance, it is not appropriate to provide those charged
with governance with copies of the auditor's report. Since such circumstances will
be exceptional and extreme, the auditor may wish to seek legal advice as to the
auditor's responsibilities and the appropriate course of action.

The Auditor's Right to Report Direct to Regulators (Ref: Para. 15)

The auditor may become aware of matters which the auditor concludes are   **A36**
relevant to the exercise of the regulator's functions even though they fall outside
the statutory definition of matters which must be reported to a regulator. In such
circumstances, the Acts in the UK provide the auditor with protection for making
disclosure of the matter to the appropriate regulator[6].

---

[6] *There is no statutory provision of protection for a voluntary report under the Acts in the Republic of Ireland.*

A37   Where the auditor considers that a matter which does not give rise to a statutory duty to report is nevertheless, in the auditor's professional judgment, such that it should be brought to the attention of the regulator, it is normally appropriate for the auditor to request those charged with governance of the regulated entity in writing to draw it to the attention of the regulator.

Contents of a Report Initiated by the Auditor (Ref: Para. 16)

A38   Such a report is a by-product of other work undertaken by the auditor. As a result it is not possible for the auditor or the regulator to conclude that all matters relevant to the regulator were encountered in the course of the auditor's work. The auditor's report therefore sets out the context in which the information reported was identified and indicates the extent to which the matter has been investigated and discussed with those charged with governance.

A39   Matters to which the auditor may wish to refer when describing the context in which a report is made direct to a regulator include:

- The nature of the appointment from which the report derives. For example, it may be appropriate to distinguish between a report made in the course of an audit of financial statements and one which arises in the course of a more limited engagement, such as an appointment to report on specified matters by the FSA or IFSRA;
- The applicable legislative requirements and interpretations of those requirements which have informed the auditor's judgment;
- The extent to which the auditor has investigated the circumstances giving rise to the matter reported;
- Whether the matter reported has been discussed with those charged with governance;
- Whether steps to rectify the matter have been taken.

Relationship With Other Reporting Responsibilities (Ref: Para. 17)

A40   The circumstances which give rise to a report direct to a regulator may involve an uncertainty or other matter which requires disclosure in the financial statements. The auditor will therefore need to consider whether the disclosures made in the financial statements are adequate for the purposes of giving a true and fair view of the regulated entity's state of affairs and profit or loss. Where the auditor considers it necessary to draw users' attention to a matter presented or disclosed in the financial statements that, in the auditor's judgment, is of such importance that it is fundamental to users' understanding of the financial statements, the auditor is required to include an emphasis of matter paragraph in the auditor's report[7].

A41   Similarly, circumstances giving rise to a report direct to a regulator may also require reflection in the auditor's reports on other matters required by legislation or another regulator.

A42   In fulfilling the responsibility to report direct to a regulator, it is important that the auditor not only assess the significance of individual transactions or events but also consider whether a combination of such items over the course of the work undertaken for the auditor's primary reporting responsibilities may give the

---

[7] *ISA (UK and Ireland) 706 "Emphasis of Matter Paragraphs and Other Matter Paragraphs in the Independent Auditor's Report," paragraph 6.*

auditor reasonable grounds to believe that they constitute a matter of material significance to the regulator, and so give rise to a statutory duty to make a report.

As there is no requirement for the auditor to extend the scope of the audit work to search for matters which may give rise to a statutory duty to report, such an assessment of the cumulative effect of evidence obtained in the course of an audit would be made when reviewing the evidence in support of the opinions to be expressed in the reports the auditor has been appointed to make. Where such a review leads to the conclusion that the cumulative effect of matters noted in the course of the audit is of material significance to the regulator, it will be appropriate for a report to be made as set out in paragraph 16 above. However, reports indicating a 'nil return' are not appropriate.

A43

Communication of Information by the Regulator

The Acts provide that, in certain exceptional circumstances, regulators may pass confidential information to another party. The precise circumstances in which regulators may disclose information varies, but in general they may do so if considered necessary to fulfil their own obligations under the appropriate Act, or, in some cases, to enable the auditor to fulfil the auditor's duties either to the regulated entity or, in other cases, to the regulator. Confidential information remains confidential in the hands of the recipient.

A44

In so far as the law permits, regulators have confirmed that they will consider taking the initiative in bringing a matter to the attention of the auditor of a regulated entity in circumstances where:

A45

(a) They believe the matter is of such importance that the auditor's knowledge of it could significantly affect the form of the auditor's report on the entity's financial statements or other matters on which the auditor is required to report, or the way in which the auditor discharges the auditor's reporting responsibilities; and

(b) The disclosure is for the purpose of enabling or assisting the regulator to discharge its functions under the Acts.

The auditor needs to be aware that there may be circumstances in which the regulators are unable to disclose such information. Where the auditor of a regulated entity is not informed by the regulator of any matter, therefore, the auditor cannot assume that there are no matters known to the regulator which could affect the auditor's judgment as to whether information is of material significance. However, in the absence of disclosure by the regulator, the auditor can only form a judgment in the light of evidence to which the auditor has access.

A46

Appendix 1

The Regulatory Framework

In both the UK and Ireland, legislation exists in the principal areas of financial services to protect the interests of investors, depositors in banks and other users of financial services. Regulated entities operating in the financial sector are required to comply with legal and regulatory requirements concerning the way their business is conducted. Compliance with those rules is monitored in four principal ways:

1

- Internal monitoring by those charged with governance of the regulated entity;
- Submission of regular returns by the regulated entity to the regulator;
- Monitoring and, in some cases, inspection of the entity by the regulator;
- Reports[2] by the reporting entity's auditor on its financial statements and other specified matters required by legislation or by the regulator.

Responsibility for Ensuring Compliance

2   Ensuring compliance with the requirements with which a regulated entity is required to comply in carrying out its business is the responsibility of those charged with governance of a regulated entity. It requires adequate organisation and systems of controls. The regulatory framework provides that adequate procedures for compliance must be established and maintained. Those charged with governance of a regulated entity are also normally required to undertake regular reviews of compliance and to inform the regulator of any breach of the rules and regulations applicable to its regulated business. In addition, regulators may undertake compliance visits.

3   The auditor of a regulated entity normally has responsibilities for reporting[2] on particular aspects of its compliance with the regulator's requirements. However, the auditor has no direct responsibility for expressing an opinion on an entity's overall compliance with the requirements for the conduct of its business, nor does an audit provide any assurance that breaches of requirements which are not the subject of regular auditors' reports will be detected.

The Role of Auditors

4   Those charged with governance of regulated entities have primary responsibility for ensuring that all appropriate information is made available to regulators. Normal reporting procedures (including auditor's reports on records, systems and returns, and regular meetings with those charged with governance and/or management and auditors) supplemented by any inspection visits considered necessary by the regulators should provide the regulators with all the information they need to carry out their responsibilities under the relevant Act.

Routine Reporting by Auditors

5   Regulators' requirements for reports by auditors vary. In general terms, however, such reports may include opinions on:

- The regulated entity's annual financial statements;
- The regulated entity's compliance with requirements for financial resources; and
- The adequacy of the regulated entity's system of controls over its transactions and in particular over its clients' money and other property.

6   As a result of performing the work necessary to discharge their routine reporting responsibilities, or those arising from an appointment to provide a special report required by the regulator, the auditor of a regulated entity may become aware of matters which the auditor considers need to be brought to the regulator's attention sooner than would be achieved by routine reports by the entity or its auditor.

The auditor of a regulated entity normally has a right to communicate in good faith[2] information the auditor considers is relevant to the regulators' functions.   **7**

The Auditor's Statutory Duty to Report to the Regulator

In addition, the auditor is required by law to report[2] direct to a regulator when the auditor concludes that there is reasonable cause to believe that a matter is or may be of material significance to the regulator. The precise matters which result in a statutory duty to make such a report vary, depending upon the specific requirements of relevant legislation and the regulator's rules. In general, however, a duty to report to a regulator arises when the auditor becomes aware that: **8**

- The regulated entity is in serious breach of:
  - Requirements to maintain adequate financial resources; or
  - Requirements for those charged with governance to conduct its business in a sound and prudent manner (including the maintenance of systems of control over transactions and over any clients' assets held by the business); or
- There are circumstances which give reason to doubt the status of those charged with governance or senior management as fit and proper persons.

Confidentiality

Confidentiality is an implied term of the auditor's contracts with client entities. However[2] in the circumstances leading to a right or duty to report, the auditor is entitled to communicate to regulators in good faith information or opinions relating to the business or affairs of the entity or any associated body without contravening the duty of confidence owed to the entity and, in the case of a bank, building society and friendly society, its associated bodies.   **9**

The statutory provisions permitting the auditor to communicate information to regulators relate to information obtained in the auditor's capacity as auditor of the regulated entity concerned. Auditors and regulators therefore should be aware that confidential information obtained in other capacities may not normally be disclosed to another party.   **10**

Appendix 2

The Application of the Statutory Duty to Report to Regulators

Introduction

The statutory duty to report to a regulator[2] applies to information which comes to the attention of the auditor in the auditor's capacity as auditor. However, neither the term 'auditor' nor the phrase "in the capacity of auditor" are defined in the legislation, nor has the court determined how these expressions should be construed.   **1**

As a result, it is not always clearly apparent when an accounting firm should regard itself as having a duty to report to a regulator. For example, information about a regulated entity may be obtained when partners or staff of the firm which is appointed as its auditor carry out work for another client entity; or when the firm undertakes other work for the regulated entity. Auditors, regulated entities   **2** and regulators need to be clear as to when the normal duty of confidentiality will be overridden by the auditor's statutory duty to report to the regulator.

3   In order to clarify whether or not an accounting firm should regard itself as bound by the duty, the APB has developed, in conjunction with HM Treasury, the IFSRA and the regulators, guidance on the interpretation of the key conditions for the existence of that duty, namely that the firm is to be regarded as auditor of a regulated entity and that information is obtained in the capacity of auditor.

4   Guidance on the interpretation of the term 'auditor' in the context of each Act is contained in the separate Practice Notes dealing with each area affected by the legislation.

5   This appendix sets out guidance on the interpretation of the phrase "in the capacity of auditor". The Board nevertheless continues to hold the view that the meaning of the phrase should be clarified in legislation in the longer term.

In the Capacity of Auditor

6   In determining whether information is obtained in the capacity of auditor, two criteria in particular should be considered:

(a)   Whether the person who obtained the information also undertook the audit work; and if so
(b)   Whether it was obtained in the course of or as a result of undertaking the audit work.

7   It is then necessary to apply these criteria to information about a regulated entity which may become known from a number of sources, and by a number of different individuals within an accounting firm. Within a large firm, for example, information may come to the attention of the partner responsible for the audit of a regulated entity, a partner in another office who undertakes a different type of work, or members of the firm's staff at any level. In the case of a sole practitioner who is the auditor of a regulated entity, information about a regulated entity may also be obtained by the practitioner in the course of work other than its audit.

Non-Audit Work Carried out in Relation to a Regulated Entity

8   Where partners or staff involved in the audit of a regulated entity carry out work other than its audit (non-audit work) information about the regulated entity will be known to them as individuals. In circumstances which suggest that a matter would otherwise give rise to a statutory duty to report[2] if obtained in the capacity of auditor, it will be prudent for them to make enquiries in the course of their audit work in order to establish whether this is the case from information obtained in that capacity.

9   However where non-audit work is carried out by other partners or staff, neither of the criteria set out in paragraph 6 is met in respect of information which becomes known to them. Nevertheless the firm should take proper account of such information when it could affect the audit so that it is treated in a responsible manner, particularly since in partnership law the knowledge obtained by one partner in the course of the partnership business may be imputed to the entire partnership. In doing so, two types of work may be distinguished: first, work

which could affect the firm's work as auditor and, secondly, work which is undertaken purely in an advisory capacity.

A firm appointed as auditor of a regulated entity needs to have in place appropriate procedures to ensure that the partner responsible for the audit function is made aware of any other relationship which exists between any department of the firm and the regulated entity when that relationship could affect the firm's work as auditor. Common examples of such work include accounting work, particularly for smaller entities, and provision of tax services to the regulated entity.   **10**

Prima facie, information obtained in the course of non-audit work is not covered by either the right or the duty to report to a regulator. However, the firm appointed as auditor needs to consider whether the results of other work undertaken for a regulated entity need to be assessed as part of the audit process. In principle, this is no different to seeking to review a report prepared by outside consultants on, say, the entity's accounting systems so as to ensure that the auditor makes a proper assessment of the risks of misstatement in the financial statements and of the work needed to form an opinion. Consequently, the partner responsible for the audit needs to make appropriate enquiries in the process of planning and completing the audit (see paragraph 17 above). Such enquiries would be directed to those aspects of the non-audit work which might reasonably be expected to be relevant to the audit. When, as a result of such enquiries, those involved in the audit become aware of issues which may be of material significance to a regulator such issues should be considered, and if appropriate reported[2] following the requirements set out in this Section of this ISA (UK and Ireland).   **11**

Work which is undertaken in an advisory capacity, for example to assist the directors of a regulated entity to determine effective and efficient methods of discharging their duties, would not normally affect the work undertaken for the audit. Nevertheless, in rare instances, the partner responsible for such advisory work may conclude that steps considered necessary in order to comply with the regulator's requirements have not been taken by the directors or that the directors intend in some respect not to comply with the regulator's requirements. Such circumstances would require consideration in the course of work undertaken for the audit, both to consider the effect on the auditor's routine reports and to determine whether the possible non-compliance is or is likely to be of material significance to the regulator.   **12**

Work Relating to a Separate Entity

Information obtained in the course of work relating to another entity audited by the same firm (or the same practitioner) is confidential to that other entity. The auditor is not required, and has no right, to report to a regulator confidential information which arises from work undertaken by the same auditing firm for another client. However, as a matter of sound practice, individuals involved in the audit of a regulated entity who become aware (in a capacity other than that of auditor of a regulated entity) of a matter which could otherwise give rise to a statutory duty to report would normally make enquiries in the course of their audit of the regulated entity to establish whether the information concerned is substantiated.   **13**

In carrying out the audit work, the auditor is required to have due regard to whether disclosure of non-compliance with laws and regulations to a proper authority is appropriate in the public interest. standards and guidance on this   **14** general professional obligation is set out in Section A of this ISA (UK and Ireland).

Conclusion

15   The phrase "in his capacity as auditor" limits information subject to the duty to report to matters of which the auditor becomes aware in the auditor's capacity as such. Consequently, it is unlikely that a partnership can be said to be acting in its capacity as auditor of a particular regulated entity whenever any apparently unrelated material comes to the attention of a partner or member of staff not engaged in that audit, particularly if that material is confidential to another client.

16   The statutory duty to report to a regulator[2] therefore does not extend automatically to any information obtained by an accounting firm regardless of its source. Accounting firms undertaking audits of regulated entities need, however, to establish lines of communication, commensurate with their size and organisational structure, sufficient to ensure that non-audit work undertaken for a regulated entity which is likely to have an effect on the audit is brought to the attention of the partner responsible for the audit and to establish procedures for the partner responsible for the audit to make appropriate enquiries of those conducting such other work as part of the process of planning and completing the audit.

Appendix 3

Action by the Auditor on Discovery of a Breach of a Regulator's Requirements

1   This appendix sets out in the form of a flowchart the steps involved in assessing whether a report to a regulator is required when a breach of the regulator's requirements comes to the attention of the auditor.

2   The flowchart is intended to provide guidance to readers in understanding this Section of this ISA (UK and Ireland). It does not form part of the auditing standards contained in the ISA (UK and Ireland).

Action by the Auditor on Discovery of a Breach of a Regulator's Requirement

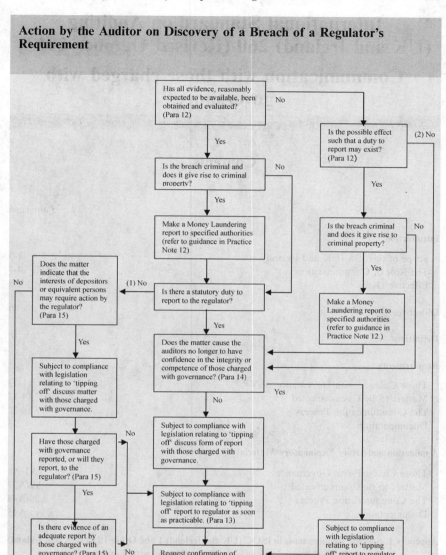

Has all evidence, reasonably expected to be available, been obtained and evaluated? (Para 12) — No

Is the possible effect such that a duty to report may exist? (Para 12) — (2) No

Yes

Is the breach criminal and does it give rise to criminal property? — No

Yes

Is the breach criminal and does it give rise to criminal property? — No

Yes

Make a Money Laundering report to specified authorities (refer to guidance in Practice Note 12)

Make a Money Laundering report to specified authorities (refer to guidance in Practice Note 12)

Does the matter indicate that the interests of depositors or equivalent persons may require action by the regulator? (Para 15) — No

(1) No

Is there a statutory duty to report to the regulator?

Yes

Yes

Subject to compliance with legislation relating to 'tipping off' discuss matter with those charged with governance.

Does the matter cause the auditors no longer to have confidence in the integrity or competence of those charged with governance? (Para 14)

Yes

No

Have those charged with governance reported, or will they report, to the regulator? (Para 15) — No

Subject to compliance with legislation relating to 'tipping off' discuss form of report with those charged with governance.

Yes

Subject to compliance with legislation relating to 'tipping off' report to regulator as soon as practicable. (Para 13)

Is there evidence of an adequate report by those charged with governance? (Para 15) — No

Subject to compliance with legislation relating to 'tipping off' report to regulator without informing those charged with governance. (Para 14)

Request confirmation of report's receipt. (Para 16)

Yes

Subject to compliance with legislation relating to 'tipping off' consider effect on other opinions. (Para 17)

(1) This route would be only followed when a distinct right to report to the regulator exists. Otherwise, where no duty to report exists, the auditor would next consider the effect on other opinions.

(2) Where the auditor considers that a distinct right to report to the regulator exists, the auditor would next consider the question marked (1).

International Standard on Auditing (UK and Ireland) 260 (Revised October 2012) Communication with those charged with governance

(Effective for audits of financial statements for periods commencing on or after 1 October 2012)[1a]

Contents

International Standard on Auditing (UK and Ireland) (ISA (UK and Ireland)) 260, "Communication with Those Charged with Governance" should be read in conjunction with ISA (UK and Ireland) 200, "Overall Objectives of the Independent Auditor and the Conduct of an Audit in Accordance with International Standards on Auditing (UK and Ireland)."

[1a] *Conforming amendments to this standard as a result of ISA (UK and Ireland) 610 (Revised June 2013), Using the Work of Internal Auditors, are included that are effective for audits of financial statements for periods ending on or after 15 June 2014. Details of the amendments are given in the Annexure to ISA (UK and Ireland) 610 (Revised June 2013).*

Introduction

Scope of this ISA (UK and Ireland)

This International Standard on Auditing (UK and Ireland) (ISA (UK and Ireland)) **1**
deals with the auditor's responsibility to communicate with those charged with
governance in an audit of financial statements. Although this ISA (UK and Ireland)
applies irrespective of an entity's governance structure or size, particular considerations apply where all of those charged with governance are involved in
managing an entity, and for listed entities. This ISA (UK and Ireland) does not
establish requirements regarding the auditor's communication with an entity's
management or owners unless they are also charged with a governance role.

This ISA (UK and Ireland) is written in the context of an audit of financial state- **2**
ments, but may also be applicable, adapted as necessary in the circumstances, to
audits of other historical financial information when those charged with governance
have a responsibility to oversee the preparation of the other historical financial
information.

Recognizing the importance of effective two-way communication in an audit of **3**
financial statements, this ISA (UK and Ireland) provides an overarching framework
for the auditor's communication with those charged with governance, and identifies
some specific matters to be communicated with them. Additional matters to be
communicated, which complement the requirements of this ISA (UK and Ireland),
are identified in other ISAs (UK and Ireland) (see Appendix 1). In addition, ISA
(UK and Ireland) 265[1] establishes specific requirements regarding the communication of significant deficiencies in internal control the auditor has identified during the
audit to those charged with governance. Further matters, not required by this or
other ISAs (UK and Ireland), may be required to be communicated by law or
regulation, by agreement with the entity, or by additional requirements applicable to
the engagement, for example, the standards of a national professional accountancy
body. Nothing in this ISA (UK and Ireland) precludes the auditor from communicating any other matters to those charged with governance. (Ref: Para. A24-A27)

The Role of Communication

This ISA (UK and Ireland) focuses primarily on communications from the auditor **4**
to those charged with governance. Nevertheless, effective two-way communication is
important in assisting:

(a) The auditor and those charged with governance in understanding matters
related to the audit in context, and in developing a constructive working relationship. This relationship is developed while maintaining the auditor's
independence and objectivity;

(b) The auditor in obtaining from those charged with governance information
relevant to the audit[1b]. For example, those charged with governance may assist
the auditor in understanding the entity and its environment, in identifying
appropriate sources of audit evidence, and in providing information about
specific transactions or events; and

---

[1] *ISA (UK and Ireland) 265, "Communicating Deficiencies in Internal Control to Those Charged with Governance and Management."*

[1b] *Sections 499 and 500 of the Companies Act 2006 set legal requirements in relation to the auditor's right to
obtain information. For the Republic of Ireland, relevant requirements are set out in Sections 193(3) and 196,
Companies Act 1990.*

(c) Those charged with governance in fulfilling their responsibility to oversee the financial reporting process, thereby reducing the risks of material misstatement of the financial statements.

5   Although the auditor is responsible for communicating matters required by this ISA (UK and Ireland), management also has a responsibility to communicate matters of governance interest to those charged with governance. Communication by the auditor does not relieve management of this responsibility. Similarly, communication by management with those charged with governance of matters that the auditor is required to communicate does not relieve the auditor of the responsibility to also communicate them. Communication of these matters by management may, however, affect the form or timing of the auditor's communication with those charged with governance.

6   Clear communication of specific matters required to be communicated by ISAs (UK and Ireland) is an integral part of every audit. ISAs (UK and Ireland) do not, however, require the auditor to perform procedures specifically to identify any other matters to communicate with those charged with governance.

7   Law or regulation may restrict the auditor's communication of certain matters with those charged with governance. For example, laws or regulations may specifically prohibit a communication, or other action, that might prejudice an investigation by an appropriate authority into an actual, or suspected, illegal act. In some circumstances, potential conflicts between the auditor's obligations of confidentiality and obligations to communicate may be complex. In such cases, the auditor may consider obtaining legal advice.

Effective Date

8   This ISA (UK and Ireland) is effective for audits of financial statements for periods commencing on or after 1 October 2012.[1a]

Objectives

9   The objectives of the auditor are:

(a) To communicate clearly with those charged with governance the responsibilities of the auditor in relation to the financial statement audit, and an overview of the planned scope and timing of the audit;

(b) To obtain from those charged with governance information relevant to the audit;

(c) To provide those charged with governance with timely observations arising from the audit that are significant and relevant to their responsibility to oversee the financial reporting process; and

(d) To promote effective two-way communication between the auditor and those charged with governance.

Definitions

10 For purposes of the ISAs (UK and Ireland), the following terms have the meanings attributed below:

(a) Those charged with governance – The person(s) or organization(s) (for example, a corporate trustee) with responsibility for overseeing the strategic direction of the entity and obligations related to the accountability of the entity. This includes overseeing the financial reporting process. For some entities in some jurisdictions, those charged with governance may include management personnel, for example, executive members of a governance board of a private or public sector entity, or an owner-manager.For discussion of the diversity of governance structures, see paragraphs A1-A8.

In the UK and Ireland, those charged with governance include the directors (executive and non-executive) of a company and the members of an audit committee where one exists. For other types of entity it usually includes equivalent persons such as the partners, proprietors, committee of management or trustees.

(b)   Management – The person(s) with executive responsibility for the conduct of the entity's operations. For some entities in some jurisdictions, management includes some or all of those charged with governance, for example, executive members of a governance board, or an owner-manager.

In the UK and Ireland, management will not normally include non-executive directors.

Requirements

Those Charged with Governance

The auditor shall determine the appropriate person(s) within the entity's governance structure with whom to communicate. (Ref: Para. A1-A4)   **11**

Communication with a Subgroup of Those Charged with Governance

If the auditor communicates with a subgroup of those charged with governance, for example, an audit committee, or an individual, the auditor shall determine whether the auditor also needs to communicate with the governing body. (Ref: Para. A5-A7)   **12**

When All of Those Charged with Governance Are Involved in Managing the Entity

In some cases, all of those charged with governance are involved in managing the entity, for example, a small business where a single owner manages the entity and no one else has a governance role. In these cases, if matters required by this ISA (UK and Ireland) are communicated with person(s) with management responsibilities, and those person(s) also have governance responsibilities, the matters need not be communicated again with those same person(s) in their governance role. These matters are noted in paragraph 16(c). The auditor shall nonetheless be satisfied that communication with person(s) with management responsibilities adequately informs all of those with whom the auditor would otherwise communicate in their governance capacity. (Ref: Para. A8)   **13**

Matters to Be Communicated

The Auditor's Responsibilities in Relation to the Financial Statement Audit

14   The auditor shall communicate with those charged with governance the responsibilities of the auditor in relation to the financial statement audit, including that:

(a) The auditor is responsible for forming and expressing an opinion on the financial statements that have been prepared by management[1c] with the oversight of those charged with governance; and

(b) The audit of the financial statements does not relieve management or those charged with governance of their responsibilities. (Ref: Para. A9-A10)

Planned Scope and Timing of the Audit

15   The auditor shall communicate with those charged with governance an overview of the planned scope and timing of the audit. (Ref: Para. A11-A15)

Significant Findings from the Audit

16   The auditor shall communicate with those charged with governance: (Ref: Para. A16)

(a) The auditor's views about significant qualitative aspects of the entity's accounting practices, including accounting policies, accounting estimates and financial statement disclosures. When applicable, the auditor shall explain to those charged with governance why the auditor considers a significant accounting practice, that is acceptable under the applicable financial reporting framework, not to be most appropriate to the particular circumstances of the entity; (Ref: Para. A17)

(b) Significant difficulties, if any, encountered during the audit; (Ref: Para. A18)

(c) Unless all of those charged with governance are involved in managing the entity:
   (i) Significant matters, if any, arising from the audit that were discussed, or subject to correspondence with management; and (Ref: Para. A19)
   (ii) Written representations the auditor is requesting; and

(d) Other matters, if any, arising from the audit that, in the auditor's professional judgment, are significant to the oversight of the financial reporting process. (Ref: Para. A20)

Entities that Report on Application of the UK Corporate Governance Code

16-1   In the case of entities that are required[1d], and those that choose voluntarily, to report on how they have applied the UK Corporate Governance Code, or to explain why they have not, the auditor shall communicate to the audit committee the information that the auditor believes will be relevant to: (Ref: Para. A20-1)

   • The board (in the context of fulfilling its responsibilities under Code provisions C.1.1 and C.2.1) and, where applicable, the audit committee (in the context of fulfilling its responsibilities under Code provision C.3.4); and

[1c] *In the UK and Ireland those charged with governance are responsible for the preparation of the financial statements.*

[1d] *In the UK, these include companies with a Premium listing of equity shares regardless of whether they are incorporated in the UK or elsewhere. In Ireland, these include Irish incorporated companies with a primary or secondary listing of equity shares on the Irish Stock Exchange.*

- The audit committee (in the context of fulfilling its responsibilities under Code provision C.3.2) in order to understand the rationale and the supporting evidence the auditor has relied on when making significant professional judgments in the course of the audit and in reaching an opinion on the financial statements.

   If not already covered by communications under paragraphs 15 and 16 above, this information shall include the auditor's views: (Ref: Para. A20-2 – A20-5)

(a) About business risks relevant to financial reporting objectives, the application of materiality and the implications of their judgments in relation to these for the overall audit strategy, the audit plan and the evaluation of misstatements identified;

(b) On the significant accounting policies (both individually and in aggregate);

(c) On management's valuations of the entity's material assets and liabilities and the related disclosures provided by management;

(d) Without expressing an opinion on the effectiveness of the entity's system of internal control as a whole, and based solely on the audit procedures performed in the audit of the financial statements, about:

   (i) The effectiveness of the entity's system of internal control relevant to risks that may affect financial reporting; and

   (ii) Other risks arising from the entity's business model and the effectiveness of related internal controls to the extent, if any, the auditor has obtained an understanding of these matters; and

(e) On any other matters identified in the course of the audit that the auditor believes will be relevant to the board or the audit committee in the context of fulfilling their responsibilities referred to above.

The auditor shall include with this communication sufficient explanation to enable the audit committee to understand the context within which the auditor's views relating to the matters in paragraph (d) above are expressed, including the extent to which the auditor has developed an understanding of these matters in the course of the audit and, if not already communicated to the audit committee, that the audit included consideration of internal control relevant to the preparation of the financial statements only in order to design audit procedures that are appropriate in the circumstances, and not for the purpose of expressing an opinion on the effectiveness of internal control.

Auditor Independence

In the case of listed entities, the auditor shall communicate with those charged with governance: **17**

(a) A statement that the engagement team and others in the firm as appropriate, the firm and, when applicable, network firms have complied with relevant ethical requirements regarding independence[1e]; and

(b) (i) All relationships and other matters between the firm, network firms, and the entity that, in the auditor's professional judgment, may reasonably be thought to bear on independence. This shall include total fees charged during the period covered by the financial statements for audit and non-

---

[1e] *In the UK and Ireland, auditors are subject to ethical requirements from two sources: the APB's Ethical Standards for Auditors (ESs), including ES 1 (Revised). "Integrity, Objectivity and Independence," and the ethical pronouncements established by the auditor's relevant professional body. In the case of listed companies, ES 1 (Revised) specifies information to be communicated to those charged with governance (see Para A21-1 in this ISA (UK and Ireland)).*

audit services provided by the firm and network firms to the entity and components controlled by the entity. These fees shall be allocated to categories that are appropriate to assist those charged with governance in assessing the effect of services on the independence of the auditor; and

(ii) The related safeguards that have been applied to eliminate identified threats to independence or reduce them to an acceptable level. (Ref: Para. A21-A23)

The Communication Process

Establishing the Communication Process

18   The auditor shall communicate with those charged with governance the form, timing and expected general content of communications. (Ref: Para. A28-A36)

Forms of Communication

19   The auditor shall communicate in writing with those charged with governance regarding significant findings from the audit if, in the auditor's professional judgment, oral communication would not be adequate. Written communications need not include all matters that arose during the course of the audit. (Ref: Para. A37-A39)

20   The auditor shall communicate in writing with those charged with governance regarding auditor independence when required by paragraph 17.

Timing of Communications

21   The auditor shall communicate with those charged with governance on a timely basis. (Ref: Para. A40 - A41-1)

Adequacy of the Communication Process

22   The auditor shall evaluate whether the two-way communication between the auditor and those charged with governance has been adequate for the purpose of the audit. If it has not, the auditor shall evaluate the effect, if any, on the auditor's assessment of the risks of material misstatement and ability to obtain sufficient appropriate audit evidence, and shall take appropriate action. (Ref: Para. A42-A44)

Documentation

23   Where matters required by this ISA (UK and Ireland) to be communicated are communicated orally, the auditor shall include them in the audit documentation, and when and to whom they were communicated. Where matters have been communicated in writing, the auditor shall retain a copy of the communication as part of the audit documentation.[2] (Ref: Para. A45)

***

---

[2] ISA (UK and Ireland) 230, "Audit Documentation," paragraphs 8-11, and paragraph A6.

Application and Other Explanatory Material

Those Charged with Governance (Ref: Para. 11)

Governance structures vary by jurisdiction and by entity, reflecting influences such as   **A1**
different cultural and legal backgrounds, and size and ownership characteristics. For
example:

- In some jurisdictions a supervisory (wholly or mainly non-executive) board
  exists that is legally separate from an executive (management) board (a "two-tier
  board" structure). In other jurisdictions, both the supervisory and executive
  functions are the legal responsibility of a single, or unitary, board (a "one-tier
  board" structure).
- In some entities, those charged with governance hold positions that are an
  integral part of the entity's legal structure, for example, company directors. In
  others, for example, some government entities, a body that is not part of the
  entity is charged with governance.
- In some cases, some or all of those charged with governance are involved in
  managing the entity. In others, those charged with governance and management
  comprise different persons.
- In some cases, those charged with governance are responsible for approving[3] the
  entity's financial statements (in other cases management has this responsibility).

In most entities, governance is the collective responsibility of a governing body, such   **A2**
as a board of directors, a supervisory board, partners, proprietors, a committee of
management, a council of governors, trustees, or equivalent persons. In some smaller
entities, however, one person may be charged with governance, for example, the
owner-manager where there are no other owners, or a sole trustee. When governance
is a collective responsibility, a subgroup such as an audit committee or even an
individual, may be charged with specific tasks to assist the governing body in meeting
its responsibilities. Alternatively, a subgroup or individual may have specific, legally
identified responsibilities that differ from those of the governing body.

Such diversity means that it is not possible for this ISA (UK and Ireland) to specify   **A3**
for all audits the person(s) with whom the auditor is to communicate particular
matters. Also, in some cases the appropriate person(s) with whom to communicate
may not be clearly identifiable from the applicable legal framework or other
engagement circumstances, for example, entities where the governance structure is
not formally defined, such as some family-owned entities, some not-for-profit
organizations, and some government entities. In such cases, the auditor may need to
discuss and agree with the engaging party the relevant person(s) with whom to
communicate. In deciding with whom to communicate, the auditor's understanding
of an entity's governance structure and processes obtained in accordance with ISA
(UK and Ireland) 315[4] is relevant. The appropriate person(s) with whom to communicate may vary depending on the matter to be communicated.

---

[3] *As described at paragraph A40 of ISA 700, "Forming an Opinion and Reporting on Financial Statements,"
having responsibility for approving in this context means having the authority to conclude that all the statements
that comprise the financial statements, including the related notes, have been prepared.*
*In the UK and Ireland, those charged with governance are responsible for the approval of the financial state-
ments.*
*The FRC has not promulgated ISA 700 as issued by the IAASB for application in the UK and Ireland. In the UK
and Ireland the applicable auditing standard is ISA (UK and Ireland) 700, "The Auditor's Report on Financial
Statements."*

[4] *ISA (UK and Ireland) 315, "Identifying and Assessing the Risks of Material Misstatement through Understanding the Entity and Its Environment."*

A4   ISA (UK and Ireland) 600 includes specific matters to be communicated by group auditors with those charged with governance.[5] When the entity is a component of a group, the appropriate person(s) with whom the component auditor communicates depends on the engagement circumstances and the matter to be communicated. In some cases, a number of components may be conducting the same businesses within the same system of internal control and using the same accounting practices. Where those charged with governance of those components are the same (for example, common board of directors), duplication may be avoided by dealing with these components concurrently for the purpose of communication.

A4-1   In the UK and Ireland there are statutory obligations on corporate subsidiary undertakings, and their auditors and other parties, to provide the auditor of a corporate parent undertaking with such information and explanations as that auditor may reasonably require for the purposes of the audit[5a]. Where there is no such statutory obligation (e.g. for non corporate entities), permission may be needed by the auditors of the subsidiary undertakings, from those charged with governance of the subsidiary undertakings, to disclose the contents of any communication to them to the auditor of the parent undertaking and also for the auditor of the parent undertaking to pass those disclosures onto those charged with governance of the parent undertaking. The auditor of the parent undertaking seeks to ensure that appropriate arrangements are made at the planning stage for these disclosures. Normally, such arrangements for groups are recorded in the instructions to the auditors of subsidiary undertakings and relevant engagement letters.

Communication with a Subgroup of Those Charged with Governance (Ref: Para. 12)

A5   When considering communicating with a subgroup of those charged with governance, the auditor may take into account such matters as:

- The respective responsibilities of the subgroup and the governing body.
- The nature of the matter to be communicated.
- Relevant legal or regulatory requirements.
- Whether the subgroup has the authority to take action in relation to the information communicated, and can provide further information and explanations the auditor may need.

A6.   When deciding whether there is also a need to communicate information, in full or in summary form, with the governing body, the auditor may be influenced by the auditor's assessment of how effectively and appropriately the subgroup communicates relevant information with the governing body. The auditor may make explicit in agreeing the terms of engagement that, unless prohibited by law

---

[5] ISA (UK and Ireland) 600, "Special Considerations—Audits of Group Financial Statements (Including the Work of Component Auditors)," paragraphs 46-49.

[5a] In the UK, Section 499 of the Companies Act 2006 specifies that the auditor of a company may require any subsidiary undertaking of the company which is a body corporate incorporated in the UK, and any officer, employee or auditor of any such subsidiary undertaking or any person holding or accountable for any books, accounts or vouchers of any such subsidiary undertaking, to provide him with such information or explanations as he thinks necessary for the performance of his duties as auditor. If a parent company has a subsidiary undertaking that is not a body corporate incorporated in the UK, Section 500 of the Companies Act 2006 specifies that the auditor of the parent company may require it to take all such steps as are reasonably open to it to obtain from the subsidiary undertaking, any officer, employee or auditor of the undertaking, or any person holding or accountable for any of the undertaking's books, accounts or vouchers, such information and explanations as he may reasonably require for the purposes of his duties as auditor. Similar obligations regarding companies incorporated in the Republic of Ireland are set out in Section 196, Companies Act 1990.

or regulation, the auditor retains the right to communicate directly with the governing body.

Audit committees report to the board on various matters related to the discharge   **A6-1**
of their responsibilities, including those related to the financial statements, the
annual report and the audit process (see paragraph A20-1 below). The auditor,
when assessing whether there is a need to communicate with the full board
regarding matters communicated by the auditor to the audit committee, takes
into consideration the adequacy of the communications between the audit committee and the board, including whether they appropriately address relevant
matters communicated to the audit committee by the auditor. This may be
achieved in one or more ways including: where judged appropriate attending the
relevant part of a board meeting where the audit committee reports to the board,
holding discussions with individual board members, or reviewing any written
reports from the audit committee to the board.

Audit committees (or similar subgroups with different names) exist in many jur-   **A7**
isdictions. Although their specific authority and functions may differ,
communication with the audit committee, where one exists, has become a key element in the auditor's communication with those charged with governance. Good
governance principles suggest that:

- The auditor will be invited to regularly attend meetings of the audit committee.
- The chair of the audit committee and, when relevant, the other members of the
  audit committee, will liaise with the auditor periodically.
- The audit committee will meet the auditor without management present at least
  annually.

When All of Those Charged with Governance Are Involved in Managing the Entity
(Ref: Para.13)

In some cases, all of those charged with governance are involved in managing the   **A8**
entity, and the application of communication requirements is modified to recognize
this position. In such cases, communication with person(s) with management
responsibilities may not adequately inform all of those with whom the auditor would
otherwise communicate in their governance capacity. For example, in a company
where all directors are involved in managing the entity, some of those directors (for
example, one responsible for marketing) may be unaware of significant matters
discussed with another director (for example, one responsible for the preparation of
the financial statements).

Matters to Be Communicated

The Auditor's Responsibilities in Relation to the Financial Statement Audit (Ref: Para. 14)

The auditor's responsibilities in relation to the financial statement audit are often   **A9**
included in the engagement letter or other suitable form of written agreement that
records the agreed terms of the engagement. Providing those charged with governance with a copy of that engagement letter or other suitable form of written
agreement may be an appropriate way to communicate with them regarding such
matters as:

- The auditor's responsibility for performing the audit in accordance with ISAs (UK and Ireland), which is directed towards the expression of an opinion on the financial statements. The matters that ISAs (UK and Ireland) require to be communicated, therefore, include significant matters arising from the audit of the financial statements that are relevant to those charged with governance in overseeing the financial reporting process.
- The fact that ISAs (UK and Ireland) do not require the auditor to design procedures for the purpose of identifying supplementary matters to communicate with those charged with governance.
- When applicable, the auditor's responsibility for communicating particular matters required by law or regulation, by agreement with the entity or by additional requirements applicable to the engagement, for example, the standards of a national professional accountancy body.

A9-1   The provision of copies of the audit engagement letter to the audit committees of listed companies facilitates their review and agreement of the audit engagement letter as recommended by the FRC Guidance on Audit Committees. As part of their review, the guidance further recommends the audit committee to consider whether the audit engagement letter has been updated to reflect changes in circumstances since the previous year.

A10   Law or regulation, an agreement with the entity or additional requirements applicable to the engagement may provide for broader communication with those charged with governance. For example, (a) an agreement with the entity may provide for particular matters to be communicated when they arise from services provided by a firm or network firm other than the financial statement audit; or (b) the mandate of a public sector auditor may provide for matters to be communicated that come to the auditor's attention as a result of other work, such as performance audits.

Planned Scope and Timing of the Audit (Ref: Para. 15)

A11   Communication regarding the planned scope and timing of the audit may:

(a) Assist those charged with governance to understand better the consequences of the auditor's work, to discuss issues of risk and the concept of materiality with the auditor, and to identify any areas in which they may request the auditor to undertake additional procedures[5b]; and

(b) Assist the auditor to understand better the entity and its environment.

A11-1   The communication of the planned scope of the audit includes, where relevant, any limitations on the work the auditor proposes to undertake (e.g. if limitations are imposed by management)[5c].

A12   Care is required when communicating with those charged with governance about the planned scope and timing of the audit so as not to compromise the effectiveness of

---

[5b] *The UK Corporate Governance Code and the FRC Guidance on Audit Committees contain, inter alia, recommendations about the audit committee's relationship with the auditor*

[5c] *ISA (UK and Ireland) 210, "Agreeing the Terms of Audit Engagements," paragraph 7 requires that if management or those charged with governance impose a limitation on the scope of the auditor's work in the terms of a proposed audit engagement such that the auditor believes the limitation will result in the auditor disclaiming an opinion on the financial statements, the auditor shall not accept such a limited engagement as an audit engagement, unless required by law or regulation to do so.*

the audit, particularly where some or all of those charged with governance are involved in managing the entity. For example, communicating the nature and timing of detailed audit procedures may reduce the effectiveness of those procedures by making them too predictable.

Matters communicated may include: **A13**

- How the auditor proposes to address the significant risks of material misstatement, whether due to fraud or error.
- The auditor's approach to internal control relevant to the audit.
- The application of the concept of materiality in the context of an audit.[6]

The nature and detail of the planning information communicated will reflect the size and nature of the entity and the manner in which those charged with governance operate.   **A13-1**

In any particular year, the auditor may decide that there are no significant changes in the planned scope and timing of the audit that have been communicated previously and judge that it is unnecessary to remind those charged with governance of all or part of that information. In these circumstances, the auditor need only make those charged with governance aware that the auditor has no new matters to communicate concerning the planned scope and timing of the audit. Matters that are included in the audit engagement letter need not be repeated.   **A13-2**

Other planning matters that it may be appropriate to discuss with those charged with governance include: **A14**

- Where the entity has an internal audit function, how the external auditor and internal auditors can work in a constructive and complementary manner, including any planned use of the work of the internal audit function, and the nature and extent of any planned use of internal auditors to provide direct assistance.[7]
- The views of those charged with governance of:
  - The appropriate person(s) in the entity's governance structure with whom to communicate.
  - The allocation of responsibilities between those charged with governance and management.
  - The entity's objectives and strategies, and the related business risks that may result in material misstatements.
  - Matters those charged with governance consider warrant particular attention during the audit, and any areas where they request additional procedures to be undertaken.
  - Significant communications with regulators.
  - Other matters those charged with governance consider may influence the audit of the financial statements.
- The attitudes, awareness, and actions of those charged with governance concerning (a) the entity's internal control and its importance in the entity, including how those charged with governance oversee the effectiveness of internal control, and (b) the detection or possibility of fraud.

[6] ISA (UK and Ireland) 320, "Materiality in Planning and Performing an Audit."

[7] ISA (UK and Ireland) 610 (Revised June 2013), "Using the Work of Internal Auditors", paragraphs 20 and 31.

The use of internal auditors to provide direct assistance is prohibited in an audit conducted in accordance with ISAs (UK and Ireland) – see ISA (UK and Ireland) 610 (Revised June 2013), paragraph 5-1.

- The actions of those charged with governance in response to developments in accounting standards, corporate governance practices, exchange listing rules, and related matters.
- The responses of those charged with governance to previous communications with the auditor.

A15   While communication with those charged with governance may assist the auditor to plan the scope and timing of the audit, it does not change the auditor's sole responsibility to establish the overall audit strategy and the audit plan, including the nature, timing and extent of procedures necessary to obtain sufficient appropriate audit evidence.

Significant Findings from the Audit (Ref: Para. 16)

A16   The communication of findings from the audit may include requesting further information from those charged with governance in order to complete the audit evidence obtained. For example, the auditor may confirm that those charged with governance have the same understanding of the facts and circumstances relevant to specific transactions or events.

Significant Qualitative Aspects of Accounting Practices (Ref: Para. 16(a))

A17   Financial reporting frameworks ordinarily allow for the entity to make accounting estimates, and judgments about accounting policies and financial statement disclosures. Open and constructive communication about significant qualitative aspects of the entity's accounting practices may include comment on the acceptability of significant accounting practices. Appendix 2 identifies matters that may be included in this communication.

Significant Difficulties Encountered during the Audit (Ref: Para. 16(b))

A18   Significant difficulties encountered during the audit may include such matters as:

- Significant delays in management providing required information.
- An unnecessarily brief time within which to complete the audit.
- Extensive unexpected effort required to obtain sufficient appropriate audit evidence.
- The unavailability of expected information.
- Restrictions imposed on the auditor by management.
- Management's unwillingness to make or extend its assessment of the entity's ability to continue as a going concern when requested.
  In some circumstances, such difficulties may constitute a scope limitation that leads to a modification of the auditor's opinion.[8]

Significant Matters Discussed, or Subject to Correspondence with Management (Ref: Para. 16(c)(i))

A19   Significant matters discussed, or subject to correspondence with management may include such matters as:

- Business conditions affecting the entity, and business plans and strategies that may affect the risks of material misstatement.

---

[8] ISA (UK and Ireland) 705, "Modifications to the Opinion in the Independent Auditor's Report."

- Concerns about management's consultations with other accountants on accounting or auditing matters.
- Discussions or correspondence in connection with the initial or recurring appointment of the auditor regarding accounting practices, the application of auditing standards, or fees for audit or other services.

Other Significant Matters Relevant to the Financial Reporting Process (Ref: Para. 16(d))

Other significant matters arising from the audit that are directly relevant to those charged with governance in overseeing the financial reporting process may include such matters as material misstatements of fact or material inconsistencies in information accompanying the audited financial statements that have been corrected.   **A20**

Entities that Report on Application of the UK Corporate Governance Code (Ref: Para. 16-1)

Under the UK Corporate Governance Code, the responsibilities of the directors under Code provision C.1.1 include making a statement that they consider the annual report and accounts taken as a whole is fair, balanced and understandable and provides the information necessary for shareholders to assess the entity's performance, business model and strategy. The responsibilities of the audit committee under Code provision C.3.4 include, where requested by the board, providing advice in relation to that statement[8a]. The responsibilities of the board under Code provision C.2.1 include conducting, at least annually, a review of the effectiveness of the company's risk management and internal control systems[8b]. The responsibilities of the audit committee under Code provision C.3.2 include: monitoring the integrity of the financial statements of the entity and any formal announcements relating to the entity's financial performance, reviewing significant financial reporting judgments contained in them; reviewing the entity's internal financial controls and, unless expressly addressed by a separate board risk committee composed of independent directors or by the board itself, the entity's internal control and risk management systems[8c]; assessing the effectiveness of the audit process; and reporting to the board on how it has discharged its responsibilities. The supporting Guidance on Audit Committees indicates that the report to the board should include, inter alia[8d]:   **A20-1**

- The significant issues that the audit committee considered in relation to the financial statements and how these issues were addressed; and

[8a] *Responsibility for ensuring the annual report is fair, balanced and understandable rests with the board as a whole. The board may ask the audit committee to provide advice on this.*

[8b] *In addition, FSA Rule DTR 7.2.5 R requires companies to describe the main features of the internal control and risk management systems in relation to the financial reporting process.*

[8c] *The FRC issues guidance for directors on their responsibilities with regard to internal control under the UK Corporate Governance Code (generally referred to as 'The Turnbull guidance'). The guidance indicates that the board takes responsibility for the disclosures on internal control and that the role of board committees in the review process is for the board to decide. The guidance also indicates the nature of the information the board may include in its narrative statement of how the company has applied Code Principle C.2.1.*

[8d] *The Guidance on Audit Committees also sets out other matters the audit committee should consider in relation to the annual audit cycle, including in relation to the audit plan and the auditor's findings.*

- The basis for its advice, where requested by the board, that the annual report and accounts taken as a whole is fair, balanced and understandable and provides the information necessary for shareholders to assess the entity's performance, business model and strategy.

A20-2   In fulfilling these responsibilities, the audit committee and the board will be assisted by an understanding of:

(a) Issues that involve significant judgment; and
(b) Other matters communicated to them by the auditor relevant to those responsibilities.

This will include an understanding of the rationale and supporting evidence for the auditor's significant professional judgments made in the course of the audit and in reaching the opinion on the financial statements, and of other matters communicated to the audit committee by the auditor in accordance with the requirements of paragraph 16-1, including relevant information communicated in accordance with the requirements of paragraphs 15 and 16. The auditor's communications include information regarding separate components of a group where relevant. In fulfilling its responsibilities set out above, the board will be assisted by the report from the audit committee on how the audit committee has discharged its responsibilities.

A20-3   The audit procedures that the auditor designs as part of the audit of the financial statements are not designed for the purpose of expressing an opinion on the effectiveness of the entity's system of internal control as a whole and accordingly the auditor does not express such an opinion on the basis of those procedures. However, communication of the auditor's views about the effectiveness of elements of the entity's system of internal control, based on the audit procedures performed in the audit of the financial statements, may help the audit committee and the board fulfil their respective responsibilities with respect to the entity's internal control and risk management systems.

A20-4   The auditor's understanding of the entity includes the entity's objectives and strategies and those related business risks that may result in risks of material misstatement, obtained in compliance with ISA (UK and Ireland) 315[*], and may also include other risks arising from the entity's business model that are relevant to an understanding of that model and the entity's strategy. To the extent that the auditor has obtained an understanding of such risks and the effectiveness of the entity's system of internal control in addressing them, communicating its views on those matters may be helpful to the audit committee and the board in their evaluation of whether the annual report is fair, balanced and understandable and provides the information necessary for users to assess the entity's performance, business model and strategy. However, the auditor is not required to design and perform audit procedures expressly for the purpose of forming views about the effectiveness of the entity's internal control in addressing such risks. Accordingly, to the extent applicable, the auditor may communicate that they have not obtained an understanding of, and therefore are not able to express views about, such risks and related aspects of the entity's internal control.

A20-5   The auditor's communication of views about the effectiveness of the entity's internal control may include, or refer to, the communication of significant deficiencies in internal control, if any, that is required by ISA (UK and Ireland) 265. However, views about effectiveness can go beyond just identifying such

---

[*] *ISA (UK and Ireland) 315, paragraph 11(d).*

deficiencies. For example they may include views about such matters as the entity's strategies for identifying and responding quickly to significant new financial or operational risks; the quality of the reports that the board receives to provide them with information about risks and the operation of internal control; or how the entity's systems compare in general terms with those of other relevant entities of which the auditor has knowledge, such as the impact on internal control effectiveness that may result from different approaches to maintaining an appropriate control environment. The auditor's communications include its views relating to separate components of a group where relevant.

Auditor Independence (Ref: Para. 17)

The auditor is required to comply with relevant ethical requirements, including those pertaining to independence, relating to financial statement audit engagements.[9]   **A21**

In the UK and Ireland, auditors are subject to ethical requirements from two sources: the APB's Ethical Standards for Auditors (ESs), including ES 1 (Revised), "Integrity, Objectivity and Independence," and the ethical pronouncements established by the auditor's relevant professional body. In the case of listed companies ES 1 (Revised) requires that: **A21-1**

> "The audit engagement partner shall ensure that those charged with the governance of the audited entity are appropriately informed on a timely basis of all significant facts and matters that bear upon the auditor's objectivity and independence." and

> "In the case of listed companies, the audit engagement partner shall ensure that the audit committee is provided with:

> (a) a written disclosure of relationships (including the provision of non-audit services) that bear on the auditor's objectivity and independence, the threats to auditor independence that these create, any safeguards that have been put in place and why they address such threats, together with any other information necessary to enable the auditor's objectivity and independence to be assessed;
> (b) details of non-audit services provided to the audited entity and the fees charged in relation thereto;
> (c) written confirmation that the auditor is independent;
> (d) details of any inconsistencies between APB Ethical Standards and the company's policy for the supply of non-audit services by the audit firm and any apparent breach of that policy.
> (e) an opportunity to discuss auditor independence issues."

The relationships and other matters, and safeguards to be communicated, vary with the circumstances of the engagement, but generally address: **A22**

(a) Threats to independence, which may be categorized as: self-interest threats, self-review threats, advocacy threats, familiarity threats, and intimidation threats; and
(b) Safeguards created by the profession, legislation or regulation, safeguards within the entity, and safeguards within the firm's own systems and procedures.

---

[9] *ISA (UK and Ireland) 200, "Overall Objectives of the Independent Auditor and the Conduct of an Audit in Accordance with International Standards on Auditing," paragraph 14.*

The communication required by paragraph 17(a) may include an inadvertent violation of relevant ethical requirements as they relate to auditor independence, and any remedial action taken or proposed.

A23   The communication requirements relating to auditor independence that apply in the case of listed entities may also be relevant in the case of some other entities, particularly those that may be of significant public interest because, as a result of their business, their size or their corporate status, they have a wide range of stakeholders. Examples of entities that are not listed entities, but where communication of auditor independence may be appropriate, include public sector entities, credit institutions, insurance companies, and retirement benefit funds. On the other hand, there may be situations where communications regarding independence may not be relevant, for example, where all of those charged with governance have been informed of relevant facts through their management activities. This is particularly likely where the entity is owner-managed, and the auditor's firm and network firms have little involvement with the entity beyond a financial statement audit.

Supplementary Matters (Ref: Para. 3)

A24   The oversight of management by those charged with governance includes ensuring that the entity designs, implements and maintains appropriate internal control with regard to reliability of financial reporting, effectiveness and efficiency of operations and compliance with applicable laws and regulations.

A25   The auditor may become aware of supplementary matters that do not necessarily relate to the oversight of the financial reporting process but which are, nevertheless, likely to be significant to the responsibilities of those charged with governance in overseeing the strategic direction of the entity or the entity's obligations related to accountability. Such matters may include, for example, significant issues regarding governance structures or processes, and significant decisions or actions by senior management that lack appropriate authorization.

A26   In determining whether to communicate supplementary matters with those charged with governance, the auditor may discuss matters of this kind of which the auditor has become aware with the appropriate level of management, unless it is inappropriate to do so in the circumstances.

A27   If a supplementary matter is communicated, it may be appropriate for the auditor to make those charged with governance aware that:

(a) Identification and communication of such matters is incidental to the purpose of the audit, which is to form an opinion on the financial statements;
(b) No procedures were carried out with respect to the matter other than any that were necessary to form an opinion on the financial statements; and
(c) No procedures were carried out to determine whether other such matters exist.

The Communication Process

Establishing the Communication Process (Ref: Para. 18)

A28   Clear communication of the auditor's responsibilities, the planned scope and timing of the audit, and the expected general content of communications helps establish the basis for effective two-way communication.

Matters that may also contribute to effective two-way communication include discussion of: **A29**

- The purpose of communications. When the purpose is clear, the auditor and those charged with governance are better placed to have a mutual understanding of relevant issues and the expected actions arising from the communication process.
- The form in which communications will be made.
- The person(s) in the engagement team and amongst those charged with governance who will communicate regarding particular matters.
- The auditor's expectation that communication will be two-way, and that those charged with governance will communicate with the auditor matters they consider relevant to the audit, for example, strategic decisions that may significantly affect the nature, timing and extent of audit procedures, the suspicion or the detection of fraud, and concerns with the integrity or competence of senior management.
- The process for taking action and reporting back on matters communicated by the auditor.
- The process for taking action and reporting back on matters communicated by those charged with governance.

The communication process will vary with the circumstances, including the size and   **A30**
governance structure of the entity, how those charged with governance operate, and the auditor's view of the significance of matters to be communicated. Difficulty in establishing effective two-way communication may indicate that the communication between the auditor and those charged with governance is not adequate for the purpose of the audit (see paragraph A44).

Considerations Specific to Smaller Entities

In the case of audits of smaller entities, the auditor may communicate in a less   **A31**
structured manner with those charged with governance than in the case of listed or larger entities.

Communication with Management

Many matters may be discussed with management in the ordinary course of an audit,   **A32**
including matters required by this ISA (UK and Ireland) to be communicated with those charged with governance. Such discussions recognize management's executive responsibility for the conduct of the entity's operations and, in particular, management's responsibility for the preparation of the financial statements.

Before communicating matters with those charged with governance, the auditor may   **A33**
discuss them with management, unless that is inappropriate. For example, it may not be appropriate to discuss questions of management's competence or integrity with management. In addition to recognizing management's executive responsibility, these initial discussions may clarify facts and issues, and give management an opportunity to provide further information and explanations. Similarly, when the entity has an internal audit function, the auditor may discuss matters with appropriate individuals within the function before communicating with those charged with governance.

Communication with Third Parties

A34   Those charged with governance may wish to provide third parties, for example, bankers or certain regulatory authorities, with copies of a written communication from the auditor. In some cases, disclosure to third parties may be illegal or otherwise inappropriate. When a written communication prepared for those charged with governance is provided to third parties, it may be important in the circumstances that the third parties be informed that the communication was not prepared with them in mind, for example, by stating in written communications with those charged with governance:

(a)   That the communication has been prepared for the sole use of those charged with governance and, where applicable, the group management and the group auditor, and should not be relied upon by third parties;

(b)   That no responsibility is assumed by the auditor to third parties; and

(c)   Any restrictions on disclosure or distribution to third parties.

A35   In some jurisdictions the auditor may be required by law or regulation to, for example:

- Notify a regulatory or enforcement body of certain matters communicated with those charged with governance. For example, in some countries the auditor has a duty to report misstatements to authorities where management and those charged with governance fail to take corrective action;
- Submit copies of certain reports prepared for those charged with governance to relevant regulatory or funding bodies, or other bodies such as a central authority in the case of some public sector entities; or
- Make reports prepared for those charged with governance publicly available.

A36   Unless required by law or regulation to provide a third party with a copy of the auditor's written communications with those charged with governance, the auditor may need the prior consent of those charged with governance before doing so.

Forms of Communication (Ref: Para. 19-20)

A37   Effective communication may involve structured presentations and written reports as well as less structured communications, including discussions. The auditor may communicate matters other than those identified in paragraphs 19 and 20 either orally or in writing. Written communications may include an engagement letter that is provided to those charged with governance.

A37-1   The auditor discusses issues clearly and unequivocally with those charged with governance so that the implications of those issues are likely to be fully comprehended by them.

A38   In addition to the significance of a particular matter, the form of communication (for example, whether to communicate orally or in writing, the extent of detail or summarization in the communication, and whether to communicate in a structured or unstructured manner) may be affected by such factors as:

- Whether the matter has been satisfactorily resolved.
- Whether management has previously communicated the matter.
- The size, operating structure, control environment, and legal structure of the entity.

- In the case of an audit of special purpose financial statements, whether the auditor also audits the entity's general purpose financial statements.
- Legal requirements. In some jurisdictions, a written communication with those charged with governance is required in a prescribed form by local law.
- The expectations of those charged with governance, including arrangements made for periodic meetings or communications with the auditor.
- The amount of ongoing contact and dialogue the auditor has with those charged with governance.
- Whether there have been significant changes in the membership of a governing body.

The judgment of whether to communicate significant matters orally or in writing **A38-1** may also be affected by the evaluation, required by paragraph 22, of whether the two-way communication between the auditor and those charged with governance has been adequate for the purpose of the audit. The auditor may judge also that for effective communication a written communication is issued even if its content is limited to explaining that there is nothing the auditor wishes to draw to the attention of those charged with governance. To avoid doubt where there are no matters the auditor wishes to communicate in writing, the auditor may communicate that fact in writing to those charged with governance.

When a significant matter is discussed with an individual member of those charged **A39** with governance, for example, the chair of an audit committee, it may be appropriate for the auditor to summarize the matter in later communications so that all of those charged with governance have full and balanced information.

Timing of Communications (Ref: Para. 21)

The appropriate timing for communications will vary with the circumstances of the **A40** engagement. Relevant circumstances include the significance and nature of the matter, and the action expected to be taken by those charged with governance. For example:

- Communications regarding planning matters may often be made early in the audit engagement and, for an initial engagement, may be made as part of agreeing the terms of the engagement.
- It may be appropriate to communicate a significant difficulty encountered during the audit as soon as practicable if those charged with governance are able to assist the auditor to overcome the difficulty, or if it is likely to lead to a modified opinion. Similarly, the auditor may communicate orally to those charged with governance as soon as practicable significant deficiencies in internal control that the auditor has identified, prior to communicating these in writing as required by ISA (UK and Ireland) 265.[10] Communications regarding independence may be appropriate whenever significant judgments are made about threats to independence and related safeguards, for example, when accepting an engagement to provide non-audit services, and at a concluding discussion. A concluding discussion may also be an appropriate time to communicate findings from the audit, including the auditor's views about the qualitative aspects of the entity's accounting practices.
- When auditing both general purpose and special purpose financial statements, it may be appropriate to coordinate the timing of communications.

---

[10] *ISA (UK and Ireland) 265, paragraphs 9 and A14.*

A41   Other factors that may be relevant to the timing of communications include:

- The size, operating structure, control environment, and legal structure of the entity being audited.
- Any legal obligation to communicate certain matters within a specified timeframe.
- The expectations of those charged with governance, including arrangements made for periodic meetings or communications with the auditor.
- The time at which the auditor identifies certain matters, for example, the auditor may not identify a particular matter (for example, noncompliance with a law) in time for preventive action to be taken, but communication of the matter may enable remedial action to be taken.

A41-1   Findings from the audit that are relevant to the financial statements, including the auditor's views about the qualitative aspects of the entity's accounting and financial reporting, are ordinarily communicated to those charged with governance before they approve the financial statements.

Adequacy of the Communication Process (Ref: Para. 22)

A42   The auditor need not design specific procedures to support the evaluation of the two-way communication between the auditor and those charged with governance; rather, that evaluation may be based on observations resulting from audit procedures performed for other purposes. Such observations may include:

- The appropriateness and timeliness of actions taken by those charged with governance in response to matters raised by the auditor. Where significant matters raised in previous communications have not been dealt with effectively, it may be appropriate for the auditor to inquire as to why appropriate action has not been taken, and to consider raising the point again. This avoids the risk of giving an impression that the auditor is satisfied that the matter has been adequately addressed or is no longer significant.
- The apparent openness of those charged with governance in their communications with the auditor.
- The willingness and capacity of those charged with governance to meet with the auditor without management present.
- The apparent ability of those charged with governance to fully comprehend matters raised by the auditor, for example, the extent to which those charged with governance probe issues, and question recommendations made to them.
- Difficulty in establishing with those charged with governance a mutual understanding of the form, timing and expected general content of communications.
- Where all or some of those charged with governance are involved in managing the entity, their apparent awareness of how matters discussed with the auditor affect their broader governance responsibilities, as well as their management responsibilities.
- Whether the two-way communication between the auditor and those charged with governance meets applicable legal and regulatory requirements.

A43   As noted in paragraph 4, effective two-way communication assists both the auditor and those charged with governance. Further, ISA (UK and Ireland) 315 (Revised June 2013) identifies participation by those charged with governance, including their interaction with the internal audit function, if any, and external auditors, as an element of the entity's control environment.[11] Inadequate two-way communication may indicate an unsatisfactory control environment and influence the auditor's assessment of the risks of material misstatements. There is also a risk that the auditor may not have obtained sufficient appropriate audit evidence to form an opinion on the financial statements.

If the two-way communication between the auditor and those charged with governance is not adequate and the situation cannot be resolved, the auditor may take such actions as:

A44

- Modifying the auditor's opinion on the basis of a scope limitation.
- Obtaining legal advice about the consequences of different courses of action.
- Communicating with third parties (for example, a regulator), or a higher authority in the governance structure that is outside the entity, such as the owners of a business (for example, shareholders in a general meeting), or the responsible government minister or parliament in the public sector.
- Withdrawing from the engagement, where withdrawal is possible under applicable law or regulation.

Documentation (Ref: Para. 23)

Documentation of oral communication may include a copy of minutes prepared by the entity retained as part of the audit documentation where those minutes are an appropriate record of the communication.

A45

Appendix 1 (Ref: Para. 3)

Specific Requirements in ISQC (UK and Ireland) 1 and Other ISAs (UK and Ireland) that Refer to Communications with Those Charged With Governance

This appendix identifies paragraphs in ISQC (UK and Ireland) 1[12] and other ISAs (UK and Ireland) in effect for audits of financial statements for periods ending on or after 15 December 2010 that require communication of specific matters with those charged with governance. The list is not a substitute for considering the requirements and related application and other explanatory material in ISAs (UK and Ireland).

- ISQC (UK and Ireland) 1, "Quality Control for Firms that Perform Audits and Reviews of Financial Statements, and Other Assurance and Related Services Engagements" – paragraph 30(a)
- ISA (UK and Ireland) 240, "The Auditor's Responsibilities Relating to Fraud in an Audit of Financial Statements" – paragraphs 21, 38(c)(i) and 40-42
- ISA (UK and Ireland) 250, "Consideration of Laws and Regulations in an Audit of Financial Statements" – paragraphs 14, 19 and 22-24
- ISA (UK and Ireland) 265, "Communicating Deficiencies in Internal Control to Those Charged with Governance and Management" – paragraph 9
- ISA (UK and Ireland) 450, "Evaluation of Misstatements Identified during the Audit" – paragraphs 12-13

---

[11] *ISA (UK and Ireland) 315 (Revised June 2013), paragraph A77.*

[12] *ISQC (UK and Ireland) 1, "Quality Control for Firms that Perform Audits and Reviews of Financial Statements, and Other Assurance and Related Services Engagements."*

- ISA (UK and Ireland) 505, "External Confirmations" – paragraph 9
- ISA (UK and Ireland) 510, "Initial Audit Engagements—Opening Balances" – paragraph 7
- ISA (UK and Ireland) 550, "Related Parties" – paragraph 27
- ISA (UK and Ireland) 560, "Subsequent Events" – paragraphs 7(b)-(c), 10(a), 13(b), 14(a) and 17
- ISA (UK and Ireland) 570, "Going Concern" – paragraph 23
- ISA (UK and Ireland) 600, "Special Considerations – Audits of Group Financial Statements (Including the Work of Component Auditors)" – paragraph 49
- ISA (UK and Ireland) 705, "Modifications to the Opinion in the Independent Auditor's Report" – paragraphs 12, 14, 19(a) and 28
- ISA (UK and Ireland) 706, "Emphasis of Matter Paragraphs and Other Matter Paragraphs in the Independent Auditor's Report" – paragraph 9
- ISA (UK and Ireland) 710, "Comparative Information—Corresponding Figures and Comparative Financial Statements" – paragraph 18
- ISA (UK and Ireland) 720, "The Auditor's Responsibilities Relating to Other Information in Documents Containing Audited Financial Statements" – paragraphs 10, 13 and 16

Appendix 2 (Ref: Para. 16(a), A17)

Qualitative Aspects of Accounting Practices

The communication required by paragraph 16(a), and discussed in paragraph A17, may include such matters as:

Accounting Policies

- The appropriateness of the accounting policies to the particular circumstances of the entity, having regard to the need to balance the cost of providing information with the likely benefit to users of the entity's financial statements. Where acceptable alternative accounting policies exist, the communication may include identification of the financial statement items that are affected by the choice of significant accounting policies as well as information on accounting policies used by similar entities.
- The initial selection of, and changes in significant accounting policies, including the application of new accounting pronouncements. The communication may include: the effect of the timing and method of adoption of a change in accounting policy on the current and future earnings of the entity; and the timing of a change in accounting policies in relation to expected new accounting pronouncements.
- The effect of significant accounting policies in controversial or emerging areas (or those unique to an industry, particularly when there is a lack of authoritative guidance or consensus).
- The effect of the timing of transactions in relation to the period in which they are recorded.

Accounting Estimates

- For items for which estimates are significant, issues discussed in ISA (UK and Ireland) 540,[13] including, for example:
  - ○ Management's identification of accounting estimates.
  - ○ Management's process for making accounting estimates.
  - ○ Risks of material misstatement.
  - ○ Indicators of possible management bias.
  - ○ Disclosure of estimation uncertainty in the financial statements.

Financial Statement Disclosures

- The issues involved, and related judgments made, in formulating particularly sensitive financial statement disclosures (for example, disclosures related to revenue recognition, remuneration, going concern, subsequent events, and contingency issues).
- The overall neutrality, consistency and clarity of the disclosures in the financial statements.

Related Matters

- The potential effect on the financial statements of significant risks, exposures and uncertainties, such as pending litigation, that are disclosed in the financial statements.
- The extent to which the financial statements are affected by unusual transactions, including non-recurring amounts recognized during the period, and the extent to which such transactions are separately disclosed in the financial statements.
- The factors affecting asset and liability carrying values, including the entity's bases for determining useful lives assigned to tangible and intangible assets. The communication may explain how factors affecting carrying values were selected and how alternative selections would have affected the financial statements.
- The selective correction of misstatements, for example, correcting misstatements with the effect of increasing reported earnings, but not those that have the effect of decreasing reported earnings.

---

[13] *ISA (UK and Ireland) 540, "Auditing Accounting Estimates, Including Fair Value Accounting Estimates, and Related Disclosures."*

International Standard on Auditing (UK and Ireland) 265

Communicating deficiencies in internal control to those charged with governance and management

(Effective for audits of financial statements for periods ending on or after 15 December 2010)[1a]

Contents

International Standard on Auditing (UK and Ireland) (ISA (UK and Ireland)) 265, "Communicating Deficiencies in Internal Control to Those Charged with Governance and Management" should be read in conjunction with ISA (UK and Ireland) 200, "Overall Objectives of the Independent Auditor and the Conduct of an Audit in Accordance with International Standards on Auditing (UK and Ireland)."

[1a] *Conforming amendments to this standard as a result of ISA (UK and Ireland) 610 (Revised June 2013),* Using the Work of Internal Auditors, *are included that are effective for audits of financial statements for periods ending on or after 15 June 2014. Details of the amendments are given in the Annexure to ISA (UK and Ireland) 610 (Revised June 2013).*

Introduction

Scope of this ISA (UK and Ireland)

This International Standard on Auditing (UK and Ireland) (ISA (UK and Ireland)) deals with the auditor's responsibility to communicate appropriately to those charged with governance and management deficiencies in internal control[1] that the auditor has identified in an audit of financial statements. This ISA (UK and Ireland) does not impose additional responsibilities on the auditor regarding obtaining an understanding of internal control and designing and performing tests of controls over and above the requirements of ISA (UK and Ireland) 315 and ISA (UK and Ireland) 330.[2] ISA (UK and Ireland) 260[3] establishes further requirements and provides guidance regarding the auditor's responsibility to communicate with those charged with governance in relation to the audit.

1

The auditor is required to obtain an understanding of internal control relevant to the audit when identifying and assessing the risks of material misstatement.[4] In making those risk assessments, the auditor considers internal control in order to design audit procedures that are appropriate in the circumstances, but not for the purpose of expressing an opinion on the effectiveness of internal control. The auditor may identify deficiencies in internal control not only during this risk assessment process but also at any other stage of the audit. This ISA (UK and Ireland) specifies which identified deficiencies the auditor is required to communicate to those charged with governance and management.

2

Nothing in this ISA (UK and Ireland) precludes the auditor from communicating to those charged with governance and management other internal control matters that the auditor has identified during the audit.

3

Effective Date

This ISA (UK and Ireland) is effective for audits of financial statements for periods ending on or after 15 December 2010.[1a]

4

Objective

The objective of the auditor is to communicate appropriately to those charged with governance and management deficiencies in internal control that the auditor has identified during the audit and that, in the auditor's professional judgment, are of sufficient importance to merit their respective attentions.

5

---

[1] *ISA (UK and Ireland) 315, "Identifying and Assessing the Risks of Material Misstatement through Understanding the Entity and Its Environment," paragraphs 4 and 12.*

[2] *ISA (UK and Ireland) 330, "The Auditor's Responses to Assessed Risks."*

[3] *ISA (UK and Ireland) 260, "Communication with Those Charged with Governance."*

[4] *ISA (UK and Ireland) 315, paragraph 12. Paragraphs A60-A65 provide guidance on controls relevant to the audit.*

Definitions

6   For purposes of the ISAs (UK and Ireland), the following terms have the meanings attributed below:

(a) Deficiency in internal control – This exists when:
   (i)   A control is designed, implemented or operated in such a way that it is unable to prevent, or detect and correct, misstatements in the financial statements on a timely basis; or
   (ii) A control necessary to prevent, or detect and correct, misstatements in the financial statements on a timely basis is missing.

(b) Significant deficiency in internal control – A deficiency or combination of deficiencies in internal control that, in the auditor's professional judgment, is of sufficient importance to merit the attention of those charged with governance. (Ref: Para. A5)

Requirements

7   The auditor shall determine whether, on the basis of the audit work performed, the auditor has identified one or more deficiencies in internal control. (Ref: Para. A1-A4)

8   If the auditor has identified one or more deficiencies in internal control, the auditor shall determine, on the basis of the audit work performed, whether, individually or in combination, they constitute significant deficiencies. (Ref: Para. A5-A11)

9   The auditor shall communicate in writing significant deficiencies in internal control identified during the audit to those charged with governance on a timely basis. (Ref: Para. A12-A18, A27)

10   The auditor shall also communicate to management at an appropriate level of responsibility on a timely basis: (Ref: Para. A19, A27)

(a) In writing, significant deficiencies in internal control that the auditor has communicated or intends to communicate to those charged with governance, unless it would be inappropriate to communicate directly to management in the circumstances; and (Ref: Para. A14, A20-A21)

(b) Other deficiencies in internal control identified during the audit that have not been communicated to management by other parties and that, in the auditor's professional judgment, are of sufficient importance to merit management's attention. (Ref: Para. A22-A26)

11   The auditor shall include in the written communication of significant deficiencies in internal control:

(a) A description of the deficiencies and an explanation of their potential effects; and (Ref: Para. A28)

(b) Sufficient information to enable those charged with governance and management to understand the context of the communication. In particular, the auditor shall explain that: (Ref: Para. A29-A30)
   (i)   The purpose of the audit was for the auditor to express an opinion on the financial statements;
   (ii) The audit included consideration of internal control relevant to the preparation of the financial statements in order to design audit procedures that are appropriate in the circumstances, but not for the purpose of expressing an opinion on the effectiveness of internal control; and

(iii) The matters being reported are limited to those deficiencies that the auditor has identified during the audit and that the auditor has concluded are of sufficient importance to merit being reported to those charged with governance.

***

Application and Other Explanatory Material

Determination of Whether Deficiencies in Internal Control Have Been Identified (Ref: Para. 7)

In determining whether the auditor has identified one or more deficiencies in internal control, the auditor may discuss the relevant facts and circumstances of the auditor's findings with the appropriate level of management. This discussion provides an opportunity for the auditor to alert management on a timely basis to the existence of deficiencies of which management may not have been previously aware. The level of management with whom it is appropriate to discuss the findings is one that is familiar with the internal control area concerned and that has the authority to take remedial action on any identified deficiencies in internal control. In some circumstances, it may not be appropriate for the auditor to discuss the auditor's findings directly with management, for example, if the findings appear to call management's integrity or competence into question (see paragraph A20).   **A1**

In discussing the facts and circumstances of the auditor's findings with management, the auditor may obtain other relevant information for further consideration, such as: **A2**

- Management's understanding of the actual or suspected causes of the deficiencies.
- Exceptions arising from the deficiencies that management may have noted, for example, misstatements that were not prevented by the relevant information technology (IT) controls.
- A preliminary indication from management of its response to the findings.

Considerations Specific to Smaller Entities

While the concepts underlying control activities in smaller entities are likely to be similar to those in larger entities, the formality with which they operate will vary. Further, smaller entities may find that certain types of control activities are not necessary because of controls applied by management. For example, management's sole authority for granting credit to customers and approving significant purchases can provide effective control over important account balances and transactions, lessening or removing the need for more detailed control activities.   **A3**

Also, smaller entities often have fewer employees which may limit the extent to which segregation of duties is practicable. However, in a small owner-managed entity, the owner-manager may be able to exercise more effective oversight than in a larger entity. This higher level of management oversight needs to be balanced against the greater potential for management override of controls.   **A4**

Significant Deficiencies in Internal Control (Ref: Para. 6(b), 8)

The significance of a deficiency or a combination of deficiencies in internal control depends not only on whether a misstatement has actually occurred, but also on the   **A5** likelihood that a misstatement could occur and the potential magnitude of the misstatement. Significant deficiencies may therefore exist even though the auditor has not identified misstatements during the audit.

A6   Examples of matters that the auditor may consider in determining whether a deficiency or combination of deficiencies in internal control constitutes a significant deficiency include:

- The likelihood of the deficiencies leading to material misstatements in the financial statements in the future.
- The susceptibility to loss or fraud of the related asset or liability.
- The subjectivity and complexity of determining estimated amounts, such as fair value accounting estimates.
- The financial statement amounts exposed to the deficiencies.
- The volume of activity that has occurred or could occur in the account balance or class of transactions exposed to the deficiency or deficiencies.
- The importance of the controls to the financial reporting process; for example:
  - General monitoring controls (such as oversight of management).
  - Controls over the prevention and detection of fraud.
  - Controls over the selection and application of significant accounting policies.
  - Controls over significant transactions with related parties.
  - Controls over significant transactions outside the entity's normal course of business.
  - Controls over the period-end financial reporting process (such as controls over non-recurring journal entries).
- The cause and frequency of the exceptions detected as a result of the deficiencies in the controls.
- The interaction of the deficiency with other deficiencies in internal control.

A7   Indicators of significant deficiencies in internal control include, for example:

- Evidence of ineffective aspects of the control environment, such as:
  - Indications that significant transactions in which management is financially interested are not being appropriately scrutinized by those charged with governance.
  - Identification of management fraud, whether or not material, that was not prevented by the entity's internal control.
  - Management's failure to implement appropriate remedial action on significant deficiencies previously communicated.
- Absence of a risk assessment process within the entity where such a process would ordinarily be expected to have been established.
- Evidence of an ineffective entity risk assessment process, such as management's failure to identify a risk of material misstatement that the auditor would expect the entity's risk assessment process to have identified.
- Evidence of an ineffective response to identified significant risks (for example, absence of controls over such a risk).
- Misstatements detected by the auditor's procedures that were not prevented, or detected and corrected, by the entity's internal control.
- Restatement of previously issued financial statements to reflect the correction of a material misstatement due to error or fraud.
- Evidence of management's inability to oversee the preparation of the financial statements.

Controls may be designed to operate individually or in combination to effectively   **A8**
prevent, or detect and correct, misstatements.[5] For example, controls over accounts
receivable may consist of both automated and manual controls designed to operate
together to prevent, or detect and correct, misstatements in the account balance. A
deficiency in internal control on its own may not be sufficiently important to constitute a significant deficiency. However, a combination of deficiencies affecting the
same account balance or disclosure, relevant assertion, or component of internal
control may increase the risks of misstatement to such an extent as to give rise to a
significant deficiency.

Law or regulation in some jurisdictions may establish a requirement (particularly for   **A9**
audits of listed entities) for the auditor to communicate to those charged with
governance or to other relevant parties (such as regulators) one or more specific types
of deficiency in internal control that the auditor has identified during the audit.
Where law or regulation has established specific terms and definitions for these types
of deficiency and requires the auditor to use these terms and definitions for the
purpose of the communication, the auditor uses such terms and definitions when
communicating in accordance with the legal or regulatory requirement.

Where the jurisdiction has established specific terms for the types of deficiency in   **A10**
internal control to be communicated but has not defined such terms, it may be
necessary for the auditor to use judgment to determine the matters to be communicated further to the legal or regulatory requirement. In doing so, the auditor may
consider it appropriate to have regard to the requirements and guidance in this ISA
(UK and Ireland). For example, if the purpose of the legal or regulatory requirement
is to bring to the attention of those charged with governance certain internal control
matters of which they should be aware, it may be appropriate to regard such matters
as being generally equivalent to the significant deficiencies required by this ISA (UK
and Ireland) to be communicated to those charged with governance.

The requirements of this ISA (UK and Ireland) remain applicable notwithstanding   **A11**
that law or regulation may require the auditor to use specific terms or definitions.

Communication of Deficiencies in Internal Control

*Communication of Significant Deficiencies in Internal Control to Those Charged with
Governance* (Ref: Para. 9)

Communicating significant deficiencies in writing to those charged with governance   **A12**
reflects the importance of these matters, and assists those charged with governance in
fulfilling their oversight responsibilities. ISA (UK and Ireland) 260 establishes relevant considerations regarding communication with those charged with governance
when all of them are involved in managing the entity.[6]

In the UK and Ireland, where applicable, timely communication of significant   **A12-1**
deficiencies in writing to directors of listed entities can assist them apply the
revised "Turnbull Guidance"[6a] on the requirements of the Combined Code
relating to internal control and reporting to shareholders thereon.

---

[5] *ISA (UK and Ireland) 315, paragraph A66.*

[6] *ISA (UK and Ireland) 260, paragraph 13.*

[6a] *"Internal Control – Revised Guidance for Directors on the Combined Code" issued by the Financial Reporting
Council, October 2005.*

A13   In determining when to issue the written communication, the auditor may consider whether receipt of such communication would be an important factor in enabling those charged with governance to discharge their oversight responsibilities. In addition, for listed entities in certain jurisdictions, those charged with governance may need to receive the auditor's written communication before the date of approval of the financial statements in order to discharge specific responsibilities in relation to internal control for regulatory or other purposes. For other entities, the auditor may issue the written communication at a later date. Nevertheless, in the latter case, as the auditor's written communication of significant deficiencies forms part of the final audit file, the written communication is subject to the overriding requirement[7] for the auditor to complete the assembly of the final audit file on a timely basis. ISA (UK and Ireland) 230 states that an appropriate time limit within which to complete the assembly of the final audit file is ordinarily not more than 60 days after the date of the auditor's report.[8]

A14   Regardless of the timing of the written communication of significant deficiencies, the auditor may communicate these orally in the first instance to management and, when appropriate, to those charged with governance to assist them in taking timely remedial action to minimize the risks of material misstatement. Doing so, however, does not relieve the auditor of the responsibility to communicate the significant deficiencies in writing, as this ISA (UK and Ireland) requires.

A15   The level of detail at which to communicate significant deficiencies is a matter of the auditor's professional judgment in the circumstances. Factors that the auditor may consider in determining an appropriate level of detail for the communication include, for example:

● The nature of the entity. For instance, the communication required for a public interest entity may be different from that for a non-public interest entity.
● The size and complexity of the entity. For instance, the communication required for a complex entity may be different from that for an entity operating a simple business.
● The nature of significant deficiencies that the auditor has identified.
● The entity's governance composition. For instance, more detail may be needed if those charged with governance include members who do not have significant experience in the entity's industry or in the affected areas.
● Legal or regulatory requirements regarding the communication of specific types of deficiency in internal control.

A16   Management and those charged with governance may already be aware of significant deficiencies that the auditor has identified during the audit and may have chosen not to remedy them because of cost or other considerations. The responsibility for evaluating the costs and benefits of implementing remedial action rests with management and those charged with governance. Accordingly, the requirement in paragraph 9 applies regardless of cost or other considerations that management and those charged with governance may consider relevant in determining whether to remedy such deficiencies.

A17   The fact that the auditor communicated a significant deficiency to those charged with governance and management in a previous audit does not eliminate the need for the auditor to repeat the communication if remedial action has not yet been taken. If a previously communicated significant deficiency remains, the current year's

---

[7] *ISA (UK and Ireland) 230, "Audit Documentation," paragraph 14.*

[8] *ISA (UK and Ireland) 230, paragraph A21.*

communication may repeat the description from the previous communication, or simply reference the previous communication. The auditor may ask management or, where appropriate, those charged with governance, why the significant deficiency has not yet been remedied. A failure to act, in the absence of a rational explanation, may in itself represent a significant deficiency.

Considerations Specific to Smaller Entities

In the case of audits of smaller entities, the auditor may communicate in a less **A18** structured manner with those charged with governance than in the case of larger entities.

Communication of Deficiencies in Internal Control to Management (Ref: Para. 10)

Ordinarily, the appropriate level of management is the one that has responsibility **A19** and authority to evaluate the deficiencies in internal control and to take the necessary remedial action. For significant deficiencies, the appropriate level is likely to be the chief executive officer or chief financial officer (or equivalent) as these matters are also required to be communicated to those charged with governance. For other deficiencies in internal control, the appropriate level may be operational management with more direct involvement in the control areas affected and with the authority to take appropriate remedial action.

Communication of Significant Deficiencies in Internal Control to Management (Ref: Para. 10(a))

Certain identified significant deficiencies in internal control may call into question **A20** the integrity or competence of management. For example, there may be evidence of fraud or intentional non-compliance with laws and regulations by management, or management may exhibit an inability to oversee the preparation of adequate financial statements that may raise doubt about management's competence. Accordingly, it may not be appropriate to communicate such deficiencies directly to management.

ISA (UK and Ireland) 250 establishes requirements and provides guidance on the **A21** reporting of identified or suspected non-compliance with laws and regulations, including when those charged with governance are themselves involved in such non-compliance.[9] ISA (UK and Ireland) 240 establishes requirements and provides guidance regarding communication to those charged with governance when the auditor has identified fraud or suspected fraud involving management.[10]

Communication of Other Deficiencies in Internal Control to Management (Ref: Para. 10(b))

During the audit, the auditor may identify other deficiencies in internal control that **A22** are not significant deficiencies but that may be of sufficient importance to merit management's attention. The determination as to which other deficiencies in internal control merit management's attention is a matter of professional judgment in the

[9] *ISA (UK and Ireland) 250, "Consideration of Laws and Regulations in an Audit of Financial Statements," paragraphs 22-28.*

[10] *ISA (UK and Ireland) 240, "The Auditor's Responsibilities Relating to Fraud in an Audit of Financial Statements," paragraph 41.*

circumstances, taking into account the likelihood and potential magnitude of mis-statements that may arise in the financial statements as a result of those deficiencies.

A23   The communication of other deficiencies in internal control that merit management's attention need not be in writing but may be oral. Where the auditor has discussed the facts and circumstances of the auditor's findings with management, the auditor may consider an oral communication of the other deficiencies to have been made to management at the time of these discussions. Accordingly, a formal communication need not be made subsequently.

A24   If the auditor has communicated deficiencies in internal control other than significant deficiencies to management in a prior period and management has chosen not to remedy them for cost or other reasons, the auditor need not repeat the communication in the current period. The auditor is also not required to repeat information about such deficiencies if it has been previously communicated to management by other parties, such as the internal audit function or regulators. It may, however, be appropriate for the auditor to re-communicate these other deficiencies if there has been a change of management, or if new information has come to the auditor's attention that alters the prior understanding of the auditor and management regarding the deficiencies. Nevertheless, the failure of management to remedy other deficiencies in internal control that were previously communicated may become a significant deficiency requiring communication with those charged with governance. Whether this is the case depends on the auditor's judgment in the circumstances.

A25   In some circumstances, those charged with governance may wish to be made aware of the details of other deficiencies in internal control the auditor has communicated to management, or be briefly informed of the nature of the other deficiencies. Alternatively, the auditor may consider it appropriate to inform those charged with governance of the communication of the other deficiencies to management. In either case, the auditor may report orally or in writing to those charged with governance as appropriate.

A26   ISA (UK and Ireland) 260 establishes relevant considerations regarding communication with those charged with governance when all of them are involved in managing the entity.[11]

Considerations Specific to Public Sector Entities (Ref: Para. 9-10)

A27   Public sector auditors may have additional responsibilities to communicate deficiencies in internal control that the auditor has identified during the audit, in ways, at a level of detail and to parties not envisaged in this ISA (UK and Ireland). For example, significant deficiencies may have to be communicated to the legislature or other governing body. Law, regulation or other authority may also mandate that public sector auditors report deficiencies in internal control, irrespective of the significance of the potential effects of those deficiencies. Further, legislation may require public sector auditors to report on broader internal control-related matters than the deficiencies in internal control required to be communicated by this ISA (UK and Ireland), for example, controls related to compliance with legislative authorities, regulations, or provisions of contracts or grant agreements.

---

[11] *ISA (UK and Ireland) 260, paragraph 13.*

Content of Written Communication of Significant Deficiencies in Internal Control (Ref: Para. 11)

In explaining the potential effects of the significant deficiencies, the auditor need not **A28** quantify those effects. The significant deficiencies may be grouped together for reporting purposes where it is appropriate to do so. The auditor may also include in the written communication suggestions for remedial action on the deficiencies, management's actual or proposed responses, and a statement as to whether or not the auditor has undertaken any steps to verify whether management's responses have been implemented.

The auditor may consider it appropriate to include the following information as **A29** additional context for the communication:

- An indication that if the auditor had performed more extensive procedures on internal control, the auditor might have identified more deficiencies to be reported, or concluded that some of the reported deficiencies need not, in fact, have been reported.
- An indication that such communication has been provided for the purposes of those charged with governance, and that it may not be suitable for other purposes.

Law or regulation may require the auditor or management to furnish a copy of the **A30** auditor's written communication on significant deficiencies to appropriate regulatory authorities. Where this is the case, the auditor's written communication may identify such regulatory authorities.

International Standard on Auditing (UK and Ireland) 300

Planning an audit of financial statements

(Effective for audits of financial statements for periods ending on or after 15 December 2010)[1a]

Contents

International Standard on Auditing (UK and Ireland) (ISA (UK and Ireland)) 300, "Planning an Audit of Financial Statements" should be read in conjunction with ISA (UK and Ireland) 200, "Overall Objectives of the Independent Auditor and the Conduct of an Audit in Accordance with International Standards on Auditing (UK and Ireland)."

[1a] *Conforming amendments to this standard as a result of ISA (UK and Ireland) 610 (Revised June 2013),* Using the Work of Internal Auditors, *are included that are effective for audits of financial statements for periods ending on or after 15 June 2014. Details of the amendments are given in the Annexure to ISA (UK and Ireland) 610 (Revised June 2013).*

Introduction

Scope of this ISA (UK and Ireland)

This International Standard on Auditing (UK and Ireland) (ISA (UK and Ireland))   **1**
deals with the auditor's responsibility to plan an audit of financial statements. This
ISA (UK and Ireland) is written in the context of recurring audits. Additional
considerations in an initial audit engagement are separately identified.

The Role and Timing of Planning

Planning an audit involves establishing the overall audit strategy for the engagement   **2**
and developing an audit plan. Adequate planning benefits the audit of financial
statements in several ways, including the following: (Ref: Para. A1-A3)

- Helping the auditor to devote appropriate attention to important areas of the
  audit.
- Helping the auditor identify and resolve potential problems on a timely basis.
- Helping the auditor properly organize and manage the audit engagement so that
  it is performed in an effective and efficient manner.
- Assisting in the selection of engagement team members with appropriate levels
  of capabilities and competence to respond to anticipated risks, and the proper
  assignment of work to them.
- Facilitating the direction and supervision of engagement team members and the
  review of their work.
- Assisting, where applicable, in coordination of work done by auditors of
  components and experts.

Effective Date

This ISA (UK and Ireland) is effective for audits of financial statements for periods   **3**
ending on or after 15 December 2010.[1a]

Objective

The objective of the auditor is to plan the audit so that it will be performed in an   **4**
effective manner.

Requirements

Involvement of Key Engagement Team Members

The engagement partner and other key members of the engagement team shall be   **5**
involved in planning the audit, including planning and participating in the discussion
among engagement team members. (Ref: Para. A4)

Preliminary Engagement Activities

The auditor shall undertake the following activities at the beginning of the current   **6**
audit engagement:

(a) Performing procedures required by ISA (UK and Ireland) 220 regarding the continuance of the client relationship and the specific audit engagement;[1]

(b) Evaluating compliance with relevant ethical requirements, including independence, in accordance with ISA (UK and Ireland) 220;[2] and

(c) Establishing an understanding of the terms of the engagement, as required by ISA (UK and Ireland) 210.[3] (Ref: Para. A5-A7)

Planning Activities

7   The auditor shall establish an overall audit strategy that sets the scope, timing and direction of the audit, and that guides the development of the audit plan.

8   In establishing the overall audit strategy, the auditor shall:

(a) Identify the characteristics of the engagement that define its scope;

(b) Ascertain the reporting objectives of the engagement to plan the timing of the audit and the nature of the communications required;

(c) Consider the factors that, in the auditor's professional judgment, are significant in directing the engagement team's efforts;

(d) Consider the results of preliminary engagement activities and, where applicable, whether knowledge gained on other engagements performed by the engagement partner for the entity is relevant; and

(e) Ascertain the nature, timing and extent of resources necessary to perform the engagement. (Ref: Para. A8-A11)

9   The auditor shall develop an audit plan that shall include a description of:

(a) The nature, timing and extent of planned risk assessment procedures, as determined under ISA (UK and Ireland) 315.[4]

(b) The nature, timing and extent of planned further audit procedures at the assertion level, as determined under ISA (UK and Ireland) 330.[5]

(c) Other planned audit procedures that are required to be carried out so that the engagement complies with ISAs (UK and Ireland). (Ref: Para. A12)

10   The auditor shall update and change the overall audit strategy and the audit plan as necessary during the course of the audit. (Ref: Para. A13)

11   The auditor shall plan the nature, timing and extent of direction and supervision of engagement team members and the review of their work. (Ref: Para. A14-A15)

Documentation

12   The auditor shall include in the audit documentation:[6]

(a) The overall audit strategy;

[1] *ISA (UK and Ireland) 220, "Quality Control for an Audit of Financial Statements," paragraphs 12-13.*

[2] *ISA (UK and Ireland) 220, paragraphs 9-11.*

[3] *ISA (UK and Ireland) 210, "Agreeing the Terms of Audit Engagements," paragraphs 9-13.*

[4] *ISA (UK and Ireland) 315, "Identifying and Assessing the Risks of Material Misstatement through Understanding the Entity and Its Environment."*

[5] *ISA (UK and Ireland) 330, "The Auditor's Responses to Assessed Risks."*

[6] *ISA (UK and Ireland) 230, "Audit Documentation," paragraphs 8-11, and paragraph A6.*

(b)   The audit plan; and
(c)   Any significant changes made during the audit engagement to the overall audit strategy or the audit plan, and the reasons for such changes. (Ref: Para. A16-A19)

Additional Considerations in Initial Audit Engagements

The auditor shall undertake the following activities prior to starting an initial audit: **13**

(a)   Performing procedures required by ISA (UK and Ireland) 220 regarding the acceptance of the client relationship and the specific audit engagement;[7] and
(b)   Communicating with the predecessor auditor, where there has been a change of auditors, in compliance with relevant ethical requirements. (Ref: Para. A20)

***

Application and Other Explanatory Material

The Role and Timing of Planning (Ref: Para. 2)

The nature and extent of planning activities will vary according to the size and   **A1**
complexity of the entity, the key engagement team members' previous experience with the entity, and changes in circumstances that occur during the audit engagement.

Planning is not a discrete phase of an audit, but rather a continual and iterative   **A2**
process that often begins shortly after (or in connection with) the completion of the previous audit and continues until the completion of the current audit engagement. Planning, however, includes consideration of the timing of certain activities and audit procedures that need to be completed prior to the performance of further audit procedures. For example, planning includes the need to consider, prior to the auditor's identification and assessment of the risks of material misstatement, such matters as:

- The analytical procedures to be applied as risk assessment procedures.
- Obtaining a general understanding of the legal and regulatory framework applicable to the entity and how the entity is complying with that framework.
- The determination of materiality.
- The involvement of experts.
- The performance of other risk assessment procedures.

The auditor may decide to discuss elements of planning with the entity's manage-   **A3**
ment to facilitate the conduct and management of the audit engagement (for example, to coordinate some of the planned audit procedures with the work of the entity's personnel). Although these discussions often occur, the overall audit strategy and the audit plan remain the auditor's responsibility. When discussing matters included in the overall audit strategy or audit plan, care is required in order not to compromise the effectiveness of the audit. For example, discussing the nature and timing of detailed audit procedures with management may compromise the effectiveness of the audit by making the audit procedures too predictable.

---

[7] *ISA (UK and Ireland) 220, paragraphs 12-13.*

Involvement of Key Engagement Team Members (Ref: Para. 5)

A4   The involvement of the engagement partner and other key members of the engagement team in planning the audit draws on their experience and insight, thereby enhancing the effectiveness and efficiency of the planning process.[8]

Preliminary Engagement Activities (Ref: Para. 6)

A5   Performing the preliminary engagement activities specified in paragraph 6 at the beginning of the current audit engagement assists the auditor in identifying and evaluating events or circumstances that may adversely affect the auditor's ability to plan and perform the audit engagement.

A6   Performing these preliminary engagement activities enables the auditor to plan an audit engagement for which, for example:

   ● The auditor maintains the necessary independence and ability to perform the engagement.
   ● There are no issues with management[8a] integrity that may affect the auditor's willingness to continue the engagement.
   ● There is no misunderstanding with the client as to the terms of the engagement.

A7   The auditor's consideration of client continuance and relevant ethical requirements, including independence, occurs throughout the audit engagement as conditions and changes in circumstances occur. Performing initial procedures on both client continuance and evaluation of relevant ethical requirements (including independence) at the beginning of the current audit engagement means that they are completed prior to the performance of other significant activities for the current audit engagement. For continuing audit engagements, such initial procedures often occur shortly after (or in connection with) the completion of the previous audit.

Planning Activities

The Overall Audit Strategy (Ref: Para. 7-8)

A8   The process of establishing the overall audit strategy assists the auditor to determine, subject to the completion of the auditor's risk assessment procedures, such matters as:

   ● The resources to deploy for specific audit areas, such as the use of appropriately experienced team members for high risk areas or the involvement of experts on complex matters;
   ● The amount of resources to allocate to specific audit areas, such as the number of team members assigned to observe the inventory count at material locations, the extent of review of other auditors' work in the case of group audits, or the audit budget in hours to allocate to high risk areas;
   ● When these resources are to be deployed, such as whether at an interim audit stage or at key cut-off dates; and

---

[8] *ISA (UK and Ireland) 315, paragraph 10, establishes requirements and provides guidance on the engagement team's discussion of the susceptibility of the entity to material misstatements of the financial statements. ISA (UK and Ireland) 240, "The Auditor's Responsibilities Relating to Fraud in an Audit of Financial Statements," paragraph 15, provides guidance on the emphasis given during this discussion to the susceptibility of the entity's financial statements to material misstatement due to fraud.*

[8a] *In the UK and Ireland, the auditor is also concerned to establish that there are no issues with the integrity of those charged with governance that may affect the auditor's willingness to continue the engagement.*

- How such resources are managed, directed and supervised, such as when team briefing and debriefing meetings are expected to be held, how engagement partner and manager reviews are expected to take place (for example, on-site or off-site), and whether to complete engagement quality control reviews.

The Appendix lists examples of considerations in establishing the overall audit strategy. **A9**

Once the overall audit strategy has been established, an audit plan can be developed to address the various matters identified in the overall audit strategy, taking into account the need to achieve the audit objectives through the efficient use of the auditor's resources. The establishment of the overall audit strategy and the detailed audit plan are not necessarily discrete or sequential processes, but are closely inter-related since changes in one may result in consequential changes to the other. **A10**

Considerations Specific to Smaller Entities

In audits of small entities, the entire audit may be conducted by a very small engagement team. Many audits of small entities involve the engagement partner (who may be a sole practitioner) working with one engagement team member (or without any engagement team members). With a smaller team, co-ordination of, and communication between, team members are easier. Establishing the overall audit strategy for the audit of a small entity need not be a complex or time-consuming exercise; it varies according to the size of the entity, the complexity of the audit, and the size of the engagement team. For example, a brief memorandum prepared at the completion of the previous audit, based on a review of the working papers and highlighting issues identified in the audit just completed, updated in the current period based on discussions with the owner-manager, can serve as the documented audit strategy for the current audit engagement if it covers the matters noted in paragraph 8. **A11**

The Audit Plan (Ref: Para. 9)

The audit plan is more detailed than the overall audit strategy in that it includes the nature, timing and extent of audit procedures to be performed by engagement team members. Planning for these audit procedures takes place over the course of the audit as the audit plan for the engagement develops. For example, planning of the auditor's risk assessment procedures occurs early in the audit process. However, planning the nature, timing and extent of specific further audit procedures depends on the outcome of those risk assessment procedures. In addition, the auditor may begin the execution of further audit procedures for some classes of transactions, account balances and disclosures before planning all remaining further audit procedures. **A12**

Changes to Planning Decisions during the Course of the Audit (Ref: Para. 10*)*

As a result of unexpected events, changes in conditions, or the audit evidence obtained from the results of audit procedures, the auditor may need to modify the overall audit strategy and audit plan and thereby the resulting planned nature, timing and extent of further audit procedures, based on the revised consideration of assessed risks. This may be the case when information comes to the auditor's attention that differs significantly from the information available when the auditor planned the audit procedures. For example, audit evidence obtained through the performance of **A13** substantive procedures may contradict the audit evidence obtained through tests of controls.

Direction, Supervision and Review (Ref: Para. 11)

A14   The nature, timing and extent of the direction and supervision of engagement team members and review of their work vary depending on many factors, including:

- The size and complexity of the entity.
- The area of the audit.
- The assessed risks of material misstatement (for example, an increase in the assessed risk of material misstatement for a given area of the audit ordinarily requires a corresponding increase in the extent and timeliness of direction and supervision of engagement team members, and a more detailed review of their work).
- The capabilities and competence of the individual team members performing the audit work.

ISA (UK and Ireland) 220 contains further guidance on the direction, supervision and review of audit work.[9]

Considerations Specific to Smaller Entities

A15   If an audit is carried out entirely by the engagement partner, questions of direction and supervision of engagement team members and review of their work do not arise. In such cases, the engagement partner, having personally conducted all aspects of the work, will be aware of all material issues. Forming an objective view on the appropriateness of the judgments made in the course of the audit can present practical problems when the same individual also performs the entire audit. If particularly complex or unusual issues are involved, and the audit is performed by a sole practitioner, it may be desirable to consult with other suitably-experienced auditors or the auditor's professional body.

Documentation (Ref: Para. 12)

A16   The documentation of the overall audit strategy is a record of the key decisions considered necessary to properly plan the audit and to communicate significant matters to the engagement team. For example, the auditor may summarize the overall audit strategy in the form of a memorandum that contains key decisions regarding the overall scope, timing and conduct of the audit.

A17   The documentation of the audit plan is a record of the planned nature, timing and extent of risk assessment procedures and further audit procedures at the assertion level in response to the assessed risks. It also serves as a record of the proper planning of the audit procedures that can be reviewed and approved prior to their performance. The auditor may use standard audit programs or audit completion checklists, tailored as needed to reflect the particular engagement circumstances.

A18   A record of the significant changes to the overall audit strategy and the audit plan, and resulting changes to the planned nature, timing and extent of audit procedures, explains why the significant changes were made, and the overall strategy and audit plan finally adopted for the audit. It also reflects the appropriate response to the significant changes occurring during the audit.

[9] *ISA (UK and Ireland) 220, paragraphs 15-17.*

Considerations Specific to Smaller Entities

As discussed in paragraph A11, a suitable, brief memorandum may serve as the documented strategy for the audit of a smaller entity. For the audit plan, standard audit programs or checklists (see paragraph A17) drawn up on the assumption of few relevant control activities, as is likely to be the case in a smaller entity, may be used provided that they are tailored to the circumstances of the engagement, including the auditor's risk assessments.   **A19**

Additional Considerations in Initial Audit Engagements (Ref: Para. 13)

The purpose and objective of planning the audit are the same whether the audit is an initial or recurring engagement. However, for an initial audit, the auditor may need to expand the planning activities because the auditor does not ordinarily have the previous experience with the entity that is considered when planning recurring engagements. For an initial audit engagement, additional matters the auditor may consider in establishing the overall audit strategy and audit plan include the following: **A20**

- Unless prohibited by law or regulation, arrangements to be made with the predecessor auditor, for example, to review the predecessor auditor's working papers.
- Any major issues (including the application of accounting principles or of auditing and reporting standards) discussed with management in connection with the initial selection as auditor, the communication of these matters to those charged with governance and how these matters affect the overall audit strategy and audit plan.
- The audit procedures necessary to obtain sufficient appropriate audit evidence regarding opening balances.[10]
- Other procedures required by the firm's system of quality control for initial audit engagements (for example, the firm's system of quality control may require the involvement of another partner or senior individual to review the overall audit strategy prior to commencing significant audit procedures or to review reports prior to their issuance).

Appendix (Ref: Para. 7-8, A8-A11)

Considerations in Establishing the Overall Audit Strategy

This appendix provides examples of matters the auditor may consider in establishing the overall audit strategy. Many of these matters will also influence the auditor's detailed audit plan. The examples provided cover a broad range of matters applicable to many engagements. While some of the matters referred to below may be required by other ISAs (UK and Ireland), not all matters are relevant to every audit engagement and the list is not necessarily complete.

Characteristics of the Engagement

- The financial reporting framework on which the financial information to be audited has been prepared, including any need for reconciliations to another financial reporting framework.

---

[10] *ISA (UK and Ireland) 510, "Initial Audit Engagements—Opening Balances."*

International Standard on Auditing (UK and Ireland) 315 (Revised June 2013)

Identifying and assessing the risks of material misstatement through understanding the entity and its environment

(Effective for audits of financial statements for periods ending on or after 15 June 2014)

Contents

Paragraph

International Standard on Auditing (UK and Ireland) (ISA (UK and Ireland)) 315 (Revised June 2013), "Identifying and Assessing the Risks of Material Misstatement through Understanding the Entity and Its Environment" should be read in conjunction with ISA (UK and Ireland) 200, "Overall Objectives of the Independent Auditor and the Conduct of an Audit in Accordance with International Standards on Auditing (UK and Ireland)."

Introduction

Scope of this ISA (UK and Ireland)

This International Standard on Auditing (UK and Ireland) (ISA (UK and Ireland))   **1**
deals with the auditor's responsibility to identify and assess the risks of material
misstatement in the financial statements, through understanding the entity and its
environment, including the entity's internal control.

Effective Date

This ISA (UK and Ireland) is effective for audits of financial statements for periods   **2**
ending on or after 15 June 2014.

Objective

The objective of the auditor is to identify and assess the risks of material misstate-   **3**
ment, whether due to fraud or error, at the financial statement and assertion levels,
through understanding the entity and its environment, including the entity's internal
control, thereby providing a basis for designing and implementing responses to the
assessed risks of material misstatement.

Definitions

For purposes of the ISAs (UK and Ireland), the following terms have the meanings   **4**
attributed below:

(a) Assertions – Representations by management[1a], explicit or otherwise, that are
     embodied in the financial statements, as used by the auditor to consider the
     different types of potential misstatements that may occur.
(b) Business risk – A risk resulting from significant conditions, events, circum-
     stances, actions or inactions that could adversely affect an entity's ability to
     achieve its objectives and execute its strategies, or from the setting of inap-
     propriate objectives and strategies.
(c) Internal control – The process designed, implemented and maintained by those
     charged with governance, management and other personnel to provide rea-
     sonable assurance about the achievement of an entity's objectives with regard to
     reliability of financial reporting, effectiveness and efficiency of operations, and
     compliance with applicable laws and regulations. The term "controls" refers to
     any aspects of one or more of the components of internal control.
(d) Risk assessment procedures – The audit procedures performed to obtain an
     understanding of the entity and its environment, including the entity's internal
     control, to identify and assess the risks of material misstatement, whether due to
     fraud or error, at the financial statement and assertion levels.
(e) Significant risk – An identified and assessed risk of material misstatement that,
     in the auditor's judgment, requires special audit consideration.

[1a] *In the UK and Ireland, those charged with governance are responsible for preparing the financial statements.*

Requirements

Risk Assessment Procedures and Related Activities

5   The auditor shall perform risk assessment procedures to provide a basis for the identification and assessment of risks of material misstatement at the financial statement and assertion levels. Risk assessment procedures by themselves, however, do not provide sufficient appropriate audit evidence on which to base the audit opinion. (Ref: Para. A1-A5)

6   The risk assessment procedures shall include the following:

(a)   Inquiries of management, of appropriate individuals within the internal audit function (if the function exists), and of others within the entity who in the auditor's judgment may have information that is likely to assist in identifying risks of material misstatement due to fraud or error. (Ref: Para. A6-A13)

(b)   Analytical procedures. (Ref: Para. A14-A17)

(c)   Observation and inspection. (Ref: Para. A18)

7   The auditor shall consider whether information obtained from the auditor's client acceptance or continuance process is relevant to identifying risks of material misstatement.

8   If the engagement partner has performed other engagements for the entity, the engagement partner shall consider whether information obtained is relevant to identifying risks of material misstatement.

9   Where the auditor intends to use information obtained from the auditor's previous experience with the entity and from audit procedures performed in previous audits, the auditor shall determine whether changes have occurred since the previous audit that may affect its relevance to the current audit. (Ref: Para. A19-A20)

10   The engagement partner and other key engagement team members shall discuss the susceptibility of the entity's financial statements to material misstatement, and the application of the applicable financial reporting framework to the entity's facts and circumstances. The engagement partner shall determine which matters are to be communicated to engagement team members not involved in the discussion. (Ref: Para. A21-A23)

The Required Understanding of the Entity and Its Environment, Including the Entity's Internal Control

The Entity and Its Environment

11   The auditor shall obtain an understanding of the following:

(a)   Relevant industry, regulatory, and other external factors including the applicable financial reporting framework. (Ref: Para. A24-A29)

(b)   The nature of the entity, including:

(i)   its operations;

(ii)   its ownership and governance structures;

(iii) the types of investments that the entity is making and plans to make, including investments in special-purpose entities; and

(iv)   the way that the entity is structured and how it is financed to enable the auditor to understand the classes of transactions, account balances, and disclosures to be expected in the financial statements. (Ref: Para. A30-A34)

(c) The entity's selection and application of accounting policies, including the reasons for changes thereto. The auditor shall evaluate whether the entity's accounting policies are appropriate for its business and consistent with the applicable financial reporting framework and accounting policies used in the relevant industry. (Ref: Para. A35)

(d) The entity's objectives and strategies, and those related business risks that may result in risks of material misstatement. (Ref: Para. A36-A42)

(e) The measurement and review of the entity's financial performance. (Ref: Para. A43-A48)

The Entity's Internal Control

The auditor shall obtain an understanding of internal control relevant to the audit. **12** Although most controls relevant to the audit are likely to relate to financial reporting, not all controls that relate to financial reporting are relevant to the audit. It is a matter of the auditor's professional judgment whether a control, individually or in combination with others, is relevant to the audit. (Ref: Para. A49-A72)

Nature and Extent of the Understanding of Relevant Controls

When obtaining an understanding of controls that are relevant to the audit, the **13** auditor shall evaluate the design of those controls and determine whether they have been implemented, by performing procedures in addition to inquiry of the entity's personnel. (Ref: Para. A73-A75)

Components of Internal Control

Control environment

The auditor shall obtain an understanding of the control environment. As part of **14** obtaining this understanding, the auditor shall evaluate whether:

(a) Management, with the oversight of those charged with governance, has created and maintained a culture of honesty and ethical behavior; and

(b) The strengths in the control environment elements collectively provide an appropriate foundation for the other components of internal control, and whether those other components are not undermined by deficiencies in the control environment. (Ref: Para. A76-A86)

The entity's risk assessment process

The auditor shall obtain an understanding of whether the entity has a process for: **15**

(a) Identifying business risks relevant to financial reporting objectives;
(b) Estimating the significance of the risks;
(c) Assessing the likelihood of their occurrence; and
(d) Deciding about actions to address those risks. (Ref: Para. A87)

If the entity has established such a process (referred to hereafter as the "entity's risk **16** assessment process"), the auditor shall obtain an understanding of it, and the results thereof. If the auditor identifies risks of material misstatement that management failed to identify, the auditor shall evaluate whether there was an underlying risk of a kind that the auditor expects would have been identified by the entity's risk assessment process. If there is such a risk, the auditor shall obtain an understanding of why that process failed to identify it, and evaluate whether the process is appropriate to its circumstances or determine if there is a significant deficiency in internal control with regard to the entity's risk assessment process.

17 If the entity has not established such a process or has an ad hoc process, the auditor shall discuss with management whether business risks relevant to financial reporting objectives have been identified and how they have been addressed. The auditor shall evaluate whether the absence of a documented risk assessment process is appropriate in the circumstances, or determine whether it represents a significant deficiency in internal control. (Ref: Para. A88)

The information system, including the related business processes, relevant to financial reporting, and communication

18 The auditor shall obtain an understanding of the information system, including the related business processes, relevant to financial reporting, including the following areas:

(a) The classes of transactions in the entity's operations that are significant to the financial statements;

(b) The procedures, within both information technology (IT) and manual systems, by which those transactions are initiated, recorded, processed, corrected as necessary, transferred to the general ledger and reported in the financial statements;

(c) The related accounting records, supporting information and specific accounts in the financial statements that are used to initiate, record, process and report transactions; this includes the correction of incorrect information and how information is transferred to the general ledger. The records may be in either manual or electronic form;

(d) How the information system captures events and conditions, other than transactions, that are significant to the financial statements;

(e) The financial reporting process used to prepare the entity's financial statements, including significant accounting estimates and disclosures; and

(f) Controls surrounding journal entries, including non-standard journal entries used to record non-recurring, unusual transactions or adjustments. (Ref: Para. A89-A93)

19 The auditor shall obtain an understanding of how the entity communicates financial reporting roles and responsibilities and significant matters relating to financial reporting, including: (Ref: Para. A94-A95)

(a) Communications between management and those charged with governance; and

(b) External communications, such as those with regulatory authorities.

Control activities relevant to the audit

20 The auditor shall obtain an understanding of control activities relevant to the audit, being those the auditor judges it necessary to understand in order to assess the risks of material misstatement at the assertion level and design further audit procedures responsive to assessed risks. An audit does not require an understanding of all the control activities related to each significant class of transactions, account balance, and disclosure in the financial statements or to every assertion relevant to them. (Ref: Para. A96-A102)

In understanding the entity's control activities, the auditor shall obtain an under-   **21**
standing of how the entity has responded to risks arising from IT. (Ref: Para. A103-
A105)

Monitoring of controls

The auditor shall obtain an understanding of the major activities that the entity uses   **22**
to monitor internal control relevant to financial reporting, including those related to
those control activities relevant to the audit, and how the entity initiates remedial
actions to deficiencies in its controls. (Ref: Para. A106-A108)

If the entity has an internal audit function,[1] the auditor shall obtain an under-   **23**
standing of the nature of the internal audit function's responsibilities, its
organizational status, and the activities performed, or to be performed. (Ref: Para
A109-A116)

The auditor shall obtain an understanding of the sources of the information used in   **24**
the entity's monitoring activities, and the basis upon which management considers
the information to be sufficiently reliable for the purpose. (Ref: Para. A117)

Identifying and Assessing the Risks of Material Misstatement

The auditor shall identify and assess the risks of material misstatement at: **25**

(a) the financial statement level; and (Ref: Para. A118-A121)
(b) the assertion level for classes of transactions, account balances, and disclosures
     (Ref: Para. A122-A126)
     to provide a basis for designing and performing further audit procedures.

For this purpose, the auditor shall: **26**

(a) Identify risks throughout the process of obtaining an understanding of the
     entity and its environment, including relevant controls that relate to the risks,
     and by considering the classes of transactions, account balances, and disclosures
     in the financial statements; (Ref: Para. A127-A128)
(b) Assess the identified risks, and evaluate whether they relate more pervasively to
     the financial statements as a whole and potentially affect many assertions;
(c) Relate the identified risks to what can go wrong at the assertion level, taking
     account of relevant controls that the auditor intends to test; and (Ref: Para.
     A129-A131)
(d) Consider the likelihood of misstatement, including the possibility of multiple
     misstatements, and whether the potential misstatement is of a magnitude that
     could result in a material misstatement.

Risks That Require Special Audit Consideration

As part of the risk assessment as described in paragraph 25, the auditor shall   **27**
determine whether any of the risks identified are, in the auditor's judgment, a significant risk. In exercising this judgment, the auditor shall exclude the effects of
identified controls related to the risk.

In exercising judgment as to which risks are significant risks, the auditor shall con-   **28**
sider at least the following:

---

[1] *ISA (UK and Ireland) 610 (Revised June 2013)*, Using the Work of Internal Auditors, *paragraph 14, defines
the term "internal audit function" for purposes of the ISAs (UK and Ireland).*

(a)   Whether the risk is a risk of fraud;

(b)   Whether the risk is related to recent significant economic, accounting or other developments and, therefore, requires specific attention;

(c)   The complexity of transactions;

(d)   Whether the risk involves significant transactions with related parties;

(e)   The degree of subjectivity in the measurement of financial information related to the risk, especially those measurements involving a wide range of measurement uncertainty; and

(f)   Whether the risk involves significant transactions that are outside the normal course of business for the entity, or that otherwise appear to be unusual. (Ref: Para. A132-A136)

29   If the auditor has determined that a significant risk exists, the auditor shall obtain an understanding of the entity's controls, including control activities, relevant to that risk. (Ref: Para. A137-A139)

Risks for Which Substantive Procedures Alone Do Not Provide Sufficient Appropriate Audit Evidence

30   In respect of some risks, the auditor may judge that it is not possible or practicable to obtain sufficient appropriate audit evidence only from substantive procedures. Such risks may relate to the inaccurate or incomplete recording of routine and significant classes of transactions or account balances, the characteristics of which often permit highly automated processing with little or no manual intervention. In such cases, the entity's controls over such risks are relevant to the audit and the auditor shall obtain an understanding of them. (Ref: Para. A140-A142)

Revision of Risk Assessment

31   The auditor's assessment of the risks of material misstatement at the assertion level may change during the course of the audit as additional audit evidence is obtained. In circumstances where the auditor obtains audit evidence from performing further audit procedures, or if new information is obtained, either of which is inconsistent with the audit evidence on which the auditor originally based the assessment, the auditor shall revise the assessment and modify the further planned audit procedures accordingly. (Ref: Para. A143)

Documentation

32   The auditor shall include in the audit documentation:[2]

(a)   The discussion among the engagement team where required by paragraph 10, and the significant decisions reached;

(b)   Key elements of the understanding obtained regarding each of the aspects of the entity and its environment specified in paragraph 11 and of each of the internal control components specified in paragraphs 14-24; the sources of information from which the understanding was obtained; and the risk assessment procedures performed;

(c)   The identified and assessed risks of material misstatement at the financial statement level and at the assertion level as required by paragraph 25; and

(d)   The risks identified, and related controls about which the auditor has obtained an understanding, as a result of the requirements in paragraphs 27-30. (Ref: Para. A144-A147)

---

[2] *ISA (UK and Ireland) 230*, Audit Documentation, *paragraphs 8-11, and A6.*

***

Application and Other Explanatory Material

Risk Assessment Procedures and Related Activities (Ref: Para. 5)

Obtaining an understanding of the entity and its environment, including the entity's   **A1**
internal control (referred to hereafter as an "understanding of the entity"), is a
continuous, dynamic process of gathering, updating and analyzing information
throughout the audit. The understanding establishes a frame of reference within
which the auditor plans the audit and exercises professional judgment throughout
the audit, for example, when:

- Assessing risks of material misstatement of the financial statements;
- Determining materiality in accordance with ISA (UK and Ireland) 320;[3]
- Considering the appropriateness of the selection and application of accounting
  policies, and the adequacy of financial statement disclosures;
- Identifying areas where special audit consideration may be necessary, for
  example, related party transactions, the appropriateness of management's use of
  the going concern assumption, or considering the business purpose of
  transactions;
- Developing expectations for use when performing analytical procedures;
- Responding to the assessed risks of material misstatement, including designing
  and performing further audit procedures to obtain sufficient appropriate audit
  evidence; and
- Evaluating the sufficiency and appropriateness of audit evidence obtained, such
  as the appropriateness of assumptions and of management's[3a] oral and written
  representations.

Information obtained by performing risk assessment procedures and related activ-   **A2**
ities may be used by the auditor as audit evidence to support assessments of the risks
of material misstatement. In addition, the auditor may obtain audit evidence about
classes of transactions, account balances, or disclosures and related assertions and
about the operating effectiveness of controls, even though such procedures were not
specifically planned as substantive procedures or as tests of controls. The auditor
also may choose to perform substantive procedures or tests of controls concurrently
with risk assessment procedures because it is efficient to do so.

The auditor uses professional judgment to determine the extent of the understanding   **A3**
required. The auditor's primary consideration is whether the understanding that has
been obtained is sufficient to meet the objective stated in this ISA (UK and Ireland).
The depth of the overall understanding that is required by the auditor is less than
that possessed by management in managing the entity.

The risks to be assessed include both those due to error and those due to fraud, and   **A4**
both are covered by this ISA (UK and Ireland). However, the significance of fraud is
such that further requirements and guidance are included in ISA (UK and Ireland)

---

[3] *ISA (UK and Ireland) 320, Materiality in Planning and Performing an Audit.*

[3a] *In the UK and Ireland, as explained in paragraph A2-1 of ISA (UK and Ireland) 580,* Written Representations, *it is appropriate for written representations that are critical to obtaining sufficient appropriate audit
evidence to be provided by those charged with governance, rather than other levels of the entity's management.*

240 in relation to risk assessment procedures and related activities to obtain information that is used to identify the risks of material misstatement due to fraud.[4]

A5   Although the auditor is required to perform all the risk assessment procedures described in paragraph 6 in the course of obtaining the required understanding of the entity (see paragraphs 11-24), the auditor is not required to perform all of them for each aspect of that understanding. Other procedures may be performed where the information to be obtained therefrom may be helpful in identifying risks of material misstatement. Examples of such procedures include:

- Reviewing information obtained from external sources such as trade and economic journals; reports by analysts, banks, or rating agencies; or regulatory or financial publications.
- Making inquiries of the entity's external legal counsel or of valuation experts that the entity has used.

Inquiries of Management, the Internal Audit Function and Others within the Entity (Ref: Para. 6(a))

A6   Much of the information obtained by the auditor's inquiries is obtained from management and those responsible for financial reporting. Information may also be obtained by the auditor through inquiries with the internal audit function, if the entity has such a function, and others within the entity.

A7   The auditor may also obtain information, or a different perspective in identifying risks of material misstatement, through inquiries of others within the entity and other employees with different levels of authority. For example:

- Inquiries directed towards those charged with governance may help the auditor understand the environment in which the financial statements are prepared. ISA (UK and Ireland) 260[5] identifies the importance of effective two-way communication in assisting the auditor to obtain information from those charged with governance in this regard.
- Inquiries of employees involved in initiating, processing or recording complex or unusual transactions may help the auditor to evaluate the appropriateness of the selection and application of certain accounting policies.
- Inquiries directed toward in-house legal counsel may provide information about such matters as litigation, compliance with laws and regulations, knowledge of fraud or suspected fraud affecting the entity, warranties, post-sales obligations, arrangements (such as joint ventures) with business partners and the meaning of contract terms.
- Inquiries directed towards marketing or sales personnel may provide information about changes in the entity's marketing strategies, sales trends, or contractual arrangements with its customers.
- Inquiries directed to the risk management function (or those performing such roles) may provide information about operational and regulatory risks that may affect financial reporting.
- Inquiries directed to information systems personnel may provide information about system changes, system or control failures, or other information system-related risks.

[4] *ISA (UK and Ireland) 240*, The Auditor's Responsibilities Relating to Fraud in an Audit of Financial Statements, *paragraphs 12-24*.

[5] *ISA (UK and Ireland) 260*, Communication with Those Charged with Governance, *paragraph 4(b)*.

As obtaining an understanding of the entity and its environment is a continual,   **A8**
dynamic process, the auditor's inquiries may occur throughout the audit
engagement.

Inquiries of the Internal Audit Function

If an entity has an internal audit function, inquiries of the appropriate individuals   **A9**
within the function may provide information that is useful to the auditor in obtaining
an understanding of the entity and its environment, and in identifying and assessing
risks of material misstatement at the financial statement and assertion levels. In
performing its work, the internal audit function is likely to have obtained insight into
the entity's operations and business risks, and may have findings based on its work,
such as identified control deficiencies or risks, that may provide valuable input into
the auditor's understanding of the entity, the auditor's risk assessments or other
aspects of the audit. The auditor's inquiries are therefore made whether or not the
auditor expects to use the work of the internal audit function to modify the nature or
timing, or reduce the extent, of audit procedures to be performed.[6] Inquiries of
particular relevance may be about matters the internal audit function has raised with
those charged with governance and the outcomes of the function's own risk
assessment process.

If, based on responses to the auditor's inquiries, it appears that there are findings that   **A10**
may be relevant to the entity's financial reporting and the audit, the auditor may
consider it appropriate to read related reports of the internal audit function.
Examples of reports of the internal audit function that may be relevant include the
function's strategy and planning documents and reports that have been prepared for
management or those charged with governance describing the findings of the internal
audit function's examinations.

In addition, in accordance with ISA (UK and Ireland) 240,[7] if the internal audit   **A11**
function provides information to the auditor regarding any actual, suspected or
alleged fraud, the auditor takes this into account in the auditor's identification of risk
of material misstatement due to fraud.

Appropriate individuals within the internal audit function with whom inquiries are   **A12**
made are those who, in the auditor's judgment, have the appropriate knowledge,
experience and authority, such as the chief internal audit executive or, depending on
the circumstances, other personnel within the function. The auditor may also consider it appropriate to have periodic meetings with these individuals.

Considerations specific to public sector entities (Ref: Para 6(a))

Auditors of public sector entities often have additional responsibilities with regard to   **A13**
internal control and compliance with applicable laws and regulations. Inquiries of
appropriate individuals in the internal audit function can assist the auditors in
identifying the risk of material noncompliance with applicable laws and regulations
and the risk of deficiencies in internal control over financial reporting.

---

[6] *The relevant requirements are contained in ISA (UK and Ireland) 610 (Revised June 2013).*

[7] *ISA (UK and Ireland) 240, paragraph 19.*

the susceptibility of the entity's financial statements to material misstatement due to fraud or error.

The Required Understanding of the Entity and Its Environment, Including the Entity's Internal Control

The Entity and Its Environment

Industry, Regulatory and Other External Factors (Ref: Para. 11(a))

Industry Factors

A24 Relevant industry factors include industry conditions such as the competitive environment, supplier and customer relationships, and technological developments. Examples of matters the auditor may consider include:

- The market and competition, including demand, capacity, and price competition.
- Cyclical or seasonal activity.
- Product technology relating to the entity's products.
- Energy supply and cost.

A25 The industry in which the entity operates may give rise to specific risks of material misstatement arising from the nature of the business or the degree of regulation. For example, long-term contracts may involve significant estimates of revenues and expenses that give rise to risks of material misstatement. In such cases, it is important that the engagement team include members with sufficient relevant knowledge and experience.[9]

Regulatory Factors

A26 Relevant regulatory factors include the regulatory environment. The regulatory environment encompasses, among other matters, the applicable financial reporting framework and the legal and political environment. Examples of matters the auditor may consider include:

- Accounting principles and industry specific practices.
- Regulatory framework for a regulated industry.
- Legislation and regulation that significantly affect the entity's operations, including direct supervisory activities.
- Taxation (corporate and other).
- Government policies currently affecting the conduct of the entity's business, such as monetary, including foreign exchange controls, fiscal, financial incentives (for example, government aid programs), and tariffs or trade restrictions policies.
- Environmental requirements affecting the industry and the entity's business.

A27 ISA (UK and Ireland) 250 includes some specific requirements related to the legal and regulatory framework applicable to the entity and the industry or sector in which the entity operates.[10]

---

[9] *ISA (UK and Ireland) 220, Quality Control for an Audit of Financial Statements,* paragraph 14.

[10] *ISA (UK and Ireland) 250, Consideration of Laws and Regulations in an Audit of Financial Statements,* paragraph 12.

Considerations specific to public sector entities

For the audits of public sector entities, law, regulation or other authority may affect **A28**
the entity's operations. Such elements are essential to consider when obtaining an
understanding of the entity and its environment.

Other External Factors

Examples of other external factors affecting the entity that the auditor may consider **A29**
include the general economic conditions, interest rates and availability of financing,
and inflation or currency revaluation.

Nature of the Entity (Ref: Para. 11(b))

An understanding of the nature of an entity enables the auditor to understand such **A30**
matters as:

- Whether the entity has a complex structure, for example with subsidiaries or
  other components in multiple locations. Complex structures often introduce
  issues that may give rise to risks of material misstatement. Such issues may
  include whether goodwill, joint ventures, investments, or special-purpose entities
  are accounted for appropriately.
- The ownership, and relations between owners and other people or entities. This
  understanding assists in determining whether related party transactions have
  been identified and accounted for appropriately. ISA (UK and Ireland) 550[11]
  establishes requirements and provides guidance on the auditor's considerations
  relevant to related parties.

Examples of matters that the auditor may consider when obtaining an understanding **A31**
of the nature of the entity include:

- Business operations such as:
  - Nature of revenue sources, products or services, and markets, including
    involvement in electronic commerce such as Internet sales and marketing
    activities.
  - Conduct of operations (for example, stages and methods of production, or
    activities exposed to environmental risks).
  - Alliances, joint ventures, and outsourcing activities.
  - Geographic dispersion and industry segmentation.
  - Location of production facilities, warehouses, and offices, and location and
    quantities of inventories.
  - Key customers and important suppliers of goods and services, employment
    arrangements (including the existence of union contracts, pension and
    other post employment benefits, stock option or incentive bonus arrange-
    ments, and government regulation related to employment matters).
  - Research and development activities and expenditures.
  - Transactions with related parties.
- Investments and investment activities such as:
  - Planned or recently executed acquisitions or divestitures.
  - Investments and dispositions of securities and loans.
  - Capital investment activities.
  - Investments in non-consolidated entities, including partnerships, joint
    ventures and special-purpose entities.
- Financing and financing activities such as:

---

[11] *ISA (UK and Ireland) 550, Related Parties.*

    o   Major subsidiaries and associated entities, including consolidated and non-consolidated structures.
    o   Debt structure and related terms, including off-balance-sheet financing arrangements and leasing arrangements.
    o   Beneficial owners (local, foreign, business reputation and experience) and related parties.
    o   Use of derivative financial instruments.
- Financial reporting such as:
    o   Accounting principles and industry specific practices, including industry-specific significant categories (for example, loans and investments for banks, or research and development for pharmaceuticals).
    o   Revenue recognition practices.
    o   Accounting for fair values.
    o   Foreign currency assets, liabilities and transactions.
    o   Accounting for unusual or complex transactions including those in controversial or emerging areas (for example, accounting for stock-based compensation).

A32   Significant changes in the entity from prior periods may give rise to, or change, risks of material misstatement.

Nature of Special-Purpose Entities

A33   A special-purpose entity (sometimes referred to as a special-purpose vehicle) is an entity that is generally established for a narrow and well-defined purpose, such as to effect a lease or a securitization of financial assets, or to carry out research and development activities. It may take the form of a corporation, trust, partnership or unincorporated entity. The entity on behalf of which the special-purpose entity has been created may often transfer assets to the latter (for example, as part of a derecognition transaction involving financial assets), obtain the right to use the latter's assets, or perform services for the latter, while other parties may provide the funding to the latter. As ISA (UK and Ireland) 550 indicates, in some circumstances, a special-purpose entity may be a related party of the entity.[12]

A34   Financial reporting frameworks often specify detailed conditions that are deemed to amount to control, or circumstances under which the special-purpose entity should be considered for consolidation. The interpretation of the requirements of such frameworks often demands a detailed knowledge of the relevant agreements involving the special-purpose entity.

The Entity's Selection and Application of Accounting Policies (Ref: Para. 11(c))

A35   An understanding of the entity's selection and application of accounting policies may encompass such matters as:

- The methods the entity uses to account for significant and unusual transactions.
- The effect of significant accounting policies in controversial or emerging areas for which there is a lack of authoritative guidance or consensus.
- Changes in the entity's accounting policies.
- Financial reporting standards and laws and regulations that are new to the entity and when and how the entity will adopt such requirements.

---

[12] *ISA (UK and Ireland) 550, paragraph A7.*

Objectives and Strategies and Related Business Risks (Ref: Para. 11(d))

The entity conducts its business in the context of industry, regulatory and other **A36** internal and external factors. To respond to these factors, the entity's management or those charged with governance define objectives, which are the overall plans for the entity. Strategies are the approaches by which management intends to achieve its objectives. The entity's objectives and strategies may change over time.

Business risk is broader than the risk of material misstatement of the financial **A37** statements, though it includes the latter. Business risk may arise from change or complexity. A failure to recognize the need for change may also give rise to business risk. Business risk may arise, for example, from:

- The development of new products or services that may fail;
- A market which, even if successfully developed, is inadequate to support a product or service; or
- Flaws in a product or service that may result in liabilities and reputational risk.

An understanding of the business risks facing the entity increases the likelihood of **A38** identifying risks of material misstatement, since most business risks will eventually have financial consequences and, therefore, an effect on the financial statements. However, the auditor does not have a responsibility to identify or assess all business risks because not all business risks give rise to risks of material misstatement.

Examples of matters that the auditor may consider when obtaining an understanding **A39** of the entity's objectives, strategies and related business risks that may result in a risk of material misstatement of the financial statements include:

- Industry developments (a potential related business risk might be, for example, that the entity does not have the personnel or expertise to deal with the changes in the industry).
- New products and services (a potential related business risk might be, for example, that there is increased product liability).
- Expansion of the business (a potential related business risk might be, for example, that the demand has not been accurately estimated).
- New accounting requirements (a potential related business risk might be, for example, incomplete or improper implementation, or increased costs).
- Regulatory requirements (a potential related business risk might be, for example, that there is increased legal exposure).
- Current and prospective financing requirements (a potential related business risk might be, for example, the loss of financing due to the entity's inability to meet requirements).
- Use of IT (a potential related business risk might be, for example, that systems and processes are incompatible).
- The effects of implementing a strategy, particularly any effects that will lead to new accounting requirements (a potential related business risk might be, for example, incomplete or improper implementation).

A business risk may have an immediate consequence for the risk of material mis- **A40** statement for classes of transactions, account balances, and disclosures at the assertion level or the financial statement level. For example, the business risk arising from a contracting customer base may increase the risk of material misstatement associated with the valuation of receivables. However, the same risk, particularly in combination with a contracting economy, may also have a longer-term consequence, which the auditor considers when assessing the appropriateness of the going concern assumption. Whether a business risk may result in a risk of material misstatement is, therefore, considered in light of the entity's circumstances. Examples of conditions and events that may indicate risks of material misstatement are indicated in Appendix 2.

A41   Usually, management identifies business risks and develops approaches to address them. Such a risk assessment process is part of internal control and is discussed in paragraph 15 and paragraphs A87-A88.

Considerations Specific to Public Sector Entities

A42   For the audits of public sector entities, "management objectives" may be influenced by concerns regarding public accountability and may include objectives which have their source in law, regulation or other authority.

Measurement and Review of the Entity's Financial Performance (Ref: Para.11(e))

A43   Management and others will measure and review those things they regard as important. Performance measures, whether external or internal, create pressures on the entity. These pressures, in turn, may motivate management to take action to improve the business performance or to misstate the financial statements. Accordingly, an understanding of the entity's performance measures assists the auditor in considering whether pressures to achieve performance targets may result in management actions that increase the risks of material misstatement, including those due to fraud. See ISA (UK and Ireland) 240 for requirements and guidance in relation to the risks of fraud.

A44   The measurement and review of financial performance is not the same as the monitoring of controls (discussed as a component of internal control in paragraphs A106-A117), though their purposes may overlap:

- The measurement and review of performance is directed at whether business performance is meeting the objectives set by management (or third parties).
- Monitoring of controls is specifically concerned with the effective operation of internal control.
  In some cases, however, performance indicators also provide information that enables management to identify deficiencies in internal control.

A45   Examples of internally-generated information used by management for measuring and reviewing financial performance, and which the auditor may consider, include:

- Key performance indicators (financial and non-financial) and key ratios, trends and operating statistics.
- Period-on-period financial performance analyses.
- Budgets, forecasts, variance analyses, segment information and divisional, departmental or other level performance reports.
- Employee performance measures and incentive compensation policies.
- Comparisons of an entity's performance with that of competitors.

A46   External parties may also measure and review the entity's financial performance. For example, external information such as analysts' reports and credit rating agency reports may represent useful information for the auditor. Such reports can often be obtained from the entity being audited.

A47   Internal measures may highlight unexpected results or trends requiring management to determine their cause and take corrective action (including, in some cases, the detection and correction of misstatements on a timely basis). Performance measures may also indicate to the auditor that risks of misstatement of related financial statement information do exist. For example, performance measures may indicate that the entity has unusually rapid growth or profitability when compared to that of other entities in the same industry. Such information, particularly if combined with other factors such as performance-based bonus or incentive remuneration, may indicate the potential risk of management bias in the preparation of the financial statements.

Considerations Specific to Smaller Entities

Smaller entities often do not have processes to measure and review financial performance. Inquiry of management may reveal that it relies on certain key indicators for evaluating financial performance and taking appropriate action. If such inquiry indicates an absence of performance measurement or review, there may be an increased risk of misstatements not being detected and corrected.

A48

The Entity's Internal Control (Ref: Para. 12)

An understanding of internal control assists the auditor in identifying types of potential misstatements and factors that affect the risks of material misstatement, and in designing the nature, timing, and extent of further audit procedures.

A49

The following application material on internal control is presented in four sections, as follows:

A50

- General Nature and Characteristics of Internal Control.
- Controls Relevant to the Audit.
- Nature and Extent of the Understanding of Relevant Controls.
- Components of Internal Control.

General Nature and Characteristics of Internal Control

Purpose of Internal Control

Internal control is designed, implemented and maintained to address identified business risks that threaten the achievement of any of the entity's objectives that concern:

A51

- The reliability of the entity's financial reporting;
- The effectiveness and efficiency of its operations; and
- Its compliance with applicable laws and regulations.

The way in which internal control is designed, implemented and maintained varies with an entity's size and complexity.

Considerations specific to smaller entities

Smaller entities may use less structured means and simpler processes and procedures to achieve their objectives.

A52

Limitations of Internal Control

Internal control, no matter how effective, can provide an entity with only reasonable assurance about achieving the entity's financial reporting objectives. The likelihood of their achievement is affected by the inherent limitations of internal control. These

A53

include the realities that human judgment in decision-making can be faulty and that breakdowns in internal control can occur because of human error. For example, there may be an error in the design of, or in the change to, a control. Equally, the operation of a control may not be effective, such as where information produced for the purposes of internal control (for example, an exception report) is not effectively used because the individual responsible for reviewing the information does not understand its purpose or fails to take appropriate action.

A54   Additionally, controls can be circumvented by the collusion of two or more people or inappropriate management override of internal control. For example, management may enter into side agreements with customers that alter the terms and conditions of the entity's standard sales contracts, which may result in improper revenue recognition. Also, edit checks in a software program that are designed to identify and report transactions that exceed specified credit limits may be overridden or disabled.

A55   Further, in designing and implementing controls, management may make judgments on the nature and extent of the controls it chooses to implement, and the nature and extent of the risks it chooses to assume.

Considerations specific to smaller entities

A56   Smaller entities often have fewer employees which may limit the extent to which segregation of duties is practicable. However, in a small owner-managed entity, the owner-manager may be able to exercise more effective oversight than in a larger entity. This oversight may compensate for the generally more limited opportunities for segregation of duties.

A57   On the other hand, the owner-manager may be more able to override controls because the system of internal control is less structured. This is taken into account by the auditor when identifying the risks of material misstatement due to fraud.

Division of Internal Control into Components

A58   The division of internal control into the following five components, for purposes of the ISAs (UK and Ireland), provides a useful framework for auditors to consider how different aspects of an entity's internal control may affect the audit:

(a)   The control environment;
(b)   The entity's risk assessment process;
(c)   The information system, including the related business processes, relevant to financial reporting, and communication;
(d)   Control activities; and
(e)   Monitoring of controls.
      The division does not necessarily reflect how an entity designs, implements and maintains internal control, or how it may classify any particular component. Auditors may use different terminology or frameworks to describe the various aspects of internal control, and their effect on the audit than those used in this ISA (UK and Ireland), provided all the components described in this ISA (UK and Ireland) are addressed.

A59   Application material relating to the five components of internal control as they relate to a financial statement audit is set out in paragraphs A76-A117 below. Appendix 1 provides further explanation of these components of internal control.

Characteristics of Manual and Automated Elements of Internal Control Relevant to the Auditor's Risk Assessment

An entity's system of internal control contains manual elements and often contains automated elements. The characteristics of manual or automated elements are relevant to the auditor's risk assessment and further audit procedures based thereon. **A60**

The use of manual or automated elements in internal control also affects the manner in which transactions are initiated, recorded, processed, and reported: **A61**

- Controls in a manual system may include such procedures as approvals and reviews of transactions, and reconciliations and follow-up of reconciling items. Alternatively, an entity may use automated procedures to initiate, record, process, and report transactions, in which case records in electronic format replace paper documents.
- Controls in IT systems consist of a combination of automated controls (for example, controls embedded in computer programs) and manual controls. Further, manual controls may be independent of IT, may use information produced by IT, or may be limited to monitoring the effective functioning of IT and of automated controls, and to handling exceptions. When IT is used to initiate, record, process or report transactions, or other financial data for inclusion in financial statements, the systems and programs may include controls related to the corresponding assertions for material accounts or may be critical to the effective functioning of manual controls that depend on IT.
  An entity's mix of manual and automated elements in internal control varies with the nature and complexity of the entity's use of IT.

Generally, IT benefits an entity's internal control by enabling an entity to: **A62**

- Consistently apply predefined business rules and perform complex calculations in processing large volumes of transactions or data;
- Enhance the timeliness, availability, and accuracy of information;
- Facilitate the additional analysis of information;
- Enhance the ability to monitor the performance of the entity's activities and its policies and procedures;
- Reduce the risk that controls will be circumvented; and
- Enhance the ability to achieve effective segregation of duties by implementing security controls in applications, databases, and operating systems.

IT also poses specific risks to an entity's internal control, including, for example: **A63**

- Reliance on systems or programs that are inaccurately processing data, processing inaccurate data, or both.
- Unauthorized access to data that may result in destruction of data or improper changes to data, including the recording of unauthorized or non-existent transactions, or inaccurate recording of transactions. Particular risks may arise where multiple users access a common database.
- The possibility of IT personnel gaining access privileges beyond those necessary to perform their assigned duties thereby breaking down segregation of duties.
- Unauthorized changes to data in master files.
- Unauthorized changes to systems or programs.
- Failure to make necessary changes to systems or programs.
- Inappropriate manual intervention.
- Potential loss of data or inability to access data as required.

Manual elements in internal control may be more suitable where judgment and discretion are required such as for the following circumstances: **A64**

- Large, unusual or non-recurring transactions.
- Circumstances where errors are difficult to define, anticipate or predict.
- In changing circumstances that require a control response outside the scope of an existing automated control.
- In monitoring the effectiveness of automated controls.

A65   Manual elements in internal control may be less reliable than automated elements because they can be more easily bypassed, ignored, or overridden and they are also more prone to simple errors and mistakes. Consistency of application of a manual control element cannot therefore be assumed. Manual control elements may be less suitable for the following circumstances:

- High volume or recurring transactions, or in situations where errors that can be anticipated or predicted can be prevented, or detected and corrected, by control parameters that are automated.
- Control activities where the specific ways to perform the control can be adequately designed and automated.

A66   The extent and nature of the risks to internal control vary depending on the nature and characteristics of the entity's information system. The entity responds to the risks arising from the use of IT or from use of manual elements in internal control by establishing effective controls in light of the characteristics of the entity's information system.

Controls Relevant to the Audit

A67   There is a direct relationship between an entity's objectives and the controls it implements to provide reasonable assurance about their achievement. The entity's objectives, and therefore controls, relate to financial reporting, operations and compliance; however, not all of these objectives and controls are relevant to the auditor's risk assessment.

A68   Factors relevant to the auditor's judgment about whether a control, individually or in combination with others, is relevant to the audit may include such matters as the following:

- Materiality.
- The significance of the related risk.
- The size of the entity.
- The nature of the entity's business, including its organization and ownership characteristics.
- The diversity and complexity of the entity's operations.
- Applicable legal and regulatory requirements.
- The circumstances and the applicable component of internal control.
- The nature and complexity of the systems that are part of the entity's internal control, including the use of service organizations.
- Whether, and how, a specific control, individually or in combination with others, prevents, or detects and corrects, material misstatement.

A69   Controls over the completeness and accuracy of information produced by the entity may be relevant to the audit if the auditor intends to make use of the information in designing and performing further procedures. Controls relating to operations and compliance objectives may also be relevant to an audit if they relate to data the auditor evaluates or uses in applying audit procedures.

Internal control over safeguarding of assets against unauthorized acquisition, use, or disposition may include controls relating to both financial reporting and operations objectives. The auditor's consideration of such controls is generally limited to those relevant to the reliability of financial reporting.   **A70**

An entity generally has controls relating to objectives that are not relevant to an audit and therefore need not be considered. For example, an entity may rely on a sophisticated system of automated controls to provide efficient and effective operations (such as an airline's system of automated controls to maintain flight schedules), but these controls ordinarily would not be relevant to the audit. Further, although internal control applies to the entire entity or to any of its operating units or business processes, an understanding of internal control relating to each of the entity's operating units and business processes may not be relevant to the audit.   **A71**

Considerations Specific to Public Sector Entities

Public sector auditors often have additional responsibilities with respect to internal control, for example to report on compliance with an established code of practice. Public sector auditors can also have responsibilities to report on compliance with law, regulation or other authority. As a result, their review of internal control may be broader and more detailed.   **A72**

Nature and Extent of the Understanding of Relevant Controls (Ref: Para. 13)

Evaluating the design of a control involves considering whether the control, individually or in combination with other controls, is capable of effectively preventing, or detecting and correcting, material misstatements. Implementation of a control means that the control exists and that the entity is using it. There is little point in assessing the implementation of a control that is not effective, and so the design of a control is considered first. An improperly designed control may represent a significant deficiency in internal control.   **A73**

Risk assessment procedures to obtain audit evidence about the design and implementation of relevant controls may include: **A74**

- Inquiring of entity personnel.
- Observing the application of specific controls.
- Inspecting documents and reports.
- Tracing transactions through the information system relevant to financial reporting.

Inquiry alone, however, is not sufficient for such purposes.

Obtaining an understanding of an entity's controls is not sufficient to test their operating effectiveness, unless there is some automation that provides for the consistent operation of the controls. For example, obtaining audit evidence about the implementation of a manual control at a point in time does not provide audit evidence about the operating effectiveness of the control at other times during the period under audit. However, because of the inherent consistency of IT processing (see paragraph A62), performing audit procedures to determine whether an automated control has been implemented may serve as a test of that control's operating effectiveness, depending on the auditor's assessment and testing of controls such as   **A75** those over program changes. Tests of the operating effectiveness of controls are further described in ISA (UK and Ireland) 330.[13]

Components of Internal Control—Control Environment (Ref: Para. 14)

A76   The control environment includes the governance and management functions and the attitudes, awareness, and actions of those charged with governance and management concerning the entity's internal control and its importance in the entity. The control environment sets the tone of an organization, influencing the control consciousness of its people.

A77   Elements of the control environment that may be relevant when obtaining an understanding of the control environment include the following:

(a) *Communication and enforcement of integrity and ethical values* – These are essential elements that influence the effectiveness of the design, administration and monitoring of controls.

(b) *Commitment to competence* – Matters such as management's consideration of the competence levels for particular jobs and how those levels translate into requisite skills and knowledge.

(c) *Participation by those charged with governance* – Attributes of those charged with governance such as:
● Their independence from management.
● Their experience and stature.
● The extent of their involvement and the information they receive, and the scrutiny of activities.
● The appropriateness of their actions, including the degree to which difficult questions are raised and pursued with management, and their interaction with internal and external auditors.

(d) *Management's philosophy and operating style* – Characteristics such as management's:
● Approach to taking and managing business risks.
● Attitudes and actions toward financial reporting.
● Attitudes toward information processing and accounting functions and personnel.

(e) *Organizational structure* – The framework within which an entity's activities for achieving its objectives are planned, executed, controlled, and reviewed.

(f) *Assignment of authority and responsibility* – Matters such as how authority and responsibility for operating activities are assigned and how reporting relationships and authorization hierarchies are established.

(g) *Human resource policies and practices* – Policies and practices that relate to, for example, recruitment, orientation, training, evaluation, counselling, promotion, compensation, and remedial actions.

Audit Evidence for Elements of the Control Environment

A78   Relevant audit evidence may be obtained through a combination of inquiries and other risk assessment procedures such as corroborating inquiries through observation or inspection of documents. For example, through inquiries of management and employees, the auditor may obtain an understanding of how management communicates to employees its views on business practices and ethical behavior. The auditor may then determine whether relevant controls have been implemented by

---

[13] *ISA (UK and Ireland) 330, The Auditor's Responses to Assessed Risks.*

considering, for example, whether management has a written code of conduct and whether it acts in a manner that supports the code.

The auditor may also consider how management has responded to the findings and recommendations of the internal audit function regarding identified deficiencies in internal control relevant to the audit, including whether and how such responses have been implemented, and whether they have been subsequently evaluated by the internal audit function.   **A79**

Effect of the Control Environment on the Assessment of the Risks of Material Misstatement

Some elements of an entity's control environment have a pervasive effect on assessing the risks of material misstatement. For example, an entity's control consciousness is influenced significantly by those charged with governance, because one of their roles is to counterbalance pressures on management in relation to financial reporting that may arise from market demands or remuneration schemes. The effectiveness of the design of the control environment in relation to participation by those charged with governance is therefore influenced by such matters as: **A80**

- Their independence from management and their ability to evaluate the actions of management.
- Whether they understand the entity's business transactions.
- The extent to which they evaluate whether the financial statements are prepared in accordance with the applicable financial reporting framework.

An active and independent board of directors may influence the philosophy and operating style of senior management. However, other elements may be more limited in their effect. For example, although human resource policies and practices directed toward hiring competent financial, accounting, and IT personnel may reduce the risk of errors in processing financial information, they may not mitigate a strong bias by top management to overstate earnings.   **A81**

The existence of a satisfactory control environment can be a positive factor when the auditor assesses the risks of material misstatement. However, although it may help reduce the risk of fraud, a satisfactory control environment is not an absolute deterrent to fraud. Conversely, deficiencies in the control environment may undermine the effectiveness of controls, in particular in relation to fraud. For example, management's failure to commit sufficient resources to address IT security risks may adversely affect internal control by allowing improper changes to be made to computer programs or to data, or unauthorized transactions to be processed. As explained in ISA (UK and Ireland) 330, the control environment also influences the nature, timing, and extent of the auditor's further procedures.[14]   **A82**

The control environment in itself does not prevent, or detect and correct, a material misstatement. It may, however, influence the auditor's evaluation of the effectiveness of other controls (for example, the monitoring of controls and the operation of specific control activities) and thereby, the auditor's assessment of the risks of material misstatement.   **A83**

---

[14] *ISA (UK and Ireland) 330, paragraphs A2-A3.*

Considerations Specific to Smaller Entities

A84   The control environment within small entities is likely to differ from larger entities. For example, those charged with governance in small entities may not include an independent or outside member, and the role of governance may be undertaken directly by the owner-manager where there are no other owners. The nature of the control environment may also influence the significance of other controls, or their absence. For example, the active involvement of an owner-manager may mitigate certain of the risks arising from a lack of segregation of duties in a small entity; it may, however, increase other risks, for example, the risk of override of controls.

A85   In addition, audit evidence for elements of the control environment in smaller entities may not be available in documentary form, in particular where communication between management and other personnel may be informal, yet effective. For example, small entities might not have a written code of conduct but, instead, develop a culture that emphasizes the importance of integrity and ethical behavior through oral communication and by management example.

A86   Consequently, the attitudes, awareness and actions of management or the owner-manager are of particular importance to the auditor's understanding of a smaller entity's control environment.

Components of Internal Control—The Entity's Risk Assessment Process (Ref: Para. 15)

A87   The entity's risk assessment process forms the basis for how management determines the risks to be managed. If that process is appropriate to the circumstances, including the nature, size and complexity of the entity, it assists the auditor in identifying risks of material misstatement. Whether the entity's risk assessment process is appropriate to the circumstances is a matter of judgment.

Considerations Specific to Smaller Entities (Ref: Para. 17)

A88   There is unlikely to be an established risk assessment process in a small entity. In such cases, it is likely that management will identify risks through direct personal involvement in the business. Irrespective of the circumstances, however, inquiry about identified risks and how they are addressed by management is still necessary.

Components of Internal Control—The Information System, Including Related Business Processes, Relevant to Financial Reporting, and Communication

The Information System, Including Related Business Processes, Relevant to Financial Reporting (Ref: Para. 18)

A89   The information system relevant to financial reporting objectives, which includes the accounting system, consists of the procedures and records designed and established to:

- Initiate, record, process, and report entity transactions (as well as events and conditions) and to maintain accountability for the related assets, liabilities, and equity;
- Resolve incorrect processing of transactions, for example, automated suspense files and procedures followed to clear suspense items out on a timely basis;
- Process and account for system overrides or bypasses to controls;
- Transfer information from transaction processing systems to the general ledger;

- Capture information relevant to financial reporting for events and conditions other than transactions, such as the depreciation and amortization of assets and changes in the recoverability of accounts receivables; and
- Ensure information required to be disclosed by the applicable financial reporting framework is accumulated, recorded, processed, summarized and appropriately reported in the financial statements.

Journal entries

An entity's information system typically includes the use of standard journal entries   **A90** that are required on a recurring basis to record transactions. Examples might be journal entries to record sales, purchases, and cash disbursements in the general ledger, or to record accounting estimates that are periodically made by management, such as changes in the estimate of uncollectible accounts receivable.

An entity's financial reporting process also includes the use of non-standard journal   **A91** entries to record non-recurring, unusual transactions or adjustments. Examples of such entries include consolidating adjustments and entries for a business combination or disposal or non-recurring estimates such as the impairment of an asset. In manual general ledger systems, non-standard journal entries may be identified through inspection of ledgers, journals, and supporting documentation. When automated procedures are used to maintain the general ledger and prepare financial statements, such entries may exist only in electronic form and may therefore be more easily identified through the use of computer-assisted audit techniques.

Related business processes

An entity's business processes are the activities designed to: **A92**

- Develop, purchase, produce, sell and distribute an entity's products and services;
- Ensure compliance with laws and regulations; and
- Record information, including accounting and financial reporting information. Business processes result in the transactions that are recorded, processed and reported by the information system. Obtaining an understanding of the entity's business processes, which include how transactions are originated, assists the auditor obtain an understanding of the entity's information system relevant to financial reporting in a manner that is appropriate to the entity's circumstances.

Considerations specific to smaller entities

Information systems and related business processes relevant to financial reporting in   **A93** small entities are likely to be less sophisticated than in larger entities, but their role is just as significant. Small entities with active management involvement may not need extensive descriptions of accounting procedures, sophisticated accounting records, or written policies. Understanding the entity's systems and processes may therefore be easier in an audit of smaller entities, and may be more dependent on inquiry than on review of documentation. The need to obtain an understanding, however, remains important.

Communication (Ref: Para. 19)

Communication by the entity of the financial reporting roles and responsibilities and   **A94** of significant matters relating to financial reporting involves providing an understanding of individual roles and responsibilities pertaining to internal control over financial reporting. It includes such matters as the extent to which personnel understand how their activities in the financial reporting information system relate to the work of others and the means of reporting exceptions to an appropriate higher level within the entity. Communication may take such forms as policy manuals and financial reporting manuals. Open communication channels help ensure that exceptions are reported and acted on.

Considerations specific to smaller entities

A95   Communication may be less structured and easier to achieve in a small entity than in a larger entity due to fewer levels of responsibility and management's greater visibility and availability.

Components of Internal Control—Control Activities Relevant to the Audit (Ref: Para. 20)

A96   Control activities are the policies and procedures that help ensure that management directives are carried out. Control activities, whether within IT or manual systems, have various objectives and are applied at various organizational and functional levels. Examples of specific control activities include those relating to the following:

- Authorization.
- Performance reviews.
- Information processing.
- Physical controls.
- Segregation of duties.

A97   Control activities that are relevant to the audit are:

- Those that are required to be treated as such, being control activities that relate to significant risks and those that relate to risks for which substantive procedures alone do not provide sufficient appropriate audit evidence, as required by paragraphs 29 and 30, respectively; or
- Those that are considered to be relevant in the judgment of the auditor.

A98   The auditor's judgment about whether a control activity is relevant to the audit is influenced by the risk that the auditor has identified that may give rise to a material misstatement and whether the auditor thinks it is likely to be appropriate to test the operating effectiveness of the control in determining the extent of substantive testing.

A99   The auditor's emphasis may be on identifying and obtaining an understanding of control activities that address the areas where the auditor considers that risks of material misstatement are likely to be higher. When multiple control activities each achieve the same objective, it is unnecessary to obtain an understanding of each of the control activities related to such objective.

A100   The auditor's knowledge about the presence or absence of control activities obtained from the understanding of the other components of internal control assists the auditor in determining whether it is necessary to devote additional attention to obtaining an understanding of control activities.

Considerations Specific to Smaller Entities

The concepts underlying control activities in small entities are likely to be similar to those in larger entities, but the formality with which they operate may vary. Further, small entities may find that certain types of control activities are not relevant because of controls applied by management. For example, management's sole authority for granting credit to customers and approving significant purchases can provide strong control over important account balances and transactions, lessening or removing the need for more detailed control activities.   **A101**

Control activities relevant to the audit of a smaller entity are likely to relate to the main transaction cycles such as revenues, purchases and employment expenses.   **A102**

Risks Arising from IT (Ref: Para. 21)

The use of IT affects the way that control activities are implemented. From the auditor's perspective, controls over IT systems are effective when they maintain the integrity of information and the security of the data such systems process, and include effective general IT controls and application controls.   **A103**

General IT controls are policies and procedures that relate to many applications and support the effective functioning of application controls. They apply to mainframe, miniframe, and end-user environments. General IT controls that maintain the integrity of information and security of data commonly include controls over the following: **A104**

- Data center and network operations.
- System software acquisition, change and maintenance.
- Program change.
- Access security.
- Application system acquisition, development, and maintenance.
  They are generally implemented to deal with the risks referred to in paragraph A63 above.

Application controls are manual or automated procedures that typically operate at a business process level and apply to the processing of transactions by individual applications. Application controls can be preventive or detective in nature and are designed to ensure the integrity of the accounting records. Accordingly, application controls relate to procedures used to initiate, record, process and report transactions or other financial data. These controls help ensure that transactions occurred, are authorized, and are completely and accurately recorded and processed. Examples include edit checks of input data, and numerical sequence checks with manual follow-up of exception reports or correction at the point of data entry.   **A105**

Components of Internal Control—Monitoring of Controls (Ref: Para. 22)

Monitoring of controls is a process to assess the effectiveness of internal control performance over time. It involves assessing the effectiveness of controls on a timely basis and taking necessary remedial actions. Management accomplishes monitoring of controls through ongoing activities, separate evaluations, or a combination of the two. Ongoing monitoring activities are often built into the normal recurring activities of an entity and include regular management and supervisory activities.   **A106**

A107   Management's monitoring activities may include using information from communications from external parties such as customer complaints and regulator comments that may indicate problems or highlight areas in need of improvement.

Considerations Specific to Smaller Entities

A108   Management's monitoring of control is often accomplished by management's or the owner-manager's close involvement in operations. This involvement often will identify significant variances from expectations and inaccuracies in financial data leading to remedial action to the control.

The Entity's Internal Audit Function (Ref: Para. 23)

A109   If the entity has an internal audit function, obtaining an understanding of that function contributes to the auditor's understanding of the entity and its environment, including internal control, in particular the role that the function plays in the entity's monitoring of internal control over financial reporting. This understanding, together with the information obtained from the auditor's inquiries in paragraph 6(a) of this ISA (UK and Ireland), may also provide information that is directly relevant to the auditor's identification and assessment of the risks of material misstatement.

A110   The objectives and scope of an internal audit function, the nature of its responsibilities and its status within the organization, including the function's authority and accountability, vary widely and depend on the size and structure of the entity and the requirements of management and, where applicable, those charged with governance. These matters may be set out in an internal audit charter or terms of reference.

A111   The responsibilities of an internal audit function may include performing procedures and evaluating the results to provide assurance to management and those charged with governance regarding the design and effectiveness of risk management, internal control and governance processes. If so, the internal audit function may play an important role in the entity's monitoring of internal control over financial reporting. However, the responsibilities of the internal audit function may be focused on evaluating the economy, efficiency and effectiveness of operations and, if so, the work of the function may not directly relate to the entity's financial reporting.

A112   The auditor's inquiries of appropriate individuals within the internal audit function in accordance with paragraph 6(a) of this ISA (UK and Ireland) help the auditor obtain an understanding of the nature of the internal audit function's responsibilities. If the auditor determines that the function's responsibilities are related to the entity's financial reporting, the auditor may obtain further understanding of the activities performed, or to be performed, by the internal audit function by reviewing the internal audit function's audit plan for the period, if any, and discussing that plan with the appropriate individuals within the function.

A113   If the nature of the internal audit function's responsibilities and assurance activities are related to the entity's financial reporting, the auditor may also be able to use the work of the internal audit function to modify the nature or timing, or reduce the extent, of audit procedures to be performed directly by the auditor in obtaining audit evidence. Auditors may be more likely to be able to use the work of an entity's internal audit function when it appears, for example, based on experience in previous audits or the auditor's risk assessment procedures, that the entity has an internal audit function that is adequately and appropriately resourced relative to the size of the entity and the nature of its operations, and has a direct reporting relationship to those charged with governance.

If, based on the auditor's preliminary understanding of the internal audit function, the auditor expects to use the work of the internal audit function to modify the nature or timing, or reduce the extent, of audit procedures to be performed, ISA (UK and Ireland) 610 (Revised June 2013) applies.   **A114**

As is further discussed in ISA (UK and Ireland) 610 (Revised June 2013), the activities of an internal audit function are distinct from other monitoring controls that may be relevant to financial reporting, such as reviews of management accounting information that are designed to contribute to how the entity prevents or detects misstatements.   **A115**

Establishing communications with the appropriate individuals within an entity's internal audit function early in the engagement, and maintaining such communications throughout the engagement, can facilitate effective sharing of information. It creates an environment in which the auditor can be informed of significant matters that may come to the attention of the internal audit function when such matters may affect the work of the auditor. ISA (UK and Ireland) 200 discusses the importance of the auditor planning and performing the audit with professional skepticism, including being alert to information that brings into question the reliability of documents and responses to inquiries to be used as audit evidence. Accordingly, communication with the internal audit function throughout the engagement may provide opportunities for internal auditors to bring such information to the auditor's attention. The auditor is then able to take such information into account in the auditor's identification and assessment of risks of material misstatement.   **A116**

Sources of Information (Ref: Para. 24)

Much of the information used in monitoring may be produced by the entity's information system. If management assumes that data used for monitoring are accurate without having a basis for that assumption, errors that may exist in the information could potentially lead management to incorrect conclusions from its monitoring activities. Accordingly, an understanding of: **A117**

* the sources of the information related to the entity's monitoring activities; and
* the basis upon which management considers the information to be sufficiently reliable for the purpose,

is required as part of the auditor's understanding of the entity's monitoring activities as a component of internal control.

Identifying and Assessing the Risks of Material Misstatement

Assessment of Risks of Material Misstatement at the Financial Statement Level
(Ref: Para. 25 (a))

Risks of material misstatement at the financial statement level refer to risks that relate pervasively to the financial statements as a whole and potentially affect many assertions. Risks of this nature are not necessarily risks identifiable with specific assertions at the class of transactions, account balance, or disclosure level. Rather, they represent circumstances that may increase the risks of material misstatement at the assertion level, for example, through management override of internal control. Financial statement level risks may be especially relevant to the auditor's consideration of the risks of material misstatement arising from fraud.   **A118**

A119   Risks at the financial statement level may derive in particular from a deficient control environment (although these risks may also relate to other factors, such as declining economic conditions). For example, deficiencies such as management's lack of competence may have a more pervasive effect on the financial statements and may require an overall response by the auditor.

A120   The auditor's understanding of internal control may raise doubts about the auditability of an entity's financial statements. For example:

*   Concerns about the integrity of the entity's management may be so serious as to cause the auditor to conclude that the risk of management misrepresentation in the financial statements is such that an audit cannot be conducted.

*   Concerns about the condition and reliability of an entity's records may cause the auditor to conclude that it is unlikely that sufficient appropriate audit evidence will be available to support an unmodified opinion on the financial statements.

A121   ISA (UK and Ireland) 705[15] establishes requirements and provides guidance in determining whether there is a need for the auditor to express a qualified opinion or disclaim an opinion or, as may be required in some cases, to withdraw from the engagement where withdrawal is possible under applicable law or regulation.

Assessment of Risks of Material Misstatement at the Assertion Level (Ref: Para. 25(b))

A122   Risks of material misstatement at the assertion level for classes of transactions, account balances, and disclosures need to be considered because such consideration directly assists in determining the nature, timing, and extent of further audit procedures at the assertion level necessary to obtain sufficient appropriate audit evidence. In identifying and assessing risks of material misstatement at the assertion level, the auditor may conclude that the identified risks relate more pervasively to the financial statements as a whole and potentially affect many assertions.

The Use of Assertions

A123   In representing that the financial statements are in accordance with the applicable financial reporting framework, management[1a] implicitly or explicitly makes assertions regarding the recognition, measurement, presentation and disclosure of the various elements of financial statements and related disclosures.

A124   Assertions used by the auditor to consider the different types of potential misstatements that may occur fall into the following three categories and may take the following forms:

(a) Assertions about classes of transactions and events for the period under audit:
    (i)   Occurrence—transactions and events that have been recorded have occurred and pertain to the entity.
    (ii) Completeness—all transactions and events that should have been recorded have been recorded.
    (iii) Accuracy—amounts and other data relating to recorded transactions and events have been recorded appropriately.
    (iv) Cutoff—transactions and events have been recorded in the correct accounting period.
    (v)   Classification—transactions and events have been recorded in the proper accounts.

---

[15] *ISA (UK and Ireland) 705, Modifications to the Opinion in the Independent Auditor's Report.*

(b) Assertions about account balances at the period end:
  (i) Existence—assets, liabilities, and equity interests exist.
  (ii) Rights and obligations—the entity holds or controls the rights to assets, and liabilities are the obligations of the entity.
  (iii) Completeness—all assets, liabilities and equity interests that should have been recorded have been recorded.
  (iv) Valuation and allocation—assets, liabilities, and equity interests are included in the financial statements at appropriate amounts and any resulting valuation or allocation adjustments are appropriately recorded.
(c) Assertions about presentation and disclosure:
  (i) Occurrence and rights and obligations—disclosed events, transactions, and other matters have occurred and pertain to the entity.
  (ii) Completeness—all disclosures that should have been included in the financial statements have been included.
  (iii) Classification and understandability—financial information is appropriately presented and described, and disclosures are clearly expressed.
  (iv) Accuracy and valuation—financial and other information are disclosed fairly and at appropriate amounts.

The auditor may use the assertions as described above or may express them differently provided all aspects described above have been covered. For example, the auditor may choose to combine the assertions about transactions and events with the assertions about account balances.   **A125**

Considerations specific to public sector entities

When making assertions about the financial statements of public sector entities, in addition to those assertions set out in paragraph A124, management[1a] may often assert that transactions and events have been carried out in accordance with law, regulation or other authority. Such assertions may fall within the scope of the financial statement audit.   **A126**

Process of Identifying Risks of Material Misstatement (Ref: Para. 26(a))

Information gathered by performing risk assessment procedures, including the audit evidence obtained in evaluating the design of controls and determining whether they have been implemented, is used as audit evidence to support the risk assessment. The risk assessment determines the nature, timing, and extent of further audit procedures to be performed.   **A127**

Appendix 2 provides examples of conditions and events that may indicate the existence of risks of material misstatement.   **A128**

Relating Controls to Assertions (Ref: Para. 26(c))

In making risk assessments, the auditor may identify the controls that are likely to prevent, or detect and correct, material misstatement in specific assertions. Generally, it is useful to obtain an understanding of controls and relate them to assertions in the context of processes and systems in which they exist because individual control activities often do not in themselves address a risk. Often, only multiple control activities, together with other components of internal control, will be sufficient to address a risk.   **A129**

A130   Conversely, some control activities may have a specific effect on an individual assertion embodied in a particular class of transactions or account balance. For example, the control activities that an entity established to ensure that its personnel are properly counting and recording the annual physical inventory relate directly to the existence and completeness assertions for the inventory account balance.

A131   Controls can be either directly or indirectly related to an assertion. The more indirect the relationship, the less effective that control may be in preventing, or detecting and correcting, misstatements in that assertion. For example, a sales manager's review of a summary of sales activity for specific stores by region ordinarily is only indirectly related to the completeness assertion for sales revenue. Accordingly, it may be less effective in reducing risk for that assertion than controls more directly related to that assertion, such as matching shipping documents with billing documents.

Significant Risks

Identifying Significant Risks (Ref: Para. 28)

A132   Significant risks often relate to significant non-routine transactions or judgmental matters. Non-routine transactions are transactions that are unusual, due to either size or nature, and that therefore occur infrequently. Judgmental matters may include the development of accounting estimates for which there is significant measurement uncertainty. Routine, non-complex transactions that are subject to systematic processing are less likely to give rise to significant risks.

A133   Risks of material misstatement may be greater for significant non-routine transactions arising from matters such as the following:

- Greater management intervention to specify the accounting treatment.
- Greater manual intervention for data collection and processing.
- Complex calculations or accounting principles.
- The nature of non-routine transactions, which may make it difficult for the entity to implement effective controls over the risks.

A134   Risks of material misstatement may be greater for significant judgmental matters that require the development of accounting estimates, arising from matters such as the following:

- Accounting principles for accounting estimates or revenue recognition may be subject to differing interpretation.
- Required judgment may be subjective or complex, or require assumptions about the effects of future events, for example, judgment about fair value.

A135   ISA (UK and Ireland) 330 describes the consequences for further audit procedures of identifying a risk as significant.[16]

Significant risks relating to the risks of material misstatement due to fraud

A136   ISA (UK and Ireland) 240 provides further requirements and guidance in relation to the identification and assessment of the risks of material misstatement due to fraud.[17]

---

[16] *ISA (UK and Ireland) 330, paragraphs 15 and 21.*

[17] *ISA (UK and Ireland) 240, paragraphs 25-27.*

Understanding Controls Related to Significant Risks (Ref: Para. 29)

Although risks relating to significant non-routine or judgmental matters are often **A137**
less likely to be subject to routine controls, management may have other responses
intended to deal with such risks. Accordingly, the auditor's understanding of whether
the entity has designed and implemented controls for significant risks arising from
non-routine or judgmental matters includes whether and how management responds
to the risks. Such responses might include:

- Control activities such as a review of assumptions by senior management or
  experts.
- Documented processes for estimations.
- Approval by those charged with governance.

For example, where there are one-off events such as the receipt of notice of a sig- **A138**
nificant lawsuit, consideration of the entity's response may include such matters as
whether it has been referred to appropriate experts (such as internal or external legal
counsel), whether an assessment has been made of the potential effect, and how it is
proposed that the circumstances are to be disclosed in the financial statements.

In some cases, management may not have appropriately responded to significant **A139**
risks of material misstatement by implementing controls over these significant risks.
Failure by management to implement such controls is an indicator of a significant
deficiency in internal control.[18]

Risks for Which Substantive Procedures Alone Do Not Provide Sufficient Appropriate
Audit Evidence (Ref: Para. 30)

Risks of material misstatement may relate directly to the recording of routine classes **A140**
of transactions or account balances, and the preparation of reliable financial statements. Such risks may include risks of inaccurate or incomplete processing for
routine and significant classes of transactions such as an entity's revenue, purchases,
and cash receipts or cash payments.

Where such routine business transactions are subject to highly automated processing **A141**
with little or no manual intervention, it may not be possible to perform only substantive procedures in relation to the risk. For example, the auditor may consider
this to be the case in circumstances where a significant amount of an entity's
information is initiated, recorded, processed, or reported only in electronic form such
as in an integrated system. In such cases:

- Audit evidence may be available only in electronic form, and its sufficiency and
  appropriateness usually depend on the effectiveness of controls over its accuracy
  and completeness.
- The potential for improper initiation or alteration of information to occur and
  not be detected may be greater if appropriate controls are not operating
  effectively.

The consequences for further audit procedures of identifying such risks are described **A142**
in ISA (UK and Ireland) 330.[19]

---

[18] ISA (UK and Ireland) 265, *Communicating Deficiencies in Internal Control to Those Charged with Gov-*
ernance and Management, paragraph A7.

[19] ISA (UK and Ireland) 330, paragraph 8.

that communicate prospective roles and responsibilities and include practices such as training schools and seminars illustrate expected levels of performance and behavior. Promotions driven by periodic performance appraisals demonstrate the entity's commitment to the advancement of qualified personnel to higher levels of responsibility.

Entity's Risk Assessment Process

3   For financial reporting purposes, the entity's risk assessment process includes how management identifies business risks relevant to the preparation of financial statements in accordance with the entity's applicable financial reporting framework, estimates their significance, assesses the likelihood of their occurrence, and decides upon actions to respond to and manage them and the results thereof. For example, the entity's risk assessment process may address how the entity considers the possibility of unrecorded transactions or identifies and analyzes significant estimates recorded in the financial statements.

4   Risks relevant to reliable financial reporting include external and internal events, transactions or circumstances that may occur and adversely affect an entity's ability to initiate, record, process, and report financial data consistent with the assertions of management[1a] in the financial statements. Management may initiate plans, programs, or actions to address specific risks or it may decide to accept a risk because of cost or other considerations. Risks can arise or change due to circumstances such as the following:

- *Changes in operating environment.* Changes in the regulatory or operating environment can result in changes in competitive pressures and significantly different risks.
- *New personnel.* New personnel may have a different focus on or understanding of internal control.
- *New or revamped information systems.* Significant and rapid changes in information systems can change the risk relating to internal control.
- *Rapid growth.* Significant and rapid expansion of operations can strain controls and increase the risk of a breakdown in controls.
- *New technology.* Incorporating new technologies into production processes or information systems may change the risk associated with internal control.
- *New business models, products, or activities.* Entering into business areas or transactions with which an entity has little experience may introduce new risks associated with internal control.
- *Corporate restructurings.* Restructurings may be accompanied by staff reductions and changes in supervision and segregation of duties that may change the risk associated with internal control.
- *Expanded foreign operations.* The expansion or acquisition of foreign operations carries new and often unique risks that may affect internal control, for example, additional or changed risks from foreign currency transactions.
- *New accounting pronouncements.* Adoption of new accounting principles or changing accounting principles may affect risks in preparing financial statements.

Information System, Including the Related Business Processes, Relevant to Financial Reporting, and Communication

5   An information system consists of infrastructure (physical and hardware components), software, people, procedures, and data. Many information systems make extensive use of information technology (IT).

Introduction

Scope of this ISA (UK and Ireland)

This International Standard on Auditing (UK and Ireland) (ISA (UK and Ireland)) deals with the auditor's responsibility to apply the concept of materiality in planning and performing an audit of financial statements. ISA (UK and Ireland) 450[1] explains how materiality is applied in evaluating the effect of identified misstatements on the audit and of uncorrected misstatements, if any, on the financial statements.   **1**

Materiality in the Context of an Audit

Financial reporting frameworks often discuss the concept of materiality in the context of the preparation and presentation of financial statements. Although financial reporting frameworks may discuss materiality in different terms, they generally explain that: **2**

- Misstatements, including omissions, are considered to be material if they, individually or in the aggregate, could reasonably be expected to influence the economic decisions of users taken on the basis of the financial statements;
- Judgments about materiality are made in light of surrounding circumstances, and are affected by the size or nature of a misstatement, or a combination of both; and
- Judgments about matters that are material to users of the financial statements are based on a consideration of the common financial information needs of users as a group.[2] The possible effect of misstatements on specific individual users, whose needs may vary widely, is not considered.

Such a discussion, if present in the applicable financial reporting framework, provides a frame of reference to the auditor in determining materiality for the audit. If the applicable financial reporting framework does not include a discussion of the concept of materiality, the characteristics referred to in paragraph 2 provide the auditor with such a frame of reference.   **3**

The auditor's determination of materiality is a matter of professional judgment, and is affected by the auditor's perception of the financial information needs of users of the financial statements. In this context, it is reasonable for the auditor to assume that users: **4**

(a) Have a reasonable knowledge of business and economic activities and accounting and a willingness to study the information in the financial statements with reasonable diligence;

(b) Understand that financial statements are prepared, presented and audited to levels of materiality;

(c) Recognize the uncertainties inherent in the measurement of amounts based on the use of estimates, judgment and the consideration of future events; and

(d) Make reasonable economic decisions on the basis of the information in the financial statements.

[1] *ISA (UK and Ireland) 450, "Evaluation of Misstatements Identified during the Audit."*

[2] *For example, the "Framework for the Preparation and Presentation of Financial Statements," adopted by the International Accounting Standards Board in April 2001, indicates that, for a profit-oriented entity, as investors are providers of risk capital to the enterprise, the provision of financial statements that meet their needs will also meet most of the needs of other users that financial statements can satisfy.*
The "Framework for the Preparation and Presentation of Financial Statements," has not been promulgated by the APB for application in the UK and Ireland.

5   The concept of materiality is applied by the auditor both in planning and performing the audit, and in evaluating the effect of identified misstatements on the audit and of uncorrected misstatements, if any, on the financial statements and in forming the opinion in the auditor's report. (Ref: Para. A1)

6   In planning the audit, the auditor makes judgments about the size of misstatements that will be considered material. These judgments provide a basis for:

(a)   Determining the nature, timing and extent of risk assessment procedures;

(b)   Identifying and assessing the risks of material misstatement; and

(c)   Determining the nature, timing and extent of further audit procedures.

The materiality determined when planning the audit does not necessarily establish an amount below which uncorrected misstatements, individually or in the aggregate, will always be evaluated as immaterial. The circumstances related to some misstatements may cause the auditor to evaluate them as material even if they are below materiality. Although it is not practicable to design audit procedures to detect misstatements that could be material solely because of their nature, the auditor considers not only the size but also the nature of uncorrected misstatements, and the particular circumstances of their occurrence, when evaluating their effect on the financial statements.[3]

Effective Date

7   This ISA (UK and Ireland) is effective for audits of financial statements for periods ending on or after 15 December 2010.

Objective

8   The objective of the auditor is to apply the concept of materiality appropriately in planning and performing the audit.

Definition

9   For purposes of the ISAs (UK and Ireland), performance materiality means the amount or amounts set by the auditor at less than materiality for the financial statements as a whole to reduce to an appropriately low level the probability that the aggregate of uncorrected and undetected misstatements exceeds materiality for the financial statements as a whole. If applicable, performance materiality also refers to the amount or amounts set by the auditor at less than the materiality level or levels for particular classes of transactions, account balances or disclosures.

Requirements

Determining Materiality and Performance Materiality When Planning the Audit

10   When establishing the overall audit strategy, the auditor shall determine materiality for the financial statements as a whole. If, in the specific circumstances of the entity, there is one or more particular classes of transactions, account balances or

---

[3] *ISA (UK and Ireland) 450, paragraph A16.*

disclosures for which misstatements of lesser amounts than materiality for the financial statements as a whole could reasonably be expected to influence the economic decisions of users taken on the basis of the financial statements, the auditor shall also determine the materiality level or levels to be applied to those particular classes of transactions, account balances or disclosures. (Ref: Para. A2-A11)

The auditor shall determine performance materiality for purposes of assessing the **11** risks of material misstatement and determining the nature, timing and extent of further audit procedures. (Ref: Para. A12)

Revision as the Audit Progresses

The auditor shall revise materiality for the financial statements as a whole (and, if **12** applicable, the materiality level or levels for particular classes of transactions, account balances or disclosures) in the event of becoming aware of information during the audit that would have caused the auditor to have determined a different amount (or amounts) initially. (Ref: Para. A13)

If the auditor concludes that a lower materiality for the financial statements as a **13** whole (and, if applicable, materiality level or levels for particular classes of transactions, account balances or disclosures) than that initially determined is appropriate, the auditor shall determine whether it is necessary to revise performance materiality, and whether the nature, timing and extent of the further audit procedures remain appropriate.

Documentation

The auditor shall include in the audit documentation the following amounts and the **14** factors considered in their determination:[4]

(a) Materiality for the financial statements as a whole (see paragraph 10);
(b) If applicable, the materiality level or levels for particular classes of transactions, account balances or disclosures (see paragraph 10);
(c) Performance materiality (see paragraph 11); and
(d) Any revision of (a)-(c) as the audit progressed (see paragraphs 12-13).

***

Application and Other Explanatory Material

Materiality and Audit Risk (Ref: Para. 5)

In conducting an audit of financial statements, the overall objectives of the auditor **A1** are to obtain reasonable assurance about whether the financial statements as a whole are free from material misstatement, whether due to fraud or error, thereby enabling the auditor to express an opinion on whether the financial statements are prepared, in all material respects, in accordance with an applicable financial reporting framework; and to report on the financial statements, and communicate as required by the ISAs (UK and Ireland), in accordance with the auditor's findings.[5] The auditor

[4] *ISA (UK and Ireland) 230, "Audit Documentation," paragraphs 8-11, and paragraph A6.*

[5] *ISA (UK and Ireland) 200, "Overall Objectives of the Independent Auditor and the Conduct of an Audit in Accordance with International Standards on Auditing (UK and Ireland)," paragraph 11.*

obtains reasonable assurance by obtaining sufficient appropriate audit evidence to reduce audit risk to an acceptably low level.[6] Audit risk is the risk that the auditor expresses an inappropriate audit opinion when the financial statements are materially misstated. Audit risk is a function of the risks of material misstatement and detection risk.[7] Materiality and audit risk are considered throughout the audit, in particular, when:

(a) Identifying and assessing the risks of material misstatement;[8]

(b) Determining the nature, timing and extent of further audit procedures;[9] and

(c) Evaluating the effect of uncorrected misstatements, if any, on the financial statements[10] and in forming the opinion in the auditor's report.[11]

Determining Materiality and Performance Materiality When Planning the Audit

Considerations Specific to Public Sector Entities (Ref: Para. 10)

A2   In the case of a public sector entity, legislators and regulators are often the primary users of its financial statements. Furthermore, the financial statements may be used to make decisions other than economic decisions. The determination of materiality for the financial statements as a whole (and, if applicable, materiality level or levels for particular classes of transactions, account balances or disclosures) in an audit of the financial statements of a public sector entity is therefore influenced by law, regulation or other authority, and by the financial information needs of legislators and the public in relation to public sector programs.

Use of Benchmarks in Determining Materiality for the Financial Statements as a Whole (Ref: Para. 10)

A3   Determining materiality involves the exercise of professional judgment. A percentage is often applied to a chosen benchmark as a starting point in determining materiality for the financial statements as a whole. Factors that may affect the identification of an appropriate benchmark include the following:

● The elements of the financial statements (for example, assets, liabilities, equity, revenue, expenses);

● Whether there are items on which the attention of the users of the particular entity's financial statements tends to be focused (for example, for the purpose of evaluating financial performance users may tend to focus on profit, revenue or net assets);

---

[6] *ISA (UK and Ireland) 200, paragraph 17.*

[7] *ISA (UK and Ireland) 200, paragraph 13(c).*

[8] *ISA (UK and Ireland) 315, "Identifying and Assessing the Risks of Material Misstatements through Understanding the Entity and Its Environment."*

[9] *ISA (UK and Ireland) 330, "The Auditor's Responses to Assessed Risks."*

[10] *ISA (UK and Ireland) 450.*

[11] *ISA 700, "Forming an Opinion and Reporting on Financial Statements."*
The APB has not promulgated ISA 700 as issued by the IAASB for application in the UK and Ireland. In the UK and Ireland the applicable auditing standard is ISA (UK and Ireland) 700, "The Auditor's Report on Financial Statements." Paragraph 8(b) of ISA (UK and Ireland) 700 requires evaluation of whether uncorrected misstatements are material, individually or in aggregate.

- The nature of the entity, where the entity is in its life cycle, and the industry and economic environment in which the entity operates;
- The entity's ownership structure and the way it is financed (for example, if an entity is financed solely by debt rather than equity, users may put more emphasis on assets, and claims on them, than on the entity's earnings); and
- The relative volatility of the benchmark.

Examples of benchmarks that may be appropriate, depending on the circumstances   **A4**
of the entity, include categories of reported income such as profit before tax, total revenue, gross profit and total expenses, total equity or net asset value. Profit before tax from continuing operations is often used for profit-oriented entities. When profit before tax from continuing operations is volatile, other benchmarks may be more appropriate, such as gross profit or total revenues.

In relation to the chosen benchmark, relevant financial data ordinarily includes prior   **A5**
periods' financial results and financial positions, the period-to-date financial results and financial position, and budgets or forecasts for the current period, adjusted for significant changes in the circumstances of the entity (for example, a significant business acquisition) and relevant changes of conditions in the industry or economic environment in which the entity operates. For example, when, as a starting point, materiality for the financial statements as a whole is determined for a particular entity based on a percentage of profit before tax from continuing operations, circumstances that give rise to an exceptional decrease or increase in such profit may lead the auditor to conclude that materiality for the financial statements as a whole is more appropriately determined using a normalized profit before tax from continuing operations figure based on past results.

Materiality relates to the financial statements on which the auditor is reporting.   **A6**
Where the financial statements are prepared for a financial reporting period of more or less than twelve months, such as may be the case for a new entity or a change in the financial reporting period, materiality relates to the financial statements prepared for that financial reporting period.

Determining a percentage to be applied to a chosen benchmark involves the exercise   **A7**
of professional judgment. There is a relationship between the percentage and the chosen benchmark, such that a percentage applied to profit before tax from continuing operations will normally be higher than a percentage applied to total revenue. For example, the auditor may consider five percent of profit before tax from continuing operations to be appropriate for a profit-oriented entity in a manufacturing industry, while the auditor may consider one percent of total revenue or total expenses to be appropriate for a not-for-profit entity. Higher or lower percentages, however, may be deemed appropriate in the circumstances.

Considerations Specific to Small Entities

When an entity's profit before tax from continuing operations is consistently nom-   **A8**
inal, as might be the case for an owner-managed business where the owner takes much of the profit before tax in the form of remuneration, a benchmark such as profit before remuneration and tax may be more relevant.

Considerations Specific to Public Sector Entities

In an audit of a public sector entity, total cost or net cost (expenses less revenues or   **A9**
expenditure less receipts) may be appropriate benchmarks for program activities.

Where a public sector entity has custody of public assets, assets may be an appropriate benchmark.

Materiality Level or Levels for Particular Classes of Transactions, Account Balances or Disclosures (Ref: Para. 10)

A10   Factors that may indicate the existence of one or more particular classes of transactions, account balances or disclosures for which misstatements of lesser amounts than materiality for the financial statements as a whole could reasonably be expected to influence the economic decisions of users taken on the basis of the financial statements include the following:

- Whether law, regulation or the applicable financial reporting framework affect users' expectations regarding the measurement or disclosure of certain items (for example, related party transactions, and the remuneration of management and those charged with governance).
- The key disclosures in relation to the industry in which the entity operates (for example, research and development costs for a pharmaceutical company).
- Whether attention is focused on a particular aspect of the entity's business that is separately disclosed in the financial statements (for example, a newly acquired business).

A11   In considering whether, in the specific circumstances of the entity, such classes of transactions, account balances or disclosures exist, the auditor may find it useful to obtain an understanding of the views and expectations of those charged with governance and management.

Performance Materiality (Ref: Para. 11)

A12   Planning the audit solely to detect individually material misstatements overlooks the fact that the aggregate of individually immaterial misstatements may cause the financial statements to be materially misstated, and leaves no margin for possible undetected misstatements. Performance materiality (which, as defined, is one or more amounts) is set to reduce to an appropriately low level the probability that the aggregate of uncorrected and undetected misstatements in the financial statements exceeds materiality for the financial statements as a whole. Similarly, performance materiality relating to a materiality level determined for a particular class of transactions, account balance or disclosure is set to reduce to an appropriately low level the probability that the aggregate of uncorrected and undetected misstatements in that particular class of transactions, account balance or disclosure exceeds the materiality level for that particular class of transactions, account balance or disclosure. The determination of performance materiality is not a simple mechanical calculation and involves the exercise of professional judgment. It is affected by the auditor's understanding of the entity, updated during the performance of the risk assessment procedures; and the nature and extent of misstatements identified in previous audits and thereby the auditor's expectations in relation to misstatements in the current period.

Revision as the Audit Progresses (Ref: Para. 12)

A13   Materiality for the financial statements as a whole (and, if applicable, the materiality level or levels for particular classes of transactions, account balances or disclosures) may need to be revised as a result of a change in circumstances that occurred during the audit (for example, a decision to dispose of a major part of the entity's business), new information, or a change in the auditor's understanding of the entity and its operations as a result of performing further audit procedures. For example, if during the audit it appears as though actual financial results are likely to be substantially different from the anticipated period end financial results that were used initially to determine materiality for the financial statements as a whole, the auditor revises that materiality.

International Standard on Auditing (UK and Ireland) 330
The auditor's responses to assessed risks

*(Effective for audits of financial statements for periods
ending on or after 15 December 2010)*

Contents

International Standard on Auditing (UK and Ireland) (ISA (UK and Ireland)) 330, "The Auditor's Responses to Assessed Risks" should be read in conjunction with ISA (UK and Ireland) 200, "Overall Objectives of the Independent Auditor and the Conduct of an Audit in Accordance with International Standards on Auditing (UK and Ireland)."

Introduction

Scope of this ISA (UK and Ireland)

This International Standard on Auditing (UK and Ireland) (ISA (UK and Ireland)) **1** deals with the auditor's responsibility to design and implement responses to the risks of material misstatement identified and assessed by the auditor in accordance with ISA (UK and Ireland) 315[1] in an audit of financial statements.

Effective Date

This ISA (UK and Ireland) is effective for audits of financial statements for periods **2** ending on or after 15 December 2010.

Objective

The objective of the auditor is to obtain sufficient appropriate audit evidence **3** regarding the assessed risks of material misstatement, through designing and implementing appropriate responses to those risks.

Definitions

For purposes of the ISAs (UK and Ireland), the following terms have the meanings **4** attributed below:

(a) Substantive procedure – An audit procedure designed to detect material misstatements at the assertion level. Substantive procedures comprise:
   (i) Tests of details (of classes of transactions, account balances, and disclosures); and
   (ii) Substantive analytical procedures.

(b) Test of controls – An audit procedure designed to evaluate the operating effectiveness of controls in preventing, or detecting and correcting, material misstatements at the assertion level.

Requirements

Overall Responses

The auditor shall design and implement overall responses to address the assessed **5** risks of material misstatement at the financial statement level. (Ref: Para. A1-A3)

Audit Procedures Responsive to the Assessed Risks of Material Misstatement at the Assertion Level

The auditor shall design and perform further audit procedures whose nature, timing, **6** and extent are based on and are responsive to the assessed risks of material misstatement at the assertion level. (Ref: Para. A4-A8)

In designing the further audit procedures to be performed, the auditor shall: **7**

---

[1] *ISA (UK and Ireland) 315, "Identifying and Assessing the Risks of Material Misstatement through Understanding the Entity and Its Environment."*

(a) Consider the reasons for the assessment given to the risk of material misstatement at the assertion level for each class of transactions, account balance, and
disclosure, including:
  (i)   The likelihood of material misstatement due to the particular character-
        istics of the relevant class of transactions, account balance, or disclosure
        (that is, the inherent risk); and
  (ii) Whether the risk assessment takes account of relevant controls (that is, the
        control risk), thereby requiring the auditor to obtain audit evidence to
        determine whether the controls are operating effectively (that is, the auditor
        intends to rely on the operating effectiveness of controls in determining the
        nature, timing and extent of substantive procedures); and (Ref: Para. A9-
        A18)
(b) Obtain more persuasive audit evidence the higher the auditor's assessment of
risk. (Ref: Para. A19)

Tests of Controls

8   The auditor shall design and perform tests of controls to obtain sufficient appropriate audit evidence as to the operating effectiveness of relevant controls if:

(a) The auditor's assessment of risks of material misstatement at the assertion level
includes an expectation that the controls are operating effectively (that is, the
auditor intends to rely on the operating effectiveness of controls in determining
the nature, timing and extent of substantive procedures); or
(b) Substantive procedures alone cannot provide sufficient appropriate audit evidence at the assertion level. (Ref: Para. A20-A24)

9   In designing and performing tests of controls, the auditor shall obtain more persuasive audit evidence the greater the reliance the auditor places on the effectiveness
of a control. (Ref: Para. A25)

Nature and Extent of Tests of Controls

10   In designing and performing tests of controls, the auditor shall:

(a) Perform other audit procedures in combination with inquiry to obtain audit
evidence about the operating effectiveness of the controls, including:
  (i)   How the controls were applied at relevant times during the period under
        audit;
  (ii) The consistency with which they were applied; and
  (iii) By whom or by what means they were applied. (Ref: Para. A26-29)
(b) Determine whether the controls to be tested depend upon other controls
(indirect controls) and, if so, whether it is necessary to obtain audit evidence
supporting the effective operation of those indirect controls. (Ref: Para. A30-
A31)

Timing of Tests of Controls

11   The auditor shall test controls for the particular time, or throughout the period, for
which the auditor intends to rely on those controls, subject to paragraphs 12 and 15
below, in order to provide an appropriate basis for the auditor's intended reliance.
(Ref: Para. A32)

Using audit evidence obtained during an interim period

If the auditor obtains audit evidence about the operating effectiveness of controls   **12**
during an interim period, the auditor shall:

(a) Obtain audit evidence about significant changes to those controls subsequent to
the interim period; and
(b) Determine the additional audit evidence to be obtained for the remaining period. (Ref: Para. A33-A34)

Using audit evidence obtained in previous audits

In determining whether it is appropriate to use audit evidence about the operating   **13**
effectiveness of controls obtained in previous audits, and, if so, the length of the time
period that may elapse before retesting a control, the auditor shall consider the
following:

(a) The effectiveness of other elements of internal control, including the control
environment, the entity's monitoring of controls, and the entity's risk assessment process;
(b) The risks arising from the characteristics of the control, including whether it is
manual or automated;
(c) The effectiveness of general IT-controls;
(d) The effectiveness of the control and its application by the entity, including the
nature and extent of deviations in the application of the control noted in previous audits, and whether there have been personnel changes that significantly
affect the application of the control;
(e) Whether the lack of a change in a particular control poses a risk due to changing
circumstances; and
(f) The risks of material misstatement and the extent of reliance on the control.
(Ref: Para. A35)

If the auditor plans to use audit evidence from a previous audit about the operating   **14**
effectiveness of specific controls, the auditor shall establish the continuing relevance
of that evidence by obtaining audit evidence about whether significant changes in
those controls have occurred subsequent to the previous audit. The auditor shall
obtain this evidence by performing inquiry combined with observation or inspection,
to confirm the understanding of those specific controls, and:

(a) If there have been changes that affect the continuing relevance of the audit
evidence from the previous audit, the auditor shall test the controls in the
current audit. (Ref: Para. A36)
(b) If there have not been such changes, the auditor shall test the controls at least
once in every third audit, and shall test some controls each audit to avoid the
possibility of testing all the controls on which the auditor intends to rely in a
single audit period with no testing of controls in the subsequent two audit
periods. (Ref: Para. A37-A39)

Controls over significant risks

If the auditor plans to rely on controls over a risk the auditor has determined to be a   **15**
significant risk, the auditor shall test those controls in the current period.

Evaluating the Operating Effectiveness of Controls

16   When evaluating the operating effectiveness of relevant controls, the auditor shall evaluate whether misstatements that have been detected by substantive procedures indicate that controls are not operating effectively. The absence of misstatements detected by substantive procedures, however, does not provide audit evidence that controls related to the assertion being tested are effective. (Ref: Para. A40)

17   If deviations from controls upon which the auditor intends to rely are detected, the auditor shall make specific inquiries to understand these matters and their potential consequences, and shall determine whether: (Ref: Para. A41)

(a)   The tests of controls that have been performed provide an appropriate basis for reliance on the controls;

(b)   Additional tests of controls are necessary; or

(c)   The potential risks of misstatement need to be addressed using substantive procedures.

Substantive Procedures

18   Irrespective of the assessed risks of material misstatement, the auditor shall design and perform substantive procedures for each material class of transactions, account balance, and disclosure. (Ref: Para. A42-A47)

19   The auditor shall consider whether external confirmation procedures are to be performed as substantive audit procedures. (Ref: Para. A48-A51)

Substantive Procedures Related to the Financial Statement Closing Process

20   The auditor's substantive procedures shall include the following audit procedures related to the financial statement closing process:

(a)   Agreeing or reconciling the financial statements with the underlying accounting records; and

(b)   Examining material journal entries and other adjustments made during the course of preparing the financial statements. (Ref: Para. A52)

Substantive Procedures Responsive to Significant Risks

21   If the auditor has determined that an assessed risk of material misstatement at the assertion level is a significant risk, the auditor shall perform substantive procedures that are specifically responsive to that risk. When the approach to a significant risk consists only of substantive procedures, those procedures shall include tests of details. (Ref: Para. A53)

Timing of Substantive Procedures

22   If substantive procedures are performed at an interim date, the auditor shall cover the remaining period by performing:

(a)   substantive procedures, combined with tests of controls for the intervening period; or

(b)   if the auditor determines that it is sufficient, further substantive procedures only that provide a reasonable basis for extending the audit conclusions from the interim date to the period end. (Ref: Para. A54-A57)

If misstatements that the auditor did not expect when assessing the risks of material **23** misstatement are detected at an interim date, the auditor shall evaluate whether the related assessment of risk and the planned nature, timing, or extent of substantive procedures covering the remaining period need to be modified. (Ref: Para. A58)

Adequacy of Presentation and Disclosure

The auditor shall perform audit procedures to evaluate whether the overall pre- **24** sentation of the financial statements, including the related disclosures, is in accordance with the applicable financial reporting framework. (Ref: Para. A59)

Evaluating the Sufficiency and Appropriateness of Audit Evidence

Based on the audit procedures performed and the audit evidence obtained, the **25** auditor shall evaluate before the conclusion of the audit whether the assessments of the risks of material misstatement at the assertion level remain appropriate. (Ref: Para. A60-A61)

The auditor shall conclude whether sufficient appropriate audit evidence has been **26** obtained. In forming an opinion, the auditor shall consider all relevant audit evidence, regardless of whether it appears to corroborate or to contradict the assertions in the financial statements. (Ref: Para. A62)

If the auditor has not obtained sufficient appropriate audit evidence as to a material **27** financial statement assertion, the auditor shall attempt to obtain further audit evidence. If the auditor is unable to obtain sufficient appropriate audit evidence, the auditor shall express a qualified opinion or disclaim an opinion on the financial statements.

Documentation

The auditor shall include in the audit documentation:[2] **28**

(a) The overall responses to address the assessed risks of material misstatement at the financial statement level, and the nature, timing, and extent of the further audit procedures performed;
(b) The linkage of those procedures with the assessed risks at the assertion level; and
(c) The results of the audit procedures, including the conclusions where these are not otherwise clear. (Ref: Para. A63)

If the auditor plans to use audit evidence about the operating effectiveness of con- **29** trols obtained in previous audits, the auditor shall include in the audit documentation the conclusions reached about relying on such controls that were tested in a previous audit.

The auditor's documentation shall demonstrate that the financial statements agree or **30** reconcile with the underlying accounting records.

***

[2] *ISA (UK and Ireland) 230, "Audit Documentation," paragraphs 8-11, and paragraph A6.*

Application and Other Explanatory Material

Overall Responses (Ref: Para. 5)

A1   Overall responses to address the assessed risks of material misstatement at the financial statement level may include:

- Emphasizing to the audit team the need to maintain professional skepticism.
- Assigning more experienced staff or those with special skills or using experts.
- Providing more supervision.
- Incorporating additional elements of unpredictability in the selection of further audit procedures to be performed.
- Making general changes to the nature, timing, or extent of audit procedures, for example: performing substantive procedures at the period end instead of at an interim date; or modifying the nature of audit procedures to obtain more persuasive audit evidence.

A2   The assessment of the risks of material misstatement at the financial statement level, and thereby the auditor's overall responses, is affected by the auditor's understanding of the control environment. An effective control environment may allow the auditor to have more confidence in internal control and the reliability of audit evidence generated internally within the entity and thus, for example, allow the auditor to conduct some audit procedures at an interim date rather than at the period end. Deficiencies in the control environment, however, have the opposite effect; for example, the auditor may respond to an ineffective control environment by:

- Conducting more audit procedures as of the period end rather than at an interim date.
- Obtaining more extensive audit evidence from substantive procedures.
- Increasing the number of locations to be included in the audit scope.

A3   Such considerations, therefore, have a significant bearing on the auditor's general approach, for example, an emphasis on substantive procedures (substantive approach), or an approach that uses tests of controls as well as substantive procedures (combined approach).

Audit Procedures Responsive to the Assessed Risks of Material Misstatement at the Assertion Level

The Nature, Timing, and Extent of Further Audit Procedures (Ref: Para. 6)

A4   The auditor's assessment of the identified risks at the assertion level provides a basis for considering the appropriate audit approach for designing and performing further audit procedures. For example, the auditor may determine that:

(a) Only by performing tests of controls may the auditor achieve an effective response to the assessed risk of material misstatement for a particular assertion;

(b) Performing only substantive procedures is appropriate for particular assertions and, therefore, the auditor excludes the effect of controls from the relevant risk assessment. This may be because the auditor's risk assessment procedures have not identified any effective controls relevant to the assertion, or because testing controls would be inefficient and therefore the auditor does not intend to rely on the operating effectiveness of controls in determining the nature, timing and extent of substantive procedures; or

(c)   A combined approach using both tests of controls and substantive procedures is an effective approach.

However, as required by paragraph 18, irrespective of the approach selected, the auditor designs and performs substantive procedures for each material class of transactions, account balance, and disclosure.

The nature of an audit procedure refers to its purpose (i.e., test of controls or substantive procedure) and its type (that is, inspection, observation, inquiry, confirmation, recalculation, reperformance, or analytical procedure). The nature of the audit procedures is of most importance in responding to the assessed risks.   **A5**

Timing of an audit procedure refers to when it is performed, or the period or date to which the audit evidence applies.   **A6**

Extent of an audit procedure refers to the quantity to be performed, for example, a sample size or the number of observations of a control activity.   **A7**

Designing and performing further audit procedures whose nature, timing, and extent are based on and are responsive to the assessed risks of material misstatement at the assertion level provides a clear linkage between the auditor's further audit procedures and the risk assessment.   **A8**

Responding to the Assessed Risks at the Assertion Level (Ref: Para. 7(a))

Nature

The auditor's assessed risks may affect both the types of audit procedures to be performed and their combination. For example, when an assessed risk is high, the auditor may confirm the completeness of the terms of a contract with the counterparty, in addition to inspecting the document. Further, certain audit procedures may be more appropriate for some assertions than others. For example, in relation to revenue, tests of controls may be most responsive to the assessed risk of misstatement of the completeness assertion, whereas substantive procedures may be most responsive to the assessed risk of misstatement of the occurrence assertion.   **A9**

The reasons for the assessment given to a risk are relevant in determining the nature of audit procedures. For example, if an assessed risk is lower because of the particular characteristics of a class of transactions without consideration of the related controls, then the auditor may determine that substantive analytical procedures alone provide sufficient appropriate audit evidence. On the other hand, if the assessed risk is lower because of internal controls, and the auditor intends to base the substantive procedures on that low assessment, then the auditor performs tests of those controls, as required by paragraph 8(a). This may be the case, for example, for a class of transactions of reasonably uniform, non-complex characteristics that are routinely processed and controlled by the entity's information system.   **A10**

Timing

The auditor may perform tests of controls or substantive procedures at an interim date or at the period end. The higher the risk of material misstatement, the more likely it is that the auditor may decide it is more effective to perform substantive procedures nearer to, or at, the period end rather than at an earlier date, or to perform audit procedures unannounced or at unpredictable times (for example, performing audit procedures at selected locations on an unannounced basis). This is   **A11** particularly relevant when considering the response to the risks of fraud. For example, the auditor may conclude that, when the risks of intentional misstatement or manipulation have been identified, audit procedures to extend audit conclusions from interim date to the period end would not be effective.

A12   On the other hand, performing audit procedures before the period end may assist the auditor in identifying significant matters at an early stage of the audit, and consequently resolving them with the assistance of management or developing an effective audit approach to address such matters.

A13   In addition, certain audit procedures can be performed only at or after the period end, for example:

- Agreeing the financial statements to the accounting records;
- Examining adjustments made during the course of preparing the financial statements; and
- Procedures to respond to a risk that, at the period end, the entity may have entered into improper sales contracts, or transactions may not have been finalized.

A14   Further relevant factors that influence the auditor's consideration of when to perform audit procedures include the following:

- The control environment.
- When relevant information is available (for example, electronic files may subsequently be overwritten, or procedures to be observed may occur only at certain times).
- The nature of the risk (for example, if there is a risk of inflated revenues to meet earnings expectations by subsequent creation of false sales agreements, the auditor may wish to examine contracts available on the date of the period end).
- The period or date to which the audit evidence relates.

Extent

A15   The extent of an audit procedure judged necessary is determined after considering the materiality, the assessed risk, and the degree of assurance the auditor plans to obtain. When a single purpose is met by a combination of procedures, the extent of each procedure is considered separately. In general, the extent of audit procedures increases as the risk of material misstatement increases. For example, in response to the assessed risk of material misstatement due to fraud, increasing sample sizes or performing substantive analytical procedures at a more detailed level may be appropriate. However, increasing the extent of an audit procedure is effective only if the audit procedure itself is relevant to the specific risk.

A16   The use of computer-assisted audit techniques (CAATs) may enable more extensive testing of electronic transactions and account files, which may be useful when the auditor decides to modify the extent of testing, for example, in responding to the risks of material misstatement due to fraud. Such techniques can be used to select sample transactions from key electronic files, to sort transactions with specific characteristics, or to test an entire population instead of a sample.

Considerations specific to public sector entities

A17   For the audits of public sector entities, the audit mandate and any other special auditing requirements may affect the auditor's consideration of the nature, timing and extent of further audit procedures.

Considerations specific to smaller entities

In the case of very small entities, there may not be many control activities that could   **A18**
be identified by the auditor, or the extent to which their existence or operation have
been documented by the entity may be limited. In such cases, it may be more efficient
for the auditor to perform further audit procedures that are primarily substantive
procedures. In some rare cases, however, the absence of control activities or of other
components of control may make it impossible to obtain sufficient appropriate audit
evidence.

Higher Assessments of Risk (Ref: Para 7(b))

When obtaining more persuasive audit evidence because of a higher assessment of   **A19**
risk, the auditor may increase the quantity of the evidence, or obtain evidence that is
more relevant or reliable, for example, by placing more emphasis on obtaining third
party evidence or by obtaining corroborating evidence from a number of independent sources.

Tests of Controls

Designing and Performing Tests of Controls (Ref: Para. 8)

Tests of controls are performed only on those controls that the auditor has deter-   **A20**
mined are suitably designed to prevent, or detect and correct, a material
misstatement in an assertion. If substantially different controls were used at different
times during the period under audit, each is considered separately.

Testing the operating effectiveness of controls is different from obtaining an   **A21**
understanding of and evaluating the design and implementation of controls. However, the same types of audit procedures are used. The auditor may, therefore, decide
it is efficient to test the operating effectiveness of controls at the same time as
evaluating their design and determining that they have been implemented.

Further, although some risk assessment procedures may not have been specifically   **A22**
designed as tests of controls, they may nevertheless provide audit evidence about the
operating effectiveness of the controls and, consequently, serve as tests of controls.
For example, the auditor's risk assessment procedures may have included:

- Inquiring about management's use of budgets.
- Observing management's comparison of monthly budgeted and actual expenses.
- Inspecting reports pertaining to the investigation of variances between budgeted
  and actual amounts.

These audit procedures provide knowledge about the design of the entity's budgeting
policies and whether they have been implemented, but may also provide audit evidence about the effectiveness of the operation of budgeting policies in preventing or
detecting material misstatements in the classification of expenses.

In addition, the auditor may design a test of controls to be performed concurrently   **A23**
with a test of details on the same transaction. Although the purpose of a test of
controls is different from the purpose of a test of details, both may be accomplished
concurrently by performing a test of controls and a test of details on the same
transaction, also known as a dual-purpose test. For example, the auditor may design,
and evaluate the results of, a test to examine an invoice to determine whether it has
been approved and to provide substantive audit evidence of a transaction.

A dual-purpose test is designed and evaluated by considering each purpose of the test separately.

A24   In some cases, the auditor may find it impossible to design effective substantive procedures that by themselves provide sufficient appropriate audit evidence at the assertion level.[3] This may occur when an entity conducts its business using IT and no documentation of transactions is produced or maintained, other than through the IT system. In such cases, paragraph 8(b) requires the auditor to perform tests of relevant controls.

Audit Evidence and Intended Reliance (Ref: Para. 9)

A25   A higher level of assurance may be sought about the operating effectiveness of controls when the approach adopted consists primarily of tests of controls, in particular where it is not possible or practicable to obtain sufficient appropriate audit evidence only from substantive procedures.

Nature and Extent of Tests of Controls

Other audit procedures in combination with inquiry (Ref: Para. 10(a))

A26   Inquiry alone is not sufficient to test the operating effectiveness of controls. Accordingly, other audit procedures are performed in combination with inquiry. In this regard, inquiry combined with inspection or reperformance may provide more assurance than inquiry and observation, since an observation is pertinent only at the point in time at which it is made.

A27   The nature of the particular control influences the type of procedure required to obtain audit evidence about whether the control was operating effectively. For example, if operating effectiveness is evidenced by documentation, the auditor may decide to inspect it to obtain audit evidence about operating effectiveness. For other controls, however, documentation may not be available or relevant. For example, documentation of operation may not exist for some factors in the control environment, such as assignment of authority and responsibility, or for some types of control activities, such as control activities performed by a computer. In such circumstances, audit evidence about operating effectiveness may be obtained through inquiry in combination with other audit procedures such as observation or the use of CAATs.

Extent of tests of controls

A28   When more persuasive audit evidence is needed regarding the effectiveness of a control, it may be appropriate to increase the extent of testing of the control. As well as the degree of reliance on controls, matters the auditor may consider in determining the extent of tests of controls include the following:

- The frequency of the performance of the control by the entity during the period.
- The length of time during the audit period that the auditor is relying on the operating effectiveness of the control.
- The expected rate of deviation from a control.
- The relevance and reliability of the audit evidence to be obtained regarding the operating effectiveness of the control at the assertion level.

[3] *ISA (UK and Ireland) 315, paragraph 30.*

- The extent to which audit evidence is obtained from tests of other controls related to the assertion.

ISA (UK and Ireland) 530[4] contains further guidance on the extent of testing.

Because of the inherent consistency of IT processing, it may not be necessary to increase the extent of testing of an automated control. An automated control can be expected to function consistently unless the program (including the tables, files, or other permanent data used by the program) is changed. Once the auditor determines that an automated control is functioning as intended (which could be done at the time the control is initially implemented or at some other date), the auditor may consider performing tests to determine that the control continues to function effectively. Such tests might include determining that:

    A29

- Changes to the program are not made without being subject to the appropriate program change controls;
- The authorized version of the program is used for processing transactions; and
- Other relevant general controls are effective.

Such tests also might include determining that changes to the programs have not been made, as may be the case when the entity uses packaged software applications without modifying or maintaining them. For example, the auditor may inspect the record of the administration of IT security to obtain audit evidence that unauthorized access has not occurred during the period.

Testing of indirect controls (Ref: Para. 10(b))

In some circumstances, it may be necessary to obtain audit evidence supporting the effective operation of indirect controls. For example, when the auditor decides to test the effectiveness of a user review of exception reports detailing sales in excess of authorized credit limits, the user review and related follow up is the control that is directly of relevance to the auditor. Controls over the accuracy of the information in the reports (for example, the general IT-controls) are described as "indirect" controls.

    A30

Because of the inherent consistency of IT processing, audit evidence about the implementation of an automated application control, when considered in combination with audit evidence about the operating effectiveness of the entity's general controls (in particular, change controls), may also provide substantial audit evidence about its operating effectiveness.

    A31

Timing of Tests of Controls

Intended period of reliance (Ref: Para. 11)

Audit evidence pertaining only to a point in time may be sufficient for the auditor's purpose, for example, when testing controls over the entity's physical inventory counting at the period end. If, on the other hand, the auditor intends to rely on a control over a period, tests that are capable of providing audit evidence that the control operated effectively at relevant times during that period are appropriate. Such tests may include tests of the entity's monitoring of controls.

    A32

---

[4] *ISA (UK and Ireland) 530, "Audit Sampling."*

Using audit evidence obtained during an interim period (Ref: Para. 12b)

A33   Relevant factors in determining what additional audit evidence to obtain about controls that were operating during the period remaining after an interim period, include:

- The significance of the assessed risks of material misstatement at the assertion level.
- The specific controls that were tested during the interim period, and significant changes to them since they were tested, including changes in the information system, processes, and personnel.
- The degree to which audit evidence about the operating effectiveness of those controls was obtained.
- The length of the remaining period.
- The extent to which the auditor intends to reduce further substantive procedures based on the reliance of controls.
- The control environment.

A34   Additional audit evidence may be obtained, for example, by extending tests of controls over the remaining period or testing the entity's monitoring of controls.

Using audit evidence obtained in previous audits (Ref: Para. 13)

A35   In certain circumstances, audit evidence obtained from previous audits may provide audit evidence where the auditor performs audit procedures to establish its continuing relevance. For example, in performing a previous audit, the auditor may have determined that an automated control was functioning as intended. The auditor may obtain audit evidence to determine whether changes to the automated control have been made that affect its continued effective functioning through, for example, inquiries of management and the inspection of logs to indicate what controls have been changed. Consideration of audit evidence about these changes may support either increasing or decreasing the expected audit evidence to be obtained in the current period about the operating effectiveness of the controls.

Controls that have changed from previous audits (Ref: Para. 14(a))

A36   Changes may affect the relevance of the audit evidence obtained in previous audits such that there may no longer be a basis for continued reliance. For example, changes in a system that enable an entity to receive a new report from the system probably do not affect the relevance of audit evidence from a previous audit; however, a change that causes data to be accumulated or calculated differently does affect it.

Controls that have not changed from previous audits (Ref: Para. 14(b))

A37   The auditor's decision on whether to rely on audit evidence obtained in previous audits for controls that:

(a) have not changed since they were last tested; and
(b) are not controls that mitigate a significant risk,

is a matter of professional judgment. In addition, the length of time between retesting such controls is also a matter of professional judgment, but is required by paragraph 14 (b) to be at least once in every third year.

In general, the higher the risk of material misstatement, or the greater the reliance on   **A38**
controls, the shorter the time period elapsed, if any, is likely to be. Factors that may
decrease the period for retesting a control, or result in not relying on audit evidence
obtained in previous audits at all, include the following:

- A deficient control environment.
- Deficient monitoring of controls.
- A significant manual element to the relevant controls.
- Personnel changes that significantly affect the application of the control.
- Changing circumstances that indicate the need for changes in the control.
- Deficient general IT-controls.

When there are a number of controls for which the auditor intends to rely on audit   **A39**
evidence obtained in previous audits, testing some of those controls in each audit
provides corroborating information about the continuing effectiveness of the control
environment. This contributes to the auditor's decision about whether it is appropriate to rely on audit evidence obtained in previous audits.

Evaluating the Operating Effectiveness of Controls (Ref: Para. 16-17)

A material misstatement detected by the auditor's procedures is a strong indicator of   **A40**
the existence of a significant deficiency in internal control.

The concept of effectiveness of the operation of controls recognizes that some   **A41**
deviations in the way controls are applied by the entity may occur. Deviations from
prescribed controls may be caused by such factors as changes in key personnel,
significant seasonal fluctuations in volume of transactions and human error. The
detected rate of deviation, in particular in comparison with the expected rate, may
indicate that the control cannot be relied on to reduce risk at the assertion level to
that assessed by the auditor.

Substantive Procedures (Ref: Para. 18)

Paragraph 18 requires the auditor to design and perform substantive procedures for   **A42**
each material class of transactions, account balance, and disclosure, irrespective of
the assessed risks of material misstatement. This requirement reflects the facts that:
(a) the auditor's assessment of risk is judgmental and so may not identify all risks of
material misstatement; and (b) there are inherent limitations to internal control,
including management override.

Nature and Extent of Substantive Procedures

Depending on the circumstances, the auditor may determine that: **A43**

- Performing only substantive analytical procedures will be sufficient to reduce
  audit risk to an acceptably low level. For example, where the auditor's assessment of risk is supported by audit evidence from tests of controls.
- Only tests of details are appropriate.
- A combination of substantive analytical procedures and tests of details are most
  responsive to the assessed risks.

Substantive analytical procedures are generally more applicable to large volumes of   **A44**
transactions that tend to be predictable over time. ISA (UK and Ireland) 520[5]

---

[5] *ISA (UK and Ireland) 520, "Analytical Procedures."*

establishes requirements and provides guidance on the application of analytical procedures during an audit.

A45   The nature of the risk and assertion is relevant to the design of tests of details. For example, tests of details related to the existence or occurrence assertion may involve selecting from items contained in a financial statement amount and obtaining the relevant audit evidence. On the other hand, tests of details related to the completeness assertion may involve selecting from items that are expected to be included in the relevant financial statement amount and investigating whether they are included.

A46   Because the assessment of the risk of material misstatement takes account of internal control, the extent of substantive procedures may need to be increased when the results from tests of controls are unsatisfactory. However, increasing the extent of an audit procedure is appropriate only if the audit procedure itself is relevant to the specific risk.

A47   In designing tests of details, the extent of testing is ordinarily thought of in terms of the sample size. However, other matters are also relevant, including whether it is more effective to use other selective means of testing. See ISA (UK and Ireland) 500.[6]

Considering Whether External Confirmation Procedures Are to Be Performed (Ref: Para. 19)

A48   External confirmation procedures frequently are relevant when addressing assertions associated with account balances and their elements, but need not be restricted to these items. For example, the auditor may request external confirmation of the terms of agreements, contracts, or transactions between an entity and other parties. External confirmation procedures also may be performed to obtain audit evidence about the absence of certain conditions. For example, a request may specifically seek confirmation that no "side agreement" exists that may be relevant to an entity's revenue cut-off assertion. Other situations where external confirmation procedures may provide relevant audit evidence in responding to assessed risks of material misstatement include:

- Bank balances and other information relevant to banking relationships.
- Accounts receivable balances and terms.
- Inventories held by third parties at bonded warehouses for processing or on consignment.
- Property title deeds held by lawyers or financiers for safe custody or as security.
- Investments held for safekeeping by third parties, or purchased from stock-brokers but not delivered at the balance sheet date.
- Amounts due to lenders, including relevant terms of repayment and restrictive covenants.
- Accounts payable balances and terms.

A49   Although external confirmations may provide relevant audit evidence relating to certain assertions, there are some assertions for which external confirmations provide less relevant audit evidence. For example, external confirmations provide less relevant audit evidence relating to the recoverability of accounts receivable balances, than they do of their existence.

A50   The auditor may determine that external confirmation procedures performed for one purpose provide an opportunity to obtain audit evidence about other matters. For example, confirmation requests for bank balances often include requests for

---

[6] ISA (UK and Ireland) 500, "Audit Evidence," paragraph 10.

information relevant to other financial statement assertions. Such considerations may influence the auditor's decision about whether to perform external confirmation procedures.

Factors that may assist the auditor in determining whether external confirmation **A51** procedures are to be performed as substantive audit procedures include:

- The confirming party's knowledge of the subject matter – responses may be more reliable if provided by a person at the confirming party who has the requisite knowledge about the information being confirmed.
- The ability or willingness of the intended confirming party to respond – for example, the confirming party:
  o May not accept responsibility for responding to a confirmation request;
  o May consider responding too costly or time consuming;
  o May have concerns about the potential legal liability resulting from responding;
  o May account for transactions in different currencies; or
  o May operate in an environment where responding to confirmation requests is not a significant aspect of day-to-day operations.
  In such situations, confirming parties may not respond, may respond in a casual manner or may attempt to restrict the reliance placed on the response.
- The objectivity of the intended confirming party – if the confirming party is a related party of the entity, responses to confirmation requests may be less reliable.

Substantive Procedures Related to the Financial Statement Closing Process (Ref: Para. 20(b))

The nature, and also the extent, of the auditor's examination of journal entries and **A52** other adjustments depends on the nature and complexity of the entity's financial reporting process and the related risks of material misstatement.

Substantive Procedures Responsive to Significant Risks (Ref: Para. 21)

Paragraph 21 of this ISA (UK and Ireland) requires the auditor to perform sub- **A53** stantive procedures that are specifically responsive to risks the auditor has determined to be significant risks. Audit evidence in the form of external confirmations received directly by the auditor from appropriate confirming parties may assist the auditor in obtaining audit evidence with the high level of reliability that the auditor requires to respond to significant risks of material misstatement, whether due to fraud or error. For example, if the auditor identifies that management is under pressure to meet earnings expectations, there may be a risk that management is inflating sales by improperly recognizing revenue related to sales agreements with terms that preclude revenue recognition or by invoicing sales before shipment. In these circumstances, the auditor may, for example, design external confirmation procedures not only to confirm outstanding amounts, but also to confirm the details of the sales agreements, including date, any rights of return and delivery terms. In addition, the auditor may find it effective to supplement such external confirmation procedures with inquiries of non-financial personnel in the entity regarding any changes in sales agreements and delivery terms.

Timing of Substantive Procedures (Ref: Para. 22-23)

In most cases, audit evidence from a previous audit's substantive procedures pro- **A54** vides little or no audit evidence for the current period. There are, however, exceptions, for example, a legal opinion obtained in a previous audit related to the structure of a securitization to which no changes have occurred, may be relevant in the current period. In such cases, it may be appropriate to use audit evidence from a previous audit's substantive procedures if that evidence and the related subject matter have not fundamentally changed, and audit procedures have been performed during the current period to establish its continuing relevance.

Using audit evidence obtained during an interim period (Ref: Para. 22)

A55   In some circumstances, the auditor may determine that it is effective to perform substantive procedures at an interim date, and to compare and reconcile information concerning the balance at the period end with the comparable information at the interim date to:

(a)   Identify amounts that appear unusual;

(b)   Investigate any such amounts; and

(c)   Perform substantive analytical procedures or tests of details to test the intervening period.

A56   Performing substantive procedures at an interim date without undertaking additional procedures at a later date increases the risk that the auditor will not detect misstatements that may exist at the period end. This risk increases as the remaining period is lengthened. Factors such as the following may influence whether to perform substantive procedures at an interim date:

- The control environment and other relevant controls.
- The availability at a later date of information necessary for the auditor's procedures.
- The purpose of the substantive procedure.
- The assessed risk of material misstatement.
- The nature of the class of transactions or account balance and related assertions.
- The ability of the auditor to perform appropriate substantive procedures or substantive procedures combined with tests of controls to cover the remaining period in order to reduce the risk that misstatements that may exist at the period end will not be detected.

A57   Factors such as the following may influence whether to perform substantive analytical procedures with respect to the period between the interim date and the period end:

- Whether the period end balances of the particular classes of transactions or account balances are reasonably predictable with respect to amount, relative significance, and composition.
- Whether the entity's procedures for analyzing and adjusting such classes of transactions or account balances at interim dates and for establishing proper accounting cutoffs are appropriate.
- Whether the information system relevant to financial reporting will provide information concerning the balances at the period end and the transactions in the remaining period that is sufficient to permit investigation of:
  (a)   Significant unusual transactions or entries (including those at or near the period end);
  (b)   Other causes of significant fluctuations, or expected fluctuations that did not occur; and
  (c)   Changes in the composition of the classes of transactions or account balances.

Misstatements detected at an interim date (Ref: Para. 23)

When the auditor concludes that the planned nature, timing, or extent of substantive **A58** procedures covering the remaining period need to be modified as a result of unexpected misstatements detected at an interim date, such modification may include extending or repeating the procedures performed at the interim date at the period end.

Adequacy of Presentation and Disclosure (Ref: Para. 24)

Evaluating the overall presentation of the financial statements, including the related **A59** disclosures, relates to whether the individual financial statements are presented in a manner that reflects the appropriate classification and description of financial information, and the form, arrangement, and content of the financial statements and their appended notes. This includes, for example, the terminology used, the amount of detail given, the classification of items in the statements, and the bases of amounts set forth.

Evaluating the Sufficiency and Appropriateness of Audit Evidence (Ref: Para. 25-27)

An audit of financial statements is a cumulative and iterative process. As the auditor **A60** performs planned audit procedures, the audit evidence obtained may cause the auditor to modify the nature, timing or extent of other planned audit procedures. Information may come to the auditor's attention that differs significantly from the information on which the risk assessment was based. For example:

- The extent of misstatements that the auditor detects by performing substantive procedures may alter the auditor's judgment about the risk assessments and may indicate a significant deficiency in internal control.
- The auditor may become aware of discrepancies in accounting records, or conflicting or missing evidence.
- Analytical procedures performed at the overall review stage of the audit may indicate a previously unrecognized risk of material misstatement.

In such circumstances, the auditor may need to reevaluate the planned audit procedures, based on the revised consideration of assessed risks for all or some of the classes of transactions, account balances, or disclosures and related assertions. ISA (UK and Ireland) 315 contains further guidance on revising the auditor's risk assessment.[7]

The auditor cannot assume that an instance of fraud or error is an isolated occur- **A61** rence. Therefore, the consideration of how the detection of a misstatement affects the assessed risks of material misstatement is important in determining whether the assessment remains appropriate.

The auditor's judgment as to what constitutes sufficient appropriate audit evidence is **A62** influenced by such factors as the following:

- Significance of the potential misstatement in the assertion and the likelihood of its having a material effect, individually or aggregated with other potential misstatements, on the financial statements.
- Effectiveness of management's responses and controls to address the risks.

---

[7] *ISA (UK and Ireland) 315, paragraph 31.*

- Experience gained during previous audits with respect to similar potential misstatements.
- Results of audit procedures performed, including whether such audit procedures identified specific instances of fraud or error.
- Source and reliability of the available information.
- Persuasiveness of the audit evidence.
- Understanding of the entity and its environment, including the entity's internal control.

Documentation (Ref: Para. 28)

A63 The form and extent of audit documentation is a matter of professional judgment, and is influenced by the nature, size and complexity of the entity and its internal control, availability of information from the entity and the audit methodology and technology used in the audit.

International Standard on Auditing (UK and Ireland) 402

Audit considerations relating to an entity using a service organization

*(Effective for audits of financial statements for periods
ending on or after 15 December 2010)*[1a]

Contents

International Standard on Auditing (UK and Ireland) (ISA (UK and Ireland))
402, "Audit Considerations Relating to an Entity Using a Service Organization"
should be read in conjunction with ISA (UK and Ireland) 200, "Overall Objectives of the Independent Auditor and the Conduct of an Audit in Accordance
with International Standards on Auditing (UK and Ireland)."

[1a] *Conforming amendments to this standard as a result of ISA (UK and Ireland) 610 (Revised June 2013),
Using the Work of Internal Auditors, are included that are effective for audits of financial statements for
periods ending on or after 15 June 2014. Details of the amendments are given in the Annexure to ISA (UK and
Ireland) 610 (Revised June 2013).*

Introduction

Scope of this ISA (UK and Ireland)

1 This International Standard on Auditing (UK and Ireland) (ISA (UK and Ireland)) deals with the user auditor's responsibility to obtain sufficient appropriate audit evidence when a user entity uses the services of one or more service organizations. Specifically, it expands on how the user auditor applies ISA (UK and Ireland) 315[1] and ISA (UK and Ireland) 330[2] in obtaining an understanding of the user entity, including internal control relevant to the audit, sufficient to identify and assess the risks of material misstatement and in designing and performing further audit procedures responsive to those risks.

2 Many entities outsource aspects of their business to organizations that provide services ranging from performing a specific task under the direction of an entity to replacing an entity's entire business units or functions, such as the tax compliance function. Many of the services provided by such organizations are integral to the entity's business operations; however, not all those services are relevant to the audit.

3 Services provided by a service organization are relevant to the audit of a user entity's financial statements when those services, and the controls over them, are part of the user entity's information system, including related business processes, relevant to financial reporting. Although most controls at the service organization are likely to relate to financial reporting, there may be other controls that may also be relevant to the audit, such as controls over the safeguarding of assets. A service organization's services are part of a user entity's information system, including related business processes, relevant to financial reporting if these services affect any of the following:

(a) The classes of transactions in the user entity's operations that are significant to the user entity's financial statements;

(b) The procedures, within both information technology (IT) and manual systems, by which the user entity's transactions are initiated, recorded, processed, corrected as necessary, transferred to the general ledger and reported in the financial statements;

(c) The related accounting records, either in electronic or manual form, supporting information and specific accounts in the user entity's financial statements that are used to initiate, record, process and report the user entity's transactions; this includes the correction of incorrect information and how information is transferred to the general ledger;

(d) How the user entity's information system captures events and conditions, other than transactions, that are significant to the financial statements;

(e) The financial reporting process used to prepare the user entity's financial statements, including significant accounting estimates and disclosures; and

(f) Controls surrounding journal entries, including non-standard journal entries used to record non-recurring, unusual transactions or adjustments.

4 The nature and extent of work to be performed by the user auditor regarding the services provided by a service organization depend on the nature and significance of those services to the user entity and the relevance of those services to the audit.

---

[1] *ISA (UK and Ireland) 315, "Identifying and Assessing the Risks of Material Misstatement through Understanding the Entity and Its Environment."*

[2] *ISA (UK and Ireland) 330, "The Auditor's Responses to Assessed Risks."*

This ISA (UK and Ireland) does not apply to services provided by financial insti- **5**
tutions that are limited to processing, for an entity's account held at the financial
institution, transactions that are specifically authorized by the entity, such as the
processing of checking account transactions by a bank or the processing of securities
transactions by a broker. In addition, this ISA (UK and Ireland) does not apply to
the audit of transactions arising from proprietary financial interests in other entities,
such as partnerships, corporations and joint ventures, when proprietary interests are
accounted for and reported to interest holders.

Effective Date

This ISA (UK and Ireland) is effective for audits of financial statements for periods **6**
ending on or after 15 December 2010.[1a]

Objectives

The objectives of the user auditor, when the user entity uses the services of a service **7**
organization, are:

(a)   To obtain an understanding of the nature and significance of the services provided by the service organization and their effect on the user entity's internal
control relevant to the audit, sufficient to identify and assess the risks of material
misstatement; and
(b)   To design and perform audit procedures responsive to those risks.

Definitions

For purposes of the ISAs (UK and Ireland), the following terms have the meanings **8**
attributed below:

(a)   Complementary user entity controls – Controls that the service organization
assumes, in the design of its service, will be implemented by user entities, and
which, if necessary to achieve control objectives, are identified in the description
of its system.
(b)   Report on the description and design of controls at a service organization
(referred to in this ISA (UK and Ireland) as a type 1 report) – A report that
comprises:
  (i)   A description, prepared by management of the service organization, of the
service organization's system, control objectives and related controls that
have been designed and implemented as at a specified date; and
  (ii) A report by the service auditor with the objective of conveying reasonable
assurance that includes the service auditor's opinion on the description of
the service organization's system, control objectives and related controls
and the suitability of the design of the controls to achieve the specified
control objectives.
(c)   Report on the description, design, and operating effectiveness of controls at a
service organization (referred to in this ISA (UK and Ireland) as a type 2 report)
– A report that comprises:
  (i)   A description, prepared by management of the service organization, of the
service organization's system, control objectives and related controls, their
design and implementation as at a specified date or throughout a specified
period and, in some cases, their operating effectiveness throughout a specified period; and

    (ii) A report by the service auditor with the objective of conveying reasonable assurance that includes:

        a.   The service auditor's opinion on the description of the service organization's system, control objectives and related controls, the suitability of the design of the controls to achieve the specified control objectives, and the operating effectiveness of the controls; and

        b.   A description of the service auditor's tests of the controls and the results thereof.

(d) Service auditor – An auditor who, at the request of the service organization, provides an assurance report on the controls of a service organization.

(e) Service organization – A third-party organization (or segment of a third-party organization) that provides services to user entities that are part of those entities' information systems relevant to financial reporting.

(f) Service organization's system – The policies and procedures designed, implemented and maintained by the service organization to provide user entities with the services covered by the service auditor's report.

(g) Subservice organization – A service organization used by another service organization to perform some of the services provided to user entities that are part of those user entities' information systems relevant to financial reporting.

(h) User auditor – An auditor who audits and reports on the financial statements of a user entity.

(i) User entity – An entity that uses a service organization and whose financial statements are being audited.

Requirements

Obtaining an Understanding of the Services Provided by a Service Organization, Including Internal Control

9   When obtaining an understanding of the user entity in accordance with ISA (UK and Ireland) 315,[3] the user auditor shall obtain an understanding of how a user entity uses the services of a service organization in the user entity's operations, including: (Ref: Para. A1-A2)

(a) The nature of the services provided by the service organization and the significance of those services to the user entity, including the effect thereof on the user entity's internal control; (Ref: Para. A3-A5)

(b) The nature and materiality of the transactions processed or accounts or financial reporting processes affected by the service organization; (Ref: Para. A6)

(c) The degree of interaction between the activities of the service organization and those of the user entity; and (Ref: Para. A7)

(d) The nature of the relationship between the user entity and the service organization, including the relevant contractual terms for the activities undertaken by the service organization. (Ref: Para. A8-A11)

(e) If the service organisation maintains all or part of a user entity's accounting records, whether those arrangements impact the work the auditor performs to fulfil reporting responsibilities in relation to accounting records that are established in law or regulation. (Ref: Para. A11-1 – A11-3)

---

[3] *ISA (UK and Ireland) 315, paragraph 11.*

When obtaining an understanding of internal control relevant to the audit in accordance with ISA (UK and Ireland) 315,[4] the user auditor shall evaluate the design and implementation of relevant controls at the user entity that relate to the services provided by the service organization, including those that are applied to the transactions processed by the service organization. (Ref: Para. A12-A14)   **10**

The user auditor shall determine whether a sufficient understanding of the nature and significance of the services provided by the service organization and their effect on the user entity's internal control relevant to the audit has been obtained to provide a basis for the identification and assessment of risks of material misstatement.   **11**

If the user auditor is unable to obtain a sufficient understanding from the user entity, the user auditor shall obtain that understanding from one or more of the following procedures: **12**

(a) Obtaining a type 1 or type 2 report, if available;
(b) Contacting the service organization, through the user entity, to obtain specific information;
(c) Visiting the service organization and performing procedures that will provide the necessary information about the relevant controls at the service organization; or
(d) Using another auditor to perform procedures that will provide the necessary information about the relevant controls at the service organization. (Ref: Para. A15-A20)

Using a Type 1 or Type 2 Report to Support the User Auditor's Understanding of the Service Organization

In determining the sufficiency and appropriateness of the audit evidence provided by a type 1 or type 2 report, the user auditor shall be satisfied as to: **13**

(a) The service auditor's professional competence and independence from the service organization; and
(b) The adequacy of the standards under which the type 1 or type 2 report was issued. (Ref: Para. A21)

If the user auditor plans to use a type 1 or type 2 report as audit evidence to support the user auditor's understanding about the design and implementation of controls at the service organization, the user auditor shall: **14**

(a) Evaluate whether the description and design of controls at the service organization is at a date or for a period that is appropriate for the user auditor's purposes;
(b) Evaluate the sufficiency and appropriateness of the evidence provided by the report for the understanding of the user entity's internal control relevant to the audit; and
(c) Determine whether complementary user entity controls identified by the service organization are relevant to the user entity and, if so, obtain an understanding of whether the user entity has designed and implemented such controls. (Ref: Para. A22-A23)

---

[4] *ISA (UK and Ireland) 315, paragraph 12.*

Responding to the Assessed Risks of Material Misstatement

15   In responding to assessed risks in accordance with ISA (UK and Ireland) 330, the user auditor shall:

(a)   Determine whether sufficient appropriate audit evidence concerning the relevant financial statement assertions is available from records held at the user entity; and, if not,

(b)   Perform further audit procedures to obtain sufficient appropriate audit evidence or use another auditor to perform those procedures at the service organization on the user auditor's behalf. (Ref: Para. A24-A28)

Tests of Controls

16   When the user auditor's risk assessment includes an expectation that controls at the service organization are operating effectively, the user auditor shall obtain audit evidence about the operating effectiveness of those controls from one or more of the following procedures:

(a)   Obtaining a type 2 report, if available;

(b)   Performing appropriate tests of controls at the service organization; or

(c)   Using another auditor to perform tests of controls at the service organization on behalf of the user auditor. (Ref: Para. A29-A30)

Using a Type 2 Report as Audit Evidence that Controls at the Service Organization Are Operating Effectively

17   If, in accordance with paragraph 16(a), the user auditor plans to use a type 2 report as audit evidence that controls at the service organization are operating effectively, the user auditor shall determine whether the service auditor's report provides sufficient appropriate audit evidence about the effectiveness of the controls to support the user auditor's risk assessment by:

(a)   Evaluating whether the description, design and operating effectiveness of controls at the service organization is at a date or for a period that is appropriate for the user auditor's purposes;

(b)   Determining whether complementary user entity controls identified by the service organization are relevant to the user entity and, if so, obtaining an understanding of whether the user entity has designed and implemented such controls and, if so, testing their operating effectiveness;

(c)   Evaluating the adequacy of the time period covered by the tests of controls and the time elapsed since the performance of the tests of controls; and

(d)   Evaluating whether the tests of controls performed by the service auditor and the results thereof, as described in the service auditor's report, are relevant to the assertions in the user entity's financial statements and provide sufficient appropriate audit evidence to support the user auditor's risk assessment. (Ref: Para. A31-A39)

Type 1 and Type 2 Reports that Exclude the Services of a Subservice Organization

18   If the user auditor plans to use a type 1 or a type 2 report that excludes the services provided by a subservice organization and those services are relevant to the audit of the user entity's financial statements, the user auditor shall apply the requirements of this ISA (UK and Ireland) with respect to the services provided by the subservice organization. (Ref: Para. A40)

Fraud, Non-Compliance with Laws and Regulations and Uncorrected Misstatements in Relation to Activities at the Service Organization

The user auditor shall inquire of management of the user entity whether the service **19** organization has reported to the user entity, or whether the user entity is otherwise aware of, any fraud, non-compliance with laws and regulations or uncorrected misstatements affecting the financial statements of the user entity. The user auditor shall evaluate how such matters affect the nature, timing and extent of the user auditor's further audit procedures, including the effect on the user auditor's conclusions and user auditor's report. (Ref: Para. A41)

Reporting by the User Auditor

The user auditor shall modify the opinion in the user auditor's report in accordance **20** with ISA (UK and Ireland) 705[5] if the user auditor is unable to obtain sufficient appropriate audit evidence regarding the services provided by the service organization relevant to the audit of the user entity's financial statements. (Ref: Para. A42)

The user auditor shall not refer to the work of a service auditor in the user auditor's **21** report containing an unmodified opinion unless required by law or regulation to do so. If such reference is required by law or regulation, the user auditor's report shall indicate that the reference does not diminish the user auditor's responsibility for the audit opinion. (Ref: Para. A43)

If reference to the work of a service auditor is relevant to an understanding of a **22** modification to the user auditor's opinion, the user auditor's report shall indicate that such reference does not diminish the user auditor's responsibility for that opinion. (Ref: Para. A44)

***

Application and Other Explanatory Material

Obtaining an Understanding of the Services Provided by a Service Organization, Including Internal Control

Sources of Information (Ref: Para. 9)

Information on the nature of the services provided by a service organization may be **A1** available from a wide variety of sources, such as:

- User manuals.
- System overviews.
- Technical manuals.
- The contract or service level agreement between the user entity and the service organization.
- Reports by service organizations, the internal audit function or regulatory authorities on controls at the service organization.
- Reports by the service auditor, including management letters, if available.

Knowledge obtained through the user auditor's experience with the service organi- **A2** zation, for example through experience with other audit engagements, may also be helpful in obtaining an understanding of the nature of the services provided by the

[5] *ISA (UK and Ireland) 705, "Modifications to the Opinion in the Independent Auditor's Report," paragraph 6.*

service organization. This may be particularly helpful if the services and controls at the service organization over those services are highly standardized.

Nature of the Services Provided by the Service Organization (Ref: Para. 9(a))

A3   A user entity may use a service organization such as one that processes transactions and maintains related accountability, or records transactions and processes related data. Service organizations that provide such services include, for example, bank trust departments that invest and service assets for employee benefit plans or for others; mortgage bankers that service mortgages for others; and application service providers that provide packaged software applications and a technology environment that enables customers to process financial and operational transactions.

A4   Examples of service organization services that are relevant to the audit include:

- Maintenance of the user entity's accounting records.
- Management of assets.
- Initiating, recording or processing transactions as agent of the user entity.

Compliance with Law and Regulations

A4-1   The user auditor considers whether the activities undertaken by the service organisation are in an area in which the user entity is required to comply with requirements of law and regulations (for example, there are legal requirements relating to the maintenance of accounting records by companies – see paragraphs A11-1 – A11-3). In such circumstances, non-compliance may have a significant effect on the financial statements. The user auditor therefore determines whether the law and regulations concerned are to be regarded as relevant to the audit[5a] in order to meet the requirements of ISA (UK and Ireland) 250 Section A "Consideration of Laws and Regulations in an Audit of Financial Statements" and undertake procedures to assess the risk of a misstatement arising from non-compliance as set out in that ISA (UK and Ireland).

Considerations Specific to Smaller Entities

A5   Smaller entities may use external bookkeeping services ranging from the processing of certain transactions (for example, payment of payroll taxes) and maintenance of their accounting records to the preparation of their financial statements. The use of such a service organization for the preparation of its financial statements does not relieve management of the smaller entity and, where appropriate, those charged with governance of their responsibilities for the financial statements.[6]

[5a] *Laws and regulations are relevant to the audit when they either relate directly to the preparation of the financial statements of the entity, or are fundamental to the operating aspects of its business (ISA (UK and Ireland) 250 Section A, "Consideration of Laws and Regulations in an Audit of Financial Statements," paragraph 6).*

[6] ISA (UK and Ireland) 200, "Overall Objectives of the Independent Auditor and the Conduct of an Audit in Accordance with International Standards on Auditing," paragraphs 4 and A2-A3.

Nature and Materiality of Transactions Processed by the Service Organization (Ref: Para. 9(b))

A service organization may establish policies and procedures that affect the user **A6** entity's internal control. These policies and procedures are at least in part physically and operationally separate from the user entity. The significance of the controls of the service organization to those of the user entity depends on the nature of the services provided by the service organization, including the nature and materiality of the transactions it processes for the user entity. In certain situations, the transactions processed and the accounts affected by the service organization may not appear to be material to the user entity's financial statements, but the nature of the transactions processed may be significant and the user auditor may determine that an under-standing of those controls is necessary in the circumstances.

The Degree of Interaction between the Activities of the Service Organization and the User Entity (Ref: Para. 9(c))

The significance of the controls of the service organization to those of the user entity **A7** also depends on the degree of interaction between its activities and those of the user entity. The degree of interaction refers to the extent to which a user entity is able to and elects to implement effective controls over the processing performed by the service organization. For example, a high degree of interaction exists between the activities of the user entity and those at the service organization when the user entity authorizes transactions and the service organization processes and does the accounting for those transactions. In these circumstances, it may be practicable for the user entity to implement effective controls over those transactions. On the other hand, when the service organization initiates or initially records, processes, and does the accounting for the user entity's transactions, there is a lower degree of interaction between the two organizations. In these circumstances, the user entity may be unable to, or may elect not to, implement effective controls over these transactions at the user entity and may rely on controls at the service organization.

Nature of the Relationship between the User Entity and the Service Organization (Ref: Para. 9(d))

The contract or service level agreement between the user entity and the service **A8** organization may provide for matters such as:

- The information to be provided to the user entity and responsibilities for initiating transactions relating to the activities undertaken by the service organization;
- The application of requirements of regulatory bodies concerning the form of records to be maintained, or access to them;
- The indemnification, if any, to be provided to the user entity in the event of a performance failure;
- Whether the service organization will provide a report on its controls and, if so, whether such report would be a type 1 or type 2 report;
- Whether the user auditor has rights of access to the accounting records of the user entity maintained by the service organization and other information necessary for the conduct of the audit; and
- Whether the agreement allows for direct communication between the user auditor and the service auditor.

A8-1   Other matters which the auditor may consider include:

- The way that accounting records relating to relevant activities are maintained.
- Whether the entity has rights of access to accounting records prepared by the service organisation concerning the activities undertaken, and relevant underlying information held by it, and the conditions in which such access may be sought.
- The nature of relevant performance standards.
- The way in which the entity monitors performance of relevant activities and the extent to which its monitoring process relies on controls operated by the service organization.

A8-2   Agreement by a service organisation to provide an indemnity does not provide information directly relevant to the user auditor's assessment of the risk of material misstatements relating to financial statement assertions. However, such agreements may help to inform the user auditor's judgment concerning the effect of performance failure on the user entity's financial statements: this may be relevant in instances of performance failure, when the existence of an indemnity may help to ensure that the user entity's status as a going concern is not threatened. Where the user auditor wishes to rely on the operation of the indemnity for this purpose, the resources available to the service organisation also need to be considered.

A8-3   The financial standing of a service organisation is relevant to the audit insofar as the user auditor considers it necessary to rely on the operation of an indemnity from the service organisation in assessing the entity's status as a going concern (see paragraph A8-2). However, a service organisation whose cash and/or capital resources are low in relation to the nature of services provided or the volume of its customers may be susceptible to pressures resulting in errors or deliberate misstatements in reporting to the entity, or fraud. If the user auditor considers that this factor may be relevant to the assessment of risk, the user auditor also takes into account the existence of binding arrangements to provide resources to the service organisations from a holding company or other group company, and the financial strength of the group as a whole.

A9   There is a direct relationship between the service organization and the user entity and between the service organization and the service auditor. These relationships do not necessarily create a direct relationship between the user auditor and the service auditor. When there is no direct relationship between the user auditor and the service auditor, communications between the user auditor and the service auditor are usually conducted through the user entity and the service organization. A direct relationship may also be created between a user auditor and a service auditor, taking into account the relevant ethical and confidentiality considerations. A user auditor, for example, may use a service auditor to perform procedures on the user auditor's behalf, such as:

(a)   Tests of controls at the service organization; or
(b)   Substantive procedures on the user entity's financial statement transactions and balances maintained by a service organization.

Considerations Specific to Public Sector Entities

A10   Public sector auditors generally have broad rights of access established by legislation. However, there may be situations where such rights of access are not available, for example when the service organization is located in a different jurisdiction. In such cases, a public sector auditor may need to obtain an understanding of the legislation applicable in the different jurisdiction to determine whether appropriate access rights can be obtained. A public sector auditor may also obtain or ask the user entity to incorporate rights of access in any contractual arrangements between the user entity and the service organization.

Public sector auditors may also use another auditor to perform tests of controls or substantive procedures in relation to compliance with law, regulation or other authority.   A11

Accounting Records (Ref: Para. 9(e))

Use of a service organisation does not diminish the ultimate responsibility of those charged with governance of a user entity for conducting its business in a manner which meets their legal responsibilities, including those of safeguarding the user entity's assets, maintaining adequate accounting records and preparing financial statements which provide information about its economic activities and financial position. Practical issues, including the way in which accounting records will be kept and the manner in which those charged with governance assess the quality of the service, need to be addressed.   A11-1

An auditor of an entity incorporated under company law has statutory reporting obligations relating to compliance with requirements for companies to maintain adequate accounting records. Where such an entity outsources the preparation of its accounting records to a service organisation, issues relating to whether the arrangements with the service organisation are such as to permit the user entity to meet its statutory obligations may require careful consideration, by both those charged with governance and the user auditor. Where there is doubt, the user auditor may wish to encourage those charged with governance to take legal advice before issuing the auditor's report on its financial statements.   A11-2

A particular issue arises in relation to companies incorporated in the United Kingdom. The wording of UK company law appears to be prescriptive and to require the company itself to keep accounting records. Consequently, whether a company 'keeps' records (as opposed to 'causes records to be kept') will depend upon the particular terms of the outsourcing arrangements and, in particular, the extent to which the company retains ownership of, has access to, or holds copies of, those records[6b].   A11-3

Understanding the Controls Relating to Services Provided by the Service Organization (Ref: Para. 10)

The user entity may establish controls over the service organization's services that may be tested by the user auditor and that may enable the user auditor to conclude that the user entity's controls are operating effectively for some or all of the related assertions, regardless of the controls in place at the service organization. If a user entity, for example, uses a service organization to process its payroll transactions, the user entity may establish controls over the submission and receipt of payroll information that could prevent or detect material misstatements. These controls may include: A12

[6b] *In Ireland, company law requires that companies shall cause records to be kept in accordance with its requirements.*

- Comparing the data submitted to the service organization with reports of information received from the service organization after the data has been processed.
- Recomputing a sample of the payroll amounts for clerical accuracy and reviewing the total amount of the payroll for reasonableness.

A13   In this situation, the user auditor may perform tests of the user entity's controls over payroll processing that would provide a basis for the user auditor to conclude that the user entity's controls are operating effectively for the assertions related to payroll transactions.

A14   As noted in ISA (UK and Ireland) 315,[7] in respect of some risks, the user auditor may judge that it is not possible or practicable to obtain sufficient appropriate audit evidence only from substantive procedures. Such risks may relate to the inaccurate or incomplete recording of routine and significant classes of transactions and account balances, the characteristics of which often permit highly automated processing with little or no manual intervention. Such automated processing characteristics may be particularly present when the user entity uses service organizations. In such cases, the user entity's controls over such risks are relevant to the audit and the user auditor is required to obtain an understanding of, and to evaluate, such controls in accordance with paragraphs 9 and 10 of this ISA (UK and Ireland).

Further Procedures When a Sufficient Understanding Cannot Be Obtained from the User Entity (Ref: Para. 12)

A15   The user auditor's decision as to which procedure, individually or in combination, in paragraph 12 to undertake, in order to obtain the information necessary to provide a basis for the identification and assessment of the risks of material misstatement in relation to the user entity's use of the service organization, may be influenced by such matters as:

- The size of both the user entity and the service organization;
- The complexity of the transactions at the user entity and the complexity of the services provided by the service organization;
- The location of the service organization (for example, the user auditor may decide to use another auditor to perform procedures at the service organization on the user auditor's behalf if the service organization is in a remote location);
- Whether the procedure(s) is expected to effectively provide the user auditor with sufficient appropriate audit evidence; and
- The nature of the relationship between the user entity and the service organization.

A16   A service organization may engage a service auditor to report on the description and design of its controls (type 1 report) or on the description and design of its controls and their operating effectiveness (type 2 report). Type 1 or type 2 reports may be issued under [proposed] International Standard on Assurance Engagements (ISAE) 3402[8] or under standards established by an authorized or recognized standards setting organization (which may identify them by different names, such as Type A or Type B reports).

A17   The availability of a type 1 or type 2 report will generally depend on whether the contract between a service organization and a user entity includes the provision of

---

[7] *ISA (UK and Ireland) 315, paragraph 30.*

[8] *[Proposed] ISAE 3402, "Assurance Reports on Controls at a Third Party Service Organization."*

such a report by the service organization. A service organization may also elect, for practical reasons, to make a type 1 or type 2 report available to the user entities. However, in some cases, a type 1 or type 2 report may not be available to user entities.

In some circumstances, a user entity may outsource one or more significant business units or functions, such as its entire tax planning and compliance functions, or finance and accounting or the controllership function to one or more service organizations. As a report on controls at the service organization may not be available in these circumstances, visiting the service organization may be the most effective procedure for the user auditor to gain an understanding of controls at the service organization, as there is likely to be direct interaction of management of the user entity with management at the service organization.   **A18**

Another auditor may be used to perform procedures that will provide the necessary information about the relevant controls at the service organization. If a type 1 or type 2 report has been issued, the user auditor may use the service auditor to perform these procedures as the service auditor has an existing relationship with the service organization. The user auditor using the work of another auditor may find the guidance in ISA (UK and Ireland) 600[9] useful as it relates to understanding another auditor (including that auditor's independence and professional competence), involvement in the work of another auditor in planning the nature, extent and timing of such work, and in evaluating the sufficiency and appropriateness of the audit evidence obtained.   **A19**

A user entity may use a service organization that in turn uses a subservice organization to provide some of the services provided to a user entity that are part of the user entity's information system relevant to financial reporting. The subservice organization may be a separate entity from the service organization or may be related to the service organization. A user auditor may need to consider controls at the subservice organization. In situations where one or more subservice organizations are used, the interaction between the activities of the user entity and those of the service organization is expanded to include the interaction between the user entity, the service organization and the subservice organizations. The degree of this interaction, as well as the nature and materiality of the transactions processed by the service organization and the subservice organizations are the most important factors for the user auditor to consider in determining the significance of the service organization's and subservice organization's controls to the user entity's controls.   **A20**

Using a Type 1 or Type 2 Report to Support the User Auditor's Understanding of the Service Organization (Ref: Para. 13-14)

The user auditor may make inquiries about the service auditor to the service auditor's professional organization or other practitioners and inquire whether the service auditor is subject to regulatory oversight. The service auditor may be practicing in a jurisdiction where different standards are followed in respect of reports on controls at a service organization, and the user auditor may obtain information about the standards used by the service auditor from the standard setting organization.   **A21**

---

[9] ISA (UK and Ireland) 600, "Special Considerations-Audits of Group Financial Statements (Including the Work of Component Auditors)," paragraph 2, states: "An auditor may find this ISA (UK and Ireland), adapted as necessary in the circumstances, useful when that auditor involves other auditors in the audit of financial statements that are not group financial statements ..." See also paragraph 19 of ISA (UK and Ireland) 600.

A22   A type 1 or type 2 report, along with information about the user entity, may assist the user auditor in obtaining an understanding of:

(a)   The aspects of controls at the service organization that may affect the processing of the user entity's transactions, including the use of subservice organizations;

(b)   The flow of significant transactions through the service organization to determine the points in the transaction flow where material misstatements in the user entity's financial statements could occur;

(c)   The control objectives at the service organization that are relevant to the user entity's financial statement assertions; and

(d)   Whether controls at the service organization are suitably designed and implemented to prevent or detect processing errors that could result in material misstatements in the user entity's financial statements.

A type 1 or type 2 report may assist the user auditor in obtaining a sufficient understanding to identify and assess the risks of material misstatement. A type 1 report, however, does not provide any evidence of the operating effectiveness of the relevant controls.

A23   A type 1 or type 2 report that is as of a date or for a period that is outside of the reporting period of a user entity may assist the user auditor in obtaining a preliminary understanding of the controls implemented at the service organization if the report is supplemented by additional current information from other sources. If the service organization's description of controls is as of a date or for a period that precedes the beginning of the period under audit, the user auditor may perform procedures to update the information in a type 1 or type 2 report, such as:

● Discussing the changes at the service organization with user entity personnel who would be in a position to know of such changes;

● Reviewing current documentation and correspondence issued by the service organization; or

● Discussing the changes with service organization personnel.

Responding to the Assessed Risks of Material Misstatement (Ref: Para. 15)

A24   Whether the use of a service organization increases a user entity's risk of material misstatement depends on the nature of the services provided and the controls over these services; in some cases, the use of a service organization may decrease a user entity's risk of material misstatement, particularly if the user entity itself does not possess the expertise necessary to undertake particular activities, such as initiating, processing, and recording transactions, or does not have adequate resources (for example, an IT system).

A25   When the service organization maintains material elements of the accounting records of the user entity, direct access to those records may be necessary in order for the user auditor to obtain sufficient appropriate audit evidence relating to the operations of controls over those records or to substantiate transactions and balances recorded in them, or both. Such access may involve either physical inspection of records at the service organization's premises or interrogation of records maintained electronically from the user entity or another location, or both. Where direct access is achieved electronically, the user auditor may thereby obtain evidence as to the adequacy of controls operated by the service organization over the completeness and integrity of the user entity's data for which the service organization is responsible.

A26   In determining the nature and extent of audit evidence to be obtained in relation to balances representing assets held or transactions undertaken by a service organization on behalf of the user entity, the following procedures may be considered by the user auditor:

(a) Inspecting records and documents held by the user entity: the reliability of this source of evidence is determined by the nature and extent of the accounting records and supporting documentation retained by the user entity. In some cases, the user entity may not maintain independent detailed records or documentation of specific transactions undertaken on its behalf.

(b) Inspecting records and documents held by the service organization: the user auditor's access to the records of the service organization may be established as part of the contractual arrangements between the user entity and the service organization. The user auditor may also use another auditor, on its behalf, to gain access to the user entity's records maintained by the service organization.

(c) Obtaining confirmations of balances and transactions from the service organization: where the user entity maintains independent records of balances and transactions, confirmation from the service organization corroborating the user entity's records may constitute reliable audit evidence concerning the existence of the transactions and assets concerned. For example, when multiple service organizations are used, such as an investment manager and a custodian, and these service organizations maintain independent records, the user auditor may confirm balances with these organizations in order to compare this information with the independent records of the user entity.

If the user entity does not maintain independent records, information obtained in confirmations from the service organization is merely a statement of what is reflected in the records maintained by the service organization. Therefore, such confirmations do not, taken alone, constitute reliable audit evidence. In these circumstances, the user auditor may consider whether an alternative source of independent evidence can be identified.

(d) Performing analytical procedures on the records maintained by the user entity or on the reports received from the service organization: the effectiveness of analytical procedures is likely to vary by assertion and will be affected by the extent and detail of information available.

Another auditor may perform procedures that are substantive in nature for the benefit of user auditors. Such an engagement may involve the performance, by another auditor, of procedures agreed upon by the user entity and its user auditor and by the service organization and its service auditor. The findings resulting from the procedures performed by another auditor are reviewed by the user auditor to determine whether they constitute sufficient appropriate audit evidence. In addition, there may be requirements imposed by governmental authorities or through contractual arrangements whereby a service auditor performs designated procedures that are substantive in nature. The results of the application of the required procedures to balances and transactions processed by the service organization may be used by user auditors as part of the evidence necessary to support their audit opinions. In these circumstances, it may be useful for the user auditor and the service auditor to agree, prior to the performance of the procedures, to the audit documentation or access to audit documentation that will be provided to the user auditor. **A27**

In certain circumstances, in particular when a user entity outsources some or all of its finance function to a service organization, the user auditor may face a situation where a significant portion of the audit evidence resides at the service organization. Substantive procedures may need to be performed at the service organization by the user auditor or another auditor on its behalf. A service auditor may provide a type 2 report and, in addition, may perform substantive procedures on behalf of the user auditor. The involvement of another auditor does not alter the user auditor's responsibility to obtain sufficient appropriate audit evidence to afford a reasonable **A28** basis to support the user auditor's opinion. Accordingly, the user auditor's consideration of whether sufficient appropriate audit evidence has been obtained and whether the user auditor needs to perform further substantive procedures includes the user auditor's involvement with, or evidence of, the direction, supervision and performance of the substantive procedures performed by another auditor.

Tests of Controls (Ref: Para. 16)

A29   The user auditor is required by ISA (UK and Ireland) 330[10] to design and perform tests of controls to obtain sufficient appropriate audit evidence as to the operating effectiveness of relevant controls in certain circumstances. In the context of a service organization, this requirement applies when:

(a)   The user auditor's assessment of risks of material misstatement includes an expectation that the controls at the service organization are operating effectively (that is, the user auditor intends to rely on the operating effectiveness of controls at the service organization in determining the nature, timing and extent of substantive procedures); or

(b)   Substantive procedures alone, or in combination with tests of the operating effectiveness of controls at the user entity, cannot provide sufficient appropriate audit evidence at the assertion level.

A30   If a type 2 report is not available, a user auditor may contact the service organization, through the user entity, to request that a service auditor be engaged to provide a type 2 report that includes tests of the operating effectiveness of the relevant controls or the user auditor may use another auditor to perform procedures at the service organization that test the operating effectiveness of those controls. A user auditor may also visit the service organization and perform tests of relevant controls if the service organization agrees to it. The user auditor's risk assessments are based on the combined evidence provided by the work of another auditor and the user auditor's own procedures.

Using a Type 2 Report as Audit Evidence that Controls at the Service Organization Are Operating Effectively (Ref: Para. 17)

A31   A type 2 report may be intended to satisfy the needs of several different user auditors; therefore tests of controls and results described in the service auditor's report may not be relevant to assertions that are significant in the user entity's financial statements. The relevant tests of controls and results are evaluated to determine that the service auditor's report provides sufficient appropriate audit evidence about the effectiveness of the controls to support the user auditor's risk assessment. In doing so, the user auditor may consider the following factors:

(a)   The time period covered by the tests of controls and the time elapsed since the performance of the tests of controls;

(b)   The scope of the service auditor's work and the services and processes covered, the controls tested and tests that were performed, and the way in which tested controls relate to the user entity's controls; and

(c)   The results of those tests of controls and the service auditor's opinion on the operating effectiveness of the controls.

A32   For certain assertions, the shorter the period covered by a specific test and the longer the time elapsed since the performance of the test, the less audit evidence the test may provide. In comparing the period covered by the type 2 report to the user entity's

---

[10] *ISA (UK and Ireland) 330, paragraph 8.*

financial reporting period, the user auditor may conclude that the type 2 report offers less audit evidence if there is little overlap between the period covered by the type 2 report and the period for which the user auditor intends to rely on the report. When this is the case, a type 2 report covering a preceding or subsequent period may provide additional audit evidence. In other cases, the user auditor may determine it is necessary to perform, or use another auditor to perform, tests of controls at the service organization in order to obtain sufficient appropriate audit evidence about the operating effectiveness of those controls.

It may also be necessary for the user auditor to obtain additional evidence about significant changes to the relevant controls at the service organization outside of the period covered by the type 2 report or determine additional audit procedures to be performed. Relevant factors in determining what additional audit evidence to obtain about controls at the service organization that were operating outside of the period covered by the service auditor's report may include: **A33**

- The significance of the assessed risks of material misstatement at the assertion level;
- The specific controls that were tested during the interim period, and significant changes to them since they were tested, including changes in the information system, processes, and personnel;
- The degree to which audit evidence about the operating effectiveness of those controls was obtained;
- The length of the remaining period;
- The extent to which the user auditor intends to reduce further substantive procedures based on the reliance on controls; and
- The effectiveness of the control environment and monitoring of controls at the user entity.

Additional audit evidence may be obtained, for example, by extending tests of controls over the remaining period or testing the user entity's monitoring of controls. **A34**

If the service auditor's testing period is completely outside the user entity's financial reporting period, the user auditor will be unable to rely on such tests for the user auditor to conclude that the user entity's controls are operating effectively because they do not provide current audit period evidence of the effectiveness of the controls, unless other procedures are performed. **A35**

In certain circumstances, a service provided by the service organization may be designed with the assumption that certain controls will be implemented by the user entity. For example, the service may be designed with the assumption that the user entity will have controls in place for authorizing transactions before they are sent to the service organization for processing. In such a situation, the service organization's description of controls may include a description of those complementary user entity controls. The user auditor considers whether those complementary user entity controls are relevant to the service provided to the user entity. **A36**

If the user auditor believes that the service auditor's report may not provide sufficient appropriate audit evidence, for example, if a service auditor's report does not contain a description of the service auditor's tests of controls and results thereon, the user auditor may supplement the understanding of the service auditor's procedures and conclusions by contacting the service organization, through the user entity, to request a discussion with the service auditor about the scope and results of the service auditor's work. Also, if the user auditor believes it is necessary, the user auditor may contact the service organization, through the user entity, to request that the service auditor perform procedures at the service organization. Alternatively, the user **A37** auditor, or another auditor at the request of the user auditor, may perform such procedures.

A38 The service auditor's type 2 report identifies results of tests, including exceptions and other information that could affect the user auditor's conclusions. Exceptions noted by the service auditor or a modified opinion in the service auditor's type 2 report do not automatically mean that the service auditor's type 2 report will not be useful for the audit of the user entity's financial statements in assessing the risks of material misstatement. Rather, the exceptions and the matter giving rise to a modified opinion in the service auditor's type 2 report are considered in the user auditor's assessment of the testing of controls performed by the service auditor. In considering the exceptions and matters giving rise to a modified opinion, the user auditor may discuss such matters with the service auditor. Such communication is dependent upon the user entity contacting the service organization, and obtaining the service organization's approval for the communication to take place.

Communication of deficiencies in internal control identified during the audit

A39 The user auditor is required to communicate in writing significant deficiencies identified during the audit to both management and those charged with governance on a timely basis.[11] The user auditor is also required to communicate to management at an appropriate level of responsibility on a timely basis other deficiencies in internal control identified during the audit that, in the user auditor's professional judgment, are of sufficient importance to merit management's attention.[12] Matters that the user auditor may identify during the audit and may communicate to management and those charged with governance of the user entity include:

- Any monitoring of controls that could be implemented by the user entity, including those identified as a result of obtaining a type 1 or type 2 report;
- Instances where complementary user entity controls are noted in the type 1 or type 2 report and are not implemented at the user entity; and
- Controls that may be needed at the service organization that do not appear to have been implemented or that are not specifically covered by a type 2 report.

Type 1 and Type 2 Reports that Exclude the Services of a Subservice Organization (Ref: Para. 18)

A40 If a service organization uses a subservice organization, the service auditor's report may either include or exclude the subservice organization's relevant control objectives and related controls in the service organization's description of its system and in the scope of the service auditor's engagement. These two methods of reporting are known as the inclusive method and the carve-out method, respectively. If the type 1 or type 2 report excludes the controls at a subservice organization, and the services provided by the subservice organization are relevant to the audit of the user entity's financial statements, the user auditor is required to apply the requirements of this ISA (UK and Ireland) in respect of the subservice organization. The nature and extent of work to be performed by the user auditor regarding the services provided by a subservice organization depend on the nature and significance of those services to the user entity and the relevance of those services to the audit. The application of

---

[11] *ISA (UK and Ireland) 265, "Communicating Deficiencies in Internal Control to Those Charged with Governance and Management," paragraphs 9-10.*

[12] *ISA (UK and Ireland) 265, paragraph 10.*

the requirement in paragraph 9 assists the user auditor in determining the effect of the subservice organization and the nature and extent of work to be performed.

Fraud, Non-Compliance with Laws and Regulations and Uncorrected Misstatements in Relation to Activities at the Service Organization (Ref: Para. 19)

A service organization may be required under the terms of the contract with user **A41** entities to disclose to affected user entities any fraud, non-compliance with laws and regulations or uncorrected misstatements attributable to the service organization's management or employees. As required by paragraph 19, the user auditor makes inquiries of the user entity management regarding whether the service organization has reported any such matters and evaluates whether any matters reported by the service organization affect the nature, timing and extent of the user auditor's further audit procedures. In certain circumstances, the user auditor may require additional information to perform this evaluation, and may request the user entity to contact the service organization to obtain the necessary information.

Reporting by the User Auditor (Ref: Para. 20)

When a user auditor is unable to obtain sufficient appropriate audit evidence **A42** regarding the services provided by the service organization relevant to the audit of the user entity's financial statements, a limitation on the scope of the audit exists. This may be the case when:

- The user auditor is unable to obtain a sufficient understanding of the services provided by the service organization and does not have a basis for the identification and assessment of the risks of material misstatement;
- A user auditor's risk assessment includes an expectation that controls at the service organization are operating effectively and the user auditor is unable to obtain sufficient appropriate audit evidence about the operating effectiveness of these controls; or
- Sufficient appropriate audit evidence is only available from records held at the service organization, and the user auditor is unable to obtain direct access to these records.

Whether the user auditor expresses a qualified opinion or disclaims an opinion depends on the user auditor's conclusion as to whether the possible effects on the financial statements are material or pervasive.

Reference to the Work of a Service Auditor (Ref: Para. 21-22)

In some cases, law or regulation may require a reference to the work of a service **A43** auditor in the user auditor's report, for example, for the purposes of transparency in the public sector. In such circumstances, the user auditor may need the consent of the service auditor before making such a reference.

The fact that a user entity uses a service organization does not alter the user auditor's **A44** responsibility under ISAs (UK and Ireland) to obtain sufficient appropriate audit evidence to afford a reasonable basis to support the user auditor's opinion. Therefore, the user auditor does not make reference to the service auditor's report as a basis, in part, for the user auditor's opinion on the user entity's financial statements. However, when the user auditor expresses a modified opinion because of a modified opinion in a service auditor's report, the user auditor is not precluded from referring to the service auditor's report if such reference assists in explaining the reason for the user auditor's modified opinion. In such circumstances, the user auditor may need the consent of the service auditor before making such a reference.

International Standard on Auditing (UK and Ireland) 450

Evaluation of misstatements identified during the audit

(Effective for audits of financial statements for periods ending on or after 15 December 2010)

Contents

International Standard on Auditing (UK and Ireland) (ISA (UK and Ireland)) 450, "Evaluation of Misstatements Identified during the Audit" should be read in the context of ISA (UK and Ireland) 200, "Overall Objectives of the Independent Auditor and the Conduct of an Audit in Accordance with International Standards on Auditing (UK and Ireland)."

Introduction

Scope of this ISA (UK and Ireland)

1   This International Standard on Auditing (UK and Ireland) (ISA (UK and Ireland)) deals with the auditor's responsibility to evaluate the effect of identified misstatements on the audit and of uncorrected misstatements, if any, on the financial statements. ISA (UK and Ireland) 700 deals with the auditor's responsibility, in forming an opinion on the financial statements, to conclude whether reasonable assurance has been obtained about whether the financial statements as a whole are free from material misstatement. The auditor's conclusion required by ISA (UK and Ireland) 700 takes into account the auditor's evaluation of uncorrected misstatements, if any, on the financial statements, in accordance with this ISA (UK and Ireland).[1] ISA (UK and Ireland) 320[2] deals with the auditor's responsibility to apply the concept of materiality appropriately in planning and performing an audit of financial statements.

Effective Date

2   This ISA (UK and Ireland) is effective for audits of financial statements for periods ending on or after 15 December 2010.

Objective

3   The objective of the auditor is to evaluate:

(a)   The effect of identified misstatements on the audit; and

(b)   The effect of uncorrected misstatements, if any, on the financial statements.

Definitions

4   For purposes of the ISAs (UK and Ireland), the following terms have the meanings attributed below:

(a)   Misstatement – A difference between the amount, classification, presentation, or disclosure of a reported financial statement item and the amount, classification, presentation, or disclosure that is required for the item to be in accordance with the applicable financial reporting framework. Misstatements can arise from error or fraud. (Ref: Para. A1)

When the auditor expresses an opinion on whether the financial statements are presented fairly, in all material respects, or give a true and fair view, misstatements also include those adjustments of amounts, classifications, presentation, or disclosures that, in the auditor's judgment, are necessary for the financial statements to be presented fairly, in all material respects, or to give a true and fair view.

---

[1] *ISA 700, "Forming an Opinion and Reporting on Financial Statements," paragraphs 10-11.*

The APB has not promulgated ISA 700 as issued by the IAASB for application in the UK and Ireland. In the UK and Ireland the applicable auditing standard is ISA (UK and Ireland) 700, "The Auditor's Report on Financial Statements." Paragraph 8(b) of ISA (UK and Ireland) 700 requires evaluation of whether uncorrected misstatements are material, individually or in aggregate.

[2] *ISA (UK and Ireland) 320, "Materiality in Planning and Performing an Audit."*

(b) Uncorrected misstatements – Misstatements that the auditor has accumulated during the audit and that have not been corrected.

Requirements

Accumulation of Identified Misstatements

The auditor shall accumulate misstatements identified during the audit, other than those that are clearly trivial. (Ref: Para. A2-A3)   **5**

Consideration of Identified Misstatements as the Audit Progresses

The auditor shall determine whether the overall audit strategy and audit plan need to be revised if: **6**

(a) The nature of identified misstatements and the circumstances of their occurrence indicate that other misstatements may exist that, when aggregated with misstatements accumulated during the audit, could be material; or (Ref: Para. A4)
(b) The aggregate of misstatements accumulated during the audit approaches materiality determined in accordance with ISA (UK and Ireland) 320. (Ref: Para. A5)

If, at the auditor's request, management has examined a class of transactions, account balance or disclosure and corrected misstatements that were detected, the auditor shall perform additional audit procedures to determine whether misstatements remain. (Ref: Para. A6)   **7**

Communication and Correction of Misstatements

The auditor shall communicate on a timely basis all misstatements accumulated during the audit with the appropriate level of management, unless prohibited by law or regulation.[3] The auditor shall request management to correct those misstatements. (Ref: Para. A7-A9)   **8**

If management refuses to correct some or all of the misstatements communicated by the auditor, the auditor shall obtain an understanding of management's reasons for not making the corrections and shall take that understanding into account when evaluating whether the financial statements as a whole are free from material misstatement. (Ref: Para. A10)   **9**

Evaluating the Effect of Uncorrected Misstatements

Prior to evaluating the effect of uncorrected misstatements, the auditor shall reassess materiality determined in accordance with ISA (UK and Ireland) 320 to confirm whether it remains appropriate in the context of the entity's actual financial results. (Ref: Para. A11-A12)   **10**

The auditor shall determine whether uncorrected misstatements are material, individually or in aggregate. In making this determination, the auditor shall consider: **11**

(a) The size and nature of the misstatements, both in relation to particular classes of transactions, account balances or disclosures and the financial statements as a

---

[3] *ISA (UK and Ireland) 260, "Communication with Those Charged with Governance," paragraph 7.*

whole, and the particular circumstances of their occurrence; and (Ref: Para. A13-A17, A19-A20)

(b) The effect of uncorrected misstatements related to prior periods on the relevant classes of transactions, account balances or disclosures, and the financial statements as a whole. (Ref: Para. A18)

Communication with Those Charged with Governance

12   The auditor shall communicate with those charged with governance uncorrected misstatements and the effect that they, individually or in aggregate, may have on the opinion in the auditor's report, unless prohibited by law or regulation.[4] The auditor's communication shall identify material uncorrected misstatements individually. The auditor shall request that uncorrected misstatements be corrected. (Ref: Para. A21-A23)

13   The auditor shall also communicate with those charged with governance the effect of uncorrected misstatements related to prior periods on the relevant classes of transactions, account balances or disclosures, and the financial statements as a whole.

Written Representation

14   The auditor shall request a written representation from management and, where appropriate, those charged with governance whether they believe the effects of uncorrected misstatements are immaterial, individually and in aggregate, to the financial statements as a whole. A summary of such items shall be included in or attached to the written representation. (Ref: Para. A24 – A24-1)

Documentation

15   The auditor shall include in the audit documentation:[5] (Ref: Para. A25)

(a) The amount below which misstatements would be regarded as clearly trivial (paragraph 5);

(b) All misstatements accumulated during the audit and whether they have been corrected (paragraphs 5, 8 and 12); and

(c) The auditor's conclusion as to whether uncorrected misstatements are material, individually or in aggregate, and the basis for that conclusion (paragraph 11).

***

Application and Other Explanatory Material

Definition of Misstatement (Ref: Para. 4(a))

A1   Misstatements may result from:

(a) An inaccuracy in gathering or processing data from which the financial statements are prepared;

(b) An omission of an amount or disclosure;

---

[4] *See footnote 3.*

[5] *ISA (UK and Ireland) 230, "Audit Documentation," paragraphs 8-11, and paragraph A6.*

(c) An incorrect accounting estimate arising from overlooking, or clear mis-interpretation of, facts; and

(d) Judgments of management concerning accounting estimates that the auditor considers unreasonable or the selection and application of accounting policies that the auditor considers inappropriate.

Examples of misstatements arising from fraud are provided in ISA (UK and Ireland) 240.[6]

Accumulation of Identified Misstatements (Ref: Para. 5)

The auditor may designate an amount below which misstatements would be clearly trivial and would not need to be accumulated because the auditor expects that the accumulation of such amounts clearly would not have a material effect on the financial statements. "Clearly trivial" is not another expression for "not material." Matters that are clearly trivial will be of a wholly different (smaller) order of magnitude than materiality determined in accordance with ISA (UK and Ireland) 320, and will be matters that are clearly inconsequential, whether taken individually or in aggregate and whether judged by any criteria of size, nature or circumstances. When there is any uncertainty about whether one or more items are clearly trivial, the matter is considered not to be clearly trivial.

A2

To assist the auditor in evaluating the effect of misstatements accumulated during the audit and in communicating misstatements to management and those charged with governance, it may be useful to distinguish between factual misstatements, judgmental misstatements and projected misstatements.

A3

• Factual misstatements are misstatements about which there is no doubt.
• Judgmental misstatements are differences arising from the judgments of management concerning accounting estimates that the auditor considers unreasonable, or the selection or application of accounting policies that the auditor considers inappropriate.
• Projected misstatements are the auditor's best estimate of misstatements in populations, involving the projection of misstatements identified in audit samples to the entire populations from which the samples were drawn. Guidance on the determination of projected misstatements and evaluation of the results is set out in ISA (UK and Ireland) 530.[7]

Consideration of Identified Misstatements as the Audit Progresses (Ref: Para. 6-7)

A misstatement may not be an isolated occurrence. Evidence that other misstatements may exist include, for example, where the auditor identifies that a misstatement arose from a breakdown in internal control or from inappropriate assumptions or valuation methods that have been widely applied by the entity.

A4

If the aggregate of misstatements accumulated during the audit approaches materiality determined in accordance with ISA (UK and Ireland) 320, there may be a greater than acceptably low level of risk that possible undetected misstatements, when taken with the aggregate of misstatements accumulated during the audit, could

A5

---

[6] *ISA (UK and Ireland) 240, "The Auditor's Responsibilities Relating to Fraud in an Audit of Financial Statements," paragraphs A1-A6.*

[7] *ISA (UK and Ireland) 530, "Audit Sampling," paragraphs 14-15.*

exceed materiality. Undetected misstatements could exist because of the presence of sampling risk and non-sampling risk.[8]

A6   The auditor may request management to examine a class of transactions, account balance or disclosure in order for management to understand the cause of a misstatement identified by the auditor, perform procedures to determine the amount of the actual misstatement in the class of transactions, account balance or disclosure, and to make appropriate adjustments to the financial statements. Such a request may be made, for example, based on the auditor's projection of misstatements identified in an audit sample to the entire population from which it was drawn.

Communication and Correction of Misstatements (Ref: Para. 8-9)

A7   Timely communication of misstatements to the appropriate level of management is important as it enables management to evaluate whether the items are misstatements, inform the auditor if it disagrees, and take action as necessary. Ordinarily, the appropriate level of management is the one that has responsibility and authority to evaluate the misstatements and to take the necessary action.

A8   Law or regulation may restrict the auditor's communication of certain misstatements to management, or others, within the entity. For example, laws or regulations may specifically prohibit a communication, or other action, that might prejudice an investigation by an appropriate authority into an actual, or suspected, illegal act. In some circumstances, potential conflicts between the auditor's obligations of confidentiality and obligations to communicate may be complex. In such cases, the auditor may consider seeking legal advice.

A9   The correction by management of all misstatements, including those communicated by the auditor, enables management to maintain accurate accounting books and records and reduces the risks of material misstatement of future financial statements because of the cumulative effect of immaterial uncorrected misstatements related to prior periods.

A10   ISA (UK and Ireland) 700 requires the auditor to evaluate whether the financial statements are prepared and presented, in all material respects, in accordance with the requirements of the applicable financial reporting framework. This evaluation includes consideration of the qualitative aspects of the entity's accounting practices, including indicators of possible bias in management's judgments,[9] which may be affected by the auditor's understanding of management's reasons for not making the corrections.

Evaluating the Effect of Uncorrected Misstatements (Ref: Para. 10-11)

A11   The auditor's determination of materiality in accordance with ISA (UK and Ireland) 320 is often based on estimates of the entity's financial results, because the actual financial results may not yet be known. Therefore, prior to the auditor's evaluation of the effect of uncorrected misstatements, it may be necessary to revise materiality

---

[8] *ISA (UK and Ireland) 530, paragraph 5(c)-(d).*

[9] *ISA 700, paragraph 12.*

The APB has not promulgated ISA 700 as issued by the IAASB for application in the UK and Ireland. In the UK and Ireland the applicable auditing standard is ISA (UK and Ireland) 700, "The Auditor's Report on Financial Statements." Paragraph 8 of ISA (UK and Ireland) 700 includes requirements equivalent to those in paragraph 12 of ISA 700.

determined in accordance with ISA (UK and Ireland) 320 based on the actual financial results.

ISA (UK and Ireland) 320 explains that, as the audit progresses, materiality for the financial statements as a whole (and, if applicable, the materiality level or levels for particular classes of transactions, account balances or disclosures) is revised in the event of the auditor becoming aware of information during the audit that would have caused the auditor to have determined a different amount (or amounts) initially.[10] Thus, any significant revision is likely to have been made before the auditor evaluates the effect of uncorrected misstatements. However, if the auditor's reassessment of materiality determined in accordance with ISA (UK and Ireland) 320 (see paragraph 10 of this ISA (UK and Ireland)) gives rise to a lower amount (or amounts), then performance materiality and the appropriateness of the nature, timing and extent of the further audit procedures are reconsidered so as to obtain sufficient appropriate audit evidence on which to base the audit opinion.   **A12**

Each individual misstatement is considered to evaluate its effect on the relevant classes of transactions, account balances or disclosures, including whether the materiality level for that particular class of transactions, account balance or disclosure, if any, has been exceeded.   **A13**

If an individual misstatement is judged to be material, it is unlikely that it can be offset by other misstatements. For example, if revenue has been materially overstated, the financial statements as a whole will be materially misstated, even if the effect of the misstatement on earnings is completely offset by an equivalent overstatement of expenses. It may be appropriate to offset misstatements within the same account balance or class of transactions; however, the risk that further undetected misstatements may exist is considered before concluding that offsetting even immaterial misstatements is appropriate.[11]   **A14**

Determining whether a classification misstatement is material involves the evaluation of qualitative considerations, such as the effect of the classification misstatement on debt or other contractual covenants, the effect on individual line items or sub-totals, or the effect on key ratios. There may be circumstances where the auditor concludes that a classification misstatement is not material in the context of the financial statements as a whole, even though it may exceed the materiality level or levels applied in evaluating other misstatements. For example, a misclassification between balance sheet line items may not be considered material in the context of the financial statements as a whole when the amount of the misclassification is small in relation to the size of the related balance sheet line items and the misclassification does not affect the income statement or any key ratios.   **A15**

The circumstances related to some misstatements may cause the auditor to evaluate them as material, individually or when considered together with other misstatements accumulated during the audit, even if they are lower than materiality for the financial statements as a whole. Circumstances that may affect the evaluation include the extent to which the misstatement: **A16**

- Affects compliance with regulatory requirements;
- Affects compliance with debt covenants or other contractual requirements;

[10] *ISA (UK and Ireland) 320, paragraph 12.*

[11] *The identification of a number of immaterial misstatements within the same account balance or class of transactions may require the auditor to reassess the risk of material misstatement for that account balance or class of transactions.*

- Relates to the incorrect selection or application of an accounting policy that has an immaterial effect on the current period's financial statements but is likely to have a material effect on future periods' financial statements;
- Masks a change in earnings or other trends, especially in the context of general economic and industry conditions;
- Affects ratios used to evaluate the entity's financial position, results of operations or cash flows;
- Affects segment information presented in the financial statements (for example, the significance of the matter to a segment or other portion of the entity's business that has been identified as playing a significant role in the entity's operations or profitability);
- Has the effect of increasing management compensation, for example, by ensuring that the requirements for the award of bonuses or other incentives are satisfied;
- Is significant having regard to the auditor's understanding of known previous communications to users, for example, in relation to forecast earnings;
- Relates to items involving particular parties (for example, whether external parties to the transaction are related to members of the entity's management);
- Is an omission of information not specifically required by the applicable financial reporting framework but which, in the judgment of the auditor, is important to the users' understanding of the financial position, financial performance or cash flows of the entity; or
- Affects other information that will be communicated in documents containing the audited financial statements (for example, information to be included in a "Management Discussion and Analysis" or an "Operating and Financial Review") that may reasonably be expected to influence the economic decisions of the users of the financial statements. ISA (UK and Ireland) 720[12] deals with the auditor's consideration of other information, on which the auditor has no obligation to report, in documents containing audited financial statements.

These circumstances are only examples; not all are likely to be present in all audits nor is the list necessarily complete. The existence of any circumstances such as these does not necessarily lead to a conclusion that the misstatement is material.

A17   ISA (UK and Ireland) 240[13] explains how the implications of a misstatement that is, or may be, the result of fraud ought to be considered in relation to other aspects of the audit, even if the size of the misstatement is not material in relation to the financial statements.

A18   The cumulative effect of immaterial uncorrected misstatements related to prior periods may have a material effect on the current period's financial statements. There are different acceptable approaches to the auditor's evaluation of such uncorrected misstatements on the current period's financial statements. Using the same evaluation approach provides consistency from period to period.

Considerations Specific to Public Sector Entities

A19   In the case of an audit of a public sector entity, the evaluation whether a misstatement is material may also be affected by the auditor's responsibilities established by

---

[12] *ISA (UK and Ireland) 720, "The Auditor's Responsibilities Relating to Other Information in Documents Containing Audited Financial Statements."*

[13] *ISA (UK and Ireland) 240, paragraph 35.*

law, regulation or other authority to report specific matters, including, for example, fraud.

Furthermore, issues such as public interest, accountability, probity and ensuring effective legislative oversight, in particular, may affect the assessment whether an item is material by virtue of its nature. This is particularly so for items that relate to compliance with law, regulation or other authority.

A20

Communication with Those Charged with Governance (Ref: Para. 12)

If uncorrected misstatements have been communicated with person(s) with management responsibilities, and those person(s) also have governance responsibilities, they need not be communicated again with those same person(s) in their governance role. The auditor nonetheless has to be satisfied that communication with person(s) with management responsibilities adequately informs all of those with whom the auditor would otherwise communicate in their governance capacity.[14]

A21

Where there is a large number of individual immaterial uncorrected misstatements, the auditor may communicate the number and overall monetary effect of the uncorrected misstatements, rather than the details of each individual uncorrected misstatement.

A22

ISA (UK and Ireland) 260 requires the auditor to communicate with those charged with governance the written representations the auditor is requesting (see paragraph 14 of this ISA (UK and Ireland)).[15] The auditor may discuss with those charged with governance the reasons for, and the implications of, a failure to correct misstatements, having regard to the size and nature of the misstatement judged in the surrounding circumstances, and possible implications in relation to future financial statements.

A23

If management have corrected material misstatements, communicating those corrections of which the auditor is aware to those charged with governance may assist them to fulfill their governance responsibilities, including reviewing the effectiveness of the system of internal control.

A23-1

Written Representation (Ref: Para. 14)

Because the preparation of the financial statements requires management and, where appropriate, those charged with governance to adjust the financial statements to correct material misstatements, the auditor is required to request them to provide a written representation about uncorrected misstatements. In some circumstances, management and, where appropriate, those charged with governance may not believe that certain uncorrected misstatements are misstatements. For that reason, they may want to add to their written representation words such as: "We do not agree that items ... and ... constitute misstatements because [description of reasons]." Obtaining this representation does not, however, relieve the auditor of the need to form a conclusion on the effect of uncorrected misstatements.

A24

[14] *ISA (UK and Ireland) 260, paragraph 13.*

[15] *ISA (UK and Ireland) 260, paragraph 16(c)(ii).*

A24-1   Requesting those charged with governance to provide written representations that set out their reasons for not correcting misstatements brought to their attention by the auditor may help focus the attention of those charged with governance on those misstatements and the circumstances giving rise to them.

Documentation (Ref: Para. 15)

A25   The auditor's documentation of uncorrected misstatements may take into account:

(a)   The consideration of the aggregate effect of uncorrected misstatements;

(b)   The evaluation of whether the materiality level or levels for particular classes of transactions, account balances or disclosures, if any, have been exceeded; and

(c)   The evaluation of the effect of uncorrected misstatements on key ratios or trends, and compliance with legal, regulatory and contractual requirements (for example, debt covenants).

International Standard on Auditing (UK and Ireland) 500

Audit evidence

(Effective for audits of financial statements for periods ending on or after 15 December 2010)[1a]

Contents

International Standard on Auditing (UK and Ireland) (ISA (UK and Ireland)) 500, "Audit Evidence" should be read in conjunction with ISA (UK and Ireland) 200, "Overall Objectives of the Independent Auditor and the Conduct of an Audit in Accordance with International Standards on Auditing (UK and Ireland)."

[1a] *Conforming amendments to this standard as a result of ISA (UK and Ireland) 610 (Revised June 2013),* Using the Work of Internal Auditors, *are included that are effective for audits of financial statements for periods ending on or after 15 June 2014. Details of the amendments are given in the Annexure to ISA (UK and Ireland) 610 (Revised June 2013).*

Introduction

Scope of this ISA (UK and Ireland)

1   This International Standard on Auditing (UK and Ireland) (ISA (UK and Ireland)) explains what constitutes audit evidence in an audit of financial statements, and deals with the auditor's responsibility to design and perform audit procedures to obtain sufficient appropriate audit evidence to be able to draw reasonable conclusions on which to base the auditor's opinion.

2   This ISA (UK and Ireland) is applicable to all the audit evidence obtained during the course of the audit. Other ISAs (UK and Ireland) deal with specific aspects of the audit (for example, ISA (UK and Ireland) 315[1]), the audit evidence to be obtained in relation to a particular topic (for example, ISA (UK and Ireland) 570[2]), specific procedures to obtain audit evidence (for example, ISA (UK and Ireland) 520[3]), and the evaluation of whether sufficient appropriate audit evidence has been obtained (ISA (UK and Ireland) 200[4] and ISA (UK and Ireland) 330[5]).

Effective Date

3   This ISA (UK and Ireland) is effective for audits of financial statements for periods ending on or after 15 December 2010.[1a]

Objective

4   The objective of the auditor is to design and perform audit procedures in such a way as to enable the auditor to obtain sufficient appropriate audit evidence to be able to draw reasonable conclusions on which to base the auditor's opinion.

Definitions

5   For purposes of the ISAs (UK and Ireland), the following terms have the meanings attributed below:

(a)   Accounting records – The records of initial accounting entries and supporting records, such as checks and records of electronic fund transfers; invoices; contracts; the general and subsidiary ledgers, journal entries and other adjustments to the financial statements that are not reflected in journal entries; and records such as work sheets and spreadsheets supporting cost allocations, computations, reconciliations and disclosures.

(b)   Appropriateness (of audit evidence) – The measure of the quality of audit evidence; that is, its relevance and its reliability in providing support for the conclusions on which the auditor's opinion is based.

---

[1] *ISA (UK and Ireland) 315, "Identifying and Assessing the Risks of Material Misstatement through Understanding the Entity and Its Environment."*

[2] *ISA (UK and Ireland) 570, "Going Concern."*

[3] *ISA (UK and Ireland) 520, "Analytical Procedures."*

[4] *ISA (UK and Ireland) 200, "Overall Objectives of the Independent Auditor and the Conduct of an Audit in Accordance with International Standards on Auditing (UK and Ireland)."*

[5] *ISA (UK and Ireland) 330, "The Auditor's Responses to Assessed Risks."*

(c) Audit evidence – Information used by the auditor in arriving at the conclusions on which the auditor's opinion is based. Audit evidence includes both information contained in the accounting records underlying the financial statements and other information.

(d) Management's expert – An individual or organization possessing expertise in a field other than accounting or auditing, whose work in that field is used by the entity to assist the entity in preparing the financial statements.

(e) Sufficiency (of audit evidence) – The measure of the quantity of audit evidence. The quantity of the audit evidence needed is affected by the auditor's assessment of the risks of material misstatement and also by the quality of such audit evidence.

Requirements

Sufficient Appropriate Audit Evidence

The auditor shall design and perform audit procedures that are appropriate in the circumstances for the purpose of obtaining sufficient appropriate audit evidence. (Ref: Para. A1-A25) **6**

Information to Be Used as Audit Evidence

When designing and performing audit procedures, the auditor shall consider the relevance and reliability of the information to be used as audit evidence. (Ref: Para. A26-A33) **7**

If information to be used as audit evidence has been prepared using the work of a management's expert, the auditor shall, to the extent necessary, having regard to the significance of that expert's work for the auditor's purposes,: (Ref: Para. A34-A36) **8**

(a) Evaluate the competence, capabilities and objectivity of that expert; (Ref: Para. A37-A43)

(b) Obtain an understanding of the work of that expert; and (Ref: Para. A44-A47)

(c) Evaluate the appropriateness of that expert's work as audit evidence for the relevant assertion. (Ref: Para. A48)

When using information produced by the entity, the auditor shall evaluate whether the information is sufficiently reliable for the auditor's purposes, including as necessary in the circumstances: **9**

(a) Obtaining audit evidence about the accuracy and completeness of the information; and (Ref: Para. A49-A50)

(b) Evaluating whether the information is sufficiently precise and detailed for the auditor's purposes. (Ref: Para. A51)

Selecting Items for Testing to Obtain Audit Evidence

When designing tests of controls and tests of details, the auditor shall determine means of selecting items for testing that are effective in meeting the purpose of the audit procedure. (Ref: Para. A52-A56) **10**

Inconsistency in, or Doubts over Reliability of, Audit Evidence

11   If:

(a)   audit evidence obtained from one source is inconsistent with that obtained from another; or

(b)   the auditor has doubts over the reliability of information to be used as audit evidence,

the auditor shall determine what modifications or additions to audit procedures are necessary to resolve the matter, and shall consider the effect of the matter, if any, on other aspects of the audit. (Ref: Para. A57)

***

Application and Other Explanatory Material

Sufficient Appropriate Audit Evidence (Ref: Para. 6)

A1   Audit evidence is necessary to support the auditor's opinion and report. It is cumulative in nature and is primarily obtained from audit procedures performed during the course of the audit. It may, however, also include information obtained from other sources such as previous audits (provided the auditor has determined whether changes have occurred since the previous audit that may affect its relevance to the current audit[6]) or a firm's quality control procedures for client acceptance and continuance. In addition to other sources inside and outside the entity, the entity's accounting records are an important source of audit evidence. Also, information that may be used as audit evidence may have been prepared using the work of a management's expert. Audit evidence comprises both information that supports and corroborates management's assertions, and any information that contradicts such assertions. In addition, in some cases the absence of information (for example, management's refusal to provide a requested representation) is used by the auditor, and therefore, also constitutes audit evidence.

A2   Most of the auditor's work in forming the auditor's opinion consists of obtaining and evaluating audit evidence. Audit procedures to obtain audit evidence can include inspection, observation, confirmation, recalculation, reperformance and analytical procedures, often in some combination, in addition to inquiry. Although inquiry may provide important audit evidence, and may even produce evidence of a misstatement, inquiry alone ordinarily does not provide sufficient audit evidence of the absence of a material misstatement at the assertion level, nor of the operating effectiveness of controls.

A3   As explained in ISA (UK and Ireland) 200,[7] reasonable assurance is obtained when the auditor has obtained sufficient appropriate audit evidence to reduce audit risk (that is, the risk that the auditor expresses an inappropriate opinion when the financial statements are materially misstated) to an acceptably low level.

A4   The sufficiency and appropriateness of audit evidence are interrelated. Sufficiency is the measure of the quantity of audit evidence. The quantity of audit evidence needed is affected by the auditor's assessment of the risks of misstatement (the higher the

---

[6] *ISA (UK and Ireland) 315, paragraph 9.*

[7] *ISA (UK and Ireland) 200, paragraph 5.*

assessed risks, the more audit evidence is likely to be required) and also by the quality of such audit evidence (the higher the quality, the less may be required). Obtaining more audit evidence, however, may not compensate for its poor quality.

Appropriateness is the measure of the quality of audit evidence; that is, its relevance and its reliability in providing support for the conclusions on which the auditor's opinion is based. The reliability of evidence is influenced by its source and by its nature, and is dependent on the individual circumstances under which it is obtained.   **A5**

ISA (UK and Ireland) 330 requires the auditor to conclude whether sufficient appropriate audit evidence has been obtained.[8] Whether sufficient appropriate audit evidence has been obtained to reduce audit risk to an acceptably low level, and thereby enable the auditor to draw reasonable conclusions on which to base the auditor's opinion, is a matter of professional judgment. ISA (UK and Ireland) 200 contains discussion of such matters as the nature of audit procedures, the timeliness of financial reporting, and the balance between benefit and cost, which are relevant factors when the auditor exercises professional judgment regarding whether sufficient appropriate audit evidence has been obtained.   **A6**

Sources of Audit Evidence

Some audit evidence is obtained by performing audit procedures to test the accounting records, for example, through analysis and review, reperforming procedures followed in the financial reporting process, and reconciling related types and applications of the same information. Through the performance of such audit procedures, the auditor may determine that the accounting records are internally consistent and agree to the financial statements.   **A7**

More assurance is ordinarily obtained from consistent audit evidence obtained from different sources or of a different nature than from items of audit evidence considered individually. For example, corroborating information obtained from a source independent of the entity may increase the assurance the auditor obtains from audit evidence that is generated internally, such as evidence existing within the accounting records, minutes of meetings, or a management representation.   **A8**

Information from sources independent of the entity that the auditor may use as audit evidence may include confirmations from third parties, analysts' reports, and comparable data about competitors (benchmarking data).   **A9**

Audit Procedures for Obtaining Audit Evidence

As required by, and explained further in, ISA (UK and Ireland) 315 and ISA (UK and Ireland) 330, audit evidence to draw reasonable conclusions on which to base the auditor's opinion is obtained by performing: **A10**

(a) Risk assessment procedures; and
(b) Further audit procedures, which comprise:
    (i) Tests of controls, when required by the ISAs (UK and Ireland) or when the auditor has chosen to do so; and
    (ii) Substantive procedures, including tests of details and substantive analytical procedures.

---

[8] *ISA (UK and Ireland) 330, paragraph 26.*

A11   The audit procedures described in paragraphs A14-A25 below may be used as risk assessment procedures, tests of controls or substantive procedures, depending on the context in which they are applied by the auditor. As explained in ISA (UK and Ireland) 330, audit evidence obtained from previous audits may, in certain circumstances, provide appropriate audit evidence where the auditor performs audit procedures to establish its continuing relevance.[9]

A12   The nature and timing of the audit procedures to be used may be affected by the fact that some of the accounting data and other information may be available only in electronic form or only at certain points or periods in time. For example, source documents, such as purchase orders and invoices, may exist only in electronic form when an entity uses electronic commerce, or may be discarded after scanning when an entity uses image processing systems to facilitate storage and reference.

A13   Certain electronic information may not be retrievable after a specified period of time, for example, if files are changed and if backup files do not exist. Accordingly, the auditor may find it necessary as a result of an entity's data retention policies to request retention of some information for the auditor's review or to perform audit procedures at a time when the information is available.

Inspection

A14   Inspection involves examining records or documents, whether internal or external, in paper form, electronic form, or other media, or a physical examination of an asset. Inspection of records and documents provides audit evidence of varying degrees of reliability, depending on their nature and source and, in the case of internal records and documents, on the effectiveness of the controls over their production. An example of inspection used as a test of controls is inspection of records for evidence of authorization.

A15   Some documents represent direct audit evidence of the existence of an asset, for example, a document constituting a financial instrument such as a stock or bond. Inspection of such documents may not necessarily provide audit evidence about ownership or value. In addition, inspecting an executed contract may provide audit evidence relevant to the entity's application of accounting policies, such as revenue recognition.

A16   Inspection of tangible assets may provide reliable audit evidence with respect to their existence, but not necessarily about the entity's rights and obligations or the valuation of the assets. Inspection of individual inventory items may accompany the observation of inventory counting.

Observation

A17   Observation consists of looking at a process or procedure being performed by others, for example, the auditor's observation of inventory counting by the entity's personnel, or of the performance of control activities. Observation provides audit evidence about the performance of a process or procedure, but is limited to the point in time at which the observation takes place, and by the fact that the act of being observed may affect how the process or procedure is performed. See ISA (UK and Ireland) 501 for further guidance on observation of the counting of inventory.[10]

[9] *ISA (UK and Ireland) 330, paragraph A35.*

[10] *ISA (UK and Ireland) 501, "Audit Evidence—Specific Considerations for Selected Items."*

External Confirmation

An external confirmation represents audit evidence obtained by the auditor as a **A18** direct written response to the auditor from a third party (the confirming party), in paper form, or by electronic or other medium. External confirmation procedures frequently are relevant when addressing assertions associated with certain account balances and their elements. However, external confirmations need not be restricted to account balances only. For example, the auditor may request confirmation of the terms of agreements or transactions an entity has with third parties; the confirmation request may be designed to ask if any modifications have been made to the agreement and, if so, what the relevant details are. External confirmation procedures also are used to obtain audit evidence about the absence of certain conditions, for example, the absence of a "side agreement" that may influence revenue recognition. See ISA (UK and Ireland) 505 for further guidance.[11]

Recalculation

Recalculation consists of checking the mathematical accuracy of documents or **A19** records. Recalculation may be performed manually or electronically.

Reperformance

Reperformance involves the auditor's independent execution of procedures or con- **A20** trols that were originally performed as part of the entity's internal control.

Analytical Procedures

Analytical procedures consist of evaluations of financial information through ana- **A21** lysis of plausible relationships among both financial and non-financial data. Analytical procedures also encompass such investigation as is necessary of identified fluctuations or relationships that are inconsistent with other relevant information or that differ from expected values by a significant amount. See ISA (UK and Ireland) 520 for further guidance.

Inquiry

Inquiry consists of seeking information of knowledgeable persons, both financial and **A22** non-financial, within the entity or outside the entity. Inquiry is used extensively throughout the audit in addition to other audit procedures. Inquiries may range from formal written inquiries to informal oral inquiries. Evaluating responses to inquiries is an integral part of the inquiry process.

Responses to inquiries may provide the auditor with information not previously **A23** possessed or with corroborative audit evidence. Alternatively, responses might provide information that differs significantly from other information that the auditor has obtained, for example, information regarding the possibility of management override of controls. In some cases, responses to inquiries provide a basis for the auditor to modify or perform additional audit procedures.

Although corroboration of evidence obtained through inquiry is often of particular **A24** importance, in the case of inquiries about management intent, the information available to support management's intent may be limited. In these cases,

---

[11] *ISA (UK and Ireland) 505, "External Confirmations."*

understanding management's past history of carrying out its stated intentions, management's stated reasons for choosing a particular course of action, and management's ability to pursue a specific course of action may provide relevant information to corroborate the evidence obtained through inquiry.

A25   In respect of some matters, the auditor may consider it necessary to obtain written representations from management and, where appropriate, those charged with governance to confirm responses to oral inquiries. See ISA (UK and Ireland) 580 for further guidance.[12]

Information to Be Used as Audit Evidence

Relevance and Reliability (Ref: Para. 7)

A26   As noted in paragraph A1, while audit evidence is primarily obtained from audit procedures performed during the course of the audit, it may also include information obtained from other sources such as, for example, previous audits, in certain circumstances, and a firm's quality control procedures for client acceptance and continuance. The quality of all audit evidence is affected by the relevance and reliability of the information upon which it is based.

Relevance

A27   Relevance deals with the logical connection with, or bearing upon, the purpose of the audit procedure and, where appropriate, the assertion under consideration. The relevance of information to be used as audit evidence may be affected by the direction of testing. For example, if the purpose of an audit procedure is to test for overstatement in the existence or valuation of accounts payable, testing the recorded accounts payable may be a relevant audit procedure. On the other hand, when testing for understatement in the existence or valuation of accounts payable, testing the recorded accounts payable would not be relevant, but testing such information as subsequent disbursements, unpaid invoices, suppliers' statements, and unmatched receiving reports may be relevant.

A28   A given set of audit procedures may provide audit evidence that is relevant to certain assertions, but not others. For example, inspection of documents related to the collection of receivables after the period end may provide audit evidence regarding existence and valuation, but not necessarily cutoff. Similarly, obtaining audit evidence regarding a particular assertion, for example, the existence of inventory, is not a substitute for obtaining audit evidence regarding another assertion, for example, the valuation of that inventory. On the other hand, audit evidence from different sources or of a different nature may often be relevant to the same assertion.

A29   Tests of controls are designed to evaluate the operating effectiveness of controls in preventing, or detecting and correcting, material misstatements at the assertion level. Designing tests of controls to obtain relevant audit evidence includes identifying conditions (characteristics or attributes) that indicate performance of a control, and deviation conditions which indicate departures from adequate performance. The presence or absence of those conditions can then be tested by the auditor.

A30   Substantive procedures are designed to detect material misstatements at the assertion level. They comprise tests of details and substantive analytical procedures. Designing

---

[12] *ISA (UK and Ireland) 580, "Written Representations."*

substantive procedures includes identifying conditions relevant to the purpose of the test that constitute a misstatement in the relevant assertion.

Reliability

The reliability of information to be used as audit evidence, and therefore of the audit evidence itself, is influenced by its source and its nature, and the circumstances under which it is obtained, including the controls over its preparation and maintenance where relevant. Therefore, generalizations about the reliability of various kinds of audit evidence are subject to important exceptions. Even when information to be used as audit evidence is obtained from sources external to the entity, circumstances may exist that could affect its reliability. For example, information obtained from an independent external source may not be reliable if the source is not knowledgeable, or a management's expert may lack objectivity. While recognizing that exceptions may exist, the following generalizations about the reliability of audit evidence may be useful:

A31

- The reliability of audit evidence is increased when it is obtained from independent sources outside the entity.
- The reliability of audit evidence that is generated internally is increased when the related controls, including those over its preparation and maintenance, imposed by the entity are effective.
- Audit evidence obtained directly by the auditor (for example, observation of the application of a control) is more reliable than audit evidence obtained indirectly or by inference (for example, inquiry about the application of a control).
- Audit evidence in documentary form, whether paper, electronic, or other medium, is more reliable than evidence obtained orally (for example, a contemporaneously written record of a meeting is more reliable than a subsequent oral representation of the matters discussed).
- Audit evidence provided by original documents is more reliable than audit evidence provided by photocopies or facsimiles, or documents that have been filmed, digitized or otherwise transformed into electronic form, the reliability of which may depend on the controls over their preparation and maintenance.

ISA (UK and Ireland) 520 provides further guidance regarding the reliability of data used for purposes of designing analytical procedures as substantive procedures.[13]

A32

ISA (UK and Ireland) 240 deals with circumstances where the auditor has reason to believe that a document may not be authentic, or may have been modified without that modification having been disclosed to the auditor.[14]

A33

Reliability of Information Produced by a Management's Expert (Ref: Para. 8)

The preparation of an entity's financial statements may require expertise in a field other than accounting or auditing, such as actuarial calculations, valuations, or engineering data. The entity may employ or engage experts in these fields to obtain the needed expertise to prepare the financial statements. Failure to do so when such expertise is necessary increases the risks of material misstatement.

A34

---

[13] *ISA (UK and Ireland) 520, paragraph 5(a).*

[14] *ISA (UK and Ireland) 240, "The Auditor's Responsibilities Relating to Fraud in an Audit of Financial Statements," paragraph 13.*

A35 When information to be used as audit evidence has been prepared using the work of a management's expert, the requirement in paragraph 8 of this ISA (UK and Ireland) applies. For example, an individual or organization may possess expertise in the application of models to estimate the fair value of securities for which there is no observable market. If the individual or organization applies that expertise in making an estimate which the entity uses in preparing its financial statements, the individual or organization is a management's expert and paragraph 8 applies. If, on the other hand, that individual or organization merely provides price data regarding private transactions not otherwise available to the entity which the entity uses in its own estimation methods, such information, if used as audit evidence, is subject to paragraph 7 of this ISA (UK and Ireland), but is not the use of a management's expert by the entity.

A36 The nature, timing and extent of audit procedures in relation to the requirement in paragraph 8 of this ISA (UK and Ireland), may be affected by such matters as:

- The nature and complexity of the matter to which the management's expert relates.
- The risks of material misstatement in the matter.
- The availability of alternative sources of audit evidence.
- The nature, scope and objectives of the management's expert's work.
- Whether the management's expert is employed by the entity, or is a party engaged by it to provide relevant services.
- The extent to which management can exercise control or influence over the work of the management's expert.
- Whether the management's expert is subject to technical performance standards or other professional or industry requirements.
- The nature and extent of any controls within the entity over the management's expert's work.
- The auditor's knowledge and experience of the management's expert's field of expertise.
- The auditor's previous experience of the work of that expert.

The Competence, Capabilities and Objectivity of a Management's Expert (Ref: Para. 8(a))

A37 Competence relates to the nature and level of expertise of the management's expert. Capability relates the ability of the management's expert to exercise that competence in the circumstances. Factors that influence capability may include, for example, geographic location, and the availability of time and resources. Objectivity relates to the possible effects that bias, conflict of interest or the influence of others may have on the professional or business judgment of the management's expert. The competence, capabilities and objectivity of a management's expert, and any controls within the entity over that expert's work, are important factors in relation to the reliability of any information produced by a management's expert.

A38 Information regarding the competence, capabilities and objectivity of a management's expert may come from a variety of sources, such as:

- Personal experience with previous work of that expert.
- Discussions with that expert.
- Discussions with others who are familiar with that expert's work.
- Knowledge of that expert's qualifications, membership of a professional body or industry association, license to practice, or other forms of external recognition.
- Published papers or books written by that expert.

- An auditor's expert, if any, who assists the auditor in obtaining sufficient appropriate audit evidence with respect to information produced by the management's expert.

Matters relevant to evaluating the competence, capabilities and objectivity of a management's expert include whether that expert's work is subject to technical performance standards or other professional or industry requirements, for example, ethical standards and other membership requirements of a professional body or industry association, accreditation standards of a licensing body, or requirements imposed by law or regulation.　**A39**

Other matters that may be relevant include:　**A40**

- The relevance of the management's expert's competence to the matter for which that expert's work will be used, including any areas of specialty within that expert's field. For example, a particular actuary may specialize in property and casualty insurance, but have limited expertise regarding pension calculations.
- The management's expert's competence with respect to relevant accounting requirements, for example, knowledge of assumptions and methods, including models where applicable, that are consistent with the applicable financial reporting framework.
- Whether unexpected events, changes in conditions, or the audit evidence obtained from the results of audit procedures indicate that it may be necessary to reconsider the initial evaluation of the competence, capabilities and objectivity of the management's expert as the audit progresses.

A broad range of circumstances may threaten objectivity, for example, self-interest threats, advocacy threats, familiarity threats, self-review threats and intimidation threats. Safeguards may reduce such threats, and may be created either by external structures (for example, the management's expert's profession, legislation or regulation), or by the management's expert's work environment (for example, quality control policies and procedures).　**A41**

Although safeguards cannot eliminate all threats to a management's expert's objectivity, threats such as intimidation threats may be of less significance to an expert engaged by the entity than to an expert employed by the entity, and the effectiveness of safeguards such as quality control policies and procedures may be greater. Because the threat to objectivity created by being an employee of the entity will always be present, an expert employed by the entity cannot ordinarily be regarded as being more likely to be objective than other employees of the entity.　**A42**

When evaluating the objectivity of an expert engaged by the entity, it may be relevant to discuss with management and that expert any interests and relationships that may create threats to the expert's objectivity, and any applicable safeguards, including any professional requirements that apply to the expert; and to evaluate whether the safeguards are adequate. Interests and relationships creating threats may include:　**A43**

- Financial interests.
- Business and personal relationships.
- Provision of other services.

Obtaining an Understanding of the Work of the Management's Expert (Ref: Para. 8(b))

An understanding of the work of the management's expert includes an understanding of the relevant field of expertise. An understanding of the relevant field of　**A44** expertise may be obtained in conjunction with the auditor's determination of whether the auditor has the expertise to evaluate the work of the management's expert, or whether the auditor needs an auditor's expert for this purpose.[15]

A45   Aspects of the management's expert's field relevant to the auditor's understanding may include:

- Whether that expert's field has areas of specialty within it that are relevant to the audit.
- Whether any professional or other standards, and regulatory or legal requirements apply.
- What assumptions and methods are used by the management's expert, and whether they are generally accepted within that expert's field and appropriate for financial reporting purposes.
- The nature of internal and external data or information the auditor's expert uses.

A46   In the case of a management's expert engaged by the entity, there will ordinarily be an engagement letter or other written form of agreement between the entity and that expert. Evaluating that agreement when obtaining an understanding of the work of the management's expert may assist the auditor in determining the appropriateness of the following for the auditor's purposes:

- The nature, scope and objectives of that expert's work;
- The respective roles and responsibilities of management and that expert; and
- The nature, timing and extent of communication between management and that expert, including the form of any report to be provided by that expert.

A47   In the case of a management's expert employed by the entity, it is less likely there will be a written agreement of this kind. Inquiry of the expert and other members of management may be the most appropriate way for the auditor to obtain the necessary understanding.

Evaluating the Appropriateness of the Management's Expert's Work (Ref: Para. 8(c))

A48   Considerations when evaluating the appropriateness of the management's expert's work as audit evidence for the relevant assertion may include:

- The relevance and reasonableness of that expert's findings or conclusions, their consistency with other audit evidence, and whether they have been appropriately reflected in the financial statements;
- If that expert's work involves use of significant assumptions and methods, the relevance and reasonableness of those assumptions and methods; and
- If that expert's work involves significant use of source data the relevance, completeness, and accuracy of that source data.

Information Produced by the Entity and Used for the Auditor's Purposes (Ref: Para. 9(a)-(b))

A49   In order for the auditor to obtain reliable audit evidence, information produced by the entity that is used for performing audit procedures needs to be sufficiently complete and accurate. For example, the effectiveness of auditing revenue by applying standard prices to records of sales volume is affected by the accuracy of the

---

[15] *ISA (UK and Ireland) 620, "Using the Work of an Auditor's Expert," paragraph 7.*

price information and the completeness and accuracy of the sales volume data. Similarly, if the auditor intends to test a population (for example, payments) for a certain characteristic (for example, authorization), the results of the test will be less reliable if the population from which items are selected for testing is not complete.

Obtaining audit evidence about the accuracy and completeness of such information may be performed concurrently with the actual audit procedure applied to the information when obtaining such audit evidence is an integral part of the audit procedure itself. In other situations, the auditor may have obtained audit evidence of the accuracy and completeness of such information by testing controls over the preparation and maintenance of the information. In some situations, however, the auditor may determine that additional audit procedures are needed.   **A50**

In some cases, the auditor may intend to use information produced by the entity for other audit purposes. For example, the auditor may intend to make use of the entity's performance measures for the purpose of analytical procedures, or to make use of the entity's information produced for monitoring activities, such as reports of the internal audit function. In such cases, the appropriateness of the audit evidence obtained is affected by whether the information is sufficiently precise or detailed for the auditor's purposes. For example, performance measures used by management may not be precise enough to detect material misstatements.   **A51**

Selecting Items for Testing to Obtain Audit Evidence (Ref: Para. 10)

An effective test provides appropriate audit evidence to an extent that, taken with other audit evidence obtained or to be obtained, will be sufficient for the auditor's purposes. In selecting items for testing, the auditor is required by paragraph 7 to determine the relevance and reliability of information to be used as audit evidence; the other aspect of effectiveness (sufficiency) is an important consideration in selecting items to test. The means available to the auditor for selecting items for testing are: **A52**

(a) Selecting all items (100% examination);
(b) Selecting specific items; and
(c) Audit sampling.

The application of any one or combination of these means may be appropriate depending on the particular circumstances, for example, the risks of material misstatement related to the assertion being tested, and the practicality and efficiency of the different means.

Selecting All Items

The auditor may decide that it will be most appropriate to examine the entire population of items that make up a class of transactions or account balance (or a stratum within that population). 100% examination is unlikely in the case of tests of controls; however, it is more common for tests of details. 100% examination may be appropriate when, for example: **A53**

● The population constitutes a small number of large value items;
● There is a significant risk and other means do not provide sufficient appropriate audit evidence; or
● The repetitive nature of a calculation or other process performed automatically by an information system makes a 100% examination cost effective.

Selecting Specific Items

A54   The auditor may decide to select specific items from a population. In making this decision, factors that may be relevant include the auditor's understanding of the entity, the assessed risks of material misstatement, and the characteristics of the population being tested. The judgmental selection of specific items is subject to non-sampling risk. Specific items selected may include:

- *High value or key items.* The auditor may decide to select specific items within a population because they are of high value, or exhibit some other characteristic, for example, items that are suspicious, unusual, particularly risk-prone or that have a history of error.
- *All items over a certain amount.* The auditor may decide to examine items whose recorded values exceed a certain amount so as to verify a large proportion of the total amount of a class of transactions or account balance.
- *Items to obtain information.* The auditor may examine items to obtain information about matters such as the nature of the entity or the nature of transactions.

A55   While selective examination of specific items from a class of transactions or account balance will often be an efficient means of obtaining audit evidence, it does not constitute audit sampling. The results of audit procedures applied to items selected in this way cannot be projected to the entire population; accordingly, selective examination of specific items does not provide audit evidence concerning the remainder of the population.

Audit Sampling

A56   Audit sampling is designed to enable conclusions to be drawn about an entire population on the basis of testing a sample drawn from it. Audit sampling is discussed in ISA (UK and Ireland) 530.[16]

Inconsistency in, or Doubts over Reliability of, Audit Evidence (Ref: Para. 11)

A57   Obtaining audit evidence from different sources or of a different nature may indicate that an individual item of audit evidence is not reliable, such as when audit evidence obtained from one source is inconsistent with that obtained from another. This may be the case when, for example, responses to inquiries of management, internal auditors, and others are inconsistent, or when responses to inquiries of those charged with governance made to corroborate the responses to inquiries of management are inconsistent with the response by management. ISA (UK and Ireland) 230 includes a specific documentation requirement if the auditor identified information that is inconsistent with the auditor's final conclusion regarding a significant matter.[17]

---

[16] *ISA (UK and Ireland) 530, "Audit Sampling."*

[17] *ISA (UK and Ireland) 230,* Audit Documentation, *paragraph 11.*

International Standard on Auditing (UK and Ireland) 501

Audit evidence—specific considerations for selected items

(Effective for audits of financial statements for periods ending on or after 15 December 2010)

Contents

International Standard on Auditing (UK and Ireland) (ISA (UK and Ireland)) 501, "Audit Evidence—Specific Considerations for Selected Items" should be read in conjunction with ISA (UK and Ireland) 200, "Overall Objectives of the Independent Auditor and the Conduct of an Audit in Accordance with International Standards on Auditing (UK and Ireland)."

Introduction

Scope of this ISA (UK and Ireland)

1   This International Standard on Auditing (UK and Ireland) (ISA (UK and Ireland)) deals with specific considerations by the auditor in obtaining sufficient appropriate audit evidence in accordance with ISA (UK and Ireland) 330,[1] ISA (UK and Ireland) 500[2] and other relevant ISAs (UK and Ireland), with respect to certain aspects of inventory, litigation and claims involving the entity, and segment information in an audit of financial statements.

Effective Date

2   This ISA (UK and Ireland) is effective for audits of financial statements for periods ending on or after 15 December 2010.

Objective

3   The objective of the auditor is to obtain sufficient appropriate audit evidence regarding the:

(a) Existence and condition of inventory;
(b) Completeness of litigation and claims involving the entity; and
(c) Presentation and disclosure of segment information in accordance with the applicable financial reporting framework.

Requirements

Inventory

4   If inventory is material to the financial statements, the auditor shall obtain sufficient appropriate audit evidence regarding the existence and condition of inventory by:

(a) Attendance at physical inventory counting, unless impracticable, to: (Ref: Para. A1-A3)
   (i) Evaluate management's instructions and procedures for recording and controlling the results of the entity's physical inventory counting; (Ref: Para. A4)
   (ii) Observe the performance of management's count procedures; (Ref: Para. A5)
   (iii) Inspect the inventory; and (Ref: Para. A6)
   (iv) Perform test counts; and (Ref: Para. A7-A8)
(b) Performing audit procedures over the entity's final inventory records to determine whether they accurately reflect actual inventory count results.

5   If physical inventory counting is conducted at a date other than the date of the financial statements, the auditor shall, in addition to the procedures required by paragraph 4, perform audit procedures to obtain audit evidence about whether changes in inventory between the count date and the date of the financial statements are properly recorded. (Ref: Para. A9-A11)

---

[1] *ISA (UK and Ireland) 330, "The Auditor's Responses to Assessed Risks."*

[2] *ISA (UK and Ireland) 500, "Audit Evidence."*

If the auditor is unable to attend physical inventory counting due to unforeseen   **6**
circumstances, the auditor shall make or observe some physical counts on an
alternative date, and perform audit procedures on intervening transactions.

If attendance at physical inventory counting is impracticable, the auditor shall   **7**
perform alternative audit procedures to obtain sufficient appropriate audit evidence
regarding the existence and condition of inventory. If it is not possible to do so, the
auditor shall modify the opinion in the auditor's report in accordance with ISA (UK
and Ireland) 705.[3] (Ref: Para. A12-A14)

If inventory under the custody and control of a third party is material to the financial   **8**
statements, the auditor shall obtain sufficient appropriate audit evidence regarding
the existence and condition of that inventory by performing one or both of the
following:

(a)   Request confirmation from the third party as to the quantities and condition of
      inventory held on behalf of the entity. (Ref: Para. A15)
(b)   Perform inspection or other audit procedures appropriate in the circumstances.
      (Ref: Para. A16)

Litigation and Claims

The auditor shall design and perform audit procedures in order to identify litigation   **9**
and claims involving the entity which may give rise to a risk of material misstatement, including: (Ref: Para. A17-A19)

(a)   Inquiry of management[3a] and, where applicable, others within the entity,
      including in-house legal counsel;
(b)   Reviewing minutes of meetings of those charged with governance and corre-
      spondence between the entity and its external legal counsel; and
(c)   Reviewing legal expense accounts. (Ref: Para. A20)

If the auditor assesses a risk of material misstatement regarding litigation or claims   **10**
that have been identified, or when audit procedures performed indicate that other
material litigation or claims may exist, the auditor shall, in addition to the procedures required by other ISAs (UK and Ireland), seek direct communication with the
entity's external legal counsel. The auditor shall do so through a letter of inquiry,
prepared by management[3b] and sent by the auditor, requesting the entity's external
legal counsel to communicate directly with the auditor. If law, regulation or the
respective legal professional body prohibits the entity's external legal counsel from
communicating directly with the auditor, the auditor shall perform alternative audit
procedures. (Ref: Para. A21-A25)

If: **11**

(a)   management[3c] refuses to give the auditor permission to communicate or meet
      with the entity's external legal counsel, or the entity's external legal counsel
      refuses to respond appropriately to the letter of inquiry, or is prohibited from
      responding; and

---

[3] *ISA (UK and Ireland) 705, "Modifications to the Opinion in the Independent Auditor's Report."*

[3a] *In the UK and Ireland the auditor also makes appropriate inquiry of those charged with governance.*

[3b] *In the UK and Ireland the letter may need to be prepared by those charged with governance.*

[3c] *In the UK and Ireland permission may be denied by those charged with governance.*

(b) the auditor is unable to obtain sufficient appropriate audit evidence by performing alternative audit procedures,

the auditor shall modify the opinion in the auditor's report in accordance with ISA (UK and Ireland) 705.

Written Representations

12   The auditor shall request management and, where appropriate, those charged with governance to provide written representations that all known actual or possible litigation and claims whose effects should be considered when preparing the financial statements have been disclosed to the auditor and accounted for and disclosed in accordance with the applicable financial reporting framework.

Segment Information

13   The auditor shall obtain sufficient appropriate audit evidence regarding the presentation and disclosure of segment information in accordance with the applicable financial reporting framework by: (Ref: Para. A26)

(a) Obtaining an understanding of the methods used by management in determining segment information, and: (Ref: Para. A27)

(i) Evaluating whether such methods are likely to result in disclosure in accordance with the applicable financial reporting framework; and

(ii) Where appropriate, testing the application of such methods; and

(b) Performing analytical procedures or other audit procedures appropriate in the circumstances.

***

Application and Other Explanatory Material

Inventory[3d]

Attendance at Physical Inventory Counting (Ref: Para. 4(a))

A1   Management ordinarily establishes procedures under which inventory is physically counted at least once a year to serve as a basis for the preparation of the financial statements and, if applicable, to ascertain the reliability of the entity's perpetual inventory system.

A2   Attendance at physical inventory counting involves:

- Inspecting the inventory to ascertain its existence and evaluate its condition, and performing test counts;
- Observing compliance with management's instructions and the performance of procedures for recording and controlling the results of the physical inventory count; and
- Obtaining audit evidence as to the reliability of management's count procedures.

[3d] *For auditors in the UK and Ireland further guidance has been promulgated by the APB in Practice Note 25, "Attendance at Stocktaking."*

These procedures may serve as test of controls or substantive procedures depending on the auditor's risk assessment, planned approach and the specific procedures carried out.

Matters relevant in planning attendance at physical inventory counting (or in designing and performing audit procedures pursuant to paragraphs 4-8 of this ISA (UK and Ireland)) include, for example:

A3

- The risks of material misstatement related to inventory.
- The nature of the internal control related to inventory.
- Whether adequate procedures are expected to be established and proper instructions issued for physical inventory counting.
- The timing of physical inventory counting.
- Whether the entity maintains a perpetual inventory system.
- The locations at which inventory is held, including the materiality of the inventory and the risks of material misstatement at different locations, in deciding at which locations attendance is appropriate. ISA (UK and Ireland) 600[4] deals with the involvement of other auditors and accordingly may be relevant if such involvement is with regards to attendance of physical inventory counting at a remote location.
- Whether the assistance of an auditor's expert is needed. ISA (UK and Ireland) 620[5] deals with the use of an auditor's expert to assist the auditor to obtain sufficient appropriate audit evidence.

Evaluate Management's Instructions and Procedures (Ref: Para. 4(a)(i))

Matters relevant in evaluating management's instructions and procedures for recording and controlling the physical inventory counting include whether they address, for example:

A4

- The application of appropriate control activities, for example, collection of used physical inventory count records, accounting for unused physical inventory count records, and count and re-count procedures.
- The accurate identification of the stage of completion of work in progress, of slow moving, obsolete or damaged items and of inventory owned by a third party, for example, on consignment.
- The procedures used to estimate physical quantities, where applicable, such as may be needed in estimating the physical quantity of a coal pile.
- Control over the movement of inventory between areas and the shipping and receipt of inventory before and after the cutoff date.

Observe the Performance of Management's Count Procedures (Ref: Para. 4(a)(ii))

Observing the performance of management's count procedures, for example those relating to control over the movement of inventory before, during and after the count, assists the auditor in obtaining audit evidence that management's instructions and count procedures are adequately designed and implemented. In addition, the auditor may obtain copies of cutoff information, such as details of the movement of inventory, to assist the auditor in performing audit procedures over the accounting for such movements at a later date.

A5

---

[4] *ISA (UK and Ireland) 600, "Special Considerations—Audits of Group Financial Statements (Including the Work of Component Auditors)."*

[5] *ISA (UK and Ireland) 620, "Using the Work of an Auditor's Expert."*

Inspect the Inventory (Ref: Para. 4(a)(iii))

A6   Inspecting inventory when attending physical inventory counting assists the auditor in ascertaining the existence of the inventory (though not necessarily its ownership), and in identifying, for example, obsolete, damaged or ageing inventory.

Perform Test Counts (Ref: Para. 4(a)(iv))

A7   Performing test counts, for example by tracing items selected from management's count records to the physical inventory and tracing items selected from the physical inventory to management's count records, provides audit evidence about the completeness and the accuracy of those records.

A8   In addition to recording the auditor's test counts, obtaining copies of management's completed physical inventory count records assists the auditor in performing subsequent audit procedures to determine whether the entity's final inventory records accurately reflect actual inventory count results.

Physical Inventory Counting Conducted Other than At the Date of the Financial Statements (Ref: Para. 5)

A9   For practical reasons, the physical inventory counting may be conducted at a date, or dates, other than the date of the financial statements. This may be done irrespective of whether management determines inventory quantities by an annual physical inventory counting or maintains a perpetual inventory system. In either case, the effectiveness of the design, implementation and maintenance of controls over changes in inventory determines whether the conduct of physical inventory counting at a date, or dates, other than the date of the financial statements is appropriate for audit purposes. ISA (UK and Ireland) 330 establishes requirements and provides guidance on substantive procedures performed at an interim date.[6]

A10   Where a perpetual inventory system is maintained, management may perform physical counts or other tests to ascertain the reliability of inventory quantity information included in the entity's perpetual inventory records. In some cases, management or the auditor may identify differences between the perpetual inventory records and actual physical inventory quantities on hand; this may indicate that the controls over changes in inventory are not operating effectively.

A11   Relevant matters for consideration when designing audit procedures to obtain audit evidence about whether changes in inventory amounts between the count date, or dates, and the final inventory records are properly recorded include:

● Whether the perpetual inventory records are properly adjusted.
● Reliability of the entity's perpetual inventory records.
● Reasons for significant differences between the information obtained during the physical count and the perpetual inventory records.

Attendance at Physical Inventory Counting Is Impracticable (Ref: Para. 7)

A12   In some cases, attendance at physical inventory counting may be impracticable. This may be due to factors such as the nature and location of the inventory, for example, where inventory is held in a location that may pose threats to the safety of the auditor. The matter of general inconvenience to the auditor, however, is not

---

[6] *ISA (UK and Ireland) 330, paragraphs 22-23.*

sufficient to support a decision by the auditor that attendance is impracticable. Further, as explained in ISA (UK and Ireland) 200,[7] the matter of difficulty, time, or cost involved is not in itself a valid basis for the auditor to omit an audit procedure for which there is no alternative or to be satisfied with audit evidence that is less than persuasive.

In some cases where attendance is impracticable, alternative audit procedures, for   **A13** example inspection of documentation of the subsequent sale of specific inventory items acquired or purchased prior to the physical inventory counting, may provide sufficient appropriate audit evidence about the existence and condition of inventory.

In other cases, however, it may not be possible to obtain sufficient appropriate audit   **A14** evidence regarding the existence and condition of inventory by performing alternative audit procedures. In such cases, ISA (UK and Ireland) 705 requires the auditor to modify the opinion in the auditor's report as a result of the scope limitation.[8]

Inventory under the Custody and Control of a Third Party

Confirmation (Ref: Para. 8(a))

ISA (UK and Ireland) 505[9] establishes requirements and provides guidance for   **A15** performing external confirmation procedures.

Other Audit Procedures (Ref: Para. 8(b))

Depending on the circumstances, for example where information is obtained that   **A16** raises doubt about the integrity and objectivity of the third party, the auditor may consider it appropriate to perform other audit procedures instead of, or in addition to, confirmation with the third party. Examples of other audit procedures include:

- Attending, or arranging for another auditor to attend, the third party's physical counting of inventory, if practicable.
- Obtaining another auditor's report, or a service auditor's report, on the adequacy of the third party's internal control for ensuring that inventory is properly counted and adequately safeguarded.
- Inspecting documentation regarding inventory held by third parties, for example, warehouse receipts.
- Requesting confirmation from other parties when inventory has been pledged as collateral.

Litigation and Claims

Completeness of Litigations and Claims (Ref: Para. 9)

Litigation and claims involving the entity may have a material effect on the financial   **A17** statements and thus may be required to be disclosed or accounted for in the financial statements.

---

[7] *ISA (UK and Ireland) 200, "Overall Objectives of the Independent Auditor and the Conduct of an Audit in Accordance with International Standards on Auditing (UK and Ireland)," paragraph A48.*

[8] *ISA (UK and Ireland) 705, paragraph 13.*

[9] *ISA (UK and Ireland) 505, "External Confirmations."*

A18   In addition to the procedures identified in paragraph 9, other relevant procedures include, for example, using information obtained through risk assessment procedures carried out as part of obtaining an understanding of the entity and its environment to assist the auditor to become aware of litigation and claims involving the entity.

A19   Audit evidence obtained for purposes of identifying litigation and claims that may give rise to a risk of material misstatement also may provide audit evidence regarding other relevant considerations, such as valuation or measurement, regarding litigation and claims. ISA (UK and Ireland) 540[10] establishes requirements and provides guidance relevant to the auditor's consideration of litigation and claims requiring accounting estimates or related disclosures in the financial statements.

Reviewing Legal Expense Accounts (Ref: Para. 9(c))

A20   Depending on the circumstances, the auditor may judge it appropriate to examine related source documents, such as invoices for legal expenses, as part of the auditor's review of legal expense accounts.

Communication with the Entity's External Legal Counsel (Ref: Para. 10-11)

A21   Direct communication with the entity's external legal counsel assists the auditor in obtaining sufficient appropriate audit evidence as to whether potentially material litigation and claims are known and management's estimates of the financial implications, including costs, are reasonable.

A22   In some cases, the auditor may seek direct communication with the entity's external legal counsel through a letter of general inquiry. For this purpose, a letter of general inquiry requests the entity's external legal counsel to inform the auditor of any litigation and claims that the counsel is aware of, together with an assessment of the outcome of the litigation and claims, and an estimate of the financial implications, including costs involved.

A23   If it is considered unlikely that the entity's external legal counsel will respond appropriately to a letter of general inquiry, for example if the professional body to which the external legal counsel belongs prohibits response to such a letter[10a], the auditor may seek direct communication through a letter of specific inquiry. For this purpose, a letter of specific inquiry includes:

(a)   A list of litigation and claims;

(b)   Where available, management's assessment of the outcome of each of the identified litigation and claims and its estimate of the financial implications, including costs involved; and

(c)   A request that the entity's external legal counsel confirm the reasonableness of management's assessments and provide the auditor with further information if the list is considered by the entity's external legal counsel to be incomplete or incorrect.

A24   In certain circumstances, the auditor also may judge it necessary to meet with the entity's external legal counsel to discuss the likely outcome of the litigation or claims. This may be the case, for example, where:

---

[10] *ISA (UK and Ireland) 540, "Auditing Accounting Estimates, Including Fair Value Accounting Estimates, and Related Disclosures."*

[10a] *In the UK, the Council of the Law Society has advised solicitors that it is unable to recommend them to comply with non-specific requests for information.*

- The auditor determines that the matter is a significant risk.
- The matter is complex.
- There is disagreement between management and the entity's external legal counsel.

Ordinarily, such meetings require management's permission[3c] and are held with a representative of management in attendance.

In accordance with ISA (UK and Ireland) 700,[11] the auditor is required to date the   **A25**
auditor's report no earlier than the date on which the auditor has obtained sufficient appropriate audit evidence on which to base the auditor's opinion on the financial statements. Audit evidence about the status of litigation and claims up to the date of the auditor's report may be obtained by inquiry of management[3a], including in-house legal counsel, responsible for dealing with the relevant matters. In some instances, the auditor may need to obtain updated information from the entity's external legal counsel.

Segment Information (Ref: Para. 13)

Depending on the applicable financial reporting framework, the entity may be   **A26**
required or permitted to disclose segment information in the financial statements. The auditor's responsibility regarding the presentation and disclosure of segment information is in relation to the financial statements taken as a whole. Accordingly, the auditor is not required to perform audit procedures that would be necessary to express an opinion on the segment information presented on a stand alone basis.

Understanding of the Methods Used by Management (Ref: Para. 13(a))

Depending on the circumstances, example of matters that may be relevant when   **A27**
obtaining an understanding of the methods used by management in determining segment information and whether such methods are likely to result in disclosure in accordance with the applicable financial reporting framework include:

- Sales, transfers and charges between segments, and elimination of inter-segment amounts.
- Comparisons with budgets and other expected results, for example, operating profits as a percentage of sales.
- The allocation of assets and costs among segments.
- Consistency with prior periods, and the adequacy of the disclosures with respect to inconsistencies.

---

[11] *ISA 700, "Forming an Opinion and Reporting on Financial Statements," paragraph 41.*
The APB has not promulgated ISA 700 as issued by the IAASB for application in the UK and Ireland. In the UK and Ireland the applicable auditing standard is ISA (UK and Ireland) 700, "The Auditor's Report on Financial Statements." Paragraphs 23 and 24 of ISA (UK and Ireland) 700 establish requirements regarding dating of the auditor's report.

International Standard on Auditing (UK and Ireland) 505
External confirmations

*(Effective for audits of financial statements for periods
ending on or after 15 December 2010)*

Contents

International Standard on Auditing (UK and Ireland) (ISA (UK and Ireland))
505, "External Confirmations" should be read in conjunction with ISA (UK and
Ireland) 200, "Overall Objectives of the Independent Auditor and the Conduct of
an Audit in Accordance with International Standards on Auditing (UK and
Ireland)."

Introduction

Scope of this ISA (UK and Ireland)

This International Standard on Auditing (UK and Ireland) (ISA (UK and Ireland))   **1**
deals with the auditor's use of external confirmation procedures to obtain audit
evidence in accordance with the requirements of ISA (UK and Ireland) 330[1] and ISA
(UK and Ireland) 500.[2] It does not address inquiries regarding litigation and claims,
which are dealt with in ISA (UK and Ireland) 501.[3]

External Confirmation Procedures to Obtain Audit Evidence

ISA (UK and Ireland) 500 indicates that the reliability of audit evidence is influenced   **2**
by its source and by its nature, and is dependent on the individual circumstances
under which it is obtained.[4] That ISA (UK and Ireland) also includes the following
generalizations applicable to audit evidence:[5]

- Audit evidence is more reliable when it is obtained from independent sources
  outside the entity.
- Audit evidence obtained directly by the auditor is more reliable than audit
  evidence obtained indirectly or by inference.
- Audit evidence is more reliable when it exists in documentary form, whether
  paper, electronic or other medium.

Accordingly, depending on the circumstances of the audit, audit evidence in the form
of external confirmations received directly by the auditor from confirming parties
may be more reliable than evidence generated internally by the entity. This ISA (UK
and Ireland) is intended to assist the auditor in designing and performing external
confirmation procedures to obtain relevant and reliable audit evidence.

Other ISAs (UK and Ireland) recognize the importance of external confirmations as   **3**
audit evidence, for example:

- ISA (UK and Ireland) 330 discusses the auditor's responsibility to design and
  implement overall responses to address the assessed risks of material misstatement at the financial statement level, and to design and perform further audit
  procedures whose nature, timing and extent are based on, and are responsive to,
  the assessed risks of material misstatement at the assertion level.[6] In addition,
  ISA (UK and Ireland) 330 requires that, irrespective of the assessed risks of
  material misstatement, the auditor designs and performs substantive procedures
  for each material class of transactions, account balance, and disclosure. The
  auditor is also required to consider whether external confirmation procedures
  are to be performed as substantive audit procedures.[7]

---

[1] *ISA (UK and Ireland) 330, "The Auditor's Responses to Assessed Risks."*

[2] *ISA (UK and Ireland) 500, "Audit Evidence."*

[3] *ISA (UK and Ireland) 501, "Audit Evidence—Specific Considerations for Selected Items."*

[4] *ISA (UK and Ireland) 500, paragraph A5.*

[5] *ISA (UK and Ireland) 500, paragraph A31.*

[6] *ISA (UK and Ireland) 330, paragraphs 5-6.*

[7] *ISA (UK and Ireland) 330, paragraphs 18-19.*

- ISA (UK and Ireland) 330 requires that the auditor obtain more persuasive audit evidence the higher the auditor's assessment of risk.[8] To do this, the auditor may increase the quantity of the evidence or obtain evidence that is more relevant or reliable, or both. For example, the auditor may place more emphasis on obtaining evidence directly from third parties or obtaining corroborating evidence from a number of independent sources. ISA (UK and Ireland) 330 also indicates that external confirmation procedures may assist the auditor in obtaining audit evidence with the high level of reliability that the auditor requires to respond to significant risks of material misstatement, whether due to fraud or error.[9]
- ISA (UK and Ireland) 240 indicates that the auditor may design confirmation requests to obtain additional corroborative information as a response to address the assessed risks of material misstatement due to fraud at the assertion level.[10]
- ISA (UK and Ireland) 500 indicates that corroborating information obtained from a source independent of the entity, such as external confirmations, may increase the assurance the auditor obtains from evidence existing within the accounting records or from representations made by management.[11]

Effective Date

4   This ISA (UK and Ireland) is effective for audits of financial statements for periods ending on or after 15 December 2010.

Objective

5   The objective of the auditor, when using external confirmation procedures, is to design and perform such procedures to obtain relevant and reliable audit evidence.

Definitions

6   For purposes of the ISAs (UK and Ireland), the following terms have the meanings attributed below:

(a) External confirmation – Audit evidence obtained as a direct written response to the auditor from a third party (the confirming party), in paper form, or by electronic or other medium.

(b) Positive confirmation request – A request that the confirming party respond directly to the auditor indicating whether the confirming party agrees or disagrees with the information in the request, or providing the requested information.

(c) Negative confirmation request – A request that the confirming party respond directly to the auditor only if the confirming party disagrees with the information provided in the request.

---

[8] *ISA (UK and Ireland) 330, paragraph 7(b).*

[9] *ISA (UK and Ireland) 330, paragraph A53.*

[10] *ISA (UK and Ireland) 240, "The Auditor's Responsibilities Relating to Fraud in an Audit of Financial Statements," paragraph A37.*

[11] *ISA (UK and Ireland) 500, paragraph A8-A9.*

(d) Non-response – A failure of the confirming party to respond, or fully respond, to a positive confirmation request, or a confirmation request returned undelivered.

(e) Exception – A response that indicates a difference between information requested to be confirmed, or contained in the entity's records, and information provided by the confirming party.

Requirements

External Confirmation Procedures

When using external confirmation procedures, the auditor shall maintain control **7** over external confirmation requests, including:

(a) Determining the information to be confirmed or requested; (Ref: Para. A1)
(b) Selecting the appropriate confirming party; (Ref: Para. A2)
(c) Designing the confirmation requests, including determining that requests are properly addressed and contain return information for responses to be sent directly to the auditor; and (Ref: Para. A3-A6)
(d) Sending the requests, including follow-up requests when applicable, to the confirming party. (Ref: Para. A7)

Management's Refusal to Allow the Auditor to Send a Confirmation Request

If management refuses to allow the auditor to send a confirmation request, the **8** auditor shall:

(a) Inquire as to management's reasons for the refusal, and seek audit evidence as to their validity and reasonableness; (Ref: Para. A8)
(b) Evaluate the implications of management's refusal on the auditor's assessment of the relevant risks of material misstatement, including the risk of fraud, and on the nature, timing and extent of other audit procedures; and (Ref: Para. A9)
(c) Perform alternative audit procedures designed to obtain relevant and reliable audit evidence. (Ref: Para. A10)

If the auditor concludes that management's refusal to allow the auditor to send a **9** confirmation request is unreasonable, or the auditor is unable to obtain relevant and reliable audit evidence from alternative audit procedures, the auditor shall communicate with those charged with governance in accordance with ISA (UK and Ireland) 260.[12] The auditor also shall determine the implications for the audit and the auditor's opinion in accordance with ISA (UK and Ireland) 705.[13]

Results of the External Confirmation Procedures

Reliability of Responses to Confirmation Requests

If the auditor identifies factors that give rise to doubts about the reliability of the **10** response to a confirmation request, the auditor shall obtain further audit evidence to resolve those doubts. (Ref: Para. A11-A16)

[12] *ISA (UK and Ireland) 260, "Communication with Those Charged with Governance," paragraph 16.*

[13] *ISA (UK and Ireland) 705, "Modifications to the Opinion in the Independent Auditor's Report."*

11   If the auditor determines that a response to a confirmation request is not reliable, the auditor shall evaluate the implications on the assessment of the relevant risks of material misstatement, including the risk of fraud, and on the related nature, timing and extent of other audit procedures. (Ref: Para. A17)

Non-Responses

12   In the case of each non-response, the auditor shall perform alternative audit procedures to obtain relevant and reliable audit evidence. (Ref: Para A18-A19)

When a Response to a Positive Confirmation Request Is Necessary to Obtain Sufficient Appropriate Audit Evidence

13   If the auditor has determined that a response to a positive confirmation request is necessary to obtain sufficient appropriate audit evidence, alternative audit procedures will not provide the audit evidence the auditor requires. If the auditor does not obtain such confirmation, the auditor shall determine the implications for the audit and the auditor's opinion in accordance with ISA (UK and Ireland) 705. (Ref: Para A20)

Exceptions

14   The auditor shall investigate exceptions to determine whether or not they are indicative of misstatements. (Ref: Para. A21-A22)

Negative Confirmations

15   Negative confirmations provide less persuasive audit evidence than positive confirmations. Accordingly, the auditor shall not use negative confirmation requests as the sole substantive audit procedure to address an assessed risk of material misstatement at the assertion level unless all of the following are present: (Ref: Para. A23)

(a)   The auditor has assessed the risk of material misstatement as low and has obtained sufficient appropriate audit evidence regarding the operating effectiveness of controls relevant to the assertion;

(b)   The population of items subject to negative confirmation procedures comprises a large number of small, homogeneous, account balances, transactions or conditions;

(c)   A very low exception rate is expected; and

(d)   The auditor is not aware of circumstances or conditions that would cause recipients of negative confirmation requests to disregard such requests.

Evaluating the Evidence Obtained

16   The auditor shall evaluate whether the results of the external confirmation procedures provide relevant and reliable audit evidence, or whether further audit evidence is necessary. (Ref: Para A24-A25)

***

Application and Other Explanatory Material

External Confirmation Procedures

Determining the Information to Be Confirmed or Requested (Ref: Para. 7(a))

External confirmation procedures frequently are performed to confirm or request information regarding account balances and their elements. They may also be used to confirm terms of agreements, contracts, or transactions between an entity and other parties, or to confirm the absence of certain conditions, such as a "side agreement." **A1**

Selecting the Appropriate Confirming Party (Ref: Para. 7(b))

Responses to confirmation requests provide more relevant and reliable audit evidence when confirmation requests are sent to a confirming party the auditor believes is knowledgeable about the information to be confirmed. For example, a financial institution official who is knowledgeable about the transactions or arrangements for which confirmation is requested may be the most appropriate person at the financial institution from whom to request confirmation. **A2**

Designing Confirmation Requests (Ref: Para. 7(c))

The design of a confirmation request may directly affect the confirmation response rate, and the reliability and the nature of the audit evidence obtained from responses. **A3**

Factors to consider when designing confirmation requests include: **A4**

- The assertions being addressed.
- Specific identified risks of material misstatement, including fraud risks.
- The layout and presentation of the confirmation request.
- Prior experience on the audit or similar engagements.
- The method of communication (for example, in paper form, or by electronic or other medium).
- Management's authorization or encouragement to the confirming parties to respond to the auditor. Confirming parties may only be willing to respond to a confirmation request containing management's authorization.
- The ability of the intended confirming party to confirm or provide the requested information (for example, individual invoice amount versus total balance).

A positive external confirmation request asks the confirming party to reply to the auditor in all cases, either by indicating the confirming party's agreement with the given information, or by asking the confirming party to provide information. A response to a positive confirmation request ordinarily is expected to provide reliable audit evidence. There is a risk, however, that a confirming party may reply to the confirmation request without verifying that the information is correct. The auditor may reduce this risk by using positive confirmation requests that do not state the amount (or other information) on the confirmation request, and ask the confirming party to fill in the amount or furnish other information. On the other hand, use of this type of "blank" confirmation request may result in lower response rates because additional effort is required of the confirming parties. **A5**

Determining that requests are properly addressed includes testing the validity of some or all of the addresses on confirmation requests before they are sent out. **A6**

Follow-Up on Confirmation Requests (Ref: Para. 7(d))

A7   The auditor may send an additional confirmation request when a reply to a previous request has not been received within a reasonable time. For example, the auditor may, having re-verified the accuracy of the original address, send an additional or follow-up request.

Management's Refusal to Allow the Auditor to Send a Confirmation Request

Reasonableness of Management's Refusal (Ref: Para. 8(a))

A8   A refusal by management to allow the auditor to send a confirmation request is a limitation on the audit evidence the auditor may wish to obtain. The auditor is therefore required to inquire as to the reasons for the limitation. A common reason advanced is the existence of a legal dispute or ongoing negotiation with the intended confirming party, the resolution of which may be affected by an untimely confirmation request. The auditor is required to seek audit evidence as to the validity and reasonableness of the reasons because of the risk that management may be attempting to deny the auditor access to audit evidence that may reveal fraud or error.

Implications for the Assessment of Risks of Material Misstatement (Ref: Para. 8(b))

A9   The auditor may conclude from the evaluation in paragraph 8(b) that it would be appropriate to revise the assessment of the risks of material misstatement at the assertion level and modify planned audit procedures in accordance with ISA (UK and Ireland) 315.[14] For example, if management's request to not confirm is unreasonable, this may indicate a fraud risk factor that requires evaluation in accordance with ISA (UK and Ireland) 240.[15]

Alternative Audit Procedures (Ref: Para. 8(c))

A10   The alternative audit procedures performed may be similar to those appropriate for a non-response as set out in paragraphs A18-A19 of this ISA (UK and Ireland). Such procedures also would take account of the results of the auditor's evaluation in paragraph 8(b) of this ISA (UK and Ireland).

Results of the External Confirmation Procedures

Reliability of Responses to Confirmation Requests (Ref: Para. 10)

A11   ISA (UK and Ireland) 500 indicates that even when audit evidence is obtained from sources external to the entity, circumstances may exist that affect its reliability.[16] All responses carry some risk of interception, alteration or fraud. Such risk exists regardless of whether a response is obtained in paper form, or by electronic or other medium. Factors that may indicate doubts about the reliability of a response include that it:

[14] *ISA (UK and Ireland) 315, "Identifying and Assessing the Risks of Material Misstatement through Understanding the Entity and Its Environment," paragraph 31.*

[15] *ISA (UK and Ireland) 240, paragraph 24.*

[16] *ISA (UK and Ireland) 500, paragraph A31.*

- Was received by the auditor indirectly; or
- Appeared not to come from the originally intended confirming party.

Responses received electronically, for example by facsimile or electronic mail, **A12**
involve risks as to reliability because proof of origin and authority of the respondent
may be difficult to establish, and alterations may be difficult to detect. A process used
by the auditor and the respondent that creates a secure environment for responses
received electronically may mitigate these risks. If the auditor is satisfied that such a
process is secure and properly controlled, the reliability of the related responses is
enhanced. An electronic confirmation process might incorporate various techniques
for validating the identity of a sender of information in electronic form, for example,
through the use of encryption, electronic digital signatures, and procedures to verify
web site authenticity.

If a confirming party uses a third party to coordinate and provide responses to **A13**
confirmation requests, the auditor may perform procedures to address the risks that:

(a) The response may not be from the proper source;
(b) A respondent may not be authorized to respond; and
(c) The integrity of the transmission may have been compromised.

The auditor is required by ISA (UK and Ireland) 500 to determine whether to modify **A14**
or add procedures to resolve doubts over the reliability of information to be used as
audit evidence.[17] The auditor may choose to verify the source and contents of a
response to a confirmation request by contacting the confirming party. For example,
when a confirming party responds by electronic mail, the auditor may telephone the
confirming party to determine whether the confirming party did, in fact, send the
response. When a response has been returned to the auditor indirectly (for example,
because the confirming party incorrectly addressed it to the entity rather than to the
auditor), the auditor may request the confirming party to respond in writing directly
to the auditor.

On its own, an oral response to a confirmation request does not meet the definition **A15**
of an external confirmation because it is not a direct written response to the auditor.
However, upon obtaining an oral response to a confirmation request, the auditor
may, depending on the circumstances, request the confirming party to respond in
writing directly to the auditor. If no such response is received, in accordance with
paragraph 12, the auditor seeks other audit evidence to support the information in
the oral response.

A response to a confirmation request may contain restrictive language regarding its **A16**
use. Such restrictions do not necessarily invalidate the reliability of the response as
audit evidence.

Unreliable Responses (Ref: Para. 11)

When the auditor concludes that a response is unreliable, the auditor may need to **A17**
revise the assessment of the risks of material misstatement at the assertion level and
modify planned audit procedures accordingly, in accordance with ISA (UK and

---

[17] *ISA (UK and Ireland) 500, paragraph 11.*

Ireland) 315.[18] For example, an unreliable response may indicate a fraud risk factor that requires evaluation in accordance with ISA (UK and Ireland) 240.[19]

Non-Responses (Ref: Para. 12)

A18   Examples of alternative audit procedures the auditor may perform include:

- For accounts receivable balances – examining specific subsequent cash receipts, shipping documentation, and sales near the period-end.
- For accounts payable balances – examining subsequent cash disbursements or correspondence from third parties, and other records, such as goods received notes.

A19   The nature and extent of alternative audit procedures are affected by the account and assertion in question. A non-response to a confirmation request may indicate a previously unidentified risk of material misstatement. In such situations, the auditor may need to revise the assessed risk of material misstatement at the assertion level, and modify planned audit procedures, in accordance with ISA (UK and Ireland) 315.[20] For example, fewer responses to confirmation requests than anticipated, or a greater number of responses than anticipated, may indicate a previously unidentified fraud risk factor that requires evaluation in accordance with ISA (UK and Ireland) 240.[21]

When a Response to a Positive Confirmation Request Is Necessary to Obtain Sufficient Appropriate Audit Evidence (Ref. Para. 13)

A20   In certain circumstances, the auditor may identify an assessed risk of material misstatement at the assertion level for which a response to a positive confirmation request is necessary to obtain sufficient appropriate audit evidence. Such circumstances may include where:

- The information available to corroborate management's assertion(s) is only available outside the entity.
- Specific fraud risk factors, such as the risk of management override of controls, or the risk of collusion which can involve employee(s) and/or management, prevent the auditor from relying on evidence from the entity.

Exceptions (Ref: Para. 14)

A21   Exceptions noted in responses to confirmation requests may indicate misstatements or potential misstatements in the financial statements. When a misstatement is identified, the auditor is required by ISA (UK and Ireland) 240 to evaluate whether such misstatement is indicative of fraud.[22] Exceptions may provide a guide to the quality of responses from similar confirming parties or for similar accounts. Exceptions also may indicate a deficiency, or deficiencies, in the entity's internal control over financial reporting.

---

[18] *ISA (UK and Ireland) 315, paragraph 31.*

[19] *ISA (UK and Ireland) 240, paragraph 24.*

[20] *ISA (UK and Ireland) 315, paragraph 31.*

[21] *ISA (UK and Ireland) 240, paragraph 24.*

[22] *ISA (UK and Ireland) 240, paragraph 35.*

Some exceptions do not represent misstatements. For example, the auditor may conclude that differences in responses to confirmation requests are due to timing, measurement, or clerical errors in the external confirmation procedures. **A22**

Negative Confirmations (Ref: Para. 15)

The failure to receive a response to a negative confirmation request does not explicitly indicate receipt by the intended confirming party of the confirmation request or verification of the accuracy of the information contained in the request. Accordingly, a failure of a confirming party to respond to a negative confirmation request provides significantly less persuasive audit evidence than does a response to a positive confirmation request. Confirming parties also may be more likely to respond indicating their disagreement with a confirmation request when the information in the request is not in their favor, and less likely to respond otherwise. For example, holders of bank deposit accounts may be more likely to respond if they believe that the balance in their account is understated in the confirmation request, but may be less likely to respond when they believe the balance is overstated. Therefore, sending negative confirmation requests to holders of bank deposit accounts may be a useful procedure in considering whether such balances may be understated, but is unlikely to be effective if the auditor is seeking evidence regarding overstatement. **A23**

Evaluating the Evidence Obtained (Ref: Para. 16)

When evaluating the results of individual external confirmation requests, the auditor may categorize such results as follows: **A24**

(a) A response by the appropriate confirming party indicating agreement with the information provided in the confirmation request, or providing requested information without exception;
(b) A response deemed unreliable;
(c) A non-response; or
(d) A response indicating an exception.

The auditor's evaluation, when taken into account with other audit procedures the auditor may have performed, may assist the auditor in concluding whether sufficient appropriate audit evidence has been obtained or whether further audit evidence is necessary, as required by ISA (UK and Ireland) 330.[23] **A25**

---

[23] *ISA (UK and Ireland) 330, paragraphs 26-27.*

International Standard on Auditing (UK and Ireland) 510

Initial audit engagements—opening balances

*(Effective for audits of financial statements for periods
ending on or after 15 December 2010)*

Contents

International Standard on Auditing (UK and Ireland) (ISA (UK and Ireland))
510, "Initial Audit Engagements—Opening Balances" should be read in conjunction with ISA (UK and Ireland) 200, "Overall Objectives of the Independent
Auditor and the Conduct of an Audit in Accordance with International Standards on Auditing (UK and Ireland)."

Introduction

Scope of this ISA (UK and Ireland)

This International Standard on Auditing (UK and Ireland) (ISA (UK and Ireland)) deals with the auditor's responsibilities relating to opening balances in an initial audit engagement. In addition to financial statement amounts, opening balances include matters requiring disclosure that existed at the beginning of the period, such as contingencies and commitments. When the financial statements include comparative financial information, the requirements and guidance in ISA (UK and Ireland) 710[1] also apply. ISA (UK and Ireland) 300[2] includes additional requirements and guidance regarding activities prior to starting an initial audit.   **1**

Effective Date

This ISA (UK and Ireland) is effective for audits of financial statements for periods ending on or after 15 December 2010.   **2**

Objective

In conducting an initial audit engagement, the objective of the auditor with respect to opening balances is to obtain sufficient appropriate audit evidence about whether: **3**

(a) Opening balances contain misstatements that materially affect the current period's financial statements; and
(b) Appropriate accounting policies reflected in the opening balances have been consistently applied in the current period's financial statements, or changes thereto are appropriately accounted for and adequately presented and disclosed in accordance with the applicable financial reporting framework.

Definitions

For the purposes of the ISAs (UK and Ireland), the following terms have the meanings attributed below: **4**

(a) Initial audit engagement – An engagement in which either:
  (i) The financial statements for the prior period were not audited; or
  (ii) The financial statements for the prior period were audited by a predecessor auditor.
(b) Opening balances – Those account balances that exist at the beginning of the period. Opening balances are based upon the closing balances of the prior period and reflect the effects of transactions and events of prior periods and accounting policies applied in the prior period. Opening balances also include matters requiring disclosure that existed at the beginning of the period, such as contingencies and commitments.
(c) Predecessor auditor – The auditor from a different audit firm, who audited the financial statements of an entity in the prior period and who has been replaced by the current auditor.

---

[1] *ISA (UK and Ireland) 710, "Comparative Information—Corresponding Figures and Comparative Financial Statements."*

[2] *ISA 300 (UK and Ireland), "Planning an Audit of Financial Statements."*

Requirements

Audit Procedures

Opening Balances

5   The auditor shall read the most recent financial statements, if any, and the predecessor auditor's report thereon, if any, for information relevant to opening balances, including disclosures.

6   The auditor shall obtain sufficient appropriate audit evidence about whether the opening balances contain misstatements that materially affect the current period's financial statements by: (Ref: Para. A1–A2)

(a)   Determining whether the prior period's closing balances have been correctly brought forward to the current period or, when appropriate, have been restated;

(b)   Determining whether the opening balances reflect the application of appropriate accounting policies; and

(c)   Performing one or more of the following: (Ref: Para. A3–A7)

(i)   Where the prior year financial statements were audited, reviewing the predecessor auditor's working papers to obtain evidence regarding the opening balances;

(ii)   Evaluating whether audit procedures performed in the current period provide evidence relevant to the opening balances; or

(iii)   Performing specific audit procedures to obtain evidence regarding the opening balances.

7   If the auditor obtains audit evidence that the opening balances contain misstatements that could materially affect the current period's financial statements, the auditor shall perform such additional audit procedures as are appropriate in the circumstances to determine the effect on the current period's financial statements. If the auditor concludes that such misstatements exist in the current period's financial statements, the auditor shall communicate the misstatements with the appropriate level of management and those charged with governance in accordance with ISA (UK and Ireland) 450.[3]

Consistency of Accounting Policies

8   The auditor shall obtain sufficient appropriate audit evidence about whether the accounting policies reflected in the opening balances have been consistently applied in the current period's financial statements, and whether changes in the accounting policies have been appropriately accounted for and adequately presented and disclosed in accordance with the applicable financial reporting framework.

Relevant Information in the Predecessor Auditor's Report

9   If the prior period's financial statements were audited by a predecessor auditor and there was a modification to the opinion, the auditor shall evaluate the effect of the matter giving rise to the modification in assessing the risks of material misstatement

---

[3] ISA (UK and Ireland) 450, "Evaluation of Misstatements Identified during the Audit," paragraphs 8 and 12.

in the current period's financial statements in accordance with ISA (UK and Ireland) 315.[4]

Audit Conclusions and Reporting

Opening Balances

If the auditor is unable to obtain sufficient appropriate audit evidence regarding the opening balances, the auditor shall express a qualified opinion or disclaim an opinion on the financial statements, as appropriate, in accordance with ISA (UK and Ireland) 705.[5] (Ref: Para. A8)   **10**

If the auditor concludes that the opening balances contain a misstatement that materially affects the current period's financial statements, and the effect of the misstatement is not appropriately accounted for or not adequately presented or disclosed, the auditor shall express a qualified opinion or an adverse opinion, as appropriate, in accordance with ISA (UK and Ireland) 705.   **11**

Consistency of Accounting Policies

If the auditor concludes that: **12**

(a) the current period's accounting policies are not consistently applied in relation to opening balances in accordance with the applicable financial reporting framework; or

(b) a change in accounting policies is not appropriately accounted for or not adequately presented or disclosed in accordance with the applicable financial reporting framework,

the auditor shall express a qualified opinion or an adverse opinion as appropriate in accordance with ISA (UK and Ireland) 705.

Modification to the Opinion in the Predecessor Auditor's Report

If the predecessor auditor's opinion regarding the prior period's financial statements included a modification to the auditor's opinion that remains relevant and material to the current period's financial statements, the auditor shall modify the auditor's opinion on the current period's financial statements in accordance with ISA (UK and Ireland) 705 and ISA (UK and Ireland) 710. (Ref: Para. A9)   **13**

***

---

[4] *ISA (UK and Ireland) 315, "Identifying and Assessing the Risks of Material Misstatement through Understanding the Entity and Its Environment."*

[5] *ISA (UK and Ireland) 705, "Modifications to the Opinion in the Independent Auditor's Report."*

Application and Other Explanatory Material

Audit Procedures

Considerations Specific to Public Sector Entities (Ref: Para. 6)

A1   In the public sector, there may be legal or regulatory limitations on the information that the current auditor can obtain from a predecessor auditor. For example, if a public sector entity that has previously been audited by a statutorily appointed auditor (for example, an Auditor General, or other suitably qualified person appointed on behalf of the Auditor General) is privatized, the amount of access to working papers or other information that the statutorily appointed auditor can provide a newly-appointed auditor that is in the private sector may be constrained by privacy or secrecy laws or regulations. In situations where such communications are constrained, audit evidence may need to be obtained through other means and, if sufficient appropriate audit evidence cannot be obtained, consideration given to the effect on the auditor's opinion.

A2   If the statutorily appointed auditor outsources an audit of a public sector entity to a private sector audit firm, and the statutorily appointed auditor appoints an audit firm other than the firm that audited the financial statements of the public sector entity in the prior period, this is not usually regarded as a change in auditors for the statutorily appointed auditor. Depending on the nature of the outsourcing arrangement, however, the audit engagement may be considered an initial audit engagement from the perspective of the private sector auditor in fulfilling their responsibilities, and therefore this ISA (UK and Ireland) applies.

Opening Balances (Ref: Para. 6(c))

A3   The nature and extent of audit procedures necessary to obtain sufficient appropriate audit evidence regarding opening balances depend on such matters as:

- The accounting policies followed by the entity.
- The nature of the account balances, classes of transactions and disclosures and the risks of material misstatement in the current period's financial statements.
- The significance of the opening balances relative to the current period's financial statements.
- Whether the prior period's financial statements were audited and, if so, whether the predecessor auditor's opinion was modified.

A4   If the prior period's financial statements were audited by a predecessor auditor, the auditor may be able to obtain sufficient appropriate audit evidence regarding the opening balances by reviewing the predecessor auditor's working papers. Whether such a review provides sufficient appropriate audit evidence is influenced by the professional competence and independence of the predecessor auditor.

A5   Relevant ethical and professional requirements guide the current auditor's communications with the predecessor auditor.

A5-1   In the UK and Ireland the relevant ethical guidance on proposed communications with a predecessor auditor is provided by the ethical pronouncements relating to the work of auditors issued by the auditor's relevant professional body.

For current assets and liabilities, some audit evidence about opening balances may **A6** be obtained as part of the current period's audit procedures. For example, the collection (payment) of opening accounts receivable (accounts payable) during the current period will provide some audit evidence of their existence, rights and obligations, completeness and valuation at the beginning of the period. In the case of inventories, however, the current period's audit procedures on the closing inventory balance provide little audit evidence regarding inventory on hand at the beginning of the period. Therefore, additional audit procedures may be necessary, and one or more of the following may provide sufficient appropriate audit evidence:

- Observing a current physical inventory count and reconciling it to the opening inventory quantities.
- Performing audit procedures on the valuation of the opening inventory items.
- Performing audit procedures on gross profit and cutoff.

For non-current assets and liabilities, such as property plant and equipment, **A7** investments and long-term debt, some audit evidence may be obtained by examining the accounting records and other information underlying the opening balances. In certain cases, the auditor may be able to obtain some audit evidence regarding opening balances through confirmation with third parties, for example, for long-term debt and investments. In other cases, the auditor may need to carry out additional audit procedures.

Audit Conclusions and Reporting

Opening Balances (Ref: Para. 10)

ISA (UK and Ireland) 705 establishes requirements and provides guidance on cir- **A8** cumstances that may result in a modification to the auditor's opinion on the financial statements, the type of opinion appropriate in the circumstances, and the content of the auditor's report when the auditor's opinion is modified. The inability of the auditor to obtain sufficient appropriate audit evidence regarding opening balances may result in one of the following modifications to the opinion in the auditor's report:

(a) A qualified opinion or a disclaimer of opinion, as is appropriate in the circumstances; or
(b) Unless prohibited by law or regulation, an opinion which is qualified or disclaimed, as appropriate, regarding the results of operations, and cash flows, where relevant, and unmodified regarding financial position.

The Appendix includes illustrative auditors' reports.[5a]

Modification to the Opinion in the Predecessor Auditor's Report (Ref: Para. 13)

In some situations, a modification to the predecessor auditor's opinion may not be **A9** relevant and material to the opinion on the current period's financial statements. This may be the case where, for example, there was a scope limitation in the prior period, but the matter giving rise to the scope limitation has been resolved in the current period.

[5a] *With respect to companies, illustrative examples of auditor's reports tailored for use with audits conducted in accordance with ISAs (UK and Ireland) are given in the most recent versions of the APB Bulletins, "Auditor's Reports on Financial Statements in the United Kingdom"/"Auditor's Reports on Financial Statements in the Republic of Ireland." Illustrative examples for various other entities are given in other Bulletins and Practice Notes issued by the APB.*

Appendix   (Ref: Para. A8)

Illustrations of Auditors' Reports with Modified Opinions

These examples have not been tailored for the UK and Ireland. With respect to companies, illustrative examples of auditor's reports tailored for use with audits conducted in accordance with ISAs (UK and Ireland) are given in the most recent versions of the APB Bulletins, "Auditor's Reports on Financial Statements in the United Kingdom"/"Auditor's Reports on Financial Statements in the Republic of Ireland." Illustrative examples for various other entities are given in other Bulletins and Practice Notes issued by the APB.

Illustration 1:

Circumstances described in paragraph A8(a) include the following:

- The auditor did not observe the counting of the physical inventory at the beginning of the current period and was unable to obtain sufficient appropriate audit evidence regarding the opening balances of inventory.
- The possible effects of the inability to obtain sufficient appropriate audit evidence regarding opening balances of inventory are deemed to be material but not pervasive to the entity's financial performance and cash flows.[6]
- The financial position at year end is fairly presented.
- In this particular jurisdiction, law and regulation prohibit the auditor from giving an opinion which is qualified regarding the financial performance and cash flows and unmodified regarding financial position.

INDEPENDENT AUDITOR'S REPORT

[Appropriate Addressee]

Report on the Financial Statements[7]

We have audited the accompanying financial statements of ABC Company, which comprise the balance sheet as at December 31, 20X1, and the income statement, statement of changes in equity and cash flow statement for the year then ended, and a summary of significant accounting policies and other explanatory information.

Management's[8] Responsibility for the Financial Statements

Management is responsible for the preparation and fair presentation of these financial statements in accordance with International Financial Reporting

---

[6] *If the possible effects, in the auditor's judgment, are considered to be material and pervasive to the entity's financial performance and cash flows, the auditor would disclaim an opinion on the financial performance and cash flows.*

[7] *The sub-title "Report on the Financial Statements" is unnecessary in circumstances when the second sub-title "Report on Other Legal and Regulatory Requirements" is not applicable.*

[8] *Or other term that is appropriate in the context of the legal framework in the particular jurisdiction.*

Standards,[9] and for such internal control as management determines is necessary to enable the preparation of financial statements that are free from material misstatement, whether due to fraud or error.

Auditor's Responsibility

Our responsibility is to express an opinion on these financial statements based on our audit. We conducted our audit in accordance with International Standards on Auditing. Those standards require that we comply with ethical requirements and plan and perform the audit to obtain reasonable assurance about whether the financial statements are free from material misstatement.

An audit involves performing procedures to obtain audit evidence about the amounts and disclosures in the financial statements. The procedures selected depend on the auditor's judgment, including the assessment of the risks of material misstatement of the financial statements, whether due to fraud or error. In making those risk assessments, the auditor considers internal control relevant to the entity's preparation and fair presentation[10] of the financial statements in order to design audit procedures that are appropriate in the circumstances, but not for the purpose of expressing an opinion on the effectiveness of the entity's internal control.[11] An audit also includes evaluating the appropriateness of accounting policies used and the reasonableness of accounting estimates made by management, as well as evaluating the overall presentation of the financial statements.

We believe that the audit evidence we have obtained is sufficient and appropriate to provide a basis for our qualified audit opinion.

Basis for Qualified Opinion

We were appointed as auditors of the company on June 30, 20X1 and thus did not observe the counting of the physical inventories at the beginning of the year. We were unable to satisfy ourselves by alternative means concerning inventory quantities held at December 31, 20X0. Since opening inventories enter into the determination of the financial performance and cash flows, we were unable to determine whether adjustments might have been necessary in respect of the profit for the year reported in the income statement and the net cash flows from operating activities reported in the cash flow statement.

---

[9] *Where management's responsibility is to prepare financial statements that give a true and fair view, this may read: "Management is responsible for the preparation of financial statements that give a true and fair view in accordance with International Financial Reporting Standards, and for such ..."*

[10] *In the case of footnote 9, this may read: "In making those risk assessments, the auditor considers internal control relevant to the entity's preparation of financial statements that give a true and fair view in order to design audit procedures that are appropriate in the circumstances, but not for the purpose of expressing an opinion on the effectiveness of the entity's internal control."*

[11] *In circumstances when the auditor also has responsibility to express an opinion on the effectiveness of internal control in conjunction with the audit of the financial statements, this sentence would be worded as follows: "In making those risk assessments, the auditor considers internal control relevant to the entity's preparation and fair presentation of the financial statements in order to design audit procedures that are appropriate in the circumstances." In the case of footnote 9, this may read: "In making those risk assessments, the auditor considers internal control relevant to the entity's preparation of financial statements that give a true and fair view in order to design audit procedures that are appropriate in the circumstances."*

Qualified Opinion

In our opinion, except for the possible effects of the matter described in the Basis for Qualified Opinion paragraph, the financial statements present fairly, in all material respects, (or *give a true and fair view of*) the financial position of ABC Company as at December 31, 20X1, and (*of*) its financial performance and its cash flows for the year then ended in accordance with International Financial Reporting Standards.

Other Matter

The financial statements of ABC Company for the year ended December 31, 20X0 were audited by another auditor who expressed an unmodified opinion on those statements on March 31, 20X1.

Report on Other Legal and Regulatory Requirements

[Form and content of this section of the auditor's report will vary depending on the nature of the auditor's other reporting responsibilities.]

[Auditor's signature]

[Date of the auditor's report]

[Auditor's address]

> **Illustration 2:**
>
> **Circumstances described in paragraph A8(b) include the following:**
>
> - The auditor did not observe the counting of the physical inventory at the beginning of the current period and was unable to obtain sufficient appropriate audit evidence regarding the opening balances of inventory.
> - The possible effects of the inability to obtain sufficient appropriate audit evidence regarding opening balances of inventory are deemed to be material but not pervasive to the entity's financial performance and cash flows.[12]
> - The financial position at year end is fairly presented.
> - An opinion that is qualified regarding the financial performance and cash flows and unmodified regarding financial position is considered appropriate in the circumstances.

INDEPENDENT AUDITOR'S REPORT

[Appropriate Addressee]

Report on the Financial Statements[13]

We have audited the accompanying financial statements of ABC Company, which comprise the balance sheet as at December 31, 20X1, and the income statement, statement of changes in equity and cash flow statement for the year then ended, and a summary of significant accounting policies and other explanatory information.

Management's[14] Responsibility for the Financial Statements

Management is responsible for the preparation and fair presentation of these financial statements in accordance with International Financial Reporting Standards,[15] and for such internal control as management determines is necessary to enable the preparation of financial statements that are free from material misstatement, whether due to fraud or error.

Auditor's Responsibility

Our responsibility is to express an opinion on these financial statements based on our audit. We conducted our audit in accordance with International Standards on Auditing. Those standards require that we comply with ethical requirements and plan and perform the audit to obtain reasonable assurance about whether the financial statements are free from material misstatement.

---

[12] *If the possible effects, in the auditor's judgment, are considered to be material and pervasive to the entity's financial performance and cash flows, the auditor would disclaim the opinion on the financial performance and cash flows.*

[13] *The sub-title "Report on the Financial Statements" is unnecessary in circumstances when the second sub-title "Report on Other Legal and Regulatory Requirements" is not applicable.*

[14] *Or other term that is appropriate in the context of the legal framework in the particular jurisdiction.*

[15] *Where management's responsibility is to prepare financial statements that give a true and fair view, this may read: "Management is responsible for the preparation of financial statements that give a true and fair view in accordance with International Financial Reporting Standards, and for such ...."*

An audit involves performing procedures to obtain audit evidence about the amounts and disclosures in the financial statements. The procedures selected depend on the auditor's judgment, including the assessment of the risks of material misstatement of the financial statements, whether due to fraud or error. In making those risk assessments, the auditor considers internal control relevant to the entity's preparation and fair presentation[16] of the financial statements in order to design audit procedures that are appropriate in the circumstances, but not for the purpose of expressing an opinion on the effectiveness of the entity's internal control.[17] An audit also includes evaluating the appropriateness of accounting policies used and the reasonableness of accounting estimates made by management, as well as evaluating the overall presentation of the financial statements.

We believe that the audit evidence we have obtained is sufficient and appropriate to provide a basis for our unmodified opinion on the financial position and our qualified audit opinion on the financial performance and cash flows.

Basis for Qualified Opinion on the Financial Performance and Cash Flows

We were appointed as auditors of the company on June 30, 20X1 and thus did not observe the counting of the physical inventories at the beginning of the year. We were unable to satisfy ourselves by alternative means concerning inventory quantities held at December 31, 20X0. Since opening inventories enter into the determination of the financial performance and cash flows, we were unable to determine whether adjustments might have been necessary in respect of the profit for the year reported in the income statement and the net cash flows from operating activities reported in the cash flow statement.

Qualified Opinion on the Financial Performance and Cash Flows

In our opinion, except for the possible effects of the matter described in the Basis for Qualified Opinion paragraph, the Income Statement and Cash Flow Statement present fairly, in all material respects (or *give a true and fair view of*) the financial performance and cash flows of ABC Company for the year ended December 31, 20X1 in accordance with International Financial Reporting Standards.

Opinion on the financial position

In our opinion, the balance sheet presents fairly, in all material respects (or *gives a true and fair view of*) the financial position of ABC Company as at December 31, 20X1 in accordance with International Financial Reporting Standards.

---

[16] *In the case of footnote 15, this may read: "In making those risk assessments, the auditor considers internal control relevant to the entity's preparation of financial statements that give a true and fair view in order to design audit procedures that are appropriate in the circumstances, but not for the purpose of expressing an opinion on the effectiveness of the entity's internal control."*

[17] *In circumstances when the auditor also has responsibility to express an opinion on the effectiveness of internal control in conjunction with the audit of the financial statements, this sentence would be worded as follows: "In making those risk assessments, the auditor considers internal control relevant to the entity's preparation and fair presentation of the financial statements in order to design audit procedures that are appropriate in the circumstances." In the case of footnote 15, this may read: "In making those risk assessments, the auditor considers internal control relevant to the entity's preparation of financial statements that give a true and fair view in order to design audit procedures that are appropriate in the circumstances."*

Other Matter

The financial statements of ABC Company for the year ended December 31, 20X0 were audited by another auditor who expressed an unmodified opinion on those statements on March 31, 20X1.

Report on Other Legal and Regulatory Requirements

[Form and content of this section of the auditor's report will vary depending on the nature of the auditor's other reporting responsibilities.]

[Auditor's signature]

[Date of the auditor's report]

[Auditor's address]

International Standard on Auditing (UK and Ireland) 520
Analytical procedures

*(Effective for audits of financial statements for periods
ending on or after 15 December 2010)*

Contents

International Standard on Auditing (UK and Ireland) (ISA (UK and Ireland))
520, "Analytical Procedures" should be read in conjunction with ISA (UK and
Ireland) 200, "Overall Objectives of the Independent Auditor and the Conduct of
an Audit in Accordance with International Standards on Auditing (UK and
Ireland)."

Introduction

Scope of this ISA (UK and Ireland)

This International Standard on Auditing (UK and Ireland) (ISA (UK and Ireland)) 1
deals with the auditor's use of analytical procedures as substantive procedures
("substantive analytical procedures"). It also deals with the auditor's responsibility
to perform analytical procedures near the end of the audit that assist the auditor
when forming an overall conclusion on the financial statements. ISA (UK and Ireland) 315[1] deals with the use of analytical procedures as risk assessment procedures.
ISA (UK and Ireland) 330 includes requirements and guidance regarding the nature,
timing and extent of audit procedures in response to assessed risks; these audit
procedures may include substantive analytical procedures.[2]

Effective Date

This ISA (UK and Ireland) is effective for audits of financial statements for periods 2
ending on or after 15 December 2010.

Objectives

The objectives of the auditor are: 3

(a) To obtain relevant and reliable audit evidence when using substantive analytical
procedures; and
(b) To design and perform analytical procedures near the end of the audit that assist
the auditor when forming an overall conclusion as to whether the financial
statements are consistent with the auditor's understanding of the entity.

Definition

For the purposes of the ISAs (UK and Ireland), the term "analytical procedures" 4
means evaluations of financial information through analysis of plausible relationships among both financial and non-financial data. Analytical procedures also
encompass such investigation as is necessary of identified fluctuations or relationships that are inconsistent with other relevant information or that differ from
expected values by a significant amount. (Ref: Para. A1-A3)

Requirements

Substantive Analytical Procedures

When designing and performing substantive analytical procedures, either alone or in 5
combination with tests of details, as substantive procedures in accordance with ISA
(UK and Ireland) 330,[3] the auditor shall: (Ref: Para. A4-A5)

---

[1] *ISA (UK and Ireland) 315, "Identifying and Assessing the Risks of Material Misstatement through Understanding the Entity and Its Environment," paragraph 6(b).*

[2] *ISA (UK and Ireland) 330, "The Auditor's Reponses to Assessed Risks," paragraphs 6 and 18.*

[3] *ISA (UK and Ireland) 330, paragraph 18.*

(a) Determine the suitability of particular substantive analytical procedures for given assertions, taking account of the assessed risks of material misstatement and tests of details, if any, for these assertions; (Ref: Para. A6-A11)

(b) Evaluate the reliability of data from which the auditor's expectation of recorded amounts or ratios is developed, taking account of source, comparability, and nature and relevance of information available, and controls over preparation; (Ref: Para. A12-A14)

(c) Develop an expectation of recorded amounts or ratios and evaluate whether the expectation is sufficiently precise to identify a misstatement that, individually or when aggregated with other misstatements, may cause the financial statements to be materially misstated; and (Ref: Para. A15)

(d) Determine the amount of any difference of recorded amounts from expected values that is acceptable without further investigation as required by paragraph 7. (Ref: Para. A16)

Analytical Procedures that Assist When Forming an Overall Conclusion

6　The auditor shall design and perform analytical procedures near the end of the audit that assist the auditor when forming an overall conclusion as to whether the financial statements are consistent with the auditor's understanding of the entity. (Ref: Para. A17-A19)

Investigating Results of Analytical Procedures

7　If analytical procedures performed in accordance with this ISA (UK and Ireland) identify fluctuations or relationships that are inconsistent with other relevant information or that differ from expected values by a significant amount, the auditor shall investigate such differences by:

(a) Inquiring of management and obtaining appropriate audit evidence relevant to management's responses; and

(b) Performing other audit procedures as necessary in the circumstances. (Ref: Para. A20-A21)

***

Application and Other Explanatory Material

Definition of Analytical Procedures (Ref: Para. 4)

A1　Analytical procedures include the consideration of comparisons of the entity's financial information with, for example:

- Comparable information for prior periods.
- Anticipated results of the entity, such as budgets or forecasts, or expectations of the auditor, such as an estimation of depreciation.
- Similar industry information, such as a comparison of the entity's ratio of sales to accounts receivable with industry averages or with other entities of comparable size in the same industry.

A2　Analytical procedures also include consideration of relationships, for example:

- Among elements of financial information that would be expected to conform to a predictable pattern based on the entity's experience, such as gross margin percentages.

- Between financial information and relevant non-financial information, such as payroll costs to number of employees.

Various methods may be used to perform analytical procedures. These methods range from performing simple comparisons to performing complex analyses using advanced statistical techniques. Analytical procedures may be applied to consolidated financial statements, components and individual elements of information.   **A3**

Substantive Analytical Procedures (Ref: Para. 5)

The auditor's substantive procedures at the assertion level may be tests of details, substantive analytical procedures, or a combination of both. The decision about which audit procedures to perform, including whether to use substantive analytical procedures, is based on the auditor's judgment about the expected effectiveness and efficiency of the available audit procedures to reduce audit risk at the assertion level to an acceptably low level.   **A4**

The auditor may inquire of management as to the availability and reliability of information needed to apply substantive analytical procedures, and the results of any such analytical procedures performed by the entity. It may be effective to use analytical data prepared by management, provided the auditor is satisfied that such data is properly prepared.   **A5**

Suitability of Particular Analytical Procedures for Given Assertions (Ref: Para. 5(a))

Substantive analytical procedures are generally more applicable to large volumes of transactions that tend to be predictable over time. The application of planned analytical procedures is based on the expectation that relationships among data exist and continue in the absence of known conditions to the contrary. However, the suitability of a particular analytical procedure will depend upon the auditor's assessment of how effective it will be in detecting a misstatement that, individually or when aggregated with other misstatements, may cause the financial statements to be materially misstated.   **A6**

In some cases, even an unsophisticated predictive model may be effective as an analytical procedure. For example, where an entity has a known number of employees at fixed rates of pay throughout the period, it may be possible for the auditor to use this data to estimate the total payroll costs for the period with a high degree of accuracy, thereby providing audit evidence for a significant item in the financial statements and reducing the need to perform tests of details on the payroll. The use of widely recognized trade ratios (such as profit margins for different types of retail entities) can often be used effectively in substantive analytical procedures to provide evidence to support the reasonableness of recorded amounts.   **A7**

Different types of analytical procedures provide different levels of assurance. Analytical procedures involving, for example, the prediction of total rental income on a building divided into apartments, taking the rental rates, the number of apartments and vacancy rates into consideration, can provide persuasive evidence and may eliminate the need for further verification by means of tests of details, provided the elements are appropriately verified. In contrast, calculation and comparison of gross margin percentages as a means of confirming a revenue figure may provide less persuasive evidence, but may provide useful corroboration if used in combination with other audit procedures.   **A8**

A9   The determination of the suitability of particular substantive analytical procedures is influenced by the nature of the assertion and the auditor's assessment of the risk of material misstatement. For example, if controls over sales order processing are deficient, the auditor may place more reliance on tests of details rather than on substantive analytical procedures for assertions related to receivables.

A10   Particular substantive analytical procedures may also be considered suitable when tests of details are performed on the same assertion. For example, when obtaining audit evidence regarding the valuation assertion for accounts receivable balances, the auditor may apply analytical procedures to an aging of customers' accounts in addition to performing tests of details on subsequent cash receipts to determine the collectability of the receivables.

Considerations Specific to Public Sector Entities

A11   The relationships between individual financial statement items traditionally considered in the audit of business entities may not always be relevant in the audit of governments or other non-business public sector entities; for example, in many public sector entities there may be little direct relationship between revenue and expenditure. In addition, because expenditure on the acquisition of assets may not be capitalized, there may be no relationship between expenditures on, for example, inventories and fixed assets and the amount of those assets reported in the financial statements. Also, industry data or statistics for comparative purposes may not be available in the public sector. However, other relationships may be relevant, for example, variations in the cost per kilometer of road construction or the number of vehicles acquired compared with vehicles retired.

The Reliability of the Data (Ref: Para. 5(b))

A12   The reliability of data is influenced by its source and nature and is dependent on the circumstances under which it is obtained. Accordingly, the following are relevant when determining whether data is reliable for purposes of designing substantive analytical procedures:

   (a)   Source of the information available. For example, information may be more reliable when it is obtained from independent sources outside the entity;[4]

   (b)   Comparability of the information available. For example, broad industry data may need to be supplemented to be comparable to that of an entity that produces and sells specialized products;

   (c)   Nature and relevance of the information available. For example, whether budgets have been established as results to be expected rather than as goals to be achieved; and

   (d)   Controls over the preparation of the information that are designed to ensure its completeness, accuracy and validity. For example, controls over the preparation, review and maintenance of budgets.

   (e)   Prior year knowledge and understanding. For example, the knowledge gained during previous audits, together with the auditor's understanding of the effectiveness of the accounting and internal control systems and the types of problems that in prior periods have given rise to accounting adjustments.

---

[4] *ISA (UK and Ireland) 500, "Audit Evidence," paragraph A31.*

The auditor may consider testing the operating effectiveness of controls, if any, over   **A13**
the entity's preparation of information used by the auditor in performing substantive
analytical procedures in response to assessed risks. When such controls are effective,
the auditor generally has greater confidence in the reliability of the information and,
therefore, in the results of analytical procedures. The operating effectiveness of
controls over non-financial information may often be tested in conjunction with
other tests of controls. For example, in establishing controls over the processing of
sales invoices, an entity may include controls over the recording of unit sales. In these
circumstances, the auditor may test the operating effectiveness of controls over the
recording of unit sales in conjunction with tests of the operating effectiveness of
controls over the processing of sales invoices. Alternatively, the auditor may consider
whether the information was subjected to audit testing. ISA (UK and Ireland) 500
establishes requirements and provides guidance in determining the audit procedures
to be performed on the information to be used for substantive analytical procedures.[5]

The matters discussed in paragraphs A12(a)-A12(d) are relevant irrespective of   **A14**
whether the auditor performs substantive analytical procedures on the entity's period
end financial statements, or at an interim date and plans to perform substantive
analytical procedures for the remaining period. ISA (UK and Ireland) 330 establishes
requirements and provides guidance on substantive procedures performed at an
interim date. [6]

Evaluation Whether the Expectation Is Sufficiently Precise (Ref: Para. 5(c))

Matters relevant to the auditor's evaluation of whether the expectation can be   **A15**
developed sufficiently precisely to identify a misstatement that, when aggregated with
other misstatements, may cause the financial statements to be materially misstated,
include:

- The accuracy with which the expected results of substantive analytical procedures can be predicted. For example, the auditor may expect greater consistency
  in comparing gross profit margins from one period to another than in comparing discretionary expenses, such as research or advertising.
- The degree to which information can be disaggregated. For example, substantive analytical procedures may be more effective when applied to financial
  information on individual sections of an operation or to financial statements of
  components of a diversified entity, than when applied to the financial statements
  of the entity as a whole.
- The availability of the information, both financial and non-financial. For
  example, the auditor may consider whether financial information, such as
  budgets or forecasts, and non-financial information, such as the number of units
  produced or sold, is available to design substantive analytical procedures. If the
  information is available, the auditor may also consider the reliability of the
  information as discussed in paragraphs A12-A13 above.

Amount of Difference of Recorded Amounts from Expected Values that Is Acceptable
(Ref: Para. 5(d))

The auditor's determination of the amount of difference from the expectation that   **A16**
can be accepted without further investigation is influenced by materiality[7] and the

[5] *ISA (UK and Ireland) 500, paragraph 10.*

[6] *ISA (UK and Ireland) 330, paragraphs 22-23.*

[7] *ISA (UK and Ireland) 320, "Materiality in Planning and Performing an Audit," paragraph A13.*

consistency with the desired level of assurance, taking account of the possibility that a misstatement, individually or when aggregated with other misstatements, may cause the financial statements to be materially misstated. ISA (UK and Ireland) 330 requires the auditor to obtain more persuasive audit evidence the higher the auditor's assessment of risk.[8] Accordingly, as the assessed risk increases, the amount of difference considered acceptable without investigation decreases in order to achieve the desired level of persuasive evidence.[9]

Analytical Procedures that Assist When Forming an Overall Conclusion (Ref: Para. 6)

A17   The conclusions drawn from the results of analytical procedures designed and performed in accordance with paragraph 6 are intended to corroborate conclusions formed during the audit of individual components or elements of the financial statements. This assists the auditor to draw reasonable conclusions on which to base the auditor's opinion.

A17-1   Considerations when carrying out such procedures may include:

(a) Whether the financial statements adequately reflect the information and explanations previously obtained and conclusions previously reached during the course of the audit;

(b) Whether the procedures reveal any new factors which may affect the presentation of, or disclosures in, the financial statements;

(c) Whether analytical procedures applied when completing the audit, such as comparing the information in the financial statements with other pertinent data, produce results which assist in arriving at the overall conclusion as to whether the financial statements as a whole are consistent with the auditor's knowledge of the entity's business;

(d) Whether the presentation adopted in the financial statements may have been unduly influenced by the desire of those charged with governance to present matters in a favourable or unfavourable light; and

(e) The potential impact on the financial statements of the aggregate of uncorrected misstatements (including those arising from bias in making accounting estimates) identified during the course of the audit and the preceding period's audit, if any.

A18   The results of such analytical procedures may identify a previously unrecognized risk of material misstatement. In such circumstances, ISA (UK and Ireland) 315 requires the auditor to revise the auditor's assessment of the risks of material misstatement and modify the further planned audit procedures accordingly.[10]

A19   The analytical procedures performed in accordance with paragraph 6 may be similar to those that would be used as risk assessment procedures.

---

[8] *ISA (UK and Ireland) 330, paragraph 7(b).*

[9] *ISA (UK and Ireland) 330, paragraph A19.*

[10] *ISA (UK and Ireland) 315, paragraph 31.*

Nature and Cause of Deviations and Misstatements

The auditor shall investigate the nature and cause of any deviations or misstatements **12**
identified, and evaluate their possible effect on the purpose of the audit procedure
and on other areas of the audit. (Ref: Para. A17)

In the extremely rare circumstances when the auditor considers a misstatement or **13**
deviation discovered in a sample to be an anomaly, the auditor shall obtain a high
degree of certainty that such misstatement or deviation is not representative of the
population. The auditor shall obtain this degree of certainty by performing additional audit procedures to obtain sufficient appropriate audit evidence that the
misstatement or deviation does not affect the remainder of the population.

Projecting Misstatements

For tests of details, the auditor shall project misstatements found in the sample to the **14**
population. (Ref: Para. A18-A20)

Evaluating Results of Audit Sampling

The auditor shall evaluate: **15**

(a) The results of the sample; and (Ref: Para. A21-A22)
(b) Whether the use of audit sampling has provided a reasonable basis for conclusions about the population that has been tested. (Ref: Para. A23)

***

Application and Other Explanatory Material

Definitions

Non-Sampling Risk (Ref: Para. 5(d))

Examples of non-sampling risk include use of inappropriate audit procedures, or **A1**
misinterpretation of audit evidence and failure to recognize a misstatement or
deviation.

Sampling Unit (Ref: Para. 5(f))

The sampling units might be physical items (for example, checks listed on deposit **A2**
slips, credit entries on bank statements, sales invoices or debtors' balances) or
monetary units.

Tolerable Misstatement (Ref: Para. 5(i))

When designing a sample, the auditor determines tolerable misstatement in order to **A3**
address the risk that the aggregate of individually immaterial misstatements may
cause the financial statements to be materially misstated and provide a margin for
possible undetected misstatements. Tolerable misstatement is the application of
performance materiality, as defined in ISA (UK and Ireland) 320,[2] to a particular

---

[2] *ISA (UK and Ireland) 320, "Materiality in Planning and Performing an Audit," paragraph 9.*

sampling procedure. Tolerable misstatement may be the same amount or an amount lower than performance materiality.

Sample Design, Size and Selection of Items for Testing

Sample Design (Ref: Para. 6)

A4   Audit sampling enables the auditor to obtain and evaluate audit evidence about some characteristic of the items selected in order to form or assist in forming a conclusion concerning the population from which the sample is drawn. Audit sampling can be applied using either non-statistical or statistical sampling approaches.

A5   When designing an audit sample, the auditor's consideration includes the specific purpose to be achieved and the combination of audit procedures that is likely to best achieve that purpose. Consideration of the nature of the audit evidence sought and possible deviation or misstatement conditions or other characteristics relating to that audit evidence will assist the auditor in defining what constitutes a deviation or misstatement and what population to use for sampling. In fulfilling the requirement of paragraph 10 of ISA (UK and Ireland) 500, when performing audit sampling, the auditor performs audit procedures to obtain evidence that the population from which the audit sample is drawn is complete.

A6   The auditor's consideration of the purpose of the audit procedure, as required by paragraph 6, includes a clear understanding of what constitutes a deviation or misstatement so that all, and only, those conditions that are relevant to the purpose of the audit procedure are included in the evaluation of deviations or projection of misstatements. For example, in a test of details relating to the existence of accounts receivable, such as confirmation, payments made by the customer before the confirmation date but received shortly after that date by the client, are not considered a misstatement. Also, a misposting between customer accounts does not affect the total accounts receivable balance. Therefore, it may not be appropriate to consider this a misstatement in evaluating the sample results of this particular audit procedure, even though it may have an important effect on other areas of the audit, such as the assessment of the risk of fraud or the adequacy of the allowance for doubtful accounts.

A7   In considering the characteristics of a population, for tests of controls, the auditor makes an assessment of the expected rate of deviation based on the auditor's understanding of the relevant controls or on the examination of a small number of items from the population. This assessment is made in order to design an audit sample and to determine sample size. For example, if the expected rate of deviation is unacceptably high, the auditor will normally decide not to perform tests of controls. Similarly, for tests of details, the auditor makes an assessment of the expected misstatement in the population. If the expected misstatement is high, 100% examination or use of a large sample size may be appropriate when performing tests of details.

A8   In considering the characteristics of the population from which the sample will be drawn, the auditor may determine that stratification or value-weighted selection is appropriate. Appendix 1 provides further discussion on stratification and value-weighted selection.

A9   The decision whether to use a statistical or non-statistical sampling approach is a matter for the auditor's judgment; however, sample size is not a valid criterion to distinguish between statistical and non-statistical approaches.

Sample Size (Ref: Para. 7)

The level of sampling risk that the auditor is willing to accept affects the sample size **A10** required. The lower the risk the auditor is willing to accept, the greater the sample size will need to be.

The sample size can be determined by the application of a statistically-based formula **A11** or through the exercise of professional judgment. Appendices 2 and 3 indicate the influences that various factors typically have on the determination of sample size. When circumstances are similar, the effect on sample size of factors such as those identified in Appendices 2 and 3 will be similar regardless of whether a statistical or non-statistical approach is chosen.

Selection of Items for Testing (Ref: Para. 8)

With statistical sampling, sample items are selected in a way that each sampling unit **A12** has a known probability of being selected. With non-statistical sampling, judgment is used to select sample items. Because the purpose of sampling is to provide a reasonable basis for the auditor to draw conclusions about the population from which the sample is selected, it is important that the auditor selects a representative sample, so that bias is avoided, by choosing sample items which have characteristics typical of the population.

The principal methods of selecting samples are the use of random selection, sys- **A13** tematic selection and haphazard selection. Each of these methods is discussed in Appendix 4.

Performing Audit Procedures (Ref: Para. 10-11)

An example of when it is necessary to perform the procedure on a replacement item **A14** is when a voided check is selected while testing for evidence of payment authorization. If the auditor is satisfied that the check has been properly voided such that it does not constitute a deviation, an appropriately chosen replacement is examined.

An example of when the auditor is unable to apply the designed audit procedures to **A15** a selected item is when documentation relating to that item has been lost.

An example of a suitable alternative procedure might be the examination of sub- **A16** sequent cash receipts together with evidence of their source and the items they are intended to settle when no reply has been received in response to a positive confirmation request.

Nature and Cause of Deviations and Misstatements (Ref: Para. 12)

In analyzing the deviations and misstatements identified, the auditor may observe **A17** that many have a common feature, for example, type of transaction, location, product line or period of time. In such circumstances, the auditor may decide to identify all items in the population that possess the common feature, and extend audit procedures to those items. In addition, such deviations or misstatements may be intentional, and may indicate the possibility of fraud.

Projecting Misstatements (Ref: Para. 14)

A18   The auditor is required to project misstatements for the population to obtain a broad view of the scale of misstatement but this projection may not be sufficient to determine an amount to be recorded.

A19   When a misstatement has been established as an anomaly, it may be excluded when projecting misstatements to the population. However, the effect of any such misstatement, if uncorrected, still needs to be considered in addition to the projection of the non-anomalous misstatements.

A20   For tests of controls, no explicit projection of deviations is necessary since the sample deviation rate is also the projected deviation rate for the population as a whole. ISA (UK and Ireland) 330[3] provides guidance when deviations from controls upon which the auditor intends to rely are detected.

Evaluating Results of Audit Sampling (Ref: Para. 15)

A21   For tests of controls, an unexpectedly high sample deviation rate may lead to an increase in the assessed risk of material misstatement, unless further audit evidence substantiating the initial assessment is obtained. For tests of details, an unexpectedly high misstatement amount in a sample may cause the auditor to believe that a class of transactions or account balance is materially misstated, in the absence of further audit evidence that no material misstatement exists.

A22   In the case of tests of details, the projected misstatement plus anomalous misstatement, if any, is the auditor's best estimate of misstatement in the population. When the projected misstatement plus anomalous misstatement, if any, exceeds tolerable misstatement, the sample does not provide a reasonable basis for conclusions about the population that has been tested. The closer the projected misstatement plus anomalous misstatement is to tolerable misstatement, the more likely that actual misstatement in the population may exceed tolerable misstatement. Also if the projected misstatement is greater than the auditor's expectations of misstatement used to determine the sample size, the auditor may conclude that there is an unacceptable sampling risk that the actual misstatement in the population exceeds the tolerable misstatement. Considering the results of other audit procedures helps the auditor to assess the risk that actual misstatement in the population exceeds tolerable misstatement, and the risk may be reduced if additional audit evidence is obtained.

A23   If the auditor concludes that audit sampling has not provided a reasonable basis for conclusions about the population that has been tested, the auditor may:

- Request management to investigate misstatements that have been identified and the potential for further misstatements and to make any necessary adjustments; or
- Tailor the nature, timing and extent of those further audit procedures to best achieve the required assurance. For example, in the case of tests of controls, the auditor might extend the sample size, test an alternative control or modify related substantive procedures.

---

[3] ISA (UK and Ireland) 330, *"The Auditor's Responses to Assessed Risks,"* paragraph 17.

Appendix 1

Stratification and Value-Weighted Selection

In considering the characteristics of the population from which the sample will be drawn, the auditor may determine that stratification or value-weighted selection is appropriate. This Appendix provides guidance to the auditor on the use of stratification and value-weighted sampling techniques.

Stratification

Audit efficiency may be improved if the auditor stratifies a population by dividing it into discrete sub-populations which have an identifying characteristic. The objective of stratification is to reduce the variability of items within each stratum and therefore allow sample size to be reduced without increasing sampling risk.   **1**

When performing tests of details, the population is often stratified by monetary value. This allows greater audit effort to be directed to the larger value items, as these items may contain the greatest potential misstatement in terms of overstatement. Similarly, a population may be stratified according to a particular characteristic that indicates a higher risk of misstatement, for example, when testing the allowance for doubtful accounts in the valuation of accounts receivable, balances may be stratified by age.   **2**

The results of audit procedures applied to a sample of items within a stratum can only be projected to the items that make up that stratum. To draw a conclusion on the entire population, the auditor will need to consider the risk of material misstatement in relation to whatever other strata make up the entire population. For example, 20% of the items in a population may make up 90% of the value of an account balance. The auditor may decide to examine a sample of these items. The auditor evaluates the results of this sample and reaches a conclusion on the 90% of value separately from the remaining 10% (on which a further sample or other means of gathering audit evidence will be used, or which may be considered immaterial).   **3**

If a class of transactions or account balance has been divided into strata, the misstatement is projected for each stratum separately. Projected misstatements for each stratum are then combined when considering the possible effect of misstatements on the total class of transactions or account balance.   **4**

Value-Weighted Selection

When performing tests of details it may be efficient to identify the sampling unit as the individual monetary units that make up the population. Having selected specific monetary units from within the population, for example, the accounts receivable balance, the auditor may then examine the particular items, for example, individual balances, that contain those monetary units. One benefit of this approach to defining the sampling unit is that audit effort is directed to the larger value items because they have a greater chance of selection, and can result in smaller sample sizes. This approach may be used in conjunction with the systematic method of sample selection (described in Appendix 4) and is most efficient when selecting items using random selection.   **5**

Appendix 2   (Ref: Para. A11)

Examples of Factors Influencing Sample Size for Tests of Controls

The following are factors that the auditor may consider when determining the sample size for tests of controls. These factors, which need to be considered together, assume the auditor does not modify the nature or timing of tests of controls or otherwise modify the approach to substantive procedures in response to assessed risks.

FACTOR	EFFECT ON SAMPLE SIZE	
1. An increase in the extent to which the auditor's risk assessment takes into account relevant controls	Increase	The more assurance the auditor intends to obtain from the operating effectiveness of controls, the lower the auditor's assessment of the risk of material misstatement will be, and the larger the sample size will need to be. When the auditor's assessment of the risk of material misstatement at the assertion level includes an expectation of the operating effectiveness of controls, the auditor is required to perform tests of controls. Other things being equal, the greater the reliance the auditor places on the operating effectiveness of controls in the risk assessment, the greater is the extent of the auditor's tests of controls (and therefore, the sample size is increased).
2. An increase in the tolerable rate of deviation	Decrease	The lower the tolerable rate of deviation, the larger the sample size needs to be.

FACTOR	EFFECT ON SAMPLE SIZE	
3. An increase in the expected rate of deviation of the population to be tested	Increase	The higher the expected rate of deviation, the larger the sample size needs to be so that the auditor is in a position to make a reasonable estimate of the actual rate of deviation. Factors relevant to the auditor's consideration of the expected rate of deviation include the auditor's understanding of the business (in particular, risk assessment procedures undertaken to obtain an understanding of internal control), changes in personnel or in internal control, the results of audit procedures applied in prior periods and the results of other audit procedures. High expected control deviation rates ordinarily warrant little, if any, reduction of the assessed risk of material misstatement.
4. An increase in the auditor's desired level of assurance that the tolerable rate of deviation is not exceeded by the actual rate of deviation in the population	Increase	The greater the level of assurance that the auditor desires that the results of the sample are in fact indicative of the actual incidence of deviation in the population, the larger the sample size needs to be.
5. An increase in the number of sampling units in the population	Negligible effect	For large populations, the actual size of the population has little, if any, effect on sample size. For small populations however, audit sampling may not be as efficient as alternative means of obtaining sufficient appropriate audit evidence.

Appendix 3

(Ref: Para. A11)

Examples of Factors Influencing Sample Size for Tests of Details

The following are factors that the auditor may consider when determining the sample size for tests of details. These factors, which need to be considered together, assume the auditor does not modify the approach to tests of controls or otherwise modify the nature or timing of substantive procedures in response to the assessed risks.

FACTOR	EFFECT ON SAMPLE SIZE	
1. An increase in the auditor's assessment of the risk of material misstatement	Increase	The higher the auditor's assessment of the risk of material misstatement, the larger the sample size needs to be. The auditor's assessment of the risk of material misstatement is affected by inherent risk and control risk. For example, if the auditor does not perform tests of controls, the auditor's risk assessment cannot be reduced for the effective operation of internal controls with respect to the particular assertion. Therefore, in order to reduce audit risk to an acceptably low level, the auditor needs a low detection risk and will rely more on substantive procedures. The more audit evidence that is obtained from tests of details (that is, the lower the detection risk), the larger the sample size will need to be.
2. An increase in the use of other substantive procedures directed at the same assertion	Decrease	The more the auditor is relying on other substantive procedures (tests of details or substantive analytical procedures) to reduce to an acceptable level the detection risk regarding a particular population, the less assurance the auditor will require from sampling and, therefore, the smaller the sample size can be.
3. An increase in the auditor's desired level of assurance that tolerable misstatement is not exceeded by actual misstatement in the population	Increase	The greater the level of assurance that the auditor requires that the results of the sample are in fact indicative of the actual amount of misstatement in the population, the larger the sample size needs to be.

FACTOR	EFFECT ON SAMPLE SIZE	
4. An increase in tolerable misstatement	Decrease	The lower the tolerable misstatement, the larger the sample size needs to be.
5. An increase in the amount of misstatement the auditor expects to find in the population	Increase	The greater the amount of misstatement the auditor expects to find in the population, the larger the sample size needs to be in order to make a reasonable estimate of the actual amount of misstatement in the population. Factors relevant to the auditor's consideration of the expected misstatement amount include the extent to which item values are determined subjectively, the results of risk assessment procedures, the results of tests of control, the results of audit procedures applied in prior periods, and the results of other substantive procedures.
6. Stratification of the population when appropriate	Decrease	When there is a wide range (variability) in the monetary size of items in the population, it may be useful to stratify the population. When a population can be appropriately stratified, the aggregate of the sample sizes from the strata generally will be less than the sample size that would have been required to attain a given level of sampling risk, had one sample been drawn from the whole population.

FACTOR	EFFECT ON SAMPLE SIZE	
7. The number of sampling units in the population	Negligible effect	For large populations, the actual size of the population has little, if any, effect on sample size. Thus, for small populations, audit sampling is often not as efficient as alternative means of obtaining sufficient appropriate audit evidence. (However, when using monetary unit sampling, an increase in the monetary value of the population increases sample size, unless this is offset by a proportional increase in materiality for the financial statements as a whole [and, if applicable, materiality level or levels for particular classes of transactions, account balances or disclosures].)

Appendix 4   (Ref: Para. A13)

Sample Selection Methods

There are many methods of selecting samples. The principal methods are as follows:

(a) Random selection (applied through random number generators, for example, random number tables).

(b) Systematic selection, in which the number of sampling units in the population is divided by the sample size to give a sampling interval, for example 50, and having determined a starting point within the first 50, each 50th sampling unit thereafter is selected. Although the starting point may be determined haphazardly, the sample is more likely to be truly random if it is determined by use of a computerized random number generator or random number tables. When using systematic selection, the auditor would need to determine that sampling units within the population are not structured in such a way that the sampling interval corresponds with a particular pattern in the population.

(c) Monetary Unit Sampling is a type of value-weighted selection (as described in Appendix 1) in which sample size, selection and evaluation results in a conclusion in monetary amounts.

(d) Haphazard selection, in which the auditor selects the sample without following a structured technique. Although no structured technique is used, the auditor would nonetheless avoid any conscious bias or predictability (for example, avoiding difficult to locate items, or always choosing or avoiding the first or last entries on a page) and thus attempt to ensure that all items in the population have a chance of selection. Haphazard selection is not appropriate when using statistical sampling.

(e) Block selection involves selection of a block(s) of contiguous items from within the population. Block selection cannot ordinarily be used in audit sampling because most populations are structured such that items in a sequence can be expected to have similar characteristics to each other, but different characteristics from items elsewhere in the population. Although in some circumstances it may be an appropriate audit procedure to examine a block of items, it would rarely be an appropriate sample selection technique when the auditor intends to draw valid inferences about the entire population based on the sample.

International Standard on Auditing (UK and Ireland) 540

Auditing accounting estimates, including fair value accounting estimates, and related disclosures

(Effective for audits of financial statements for periods ending on or after 15 December 2010)

Contents

International Standard on Auditing (UK and Ireland) (ISA (UK and Ireland)) 540, "Auditing Accounting Estimates, Including Fair Value Accounting Estimates, and Related Disclosures" should be read in conjunction with ISA (UK and Ireland) 200, "Overall Objectives of the Independent Auditor and the Conduct of an Audit in Accordance with International Standards on Auditing (UK and Ireland)."

Introduction

Scope of this ISA (UK and Ireland)

1   This International Standard on Auditing (UK and Ireland) (ISA (UK and Ireland)) deals with the auditor's responsibilities relating to accounting estimates, including fair value accounting estimates, and related disclosures in an audit of financial statements. Specifically, it expands on how ISA (UK and Ireland) 315[1] and ISA (UK and Ireland) 330[2] and other relevant ISAs (UK and Ireland) are to be applied in relation to accounting estimates. It also includes requirements and guidance on misstatements of individual accounting estimates, and indicators of possible management bias.

Nature of Accounting Estimates

2   Some financial statement items cannot be measured precisely, but can only be estimated. For purposes of this ISA (UK and Ireland), such financial statement items are referred to as accounting estimates. The nature and reliability of information available to management to support the making of an accounting estimate varies widely, which thereby affects the degree of estimation uncertainty associated with accounting estimates. The degree of estimation uncertainty affects, in turn, the risks of material misstatement of accounting estimates, including their susceptibility to unintentional or intentional management bias. (Ref: Para. A1-A11)

3   The measurement objective of accounting estimates can vary depending on the applicable financial reporting framework and the financial item being reported. The measurement objective for some accounting estimates is to forecast the outcome of one or more transactions, events or conditions giving rise to the need for the accounting estimate. For other accounting estimates, including many fair value accounting estimates, the measurement objective is different, and is expressed in terms of the value of a current transaction or financial statement item based on conditions prevalent at the measurement date, such as estimated market price for a particular type of asset or liability. For example, the applicable financial reporting framework may require fair value measurement based on an assumed hypothetical current transaction between knowledgeable, willing parties (sometimes referred to as "marketplace participants" or equivalent) in an arm's length transaction, rather than the settlement of a transaction at some past or future date.[3]

4   A difference between the outcome of an accounting estimate and the amount originally recognized or disclosed in the financial statements does not necessarily represent a misstatement of the financial statements. This is particularly the case for fair value accounting estimates, as any observed outcome is invariably affected by events or conditions subsequent to the date at which the measurement is estimated for purposes of the financial statements.

---

[1] *ISA (UK and Ireland) 315, "Identifying and Assessing the Risks of Material Misstatement through Understanding the Entity and Its Environment."*

[2] *ISA (UK and Ireland) 330, "The Auditor's Responses to Assessed Risks."*

[3] *Different definitions of fair value may exist among financial reporting frameworks.*

Effective Date

This ISA (UK and Ireland) is effective for audits of financial statements for periods   5
ending on or after 15 December 2010.

Objective

The objective of the auditor is to obtain sufficient appropriate audit evidence about   6
whether:

(a) accounting estimates, including fair value accounting estimates, in the financial
     statements, whether recognized or disclosed, are reasonable; and
(b) related disclosures in the financial statements are adequate,

in the context of the applicable financial reporting framework.

Definitions

For purposes of the ISAs (UK and Ireland), the following terms have the meanings   7
attributed below:

(a) Accounting estimate – An approximation of a monetary amount in the absence
     of a precise means of measurement. This term is used for an amount measured
     at fair value where there is estimation uncertainty, as well as for other amounts
     that require estimation. Where this ISA (UK and Ireland) addresses only
     accounting estimates involving measurement at fair value, the term "fair value
     accounting estimates" is used.
(b) Auditor's point estimate or auditor's range – The amount, or range of amounts,
     respectively, derived from audit evidence for use in evaluating management's
     point estimate.
(c) Estimation uncertainty – The susceptibility of an accounting estimate and
     related disclosures to an inherent lack of precision in its measurement.
(d) Management bias – A lack of neutrality by management in the preparation of
     information.
(e) Management's point estimate – The amount selected by management for
     recognition or disclosure in the financial statements as an accounting estimate.
(f) Outcome of an accounting estimate – The actual monetary amount which
     results from the resolution of the underlying transaction(s), event(s) or condi-
     tion(s) addressed by the accounting estimate.

Requirements

Risk Assessment Procedures and Related Activities

When performing risk assessment procedures and related activities to obtain an   8
understanding of the entity and its environment, including the entity's internal
control, as required by ISA (UK and Ireland) 315,[4] the auditor shall obtain an
understanding of the following in order to provide a basis for the identification and
assessment of the risks of material misstatement for accounting estimates: (Ref: Para.
A12)

---

[4] *ISA (UK and Ireland) 315, paragraphs 5-6 and 11-12.*

(a) The requirements of the applicable financial reporting framework relevant to accounting estimates, including related disclosures. (Ref: Para. A13-A15)

(b) How management identifies those transactions, events and conditions that may give rise to the need for accounting estimates to be recognized or disclosed in the financial statements. In obtaining this understanding, the auditor shall make inquiries of management about changes in circumstances that may give rise to new, or the need to revise existing, accounting estimates. (Ref: Para. A16-A21)

(c) How management makes the accounting estimates, and an understanding of the data on which they are based, including: (Ref: Para. A22-A23)

    (i) The method, including where applicable the model, used in making the accounting estimate; (Ref: Para. A24-A26)

    (ii) Relevant controls; (Ref: Para. A27-A28)

    (iii) Whether management has used an expert; (Ref: Para. A29-A30)

    (iv) The assumptions underlying the accounting estimates; (Ref: Para. A31-A36)

    (v) Whether there has been or ought to have been a change from the prior period in the methods for making the accounting estimates, and if so, why; and (Ref: Para. A37)

    (vi) Whether and, if so, how management has assessed the effect of estimation uncertainty. (Ref: Para. A38)

9   The auditor shall review the outcome of accounting estimates included in the prior period financial statements, or, where applicable, their subsequent re-estimation for the purpose of the current period. The nature and extent of the auditor's review takes account of the nature of the accounting estimates, and whether the information obtained from the review would be relevant to identifying and assessing risks of material misstatement of accounting estimates made in the current period financial statements. However, the review is not intended to call into question the judgments made in the prior periods that were based on information available at the time. (Ref: Para. A39-A44)

Identifying and Assessing the Risks of Material Misstatement

10   In identifying and assessing the risks of material misstatement, as required by ISA (UK and Ireland) 315,[5] the auditor shall evaluate the degree of estimation uncertainty associated with an accounting estimate. (Ref: Para. A45-A46)

11   The auditor shall determine whether, in the auditor's judgment, any of those accounting estimates that have been identified as having high estimation uncertainty give rise to significant risks. (Ref: Para. A47-A51)

Responses to the Assessed Risks of Material Misstatement

12   Based on the assessed risks of material misstatement, the auditor shall determine: (Ref: Para. A52)

(a) Whether management has appropriately applied the requirements of the applicable financial reporting framework relevant to the accounting estimate; and (Ref: Para. A53-A56)

(b) Whether the methods for making the accounting estimates are appropriate and have been applied consistently, and whether changes, if any, in accounting estimates or in the method for making them from the prior period are appropriate in the circumstances. (Ref: Para. A57-A58)

---

[5] *ISA (UK and Ireland) 315, paragraph 25.*

In responding to the assessed risks of material misstatement, as required by ISA (UK **13**
and Ireland) 330,[6] the auditor shall undertake one or more of the following, taking
account of the nature of the accounting estimate: (Ref: Para. A59-A61)

(a) Determine whether events occurring up to the date of the auditor's report
provide audit evidence regarding the accounting estimate. (Ref: Para. A62-A67)
(b) Test how management made the accounting estimate and the data on which it is
based. In doing so, the auditor shall evaluate whether: (Ref: Para. A68-A70)
    (i) The method of measurement used is appropriate in the circumstances; and
       (Ref: Para. A71-A76)
    (ii) The assumptions used by management are reasonable in light of the mea-
       surement objectives of the applicable financial reporting framework. (Ref:
       Para. A77-A83)
(c) Test the operating effectiveness of the controls over how management made the
accounting estimate, together with appropriate substantive procedures. (Ref:
Para. A84-A86)
(d) Develop a point estimate or a range to evaluate management's point estimate.
For this purpose: (Ref: Para. A87-A91)
    (i) If the auditor uses assumptions or methods that differ from management's,
       the auditor shall obtain an understanding of management's assumptions or
       methods sufficient to establish that the auditor's point estimate or range
       takes into account relevant variables and to evaluate any significant dif-
       ferences from management's point estimate. (Ref: Para. A92)
    (ii) If the auditor concludes that it is appropriate to use a range, the auditor
       shall narrow the range, based on audit evidence available, until all out-
       comes within the range are considered reasonable. (Ref: Para. A93-A95)

In determining the matters identified in paragraph 12 or in responding to the assessed **14**
risks of material misstatement in accordance with paragraph 13, the auditor shall
consider whether specialized skills or knowledge in relation to one or more aspects of
the accounting estimates are required in order to obtain sufficient appropriate audit
evidence. (Ref: Para. A96-A101)

Further Substantive Procedures to Respond to Significant Risks

Estimation Uncertainty

For accounting estimates that give rise to significant risks, in addition to other **15**
substantive procedures performed to meet the requirements of ISA (UK and Ireland)
330,[7] the auditor shall evaluate the following: (Ref: Para. A102)

(a) How management has considered alternative assumptions or outcomes, and
why it has rejected them, or how management has otherwise addressed estimation uncertainty in making the accounting estimate. (Ref: Para. A103-A106)
(b) Whether the significant assumptions used by management are reasonable. (Ref:
Para. A107-A109)
(c) Where relevant to the reasonableness of the significant assumptions used by
management or the appropriate application of the applicable financial reporting
framework, management's intent to carry out specific courses of action and its
ability to do so. (Ref: Para. A110)

---

[6] *ISA (UK and Ireland) 330, paragraph 5.*

[7] *ISA (UK and Ireland) 330, paragraph 18.*

16 If, in the auditor's judgment, management has not adequately addressed the effects of estimation uncertainty on the accounting estimates that give rise to significant risks, the auditor shall, if considered necessary, develop a range with which to evaluate the reasonableness of the accounting estimate. (Ref: Para. A111-A112)

Recognition and Measurement Criteria

17 For accounting estimates that give rise to significant risks, the auditor shall obtain sufficient appropriate audit evidence about whether:

(a) management's decision to recognize, or to not recognize, the accounting estimates in the financial statements; and (Ref: Para. A113-A114)

(b) the selected measurement basis for the accounting estimates, (Ref: Para. A115)

are in accordance with the requirements of the applicable financial reporting framework.

Evaluating the Reasonableness of the Accounting Estimates, and Determining Misstatements

18 The auditor shall evaluate, based on the audit evidence, whether the accounting estimates in the financial statements are either reasonable in the context of the applicable financial reporting framework, or are misstated. (Ref: Para. A116-A119)

Disclosures Related to Accounting Estimates

19 The auditor shall obtain sufficient appropriate audit evidence about whether the disclosures in the financial statements related to accounting estimates are in accordance with the requirements of the applicable financial reporting framework. (Ref: Para. A120-A121)

20 For accounting estimates that give rise to significant risks, the auditor shall also evaluate the adequacy of the disclosure of their estimation uncertainty in the financial statements in the context of the applicable financial reporting framework. (Ref: Para. A122-A123)

Indicators of Possible Management Bias

21 The auditor shall review the judgments and decisions made by management in the making of accounting estimates to identify whether there are indicators of possible management bias. Indicators of possible management bias do not themselves constitute misstatements for the purposes of drawing conclusions on the reasonableness of individual accounting estimates. (Ref: Para. A124-A125)

Written Representations

22 The auditor shall obtain written representations from management and, where appropriate, those charged with governance whether they believe significant assumptions used in making accounting estimates are reasonable. (Ref: Para. A126-A127)

Documentation

The auditor shall include in the audit documentation:[8] **23**

(a) The basis for the auditor's conclusions about the reasonableness of accounting estimates and their disclosure that give rise to significant risks; and

(b) Indicators of possible management bias, if any. (Ref: Para. A128)

***

Application and Other Explanatory Material

Nature of Accounting Estimates (Ref: Para. 2)

Because of the uncertainties inherent in business activities, some financial statement **A1**
items can only be estimated. Further, the specific characteristics of an asset, liability or component of equity, or the basis of or method of measurement prescribed by the financial reporting framework, may give rise to the need to estimate a financial statement item. Some financial reporting frameworks prescribe specific methods of measurement and the disclosures that are required to be made in the financial statements, while other financial reporting frameworks are less specific. The Appendix to this ISA (UK and Ireland) discusses fair value measurements and disclosures under different financial reporting frameworks.

Some accounting estimates involve relatively low estimation uncertainty and may **A2**
give rise to lower risks of material misstatements, for example:

- Accounting estimates arising in entities that engage in business activities that are not complex.
- Accounting estimates that are frequently made and updated because they relate to routine transactions.
- Accounting estimates derived from data that is readily available, such as published interest rate data or exchange-traded prices of securities. Such data may be referred to as "observable" in the context of a fair value accounting estimate.
- Fair value accounting estimates where the method of measurement prescribed by the applicable financial reporting framework is simple and applied easily to the asset or liability requiring measurement at fair value.
- Fair value accounting estimates where the model used to measure the accounting estimate is well-known or generally accepted, provided that the assumptions or inputs to the model are observable.

For some accounting estimates, however, there may be relatively high estimation **A3**
uncertainty, particularly where they are based on significant assumptions, for example:

- Accounting estimates relating to the outcome of litigation.
- Fair value accounting estimates for derivative financial instruments not publicly traded.
- Fair value accounting estimates for which a highly specialized entity-developed model is used or for which there are assumptions or inputs that cannot be observed in the marketplace.

The degree of estimation uncertainty varies based on the nature of the accounting **A4**
estimate, the extent to which there is a generally accepted method or model used to

[8] *ISA (UK and Ireland) 230, "Audit Documentation," paragraphs 8-11, and paragraph A6.*

make the accounting estimate, and the subjectivity of the assumptions used to make the accounting estimate. In some cases, estimation uncertainty associated with an accounting estimate may be so great that the recognition criteria in the applicable financial reporting framework are not met and the accounting estimate cannot be made.

A5   Not all financial statement items requiring measurement at fair value, involve estimation uncertainty. For example, this may be the case for some financial statement items where there is an active and open market that provides readily available and reliable information on the prices at which actual exchanges occur, in which case the existence of published price quotations ordinarily is the best audit evidence of fair value. However, estimation uncertainty may exist even when the valuation method and data are well defined. For example, valuation of securities quoted on an active and open market at the listed market price may require adjustment if the holding is significant in relation to the market or is subject to restrictions in marketability. In addition, general economic circumstances prevailing at the time, for example, illiquidity in a particular market, may impact estimation uncertainty.

A6   Additional examples of situations where accounting estimates, other than fair value accounting estimates, may be required include:

- Allowance for doubtful accounts.
- Inventory obsolescence.
- Warranty obligations.
- Depreciation method or asset useful life.
- Provision against the carrying amount of an investment where there is uncertainty regarding its recoverability.
- Outcome of long term contracts.
- Costs arising from litigation settlements and judgments.

A7   Additional examples of situations where fair value accounting estimates may be required include:

- Complex financial instruments, which are not traded in an active and open market.
- Share-based payments.
- Property or equipment held for disposal.
- Certain assets or liabilities acquired in a business combination, including goodwill and intangible assets.
- Transactions involving the exchange of assets or liabilities between independent parties without monetary consideration, for example, a non-monetary exchange of plant facilities in different lines of business.

A8   Estimation involves judgments based on information available when the financial statements are prepared. For many accounting estimates, these include making assumptions about matters that are uncertain at the time of estimation. The auditor is not responsible for predicting future conditions, transactions or events that, if known at the time of the audit, might have significantly affected management's actions or the assumptions used by management.

Management Bias

A9   Financial reporting frameworks often call for neutrality, that is, freedom from bias. Accounting estimates are imprecise, however, and can be influenced by management judgment. Such judgment may involve unintentional or intentional management bias (for example, as a result of motivation to achieve a desired result). The susceptibility of an accounting estimate to management bias increases with the subjectivity involved in making it. Unintentional management bias and the potential for intentional management bias are inherent in subjective decisions that are often required in making an accounting estimate. For continuing audits, indicators of possible management bias identified during the audit of the preceding periods influence the planning and risk identification and assessment activities of the auditor in the current period.

Management bias can be difficult to detect at an account level. It may only be   **A10**
identified when considered in the aggregate of groups of accounting estimates or all accounting estimates, or when observed over a number of accounting periods. Although some form of management bias is inherent in subjective decisions, in making such judgments there may be no intention by management to mislead the users of financial statements. Where, however, there is intention to mislead, management bias is fraudulent in nature.

Considerations Specific to Public Sector Entities

Public sector entities may have significant holdings of specialized assets for which   **A11**
there are no readily available and reliable sources of information for purposes of measurement at fair value or other current value bases, or a combination of both. Often specialized assets held do not generate cash flows and do not have an active market. Measurement at fair value therefore ordinarily requires estimation and may be complex, and in some rare cases may not be possible at all.

Risk Assessment Procedures and Related Activities (Ref: Para. 8)

The risk assessment procedures and related activities required by paragraph 8 of this   **A12**
ISA (UK and Ireland) assist the auditor in developing an expectation of the nature and type of accounting estimates that an entity may have. The auditor's primary consideration is whether the understanding that has been obtained is sufficient to identify and assess the risks of material misstatement in relation to accounting estimates, and to plan the nature, timing and extent of further audit procedures.

Obtaining an Understanding of the Requirements of the Applicable Financial Reporting Framework (Ref: Para. 8(a))

Obtaining an understanding of the requirements of the applicable financial reporting   **A13**
framework assists the auditor in determining whether it, for example:

- Prescribes certain conditions for the recognition,[9] or methods for the measurement, of accounting estimates.
- Specifies certain conditions that permit or require measurement at a fair value, for example, by referring to management's intentions to carry out certain courses of action with respect to an asset or liability.
- Specifies required or permitted disclosures.

Obtaining this understanding also provides the auditor with a basis for discussion with management about how management has applied those requirements relevant to the accounting estimate, and the auditor's determination of whether they have been applied appropriately.

---

[9] *Most financial reporting frameworks require incorporation in the balance sheet or income statement of items that satisfy their criteria for recognition. Disclosure of accounting policies or adding notes to the financial statements does not rectify a failure to recognize such items, including accounting estimates.*

A14 Financial reporting frameworks may provide guidance for management on determining point estimates where alternatives exist. Some financial reporting frameworks, for example, require that the point estimate selected be the alternative that reflects management's judgment of the most likely outcome.[10] Others may require, for example, use of a discounted probability-weighted expected value. In some cases, management may be able to make a point estimate directly. In other cases, management may be able to make a reliable point estimate only after considering alternative assumptions or outcomes from which it is able to determine a point estimate.

A15 Financial reporting frameworks may require the disclosure of information concerning the significant assumptions to which the accounting estimate is particularly sensitive. Furthermore, where there is a high degree of estimation uncertainty, some financial reporting frameworks do not permit an accounting estimate to be recognized in the financial statements, but certain disclosures may be required in the notes to the financial statements.

Obtaining an Understanding of How Management Identifies the Need for Accounting Estimates (Ref: Para. 8(b))

A16 The preparation of the financial statements requires management to determine whether a transaction, event or condition gives rise to the need to make an accounting estimate, and that all necessary accounting estimates have been recognized, measured and disclosed in the financial statements in accordance with the applicable financial reporting framework.

A17 Management's identification of transactions, events and conditions that give rise to the need for accounting estimates is likely to be based on:

- Management's knowledge of the entity's business and the industry in which it operates.
- Management's knowledge of the implementation of business strategies in the current period.
- Where applicable, management's cumulative experience of preparing the entity's financial statements in prior periods.

In such cases, the auditor may obtain an understanding of how management identifies the need for accounting estimates primarily through inquiry of management. In other cases, where management's process is more structured, for example, when management has a formal risk management function, the auditor may perform risk assessment procedures directed at the methods and practices followed by management for periodically reviewing the circumstances that give rise to the accounting estimates and re-estimating the accounting estimates as necessary. The completeness of accounting estimates is often an important consideration of the auditor, particularly accounting estimates relating to liabilities.

A18 The auditor's understanding of the entity and its environment obtained during the performance of risk assessment procedures, together with other audit evidence obtained during the course of the audit, assist the auditor in identifying circumstances, or changes in circumstances, that may give rise to the need for an accounting estimate.

[10] *Different financial reporting frameworks may use different terminology to describe point estimates determined in this way.*

Inquiries of management about changes in circumstances may include, for example, inquiries about whether: **A19**

- The entity has engaged in new types of transactions that may give rise to accounting estimates.
- Terms of transactions that gave rise to accounting estimates have changed.
- Accounting policies relating to accounting estimates have changed, as a result of changes to the requirements of the applicable financial reporting framework or otherwise.
- Regulatory or other changes outside the control of management have occurred that may require management to revise, or make new, accounting estimates.
- New conditions or events have occurred that may give rise to the need for new or revised accounting estimates.

During the audit, the auditor may identify transactions, events and conditions that give rise to the need for accounting estimates that management failed to identify. ISA (UK and Ireland) 315 deals with circumstances where the auditor identifies risks of material misstatement that management failed to identify, including determining whether there is a significant deficiency in internal control with regard to the entity's risk assessment processes.[11]   **A20**

Considerations Specific to Smaller Entities

Obtaining this understanding for smaller entities is often less complex as their business activities are often limited and transactions are less complex. Further, often a single person, for example the owner-manager, identifies the need to make an accounting estimate and the auditor may focus inquiries accordingly.   **A21**

Obtaining an Understanding of How Management Makes the Accounting Estimates
(Ref: Para. 8(c))

The preparation of the financial statements also requires management to establish financial reporting processes for making accounting estimates, including adequate internal control. Such processes include the following: **A22**

- Selecting appropriate accounting policies and prescribing estimation processes, including appropriate estimation or valuation methods, including, where applicable, models.
- Developing or identifying relevant data and assumptions that affect accounting estimates.
- Periodically reviewing the circumstances that give rise to the accounting estimates and re-estimating the accounting estimates as necessary.

Matters that the auditor may consider in obtaining an understanding of how management makes the accounting estimates include, for example: **A23**

- The types of accounts or transactions to which the accounting estimates relate (for example, whether the accounting estimates arise from the recording of routine and recurring transactions or whether they arise from non-recurring or unusual transactions).
- Whether and, if so, how management has used recognized measurement techniques for making particular accounting estimates.
- Whether the accounting estimates were made based on data available at an interim date and, if so, whether and how management has taken into account

---

[11] *ISA (UK and Ireland) 315, paragraph 16.*

the effect of events, transactions and changes in circumstances occurring between that date and the period end.

Method of Measurement, Including the Use of Models (Ref: Para. 8(c)(i))

A24   In some cases, the applicable financial reporting framework may prescribe the method of measurement for an accounting estimate, for example, a particular model that is to be used in measuring a fair value estimate. In many cases, however, the applicable financial reporting framework does not prescribe the method of measurement, or may specify alternative methods for measurement.

A25   When the applicable financial reporting framework does not prescribe a particular method to be used in the circumstances, matters that the auditor may consider in obtaining an understanding of the method or, where applicable the model, used to make accounting estimates include, for example:

- How management considered the nature of the asset or liability being estimated when selecting a particular method.
- Whether the entity operates in a particular business, industry or environment in which there are methods commonly used to make the particular type of accounting estimate.

A26   There may be greater risks of material misstatement, for example, in cases when management has internally developed a model to be used to make the accounting estimate or is departing from a method commonly used in a particular industry or environment.

Relevant Controls (Ref: Para. 8(c)(ii))

A27   Matters that the auditor may consider in obtaining an understanding of relevant controls include, for example, the experience and competence of those who make the accounting estimates, and controls related to:

- How management determines the completeness, relevance and accuracy of the data used to develop accounting estimates.
- The review and approval of accounting estimates, including the assumptions or inputs used in their development, by appropriate levels of management and, where appropriate, those charged with governance.
- The segregation of duties between those committing the entity to the underlying transactions and those responsible for making the accounting estimates, including whether the assignment of responsibilities appropriately takes account of the nature of the entity and its products or services (for example, in the case of a large financial institution, relevant segregation of duties may include an independent function responsible for estimation and validation of fair value pricing of the entity's proprietary financial products staffed by individuals whose remuneration is not tied to such products).

A28   Other controls may be relevant to making the accounting estimates depending on the circumstances. For example, if the entity uses specific models for making accounting estimates, management may put into place specific policies and procedures around such models. Relevant controls may include, for example, those established over:

- The design and development, or selection, of a particular model for a particular purpose.
- The use of the model.
- The maintenance and periodic validation of the integrity of the model.

Management's Use of Experts (Ref: Para. 8(c)(iii))

Management may have, or the entity may employ individuals with, the experience **A29** and competence necessary to make the required point estimates. In some cases, however, management may need to engage an expert to make, or assist in making, them. This need may arise because of, for example:

- The specialized nature of the matter requiring estimation, for example, the measurement of mineral or hydrocarbon reserves in extractive industries.
- The technical nature of the models required to meet the relevant requirements of the applicable financial reporting framework, as may be the case in certain measurements at fair value.
- The unusual or infrequent nature of the condition, transaction or event requiring an accounting estimate.

Considerations specific to smaller entities

In smaller entities, the circumstances requiring an accounting estimate often are such **A30** that the owner-manager is capable of making the required point estimate. In some cases, however, an expert will be needed. Discussion with the owner-manager early in the audit process about the nature of any accounting estimates, the completeness of the required accounting estimates, and the adequacy of the estimating process may assist the owner-manager in determining the need to use an expert.

Assumptions (Ref: Para. 8(c)(iv))

Assumptions are integral components of accounting estimates. Matters that the **A31** auditor may consider in obtaining an understanding of the assumptions underlying the accounting estimates include, for example:

- The nature of the assumptions, including which of the assumptions are likely to be significant assumptions.
- How management assesses whether the assumptions are relevant and complete (that is, that all relevant variables have been taken into account).
- Where applicable, how management determines that the assumptions used are internally consistent.
- Whether the assumptions relate to matters within the control of management (for example, assumptions about the maintenance programs that may affect the estimation of an asset's useful life), and how they conform to the entity's business plans and the external environment, or to matters that are outside its control (for example, assumptions about interest rates, mortality rates, potential judicial or regulatory actions, or the variability and the timing of future cash flows).
- The nature and extent of documentation, if any, supporting the assumptions.

Assumptions may be made or identified by an expert to assist management in making the accounting estimates. Such assumptions, when used by management, become management's assumptions.

In some cases, assumptions may be referred to as inputs, for example, where man- **A32** agement uses a model to make an accounting estimate, though the term inputs may also be used to refer to the underlying data to which specific assumptions are applied.

Management may support assumptions with different types of information drawn **A33** from internal and external sources, the relevance and reliability of which will vary. In some cases, an assumption may be reliably based on applicable information from either external sources (for example, published interest rate or other statistical data) or internal sources (for example, historical information or previous conditions experienced by the entity). In other cases, an assumption may be more subjective, for example, where the entity has no experience or external sources from which to draw.

A34   In the case of fair value accounting estimates, assumptions reflect, or are consistent with, what knowledgeable, willing arm's length parties (sometimes referred to as "marketplace participants" or equivalent) would use in determining fair value when exchanging an asset or settling a liability. Specific assumptions will also vary with the characteristics of the asset or liability being valued, the valuation method used (for example, a market approach, or an income approach) and the requirements of the applicable financial reporting framework.

A35   With respect to fair value accounting estimates, assumptions or inputs vary in terms of their source and bases, as follows:

(a)   Those that reflect what marketplace participants would use in pricing an asset or liability developed based on market data obtained from sources independent of the reporting entity (sometimes referred to as "observable inputs" or equivalent).

(b)   Those that reflect the entity's own judgments about what assumptions marketplace participants would use in pricing the asset or liability developed based on the best information available in the circumstances (sometimes referred to as "unobservable inputs" or equivalent).

In practice, however, the distinction between (a) and (b) is not always apparent. Further, it may be necessary for management to select from a number of different assumptions used by different marketplace participants.

A36   The extent of subjectivity, such as whether an assumption or input is observable, influences the degree of estimation uncertainty and thereby the auditor's assessment of the risks of material misstatement for a particular accounting estimate.

Changes in Methods for Making Accounting Estimates (Ref: Para. 8(c)(v))

A37   In evaluating how management makes the accounting estimates, the auditor is required to understand whether there has been or ought to have been a change from the prior period in the methods for making the accounting estimates. A specific estimation method may need to be changed in response to changes in the environment or circumstances affecting the entity or in the requirements of the applicable financial reporting framework. If management has changed the method for making an accounting estimate, it is important that management can demonstrate that the new method is more appropriate, or is itself a response to such changes. For example, if management changes the basis of making an accounting estimate from a mark-to-market approach to using a model, the auditor challenges whether management's assumptions about the marketplace are reasonable in light of economic circumstances.

Estimation Uncertainty (Ref: Para. 8(c)(vi))

A38   Matters that the auditor may consider in obtaining an understanding of whether and, if so, how management has assessed the effect of estimation uncertainty include, for example:

- Whether and, if so, how management has considered alternative assumptions or outcomes by, for example, performing a sensitivity analysis to determine the effect of changes in the assumptions on an accounting estimate.
- How management determines the accounting estimate when analysis indicates a number of outcome scenarios.
- Whether management monitors the outcome of accounting estimates made in the prior period, and whether management has appropriately responded to the outcome of that monitoring procedure.

Reviewing Prior Period Accounting Estimates (Ref: Para. 9)

The outcome of an accounting estimate will often differ from the accounting estimate recognized in the prior period financial statements. By performing risk assessment procedures to identify and understand the reasons for such differences, the auditor may obtain:

A39

- Information regarding the effectiveness of management's prior period estimation process, from which the auditor can judge the likely effectiveness of management's current process.
- Audit evidence that is pertinent to the re-estimation, in the current period, of prior period accounting estimates.
- Audit evidence of matters, such as estimation uncertainty, that may be required to be disclosed in the financial statements.

The review of prior period accounting estimates may also assist the auditor, in the current period, in identifying circumstances or conditions that increase the susceptibility of accounting estimates to, or indicate the presence of, possible management bias. The auditor's professional skepticism assists in identifying such circumstances or conditions and in determining the nature, timing and extent of further audit procedures.

A40

A retrospective review of management judgments and assumptions related to significant accounting estimates is also required by ISA (UK and Ireland) 240.[12] That review is conducted as part of the requirement for the auditor to design and perform procedures to review accounting estimates for biases that could represent a risk of material misstatement due to fraud, in response to the risks of management override of controls. As a practical matter, the auditor's review of prior period accounting estimates as a risk assessment procedure in accordance with this ISA (UK and Ireland) may be carried out in conjunction with the review required by ISA (UK and Ireland) 240.

A41

The auditor may judge that a more detailed review is required for those accounting estimates that were identified during the prior period audit as having high estimation uncertainty, or for those accounting estimates that have changed significantly from the prior period. On the other hand, for example, for accounting estimates that arise from the recording of routine and recurring transactions, the auditor may judge that the application of analytical procedures as risk assessment procedures is sufficient for purposes of the review.

A42

For fair value accounting estimates and other accounting estimates based on current conditions at the measurement date, more variation may exist between the fair value amount recognized in the prior period financial statements and the outcome or the amount re-estimated for the purpose of the current period. This is because the

A43

---

[12] *ISA (UK and Ireland) 240, "The Auditor's Responsibilities Relating to Fraud in an Audit of Financial Statements," paragraph 32(b)(ii).*

measurement objective for such accounting estimates deals with perceptions about value at a point in time, which may change significantly and rapidly as the environment in which the entity operates changes. The auditor may therefore focus the review on obtaining information that would be relevant to identifying and assessing risks of material misstatement. For example, in some cases obtaining an understanding of changes in marketplace participant assumptions which affected the outcome of a prior period fair value accounting estimate may be unlikely to provide relevant information for audit purposes. If so, then the auditor's consideration of the outcome of prior period fair value accounting estimates may be directed more towards understanding the effectiveness of management's prior estimation process, that is, management's track record, from which the auditor can judge the likely effectiveness of management's current process.

A44   A difference between the outcome of an accounting estimate and the amount recognized in the prior period financial statements does not necessarily represent a misstatement of the prior period financial statements. However, it may do so if, for example, the difference arises from information that was available to management when the prior period's financial statements were finalized, or that could reasonably be expected to have been obtained and taken into account in the preparation of those financial statements. Many financial reporting frameworks contain guidance on distinguishing between changes in accounting estimates that constitute misstatements and changes that do not, and the accounting treatment required to be followed.

Identifying and Assessing the Risks of Material Misstatement

Estimation Uncertainty (Ref: Para. 10)

A45   The degree of estimation uncertainty associated with an accounting estimate may be influenced by factors such as:

- The extent to which the accounting estimate depends on judgment.
- The sensitivity of the accounting estimate to changes in assumptions.
- The existence of recognized measurement techniques that may mitigate the estimation uncertainty (though the subjectivity of the assumptions used as inputs may nevertheless give rise to estimation uncertainty).
- The length of the forecast period, and the relevance of data drawn from past events to forecast future events.
- The availability of reliable data from external sources.
- The extent to which the accounting estimate is based on observable or unobservable inputs.

The degree of estimation uncertainty associated with an accounting estimate may influence the estimate's susceptibility to bias.

A46   Matters that the auditor considers in assessing the risks of material misstatement may also include:

- The actual or expected magnitude of an accounting estimate.
- The recorded amount of the accounting estimate (that is, management's point estimate) in relation to the amount expected by the auditor to be recorded.
- Whether management has used an expert in making the accounting estimate.
- The outcome of the review of prior period accounting estimates.

High Estimation Uncertainty and Significant Risks (Ref: Para. 11)

Examples of accounting estimates that may have high estimation uncertainty include the following:

A47

- Accounting estimates that are highly dependent upon judgment, for example, judgments about the outcome of pending litigation or the amount and timing of future cash flows dependent on uncertain events many years in the future.
- Accounting estimates that are not calculated using recognized measurement techniques.
- Accounting estimates where the results of the auditor's review of similar accounting estimates made in the prior period financial statements indicate a substantial difference between the original accounting estimate and the actual outcome.
- Fair value accounting estimates for which a highly specialized entity-developed model is used or for which there are no observable inputs.

A seemingly immaterial accounting estimate may have the potential to result in a material misstatement due to the estimation uncertainty associated with the estimation; that is, the size of the amount recognized or disclosed in the financial statements for an accounting estimate may not be an indicator of its estimation uncertainty.

A48

In some circumstances, the estimation uncertainty is so high that a reasonable accounting estimate cannot be made. The applicable financial reporting framework may, therefore, preclude recognition of the item in the financial statements, or its measurement at fair value. In such cases, the significant risks relate not only to whether an accounting estimate should be recognized, or whether it should be measured at fair value, but also to the adequacy of the disclosures. With respect to such accounting estimates, the applicable financial reporting framework may require disclosure of the accounting estimates and the high estimation uncertainty associated with them (see paragraphs A120-A123).

A49

If the auditor determines that an accounting estimate gives rise to a significant risk, the auditor is required to obtain an understanding of the entity's controls, including control activities.[13]

A50

In some cases, the estimation uncertainty of an accounting estimate may cast significant doubt about the entity's ability to continue as a going concern. ISA (UK and Ireland) 570[14] establishes requirements and provides guidance in such circumstances.

A51

Responses to the Assessed Risks of Material Misstatement (Ref: Para. 12)

ISA (UK and Ireland) 330 requires the auditor to design and perform audit procedures whose nature, timing and extent are responsive to the assessed risks of material misstatement in relation to accounting estimates at both the financial statement and assertion levels.[15] Paragraphs A53-A115 focus on specific responses at the assertion level only.

A52

[13] *ISA (UK and Ireland) 315, paragraph 29.*

[14] *ISA (UK and Ireland) 570, "Going Concern."*

[15] *ISA (UK and Ireland) 330, paragraphs 5-6.*

Application of the Requirements of the Applicable Financial Reporting Framework
(Ref: Para. 12(a))

A53   Many financial reporting frameworks prescribe certain conditions for the recognition of accounting estimates and specify the methods for making them and required disclosures. Such requirements may be complex and require the application of judgment. Based on the understanding obtained in performing risk assessment procedures, the requirements of the applicable financial reporting framework that may be susceptible to misapplication or differing interpretations become the focus of the auditor's attention.

A54   Determining whether management has appropriately applied the requirements of the applicable financial reporting framework is based, in part, on the auditor's understanding of the entity and its environment. For example, the measurement of the fair value of some items, such as intangible assets acquired in a business combination, may involve special considerations that are affected by the nature of the entity and its operations.

A55   In some situations, additional audit procedures, such as the inspection by the auditor of the current physical condition of an asset, may be necessary to determine whether management has appropriately applied the requirements of the applicable financial reporting framework.

A56   The application of the requirements of the applicable financial reporting framework requires management to consider changes in the environment or circumstances that affect the entity. For example, the introduction of an active market for a particular class of asset or liability may indicate that the use of discounted cash flows to estimate the fair value of such asset or liability is no longer appropriate.

Consistency in Methods and Basis for Changes (Ref: Para. 12(b))

A57   The auditor's consideration of a change in an accounting estimate, or in the method for making it from the prior period, is important because a change that is not based on a change in circumstances or new information is considered arbitrary. Arbitrary changes in an accounting estimate result in inconsistent financial statements over time and may give rise to a financial statement misstatement or be an indicator of possible management bias.

A58   Management often is able to demonstrate good reason for a change in an accounting estimate or the method for making an accounting estimate from one period to another based on a change in circumstances. What constitutes a good reason, and the adequacy of support for management's contention that there has been a change in circumstances that warrants a change in an accounting estimate or the method for making an accounting estimate, are matters of judgment.

Responses to the Assessed Risks of Material Misstatements (Ref: Para. 13)

A59   The auditor's decision as to which response, individually or in combination, in paragraph 13 to undertake to respond to the risks of material misstatement may be influenced by such matters as:

- The nature of the accounting estimate, including whether it arises from routine or non routine transactions.
- Whether the procedure(s) is expected to effectively provide the auditor with sufficient appropriate audit evidence.

- The assessed risk of material misstatement, including whether the assessed risk is a significant risk.

For example, when evaluating the reasonableness of the allowance for doubtful accounts, an effective procedure for the auditor may be to review subsequent cash collections in combination with other procedures. Where the estimation uncertainty associated with an accounting estimate is high, for example, an accounting estimate based on a proprietary model for which there are unobservable inputs, it may be that a combination of the responses to assessed risks in paragraph 13 is necessary in order to obtain sufficient appropriate audit evidence. **A60**

Additional guidance explaining the circumstances in which each of the responses may be appropriate is provided in paragraphs A62-A95. **A61**

Events Occurring Up to the Date of the Auditor's Report (Ref: Para. 13(a))

Determining whether events occurring up to the date of the auditor's report provide audit evidence regarding the accounting estimate may be an appropriate response when such events are expected to: **A62**

- Occur; and
- Provide audit evidence that confirms or contradicts the accounting estimate.

Events occurring up to the date of the auditor's report may sometimes provide sufficient appropriate audit evidence about an accounting estimate. For example, sale of the complete inventory of a superseded product shortly after the period end may provide audit evidence relating to the estimate of its net realizable value. In such cases, there may be no need to perform additional audit procedures on the accounting estimate, provided that sufficient appropriate evidence about the events is obtained. **A63**

For some accounting estimates, events occurring up to the date of the auditor's report are unlikely to provide audit evidence regarding the accounting estimate. For example, the conditions or events relating to some accounting estimates develop only over an extended period. Also, because of the measurement objective of fair value accounting estimates, information after the period-end may not reflect the events or conditions existing at the balance sheet date and therefore may not be relevant to the measurement of the fair value accounting estimate. Paragraph 13 identifies other responses to the risks of material misstatement that the auditor may undertake. **A64**

In some cases, events that contradict the accounting estimate may indicate that management has ineffective processes for making accounting estimates, or that there is management bias in the making of accounting estimates. **A65**

Even though the auditor may decide not to undertake this approach in respect of specific accounting estimates, the auditor is required to comply with ISA (UK and Ireland) 560.[16] The auditor is required to perform audit procedures designed to obtain sufficient appropriate audit evidence that all events occurring between the date of the financial statements and the date of the auditor's report that require adjustment of, or disclosure in, the financial statements have been identified[17] and **A66**

---

[16] *ISA (UK and Ireland) 560, "Subsequent Events."*

[17] *ISA (UK and Ireland) 560, paragraph 6.*

appropriately reflected in the financial statements.[18] Because the measurement of many accounting estimates, other than fair value accounting estimates, usually depends on the outcome of future conditions, transactions or events, the auditor's work under ISA (UK and Ireland) 560 is particularly relevant.

Considerations specific to smaller entities

A67   When there is a longer period between the balance sheet date and the date of the auditor's report, the auditor's review of events in this period may be an effective response for accounting estimates other than fair value accounting estimates. This may particularly be the case in some smaller owner-managed entities, especially when management does not have formalized control procedures over accounting estimates.

Testing How Management Made the Accounting Estimate (Ref: Para. 13(b))

A68   Testing how management made the accounting estimate and the data on which it is based may be an appropriate response when the accounting estimate is a fair value accounting estimate developed on a model that uses observable and unobservable inputs. It may also be appropriate when, for example:

* The accounting estimate is derived from the routine processing of data by the entity's accounting system.
* The auditor's review of similar accounting estimates made in the prior period financial statements suggests that management's current period process is likely to be effective.
* The accounting estimate is based on a large population of items of a similar nature that individually are not significant.

A69   Testing how management made the accounting estimate may involve, for example:

* Testing the extent to which data on which the accounting estimate is based is accurate, complete and relevant, and whether the accounting estimate has been properly determined using such data and management assumptions.
* Considering the source, relevance and reliability of external data or information, including that received from external experts engaged by management to assist in making an accounting estimate.
* Recalculating the accounting estimate, and reviewing information about an accounting estimate for internal consistency.
* Considering management's review and approval processes.

Considerations specific to smaller entities

A70   In smaller entities, the process for making accounting estimates is likely to be less structured than in larger entities. Smaller entities with active management involvement may not have extensive descriptions of accounting procedures, sophisticated accounting records, or written policies. Even if the entity has no formal established process, it does not mean that management is not able to provide a basis upon which the auditor can test the accounting estimate.

---

[18] *ISA (UK and Ireland) 560, paragraph 8.*

Evaluating the method of measurement (Ref: Para. 13(b)(i))

When the applicable financial reporting framework does not prescribe the method of measurement, evaluating whether the method used, including any applicable model, is appropriate in the circumstances is a matter of professional judgment.   **A71**

For this purpose, matters that the auditor may consider include, for example, whether: **A72**

- Management's rationale for the method selected is reasonable.
- Management has sufficiently evaluated and appropriately applied the criteria, if any, provided in the applicable financial reporting framework to support the selected method.
- The method is appropriate in the circumstances given the nature of the asset or liability being estimated and the requirements of the applicable financial reporting framework relevant to accounting estimates.
- The method is appropriate in relation to the business, industry and environment in which the entity operates.

In some cases, management may have determined that different methods result in a range of significantly different estimates. In such cases, obtaining an understanding of how the entity has investigated the reasons for these differences may assist the auditor in evaluating the appropriateness of the method selected.   **A73**

Evaluating the use of models

In some cases, particularly when making fair value accounting estimates, management may use a model. Whether the model used is appropriate in the circumstances may depend on a number of factors, such as the nature of the entity and its environment, including the industry in which it operates, and the specific asset or liability being measured.   **A74**

The extent to which the following considerations are relevant depends on the circumstances, including whether the model is one that is commercially available for use in a particular sector or industry, or a proprietary model. In some cases, an entity may use an expert to develop and test a model.   **A75**

Depending on the circumstances, matters that the auditor may also consider in testing the model include, for example, whether: **A76**

- The model is validated prior to usage, with periodic reviews to ensure it is still suitable for its intended use. The entity's validation process may include evaluation of:
  - The model's theoretical soundness and mathematical integrity, including the appropriateness of model parameters.
  - The consistency and completeness of the model's inputs with market practices.
  - The model's output as compared to actual transactions.
- Appropriate change control policies and procedures exist.
- The model is periodically calibrated and tested for validity, particularly when inputs are subjective.
- Adjustments are made to the output of the model, including in the case of fair value accounting estimates, whether such adjustments reflect the assumptions marketplace participants would use in similar circumstances.

- The model is adequately documented, including the model's intended applications and limitations and its key parameters, required inputs, and results of any validation analysis performed.

Assumptions used by management (Ref: Para. 13(b)(ii))

A77   The auditor's evaluation of the assumptions used by management is based only on information available to the auditor at the time of the audit. Audit procedures dealing with management assumptions are performed in the context of the audit of the entity's financial statements, and not for the purpose of providing an opinion on assumptions themselves.

A78   Matters that the auditor may consider in evaluating the reasonableness of the assumptions used by management include, for example:

- Whether individual assumptions appear reasonable.
- Whether the assumptions are interdependent and internally consistent.
- Whether the assumptions appear reasonable when considered collectively or in conjunction with other assumptions, either for that accounting estimate or for other accounting estimates.
- In the case of fair value accounting estimates, whether the assumptions appropriately reflect observable marketplace assumptions.

A79   The assumptions on which accounting estimates are based may reflect what management expects will be the outcome of specific objectives and strategies. In such cases, the auditor may perform audit procedures to evaluate the reasonableness of such assumptions by considering, for example, whether the assumptions are consistent with:

- The general economic environment and the entity's economic circumstances.
- The plans of the entity.
- Assumptions made in prior periods, if relevant.
- Experience of, or previous conditions experienced by, the entity, to the extent this historical information may be considered representative of future conditions or events.
- Other assumptions used by management relating to the financial statements.

A80   The reasonableness of the assumptions used may depend on management's intent and ability to carry out certain courses of action. Management often documents plans and intentions relevant to specific assets or liabilities and the financial reporting framework may require it to do so. Although the extent of audit evidence to be obtained about management's intent and ability is a matter of professional judgment, the auditor's procedures may include the following:

- Review of management's history of carrying out its stated intentions.
- Review of written plans and other documentation, including, where applicable, formally approved budgets, authorizations or minutes.
- Inquiry of management about its reasons for a particular course of action.
- Review of events occurring subsequent to the date of the financial statements and up to the date of the auditor's report.
- Evaluation of the entity's ability to carry out a particular course of action given the entity's economic circumstances, including the implications of its existing commitments.

Certain financial reporting frameworks, however, may not permit management's intentions or plans to be taken into account when making an accounting estimate.

This is often the case for fair value accounting estimates because their measurement objective requires that assumptions reflect those used by marketplace participants.

Matters that the auditor may consider in evaluating the reasonableness of assumptions used by management underlying fair value accounting estimates, in addition to those discussed above where applicable, may include, for example: **A81**

- Where relevant, whether and, if so, how management has incorporated market-specific inputs into the development of assumptions.
- Whether the assumptions are consistent with observable market conditions, and the characteristics of the asset or liability being measured at fair value.
- Whether the sources of market-participant assumptions are relevant and reliable, and how management has selected the assumptions to use when a number of different market participant assumptions exist.
- Where appropriate, whether and, if so, how management considered assumptions used in, or information about, comparable transactions, assets or liabilities.

Further, fair value accounting estimates may comprise observable inputs as well as unobservable inputs. Where fair value accounting estimates are based on unobservable inputs, matters that the auditor may consider include, for example, how management supports the following: **A82**

- The identification of the characteristics of marketplace participants relevant to the accounting estimate.
- Modifications it has made to its own assumptions to reflect its view of assumptions marketplace participants would use.
- Whether it has incorporated the best information available in the circumstances.
- Where applicable, how its assumptions take account of comparable transactions, assets or liabilities.

If there are unobservable inputs, it is more likely that the auditor's evaluation of the assumptions will need to be combined with other responses to assessed risks in paragraph 13 in order to obtain sufficient appropriate audit evidence. In such cases, it may be necessary for the auditor to perform other audit procedures, for example, examining documentation supporting the review and approval of the accounting estimate by appropriate levels of management and, where appropriate, by those charged with governance.

In evaluating the reasonableness of the assumptions supporting an accounting estimate, the auditor may identify one or more significant assumptions. If so, it may indicate that the accounting estimate has high estimation uncertainty and may, therefore, give rise to a significant risk. Additional responses to significant risks are described in paragraphs A102-A115. **A83**

Testing the Operating Effectiveness of Controls (Ref: Para. 13(c))

Testing the operating effectiveness of the controls over how management made the accounting estimate may be an appropriate response when management's process has been well-designed, implemented and maintained, for example: **A84**

- Controls exist for the review and approval of the accounting estimates by appropriate levels of management and, where appropriate, by those charged with governance.
- The accounting estimate is derived from the routine processing of data by the entity's accounting system.

A85   Testing the operating effectiveness of the controls is required when:

(a)   The auditor's assessment of risks of material misstatement at the assertion level includes an expectation that controls over the process are operating effectively; or

(b)   Substantive procedures alone do not provide sufficient appropriate audit evidence at the assertion level.[19]

Considerations specific to smaller entities

A86   Controls over the process to make an accounting estimate may exist in smaller entities, but the formality with which they operate varies. Further, smaller entities may determine that certain types of controls are not necessary because of active management involvement in the financial reporting process. In the case of very small entities, however, there may not be many controls that the auditor can identify. For this reason, the auditor's response to the assessed risks is likely to be substantive in nature, with the auditor performing one or more of the other responses in paragraph 13.

Developing a Point Estimate or Range (Ref: Para. 13(d))

A87   Developing a point estimate or a range to evaluate management's point estimate may be an appropriate response where, for example:

*   An accounting estimate is not derived from the routine processing of data by the accounting system.
*   The auditor's review of similar accounting estimates made in the prior period financial statements suggests that management's current period process is unlikely to be effective.
*   The entity's controls within and over management's processes for determining accounting estimates are not well designed or properly implemented.
*   Events or transactions between the period end and the date of the auditor's report contradict management's point estimate.
*   There are alternative sources of relevant data available to the auditor which can be used in making a point estimate or a range.

A88   Even where the entity's controls are well designed and properly implemented, developing a point estimate or a range may be an effective or efficient response to the assessed risks. In other situations, the auditor may consider this approach as part of determining whether further procedures are necessary and, if so, their nature and extent.

A89   The approach taken by the auditor in developing either a point estimate or a range may vary based on what is considered most effective in the circumstances. For example, the auditor may initially develop a preliminary point estimate, and then assess its sensitivity to changes in assumptions to ascertain a range with which to evaluate management's point estimate. Alternatively, the auditor may begin by developing a range for purposes of determining, where possible, a point estimate.

A90   The ability of the auditor to make a point estimate, as opposed to a range, depends on several factors, including the model used, the nature and extent of data available and the estimation uncertainty involved with the accounting estimate. Further, the decision to develop a point estimate or range may be influenced by the applicable financial reporting framework, which may prescribe the point estimate that is to be

[19] *ISA (UK and Ireland) 330, paragraph 8.*

Recognition and Measurement Criteria

Recognition of the Accounting Estimates in the Financial Statements (Ref: Para. 17(a))

Where management has recognized an accounting estimate in the financial state-   **A113**
ments, the focus of the auditor's evaluation is on whether the measurement of the
accounting estimate is sufficiently reliable to meet the recognition criteria of the
applicable financial reporting framework.

With respect to accounting estimates that have not been recognized, the focus of the   **A114**
auditor's evaluation is on whether the recognition criteria of the applicable financial
reporting framework have in fact been met. Even where an accounting estimate has
not been recognized, and the auditor concludes that this treatment is appropriate,
there may be a need for disclosure of the circumstances in the notes to the financial
statements. The auditor may also determine that there is a need to draw the reader's
attention to a significant uncertainty by adding an Emphasis of Matter paragraph to
the auditor's report. ISA (UK and Ireland) 706[23] establishes requirements and provides guidance concerning such paragraphs.

Measurement Basis for the Accounting Estimates (Ref: Para. 17(b))

With respect to fair value accounting estimates, some financial reporting frameworks   **A115**
presume that fair value can be measured reliably as a prerequisite to either requiring
or permitting fair value measurements and disclosures. In some cases, this presumption may be overcome when, for example, there is no appropriate method or
basis for measurement. In such cases, the focus of the auditor's evaluation is on
whether management's basis for overcoming the presumption relating to the use of
fair value set forth under the applicable financial reporting framework is
appropriate.

**Evaluating the Reasonableness of the Accounting Estimates, and Determining
Misstatements** (Ref: Para. 18)

Based on the audit evidence obtained, the auditor may conclude that the evidence   **A116**
points to an accounting estimate that differs from management's point estimate.
Where the audit evidence supports a point estimate, the difference between the
auditor's point estimate and management's point estimate constitutes a misstatement. Where the auditor has concluded that using the auditor's range provides
sufficient appropriate audit evidence, a management point estimate that lies outside
the auditor's range would not be supported by audit evidence. In such cases, the
misstatement is no less than the difference between management's point estimate and
the nearest point of the auditor's range.

Where management has changed an accounting estimate, or the method in making it,   **A117**
from the prior period based on a subjective assessment that there has been a change
in circumstances, the auditor may conclude based on the audit evidence that the
accounting estimate is misstated as a result of an arbitrary change by management,
or may regard it as an indicator of possible management bias (see paragraphs A124-
A125).

[23] *ISA (UK and Ireland) 706, "Emphasis of Matter Paragraphs and Other Matter Paragraphs in the Independent Auditor's Report."*

A118   ISA (UK and Ireland) 450[24] provides guidance on distinguishing misstatements for purposes of the auditor's evaluation of the effect of uncorrected misstatements on the financial statements. In relation to accounting estimates, a misstatement, whether caused by fraud or error, may arise as a result of:

- Misstatements about which there is no doubt (factual misstatements).
- Differences arising from management's judgments concerning accounting estimates that the auditor considers unreasonable, or the selection or application of accounting policies that the auditor considers inappropriate (judgmental misstatements).
- The auditor's best estimate of misstatements in populations, involving the projection of misstatements identified in audit samples to the entire populations from which the samples were drawn (projected misstatements).

In some cases involving accounting estimates, a misstatement could arise as a result of a combination of these circumstances, making separate identification difficult or impossible.

A119   Evaluating the reasonableness of accounting estimates and related disclosures included in the notes to the financial statements, whether required by the applicable financial reporting framework or disclosed voluntarily, involves essentially the same types of considerations applied when auditing an accounting estimate recognized in the financial statements.

Disclosures Related to Accounting Estimates

Disclosures in Accordance with the Applicable Financial Reporting Framework (Ref: Para. 19)

A120   The presentation of financial statements in accordance with the applicable financial reporting framework includes adequate disclosure of material matters. The applicable financial reporting framework may permit, or prescribe, disclosures related to accounting estimates, and some entities may disclose voluntarily additional information in the notes to the financial statements. These disclosures may include, for example:

- The assumptions used.
- The method of estimation used, including any applicable model.
- The basis for the selection of the method of estimation.
- The effect of any changes to the method of estimation from the prior period.
- The sources and implications of estimation uncertainty.

Such disclosures are relevant to users in understanding the accounting estimates recognized or disclosed in the financial statements, and sufficient appropriate audit evidence needs to be obtained about whether the disclosures are in accordance with the requirements of the applicable financial reporting framework.

A121   In some cases, the applicable financial reporting framework may require specific disclosures regarding uncertainties. For example, some financial reporting frameworks prescribe:

- The disclosure of key assumptions and other sources of estimation uncertainty that have a significant risk of causing a material adjustment to the carrying amounts of assets and liabilities. Such requirements may be described using

---

[24] *ISA (UK and Ireland) 450, "Evaluation of Misstatements Identified during the Audit."*

terms such as "Key Sources of Estimation Uncertainty" or "Critical Accounting Estimates."

- The disclosure of the range of possible outcomes, and the assumptions used in determining the range.
- The disclosure of information regarding the significance of fair value accounting estimates to the entity's financial position and performance.
- Qualitative disclosures such as the exposures to risk and how they arise, the entity's objectives, policies and procedures for managing the risk and the methods used to measure the risk and any changes from the previous period of these qualitative concepts.
- Quantitative disclosures such as the extent to which the entity is exposed to risk, based on information provided internally to the entity's key management personnel, including credit risk, liquidity risk and market risk.

Disclosures of Estimation Uncertainty for Accounting Estimates that Give Rise to Significant Risks (Ref: Para. 20)

In relation to accounting estimates having significant risk, even where the disclosures are in accordance with the applicable financial reporting framework, the auditor may conclude that the disclosure of estimation uncertainty is inadequate in light of the circumstances and facts involved. The auditor's evaluation of the adequacy of disclosure of estimation uncertainty increases in importance the greater the range of possible outcomes of the accounting estimate is in relation to materiality (see related discussion in paragraph A94). **A122**

In some cases, the auditor may consider it appropriate to encourage management to describe, in the notes to the financial statements, the circumstances relating to the estimation uncertainty. ISA (UK and Ireland) 705[25] provides guidance on the implications for the auditor's opinion when the auditor believes that management's disclosure of estimation uncertainty in the financial statements is inadequate or misleading. **A123**

Indicators of Possible Management Bias (Ref: Para. 21)

During the audit, the auditor may become aware of judgments and decisions made by management which give rise to indicators of possible management bias. Such indicators may affect the auditor's conclusion as to whether the auditor's risk assessment and related responses remain appropriate, and the auditor may need to consider the implications for the rest of the audit. Further, they may affect the auditor's evaluation of whether the financial statements as a whole are free from material misstatement, as discussed in ISA (UK and Ireland) 700.[26] **A124**

Examples of indicators of possible management bias with respect to accounting estimates include: **A125**

---

[25] *ISA (UK and Ireland) 705, "Modifications to the Opinion in the Independent Auditor's Report."*

[26] *ISA 700, "Forming an Opinion and Reporting on Financial Statements."*
The APB has not promulgated ISA 700 as issued by the IAASB for application in the UK and Ireland. In the UK and Ireland the applicable auditing standard is ISA (UK and Ireland) 700, "The Auditor's Report on Financial Statements." Paragraph 8(b) of ISA (UK and Ireland) requires the auditor's evaluation of whether uncorrected misstatements are material. This evaluation is required to include consideration of possible indicators of management bias.

- Changes in an accounting estimate, or the method for making it, where management has made a subjective assessment that there has been a change in circumstances.
- Use of an entity's own assumptions for fair value accounting estimates when they are inconsistent with observable marketplace assumptions.
- Selection or construction of significant assumptions that yield a point estimate favorable for management objectives.
- Selection of a point estimate that may indicate a pattern of optimism or pessimism.

Written Representations (Ref: Para. 22)

A126   ISA (UK and Ireland) 580[27] discusses the use of written representations. Depending on the nature, materiality and extent of estimation uncertainty, written representations about accounting estimates recognized or disclosed in the financial statements may include representations:

- About the appropriateness of the measurement processes, including related assumptions and models, used by management in determining accounting estimates in the context of the applicable financial reporting framework, and the consistency in application of the processes.
- That the assumptions appropriately reflect management's intent and ability to carry out specific courses of action on behalf of the entity, where relevant to the accounting estimates and disclosures.
- That disclosures related to accounting estimates are complete and appropriate under the applicable financial reporting framework.
- That no subsequent event requires adjustment to the accounting estimates and disclosures included in the financial statements.

A127   For those accounting estimates not recognized or disclosed in the financial statements, written representations may also include representations about:

- The appropriateness of the basis used by management for determining that the recognition or disclosure criteria of the applicable financial reporting framework have not been met (see paragraph A114).
- The appropriateness of the basis used by management to overcome the presumption relating to the use of fair value set forth under the entity's applicable financial reporting framework, for those accounting estimates not measured or disclosed at fair value (see paragraph A115).

Documentation (Ref: Para. 23)

A128   Documentation of indicators of possible management bias identified during the audit assists the auditor in concluding whether the auditor's risk assessment and related responses remain appropriate, and in evaluating whether the financial statements as a whole are free from material misstatement. See paragraph A125 for examples of indicators of possible management bias.

---

[27] ISA (UK and Ireland) 580, "Written Representations."

Appendix

(Ref: Para. A1)

Fair Value Measurements and Disclosures under Different Financial Reporting Frameworks

The purpose of this appendix is only to provide a general discussion of fair value measurements and disclosures under different financial reporting frameworks, for background and context.

Different financial reporting frameworks require or permit a variety of fair value measurements and disclosures in financial statements. They also vary in the level of guidance that they provide on the basis for measuring assets and liabilities or the related disclosures. Some financial reporting frameworks give prescriptive guidance, others give general guidance, and some give no guidance at all. In addition, certain industry-specific measurement and disclosure practices for fair values also exist.   1

Definitions of fair value may differ among financial reporting frameworks, or for different assets, liabilities or disclosures within a particular framework. For example, International Accounting Standard (IAS) 39[28] defines fair value as "the amount for which an asset could be exchanged, or a liability settled, between knowledgeable, willing parties in an arm's length transaction." The concept of fair value ordinarily assumes a current transaction, rather than settlement at some past or future date. Accordingly, the process of measuring fair value would be a search for the estimated price at which that transaction would occur. Additionally, different financial reporting frameworks may use such terms as "entity-specific value," "value in use," or similar terms, but may still fall within the concept of fair value in this ISA (UK and Ireland).   2

Financial reporting frameworks may treat changes in fair value measurements that occur over time in different ways. For example, a particular financial reporting framework may require that changes in fair value measurements of certain assets or liabilities be reflected directly in equity, while such changes might be reflected in income under another framework. In some frameworks, the determination of whether to use fair value accounting or how it is applied is influenced by management's intent to carry out certain courses of action with respect to the specific asset or liability.   3

Different financial reporting frameworks may require certain specific fair value measurements and disclosures in financial statements and prescribe or permit them in varying degrees. The financial reporting frameworks may: 4

- Prescribe measurement, presentation and disclosure requirements for certain information included in the financial statements or for information disclosed in notes to financial statements or presented as supplementary information;
- Permit certain measurements using fair values at the option of an entity or only when certain criteria have been met;
- Prescribe a specific method for determining fair value, for example, through the use of an independent appraisal or specified ways of using discounted cash flows;
- Permit a choice of method for determining fair value from among several alternative methods (the criteria for selection may or may not be provided by the financial reporting framework); or

[28] *IAS 39, "Financial Instruments: Recognition and Measurement."*

- Provide no guidance on the fair value measurements or disclosures of fair value other than their use being evident through custom or practice, for example, an industry practice.

5   Some financial reporting frameworks presume that fair value can be measured reliably for assets or liabilities as a prerequisite to either requiring or permitting fair value measurements or disclosures. In some cases, this presumption may be overcome when an asset or liability does not have a quoted market price in an active market and for which other methods of reasonably estimating fair value are clearly inappropriate or unworkable. Some financial reporting frameworks may specify a fair value hierarchy that distinguishes inputs for use in arriving at fair values ranging from those that involve clearly "observable inputs" based on quoted prices and active markets and those "unobservable inputs" that involve an entity's own judgments about assumptions that marketplace participants would use.

6   Some financial reporting frameworks require certain specified adjustments or modifications to valuation information, or other considerations unique to a particular asset or liability. For example, accounting for investment properties may require adjustments to be made to an appraised market value, such as adjustments for estimated closing costs on sale, adjustments related to the property's condition and location, and other matters. Similarly, if the market for a particular asset is not an active market, published price quotations may have to be adjusted or modified to arrive at a more suitable measure of fair value. For example, quoted market prices may not be indicative of fair value if there is infrequent activity in the market, the market is not well established, or small volumes of units are traded relative to the aggregate number of trading units in existence. Accordingly, such market prices may have to be adjusted or modified. Alternative sources of market information may be needed to make such adjustments or modifications. Further, in some cases, collateral assigned (for example, when collateral is assigned for certain types of investment in debt) may need to be considered in determining the fair value or possible impairment of an asset or liability.

7   In most financial reporting frameworks, underlying the concept of fair value measurements is a presumption that the entity is a going concern without any intention or need to liquidate, curtail materially the scale of its operations, or undertake a transaction on adverse terms. Therefore, in this case, fair value would not be the amount that an entity would receive or pay in a forced transaction, involuntary liquidation, or distress sale. On the other hand, general economic conditions or economic conditions specific to certain industries may cause illiquidity in the marketplace and require fair values to be predicated upon depressed prices, potentially significantly depressed prices. An entity, however, may need to take its current economic or operating situation into account in determining the fair values of its assets and liabilities if prescribed or permitted to do so by its financial reporting framework and such framework may or may not specify how that is done. For example, management's plan to dispose of an asset on an accelerated basis to meet specific business objectives may be relevant to the determination of the fair value of that asset.

Prevalence of Fair Value Measurements

8   Measurements and disclosures based on fair value are becoming increasingly prevalent in financial reporting frameworks. Fair values may occur in, and affect the determination of, financial statements in a number of ways, including the measurement at fair value of the following:

- Specific assets or liabilities, such as marketable securities or liabilities to settle an obligation under a financial instrument, routinely or periodically "marked-to-market."
- Specific components of equity, for example when accounting for the recognition, measurement and presentation of certain financial instruments with equity features, such as a bond convertible by the holder into common shares of the issuer.
- Specific assets or liabilities acquired in a business combination. For example, the initial determination of goodwill arising on the purchase of an entity in a business combination usually is based on the fair value measurement of the identifiable assets and liabilities acquired and the fair value of the consideration given.
- Specific assets or liabilities adjusted to fair value on a one-time basis. Some financial reporting frameworks may require the use of a fair value measurement to quantify an adjustment to an asset or a group of assets as part of an asset impairment determination, for example, a test of impairment of goodwill acquired in a business combination based on the fair value of a defined operating entity or reporting unit, the value of which is then allocated among the entity's or unit's group of assets and liabilities in order to derive an implied goodwill for comparison to the recorded goodwill.
- Aggregations of assets and liabilities. In some circumstances, the measurement of a class or group of assets or liabilities calls for an aggregation of fair values of some of the individual assets or liabilities in such class or group. For example, under an entity's applicable financial reporting framework, the measurement of a diversified loan portfolio might be determined based on the fair value of some categories of loans comprising the portfolio.
- Information disclosed in notes to financial statements or presented as supplementary information, but not recognized in the financial statements.

International Standard on Auditing (UK and Ireland) 550

Related parties

(Effective for audits of financial statements for periods ending on or after 15 December 2010)[a]

Contents

[a] *Conforming amendments to this standard as a result of ISA (UK and Ireland) 610 (Revised June 2013), Using the Work of Internal Auditors, are included that are effective for audits of financial statements for periods ending on or after 15 June 2014. Details of the amendments are given in the Annexure to ISA (UK and Ireland) 610 (Revised June 2013).*

International Standard on Auditing (UK and Ireland) (ISA (UK and Ireland))
550, "Related Parties" should be read in conjunction with ISA (UK and Ireland)
200, "Overall Objectives of the Independent Auditor and the Conduct of an
Audit in Accordance with International Standards on Auditing (UK and
Ireland)."

Introduction

Scope of this ISA (UK and Ireland)

1   This International Standard on Auditing (UK and Ireland) (ISA (UK and Ireland)) deals with the auditor's responsibilities relating to related party relationships and transactions in an audit of financial statements. Specifically, it expands on how ISA (UK and Ireland) 315,[1] ISA (UK and Ireland) 330,[2] and ISA (UK and Ireland) 240[3] are to be applied in relation to risks of material misstatement associated with related party relationships and transactions.

Nature of Related Party Relationships and Transactions

2   Many related party transactions are in the normal course of business. In such circumstances, they may carry no higher risk of material misstatement of the financial statements than similar transactions with unrelated parties. However, the nature of related party relationships and transactions may, in some circumstances, give rise to higher risks of material misstatement of the financial statements than transactions with unrelated parties. For example:

- Related parties may operate through an extensive and complex range of relationships and structures, with a corresponding increase in the complexity of related party transactions.
- Information systems may be ineffective at identifying or summarizing transactions and outstanding balances between an entity and its related parties.
- Related party transactions may not be conducted under normal market terms and conditions; for example, some related party transactions may be conducted with no exchange of consideration.

Responsibilities of the Auditor

3   Because related parties are not independent of each other, many financial reporting frameworks establish specific accounting and disclosure requirements for related party relationships, transactions and balances to enable users of the financial statements to understand their nature and actual or potential effects on the financial statements. Where the applicable financial reporting framework establishes such requirements[3a], the auditor has a responsibility to perform audit procedures to identify, assess and respond to the risks of material misstatement arising from the entity's failure to appropriately account for or disclose related party relationships, transactions or balances in accordance with the requirements of the framework.

4   Even if the applicable financial reporting framework establishes minimal or no related party requirements, the auditor nevertheless needs to obtain an understanding of the entity's related party relationships and transactions sufficient to be

---

[1] *ISA (UK and Ireland) 315, "Identifying and Assessing the Risks of Material Misstatement through Understanding the Entity and Its Environment."*

[2] *ISA (UK and Ireland) 330, "The Auditor's Responses to Assessed Risks."*

[3] *ISA (UK and Ireland) 240, "The Auditor's Responsibilities Relating to Fraud in an Audit of Financial Statements."*

[3a] *In the UK and Ireland, specific accounting and disclosure requirements for related party relationships, transactions and balances are established in accounting standards and in law and regulations.*

able to conclude whether the financial statements, insofar as they are affected by those relationships and transactions: (Ref: Para. A1)

(a) Achieve fair presentation (for fair presentation frameworks); or (Ref: Para. A2)
(b) Are not misleading (for compliance frameworks). (Ref: Para. A3)

In addition, an understanding of the entity's related party relationships and trans-   5
actions is relevant to the auditor's evaluation of whether one or more fraud risk factors are present as required by ISA (UK and Ireland) 240,[4] because fraud may be more easily committed through related parties.

Owing to the inherent limitations of an audit, there is an unavoidable risk that some   6
material misstatements of the financial statements may not be detected, even though the audit is properly planned and performed in accordance with the ISAs (UK and Ireland).[5] In the context of related parties, the potential effects of inherent limitations on the auditor's ability to detect material misstatements are greater for such reasons as the following:

- Management may be unaware of the existence of all related party relationships and transactions, particularly if the applicable financial reporting framework does not establish related party requirements.
- Related party relationships may present a greater opportunity for collusion, concealment or manipulation by management.

Planning and performing the audit with professional skepticism as required by ISA   7
(UK and Ireland) 200[6] is therefore particularly important in this context, given the potential for undisclosed related party relationships and transactions. The requirements in this ISA (UK and Ireland) are designed to assist the auditor in identifying and assessing the risks of material misstatement associated with related party relationships and transactions, and in designing audit procedures to respond to the assessed risks.

Effective Date

This ISA (UK and Ireland) is effective for audits of financial statements for periods   8
ending on or after 15 December 2010.[1a]

Objectives

The objectives of the auditor are: 9

(a) Irrespective of whether the applicable financial reporting framework establishes related party requirements, to obtain an understanding of related party relationships and transactions sufficient to be able:
   (i) To recognize fraud risk factors, if any, arising from related party relationships and transactions that are relevant to the identification and assessment of the risks of material misstatement due to fraud; and

---

[4] *ISA (UK and Ireland) 240, paragraph 24.*

[5] *ISA (UK and Ireland) 200, "Overall Objectives of the Independent Auditor and the Conduct of an Audit in Accordance with International Standards on Auditing," paragraphs A51-A52.*

[6] *ISA (UK and Ireland) 200, paragraph 15.*

(ii)   To conclude, based on the audit evidence obtained, whether the financial statements, insofar as they are affected by those relationships and transactions:

    a.   Achieve fair presentation (for fair presentation frameworks); or

    b.   Are not misleading (for compliance frameworks); and

(b)   In addition, where the applicable financial reporting framework establishes related party requirements, to obtain sufficient appropriate audit evidence about whether related party relationships and transactions have been appropriately identified, accounted for and disclosed in the financial statements in accordance with the framework.

Definitions

10   For purposes of the ISAs (UK and Ireland), the following terms have the meanings attributed below:

(a)   Arm's length transaction – A transaction conducted on such terms and conditions as between a willing buyer and a willing seller who are unrelated and are acting independently of each other and pursuing their own best interests.

(b)   Related party – A party that is either: (Ref: Para. A4-A7)

    (i)   A related party as defined in the applicable financial reporting framework; or

    (ii)   Where the applicable financial reporting framework establishes minimal or no related party requirements:

        a.   A person or other entity that has control or significant influence, directly or indirectly through one or more intermediaries, over the reporting entity;

        b.   Another entity over which the reporting entity has control or significant influence, directly or indirectly through one or more intermediaries; or

        c.   Another entity that is under common control with the reporting entity through having:

            i.   Common controlling ownership;

            ii.   Owners who are close family members; or

            iii.   Common key management.

        However, entities that are under common control by a state (that is, a national, regional or local government) are not considered related unless they engage in significant transactions or share resources to a significant extent with one another.

Requirements

Risk Assessment Procedures and Related Activities

11   As part of the risk assessment procedures and related activities that ISA (UK and Ireland) 315 and ISA (UK and Ireland) 240 require the auditor to perform during the audit,[7] the auditor shall perform the audit procedures and related activities set out in paragraphs 12-17 to obtain information relevant to identifying the risks of material misstatement associated with related party relationships and transactions. (Ref: Para. A8)

---

[7] *ISA (UK and Ireland) 315, paragraph 5; ISA 240, paragraph 16.*

Understanding the Entity's Related Party Relationships and Transactions

The engagement team discussion that ISA (UK and Ireland) 315 and ISA (UK and **12**
Ireland) 240 require[8] shall include specific consideration of the susceptibility of the
financial statements to material misstatement due to fraud or error that could result
from the entity's related party relationships and transactions. (Ref: Para. A9-A10)

The auditor shall inquire of management regarding: **13**

(a) The identity of the entity's related parties, including changes from the prior
    period; (Ref: Para. A11-A14)
(b) The nature of the relationships between the entity and these related parties; and
(c) Whether the entity entered into any transactions with these related parties
    during the period and, if so, the type and purpose of the transactions.

The auditor shall inquire of management and others within the entity, and perform **14**
other risk assessment procedures considered appropriate, to obtain an understanding
of the controls, if any, that management has established to: (Ref: Para. A15-A20)

(a) Identify, account for, and disclose related party relationships and transactions
    in accordance with the applicable financial reporting framework;
(b) Authorize and approve significant transactions and arrangements with related
    parties; and (Ref: Para. A21)
(c) Authorize and approve significant transactions and arrangements outside the
    normal course of business.

Maintaining Alertness for Related Party Information When Reviewing Records or
Documents

During the audit, the auditor shall remain alert, when inspecting records or docu- **15**
ments, for arrangements or other information that may indicate the existence of
related party relationships or transactions that management has not previously
identified or disclosed to the auditor. (Ref: Para. A22-A23)

In particular, the auditor shall inspect the following for indications of the existence
of related party relationships or transactions that management has not previously
identified or disclosed to the auditor:

(a) Bank and legal confirmations obtained as part of the auditor's procedures;
(b) Minutes of meetings of shareholders and of those charged with governance; and
(c) Such other records or documents as the auditor considers necessary in the
    circumstances of the entity.

If the auditor identifies significant transactions outside the entity's normal course of **16**
business when performing the audit procedures required by paragraph 15 or through
other audit procedures, the auditor shall inquire of management about: (Ref: Para.
A24-A25)

(a) The nature of these transactions; and (Ref: Para. A26)
(b) Whether related parties could be involved. (Ref: Para. A27)

Sharing Related Party Information with the Engagement Team

The auditor shall share relevant information obtained about the entity's related **17**
parties with the other members of the engagement team. (Ref: Para. A28)

---

[8] *ISA (UK and Ireland) 315, paragraph 10; ISA 240, paragraph 15.*

Identification and Assessment of the Risks of Material Misstatement Associated with Related Party Relationships and Transactions

18   In meeting the ISA (UK and Ireland) 315 requirement to identify and assess the risks of material misstatement,[9] the auditor shall identify and assess the risks of material misstatement associated with related party relationships and transactions and determine whether any of those risks are significant risks. In making this determination, the auditor shall treat identified significant related party transactions outside the entity's normal course of business as giving rise to significant risks.

19   If the auditor identifies fraud risk factors (including circumstances relating to the existence of a related party with dominant influence) when performing the risk assessment procedures and related activities in connection with related parties, the auditor shall consider such information when identifying and assessing the risks of material misstatement due to fraud in accordance with ISA (UK and Ireland) 240. (Ref: Para. A6 and A29-A30)

Responses to the Risks of Material Misstatement Associated with Related Party Relationships and Transactions

20   As part of the ISA (UK and Ireland) 330 requirement that the auditor respond to assessed risks,[10] the auditor designs and performs further audit procedures to obtain sufficient appropriate audit evidence about the assessed risks of material misstatement associated with related party relationships and transactions. These audit procedures shall include those required by paragraphs 21-24. (Ref: Para. A31-A34)

Identification of Previously Unidentified or Undisclosed Related Parties or Significant Related Party Transactions

21   If the auditor identifies arrangements or information that suggests the existence of related party relationships or transactions that management has not previously identified or disclosed to the auditor, the auditor shall determine whether the underlying circumstances confirm the existence of those relationships or transactions.

22   If the auditor identifies related parties or significant related party transactions that management has not previously identified or disclosed to the auditor, the auditor shall:

(a) Promptly communicate the relevant information to the other members of the engagement team; (Ref: Para. A35)

(b) Where the applicable financial reporting framework establishes related party requirements:
   (i) Request management to identify all transactions with the newly identified related parties for the auditor's further evaluation; and
   (ii) Inquire as to why the entity's controls over related party relationships and transactions failed to enable the identification or disclosure of the related party relationships or transactions;

(c) Perform appropriate substantive audit procedures relating to such newly identified related parties or significant related party transactions; (Ref: Para. A36)

---

[9] *ISA (UK and Ireland) 315, paragraph 25.*

[10] *ISA (UK and Ireland) 330, paragraphs 5-6.*

(d) Reconsider the risk that other related parties or significant related party transactions may exist that management has not previously identified or disclosed to the auditor, and perform additional audit procedures as necessary; and

(e) If the non-disclosure by management appears intentional (and therefore indicative of a risk of material misstatement due to fraud), evaluate the implications for the audit. (Ref: Para. A37)

Identified Significant Related Party Transactions outside the Entity's Normal Course of Business

For identified significant related party transactions outside the entity's normal course of business, the auditor shall: **23**

(a) Inspect the underlying contracts or agreements, if any, and evaluate whether:
  (i) The business rationale (or lack thereof) of the transactions suggests that they may have been entered into to engage in fraudulent financial reporting or to conceal misappropriation of assets;[11](Ref: Para. A38-A39)
  (ii) The terms of the transactions are consistent with management's explanations; and
  (iii) The transactions have been appropriately accounted for and disclosed in accordance with the applicable financial reporting framework; and
(b) Obtain audit evidence that the transactions have been appropriately authorized and approved. (Ref: Para. A40-A41)

Assertions That Related Party Transactions Were Conducted on Terms Equivalent to Those Prevailing in an Arm's Length Transaction

If management has made an assertion in the financial statements to the effect that a **24**
related party transaction was conducted on terms equivalent to those prevailing in an arm's length transaction, the auditor shall obtain sufficient appropriate audit evidence about the assertion. (Ref: Para. A42-A45)

Evaluation of the Accounting for and Disclosure of Identified Related Party Relationships and Transactions

In forming an opinion on the financial statements in accordance with ISA (UK and **25**
Ireland) 700,[12] the auditor shall evaluate: (Ref: Para. A46)

(a) Whether the identified related party relationships and transactions have been appropriately accounted for and disclosed in accordance with the applicable financial reporting framework; and (Ref: Para. A47 – A47-1)
(b) Whether the effects of the related party relationships and transactions:
  (i) Prevent the financial statements from achieving fair presentation (for fair presentation frameworks); or
  (ii) Cause the financial statements to be misleading (for compliance frameworks).

---

[11] *ISA (UK and Ireland) 240, paragraph 32(c).*

[12] *ISA 700, "Forming an Opinion and Reporting on Financial Statements," paragraphs 10-15.*
The APB has not promulgated ISA 700 as issued by the IAASB for application in the UK and Ireland. In the UK and Ireland the applicable auditing standard is ISA (UK and Ireland) 700, "The Auditor's Report on Financial Statements." Paragraphs 8 - 11 of ISA (UK and Ireland) 700 establish requirements regarding forming an opinion on the financial statements.

Written Representations

26   Where the applicable financial reporting framework establishes related party requirements, the auditor shall obtain written representations from management and, where appropriate, those charged with governance that: (Ref: Para. A48 - A49-1)

(a)   They have disclosed to the auditor the identity of the entity's related parties and all the related party relationships and transactions of which they are aware; and

(b)   They have appropriately accounted for and disclosed such relationships and transactions in accordance with the requirements of the framework.

Communication with Those Charged with Governance

27   Unless all of those charged with governance are involved in managing the entity,[13] the auditor shall communicate with those charged with governance significant matters arising during the audit in connection with the entity's related parties. (Ref: Para. A50)

Documentation

28   The auditor shall include in the audit documentation the names of the identified related parties and the nature of the related party relationships.[14]

***

Application and Other Explanatory Material

Responsibilities of the Auditor

Financial Reporting Frameworks That Establish Minimal Related Party Requirements (Ref: Para. 4)

A1   An applicable financial reporting framework that establishes minimal related party requirements is one that defines the meaning of a related party but that definition has a substantially narrower scope than the definition set out in paragraph 10(b)(ii) of this ISA (UK and Ireland), so that a requirement in the framework to disclose related party relationships and transactions would apply to substantially fewer related party relationships and transactions.

Fair Presentation Frameworks (Ref: Para. 4(a))

A2   In the context of a fair presentation framework,[15] related party relationships and transactions may cause the financial statements to fail to achieve fair presentation if, for example, the economic reality of such relationships and transactions is not appropriately reflected in the financial statements. For instance, fair presentation may not be achieved if the sale of a property by the entity to a controlling share-holder at a price above or below fair market value has been accounted for as a

---

[13] *ISA (UK and Ireland) 260, "Communication with Those Charged with Governance," paragraph 13.*

[14] *ISA (UK and Ireland) 230, "Audit Documentation," paragraphs 8-11, and paragraph A6.*

[15] *ISA 200, paragraph 13(a), defines the meaning of fair presentation and compliance frameworks.*

transaction involving a profit or loss for the entity when it may constitute a contribution or return of capital or the payment of a dividend.

Compliance Frameworks (Ref: Para. 4(b))

In the context of a compliance framework, whether related party relationships and **A3** transactions cause the financial statements to be misleading as discussed in ISA (UK and Ireland) 700 depends upon the particular circumstances of the engagement. For example, even if non-disclosure of related party transactions in the financial statements is in compliance with the framework and applicable law or regulation, the financial statements could be misleading if the entity derives a very substantial portion of its revenue from transactions with related parties, and that fact is not disclosed. However, it will be extremely rare for the auditor to consider financial statements that are prepared and presented in accordance with a compliance framework to be misleading if in accordance with ISA (UK and Ireland) 210[16] the auditor determined that the framework is acceptable.[17]

Definition of a Related Party (Ref: Para. 10(b))

Many financial reporting frameworks discuss the concepts of control and significant **A4** influence. Although they may discuss these concepts using different terms, they generally explain that:

(a) Control is the power to govern the financial and operating policies of an entity so as to obtain benefits from its activities; and

(b) Significant influence (which may be gained by share ownership, statute or agreement) is the power to participate in the financial and operating policy decisions of an entity, but is not control over those policies.

The existence of the following relationships may indicate the presence of control or **A5** significant influence:

(a) Direct or indirect equity holdings or other financial interests in the entity.

(b) The entity's holdings of direct or indirect equity or other financial interests in other entities.

(c) Being part of those charged with governance or key management (that is, those members of management who have the authority and responsibility for planning, directing and controlling the activities of the entity).

(d) Being a close family member of any person referred to in subparagraph (c).

(e) Having a significant business relationship with any person referred to in subparagraph (c).

Related Parties with Dominant Influence

Related parties, by virtue of their ability to exert control or significant influence, may **A6** be in a position to exert dominant influence over the entity or its management.

---

[16] *ISA (UK and Ireland) 210, "Agreeing the Terms of Audit Engagements," paragraph 6(a).*

[17] *ISA 700, paragraph A12.*

The APB has not promulgated ISA 700 as issued by the IAASB for application in the UK and Ireland. In the UK and Ireland the applicable auditing standard is ISA (UK and Ireland) 700, "The Auditor's Report on Financial Statements." Paragraph A12 of ISA 700 states "It will be extremely rare for the auditor to consider financial statements that are prepared in accordance with a compliance framework to be misleading if, in accordance with ISA 210, the auditor determined that the framework is acceptable."

Consideration of such behavior is relevant when identifying and assessing the risks of material misstatement due to fraud, as further explained in paragraphs A29-A30.

Special-Purpose Entities as Related Parties

A7   In some circumstances, a special-purpose entity[18] may be a related party of the entity because the entity may in substance control it, even if the entity owns little or none of the special-purpose entity's equity.

Risk Assessment Procedures and Related Activities

Risks of Material Misstatement Associated with Related Party Relationships and Transactions (Ref: Para. 11)

Considerations Specific to Public Sector Entities

A8   The public sector auditor's responsibilities regarding related party relationships and transactions may be affected by the audit mandate, or by obligations on public sector entities arising from law, regulation or other authority. Consequently, the public sector auditor's responsibilities may not be limited to addressing the risks of material misstatement associated with related party relationships and transactions, but may also include a broader responsibility to address the risks of non-compliance with law, regulation and other authority governing public sector bodies that lay down specific requirements in the conduct of business with related parties. Further, the public sector auditor may need to have regard to public sector financial reporting requirements for related party relationships and transactions that may differ from those in the private sector.

Understanding the Entity's Related Party Relationships and Transactions

Discussion among the Engagement Team (Ref: Para. 12)

A9   Matters that may be addressed in the discussion among the engagement team include:

- The nature and extent of the entity's relationships and transactions with related parties (using, for example, the auditor's record of identified related parties updated after each audit).
- An emphasis on the importance of maintaining professional skepticism throughout the audit regarding the potential for material misstatement associated with related party relationships and transactions.
- The circumstances or conditions of the entity that may indicate the existence of related party relationships or transactions that management has not identified or disclosed to the auditor for example, a complex organizational structure, use of special-purpose entities for off-balance sheet transactions, or an inadequate information system).
- The records or documents that may indicate the existence of related party relationships or transactions.
- The importance that management and those charged with governance attach to the identification, appropriate accounting for, and disclosure of related party relationships and transactions (if the applicable financial reporting framework

---

[18] *ISA (UK and Ireland) 315, paragraphs A26-A27, provides guidance regarding the nature of a special-purpose entity.*

establishes related party requirements), and the related risk of management override of relevant controls.

In addition, the discussion in the context of fraud may include specific consideration of how related parties may be involved in fraud. For example: **A10**

- How special-purpose entities controlled by management might be used to facilitate earnings management.
- How transactions between the entity and a known business partner of a key member of management could be arranged to facilitate misappropriation of the entity's assets.

The Identity of the Entity's Related Parties (Ref: Para. 13(a))

Where the applicable financial reporting framework establishes related party requirements, information regarding the identity of the entity's related parties is likely to be readily available to management because the entity's information systems will need to record, process and summarize related party relationships and transactions to enable the entity to meet the accounting and disclosure requirements of the framework. Management is therefore likely to have a comprehensive list of related parties and changes from the prior period. For recurring engagements, making the inquiries provides a basis for comparing the information supplied by management with the auditor's record of related parties noted in previous audits. **A11**

However, where the framework does not establish related party requirements, the entity may not have such information systems in place. Under such circumstances, it is possible that management may not be aware of the existence of all related parties. Nevertheless, the requirement to make the inquiries specified by paragraph 13 still applies because management may be aware of parties that meet the related party definition set out in this ISA (UK and Ireland). In such a case, however, the auditor's inquiries regarding the identity of the entity's related parties are likely to form part of the auditor's risk assessment procedures and related activities performed in accordance with ISA (UK and Ireland) 315 to obtain information regarding: **A12**

- The entity's ownership and governance structures;
- The types of investments that the entity is making and plans to make; and
- The way the entity is structured and how it is financed.

In the particular case of common control relationships, as management is more likely to be aware of such relationships if they have economic significance to the entity, the auditor's inquiries are likely to be more effective if they are focused on whether parties with which the entity engages in significant transactions, or shares resources to a significant degree, are related parties.

In the context of a group audit, ISA (UK and Ireland) 600 requires the group engagement team to provide each component auditor with a list of related parties prepared by group management and any other related parties of which the group engagement team is aware.[19] Where the entity is a component within a group, this information provides a useful basis for the auditor's inquiries of management regarding the identity of the entity's related parties. **A13**

---

[19] ISA (UK and Ireland) 600, "Special Considerations—Audits of Group Financial Statements (Including the Work of Component Auditors)," paragraph 40(e).

A14   The auditor may also obtain some information regarding the identity of the entity's related parties through inquiries of management during the engagement acceptance or continuance process.

The Entity's Controls over Related Party Relationships and Transactions (Ref: Para. 14)

A15   Others within the entity are those considered likely to have knowledge of the entity's related party relationships and transactions, and the entity's controls over such relationships and transactions. These may include, to the extent that they do not form part of management:

- Those charged with governance;
- Personnel in a position to initiate, process, or record transactions that are both significant and outside the entity's normal course of business, and those who supervise or monitor such personnel;
- The internal audit function;
- In-house legal counsel; and
- The chief ethics officer or equivalent person.

A16   The audit is conducted on the premise that management and, where appropriate, those charged with governance have acknowledged and understand that they have responsibility for the preparation of the financial statements in accordance with the applicable financial reporting framework, including where relevant their fair presentation, and for such internal control as management and, where appropriate, those charged with governance determine is necessary to enable the preparation of financial statements that are free from material misstatement, whether due to fraud or error.[20] Accordingly, where the framework establishes related party requirements, the preparation of the financial statements requires management, with oversight from those charged with governance, to design, implement and maintain adequate controls over related party relationships and transactions so that these are identified and appropriately accounted for and disclosed in accordance with the framework. In their oversight role, those charged with governance monitor how management is discharging its responsibility for such controls. Regardless of any related party requirements the framework may establish, those charged with governance may, in their oversight role, obtain information from management to enable them to understand the nature and business rationale of the entity's related party relationships and transactions.

A17   In meeting the ISA (UK and Ireland) 315 (Revised June 2013) requirement to obtain an understanding of the control environment,[21] the auditor may consider features of the control environment relevant to mitigating the risks of material misstatement associated with related party relationships and transactions, such as:

- Internal ethical codes, appropriately communicated to the entity's personnel and enforced, governing the circumstances in which the entity may enter into specific types of related party transactions.
- Policies and procedures for open and timely disclosure of the interests that management and those charged with governance have in related party transactions.
- The assignment of responsibilities within the entity for identifying, recording, summarizing, and disclosing related party transactions.

[20] *ISA (UK and Ireland) 200, paragraph A2.*

[21] *ISA (UK and Ireland) 315 (Revised June 2013), paragraph 14.*

- Timely disclosure and discussion between management and those charged with governance of significant related party transactions outside the entity's normal course of business, including whether those charged with governance have appropriately challenged the business rationale of such transactions (for example, by seeking advice from external professional advisors).
- Clear guidelines for the approval of related party transactions involving actual or perceived conflicts of interest, such as approval by a subcommittee of those charged with governance comprising individuals independent of management.
- Periodic reviews by the internal audit function, where applicable.
- Proactive action taken by management to resolve related party disclosure issues, such as by seeking advice from the auditor or external legal counsel.
- The existence of whistle-blowing policies and procedures, where applicable.

Controls over related party relationships and transactions within some entities may be deficient or non-existent for a number of reasons, such as: **A18**

- The low importance attached by management to identifying and disclosing related party relationships and transactions.
- The lack of appropriate oversight by those charged with governance.
- An intentional disregard for such controls because related party disclosures may reveal information that management considers sensitive, for example, the existence of transactions involving family members of management.
- An insufficient understanding by management of the related party requirements of the applicable financial reporting framework.
- The absence of disclosure requirements under the applicable financial reporting framework.

Where such controls are ineffective or non-existent, the auditor may be unable to obtain sufficient appropriate audit evidence about related party relationships and transactions. If this were the case, the auditor would, in accordance with ISA (UK and Ireland) 705,[22] consider the implications for the audit, including the opinion in the auditor's report.

Fraudulent financial reporting often involves management override of controls that otherwise may appear to be operating effectively.[23] The risk of management override of controls is higher if management has relationships that involve control or significant influence with parties with which the entity does business because these relationships may present management with greater incentives and opportunities to perpetrate fraud. For example, management's financial interests in certain related parties may provide incentives for management to override controls by (a) directing the entity, against its interests, to conclude transactions for the benefit of these parties, or (b) colluding with such parties or controlling their actions. Examples of possible fraud include: **A19**

- Creating fictitious terms of transactions with related parties designed to misrepresent the business rationale of these transactions.
- Fraudulently organizing the transfer of assets from or to management or others at amounts significantly above or below market value.
- Engaging in complex transactions with related parties, such as special-purpose entities, that are structured to misrepresent the financial position or financial performance of the entity.

---

[22] ISA (UK and Ireland) 705, "Modifications to the Opinion in the Independent Auditor's Report."

[23] ISA (UK and Ireland) 240, paragraphs 31 and A4.

Considerations specific to smaller entities

A20   Control activities in smaller entities are likely to be less formal and smaller entities may have no documented processes for dealing with related party relationships and transactions. An owner-manager may mitigate some of the risks arising from related party transactions, or potentially increase those risks, through active involvement in all the main aspects of the transactions. For such entities, the auditor may obtain an understanding of the related party relationships and transactions, and any controls that may exist over these, through inquiry of management combined with other procedures, such as observation of management's oversight and review activities, and inspection of available relevant documentation.

Authorization and approval of significant transactions and arrangements (Ref: Para. 14(b))

A21   Authorization involves the granting of permission by a party or parties with the appropriate authority (whether management, those charged with governance or the entity's shareholders) for the entity to enter into specific transactions in accordance with pre-determined criteria, whether judgmental or not. Approval involves those parties' acceptance of the transactions the entity has entered into as having satisfied the criteria on which authorization was granted. Examples of controls the entity may have established to authorize and approve significant transactions and arrangements with related parties or significant transactions and arrangements outside the normal course of business include:

- Monitoring controls to identify such transactions and arrangements for authorization and approval.
- Approval of the terms and conditions of the transactions and arrangements by management, those charged with governance or, where applicable, shareholders.

Maintaining Alertness for Related Party Information When Reviewing Records or Documents

Records or Documents That the Auditor May Inspect (Ref: Para. 15)

A22   During the audit, the auditor may inspect records or documents that may provide information about related party relationships and transactions, for example:

- Third-party confirmations obtained by the auditor (in addition to bank and legal confirmations).
- Entity income tax returns.
- Information supplied by the entity to regulatory authorities.
- Shareholder registers to identify the entity's principal shareholders.
- Statements of conflicts of interest from management and those charged with governance.
- Records of the entity's investments and those of its pension plans.
- Contracts and agreements with key management or those charged with governance.
- Significant contracts and agreements not in the entity's ordinary course of business.
- Specific invoices and correspondence from the entity's professional advisors.
- Life insurance policies acquired by the entity.
- Significant contracts re-negotiated by the entity during the period.
- Reports of the internal audit function.
- Documents associated with the entity's filings with a securities regulator (for example, prospectuses).

Arrangements that may indicate the existence of previously unidentified or undisclosed related party relationships or transactions

An arrangement involves a formal or informal agreement between the entity and one or more other parties for such purposes as:　　**A23**

- The establishment of a business relationship through appropriate vehicles or structures.
- The conduct of certain types of transactions under specific terms and conditions.
- The provision of designated services or financial support.

Examples of arrangements that may indicate the existence of related party relationships or transactions that management has not previously identified or disclosed to the auditor include:

- Participation in unincorporated partnerships with other parties.
- Agreements for the provision of services to certain parties under terms and conditions that are outside the entity's normal course of business.
- Guarantees and guarantor relationships.

Identification of Significant Transactions outside the Normal Course of Business (Ref: Para. 16)

Obtaining further information on significant transactions outside the entity's normal　　**A24**
course of business enables the auditor to evaluate whether fraud risk factors, if any, are present and, where the applicable financial reporting framework establishes related party requirements, to identify the risks of material misstatement.

Examples of transactions outside the entity's normal course of business may include:　　**A25**

- Complex equity transactions, such as corporate restructurings or acquisitions.
- Transactions with offshore entities in jurisdictions with weak corporate laws.
- The leasing of premises or the rendering of management services by the entity to another party if no consideration is exchanged.
- Sales transactions with unusually large discounts or returns.
- Transactions with circular arrangements, for example, sales with a commitment to repurchase.
- Transactions under contracts whose terms are changed before expiry.

Understanding the nature of significant transactions outside the normal course of business (Ref: Para. 16(a))

Inquiring into the nature of the significant transactions outside the entity's normal　　**A26**
course of business involves obtaining an understanding of the business rationale of the transactions, and the terms and conditions under which these have been entered into.

Inquiring into whether related parties could be involved (Ref: Para. 16(b))

A related party could be involved in a significant transaction outside the entity's　　**A27**
normal course of business not only by directly influencing the transaction through being a party to the transaction, but also by indirectly influencing it through an intermediary. Such influence may indicate the presence of a fraud risk factor.

Sharing Related Party Information with the Engagement Team (Ref: Para. 17)

A28   Relevant related party information that may be shared among the engagement team members includes, for example:

- The identity of the entity's related parties.
- The nature of the related party relationships and transactions.
- Significant or complex related party relationships or transactions that may require special audit consideration, in particular transactions in which management or those charged with governance are financially involved.

Identification and Assessment of the Risks of Material Misstatement Associated with Related Party Relationships and Transactions

Fraud Risk Factors Associated with a Related Party with Dominant Influence (Ref: Para. 19)

A29   Domination of management by a single person or small group of persons without compensating controls is a fraud risk factor.[24] Indicators of dominant influence exerted by a related party include:

- The related party has vetoed significant business decisions taken by management or those charged with governance.
- Significant transactions are referred to the related party for final approval.
- There is little or no debate among management and those charged with governance regarding business proposals initiated by the related party.
- Transactions involving the related party (or a close family member of the related party) are rarely independently reviewed and approved.

Dominant influence may also exist in some cases if the related party has played a leading role in founding the entity and continues to play a leading role in managing the entity.

A30   In the presence of other risk factors, the existence of a related party with dominant influence may indicate significant risks of material misstatement due to fraud. For example:

- An unusually high turnover of senior management or professional advisors may suggest unethical or fraudulent business practices that serve the related party's purposes.
- The use of business intermediaries for significant transactions for which there appears to be no clear business justification may suggest that the related party could have an interest in such transactions through control of such intermediaries for fraudulent purposes.
- Evidence of the related party's excessive participation in or preoccupation with the selection of accounting policies or the determination of significant estimates may suggest the possibility of fraudulent financial reporting.

Responses to the Risks of Material Misstatement Associated with Related Party Relationships and Transactions (Ref: Para. 20)

A31   The nature, timing and extent of the further audit procedures that the auditor may select to respond to the assessed risks of material misstatement associated with

---

[24] *ISA (UK and Ireland) 240, Appendix 1.*

related party relationships and transactions depend upon the nature of those risks and the circumstances of the entity.[25]

Examples of substantive audit procedures that the auditor may perform when the auditor has assessed a significant risk that management has not appropriately accounted for or disclosed specific related party transactions in accordance with the applicable financial reporting framework (whether due to fraud or error) include: **A32**

- Confirming or discussing specific aspects of the transactions with intermediaries such as banks, law firms, guarantors, or agents, where practicable and not prohibited by law, regulation or ethical rules.
- Confirming the purposes, specific terms or amounts of the transactions with the related parties (this audit procedure may be less effective where the auditor judges that the entity is likely to influence the related parties in their responses to the auditor).
- Where applicable, reading the financial statements or other relevant financial information, if available, of the related parties for evidence of the accounting of the transactions in the related parties' accounting records.

If the auditor has assessed a significant risk of material misstatement due to fraud as a result of the presence of a related party with dominant influence, the auditor may, in addition to the general requirements of ISA (UK and Ireland) 240, perform audit procedures such as the following to obtain an understanding of the business relationships that such a related party may have established directly or indirectly with the entity and to determine the need for further appropriate substantive audit procedures: **A33**

- Inquiries of, and discussion with, management and those charged with governance.
- Inquiries of the related party.
- Inspection of significant contracts with the related party.
- Appropriate background research, such as through the Internet or specific external business information databases.
- Review of employee whistle-blowing reports where these are retained.

Depending upon the results of the auditor's risk assessment procedures, the auditor may consider it appropriate to obtain audit evidence without testing the entity's controls over related party relationships and transactions. In some circumstances, however, it may not be possible to obtain sufficient appropriate audit evidence from substantive audit procedures alone in relation to the risks of material misstatement associated with related party relationships and transactions. For example, where intra-group transactions between the entity and its components are numerous and a significant amount of information regarding these transactions is initiated, recorded, processed or reported electronically in an integrated system, the auditor may determine that it is not possible to design effective substantive audit procedures that by themselves would reduce the risks of material misstatement associated with these transactions to an acceptably low level. In such a case, in meeting the ISA (UK and Ireland) 330 requirement to obtain sufficient appropriate audit evidence as to the operating effectiveness of relevant controls,[26] the auditor is required to test the entity's controls over the completeness and accuracy of the recording of the related party relationships and transactions. **A34**

---

[25] *ISA (UK and Ireland) 330 provides further guidance on considering the nature, timing and extent of further audit procedures. ISA 240 establishes requirements and provides guidance on appropriate responses to assessed risks of material misstatement due to fraud.*

[26] *ISA (UK and Ireland) 330, paragraph 8(b).*

Identification of Previously Unidentified or Undisclosed Related Parties or Significant Related Party Transactions

Communicating Newly Identified Related Party Information to the Engagement Team (Ref: Para. 22(a))

A35   Communicating promptly any newly identified related parties to the other members of the engagement team assists them in determining whether this information affects the results of, and conclusions drawn from, risk assessment procedures already performed, including whether the risks of material misstatement need to be reassessed.

Substantive Procedures Relating to Newly Identified Related Parties or Significant Related Party Transactions (Ref: Para. 22(c))

A36   Examples of substantive audit procedures that the auditor may perform relating to newly identified related parties or significant related party transactions include:

- Making inquiries regarding the nature of the entity's relationships with the newly identified related parties, including (where appropriate and not prohibited by law, regulation or ethical rules) inquiring of parties outside the entity who are presumed to have significant knowledge of the entity and its business, such as legal counsel, principal agents, major representatives, consultants, guarantors, or other close business partners.
- Conducting an analysis of accounting records for transactions with the newly identified related parties. Such an analysis may be facilitated using computer-assisted audit techniques.
- Verifying the terms and conditions of the newly identified related party transactions, and evaluating whether the transactions have been appropriately accounted for and disclosed in accordance with the applicable financial reporting framework.

Intentional Non-Disclosure by Management (Ref: Para. 22(e))

A37   The requirements and guidance in ISA (UK and Ireland) 240 regarding the auditor's responsibilities relating to fraud in an audit of financial statements are relevant where management appears to have intentionally failed to disclose related parties or significant related party transactions to the auditor. The auditor may also consider whether it is necessary to re-evaluate the reliability of management's responses to the auditor's inquiries and management's representations to the auditor.

Identified Significant Related Party Transactions outside the Entity's Normal Course of Business

Evaluating the Business Rationale of Significant Related Party Transactions (Ref: Para. 23)

A38   In evaluating the business rationale of a significant related party transaction outside the entity's normal course of business, the auditor may consider the following:

- Whether the transaction:
  - Is overly complex (for example, it may involve multiple related parties within a consolidated group).
  - Has unusual terms of trade, such as unusual prices, interest rates, guarantees and repayment terms.

    ○ Lacks an apparent logical business reason for its occurrence.
    ○ Involves previously unidentified related parties.
    ○ Is processed in an unusual manner.
- Whether management has discussed the nature of, and accounting for, such a transaction with those charged with governance.
- Whether management is placing more emphasis on a particular accounting treatment rather than giving due regard to the underlying economics of the transaction.

If management's explanations are materially inconsistent with the terms of the related party transaction, the auditor is required, in accordance with ISA (UK and Ireland) 500,[27] to consider the reliability of management's explanations and representations on other significant matters.

The auditor may also seek to understand the business rationale of such a transaction **A39** from the related party's perspective, as this may help the auditor to better understand the economic reality of the transaction and why it was carried out. A business rationale from the related party's perspective that appears inconsistent with the nature of its business may represent a fraud risk factor.

Authorization and Approval of Significant Related Party Transactions (Ref: Para. 23(b))

Authorization and approval by management, those charged with governance, or, **A40** where applicable, the shareholders of significant related party transactions outside the entity's normal course of business may provide audit evidence that these have been duly considered at the appropriate levels within the entity and that their terms and conditions have been appropriately reflected in the financial statements. The existence of transactions of this nature that were not subject to such authorization and approval, in the absence of rational explanations based on discussion with management or those charged with governance, may indicate risks of material misstatement due to error or fraud. In these circumstances, the auditor may need to be alert for other transactions of a similar nature. Authorization and approval alone, however, may not be sufficient in concluding whether risks of material misstatement due to fraud are absent because authorization and approval may be ineffective if there has been collusion between the related parties or if the entity is subject to the dominant influence of a related party.

Considerations specific to smaller entities

A smaller entity may not have the same controls provided by different levels of **A41** authority and approval that may exist in a larger entity. Accordingly, when auditing a smaller entity, the auditor may rely to a lesser degree on authorization and approval for audit evidence regarding the validity of significant related party transactions outside the entity's normal course of business. Instead, the auditor may consider performing other audit procedures such as inspecting relevant documents, confirming specific aspects of the transactions with relevant parties, or observing the owner-manager's involvement with the transactions.

---

[27] *ISA (UK and Ireland) 500, "Audit Evidence," paragraph 11.*

Assertions That Related Party Transactions Were Conducted on Terms Equivalent to Those Prevailing in an Arm's Length Transaction (Ref: Para. 24)

A42   Although audit evidence may be readily available regarding how the price of a related party transaction compares to that of a similar arm's length transaction, there are ordinarily practical difficulties that limit the auditor's ability to obtain audit evidence that all other aspects of the transaction are equivalent to those of the arm's length transaction. For example, although the auditor may be able to confirm that a related party transaction has been conducted at a market price, it may be impracticable to confirm whether other terms and conditions of the transaction (such as credit terms, contingencies and specific charges) are equivalent to those that would ordinarily be agreed between independent parties. Accordingly, there may be a risk that management's assertion that a related party transaction was conducted on terms equivalent to those prevailing in an arm's length transaction may be materially misstated.

A43   The preparation of the financial statements requires management to substantiate an assertion that a related party transaction was conducted on terms equivalent to those prevailing in an arm's length transaction. Management's support for the assertion may include:

- Comparing the terms of the related party transaction to those of an identical or similar transaction with one or more unrelated parties.
- Engaging an external expert to determine a market value and to confirm market terms and conditions for the transaction.
- Comparing the terms of the transaction to known market terms for broadly similar transactions on an open market.

A44   Evaluating management's support for this assertion may involve one or more of the following:

- Considering the appropriateness of management's process for supporting the assertion.
- Verifying the source of the internal or external data supporting the assertion, and testing the data to determine their accuracy, completeness and relevance.
- Evaluating the reasonableness of any significant assumptions on which the assertion is based.

A45   Some financial reporting frameworks require the disclosure of related party transactions not conducted on terms equivalent to those prevailing in arm's length transactions. In these circumstances, if management has not disclosed a related party transaction in the financial statements, there may be an implicit assertion that the transaction was conducted on terms equivalent to those prevailing in an arm's length transaction.

Evaluation of the Accounting for and Disclosure of Identified Related Party Relationships and Transactions

Materiality Considerations in Evaluating Misstatements (Ref: Para. 25)

A46   ISA (UK and Ireland) 450 requires the auditor to consider both the size and the nature of a misstatement, and the particular circumstances of its occurrence, when evaluating whether the misstatement is material.[28] The significance of the transaction

---

[28] *ISA (UK and Ireland) 450, "Evaluation of Misstatements Identified during the Audit," paragraph 11(a). Paragraph A16 of ISA 450 provides guidance on the circumstances that may affect the evaluation of a misstatement.*

to the financial statement users may not depend solely on the recorded amount of the transaction but also on other specific relevant factors, such as the nature of the related party relationship.

Evaluation of Related Party Disclosures (Ref: Para. 25(a))

Evaluating the related party disclosures in the context of the disclosure requirements of the applicable financial reporting framework means considering whether the facts and circumstances of the entity's related party relationships and transactions have been appropriately summarized and presented so that the disclosures are understandable. Disclosures of related party transactions may not be understandable if:

A47

(a) The business rationale and the effects of the transactions on the financial statements are unclear or misstated; or
(b) Key terms, conditions, or other important elements of the transactions necessary for understanding them are not appropriately disclosed.

Accounting standards and corporate law applicable in the UK and Ireland include requirements for many entities for disclosures relating to control of the entity. The auditor may only be able to determine the name of the entity's ultimate controlling party through specific inquiry of management or those charged with governance. When the auditor considers it necessary, the auditor obtains corroboration from the ultimate controlling party confirming representations received in this regard.

A47-1

Written Representations (Ref: Para. 26)

Circumstances in which it may be appropriate to obtain written representations from those charged with governance include:

A48

- When they have approved specific related party transactions that (a) materially affect the financial statements, or (b) involve management.
- When they have made specific oral representations to the auditor on details of certain related party transactions.
- When they have financial or other interests in the related parties or the related party transactions.

The auditor may also decide to obtain written representations regarding specific assertions that management may have made, such as a representation that specific related party transactions do not involve undisclosed side agreements.

A49

An entity may require its management and those charged with governance to sign individual declarations in relation to related party matters. It may be helpful if any such declarations are addressed jointly to a designated official of the entity and also to the auditor. In other cases, the auditor may wish to obtain written representations directly from each of those charged with governance and from members of management.

A49-1

Communication with Those Charged with Governance (Ref: Para. 27)

A50   Communicating significant matters arising during the audit[29] in connection with the entity's related parties helps the auditor to establish a common understanding with those charged with governance of the nature and resolution of these matters. Examples of significant related party matters include:

- Non-disclosure (whether intentional or not) by management to the auditor of related parties or significant related party transactions, which may alert those charged with governance to significant related party relationships and transactions of which they may not have been previously aware.
- The identification of significant related party transactions that have not been appropriately authorized and approved, which may give rise to suspected fraud.
- Disagreement with management regarding the accounting for and disclosure of significant related party transactions in accordance with the applicable financial reporting framework.
- Non-compliance with applicable law or regulations prohibiting or restricting specific types of related party transactions.
- Difficulties in identifying the party that ultimately controls the entity.

---

[29] *ISA (UK and Ireland) 230, paragraph A8, provides further guidance on the nature of significant matters arising during the audit.*

International Standard on Auditing (UK and Ireland) 560

Subsequent events

(Effective for audits of financial statements for periods ending on or after 15 December 2010)

Contents

International Standard on Auditing (UK and Ireland) (ISA (UK and Ireland)) 560, "Subsequent Events" should be read in conjunction with ISA (UK and Ireland) 200, "Overall Objectives of the Independent Auditor and the Conduct of an Audit in Accordance with International Standards on Auditing (UK and Ireland)."

Introduction

Scope of this ISA (UK and Ireland)

1   This International Standard on Auditing (UK and Ireland) (ISA (UK and Ireland)) deals with the auditor's responsibilities relating to subsequent events in an audit of financial statements. (Ref: Para. A1)

Subsequent Events

2   Financial statements may be affected by certain events that occur after the date of the financial statements. Many financial reporting frameworks specifically refer to such events.[1] Such financial reporting frameworks ordinarily identify two types of events:

(a)   Those that provide evidence of conditions that existed at the date of the financial statements; and

(b)   Those that provide evidence of conditions that arose after the date of the financial statements.

ISA (UK and Ireland) 700 explains that the date of the auditor's report informs the reader that the auditor has considered the effect of events and transactions of which the auditor becomes aware and that occurred up to that date.[2]

Effective Date

3   This ISA (UK and Ireland) is effective for audits of financial statements for periods ending on or after 15 December 2010.

Objectives

4   The objectives of the auditor are:

(a)   To obtain sufficient appropriate audit evidence about whether events occurring between the date of the financial statements and the date of the auditor's report that require adjustment of, or disclosure in, the financial statements are appropriately reflected in those financial statements in accordance with the applicable financial reporting framework; and

(b)   To respond appropriately to facts that become known to the auditor after the date of the auditor's report, that, had they been known to the auditor at that date, may have caused the auditor to amend the auditor's report.

---

[1] *For example, International Accounting Standard (IAS) 10, "Events After the Reporting Period" deals with the treatment in financial statements of events, both favorable and unfavorable, that occur between the date of the financial statements (referred to as the "end of the reporting period" in the IAS) and the date when financial statements are authorized for issue.*

[2] *ISA (UK and Ireland) 700, "Forming an Opinion and Reporting on Financial Statements," paragraph A38. The APB has not promulgated ISA 700 as issued by the IAASB for application in the UK and Ireland. In the UK and Ireland the applicable auditing standard is ISA (UK and Ireland) 700, "The Auditor's Report on Financial Statements." Paragraph A19 of ISA (UK and Ireland) 700 explains that the date of the auditor's report informs the reader that the auditor has considered the effect of events and transactions of which the auditor becomes aware and that occurred up to that date.*

Definitions

For purposes of the ISAs (UK and Ireland), the following terms have the meanings **5** attributed below:

(a) Date of the financial statements – The date of the end of the latest period covered by the financial statements.

(b) Date of approval of the financial statements – The date on which all the statements that comprise the financial statements, including the related notes, have been prepared and those with the recognized authority have asserted that they have taken responsibility for those financial statements. (Ref: Para. A2)

(c) Date of the auditor's report – The date the auditor dates the report on the financial statements in accordance with ISA (UK and Ireland) 700. (Ref: Para. A3)

(d) Date the financial statements are issued – The date that the auditor's report and audited financial statements are made available to third parties. (Ref: Para. A4-A5)

(e) Subsequent events – Events occurring between the date of the financial statements and the date of the auditor's report, and facts that become known to the auditor after the date of the auditor's report.

Requirements

Events Occurring between the Date of the Financial Statements and the Date of the Auditor's Report

The auditor shall perform audit procedures designed to obtain sufficient appropriate **6** audit evidence that all events occurring between the date of the financial statements and the date of the auditor's report that require adjustment of, or disclosure in, the financial statements have been identified. The auditor is not, however, expected to perform additional audit procedures on matters to which previously applied audit procedures have provided satisfactory conclusions. (Ref: Para. A6)

The auditor shall perform the procedures required by paragraph 6 so that they cover **7** the period from the date of the financial statements to the date of the auditor's report, or as near as practicable thereto. The auditor shall take into account the auditor's risk assessment in determining the nature and extent of such audit procedures, which shall include the following: (Ref: Para. A7-A8)

(a) Obtaining an understanding of any procedures management has established to ensure that subsequent events are identified.

(b) Inquiring of management and, where appropriate, those charged with governance as to whether any subsequent events have occurred which might affect the financial statements. (Ref: Para. A9)

(c) Reading minutes, if any, of the meetings, of the entity's owners, management and those charged with governance, that have been held after the date of the financial statements and inquiring about matters discussed at any such meetings for which minutes are not yet available. (Ref: Para. A10)

(d) Reading the entity's latest subsequent interim financial statements, if any.

If, as a result of the procedures performed as required by paragraphs 6 and 7, the **8** auditor identifies events that require adjustment of, or disclosure in, the financial statements, the auditor shall determine whether each such event is appropriately reflected in those financial statements in accordance with the applicable financial reporting framework.

Written Representations

9   The auditor shall request management and, where appropriate, those charged with governance, to provide a written representation in accordance with ISA (UK and Ireland) 580[3] that all events occurring subsequent to the date of the financial statements and for which the applicable financial reporting framework requires adjustment or disclosure have been adjusted or disclosed.

Facts Which Become Known to the Auditor after the Date of the Auditor's Report but before the Date the Financial Statements Are Issued

10   The auditor has no obligation to perform any audit procedures regarding the financial statements after the date of the auditor's report. However, if, after the date of the auditor's report but before the date the financial statements are issued, a fact becomes known to the auditor that, had it been known to the auditor at the date of the auditor's report, may have caused the auditor to amend the auditor's report, the auditor shall: (Ref: Para. A11)

    (a) Discuss the matter with management and, where appropriate, those charged with governance.

    (b) Determine whether the financial statements need amendment and, if so,

    (c) Inquire how management intends to address the matter in the financial statements.

11   If management[3a] amends the financial statements, the auditor shall:

    (a) Carry out the audit procedures necessary in the circumstances on the amendment.

    (b) Unless the circumstances in paragraph 12 apply:

        (i)   Extend the audit procedures referred to in paragraphs 6 and 7 to the date of the new auditor's report; and

        (ii) Provide a new auditor's report on the amended financial statements. The new auditor's report shall not be dated earlier than the date of approval of the amended financial statements.

12   Where law, regulation or the financial reporting framework does not prohibit management[3a] from restricting the amendment of the financial statements to the effects of the subsequent event or events causing that amendment and those responsible for approving the financial statements are not prohibited from restricting their approval to that amendment, the auditor is permitted to restrict the audit procedures on subsequent events required in paragraph 11(b)(i) to that amendment. In such cases, the auditor shall either:

    (a) Amend the auditor's report to include an additional date restricted to that amendment that thereby indicates that the auditor's procedures on subsequent events are restricted solely to the amendment of the financial statements described in the relevant note to the financial statements; or (Ref: Para. A12)

    (b) Provide a new or amended auditor's report that includes a statement in an Emphasis of Matter paragraph[4] or Other Matter paragraph that conveys that

---

[3] ISA (UK and Ireland) 580, "Written Representations."

[3a] *In the UK and Ireland the responsibility for amending the financial statements rests with those charged with governance.*

[4] See ISA (UK and Ireland) 706, "Emphasis of Matter Paragraphs and Other Matter Paragraphs in the Independent Auditor's Report."

the auditor's procedures on subsequent events are restricted solely to the amendment of the financial statements as described in the relevant note to the financial statements.

In some jurisdictions, management[3a] may not be required by law, regulation or the **13** financial reporting framework to issue amended financial statements and, accordingly, the auditor need not provide an amended or new auditor's report. However, if management does not amend the financial statements in circumstances where the auditor believes they need to be amended, then: (Ref: Para. A13-A14)

(a) If the auditor's report has not yet been provided to the entity, the auditor shall modify the opinion as required by ISA (UK and Ireland) 705[5] and then provide the auditor's report; or

(b) If the auditor's report has already been provided to the entity, the auditor shall notify management and, unless all of those charged with governance are involved in managing the entity, those charged with governance, not to issue the financial statements to third parties before the necessary amendments have been made. If the financial statements are nevertheless subsequently issued without the necessary amendments, the auditor shall take appropriate action, to seek to prevent reliance on the auditor's report. (Ref: Para: A15-A16)

Facts Which Become Known to the Auditor after the Financial Statements Have Been Issued

After the financial statements have been issued, the auditor has no obligation to **14** perform any audit procedures regarding such financial statements. However, if, after the financial statements have been issued, a fact becomes known to the auditor that, had it been known to the auditor at the date of the auditor's report, may have caused the auditor to amend the auditor's report, the auditor shall:

(a) Discuss the matter with management and, where appropriate, those charged with governance;

(b) Determine whether the financial statements need amendment; and, if so,

(c) Inquire how management intends to address the matter in the financial statements. (Ref: Para. A16-1 – A16-3)

If management[3a] amends the financial statements[5a], the auditor shall: (Ref: Para. **15** A17)

(a) Carry out the audit procedures necessary in the circumstances on the amendment.

(b) Review the steps taken by management to ensure that anyone in receipt of the previously issued financial statements together with the auditor's report thereon is informed of the situation.

(c) Unless the circumstances in paragraph 12 apply:
(i) Extend the audit procedures referred to in paragraphs 6 and 7 to the date of the new auditor's report, and date the new auditor's report no earlier than the date of approval of the amended financial statements; and
(ii) Provide a new auditor's report on the amended financial statements.

(d) When the circumstances in paragraph 12 apply, amend the auditor's report, or provide a new auditor's report as required by paragraph 12.

---

[5] ISA (UK and Ireland) 705, "Modifications to the Opinion in the Independent Auditor's Report."

[5a] *In the UK the detailed regulations governing revised financial statements and directors' reports, where the revision is voluntary, are set out in section 454 of the Companies Act 2006. There are no provisions in the Companies Acts of the Republic of Ireland for revising financial statements.*

16   The auditor shall include in the new or amended auditor's report an Emphasis of Matter paragraph or Other Matter(s) paragraph referring to a note to the financial statements that more extensively discusses the reason for the amendment of the previously issued financial statements and to the earlier report provided by the auditor.

17   If management[5b] does not take the necessary steps to ensure that anyone in receipt of the previously issued financial statements is informed of the situation and does not amend the financial statements in circumstances where the auditor believes they need to be amended, the auditor shall notify management and, unless all of those charged with governance are involved in managing the entity[6], those charged with governance, that the auditor will seek to prevent future reliance on the auditor's report. If, despite such notification, management or those charged with governance do not take these necessary steps, the auditor shall take appropriate action to seek to prevent reliance on the auditor's report. (Ref: Para. A18 – A18-1)

***

Application and Other Explanatory Material

Scope of this ISA (UK and Ireland) (Ref: Para. 1)

A1   When the audited financial statements are included in other documents subsequent to the issuance of the financial statements, the auditor may have additional responsibilities relating to subsequent events that the auditor may need to consider, such as legal or regulatory requirements involving the offering of securities to the public in jurisdictions in which the securities are being offered. For example, the auditor may be required to perform additional audit procedures to the date of the final offering document. These procedures may include those referred to in paragraphs 6 and 7 performed up to a date at or near the effective date of the final offering document, and reading the offering document to assess whether the other information in the offering document is consistent with the financial information with which the auditor is associated.[7]

Definitions

Date of Approval of the Financial Statements (Ref: Para. 5(b))

A2   In some jurisdictions, law or regulation identifies the individuals or bodies (for example, management or those charged with governance) that are responsible for concluding that all the statements that comprise the financial statements, including the related notes, have been prepared, and specifies the necessary approval process. In other jurisdictions, the approval process is not prescribed in law or regulation and the entity follows its own procedures in preparing and finalizing its financial

---

[5b] *In the UK and Ireland, those charged with governance have responsibility for taking the steps referred to in paragraph 17.*

[6] *ISA (UK and Ireland) 260, "Communication with Those Charged with Governance," paragraph 13.*

[7] *See ISA (UK and Ireland) 200, "Overall Objectives of the Independent Auditor and the Conduct of an Audit in Accordance with International Standards on Auditing," paragraph 2.*
In the UK and Ireland, standards and guidance for accountants engaged to prepare a report and/or letter for inclusion in, or in connection with, an investment circular are set out in APB's Statements of Investment Circular Reporting Standards (SIRS).

statements in view of its management and governance structures. In some jurisdictions, final approval of the financial statements by shareholders is required. In these jurisdictions, final approval by shareholders is not necessary for the auditor to conclude that sufficient appropriate audit evidence on which to base the auditor's opinion on the financial statements has been obtained. The date of approval of the financial statements for purposes of the ISAs (UK and Ireland) is the earlier date on which those with the recognized authority determine that all the statements that comprise the financial statements, including the related notes, have been prepared and that those with the recognized authority have asserted that they have taken responsibility for those financial statements.

Date of the Auditor's Report (Ref: Para. 5(c))

The auditor's report cannot be dated earlier than the date on which the auditor has   **A3** obtained sufficient appropriate audit evidence on which to base the opinion on the financial statements including evidence that all the statements that comprise the financial statements, including the related notes, have been prepared and that those with the recognized authority have asserted that they have taken responsibility for those financial statements.[8] Consequently, the date of the auditor's report cannot be earlier than the date of approval of the financial statements as defined in paragraph 5(b). A time period may elapse due to administrative issues between the date of the auditor's report as defined in paragraph 5(c) and the date the auditor's report is provided to the entity.

Date the Financial Statements Are Issued (Ref: Para. 5(d))

The date the financial statements are issued generally depends on the regulatory   **A4** environment of the entity. In some circumstances, the date the financial statements are issued may be the date that they are filed with a regulatory authority. Since audited financial statements cannot be issued without an auditor's report, the date that the audited financial statements are issued must not only be at or later than the date of the auditor's report, but must also be at or later than the date the auditor's report is provided to the entity.

Considerations Specific to Public Sector Entities

In the case of the public sector, the date the financial statements are issued may be   **A5** the date the audited financial statements and the auditor's report thereon are presented to the legislature or otherwise made public.

Events Occurring between the Date of the Financial Statements and the Date of the Auditor's Report (Ref: Para. 6-9)

Depending on the auditor's risk assessment, the audit procedures required by   **A6** paragraph 6 may include procedures, necessary to obtain sufficient appropriate audit evidence, involving the review or testing of accounting records or transactions

---

[8] *ISA 700, paragraph 41. In some cases, law or regulation also identifies the point in the financial statement reporting process at which the audit is expected to be complete.*

The APB has not promulgated ISA 700 as issued by the IAASB for application in the UK and Ireland. In the UK and Ireland the applicable auditing standard is ISA (UK and Ireland) 700, "The Auditor's Report on Financial Statements." Paragraph 24 of ISA (UK and Ireland) 700 establishes requirements regarding dating of the auditor's report, including that this shall not be earlier than the date the auditor has considered all necessary available evidence.

occurring between the date of the financial statements and the date of the auditor's report. The audit procedures required by paragraphs 6 and 7 are in addition to procedures that the auditor may perform for other purposes that, nevertheless, may provide evidence about subsequent events (for example, to obtain audit evidence for account balances as at the date of the financial statements, such as cut-off procedures or procedures in relation to subsequent receipts of accounts receivable).

A7   Paragraph 7 stipulates certain audit procedures in this context that the auditor is required to perform pursuant to paragraph 6. The subsequent events procedures that the auditor performs may, however, depend on the information that is available and, in particular, the extent to which the accounting records have been prepared since the date of the financial statements. Where the accounting records are not up-to-date, and accordingly no interim financial statements (whether for internal or external purposes) have been prepared, or minutes of meetings of management or those charged with governance have not been prepared, relevant audit procedures may take the form of inspection of available books and records, including bank statements. Paragraph A8 gives examples of some of the additional matters that the auditor may consider in the course of these inquiries.

A8   In addition to the audit procedures required by paragraph 7, the auditor may consider it necessary and appropriate to:

- Read the entity's latest available budgets, cash flow forecasts and other related management reports for periods after the date of the financial statements;
- Inquire, or extend previous oral or written inquiries, of the entity's legal counsel concerning litigation and claims; or
- Consider whether written representations covering particular subsequent events may be necessary to support other audit evidence and thereby obtain sufficient appropriate audit evidence.

Inquiry (Ref. Para. 7(b))

A9   In inquiring of management and, where appropriate, those charged with governance, as to whether any subsequent events have occurred that might affect the financial statements, the auditor may inquire as to the current status of items that were accounted for on the basis of preliminary or inconclusive data and may make specific inquiries about the following matters:

- Whether new commitments, borrowings or guarantees have been entered into.
- Whether sales or acquisitions of assets have occurred or are planned.
- Whether there have been increases in capital or issuance of debt instruments, such as the issue of new shares or debentures, or an agreement to merge or liquidate has been made or is planned.
- Whether any assets have been appropriated by government or destroyed, for example, by fire or flood.
- Whether there have been any developments regarding contingencies.
- Whether any unusual accounting adjustments have been made or are contemplated.
- Whether any events have occurred or are likely to occur that will bring into question the appropriateness of accounting policies used in the financial statements, as would be the case, for example, if such events call into question the validity of the going concern assumption.
- Whether any events have occurred that are relevant to the measurement of estimates or provisions made in the financial statements.
- Whether any events have occurred that are relevant to the recoverability of assets.

Reading Minutes (Ref. Para. 7(c))

Considerations Specific to Public Sector Entities

In the public sector, the auditor may read the official records of relevant proceedings **A10**
of the legislature and inquire about matters addressed in proceedings for which
official records are not yet available.

Facts Which Become Known to the Auditor after the Date of the Auditor's Report but before the Date the Financial Statements Are Issued

Management Responsibility towards Auditor (Ref: Para. 10)

As explained in ISA (UK and Ireland) 210, the terms of the audit engagement **A11**
include the agreement of management[8a] to inform the auditor of facts that may affect
the financial statements, of which management may become aware during the period
from the date of the auditor's report to the date the financial statements are issued.[9]

Dual Dating (Ref: Para. 12(a))

When, in the circumstances described in paragraph 12(a), the auditor amends the **A12**
auditor's report to include an additional date restricted to that amendment, the date
of the auditor's report on the financial statements prior to their subsequent
amendment by management[3a] remains unchanged because this date informs the
reader as to when the audit work on those financial statements was completed.
However, an additional date is included in the auditor's report to inform users that
the auditor's procedures subsequent to that date were restricted to the subsequent
amendment of the financial statements. The following is an illustration of such an
additional date:

> "(Date of auditor's report), except as to Note Y, which is as of (date of completion of audit procedures restricted to amendment described in Note Y)."

No Amendment of Financial Statements by Management (Ref: Para. 13)

In some jurisdictions, management[3a] may not be required by law, regulation or the **A13**
financial reporting framework to issue amended financial statements. This is often
the case when issuance of the financial statements for the following period is
imminent, provided appropriate disclosures are made in such statements.

Considerations Specific to Public Sector Entities

In the public sector, the actions taken in accordance with paragraph 13 when **A14**
management does not amend the financial statements may also include reporting
separately to the legislature, or other relevant body in the reporting hierarchy, on the
implications of the subsequent event for the financial statements and the auditor's
report.

[8a] *In the UK and Ireland the responsibility to inform the auditor of facts which may affect the financial statements usually rests with those charged with governance.*

[9] *ISA (UK and Ireland) 210, "Agreeing the Terms of Audit Engagements," paragraph A23.*

Auditor Action to Seek to Prevent Reliance on Auditor's Report (Ref: Para. 13(b))

A15   The auditor may need to fulfill additional legal obligations even when the auditor has notified management not to issue the financial statements and management has agreed to this request.

A16   Where management has issued the financial statements despite the auditor's notification not to issue the financial statements to third parties, the auditor's course of action to prevent reliance on the auditor's report on the financial statements depends upon the auditor's legal rights and obligations. Consequently, the auditor may consider it appropriate to seek legal advice.

Facts Which Become Known to the Auditor after the Financial Statements Have Been Issued

A16-1   When issuing a new report the auditor has regard to the regulations relating to reports on revised annual financial statements and directors' reports[5a].

A16-2   Where the auditor becomes aware of a fact relevant to the audited financial statements which did not exist at the date of the auditor's report there are no statutory provisions for revising financial statements. The auditor discusses with those charged with governance whether they should withdraw the financial statements and where those charged with governance decide not to do so the auditor may wish to take advice on whether it might be possible to withdraw their report. In both cases, other possible courses of action include the making of a statement by those charged with governance or the auditor at the annual general meeting. In any event legal advice may be helpful.

A16-3   In the UK or the Republic of Ireland the auditor of a company has a statutory right to attend the Annual General Meeting and be heard on any part of the business of the meeting which concerns them as auditor. This right could include making a statement about facts discovered after the date of the auditor's report and where subsequent events come to the attention of the auditor, the auditor needs to consider what to do in relation to them.

No Amendment of Financial Statements by Management (Ref: Para. 15)

Considerations Specific to Public Sector Entities

A17   In some jurisdictions, entities in the public sector may be prohibited from issuing amended financial statements by law or regulation. In such circumstances, the appropriate course of action for the auditor may be to report to the appropriate statutory body.

Auditor Action to Seek to Prevent Reliance on Auditor's Report (Ref: Para. 17)

A18   Where the auditor believes that management, or those charged with governance, have failed to take the necessary steps to prevent reliance on the auditor's report on financial statements previously issued by the entity despite the auditor's prior notification that the auditor will take action to seek to prevent such reliance, the auditor's course of action depends upon the auditor's legal rights and obligations. Consequently, the auditor may consider it appropriate to seek legal advice.

Where the financial statements of companies are issued but have not yet been laid before the members or equivalent, or if those charged with governance do not intend to make an appropriate statement at the annual general meeting, then the auditor may consider making an appropriate statement at the annual general meeting. The auditor does not have a statutory right to communicate directly in writing with the members although, if the auditor resigns or is removed or is not reappointed, the auditor has, for example, various duties under company law[9a].

A18-1

[9a] *The auditor of a limited company in Great Britain who ceases to hold office as auditor is required to comply with the requirements of section 519 of the Companies Act 2006 regarding the statement to be made by the auditor in relation to ceasing to hold office. Equivalent requirements for the Republic of Ireland, are contained in section 185 of the Companies Act 1990.*

International Standard on Auditing (UK and Ireland) 570
Going concern

(Effective for audits of financial statements for periods ending on or after 15 December 2010)

Contents

International Standard on Auditing (UK and Ireland) (ISA (UK and Ireland)) 570, "Going Concern" should be read in conjunction with ISA (UK and Ireland) 200, "Overall Objectives of the Independent Auditor and the Conduct of an Audit in Accordance with International Standards on Auditing (UK and Ireland)."

Introduction

Scope of this ISA (UK and Ireland)

1   This International Standard on Auditing (UK and Ireland) (ISA (UK and Ireland)) deals with the auditor's responsibilities in the audit of financial statements relating to management's use of the going concern assumption in the preparation of the financial statements.

Going Concern Assumption

2   Under the going concern assumption, an entity is viewed as continuing in business for the foreseeable future. General purpose financial statements are prepared on a going concern basis, unless management either intends to liquidate the entity or to cease operations, or has no realistic alternative but to do so. Special purpose financial statements may or may not be prepared in accordance with a financial reporting framework for which the going concern basis is relevant for example, the going concern basis is not relevant for some financial statements prepared on a tax basis in particular jurisdictions). When the use of the going concern assumption is appropriate, assets and liabilities are recorded on the basis that the entity will be able to realize its assets and discharge its liabilities in the normal course of business. (Ref: Para. A1)

Responsibility for Assessment of the Entity's Ability to Continue as a Going Concern

3   Some financial reporting frameworks contain an explicit requirement for management[1a] to make a specific assessment of the entity's ability to continue as a going concern, and standards regarding matters to be considered and disclosures to be made in connection with going concern. For example, International Accounting Standard (IAS) 1 requires management to make an assessment of an entity's ability to continue as a going concern.[1] The detailed requirements regarding management's responsibility to assess the entity's ability to continue as a going concern and related financial statement disclosures may also be set out in law or regulation.

4   In other financial reporting frameworks, there may be no explicit requirement for management to make a specific assessment of the entity's ability to continue as a going concern. Nevertheless, since the going concern assumption is a fundamental principle in the preparation of financial statements as discussed in paragraph 2, the preparation of the financial statements requires management to assess the entity's ability to continue as a going concern even if the financial reporting framework does not include an explicit requirement to do so.

5   Management's[1a] assessment of the entity's ability to continue as a going concern involves making a judgment, at a particular point in time, about inherently uncertain future outcomes of events or conditions. The following factors are relevant to that judgment:

- The degree of uncertainty associated with the outcome of an event or condition increases significantly the further into the future an event or condition or the

---

[1a] *In the UK and Ireland those charged with governance are responsible for the preparation of the financial statements and the assessment of the entity's ability to continue as a going concern.*

[1] *IAS 1, "Presentation of Financial Statements" as at 1 January 2009, paragraphs 25-26.*

outcome occurs. For that reason, most financial reporting frameworks that require an explicit management assessment specify the period for which management is required to take into account all available information.

- The size and complexity of the entity, the nature and condition of its business and the degree to which it is affected by external factors affect the judgment regarding the outcome of events or conditions.
- Any judgment about the future is based on information available at the time at which the judgment is made. Subsequent events may result in outcomes that are inconsistent with judgments that were reasonable at the time they were made.

Responsibilities of the Auditor

The auditor's responsibility is to obtain sufficient appropriate audit evidence about the appropriateness of management's[1a] use of the going concern assumption in the preparation and presentation of the financial statements and to conclude whether there is a material uncertainty about the entity's ability to continue as a going concern. This responsibility exists even if the financial reporting framework used in the preparation of the financial statements does not include an explicit requirement for management to make a specific assessment of the entity's ability to continue as a going concern.   **6**

However, as described in ISA (UK and Ireland) 200,[2] the potential effects of inherent limitations on the auditor's ability to detect material misstatements are greater for future events or conditions that may cause an entity to cease to continue as a going concern. The auditor cannot predict such future events or conditions. Accordingly, the absence of any reference to going concern uncertainty in an auditor's report cannot be viewed as a guarantee as to the entity's ability to continue as a going concern.   **7**

Effective Date

This ISA (UK and Ireland) is effective for audits of financial statements for periods ending on or after 15 December 2010.   **8**

Objectives

The objectives of the auditor are: **9**

(a) To obtain sufficient appropriate audit evidence regarding the appropriateness of management's[1a] use of the going concern assumption in the preparation of the financial statements;

(b) To conclude, based on the audit evidence obtained, whether a material uncertainty exists related to events or conditions that may cast significant doubt on the entity's ability to continue as a going concern; and

(c) To determine the implications for the auditor's report.

---

[2] ISA (UK and Ireland) 200, "Overall Objectives of the Independent Auditor and the Conduct of an Audit in Accordance with International Standards on Auditing."

Requirements

Risk Assessment Procedures and Related Activities

10   When performing risk assessment procedures as required by ISA (UK and Ireland) 315,[3] the auditor shall consider whether there are events or conditions that may cast significant doubt on the entity's ability to continue as a going concern. In so doing, the auditor shall determine whether management[1a] has already performed a preliminary assessment of the entity's ability to continue as a going concern, and: (Ref: Para. A2-A5)

     (a) If such an assessment has been performed, the auditor shall discuss the assessment with management and determine whether management has identified events or conditions that, individually or collectively, may cast significant doubt on the entity's ability to continue as a going concern and, if so, management's plans to address them; or

     (b) If such an assessment has not yet been performed, the auditor shall discuss with management the basis for the intended use of the going concern assumption, and inquire of management whether events or conditions exist that, individually or collectively, may cast significant doubt on the entity's ability to continue as a going concern.

11   The auditor shall remain alert throughout the audit for audit evidence of events or conditions that may cast significant doubt on the entity's ability to continue as a going concern. (Ref: Para. A6)

Evaluating Management's Assessment

12   The auditor shall evaluate management's[1a] assessment of the entity's ability to continue as a going concern. (Ref: Para. A7-A9; A11-A12)

13   In evaluating management's[1a] assessment of the entity's ability to continue as a going concern, the auditor shall cover the same period as that used by management to make its assessment as required by the applicable financial reporting framework, or by law or regulation if it specifies a longer period. If management's assessment of the entity's ability to continue as a going concern covers less than twelve months from the date of the financial statements as defined in ISA 560,[4] the auditor shall request management to extend its assessment period to at least twelve months from that date[4a]. (Ref: Para. A10-A12)

14   In evaluating management's[1a] assessment, the auditor shall consider whether management's assessment includes all relevant information of which the auditor is aware as a result of the audit.

---

[3] *ISA (UK and Ireland) 315, "Identifying and Assessing the Risks of Material Misstatement through Understanding the Entity and Its Environment," paragraph 5.*

[4] *ISA (UK and Ireland) 560, "Subsequent Events," paragraph 5(a).*

[4a] *In the UK and Ireland the period used by those charged with governance in making their assessment is usually at least one year from the date of approval of the financial statements.*

Period beyond Management's[1a] Assessment

The auditor shall inquire of management as to its knowledge of events or conditions **15** beyond the period of management's[1a] assessment that may cast significant doubt on the entity's ability to continue as a going concern. (Ref: Para. A13–A14)

Additional Audit Procedures When Events or Conditions Are Identified

If events or conditions have been identified that may cast significant doubt on the **16** entity's ability to continue as a going concern, the auditor shall obtain sufficient appropriate audit evidence to determine whether or not a material uncertainty exists through performing additional audit procedures, including consideration of mitigating factors. These procedures shall include: (Ref: Para. A15)

(a) Where management[1a] has not yet performed an assessment of the entity's ability to continue as a going concern, requesting management to make its assessment.
(b) Evaluating management's[1a] plans for future actions in relation to its going concern assessment, whether the outcome of these plans is likely to improve the situation and whether management's plans are feasible in the circumstances. (Ref: Para. A16)
(c) Where the entity has prepared a cash flow forecast, and analysis of the forecast is a significant factor in considering the future outcome of events or conditions in the evaluation of management's[1a] plans for future action: (Ref: Para. A17–A18)
    (i) Evaluating the reliability of the underlying data generated to prepare the forecast; and
    (ii) Determining whether there is adequate support for the assumptions underlying the forecast.
(d) Considering whether any additional facts or information have become available since the date on which management made its assessment.
(e) Requesting written representations from management and, where appropriate, those charged with governance, regarding their plans for future action and the feasibility of these plans[1a].

Audit Conclusions and Reporting

Based on the audit evidence obtained, the auditor shall conclude whether, in the **17** auditor's judgment, a material uncertainty exists related to events or conditions that, individually or collectively, may cast significant doubt on the entity's ability to continue as a going concern. A material uncertainty exists when the magnitude of its potential impact and likelihood of occurrence is such that, in the auditor's judgment, appropriate disclosure of the nature and implications of the uncertainty is necessary for: (Ref: Para. A19 – A19-2)

(a) In the case of a fair presentation financial reporting framework, the fair presentation of the financial statements, or
(b) In the case of a compliance framework, the financial statements not to be misleading.

If the period to which those charged with governance have paid particular **17-1** attention in assessing going concern is less than one year from the date of approval of the financial statements, and those charged with governance have not disclosed that fact, the auditor shall do so within the auditor's report[4b]. (Ref: Para A19-1)

Use of Going Concern Assumption Appropriate but a Material Uncertainty Exists

18 If the auditor concludes that the use of the going concern assumption is appropriate in the circumstances but a material uncertainty exists, the auditor shall determine whether the financial statements:

   (a) Adequately describe the principal events or conditions that may cast significant doubt on the entity's ability to continue as a going concern and management's[1a] plans to deal with these events or conditions; and

   (b) Disclose clearly that there is a material uncertainty related to events or conditions that may cast significant doubt on the entity's ability to continue as a going concern and, therefore, that it may be unable to realize its assets and discharge its liabilities in the normal course of business. (Ref: Para. A20)

19 If adequate disclosure is made in the financial statements, the auditor shall express an unmodified opinion and include an Emphasis of Matter paragraph in the auditor's report to:

   (a) Highlight the existence of a material uncertainty relating to the event or condition that may cast significant doubt on the entity's ability to continue as a going concern; and to

   (b) Draw attention to the note in the financial statements that discloses the matters set out in paragraph 18. (See ISA (UK and Ireland) 706.[5]) (Ref: Para. A21-A22)

20 If adequate disclosure is not made in the financial statements, the auditor shall express a qualified opinion or adverse opinion, as appropriate, in accordance with ISA (UK and Ireland) 705.[6] The auditor shall state in the auditor's report that there is a material uncertainty that may cast significant doubt about the entity's ability to continue as a going concern. (Ref: Para. A23-A24)

Use of Going Concern Assumption Inappropriate

21 If the financial statements have been prepared on a going concern basis but, in the auditor's judgment, management's[1a] use of the going concern assumption in the financial statements is inappropriate, the auditor shall express an adverse opinion. (Ref: Para. A25-A26)

Management Unwilling to Make or Extend Its Assessment

22 If management[1a] is unwilling to make or extend its assessment when requested to do so by the auditor, the auditor shall consider the implications for the auditor's report. (Ref: Para. A27)

[4b] *If the non-disclosure of the fact in the financial statements is a departure from the requirements of the applicable financial reporting framework, the auditor would give a qualified opinion ("except for").*

[5] *ISA (UK and Ireland) 706, "Emphasis of Matter Paragraphs and Other Matter Paragraphs in the Independent Auditor's Report."*

[6] *ISA (UK and Ireland) 705, "Modifications to the Opinion in the Independent Auditor's Report."*

Communication with Those Charged with Governance

Unless all those charged with governance are involved in managing the entity,[7] the auditor shall communicate with those charged with governance events or conditions identified that may cast significant doubt on the entity's ability to continue as a going concern. Such communication with those charged with governance shall include the following: **23**

(a) Whether the events or conditions constitute a material uncertainty;
(b) Whether the use of the going concern assumption is appropriate in the preparation and presentation of the financial statements; and
(c) The adequacy of related disclosures in the financial statements.

Significant Delay in the Approval of Financial Statements

If there is significant delay in the approval of the financial statements by management or those charged with governance after the date of the financial statements, the auditor shall inquire as to the reasons for the delay. If the auditor believes that the delay could be related to events or conditions relating to the going concern assessment, the auditor shall perform those additional audit procedures necessary, as described in paragraph 16, as well as consider the effect on the auditor's conclusion regarding the existence of a material uncertainty, as described in paragraph 17. **24**

***

Application and Other Explanatory Material

Going Concern Assumption (Ref: Para. 2)

Considerations Specific to Public Sector Entities

Management's[1a] use of the going concern assumption is also relevant to public sector entities. For example, International Public Sector Accounting Standard (IPSAS) 1 addresses the issue of the ability of public sector entities to continue as going concerns.[8] Going concern risks may arise, but are not limited to, situations where public sector entities operate on a for-profit basis, where government support may be reduced or withdrawn, or in the case of privatization. Events or conditions that may cast significant doubt on an entity's ability to continue as a going concern in the public sector may include situations where the public sector entity lacks funding for its continued existence or when policy decisions are made that affect the services provided by the public sector entity. **A1**

Risk Assessment Procedures and Related Activities

Events or Conditions That May Cast Doubt about Going Concern Assumption (Ref: Para. 10)

The following are examples of events or conditions that, individually or collectively, may cast significant doubt about the going concern assumption. This listing is not **A2**

[7] *ISA (UK and Ireland) 260, "Communication with Those Charged with Governance," paragraph 13.*

[8] *IPSAS 1, "Presentation of Financial Statements" as at 1 January 2009, paragraphs 38-41.*

all-inclusive nor does the existence of one or more of the items always signify that a material uncertainty exists.

Financial

- Net liability or net current liability position.
- Fixed-term borrowings approaching maturity without realistic prospects of renewal or repayment; or excessive reliance on short-term borrowings to finance long-term assets.
- Indications of withdrawal of financial support by creditors.
- Negative operating cash flows indicated by historical or prospective financial statements.
- Adverse key financial ratios.
- Substantial operating losses or significant deterioration in the value of assets used to generate cash flows.
- Arrears or discontinuance of dividends.
- Inability to pay creditors on due dates.
- Inability to comply with the terms of loan agreements.
- Change from credit to cash-on-delivery transactions with suppliers.
- Inability to obtain financing for essential new product development or other essential investments.

Operating

- Management intentions to liquidate the entity or to cease operations.
- Loss of key management without replacement.
- Loss of a major market, key customer(s), franchise, license, or principal supplier(s).
- Labor difficulties.
- Shortages of important supplies.
- Emergence of a highly successful competitor.

Other

- Non-compliance with capital or other statutory requirements.
- Pending legal or regulatory proceedings against the entity that may, if successful, result in claims that the entity is unlikely to be able to satisfy.
- Changes in law or regulation or government policy expected to adversely affect the entity.
- Uninsured or underinsured catastrophes when they occur.

The significance of such events or conditions often can be mitigated by other factors. For example, the effect of an entity being unable to make its normal debt repayments may be counterbalanced by management's plans to maintain adequate cash flows by alternative means, such as by disposing of assets, rescheduling loan repayments, or obtaining additional capital. Similarly, the loss of a principal supplier may be mitigated by the availability of a suitable alternative source of supply.

A3 The risk assessment procedures required by paragraph 10 help the auditor to determine whether management's use of the going concern assumption is likely to be an important issue and its impact on planning the audit. These procedures also allow for more timely discussions with management, including a discussion of management's[1a] plans and resolution of any identified going concern issues.

Considerations Specific to Smaller Entities

The size of an entity may affect its ability to withstand adverse conditions. Small **A4** entities may be able to respond quickly to exploit opportunities, but may lack reserves to sustain operations.

Conditions of particular relevance to small entities include the risk that banks and **A5** other lenders may cease to support the entity, as well as the possible loss of a principal supplier, major customer, key employee, or the right to operate under a license, franchise or other legal agreement.

Remaining Alert throughout the Audit for Audit Evidence about Events or Conditions (Ref: Para. 11)

ISA (UK and Ireland) 315 requires the auditor to revise the auditor's risk assessment **A6** and modify the further planned audit procedures accordingly when additional audit evidence is obtained during the course of the audit that affects the auditor's assessment of risk.[9] If events or conditions that may cast significant doubt on the entity's ability to continue as a going concern are identified after the auditor's risk assessments are made, in addition to performing the procedures in paragraph 16, the auditor's assessment of the risks of material misstatement may need to be revised. The existence of such events or conditions may also affect the nature, timing and extent of the auditor's further procedures in response to the assessed risks. ISA (UK and Ireland) 330[10] establishes requirements and provides guidance on this issue.

Evaluating Management's Assessment

Management's[1a] Assessment and Supporting Analysis and the Auditor's Evaluation (Ref: Para. 12)

Management's[1a] assessment of the entity's ability to continue as a going concern is a **A7** key part of the auditor's consideration of management's use of the going concern assumption.

It is not the auditor's responsibility to rectify the lack of analysis by management[1a]. **A8** In some circumstances, however, the lack of detailed analysis by management to support its assessment may not prevent the auditor from concluding whether management's use of the going concern assumption is appropriate in the circumstances. For example, when there is a history of profitable operations and a ready access to financial resources, management may make its assessment without detailed analysis. In this case, the auditor's evaluation of the appropriateness of management's assessment may be made without performing detailed evaluation procedures if the auditor's other audit procedures are sufficient to enable the auditor to conclude whether management's use of the going concern assumption in the preparation of the financial statements is appropriate in the circumstances.

In other circumstances, evaluating management's[1a] assessment of the entity's ability **A9** to continue as a going concern, as required by paragraph 12, may include an evaluation of the process management followed to make its assessment, the assumptions on which the assessment is based and management's plans for future action and whether management's plans are feasible in the circumstances.

---

[9] *ISA (UK and Ireland) 315, paragraph 31.*

[10] *ISA (UK and Ireland) 330, "The Auditor's Responses to Assessed Risks."*

The Period of Management's[1a] Assessment (Ref: Para. 13)

A10   Most financial reporting frameworks requiring an explicit management[1a] assessment specify the period for which management is required to take into account all available information.[11]

A10-1   If the future period to which those charged with governance have paid particular attention has been limited, for example, to a period of less than one year from the date of approval of the financial statements, those charged with governance will have determined whether, in their opinion, the financial statements require any additional disclosures to explain adequately the assumptions that underlie the adoption of the going concern basis.

A10-2   The auditor assesses whether to concur with the judgments of those charged with governance regarding the need for additional disclosures and their adequacy. Disclosure, however, does not eliminate the need to make appropriate judgments about the suitability of the future period as an adequate basis for assessing the going concern position. Paragraph 17-1 requires the auditor to disclose in the auditor's report if the period to which those charged with governance have paid particular attention in assessing going concern is less than one year from the date of approval of the financial statements, and those charged with governance have not disclosed that fact. The auditor through discussion with those charged with governance of their plans and expectations may be able to obtain satisfaction that those charged with governance have in fact paid particular attention to a period of one year from the date of approval of the financial statements.

Procedures to Identify Material Matters Indicating Concern

A10-3   Having regard to the future period to which those charged with governance have paid particular attention in assessing going concern, the auditor plans and performs procedures specifically designed to identify any material matters which could indicate concern about the entity's ability to continue as a going concern.

A10-4   The extent of the auditor's procedures is influenced primarily by the excess of the financial resources available to the entity over the financial resources that it requires. The entity's procedures (and the auditor's procedures) need not always be elaborate in order to provide sufficient appropriate audit evidence. A determination of the sufficiency of the evidence supplied to the auditor by those charged with governance will depend on the particular circumstances. For example, to be sufficient the evidence may not require formal cash flow forecasts and budgets to have been prepared for the period ending one year from the date of approval of the financial statements. Although such forecasts and budgets are

---

[11] *Accounting frameworks do not normally specify a maximum period that should be reviewed as part of the assessment of going concern. However, IAS 1 and FRS 18 both provide that management takes into account all available information about the future.*

For example, IAS 1 defines this as a period that should be at least, but is not limited to, twelve months from the end of the reporting period.

FRS 18 does not specify a period but does require that where the foreseeable future considered by the directors has been limited to a period of less than one year from the date of approval of the financial statements, that fact should be disclosed in the financial statements.

Guidance issued by the FRC for directors of listed companies in "An Update for Directors of Listed Companies: Going Concern and Liquidity Risk" (November 2008) states that "Where the period considered by the directors has been limited, for example to a period of less than twelve months from the date of approval of the annual report and accounts, the directors need to consider whether additional disclosures are necessary to explain adequately the assumptions that underlie the adoption of the going concern basis."

likely to provide the most persuasive evidence, alternative sources of evidence may also be acceptable. This is particularly likely to be the case in respect of entities with uncomplicated circumstances. Many smaller companies fall into this category.

Considerations Specific to Smaller Entities (Ref: Para. 12-13)

In many cases, the management[1a] of smaller entities may not have prepared a detailed assessment of the entity's ability to continue as a going concern, but instead may rely on in-depth knowledge of the business and anticipated future prospects. Nevertheless, in accordance with the requirements of this ISA (UK and Ireland), the auditor needs to evaluate management's assessment of the entity's ability to continue as a going concern. For smaller entities, it may be appropriate to discuss the medium and long-term financing of the entity with management, provided that management's contentions can be corroborated by sufficient documentary evidence and are not inconsistent with the auditor's understanding of the entity. Therefore, the requirement in paragraph 13 for the auditor to request management to extend its assessment may, for example, be satisfied by discussion, inquiry and inspection of supporting documentation, for example, orders received for future supply, evaluated as to their feasibility or otherwise substantiated.

A11

Continued support by owner-managers is often important to smaller entities' ability to continue as a going concern. Where a small entity is largely financed by a loan from the owner-manager, it may be important that these funds are not withdrawn. For example, the continuance of a small entity in financial difficulty may be dependent on the owner-manager subordinating a loan to the entity in favor of banks or other creditors, or the owner manager supporting a loan for the entity by providing a guarantee with his or her personal assets as collateral. In such circumstances the auditor may obtain appropriate documentary evidence of the subordination of the owner-manager's loan or of the guarantee. Where an entity is dependent on additional support from the owner-manager, the auditor may evaluate the owner-manager's ability to meet the obligation under the support arrangement. In addition, the auditor may request written confirmation of the terms and conditions attaching to such support and the owner-manager's intention or understanding.

A12

Period beyond Management's[1a] Assessment (Ref: Para. 15)

As required by paragraph 11, the auditor remains alert to the possibility that there may be known events, scheduled or otherwise, or conditions that will occur beyond the period of assessment used by management[1a] that may bring into question the appropriateness of management's use of the going concern assumption in preparing the financial statements. Since the degree of uncertainty associated with the outcome of an event or condition increases as the event or condition is further into the future, in considering events or conditions further in the future, the indications of going concern issues need to be significant before the auditor needs to consider taking further action. If such events or conditions are identified, the auditor may need to request management to evaluate the potential significance of the event or condition on its assessment of the entity's ability to continue as a going concern. In these circumstances the procedures in paragraph 16 apply.

A13

Other than inquiry of management, the auditor does not have a responsibility to perform any other audit procedures to identify events or conditions that may cast significant doubt on the entity's ability to continue as a going concern beyond the

A14

period assessed by management[1a], which, as discussed in paragraph 13, would be at least twelve months from the date of the financial statements.

Additional Audit Procedures When Events or Conditions Are Identified (Ref: Para. 16)

A15   Audit procedures that are relevant to the requirement in paragraph 16 may include the following:

- Analyzing and discussing cash flow, profit and other relevant forecasts with management.
- Analyzing and discussing the entity's latest available interim financial statements.
- Reading the terms of debentures and loan agreements and determining whether any have been breached.
- Reading minutes of the meetings of shareholders, those charged with governance and relevant committees for reference to financing difficulties.
- Inquiring of the entity's legal counsel regarding the existence of litigation and claims and the reasonableness of management's[1a] assessments of their outcome and the estimate of their financial implications.
- Confirming the existence, legality and enforceability of arrangements to provide or maintain financial support with related and third parties and assessing the financial ability of such parties to provide additional funds.
- Evaluating the entity's plans to deal with unfilled customer orders.
- Performing audit procedures regarding subsequent events to identify those that either mitigate or otherwise affect the entity's ability to continue as a going concern.
- Confirming the existence, terms and adequacy of borrowing facilities.
- Obtaining and reviewing reports of regulatory actions.
- Determining the adequacy of support for any planned disposals of assets.

Evaluating Management's Plans for Future Actions (Ref: Para. 16(b))

A16   Evaluating management's[1a] plans for future actions may include inquiries of management as to its plans for future action, including, for example, its plans to liquidate assets, borrow money or restructure debt, reduce or delay expenditures, or increase capital.

The Period of Management's[1a] Assessment (Ref: Para. 16(c))

A17   In addition to the procedures required in paragraph 16(c), the auditor may compare:

- The prospective financial information for recent prior periods with historical results; and
- The prospective financial information for the current period with results achieved to date.

A18   Where management's[1a] assumptions include continued support by third parties, whether through the subordination of loans, commitments to maintain or provide additional funding, or guarantees, and such support is important to an entity's ability to continue as a going concern, the auditor may need to consider requesting written confirmation (including of terms and conditions) from those third parties and to obtain evidence of their ability to provide such support.

Audit Conclusions and Reporting (Ref: Para. 17 – 17-1)

The phrase "material uncertainty" is used in IAS 1 in discussing the uncertainties   **A19**
related to events or conditions which may cast significant doubt on the entity's ability
to continue as a going concern that should be disclosed in the financial statements. In
some other financial reporting frameworks the phrase "significant uncertainty" is
used in similar circumstances.

Where, in forming their opinion, the auditor's assessment of going concern is   **A19-1**
based on a period to which those charged with governance have paid particular
attention which is less than one year from the date of approval of the financial
statements, it is appropriate for the auditor to disclose that fact within the basis of
the audit opinion, unless it is disclosed in the financial statements or accompanying information (for example, a Corporate Governance Statement). In
deciding whether to disclose the fact, the auditor assesses whether the evidence
supplied by those charged with governance is sufficient to demonstrate that those
charged with governance have, in assessing going concern, paid particular
attention to a period of one year from the date of approval of the financial
statements (see paragraph A10-3).

In complying with the requirements of ISA (UK and Ireland) 230 to document   **A19-2**
significant matters arising during the audit,[11a] the auditor documents concerns (if
any) about the entity's ability to continue as a going concern.

Use of Going Concern Assumption Appropriate but a Material Uncertainty Exists

Adequacy of Disclosure of Material Uncertainty (Ref: Para. 18)

The determination of the adequacy of the financial statement disclosure may involve   **A20**
determining whether the information explicitly draws the reader's attention to the
possibility that the entity may be unable to continue realizing its assets and discharging its liabilities in the normal course of business.

Audit Reporting When Disclosure of Material Uncertainty Is Adequate (Ref: Para. 19)

The following is an illustration of an Emphasis of Matter paragraph when the   **A21**
auditor is satisfied as to the adequacy of the note disclosure:[11b]

Emphasis of Matter

Without qualifying our opinion, we draw attention to Note X in the financial
statements which indicates that the Company incurred a net loss of ZZZ during
the year ended December 31, 20X1 and, as of that date, the Company's current
liabilities exceeded its total assets by YYY. These conditions, along with other
matters as set forth in Note X, indicate the existence of a material uncertainty

---

[11a] *ISA (UK and Ireland) 230, "Audit Documentation," paragraph 8(c).*

[11b] *With respect to companies, illustrative examples of auditor's reports tailored for use with audits conducted in
accordance with ISAs (UK and Ireland) are given in the most recent versions of the APB Bulletins, "Auditor's
Reports on Financial Statements in the United Kingdom"/"Auditor's Reports on Financial Statements in the
Republic of Ireland." Illustrative examples for various other entities are given in other Bulletins and Practice
Notes issued by the APB.*

that may cast significant doubt about the Company's ability to continue as a going concern.

A22   In situations involving multiple material uncertainties that are significant to the financial statements as a whole, the auditor may consider it appropriate in extremely rare cases to express a disclaimer of opinion instead of adding an Emphasis of Matter paragraph. ISA (UK and Ireland) 705 provides guidance on this issue.

Audit Reporting When Disclosure of Material Uncertainty Is Inadequate (Ref: Para. 20)

A23   The following is an illustration of the relevant paragraphs when a qualified opinion is to be expressed:[11b]

Basis for Qualified Opinion

The Company's financing arrangements expire and amounts outstanding are payable on March 19, 20X1. The Company has been unable to re-negotiate or obtain replacement financing. This situation indicates the existence of a material uncertainty that may cast significant doubt on the Company's ability to continue as a going concern and therefore the Company may be unable to realize its assets and discharge its liabilities in the normal course of business. The financial statements (and notes thereto) do not fully disclose this fact.

Qualified Opinion

In our opinion, except for the incomplete disclosure of the information referred to in the Basis for Qualified Opinion paragraph, the financial statements present fairly, in all material respects (or "give a true and fair view of") the financial position of the Company at December 31, 20X0 and of its financial performance and its cash flows for the year then ended in accordance with ...

A24   The following is an illustration of the relevant paragraphs when an adverse opinion is to be expressed:[11b]

Basis for Adverse Opinion

The Company's financing arrangements expired and the amount outstanding was payable on December 31, 20X0. The Company has been unable to re-negotiate or obtain replacement financing and is considering filing for bankruptcy. These events indicate a material uncertainty that may cast significant doubt on the Company's ability to continue as a going concern and therefore it may be unable to realize its assets and discharge its liabilities in the normal course of business. The financial statements (and notes thereto) do not disclose this fact.

Adverse Opinion

In our opinion, because of the omission of the information mentioned in the Basis for Adverse Opinion paragraph, the financial statements do not present fairly (or "give a true and fair view of") the financial position of the Company as at December 31, 20X0, and of its financial performance and its cash flows for the year then ended in accordance with...

Use of Going Concern Assumption Inappropriate (Ref: Para. 21)

A25   If the financial statements have been prepared on a going concern basis but, in the auditor's judgment, management's use of the going concern assumption in the financial statements is inappropriate, the requirement of paragraph 21 for the auditor to express an adverse opinion applies regardless of whether or not the financial statements include disclosure of the inappropriateness of management's[1a] use of the going concern assumption.

If the entity's management[1a] is required, or elects, to prepare financial statements when the use of the going concern assumption is not appropriate in the circumstances, the financial statements are prepared on an alternative basis (for example, liquidation basis). The auditor may be able to perform an audit of those financial statements provided that the auditor determines that the alternative basis is an acceptable financial reporting framework in the circumstances. The auditor may be able to express an unmodified opinion on those financial statements, provided there is adequate disclosure therein but may consider it appropriate or necessary to include an Emphasis of Matter paragraph in the auditor's report to draw the user's attention to that alternative basis and the reasons for its use.

A26

Management[1a] Unwilling to Make or Extend Its Assessment (Ref: Para. 22)

In certain circumstances, the auditor may believe it necessary to request management[1a] to make or extend its assessment. If management is unwilling to do so, a qualified opinion or a disclaimer of opinion in the auditor's report may be appropriate, because it may not be possible for the auditor to obtain sufficient appropriate audit evidence regarding the use of the going concern assumption in the preparation of the financial statements, such as audit evidence regarding the existence of plans management has put in place or the existence of other mitigating factors.

A27

Regulated Entities

When the auditor of a regulated financial entity considers that it might be necessary to either qualify the audit opinion or add an explanatory paragraph to the audit report, the auditor may have a duty to inform the appropriate regulator at an early stage in the audit. In such cases the regulator might, if it has not already done so, specify corrective action to be taken by the entity. At the time at which the auditor formulates the audit report, the auditor takes account of matters such as:

A27-1

- Any views expressed by the regulator.
- Any legal advice obtained by those charged with governance.
- The actual and planned corrective action.

International Standard on Auditing (UK and Ireland) 580
Written representations

(Effective for audits of financial statements for periods ending on or after 15 December 2010)

Contents

International Standard on Auditing (UK and Ireland) (ISA (UK and Ireland)) 580, "Written Representations" should be read in conjunction with ISA (UK and Ireland) 200, "Overall Objectives of the Independent Auditor and the Conduct of an Audit in Accordance with International Standards on Auditing (UK and Ireland)."

Introduction

1. This International Standard on Auditing (UK and Ireland) (ISA (UK and Ireland)) deals with the auditor's responsibility to obtain written representations from management and, where appropriate, those charged with governance in an audit of financial statements.

2. Appendix 1 lists other ISAs (UK and Ireland) containing subject-matter specific requirements for written representations. The specific requirements for written representations of other ISAs (UK and Ireland) do not limit the application of this ISA (UK and Ireland).

Written Representations as Audit Evidence

3. Audit evidence is the information used by the auditor in arriving at the conclusions on which the auditor's opinion is based. Written representations are necessary information that the auditor requires in connection with the audit of the entity's financial statements. Accordingly, similar to responses to inquiries, written representations are audit evidence. (Ref: Para. A1)

4. Although written representations provide necessary audit evidence, they do not provide sufficient appropriate audit evidence on their own about any of the matters with which they deal. Furthermore, the fact that management has provided reliable written representations does not affect the nature or extent of other audit evidence that the auditor obtains about the fulfilment of management's responsibilities, or about specific assertions.

Effective Date

5. This ISA (UK and Ireland) is effective for audits of financial statements for periods ending on or after 15 December 2010.

Objectives

6. The objectives of the auditor are:

   (a) To obtain written representations from management and, where appropriate, those charged with governance that they believe that they have fulfilled their responsibility for the preparation of the financial statements and for the completeness of the information provided to the auditor;

   (b) To support other audit evidence relevant to the financial statements or specific assertions in the financial statements by means of written representations if determined necessary by the auditor or required by other ISAs (UK and Ireland); and

   (c) To respond appropriately to written representations provided by management and, where appropriate, those charged with governance, or if management or those charged with governance do not provide the written representations requested by the auditor.

Introduction

Scope of this ISA (UK and Ireland)

1 This International Standard on Auditing (UK and Ireland) (ISA (UK and Ireland)) deals with the auditor's responsibility to obtain written representations from management and, where appropriate, those charged with governance in an audit of financial statements.

2 Appendix 1 lists other ISAs (UK and Ireland) containing subject-matter specific requirements for written representations. The specific requirements for written representations of other ISAs (UK and Ireland) do not limit the application of this ISA (UK and Ireland).

Written Representations as Audit Evidence

3 Audit evidence is the information used by the auditor in arriving at the conclusions on which the auditor's opinion is based.[1] Written representations are necessary information that the auditor requires in connection with the audit of the entity's financial statements. Accordingly, similar to responses to inquiries, written representations are audit evidence. (Ref: Para. A1)

4 Although written representations provide necessary audit evidence, they do not provide sufficient appropriate audit evidence on their own about any of the matters with which they deal. Furthermore, the fact that management has provided reliable written representations does not affect the nature or extent of other audit evidence that the auditor obtains about the fulfillment of management's responsibilities, or about specific assertions.

Effective Date

5 This ISA (UK and Ireland) is effective for audits of financial statements for periods ending on or after 15 December 2010.

Objectives

6 The objectives of the auditor are:

(a) To obtain written representations from management and, where appropriate, those charged with governance that they believe that they have fulfilled their responsibility for the preparation of the financial statements and for the completeness of the information provided to the auditor;

(b) To support other audit evidence relevant to the financial statements or specific assertions in the financial statements by means of written representations if determined necessary by the auditor or required by other ISAs (UK and Ireland); and

(c) To respond appropriately to written representations provided by management and, where appropriate, those charged with governance, or if management or, where appropriate, those charged with governance do not provide the written representations requested by the auditor.

---

[1] ISA (UK and Ireland) 500, "Audit Evidence," paragraph 5(c).

Definitions

For purposes of the ISAs (UK and Ireland), the following term has the meaning attributed below: **7**

Written representation – A written statement by management provided to the auditor to confirm certain matters or to support other audit evidence. Written representations in this context do not include financial statements, the assertions therein, or supporting books and records.

For purposes of this ISA (UK and Ireland), references to "management" should be read as "management and, where appropriate, those charged with governance." Furthermore, in the case of a fair presentation framework, management is responsible for the preparation and *fair* presentation of the financial statements in accordance with the applicable financial reporting framework; or the preparation of financial statements *that give a true and fair view* in accordance with the applicable financial reporting framework.   **8**

Requirements

Management from whom Written Representations Requested

The auditor shall request written representations from management with appropriate responsibilities for the financial statements and knowledge of the matters concerned. (Ref: Para. A2-A6)   **9**

Written Representations about Management's Responsibilities

Preparation of the Financial Statements

The auditor shall request management to provide a written representation that it has fulfilled its responsibility for the preparation of the financial statements in accordance with the applicable financial reporting framework, including where relevant their fair presentation, as set out in the terms of the audit engagement.[2] (Ref: Para. A7-A9, A14, A22)   **10**

Information Provided and Completeness of Transactions

The auditor shall request management to provide a written representation that: **11**

(a) It has provided the auditor with all relevant information and access as agreed in the terms of the audit engagement,[3] and

(b) All transactions have been recorded and are reflected in the financial statements. (Ref: Para. A7-A9, A14, A22 – A22-1)

Management may include in the written representations required by paragraphs 10 and 11 qualifying language to the effect that the representations are made to the best of its knowledge and belief. Such qualifying language does not cause paragraph 20 to apply if, during the audit, the auditor found no evidence that the representations are incorrect. (Ref; Para A5, A8-1)   **11-1**

[2] ISA (UK and Ireland) 210, "Agreeing the Terms of Audit Engagements," paragraph 6(b)(i).

[3] ISA (UK and Ireland) 210, paragraph 6(b)(iii).

Description of Management's Responsibilities in the Written Representations

12   Management's responsibilities shall be described in the written representations required by paragraphs 10 and 11 in the manner in which these responsibilities are described in the terms of the audit engagement.

Other Written Representations

13   Other ISAs (UK and Ireland) require the auditor to request written representations. If, in addition to such required representations, the auditor determines that it is necessary to obtain one or more written representations to support other audit evidence relevant to the financial statements or one or more specific assertions in the financial statements, the auditor shall request such other written representations. (Ref: Para. A10-A13, A14, A22 – A22-1)

Date of and Period(s) Covered by Written Representations

14   The date of the written representations shall be as near as practicable to, but not after, the date of the auditor's report on the financial statements. The written representations shall be for all financial statements and period(s) referred to in the auditor's report. (Ref: Para. A15-A18)

Form of Written Representations

15   The written representations shall be in the form of a representation letter addressed to the auditor. If law or regulation requires management to make written public statements about its responsibilities, and the auditor determines that such statements provide some or all of the representations required by paragraphs 10 or 11, the relevant matters covered by such statements need not be included in the representation letter. (Ref: Para. A19-A21)

Doubt as to the Reliability of Written Representations and Requested Written Representations Not Provided

Doubt as to the Reliability of Written Representations

16   If the auditor has concerns about the competence, integrity, ethical values or diligence of management, or about its commitment to or enforcement of these, the auditor shall determine the effect that such concerns may have on the reliability of representations (oral or written) and audit evidence in general. (Ref: Para. A24-A25)

17   In particular, if written representations are inconsistent with other audit evidence, the auditor shall perform audit procedures to attempt to resolve the matter. If the matter remains unresolved, the auditor shall reconsider the assessment of the competence, integrity, ethical values or diligence of management, or of its commitment to or enforcement of these, and shall determine the effect that this may have on the reliability of representations (oral or written) and audit evidence in general. (Ref: Para. A23)

18   If the auditor concludes that the written representations are not reliable, the auditor shall take appropriate actions, including determining the possible effect on the opinion in the auditor's report in accordance with ISA (UK and Ireland) 705,[4] having regard to the requirement in paragraph 20 of this ISA (UK and Ireland).

Requested Written Representations Not Provided

If management does not provide one or more of the requested written representa- **19** tions, the auditor shall:

(a) Discuss the matter with management;
(b) Reevaluate the integrity of management and evaluate the effect that this may have on the reliability of representations (oral or written) and audit evidence in general; and
(c) Take appropriate actions, including determining the possible effect on the opinion in the auditor's report in accordance with ISA (UK and Ireland) 705, having regard to the requirement in paragraph 20 of this ISA (UK and Ireland).

Written Representations about Management's Responsibilities

The auditor shall disclaim an opinion on the financial statements in accordance with **20** ISA (UK and Ireland) 705 if:

(a) The auditor concludes that there is sufficient doubt about the integrity of management such that the written representations required by paragraphs 10 and 11 are not reliable; or
(b) Management does not provide the written representations required by paragraphs 10 and 11. (Ref: Para. A26-A27)

***

Application and Other Explanatory Material

Written Representations as Audit Evidence (Ref: Para. 3)

Written representations are an important source of audit evidence. If management **A1** modifies or does not provide the requested written representations, it may alert the auditor to the possibility that one or more significant issues may exist. Further, a request for written, rather than oral, representations in many cases may prompt management to consider such matters more rigorously, thereby enhancing the quality of the representations.

Management from whom Written Representations Requested (Ref: Para. 9)

Written representations are requested from those responsible for the preparation of **A2** the financial statements. Those individuals may vary depending on the governance structure of the entity, and relevant law or regulation; however, management (rather than those charged with governance) is often the responsible party. Written representations may therefore be requested from the entity's chief executive officer and chief financial officer, or other equivalent persons in entities that do not use such titles. In some circumstances, however, other parties, such as those charged with

---

[4] ISA (UK and Ireland) 705, "Modifications to the Opinion in the Independent Auditor's Report."

governance, are also responsible for the preparation and presentation of the financial statements[4a].

A2-1   In view of their importance, it is appropriate for written representations that are critical to obtaining sufficient appropriate audit evidence to be provided by those charged with governance rather than the entity's management.

A3   Due to its responsibility for the preparation of the financial statements, and its responsibilities for the conduct of the entity's business, management would be expected to have sufficient knowledge of the process followed by the entity in preparing and presenting the financial statements and the assertions therein on which to base the written representations.

A4   In some cases, however, management may decide to make inquiries of others who participate in preparing and presenting the financial statements and assertions therein, including individuals who have specialized knowledge relating to the matters about which written representations are requested. Such individuals may include:

● An actuary responsible for actuarially determined accounting measurements.
● Staff engineers who may have responsibility for and specialized knowledge about environmental liability measurements.
● Internal counsel who may provide information essential to provisions for legal claims.

A5   In some cases, management may include in the written representations qualifying language to the effect that representations are made to the best of its knowledge and belief. It is reasonable for the auditor to accept such wording if the auditor is satisfied that the representations are being made by those with appropriate responsibilities and knowledge of the matters included in the representations.

A6   To reinforce the need for management to make informed representations, the auditor may request that management include in the written representations confirmation that it has made such inquiries as it considered appropriate to place it in the position to be able to make the requested written representations. It is not expected that such inquiries would usually require a formal internal process beyond those already established by the entity.

Written Representations about Management's Responsibilities (Ref: Para. 10-11)

A7   Audit evidence obtained during the audit that management has fulfilled the responsibilities referred to in paragraphs 10 and 11 is not sufficient without obtaining confirmation from management that it believes that it has fulfilled those responsibilities. This is because the auditor is not able to judge solely on other audit evidence whether management has prepared and presented the financial statements and provided information to the auditor on the basis of the agreed acknowledgement and understanding of its responsibilities. For example, the auditor could not conclude that management has provided the auditor with all relevant information agreed in the terms of the audit engagement without asking it whether, and receiving confirmation that, such information has been provided.

[4a] *In the UK and Ireland, those charged with governance are responsible for the preparation of the financial statements.*

A signed copy of the financial statements for a company may be sufficient evidence of the directors' acknowledgement of their collective responsibility for the preparation of the financial statements where it incorporates a statement to that effect. A signed copy of the financial statements, however, is not, by itself, sufficient appropriate evidence to confirm other representations given to the auditor as it does not, ordinarily, clearly identify and explain the specific separate representations.

A7-1

The written representations required by paragraphs 10 and 11 draw on the agreed acknowledgement and understanding of management of its responsibilities in the terms of the audit engagement by requesting confirmation that it has fulfilled them. The auditor may also ask management to reconfirm its acknowledgement and understanding of those responsibilities in written representations. This is common in certain jurisdictions, but in any event may be particularly appropriate when:

A8

- Those who signed the terms of the audit engagement on behalf of the entity no longer have the relevant responsibilities;
- The terms of the audit engagement were prepared in a previous year;
- There is any indication that management misunderstands those responsibilities; or
- Changes in circumstances make it appropriate to do so.

Consistent with the requirement of ISA (UK and Ireland) 210,[5] such reconfirmation of management's acknowledgement and understanding of its responsibilities is not made subject to the best of management's knowledge and belief (as discussed in paragraph A5 of this ISA (UK and Ireland)).

Although reconfirmation of management's acknowledgement and understanding of its responsibilities is not made subject to the best of management's knowledge and belief, as discussed in paragraph A8, this does not prevent management from stating that the written representations required by paragraphs 10 and 11 relating to the fulfillment of its responsibilities are given to the best of its knowledge and belief.

A8-1

Considerations Specific to Public Sector Entities

The mandates for audits of the financial statements of public sector entities may be broader than those of other entities. As a result, the premise, relating to management's responsibilities, on which an audit of the financial statements of a public sector entity is conducted may give rise to additional written representations. These may include written representations confirming that transactions and events have been carried out in accordance with law, regulation or other authority.

A9

Other Written Representations (Ref: Para. 13)

Additional Written Representations about the Financial Statements

In addition to the written representation required by paragraph 10, the auditor may consider it necessary to request other written representations about the financial statements. Such written representations may supplement, but do not form part of,

A10

---

[5] *ISA (UK and Ireland) 210, paragraph 6(b).*

the written representation required by paragraph 10. They may include representations about the following:

- Whether the selection and application of accounting policies are appropriate; and
- Whether matters such as the following, where relevant under the applicable financial reporting framework, have been recognized, measured, presented or disclosed in accordance with that framework:
    o Plans or intentions that may affect the carrying value or classification of assets and liabilities;
    o Liabilities, both actual and contingent;
    o Title to, or control over, assets, the liens or encumbrances on assets, and assets pledged as collateral; and
    o Aspects of laws, regulations and contractual agreements that may affect the financial statements, including non-compliance.

Additional Written Representations about Information Provided to the Auditor

A11   In addition to the written representation required by paragraph 11, the auditor may consider it necessary to request management to provide a written representation that it has communicated to the auditor all deficiencies in internal control of which management is aware.

Written Representations about Specific Assertions

A12   When obtaining evidence about, or evaluating, judgments and intentions, the auditor may consider one or more of the following:

- The entity's past history in carrying out its stated intentions.
- The entity's reasons for choosing a particular course of action.
- The entity's ability to pursue a specific course of action.
- The existence or lack of any other information that might have been obtained during the course of the audit that may be inconsistent with management's judgment or intent.

A13   In addition, the auditor may consider it necessary to request management to provide written representations about specific assertions in the financial statements; in particular, to support an understanding that the auditor has obtained from other audit evidence of management's judgment or intent in relation to, or the completeness of, a specific assertion. For example, if the intent of management is important to the valuation basis for investments, it may not be possible to obtain sufficient appropriate audit evidence without a written representation from management about its intentions. Although such written representations provide necessary audit evidence, they do not provide sufficient appropriate audit evidence on their own for that assertion.

Communicating a Threshold Amount (Ref: Para. 10-11, 13)

A14   ISA (UK and Ireland) 450 requires the auditor to accumulate misstatements identified during the audit, other than those that are clearly trivial.[6] The auditor may determine a threshold above which misstatements cannot be regarded as clearly trivial. In the same way, the auditor may consider communicating to management a threshold for purposes of the requested written representations.

[6] ISA (UK and Ireland) 450, "Evaluation of Misstatements Identified during the Audit," paragraph 5.

Date of and Period(s) Covered by Written Representations (Ref: Para. 14)

Because written representations are necessary audit evidence, the auditor's opinion cannot be expressed, and the auditor's report cannot be dated, before the date of the written representations. Furthermore, because the auditor is concerned with events occurring up to the date of the auditor's report that may require adjustment to or disclosure in the financial statements, the written representations are dated as near as practicable to, but not after, the date of the auditor's report on the financial statements. **A15**

In some circumstances it may be appropriate for the auditor to obtain a written representation about a specific assertion in the financial statements during the course of the audit. Where this is the case, it may be necessary to request an updated written representation. **A16**

The written representations are for all periods referred to in the auditor's report because management needs to reaffirm that the written representations it previously made with respect to the prior periods remain appropriate. The auditor and management may agree to a form of written representation that updates written representations relating to the prior periods by addressing whether there are any changes to such written representations and, if so, what they are. **A17**

Situations may arise where current management were not present during all periods referred to in the auditor's report. Such persons may assert that they are not in a position to provide some or all of the written representations because they were not in place during the period. This fact, however, does not diminish such persons' responsibilities for the financial statements as a whole. Accordingly, the requirement for the auditor to request from them written representations that cover the whole of the relevant period(s) still applies. **A18**

Form of Written Representations (Ref: Para. 15)

Written representations are required to be included in a representation letter addressed to the auditor. In some jurisdictions, however, management may be required by law or regulation to make a written public statement about its responsibilities. Although such statement is a representation to the users of the financial statements, or to relevant authorities, the auditor may determine that it is an appropriate form of written representation in respect of some or all of the representations required by paragraph 10 or 11. Consequently, the relevant matters covered by such statement need not be included in the representation letter. Factors that may affect the auditor's determination include: **A19**

- Whether the statement includes confirmation of the fulfillment of the responsibilities referred to in paragraphs 10 and 11.
- Whether the statement has been given or approved by those from whom the auditor requests the relevant written representations.
- Whether a copy of the statement is provided to the auditor as near as practicable to, but not after, the date of the auditor's report on the financial statements (see paragraph 14).

A formal statement of compliance with law or regulation, or of approval of the financial statements, would not contain sufficient information for the auditor to be satisfied that all necessary representations have been consciously made. The expression of management's responsibilities in law or regulation is also not a substitute for the requested written representations. **A20**

A21   Appendix 2 provides an illustrative example of a representation letter.

Communication with Those Charged with Governance (Ref: Para. 10-11, 13)

A22   ISA (UK and Ireland) 260 requires the auditor to communicate with those charged with governance the written representations which the auditor has requested from management.[7]

A22-1   In the UK and Ireland these communications are made before those charged with governance approve the financial statements, to ensure that they are aware of the representations on which the auditor intends to rely in expressing the auditor's opinion on those financial statements.

Doubt as to the Reliability of Written Representations and Requested Written Representations Not Provided

Doubt as to the Reliability of Written Representations (Ref: Para. 16-17)

A23   In the case of identified inconsistencies between one or more written representations and audit evidence obtained from another source, the auditor may consider whether the risk assessment remains appropriate and, if not, revise the risk assessment and determine the nature, timing and extent of further audit procedures to respond to the assessed risks.

A24   Concerns about the competence, integrity, ethical values or diligence of management, or about its commitment to or enforcement of these, may cause the auditor to conclude that the risk of management misrepresentation in the financial statements is such that an audit cannot be conducted. In such a case, the auditor may consider withdrawing from the engagement, where withdrawal is possible under applicable law or regulation, unless those charged with governance put in place appropriate corrective measures. Such measures, however, may not be sufficient to enable the auditor to issue an unmodified audit opinion.

A25   ISA (UK and Ireland) 230 requires the auditor to document significant matters arising during the audit, the conclusions reached thereon, and significant professional judgments made in reaching those conclusions.[8] The auditor may have identified significant issues relating to the competence, integrity, ethical values or diligence of management, or about its commitment to or enforcement of these, but concluded that the written representations are nevertheless reliable. In such a case, this significant matter is documented in accordance with ISA (UK and Ireland) 230.

Written Representations about Management's Responsibilities (Ref: Para. 20)

A26   As explained in paragraph A7, the auditor is not able to judge solely on other audit evidence whether management has fulfilled the responsibilities referred to in paragraphs 10 and 11. Therefore, if, as described in paragraph 20(a), the auditor concludes that the written representations about these matters are unreliable, or if management does not provide those written representations, the auditor is unable to obtain sufficient appropriate audit evidence. The possible effects on the financial

---

[7] *ISA (UK and Ireland) 260, "Communication with Those Charged with Governance," paragraph 16(c)(ii).*

[8] *ISA (UK and Ireland) 230, "Audit Documentation," paragraphs 8(c) and 10.*

statements of such inability are not confined to specific elements, accounts or items of the financial statements and are hence pervasive. ISA (UK and Ireland) 705 requires the auditor to disclaim an opinion on the financial statements in such circumstances.[9]

A written representation that has been modified from that requested by the auditor does not necessarily mean that management did not provide the written representation. However, the underlying reason for such modification may affect the opinion in the auditor's report. For example:

A27

- The written representation about management's fulfillment of its responsibility for the preparation of the financial statements may state that management believes that, except for material non-compliance with a particular requirement of the applicable financial reporting framework, the financial statements are prepared in accordance with that framework. The requirement in paragraph 20 does not apply because the auditor concluded that management has provided reliable written representations. However, the auditor is required to consider the effect of the non-compliance on the opinion in the auditor's report in accordance with ISA (UK and Ireland) 705.
- The written representation about the responsibility of management to provide the auditor with all relevant information agreed in the terms of the audit engagement may state that management believes that, except for information destroyed in a fire, it has provided the auditor with such information. The requirement in paragraph 20 does not apply because the auditor concluded that management has provided reliable written representations. However, the auditor is required to consider the effects of the pervasiveness of the information destroyed in the fire on the financial statements and the effect thereof on the opinion in the auditor's report in accordance with ISA (UK and Ireland) 705.
- The written representation that all transactions have been recorded and are reflected in the financial statements may be modified, for example to refer a threshold amount agreed with the auditor (see paragraph A14) or to state that all transactions that may have a material effect on the financial statements have been recorded.

Appendix 1 (Ref: Para. 2)

List of ISAs (UK and Ireland) Containing Requirements for Written Representations

This appendix identifies paragraphs in other ISAs (UK and Ireland) in effect for audits of financial statements for periods ending on or after 15 December 2010 that require subject-matter specific written representations. The list is not a substitute for considering the requirements and related application and other explanatory material in ISAs (UK and Ireland).

- ISA 240 (UK and Ireland), "The Auditor's Responsibilities Relating to Fraud in an Audit of Financial Statements" – paragraph 39
- ISA 250 (UK and Ireland), "Consideration of Laws and Regulations in an Audit of Financial Statements" – paragraph 16
- ISA 450 (UK and Ireland), "Evaluation of Misstatements Identified during the Audit" – paragraph 14

[9] *ISA (UK and Ireland) 705, paragraph 9.*

- ISA 501 (UK and Ireland), "Audit Evidence—Specific Considerations for Selected Items" – paragraph 12
- ISA 540 (UK and Ireland), "Auditing Accounting Estimates, Including Fair Value Accounting Estimates, and Related Disclosures" – paragraph 22
- ISA 550 (UK and Ireland), "Related Parties" – paragraph 26
- ISA 560 (UK and Ireland), "Subsequent Events" – paragraph 9
- ISA 570 (UK and Ireland), "Going Concern" – paragraph 16(e)
- ISA 710 (UK and Ireland), "Comparative Information—Corresponding Figures and Comparative Financial Statements" – paragraph 9

Appendix 2 (Ref: Para. A21)

This illustrative representation letter has not been tailored for the UK and Ireland. For example, when describing the responsibilities of management and those charged with governance for the financial statements and providing information to the auditor, the auditor has regard to the manner in which those responsibilities are described in the terms of the audit engagement (see ISA (UK and Ireland) 210).

Illustrative Representation Letter

The following illustrative letter includes written representations that are required by this and other ISAs in effect for audits of financial statements for periods ending on or after 15 December 2010. It is assumed in this illustration that the applicable financial reporting framework is International Financial Reporting Standards; the requirement of ISA 570[10] to obtain a written representation is not relevant; and that there are no exceptions to the requested written representations. If there were exceptions, the representations would need to be modified to reflect the exceptions.

(Entity Letterhead)

(To Auditor) (Date)

This representation letter is provided in connection with your audit of the financial statements of ABC Company for the year ended December 31, 20XX[11] for the purpose of expressing an opinion as to whether the financial statements are presented fairly, in all material respects, (or *give a true and fair view*) in accordance with International Financial Reporting Standards.

We confirm that (*, to the best of our knowledge and belief, having made such inquiries as we considered necessary for the purpose of appropriately informing ourselves*):

Financial Statements

- We have fulfilled our responsibilities, as set out in the terms of the audit engagement dated [insert date], for the preparation of the financial statements in accordance with International Financial Reporting Standards; in particular the financial statements are fairly presented (or *give a true and fair view*) in accordance therewith.

---

[10] *ISA 570, "Going Concern."*

[11] *Where the auditor reports on more than one period, the auditor adjusts the date so that the letter pertains to all periods covered by the auditor's report.*

- Significant assumptions used by us in making accounting estimates, including those measured at fair value, are reasonable. (ISA 540)
- Related party relationships and transactions have been appropriately accounted for and disclosed in accordance with the requirements of International Financial Reporting Standards. (ISA 550)
- All events subsequent to the date of the financial statements and for which International Financial Reporting Standards require adjustment or disclosure have been adjusted or disclosed. (ISA 560)
- The effects of uncorrected misstatements are immaterial, both individually and in the aggregate, to the financial statements as a whole. A list of the uncorrected misstatements is attached to the representation letter. (ISA 450)
- [Any other matters that the auditor may consider appropriate (see paragraph A10 of this ISA).]

Information Provided

- We have provided you with:
  - Access to all information of which we are aware that is relevant to the preparation of the financial statements such as records, documentation and other matters;
  - Additional information that you have requested from us for the purpose of the audit; and
  - Unrestricted access to persons within the entity from whom you determined it necessary to obtain audit evidence.
- All transactions have been recorded in the accounting records and are reflected in the financial statements.
- We have disclosed to you the results of our assessment of the risk that the financial statements may be materially misstated as a result of fraud. (ISA 240)
- We have disclosed to you all information in relation to fraud or suspected fraud that we are aware of and that affects the entity and involves:
  - Management;
  - Employees who have significant roles in internal control; or
  - Others where the fraud could have a material effect on the financial statements. (ISA 240)
- We have disclosed to you all information in relation to allegations of fraud, or suspected fraud, affecting the entity's financial statements communicated by employees, former employees, analysts, regulators or others. (ISA 240)
- We have disclosed to you all known instances of non-compliance or suspected non-compliance with laws and regulations whose effects should be considered when preparing financial statements. (ISA 250)
- We have disclosed to you the identity of the entity's related parties and all the related party relationships and transactions of which we are aware. 550)
- [Any other matters that the auditor may consider necessary (see paragraph A11 of this ISA).]

Management   Management

International Standard on Auditing (UK and Ireland) 600

Special considerations—audits of group financial statements (including the work of component auditors)

(Effective for audits of group financial statements for periods ending on or after 15 December 2010)[1a]

Contents

[1a] *Conforming amendments to this standard as a result of ISA (UK and Ireland) 610 (Revised June 2013), Using the Work of Internal Auditors, are included that are effective for audits of financial statements for periods ending on or after 15 June 2014. Details of the amendments are given in the Annexure to ISA (UK and Ireland) 610 (Revised June 2013).*

Appendix 1: Example of a Qualified Opinion Where the Group Engagement Team Is Not Able to Obtain Sufficient Appropriate Audit Evidence on Which to Base the Group Audit Opinion

Appendix 2: Examples of Matters about Which the Group Engagement Team Obtains an Understanding

Appendix 3: Examples of Conditions or Events that May Indicate Risks of Material Misstatement of the Group Financial Statements

Appendix 4: Examples of a Component Auditor's Confirmations

Appendix 5: Required and Additional Matters Included in the Group Engagement Team's Letter of Instruction

---

International Standard on Auditing (UK and Ireland) (ISA (UK and Ireland)) 600, "Special Considerations—Audits of Group Financial Statements (Including the Work of Component Auditors)" should be read in conjunction with ISA (UK and Ireland) 200, "Overall Objectives of the Independent Auditor and the Conduct of an Audit in Accordance with International Standards on Auditing (UK and Ireland)."

Introduction

Scope of this ISA (UK and Ireland)

1   The International Standards on Auditing (UK and Ireland) (ISAs (UK and Ireland)) apply to group audits. This ISA (UK and Ireland) deals with special considerations that apply to group audits, in particular those that involve component auditors.

2   An auditor may find this ISA (UK and Ireland), adapted as necessary in the circumstances, useful when that auditor involves other auditors in the audit of financial statements that are not group financial statements. For example, an auditor may involve another auditor to observe the inventory count or inspect physical fixed assets at a remote location.

3   A component auditor may be required by statute, regulation or for another reason, to express an audit opinion on the financial statements of a component. The group engagement team may decide to use the audit evidence on which the audit opinion on the financial statements of the component is based to provide audit evidence for the group audit, but the requirements of this ISA (UK and Ireland) nevertheless apply. (Ref: Para. A1)

4   In accordance with ISA (UK and Ireland) 220,[1] the group engagement partner is required to be satisfied that those performing the group audit engagement, including component auditors, collectively have the appropriate competence and capabilities. The group engagement partner is also responsible for the direction, supervision and performance of the group audit engagement.

5   The group engagement partner applies the requirements of ISA (UK and Ireland) 220 regardless of whether the group engagement team or a component auditor performs the work on the financial information of a component. This ISA (UK and Ireland) assists the group engagement partner to meet the requirements of ISA (UK and Ireland) 220 where component auditors perform work on the financial information of components.

6   Audit risk is a function of the risk of material misstatement of the financial statements and the risk that the auditor will not detect such misstatements.[2] In a group audit, this includes the risk that the component auditor may not detect a misstatement in the financial information of the component that could cause a material misstatement of the group financial statements, and the risk that the group engagement team may not detect this misstatement. This ISA (UK and Ireland) explains the matters that the group engagement team considers when determining the nature, timing and extent of its involvement in the risk assessment procedures and further audit procedures performed by the component auditors on the financial information of the components. The purpose of this involvement is to obtain sufficient appropriate audit evidence on which to base the audit opinion on the group financial statements.

---

[1] *ISA (UK and Ireland) 220, "Quality Control for an Audit of Financial Statements," paragraphs 14 and 15.*

[2] *ISA (UK and Ireland) 200, "Overall Objectives of the Independent Auditor and the Conduct of an Audit in Accordance with International Standards on Auditing (UK and Ireland)," paragraph A32.*

Effective Date

This ISA (UK and Ireland) is effective for audits of group financial statements for   7
periods ending on or after 15 December 2010.[1a]

Objectives

The objectives of the auditor are: 8

(a) To determine whether to act as the auditor of the group financial statements;
    and
(b) If acting as the auditor of the group financial statements:
    (i) To communicate clearly with component auditors about the scope and
         timing of their work on financial information related to components and
         their findings; and
    (ii) To obtain sufficient appropriate audit evidence regarding the financial
         information of the components and the consolidation process to express an
         opinion on whether the group financial statements are prepared, in all
         material respects, in accordance with the applicable financial reporting
         framework.

Definitions

For purposes of the ISAs (UK and Ireland), the following terms have the meanings   9
attributed below:

(a) Component – An entity or business activity for which group or component
    management prepares financial information that should be included in the
    group financial statements. (Ref: Para. A2-A4)
(b) Component auditor – An auditor who, at the request of the group engagement
    team, performs work on financial information related to a component for the
    group audit. (Ref: Para. A7)
(c) Component management – Management responsible for the preparation of the
    financial information of a component.
(d) Component materiality – The materiality for a component determined by the
    group engagement team.
(e) Group – All the components whose financial information is included in the
    group financial statements. A group always has more than one component.
(f) Group audit – The audit of group financial statements.
(g) Group audit opinion – The audit opinion on the group financial statements.
(h) Group engagement partner – The partner or other person in the firm who is
    responsible for the group audit engagement and its performance, and for the
    auditor's report on the group financial statements that is issued on behalf of the
    firm. Where joint auditors conduct the group audit, the joint engagement
    partners and their engagement teams collectively constitute the group engage-
    ment partner and the group engagement team. This ISA (UK and Ireland) does
    not, however, deal with the relationship between joint auditors or the work that
    one joint auditor performs in relation to the work of the other joint auditor.
(i) Group engagement team – Partners, including the group engagement partner,
    and staff who establish the overall group audit strategy, communicate with
    component auditors, perform work on the consolidation process, and evaluate
    the conclusions drawn from the audit evidence as the basis for forming an
    opinion on the group financial statements.

(j) Group financial statements – Financial statements that include the financial information of more than one component. The term "group financial statements" also refers to combined financial statements aggregating the financial information prepared by components that have no parent but are under common control.

(k) Group management – Management responsible for the preparation of the group financial statements.

(l) Group-wide controls – Controls designed, implemented and maintained by group management over group financial reporting.

(m) Significant component – A component identified by the group engagement team (i) that is of individual financial significance to the group, or (ii) that, due to its specific nature or circumstances, is likely to include significant risks of material misstatement of the group financial statements. (Ref: Para. A5-A6)

10   Reference to "the applicable financial reporting framework" means the financial reporting framework that applies to the group financial statements. Reference to "the consolidation process" includes:

(a) The recognition, measurement, presentation, and disclosure of the financial information of the components in the group financial statements by way of consolidation, proportionate consolidation, or the equity or cost methods of accounting; and

(b) The aggregation in combined financial statements of the financial information of components that have no parent but are under common control.

Requirements

Responsibility

11   The group engagement partner is responsible for the direction, supervision and performance of the group audit engagement in compliance with professional standards and applicable legal and regulatory requirements, and whether the auditor's report that is issued is appropriate in the circumstances.[3]; As a result, the auditor's report on the group financial statements shall not refer to a component auditor, unless required by law or regulation to include such reference. If such reference is required by law or regulation, the auditor's report shall indicate that the reference does not diminish the group engagement partner's or the group engagement partner's firm's responsibility for the group audit opinion. (Ref: Para. A8-A9)

Acceptance and Continuance

12   In applying ISA (UK and Ireland) 220, the group engagement partner shall determine whether sufficient appropriate audit evidence can reasonably be expected to be obtained in relation to the consolidation process and the financial information of the components on which to base the group audit opinion. For this purpose, the group engagement team shall obtain an understanding of the group, its components, and their environments that is sufficient to identify components that are likely to be significant components. Where component auditors will perform work on the financial information of such components, the group engagement partner shall evaluate whether the group engagement team will be able to be involved in the work of those component auditors to the extent necessary to obtain sufficient appropriate audit evidence. (Ref: Para. A10-A12)

---

[3] *ISA (UK and Ireland) 220, paragraph 15.*

If the group engagement partner concludes that: **13**

(a) it will not be possible for the group engagement team to obtain sufficient appropriate audit evidence due to restrictions imposed by group management; and

(b) the possible effect of this inability will result in a disclaimer of opinion on the group financial statements),[4]

the group engagement partner shall either:

- in the case of a new engagement, not accept the engagement, or, in the case of a continuing engagement, withdraw from the engagement, where withdrawal is possible under applicable law or regulation; or
- where law or regulation prohibits an auditor from declining an engagement or where withdrawal from an engagement is not otherwise possible, having performed the audit of the group financial statements to the extent possible, disclaim an opinion on the group financial statements. (Ref: Para. A13-A19)

Terms of Engagement

The group engagement partner shall agree on the terms of the group audit engagement in accordance with ISA (UK and Ireland) 210.[5] (Ref: Para. A20-A21) **14**

Overall Audit Strategy and Audit Plan

The group engagement team shall establish an overall group audit strategy and shall develop a group audit plan in accordance with ISA (UK and Ireland) 300.[6] **15**

The group engagement partner shall review the overall group audit strategy and group audit plan. (Ref: Para. A22) **16**

Understanding the Group, Its Components and Their Environments

The auditor is required to identify and assess the risks of material misstatement through obtaining an understanding of the entity and its environment.[7] The group engagement team shall: **17**

(a) Enhance its understanding of the group, its components, and their environments, including group-wide controls, obtained during the acceptance or continuance stage; and

(b) Obtain an understanding of the consolidation process, including the instructions issued by group management to components. (Ref: Para. A23-A29)

The group engagement team shall obtain an understanding that is sufficient to: **18**

(a) Confirm or revise its initial identification of components that are likely to be significant; and

---

[4] *ISA (UK and Ireland) 705, "Modifications to the Opinion in the Independent Auditor's Report."*

[5] *ISA (UK and Ireland) 210, "Agreeing the Terms of Audit Engagements."*

[6] *ISA (UK and Ireland) 300, "Planning an Audit of Financial Statements," paragraphs 7-12.*

[7] *ISA (UK and Ireland) 315, "Identifying and Assessing the Risks of Material Misstatement through Understanding the Entity and Its Environment."*

(b) Assess the risks of material misstatement of the group financial statements, whether due to fraud or error.[8] (Ref: Para. A30-A31)

Understanding the Component Auditor

19   If the group engagement team plans to request a component auditor to perform work on the financial information of a component, the group engagement team shall obtain an understanding of the following: (Ref: Para. A32-A35)

(a) Whether the component auditor understands and will comply with the ethical requirements that are relevant to the group audit and, in particular, is independent. (Ref: Para. A37)

(b) The component auditor's professional competence. (Ref: Para. A38)

(c) Whether the group engagement team will be able to be involved in the work of the component auditor to the extent necessary to obtain sufficient appropriate audit evidence.

(d) Whether the component auditor operates in a regulatory environment that actively oversees auditors. (Ref: Para. A36)

20   If a component auditor does not meet the independence requirements that are relevant to the group audit, or the group engagement team has serious concerns about the other matters listed in paragraph 19(a)-(c), the group engagement team shall obtain sufficient appropriate audit evidence relating to the financial information of the component without requesting that component auditor to perform work on the financial information of that component. (Ref: Para. A39-A41)

Materiality

21   The group engagement team shall determine the following: (Ref: Para. A42)

(a) Materiality for the group financial statements as a whole when establishing the overall group audit strategy.

(b) If, in the specific circumstances of the group, there are particular classes of transactions, account balances or disclosures in the group financial statements for which misstatements of lesser amounts than materiality for the group financial statements as a whole could reasonably be expected to influence the economic decisions of users taken on the basis of the group financial statements, the materiality level or levels to be applied to those particular classes of transactions, account balances or disclosures.

(c) Component materiality for those components where component auditors will perform an audit or a review for purposes of the group audit. To reduce to an appropriately low level the probability that the aggregate of uncorrected and undetected misstatements in the group financial statements exceeds materiality for the group financial statements as a whole, component materiality shall be lower than materiality for the group financial statements as a whole. (Ref: Para. A43-A44)

(d) The threshold above which misstatements cannot be regarded as clearly trivial to the group financial statements. (Ref: Para. A45)

22   Where component auditors will perform an audit for purposes of the group audit, the group engagement team shall evaluate the appropriateness of performance materiality determined at the component level. (Ref: Para. A46)

---

[8] *ISA (UK and Ireland) 315.*

If a component is subject to audit by statute, regulation or other reason, and the group engagement team decides to use that audit to provide audit evidence for the group audit, the group engagement team shall determine whether: **23**

(a) materiality for the component financial statements as a whole; and
(b) performance materiality at the component level

meet the requirements of this ISA (UK and Ireland).

Responding to Assessed Risks

The auditor is required to design and implement appropriate responses to address   **24**
the assessed risks of material misstatement of the financial statements.[9] The group
engagement team shall determine the type of work to be performed by the group
engagement team, or the component auditors on its behalf, on the financial information of the components (see paragraphs 26-29). The group engagement team shall
also determine the nature, timing and extent of its involvement in the work of the
component auditors (see paragraphs 30-31).

If the nature, timing and extent of the work to be performed on the consolidation   **25**
process or the financial information of the components are based on an expectation
that group-wide controls are operating effectively, or if substantive procedures alone
cannot provide sufficient appropriate audit evidence at the assertion level, the group
engagement team shall test, or request a component auditor to test, the operating
effectiveness of those controls.

Determining the Type of Work to Be Performed on the Financial Information of Components (Ref: Para. A47)

Significant Components

For a component that is significant due to its individual financial significance to the   **26**
group, the group engagement team, or a component auditor on its behalf, shall
perform an audit of the financial information of the component using component
materiality.

For a component that is significant because it is likely to include significant risks of   **27**
material misstatement of the group financial statements due to its specific nature or
circumstances, the group engagement team, or a component auditor on its behalf,
shall perform one or more of the following:

(a) An audit of the financial information of the component using component
materiality.
(b) An audit of one or more account balances, classes of transactions or disclosures
relating to the likely significant risks of material misstatement of the group
financial statements. (Ref: Para. A48)
(c) Specified audit procedures relating to the likely significant risks of material
misstatement of the group financial statements. (Ref: Para. A49)

Components that Are Not Significant Components

For components that are not significant components, the group engagement team   **28**
shall perform analytical procedures at group level. (Ref: Para. A50)

---

[9] *ISA (UK and Ireland) 330, "The Auditor's Responses to Assessed Risks."*

29 If the group engagement team does not consider that sufficient appropriate audit evidence on which to base the group audit opinion will be obtained from:

(a) the work performed on the financial information of significant components;
(b) the work performed on group-wide controls and the consolidation process; and
(c) the analytical procedures performed at group level,

the group engagement team shall select components that are not significant components and shall perform, or request a component auditor to perform, one or more of the following on the financial information of the individual components selected: (Ref: Para. A51-A53)

- An audit of the financial information of the component using component materiality.
- An audit of one or more account balances, classes of transactions or disclosures.
- A review of the financial information of the component using component materiality.
- Specified procedures.

The group engagement team shall vary the selection of components over a period of time.

Involvement in the Work Performed by Component Auditors (Ref: Para. A54-A55)

Significant Components—Risk Assessment

30 If a component auditor performs an audit of the financial information of a significant component, the group engagement team shall be involved in the component auditor's risk assessment to identify significant risks of material misstatement of the group financial statements. The nature, timing and extent of this involvement are affected by the group engagement team's understanding of the component auditor, but at a minimum shall include:

(a) Discussing with the component auditor or component management those of the component's business activities that are significant to the group;
(b) Discussing with the component auditor the susceptibility of the component to material misstatement of the financial information due to fraud or error; and
(c) Reviewing the component auditor's documentation of identified significant risks of material misstatement of the group financial statements. Such documentation may take the form of a memorandum that reflects the component auditor's conclusion with regard to the identified significant risks.

Identified Significant Risks of Material Misstatement of the Group Financial Statements—Further Audit Procedures

31 If significant risks of material misstatement of the group financial statements have been identified in a component on which a component auditor performs the work, the group engagement team shall evaluate the appropriateness of the further audit procedures to be performed to respond to the identified significant risks of material misstatement of the group financial statements. Based on its understanding of the component auditor, the group engagement team shall determine whether it is necessary to be involved in the further audit procedures.

Consolidation Process

In accordance with paragraph 17, the group engagement team obtains an understanding of group-wide controls and the consolidation process, including the instructions issued by group management to components. In accordance with paragraph 25, the group engagement team, or component auditor at the request of the group engagement team, tests the operating effectiveness of group-wide controls if the nature, timing and extent of the work to be performed on the consolidation process are based on an expectation that group-wide controls are operating effectively, or if substantive procedures alone cannot provide sufficient appropriate audit evidence at the assertion level.

32

The group engagement team shall design and perform further audit procedures on the consolidation process to respond to the assessed risks of material misstatement of the group financial statements arising from the consolidation process. This shall include evaluating whether all components have been included in the group financial statements.

33

The group engagement team shall evaluate the appropriateness, completeness and accuracy of consolidation adjustments and reclassifications, and shall evaluate whether any fraud risk factors or indicators of possible management bias exist. (Ref: Para. A56)

34

If the financial information of a component has not been prepared in accordance with the same accounting policies applied to the group financial statements, the group engagement team shall evaluate whether the financial information of that component has been appropriately adjusted for purposes of preparing and presenting the group financial statements.

35

The group engagement team shall determine whether the financial information identified in the component auditor's communication (see paragraph 41(c)) is the financial information that is incorporated in the group financial statements.

36

If the group financial statements include the financial statements of a component with a financial reporting period-end that differs from that of the group, the group engagement team shall evaluate whether appropriate adjustments have been made to those financial statements in accordance with the applicable financial reporting framework.

37

Subsequent Events

Where the group engagement team or component auditors perform audits on the financial information of components, the group engagement team or the component auditors shall perform procedures designed to identify events at those components that occur between the dates of the financial information of the components and the date of the auditor's report on the group financial statements, and that may require adjustment to or disclosure in the group financial statements.

38

Where component auditors perform work other than audits of the financial information of components, the group engagement team shall request the component auditors to notify the group engagement team if they become aware of subsequent events that may require an adjustment to or disclosure in the group financial statements.

39

Communication with the Component Auditor

40   The group engagement team shall communicate its requirements to the component auditor on a timely basis. This communication shall set out the work to be performed, the use to be made of that work, and the form and content of the component auditor's communication with the group engagement team. It shall also include the following: (Ref: Para. A57, A58, A60)

(a)   A request that the component auditor, knowing the context in which the group engagement team will use the work of the component auditor, confirms that the component auditor will cooperate with the group engagement team. (Ref: Para. A59)

(b)   The ethical requirements that are relevant to the group audit and, in particular, the independence requirements.

(c)   In the case of an audit or review of the financial information of the component, component materiality (and, if applicable, the materiality level or levels for particular classes of transactions, account balances or disclosures) and the threshold above which misstatements cannot be regarded as clearly trivial to the group financial statements.

(d)   Identified significant risks of material misstatement of the group financial statements, due to fraud or error, that are relevant to the work of the component auditor. The group engagement team shall request the component auditor to communicate on a timely basis any other identified significant risks of material misstatement of the group financial statements, due to fraud or error, in the component, and the component auditor's responses to such risks.

(e)   A list of related parties prepared by group management, and any other related parties of which the group engagement team is aware. The group engagement team shall request the component auditor to communicate on a timely basis related parties not previously identified by group management or the group engagement team. The group engagement team shall determine whether to identify such additional related parties to other component auditors.

41   The group engagement team shall request the component auditor to communicate matters relevant to the group engagement team's conclusion with regard to the group audit. Such communication shall include: (Ref: Para. A60)

(a)   Whether the component auditor has complied with ethical requirements that are relevant to the group audit, including independence and professional competence;

(b)   Whether the component auditor has complied with the group engagement team's requirements;

(c)   Identification of the financial information of the component on which the component auditor is reporting;

(d)   Information on instances of non-compliance with laws or regulations that could give rise to a material misstatement of the group financial statements;

(e)   A list of uncorrected misstatements of the financial information of the component (the list need not include misstatements that are below the threshold for clearly trivial misstatements communicated by the group engagement team (see paragraph 40(c));

(f)   Indicators of possible management bias;

(g)   Description of any identified significant deficiencies in internal control at the component level;

(h)   Other significant matters that the component auditor communicated or expects to communicate to those charged with governance of the component, including fraud or suspected fraud involving component management, employees who have significant roles in internal control at the component level or others where the fraud resulted in a material misstatement of the financial information of the component;

(i)   Any other matters that may be relevant to the group audit, or that the component auditor wishes to draw to the attention of the group engagement team, including exceptions noted in the written representations that the component auditor requested from component management; and

(j)   The component auditor's overall findings, conclusions or opinion.

Evaluating the Sufficiency and Appropriateness of Audit Evidence Obtained

Evaluating the Component Auditor's Communication and Adequacy of their Work

The group engagement team shall evaluate the component auditor's communication   **42**
(see paragraph 41). The group engagement team shall:

(a)   Discuss significant matters arising from that evaluation with the component auditor, component management or group management, as appropriate; and

(b)   Determine whether it is necessary to review other relevant parts of the component auditor's audit documentation. (Ref: Para. A61)

If the group engagement team concludes that the work of the component auditor is   **43**
insufficient, the group engagement team shall determine what additional procedures are to be performed, and whether they are to be performed by the component auditor or by the group engagement team.

Sufficiency and Appropriateness of Audit Evidence

The auditor is required to obtain sufficient appropriate audit evidence to reduce   **44**
audit risk to an acceptably low level and thereby enable the auditor to draw reasonable conclusions on which to base the auditor's opinion.[10] The group engagement team shall evaluate whether sufficient appropriate audit evidence has been obtained from the audit procedures performed on the consolidation process and the work performed by the group engagement team and the component auditors on the financial information of the components, on which to base the group audit opinion. (Ref: Para. A62)

The group engagement partner shall evaluate the effect on the group audit opinion of   **45**
any uncorrected misstatements (either identified by the group engagement team or communicated by component auditors) and any instances where there has been an inability to obtain sufficient appropriate audit evidence. (Ref: Para. A63)

Communication with Group Management and Those Charged with Governance of the Group

Communication with Group Management

The group engagement team shall determine which identified deficiencies in internal   **46**
control to communicate to those charged with governance and group management in accordance with ISA (UK and Ireland) 265.[11] In making this determination, the group engagement team shall consider:

[10] *ISA (UK and Ireland) 200, paragraph 17.*

[11] *ISA (UK and Ireland) 265, "Communicating Deficiencies in Internal Control to Those Charged with Governance and Management."*

(a) Deficiencies in group-wide internal control that the group engagement team has identified;

(b) Deficiencies in internal control that the group engagement team has identified in internal controls at components; and

(c) Deficiencies in internal control that component auditors have brought to the attention of the group engagement team.

47   If fraud has been identified by the group engagement team or brought to its attention by a component auditor (see paragraph 41(h)), or information indicates that a fraud may exist, the group engagement team shall communicate this on a timely basis to the appropriate level of group management in order to inform those with primary responsibility for the prevention and detection of fraud of matters relevant to their responsibilities. (Ref. Para. A64)

48   A component auditor may be required by statute, regulation or for another reason, to express an audit opinion on the financial statements of a component. In that case, the group engagement team shall request group management to inform component management of any matter of which the group engagement team becomes aware that may be significant to the financial statements of the component, but of which component management may be unaware. If group management refuses to communicate the matter to component management, the group engagement team shall discuss the matter with those charged with governance of the group. If the matter remains unresolved, the group engagement team, subject to legal and professional confidentiality considerations, shall consider whether to advise the component auditor not to issue the auditor's report on the financial statements of the component until the matter is resolved. (Ref: Para. A65)

Communication with Those Charged with Governance of the Group

49   The group engagement team shall communicate the following matters with those charged with governance of the group, in addition to those required by ISA (UK and Ireland) 260[12] and other ISAs (UK and Ireland): (Ref: Para. A66)

(a) An overview of the type of work to be performed on the financial information of the components.

(b) An overview of the nature of the group engagement team's planned involvement in the work to be performed by the component auditors on the financial information of significant components.

(c) Instances where the group engagement team's evaluation of the work of a component auditor gave rise to a concern about the quality of that auditor's work.

(d) Any limitations on the group audit, for example, where the group engagement team's access to information may have been restricted.

(e) Fraud or suspected fraud involving group management, component management, employees who have significant roles in group-wide controls or others where the fraud resulted in a material misstatement of the group financial statements.

---

[12] *ISA (UK and Ireland) 260, "Communication with Those Charged with Governance."*

Documentation

The group engagement team shall include in the audit documentation the following matters:[13] **50**

(a) An analysis of components, indicating those that are significant, and the type of work performed on the financial information of the components.
(b) The nature, timing and extent of the group engagement team's involvement in the work performed by the component auditors on significant components including, where applicable, the group engagement team's review of relevant parts of the component auditors' audit documentation and conclusions thereon. (Ref: Para. A66-1)
(c) Written communications between the group engagement team and the component auditors about the group engagement team's requirements.

***

Application and Other Explanatory Material

Components Subject to Audit by Statute, Regulation or Other Reason (Ref: Para. 3)

Factors that may affect the group engagement team's decision whether to use an audit required by statute, regulation or for another reason to provide audit evidence for the group audit include the following: **A1**

- Differences in the financial reporting framework applied in preparing the financial statements of the component and that applied in preparing the group financial statements.
- Differences in the auditing and other standards applied by the component auditor and those applied in the audit of the group financial statements.
- Whether the audit of the financial statements of the component will be completed in time to meet the group reporting timetable.

Considerations Specific to Public Sector Entities

In certain parts of the public sector where the responsibilities of principal and other auditors are governed by statutory provisions, these override the provisions of this ISA (UK and Ireland). **A1-1**

Definitions

Component (Ref: Para. 9(a))

The structure of a group affects how components are identified. For example, the group financial reporting system may be based on an organizational structure that provides for financial information to be prepared by a parent and one or more subsidiaries, joint ventures, or investees accounted for by the equity or cost methods of accounting; by a head office and one or more divisions or branches; or by a combination of both. Some groups, however, may organize their financial reporting system by function, process, product or service (or by groups of products or services), or geographical locations. In these cases, the entity or business activity for **A2**

[13] ISA (UK and Ireland) 230, "Audit Documentation," paragraphs 8-11, and paragraph A6.

which group or component management prepares financial information that is included in the group financial statements may be a function, process, product or service (or group of products or services), or geographical location.

A3   Various levels of components may exist within the group financial reporting system, in which case it may be more appropriate to identify components at certain levels of aggregation rather than individually.

A4   Components aggregated at a certain level may constitute a component for purposes of the group audit; however, such a component may also prepare group financial statements that incorporate the financial information of the components it encompasses (that is, a subgroup). This ISA (UK and Ireland) may therefore be applied by different group engagement partners and teams for different subgroups within a larger group.

Significant Component (Ref: Para. 9(m))

A5   As the individual financial significance of a component increases, the risks of material misstatement of the group financial statements ordinarily increase. The group engagement team may apply a percentage to a chosen benchmark as an aid to identify components that are of individual financial significance. Identifying a benchmark and determining a percentage to be applied to it involve the exercise of professional judgment. Depending on the nature and circumstances of the group, appropriate benchmarks might include group assets, liabilities, cash flows, profit or turnover. For example, the group engagement team may consider that components exceeding 15% of the chosen benchmark are significant components. A higher or lower percentage may, however, be deemed appropriate in the circumstances.

A6   The group engagement team may also identify a component as likely to include significant risks of material misstatement of the group financial statements due to its specific nature or circumstances (that is, risks that require special audit consideration[14]). For example, a component could be responsible for foreign exchange trading and thus expose the group to a significant risk of material misstatement, even though the component is not otherwise of individual financial significance to the group.

Component Auditor (Ref: Para. 9(b))

A7   A member of the group engagement team may perform work on the financial information of a component for the group audit at the request of the group engagement team. Where this is the case, such a member of the engagement team is also a component auditor.

Responsibility (Ref: Para. 11)

A8   Although component auditors may perform work on the financial information of the components for the group audit and as such are responsible for their overall findings, conclusions or opinions, the group engagement partner or the group engagement partner's firm is responsible for the group audit opinion.

A9   When the group audit opinion is modified because the group engagement team was unable to obtain sufficient appropriate audit evidence in relation to the financial information of one or more components, the Basis for Modification paragraph in the

---

[14] *ISA (UK and Ireland) 315, paragraphs 27-29.*

auditor's report on the group financial statements describes the reasons for that inability without referring to the component auditor, unless such a reference is necessary for an adequate explanation of the circumstances.[15]

Acceptance and Continuance

Obtaining an Understanding at the Acceptance or Continuance Stage (Ref: Para. 12)

In the case of a new engagement, the group engagement team's understanding of the group, its components, and their environments may be obtained from: **A10**

- Information provided by group management;
- Communication with group management; and
- Where applicable, communication with the previous group engagement team, component management, or component auditors.

The group engagement team's understanding may include matters such as the following: **A11**

- The group structure, including both the legal and organizational structure (that is, how the group financial reporting system is organized).
- Components' business activities that are significant to the group, including the industry and regulatory, economic and political environments in which those activities take place.
- The use of service organizations, including shared service centers.
- A description of group-wide controls.
- The complexity of the consolidation process.
- Whether component auditors that are not from the group engagement partner's firm or network will perform work on the financial information of any of the components, and group management's rationale for appointing more than one auditor.
- Whether the group engagement team:
  - o Will have unrestricted access to those charged with governance of the group, group management, those charged with governance of the component, component management, component information, and the component auditors (including relevant audit documentation sought by the group engagement team); and
  - o Will be able to perform necessary work on the financial information of the components.

In the case of a continuing engagement, the group engagement team's ability to obtain sufficient appropriate audit evidence may be affected by significant changes, for example: **A12**

- Changes in the group structure (for example, acquisitions, disposals, reorganizations, or changes in how the group financial reporting system is organized).
- Changes in components' business activities that are significant to the group.
- Changes in the composition of those charged with governance of the group, group management, or key management of significant components.
- Concerns the group engagement team has with regard to the integrity and competence of group or component management.
- Changes in group-wide controls.
- Changes in the applicable financial reporting framework.

---

[15] *ISA (UK and Ireland) 705, paragraph 20.*

Expectation to Obtain Sufficient Appropriate Audit Evidence (Ref: Para. 13)

A13   A group may consist only of components not considered significant components. In these circumstances, the group engagement partner can reasonably expect to obtain sufficient appropriate audit evidence on which to base the group audit opinion if the group engagement team will be able to:

(a) Perform the work on the financial information of some of these components; and

(b) Be involved in the work performed by component auditors on the financial information of other components to the extent necessary to obtain sufficient appropriate audit evidence.

Access to Information (Ref: Para. 13)

A14   The group engagement team's access to information may be restricted by circumstances that cannot be overcome by group management, for example, laws relating to confidentiality and data privacy, or denial by the component auditor of access to relevant audit documentation sought by the group engagement team. It may also be restricted by group management.

A14-1   In the UK and Ireland there are statutory obligations on corporate subsidiary undertakings, and their auditors and other parties, in the UK and Ireland to provide the auditor of a corporate parent undertaking with such information and explanations as that auditor may reasonably require for the purposes of the audit[15a]. Where there is no such statutory obligation (e.g. for non corporate entities and overseas subsidiary undertakings), permission may be needed by the auditors of the subsidiary undertakings, from those charged with governance of the subsidiary undertakings, to disclose information to the auditor of the parent undertaking. Permission may also be needed from those charged with governance of the subsidiary undertakings for the auditor of the parent undertaking to pass those disclosures on to those charged with governance of the parent undertaking. The auditor of the parent undertaking seeks to ensure that appropriate arrangements are made at the planning stage for these disclosures. Normally, such arrangements for groups are recorded in the instructions to the auditors of subsidiary undertakings and relevant engagement letters.

A15   Where access to information is restricted by circumstances, the group engagement team may still be able to obtain sufficient appropriate audit evidence; however, this is less likely as the significance of the component increases. For example, the group

---

[15a] *In the UK, Section 499 of the Companies Act 2006 specifies that the auditor of a company may require any subsidiary undertaking of the company which is a body corporate incorporated in the UK, and any officer, employee or auditor of any such subsidiary undertaking or any person holding or accountable for any books, accounts or vouchers of any such subsidiary undertaking, to provide him with such information or explanations as he thinks necessary for the performance of his duties as auditor. (Similar obligations regarding companies incorporated in the Republic of Ireland are set out in Section 196, Companies Act 1990.) If a parent company has a subsidiary undertaking that is not a body corporate incorporated in the UK, Section 500 of the Companies Act 2006 specifies that the auditor of the parent company may require it to take all such steps as are reasonably open to it to obtain from the subsidiary undertaking, any officer, employee or auditor of the undertaking, or any person holding or accountable for any of the undertaking's books, accounts or vouchers, such information and explanations as he may reasonably require for the purposes of his duties as auditor.*
Schedule 10, paragraph 10A, to the Companies Act 2006 includes provisions relating to arrangements to enable Recognised Supervisory Bodies and other bodies involved in monitoring audits to have access to the audit documentation of certain other auditors involved in the group audit. These provisions are addressed in audit regulations not in ISAs (UK and Ireland).

engagement team may not have access to those charged with governance, management, or the auditor (including relevant audit documentation sought by the group engagement team) of a component that is accounted for by the equity method of accounting. If the component is not a significant component, and the group engagement team has a complete set of financial statements of the component, including the auditor's report thereon, and has access to information kept by group management in relation to that component, the group engagement team may conclude that this information constitutes sufficient appropriate audit evidence in relation to that component. If the component is a significant component, however, the group engagement team will not be able to comply with the requirements of this ISA (UK and Ireland) relevant in the circumstances of the group audit. For example, the group engagement team will not be able to comply with the requirement in paragraphs 30-31 to be involved in the work of the component auditor. The group engagement team will not, therefore, be able to obtain sufficient appropriate audit evidence in relation to that component. The effect of the group engagement team's inability to obtain sufficient appropriate audit evidence is considered in terms of ISA (UK and Ireland) 705.

The group engagement team will not be able to obtain sufficient appropriate audit **A16** evidence if group management restricts the access of the group engagement team or a component auditor to the information of a significant component.

Although the group engagement team may be able to obtain sufficient appropriate **A17** audit evidence if such restriction relates to a component considered not a significant component, the reason for the restriction may affect the group audit opinion. For example, it may affect the reliability of group management's responses to the group engagement team's inquiries and group management's representations to the group engagement team.

Law or regulation may prohibit the group engagement partner from declining or **A18** withdrawing from an engagement. For example, in some jurisdictions the auditor is appointed for a specified period of time and is prohibited from withdrawing before the end of that period. Also, in the public sector, the option of declining or withdrawing from an engagement may not be available to the auditor due to the nature of the mandate or public interest considerations. In these circumstances, this ISA (UK and Ireland) still applies to the group audit, and the effect of the group engagement team's inability to obtain sufficient appropriate audit evidence is considered in terms of ISA (UK and Ireland) 705.

Appendix 1 contains an example of an auditor's report containing a qualified opi- **A19** nion based on the group engagement team's inability to obtain sufficient appropriate audit evidence in relation to a significant component accounted for by the equity method of accounting, but where, in the group engagement team's judgment, the effect is material but not pervasive[15b].

Terms of Engagement (Ref: Para. 14)

The terms of engagement identify the applicable financial reporting framework.[16] **A20** Additional matters may be included in the terms of a group audit engagement, such as the fact that:

[15b] *The example in the Appendix has not been tailored for the UK and Ireland. Illustrative auditor's reports tailored for use with audits conducted in accordance with ISAs (UK and Ireland) are given in the current versions of the APB Compendia Auditor's Report Bulletins.*

[16] *ISA (UK and Ireland) 210, paragraph 8.*

- The communication between the group engagement team and the component auditors should be unrestricted to the extent possible under law or regulation;
- Important communications between the component auditors, those charged with governance of the component, and component management, including communications on significant deficiencies in internal control, should be communicated as well to the group engagement team;
- Important communications between regulatory authorities and components related to financial reporting matters should be communicated to the group engagement team; and
- To the extent the group engagement team considers necessary, it should be permitted:
  - o   Access to component information, those charged with governance of components, component management, and the component auditors (including relevant audit documentation sought by the group engagement team); and
  - o   To perform work or request a component auditor to perform work on the financial information of the components.

A21   Restrictions imposed on:

- the group engagement team's access to component information, those charged with governance of components, component management, or the component auditors (including relevant audit documentation sought by the group engagement team); or
- the work to be performed on the financial information of the components

after the group engagement partner's acceptance of the group audit engagement, constitute an inability to obtain sufficient appropriate audit evidence that may affect the group audit opinion. In exceptional circumstances it may even lead to withdrawal from the engagement where withdrawal is possible under applicable law or regulation.

Overall Audit Strategy and Audit Plan (Ref: Para. 16)

A22   The group engagement partner's review of the overall group audit strategy and group audit plan is an important part of fulfilling the group engagement partner's responsibility for the direction of the group audit engagement.

Understanding the Group, Its Components and Their Environments

Matters about Which the Group Engagement Team Obtains an Understanding (Ref: Para. 17)

A23   ISA (UK and Ireland) 315 contains guidance on matters the auditor may consider when obtaining an understanding of the industry, regulatory, and other external factors that affect the entity, including the applicable financial reporting framework; the nature of the entity; objectives and strategies and related business risks; and measurement and review of the entity's financial performance.[17] Appendix 2 of this ISA (UK and Ireland) contains guidance on matters specific to a group, including the consolidation process.

---

[17] *ISA (UK and Ireland) 315, paragraphs A17-A41.*

Instructions Issued by Group Management to Components (Ref: Para. 17)

To achieve uniformity and comparability of financial information, group manage-   A24
ment ordinarily issues instructions to components. Such instructions specify the
requirements for financial information of the components to be included in the group
financial statements and often include financial reporting procedures manuals and a
reporting package. A reporting package ordinarily consists of standard formats for
providing financial information for incorporation in the group financial statements.
Reporting packages generally do not, however, take the form of complete financial
statements prepared and presented in accordance with the applicable financial
reporting framework.

The instructions ordinarily cover: A25

- The accounting policies to be applied;
- Statutory and other disclosure requirements applicable to the group financial
  statements, including:
  - The identification and reporting of segments;
  - Related party relationships and transactions;
  - Intra-group transactions and unrealized profits;
  - Intra-group account balances; and
- A reporting timetable.

The group engagement team's understanding of the instructions may include the   A26
following:

- The clarity and practicality of the instructions for completing the reporting
  package.
- Whether the instructions:
  - Adequately describe the characteristics of the applicable financial reporting
    framework;
  - Provide for disclosures that are sufficient to comply with the requirements
    of the applicable financial reporting framework, for example, disclosure of
    related party relationships and transactions, and segment information;
  - Provide for the identification of consolidation adjustments, for example,
    intra-group transactions and unrealized profits, and intra-group account
    balances; and
  - Provide for the approval of the financial information by component
    management.

Fraud (Ref: Para. 17)

The auditor is required to identify and assess the risks of material misstatement of   A27
the financial statements due to fraud, and to design and implement appropriate
responses to the assessed risks.[18] Information used to identify the risks of material
misstatement of the group financial statements due to fraud may include the
following:

- Group management's assessment of the risks that the group financial statements
  may be materially misstated as a result of fraud.
- Group management's process for identifying and responding to the risks of
  fraud in the group, including any specific fraud risks identified by group management, or account balances, classes of transactions, or disclosures for which a
  risk of fraud is likely.

---

[18] *ISA (UK and Ireland) 240*, The Auditor's Responsibilities Relating to Fraud in an Audit of Financial
Statements.

- Whether there are particular components for which a risk of fraud is likely.
- How those charged with governance of the group monitor group management's processes for identifying and responding to the risks of fraud in the group, and the controls group management has established to mitigate these risks.
- Responses of those charged with governance of the group, group management, appropriate individuals within the internal audit function (and if considered appropriate, component management, the component auditors, and others) to the group engagement team's inquiry whether they have knowledge of any actual, suspected, or alleged fraud affecting a component or the group.

Discussion among Group Engagement Team Members and Component Auditors Regarding the Risks of Material Misstatement of the Group Financial Statements, Including Risks of Fraud (Ref: Para. 17)

A28   The key members of the engagement team are required to discuss the susceptibility of an entity to material misstatement of the financial statements due to fraud or error, specifically emphasizing the risks due to fraud. In a group audit, these discussions may also include the component auditors.[19] The group engagement partner's determination of who to include in the discussions, how and when they occur, and their extent, is affected by factors such as prior experience with the group.

A29   The discussions provide an opportunity to:

- Share knowledge of the components and their environments, including group-wide controls.
- Exchange information about the business risks of the components or the group.
- Exchange ideas about how and where the group financial statements may be susceptible to material misstatement due to fraud or error, how group management and component management could perpetrate and conceal fraudulent financial reporting, and how assets of the components could be misappropriated.
- Identify practices followed by group or component management that may be biased or designed to manage earnings that could lead to fraudulent financial reporting, for example, revenue recognition practices that do not comply with the applicable financial reporting framework.
- Consider known external and internal factors affecting the group that may create an incentive or pressure for group management, component management, or others to commit fraud, provide the opportunity for fraud to be perpetrated, or indicate a culture or environment that enables group management, component management, or others to rationalize committing fraud.
- Consider the risk that group or component management may override controls.
- Consider whether uniform accounting policies are used to prepare the financial information of the components for the group financial statements and, where not, how differences in accounting policies are identified and adjusted (where required by the applicable financial reporting framework).
- Discuss fraud that has been identified in components, or information that indicates existence of a fraud in a component.
- Share information that may indicate non-compliance with national laws or regulations, for example, payments of bribes and improper transfer pricing practices.

---

[19] *ISA (UK and Ireland) 240, paragraph 15, and ISA 315, paragraph 10.*

Risk Factors (Ref: Para. 18)

Appendix 3 sets out examples of conditions or events that, individually or together, may indicate risks of material misstatement of the group financial statements, including risks due to fraud. **A30**

Risk Assessment (Ref: Para. 18)

The group engagement team's assessment at group level of the risks of material misstatement of the group financial statements is based on information such as the following: **A31**

- Information obtained from the understanding of the group, its components, and their environments, and of the consolidation process, including audit evidence obtained in evaluating the design and implementation of group-wide controls and controls that are relevant to the consolidation.
- Information obtained from the component auditors.

Understanding the Component Auditor (Ref: Para. 19)

The group engagement team obtains an understanding of a component auditor only when it plans to request the component auditor to perform work on the financial information of a component for the group audit. For example, it will not be necessary to obtain an understanding of the auditors of those components for which the group engagement team plans to perform analytical procedures at group level only. **A32**

Group Engagement Team's Procedures to Obtain an Understanding of the Component Auditor and Sources of Audit Evidence (Ref: Para. 19)

The nature, timing and extent of the group engagement team's procedures to obtain an understanding of the component auditor are affected by factors such as previous experience with or knowledge of the component auditor, and the degree to which the group engagement team and the component auditor are subject to common policies and procedures, for example: **A33**

- Whether the group engagement team and a component auditor share:
  - o Common policies and procedures for performing the work (for example, audit methodologies);
  - o Common quality control policies and procedures; or
  - o Common monitoring policies and procedures.
- The consistency or similarity of:
  - o Laws and regulations or legal system;
  - o Professional oversight, discipline, and external quality assurance;
  - o Education and training;
  - o Professional organizations and standards; or
  - o Language and culture.

These factors interact and are not mutually exclusive. For example, the extent of the group engagement team's procedures to obtain an understanding of Component Auditor A, who consistently applies common quality control and monitoring policies and procedures and a common audit methodology or operates in the same jurisdiction as the group engagement partner, may be less than the extent of the group engagement team's procedures to obtain an understanding of Component Auditor B, who is not consistently applying common quality control and monitoring policies **A34**

and procedures and a common audit methodology or operates in a foreign jurisdiction. The nature of the procedures performed in relation to Component
Auditors A and B may also be different.

A35   The group engagement team may obtain an understanding of the component auditor
in a number of ways. In the first year of involving a component auditor, the group
engagement team may, for example:

- Evaluate the results of the quality control monitoring system where the group
  engagement team and component auditor are from a firm or network that
  operates under and complies with common monitoring policies and
  procedures;[20]
- Visit the component auditor to discuss the matters in paragraph 19(a)-(c);
- Request the component auditor to confirm the matters referred to in paragraph
  19(a)-(c) in writing. Appendix 4 contains an example of written confirmations by
  a component auditor;
- Request the component auditor to complete questionnaires about the matters in
  paragraph 19(a)-(c);
- Discuss the component auditor with colleagues in the group engagement partner's firm, or with a reputable third party that has knowledge of the component
  auditor; or
- Obtain confirmations from the professional body or bodies to which the component auditor belongs, the authorities by which the component auditor is
  licensed, or other third parties.

In subsequent years, the understanding of the component auditor may be based on
the group engagement team's previous experience with the component auditor. The
group engagement team may request the component auditor to confirm whether
anything in relation to the matters listed in paragraph 19(a)-(c) has changed since the
previous year.

A36   Where independent oversight bodies have been established to oversee the auditing
profession and monitor the quality of audits, awareness of the regulatory environment may assist the group engagement team in evaluating the independence and
competence of the component auditor. Information about the regulatory environment may be obtained from the component auditor or information provided by the
independent oversight bodies.

Ethical Requirements that Are Relevant to the Group Audit (Ref: Para. 19(a))

A37   When performing work on the financial information of a component for a group
audit, the component auditor is subject to ethical requirements that are relevant to
the group audit. Such requirements may be different or in addition to those applying
to the component auditor when performing a statutory audit in the component
auditor's jurisdiction. The group engagement team therefore obtains an understanding whether the component auditor understands and will comply with the
ethical requirements that are relevant to the group audit, sufficient to fulfill the
component auditor's responsibilities in the group audit.

---

[20] *As required by ISQC (UK and Ireland) 1, "Quality Control for Firms that Perform Audits and Reviews of
Financial Statements, and Other Assurance and Related Services Engagements," paragraph 54, or national
requirements that are at least as demanding.*

The Component Auditor's Professional Competence (Ref: Para. 19(b))

The group engagement team's understanding of the component auditor's profes-   **A38**
sional competence may include whether the component auditor:

- Possesses an understanding of auditing and other standards applicable to the group audit that is sufficient to fulfill the component auditor's responsibilities in the group audit;

- Has sufficient resources (e.g. personnel with the necessary capabilities) to perform the work on the financial information of the particular component;

- Possesses the special skills (for example, industry specific knowledge) necessary to perform the work on the financial information of the particular component; and
- Where relevant, possesses an understanding of the applicable financial reporting framework that is sufficient to fulfill the component auditor's responsibilities in the group audit (instructions issued by group management to components often describe the characteristics of the applicable financial reporting framework).

Application of the Group Engagement Team's Understanding of a Component Auditor (Ref: Para. 20)

The group engagement team cannot overcome the fact that a component auditor is   **A39**
not independent by being involved in the work of the component auditor or by performing additional risk assessment or further audit procedures on the financial information of the component.

However, the group engagement team may be able to overcome less than serious   **A40**
concerns about the component auditor's professional competency (for example, lack of industry specific knowledge), or the fact that the component auditor does not operate in an environment that actively oversees auditors, by being involved in the work of the component auditor or by performing additional risk assessment or further audit procedures on the financial information of the component.

Where law or regulation prohibits access to relevant parts of the audit documenta-   **A41**
tion of the component auditor, the group engagement team may request the component auditor to overcome this by preparing a memorandum that covers the relevant information.

Materiality (Ref: Para. 21-23)

The auditor is required:[21]   **A42**

(a) When establishing the overall audit strategy, to determine:
   (i) Materiality for the financial statements as a whole; and
   (ii) If, in the specific circumstances of the entity, there are particular classes of transactions, account balances or disclosures for which misstatements of lesser amounts than materiality for the financial statements as a whole could reasonably be expected to influence the economic decisions of users taken on the basis of the financial statements, the materiality level or levels

---

[21] *ISA (UK and Ireland) 320, "Materiality in Planning and Performing an Audit," paragraphs 10-11.*

to be applied to those particular classes of transactions, account balances or disclosures; and
(b) To determine performance materiality.

In the context of a group audit, materiality is established for both the group financial statements as a whole, and for the financial information of the components. Materiality for the group financial statements as a whole is used when establishing the overall group audit strategy.

A43 To reduce to an appropriately low level the probability that the aggregate of uncorrected and undetected misstatements in the group financial statements exceeds materiality for the group financial statements as a whole, component materiality is set lower than materiality for the group financial statements as a whole. Different component materiality may be established for different components. Component materiality need not be an arithmetical portion of the materiality for the group financial statements as a whole and, consequently, the aggregate of component materiality for the different components may exceed the materiality for the group financial statements as a whole. Component materiality is used when establishing the overall audit strategy for a component.

A44 Component materiality is determined for those components whose financial information will be audited or reviewed as part of the group audit in accordance with paragraphs 26, 27(a) and 29. Component materiality is used by the component auditor to evaluate whether uncorrected detected misstatements are material, individually or in the aggregate.

A45 A threshold for misstatements is determined in addition to component materiality. Misstatements identified in the financial information of the component that are above the threshold for misstatements are communicated to the group engagement team.

A46 In the case of an audit of the financial information of a component, the component auditor (or group engagement team) determines performance materiality at the component level. This is necessary to reduce to an appropriately low level the probability that the aggregate of uncorrected and undetected misstatements in the financial information of the component exceeds component materiality. In practice, the group engagement team may set component materiality at this lower level. Where this is the case, the component auditor uses component materiality for purposes of assessing the risks of material misstatement of the financial information of the component and to design further audit procedures in response to assessed risks as well as for evaluating whether detected misstatements are material individually or in the aggregate.

Responding to Assessed Risks

Determining the Type of Work to Be Performed on the Financial Information of Components (Ref: Para. 26-27)

A47 The group engagement team's determination of the type of work to be performed on the financial information of a component and its involvement in the work of the component auditor is affected by:
(a) The significance of the component;
(b) The identified significant risks of material misstatement of the group financial statements;

(c) The group engagement team's evaluation of the design of group-wide controls and determination whether they have been implemented; and

(d) The group engagement team's understanding of the component auditor.

The diagram shows how the significance of the component affects the group engagement team's determination of the type of work to be performed on the financial information of the component.

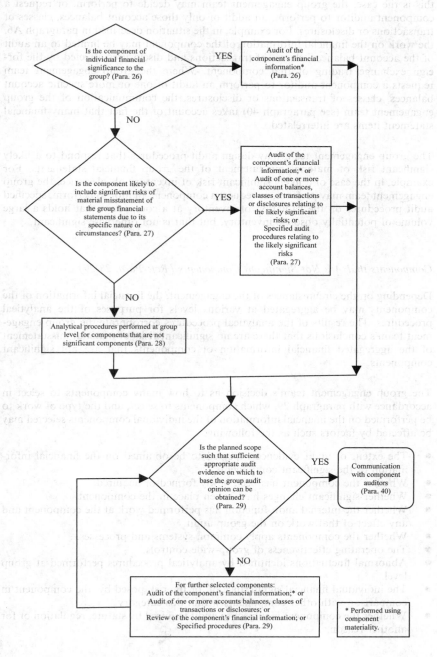

Is the component of individual financial significance to the group? (Para. 26)
— YES → Audit of the component's financial information* (Para. 26)

— NO ↓

Is the component likely to include significant risks of material misstatement of the group financial statements due to its specific nature or circumstances? (Para. 27)
— YES → Audit of the component's financial information;* or Audit of one or more account balances, classes of transactions or disclosures relating to the likely significant risks; or Specified audit procedures relating to the likely significant risks (Para. 27)

— NO ↓

Analytical procedures performed at group level for components that are not significant components (Para. 28)

Is the planned scope such that sufficient appropriate audit evidence on which to base the group audit opinion can be obtained? (Para. 29)
— YES → Communication with component auditors (Para. 40)

— NO ↓

For further selected components:
Audit of the component's financial information;* or
Audit of one or more accounts balances, classes of transactions or disclosures; or
Review of the component's financial information; or
Specified procedures (Para. 29)

* Performed using component materiality.

Significant Components (Ref: Para. 27(b)-(c))

A48   The group engagement team may identify a component as a significant component because that component is likely to include significant risks of material misstatement of the group financial statements due to its specific nature or circumstances. In that case, the group engagement team may be able to identify the account balances, classes of transactions or disclosures affected by the likely significant risks. Where this is the case, the group engagement team may decide to perform, or request a component auditor to perform, an audit of only those account balances, classes of transactions or disclosures. For example, in the situation described in paragraph A6, the work on the financial information of the component may be limited to an audit of the account balances, classes of transactions and disclosures affected by the foreign exchange trading of that component. Where the group engagement team requests a component auditor to perform an audit of one or more specific account balances, classes of transactions or disclosures, the communication of the group engagement team (see paragraph 40) takes account of the fact that many financial statement items are interrelated.

A49   The group engagement team may design audit procedures that respond to a likely significant risk of material misstatement of the group financial statements. For example, in the case of a likely significant risk of inventory obsolescence, the group engagement team may perform, or request a component auditor to perform, specified audit procedures on the valuation of inventory at a component that holds a large volume of potentially obsolete inventory, but that is not otherwise significant.

Components that Are Not Significant Components (Ref: Para. 28-29)

A50   Depending on the circumstances of the engagement, the financial information of the components may be aggregated at various levels for purposes of the analytical procedures. The results of the analytical procedures corroborate the group engagement team's conclusions that there are no significant risks of material misstatement of the aggregated financial information of components that are not significant components.

A51   The group engagement team's decision as to how many components to select in accordance with paragraph 29, which components to select, and the type of work to be performed on the financial information of the individual components selected may be affected by factors such as the following:

- The extent of audit evidence expected to be obtained on the financial information of the significant components.
- Whether the component has been newly formed or acquired.
- Whether significant changes have taken place in the component.
- Whether the internal audit function has performed work at the component and any effect of that work on the group audit.
- Whether the components apply common systems and processes.
- The operating effectiveness of group-wide controls.
- Abnormal fluctuations identified by analytical procedures performed at group level.
- The individual financial significance of, or the risk posed by, the component in comparison with other components within this category.
- Whether the component is subject to audit required by statute, regulation or for another reason.

Including an element of unpredictability in selecting components in this category may increase the likelihood of identifying material misstatement of the components' financial information. The selection of components is often varied on a cyclical basis.

A review of the financial information of a component may be performed in accordance with International Standard on Review Engagements (ISRE) 2400[22] or ISRE (UK and Ireland) 2410,[23] adapted as necessary in the circumstances. The group engagement team may also specify additional procedures to supplement this work.　**A52**

As explained in paragraph A13, a group may consist only of components that are not significant components. In these circumstances, the group engagement team can obtain sufficient appropriate audit evidence on which to base the group audit opinion by determining the type of work to be performed on the financial information of the components in accordance with paragraph 29. It is unlikely that the group engagement team will obtain sufficient appropriate audit evidence on which to base the group audit opinion if the group engagement team, or a component auditor, only tests group-wide controls and performs analytical procedures on the financial information of the components.　**A53**

Involvement in the Work Performed by Component Auditors (Ref: Para. 30-31)

Factors that may affect the group engagement team's involvement in the work of the component auditor include:　**A54**

(a) The significance of the component;
(b) The identified significant risks of material misstatement of the group financial statements; and
(c) The group engagement team's understanding of the component auditor.

In the case of a significant component or identified significant risks, the group engagement team performs the procedures described in paragraphs 30-31. In the case of a component that is not a significant component, the nature, timing and extent of the group engagement team's involvement in the work of the component auditor will vary based on the group engagement team's understanding of that component auditor. The fact that the component is not a significant component becomes secondary. For example, even though a component is not considered a significant component, the group engagement team nevertheless may decide to be involved in the component auditor's risk assessment, because it has less than serious concerns about the component auditor's professional competency (for example, lack of industry specific knowledge), or the component auditor does not operate in an environment that actively oversees auditors.

Forms of involvement in the work of a component auditor other than those described in paragraphs 30-31 and 42 may, based on the group engagement team's understanding of the component auditor, include one or more of the following:　**A55**

(a) Meeting with component management or the component auditors to obtain an understanding of the component and its environment.
(b) Reviewing the component auditors' overall audit strategy and audit plan.

---

[22] *ISRE 2400, "Engagements to Review Financial Statements."*
ISRE 2400 has not been promulgated by APB for application in the UK and Ireland.

[23] *ISRE (UK and Ireland) 2410, "Review of Interim Financial Information Performed by the Independent Auditor of the Entity."*

(c) Performing risk assessment procedures to identify and assess the risks of material misstatement at the component level. These may be performed with the component auditors, or by the group engagement team.

(d) Designing and performing further audit procedures. These may be designed and performed with the component auditors, or by the group engagement team.

(e) Participating in the closing and other key meetings between the component auditors and component management.

(f) Reviewing other relevant parts of the component auditors' audit documentation.

Consolidation Process

Consolidation Adjustments and Reclassifications (Ref: Para. 34)

A56 The consolidation process may require adjustments to amounts reported in the group financial statements that do not pass through the usual transaction processing systems, and may not be subject to the same internal controls to which other financial information is subject. The group engagement team's evaluation of the appropriateness, completeness and accuracy of the adjustments may include:

- Evaluating whether significant adjustments appropriately reflect the events and transactions underlying them;
- Determining whether significant adjustments have been correctly calculated, processed and authorized by group management and, where applicable, by component management;
- Determining whether significant adjustments are properly supported and sufficiently documented; and
- Checking the reconciliation and elimination of intra-group transactions and unrealized profits, and intra-group account balances.

Communication with the Component Auditor (Ref: Para. 40-41)

A57 If effective two-way communication between the group engagement team and the component auditors does not exist, there is a risk that the group engagement team may not obtain sufficient appropriate audit evidence on which to base the group audit opinion. Clear and timely communication of the group engagement team's requirements forms the basis of effective two-way communication between the group engagement team and the component auditor.

A58 The group engagement team's requirements are often communicated in a letter of instruction. Appendix 5 contains guidance on required and additional matters that may be included in such a letter of instruction. The component auditor's communication with the group engagement team often takes the form of a memorandum or report of work performed. Communication between the group engagement team and the component auditor, however, may not necessarily be in writing. For example, the group engagement team may visit the component auditor to discuss identified significant risks or review relevant parts of the component auditor's audit documentation. Nevertheless, the documentation requirements of this and other ISAs (UK and Ireland) apply.

A59 In cooperating with the group engagement team, the component auditor, for example, would provide the group engagement team with access to relevant audit documentation if not prohibited by law or regulation.

Where a member of the group engagement team is also a component auditor, the   **A60**
objective for the group engagement team to communicate clearly with the component auditor can often be achieved by means other than specific written
communication. For example:

- Access by the component auditor to the overall audit strategy and audit plan
  may be sufficient to communicate the group engagement team's requirements set
  out in paragraph 40; and
- A review of the component auditor's audit documentation by the group
  engagement team may be sufficient to communicate matters relevant to the
  group engagement team's conclusion set out in paragraph 41.

Evaluating the Sufficiency and Appropriateness of Audit Evidence Obtained

Reviewing the Component Auditor's Audit Documentation (Ref: Para. 42(b))

What parts of the audit documentation of the component auditor will be relevant to   **A61**
the group audit may vary depending on the circumstances. Often the focus is on
audit documentation that is relevant to the significant risks of material misstatement
of the group financial statements. The extent of the review may be affected by the
fact that the component auditor's audit documentation has been subjected to the
component auditor's firm's review procedures.

Sufficiency and Appropriateness of Audit Evidence (Ref: Para. 44-45)

If the group engagement team concludes that sufficient appropriate audit evidence   **A62**
on which to base the group audit opinion has not been obtained, the group
engagement team may request the component auditor to perform additional procedures. If this is not feasible, the group engagement team may perform its own
procedures on the financial information of the component.

The group engagement partner's evaluation of the aggregate effect of any mis-   **A63**
statements (either identified by the group engagement team or communicated by
component auditors) allows the group engagement partner to determine whether the
group financial statements as a whole are materially misstated.

Communication with Group Management and Those Charged with Governance of the Group

Communication with Group Management (Ref: Para. 46-48)

ISA (UK and Ireland) 240 contains requirements and guidance on communication of   **A64**
fraud to management and, where management may be involved in the fraud, to those
charged with governance.[24]

Group management may need to keep certain material sensitive information con-   **A65**
fidential. Examples of matters that may be significant to the financial statements of
the component of which component management may be unaware include the
following:

- Potential litigation.
- Plans for abandonment of material operating assets.

---

[24] *ISA (UK and Ireland) 240, paragraphs 40-42.*

- Subsequent events.
- Significant legal agreements.

A65-1 Information that group management has determined needs to be kept confidential would ordinarily be known to those charged with governance of the group[24a].

Communication with Those Charged with Governance of the Group (Ref: Para. 49)

A66 The matters the group engagement team communicates to those charged with governance of the group may include those brought to the attention of the group engagement team by component auditors that the group engagement team judges to be significant to the responsibilities of those charged with governance of the group. Communication with those charged with governance of the group takes place at various times during the group audit. For example, the matters referred to in paragraph 49(a)-(b) may be communicated after the group engagement team has determined the work to be performed on the financial information of the components. On the other hand, the matter referred to in paragraph 49(c) may be communicated at the end of the audit, and the matters referred to in paragraph 49(d)-(e) may be communicated when they occur.

Documentation (Ref: Para. 50(b))

A66-1 In the UK legislation[24b] has been enacted to implement Article 27(b) of the Statutory Audit Directive which requires that group auditors:

(a) review for the purposes of a group audit the audit work conducted by other persons, and
(b) record that review.

Accordingly, the documentation of the group engagement team's involvement in the work performed by the component auditors includes any review that the group engagement team undertook, for the purpose of the group audit, of the audit work conducted by component auditors.

Appendix 1   (Ref: Para. A19)

The example in this Appendix has not been tailored for the UK and Ireland. Illustrative auditor's reports tailored for use with audits conducted in accordance with ISAs (UK and Ireland) are given in the current versions of the APB Compendia Auditor's Report Bulletins.

[24a] *ISA (UK and Ireland) 260, paragraph 16(c), requires that, unless all of those charged with governance are involved in managing the entity, the auditor shall communicate with those charged with governance significant matters, if any, arising from the audit that were discussed, or subject to correspondence with management.*

[24b] *UK Companies Act 2006, Schedule 10, paragraph 10A(1).*

Example of a Qualified Opinion Where the Group Engagement Team Is Not Able to Obtain Sufficient Appropriate Audit Evidence on Which to Base the Group Audit Opinion

In this example, the group engagement team is unable to obtain sufficient appropriate audit evidence relating to a significant component accounted for by the equity method (recognized at $15 million in the balance sheet, which reflects total assets of $60 million) because the group engagement team did not have access to the accounting records, management, or auditor of the component.

The group engagement team has read the audited financial statements of the component as of December 31, 20X1, including the auditor's report thereon, and considered related financial information kept by group management in relation to the component.

In the group engagement partner's judgment, the effect on the group financial statements of this inability to obtain sufficient appropriate audit evidence is material but not pervasive.

INDEPENDENT AUDITOR'S REPORT

[Appropriate Addressee]

Report on the Consolidated Financial Statements[25]

We have audited the accompanying consolidated financial statements of ABC Company and its subsidiaries, which comprise the consolidated balance sheet as at December 31, 20X1, and the consolidated income statement, statement of changes in equity and cash flow statement for the year then ended, and a summary of significant accounting policies and other explanatory information.

Management's[26] Responsibility for the Consolidated Financial Statements

Management is responsible for the preparation and fair presentation of these consolidated financial statements in accordance with International Financial Reporting Standards,[27] and for such internal control as management determines is necessary to enable the preparation of consolidated financial statements that are free from material misstatement, whether due to fraud or error.

Auditor's Responsibility

Our responsibility is to express an opinion on these consolidated financial statements based on our audit. We conducted our audit in accordance with International Standards on Auditing. Those standards require that we comply with ethical requirements and plan and perform the audit to obtain reasonable assurance about whether the consolidated financial statements are free from material misstatement.

An audit involves performing procedures to obtain audit evidence about the amounts and disclosures in the consolidated financial statements. The procedures selected depend on the auditor's judgment, including the assessment of the risks of material misstatement of the consolidated financial statements, whether

---

[25] *The sub-title, "Report on the Consolidated Financial Statements" is unnecessary in circumstances when the second sub-title, "Report on Other Legal and Regulatory Requirements" is not applicable.*

[26] *Or other term that is appropriate in the context of the legal framework in the particular jurisdiction.*

[27] *Where management's responsibility is to prepare consolidated financial statements that give a true and fair view, this may read: "Management is responsible for the preparation of consolidated financial statements that give a true and fair view in accordance with International Financial Reporting Standards, and for such ..."*

due to fraud or error. In making those risk assessments, the auditor considers internal control relevant to the entity's preparation and fair presentation[28] of the consolidated financial statements in order to design audit procedures that are appropriate in the circumstances, but not for the purpose of expressing an opinion on the effectiveness of the entity's internal control.[29] An audit also includes evaluating the appropriateness of accounting policies used and the reasonableness of accounting estimates made by management, as well as evaluating the overall presentation of the consolidated financial statements.

We believe that the audit evidence we have obtained is sufficient and appropriate to provide a basis for our qualified audit opinion.

Basis for Qualified Opinion

ABC Company's investment in XYZ Company, a foreign associate acquired during the year and accounted for by the equity method, is carried at $15 million on the consolidated balance sheet as at December 31, 20X1, and ABC's share of XYZ's net income of $1 million is included in the consolidated income statement for the year then ended. We were unable to obtain sufficient appropriate audit evidence about the carrying amount of ABC's investment in XYZ as at December 31, 20X1 and ABC's share of XYZ's net income for the year because we were denied access to the financial information, management, and the auditors of XYZ. Consequently, we were unable to determine whether any adjustments to these amounts were necessary.

Qualified Opinion

In our opinion, except for the possible effects of the matter described in the Basis for Qualified Opinion paragraph, the consolidated financial statements present fairly, in all material respects, *(or give a true and fair view of)* the financial position of ABC Company and its subsidiaries as at December 31, 20X1, and *(of)* their financial performance and cash flows for the year then ended in accordance with International Financial Reporting Standards.

Report on Other Legal and Regulatory Requirements

[Form and content of this section of the auditor's report will vary depending on the nature of the auditor's other reporting responsibilities.]

[Auditor's signature]

[Date of the auditor's report]

[Auditor's address]

If, in the group engagement partner's judgment, the effect on the group financial statements of the inability to obtain sufficient appropriate audit evidence is material

---

[28] *In the case of footnote 27, this may read: "In making those risk assessments, the auditor considers internal control relevant to the entity's preparation of consolidated financial statements that give a true and fair view in order to design audit procedures that are appropriate in the circumstances, but not for the purpose of expressing an opinion on the effectiveness of the entity's internal control."*

[29] *In circumstances when the auditor also has responsibility to express an opinion on the effectiveness of internal control in conjunction with the audit of the consolidated financial statements, this sentence would be worded as follows: "In making those risk assessments, the auditor considers internal control relevant to the entity's preparation and fair presentation of the consolidated financial statements in order to design audit procedures that are appropriate in the circumstances." In the case of footnote 27, this may read: "In making those risk assessments, the auditor considers internal control relevant to the entity's preparation of consolidated financial statements that give a true and fair view in order to design audit procedures that are appropriate in the circumstances."*

and pervasive, the group engagement partner would disclaim an opinion in accordance with ISA (UK and Ireland) 705.

Appendix 2 (Ref: Para. A23)

Examples of Matters about Which the Group Engagement Team Obtains an Understanding

The examples provided cover a broad range of matters; however, not all matters are relevant to every group audit engagement and the list of examples is not necessarily complete.

Group-Wide Controls

Group-wide controls may include a combination of the following: **1**

- Regular meetings between group and component management to discuss business developments and to review performance.
- Monitoring of components' operations and their financial results, including regular reporting routines, which enables group management to monitor components' performance against budgets, and to take appropriate action.
- Group management's risk assessment process, that is, the process for identifying, analyzing and managing business risks, including the risk of fraud, that may result in material misstatement of the group financial statements.
- Monitoring, controlling, reconciling, and eliminating intra-group transactions and unrealized profits, and intra-group account balances at group level.
- A process for monitoring the timeliness and assessing the accuracy and completeness of financial information received from components.
- A central IT system controlled by the same general IT controls for all or part of the group.
- Control activities within an IT system that is common for all or some components.
- Monitoring of controls, including activities of the internal audit function and self-assessment programs.
- Consistent policies and procedures, including a group financial reporting procedures manual.
- Group-wide programs, such as codes of conduct and fraud prevention programs.
- Arrangements for assigning authority and responsibility to component management.

The internal audit function may be regarded as part of group-wide controls, for   **2**
example, when the function is centralized. ISA (UK and Ireland) 610 (Revised June 2013)[30] deals with the group engagement team's evaluation of whether the internal audit function's organizational status and relevant policies and procedures adequately supports the objectivity of internal auditors, the level of competence of the internal audit function, and whether the function applies a systematic and disciplined approach where the group engagement team expects to use the function's work.

Consolidation Process

The group engagement team's understanding of the consolidation process may   **3**
include matters such as the following:

[30] *ISA (UK and Ireland) 610 (Revised June 2013), Using the Work of Internal Auditors, paragraphs 15–16.*

Matters relating to the applicable financial reporting framework:

- The extent to which component management has an understanding of the applicable financial reporting framework.
- The process for identifying and accounting for components in accordance with the applicable financial reporting framework.
- The process for identifying reportable segments for segment reporting in accordance with the applicable financial reporting framework.
- The process for identifying related party relationships and related party transactions for reporting in accordance with the applicable financial reporting framework.
- The accounting policies applied to the group financial statements, changes from those of the previous financial year, and changes resulting from new or revised standards under the applicable financial reporting framework.
- The procedures for dealing with components with financial year-ends different from the group's year-end.

Matters relating to the consolidation process:

- Group management's process for obtaining an understanding of the accounting policies used by components, and, where applicable, ensuring that uniform accounting policies are used to prepare the financial information of the components for the group financial statements, and that differences in accounting policies are identified, and adjusted where required in terms of the applicable financial reporting framework. Uniform accounting policies are the specific principles, bases, conventions, rules, and practices adopted by the group, based on the applicable financial reporting framework, that the components use to report similar transactions consistently. These policies are ordinarily described in the financial reporting procedures manual and reporting package issued by group management.
- Group management's process for ensuring complete, accurate and timely financial reporting by the components for the consolidation.
- The process for translating the financial information of foreign components into the currency of the group financial statements.
- How IT is organized for the consolidation, including the manual and automated stages of the process, and the manual and programmed controls in place at various stages of the consolidation process.
- Group management's process for obtaining information on subsequent events.

Matters relating to consolidation adjustments:

- The process for recording consolidation adjustments, including the preparation, authorization and processing of related journal entries, and the experience of personnel responsible for the consolidation.
- The consolidation adjustments required by the applicable financial reporting framework.
- Business rationale for the events and transactions that gave rise to the consolidation adjustments.
- Frequency, nature and size of transactions between components.
- Procedures for monitoring, controlling, reconciling and eliminating intra-group transactions and unrealized profits, and intra-group account balances.
- Steps taken to arrive at the fair value of acquired assets and liabilities, procedures for amortizing goodwill (where applicable), and impairment testing of goodwill, in accordance with the applicable financial reporting framework.
- Arrangements with a majority owner or minority interests regarding losses incurred by a component (for example, an obligation of the minority interest to make good such losses).

Appendix 3

(Ref: Para. A30)

Examples of Conditions or Events that May Indicate Risks of Material Misstatement of the Group Financial Statements

The examples provided cover a broad range of conditions or events; however, not all conditions or events are relevant to every group audit engagement and the list of examples is not necessarily complete.

- A complex group structure, especially where there are frequent acquisitions, disposals or reorganizations.
- Poor corporate governance structures, including decision-making processes, that are not transparent.
- Non-existent or ineffective group-wide controls, including inadequate group management information on monitoring of components' operations and their results.
- Components operating in foreign jurisdictions that may be exposed to factors such as unusual government intervention in areas such as trade and fiscal policy, and restrictions on currency and dividend movements; and fluctuations in exchange rates.
- Business activities of components that involve high risk, such as long-term contracts or trading in innovative or complex financial instruments.
- Uncertainties regarding which components' financial information require incorporation in the group financial statements in accordance with the applicable financial reporting framework, for example, whether any special-purpose entities or non-trading entities exist and require incorporation.
- Unusual related party relationships and transactions.
- Prior occurrences of intra-group account balances that did not balance or reconcile on consolidation.
- The existence of complex transactions that are accounted for in more than one component.
- Components' application of accounting policies that differ from those applied to the group financial statements.
- Components with different financial year-ends, which may be utilized to manipulate the timing of transactions.
- Prior occurrences of unauthorized or incomplete consolidation adjustments.
- Aggressive tax planning within the group, or large cash transactions with entities in tax havens.
- Frequent changes of auditors engaged to audit the financial statements of components.

Appendix 4

(Ref: Para. A35)

Examples of a Component Auditor's Confirmations

The following is not intended to be a standard letter. Confirmations may vary from one component auditor to another and from one period to the next.

Confirmations often are obtained before work on the financial information of the component commences.

[Component Auditor Letterhead]

[Date]

[To Group Engagement Partner]

This letter is provided in connection with your audit of the group financial statements of [name of parent] for the year ended [date] for the purpose of expressing an opinion on whether the group financial statements present fairly, in all material respects (give a true and fair view of) the financial position of the group as of [date] and of its financial performance and cash flows for the year then ended in accordance with [indicate applicable financial reporting framework].

We acknowledge receipt of your instructions dated [date], requesting us to perform the specified work on the financial information of [name of component] for the year ended [date].

We confirm that:

1.   We will be able to comply with the instructions. / We advise you that we will not be able to comply with the following instructions [specify instructions] for the following reasons [specify reasons].
2.   The instructions are clear and we understand them. / We would appreciate it if you could clarify the following instructions [specify instructions].
3.   We will cooperate with you and provide you with access to relevant audit documentation.

We acknowledge that:

1.   The financial information of [name of component] will be included in the group financial statements of [name of parent].
2.   You may consider it necessary to be involved in the work you have requested us to perform on the financial information of [name of component] for the year ended [date].
3.   You intend to evaluate and, if considered appropriate, use our work for the audit of the group financial statements of [name of parent].

In connection with the work that we will perform on the financial information of [name of component], a [describe component, for example, wholly-owned subsidiary, subsidiary, joint venture, investee accounted for by the equity or cost methods of accounting] of [name of parent], we confirm the following:

1.   We have an understanding of [indicate relevant ethical requirements] that is sufficient to fulfill our responsibilities in the audit of the group financial statements, and will comply therewith. In particular, and with respect to [name of parent] and the other components in the group, we are independent within the meaning of [indicate relevant ethical requirements] and comply with the applicable requirements of [refer to rules] promulgated by [name of regulatory agency].
2.   We have an understanding of International Standards on Auditing and [indicate other national standards applicable to the audit of the group financial statements] that is sufficient to fulfill our responsibilities in the audit of the group financial statements and will conduct our work on the financial information of [name of component] for the year ended [date] in accordance with those standards.

3. We possess the special skills (for example, industry specific knowledge) necessary to perform the work on the financial information of the particular component.
4. We have an understanding of [indicate applicable financial reporting framework or group financial reporting procedures manual] that is sufficient to fulfill our responsibilities in the audit of the group financial statements.

We will inform you of any changes in the above representations during the course of our work on the financial information of [name of component].

[Auditor's signature]

[Date]

[Auditor's address]

Appendix 5 (Ref: Para. A58)

Required and Additional Matters Included in the Group Engagement Team's Letter of Instruction

Matters required by this ISA (UK and Ireland) to be communicated to the component auditor are shown in italicized text.

Matters that are relevant to the planning of the work of the component auditor:

* *A request for the component auditor, knowing the context in which the group engagement team will use the work of the component auditor, to confirm that the component auditor will cooperate with the group engagement team.*
* The timetable for completing the audit.
* Dates of planned visits by group management and the group engagement team, and dates of planned meetings with component management and the component auditor.
* A list of key contacts.
* *The work to be performed by the component auditor, the use to be made of that work*, and arrangements for coordinating efforts at the initial stage of and during the audit, including the group engagement team's planned involvement in the work of the component auditor.
* *The ethical requirements that are relevant to the group audit and, in particular, the independence requirements, for example, where the group auditor is prohibited by law or regulation from using internal auditors to provide direct assistance, it is relevant for the group auditor to consider whether the prohibition also extends to component auditors and, if so, to address this in the communication to the component auditors.*[31]
* *In the case of an audit or review of the financial information of the component, component materiality (and, if applicable, the materiality level or levels for particular classes of transactions, account balances or disclosures), and the threshold above which misstatements cannot be regarded as clearly trivial to the group financial statements.*

---

[31] *ISA 610 (Revised June 2013), "Using the Work of Internal Auditors", paragraph A31.*
The use of internal auditors to provide direct assistance is prohibited in an audit conducted in accordance with ISAs (UK and Ireland). For a group audit this prohibition extends to the work of any component auditor which is relied upon by the group auditor, including for overseas components – see ISA (UK and Ireland) 610 (Revised June 2013), paragraph 5-1.

- *A list of related parties prepared by group management, and any other related parties that the group engagement team is aware of, and a request that the component auditor communicates on a timely basis to the group engagement team related parties not previously identified by group management or the group engagement team.*
- Work to be performed on intra-group transactions and unrealized profits and intra-group account balances.
- Guidance on other statutory reporting responsibilities, for example, reporting on group management's assertion on the effectiveness of internal control.
- Where time lag between completion of the work on the financial information of the components and the group engagement team's conclusion on the group financial statements is likely, specific instructions for a subsequent events review.

Matters that are relevant to the conduct of the work of the component auditor

- The findings of the group engagement team's tests of control activities of a processing system that is common for all or some components, and tests of controls to be performed by the component auditor.
- *Identified significant risks of material misstatement of the group financial statements, due to fraud or error, that are relevant to the work of the component auditor, and a request that the component auditor communicates on a timely basis any other significant risks of material misstatement of the group financial statements, due to fraud or error, identified in the component and the component auditor's response to such risks.*
- The findings of the internal audit function, based on work performed on controls at or relevant to components.
- A request for timely communication of audit evidence obtained from performing work on the financial information of the components that contradicts the audit evidence on which the group engagement team originally based the risk assessment performed at group level.
- A request for a written representation on component management's compliance with the applicable financial reporting framework, or a statement that differences between the accounting policies applied to the financial information of the component and those applied to the group financial statements have been disclosed.
- Matters to be documented by the component auditor.

Other information

- A request that the following be reported to the group engagement team on a timely basis:
  - ○ Significant accounting, financial reporting and auditing matters, including accounting estimates and related judgments.
  - ○ Matters relating to the going concern status of the component.
  - ○ Matters relating to litigation and claims.
  - ○ Significant deficiencies in internal control that the component auditor has identified during the performance of the work on the financial information of the component, and information that indicates the existence of fraud.
- A request that the group engagement team be notified of any significant or unusual events as early as possible.
- *A request that the matters listed in paragraph 41 be communicated to the group engagement team when the work on the financial information of the component is completed.*

International Standard on Auditing (UK and Ireland) 610 (Revised June 2013)
Using the work of internal auditors

(Effective for audits of financial statements for periods ending on or after 15 June 2014)

Contents

Paragraph

International Standard on Auditing (ISA) (UK and Ireland) 610 (Revised June 2013), *Using the Work of Internal Auditors,* should be read in conjunction with ISA (UK and Ireland) 200, *Overall Objectives of the Independent Auditor and the Conduct of an Audit in Accordance with International Standards on Auditing.*

Introduction

Scope of this ISA (UK and Ireland)

1   This International Standard on Auditing (ISA) (UK and Ireland) deals with the external auditor's responsibilities if using the work of internal auditors. This includes (a) using the work of the internal audit function in obtaining audit evidence and (b) using internal auditors to provide direct assistance under the direction, supervision and review of the external auditor.

2   This ISA (UK and Ireland) does not apply if the entity does not have an internal audit function. (Ref: Para. A2)

3   If the entity has an internal audit function, the requirements in this ISA (UK and Ireland) relating to using the work of that function do not apply if:

(a)   The responsibilities and activities of the function are not relevant to the audit; or

(b)   Based on the auditor's preliminary understanding of the function obtained as a result of procedures performed under ISA (UK and Ireland) 315 (Revised June 2013),[1] the external auditor does not expect to use the work of the function in obtaining audit evidence.

Nothing in this ISA (UK and Ireland) requires the external auditor to use the work of the internal audit function to modify the nature or timing, or reduce the extent, of audit procedures to be performed directly by the external auditor; it remains a decision of the external auditor in establishing the overall audit strategy.

4   Furthermore, the requirements in this ISA (UK and Ireland) relating to direct assistance do not apply if the external auditor does not plan to use internal auditors to provide direct assistance.

5   In some jurisdictions, the external auditor may be prohibited, or restricted to some extent, by law or regulation from using the work of the internal audit function or using internal auditors to provide direct assistance. The ISAs (UK and Ireland) do not override laws or regulations that govern an audit of financial statements.[2] Such prohibitions or restrictions will therefore not prevent the external auditor from complying with the ISAs (UK and Ireland). (Ref: Para. A31)

5-1   The use of internal auditors to provide direct assistance is prohibited in an audit conducted in accordance with ISAs (UK and Ireland). For a group audit this prohibition extends to the work of any component auditor which is relied upon by the group auditor, including for overseas components. Accordingly, the requirements and related application material in this ISA (UK and Ireland) relating to direct assistance are not applicable.[2a]

---

[1] *ISA (UK and Ireland) 315 (Revised June 2013), Identifying and Assessing the Risks of Material Misstatement through Understanding the Entity and Its Environment.*

[2] *ISA (UK and Ireland) 200, Overall Objectives of the Independent Auditor and the Conduct of an Audit in Accordance with International Standards on Auditing, paragraph A55.*

[2a] *The non-applicable requirements are those set out in paragraphs 27-35 and 37. The non-applicable application material is that set out in paragraphs A32-A41.*

Relationship between ISA (UK and Ireland) 315 (Revised June 2013) and ISA (UK and Ireland) 610 (Revised June 2013)

Many entities establish internal audit functions as part of their internal control and governance structures. The objectives and scope of an internal audit function, the nature of its responsibilities and its organizational status, including the function's authority and accountability, vary widely and depend on the size and structure of the entity and the requirements of management and, where applicable, those charged with governance.   **6**

ISA (UK and Ireland) 315 (Revised June 2013) addresses how the knowledge and experience of the internal audit function can inform the external auditor's understanding of the entity and its environment and identification and assessment of risks of material misstatement. ISA (UK and Ireland) 315 (Revised 2013)[3] also explains how effective communication between the internal and external auditors also creates an environment in which the external auditor can be informed of significant matters that may affect the external auditor's work.   **7**

Depending on whether the internal audit function's organizational status and relevant policies and procedures adequately support the objectivity of the internal auditors, the level of competency of the internal audit function, and whether the function applies a systematic and disciplined approach, the external auditor may also be able to use the work of the internal audit function in a constructive and complementary manner. This ISA (UK and Ireland) addresses the external auditor's responsibilities when, based on the external auditor's preliminary understanding of the internal audit function obtained as a result of procedures performed under ISA (UK and Ireland) 315 (Revised 2013), the external auditor expects to use the work of the internal audit function as part of the audit evidence obtained.[4] Such use of that work modifies the nature or timing, or reduces the extent, of audit procedures to be performed directly by the external auditor.   **8**

In addition, this ISA (UK and Ireland) also addresses the external auditor's responsibilities if considering using internal auditors to provide direct assistance under the direction, supervision and review of the external auditor.   **9**

There may be individuals in an entity that perform procedures similar to those performed by an internal audit function. However, unless performed by an objective and competent function that applies a systematic and disciplined approach, including quality control, such procedures would be considered internal controls and obtaining evidence regarding the effectiveness of such controls would be part of the auditor's responses to assessed risks in accordance with ISA (UK and Ireland) 330.[5]   **10**

The External Auditor's Responsibility for the Audit

The external auditor has sole responsibility for the audit opinion expressed, and that responsibility is not reduced by the external auditor's use of the work of the internal audit function or internal auditors to provide direct assistance on the engagement. Although they may perform audit procedures similar to those performed by the external auditor, neither the internal audit function nor the internal auditors are independent of the entity as is required of the external auditor in an audit of financial   **11**

---

[3] *ISA UK and Ireland) 315 (Revised June 2013), paragraph A116.*

[4] *See paragraphs 15–25.*

[5] *ISA (UK and Ireland) 330, The Auditor's Responses to Assessed Risks.*

statements in accordance with ISA (UK and Ireland) 200.[6] This ISA (UK and Ireland), therefore, defines the conditions that are necessary for the external auditor to be able to use the work of internal auditors. It also defines the necessary work effort to obtain sufficient appropriate evidence that the work of the internal audit function, or internal auditors providing direct assistance, is adequate for the purposes of the audit. The requirements are designed to provide a framework for the external auditor's judgments regarding the use of the work of internal auditors to prevent over or undue use of such work.

Effective Date

12 This ISA (UK and Ireland) is effective for audits of financial statements for periods ending on or after 15 June 2014[6a].

Objectives

13 The objectives of the external auditor, where the entity has an internal audit function and the external auditor expects to use the work of the function to modify the nature or timing, or reduce the extent, of audit procedures to be performed directly by the external auditor, or to use internal auditors to provide direct assistance, are:

(a) To determine whether the work of the internal audit function or direct assistance from internal auditors can be used, and if so, in which areas and to what extent;

and having made that determination:

(b) If using the work of the internal audit function, to determine whether that work is adequate for purposes of the audit; and

(c) If using internal auditors to provide direct assistance, to appropriately direct, supervise and review their work.

Definitions

14 For purposes of the ISAs (UK and Ireland), the following terms have the meanings attributed below:

(a) Internal audit function – A function of an entity that performs assurance and consulting activities designed to evaluate and improve the effectiveness of the entity's governance, risk management and internal control processes. (Ref: Para. A1–A4)

(b) Direct assistance – The use of internal auditors to perform audit procedures under the direction, supervision and review of the external auditor.

---

[6] *ISA (UK and Ireland) 200, paragraph 14.*

[6a] *For the purpose of audits under ISAs as issued by the IAASB, the material pertaining to the use of direct assistance has an effective date of audits of financial statements for periods ending on or after 15 December 2014. However, as stated in paragraph 5-1, the use of internal auditors to provide direct assistance is prohibited in an audit conducted in accordance with ISAs (UK and Ireland) – such prohibition being effective from the effective date of this ISA (UK and Ireland), audits of financial statements for periods ending on or after 15 June 2014.*

Requirements

Determining Whether, in Which Areas, and to What Extent the Work of the Internal Audit Function Can Be Used

Evaluating the Internal Audit Function

The external auditor shall determine whether the work of the internal audit function **15** can be used for purposes of the audit by evaluating the following:

(a) The extent to which the internal audit function's organizational status and relevant policies and procedures support the objectivity of the internal auditors; (Ref: Para. A5–A9)
(b) The level of competence of the internal audit function; and (Ref: Para. A5–A9)
(c) Whether the internal audit function applies a systematic and disciplined approach, including quality control. (Ref: Para. A10–A11)

The external auditor shall not use the work of the internal audit function if the **16** external auditor determines that:

(a) The function's organizational status and relevant policies and procedures do not adequately support the objectivity of internal auditors;
(b) The function lacks sufficient competence; or
(c) The function does not apply a systematic and disciplined approach, including quality control. (Ref: Para. A12–A14)

Determining the Nature and Extent of Work of the Internal Audit Function that Can Be Used

As a basis for determining the areas and the extent to which the work of the internal **17** audit function can be used, the external auditor shall consider the nature and scope of the work that has been performed, or is planned to be performed, by the internal audit function and its relevance to the external auditor's overall audit strategy and audit plan. (Ref: Para. A15–A17)

The external auditor shall make all significant judgments in the audit engagement **18** and, to prevent undue use of the work of the internal audit function, shall plan to use less of the work of the function and perform more of the work directly: (Ref: Para. A15–A17)

(a) The more judgment is involved in:
    (i) Planning and performing relevant audit procedures; and
    (ii) Evaluating the audit evidence gathered; (Ref: Para. A18–A19)
(b) The higher the assessed risk of material misstatement at the assertion level, with special consideration given to risks identified as significant; (Ref: Para. A20–A22)
(c) The less the internal audit function's organizational status and relevant policies and procedures adequately support the objectivity of the internal auditors; and
(d) The lower the level of competence of the internal audit function.

The external auditor shall also evaluate whether, in aggregate, using the work of the **19** internal audit function to the extent planned would still result in the external auditor being sufficiently involved in the audit, given the external auditor's sole responsibility for the audit opinion expressed. (Ref: Para. A15–A22)

20   The external auditor shall, in communicating with those charged with governance an overview of the planned scope and timing of the audit in accordance with ISA (UK and Ireland) 260,[7] communicate how the external auditor has planned to use the work of the internal audit function. (Ref: Para. A23)

Using the Work of the Internal Audit Function

21   If the external auditor plans to use the work of the internal audit function, the external auditor shall discuss the planned use of its work with the function as a basis for coordinating their respective activities. (Ref: Para. A24–A26)

22   The external auditor shall read the reports of the internal audit function relating to the work of the function that the external auditor plans to use to obtain an understanding of the nature and extent of audit procedures it performed and the related findings.

23   The external auditor shall perform sufficient audit procedures on the body of work of the internal audit function as a whole that the external auditor plans to use to determine its adequacy for purposes of the audit, including evaluating whether:

(a) The work of the function had been properly planned, performed, supervised, reviewed and documented;

(b) Sufficient appropriate evidence had been obtained to enable the function to draw reasonable conclusions; and

(c) Conclusions reached are appropriate in the circumstances and the reports prepared by the function are consistent with the results of the work performed. (Ref: Para. A27–A30)

24   The nature and extent of the external auditor's audit procedures shall be responsive to the external auditor's evaluation of:

(a) The amount of judgment involved;

(b) The assessed risk of material misstatement;

(c) The extent to which the internal audit function's organizational status and relevant policies and procedures support the objectivity of the internal auditors; and

(d) The level of competence of the function;[8] (Ref: Para. A27–A29)

and shall include reperformance of some of the work. (Ref: Para. A30)

25   The external auditor shall also evaluate whether the external auditor's conclusions regarding the internal audit function in paragraph 15 of this ISA (UK and Ireland) and the determination of the nature and extent of use of the work of the function for purposes of the audit in paragraphs 18–19 of this ISA (UK and Ireland) remain appropriate.

---

[7] *ISA (UK and Ireland) 260, Communication with Those Charged with Governance*, paragraph 15.

[8] *See paragraph 18.*

Determining Whether, in Which Areas, and to What Extent Internal Auditors Can Be Used to Provide Direct Assistance

Determining Whether Internal Auditors Can Be Used to Provide Direct Assistance for Purposes of the Audit

The external auditor may be prohibited by law or regulation from obtaining direct assistance from internal auditors. If so, paragraphs 27–35 and 37 do not apply[8a]. (Ref: Para. A31) **26**

If using internal auditors to provide direct assistance is not prohibited by law or regulation, and the external auditor plans to use internal auditors to provide direct assistance on the audit, the external auditor shall evaluate the existence and significance of threats to objectivity and the level of competence of the internal auditors who will be providing such assistance. The external auditor's evaluation of the existence and significance of threats to the internal auditors' objectivity shall include inquiry of the internal auditors regarding interests and relationships that may create a threat to their objectivity. (Ref: Para. A32–A34) **27**

The external auditor shall not use an internal auditor to provide direct assistance if: **28**

(a) There are significant threats to the objectivity of the internal auditor; or
(b) The internal auditor lacks sufficient competence to perform the proposed work.
      (Ref: Para. A32–A34)

Determining the Nature and Extent of Work that Can Be Assigned to Internal Auditors Providing Direct Assistance

In determining the nature and extent of work that may be assigned to internal auditors and the nature, timing and extent of direction, supervision and review that is appropriate in the circumstances, the external auditor shall consider: **29**

(a) The amount of judgment involved in:
      (i)   Planning and performing relevant audit procedures; and
      (ii) Evaluating the audit evidence gathered;
(b) The assessed risk of material misstatement; and
(c) The external auditor's evaluation of the existence and significance of threats to the objectivity and level of competence of the internal auditors who will be providing such assistance. (Ref: Para. A35–A39)

The external auditor shall not use internal auditors to provide direct assistance to perform procedures that: **30**

(a) Involve making significant judgments in the audit; (Ref: Para. A19)
(b) Relate to higher assessed risks of material misstatement where the judgment required in performing the relevant audit procedures or evaluating the audit evidence gathered is more than limited; (Ref: Para. A38)
(c) Relate to work with which the internal auditors have been involved and which has already been, or will be, reported to management or those charged with governance by the internal audit function; or
(d) Relate to decisions the external auditor makes in accordance with this ISA (UK and Ireland) regarding the internal audit function and the use of its work or direct assistance. (Ref: Para. A35–A39)

[8a] *The use of internal auditors to provide direct assistance is prohibited in an audit conducted in accordance with ISAs (UK and Ireland). See paragraph 5-1 above of this ISA (UK and Ireland).*

31   Having appropriately evaluated whether and, if so, to what extent internal auditors can be used to provide direct assistance on the audit, the external auditor shall, in communicating with those charged with governance an overview of the planned scope and timing of the audit in accordance with ISA (UK and Ireland) 260,[9] communicate the nature and extent of the planned use of internal auditors to provide direct assistance so as to reach a mutual understanding that such use is not excessive in the circumstances of the engagement. (Ref: Para. A39)

32   The external auditor shall evaluate whether, in aggregate, using internal auditors to provide direct assistance to the extent planned, together with the planned use of the work of the internal audit function, would still result in the external auditor being sufficiently involved in the audit, given the external auditor's sole responsibility for the audit opinion expressed.

Using Internal Auditors to Provide Direct Assistance

33   Prior to using internal auditors to provide direct assistance for purposes of the audit, the external auditor shall:

(a)   Obtain written agreement from an authorized representative of the entity that the internal auditors will be allowed to follow the external auditor's instructions, and that the entity will not intervene in the work the internal auditor performs for the external auditor; and

(b)   Obtain written agreement from the internal auditors that they will keep confidential specific matters as instructed by the external auditor and inform the external auditor of any threat to their objectivity.

34   The external auditor shall direct, supervise and review the work performed by internal auditors on the engagement in accordance with ISA (UK and Ireland) 220.[10] In so doing:

(a)   The nature, timing and extent of direction, supervision, and review shall recognize that the internal auditors are not independent of the entity and be responsive to the outcome of the evaluation of the factors in paragraph 29 of this ISA (UK and Ireland); and

(b)   The review procedures shall include the external auditor checking back to the underlying audit evidence for some of the work performed by the internal auditors.

The direction, supervision and review by the external auditor of the work performed by the internal auditors shall be sufficient in order for the external auditor to be satisfied that the internal auditors have obtained sufficient appropriate audit evidence to support the conclusions based on that work. (Ref: Para. A40–A41)

35   In directing, supervising and reviewing the work performed by internal auditors, the external auditor shall remain alert for indications that the external auditor's evaluations in paragraph 27 are no longer appropriate.

Documentation

36   If the external auditor uses the work of the internal audit function, the external auditor shall include in the audit documentation:

[9] *ISA (UK and Ireland) 260, paragraph 15.*

[10] *ISA (UK and Ireland) 220, Quality Control for an Audit of Financial Statements.*

(a) The evaluation of:
    (i) Whether the function's organizational status and relevant policies and procedures adequately support the objectivity of the internal auditors;
    (ii) The level of competence of the function; and
    (iii) Whether the function applies a systematic and disciplined approach, including quality control;
(b) The nature and extent of the work used and the basis for that decision; and
(c) The audit procedures performed by the external auditor to evaluate the adequacy of the work used.

If the external auditor uses internal auditors to provide direct assistance on the audit, the external auditor shall include in the audit documentation: **37**

(a) The evaluation of the existence and significance of threats to the objectivity of the internal auditors, and the level of competence of the internal auditors used to provide direct assistance;
(b) The basis for the decision regarding the nature and extent of the work performed by the internal auditors;
(c) Who reviewed the work performed and the date and extent of that review in accordance with ISA (UK and Ireland) 230;[11]
(d) The written agreements obtained from an authorized representative of the entity and the internal auditors under paragraph 33 of this ISA (UK and Ireland); and
(e) The working papers prepared by the internal auditors who provided direct assistance on the audit engagement.

***

Application and Other Explanatory Material

Definition of Internal Audit Function (Ref: Para. 2, 14(a))

The objectives and scope of internal audit functions typically include assurance and consulting activities designed to evaluate and improve the effectiveness of the entity's governance processes, risk management and internal control such as the following: **A1**

Activities Relating to Governance

- The internal audit function may assess the governance process in its accomplishment of objectives on ethics and values, performance management and accountability, communicating risk and control information to appropriate areas of the organization and effectiveness of communication among those charged with governance, external and internal auditors, and management.

Activities Relating to Risk Management

- The internal audit function may assist the entity by identifying and evaluating significant exposures to risk and contributing to the improvement of risk management and internal control (including effectiveness of the financial reporting process).
- The internal audit function may perform procedures to assist the entity in the detection of fraud.

---

[11] *ISA (UK and Ireland) 230, Audit Documentation.*

Activities Relating to Internal Control

- Evaluation of internal control. The internal audit function may be assigned specific responsibility for reviewing controls, evaluating their operation and recommending improvements thereto. In doing so, the internal audit function provides assurance on the control. For example, the internal audit function might plan and perform tests or other procedures to provide assurance to management and those charged with governance regarding the design, implementation and operating effectiveness of internal control, including those controls that are relevant to the audit.

- Examination of financial and operating information. The internal audit function may be assigned to review the means used to identify, recognize, measure, classify and report financial and operating information, and to make specific inquiry into individual items, including detailed testing of transactions, balances and procedures.

- Review of operating activities. The internal audit function may be assigned to review the economy, efficiency and effectiveness of operating activities, including non-financial activities of an entity.

- Review of compliance with laws and regulations. The internal audit function may be assigned to review compliance with laws, regulations and other external requirements, and with management policies and directives and other internal requirements.

A2   Activities similar to those performed by an internal audit function may be conducted by functions with other titles within an entity. Some or all of the activities of an internal audit function may also be outsourced to a third-party service provider. Neither the title of the function, nor whether it is performed by the entity or a third-party service provider, are sole determinants of whether or not the external auditor can use the work of the function. Rather, it is the nature of the activities; the extent to which the internal audit function's organizational status and relevant policies and procedures support the objectivity of the internal auditors; competence; and systematic and disciplined approach of the function that are relevant. References in this ISA (UK and Ireland) to the work of the internal audit function include relevant activities of other functions or third-party providers that have these characteristics.

A3   In addition, those in the entity with operational and managerial duties and responsibilities outside of the internal audit function would ordinarily face threats to their objectivity that would preclude them from being treated as part of an internal audit function for the purpose of this ISA (UK and Ireland), although they may perform control activities that can be tested in accordance with ISA (UK and Ireland) 330.[12] For this reason, monitoring controls performed by an owner-manager would not be considered equivalent to an internal audit function.

A4   While the objectives of an entity's internal audit function and the external auditor differ, the function may perform audit procedures similar to those performed by the external auditor in an audit of financial statements. If so, the external auditor may make use of the function for purposes of the audit in one or more of the following ways:

- To obtain information that is relevant to the external auditor's assessments of the risks of material misstatement due to error or fraud. In this regard, ISA (UK and Ireland) 315 (Revised June 2013)[13] requires the external auditor to obtain an understanding of the nature of the internal audit function's responsibilities, its

---

[12] *See paragraph 10.*

[13] *ISA (UK and Ireland) 315 (Revised June 2013), paragraph 6(a).*

status within the organization, and the activities performed, or to be performed, and make inquiries of appropriate individuals within the internal audit function (if the entity has such a function); or

- Unless prohibited, or restricted to some extent, by law or regulation, the external auditor, after appropriate evaluation, may decide to use work that has been performed by the internal audit function during the period in partial substitution for audit evidence to be obtained directly by the external auditor.[14]

In addition, unless prohibited, or restricted to some extent, by law or regulation, the external auditor may use internal auditors to perform audit procedures under the direction, supervision and review of the external auditor (referred to as "direct assistance" in this ISA (UK and Ireland)).[15]

Determining Whether, in Which Areas, and to What Extent the Work of the Internal Audit Function Can Be Used

Evaluating the Internal Audit Function

Objectivity and Competence (Ref: Para. 15(a)–(b))

The external auditor exercises professional judgment in determining whether the   **A5**
work of the internal audit function can be used for purposes of the audit, and the nature and extent to which the work of the internal audit function can be used in the circumstances.

The extent to which the internal audit function's organizational status and relevant   **A6**
policies and procedures support the objectivity of the internal auditors and the level of competence of the function are particularly important in determining whether to use and, if so, the nature and extent of the use of the work of the function that is appropriate in the circumstances.

Objectivity refers to the ability to perform those tasks without allowing bias, conflict   **A7**
of interest or undue influence of others to override professional judgments. Factors that may affect the external auditor's evaluation include the following:

- Whether the organizational status of the internal audit function, including the function's authority and accountability, supports the ability of the function to be free from bias, conflict of interest or undue influence of others to override professional judgments. For example, whether the internal audit function reports to those charged with governance or an officer with appropriate authority, or if the function reports to management, whether it has direct access to those charged with governance.
- Whether the internal audit function is free of any conflicting responsibilities, for example, having managerial or operational duties or responsibilities that are outside of the internal audit function.
- Whether those charged with governance oversee employment decisions related to the internal audit function, for example, determining the appropriate remuneration policy.
- Whether there are any constraints or restrictions placed on the internal audit function by management or those charged with governance, for example, in communicating the internal audit function's findings to the external auditor.

---

[14] *See paragraphs 15–25.*

[15] *See paragraphs 26–35. The use of internal auditors to provide direct assistance is prohibited in an audit conducted in accordance with ISAs (UK and Ireland) – see paragraph 5-1.*

- Whether the internal auditors are members of relevant professional bodies and their memberships obligate their compliance with relevant professional standards relating to objectivity, or whether their internal policies achieve the same objectives.

A8   Competence of the internal audit function refers to the attainment and maintenance of knowledge and skills of the function as a whole at the level required to enable assigned tasks to be performed diligently and in accordance with applicable professional standards. Factors that may affect the external auditor's determination include the following:

- Whether the internal audit function is adequately and appropriately resourced relative to the size of the entity and the nature of its operations.
- Whether there are established policies for hiring, training and assigning internal auditors to internal audit engagements.
- Whether the internal auditors have adequate technical training and proficiency in auditing. Relevant criteria that may be considered by the external auditor in making the assessment may include, for example, the internal auditors' possession of a relevant professional designation and experience.
- Whether the internal auditors possess the required knowledge relating to the entity's financial reporting and the applicable financial reporting framework and whether the internal audit function possesses the necessary skills (for example, industry-specific knowledge) to perform work related to the entity's financial statements.
- Whether the internal auditors are members of relevant professional bodies that oblige them to comply with the relevant professional standards including continuing professional development requirements.

A9   Objectivity and competence may be viewed as a continuum. The more the internal audit function's organizational status and relevant policies and procedures adequately support the objectivity of the internal auditors and the higher the level of competence of the function, the more likely the external auditor may make use of the work of the function and in more areas. However, an organizational status and relevant policies and procedures that provide strong support for the objectivity of the internal auditors cannot compensate for the lack of sufficient competence of the internal audit function. Equally, a high level of competence of the internal audit function cannot compensate for an organizational status and policies and procedures that do not adequately support the objectivity of the internal auditors.

Application of a Systematic and Disciplined Approach (Ref: Para. 15(c))

A10   The application of a systematic and disciplined approach to planning, performing, supervising, reviewing and documenting its activities distinguishes the activities of the internal audit function from other monitoring control activities that may be performed within the entity.

A11   Factors that may affect the external auditor's determination of whether the internal audit function applies a systematic and disciplined approach include the following:

- The existence, adequacy and use of documented internal audit procedures or guidance covering such areas as risk assessments, work programs, documentation and reporting, the nature and extent of which is commensurate with the size and circumstances of an entity.

- Whether the internal audit function has appropriate quality control policies and procedures, for example, such as those policies and procedures in ISQC (UK and Ireland) 1[16] that would be applicable to an internal audit function (such as those relating to leadership, human resources and engagement performance) or quality control requirements in standards set by the relevant professional bodies for internal auditors. Such bodies may also establish other appropriate requirements such as conducting periodic external quality assessments.

Circumstances When Work of the Internal Audit Function Cannot Be Used (Ref: Para. 16)

The external auditor's evaluation of whether the internal audit function's organizational status and relevant policies and procedures adequately support the objectivity of the internal auditors, the level of competence of the internal audit function, and whether it applies a systematic and disciplined approach may indicate that the risks to the quality of the work of the function are too significant and therefore it is not appropriate to use any of the work of the function as audit evidence.   **A12**

Consideration of the factors in paragraphs A7, A8 and A11 of this ISA (UK and Ireland) individually and in aggregate is important because an individual factor is often not sufficient to conclude that the work of the internal audit function cannot be used for purposes of the audit. For example, the internal audit function's organizational status is particularly important in evaluating threats to the objectivity of the internal auditors. If the internal audit function reports to management, this would be considered a significant threat to the function's objectivity unless other factors such as those described in paragraph A7 of this ISA (UK and Ireland) collectively provide sufficient safeguards to reduce the threat to an acceptable level.   **A13**

In addition, the IESBA Code[17] states that a self-review threat is created when the external auditor accepts an engagement to provide internal audit services to an audit client, and the results of those services will be used in conducting the audit. This is because of the possibility that the engagement team will use the results of the internal audit service without properly evaluating those results or without exercising the same level of professional skepticism as would be exercised when the internal audit work is performed by individuals who are not members of the firm. The IESBA Code[18] discusses the prohibitions that apply in certain circumstances and the threats and the safeguards that can be applied to reduce the threats to an acceptable level in other circumstances.   **A14**

Auditors in the UK and Ireland are subject to ethical requirements from two sources: the APB Ethical Standards for Auditors (ESs) concerning the integrity, objectivity and independence of the auditor, and the ethical pronouncements established by the auditor's relevant professional body. Requirements and guidance concerning the provision of internal audit services, including to address the self-review threat, are set out in ES 5[18a].   **A14-1**

---

[16] *International Standard on Quality Control (ISQC) (UK and Ireland) 1, Quality Control for Firms that Perform Audits and Reviews of Financial Statements, and Other Assurance and Related Services Engagements.*

[17] *The International Ethics Standards Board for Accountants' (IESBA) Code of Ethics for Professional Accountants* (IESBA Code), Section 290.199.

[18] *IESBA Code*, Section 290.195–290.200.

[18a] *ES 5, Non-audit services provided to audited entities*, paragraphs 58-69.

Determining the Nature and Extent of Work of the Internal Audit Function that Can Be Used

Factors Affecting the Determination of the Nature and Extent of the Work of the Internal Audit Function that Can Be Used (Ref: Para. 17–19)

A15   Once the external auditor has determined that the work of the internal audit function can be used for purposes of the audit, a first consideration is whether the planned nature and scope of the work of the internal audit function that has been performed, or is planned to be performed, is relevant to the overall audit strategy and audit plan that the external auditor has established in accordance with ISA (UK and Ireland) 300.[19]

A16   Examples of work of the internal audit function that can be used by the external auditor include the following:

- Testing of the operating effectiveness of controls.
- Substantive procedures involving limited judgment.
- Observations of inventory counts.
- Tracing transactions through the information system relevant to financial reporting.
- Testing of compliance with regulatory requirements.
- In some circumstances, audits or reviews of the financial information of subsidiaries that are not significant components to the group (where this does not conflict with the requirements of ISA (UK and Ireland) 600).[20]

A17   The external auditor's determination of the planned nature and extent of use of the work of the internal audit function will be influenced by the external auditor's evaluation of the extent to which the internal audit function's organizational status and relevant policies and procedures adequately support the objectivity of the internal auditors and the level of competence of the internal audit function in paragraph 18 of this ISA (UK and Ireland). In addition, the amount of judgment needed in planning, performing and evaluating such work and the assessed risk of material misstatement at the assertion level are inputs to the external auditor's determination. Further, there are circumstances in which the external auditor cannot use the work of the internal audit function for purpose of the audit as described in paragraph 16 of this ISA (UK and Ireland).

Judgments in planning and performing audit procedures and evaluating results (Ref: Para. 18(a), 30(a))

A18   The greater the judgment needed to be exercised in planning and performing the audit procedures and evaluating the audit evidence, the external auditor will need to perform more procedures directly in accordance with paragraph 18 of this ISA (UK and Ireland), because using the work of the internal audit function alone will not provide the external auditor with sufficient appropriate audit evidence.

A19   Since the external auditor has sole responsibility for the audit opinion expressed, the external auditor needs to make the significant judgments in the audit engagement in accordance with paragraph 18. Significant judgments include the following:

---

[19] *ISA (UK and Ireland) 300, Planning an Audit of Financial Statements.*

[20] *ISA (UK and Ireland) 600, Special Considerations—Audits of Group Financial Statements (Including the Work of Component Auditors).*

- Assessing the risks of material misstatement;
- Evaluating the sufficiency of tests performed;
- Evaluating the appropriateness of management's use of the going concern assumption;
- Evaluating significant accounting estimates; and
- Evaluating the adequacy of disclosures in the financial statements, and other matters affecting the auditor's report.

Assessed risk of material misstatement (Ref: Para. 18(b))

For a particular account balance, class of transaction or disclosure, the higher an assessed risk of material misstatement at the assertion level, the more judgment is often involved in planning and performing the audit procedures and evaluating the results thereof. In such circumstances, the external auditor will need to perform more procedures directly in accordance with paragraph 18 of this ISA (UK and Ireland), and accordingly, make less use of the work of the internal audit function in obtaining sufficient appropriate audit evidence. Furthermore, as explained in ISA (UK and Ireland) 200,[21] the higher the assessed risks of material misstatement, the more persuasive the audit evidence required by the external auditor will need to be, and, therefore, the external auditor will need to perform more of the work directly.   **A20**

As explained in ISA (UK and Ireland) 315 (Revised June 2013),[22] significant risks require special audit consideration and therefore the external auditor's ability to use the work of the internal audit function in relation to significant risks will be restricted to procedures that involve limited judgment. In addition, where the risk of material misstatement is other than low, the use of the work of the internal audit function alone is unlikely to reduce audit risk to an acceptably low level and eliminate the need for the external auditor to perform some tests directly.   **A21**

Carrying out procedures in accordance with this ISA (UK and Ireland) may cause the external auditor to reevaluate the external auditor's assessment of the risks of material misstatement. Consequently, this may affect the external auditor's determination of whether to use the work of the internal audit function and whether further application of this ISA (UK and Ireland) is necessary.   **A22**

Communication with Those Charged with Governance (Ref: Para. 20)

In accordance with ISA (UK and Ireland) 260,[23] the external auditor is required to communicate with those charged with governance an overview of the planned scope and timing of the audit. The planned use of the work of the internal audit function is an integral part of the external auditor's overall audit strategy and is therefore relevant to those charged with governance for their understanding of the proposed audit approach.   **A23**

---

[21] *ISA (UK and Ireland) 200, paragraph A29.*

[22] *ISA (UK and Ireland) 315 (Revised June 2013), paragraph 4(e).*

[23] *ISA (UK and Ireland) 260, paragraph 15.*

Using the Work of the Internal Audit Function

Discussion and Coordination with the Internal Audit Function (Ref: Para. 21)

A24   In discussing the planned use of their work with the internal audit function as a basis for coordinating the respective activities, it may be useful to address the following:

- The timing of such work.
- The nature of the work performed.
- The extent of audit coverage.
- Materiality for the financial statements as a whole (and, if applicable, materiality level or levels for particular classes of transactions, account balances or disclosures), and performance materiality.
- Proposed methods of item selection and sample sizes.
- Documentation of the work performed.
- Review and reporting procedures.

A25   Coordination between the external auditor and the internal audit function is effective when, for example:

- Discussions take place at appropriate intervals throughout the period.
- The external auditor informs the internal audit function of significant matters that may affect the function.
- The external auditor is advised of and has access to relevant reports of the internal audit function and is informed of any significant matters that come to the attention of the function when such matters may affect the work of the external auditor so that the external auditor is able to consider the implications of such matters for the audit engagement.

A26   ISA (UK and Ireland) 200[24] discusses the importance of the auditor planning and performing the audit with professional skepticism, including being alert to information that brings into question the reliability of documents and responses to inquiries to be used as audit evidence. Accordingly, communication with the internal audit function throughout the engagement may provide opportunities for internal auditors to bring matters that may affect the work of the external auditor to the external auditor's attention.[25] The external auditor is then able to take such information into account in the external auditor's identification and assessment of risks of material misstatement. In addition, if such information may be indicative of a heightened risk of a material misstatement of the financial statements or may be regarding any actual, suspected or alleged fraud, the external auditor can take this into account in the external auditor's identification of risk of material misstatement due to fraud in accordance with ISA (UK and Ireland) 240.[26]

Procedures to Determine the Adequacy of Work of the Internal Audit Function (Ref: Para. 23–24)

A27   The external auditor's audit procedures on the body of work of the internal audit function as a whole that the external auditor plans to use provide a basis for evaluating the overall quality of the function's work and the objectivity with which it has been performed.

---

[24] *ISA (UK and Ireland) 200, paragraphs 15 and A18.*

[25] *ISA (UK and Ireland) 315 (Revised June 2013), paragraph A116.*

[26] *ISA (UK and Ireland) 315 (Revised June 2013), paragraph A11 in relation to ISA (UK and Ireland) 240, The Auditor's Responsibilities Relating to Fraud in an Audit of Financial Statements.*

The procedures the external auditor may perform to evaluate the quality of the work   **A28**
performed and the conclusions reached by the internal audit function, in addition to
reperformance in accordance with paragraph 24, include the following:

- Making inquiries of appropriate individuals within the internal audit function.
- Observing procedures performed by the internal audit function.
- Reviewing the internal audit function's work program and working papers.

The more judgment involved, the higher the assessed risk of material misstatement,   **A29**
the less the internal audit function's organizational status and relevant policies and
procedures adequately support the objectivity of the internal auditors, or the lower
the level of competence of the internal audit function, the more audit procedures are
needed to be performed by the external auditor on the overall body of work of the
function to support the decision to use the work of the function in obtaining sufficient appropriate audit evidence on which to base the audit opinion.

Reperformance (Ref: Para. 24)

For purposes of this ISA (UK and Ireland), reperformance involves the external   **A30**
auditor's independent execution of procedures to validate the conclusions reached by
the internal audit function. This objective may be accomplished by examining items
already examined by the internal audit function, or where it is not possible to do so,
the same objective may also be accomplished by examining sufficient other similar
items not actually examined by the internal audit function. Reperformance provides
more persuasive evidence regarding the adequacy of the work of the internal audit
function compared to other procedures the external auditor may perform in paragraph A28. While it is not necessary for the external auditor to do reperformance in
each area of work of the internal audit function that is being used, some reperformance is required on the body of work of the internal audit function as a whole that
the external auditor plans to use in accordance with paragraph 24. The external
auditor is more likely to focus reperformance in those areas where more judgment
was exercised by the internal audit function in planning, performing and evaluating
the results of the audit procedures and in areas of higher risk of material
misstatement.

Determining Whether, in Which Areas and to What Extent Internal Auditors Can Be Used to Provide Direct Assistance

Determining Whether Internal Auditors Can Be Used to Provide Direct Assistance for Purposes of the Audit (Ref: Para. 5, 26–28)

In jurisdictions where the external auditor is prohibited by law or regulation from   **A31**
using internal auditors to provide direct assistance, it is relevant for the group
auditors to consider whether the prohibition also extends to component auditors
and, if so, to address this in the communication to the component auditors.[27]

As stated in paragraph A7 of this ISA (UK and Ireland), objectivity refers to the   **A32**
ability to perform the proposed work without allowing bias, conflict of interest or
undue influence of others to override professional judgments. In evaluating the

---

[27] *ISA 600, paragraph 40(b). The use of internal auditors to provide direct assistance is prohibited in an audit
conducted in accordance with ISAs (UK and Ireland). For a group audit this prohibition extends to the work of
any component auditor which is relied upon by the group auditor, including for overseas components – see
paragraph 5-1 above of this ISA (UK and Ireland).*

existence and significance of threats to the objectivity of an internal auditor, the following factors may be relevant:

- The extent to which the internal audit function's organizational status and relevant policies and procedures support the objectivity of the internal auditors.[28]
- Family and personal relationships with an individual working in, or responsible for, the aspect of the entity to which the work relates.
- Association with the division or department in the entity to which the work relates.
- Significant financial interests in the entity other than remuneration on terms consistent with those applicable to other employees at a similar level of seniority.

Material issued by relevant professional bodies for internal auditors may provide additional useful guidance.

A33   There may also be some circumstances in which the significance of the threats to the objectivity of an internal auditor is such that there are no safeguards that could reduce them to an acceptable level. For example, because the adequacy of safeguards is influenced by the significance of the work in the context of the audit, paragraph 30 (a) and (b) prohibits the use of internal auditors to provide direct assistance in relation to performing procedures that involve making significant judgments in the audit or that relate to higher assessed risks of material misstatement where the judgment required in performing the relevant audit procedures or evaluating the audit evidence gathered is more than limited. This would also be the case where the work involved creates a self-review threat, which is why internal auditors are pro-hibited from performing procedures in the circumstances described in paragraph 30 (c) and (d).

A34   In evaluating the level of competence of an internal auditor, many of the factors in paragraph A8 of this ISA (UK and Ireland) may also be relevant applied in the context of individual internal auditors and the work to which they may be assigned.

Determining the Nature and Extent of Work that Can Be Assigned to Internal Auditors Providing Direct Assistance (Ref: Para. 29–31)

A35   Paragraphs A15-A22 of this ISA (UK and Ireland) provide relevant guidance in determining the nature and extent of work that may be assigned to internal auditors.

A36   In determining the nature of work that may be assigned to internal auditors, the external auditor is careful to limit such work to those areas that would be appro-priate to be assigned. Examples of activities and tasks that would not be appropriate to use internal auditors to provide direct assistance include the following:

- Discussion of fraud risks. However, the external auditors may make inquiries of internal auditors about fraud risks in the organization in accordance with ISA (UK and Ireland) 315 (Revised June 2013).[29]
- Determination of unannounced audit procedures as addressed in ISA (UK and Ireland) 240.

---

[28] *See paragraph A7.*

[29] *ISA 315 (Revised), paragraph 6(a).*

Similarly, since in accordance with ISA (UK and Ireland) 505[30] the external auditor   **A37**
is required to maintain control over external confirmation requests and evaluate the
results of external confirmation procedures, it would not be appropriate to assign
these responsibilities to internal auditors. However, internal auditors may assist in
assembling information necessary for the external auditor to resolve exceptions in
confirmation responses.

The amount of judgment involved and the risk of material misstatement are also   **A38**
relevant in determining the work that may be assigned to internal auditors providing
direct assistance. For example, in circumstances where the valuation of accounts
receivable is assessed as an area of higher risk, the external auditor could assign the
checking of the accuracy of the aging to an internal auditor providing direct assistance. However, because the evaluation of the adequacy of the provision based on
the aging would involve more than limited judgment, it would not be appropriate to
assign that latter procedure to an internal auditor providing direct assistance.

Notwithstanding the direction, supervision and review by the external auditor,   **A39**
excessive use of internal auditors to provide direct assistance may affect perceptions
regarding the independence of the external audit engagement.

Using Internal Auditors to Provide Direct Assistance (Ref: Para. 34)

As individuals in the internal audit function are not independent of the entity as is   **A40**
required of the external auditor when expressing an opinion on financial statements,
the external auditor's direction, supervision and review of the work performed by
internal auditors providing direct assistance will generally be of a different nature
and more extensive than if members of the engagement team perform the work.

In directing the internal auditors, the external auditor may for example, remind the   **A41**
internal auditors to bring accounting and auditing issues identified during the audit
to the attention of the external auditor. In reviewing the work performed by the
internal auditors, the external auditor's considerations include whether the evidence
obtained is sufficient and appropriate in the circumstances, and that it supports the
conclusions reached.

---

[30] *ISA 505, External Confirmations*, paragraphs 7 and 16.

Annexure

Conforming amendments to other ISAs (UK and Ireland)

This annexure shows the conforming amendments to ISQC (UK and Ireland) 1 and other ISAs (UK and Ireland) as a result of ISA (UK and Ireland) 610 (Revised June 2013), *Using the Work of Internal Auditors*. These amendments are effective for audits of financial statements for periods ending on or after 15 June 2014[1]. The footnote numbers within these amendments do not align with the ISAs (UK and Ireland) that will be amended, and reference should be made to those ISAs (UK and Ireland).

ISQC (UK and Ireland) 1, *Quality Control for Firms that Perform Audits and Reviews of Financial Statements, and Other Assurance and Related Services Engagements*

Definitions

12   In this ISQC (UK and Ireland), the following terms have the meanings attributed below:

(f)   Engagement team – All partners and staff performing the engagement, and any individuals engaged by the firm or a network firm who perform procedures on the engagement. This excludes an auditor's external experts engaged by the firm or by a network firm. The term "engagement team" also excludes individuals within the client's internal audit function who provide direct assistance on an audit engagement when the external auditor complies with the requirements of ISA (UK and Ireland) 610 (Revised June 2013)[2].

***

ISA (UK and Ireland) 200, *Overall Objectives of the Independent Auditor and the Conduct of an Audit in Accordance with International Standards on Auditing*

A72   In some cases, an ISA (UK and Ireland) (and therefore all of its requirements) may not be relevant in the circumstances. For example, if an entity does not have an internal audit function, nothing in ISA (UK and Ireland) 610 (Revised June 2013)[3] is relevant.

***

[1] *For the purpose of audits under ISAs as issued by the IAASB, the material pertaining to the use of direct assistance has an effective date of audits of financial statements for periods ending on or after 15 December 2014. However, as stated in paragraph 5-1 of ISA (UK and Ireland) 610 (Revised June 2013), the use of internal auditors to provide direct assistance is prohibited in an audit conducted in accordance with ISAs (UK and Ireland) – such prohibition being effective from the effective date of ISA (UK and Ireland) 610 (Revised June 2013), audits of financial statements for periods ending on or after 15 June 2014.*

[2] *ISA 610 (Revised June 2013), Using the Work of Internal Auditors, establishes limits on the use of direct assistance. It also acknowledges that the external auditor may be prohibited by law or regulation from obtaining direct assistance from internal auditors. Therefore, the use of direct assistance is restricted to situations where it is permitted. The use of internal auditors to provide direct assistance is prohibited in an audit conducted in accordance with ISAs (UK and Ireland) – see ISA (UK and Ireland) 610 (Revised June 2013), paragraph 5-1.*

[3] *ISA (UK and Ireland) 610 (Revised June 2013), Using the Work of Internal Auditors, paragraph 2.*

ISA (UK and Ireland) 220, *Quality Control for an Audit of Financial Statements*

Definitions

For purposes of the ISAs (UK and Ireland), the following terms have the meanings attributed below: **7**

(d) Engagement team – All partners and staff performing the engagement, and any individuals engaged by the firm or a network firm who perform audit procedures on the engagement. This excludes an auditor's external expert engaged by the firm or by a network firm.[4] The term "engagement team" also excludes individuals within the client's internal audit function who provide direct assistance on an audit engagement when the external auditor complies with the requirements of ISA (UK and Ireland) 610 (Revised June 2013).[5]

***

ISA (UK and Ireland) 230, *Audit Documentation*

The documentation requirement applies only to requirements that are relevant in the circumstances. A requirement is not relevant[6] only in the cases where: **A19**

(a) The entire ISA (UK and Ireland) is not relevant (for example, if an entity does not have an internal audit function, nothing in ISA (UK and Ireland) 610 (Revised June 2013)[7] is relevant); or

(b) The requirement is conditional and the condition does not exist (for example, the requirement to modify the auditor's opinion where there is an inability to obtain sufficient appropriate audit evidence, and there is no such inability).

***

ISA (UK and Ireland) 240, *The Auditor's Responsibilities Relating to Fraud in an Audit of Financial Statements*

For those entities that have an internal audit function, the auditor shall make inquiries of appropriate individuals within the function ~~internal audit~~ to determine whether ~~it~~ they ~~ha~~ves knowledge of any actual, suspected or alleged fraud affecting the entity, and to obtain its views about the risks of fraud. (Ref: Para. A18)   **19**

---

[4] *ISA (UK and Ireland) 620, Using the Work of an Auditor's Expert*, paragraph 6(a), defines the term "auditor's expert."

[5] *ISA 610 (Revised June 2013)*, Using the Work of Internal Auditors, *establishes limits on the use of direct assistance. It also acknowledges that the external auditor may be prohibited by law or regulation from obtaining direct assistance from internal auditors. Therefore, the use of direct assistance is restricted to situations where it is permitted. The use of internal auditors to provide direct assistance is prohibited in an audit conducted in accordance with ISAs (UK and Ireland) – see ISA (UK and Ireland) 610 (Revised June 2013), paragraph 5-1.*

[6] *ISA (UK and Ireland) 200, paragraph 22.*

[7] *ISA (UK and Ireland) 610 (Revised June 2013), Using the Work of Internal Auditors, paragraph 2.*

Inquiries~~y~~ of ~~the~~ Internal Audit Function (Ref: Para. 19)

A18   ISA (UK and Ireland) 315 (Revised June 2013) and ISA (UK and Ireland) 610 (Revised June 2013) establish requirements and provide guidance relevant to ~~in~~ audits of those entities that have an internal audit function.[8] In carrying out the requirements of those ISAs (UK and Ireland) in the context of fraud, the auditor may inquire about specific activities of the function ~~internal audit activities~~ including, for example:

- The procedures performed, if any, by the internal audit~~ors~~ function during the year to detect fraud.
- Whether management has satisfactorily responded to any findings resulting from those procedures.

Appendix 1

Examples of Fraud Risk Factors

Internal control components are deficient as a result of the following:
- Inadequate monitoring of controls, including automated controls and controls over interim financial reporting (where external reporting is required).
- High turnover rates or employment of staff in accounting, ~~internal audit, or~~ information technology, or the internal audit function ~~staff~~ that are not effective.

***

ISA (UK and Ireland) 260, *Communication with Those Charged with Governance*

A14   Other planning matters that it may be appropriate to discuss with those charged with governance include:

- Where the entity has an internal audit function, ~~the extent to which~~ how the external auditor ~~will use the work of internal audit, and how the external~~ and internal auditors can ~~best~~ work ~~together~~ in a constructive and complementary manner, including any planned use of the work of the internal audit function, and the nature and extent of any planned use of internal auditors to provide direct assistance.[9]
- ...

A33   Before communicating matters with those charged with governance, the auditor may discuss them with management, unless that is inappropriate. For example, it may not be appropriate to discuss questions of management's competence or integrity with management. In addition to recognizing management's executive responsibility, these initial discussions may clarify facts and issues, and give management an opportunity to provide further information and explanations. Similarly, when the entity has an internal audit function, the auditor may discuss matters with ~~the~~ appropriate individuals within the function ~~internal auditor~~ before communicating with those charged with governance.

---

[8] *ISA (UK and Ireland) 315 (Revised June 2013), paragraphs 6(a) and 23, and ISA (UK and Ireland) 610 (Revised June 2013)*, Using the Work of Internal Auditors.

[9] *ISA (UK and Ireland) 610 (Revised June 2013)*, Using the Work of Internal Auditors, *paragraphs 20 and 31. The use of internal auditors to provide direct assistance is prohibited in an audit conducted in accordance with ISAs (UK and Ireland) – see ISA (UK and Ireland) 610 (Revised June 2013), paragraph 5-1.*

As noted in paragraph 4, effective two-way communication assists both the auditor **A43** and those charged with governance. Further, ISA (UK and Ireland) 315 (Revised June 2013) identifies participation by those charged with governance, including their interaction with the internal audit function, if any, and external auditors, as an element of the entity's control environment.[10] Inadequate two-way communication may indicate an unsatisfactory control environment and influence the auditor's assessment of the risks of material misstatements. There is also a risk that the auditor may not have obtained sufficient appropriate audit evidence to form an opinion on the financial statements.

***

ISA (UK and Ireland) 265, *Communicating Deficiencies in Internal Control to Those Charged with Governance and Management*

If the auditor has communicated deficiencies in internal control other than significant **A24** deficiencies to management in a prior period and management has chosen not to remedy them for cost or other reasons, the auditor need not repeat the communication in the current period. The auditor is also not required to repeat information about such deficiencies if it has been previously communicated to management by other parties, such as the internal auditors function or regulators. It may, however, be appropriate for the auditor to re-communicate these other deficiencies if there has been a change of management, or if new information has come to the auditor's attention that alters the prior understanding of the auditor and management regarding the deficiencies. ...

***

ISA (UK and Ireland) 300, *Planning an Audit of Financial Statements*

Appendix

Characteristics of the Engagement

...

- The need for a statutory audit of standalone financial statements in addition to an audit for consolidation purposes.
- ~~The availability of the work of internal auditors and the extent of the auditor's potential reliance on such work~~ Whether the entity has an internal audit function and if so, whether, in which areas and to what extent, the work of the function can be used, or internal auditors can be used to provide direct assistance[11], for purposes of the audit.
  ...

***

---

[10] *ISA (UK and Ireland) 315 (Revised June 2013), paragraph* A77~~70~~.

[11] *The use of internal auditors to provide direct assistance is prohibited in an audit conducted in accordance with ISAs (UK and Ireland) – see ISA (UK and Ireland) 610 (Revised June 2013), Using the Work of Internal Auditors, paragraph 5-1.*

ISA (UK and Ireland) 402, *Audit Considerations Relating to an Entity Using a Service Organization*

A1   Information on the nature of the services provided by a service organization may be available from a wide variety of sources, such as:

- User manuals.
- System overviews.
- Technical manuals.
- The contract or service level agreement between the user entity and the service organization.
- Reports by service organizations, the internal ~~auditors~~ function or regulatory authorities on controls at the service organization.
- Reports by the service auditor, including management letters, if available.

***

ISA (UK and Ireland) 500, *Audit Evidence*

A51   In some cases, the auditor may intend to use information produced by the entity for other audit purposes. For example, the auditor may intend to make use of the entity's performance measures for the purpose of analytical procedures, or to make use of the entity's information produced for monitoring activities, such as ~~internal auditor's~~ reports of the internal audit function. In such cases, the appropriateness of the audit evidence obtained is affected by whether the information is sufficiently precise or detailed for the auditor's purposes. For example, performance measures used by management may not be precise enough to detect material misstatements.

Inconsistency in, or Doubts over Reliability of, Audit Evidence (Ref: Para. 11)

A57   Obtaining audit evidence from different sources or of a different nature may indicate that an individual item of audit evidence is not reliable, such as when audit evidence obtained from one source is inconsistent with that obtained from another. This may be the case when, for example, responses to inquiries of management, internal auditors, and others are inconsistent, or when responses to inquiries of those charged with governance made to corroborate the responses to inquiries of management are inconsistent with the response by management. ISA (UK and Ireland) 230 includes a specific documentation requirement if the auditor identified information that is inconsistent with the auditor's final conclusion regarding a significant matter.[12]

***

ISA (UK and Ireland) 550, *Related Parties*

A15   Others within the entity are those considered likely to have knowledge of the entity's related party relationships and transactions, and the entity's controls over such relationships and transactions. These may include, to the extent that they do not form part of management:

- Those charged with governance;
- Personnel in a position to initiate, process, or record transactions that are both significant and outside the entity's normal course of business, and those who supervise or monitor such personnel;

---

[12] *ISA (UK and Ireland) 230, Audit Documentation,* paragraph 11.

- The ~~I~~internal audit~~ors~~ function;
- In-house legal counsel; and
- The chief ethics officer or equivalent person.

In meeting the ISA (UK and Ireland) 315 (Revised June 2013) requirement to obtain   **A17**
an understanding of the control environment,[13] the auditor may consider features of
the control environment relevant to mitigating the risks of material misstatement
associated with related party relationships and transactions, such as:

- Internal ethical codes, appropriately communicated to the entity's personnel
  and enforced, governing the circumstances in which the entity may enter into
  specific types of related party transactions.

...

- Periodic reviews by ~~the~~ internal audit~~ors~~ function, where applicable.

...

During the audit, the auditor may inspect records or documents that may provide   **A22**
information about related party relationships and transactions, for example:

- Third-party confirmations obtained by the auditor (in addition to bank and
  legal confirmations).

...

- ~~Internal auditors' r~~Reports of the internal audit function.

...

***

ISA (UK and Ireland) 600, *Special Considerations—Audits of Group Financial Statements (Including the Work of Component Auditors)*

The auditor is required to identify and assess the risks of material misstatement of   **A27**
the financial statements due to fraud, and to design and implement appropriate
responses to the assessed risks.[14] Information used to identify the risks of material
misstatement of the group financial statements due to fraud may include the
following:

...

- Responses of those charged with governance of the group, group management,
  appropriate individuals within the internal audit function (and if considered
  appropriate, component management, the component auditors, and others) to
  the group engagement team's *inquiry* whether they have knowledge of any
  actual, suspected, or alleged fraud affecting a component or the group.

---

[13] *ISA (UK and Ireland) 315 (Revised June 2013), paragraph 14.*

[14] *ISA (UK and Ireland) 240, The Auditor's Responsibilities Relating to Fraud in an Audit of Financial Statements.*

A51 The group engagement team's decision as to how many components to select in accordance with paragraph 29, which components to select, and the type of work to be performed on the financial information of the individual components selected may be affected by factors such as the following:

- ...
- Whether the internal audit function has performed work at the component and any effect of that work on the group audit.
- ...

Appendix 2

Examples of Matters about Which the Group Engagement Team Obtains an Understanding

The examples provided cover a broad range of matters; however, not all matters are relevant to every group audit engagement and the list of examples is not necessarily complete.

Group-Wide Controls

1   Group-wide controls may include a combination of the following:

- ...
- Monitoring of controls, including activities of the internal audit function and self-assessment programs.
- ...

2   The ~~I~~internal audit function may be regarded as part of group-wide controls, for example, when the ~~internal audit~~ function is centralized. ISA (UK and Ireland) 610 (Revised June 2013)[15] deals with the group engagement team's evaluation of ~~the~~ whether the internal audit function's organizational status and relevant policies and procedures adequately supports the ~~competence and~~ objectivity of ~~the~~ internal auditors, the level of competence of the internal audit function, and whether the function applies a systematic and disciplined approach where the group engagement team expects ~~it plans~~ to use ~~their~~ the function's work.

Appendix 5

Required and Additional Matters Included in the Group Engagement Team's Letter of Instruction

Matters required by this ISA (UK and Ireland) to be communicated to the component auditor are shown in italicized text.

Matters that are relevant to the planning of the work of the component auditor:

- *The ethical requirements that are relevant to the group audit and, in particular, the independence requirements, for example, where the group auditor is prohibited by law or regulation from using internal auditors to provide direct assistance, it is relevant for the group auditor to consider whether the prohibition also extends to*

---

[15] *ISA (UK and Ireland) 610 (Revised June 2013), Using the Work of Internal Auditors*, paragraphs 15-16 ~~9~~.

component auditors and, if so, to address this in the communication to the component auditors.[16]

...

Matters that are relevant to the conduct of the work of the component auditor:

- ...
- The findings of the internal audit function, based on work performed on controls at or relevant to components...

[16] ISA 610 *(Revised June 2013)*, Using the Work of Internal Auditors, *paragraph A31. The use of internal auditors to provide direct assistance is prohibited in an audit conducted in accordance with ISAs (UK and Ireland). For a group audit this prohibition extends to the work of any component auditor which is relied upon by the group auditor, including for overseas components – see ISA (UK and Ireland) 610 (Revised June 2013), paragraph 5-1.*

International Standard on Auditing (UK and Ireland) 620

Using the work of an auditor's expert

(Effective for audits of financial statements for periods ending on or after 15 December 2010)

Contents

International Standard on Auditing (UK and Ireland) (ISA (UK and Ireland)) 620, "Using the Work of an Auditor's Expert" should be read in conjunction with ISA (UK and Ireland) 200, "Overall Objectives of the Independent Auditor and the Conduct of an Audit in Accordance with International Standards on Auditing (UK and Ireland)."

Introduction

Scope of this ISA (UK and Ireland)

This International Standard on Auditing (UK and Ireland) (ISA (UK and Ireland)) **1** deals with the auditor's responsibilities relating to the work of an individual or organization in a field of expertise other than accounting or auditing, when that work is used to assist the auditor in obtaining sufficient appropriate audit evidence.

This ISA (UK and Ireland) does not deal with: **2**

(a) Situations where the engagement team includes a member, or consults an individual or organization, with expertise in a specialized area of accounting or auditing, which are dealt with in ISA (UK and Ireland) 220;[1] or
(b) The auditor's use of the work of an individual or organization possessing expertise in a field other than accounting or auditing, whose work in that field is used by the entity to assist the entity in preparing the financial statements (a management's expert), which is dealt with in ISA (UK and Ireland) 500.[2]

The Auditor's Responsibility for the Audit Opinion

The auditor has sole responsibility for the audit opinion expressed, and that **3** responsibility is not reduced by the auditor's use of the work of an auditor's expert. Nonetheless, if the auditor using the work of an auditor's expert, having followed this ISA (UK and Ireland), concludes that the work of that expert is adequate for the auditor's purposes, the auditor may accept that expert's findings or conclusions in the expert's field as appropriate audit evidence.

Effective Date

This ISA (UK and Ireland) is effective for audits of financial statements for periods **4** ending on or after 15 December 2010.

Objectives

The objectives of the auditor are: **5**

(a) To determine whether to use the work of an auditor's expert; and
(b) If using the work of an auditor's expert, to determine whether that work is adequate for the auditor's purposes.

Definitions

For purposes of the ISAs (UK and Ireland), the following terms have the meanings **6** attributed below:

(a) Auditor's expert – An individual or organization possessing expertise in a field other than accounting or auditing, whose work in that field is used by the auditor to assist the auditor in obtaining sufficient appropriate audit evidence.

---

[1] *ISA (UK and Ireland) 220, "Quality Control for an Audit of Financial Statements," paragraphs A10, A20-A22.*

[2] *ISA (UK and Ireland) 500, "Audit Evidence," paragraphs A34-A48.*

An auditor's expert may be either an auditor's internal expert (who is a partner[3] or staff, including temporary staff, of the auditor's firm or a network firm), or an auditor's external expert. (Ref: Para. A1-A3)

(b) Expertise – Skills, knowledge and experience in a particular field.

(c) Management's expert – An individual or organization possessing expertise in a field other than accounting or auditing, whose work in that field is used by the entity to assist the entity in preparing the financial statements.

Requirements

Determining the Need for an Auditor's Expert

7 If expertise in a field other than accounting or auditing is necessary to obtain sufficient appropriate audit evidence, the auditor shall determine whether to use the work of an auditor's expert. (Ref: Para. A4-A9)

Nature, Timing and Extent of Audit Procedures

8 The nature, timing and extent of the auditor's procedures with respect to the requirements in paragraphs 9-13 of this ISA (UK and Ireland) will vary depending on the circumstances. In determining the nature, timing and extent of those procedures, the auditor shall consider matters including: (Ref: Para. A10)

(a) The nature of the matter to which that expert's work relates;

(b) The risks of material misstatement in the matter to which that expert's work relates;

(c) The significance of that expert's work in the context of the audit;

(d) The auditor's knowledge of and experience with previous work performed by that expert; and

(e) Whether that expert is subject to the auditor's firm's quality control policies and procedures. (Ref: Para. A11-A13)

The Competence, Capabilities and Objectivity of the Auditor's Expert

9 The auditor shall evaluate whether the auditor's expert has the necessary competence, capabilities and objectivity for the auditor's purposes. In the case of an auditor's external expert, the evaluation of objectivity shall include inquiry regarding interests and relationships that may create a threat to that expert's objectivity. (Ref: Para. A14-A20)

Obtaining an Understanding of the Field of Expertise of the Auditor's Expert

10 The auditor shall obtain a sufficient understanding of the field of expertise of the auditor's expert to enable the auditor to: (Ref: Para. A21-A22)

(a) Determine the nature, scope and objectives of that expert's work for the auditor's purposes; and

(b) Evaluate the adequacy of that work for the auditor's purposes.

---

[3] *"Partner" and "firm" should be read as referring to their public sector equivalents where relevant.*

Agreement with the Auditor's Expert

The auditor shall agree, in writing when appropriate, on the following matters with **11**
the auditor's expert: (Ref: Para. A23-A26)

(a) The nature, scope and objectives of that expert's work; (Ref: Para. A27)
(b) The respective roles and responsibilities of the auditor and that expert; (Ref: Para. A28-A29)
(c) The nature, timing and extent of communication between the auditor and that expert, including the form of any report to be provided by that expert; and (Ref: Para. A30)
(d) The need for the auditor's expert to observe confidentiality requirements. (Ref: Para. A31)

Evaluating the Adequacy of the Auditor's Expert's Work

The auditor shall evaluate the adequacy of the auditor's expert's work for the **12**
auditor's purposes, including: (Ref: Para. A32)

(a) The relevance and reasonableness of that expert's findings or conclusions, and their consistency with other audit evidence; (Ref: Para. A33-A34)
(b) If that expert's work involves use of significant assumptions and methods, the relevance and reasonableness of those assumptions and methods in the circumstances; and (Ref: Para. A35-A37)
(c) If that expert's work involves the use of source data that is significant to that expert's work, the relevance, completeness, and accuracy of that source data. (Ref: Para. A38-A39)

If the auditor determines that the work of the auditor's expert is not adequate for the **13**
auditor's purposes, the auditor shall: (Ref: Para. A40)

(a) Agree with that expert on the nature and extent of further work to be performed by that expert; or
(b) Perform additional audit procedures appropriate to the circumstances.

Reference to the Auditor's Expert in the Auditor's Report

The auditor shall not refer to the work of an auditor's expert in an auditor's report **14**
containing an unmodified opinion unless required by law or regulation to do so. If
such reference is required by law or regulation, the auditor shall indicate in the
auditor's report that the reference does not reduce the auditor's responsibility for the
auditor's opinion. (Ref: Para. A41)

If the auditor makes reference to the work of an auditor's expert in the auditor's **15**
report because such reference is relevant to an understanding of a modification to the
auditor's opinion, the auditor shall indicate in the auditor's report that such reference does not reduce the auditor's responsibility for that opinion. (Ref: Para. A42)

***

A8   In other cases, however, the auditor may determine that it is necessary, or may choose, to use an auditor's expert to assist in obtaining sufficient appropriate audit evidence. Considerations when deciding whether to use an auditor's expert may include:

- Whether management[4a] has used a management's expert in preparing the financial statements (see paragraph A9).
- The nature and significance of the matter, including its complexity.
- The risks of material misstatement in the matter.
- The expected nature of procedures to respond to identified risks, including: the auditor's knowledge of and experience with the work of experts in relation to such matters; and the availability of alternative sources of audit evidence.

A9   When management has used a management's expert in preparing the financial statements, the auditor's decision on whether to use an auditor's expert may also be influenced by such factors as:

- The nature, scope and objectives of the management's expert's work.
- Whether the management's expert is employed by the entity, or is a party engaged by it to provide relevant services.
- The extent to which management can exercise control or influence over the work of the management's expert.
- The management's expert's competence and capabilities.
- Whether the management's expert is subject to technical performance standards or other professional or industry requirements
- Any controls within the entity over the management's expert's work.

ISA (UK and Ireland) 500[8] includes requirements and guidance regarding the effect of the competence, capabilities and objectivity of management's experts on the reliability of audit evidence.

Nature, Timing and Extent of Audit Procedures (Ref: Para. 8)

A10   The nature, timing and extent of audit procedures with respect to the requirements in paragraphs 9-13 of this ISA (UK and Ireland) will vary depending on the circumstances. For example, the following factors may suggest the need for different or more extensive procedures than would otherwise be the case:

- The work of the auditor's expert relates to a significant matter that involves subjective and complex judgments.
- The auditor has not previously used the work of the auditor's expert, and has no prior knowledge of that expert's competence, capabilities and objectivity.
- The auditor's expert is performing procedures that are integral to the audit, rather than being consulted to provide advice on an individual matter.
- The expert is an auditor's external expert and is not, therefore, subject to the firm's quality control policies and procedures.

The Auditor's Firm's Quality Control Policies and Procedures (Ref: Para. 8(e))

A11   An auditor's internal expert may be a partner or staff, including temporary staff, of the auditor's firm, and therefore subject to the quality control policies and

---

[8] *ISA (UK and Ireland) 500, paragraph 8.*

procedures of that firm in accordance with ISQC (UK and Ireland) 1[9] or national requirements that are at least as demanding.[10] Alternatively, an auditor's internal expert may be a partner or staff, including temporary staff, of a network firm, which may share common quality control policies and procedures with the auditor's firm.

An auditor's external expert is not a member of the engagement team and is not subject to quality control policies and procedures in accordance with ISQC (UK and Ireland) 1.[11] In some jurisdictions, however, law or regulation may require that an auditor's external expert be treated as a member of the engagement team, and may therefore be subject to relevant ethical requirements, including those pertaining to independence, and other professional requirements, as determined by that law or regulation.   **A12**

Engagement teams are entitled to rely on the firm's system of quality control, unless information provided by the firm or other parties suggests otherwise.[12] The extent of that reliance will vary with the circumstances, and may affect the nature, timing and extent of the auditor's procedures with respect to such matters as: **A13**

- Competence and capabilities, through recruitment and training programs.
- Objectivity. Auditor's internal experts are subject to relevant ethical requirements, including those pertaining to independence.
- The auditor's evaluation of the adequacy of the auditor's expert's work. For example, the firm's training programs may provide auditor's internal experts with an appropriate understanding of the interrelationship of their expertise with the audit process. Reliance on such training and other firm processes, such as protocols for scoping the work of auditor's internal experts, may affect the nature, timing and extent of the auditor's procedures to evaluate the adequacy of the auditor's expert's work.
- Adherence to regulatory and legal requirements, through monitoring processes.
- Agreement with the auditor's expert.

Such reliance does not reduce the auditor's responsibility to meet the requirements of this ISA (UK and Ireland).

The Competence, Capabilities and Objectivity of the Auditor's Expert (Ref: Para. 9)

The competence, capabilities and objectivity of an auditor's expert are factors that significantly affect whether the work of the auditor's expert will be adequate for the auditor's purposes. Competence relates to the nature and level of expertise of the auditor's expert. Capability relates to the ability of the auditor's expert to exercise that competence in the circumstances of the engagement. Factors that influence capability may include, for example, geographic location, and the availability of time and resources. Objectivity relates to the possible effects that bias, conflict of interest, or the influence of others may have on the professional or business judgment of the auditor's expert.   **A14**

---

[9] ISQC (UK and Ireland) 1, "*Quality Control for Firms that Perform Audits and Reviews of Financial Statements, and Other Assurance and Related Services Engagements,*" *paragraph 12(f).*

[10] *ISA (UK and Ireland) 220, paragraph 2.*

[11] *ISQC (UK and Ireland) 1, paragraph 12(f).*

[12] *ISA (UK and Ireland) 220, paragraph 4.*

A15   Information regarding the competence, capabilities and objectivity of an auditor's expert may come from a variety of sources, such as:

- Personal experience with previous work of that expert.
- Discussions with that expert.
- Discussions with other auditors or others who are familiar with that expert's work.
- Knowledge of that expert's qualifications, membership of a professional body or industry association, license to practice, or other forms of external recognition.
- Published papers or books written by that expert.
- The auditor's firm's quality control policies and procedures (see paragraphs A11-A13).

A16   Matters relevant to evaluating the competence, capabilities and objectivity of the auditor's expert include whether that expert's work is subject to technical performance standards or other professional or industry requirements, for example, ethical standards and other membership requirements of a professional body or industry association, accreditation standards of a licensing body, or requirements imposed by law or regulation.

A17   Other matters that may be relevant include:

- The relevance of the auditor's expert's competence to the matter for which that expert's work will be used, including any areas of specialty within that expert's field. For example, a particular actuary may specialize in property and casualty insurance, but have limited expertise regarding pension calculations.
- The auditor's expert's competence with respect to relevant accounting and auditing requirements, for example, knowledge of assumptions and methods, including models where applicable, that are consistent with the applicable financial reporting framework.
- Whether unexpected events, changes in conditions, or the audit evidence obtained from the results of audit procedures indicate that it may be necessary to reconsider the initial evaluation of the competence, capabilities and objectivity of the auditor's expert as the audit progresses.

A18   A broad range of circumstances may threaten objectivity, for example, self-interest threats, advocacy threats, familiarity threats, self-review threats, and intimidation threats. Safeguards may eliminate or reduce such threats, and may be created by external structures (for example, the auditor's expert's profession, legislation or regulation), or by the auditor's expert's work environment (for example, quality control policies and procedures). There may also be safeguards specific to the audit engagement.

A19   The evaluation of the significance of threats to objectivity and of whether there is a need for safeguards may depend upon the role of the auditor's expert and the significance of the expert's work in the context of the audit. There may be some circumstances in which safeguards cannot reduce threats to an acceptable level, for example, if a proposed auditor's expert is an individual who has played a significant role in preparing the information that is being audited, that is, if the auditor's expert is a management's expert.

A20   When evaluating the objectivity of an auditor's external expert, it may be relevant to:

(a) Inquire of the entity about any known interests or relationships that the entity has with the auditor's external expert that may affect that expert's objectivity.

(b) Discuss with that expert any applicable safeguards, including any professional requirements that apply to that expert; and evaluate whether the safeguards are adequate to reduce threats to an acceptable level. Interests and relationships that it may be relevant to discuss with the auditor's expert include:

- Financial interests.
- Business and personal relationships.
- Provision of other services by the expert, including by the organization in the case of an external expert that is an organization.

In some cases, it may also be appropriate for the auditor to obtain a written representation from the auditor's external expert about any interests or relationships with the entity of which that expert is aware.

Obtaining an Understanding of the Field of Expertise of the Auditor's Expert (Ref: Para. 10)

The auditor may obtain an understanding of the auditor's expert's field of expertise through the means described in paragraph A7, or through discussion with that expert. **A21**

Aspects of the auditor's expert's field relevant to the auditor's understanding may include: **A22**

- Whether that expert's field has areas of specialty within it that are relevant to the audit (see paragraph A17).
- Whether any professional or other standards, and regulatory or legal requirements apply.
- What assumptions and methods, including models where applicable, are used by the auditor's expert, and whether they are generally accepted within that expert's field and appropriate for financial reporting purposes.
- The nature of internal and external data or information the auditor's expert uses.

Agreement with the Auditor's Expert (Ref: Para. 11)

The nature, scope and objectives of the auditor's expert's work may vary considerably with the circumstances, as may the respective roles and responsibilities of the auditor and the auditor's expert, and the nature, timing and extent of communication between the auditor and the auditor's expert. It is therefore required that these matters are agreed between the auditor and the auditor's expert regardless of whether the expert is an auditor's external expert or an auditor's internal expert. **A23**

The matters noted in paragraph 8 may affect the level of detail and formality of the agreement between the auditor and the auditor's expert, including whether it is appropriate that the agreement be in writing. For example, the following factors may suggest the need for more a detailed agreement than would otherwise be the case, or for the agreement to be set out in writing: **A24**

- The auditor's expert will have access to sensitive or confidential entity information.
- The respective roles or responsibilities of the auditor and the auditor's expert are different from those normally expected.
- Multi-jurisdictional legal or regulatory requirements apply.
- The matter to which the auditor's expert's work relates is highly complex.
- The auditor has not previously used work performed by that expert.
- The greater the extent of the auditor's expert's work, and its significance in the context of the audit.

A25   The agreement between the auditor and an auditor's external expert is often in the form of an engagement letter. The Appendix lists matters that the auditor may consider for inclusion in such an engagement letter, or in any other form of agreement with an auditor's external expert.

A26   When there is no written agreement between the auditor and the auditor's expert, evidence of the agreement may be included in, for example:

- Planning memoranda, or related working papers such as the audit program.
- The policies and procedures of the auditor's firm. In the case of an auditor's internal expert, the established policies and procedures to which that expert is subject may include particular policies and procedures in relation to that expert's work. The extent of documentation in the auditor's working papers depends on the nature of such policies and procedures. For example, no documentation may be required in the auditor's working papers if the auditor's firm has detailed protocols covering the circumstances in which the work of such an expert is used.

Nature, Scope and Objectives of Work (Ref: Para. 11(a))

A27   It may often be relevant when agreeing on the nature, scope and objectives of the auditor's expert's work to include discussion of any relevant technical performance standards or other professional or industry requirements that the expert will follow.

Respective Roles and Responsibilities (Ref: Para. 11(b))

A28   Agreement on the respective roles and responsibilities of the auditor and the auditor's expert may include:

- Whether the auditor or the auditor's expert will perform detailed testing of source data.
- Consent for the auditor to discuss the auditor's expert's findings or conclusions with the entity and others, and to include details of that expert's findings or conclusions in the basis for a modified opinion in the auditor's report, if necessary (see paragraph A42).
- Any agreement to inform the auditor's expert of the auditor's conclusions concerning that expert's work.

Working Papers

A29   Agreement on the respective roles and responsibilities of the auditor and the auditor's expert may also include agreement about access to, and retention of, each other's working papers. When the auditor's expert is a member of the engagement team, that expert's working papers form part of the audit documentation. Subject to any agreement to the contrary, auditor's external experts' working papers are their own and do not form part of the audit documentation.

Communication (Ref: Para. 11(c))

A30   Effective two-way communication facilitates the proper integration of the nature, timing and extent of the auditor's expert's procedures with other work on the audit, and appropriate modification of the auditor's expert's objectives during the course of the audit. For example, when the work of the auditor's expert relates to the auditor's conclusions regarding a significant risk, both a formal written report at the conclusion of that expert's work, and oral reports as the work progresses, may be appropriate. Identification of specific partners or staff who will liaise with the auditor's expert, and procedures for communication between that expert and the entity, assists timely and effective communication, particularly on larger engagements.

Confidentiality (Ref: Para. 11(d))

It is necessary for the confidentiality provisions of relevant ethical requirements that apply to the auditor also to apply to the auditor's expert. Additional requirements may be imposed by law or regulation. The entity may also have requested that specific confidentiality provisions be agreed with auditor's external experts. **A31**

Evaluating the Adequacy of the Auditor's Expert's Work (Ref: Para. 12)

The auditor's evaluation of the auditor's expert's competence, capabilities and objectivity, the auditor's familiarity with the auditor's expert's field of expertise, and the nature of the work performed by the auditor's expert affect the nature, timing and extent of audit procedures to evaluate the adequacy of that expert's work for the auditor's purposes. **A32**

The Findings and Conclusions of the Auditor's Expert (Ref: Para. 12(a))

Specific procedures to evaluate the adequacy of the auditor's expert's work for the auditor's purposes may include: **A33**

- Inquiries of the auditor's expert.
- Reviewing the auditor's expert's working papers and reports.
- Corroborative procedures, such as:
  - Observing the auditor's expert's work;
  - Examining published data, such as statistical reports from reputable, authoritative sources;
  - Confirming relevant matters with third parties;
  - Performing detailed analytical procedures; and
  - Reperforming calculations.
- Discussion with another expert with relevant expertise when, for example, the findings or conclusions of the auditor's expert are not consistent with other audit evidence.
- Discussing the auditor's expert's report with management.

Relevant factors when evaluating the relevance and reasonableness of the findings or conclusions of the auditor's expert, whether in a report or other form, may include whether they are: **A34**

- Presented in a manner that is consistent with any standards of the auditor's expert's profession or industry;
- Clearly expressed, including reference to the objectives agreed with the auditor, the scope of the work performed and standards applied;
- Based on an appropriate period and take into account subsequent events, where relevant;
- Subject to any reservation, limitation or restriction on use, and if so, whether this has implications for the auditor; and
- Based on appropriate consideration of errors or deviations encountered by the auditor's expert.

Assumptions, Methods and Source Data

Assumptions and Methods (Ref: Para. 12(b))

A35   When the auditor's expert's work is to evaluate underlying assumptions and methods, including models where applicable, used by management in developing an accounting estimate, the auditor's procedures are likely to be primarily directed to evaluating whether the auditor's expert has adequately reviewed those assumptions and methods. When the auditor's expert's work is to develop an auditor's point estimate or an auditor's range for comparison with management's point estimate, the auditor's procedures may be primarily directed to evaluating the assumptions and methods, including models where appropriate, used by the auditor's expert.

A36   ISA (UK and Ireland) 540[13] discusses the assumptions and methods used by management in making accounting estimates, including the use in some cases of highly specialized, entity-developed models. Although that discussion is written in the context of the auditor obtaining sufficient appropriate audit evidence regarding management's assumptions and methods, it may also assist the auditor when evaluating an auditor's expert's assumptions and methods.

A37   When an auditor's expert's work involves the use of significant assumptions and methods, factors relevant to the auditor's evaluation of those assumptions and methods include whether they are:

- Generally accepted within the auditor's expert's field;
- Consistent with the requirements of the applicable financial reporting framework;
- Dependent on the use of specialized models; and
- Consistent with those of management, and if not, the reason for, and effects of, the differences.

Source Data Used by the Auditor's Expert (Ref: Para. 12(c))

A38   When an auditor's expert's work involves the use of source data that is significant to that expert's work, procedures such as the following may be used to test that data:

- Verifying the origin of the data, including obtaining an understanding of, and where applicable testing, the internal controls over the data and, where relevant, its transmission to the expert.
- Reviewing the data for completeness and internal consistency.

A39   In many cases, the auditor may test source data. However, in other cases, when the nature of the source data used by an auditor's expert is highly technical in relation to the expert's field, that expert may test the source data. If the auditor's expert has tested the source data, inquiry of that expert by the auditor, or supervision or review of that expert's tests may be an appropriate way for the auditor to evaluate that data's relevance, completeness, and accuracy.

Inadequate Work (Ref: Para. 13)

A40   If the auditor concludes that the work of the auditor's expert is not adequate for the auditor's purposes and the auditor cannot resolve the matter through the additional audit procedures required by paragraph 13, which may involve further work being performed by both the expert and the auditor, or include employing or engaging

---

[13] *ISA (UK and Ireland) 540, "Auditing Accounting Estimates, Including Fair Value Accounting Estimates, and Related Disclosures," paragraphs 8, 13 and 15.*

another expert, it may be necessary to express a modified opinion in the auditor's report in accordance with ISA (UK and Ireland) 705 because the auditor has not obtained sufficient appropriate audit evidence.[14]

Reference to the Auditor's Expert in the Auditor's Report (Ref: Para. 14-15)

In some cases, law or regulation may require a reference to the work of an auditor's expert, for example, for the purposes of transparency in the public sector.   **A41**

It may be appropriate in some circumstances to refer to the auditor's expert in an auditor's report containing a modified opinion, to explain the nature of the modification. In such circumstances, the auditor may need the permission of the auditor's expert before making such a reference.   **A42**

Appendix   (Ref: Para. A25)

Considerations for Agreement between the Auditor and an Auditor's External Expert

This Appendix lists matters that the auditor may consider for inclusion in any agreement with an auditor's external expert. The following list is illustrative and is not exhaustive; it is intended only to be a guide that may be used in conjunction with the considerations outlined in this ISA (UK and Ireland). Whether to include particular matters in the agreement depends on the circumstances of the engagement. The list may also be of assistance in considering the matters to be included in an agreement with an auditor's internal expert.

Nature, Scope and Objectives of the Auditor's External Expert's Work

- The nature and scope of the procedures to be performed by the auditor's external expert.
- The objectives of the auditor's external expert's work in the context of materiality and risk considerations concerning the matter to which the auditor's external expert's work relates, and, when relevant, the applicable financial reporting framework.
- Any relevant technical performance standards or other professional or industry requirements the auditor's external expert will follow.
- The assumptions and methods, including models where applicable, the auditor's external expert will use, and their authority.
- The effective date of, or when applicable the testing period for, the subject matter of the auditor's external expert's work, and requirements regarding subsequent events.

The Respective Roles and Responsibilities of the Auditor and the Auditor's External Expert

- Relevant auditing and accounting standards, and relevant regulatory or legal requirements.
- The auditor's external expert's consent to the auditor's intended use of that expert's report, including any reference to it, or disclosure of it, to others, for

---

[14] *ISA (UK and Ireland) 705, "Modifications to the Opinion in the Independent Auditor's Report," paragraph 6(b).*

example reference to it in the basis for a modified opinion in the auditor's report, if necessary, or disclosure of it to management or an audit committee.

- The nature and extent of the auditor's review of the auditor's external expert's work.
- Whether the auditor or the auditor's external expert will test source data.
- The auditor's external expert's access to the entity's records, files, personnel and to experts engaged by the entity.
- Procedures for communication between the auditor's external expert and the entity.
- The auditor's and the auditor's external expert's access to each other's working papers.
- Ownership and control of working papers during and after the engagement, including any file retention requirements.
- The auditor's external expert's responsibility to perform work with due skill and care.
- The auditor's external expert's competence and capability to perform the work.
- The expectation that the auditor's external expert will use all knowledge that expert has that is relevant to the audit or, if not, will inform the auditor.
- Any restriction on the auditor's external expert's association with the auditor's report.
- Any agreement to inform the auditor's external expert of the auditor's conclusions concerning that expert's work.

Communications and Reporting

- Methods and frequency of communications, including:
  - How the auditor's external expert's findings or conclusions will be reported (written report, oral report, ongoing input to the engagement team, for example.).
  - Identification of specific persons within the engagement team who will liaise with the auditor's external expert.
- When the auditor's external expert will complete the work and report findings or conclusions to the auditor.
- The auditor's external expert's responsibility to communicate promptly any potential delay in completing the work, and any potential reservation or limitation on that expert's findings or conclusions.
- The auditor's external expert's responsibility to communicate promptly instances in which the entity restricts that expert's access to records, files, personnel or experts engaged by the entity.
- The auditor's external expert's responsibility to communicate to the auditor all information that expert believes may be relevant to the audit, including any changes in circumstances previously communicated.
- The auditor's external expert's responsibility to communicate circumstances that may create threats to that expert's objectivity, and any relevant safeguards that may eliminate or reduce such threats to an acceptable level.

Confidentiality

- The need for the auditor's expert to observe confidentiality requirements, including:
  - The confidentiality provisions of relevant ethical requirements that apply to the auditor.
  - Additional requirements that may be imposed by law or regulation, if any.
  - Specific confidentiality provisions requested by the entity, if any.

International Standard on Auditing (UK and Ireland) 700 (Revised June 2013)
The independent auditor's report on financial statements

*(Effective for audits of financial statements for periods
commencing on or after 1 October 2012)*

Contents

International Standard on Auditing (UK and Ireland) (ISA (UK and Ireland)
700, "The Independent Auditor's Report on Financial Statements (Revised
June 2013)" should be read in conjunction with ISA (UK and Ireland) 200,
"Overall Objectives of the Independent Auditor and the Conduct of an Audit
in Accordance with International Standards on Auditing (UK and Ireland)."

*NOTE: The FRC has not at this time adopted ISA 700 "Forming an Opinion and
Reporting on Financial Statements". The FRC has instead issued ISA (UK and
Ireland) 700 "The Independent Auditor's Report on Financial Statements (Revised
June 2013)". The main effect of this is that the form of auditor's reports may not be
exactly aligned with the precise format required by ISA 700 issued by the IAASB.
However, ISA (UK and Ireland) 700 (Revised June 2013) has been drafted such
that compliance with it will not preclude the auditor from being able to assert
compliance with the ISAs issued by the IAASB.*

Introduction

Scope of this ISA (UK and Ireland)

1   This International Standard on Auditing (UK and Ireland) (ISA (UK and Ireland)) establishes standards and provides guidance on the form and content of the auditor's report issued as a result of an audit performed by an independent auditor of the financial statements.

2   This ISA (UK and Ireland) is written to address both "true and fair frameworks[1]" and "compliance frameworks". A "true and fair framework" is one that requires compliance with the framework but which acknowledges that to achieve a true and fair view:

(a) It may be necessary to provide disclosures additional to those specifically required by the framework[2]; and

(b) It may be necessary to depart from a requirement of the framework[3].

A "compliance framework" is one that requires compliance with the framework and does not contain the acknowledgements in (a) or (b) above.

3   Illustrative examples of auditor's reports tailored for use with audits conducted in accordance with ISAs (UK and Ireland) are provided in compendia Bulletins issued by the FRC[4]. Illustrative examples of auditor's reports on regulatory returns are provided in various Practice Notes issued by the FRC.

4   ISA (UK and Ireland) 705 and ISA (UK and Ireland) 706 deal with how the form and content of the auditor's report are affected when the auditor expresses a modified opinion or includes an Emphasis of Matter paragraph or an Other Matter paragraph in the auditor's report.

Status of this ISA (UK and Ireland)

5   Paragraph 43 of ISA 700, "Forming an opinion and reporting on financial statements," as issued by the IAASB specifies the minimum elements of auditor's reports where the regulation of a specific jurisdiction specify wording of the auditor's report. Reports prepared in accordance with ISA (UK and Ireland) 700 contain those minimum elements and consequently compliance with this ISA

---

[1] *True and fair frameworks are sometimes referred to as "fair presentation frameworks".*

[2] *In the IFRS Framework this is acknowledged in paragraph 17(c) of IAS 1. In UK GAAP this is acknowledged in Sections 396(4) and 404(4) of the Companies Act 2006. Under Generally Accepted Accounting Practice in Ireland this is acknowledged, for example, in Section 3(c) of the Companies (Amendment) Act 1986 and Regulation 14 of the European Communities (Companies: Group Accounts) Regulations 1992.*

[3] *This is sometimes referred to as the "true and fair override". In the IFRS Framework this is acknowledged in paragraph 19 of IAS 1. In UK GAAP this is acknowledged in Sections 396(5) and 404(5) of the Companies Act 2006. Under Generally Accepted Accounting Practice in Ireland this is acknowledged, for example, in Section 3(d) of the Companies (Amendment) Act 1986 and Regulation 14(3) of the European Communities (Companies: Group Accounts) Regulations 1992.*

[4] *At the date of publication of this ISA (UK and Ireland), Bulletins 2010/2 (Revised) "Compendium of Illustrative Auditor's Reports on United Kingdom Private Sector Financial Statements for periods ended on or after 15 December 2010" and 1(I) "Compendium of Illustrative Auditor's Reports on Irish Financial Statements" were the current compendia Bulletins.*

(UK and Ireland) does not preclude the auditor from being able to assert compliance with International Standards on Auditing issued by the IAASB.

Effective Date

This ISA (UK and Ireland) is effective for audits of financial statements for periods commencing on or after 1 October 2012. Except for the requirements in paragraphs 22A and 22B, earlier adoption is permitted.

6

Objectives

The objectives of the auditor are to:

7

(a) Form an opinion on the financial statements based on an evaluation of the conclusions drawn from the audit evidence obtained; and

(b) Express clearly that opinion through a written report that also describes the basis for the opinion.

Requirements

Forming an Opinion on the Financial Statements

The auditor's report on the financial statements shall contain a clear written expression of opinion on the financial statements taken as a whole, based on the auditor evaluating the conclusions drawn from the audit evidence obtained, including evaluating whether:

8

(a) Sufficient appropriate audit evidence as to whether the financial statements as a whole are free from material misstatement, whether due to fraud or error has been obtained;

(b) Uncorrected misstatements are material, individually or in aggregate. This evaluation shall include consideration of the qualitative aspects of the entity's accounting practices, including indicators of possible bias in management's judgments; (Ref: Para. A1-A3)

(c) In respect of a true and fair framework, the financial statements, including the related notes, give a true and fair view; and

(d) In respect of all frameworks the financial statements have been prepared in all material respects in accordance with the framework, including the requirements of applicable law.

In particular, the auditor shall evaluate whether:

9

(a) The financial statements adequately refer to or describe the relevant financial reporting framework;

(b) The financial statements adequately disclose the significant accounting policies selected and applied;

(c) The accounting policies selected and applied are consistent with the applicable financial reporting framework, and are appropriate in the circumstances;

(d) Accounting estimates are reasonable;

(e) The information presented in the financial statements is relevant, reliable, comparable and understandable;

(f) The financial statements provide adequate disclosures to enable the intended users to understand the effect of material transactions and events on the information conveyed in the financial statements; and

(g) The terminology used in the financial statements, including the title of each financial statement, is appropriate.

10   With respect to compliance frameworks an unqualified opinion on the financial statements shall be expressed only when the auditor concludes that they have been prepared in accordance with the identified financial reporting framework, including the requirements of applicable law.

11   With respect to true and fair frameworks an unqualified opinion on the financial statements shall be expressed only when the auditor concludes that they have been prepared in accordance with the identified financial reporting framework, including the requirements of applicable law, and the financial statements give a true and fair view.

Auditor's Report

Title

12   The auditor's report shall have an appropriate title. (Ref: Para A4)

Addressee

13   The auditor's report shall be appropriately addressed as required by the circumstances of the engagement. (Ref: Para A5)

Introductory Paragraph

14   The auditor's report shall identify the financial statements of the entity that have been audited, including the date of, and period covered by, the financial statements.

Respective Responsibilities of Those Charged with Governance and Auditors

15   The auditor's report shall include a statement that those charged with governance are responsible for the preparation of the financial statements and a statement that the responsibility of the auditor is to audit and express an opinion on the financial statements in accordance with applicable legal requirements and International Standards on Auditing (UK and Ireland). The report shall also state that those standards require the auditor to comply with the APB's Ethical Standards for Auditors. (Ref: Para A6 – A7)

Description of the Generic Scope of an Audit

16   The auditor's report shall include a description of the generic scope of an audit by either:

(a) Cross referring to the applicable version of a "Statement of the Scope of an Audit" that is maintained on the FRC's web-site; or

(b) Cross referring to a "Statement of the Scope of an Audit" that is included elsewhere within the Annual Report; or

(c) Including verbatim within the report the following:
"An audit involves obtaining evidence about the amounts and disclosures in the financial statements sufficient to give reasonable assurance that the financial statements are free from material misstatement, whether caused by fraud or error. This includes an assessment of: whether the accounting policies are appropriate to the *[describe nature of entity]* circumstances and have been consistently applied and adequately disclosed; the reasonableness of significant accounting estimates made by *[describe those charged with governance]*; and the overall presentation of the financial statements. In addition, we read all the financial and non-financial information in the *[describe the annual report]* to identify material inconsistencies with the audited financial statements and to identify any information that is apparently materially incorrect based on, or materially inconsistent with, the knowledge acquired by us in the course of performing the audit. If we become aware of any apparent material misstatements or inconsistencies we consider the implications for our report." (Ref: Para A8 – A9)

Opinion on the Financial Statements

The opinion paragraph of the auditor's report shall clearly state the auditor's opinion as required by the relevant financial reporting framework used to prepare the financial statements, including applicable law.

17

When expressing an unqualified opinion on financial statements prepared in accordance with a true and fair framework the opinion paragraph shall clearly state that the financial statements give a true and fair view[5]. It is not sufficient for the auditor to conclude that the financial statements give a true and fair view solely on the basis that the financial statements were prepared in accordance with accounting standards and any other applicable legal requirements. (Ref: Para A10 – A12)

18

Opinion in Respect of an Additional Financial Reporting Framework

When an auditor is engaged to issue an opinion on the compliance of the financial statements with an additional financial reporting framework the second opinion shall be clearly separated from the first opinion on the financial statements, by use of an appropriate heading. (Ref: Para A13)

19

---

[5] *United Kingdom auditor's reports prepared in accordance with section 495(3) of the UK Companies Act 2006 will meet this requirement. Irish auditor's reports prepared in accordance with Section 193(4C) of the Irish Companies Act 1990 and, therefore, expressing an opinion in terms of "true and fair view, in accordance with the relevant financial reporting framework" also meets this requirement. This is supported by recital 10 of EU Directive 2003/51/EC which states "The fundamental requirement that an audit opinion states whether the annual or consolidated accounts give a true and fair view in accordance with the relevant financial reporting framework does not represent a restriction of the scope of that opinion but clarifies the context in which it is expressed".*

Entities that Report on Application of the UK Corporate Governance Code

19A In the case of entities[6] that are required, and those that choose voluntarily, to report on how they have applied the UK Corporate Governance Code, or to explain why they have not, the auditor's report shall:

(a) Describe those assessed risks of material misstatement that were identified by the auditor and which had the greatest effect on: the overall audit strategy; the allocation of resources in the audit; and directing the efforts of the engagement team;

(b) Provide an explanation of how the auditor applied the concept of materiality in planning and performing the audit. Such explanation shall specify the threshold used by the auditor as being materiality for the financial statements as a whole[7]; and

(c) Provide an overview of the scope of the audit[8], including an explanation of how such scope addressed the assessed risks of material misstatement disclosed in accordance with (a) and was influenced by the auditor's application of materiality disclosed in accordance with (b). (Ref. Para A13A – A13C)

19B In order to be useful to users of the financial statements, the explanations of the matters required to be set out in the auditor's report by paragraph 19A shall be described:

● So as to enable a user to understand their significance in the context of the audit of the financial statements as a whole and not as discrete opinions on separate elements of the financial statements.

● In a way that enables them to be related directly to the specific circumstances of the audited entity and are not, therefore, generic or abstract matters expressed in standardised language.

● In a manner that complements the description of significant issues relating to the financial statements, required to be set out in the separate section of the annual report describing the work of the audit committee in discharging its responsibilities[9]. The auditor seeks to coordinate descriptions of overlapping topics addressed in these communications, to avoid duplication of reporting about them, whilst having appropriate regard to the separate responsibilities of the auditor and the board for directly communicating information primarily in their respective domains.

Requirement Specific to Public Sector Entities where an Opinion on Regularity is Given.

20 The auditor shall address other reporting responsibilities in [a] separate section[s] of the auditor's report following the opinion[s] on the financial statements and, where there is one, the opinion on regularity. (Ref: Para A14)

---

[6] *In the UK, these include companies with a Premium listing of equity shares regardless of whether they are incorporated in the UK or elsewhere. In Ireland, these include Irish incorporated companies with a primary or secondary listing of equity shares on the Irish Stock Exchange.*

[7] *As required by paragraph 10 of ISA (UK and Ireland) 320 "Materiality in Planning and Performing an Audit".*

[8] *See also paragraphs 15 and A11 to A15 of ISA (UK and Ireland) 260 "Communication with Those Charged with Governance" and paragraph 49 of ISA (UK and Ireland) 600 "Special considerations – Audits of Group Financial Statements (Including the Work of Component Auditors).*

[9] *In accordance with provision C.3.8 of the UK Corporate Governance Code.*

Opinions on Other Matters

When the auditor addresses other reporting responsibilities within the auditor's report on the financial statements, the opinion arising from such other responsibilities shall be set out in a separate section of the auditor's report following the opinion[s] on the financial statements or, where there is one, the opinion on regularity. (Ref: Para A15 – A16)   **21**

If the auditor is required to report on certain matters by exception the auditor shall describe its responsibilities under the heading "Matters on which we are required to report by exception" and incorporate a suitable conclusion in respect of such matters. (Ref: Para A17 – A18)   **22**

In the case of entities that are required[6], and those that choose voluntarily, to report on how they have applied the UK Corporate Governance Code or to explain why they have not, the auditor shall report by exception if, when reading the other financial and non-financial information included in the annual report, the auditor has identified information that is materially inconsistent with the information in the audited financial statements or is apparently materially incorrect based on, or materially inconsistent with, the knowledge acquired by the auditor in the course of performing the audit or that is otherwise misleading. (Ref: Para A18A)   **22A**

Matters that the auditor shall report on by exception in accordance with paragraph 22A include circumstances where the annual report includes: **22B**

(a) A statement given by the directors that they consider the annual report and accounts taken as a whole is fair, balanced and understandable and provides the information necessary for shareholders to assess the entity's performance, business model and strategy, that is inconsistent with the knowledge acquired by the auditor in the course of performing the audit; or

(b) A section describing the work of the audit committee that does not appropriately address matters communicated by the auditor to the audit committee; or

(c) An explanation, as to why the annual report does not include such a statement or section, that is materially inconsistent with the knowledge acquired by the auditor in the course of performing the audit; or

(d) Other information that, in the auditor's judgment, contains a material inconsistency or a material misstatement of fact.

The auditor shall include a suitable conclusion on these matters in the auditor's report in accordance with paragraph 22 and, if applicable, shall describe why the auditor believes that any such statement, section, explanation or other information is materially inconsistent with the knowledge acquired by the auditor in the course of performing the audit or otherwise contains a material inconsistency or a material misstatement of fact. If a section of the annual report describing the work of the audit committee does not appropriately disclose any matters communicated by the auditor to the audit committee that in the auditor's judgment should have been disclosed, or if the annual report does not contain such a section, the auditor's report shall also include any such information.

Date of Report

23   The date of an auditor's report on a reporting entity's financial statements shall be the date on which the auditor signed the report expressing an opinion on those financial statements. (Ref. Para A19)

24   The auditor shall not sign, and hence date, the report earlier than the date on which all other information contained in a report of which the audited financial statements form a part have been approved by those charged with governance and the auditor has considered all necessary available evidence. (Ref. Para A20 – A23)

Location of Auditor's Office

25   The report shall name the location of the office where the auditor is based.

Auditor's Signature

26   The auditor's report shall state the name of the auditor and be signed and dated. (Ref. Para A24)

***

Application and Other Explanatory Material

Qualitative Aspects of the Entity's Accounting Practices (Ref: Para 8)

A1   Management makes a number of judgments about the amounts and disclosures in the financial statements.

A2   ISA (UK and Ireland) 260 contains a discussion of the qualitative aspects of accounting practices.[10] In considering the qualitative aspects of the entity's accounting practices, the auditor may become aware of possible bias in management's judgments. The auditor may conclude that the cumulative effect of a lack of neutrality, together with the effect of uncorrected misstatements, causes the financial statements as a whole to be materially misstated. Indicators of a lack of neutrality that may affect the auditor's evaluation of whether the financial statements as a whole are materially misstated include the following:

- The selective correction of misstatements brought to management's attention during the audit (e.g., correcting misstatements with the effect of increasing reported earnings, but not correcting misstatements that have the effect of decreasing reported earnings).
- Possible management bias in the making of accounting estimates.

A3   ISA (UK and Ireland) 540 addresses possible management bias in making accounting estimates.[11] Indicators of possible management bias do not constitute misstatements for purposes of drawing conclusions on the reasonableness of individual accounting estimates. They may, however, affect the auditor's

---

[10] *ISA (UK and Ireland) 260, "Communication with Those Charged with Governance," Appendix 2.*

[11] *ISA (UK and Ireland) 540, "Auditing Accounting Estimates, Including Fair Value Accounting Estimates, and Related Disclosures," paragraph 21.*

evaluation of whether the financial statements as a whole are free from material misstatement.

Auditor's Report

Title (Ref: Para 12)

The term "Independent Auditor" is usually used in the title in order to distinguish the auditor's report from reports that might be issued by others, such as by those charged with governance, or from the reports of other auditors who may not have to comply with the APB's Ethical Standards for Auditors.

A4

Addressee (Ref: Para 13)

The Companies Acts[12] require the auditor to report to the company's members because the audit is undertaken on their behalf. Such auditor's reports are, therefore, typically addressed to either the members or the shareholders of the company. The auditor's report on financial statements of other types of reporting entity is addressed to the appropriate person or persons, as defined by statute or by the terms of the individual engagement.

A5

Respective Responsibilities of Those Charged with Governance and Auditors(Ref: Para 15)

An appreciation of the interrelationship between the responsibilities of those who prepare financial statements and those who audit them facilitates an understanding of the nature and context of the opinion expressed by the auditor.

A6

The preparation of financial statements requires those charged with governance to make significant accounting estimates and judgments, as well as to determine the appropriate accounting principles and methods used in preparation of the financial statements. This determination will be made in the context of the financial reporting framework that those charged with governance choose, or are required, to use. In contrast, the auditor's responsibility is to audit the financial statements in order to express an opinion on them.

A7

Description of the Generic Scope of an Audit (Ref: Para 16)

The FRC maintains on its web-site generic descriptions of the scope of an audit of the financial statements of private sector entities[13]. These descriptions address the auditor's responsibilities under ISAs (UK and Ireland).

A8

Where the generic scope of the audit is described within the Annual Report but not in the auditor's report, such description includes the prescribed text set out in paragraph 16 (c). The content of the description of the generic scope of the audit is determined by the auditor regardless of whether it is incorporated into the auditor's report or published as a separate statement elsewhere in the annual report.

A9

---

[12] *In the United Kingdom the Companies Act 2006 establishes this requirement. In Ireland the Companies Acts 1963 to 2006 establish this requirement.*

---

[13] *The web-site reference relevant to the UK is www.frc.org.uk/apb/scope/private.cfm and the web-site reference relevant to Ireland is www.frc.org.uk/audit-scope-ireland.*

Opinion on the Financial Statements (Ref: Para 18)

A10   Although the "true and fair" concept has been central to accounting and auditing practice in the UK and Ireland for many years it is not defined in legislation. In 2008, the Financial Reporting Council published a legal opinion, that it had commissioned, entitled "The true and fair requirement revisited" (The Opinion)[14]. The Opinion confirms the overarching nature of the true and fair requirement to the preparation of financial statements in the United Kingdom, whether they are prepared in accordance with international or national accounting standards[15].

A11   The Opinion states that "The preparation of financial statements is not a mechanical process where compliance with relevant accounting standards will automatically ensure that those financial statements show a true and fair view, or a fair presentation. Such compliance may be highly likely to produce such an outcome; but it does not guarantee it".

A12   To advise the reader of the context in which the auditor's opinion is expressed, the auditor's opinion indicates the financial reporting framework upon which the financial statements are based. The financial reporting framework is normally one of:

   ● "International Financial Reporting Standards (IFRSs) as adopted by the European Union", and the national law that is applicable when using IFRSs and, in the case of consolidated financial statements of publicly traded companies[16], Article 4 of the IAS Regulation (1606/2002/EC); or
   ● "Generally Accepted Accounting Practice in Ireland", which comprises applicable Irish law and accounting standards issued by the Financial Reporting Council (FRC) and promulgated by the Institute of Chartered Accountants in Ireland; or
   ● "UK Generally Accepted Accounting Practice", which comprises applicable UK law and UK Accounting Standards as issued by the FRC.

Opinion in Respect of an Additional Financial Reporting Framework (Ref: Para 19)

A13   The financial statements of some entities may comply with two financial reporting frameworks (for example "IFRSs as issued by the IASB" and "IFRSs as adopted by the European Union" and those charged with governance may engage the auditor to express an opinion in respect of both frameworks. Once the auditor is satisfied that there are no differences between the two financial reporting frameworks that affect the financial statements being reported on, the auditor states a second separate opinion with regard to the other financial reporting framework.

---

[14] *The opinion can be downloaded from the FRC web-site at http://www.frc.org.uk/about/trueandfair.cfm*

[15] *UK and Irish law differ but follow similar principles.*

[16] *A publicly traded company is one whose securities are admitted to trading on a regulated market in any Member State in the European Union.*

Entities that Report on Application of the UK Corporate Governance Code (Ref: Para 19A)

Such assessed risks of material misstatement are likely to have been identified by the auditor in meeting the requirements of ISA (UK and Ireland) 315 "Identifying and assessing the risks of material misstatement through understanding the entity and its environment"[17], including those relating to significant risks. However, the auditor uses its judgment to determine which, if any, of the significant risks and which, if any, of the other identified risks meet the criteria set out in paragraph 19A(a) and are to be described in the auditor's report. If the auditor significantly revises its risk assessment during the audit the auditor considers whether to disclose that fact and the circumstances giving rise to the changed assessment.

A13A

The explanation, of how the auditor applied the concept of materiality in planning and performing the audit, is tailored to the particular circumstances and complexity of the audit and, in addition to specifying the threshold used by the auditor as being materiality for the financial statements as a whole, might include, for example:

A13B

- Materiality level or levels for those classes of transactions, account balances or disclosures where such materiality levels are lower than materiality for the financial statements as a whole (as described in paragraph 10 of ISA (UK and Ireland) 320).
- Performance materiality (as described in paragraph 11 of ISA (UK and Ireland) 320).
- Any significant revisions of materiality thresholds that were made as the audit progressed.
- The threshold used for reporting unadjusted differences to the audit committee.
- Significant qualitative considerations relating to the auditor's evaluation of materiality.

The content of the overview of the scope of the audit is tailored to the particular circumstances of the audit and how the scope was influenced by the auditor's application of materiality and addressed the assessed risks of material misstatement described in the auditor's report. Such a summary might also include, for example:

A13C

- The coverage of revenue, total assets and profit before tax achieved.
- The coverage of revenue, total assets and profit before tax of reportable segments achieved.
- The number of locations visited by the auditor as a proportion of the total number of locations, and the rationale underlying any programme of visits.
- The effect of the group structure on the scope. The audit approach to a group consisting of autonomous subsidiary companies may differ from that applied to one which consists of a number of non-autonomous divisions.
- The nature and extent of the group auditor's involvement in the work of component auditors.

[17] *The relevant section of the ISA (UK and Ireland) is "Identifying and Assessing the Risks of Material Misstatement" (paragraphs 25 to 31).*

Requirement Specific to Public Sector Entities where an Opinion on Regularity is Given (Ref: Para 20)

A14   For the audit of certain public sector entities the audit mandate may require the auditor to express an opinion on regularity[18]. Regularity is the requirement that financial transactions are in accordance with the legislation authorising them.

Opinion on Other Matters (Ref: Para 21 – 22B)

A15   The auditor sets out its opinion[s] on these other reporting responsibilities in [a] separate section[s] of the report in order to clearly distinguish it from the auditor's opinion[s] on the financial statements.

A16   Other reporting responsibilities may be determined by specific statutory requirements applicable to the reporting entity, or, in some circumstances, by the terms of the auditor's engagement[19]. Such matters may be required to be dealt with by either:

(a) a positive statement in the auditor's report; or
(b) by exception.

An example of (a) arises where the auditor of a company is required to state whether, in the auditor's opinion, the information given in the directors' report for the financial year for which the accounts are prepared is consistent with those accounts[20]. An example of (b) arises in the United Kingdom where company legislation requires the auditor of a company to report when a company has not maintained adequate accounting records[21]. An example of (b) arises in Ireland where company legislation requires the auditor to report when the disclosures of directors' remuneration and transactions specified by law are not made[22].

A17   Where the auditor has discharged such responsibilities and has nothing to report in respect of them, the conclusion could be expressed in the form of the following phrase: "We have nothing to report in respect of the following".

A18   Where the auditor expresses a modified conclusion in respect of other reporting responsibilities (including those on which they are required to report by exception) this may give rise to a modification of the auditor's opinion on the financial statements. For example, if adequate accounting records have not been maintained and as a result it proves impracticable for the auditor to obtain sufficient

---

[18] *Guidance for auditors of public sector bodies in the UK and Ireland is given in Practice Note 10 "Audit of Financial Statements of Public Sector Bodies in the United Kingdom (Revised)" and Practice Note 10 (I) "Audit of Central Government Financial Statements in the Republic of Ireland".*

[19] *An example of a reporting responsibility determined by the terms of the auditor's engagement is where the directors of a listed company are required by the rules of a Listing Authority to ensure that the auditor reviews certain statements made by the directors before the annual report is published.*

[20] *In the UK section 496 of the Companies Act 2006 and in Ireland section 15 of Companies (Amendment Act) 1986.*

[21] *Section 498(2) of the Companies Act 2006*

[22] *Section 191(8) of the Companies Act 1963 and section 46 of the Companies Act 1990.*

appropriate evidence concerning material matters in the financial statements, the auditor's report on the financial statements includes a qualified opinion or disclaimer of opinion arising from that limitation.[23]

For entities that apply the UK Corporate Governance Code, the directors are required to give a statement in the annual report that they consider the annual report and accounts taken as a whole is fair, balanced and understandable and provides the information necessary for shareholders to assess the entity's performance, business model and strategy. Such entities are also required to include a separate section of the annual report that describes the work of the audit committee in discharging its responsibilities. This should include, inter alia, the significant issues that the audit committee considered in relation to the financial statements, including appropriate matters considered that were communicated to it by the auditor, and how these issues were addressed.

A18A

Date of Report (Ref: Para 23 – 24)

This informs the reader that the auditor has considered the effect on the financial statements and on the auditor's report of events and transactions of which the auditor became aware and that occurred up to that date.

A19

The auditor is not in a position to form the opinion until the financial statements (and any other information contained in a report of which the audited financial statements form a part) have been approved by those charged with governance and the auditor has completed the assessment of all the evidence the auditor considers necessary for the opinion or opinions to be given in the auditor's report. This assessment includes events occurring up to the date the opinion is expressed. The auditor, therefore, plans the conduct of the audit to take account of the need to ensure, before expressing an opinion on financial statements, that those charged with governance have approved the financial statements and any accompanying other information and that the auditor has completed a sufficient review of post balance sheet events.

A20

The date of the auditor's report is, therefore, the date on which the auditor signs the auditor's report expressing an opinion on the financial statements for distribution with those financial statements, following:

A21

(a) Receipt of the financial statements and accompanying documents in the form approved by those charged with governance for release;
(b) Review of all documents which the auditor is required to consider in addition to the financial statements (for example the directors' report, chairman's statement or other review of an entity's affairs which will accompany the financial statements); and
(c) Completion of all procedures necessary to form an opinion on the financial statements (and any other opinions required by law or regulation) including a review of post balance sheet events,

---

[23] *ISA (UK and Ireland) 705 "Modifications to the opinion in the independent auditor's report" sets out the requirements relating to qualified opinions and disclaimer of opinions on financial statements.*

A22   The form of the financial statements and other information approved by those charged with governance, and considered by the auditor when signing a report expressing the auditor's opinion, may be in the form of final drafts from which printed documents will be prepared. Subsequent production of printed copies of the financial statements and the auditor's report does not constitute the creation of a new document. Copies of the report produced for circulation to shareholders or others may, therefore, reproduce a printed version of the auditor's signature showing the date of actual signature.

A23   If the date on which the auditor signs the report is later than that on which those charged with governance approved the financial statements, the auditor takes such steps as are appropriate:

(a)   To obtain assurance that those charged with governance would have approved the financial statements on that later date (for example, by obtaining confirmation from specified individual members of the Board to whom authority has been delegated for this purpose); and

(b)   To ensure that its procedures for reviewing subsequent events cover the period up to that date.

Auditor's Signature   (Ref: Para 26)

A24   The report is signed in the name of the audit firm, the personal name of the auditor or both, as required by law. In the case of a UK company and certain other entities UK law requires:

(a)   where the auditor is an individual that the report is signed by the individual; or

(b)   where the auditor is a firm that the report is signed by the senior statutory auditor[24] in his or her own name, for and on behalf of the auditor.

In the case of an Irish company and certain other entities Irish law requires:

●   where the auditor is a statutory auditor (a natural person) that the report is signed by that person; or

●   where the auditor is a statutory audit firm:

○   that the report is signed by the statutory auditor designated by the statutory audit firm as being primarily responsible for carrying out the statutory audit on behalf of the audit firm; or

○   in the case of a group audit at least the statutory auditor designated by the statutory audit firm as being primarily responsible for carrying out the statutory audit at the level of the group;

in his or her own name, for and on behalf of, the audit firm[25].

---

[24] *See Bulletin 2008/6 "The "Senior Statutory Auditor" under the United Kingdom Companies Act 2006". That Bulletin at paragraphs 8-10 also explains the meaning of "signing the auditor's report" in a UK context.*

[25] *See Statutory Instrument 220 of 2010.*

International Standard on Auditing (UK and Ireland) 705 (Revised October 2012)

Modifications to the opinion in the independent auditor's report

(Effective for audits of financial statements for periods commencing on or after 1 October 2012)

Contents

International Standard on Auditing (UK and Ireland) (ISA (UK and Ireland)) 705, "Modifications to the Opinion in the Independent Auditor's Report" should be read in conjunction with ISA (UK and Ireland) 200, "Overall Objectives of the Independent Auditor and the Conduct of an Audit in Accordance with International Standards on Auditing (UK and Ireland)."

Introduction

Scope of this ISA (UK and Ireland)

1   This International Standard on Auditing (UK and Ireland) (ISA (UK and Ireland)) deals with the auditor's responsibility to issue an appropriate report in circumstances when, in forming an opinion in accordance with ISA (UK and Ireland) 700,[1] the auditor concludes that a modification to the auditor's opinion on the financial statements is necessary.

Types of Modified Opinions

2   This ISA (UK and Ireland) establishes three types of modified opinions, namely, a qualified opinion, an adverse opinion, and a disclaimer of opinion. The decision regarding which type of modified opinion is appropriate depends upon:

(a)   The nature of the matter giving rise to the modification, that is, whether the financial statements are materially misstated or, in the case of an inability to obtain sufficient appropriate audit evidence, may be materially misstated; and

(b)   The auditor's judgment about the pervasiveness of the effects or possible effects of the matter on the financial statements. (Ref: Para. A1)

Effective Date

3   This ISA (UK and Ireland) is effective for audits of financial statements for periods commencing on or after 1 October 2012. Earlier adoption is permitted.

Objective

4   The objective of the auditor is to express clearly an appropriately modified opinion on the financial statements that is necessary when:

(a)   The auditor concludes, based on the audit evidence obtained, that the financial statements as a whole are not free from material misstatement; or

(b)   The auditor is unable to obtain sufficient appropriate audit evidence to conclude that the financial statements as a whole are free from material misstatement.

Definitions

5   For purposes of the ISAs (UK and Ireland), the following terms have the meanings attributed below:

(a)   Pervasive – A term used, in the context of misstatements, to describe the effects on the financial statements of misstatements or the possible effects on the financial statements of misstatements, if any, that are undetected due to an inability to obtain sufficient appropriate audit evidence. Pervasive effects on the financial statements are those that, in the auditor's judgment:

(i)   Are not confined to specific elements, accounts or items of the financial statements;

(ii)   If so confined, represent or could represent a substantial proportion of the financial statements; or

---

[1]   *ISA (UK and Ireland) 700, "The Auditor's Report on Financial Statements."*

  (iii) In relation to disclosures, are fundamental to users' understanding of the financial statements.

(b) Modified opinion – A qualified opinion, an adverse opinion or a disclaimer of opinion.

Requirements

Circumstances When a Modification to the Auditor's Opinion Is Required

The auditor shall modify the opinion in the auditor's report when: 6

(a) The auditor concludes that, based on the audit evidence obtained, the financial statements as a whole are not free from material misstatement; or
  (Ref: Para. A2-A7)
(b) The auditor is unable to obtain sufficient appropriate audit evidence to conclude that the financial statements as a whole are free from material misstatement.
  (Ref: Para. A8-A12)

Determining the Type of Modification to the Auditor's Opinion

Qualified Opinion

The auditor shall express a qualified opinion when: 7

(a) The auditor, having obtained sufficient appropriate audit evidence, concludes that misstatements, individually or in the aggregate, are material, but not pervasive, to the financial statements; or
(b) The auditor is unable to obtain sufficient appropriate audit evidence on which to base the opinion, but the auditor concludes that the possible effects on the financial statements of undetected misstatements, if any, could be material but not pervasive.

Adverse Opinion

The auditor shall express an adverse opinion when the auditor, having obtained 8
sufficient appropriate audit evidence, concludes that misstatements, individually or in the aggregate, are both material and pervasive to the financial statements.

Disclaimer of Opinion

The auditor shall disclaim an opinion when the auditor is unable to obtain sufficient 9
appropriate audit evidence on which to base the opinion, and the auditor concludes that the possible effects on the financial statements of undetected misstatements, if any, could be both material and pervasive.

The auditor shall disclaim an opinion when, in extremely rare circumstances invol- 10
ving multiple uncertainties, the auditor concludes that, notwithstanding having obtained sufficient appropriate audit evidence regarding each of the individual uncertainties, it is not possible to form an opinion on the financial statements due to the potential interaction of the uncertainties and their possible cumulative effect on the financial statements.

(a) The financial statements present fairly, in all material respects (or give a true and fair view when reporting in accordance with a fair presentation framework[3a]; or

(b) The financial statements have been prepared, in all material respects, in accordance with the applicable financial reporting framework when reporting in accordance with a compliance framework.

When the modification arises from an inability to obtain sufficient appropriate audit evidence, the auditor shall use the corresponding phrase "except for the possible effects of the matter(s) ..." for the modified opinion. (Ref: Para. A22)

24   When the auditor expresses an adverse opinion, the auditor shall state in the Qualified Opinion on Financial Statements paragraph that, in the auditor's opinion, because of the significance of the matter(s) described in the Basis for Adverse Opinion paragraph:

(a) The financial statements do not present fairly (or give a true and fair view) when reporting in accordance with a fair presentation framework[4]; or

(b) The financial statements have not been prepared, in all material respects, in accordance with the applicable financial reporting framework when reporting in accordance with a compliance framework.

25   When the auditor disclaims an opinion due to an inability to obtain sufficient appropriate audit evidence, the auditor shall state in the Qualified Opinion on Financial Statements paragraph that:

(a) Because of the significance of the matter(s) described in the Basis for Disclaimer of Opinion paragraph, the auditor has not been able to obtain sufficient appropriate audit evidence to provide a basis for an audit opinion; and, accordingly,

(b) The auditor does not express an opinion on the financial statements.

26   *[Deliberately left blank]*

Description of Auditor's Responsibility When the Auditor Disclaims an Opinion

27   When the auditor disclaims an opinion due to an inability to obtain sufficient appropriate audit evidence, the auditor shall amend the introductory paragraph of the auditor's report to state that the auditor was engaged to audit the financial statements.

Communication with Those Charged with Governance

28   When the auditor expects to modify the opinion in the auditor's report, the auditor shall communicate with those charged with governance the circumstances that led to the expected modification and the proposed wording of the modification. (Ref: Para. A25)

***

[3a] *Auditor's reports prepared in accordance with Section 193 (4C) of the Irish Companies Act 1990 will express the opinion in terms of "true and fair view in accordance with the relevant financial reporting framework".*

Application and Other Explanatory Material

Types of Modified Opinions (Ref: Para. 2)

The table below illustrates how the auditor's judgment about the nature of the matter A1 giving rise to the modification, and the pervasiveness of its effects or possible effects on the financial statements, affects the type of opinion to be expressed.

	Auditor's Judgment about the Pervasiveness of the Effects or Possible Effects on the Financial Statements	
Nature of Matter Giving Rise to the Modification	*Material but Not Pervasive*	*Material and Pervasive*
Financial statements are materially misstated	Qualified opinion	Adverse opinion
Inability to obtain sufficient appropriate audit evidence	Qualified opinion	Disclaimer of opinion

Nature of Material Misstatements (Ref: Para. 6(a))

ISA (UK and Ireland) 700 requires the auditor, in order to form an opinion on the A2 financial statements, to conclude as to whether reasonable assurance has been obtained about whether the financial statements as a whole are free from material misstatement.[4] This conclusion takes into account the auditor's evaluation of uncorrected misstatements, if any, on the financial statements in accordance with ISA (UK and Ireland) 450.[5]

ISA (UK and Ireland) 450 defines a misstatement as a difference between the A3 amount, classification, presentation, or disclosure of a reported financial statement item and the amount, classification, presentation, or disclosure that is required for the item to be in accordance with the applicable financial reporting framework. Accordingly, a material misstatement of the financial statements may arise in relation to:

(a) The appropriateness of the selected accounting policies;
(b) The application of the selected accounting policies; or
(c) The appropriateness or adequacy of disclosures in the financial statements.

Appropriateness of the Selected Accounting Policies

In relation to the appropriateness of the accounting policies management has A4 selected, material misstatements of the financial statements may arise when:

(a) The selected accounting policies are not consistent with the applicable financial reporting framework; or
(b) The financial statements, including the related notes, do not represent the underlying transactions and events in a manner that achieves fair presentation.

---

[4] *ISA 700, paragraph 11.*

The FRC has not promulgated ISA 700 as issued by the IAASB for application in the UK and Ireland. In the UK and Ireland the applicable auditing standard is ISA (UK and Ireland) 700, "The Auditor's Report on Financial Statements." Paragraph 8 of ISA (UK and Ireland) 700 requires evaluation of whether sufficient appropriate audit evidence has been obtained.

[5] *ISA (UK and Ireland) 450, "Evaluation of Misstatements Identified during the Audit," paragraph 11.*

A5   Financial reporting frameworks often contain requirements for the accounting for, and disclosure of, changes in accounting policies. Where the entity has changed its selection of significant accounting policies, a material misstatement of the financial statements may arise when the entity has not complied with these requirements.

Application of the Selected Accounting Policies

A6   In relation to the application of the selected accounting policies, material misstatements of the financial statements may arise:

(a)   When management has not applied the selected accounting policies consistently with the financial reporting framework, including when management has not applied the selected accounting policies consistently between periods or to similar transactions and events (consistency in application); or

(b)   Due to the method of application of the selected accounting policies (such as an unintentional error in application).

Appropriateness or Adequacy of Disclosures in the Financial Statements

A7   In relation to the appropriateness or adequacy of disclosures in the financial statements, material misstatements of the financial statements may arise when:

(a)   The financial statements do not include all of the disclosures required by the applicable financial reporting framework;

(b)   The disclosures in the financial statements are not presented in accordance with the applicable financial reporting framework; or

(c)   The financial statements do not provide the disclosures necessary to achieve fair presentation.

Nature of an Inability to Obtain Sufficient Appropriate Audit Evidence
(Ref: Para. 6(b))

A8   The auditor's inability to obtain sufficient appropriate audit evidence (also referred to as a limitation on the scope of the audit) may arise from:

(a)   Circumstances beyond the control of the entity;

(b)   Circumstances relating to the nature or timing of the auditor's work; or

(c)   Limitations imposed by management.

A9   An inability to perform a specific procedure does not constitute a limitation on the scope of the audit if the auditor is able to obtain sufficient appropriate audit evidence by performing alternative procedures. If this is not possible, the requirements of paragraphs 7(b) and 10 apply as appropriate. Limitations imposed by management may have other implications for the audit, such as for the auditor's assessment of fraud risks and consideration of engagement continuance.

A10   Examples of circumstances beyond the control of the entity include when:

- The entity's accounting records have been destroyed.
- The accounting records of a significant component have been seized indefinitely by governmental authorities.

A11   Examples of circumstances relating to the nature or timing of the auditor's work include when:

- The entity is required to use the equity method of accounting for an associated entity, and the auditor is unable to obtain sufficient appropriate audit evidence about the latter's financial information to evaluate whether the equity method has been appropriately applied.

- The timing of the auditor's appointment is such that the auditor is unable to observe the counting of the physical inventories.
- The auditor determines that performing substantive procedures alone is not sufficient, but the entity's controls are not effective.

Examples of an inability to obtain sufficient appropriate audit evidence arising from a limitation on the scope of the audit imposed by management include when:

   A12

- Management prevents the auditor from observing the counting of the physical inventory.
- Management prevents the auditor from requesting external confirmation of specific account balances.

Consequence of an Inability to Obtain Sufficient Appropriate Audit Evidence Due to a Management-Imposed Limitation after the Auditor Has Accepted the Engagement
(Ref: Para. 13(b)-14)

The practicality of withdrawing from the audit may depend on the stage of completion of the engagement at the time that management imposes the scope limitation. If the auditor has substantially completed the audit, the auditor may decide to complete the audit to the extent possible, disclaim an opinion and explain the scope limitation in the Basis for Disclaimer of Opinion paragraph prior to withdrawing.

   A13

In certain circumstances, withdrawal from the audit may not be possible if the auditor is required by law or regulation to continue the audit engagement. This may be the case for an auditor that is appointed to audit the financial statements of public sector entities. It may also be the case in jurisdictions where the auditor is appointed to audit the financial statements covering a specific period, or appointed for a specific period and is prohibited from withdrawing before the completion of the audit of those financial statements or before the end of that period, respectively. The auditor may also consider it necessary to include an Other Matter paragraph in the auditor's report.[6]

   A14

When the auditor concludes that withdrawal from the audit is necessary because of a scope limitation, there may be a professional, legal or regulatory requirement for the auditor to communicate matters relating to the withdrawal from the engagement to regulators or the entity's owners.

   A15

Statement by Auditor on Ceasing to Hold Office

The auditor of a company in the UK who ceases to hold office as auditor is required to comply with the requirements of sections 519 and 521 of the Companies Act 2006 regarding the statement to be made by the auditor in relation to ceasing to hold office. In addition, the auditor may need to notify the appropriate audit authority in accordance with section 522 of the Companies Act 2006.

   A15-1

---

[6] *ISA (UK and Ireland) 706, "Emphasis of Matter Paragraphs and Other Matter Paragraphs in the Independent Auditor's Report," paragraph A5.*

A15-2 Auditors of Irish Companies, generally, are obliged to notify the Irish Auditing and Accounting Supervisory Authority (IAASA) within one month of ceasing to hold office on the appropriate form which includes stating the reason for resignation notwithstanding that the auditor may have nothing to report to the members or creditors regarding their ceasing to hold office[6a].

Other Considerations Relating to an Adverse Opinion or Disclaimer of Opinion (Ref: Para. 15)

A16 The following are examples of reporting circumstances that would not contradict the auditor's adverse opinion or disclaimer of opinion:

- The expression of an unmodified opinion on financial statements prepared under a given financial reporting framework and, within the same report, the expression of an adverse opinion on the same financial statements under a different financial reporting framework.[7]
- The expression of a disclaimer of opinion regarding the results of operations, and cash flows, where relevant, and an unmodified opinion regarding the financial position (see ISA (UK and Ireland) 510[8]). In this case, the auditor has not expressed a disclaimer of opinion on the financial statements as a whole.

Form and Content of the Auditor's Report When the Opinion Is Modified

Basis for Modification Paragraph (Ref: Para. 16-17, 19, 21)

A17 Consistency in the auditor's report helps to promote users' understanding and to identify unusual circumstances when they occur. Accordingly, although uniformity in the wording of a modified opinion and in the description of the basis for the modification may not be possible, consistency in both the form and content of the auditor's report is desirable.

A18 An example of the financial effects of material misstatements that the auditor may describe in the basis for modification paragraph in the auditor's report is the quantification of the effects on income tax, income before taxes, net income and equity if inventory is overstated.

A19 Disclosing the omitted information in the basis for modification paragraph would not be practicable if:

(a) The disclosures have not been prepared by management or the disclosures are otherwise not readily available to the auditor; or

(b) In the auditor's judgment, the disclosures would be unduly voluminous in relation to the auditor's report.

A20 An adverse opinion or a disclaimer of opinion relating to a specific matter described in the basis for qualification paragraph does not justify the omission of a description

---

[6a] *See section 161A. (1) of the Companies Act of 1990.*

[7] *See paragraph A32 of ISA 700 for a description of this circumstance.*
The FRC has not promulgated ISA 700 as issued by the IAASB for application in the UK and Ireland. In the UK and Ireland the applicable auditing standard is ISA (UK and Ireland) 700, "The Auditor's Report on Financial Statements." Paragraph A13 of ISA (UK and Ireland) 700 provides guidance on expressing an opinion in respect of an additional financial reporting framework.

[8] *ISA (UK and Ireland) 510, "Initial Audit Engagements – Opening Balances," paragraph 10.*

of other identified matters that would have otherwise required a modification of the auditor's opinion. In such cases, the disclosure of such other matters of which the auditor is aware may be relevant to users of the financial statements.

Opinion on the Financial Statements Paragraph (Ref: Para. 22-23)

Inclusion of this paragraph heading makes it clear to the user that the auditor's opinion is modified and indicates the type of modification.　　**A21**

When the auditor expresses a qualified opinion, it would not be appropriate to use phrases such as "with the foregoing explanation" or "subject to" in the opinion paragraph as these are not sufficiently clear or forceful.　　**A22**

Illustrative Auditors' Reports[8a]

> *Illustrative auditor's reports tailored for use with audits conducted in accordance*　**A23**
> *with ISAs (UK and Ireland) are given in the current versions of the FRC's com-*
> *pendia Auditor's Report Bulletins[8a].*
>
> *[Deliberately left blank]*　　**A24**

Communication with Those Charged with Governance (Ref: Para. 28)

Communicating with those charged with governance the circumstances that lead to　**A25**
an expected modification to the auditor's opinion and the proposed wording of the modification enables:

(a) The auditor to give notice to those charged with governance of the intended modification(s) and the reasons (or circumstances) for the modification(s);

(b) The auditor to seek the concurrence of those charged with governance regarding the facts of the matter(s) giving rise to the expected modification(s), or to confirm matters of disagreement with management as such; and

(c) Those charged with governance to have an opportunity, where appropriate, to provide the auditor with further information and explanations in respect of the matter(s) giving rise to the expected modification(s).

[8a] *At the date of publication of this ISA (UK and Ireland), Bulletins 2010/2 (Revised) "Compendium of Illustrative Auditor's Reports on United Kingdom Private Sector Financial Statements for periods ended on or after 15 December 2010" and 1(1) "Compendium of Illustrative Auditor's Reports on Irish Financial Statements" were the current compendia Bulletins.*

International Standard on Auditing (UK and Ireland) 706 (Revised October 2012)

Emphasis of matter paragraphs and other matter paragraphs in the independent auditor's report

(Effective for audits of financial statements for periods commencing on or after 1 October 2012)

Contents

International Standard on Auditing (UK and Ireland) (ISA (UK and Ireland)) 706, "Emphasis of Matter Paragraphs and Other Matter Paragraphs in the Independent Auditor's Report" should be read in conjunction with ISA (UK and Ireland) 200, "Overall Objectives of the Independent Auditor and the Conduct of an Audit in Accordance with International Standards on Auditing (UK and Ireland)."

Introduction

Scope of this ISA (UK and Ireland)

This International Standard on Auditing (UK and Ireland) (ISA (UK and Ireland))   **1**
deals with additional communication in the auditor's report when the auditor considers it necessary to:

(a) Draw users' attention to a matter or matters presented or disclosed in the
    financial statements that are of such importance that they are fundamental to
    users' understanding of the financial statements; or

(b) Draw users' attention to any matter or matters other than those presented or
    disclosed in the financial statements that are relevant to users' understanding of
    the audit, the auditor's responsibilities or the auditor's report.

Appendices 1 and 2 identify ISAs (UK and Ireland) that contain specific require-   **2**
ments for the auditor to include Emphasis of Matter paragraphs or Other Matter
paragraphs in the auditor's report. In those circumstances, the requirements in this
ISA regarding the form and placement of such paragraphs apply.

At the date of publication of this ISA (UK and Ireland) illustrative examples of   **2-1**
emphasis of matter paragraphs for UK and Irish financial statements are contained in the compendia Bulletins 2010/2 "Compendium of Illustrative Auditor's
Reports on United Kingdom Private Sector Financial Statements for periods
ended on or after 15 December 2010" (Revised) and 1(I) "Compendium of
Illustrative Auditor's Reports on Irish Financial Statements".

Effective Date

This ISA (UK and Ireland) is effective for audits of financial statements for periods   **3**
commencing on or after 1 October 2012. Earlier adoption is permitted.

Objective

The objective of the auditor, having formed an opinion on the financial statements, is   **4**
to draw users' attention, when in the auditor's judgment it is necessary to do so, by
way of clear additional communication in the auditor's report, to:

(a) A matter, although appropriately presented or disclosed in the financial statements, that is of such importance that it is fundamental to users' understanding
    of the financial statements; or

(b) As appropriate, any other matter that is relevant to users' understanding of the
    audit, the auditor's responsibilities or the auditor's report.

Definitions

For the purposes of the ISAs (UK and Ireland), the following terms have the   **5**
meanings attributed below:

(a) Emphasis of Matter paragraph – A paragraph included in the auditor's report
    that refers to a matter appropriately presented or disclosed in the financial
    statements that, in the auditor's judgment, is of such importance that it is
    fundamental to users' understanding of the financial statements.

(b) Other Matter paragraph – A paragraph included in the auditor's report that refers to a matter other than those presented or disclosed in the financial statements that, in the auditor's judgment, is relevant to users' understanding of the audit, the auditor's responsibilities or the auditor's report.

Requirements

Emphasis of Matter Paragraphs in the Auditor's Report

6   If the auditor considers it necessary to draw users' attention to a matter presented or disclosed in the financial statements that, in the auditor's judgment, is of such importance that it is fundamental to users' understanding of the financial statements, the auditor shall include an Emphasis of Matter paragraph in the auditor's report provided the auditor has obtained sufficient appropriate audit evidence that the matter is not materially misstated in the financial statements[1a]. Such a paragraph shall refer only to information presented or disclosed in the financial statements. (Ref: Para. A1-A2)

7   When the auditor includes an Emphasis of Matter paragraph in the auditor's report, the auditor shall:

(a) Include it immediately after the Opinion on Financial Statements paragraph in the auditor's report;
(b) Use the heading "Emphasis of Matter," or other appropriate heading;
(c) Include in the paragraph a clear reference to the matter being emphasized and to where relevant disclosures that fully describe the matter can be found in the financial statements; and
(d) Indicate that the auditor's opinion is not modified in respect of the matter emphasized. (Ref: Para. A3-A4)

Other Matter Paragraphs in the Auditor's Report

8   If the auditor considers it necessary to communicate a matter other than those that are presented or disclosed in the financial statements that, in the auditor's judgment, is relevant to users' understanding of the audit, the auditor's responsibilities or the auditor's report and this is not prohibited by law or regulation, the auditor shall do so in a paragraph in the auditor's report, with the heading "Other Matter," or other appropriate heading. The auditor shall include this paragraph immediately after the Opinion on Financial Statements paragraph and any Emphasis of Matter paragraph, or elsewhere in the auditor's report if the content of the Other Matter paragraph is relevant to the Other Reporting Responsibilities section. (Ref: Para. A5-A11)

Communication with Those Charged with Governance

9   If the auditor expects to include an Emphasis of Matter or an Other Matter paragraph in the auditor's report, the auditor shall communicate with those charged with governance regarding this expectation and the proposed wording of this paragraph. (Ref: Para. A12)

***

[1a] *Paragraph 19 of ISA (UK and Ireland) 570, "Going Concern," requires, where adequate disclosure is made in the financial statements, the auditor always include an Emphasis of Matter paragraph in the auditor's report to highlight the existence of a material uncertainty relating to an event or condition that may cast significant doubt on the entity's ability to continue as a going concern.*

Application and Other Explanatory Material

Emphasis of Matter Paragraphs in the Auditor's Report

Circumstances in Which an Emphasis of Matter Paragraph May Be Necessary (Ref: Para. 6)

Examples of circumstances where the auditor may consider it necessary to include an Emphasis of Matter paragraph are: **A1**

- An uncertainty relating to the future outcome of exceptional litigation or regulatory action.
- Early application (where permitted) of a new accounting standard (for example, a new International Financial Reporting Standard) that has a pervasive effect on the financial statements in advance of its effective date.
- A major catastrophe that has had, or continues to have, a significant effect on the entity's financial position.

A widespread use of Emphasis of Matter paragraphs diminishes the effectiveness of the auditor's communication of such matters. Additionally, to include more information in an Emphasis of Matter paragraph than is presented or disclosed in the financial statements may imply that the matter has not been appropriately presented or disclosed; accordingly, paragraph 6 limits the use of an Emphasis of Matter paragraph to matters presented or disclosed in the financial statements.   **A2**

Including an Emphasis of Matter Paragraph in the Auditor's Report (Ref: Para. 7)

The inclusion of an Emphasis of Matter paragraph in the auditor's report does not affect the auditor's opinion. An Emphasis of Matter paragraph is not a substitute for either: **A3**

(a) The auditor expressing a qualified opinion or an adverse opinion, or disclaiming an opinion, when required by the circumstances of a specific audit engagement (see ISA (UK and Ireland) 705[1]); or
(b) Disclosures in the financial statements that the applicable financial reporting framework requires management to make.

[Deliberately left blank].   **A4**

Other Matter Paragraphs in the Auditor's Report (Ref: Para. 8)

Circumstances in Which an Other Matter Paragraph May Be Necessary

Relevant to Users' Understanding of the Audit

In the rare circumstance where the auditor is unable to withdraw from an engagement even though the possible effect of an inability to obtain sufficient appropriate audit evidence due to a limitation on the scope of the audit imposed by management is pervasive,[2] the auditor may consider it necessary to include an Other Matter paragraph in the auditor's report to explain why it is not possible for the auditor to withdraw from the engagement.   **A5**

---

[1] *ISA (UK and Ireland) 705, "Modifications to the Opinion in the Independent Auditor's Report."*

[2] *See paragraph 13(b)(ii) of ISA (UK and Ireland) 705 for a discussion of this circumstance.*

Relevant to Users' Understanding of the Auditor's Responsibilities or the Auditor's Report

A6   Law, regulation or generally accepted practice in a jurisdiction may require or permit the auditor to elaborate on matters that provide further explanation of the auditor's responsibilities in the audit of the financial statements or of the auditor's report thereon. Where relevant, one or more sub-headings may be used that describe the content of the Other Matter paragraph.

A7   An Other Matter paragraph does not deal with circumstances where the auditor has other reporting responsibilities that are in addition to the auditor's responsibility under the ISAs (UK and Ireland) to report on the financial statements (see "Other Reporting Responsibilities" section in ISA (UK and Ireland) 700[3]), or where the auditor has been asked to perform and report on additional specified procedures, or to express an opinion on specific matters.

Reporting on more than one set of financial statements

A8   An entity may prepare one set of financial statements in accordance with a general purpose framework (for example, the national framework) and another set of financial statements in accordance with another general purpose framework (for example, International Financial Reporting Standards), and engage the auditor to report on both sets of financial statements. If the auditor has determined that the frameworks are acceptable in the respective circumstances, the auditor may include an Other Matter paragraph in the auditor's report, referring to the fact that another set of financial statements has been prepared by the same entity in accordance with another general purpose framework and that the auditor has issued a report on those financial statements.

A8-1   The situation described in paragraph A8 is differentiated from the requirement in paragraph 19 of ISA (UK and Ireland) 700 in that, in the latter case, the auditor is engaged to express in the same auditor's report an opinion on the compliance of the financial statements with an additional financial reporting framework. This is only permissible if the auditor is satisfied that there are no differences between the two financial reporting frameworks that affect the financial statements being reported on.

Restriction on distribution or use of the auditor's report

A9   Financial statements prepared for a specific purpose may be prepared in accordance with a general purpose framework because the intended users have determined that such general purpose financial statements meet their financial information needs. Since the auditor's report is intended for specific users, the auditor may consider it necessary in the circumstances to include an Other Matter paragraph, stating that the auditor's report is intended solely for the intended users, and should not be distributed to or used by other parties.

---

[3] ISA 700, "Forming an Opinion and Reporting on Financial Statements," paragraphs 38-39.
The FRC has not promulgated ISA 700 as issued by the IAASB for application in the UK and Ireland. In the UK and Ireland the applicable auditing standard is ISA (UK and Ireland) 700, "The Auditor's Report on Financial Statements." Paragraphs 21 and 22 of ISA (UK and Ireland) 700 are the equivalent paragraphs to 38 -39 of ISA 700.

Including an Other Matter Paragraph in the Auditor's Report

The content of an Other Matter paragraph reflects clearly that such other matter is **A10** not required to be presented and disclosed in the financial statements. An Other Matter paragraph does not include information that the auditor is prohibited from providing by law, regulation or other professional standards, for example, ethical standards relating to confidentiality of information. An Other Matter paragraph also does not include information that is required to be provided by management.

The placement of an Other Matter paragraph depends on the nature of the infor- **A11** mation to be communicated. When an Other Matter paragraph is included to draw users' attention to a matter relevant to their understanding of the audit of the financial statements, the paragraph is included immediately after the Opinion on Financial Statements paragraph and any Emphasis of Matter paragraph. When an Other Matter paragraph is included to draw users' attention to a matter relating to Other Reporting Responsibilities addressed in the auditor's report, the paragraph may be included in the Opinion on Other Matters (prescribed by applicable legislation under the terms of our engagement) paragraph. Alternatively, when relevant to all the auditor's responsibilities or users' understanding of the auditor's report, the Other Matter paragraph may be included as a separate section at the end of the auditor's report[3a].

Communication with Those Charged with Governance (Ref. Para. 9)

Such communication enables those charged with governance to be made aware of the **A12** nature of any specific matters that the auditor intends to highlight in the auditor's report, and provides them with an opportunity to obtain further clarification from the auditor where necessary. Where the inclusion of an Other Matter paragraph on a particular matter in the auditor's report recurs on each successive engagement, the auditor may determine that it is unnecessary to repeat the communication on each engagement.

Appendix 1 (Ref: Para. 2)

List of ISAs (UK and Ireland) Containing Requirements for Emphasis of Matter Paragraphs

This appendix identifies paragraphs in other ISAs (UK and Ireland) in effect for audits of financial statements for periods ending on or after 15 December 2010 that require the auditor to include an Emphasis of Matter paragraph in the auditor's report in certain circumstances. The list is not a substitute for considering the requirements and related application and other explanatory material in ISAs.

- ISA (UK and Ireland) 210, "Agreeing the Terms of Audit Engagements" – paragraph 19(b)
- ISA (UK and Ireland) 560, "Subsequent Events" – paragraphs 12(b) and 16
- ISA (UK and Ireland) 570, "Going Concern" – paragraph 19

[3a] *In the UK and Ireland separate auditor's reports may be provided where the consolidated financial statements of a group of companies and the financial statements of the parent company are presented separately. In such cases, an "Other Matter" paragraph explaining that separate auditor's reports have been provided is usually included as the final paragraph of both of the auditor's reports.*

- ISA 800[36], "Special Considerations—Audits of Financial Statements Prepared in Accordance with Special Purpose Frameworks" – paragraph 14

Appendix 2 (Ref: Para. 2)

List of ISAs (UK and Ireland) Containing Requirements for Other Matter Paragraphs

This appendix identifies paragraphs in other ISAs (UK and Ireland) in effect for audits of financial statements for periods ending on or after 15 December 2010 that require the auditor to include an Other Matter paragraph in the auditor's report in certain circumstances. The list is not a substitute for considering the requirements and related application and other explanatory material in ISAs.

- ISA (UK and Ireland) 560, "Subsequent Events" – paragraphs 12(b) and 16
- ISA (UK and Ireland) 710, "Comparative Information—Corresponding Figures and Comparative Financial Statements" – paragraphs 13-14, 16-17 and 19
- ISA (UK and Ireland) 720 Section A, "The Auditor's Responsibilities Relating to Other Information in Documents Containing Audited Financial Statements" – paragraph 10(a)

International Standard on Auditing (UK and Ireland) 710

Comparative information—corresponding figures and comparative financial statements

(Effective for audits of financial statements for periods ending on or after 15 December 2010)

Contents

International Standard on Auditing (UK and Ireland) (ISA (UK and Ireland)) 710, "Comparative Information—Corresponding Figures and Comparative Financial Statements" should be read in conjunction with ISA (UK and Ireland) 200, "Overall Objectives of the Independent Auditor and the Conduct of an Audit in Accordance with International Standards on Auditing (UK and Ireland)."

Introduction

Scope of this ISA (UK and Ireland)

1   This International Standard on Auditing (UK and Ireland) (ISA (UK and Ireland)) deals with the auditor's responsibilities relating to comparative information in an audit of financial statements. When the financial statements of the prior period have been audited by a predecessor auditor or were not audited, the requirements and guidance in ISA (UK and Ireland) 510[1] regarding opening balances also apply.

The Nature of Comparative Information

2   The nature of the comparative information that is presented in an entity's financial statements depends on the requirements of the applicable financial reporting framework. There are two different broad approaches to the auditor's reporting responsibilities in respect of such comparative information: corresponding figures and comparative financial statements. The approach to be adopted is often specified by law or regulation but may also be specified in the terms of engagement.

2-1   In the UK and Ireland the corresponding figures method of presentation is usually required.

3   The essential audit reporting differences between the approaches are:

    (a)   For corresponding figures, the auditor's opinion on the financial statements refers to the current period only; whereas

    (b)   For comparative financial statements, the auditor's opinion refers to each period for which financial statements are presented.

This ISA (UK and Ireland) addresses separately the auditor's reporting requirements for each approach.

Effective Date

4   This ISA (UK and Ireland) is effective for audits of financial statements for periods ending on or after 15 December 2010.

Objectives

5   The objectives of the auditor are:

    (a)   To obtain sufficient appropriate audit evidence about whether the comparative information included in the financial statements has been presented, in all material respects, in accordance with the requirements for comparative information in the applicable financial reporting framework; and

    (b)   To report in accordance with the auditor's reporting responsibilities.

---

[1] *ISA (UK and Ireland) 510, "Initial Audit Engagements—Opening Balances."*

Definitions

For purposes of the ISAs (UK and Ireland), the following terms have the meanings attributed below: **6**

(a) Comparative information – The amounts and disclosures included in the financial statements in respect of one or more prior periods in accordance with the applicable financial reporting framework.

(b) Corresponding figures – Comparative information where amounts and other disclosures for the prior period are included as an integral part of the current period financial statements, and are intended to be read only in relation to the amounts and other disclosures relating to the current period (referred to as "current period figures"). The level of detail presented in the corresponding amounts and disclosures is dictated primarily by its relevance to the current period figures.

(c) Comparative financial statements – Comparative information where amounts and other disclosures for the prior period are included for comparison with the financial statements of the current period but, if audited, are referred to in the auditor's opinion. The level of information included in those comparative financial statements is comparable with that of the financial statements of the current period.

For purposes of this ISA (UK and Ireland), references to "prior period" should be read as "prior periods" when the comparative information includes amounts and disclosures for more than one period.

Requirements

Audit Procedures

The auditor shall determine whether the financial statements include the comparative information required by the applicable financial reporting framework and whether such information is appropriately classified. For this purpose, the auditor shall evaluate whether: **7**

(a) The comparative information agrees with the amounts and other disclosures presented in the prior period or, when appropriate, have been restated; (Ref: Para. A1-1) and

(b) The accounting policies reflected in the comparative information are consistent with those applied in the current period or, if there have been changes in accounting policies, whether those changes have been properly accounted for and adequately presented and disclosed.

If the auditor becomes aware of a possible material misstatement in the comparative information while performing the current period audit, the auditor shall perform such additional audit procedures as are necessary in the circumstances to obtain sufficient appropriate audit evidence to determine whether a material misstatement exists. If the auditor had audited the prior period's financial statements, the auditor shall also follow the relevant requirements of ISA (UK and Ireland) 560.[2] If the prior period financial statements are amended, the auditor shall determine that the comparative information agrees with the amended financial statements. **8**

---

[2] *ISA (UK and Ireland) 560, "Subsequent Events," paragraphs 14-17.*

9   As required by ISA (UK and Ireland) 580,[3] the auditor shall request written representations for all periods referred to in the auditor's opinion. The auditor shall also obtain a specific written representation regarding any restatement made to correct a material misstatement in prior period financial statements that affect the comparative information. (Ref: Para. A1)

Audit Reporting

Corresponding Figures

10   When corresponding figures are presented, the auditor's opinion shall not refer to the corresponding figures except in the circumstances described in paragraphs 11, 12, and 14. (Ref: Para. A2)

11   If the auditor's report on the prior period, as previously issued, included a qualified opinion, a disclaimer of opinion, or an adverse opinion and the matter which gave rise to the modification is unresolved, the auditor shall modify the auditor's opinion on the current period's financial statements. In the Basis for Modification paragraph in the auditor's report, the auditor shall either:

(a)   Refer to both the current period's figures and the corresponding figures in the description of the matter giving rise to the modification when the effects or possible effects of the matter on the current period's figures are material; or

(b)   In other cases, explain that the audit opinion has been modified because of the effects or possible effects of the unresolved matter on the comparability of the current period's figures and the corresponding figures. (Ref: Para. A3-A5)

12   If the auditor obtains audit evidence that a material misstatement exists in the prior period financial statements on which an unmodified opinion has been previously issued, and the corresponding figures have not been properly restated or appropriate disclosures have not been made, the auditor shall express a qualified opinion or an adverse opinion in the auditor's report on the current period financial statements, modified with respect to the corresponding figures included therein. (Ref: Para. A6)

Prior Period Financial Statements Audited by a Predecessor Auditor

13   If the financial statements of the prior period were audited by a predecessor auditor and the auditor is not prohibited by law or regulation from referring to the predecessor auditor's report on the corresponding figures and decides to do so, the auditor shall state in an Other Matter paragraph in the auditor's report:

(a)   That the financial statements of the prior period were audited by the predecessor auditor;

(b)   The type of opinion expressed by the predecessor auditor and, if the opinion was modified, the reasons therefore; and

(c)   The date of that report. (Ref: Para. A7 – A7-2)

Prior Period Financial Statements Not Audited

14   If the prior period financial statements were not audited, the auditor shall state in an Other Matter paragraph in the auditor's report that the corresponding figures are unaudited. Such a statement does not, however, relieve the auditor of the requirement to obtain sufficient appropriate audit evidence that the opening balances do not

---

[3] ISA (UK and Ireland) 580, "Written Representations," paragraph 14.

contain misstatements that materially affect the current period's financial statements.[4]

Comparative Financial Statements

When comparative financial statements are presented, the auditor's opinion shall refer to each period for which financial statements are presented and on which an audit opinion is expressed. (Ref: Para. A8-A9) **15**

When reporting on prior period financial statements in connection with the current period's audit, if the auditor's opinion on such prior period financial statements differs from the opinion the auditor previously expressed, the auditor shall disclose the substantive reasons for the different opinion in an Other Matter paragraph in accordance with ISA (UK and Ireland) 706.[5] (Ref: Para. A10) **16**

Prior Period Financial Statements Audited by a Predecessor Auditor

If the financial statements of the prior period were audited by a predecessor auditor, in addition to expressing an opinion on the current period's financial statements, the auditor shall state in an Other Matter paragraph: **17**

(a) that the financial statements of the prior period were audited by a predecessor auditor;
(b) the type of opinion expressed by the predecessor auditor and, if the opinion was modified, the reasons therefore; and
(c) the date of that report,

unless the predecessor auditor's report on the prior period's financial statements is reissued with the financial statements.

If the auditor concludes that a material misstatement exists that affects the prior period financial statements on which the predecessor auditor had previously reported without modification, the auditor shall communicate the misstatement with the appropriate level of management and, unless all of those charged with governance are involved in managing the entity,[6] those charged with governance and request that the predecessor auditor be informed. If the prior period financial statements are amended, and the predecessor auditor agrees to issue a new auditor's report on the amended financial statements of the prior period, the auditor shall report only on the current period. (Ref: Para. A11) **18**

Prior Period Financial Statements Not Audited

If the prior period financial statements were not audited, the auditor shall state in an Other Matter paragraph that the comparative financial statements are unaudited. Such a statement does not, however, relieve the auditor of the requirement to obtain sufficient appropriate audit evidence that the opening balances do not contain misstatements that materially affect the current period's financial statements.[7] **19**

[4] *ISA (UK and Ireland) 510, paragraph 6.*

[5] *ISA (UK and Ireland) 706, "Emphasis of Matter Paragraphs and Other Matter Paragraphs in the Independent Auditor's Report," paragraph 8.*

[6] *ISA (UK and Ireland) 260, "Communication with Those Charged with Governance," paragraph 13.*

[7] *ISA (UK and Ireland) 510, paragraph 6.*

***

Application and Other Explanatory Material

Audit Procedures (Ref: Para. 7(a))

A1-1   When evaluating whether the comparative information agrees with the amounts and other disclosures presented in the prior period or, where appropriate, have been restated, the auditor's procedures include checking whether the related opening balances in the accounting records were appropriately brought forward.

Written Representations (Ref: Para. 9)

A1   In the case of comparative financial statements, the written representations are requested for all periods referred to in the auditor's opinion because management needs to reaffirm that the written representations it previously made with respect to the prior period remain appropriate. In the case of corresponding figures, the written representations are requested for the financial statements of the current period only because the auditor's opinion is on those financial statements, which include the corresponding figures. However, the auditor requests a specific written representation regarding any restatement made to correct a material misstatement in the prior period financial statements that affect the comparative information.

Audit Reporting

Corresponding Figures

No Reference in Auditor's Opinion (Ref: Para. 10)

A2   The auditor's opinion does not refer to the corresponding figures because the auditor's opinion is on the current period financial statements as a whole, including the corresponding figures.

Modification in Auditor's Report on the Prior Period Unresolved (Ref: Para. 11)

A3   When the auditor's report on the prior period, as previously issued, included a qualified opinion, a disclaimer of opinion, or an adverse opinion and the matter which gave rise to the modified opinion is resolved and properly accounted for or disclosed in the financial statements in accordance with the applicable financial reporting framework, the auditor's opinion on the current period need not refer to the previous modification.

A3-1   In some circumstances the auditor may consider it appropriate to qualify the audit opinion on the current period's financial statements. For example, if a provision which the auditor considered should have been made in the previous period is made in the current period.

A4   When the auditor's opinion on the prior period, as previously expressed, was modified, the unresolved matter that gave rise to the modification may not be relevant to the current period figures. Nevertheless, a qualified opinion, a disclaimer of

Example A – Corresponding Figures (Ref: Para. A5)

> **Report illustrative of the circumstances described in paragraph 11(a), as follows:**
>
> - **The auditor's report on the prior period, as previously issued, included a qualified opinion.**
> - **The matter giving rise to the modification is unresolved.**
> - **The effects or possible effects of the matter on the current period's figures are material and require a modification to the auditor's opinion regarding the current period figures.**

INDEPENDENT AUDITOR'S REPORT

[Appropriate Addressee]

Report on the Financial Statements[8]

We have audited the accompanying financial statements of ABC Company, which comprise the balance sheet as at December 31, 20X1, and the income statement, statement of changes in equity and cash flow statement for the year then ended, and a summary of significant accounting policies and other explanatory information.

Management's[9] Responsibility for the Financial Statements

Management is responsible for the preparation and fair presentation of these financial statements in accordance with International Financial Reporting Standards,[10] and for such internal control as management determines is necessary to enable the preparation of financial statements that are free from material misstatement, whether due to fraud or error.

Auditor's Responsibility

Our responsibility is to express an opinion on these financial statements based on our audit. We conducted our audit in accordance with International Standards on Auditing. Those standards require that we comply with ethical requirements and plan and perform the audit to obtain reasonable assurance about whether the financial statements are free from material misstatement.

An audit involves performing procedures to obtain audit evidence about the amounts and disclosures in the financial statements. The procedures selected depend on the auditor's judgment, including the assessment of the risks of material

---

[8] The sub-title "Report on the Financial Statements" is unnecessary in circumstances when the second sub-title "Report on Other Legal and Regulatory Requirements" is not applicable.

[9] Or other term that is appropriate in the context of the legal framework in the particular jurisdiction.

[10] Where management's responsibility is to prepare financial statements that give a true and fair view, this may read: "Management is responsible for the preparation of financial statements that give a true and fair view in accordance with International Financial Reporting Standards, and for such ..."

misstatement of the financial statements, whether due to fraud or error. In making those risk assessments, the auditor considers internal control relevant to the entity's preparation and fair presentation[11] of the financial statements in order to design audit procedures that are appropriate in the circumstances, but not for the purpose of expressing an opinion on the effectiveness of the entity's internal control.[12] An audit also includes evaluating the appropriateness of accounting policies used and the reasonableness of accounting estimates made by management, as well as evaluating the overall presentation of the financial statements.

We believe that the audit evidence we have obtained is sufficient and appropriate to provide a basis for our qualified audit opinion.

Basis for Qualified Opinion

As discussed in Note X to the financial statements, no depreciation has been provided in the financial statements, which constitutes a departure from International Financial Reporting Standards. This is the result of a decision taken by management at the start of the preceding financial year and caused us to qualify our audit opinion on the financial statements relating to that year. Based on the straight-line method of depreciation and annual rates of 5% for the building and 20% for the equipment, the loss for the year should be increased by xxx in 20X1 and xxx in 20X0, property, plant and equipment should be reduced by accumulated depreciation of xxx in 20X1 and xxx in 20X0, and the accumulated loss should be increased by xxx in 20X1 and xxx in 20X0.

Qualified Opinion

In our opinion, except for the effects of the matter described in the Basis for Qualified Opinion paragraph, the financial statements present fairly, in all material respects, (or *give a true and fair view of*) the financial position of ABC Company as at December 31, 20X1, and (*of*) its financial performance and its cash flows for the year then ended in accordance with International Financial Reporting Standards.

Report on Other Legal and Regulatory Requirements

[Form and content of this section of the auditor's report will vary depending on the nature of the auditor's other reporting responsibilities.]

[Auditor's signature]

[Date of the auditor's report]

[Auditor's address]

---

[11] *In the case of footnote 10, this may read: "In making those risk assessments, the auditor considers internal control relevant to the entity's preparation of financial statements that give a true and fair view in order to design audit procedures that are appropriate in the circumstances, but not for the purpose of expressing an opinion on the effectiveness of the entity's internal control."*

[12] *In circumstances when the auditor also has responsibility to express an opinion on the effectiveness of internal control in conjunction with the audit of the financial statements, this sentence would be worded as follows: "In making those risk assessments, the auditor considers internal control relevant to the entity's preparation and fair presentation of the financial statements in order to design audit procedures that are appropriate in the circumstances." In the case of footnote 10, this may read: "In making those risk assessments, the auditor considers internal control relevant to the entity's preparation of financial statements that give a true and fair view in order to design audit procedures that are appropriate in the circumstances."*

Example B – Corresponding Figures (Ref: Para. A5)

> **Report illustrative of the circumstances described in paragraph 11(b), as follows:**
>
> - **The auditor's report on the prior period, as previously issued, included a qualified opinion.**
>
> - **The matter giving rise to the modification is unresolved.**
>
> - **The effects or possible effects of the matter on the current period's figures are immaterial but require a modification to the auditor's opinion because of the effects or possible effects of the unresolved matter on the comparability of the current period's figures and the corresponding figures.**

INDEPENDENT AUDITOR'S REPORT

[Appropriate Addressee]

Report on the Financial Statements[13]

We have audited the accompanying financial statements of ABC Company, which comprise the balance sheet as at December 31, 20X1, and the income statement, statement of changes in equity and cash flow statement for the year then ended, and a summary of significant accounting policies and other explanatory information.

Management's[14] *Responsibility for the Financial Statements*

Management is responsible for the preparation and fair presentation of these financial statements in accordance with International Financial Reporting Standards,[15] and for such internal control as management determines is necessary to enable the preparation of financial statements that are free from material misstatement, whether due to fraud or error.

Auditor's Responsibility

Our responsibility is to express an opinion on these financial statements based on our audit. We conducted our audit in accordance with International Standards on Auditing. Those standards require that we comply with ethical requirements and plan and perform the audit to obtain reasonable assurance about whether the financial statements are free from material misstatement.

An audit involves performing procedures to obtain audit evidence about the amounts and disclosures in the financial statements. The procedures selected depend on the auditor's judgment, including the assessment of the risks of material misstatement of the financial statements, whether due to fraud or error. In making those

---

[13] *The sub-title "Report on the Financial Statements" is unnecessary in circumstances when the second sub-title "Report on Other Legal and Regulatory Requirements" is not applicable.*

[14] *Or other term that is appropriate in the context of the legal framework in the particular jurisdiction.*

[15] *Where management's responsibility is to prepare financial statements that give a true and fair view, this may read: "Management is responsible for the preparation of financial statements that give a true and fair view in accordance with International Financial Reporting Standards, and for such ..."*

risk assessments, the auditor considers internal control relevant to the entity's pre-paration and fair presentation[16] of the financial statements in order to design audit procedures that are appropriate in the circumstances, but not for the purpose of expressing an opinion on the effectiveness of the entity's internal control.[17] An audit also includes evaluating the appropriateness of accounting policies used and the reasonableness of accounting estimates made by management, as well as evaluating the overall presentation of the financial statements.

We believe that the audit evidence we have obtained is sufficient and appropriate to provide a basis for our qualified audit opinion.

Basis for Qualified Opinion

Because we were appointed auditors of ABC Company during 20X0, we were not able to observe the counting of the physical inventories at the beginning of that period or satisfy ourselves concerning those inventory quantities by alternative means. Since opening inventories affect the determination of the results of opera-tions, we were unable to determine whether adjustments to the results of operations and opening retained earnings might be necessary for 20X0. Our audit opinion on the financial statements for the period ended December 31, 20X0 was modified accordingly. Our opinion on the current period's financial statements is also modified because of the possible effect of this matter on the comparability of the current period's figures and the corresponding figures.

Qualified Opinion

In our opinion, except for the possible effects on the corresponding figures of the matter described in the Basis for Qualified Opinion paragraph, the financial state-ments present fairly, in all material respects, (or *give a true and fair view of*) the financial position of ABC Company as at December 31, 20X1, and (*of*) its financial performance and its cash flows for the year then ended in accordance with Inter-national Financial Reporting Standards.

Report on Other Legal and Regulatory Requirements

[Form and content of this section of the auditor's report will vary depending on the nature of the auditor's other reporting responsibilities.]

[Auditor's signature]

[Date of the auditor's report]

[Auditor's address]

---

[16] *In the case of footnote 15, this may read: "In making those risk assessments, the auditor considers internal control relevant to the entity's preparation of financial statements that give a* true and fair view *in order to design audit procedures that are appropriate in the circumstances, but not for the purpose of expressing an opinion on the effectiveness of the entity's internal control."*

[17] *In circumstances when the auditor also has responsibility to express an opinion on the effectiveness of internal control in conjunction with the audit of the financial statements, this sentence would be worded as follows: "In making those risk assessments, the auditor considers internal control relevant to the entity's preparation and fair presentation of the financial statements in order to design audit procedures that are appropriate in the cir-cumstances." In the case of footnote 15, this may read: "In making those risk assessments, the auditor considers internal control relevant to the entity's preparation of financial statements that give a true and fair view in order to design audit procedures that are appropriate in the circumstances."*

Example C – Corresponding Figures: (Ref: Para. A7)

Report illustrative of the circumstances described in paragraph 13, as follows:

- **The prior period's financial statements were audited by a predecessor auditor.**

- **The auditor is not prohibited by law or regulation from referring to the predecessor auditor's report on the corresponding figures and decides to do so.**

INDEPENDENT AUDITOR'S REPORT

[Appropriate Addressee]

Report on the Financial Statements[18]

We have audited the accompanying financial statements of ABC Company, which comprise the balance sheet as at December 31, 20X1, and the income statement, statement of changes in equity and cash flow statement for the year then ended, and a summary of significant accounting policies and other explanatory information.

Management's[19] Responsibility for the Financial Statements

Management is responsible for the preparation and fair presentation of these financial statements in accordance with International Financial Reporting Standards,[20] and for such internal control as management determines is necessary to enable the preparation of financial statements that are free from material misstatement, whether due to fraud or error.

Auditor's Responsibility

Our responsibility is to express an opinion on these financial statements based on our audit. We conducted our audit in accordance with International Standards on Auditing. Those standards require that we comply with ethical requirements and plan and perform the audit to obtain reasonable assurance about whether the financial statements are free from material misstatement.

An audit involves performing procedures to obtain audit evidence about the amounts and disclosures in the financial statements. The procedures selected depend on the auditor's judgment, including the assessment of the risks of material misstatement of the financial statements, whether due to fraud or error. In making those risk assessments, the auditor considers internal control relevant to the entity's preparation and fair presentation[21] of the financial statements in order to design audit procedures that are appropriate in the circumstances, but not for the purpose of

---

[18] *The sub-title "Report on the Financial Statements" is unnecessary in circumstances when the second sub-title "Report on Other Legal and Regulatory Requirements" is not applicable.*

[19] *Or other term that is appropriate in the context of the legal framework in the particular jurisdiction.*

[20] *Where management's responsibility is to prepare financial statements that give a true and fair view, this may read: "Management is responsible for the preparation of financial statements that give a true and fair view in accordance with International Financial Reporting Standards, and for such ..."*

[21] *In the case of footnote 20, this may read: "In making those risk assessments, the auditor considers internal control relevant to the entity's preparation of financial statements that give a true and fair view in order to design audit procedures that are appropriate in the circumstances, but not for the purpose of expressing an opinion on the effectiveness of the entity's internal control."*

expressing an opinion on the effectiveness of the entity's internal control.[22] An audit also includes evaluating the appropriateness of accounting policies used and the reasonableness of accounting estimates made by management, as well as evaluating the overall presentation of the financial statements.

We believe that the audit evidence we have obtained is sufficient and appropriate to provide a basis for our audit opinion.

Opinion

In our opinion, the financial statements present fairly, in all material respects, (or *give a true and fair view of*) the financial position of ABC Company as at December 31, 20X1, and (*of*) its financial performance and its cash flows for the year then ended in accordance with International Financial Reporting Standards.

Other Matter

The financial statements of ABC Company for the year ended December 31, 20X0, were audited by another auditor who expressed an unmodified opinion on those statements on March 31, 20X1.

Report on Other Legal and Regulatory Requirements

[Form and content of this section of the auditor's report will vary depending on the nature of the auditor's other reporting responsibilities.]

[Auditor's signature]

[Date of the auditor's report]

[Auditor's address]

---

[22] *In circumstances when the auditor also has responsibility to express an opinion on the effectiveness of internal control in conjunction with the audit of the financial statements, this sentence would be worded as follows: "In making those risk assessments, the auditor considers internal control relevant to the entity's preparation and fair presentation of the financial statements in order to design audit procedures that are appropriate in the circumstances." In the case of footnote 20, this may read: "In making those risk assessments, the auditor considers internal control relevant to the entity's preparation of financial statements that give a true and fair view in order to design audit procedures that are appropriate in the circumstances."*

Example D – Comparative Financial Statements: (Ref: Para. A9)

> **Report illustrative of the circumstances described in paragraph 15, as follows:**
>
> - **Auditor is required to report on both the current period financial statements and the prior period financial statements in connection with the current year's audit.**
>
> - **The auditor's report on the prior period, as previously issued, included a qualified opinion.**
>
> - **The matter giving rise to the modification is unresolved.**
>
> - **The effects or possible effects of the matter on the current period's figures are material to both the current period financial statements and prior period financial statements and require a modification to the auditor's opinion.**

INDEPENDENT AUDITOR'S REPORT

[Appropriate Addressee]

Report on the Financial Statements[23]

We have audited the accompanying financial statements of ABC Company, which comprise the balance sheets as at December 31, 20X1 and 20X0, and the income statements, statements of changes in equity and cash flow statements for the years then ended, and a summary of significant accounting policies and other explanatory information.

Management's[24] Responsibility for the Financial Statements

Management is responsible for the preparation and fair presentation of these financial statements in accordance with International Financial Reporting Standards,[25] and for such internal control as management determines is necessary to enable the preparation of financial statements that are free from material misstatement, whether due to fraud or error.

Auditor's Responsibility

Our responsibility is to express an opinion on these financial statements based on our audits. We conducted our audits in accordance with International Standards on Auditing. Those standards require that we comply with ethical requirements and plan and perform the audit to obtain reasonable assurance about whether the financial statements are free from material misstatement.

An audit involves performing procedures to obtain audit evidence about the amounts and disclosures in the financial statements. The procedures selected depend on the auditor's judgment, including the assessment of the risks of material misstatement of the financial statements, whether due to fraud or error. In making those

---

[23] *The sub-title "Report on the Financial Statements" is unnecessary in circumstances when the second sub-title "Report on Other Legal and Regulatory Requirements" is not applicable.*

[24] *Or other term that is appropriate in the context of the legal framework in the particular jurisdiction.*

[25] *Where management's responsibility is to prepare financial statements that give a true and fair view, this may read: "Management is responsible for the preparation of financial statements that give a true and fair view in accordance with International Financial Reporting Standards, and for such ..."*

risk assessments, the auditor considers internal control relevant to the entity's preparation and fair presentation[26] of the financial statements in order to design audit procedures that are appropriate in the circumstances, but not for the purpose of expressing an opinion on the effectiveness of the entity's internal control.[27] An audit also includes evaluating the appropriateness of accounting policies used and the reasonableness of accounting estimates made by management, as well as evaluating the overall presentation of the financial statements.

We believe that the audit evidence we have obtained in our audits is sufficient and appropriate to provide a basis for our qualified audit opinion.

Basis for Qualified Opinion

As discussed in Note X to the financial statements, no depreciation has been provided in the financial statements, which constitutes a departure from International Financial Reporting Standards. Based on the straight-line method of depreciation and annual rates of 5% for the building and 20% for the equipment, the loss for the year should be increased by xxx in 20X1 and xxx in 20X0, property, plant and equipment should be reduced by accumulated depreciation of xxx in 20X1 and xxx in 20X0, and the accumulated loss should be increased by xxx in 20X1 and xxx in 20X0.

Qualified Opinion

In our opinion, except for the effects of the matter described in the Basis for Qualified Opinion paragraph, the financial statements present fairly, in all material respects, (or *give a true and fair view of*) the financial position of ABC Company as at December 31, 20X1 and 20X0 and (*of*) its financial performance and its cash flows for the years then ended in accordance with International Financial Reporting Standards.

Report on Other Legal and Regulatory Requirements

[Form and content of this section of the auditor's report will vary depending on the nature of the auditor's other reporting responsibilities.]

[Auditor's signature]

[Date of the auditor's report]

[Auditor's address]

---

[26] *In the case of footnote 25, this may read: "In making those risk assessments, the auditor considers internal control relevant to the entity's preparation of financial statements that give a true and fair view in order to design audit procedures that are appropriate in the circumstances, but not for the purpose of expressing an opinion on the effectiveness of the entity's internal control."*

[27] *In circumstances when the auditor also has responsibility to express an opinion on the effectiveness of internal control in conjunction with the audit of the financial statements, this sentence would be worded as follows: "In making those risk assessments, the auditor considers internal control relevant to the entity's preparation and fair presentation of the financial statements in order to design audit procedures that are appropriate in the circumstances." In the case of footnote 25, this may read: "In making those risk assessments, the auditor considers internal control relevant to the entity's preparation of financial statements that give a true and fair view in order to design audit procedures that are appropriate in the circumstances."*

International Standard on Auditing (UK and Ireland) 720 (Revised October 2012)

Section A – The auditor's responsibilities relating to other information in documents containing audited financial statements

(Effective for audits of financial statements for periods commencing on or after 1 October 2012)

Contents

International Standard on Auditing (UK and Ireland) (ISA (UK and Ireland)) 720 Section A, "The Auditor's Responsibilities Relating to Other Information in Documents Containing Audited Financial Statements" should be read in conjunction with ISA (UK and Ireland) 200, "Overall Objectives of the Independent Auditor and the Conduct of an Audit in Accordance with International Standards on Auditing (UK and Ireland)."

Introduction

Scope of this ISA (UK and Ireland)

1   This International Standard on Auditing (UK and Ireland) (ISA (UK and Ireland)) deals with the auditor's responsibilities relating to other information in documents containing audited financial statements and the auditor's report thereon. In the absence of any separate requirement in the particular circumstances of the engagement, the auditor's opinion does not cover other information and the auditor has no specific responsibility for determining whether or not other information is properly stated. However, the auditor reads the other information because the credibility of the audited financial statements may be undermined by material inconsistencies between the audited financial statements and other information. (Ref: Para. A1)

1-1   The standards and guidance in this Section apply to all other information included in documents containing audited financial statements, including the directors' report. Further standards and guidance on the auditor's statutory reporting obligations in relation to directors' reports are set out in Section B.

2   In this ISA (UK and Ireland) "documents containing audited financial statements" refers to annual reports (or similar documents), that are issued to owners (or similar stakeholders), containing audited financial statements and the auditor's report thereon. This ISA (UK and Ireland) may also be applied, adapted as necessary in the circumstances, to other documents containing audited financial statements, such as those used in securities offerings.[1] (Ref: Para. A2)

Effective Date

3   This ISA (UK and Ireland) is effective for audits of financial statements for periods commencing on or after 1 October 2012.

Objective

4   The objective of the auditor is to respond appropriately when documents containing audited financial statements and the auditor's report thereon include other information that could undermine the credibility of those financial statements and the auditor's report.

---

[1] See ISA (UK and Ireland) 200, "Overall Objectives of the Independent Auditor and the Conduct of an Audit in Accordance with International Standards on Auditing," paragraph 2.

Paragraph 2 of ISA (UK and Ireland) 200 includes the statement that "ISAs (UK and Ireland) do not address the responsibilities of the auditor that may exist in legislation, regulation or otherwise in connection with, for example, the offering of securities to the public. Such responsibilities may differ from those established in the ISAs (UK and Ireland). Accordingly, while the auditor may find aspects of the ISAs (UK and Ireland) helpful in such circumstances, it is the responsibility of the auditor to ensure compliance with all relevant legal, regulatory or professional obligations." Guidance on other information issued with investment circulars is covered in the FRC's Statement of Investment Reporting Standard (SIR) 1000. Accordingly, the guidance in this ISA (UK and Ireland) is limited to Annual Reports and statutory audits.

Definitions

For purposes of the ISAs (UK and Ireland) the following terms have the meanings attributed below: **5**

(a) Other information – Financial and non-financial information (other than the financial statements and the auditor's report thereon) which is included, either by law, regulation or custom, in a document containing audited financial statements and the auditor's report thereon. (Ref: Para. A3-A4)

(b) Inconsistency – Other information that contradicts information contained in the audited financial statements. A material inconsistency may raise doubt about the audit conclusions drawn from audit evidence previously obtained and, possibly, about the basis for the auditor's opinion on the financial statements.

(c) Misstatement of fact – Other information that is unrelated to matters appearing in the audited financial statements that is incorrectly stated or presented. A material misstatement of fact may undermine the credibility of the document containing audited financial statements.

> In the context of an audit conducted in accordance with ISAs (UK and Ireland), other information that is incorrectly stated or presented includes other information that is apparently incorrect based on, or inconsistent with, the knowledge acquired by the auditor in the course of performing the audit or that is otherwise misleading.

Requirements

Reading Other Information

The auditor shall read the other information to identify material inconsistencies, if any, with the audited financial statements. (Ref: Para. A4-1 – A4-2)   **6**

> The auditor shall also read the other information to identify any information that is apparently materially incorrect based on, or materially inconsistent with, the knowledge acquired by the auditor in the course of performing the audit. (Ref: Para. A4-1 – A4-2)   **6-1**

The auditor shall make appropriate arrangements with management or those charged with governance to obtain the other information prior to the date of the auditor's report. If it is not possible to obtain all the other information prior to the date of the auditor's report, the auditor shall read such other information as soon as practicable[1a]. (Ref: Para. A5)   **7**

Material Inconsistencies

If, on reading the other information, the auditor identifies a material inconsistency, the auditor shall determine whether the audited financial statements or the other information needs to be revised.   **8**

[1a] *ISA (UK and Ireland) 700 requires that "The auditor shall not sign, and hence date, the report earlier than the date on which all other information contained in a report of which the audited financial statements form a part have been approved by those charged with governance and the auditor has considered all necessary available evidence."*

Material Inconsistencies Identified in Other Information Obtained Prior to the Date of the Auditor's Report

9   If revision of the audited financial statements is necessary and management[1b] refuses to make the revision, the auditor shall modify the opinion in the auditor's report in accordance with ISA (UK and Ireland) 705.[2]

10   If revision of the other information is necessary and management refuses to make the revision, the auditor shall communicate this matter to those charged with governance, unless all of those charged with governance are involved in managing the entity;[3] and

(a) Include in the auditor's report an Other Matter(s) paragraph describing the material inconsistency in accordance with ISA (UK and Ireland) 706;[4] or

(b) Withhold the auditor's report; or

(c) Withdraw from the engagements, where withdrawal is possible under applicable law or regulation. (Ref: Para. A6-A7, A11-2 – A11-3)

Material Inconsistencies Identified in Other Information Obtained Subsequent to the Date of the Auditor's Report

> *Paragraphs 11 to 13 deal with other information obtained subsequent to the date of the auditor's report. These are not applicable in an audit conducted in accordance with ISAs (UK and Ireland) because ISA (UK and Ireland) 700, "The Auditor's Report on Financial Statements" requires that "The auditor shall not sign, and hence date, the report earlier than the date on which all other information contained in a report of which the audited financial statements forma part have been approved by those charged with governance and the auditor has considered all necessary available evidence."*

11   *If revision of the audited financial statements is necessary, the auditor shall follow the relevant requirements in ISA (UK and Ireland) 560.[5]*

12   *If revision of the other information is necessary and management agrees to make the revision, the auditor shall carry out the procedures necessary under the circumstances. (Ref: Para. A8)*

13   *If revision of the other information is necessary, but management refuses to make the revision, the auditor shall notify those charged with governance, unless all of those charged with governance are involved in managing the entity, of the auditor's concern regarding the other information and take any further appropriate action. (Ref: Para. A9)*

[1b] In the UK and Ireland those charged with governance are responsible for the preparation of the financial statements.

[2] ISA (UK and Ireland) 705, "Modifications to the Opinion in the Independent Auditor's Report."

[3] ISA (UK and Ireland) 260, "Communication with Those Charged with Governance," paragraph 13.

[4] ISA (UK and Ireland) 706, "Emphasis of Matter Paragraphs and Other Matter Paragraphs in the Independent Auditor's Report," paragraph 8.

[5] ISA (UK and Ireland) 560, "Subsequent Events," paragraphs 10-17.

Material Misstatements of Fact

If, on reading the other information for the purpose of identifying material incon-   **14**
sistencies, the auditor becomes aware of an apparent material misstatement of fact,
the auditor shall discuss the matter with management. (Ref: Para. A10)

If, on reading the other information for the purpose of identifying any infor-   **14-1**
mation that is apparently materially incorrect based on, or materially inconsistent
with, the knowledge acquired by the auditor in the course of performing the audit,
the auditor becomes aware of an apparent misstatement of fact, the auditor shall
discuss the matter with management. (Ref: Para. A10 – A10-2)

If, following such discussions, the auditor still considers that there is an apparent   **15**
material misstatement of fact, the auditor shall request management to consult with
a qualified third party, such as the entity's legal counsel, and the auditor shall
consider the advice received.

If the auditor concludes that there is a material misstatement of fact in the other   **16**
information which management refuses to correct, the auditor shall notify those
charged with governance, unless all of those charged with governance are involved in
managing the entity, of the auditor's concern regarding the other information and
take any further appropriate action. (Ref: Para. A11 – A11-3)

***

Application and Other Explanatory Material

Scope of this ISA (UK and Ireland)

*Additional Responsibilities, through Statutory or Other Regulatory Requirements, in
Relation to Other Information* (Ref: Para. 1)

The auditor may have additional responsibilities, through statutory or other reg-   **A1**
ulatory requirements, in relation to other information that are beyond the scope of
this ISA (UK and Ireland). For example, some jurisdictions may require the auditor
to apply specific procedures to certain of the other information such as required
supplementary data or to express an opinion on the reliability of performance
indicators described in the other information. Where there are such obligations, the
auditor's additional responsibilities are determined by the nature of the engagement
and by law, regulation and professional standards. If such other information is
omitted or contains deficiencies, the auditor may be required by law or regulation to
refer to the matter in the auditor's report.

In the UK and Ireland an example of an auditor's additional responsibilities for a   **A1-1**
listed company would include the auditor's review of whether the Corporate
Governance Statement reflects the company's compliance with the provisions of
the UK Corporate Governance Code specified by the Listing Rules for review by
the auditor.

Documents Containing Audited Financial Statements (Ref: Para. 2)

Considerations Specific to Smaller Entities

A2   Unless required by law or regulation, smaller entities are less likely to issue documents containing audited financial statements. However, an example of such a document would be where a legal requirement exists for an accompanying report by those charged with governance. Examples of other information that may be included in a document containing the audited financial statements of a smaller entity are a detailed income statement and a management report.

Definition of Other Information (Ref: Para. 5(a))

A3   Other information may comprise, for example:

- A report by management or those charged with governance on operations.
- Financial summaries or highlights.
- Employment data.
- Planned capital expenditures.
- Financial ratios.
- Names of officers and directors.
- Selected quarterly data.

A3-1   Further examples relevant in the UK and Ireland are a directors' report required by statute (see Section B), statements relating to corporate governance, as required by the Listing Rules, a chairman's statement, a voluntary Operating and Financial Review and non-statutory financial information included within the annual report[5a].

A4   For purposes of the ISAs (UK and Ireland), other information does not encompass, for example:

- A press release or a transmittal memorandum, such as a covering letter, accompanying the document containing audited financial statements and the auditor's report thereon.
- Information contained in analyst briefings.
- Information contained on the entity's website.

Reading Other Information (Ref: Para. 6-7)

A4-1   When the auditor reads the other information, the auditor does so in the light of the knowledge the auditor has acquired during the audit. The auditor is not expected to verify any of the other information. The audit engagement partner (and, where appropriate, other senior members of the engagement team who can reasonably be expected to be aware of the more important matters arising during

---

[5a] *The FRC recognises that in some circumstances the presentation of non-statutory financial information and associated narrative explanations with the statutory results may help shareholders understand better the financial performance of a company. However, the FRC is concerned that in other circumstances such non-statutory information in annual reports has the potential to be misleading and shareholders may sometimes be misinformed by the manner in which non-statutory information is presented. The FRC believes that the potential for non-statutory information to be misleading is considerable when undue and inappropriate prominence is given to the non-statutory information, when there is no description of the non-statutory information and, where appropriate, the adjusted numbers are not reconciled to the statutory financial information.*

the audit and to have a general understanding of the entity's affairs), reads the other information with a view to identifying significant misstatements therein or matters which are inconsistent with the financial statements or the knowledge acquired by the auditor in the course of performing the audit.

If the auditor believes that the other information contains a material misstate-ment of fact, is materially inconsistent with the financial statements, or is otherwise misleading, and the auditor is unable to resolve the matter with man-agement and those charged with governance, the auditor considers the implications for the auditor's report and what further actions may be appropriate. The auditor has regard to the guidance in paragraphs A11-1 and A11-2 below and, for entities that are required, and those that choose voluntarily, to report on how they have applied the UK Corporate Governance Code, the requirements in paragraphs 22A and 22B, and related guidance in paragraph A18A, of ISA (UK and Ireland) 700 (Revised) to report on matters by exception.

A4-2

Obtaining the other information prior to the date of the auditor's report enables the auditor to resolve possible material inconsistencies and apparent material misstate-ments of fact with management on a timely basis. An agreement with management as to when the other information will be available may be helpful.

A5

Guidance to auditors in the UK and Ireland on the consideration of other information where the annual financial statements accompanied by the auditor's report are published on an entity's website, or in the UK where companies can meet their statutory reporting obligations to shareholders by distributing annual financial statements and certain other reports electronically, is given in the Appendix to this Section[5b].

A5-1

Material Inconsistencies

Material Inconsistencies Identified in Other Information Obtained Prior to the Date of the Auditor's Report (Ref: Para. 10)

When management refuses to revise the other information, the auditor may base any decision on what further action to take on advice from the auditor's legal counsel.

A6

If the auditor concludes that the other information contains inconsistencies with the financial statements, and the auditor is unable to resolve them through dis-cussion with those charged with governance, the auditor considers requesting those charged with governance to consult with a qualified third party, such as the entity's legal counsel and considers the advice received.

A6-1

[5b] *In the UK, the Companies Act 2006 enables companies, subject to certain conditions set out in Schedule 5 thereto, to make communications in electronic form, including by means of a website. Further, section 430 of the Companies Act 2006 requires that a quoted company must ensure that its annual accounts and reports are made available on a website.*

Considerations Specific to Public Sector Entities

A7   In the public sector, withdrawal from the engagement or withholding the auditor's report may not be options. In such cases, the auditor may issue a report to the appropriate statutory body giving details of the inconsistency.

Material Inconsistencies Identified in Other Information Obtained Subsequent to the Date of the Auditor's Report (Ref: Para. 12-13)

A8   *When management agrees to revise the other information, the auditor's procedures may include reviewing the steps taken by management to ensure that individuals in receipt of the previously issued financial statements, the auditor's report thereon, and the other information are informed of the revision.*

A9   *When management refuses to make the revision of such other information that the auditor concludes is necessary, appropriate further actions by the auditor may include obtaining advice from the auditor's legal counsel.*

Material Misstatements of Fact (Ref: Para. 14-16)

A10   When discussing an apparent material misstatement of fact with management, the auditor may not be able to evaluate the validity of some disclosures included within the other information and management's responses to the auditor's inquiries, and may conclude that valid differences of judgment or opinion exist.

A10-1   A material misstatement of fact in other information would potentially include an inconsistency between information obtained by the auditor during the audit (such as information obtained as part of the planning process or analytical procedures, or as written representations) and information which is included in the other information.

A10-2   The auditor has regard to the nature of the inconsistency or misstatement that in the auditor's opinion exists. A distinction may be drawn between a matter of fact and one of judgment. It is generally more difficult for the auditor to take issue with a matter of judgment (such as the view of those charged with governance of the likely out-turn for the following year) than a factual error. Although an auditor does not substitute the auditor's judgment for that of management and those charged with governance in such matters, there may be circumstances in which the auditor is aware that the expressed view of management and those charged with governance is significantly at variance with the entity's internal assessment or is so unreasonable as not to be credible to someone with the auditor's knowledge.

A11   When the auditor concludes that there is a material misstatement of fact that management refuses to correct, appropriate further actions by the auditor may include obtaining advice from the auditor's legal counsel.

When the auditor concludes that there is a material misstatement of fact that management refuses to correct, appropriate further actions may also include including in the auditor's report an Other Matter(s) paragraph describing the material misstatement of fact.

A11-1

Further Actions Available to the Auditor when a Material Inconsistency or Material Misstatement of Fact in Other Information is not Corrected

The auditor of a limited company in the United Kingdom or the Republic of Ireland may use the auditor's right to be heard at any general meeting of the members on any part of the business of the meeting which concerns the auditor as auditor[5c].

A11-2

The auditor may also consider resigning from the audit engagement. In the case of auditors of limited companies in the United Kingdom or the Republic of Ireland, the requirements for the auditor to make a statement on ceasing to hold office as auditor apply[5d]. When making a statement in these circumstances, the considerations set out in paragraph A10-2 above would normally be applicable. In addition, in the UK the auditor may need to notify the relevant audit authority.

A11-3

Appendix

Electronic Publication of the Auditor's Report

Introduction

In the UK, section 430 of the Companies Act 2006 requires that a quoted company must ensure that its annual accounts and reports are made available on a website. The Companies Act 2006 also enables all companies, subject to certain conditions set out in Schedule 5 thereto, to make communications in electronic form, including by means of a website.

1

Various types of financial information can be found on websites including information that has been audited (for example the annual financial statements), information which the auditor may have reviewed (for example interim financial information) and information with which the auditor has had no direct involvement, such as financial highlights from a company's Annual Report or may never have seen, such as presentations for analysts. In addition, websites typically contain a considerable amount of non-financial information.

2

The purpose of this Appendix is to provide guidance to auditors on the consideration of other information in situations where the annual financial statements accompanied by the auditor's report are published on an entity's website[5e].

3

[5c] *The relevant reference for the UK is section 502 of the Companies Act 2006, and for the Republic of Ireland is section 193(5) of the Companies Act 1990.*

[5d] *The relevant reference for the UK is section 519 of the Companies Act 2006, and for the Republic of Ireland is section 185 of the Companies Act 1990.*

[5e] *This guidance is generally applicable both to auditors in the UK (where the provisions of the Companies Act 2006 apply) and the Republic of Ireland (where they do not).*

differentiation would normally also be clearly stated in an introduction page within the website.

15   During the course of the audit, the auditor discusses with those charged with governance or, where appropriate, the audit committee how the financial statements and auditor's report will be presented on the entity's website with a view to minimizing the possibility that the auditor's report is inappropriately associated with other information. If the auditor is not satisfied with the proposed electronic presentation of the audited financial statements and auditor's report, the auditor requests that the presentation be amended. If the presentation is not amended the auditor will, in accordance with the terms of the engagement, not give consent for the electronic release of the audit opinion.

16   If the auditor's report is used without the auditor's consent, and the auditor has concerns about the electronic presentation of the audited financial statements or the auditor's report and appropriate action is not taken by those charged with governance, the auditor seeks legal advice as necessary. The auditor also considers whether it would be appropriate to resign.

International Standard on Auditing (UK and Ireland) 720

Section B – The auditor's statutory reporting responsibility in relation to directors' reports

(Effective for audits of financial statements for periods ending on or after 15 December 2010)

Contents

International Standard on Auditing (UK and Ireland) (ISA (UK and Ireland)) 720 Section B, "The Auditor's Statutory Reporting Responsibility in Relation to Directors' Reports" should be read in conjunction with ISA (UK and Ireland) 200, "Overall Objectives of the Independent Auditor and the Conduct of an Audit in Accordance with International Standards on Auditing (UK and Ireland)."

Introduction

Scope of this Section

1   This Section of International Standard on Auditing (UK and Ireland) (ISA (UK and Ireland)) 720 deals with the auditor's statutory reporting responsibility in relation to directors' reports.

2   In the United Kingdom and the Republic of Ireland, legislation[1] requires the auditor of a company to state in the auditor's report whether, in the auditor's opinion, the information given in the directors' report is consistent with the financial statements.

3   "Information given in the directors' report" includes information that is included by way of cross reference to other information presented separately from the directors' report. For example, a UK company may decide to present a voluntary Operating and Financial Review (OFR) which includes some or all of the matters required for the Business Review section of the directors' report. Rather than duplicate the information, the company may cross refer from the Business Review section in the directors' report to the relevant information provided in the OFR.

4   The auditor is not required to verify, or report on, the completeness of the information in the directors' report. If, however, the auditor becomes aware that information that is required by law or regulations to be in the directors' report has been omitted the auditor communicates the matter to those charged with governance. This communication includes situations where the required information is presented separately from the directors' report without appropriate cross references.

5   Illustrative examples of wording to include auditor's reports tailored for use with audits conducted in accordance with ISAs (UK and Ireland) are provided in the most recent versions of the APB Bulletins, "Auditor's Reports on Financial Statements in the United Kingdom"/"Auditor's Reports on Financial Statements in the Republic of Ireland".

Effective Date

6   This Section of ISA (UK and Ireland) 720 is effective for audits of financial statements for periods ending on or after 15 December 2010.

Objective

7   The objective of the auditor is to form an opinion on whether the information given in the directors' report is consistent with the financial statements and to respond appropriately if it is not consistent.

---

[1] *Relevant legislation includes:*
- *In the UK, Section 496 of the Companies Act 2006*
- *In the Republic of Ireland, Section 15 of the Companies (Amendment) Act 1986.*

Requirements

Reading the Directors' Report

The auditor shall read the information in the directors' report and assess whether it is consistent with the financial statements. (Ref: Para. A1)   **8**

Inconsistencies

If the auditor identifies any inconsistencies between the information in the directors' report and the financial statements the auditor shall seek to resolve them. (Ref: Para. A2)   **9**

If the auditor is of the opinion that the information in the directors' report is materially inconsistent[2] with the financial statements, and has been unable to resolve the inconsistency, the auditor shall state that opinion and describe the inconsistency in the auditor's report.   **10**

If an amendment is necessary to the financial statements and management and those charged with governance refuse to make the amendment, the auditor shall express a qualified or adverse opinion on the financial statements.   **11**

Documentation

The auditor shall document: **12**

(a)   The results of those procedures performed to assess whether the information in the directors' report is consistent with the financial statements, including details of any material inconsistencies identified and how they were resolved; and

(b)   The conclusion reached as to whether the information in the directors' report is consistent with the financial statements.

***

Application and Other Explanatory Material

Reading the Directors' Report (Ref: Para. 8)

Much of the information in the directors' report is likely to be extracted or directly derived from the financial statements and will therefore be directly comparable with them. Some financial information may, however, be more detailed or prepared on a different basis from that in the financial statements. Where the financial information is more detailed, the auditor agrees the information to the auditor's working papers or the entity's accounting records. Where the financial information has been prepared on a different basis, the auditor considers whether there is adequate disclosure of the differences in the bases of preparation to enable an understanding of the differences in the information, and checks the reconciliation of the information to the financial statements.   **A1**

---

[2] *Materiality is addressed in ISA (UK and Ireland) 320 "Audit Materiality". An inconsistency is "material" if it could influence the economic decisions of users.*

Inconsistencies (Ref: Para. 9)

A2   Inconsistencies include:

- Differences between amounts or narrative appearing in the financial statements and the directors' report.
- Differences between the bases of preparation of related items appearing in the financial statements and the directors' report, where the figures themselves are not directly comparable and the different bases are not disclosed.
- Contradictions between figures contained in the financial statements and narrative explanations of those figures in the directors' report.

The auditor ordinarily seeks to resolve inconsistencies through discussion with management and those charged with governance.

Part Two

International Standards on Auditing

International Standard on Auditing 800

Special considerations—audits of financial statements prepared in accordance with special purpose frameworks

*(Effective for audits of financial statements for periods
beginning on or after December 15, 2009)*

Contents

International Standard on Auditing (ISA) 800, "Special Considerations—Audits of Financial Statements Prepared in Accordance with Special Purpose Frameworks" should be read in conjunction with ISA 200, "Overall Objectives of the Independent Auditor and the Conduct of an Audit in Accordance with International Standards on Auditing."

Introduction

Scope of this ISA

1   The International Standards on Auditing (ISAs) in the 100-700 series apply to an audit of financial statements. This ISA deals with special considerations in the application of those ISAs to an audit of financial statements prepared in accordance with a special purpose framework.

2   This ISA is written in the context of a complete set of financial statements prepared in accordance with a special purpose framework. ISA 805[1] deals with special considerations relevant to an audit of a single financial statement or of a specific element, account or item of a financial statement.

3   This ISA does not override the requirements of the other ISAs; nor does it purport to deal with all special considerations that may be relevant in the circumstances of the engagement.

Effective Date

4   This ISA is effective for audits of financial statements for periods beginning on or after December 15, 2009.

Objective

5   The objective of the auditor, when applying ISAs in an audit of financial statements prepared in accordance with a special purpose framework, is to address appropriately the special considerations that are relevant to:

    (a)   The acceptance of the engagement;
    (b)   The planning and performance of that engagement; and
    (c)   Forming an opinion and reporting on the financial statements.

Definitions

6   For purposes of the ISAs, the following terms have the meanings attributed below:

    (a)   Special purpose financial statements – Financial statements prepared in accordance with a special purpose framework. (Ref: Para. A4)
    (b)   Special purpose framework – A financial reporting framework designed to meet the financial information needs of specific users. The financial reporting framework may be a fair presentation framework or a compliance framework.[2] (Ref: Para. A1-A4)

7   Reference to "financial statements" in this ISA means "a complete set of special purpose financial statements, including the related notes." The related notes ordinarily comprise a summary of significant accounting policies and other explanatory information. The requirements of the applicable financial reporting framework

---

[1] *ISA 805, "Special Considerations—Audits of Single Financial Statements and Specific Elements, Accounts or Items of a Financial Statement."*

[2] *ISA 200, "Overall Objectives of the Independent Auditor and the Conduct of an Audit in Accordance with International Standards on Auditing," paragraph 13(a).*

determine the form and content of the financial statements, and what constitutes a complete set of financial statements.

Requirements

Considerations When Accepting the Engagement

Acceptability of the Financial Reporting Framework

ISA 210 requires the auditor to determine the acceptability of the financial reporting **8** framework applied in the preparation of the financial statements.[3] In an audit of special purpose financial statements, the auditor shall obtain an understanding of: (Ref: Para. A5-A8)

(a) The purpose for which the financial statements are prepared;
(b) The intended users; and
(c) The steps taken by management to determine that the applicable financial reporting framework is acceptable in the circumstances.

Considerations When Planning and Performing the Audit

ISA 200 requires the auditor to comply with all ISAs relevant to the audit.[4] In **9** planning and performing an audit of special purpose financial statements, the auditor shall determine whether application of the ISAs requires special consideration in the circumstances of the engagement. (Ref: Para. A9-A12)

ISA 315 requires the auditor to obtain an understanding of the entity's selection and **10** application of accounting policies.[5] In the case of financial statements prepared in accordance with the provisions of a contract, the auditor shall obtain an understanding of any significant interpretations of the contract that management made in the preparation of those financial statements. An interpretation is significant when adoption of another reasonable interpretation would have produced a material difference in the information presented in the financial statements.

Forming an Opinion and Reporting Considerations

When forming an opinion and reporting on special purpose financial statements, the **11** auditor shall apply the requirements in ISA 700.[6] (Ref: Para. A13)

Description of the Applicable Financial Reporting Framework

ISA 700 requires the auditor to evaluate whether the financial statements adequately **12** refer to or describe the applicable financial reporting framework.[7] In the case of financial statements prepared in accordance with the provisions of a contract, the

---

[3] *ISA 210, "Agreeing the Terms of Audit Engagements," paragraph 6(a).*

[4] *ISA 200, paragraph 18.*

[5] *ISA 315, "Identifying and Assessing the Risks of Material Misstatement through Understanding the Entity and Its Environment," paragraph 11(c).*

[6] *ISA 700, "Forming an Opinion and Reporting on Financial Statements."*

[7] *ISA 700, paragraph 15.*

auditor shall evaluate whether the financial statements adequately describe any significant interpretations of the contract on which the financial statements are based.

13   ISA 700 deals with the form and content of the auditor's report. In the case of an auditor's report on special purpose financial statements:

(a)   The auditor's report shall also describe the purpose for which the financial statements are prepared and, if necessary, the intended users, or refer to a note in the special purpose financial statements that contains that information; and

(b)   If management has a choice of financial reporting frameworks in the preparation of such financial statements, the explanation of management's[8] responsibility for the financial statements shall also make reference to its responsibility for determining that the applicable financial reporting framework is acceptable in the circumstances.

Alerting Readers that the Financial Statements Are Prepared in Accordance with a Special Purpose Framework

14   The auditor's report on special purpose financial statements shall include an Emphasis of Matter paragraph alerting users of the auditor's report that the financial statements are prepared in accordance with a special purpose framework and that, as a result, the financial statements may not be suitable for another purpose. The auditor shall include this paragraph under an appropriate heading. (Ref: Para. A14-A15)

***

Application and Other Explanatory Material

Definition of Special Purpose Framework (Ref: Para. 6)

A1   Examples of special purpose frameworks are:

- A tax basis of accounting for a set of financial statements that accompany an entity's tax return;
- The cash receipts and disbursements basis of accounting for cash flow information that an entity may be requested to prepare for creditors;
- The financial reporting provisions established by a regulator to meet the requirements of that regulator; or
- The financial reporting provisions of a contract, such as a bond indenture, a loan agreement, or a project grant.

A2   There may be circumstances where a special purpose framework is based on a financial reporting framework established by an authorized or recognized standards setting organization or by law or regulation, but does not comply with all the requirements of that framework. An example is a contract that requires financial statements to be prepared in accordance with most, but not all, of the Financial Reporting Standards of Jurisdiction X. When this is acceptable in the circumstances of the engagement, it is inappropriate for the description of the applicable financial reporting framework in the special purpose financial statements to imply full compliance with the financial reporting framework established by the authorized or recognized standards setting organization or by law or regulation. In the above

---

[8] *Or other term that is appropriate in the context of the legal framework in the particular jurisdiction.*

example of the contract, the description of the applicable financial reporting framework may refer to the financial reporting provisions of the contract, rather than make any reference to the Financial Reporting Standards of Jurisdiction X.

In the circumstances described in paragraph A2, the special purpose framework may not be a fair presentation framework even if the financial reporting framework on which it is based is a fair presentation framework. This is because the special purpose framework may not comply with all the requirements of the financial reporting framework established by the authorized or recognized standards setting organization or by law or regulation that are necessary to achieve fair presentation of the financial statements.   **A3**

Financial statements prepared in accordance with a special purpose framework may be the only financial statements an entity prepares. In such circumstances, those financial statements may be used by users other than those for whom the financial reporting framework is designed. Despite the broad distribution of the financial statements in those circumstances, the financial statements are still considered to be special purpose financial statements for purposes of the ISAs. The requirements in paragraphs 13-14 are designed to avoid misunderstandings about the purpose for which the financial statements are prepared.   **A4**

Considerations When Accepting the Engagement

Acceptability of the Financial Reporting Framework (Ref: Para. 8)

In the case of special purpose financial statements, the financial information needs of the intended users are a key factor in determining the acceptability of the financial reporting framework applied in the preparation of the financial statements.   **A5**

The applicable financial reporting framework may encompass the financial reporting standards established by an organization that is authorized or recognized to promulgate standards for special purpose financial statements. In that case, those standards will be presumed acceptable for that purpose if the organization follows an established and transparent process involving deliberation and consideration of the views of relevant stakeholders. In some jurisdictions, law or regulation may prescribe the financial reporting framework to be used by management in the preparation of special purpose financial statements for a certain type of entity. For example, a regulator may establish financial reporting provisions to meet the requirements of that regulator. In the absence of indications to the contrary, such a financial reporting framework is presumed acceptable for special purpose financial statements prepared by such entity.   **A6**

Where the financial reporting standards referred to in paragraph A6 are supplemented by legislative or regulatory requirements, ISA 210 requires the auditor to determine whether any conflicts between the financial reporting standards and the additional requirements exist, and prescribes actions to be taken by the auditor if such conflicts exist.[9]   **A7**

The applicable financial reporting framework may encompass the financial reporting provisions of a contract, or sources other than those described in paragraphs A6 and A7. In that case, the acceptability of the financial reporting framework in the circumstances of the engagement is determined by considering whether the framework exhibits attributes normally exhibited by acceptable financial reporting frameworks   **A8**

---

[9] *ISA 210, paragraph 18.*

as described in Appendix 2 of ISA 210. In the case of a special purpose framework, the relative importance to a particular engagement of each of the attributes normally exhibited by acceptable financial reporting frameworks is a matter of professional judgment. For example, for purposes of establishing the value of net assets of an entity at the date of its sale, the vendor and the purchaser may have agreed that very prudent estimates of allowances for uncollectible accounts receivable are appropriate for their needs, even though such financial information is not neutral when compared with financial information prepared in accordance with a general purpose framework.

Considerations When Planning and Performing the Audit (Ref: Para. 9)

A9   ISA 200 requires the auditor to comply with (a) relevant ethical requirements, including those pertaining to independence, relating to financial statement audit engagements, and (b) all ISAs relevant to the audit. It also requires the auditor to comply with each requirement of an ISA unless, in the circumstances of the audit, the entire ISA is not relevant or the requirement is not relevant because it is conditional and the condition does not exist. In exceptional circumstances, the auditor may judge it necessary to depart from a relevant requirement in an ISA by performing alternative audit procedures to achieve the aim of that requirement.[10]

A10   Application of some of the requirements of the ISAs in an audit of special purpose financial statements may require special consideration by the auditor. For example, in ISA 320, judgments about matters that are material to users of the financial statements are based on a consideration of the common financial information needs of users as a group.[11] In the case of an audit of special purpose financial statements, however, those judgments are based on a consideration of the financial information needs of the intended users.

A11   In the case of special purpose financial statements, such as those prepared in accordance with the requirements of a contract, management may agree with the intended users on a threshold below which misstatements identified during the audit will not be corrected or otherwise adjusted. The existence of such a threshold does not relieve the auditor from the requirement to determine materiality in accordance with ISA 320 for purposes of planning and performing the audit of the special purpose financial statements.

A12   Communication with those charged with governance in accordance with ISAs is based on the relationship between those charged with governance and the financial statements subject to audit, in particular, whether those charged with governance are responsible for overseeing the preparation of those financial statements. In the case of special purpose financial statements, those charged with governance may not have such a responsibility; for example, when the financial information is prepared solely for management's use. In such cases, the requirements of ISA 260[12] may not be relevant to the audit of the special purpose financial statements, except when the auditor is also responsible for the audit of the entity's general purpose financial statements or, for example, has agreed with those charged with governance of the entity to communicate to them relevant matters identified during the audit of the special purpose financial statements.

[10] *ISA 200, paragraphs 14, 18 and 22-23.*

[11] *ISA 320, "Materiality in Planning and Performing an Audit," paragraph 2.*

[12] *ISA 260, "Communication with Those Charged with Governance."*

Forming an Opinion and Reporting Considerations (Ref: Para. 11)

The Appendix to this ISA contains illustrations of auditors' reports on special purpose financial statements. **A13**

Alerting Readers that the Financial Statements Are Prepared in Accordance with a Special Purpose Framework (Ref: Para. 14)

The special purpose financial statements may be used for purposes other than those for which they were intended. For example, a regulator may require certain entities to place the special purpose financial statements on public record. To avoid misunderstandings, the auditor alerts users of the auditor's report that the financial statements are prepared in accordance with a special purpose framework and, therefore, may not be suitable for another purpose. **A14**

Restriction on Distribution or Use (Ref: Para. 14)

In addition to the alert required by paragraph 14, the auditor may consider it appropriate to indicate that the auditor's report is intended solely for the specific users. Depending on the law or regulation of the particular jurisdiction, this may be achieved by restricting the distribution or use of the auditor's report. In these circumstances, the paragraph referred to in paragraph 14 may be expanded to include these other matters, and the heading modified accordingly. **A15**

Appendix (Ref: Para. A13)

Illustrations of Auditors' Reports on Special Purpose Financial Statements

- Illustration 1: An auditor's report on a complete set of financial statements prepared in accordance with the financial reporting provisions of a contract (for purposes of this illustration, a compliance framework).
- Illustration 2: An auditor's report on a complete set of financial statements prepared in accordance with the tax basis of accounting in Jurisdiction X (for purposes of this illustration, a compliance framework).
- Illustration 3: An auditor's report on a complete set of financial statements prepared in accordance with the financial reporting provisions established by a regulator (for purposes of this illustration, a fair presentation framework).

Illustration 1:

Circumstances include the following:

- **The financial statements have been prepared by management of the entity in accordance with the financial reporting provisions of a contract (that is, a special purpose framework) to comply with the provisions of that contract. Management does not have a choice of financial reporting frameworks.**

- **The applicable financial reporting framework is a compliance framework.**

- **The terms of the audit engagement reflect the description of management's responsibility for the financial statements in ISA 210.**

- **Distribution and use of the auditor's report are restricted.**

INDEPENDENT AUDITOR'S REPORT

[Appropriate Addressee]

We have audited the accompanying financial statements of ABC Company, which comprise the balance sheet as at December 31, 20X1, and the income statement, statement of changes in equity and cash flow statement for the year then ended, and a summary of significant accounting policies and other explanatory information. The financial statements have been prepared by management of ABC Company based on the financial reporting provisions of Section Z of the contract dated January 1, 20X1 between ABC Company and DEF Company ("the contract").

Management's[13] Responsibility for the Financial Statements

Management is responsible for the preparation of these financial statements in accordance with the financial reporting provisions of Section Z of the contract, and for such internal control as management determines is necessary to enable the preparation of financial statements that are free from material misstatement, whether due to fraud or error.

Auditor's Responsibility

Our responsibility is to express an opinion on these financial statements based on our audit. We conducted our audit in accordance with International Standards on Auditing. Those standards require that we comply with ethical requirements and plan and perform the audit to obtain reasonable assurance about whether the financial statements are free from material misstatement.

An audit involves performing procedures to obtain audit evidence about the amounts and disclosures in the financial statements. The procedures selected depend on the auditor's judgment, including the assessment of the risks of material misstatement of the financial statements, whether due to fraud or error. In making those risk assessments, the auditor considers internal control relevant to the entity's preparation of the financial statements in order to design audit procedures that are appropriate in the circumstances, but not for the purpose of expressing an opinion on the effectiveness of the entity's internal control. An audit also includes evaluating the appropriateness of accounting policies used and the reasonableness of accounting

---

[13] *Or other term that is appropriate in the context of the legal framework in the particular jurisdiction.*

estimates made by management, as well as evaluating the overall presentation of the financial statements.

We believe that the audit evidence we have obtained is sufficient and appropriate to provide a basis for our audit opinion.

Opinion

In our opinion, the financial statements of ABC Company for the year ended December 31, 20X1 are prepared, in all material respects, in accordance with the financial reporting provisions of Section Z of the contract.

Basis of Accounting and Restriction on Distribution and Use

Without modifying our opinion, we draw attention to Note X to the financial statements, which describes the basis of accounting. The financial statements are prepared to assist ABC Company to comply with the financial reporting provisions of the contract referred to above. As a result, the financial statements may not be suitable for another purpose. Our report is intended solely for ABC Company and DEF Company and should not be distributed to or used by parties other than ABC Company or DEF Company.

[Auditor's signature]

[Date of the auditor's report]

[Auditor's address]

Illustration 2:

Circumstances include the following:

- The financial statements have been prepared by management of a partnership in accordance with the tax basis of accounting in Jurisdiction X (that is, a special purpose framework) to assist the partners in preparing their individual income tax returns. Management does not have a choice of financial reporting frameworks.

- The applicable financial reporting framework is a compliance framework.

- The terms of the audit engagement reflect the description of management's responsibility for the financial statements in ISA 210.

- Distribution of the auditor's report is restricted.

INDEPENDENT AUDITOR'S REPORT

[Appropriate Addressee]

We have audited the accompanying financial statements of ABC Partnership, which comprise the balance sheet as at December 31, 20X1 and the income statement for the year then ended, and a summary of significant accounting policies and other explanatory information. The financial statements have been prepared by management using the tax basis of accounting in Jurisdiction X.

Management's[14] Responsibility for the Financial Statements

Management is responsible for the preparation of these financial statements in accordance with the tax basis of accounting in Jurisdiction X, and for such internal control as management determines is necessary to enable the preparation of financial statements that are free from material misstatement, whether due to fraud or error.

Auditor's Responsibility

Our responsibility is to express an opinion on these financial statements based on our audit. We conducted our audit in accordance with International Standards on Auditing. Those standards require that we comply with ethical requirements and plan and perform the audit to obtain reasonable assurance about whether the financial statements are free from material misstatement.

An audit involves performing procedures to obtain audit evidence about the amounts and disclosures in the financial statements. The procedures selected depend on the auditor's judgment, including the assessment of the risks of material misstatement of the financial statements, whether due to fraud or error. In making those risk assessments, the auditor considers internal control relevant to the partnership's preparation of the financial statements in order to design audit procedures that are appropriate in the circumstances, but not for the purpose of expressing an opinion on the effectiveness of the partnership's internal control. An audit also includes evaluating the appropriateness of accounting policies used and the reasonableness of accounting estimates made by management, as well as evaluating the overall presentation of the financial statements.

---

[14] *Or other term that is appropriate in the context of the legal framework in the particular jurisdiction.*

We believe that the audit evidence we have obtained is sufficient and appropriate to provide a basis for our audit opinion.

Opinion

In our opinion, the financial statements of ABC Partnership for the year ended December 31, 20X1 are prepared, in all material respects, in accordance with [describe the applicable income tax law] of Jurisdiction X.

Basis of Accounting and Restriction on Distribution

Without modifying our opinion, we draw attention to Note X to the financial statements, which describes the basis of accounting. The financial statements are prepared to assist the partners of ABC Partnership in preparing their individual income tax returns. As a result, the financial statements may not be suitable for another purpose. Our report is intended solely for ABC Partnership and its partners and should not be distributed to parties other than ABC Partnership or its partners.

[Auditor's signature]

[Date of the auditor's report]

[Auditor's address]

Illustration 3:

Circumstances include the following:

- The financial statements have been prepared by management of the entity in accordance with the financial reporting provisions established by a regulator (that is, a special purpose framework) to meet the requirements of that regulator. Management does not have a choice of financial reporting frameworks.

- The applicable financial reporting framework is a fair presentation framework.

- The terms of the audit engagement reflect the description of management's responsibility for the financial statements in ISA 210.

- Distribution or use of the auditor's report is not restricted.

- The Other Matter paragraph refers to the fact that the auditor has also issued an auditor's report on financial statements prepared by ABC Company for the same period in accordance with a general purpose framework.

INDEPENDENT AUDITOR'S REPORT

[Appropriate Addressee]

We have audited the accompanying financial statements of ABC Company, which comprise the balance sheet as at December 31, 20X1, and the income statement, statement of changes in equity and cash flow statement for the year then ended, and a summary of significant accounting policies and other explanatory information. The financial statements have been prepared by management based on the financial reporting provisions of Section Y of Regulation Z.

Management's[15] Responsibility for the Financial Statements

Management is responsible for the preparation and fair presentation of these financial statements in accordance with the financial reporting provisions of Section Y of Regulation Z,[16] and for such internal control as management determines is necessary to enable the preparation of financial statements that are free from material misstatement, whether due to fraud or error.

Auditor's Responsibility

Our responsibility is to express an opinion on these financial statements based on our audit. We conducted our audit in accordance with International Standards on Auditing. Those standards require that we comply with ethical requirements and plan and perform the audit to obtain reasonable assurance about whether the financial statements are free from material misstatement.

An audit involves performing procedures to obtain audit evidence about the amounts and disclosures in the financial statements. The procedures selected depend on the auditor's judgment, including the assessment of the risks of material misstatement of the financial statements, whether due to fraud or error. In making those

---

[15] Or other term that is appropriate in the context of the legal framework in the particular jurisdiction.

[16] Where management's responsibility is to prepare financial statements that give a true and fair view, this may read: "Management is responsible for the preparation of financial statements that give a true and fair view in accordance with the financial reporting provisions of section Y of Regulation Z, and for such ..."

risk assessments, the auditor considers internal control relevant to the entity's preparation and fair presentation[17] of the financial statements in order to design audit procedures that are appropriate in the circumstances, but not for the purpose of expressing an opinion on the effectiveness of the entity's internal control.[18] An audit also includes evaluating the appropriateness of accounting policies used and the reasonableness of accounting estimates made by management, as well as evaluating the overall presentation of the financial statements.

We believe that the audit evidence we have obtained is sufficient and appropriate to provide a basis for our audit opinion.

Opinion

In our opinion, the financial statements present fairly, in all material respects, (or *give a true and fair view of*) the financial position of ABC Company as at December 31, 20X1, and (*of*) its financial performance and its cash flows for the year then ended in accordance with the financial reporting provisions of Section Y of Regulation Z.

Basis of Accounting

Without modifying our opinion, we draw attention to Note X to the financial statements, which describes the basis of accounting. The financial statements are prepared to assist ABC Company to meet the requirements of Regulator DEF. As a result, the financial statements may not be suitable for another purpose.

Other Matter

ABC Company has prepared a separate set of financial statements for the year ended December 31, 20X1 in accordance with International Financial Reporting Standards on which we issued a separate auditor's report to the shareholders of ABC Company dated March 31, 20X2.

[Auditor's signature]

[Date of the auditor's report]

[Auditor's address]

---

[17] *In the case of footnote 16, this may read: "In making those risk assessments, the auditor considers internal control relevant to the entity's preparation of financial statements that give a true and fair view in order to design audit procedures that are appropriate in the circumstances, but not for the purpose of expressing an opinion on the effectiveness of the entity's internal control."*

[18] *In circumstances when the auditor also has responsibility to express an opinion on the effectiveness of internal control in conjunction with the audit of the financial statements, this sentence would be worded as follows: "In making those risk assessments, the auditor considers internal control relevant to the entity's preparation and fair presentation of the financial statements in order to design audit procedures that are appropriate in the circumstances." In the case of footnote 16, this may read: "In making those risk assessments, the auditor considers internal control relevant to the entity's preparation of financial statements that give a true and fair view in order to design audit procedures that are appropriate in the circumstances."*

International Standard on Auditing 805
Special considerations—audits of single financial statements and specific elements, accounts or items of a financial statement

(Effective for audits for periods
beginning on or after December 15, 2009)

Contents

International Standard on Auditing (ISA) 805, "Special Considerations—Audits of Single Financial Statements and Specific Elements, Accounts or Items of a Financial Statement" should be read in conjunction with ISA 200, "Overall Objectives of the Independent Auditor and the Conduct of an Audit in Accordance with International Standards on Auditing."

Introduction

Scope of this ISA

The International Standards on Auditing (ISAs) in the 100-700 series apply to an audit of financial statements and are to be adapted as necessary in the circumstances when applied to audits of other historical financial information. This ISA deals with special considerations in the application of those ISAs to an audit of a single financial statement or of a specific element, account or item of a financial statement. The single financial statement or the specific element, account or item of a financial statement may be prepared in accordance with a general or special purpose framework. If prepared in accordance with a special purpose framework, ISA 800¹ also applies to the audit. (Ref: Para. A1-A4)   **1**

This ISA does not apply to the report of a component auditor, issued as a result of work performed on the financial information of a component at the request of a group engagement team for purposes of an audit of group financial statements (see ISA 600²).   **2**

This ISA does not override the requirements of the other ISAs; nor does it purport to deal with all special considerations that may be relevant in the circumstances of the engagement.   **3**

Effective Date

This ISA is effective for audits of single financial statements or of specific elements, accounts or items for periods beginning on or after December 15, 2009. In the case of audits of single financial statements or of specific elements, accounts or items of a financial statement prepared as at a specific date, this ISA is effective for audits of such information prepared as at a date on or after December 14, 2010.   **4**

Objective

The objective of the auditor, when applying ISAs in an audit of a single financial statement or of a specific element, account or item of a financial statement, is to address appropriately the special considerations that are relevant to: **5**

(a) The acceptance of the engagement;
(b) The planning and performance of that engagement; and
(c) Forming an opinion and reporting on the single financial statement or on the specific element, account or item of a financial statement.

Definitions

For purposes of this ISA, reference to: **6**

(a) "Element of a financial statement" or "element" means an "element, account or item of a financial statement;"

---

¹ ISA 800, *"Special Considerations—Audits of Financial Statements Prepared in Accordance with Special Purpose Frameworks."*

² ISA 600, *"Special Considerations—Audits of Group Financial Statements (Including the Work of Component Auditors)."*

(b) "International Financial Reporting Standards" means the International Financial Reporting Standards issued by the International Accounting Standards Board; and

(c) A single financial statement or to a specific element of a financial statement includes the related notes. The related notes ordinarily comprise a summary of significant accounting policies and other explanatory information relevant to the financial statement or to the element.

Requirements

Considerations When Accepting the Engagement

Application of ISAs

7   ISA 200 requires the auditor to comply with all ISAs relevant to the audit.[3] In the case of an audit of a single financial statement or of a specific element of a financial statement, this requirement applies irrespective of whether the auditor is also engaged to audit the entity's complete set of financial statements. If the auditor is not also engaged to audit the entity's complete set of financial statements, the auditor shall determine whether the audit of a single financial statement or of a specific element of those financial statements in accordance with ISAs is practicable. (Ref: Para. A5-A6)

Acceptability of the Financial Reporting Framework

8   ISA 210 requires the auditor to determine the acceptability of the financial reporting framework applied in the preparation of the financial statements.[4] In the case of an audit of a single financial statement or of a specific element of a financial statement, this shall include whether application of the financial reporting framework will result in a presentation that provides adequate disclosures to enable the intended users to understand the information conveyed in the financial statement or the element, and the effect of material transactions and events on the information conveyed in the financial statement or the element. (Ref: Para. A7)

Form of Opinion

9   ISA 210 requires that the agreed terms of the audit engagement include the expected form of any reports to be issued by the auditor.[5] In the case of an audit of a single financial statement or of a specific element of a financial statement, the auditor shall consider whether the expected form of opinion is appropriate in the circumstances. (Ref: Para. A8-A9)

---

[3] *ISA 200, "Overall Objectives of the Independent Auditor and the Conduct of an Audit in Accordance with International Standards on Auditing," paragraph 18.*

[4] *ISA 210, "Agreeing the Terms of Audit Engagements," paragraph 6(a).*

[5] *ISA 210, paragraph 10(e).*

Considerations When Planning and Performing the Audit

ISA 200 states that ISAs are written in the context of an audit of financial statements; they are to be adapted as necessary in the circumstances when applied to audits of other historical financial information.[6][7] In planning and performing the audit of a single financial statement or of a specific element of a financial statement, the auditor shall adapt all ISAs relevant to the audit as necessary in the circumstances of the engagement. (Ref: Para. A10-A14)

10

Forming an Opinion and Reporting Considerations

When forming an opinion and reporting on a single financial statement or on a specific element of a financial statement, the auditor shall apply the requirements in ISA 700,[8] adapted as necessary in the circumstances of the engagement. (Ref: Para. A15-A16)

11

Reporting on the Entity's Complete Set of Financial Statements and on a Single Financial Statement or on a Specific Element of Those Financial Statements

If the auditor undertakes an engagement to report on a single financial statement or on a specific element of a financial statement in conjunction with an engagement to audit the entity's complete set of financial statements, the auditor shall express a separate opinion for each engagement.

12

An audited single financial statement or an audited specific element of a financial statement may be published together with the entity's audited complete set of financial statements. If the auditor concludes that the presentation of the single financial statement or of the specific element of a financial statement does not differentiate it sufficiently from the complete set of financial statements, the auditor shall ask management to rectify the situation. Subject to paragraphs 15 and 16, the auditor shall also differentiate the opinion on the single financial statement or on the specific element of a financial statement from the opinion on the complete set of financial statements. The auditor shall not issue the auditor's report containing the opinion on the single financial statement or on the specific element of a financial statement until satisfied with the differentiation.

13

Modified Opinion, Emphasis of Matter Paragraph or Other Matter Paragraph in the Auditor's Report on the Entity's Complete Set of Financial Statements

If the opinion in the auditor's report on an entity's complete set of financial statements is modified, or that report includes an Emphasis of Matter paragraph or an Other Matter paragraph, the auditor shall determine the effect that this may have on the auditor's report on a single financial statement or on a specific element of those financial statements. When deemed appropriate, the auditor shall modify the opinion on the single financial statement or on the specific element of a financial statement, or include an Emphasis of Matter paragraph or an Other Matter paragraph in the auditor's report, accordingly. (Ref: Para. A17)

14

---

[6] *ISA 200, paragraph 2.*

[7] *ISA 200, paragraph 13(f), explains that the term "financial statements" ordinarily refers to a complete set of financial statements as determined by the requirements of the applicable financial reporting framework.*

15   If the auditor concludes that it is necessary to express an adverse opinion or disclaim an opinion on the entity's complete set of financial statements as a whole, ISA 705 does not permit the auditor to include in the same auditor's report an unmodified opinion on a single financial statement that forms part of those financial statements or on a specific element that forms part of those financial statements.[9] This is because such an unmodified opinion would contradict the adverse opinion or disclaimer of opinion on the entity's complete set of financial statements as a whole. (Ref: Para. A18)

16   If the auditor concludes that it is necessary to express an adverse opinion or disclaim an opinion on the entity's complete set of financial statements as a whole but, in the context of a separate audit of a specific element that is included in those financial statements, the auditor nevertheless considers it appropriate to express an unmodified opinion on that element, the auditor shall only do so if:

   (a)   The auditor is not prohibited by law or regulation from doing so;

   (b)   That opinion is expressed in an auditor's report that is not published together with the auditor's report containing the adverse opinion or disclaimer of opinion; and

   (c)   The specific element does not constitute a major portion of the entity's complete set of financial statements.

17   The auditor shall not express an unmodified opinion on a single financial statement of a complete set of financial statements if the auditor has expressed an adverse opinion or disclaimed an opinion on the complete set of financial statements as a whole. This is the case even if the auditor's report on the single financial statement is not published together with the auditor's report containing the adverse opinion or disclaimer of opinion. This is because a single financial statement is deemed to constitute a major portion of those financial statements.

***

Application and Other Explanatory Material

Scope of this ISA (Ref: Para. 1)

A1   ISA 200 defines the term "historical financial information" as information expressed in financial terms in relation to a particular entity, derived primarily from that entity's accounting system, about economic events occurring in past time periods or about economic conditions or circumstances at points in time in the past.[10]

A2   ISA 200 defines the term "financial statements" as a structured representation of historical financial information, including related notes, intended to communicate an entity's economic resources or obligations at a point in time or the changes therein for a period of time in accordance with a financial reporting framework. The term ordinarily refers to a complete set of financial statements as determined by the requirements of the applicable financial reporting framework.[11]

---

[9] *ISA 705, "Modifications to the Opinion in the Independent Auditor's Report," paragraph 15.*

[10] *ISA 200, paragraph 13(g).*

[11] *ISA 200, paragraph 13(f).*

ISAs are written in the context of an audit of financial statements;[12] they are to be   **A3** adapted as necessary in the circumstances when applied to an audit of other historical financial information, such as a single financial statement or a specific element of a financial statement. This ISA assists in this regard. (Appendix 1 lists examples of such other historical financial information.)

A reasonable assurance engagement other than an audit of historical financial   **A4** information is performed in accordance with International Standard on Assurance Engagements (ISAE) 3000.[13]

Considerations When Accepting the Engagement

Application of ISAs (Ref: Para. 7)

ISA 200 requires the auditor to comply with (a) relevant ethical requirements,   **A5** including those pertaining to independence, relating to financial statement audit engagements, and (b) all ISAs relevant to the audit. It also requires the auditor to comply with each requirement of an ISA unless, in the circumstances of the audit, the entire ISA is not relevant or the requirement is not relevant because it is conditional and the condition does not exist. In exceptional circumstances, the auditor may judge it necessary to depart from a relevant requirement in an ISA by performing alternative audit procedures to achieve the aim of that requirement.[14]

Compliance with the requirements of ISAs relevant to the audit of a single financial   **A6** statement or of a specific element of a financial statement may not be practicable when the auditor is not also engaged to audit the entity's complete set of financial statements. In such cases, the auditor often does not have the same understanding of the entity and its environment, including its internal control, as an auditor who also audits the entity's complete set of financial statements. The auditor also does not have the audit evidence about the general quality of the accounting records or other accounting information that would be acquired in an audit of the entity's complete set of financial statements. Accordingly, the auditor may need further evidence to corroborate audit evidence acquired from the accounting records. In the case of an audit of a specific element of a financial statement, certain ISAs require audit work that may be disproportionate to the element being audited. For example, although the requirements of ISA 570[15] are likely to be relevant in the circumstances of an audit of a schedule of accounts receivable, complying with those requirements may not be practicable because of the audit effort required. If the auditor concludes that an audit of a single financial statement or of a specific element of a financial statement in accordance with ISAs may not be practicable, the auditor may discuss with management whether another type of engagement might be more practicable.

Acceptability of the Financial Reporting Framework (Ref: Para. 8)

A single financial statement or a specific element of a financial statement may be   **A7** prepared in accordance with an applicable financial reporting framework that is based on a financial reporting framework established by an authorized or recognized

[12] *ISA 200, paragraph 2.*

[13] *ISAE 3000, "Assurance Engagements Other than Audits or Reviews of Historical Financial Information."*

[14] *ISA 200, paragraphs 14, 18 and 22-23.*

[15] *ISA 570, "Going Concern."*

standards setting organization for the preparation of a complete set of financial statements (for example, International Financial Reporting Standards). If this is the case, determination of the acceptability of the applicable framework may involve considering whether that framework includes all the requirements of the framework on which it is based that are relevant to the presentation of a single financial statement or of a specific element of a financial statement that provides adequate disclosures.

Form of Opinion (Ref: Para. 9)

A8   The form of opinion to be expressed by the auditor depends on the applicable financial reporting framework and any applicable laws or regulations.[16] In accordance with ISA 700:[17]

(a) When expressing an unmodified opinion on a complete set of financial statements prepared in accordance with a fair presentation framework, the auditor's opinion, unless otherwise required by law or regulation, uses one of the following phrases: (i) the financial statements present fairly, in all material respects, in accordance with [the applicable financial reporting framework]; or (ii) the financial statements give a true and fair view in accordance with [the applicable financial reporting framework]; and

(b) When expressing an unmodified opinion on a complete set of financial statements prepared in accordance with a compliance framework, the auditor's opinion states that the financial statements are prepared, in all material respects, in accordance with [the applicable financial reporting framework].

A9   In the case of a single financial statement or of a specific element of a financial statement, the applicable financial reporting framework may not explicitly address the presentation of the financial statement or of the element. This may be the case when the applicable financial reporting framework is based on a financial reporting framework established by an authorized or recognized standards setting organization for the preparation of a complete set of financial statements (for example, International Financial Reporting Standards). The auditor therefore considers whether the expected form of opinion is appropriate in the light of the applicable financial reporting framework. Factors that may affect the auditor's consideration as to whether to use the phrases "presents fairly, in all material respects," or "gives a true and fair view" in the auditor's opinion include:

- Whether the applicable financial reporting framework is explicitly or implicitly restricted to the preparation of a complete set of financial statements.
- Whether the single financial statement or the specific element of a financial statement will:
  - Comply fully with each of those requirements of the framework relevant to the particular financial statement or the particular element, and the presentation of the financial statement or the element include the related notes.
  - If necessary to achieve fair presentation, provide disclosures beyond those specifically required by the framework or, in exceptional circumstances, depart from a requirement of the framework.

The auditor's decision as to the expected form of opinion is a matter of professional judgment. It may be affected by whether use of the phrases "presents fairly, in all material respects," or "gives a true and fair view" in the auditor's opinion on a single

---

[16] *ISA 200, paragraph 8.*

[17] *ISA 700, paragraphs 35-36.*

financial statement or on a specific element of a financial statement prepared in accordance with a fair presentation framework is generally accepted in the particular jurisdiction.

Considerations When Planning and Performing the Audit (Ref: Para. 10)

The relevance of each of the ISAs requires careful consideration. Even when only a specific element of a financial statement is the subject of the audit, ISAs such as ISA 240,[18] ISA 550[19] and ISA 570 are, in principle, relevant. This is because the element could be misstated as a result of fraud, the effect of related party transactions, or the incorrect application of the going concern assumption under the applicable financial reporting framework.

A10

Furthermore, ISAs are written in the context of an audit of financial statements; they are to be adapted as necessary in the circumstances when applied to the audit of a single financial statement or of a specific element of a financial statement.[20] For example, written representations from management about the complete set of financial statements would be replaced by written representations about the presentation of the financial statement or the element in accordance with the applicable financial reporting framework.

A11

When auditing a single financial statement or a specific element of a financial statement in conjunction with the audit of the entity's complete set of financial statements, the auditor may be able to use audit evidence obtained as part of the audit of the entity's complete set of financial statements in the audit of the financial statement or the element. ISAs, however, require the auditor to plan and perform the audit of the financial statement or element to obtain sufficient appropriate audit evidence on which to base the opinion on the financial statement or on the element.

A12

The individual financial statements that comprise a complete set of financial statements, and many of the elements of those financial statements, including their related notes, are interrelated. Accordingly, when auditing a single financial statement or a specific element of a financial statement, the auditor may not be able to consider the financial statement or the element in isolation. Consequently, the auditor may need to perform procedures in relation to the interrelated items to meet the objective of the audit.

A13

Furthermore, the materiality determined for a single financial statement or for a specific element of a financial statement may be lower than the materiality determined for the entity's complete set of financial statements; this will affect the nature, timing and extent of the audit procedures and the evaluation of uncorrected misstatements.

A14

Forming an Opinion and Reporting Considerations (Ref: Para. 11)

ISA 700 requires the auditor, in forming an opinion, to evaluate whether the financial statements provide adequate disclosures to enable the intended users to

A15

---

[18] *ISA 240, "The Auditor's Responsibilities Relating to Fraud in an Audit of Financial Statements."*

[19] *ISA 550, "Related Parties."*

[20] *ISA 200, paragraph 2.*

understand the effect of material transactions and events on the information conveyed in the financial statements.[21] In the case of a single financial statement or of a specific element of a financial statement, it is important that the financial statement or the element, including the related notes, in view of the requirements of the applicable financial reporting framework, provides adequate disclosures to enable the intended users to understand the information conveyed in the financial statement or the element, and the effect of material transactions and events on the information conveyed in the financial statement or the element.

A16   Appendix 2 of this ISA contains illustrations of auditors' reports on a single financial statement and on a specific element of a financial statement.

Modified Opinion, Emphasis of Matter Paragraph or Other Matter Paragraph in the Auditor's Report on the Entity's Complete Set of Financial Statements (Ref: Para. 14-15)

A17   Even when the modified opinion on the entity's complete set of financial statements, Emphasis of Matter paragraph or Other Matter paragraph does not relate to the audited financial statement or the audited element, the auditor may still deem it appropriate to refer to the modification in an Other Matter paragraph in an auditor's report on the financial statement or on the element because the auditor judges it to be relevant to the users' understanding of the audited financial statement or the audited element or the related auditor's report (see ISA 706).[22]

A18   In the auditor's report on an entity's complete set of financial statements, the expression of a disclaimer of opinion regarding the results of operations and cash flows, where relevant, and an unmodified opinion regarding the financial position is permitted since the disclaimer of opinion is being issued in respect of the results of operations and cash flows only and not in respect of the financial statements as a whole.[23]

Appendix 1   (Ref: Para. A3)

Examples of Specific Elements, Accounts or Items of a Financial Statement

- Accounts receivable, allowance for doubtful accounts receivable, inventory, the liability for accrued benefits of a private pension plan, the recorded value of identified intangible assets, or the liability for "incurred but not reported" claims in an insurance portfolio, including related notes.
- A schedule of externally managed assets and income of a private pension plan, including related notes.
- A schedule of net tangible assets, including related notes.
- A schedule of disbursements in relation to a lease property, including explanatory notes.
- A schedule of profit participation or employee bonuses, including explanatory notes.

---

[21] *ISA 700, paragraph 13(e).*

[22] *ISA 706, "Emphasis of Matter Paragraphs and Other Matter Paragraphs in the Independent Auditor's Report," paragraph 6.*

[23] *ISA 510, "Initial Audit Engagements—Opening Balances," paragraph A8, and ISA 705, paragraph A16.*

Appendix 2

(Ref: Para. A16)

Illustrations of Auditors' Reports on a Single Financial Statement and on a Specific Element of a Financial Statement

- Illustration 1: An auditor's report on a single financial statement prepared in accordance with a general purpose framework (for purposes of this illustration, a fair presentation framework).
- Illustration 2: An auditor's report on a single financial statement prepared in accordance with a special purpose framework (for purposes of this illustration, a fair presentation framework).
- Illustration 3: An auditor's report on a specific element, account or item of a financial statement prepared in accordance with a special purpose framework (for purposes of this illustration, a compliance framework).

Illustration 1:

Circumstances include the following:

- Audit of a balance sheet (that is, a single financial statement).

- The balance sheet has been prepared by management of the entity in accordance with the requirements of the Financial Reporting Framework in Jurisdiction X relevant to preparing a balance sheet.

- The applicable financial reporting framework is a fair presentation framework designed to meet the common financial information needs of a wide range of users.

- The terms of the audit engagement reflect the description of management's responsibility for the financial statements in ISA 210.

- The auditor has determined that it is appropriate to use the phrase "presents fairly, in all material respects," in the auditor's opinion.

INDEPENDENT AUDITOR'S REPORT

[Appropriate Addressee]

We have audited the accompanying balance sheet of ABC Company as at December 31, 20X1 and a summary of significant accounting policies and other explanatory information (together "the financial statement").

Management's[24] Responsibility for the Financial Statement

Management is responsible for the preparation and fair presentation of this financial statement in accordance with those requirements of the Financial Reporting Framework in Jurisdiction X relevant to preparing such a financial statement, and for such internal control as management determines is necessary to enable the preparation of the financial statement that is free from material misstatement, whether due to fraud or error.

Auditor's Responsibility

Our responsibility is to express an opinion on the financial statement based on our audit. We conducted our audit in accordance with International Standards on Auditing. Those standards require that we comply with ethical requirements and plan and perform the audit to obtain reasonable assurance about whether the financial statement is free from material misstatement.

An audit involves performing procedures to obtain audit evidence about the amounts and disclosures in the financial statement. The procedures selected depend on the auditor's judgment, including the assessment of the risks of material misstatement of the financial statement, whether due to fraud or error. In making those risk assessments, the auditor considers internal control relevant to the entity's preparation and fair presentation of the financial statement in order to design audit procedures that are appropriate in the circumstances, but not for the purpose of

---

[24] *Or other term that is appropriate in the context of the legal framework in the particular jurisdiction.*

expressing an opinion on the effectiveness of the entity's internal control.[25] An audit also includes evaluating the appropriateness of accounting policies used and the reasonableness of accounting estimates, if any, made by management, as well as evaluating the overall presentation of the financial statement.

We believe that the audit evidence we have obtained is sufficient and appropriate to provide a basis for our audit opinion.

Opinion

In our opinion, the financial statement presents fairly, in all material respects, the financial position of ABC Company as at December 31, 20X1 in accordance with those requirements of the Financial Reporting Framework in Jurisdiction X relevant to preparing such a financial statement.

[Auditor's signature]

[Date of the auditor's report]

[Auditor's address]

Illustration 2:

Circumstances include the following:

- Audit of a statement of cash receipts and disbursements (that is, a single financial statement).

- The financial statement has been prepared by management of the entity in accordance with the cash receipts and disbursements basis of accounting to respond to a request for cash flow information received from a creditor. Management has a choice of financial reporting frameworks.

- The applicable financial reporting framework is a fair presentation framework designed to meet the financial information needs of specific users.[26]

- The auditor has determined that it is appropriate to use the phrase "presents fairly, in all material respects," in the auditor's opinion.

- Distribution or use of the auditor's report is not restricted.

INDEPENDENT AUDITOR'S REPORT

[Appropriate Addressee]

We have audited the accompanying statement of cash receipts and disbursements of ABC Company for the year ended December 31, 20X1 and a summary of significant accounting policies and other explanatory information (together "the financial statement"). The financial statement has been prepared by management using the cash receipts and disbursements basis of accounting described in Note X.

Management's[27] Responsibility for the Financial Statement

Management is responsible for the preparation and fair presentation of this financial statement in accordance with the cash receipts and disbursements basis of accounting described in Note X; this includes determining that the cash receipts and disbursements basis of accounting is an acceptable basis for the preparation of the financial statement in the circumstances, and for such internal control as management determines is necessary to enable the preparation of the financial statement that is free from material misstatement, whether due to fraud or error.

Auditor's Responsibility

Our responsibility is to express an opinion on the financial statement based on our audit. We conducted our audit in accordance with International Standards on Auditing. Those standards require that we comply with ethical requirements and plan and perform the audit to obtain reasonable assurance about whether the financial statement is free from material misstatement.

An audit involves performing procedures to obtain audit evidence about the amounts and disclosures in the financial statement. The procedures selected depend on the auditor's judgment, including the assessment of the risks of material

---

[26] *ISA 800 contains requirements and guidance on the form and content of financial statements prepared in accordance with a special purpose framework.*

[27] *Or other term that is appropriate in the context of the legal framework in the particular jurisdiction.*

misstatement of the financial statement, whether due to fraud or error. In making those risk assessments, the auditor considers internal control relevant to the entity's preparation and fair presentation of the financial statement in order to design audit procedures that are appropriate in the circumstances, but not for the purpose of expressing an opinion on the effectiveness of the entity's internal control. An audit also includes evaluating the appropriateness of accounting policies used and the reasonableness of accounting estimates, if any, made by management, as well as evaluating the overall presentation of the financial statement.

We believe that the audit evidence we have obtained is sufficient and appropriate to provide a basis for our audit opinion.

Opinion

In our opinion, the financial statement presents fairly, in all material respects, the cash receipts and disbursements of ABC Company for the year ended December 31, 20X1 in accordance with the cash receipts and disbursements basis of accounting described in Note X.

Basis of Accounting

Without modifying our opinion, we draw attention to Note X to the financial statement, which describes the basis of accounting. The financial statement is prepared to provide information to XYZ Creditor. As a result, the statement may not be suitable for another purpose.

[Auditor's signature]

[Date of the auditor's report]

[Auditor's address]

Illustration 3:

Circumstances include the following:

- Audit of the liability for "incurred but not reported" claims in an insurance portfolio (that is, element, account or item of a financial statement).

- The financial information has been prepared by management of the entity in accordance with the financial reporting provisions established by a regulator to meet the requirements of that regulator. Management does not have a choice of financial reporting frameworks.

- The applicable financial reporting framework is a compliance framework designed to meet the financial information needs of specific users.[28]

- The terms of the audit engagement reflect the description of management's responsibility for the financial statements in ISA 210.

- Distribution of the auditor's report is restricted.

INDEPENDENT AUDITOR'S REPORT

[Appropriate Addressee]

We have audited the accompanying schedule of the liability for "incurred but not reported" claims of ABC Insurance Company as at December 31, 20X1 ("the schedule"). The schedule has been prepared by management based on [describe the financial reporting provisions established by the regulator].

Management's[29] Responsibility for the Schedule

Management is responsible for the preparation of the schedule in accordance with [describe the financial reporting provisions established by the regulator], and for such internal control as management determines is necessary to enable the preparation of the schedule that is free from material misstatement, whether due to fraud or error.

Auditor's Responsibility

Our responsibility is to express an opinion on the schedule based on our audit. We conducted our audit in accordance with International Standards on Auditing. Those standards require that we comply with ethical requirements and plan and perform the audit to obtain reasonable assurance about whether the schedule is free from material misstatement.

An audit involves performing procedures to obtain audit evidence about the amounts and disclosures in the schedule. The procedures selected depend on the auditor's judgment, including the assessment of the risks of material misstatement of the schedule, whether due to fraud or error. In making those risk assessments, the auditor considers internal control relevant to the entity's preparation of the schedule in order to design audit procedures that are appropriate in the circumstances, but not for the purpose of expressing an opinion on the effectiveness of the entity's internal control. An audit also includes evaluating the appropriateness of accounting policies

---

[28] *ISA 800 contains requirements and guidance on the form and content of financial statements prepared in accordance with a special purpose framework.*

[29] *Or other term that is appropriate in the context of the legal framework in the particular jurisdiction.*

used and the reasonableness of accounting estimates made by management, as well as evaluating the overall presentation of the schedule.

We believe that the audit evidence we have obtained is sufficient and appropriate to provide a basis for our audit opinion.

Opinion

In our opinion, the financial information in the schedule of the liability for "incurred but not reported" claims of ABC Insurance Company as at December 31, 20X1 is prepared, in all material respects, in accordance with [describe the financial reporting provisions established by the regulator].

Basis of Accounting and Restriction on Distribution

Without modifying our opinion, we draw attention to Note X to the schedule, which describes the basis of accounting. The schedule is prepared to assist ABC Insurance Company to meet the requirements of Regulator DEF. As a result, the schedule may not be suitable for another purpose. Our report is intended solely for ABC Insurance Company and Regulator DEF and should not be distributed to parties other than ABC Insurance Company or Regulator DEF.

[Auditor's signature]

[Date of the auditor's report]

[Auditor's address]

International Standard on Auditing 810
Engagements to report on summary financial statements

*(Effective for engagements for periods
beginning on or after December 15, 2009)*

Contents

International Standard on Auditing (ISA) 810, "Engagements to Report on Summary Financial Statements" should be read in conjunction with ISA 200, "Overall Objectives of the Independent Auditor and the Conduct of an Audit in Accordance with International Standards on Auditing."

Introduction

Scope of this ISA

This International Standard on Auditing (ISA) deals with the auditor's responsi- **1**
bilities relating to an engagement to report on summary financial statements derived
from financial statements audited in accordance with ISAs by that same auditor.

Effective Date

This ISA is effective for engagements for periods beginning on or after December 15, **2**
2009.

Objectives

The objectives of the auditor are: **3**

(a) To determine whether it is appropriate to accept the engagement to report on
summary financial statements; and

(b) If engaged to report on summary financial statements:

 (i) To form an opinion on the summary financial statements based on an
evaluation of the conclusions drawn from the evidence obtained; and

 (ii) To express clearly that opinion through a written report that also describes
the basis for that opinion.

Definitions

For purposes of this ISA, the following terms have the meanings attributed below: **4**

(a) Applied criteria – The criteria applied by management in the preparation of the
summary financial statements.

(b) Audited financial statements – Financial statements[1] audited by the auditor in
accordance with ISAs, and from which the summary financial statements are
derived.

(c) Summary financial statements – Historical financial information that is derived
from financial statements but that contains less detail than the financial statements, while still providing a structured representation consistent with that
provided by the financial statements of the entity's economic resources or
obligations at a point in time or the changes therein for a period of time.[2]
Different jurisdictions may use different terminology to describe such historical
financial information.

Requirements

Engagement Acceptance

The auditor shall accept an engagement to report on summary financial statements in **5**
accordance with this ISA only when the auditor has been engaged to conduct an

---

[1] ISA 200, "Overall Objectives of the Independent Auditor and the Conduct of an Audit in Accordance with
International Standards on Auditing," paragraph 13(f), defines the term "financial statements."

[2] ISA 200, paragraph 13(f).

audit in accordance with ISAs of the financial statements from which the summary financial statements are derived. (Ref: Para. A1)

6   Before accepting an engagement to report on summary financial statements, the auditor shall: (Ref: Para. A2)

(a) Determine whether the applied criteria are acceptable; (Ref: Para. A3-A7)

(b) Obtain the agreement of management that it acknowledges and understands its responsibility:

   (i)   For the preparation of the summary financial statements in accordance with the applied criteria;

   (ii) To make the audited financial statements available to the intended users of the summary financial statements without undue difficulty (or, if law or regulation provides that the audited financial statements need not be made available to the intended users of the summary financial statements and establishes the criteria for the preparation of the summary financial statements, to describe that law or regulation in the summary financial statements); and

   (iii) To include the auditor's report on the summary financial statements in any document that contains the summary financial statements and that indicates that the auditor has reported on them.

(c) Agree with management the form of opinion to be expressed on the summary financial statements (see paragraphs 9-11).

7   If the auditor concludes that the applied criteria are unacceptable or is unable to obtain the agreement of management set out in paragraph 6(b), the auditor shall not accept the engagement to report on the summary financial statements, unless required by law or regulation to do so. An engagement conducted in accordance with such law or regulation does not comply with this ISA. Accordingly, the auditor's report on the summary financial statements shall not indicate that the engagement was conducted in accordance with this ISA. The auditor shall include appropriate reference to this fact in the terms of the engagement. The auditor shall also determine the effect that this may have on the engagement to audit the financial statements from which the summary financial statements are derived.

Nature of Procedures

8   The auditor shall perform the following procedures, and any other procedures that the auditor may consider necessary, as the basis for the auditor's opinion on the summary financial statements:

(a) Evaluate whether the summary financial statements adequately disclose their summarized nature and identify the audited financial statements.

(b) When summary financial statements are not accompanied by the audited financial statements, evaluate whether they describe clearly:

   (i)   From whom or where the audited financial statements are available; or

   (ii) The law or regulation that specifies that the audited financial statements need not be made available to the intended users of the summary financial statements and establishes the criteria for the preparation of the summary financial statements.

(c) Evaluate whether the summary financial statements adequately disclose the applied criteria.

(d) Compare the summary financial statements with the related information in the audited financial statements to determine whether the summary financial statements agree with or can be recalculated from the related information in the audited financial statements.

(e)   Evaluate whether the summary financial statements are prepared in accordance with the applied criteria.

(f)   Evaluate, in view of the purpose of the summary financial statements, whether the summary financial statements contain the information necessary, and are at an appropriate level of aggregation, so as not to be misleading in the circumstances.

(g)   Evaluate whether the audited financial statements are available to the intended users of the summary financial statements without undue difficulty, unless law or regulation provides that they need not be made available and establishes the criteria for the preparation of the summary financial statements. (Ref: Para. A8)

Form of Opinion

When the auditor has concluded that an unmodified opinion on the summary   **9** financial statements is appropriate, the auditor's opinion shall, unless otherwise required by law or regulation, use one of the following phrases: (Ref: Para. A9)

(a)   The summary financial statements are consistent, in all material respects, with the audited financial statements, in accordance with [the applied criteria]; or

(b)   The summary financial statements are a fair summary of the audited financial statements, in accordance with [the applied criteria].

If law or regulation prescribes the wording of the opinion on summary financial   **10** statements in terms that are different from those described in paragraph 9, the auditor shall:

(a)   Apply the procedures described in paragraph 8 and any further procedures necessary to enable the auditor to express the prescribed opinion; and

(b)   Evaluate whether users of the summary financial statements might misunderstand the auditor's opinion on the summary financial statements and, if so, whether additional explanation in the auditor's report on the summary financial statements can mitigate possible misunderstanding.

If, in the case of paragraph 10(b), the auditor concludes that additional explanation   **11** in the auditor's report on the summary financial statements cannot mitigate possible misunderstanding, the auditor shall not accept the engagement, unless required by law or regulation to do so. An engagement conducted in accordance with such law or regulation does not comply with this ISA. Accordingly, the auditor's report on the summary financial statements shall not indicate that the engagement was conducted in accordance with this ISA.

Timing of Work and Events Subsequent to the Date of the Auditor's Report on the Audited Financial Statements

The auditor's report on the summary financial statements may be dated later than   **12** the date of the auditor's report on the audited financial statements. In such cases, the auditor's report on the summary financial statements shall state that the summary financial statements and audited financial statements do not reflect the effects of events that occurred subsequent to the date of the auditor's report on the audited financial statements that may require adjustment of, or disclosure in, the audited financial statements. (Ref: Para. A10)

The auditor may become aware of facts that existed at the date of the auditor's   **13** report on the audited financial statements, but of which the auditor previously was unaware. In such cases, the auditor shall not issue the auditor's report on the summary financial statements until the auditor's consideration of such facts in relation to the audited financial statements in accordance with ISA 560[3] has been completed.

Auditor's Report on Summary Financial Statements

Elements of the Auditor's Report

14 The auditor's report on summary financial statements shall include the following elements:[4] (Ref: Para. A15)

(a) A title clearly indicating it as the report of an independent auditor. (Ref: Para. A11)

(b) An addressee. (Ref: Para. A12)

(c) An introductory paragraph that:

(i) Identifies the summary financial statements on which the auditor is reporting, including the title of each statement included in the summary financial statements; (Ref: Para. A13)

(ii) Identifies the audited financial statements;

(iii) Refers to the auditor's report on the audited financial statements, the date of that report, and, subject to paragraphs 17-18, the fact that an unmodified opinion is expressed on the audited financial statements;

(iv) If the date of the auditor's report on the summary financial statements is later than the date of the auditor's report on the audited financial statements, states that the summary financial statements and the audited financial statements do not reflect the effects of events that occurred subsequent to the date of the auditor's report on the audited financial statements; and

(v) A statement indicating that the summary financial statements do not contain all the disclosures required by the financial reporting framework applied in the preparation of the audited financial statements, and that reading the summary financial statements is not a substitute for reading the audited financial statements.

(d) A description of management's[5] responsibility for the summary financial statements, explaining that management[6] is responsible for the preparation of the summary financial statements in accordance with the applied criteria.

(e) A statement that the auditor is responsible for expressing an opinion on the summary financial statements based on the procedures required by this ISA.

(f) A paragraph clearly expressing an opinion (see paragraphs 9-11).

(g) The auditor's signature.

(h) The date of the auditor's report. (Ref: Para. A14)

(i) The auditor's address.

15 If the addressee of the summary financial statements is not the same as the addressee of the auditor's report on the audited financial statements, the auditor shall evaluate the appropriateness of using a different addressee. (Ref: Para. A12)

16 The auditor shall date the auditor's report on the summary financial statements no earlier than: (Ref: Para. A14)

[3] *ISA 560, "Subsequent Events."*

[4] *Paragraphs 17-18, which deal with circumstances where the auditor's report on the audited financial statements has been modified, require additional elements to those listed in this paragraph.*

[5] *Or other term that is appropriate in the context of the legal framework in the particular jurisdiction.*

[6] *Or other term that is appropriate in the context of the legal framework in the particular jurisdiction.*

(a) The date on which the auditor has obtained sufficient appropriate evidence on which to base the opinion, including evidence that the summary financial statements have been prepared and those with the recognized authority have asserted that they have taken responsibility for them; and

(b) The date of the auditor's report on the audited financial statements.

Modifications to the Opinion, Emphasis of Matter Paragraph or Other Matter Paragraph in the Auditor's Report on the Audited Financial Statements (Ref: Para. A15)

When the auditor's report on the audited financial statements contains a qualified **17** opinion, an Emphasis of Matter paragraph, or an Other Matter paragraph, but the auditor is satisfied that the summary financial statements are consistent, in all material respects, with or are a fair summary of the audited financial statements, in accordance with the applied criteria, the auditor's report on the summary financial statements shall, in addition to the elements in paragraph 14:

(a) State that the auditor's report on the audited financial statements contains a qualified opinion, an Emphasis of Matter paragraph, or an Other Matter paragraph; and

(b) Describe:
   (i) The basis for the qualified opinion on the audited financial statements, and that qualified opinion; or the Emphasis of Matter or the Other Matter paragraph in the auditor's report on the audited financial statements; and
   (ii) The effect thereof on the summary financial statements, if any.

When the auditor's report on the audited financial statements contains an adverse **18** opinion or a disclaimer of opinion, the auditor's report on the summary financial statements shall, in addition to the elements in paragraph 14:

(a) State that the auditor's report on the audited financial statements contains an adverse opinion or disclaimer of opinion;

(b) Describe the basis for that adverse opinion or disclaimer of opinion; and

(c) State that, as a result of the adverse opinion or disclaimer of opinion, it is inappropriate to express an opinion on the summary financial statements.

Modified Opinion on the Summary Financial Statements

If the summary financial statements are not consistent, in all material respects, with **19** or are not a fair summary of the audited financial statements, in accordance with the applied criteria, and management does not agree to make the necessary changes, the auditor shall express an adverse opinion on the summary financial statements. (Ref: Para. A15)

Restriction on Distribution or Use or Alerting Readers to the Basis of Accounting

When distribution or use of the auditor's report on the audited financial statements is **20** restricted, or the auditor's report on the audited financial statements alerts readers that the audited financial statements are prepared in accordance with a special purpose framework, the auditor shall include a similar restriction or alert in the auditor's report on the summary financial statements.

Comparatives

21 If the audited financial statements contain comparatives, but the summary financial statements do not, the auditor shall determine whether such omission is reasonable in the circumstances of the engagement. The auditor shall determine the effect of an unreasonable omission on the auditor's report on the summary financial statements. (Ref: Para. A16)

22 If the summary financial statements contain comparatives that were reported on by another auditor, the auditor's report on the summary financial statements shall also contain the matters that ISA 710) requires the auditor to include in the auditor's report on the audited financial statements.[7] (Ref: Para. A17)

Unaudited Supplementary Information Presented with Summary Financial Statements

23 The auditor shall evaluate whether any unaudited supplementary information presented with the summary financial statements is clearly differentiated from the summary financial statements. If the auditor concludes that the entity's presentation of the unaudited supplementary information is not clearly differentiated from the summary financial statements, the auditor shall ask management to change the presentation of the unaudited supplementary information. If management refuses to do so, the auditor shall explain in the auditor's report on the summary financial statements that such information is not covered by that report. (Ref: Para. A18)

Other Information in Documents Containing Summary Financial Statements

24 The auditor shall read other information included in a document containing the summary financial statements and related auditor's report to identify material inconsistencies, if any, with the summary financial statements. If, on reading the other information, the auditor identifies a material inconsistency, the auditor shall determine whether the summary financial statements or the other information needs to be revised. If, on reading the other information, the auditor becomes aware of an apparent material misstatement of fact, the auditor shall discuss the matter with management. (Ref: Para. A19)

Auditor Association

25 If the auditor becomes aware that the entity plans to state that the auditor has reported on summary financial statements in a document containing the summary financial statements, but does not plan to include the related auditor's report, the auditor shall request management to include the auditor's report in the document. If management does not do so, the auditor shall determine and carry out other appropriate actions designed to prevent management from inappropriately associating the auditor with the summary financial statements in that document. (Ref: Para. A20)

26 The auditor may be engaged to report on the financial statements of an entity, while not engaged to report on the summary financial statements. If, in this case, the auditor becomes aware that the entity plans to make a statement in a document that refers to the auditor and the fact that summary financial statements are derived from the financial statements audited by the auditor, the auditor shall be satisfied that:

---

[7] *ISA 710, "Comparative Information—Corresponding Figures and Comparative Financial Statements."*

(a) The reference to the auditor is made in the context of the auditor's report on the audited financial statements; and

(b) The statement does not give the impression that the auditor has reported on the summary financial statements.

If (a) or (b) are not met, the auditor shall request management to change the statement to meet them, or not to refer to the auditor in the document. Alternatively, the entity may engage the auditor to report on the summary financial statements and include the related auditor's report in the document. If management does not change the statement, delete the reference to the auditor, or include an auditor's report on the summary financial statements in the document containing the summary financial statements, the auditor shall advise management that the auditor disagrees with the reference to the auditor, and the auditor shall determine and carry out other appropriate actions designed to prevent management from inappropriately referring to the auditor. (Ref: Para. A20)

***

Application and Other Explanatory Material

Engagement Acceptance (Ref: Para. 5-6)

The audit of the financial statements from which the summary financial statements **A1** are derived provides the auditor with the necessary knowledge to discharge the auditor's responsibilities in relation to the summary financial statements in accordance with this ISA. Application of this ISA will not provide sufficient appropriate evidence on which to base the opinion on the summary financial statements if the auditor has not also audited the financial statements from which the summary financial statements are derived.

Management's agreement with the matters described in paragraph 6 may be evi- **A2** denced by its written acceptance of the terms of the engagement.

Criteria (Ref: Para. 6(a))

The preparation of summary financial statements requires management to determine **A3** the information that needs to be reflected in the summary financial statements so that they are consistent, in all material respects, with or represent a fair summary of the audited financial statements. Because summary financial statements by their nature contain aggregated information and limited disclosure, there is an increased risk that they may not contain the information necessary so as not to be misleading in the circumstances. This risk increases when established criteria for the preparation of summary financial statements do not exist.

Factors that may affect the auditor's determination of the acceptability of the **A4** applied criteria include:

- The nature of the entity;
- The purpose of the summary financial statements;
- The information needs of the intended users of the summary financial statements; and
- Whether the applied criteria will result in summary financial statements that are not misleading in the circumstances.

A5 The criteria for the preparation of summary financial statements may be established by an authorized or recognized standards setting organization or by law or regulation. Similar to the case of financial statements, as explained in ISA 210,[8] in many such cases, the auditor may presume that such criteria are acceptable.

A6 Where established criteria for the preparation of summary financial statements do not exist, criteria may be developed by management, for example, based on practice in a particular industry. Criteria that are acceptable in the circumstances will result in summary financial statements that:

(a) Adequately disclose their summarized nature and identify the audited financial statements;

(b) Clearly describe from whom or where the audited financial statements are available or, if law or regulation provides that the audited financial statements need not be made available to the intended users of the summary financial statements and establishes the criteria for the preparation of the summary financial statements, that law or regulation;

(c) Adequately disclose the applied criteria;

(d) Agree with or can be recalculated from the related information in the audited financial statements; and

(e) In view of the purpose of the summary financial statements, contain the information necessary, and are at an appropriate level of aggregation, so as not to be misleading in the circumstances.

A7 Adequate disclosure of the summarized nature of the summary financial statements and the identity of the audited financial statements, as referred to in paragraph A6(a), may, for example, be provided by a title such as "Summary Financial Statements Prepared from the Audited Financial Statements for the Year Ended December 31, 20X1."

Evaluating the Availability of the Audited Financial Statements (Ref: Para. 8(g))

A8 The auditor's evaluation whether the audited financial statements are available to the intended users of the summary financial statements without undue difficulty is affected by factors such as whether:

- The summary financial statements describe clearly from whom or where the audited financial statements are available;
- The audited financial statements are on public record; or
- Management has established a process by which the intended users of the summary financial statements can obtain ready access to the audited financial statements.

Form of Opinion (Ref: Para. 9)

A9 A conclusion, based on an evaluation of the evidence obtained by performing the procedures in paragraph 8, that an unmodified opinion on the summary financial statements is appropriate enables the auditor to express an opinion containing one of the phrases in paragraph 9. The auditor's decision as to which of the phrases to use may be affected by generally accepted practice in the particular jurisdiction.

---

[8] *ISA 210, "Agreeing the Terms of Audit Engagements," paragraphs A3 and A8-A9.*

Timing of Work and Events Subsequent to the Date of the Auditor's Report on the Audited Financial Statements (Ref: Para. 12)

The procedures described in paragraph 8 are often performed during or immediately **A10** after the audit of the financial statements. When the auditor reports on the summary financial statements after the completion of the audit of the financial statements, the auditor is not required to obtain additional audit evidence on the audited financial statements, or report on the effects of events that occurred subsequent to the date of the auditor's report on the audited financial statements since the summary financial statements are derived from the audited financial statements and do not update them.

Auditor's Report on Summary Financial Statements

Elements of the Auditor's Report

Title (Ref: Para. 14(a))

A title indicating the report is the report of an independent auditor, for example, **A11** "Report of the Independent Auditor," affirms that the auditor has met all of the relevant ethical requirements regarding independence. This distinguishes the report of the independent auditor from reports issued by others.

Addressee (Ref: Para. 14(b), 15)

Factors that may affect the auditor's evaluation of the appropriateness of the **A12** addressee of the summary financial statements include the terms of the engagement, the nature of the entity, and the purpose of the summary financial statements.

Introductory Paragraph (Ref: Para. 14(c)(i))

When the auditor is aware that the summary financial statements will be included in **A13** a document that contains other information, the auditor may consider, if the form of presentation allows, identifying the page numbers on which the summary financial statements are presented. This helps readers to identify the summary financial statements to which the auditor's report relates.

Date of the Auditor's Report (Ref: Para. 14(h), 16)

The person or persons with recognized authority to conclude that the summary **A14** financial statements have been prepared and take responsibility for them depend on the terms of the engagement, the nature of the entity, and the purpose of the summary financial statements.

Illustrations (Ref: Para.14. 17-18, 19)

The Appendix to this ISA contains illustrations of auditors' reports on summary **A15** financial statements that:

(a) Contain unmodified opinions;
(b) Are derived from audited financial statements on which the auditor issued modified opinions; and
(c) Contain a modified opinion.

Comparatives (Ref: Para. 21-22)

A16   If the audited financial statements contain comparatives, there is a presumption that the summary financial statements also would contain comparatives. Comparatives in the audited financial statements may be regarded as corresponding figures or as comparative financial information. ISA 710 describes how this difference affects the auditor's report on the financial statements, including, in particular, reference to other auditors who audited the financial statements for the prior period.

A17   Circumstances that may affect the auditor's determination whether an omission of comparatives is reasonable include the nature and objective of the summary financial statements, the applied criteria, and the information needs of the intended users of the summary financial statements.

Unaudited Supplementary Information Presented with Summary Financial Statements (Ref: Para. 23)

A18   ISA 700[9] contains requirements and guidance to be applied when unaudited supplementary information is presented with audited financial statements that, adapted as necessary in the circumstances, may be helpful in applying the requirement in paragraph 23.

Other Information in Documents Containing Summary Financial Statements (Ref: Para. 24)

A19   ISA 720[10] contains requirements and guidance relating to reading other information included in a document containing the audited financial statements and related auditor's report, and responding to material inconsistencies and material misstatements of fact. Adapted as necessary in the circumstances, they may be helpful in applying the requirement in paragraph 24.

Auditor Association (Ref: Para. 25-26)

A20   Other appropriate actions the auditor may take when management does not take the requested action may include informing the intended users and other known third-party users of the inappropriate reference to the auditor. The auditor's course of action depends on the auditor's legal rights and obligations. Consequently, the auditor may consider it appropriate to seek legal advice.

Appendix   (Ref: Para. A15)

Illustrations of Reports on Summary Financial Statements

- Illustration 1: An auditor's report on summary financial statements prepared in accordance with established criteria. An unmodified opinion is expressed on the audited financial statements. The auditor's report on the summary financial statements is dated later than the date of the auditor's report on the financial statements from which summary financial statements are derived.

[9] *ISA 700, "Forming an Opinion and Reporting on Financial Statements," paragraphs 46-47.*

[10] *ISA 720, "The Auditor's Responsibilities Relating to Other Information in Documents Containing Audited Financial Statements."*

- Illustration 2: An auditor's report on summary financial statements prepared in accordance with criteria developed by management and adequately disclosed in the summary financial statements. The auditor has determined that the applied criteria are acceptable in the circumstances. An unmodified opinion is expressed on the audited financial statements.

- Illustration 3: An auditor's report on summary financial statements prepared in accordance with criteria developed by management and adequately disclosed in the summary financial statements. The auditor has determined that the applied criteria are acceptable in the circumstances. A qualified opinion is expressed on the audited financial statements.

- Illustration 4: An auditor's report on summary financial statements prepared in accordance with criteria developed by management and adequately disclosed in the summary financial statements. The auditor has determined that the applied criteria are acceptable in the circumstances. An adverse opinion is expressed on the audited financial statements.

- Illustration 5: An auditor's report on summary financial statements prepared in accordance with established criteria. An unmodified opinion is expressed on the audited financial statements. The auditor concludes that it is not possible to express an unmodified opinion on the summary financial statements.

Illustration 1:

Circumstances include the following:

- **An unmodified opinion is expressed on the audited financial statements.**

- **Established criteria for the preparation of summary financial statements exist.**

- **The auditor's report on the summary financial statements is dated later than the date of the auditor's report on the financial statements from which the summary financial statements are derived.**

REPORT OF THE INDEPENDENT AUDITOR ON THE SUMMARY FINANCIAL STATEMENTS

[Appropriate Addressee]

The accompanying summary financial statements, which comprise the summary balance sheet as at December 31, 20X1, the summary income statement, summary statement of changes in equity and summary cash flow statement for the year then ended, and related notes, are derived from the audited financial statements of ABC Company for the year ended December 31, 20X1. We expressed an unmodified audit opinion on those financial statements in our report dated February 15, 20X2. Those financial statements, and the summary financial statements, do not reflect the effects of events that occurred subsequent to the date of our report on those financial statements.

The summary financial statements do not contain all the disclosures required by [describe financial reporting framework applied in the preparation of the audited financial statements of ABC Company]. Reading the summary financial statements, therefore, is not a substitute for reading the audited financial statements of ABC Company.

Management's[11] Responsibility for the Summary Financial Statements

Management is responsible for the preparation of a summary of the audited financial statements in accordance with [describe established criteria].

Auditor's Responsibility

Our responsibility is to express an opinion on the summary financial statements based on our procedures, which were conducted in accordance with International Standard on Auditing (ISA) 810, "Engagements to Report on Summary Financial Statements."

Opinion

In our opinion, the summary financial statements derived from the audited financial statements of ABC Company for the year ended December 31, 20X1 are consistent, in all material respects, with (or *a fair summary of*) those financial statements, in accordance with [describe established criteria].

[Auditor's signature]

[Date of the auditor's report]

[Auditor's address]

---

[11] *Or other term that is appropriate in the context of the legal framework in the particular jurisdiction.*

Illustration 2:

Circumstances include the following:

* An unmodified opinion is expressed on the audited financial statements.

* Criteria are developed by management and adequately disclosed in Note X. The auditor has determined that the criteria are acceptable in the circumstances.

REPORT OF THE INDEPENDENT AUDITOR ON THE SUMMARY FINANCIAL STATEMENTS

[Appropriate Addressee]

The accompanying summary financial statements, which comprise the summary balance sheet as at December 31, 20X1, the summary income statement, summary statement of changes in equity and summary cash flow statement for the year then ended, and related notes, are derived from the audited financial statements of ABC Company for the year ended December 31, 20X1. We expressed an unmodified audit opinion on those financial statements in our report dated February 15, 20X2.[12]

The summary financial statements do not contain all the disclosures required by [describe financial reporting framework applied in the preparation of the audited financial statements of ABC Company]. Reading the summary financial statements, therefore, is not a substitute for reading the audited financial statements of ABC Company.

Management's[13] Responsibility for the Summary Financial Statements

Management is responsible for the preparation of a summary of the audited financial statements on the basis described in Note X.

Auditor's Responsibility

Our responsibility is to express an opinion on the summary financial statements based on our procedures, which were conducted in accordance with International Standard on Auditing (ISA) 810, "Engagements to Report on Summary Financial Statements."

Opinion

In our opinion, the summary financial statements derived from the audited financial statements of ABC Company for the year ended December 31, 20X1 are consistent, in all material respects, with (or *a fair summary of*) those financial statements, on the basis described in Note X.

[Auditor's signature]

[Date of the auditor's report]

[Auditor's address]

---

[12] *When the auditor's report on the summary financial statements is dated later than the date of the auditor's report on the audited financial statements from which it is derived, the following sentence is added to this paragraph: "Those financial statements, and the summary financial statements, do not reflect the effects of events that occurred subsequent to the date of our report on those financial statements."*

[13] *Or other term that is appropriate in the context of the legal framework in the particular jurisdiction.*

> **Illustration 3:**
>
> **Circumstances include the following:**
>
> - **A qualified opinion is expressed on the audited financial statements.**
>
> - **Criteria are developed by management and adequately disclosed in Note X. The auditor has determined that the criteria are acceptable in the circumstances.**

REPORT OF THE INDEPENDENT AUDITOR ON THE SUMMARY FINANCIAL STATEMENTS

[Appropriate Addressee]

The accompanying summary financial statements, which comprise the summary balance sheet as at December 31, 20X1, the summary income statement, summary statement of changes in equity and summary cash flow statement for the year then ended, and related notes, are derived from the audited financial statements of ABC Company for the year ended December 31, 20X1.[14] We expressed a qualified audit opinion on those financial statements in our report dated February 15, 20X2 (see below).

The summary financial statements do not contain all the disclosures required by [describe financial reporting framework applied in the preparation of the audited financial statements of ABC Company]. Reading the summary financial statements, therefore, is not a substitute for reading the audited financial statements of ABC Company.

Management's[15] Responsibility for the Summary Financial Statements

Management is responsible for the preparation of a summary of the audited financial statements on the basis described in Note X.

Auditor's Responsibility

Our responsibility is to express an opinion on the summary financial statements based on our procedures, which were conducted in accordance with International Standard on Auditing (ISA) 810, "Engagements to Report on Summary Financial Statements."

Opinion

In our opinion, the summary financial statements derived from the audited financial statements of ABC Company for the year ended December 31, 20X1 are consistent, in all material respects, with (or *a fair summary of*) those financial statements, on the basis described in Note X. However, the summary financial statements are misstated to the equivalent extent as the audited financial statements of ABC Company for the year ended December 31, 20X1.

---

[14] *When the auditor's report on the summary financial statements is dated later than the date of the auditor's report on the audited financial statements from which it is derived, the following sentence is added to this paragraph: "Those financial statements, and the summary financial statements, do not reflect the effects of events that occurred subsequent to the date of our report on those financial statements."*

[15] *Or other term that is appropriate in the context of the legal framework in the particular jurisdiction.*

The misstatement of the audited financial statements is described in our qualified audit opinion in our report dated February 15, 20X2. Our qualified audit opinion is based on the fact that the company's inventories are carried in the balance sheet in those financial statements at xxx. Management has not stated the inventories at the lower of cost and net realizable value but has stated them solely at cost, which constitutes a departure from International Financial Reporting Standards. The company's records indicate that had management stated the inventories at the lower of cost and net realizable value, an amount of xxx would have been required to write the inventories down to their net realizable value. Accordingly, cost of sales would have been increased by xxx, and income tax, net income and shareholders' equity would have been reduced by xxx, xxx and xxx, respectively. Our qualified audit opinion states that, except for the effects of the described matter, those financial statements present fairly, in all material respects, (or *give a true and fair view of*) the financial position of ABC Company as at December 31, 20X1, and (*of*) its financial performance and its cash flows for the year then ended in accordance with International Financial Reporting Standards.

[Auditor's signature]

[Date of the auditor's report]

[Auditor's address]

Illustration 4:

Circumstances include the following:

- **An adverse opinion is expressed on the audited financial statements.**

- **Criteria are developed by management and adequately disclosed in Note X. The auditor has determined that the criteria are acceptable in the circumstances.**

REPORT OF THE INDEPENDENT AUDITOR ON THE SUMMARY FINANCIAL STATEMENTS

[Appropriate Addressee]

The accompanying summary financial statements, which comprise the summary balance sheet as at December 31, 20X1, the summary income statement, summary statement of changes in equity and summary cash flow statement for the year then ended, and related notes, are derived from the audited financial statements of ABC Company for the year ended December 31, 20X1.[16]

The summary financial statements do not contain all the disclosures required by [describe financial reporting framework applied in the preparation of the audited financial statements of ABC Company]. Reading the summary financial statements, therefore, is not a substitute for reading the audited financial statements of ABC Company.

Management's[17] Responsibility for the Summary Financial Statements

Management is responsible for the preparation of a summary of the audited financial statements on the basis described in Note X.

Auditor's Responsibility

Our responsibility is to express an opinion on the summary financial statements based on our procedures, which were conducted in accordance with International Standard on Auditing (ISA) 810, "Engagements to Report on Summary Financial Statements."

Denial of Opinion

In our report dated February 15, 20X2, we expressed an adverse audit opinion on the financial statements of ABC Company for the year ended December 31, 20X1. The basis for our adverse audit opinion was [describe basis for adverse audit opinion]. Our adverse audit opinion stated that [describe adverse audit opinion].

Because of the significance of the matter discussed above, it is inappropriate to express an opinion on the summary financial statements of ABC Company for the year ended December 31, 20X1.

---

[16] *When the auditor's report on the summary financial statements is dated later than the date of the auditor's report on the audited financial statements from which it is derived, the following sentence is added to this paragraph: "Those financial statements, and the summary financial statements, do not reflect the effects of events that occurred subsequent to the date of our report on those financial statements."*

[17] *Or other term that is appropriate in the context of the legal framework in the particular jurisdiction.*

[Auditor's signature]

[Date of the auditor's report]

[Auditor's address]

> **Illustration 5:**
>
> **Circumstances include the following:**
>
> - **An unmodified opinion is expressed on the audited financial statements.**
> - **Established criteria for the preparation of summary financial statements exist.**
> - **The auditor concludes that it is not possible to express an unmodified opinion on the summary financial statements.**

REPORT OF THE INDEPENDENT AUDITOR ON THE SUMMARY FINANCIAL STATEMENTS

[Appropriate Addressee]

The accompanying summary financial statements, which comprise the summary balance sheet as at December 31, 20X1, the summary income statement, summary statement of changes in equity and summary cash flow statement for the year then ended, and related notes, are derived from the audited financial statements of ABC Company for the year ended December 31, 20X1. We expressed an unmodified audit opinion on those financial statements in our report dated February 15, 20X2.[18]

The summary financial statements do not contain all the disclosures required by [describe financial reporting framework applied in the preparation of the audited financial statements of ABC Company]. Reading the summary financial statements, therefore, is not a substitute for reading the audited financial statements of ABC Company.

Management's[19] Responsibility for the Summary Audited Financial Statements

Management is responsible for the preparation of a summary of the audited financial statements in accordance with [describe established criteria].

Auditor's Responsibility

Our responsibility is to express an opinion on the summary financial statements based on our procedures, which were conducted in accordance with International Standard on Auditing (ISA) 810, "Engagements to Report on Summary Financial Statements."

Basis for Adverse Opinion

[Describe matter that caused the summary financial statements not to be consistent, in all material respects, with (or *a fair summary of*) the audited financial statements, in accordance with the applied criteria.]

---

[18] *When the auditor's report on the summary financial statements is dated later than the date of the auditor's report on the audited financial statements from which it is derived, the following sentence is added to this paragraph: "Those financial statements, and the summary financial statements, do not reflect the effects of events that occurred subsequent to the date of our report on those financial statements."*

[19] *Or other term that is appropriate in the context of the legal framework in the particular jurisdiction.*

Adverse Opinion

In our opinion, because of the significance of the matter discussed in the Basis for Adverse Opinion paragraph, the summary financial statements referred to above are not consistent with (or *a fair summary of*) the audited financial statements of ABC Company for the year ended December 31, 20X1, in accordance with [describe established criteria].

[Auditor's signature]

[Date of the auditor's report]

[Auditor's address]

Part Three

International Auditing Practice Note (IAPN)

International Auditing Practice Note 1000
Special considerations in auditing financial instruments

Contents

International Auditing Practice Note (IAPN) 1000, *Special Considerations in Auditing Financial Instruments*, should be read in conjunction with the *Preface to the International Quality Control, Auditing, Review, Other Assurance, and Related Services Pronouncements*. IAPNs do not impose additional requirements on auditors beyond those included in the International Standards on Auditing (ISAs), nor do they change the auditor's responsibility to comply with all ISAs relevant to the audit. IAPNs provide practical assistance to auditors. They are intended to be disseminated by those responsible for national standards, or used in developing corresponding national material. They also provide material that firms can use in developing their training programs and internal guidance.

Introduction

Financial instruments may be used by financial and non-financial entities of all sizes **1** for a variety of purposes. Some entities have large holdings and transaction volumes while other entities may only engage in a few financial instrument transactions. Some entities may take positions in financial instruments to assume and benefit from risk while other entities may use financial instruments to reduce certain risks by hedging or managing exposures. This International Auditing Practice Note (IAPN) is relevant to all of these situations.

The following International Standards on Auditing (ISAs) are particularly relevant **2** to audits of financial instruments:

(a) ISA 540[1] deals with the auditor's responsibilities relating to auditing accounting estimates, including accounting estimates related to financial instruments measured at fair value;

(b) ISA 315[2] and ISA 330[3] deal with identifying and assessing risks of material misstatement and responding to those risks; and

(c) ISA 500[4] explains what constitutes audit evidence and deals with the auditor's responsibility to design and perform audit procedures to obtain sufficient appropriate audit evidence to be able to draw reasonable conclusions on which to base the auditor's opinion.

The purpose of this IAPN is to provide: **3**

(a) Background information about financial instruments (Section I); and

(b) Discussion of audit considerations relating to financial instruments (Section II).

IAPNs provide practical assistance to auditors. They are intended to be disseminated by those responsible for national standards, or used in developing corresponding national material. They also provide material that firms can use in developing their training programs and internal guidance.

This IAPN is relevant to entities of all sizes, as all entities may be subject to risks of **4** material misstatement when using financial instruments.

The guidance on valuation[5] in this IAPN is likely to be more relevant for financial **5** instruments measured or disclosed at fair value, while the guidance on areas other than valuation applies equally to financial instruments either measured at fair value or amortized cost. This IAPN is also applicable to both financial assets and financial liabilities. This IAPN does not deal with instruments such as:

(a) The simplest financial instruments such as cash, simple loans, trade accounts receivable and trade accounts payable;

(b) Investments in unlisted equity instruments; or

(c) Insurance contracts.

---

[1] ISA 540, *Auditing Accounting Estimates, Including Fair Value Accounting Estimates, and Related Disclosures*

[2] ISA 315, *Identifying and Assessing the Risks of Material Misstatement through Understanding the Entity and Its Environment*

[3] ISA 330, *The Auditor's Responses to Assessed Risks*

[4] ISA 500, *Audit Evidence*

[5] In this IAPN, the terms *"valuation"* and *"measurement"* are used interchangeably.

6   Also, this IAPN does not deal with specific accounting issues relevant to financial instruments, such as hedge accounting, profit or loss on inception (often known as "Day 1" profit or loss), offsetting, risk transfers or impairment, including loan loss provisioning. Although these subject matters can relate to an entity's accounting for financial instruments, a discussion of the auditor's consideration regarding how to address specific accounting requirements is beyond the scope of this IAPN.

7   An audit in accordance with ISAs is conducted on the premise that management and, where appropriate, those charged with governance have acknowledged certain responsibilities. Such responsibilities subsume making fair value measurements. This IAPN does not impose responsibilities on management or those charged with governance nor override laws and regulation that govern their responsibilities.

8   This IAPN has been written in the context of general purpose fair presentation financial reporting frameworks, but may also be useful, as appropriate in the circumstance, in other financial reporting frameworks such as special purpose financial reporting frameworks.

9   This IAPN focuses on the assertions of valuation, and presentation and disclosure, but also covers, in less detail, completeness, accuracy, existence, and rights and obligations.

10   Financial instruments are susceptible to estimation uncertainty, which is defined in ISA 540 as "the susceptibility of an accounting estimate and related disclosures to an inherent lack of precision in its measurement."[6] Estimation uncertainty is affected by the complexity of financial instruments, among other factors. The nature and reliability of information available to support the measurement of financial instruments varies widely, which affects the estimation uncertainty associated with their measurement. This IAPN uses the term "measurement uncertainty" to refer to the estimation uncertainty associated with fair value measurements.

Section I—Background Information about Financial Instruments

11   Different definitions of financial instruments may exist among financial reporting frameworks. For example, International Financial Reporting Standards (IFRS) define a financial instrument as any contract that gives rise to a financial asset of one entity and a financial liability or equity instrument of another entity.[7] Financial instruments may be cash, the equity of another entity, the contractual right or obligation to receive or deliver cash or exchange financial assets or liabilities, certain contracts settled in an entity's own equity instruments, certain contracts on non-financial items, or certain contracts issued by insurers that do not meet the definition of an insurance contract. This definition encompasses a wide range of financial instruments from simple loans and deposits to complex derivatives, structured products, and some commodity contracts.

12   Financial instruments vary in complexity, though the complexity of the financial instrument can come from difference sources, such as:

  ● A very high volume of individual cash flows, where a lack of homogeneity requires analysis of each one or a large number of grouped cash flows to

---

[6] *ISA 540, paragraph 7(c)*

[7] *International Accounting Standard (IAS) 32, Financial Instruments: Presentation*, paragraph 11

evaluate, for example, credit risk (for example, collateralized debt obligations (CDOs)).

- Complex formulae for determining the cash flows.
- Uncertainty or variability of future cash flows, such as that arising from credit risk, option contracts or financial instruments with lengthy contractual terms.

The higher the variability of cash flows to changes in market conditions, the more complex and uncertain the fair value measurement of the financial instrument is likely to be. In addition, sometimes financial instruments that, ordinarily, are relatively easy to value become complex to value because of particular circumstances, for example, instruments for which the market has become inactive or which have lengthy contractual terms. Derivatives and structured products become more complex when they are a combination of individual financial instruments. In addition, the accounting for financial instruments under certain financial reporting frameworks or certain market conditions may be complex.

Another source of complexity is the volume of financial instruments held or traded. While a "plain vanilla" interest rate swap may not be complex, an entity holding a large number of them may use a sophisticated information system to identify, value and transact these instruments.   **13**

Purpose and Risks of Using Financial Instruments

Financial instruments are used for: **14**

- Hedging purposes (that is, to change an existing risk profile to which an entity is exposed). This includes:
  - ○ The forward purchase or sale of currency to fix a future exchange rate;
  - ○ Converting future interest rates to fixed rates or floating rates through the use of swaps; and
  - ○ The purchase of option contracts to provide an entity with protection against a particular price movement, including contracts which may contain embedded derivatives;
- Trading purposes (for example, to enable an entity to take a risk position to benefit from short term market movements); and
- Investment purposes (for example, to enable an entity to benefit from long term investment returns).

The use of financial instruments can reduce exposures to certain business risks, for example changes in exchange rates, interest rates and commodity prices, or a combination of those risks. On the other hand, the inherent complexities of some financial instruments also may result in increased risk.   **15**

Business risk and the risk of material misstatement increase when management and those charged with governance: **16**

- Do not fully understand the risks of using financial instruments and have insufficient skills and experience to manage those risks;
- Do not have the expertise to value them appropriately in accordance with the applicable financial reporting framework;
- Do not have sufficient controls in place over financial instrument activities; or
- Inappropriately hedge risks or speculate.

Management's failure to fully understand the risks inherent in a financial instrument can have a direct effect on management's ability to manage these risks appropriately, and may ultimately threaten the viability of the entity.   **17**

18 The principal types of risk applicable to financial instruments are listed below. This list is not meant to be exhaustive and different terminology may be used to describe these risks or classify the components of individual risks.

(a) Credit (or counterparty) risk is the risk that one party to a financial instrument will cause a financial loss to another party by failing to discharge an obligation and is often associated with default. Credit risk includes settlement risk, which is the risk that one side of a transaction will be settled without consideration being received from the customer or counterparty.

(b) Market risk is the risk that the fair value or future cash flows of a financial instrument will fluctuate because of changes in market prices. Examples of market risk include currency risk, interest rate risk, commodity and equity price risk.

(c) Liquidity risk includes the risk of not being able to buy or sell a financial instrument at an appropriate price in a timely manner due to a lack of marketability for that financial instrument.

(d) Operational risk relates to the specific processing required for financial instruments. Operational risk may increase as the complexity of a financial instrument increases, and poor management of operational risk may increase other types of risk. Operational risk includes:

   (i) The risk that confirmation and reconciliation controls are inadequate resulting in incomplete or inaccurate recording of financial instruments;

   (ii) The risks that there is inappropriate documentation of transactions and insufficient monitoring of these transactions;

   (iii) The risk that transactions are incorrectly recorded, processed or risk managed and, therefore, do not reflect the economics of the overall trade;

   (iv) The risk that undue reliance is placed by staff on the accuracy of valuation techniques, without adequate review, and transactions are therefore incorrectly valued or their risk is improperly measured;

   (v) The risk that the use of financial instruments is not adequately incorporated into the entity's risk management policies and procedures;

   (vi) The risk of loss resulting from inadequate or failed internal processes and systems, or from external events, including the risk of fraud from both internal and external sources;

   (vii) The risk that there is inadequate or non-timely maintenance of valuation techniques used to measure financial instruments; and

   (viii) Legal risk, which is a component of operational risk, and relates to losses resulting from a legal or regulatory action that invalidates or otherwise precludes performance by the end user or its counterparty under the terms of the contract or related netting arrangements. For example, legal risk could arise from insufficient or incorrect documentation for the contract, an inability to enforce a netting arrangement in bankruptcy, adverse changes in tax laws, or statutes that prohibit entities from investing in certain types of financial instruments.

19 Other considerations relevant to risks of using financial instruments include:

   ● The risk of fraud that may be increased if, for example, an employee in a position to perpetrate a financial fraud understands both the financial instruments and the processes for accounting for them, but management and those charged with governance have a lesser degree of understanding.

   ● The risk that master netting arrangements[8] may not be properly reflected in the financial statements.

---

[8] *An entity that undertakes a number of financial instrument transactions with a single counterparty may enter into a master netting arrangement with that counterparty. Such an agreement provides for a single net settlement of all financial instruments covered by the agreement in the event of default of any one contract.*

- The risk that some financial instruments may change between being assets or liabilities during their term and that such change may occur rapidly.

Controls Relating to Financial Instruments

The extent of an entity's use of financial instruments and the degree of complexity of the instruments are important determinants of the necessary level of sophistication of the entity's internal control. For example, smaller entities may use less structured products and simple processes and procedures to achieve their objectives.   **20**

Often, it is the role of those charged with governance to set the tone regarding, and approve and oversee the extent of use of, financial instruments while it is management's role to manage and monitor the entity's exposures to those risks. Management and, where appropriate, those charged with governance are also responsible for designing and implementing a system of internal control to enable the preparation of financial statements in accordance with the applicable financial reporting framework. An entity's internal control over financial instruments is more likely to be effective when management and those charged with governance have: **21**

(a) Established an appropriate control environment, active participation by those charged with governance in controlling the use of financial instruments, a logical organizational structure with clear assignment of authority and responsibility, and appropriate human resource policies and procedures. In particular, clear rules are needed on the extent to which those responsible for financial instrument activities are permitted to act. Such rules have regard to any legal or regulatory restrictions on using financial instruments. For example, certain public sector entities may not have the power to conduct business using derivatives;

(b) Established a risk management process relative to the size of the entity and the complexity of its financial instruments (for example, in some entities a formal risk management function may exist);

(c) Established information systems that provide those charged with governance with an understanding of the nature of the financial instrument activities and the associated risks, including adequate documentation of transactions;

(d) Designed, implemented and documented a system of internal control to:
    ○ Provide reasonable assurance that the entity's use of financial instruments is within its risk management policies;
    ○ Properly present financial instruments in the financial statements;
    ○ Ensure that the entity is in compliance with applicable laws and regulations; and
    ○ Monitor risk.

    The Appendix provides examples of controls that may exist in an entity that deals in a high volume of financial instrument transactions; and

(e) Established appropriate accounting policies, including valuation policies, in accordance with the applicable financial reporting framework.

Key elements of risk management processes and internal control relating to an entity's financial instruments include: **22**

- Setting an approach to define the amount of risk exposure that the entity is willing to accept when engaging in financial instrument transactions (this may be referred to as its "risk appetite"), including policies for investing in financial instruments, and the control framework in which the financial instrument activities are conducted;

- Establishing processes for the documentation and authorization of new types of financial instrument transactions which consider the accounting, regulatory, legal, financial and operational risks that are associated with such instruments;
- Processing financial instrument transactions, including confirmation and reconciliation of cash and asset holdings to external statements, and the payments process;
- Segregation of duties between those investing or trading in the financial instruments and those responsible for processing, valuing and confirming such instruments. For example, a model development function that is involved in assisting in pricing deals is less objective than one that is functionally and organizationally separate from the front office;
- Valuation processes and controls, including controls over data obtained from third-party pricing sources; and
- Monitoring of controls.

23   The nature of risks often differs between entities with a high volume and variety of financial instruments and those with only a few financial instrument transactions. This results in different approaches to internal control. For example:

- Typically, an institution with high volumes of financial instruments will have a dealing room type environment in which there are specialist traders and segregation of duties between those traders and the back office (which refers to the operations function that data-checks trades that have been conducted, ensuring that they are not erroneous, and transacting the required transfers). In such environments, the traders will typically initiate contracts verbally over the phone or via an electronic trading platform. Capturing relevant transactions and accurately recording financial instruments in such an environment is significantly more challenging than for an entity with only a few financial instruments, whose existence and completeness often can be confirmed with a bank confirmation to a few banks.
- On the other hand, entities with only a small number of financial instruments often do not have segregation of duties, and access to the market is limited. In such cases, although it may be easier to identify financial instrument transactions, there is a risk that management may rely on a limited number of personnel, which may increase the risk that unauthorized transactions may be initiated or transactions may not be recorded.

Completeness, Accuracy, and Existence

24   Paragraphs 25–33 describe controls and processes which may be in place in entities with a high volume of financial instrument transactions, including those with trading rooms. By contrast, an entity that does not have a high volume of financial instrument transactions may not have these controls and processes but may instead confirm their transactions with the counterparty or clearing house. Doing so may be relatively straightforward in that the entity may only transact with one or two counterparties.

Trade Confirmations and Clearing Houses

25   Generally, for transactions undertaken by financial institutions, the terms of financial instruments are documented in confirmations exchanged between counterparties and legal agreements. Clearing houses serve to monitor the exchange of confirmations by matching trades and settling them. A central clearing house is associated with an exchange and entities that clear through clearing houses typically have processes to manage the information delivered to the clearing house.

Not all transactions are settled through such an exchange. In many other markets **26** there is an established practice of agreeing the terms of transactions before settlement begins. To be effective, this process needs to be run separately from those who trade the financial instruments to minimize the risk of fraud. In other markets, transactions are confirmed after settlement has begun and sometimes confirmation backlogs result in settlement beginning before all terms have been fully agreed. This presents additional risk because the transacting entities need to rely on alternative means of agreeing trades. These may include:

- Enforcing rigorous reconciliations between the records of those trading the financial instruments and those settling them (strong segregation of duties between the two are important), combined with strong supervisory controls over those trading the financial instruments to ensure the integrity of the transactions;
- Reviewing summary documentation from counterparties that highlights the key terms even if the full terms have not been agreed; and
- Thorough review of traders' profits and losses to ensure that they reconcile to what the back office has calculated.

Reconciliations with Banks and Custodians

Some components of financial instruments, such as bonds and shares, may be held in **27** separate depositories. In addition, most financial instruments result in payments of cash at some point and often these cash flows begin early in the contract's life. These cash payments and receipts will pass through an entity's bank account. Regular reconciliation of the entity's records to external banks' and custodians' records enables the entity to ensure transactions are properly recorded.

It should be noted that not all financial instruments result in a cash flow in the early **28** stages of the contract's life or are capable of being recorded with an exchange or custodian. Where this is the case, reconciliation processes will not identify an omitted or inaccurately recorded trade and confirmation controls are more important. Even where such a cash flow is accurately recorded in the early stages of an instrument's life, this does not ensure that all characteristics or terms of the instrument (for example, the maturity or an early termination option) have been recorded accurately.

In addition, cash movements may be quite small in the context of the overall size of **29** the trade or the entity's own balance sheet and may therefore be difficult to identify. The value of reconciliations is enhanced when finance, or other back office staff, review entries in all general ledger accounts to ensure that they are valid and supportable. This process will help identify if the other side to cash entries relating to financial instruments has not been properly recorded. Reviewing suspense and clearing accounts is important regardless of the account balance, as there may be offsetting reconciling items in the account.

In entities with a high volume of financial instrument transactions, reconciliation and **30** confirmation controls may be automated and, if so, adequate IT controls need to be in place to support them. In particular, controls are needed to ensure that data is completely and accurately picked up from external sources (such as banks and custodians) and from the entity's records and is not tampered with before or during reconciliation. Controls are also needed to ensure that the criteria on which entries are matched are sufficiently restrictive to prevent inaccurate clearance of reconciling items.

Other Controls over Completeness, Accuracy, and Existence

31   The complexity inherent in some financial instruments means that it will not always be obvious how they should be recorded in the entity's systems. In such cases, management may set up control processes to monitor policies that prescribe how particular types of transactions are measured, recorded and accounted for. These policies are typically established and reviewed in advance by suitably qualified personnel who are capable of understanding the full effects of the financial instruments being booked.

32   Some transactions may be cancelled or amended after initial execution. Application of appropriate controls relating to cancellation or amendment can mitigate the risks of material misstatement due to fraud or error. In addition, an entity may have a process in place to reconfirm trades that are cancelled or amended.

33   In financial institutions with a high volume of trading, a senior employee typically reviews daily profits and losses on individual traders' books to evaluate whether they are reasonable based on the employee's knowledge of the market. Doing so may enable management to determine that particular trades were not completely or accurately recorded, or may identify fraud by a particular trader. It is important that there are transaction authorization procedures that support the more senior review.

Valuation of Financial Instruments

Financial Reporting Requirements

34   In many financial reporting frameworks, financial instruments, including embedded derivatives, are often measured at fair value for the purpose of balance sheet presentation, calculating profit or loss, and/or disclosure. In general, the objective of fair value measurement is to arrive at the price at which an orderly transaction would take place between market participants at the measurement date under current market conditions; that is, it is not the transaction price for a forced liquidation or distressed sale. In meeting this objective, all relevant available market information is taken into account.

35   Fair value measurements of financial assets and financial liabilities may arise both at the initial recording of transactions and later when there are changes in value. Changes in fair value measurements that occur over time may be treated in different ways under different financial reporting frameworks. For example, such changes may be recorded as profit or loss, or may be recorded in the other comprehensive income. Also, depending on the applicable financial reporting framework, the whole financial instrument or only a component of it (for example, an embedded derivative when it is separately accounted for) may be required to be measured at fair value.

36   Some financial reporting frameworks establish a fair value hierarchy to develop increased consistency and comparability in fair value measurements and related disclosures. The inputs may be classified into different levels such as:

- Level 1 inputs—Quoted prices (unadjusted) in active markets for identical financial assets or financial liabilities that the entity can access at the measurement date.
- Level 2 inputs—Inputs other than quoted prices included within level 1 that are observable for the financial asset or financial liability, either directly or indirectly. If the financial asset or financial liability has a specified (contractual) term, a level 2 input must be observable for substantially the full term of the financial asset or financial liability. Level 2 inputs include the following:

○ Quoted prices for similar financial assets or financial liabilities in active markets.

○ Quoted prices for identical or similar financial assets or financial liabilities in markets that are not active.

○ Inputs other than quoted prices that are observable for the financial asset or financial liability (for example, interest rates and yield curves observable at commonly quoted intervals, implied volatilities and credit spreads).

○ Inputs that are derived principally from, or corroborated by, observable market data by correlation or other means (market-corroborated inputs).

• Level 3 inputs—Unobservable inputs for the financial asset or financial liability. Unobservable inputs are used to measure fair value to the extent that relevant observable inputs are not available, thereby allowing for situations in which there is little, if any, market activity for the financial asset or financial liability at the measurement date.

In general, measurement uncertainty increases as a financial instrument moves from level 1 to level 2, or level 2 to level 3. Also, within level 2 there may be a wide range of measurement uncertainty depending on the observability of inputs, the complexity of the financial instrument, its valuation, and other factors.

Certain financial reporting frameworks may require or permit the entity to adjust for   **37** measurement uncertainties, in order to adjust for risks that a market participant would make in the pricing to take account of the uncertainties of the risks associated with the pricing or cash flows of the financial instrument. For example:

• Model adjustments. Some models may have a known deficiency or the result of calibration may highlight the deficiency for the fair value measurement in accordance with the financial reporting framework.

• Credit-risk adjustments. Some models do not take into account credit risk, including counterparty risk or own credit risk.

• Liquidity adjustments. Some models calculate a mid-market price, even though the financial reporting framework may require use of a liquidity adjusted amount such as a bid/offer spread. Another, more judgmental, liquidity adjustment recognizes that some financial instruments are illiquid which affects the valuation.

• Other risk adjustments. A value measured using a model that does not take into account all other factors that market participants would consider in pricing the financial instrument may not represent fair value on the measurement date, and therefore may need to be adjusted separately to comply with the applicable financial reporting framework.

Adjustments are not appropriate if they adjust the measurement and valuation of the financial instrument away from fair value as defined by the applicable financial reporting framework, for example for conservatism.

Observable and Unobservable Inputs

As mentioned above, financial reporting frameworks often categorize inputs   **38** according to the degree of observability. As activity in a market for financial instruments declines and the observability of inputs declines, measurement uncertainty increases. The nature and reliability of information available to support valuation of financial instruments varies depending on the observability of inputs to its measurement, which is influenced by the nature of the market (for example, the level of market activity and whether it is through an exchange or over-the-counter (OTC)). Accordingly, there is a continuum of the nature and reliability of evidence used to support valuation, and it becomes more difficult for management to obtain information to support a valuation when markets become inactive and inputs become less observable.

39   When observable inputs are not available, an entity uses unobservable inputs (level 3 inputs) that reflect the assumption that market participants would use when pricing the financial asset or the financial liability, including assumptions about risk. Unobservable inputs are developed using the best information available in the circumstances. In developing unobservable inputs, an entity may begin with its own data, which is adjusted if reasonably available information indicates that (a) other market participants would use different data or (b) there is something particular to the entity that is not available to other market participants (for example, an entity-specific synergy).

Effects of Inactive Markets

40   Measurement uncertainty increases and valuation is more complicated when the markets in which financial instruments or their component parts are traded become inactive. There is no clear point at which an active market becomes inactive, though financial reporting frameworks may provide guidance on this issue. Characteristics of an inactive market include a significant decline in the volume and level of trading activity, available prices vary significantly over time or among market participants or the prices are not current. However, assessing whether a market is inactive requires judgment.

41   When markets are inactive, prices quoted may be stale (that is, out of date), may not represent prices at which market participants may trade or may represent forced transactions (such as when a seller is required to sell an asset to meet regulatory or legal requirements, needs to dispose of an asset immediately to create liquidity or the existence of a single potential buyer as a result of the legal or time restrictions imposed). Accordingly, valuations are developed based on level 2 and level 3 inputs. Under such circumstances, entities may have:

- A valuation policy that includes a process for determining whether level 1 inputs are available;
- An understanding of how particular prices or inputs from external sources used as inputs to valuation techniques were calculated in order to assess their reliability. For example, in an active market, a broker quote on a financial instrument that has not traded is likely to reflect actual transactions on a similar financial instrument, but, as the market becomes less active, the broker quote may rely more on proprietary valuation techniques to determine prices;
- An understanding of how deteriorating business conditions affect the counterparty, as well as whether deteriorating business conditions in entities similar to the counterparty may indicate that the counterparty may not fulfill its obligations (that is, non-performance risk);
- Policies for adjusting for measurement uncertainties. Such adjustments can include model adjustments, lack of liquidity adjustments, credit risk adjustments, and other risk adjustments;
- The capability to calculate the range of realistic outcomes given the uncertainties involved, for example by performing a sensitivity analysis; and
- Policies for identifying when a fair value measurement input moves to a different level of the fair value hierarchy.

42   Particular difficulties may develop where there is severe curtailment or even cessation of trading in particular financial instruments. In these circumstances, financial instruments that have previously been valued using market prices may need to be valued using a model.

Management's Valuation Process

Techniques that management may use to value their financial instruments include 43 observable prices, recent transactions, and models that use observable or unobservable inputs. Management may also make use of:

(a) A third-party pricing source, such as a pricing service or broker quote; or
(b) A valuation expert.

Third-party pricing sources and valuation experts may use one or more of these valuation techniques.

In many financial reporting frameworks, the best evidence of a financial instrument's 44 fair value is found in contemporaneous transactions in an active market (that is, level 1 inputs). In such cases, the valuation of a financial instrument may be relatively simple. Quoted prices for financial instruments that are listed on exchanges or traded in liquid over-the-counter markets may be available from sources such as financial publications, the exchanges themselves or third-party pricing sources. When using quoted prices, it is important that management understand the basis on which the quote is given to ensure that the price reflects market conditions at the measurement date. Quoted prices obtained from publications or exchanges may provide sufficient evidence of fair value when, for example:

(a) The prices are not out of date or "stale" (for example, if the quote is based on the last traded price and the trade occurred some time ago); and
(b) The quotes are prices at which dealers would actually trade the financial instrument with sufficient frequency and volume.

Where there is no current observable market price for the financial instrument (that 45 is, a level 1 input), it will be necessary for the entity to gather other price indicators to use in a valuation technique to value the financial instrument. Price indicators may include:

- Recent transactions, including transactions after the date of the financial statements in the same instrument. Consideration is given to whether an adjustment needs to be made for changes in market conditions between the measurement date and the date the transaction was made, as these transactions are not necessarily indicative of the market conditions that existed at the date of the financial statements. In addition it is possible that the transaction represents a forced transaction and is therefore not indicative of a price in an orderly trade.
- Current or recent transactions in similar instruments, often known as "proxy pricing." Adjustments will need to be made to the price of the proxy to reflect the differences between them and the instrument being priced, for example, to take account of differences in liquidity or credit risk between the two instruments.
- Indices for similar instruments. As with transactions in similar instruments, adjustments will need to be made to reflect the difference between the instrument being priced and the instrument(s) from which the index used is derived.

It is expected that management will document its valuation policies and model used 46 to value a particular financial instrument, including the rationale for the model(s) used, the selection of assumptions in the valuation methodology, and the entity's consideration of whether adjustments for measurement uncertainty are necessary.

Models

Models may be used to value financial instruments when the price cannot be directly 47 observed in the market. Models can be as simple as a commonly used bond pricing formula or involve complex, specifically developed software tools to value financial instruments with level 3 inputs. Many models are based on discounted cash flow calculations.

48   Models comprise a methodology, assumptions and data. The methodology describes rules or principles governing the relationship between the variables in the valuation. Assumptions include estimates of uncertain variables which are used in the model. Data may comprise actual or hypothetical information about the financial instrument, or other inputs to the financial instrument.

49   Depending on the circumstances, matters that the entity may address when establishing or validating a model for a financial instrument include whether:

- The model is validated prior to usage, with periodic reviews to ensure it is still suitable for its intended use. The entity's validation process may include evaluation of:
  - o   The methodology's theoretical soundness and mathematical integrity, including the appropriateness of parameters and sensitivities.
  - o   The consistency and completeness of the model's inputs with market practices, and whether the appropriate inputs are available for use in the model.
- There are appropriate change control policies, procedures and security controls over the model.
- The model is appropriately changed or adjusted on a timely basis for changes in market conditions.
- The model is periodically calibrated, reviewed and tested for validity by a separate and objective function. Doing so is a means of ensuring that the model's output is a fair representation of the value that marketplace participants would ascribe to a financial instrument.
- The model maximizes the use of relevant observable inputs and minimizes the use of unobservable inputs.
- Adjustments are made to the output of the model to reflect the assumptions marketplace participants would use in similar circumstances.
- The model is adequately documented, including the model's intended applications and limitations and its key parameters, required data, results of any validation analysis performed and any adjustments made to the output of the model.

An Example of a Common Financial Instrument

50   The following describes how models may be applied to value a common financial instrument, known as an asset backed security.[9] Because asset backed securities are often valued based on level 2 or 3 inputs, they are frequently valued using models and involve:

- Understanding the type of security—considering (a) the underlying collateral; and (b) the terms of the security. The underlying collateral is used to estimate the timing and amounts of cash flows such as mortgage or credit card interest and principal payments.
- Understanding the terms of the security—this includes evaluating contractual cash flow rights, such as the order of repayment, and any default events. The order of repayment, often known as seniority, refers to terms which require that some classes of security holders (senior debt) are repaid before others

---

[9] *An asset backed security is a financial instrument which is backed by a pool of underlying assets (known as the collateral, such as credit card receivables or vehicle loans) and derives value and income from those underlying assets.*

(subordinated debt). The rights of each class of security holder to the cash flows, frequently referred to as the cash flow "waterfall," together with assumptions of the timing and amount of cash flows are used to derive a set of estimated cash flows for each class of security holder. The expected cash flows are then discounted to derive an estimated fair value.

The cash flows of an asset backed security may be affected by prepayments of the underlying collateral and by potential default risk and resulting estimated loss severities. Prepayment assumptions, if applicable, are generally based on evaluating market interest rates for similar collateral to the rates on the collateral underlying the security. For example, if market interest rates for mortgages have declined then the underlying mortgages in a security may experience higher prepayment rates than originally expected. Estimating potential default and loss severity involves close evaluation of the underlying collateral and borrowers to estimate default rates. For example, when the underlying collateral comprises residential mortgages, loss severities may be affected by estimates of residential housing prices over the term of the security.   **51**

Third-Party Pricing Sources

Entities may use third-party pricing sources in order to obtain fair value information. The preparation of an entity's financial statements, including the valuation of financial instruments and the preparation of financial statement disclosures relating to these instruments, may require expertise that management does not possess. Entities may not be able to develop appropriate valuation techniques, including models that may be used in a valuation, and may use a third-party pricing source to arrive at a valuation or to provide disclosures for the financial statements. This may particularly be the case in smaller entities or in entities that do not engage in a high volume of financial instruments transactions (for example, non-financial institutions with treasury departments). Even though management has used a third-party pricing source, management is ultimately responsible for the valuation.   **52**

Third-party pricing sources may also be used because the volume of securities to price over a short timeframe may not be possible by the entity. This is often the case for traded investment funds that must determine a net asset value each day. In other cases, management may have their own pricing process but use third-party pricing sources to corroborate their own valuations.   **53**

For one or more of these reasons most entities use third-party pricing sources when valuing securities either as a primary source or as a source of corroboration for their own valuations. Third-party pricing sources generally fall into the following categories: **54**

- Pricing services, including consensus pricing services; and
- Brokers proving broker quotes.

Pricing services

Pricing services provide entities with prices and price-related data for a variety of financial instruments, often performing daily valuations of large numbers of financial instruments. These valuations may be made by collecting market data and prices from a wide variety of sources, including market makers, and, in certain instances, using internal valuations techniques to derive estimated fair values. Pricing services may combine a number of approaches to arrive at a price. Pricing services are often used as a source of prices based on level 2 inputs. Pricing services may have strong controls around how prices are developed and their customers often include a wide   **55** variety of parties, including buy and sell side investors, back and middle office functions, auditors and others.

56   Pricing services often have a formalized process for customers to challenge the prices received from the pricing services. These challenge processes usually require the customer to provide evidence to support an alternative price, with challenges categorized based on the quality of evidence provided. For example, a challenge based on a recent sale of that instrument that the pricing service was not aware of may be upheld, whereas a challenge based on a customer's own valuation technique may be more heavily scrutinized. In this way, a pricing service with a large number of leading participants, both buy and sell side, may be able to constantly correct prices to more fully reflect the information available to market participants.

Consensus pricing services

57   Some entities may use pricing data from consensus pricing services which differ from other pricing services. Consensus pricing services obtain pricing information about an instrument from several participating entities (subscribers). Each subscriber submits prices to the pricing service. The pricing service treats this information confidentially and returns to each subscriber the consensus price, which is usually an arithmetical average of the data after a data cleansing routine has been employed to eliminate outliers. For some markets, such as for exotic derivatives, consensus prices might constitute the best available data. However, many factors are considered when assessing the representational faithfulness of the consensus prices including, for example:

- Whether the prices submitted by the subscribers reflect actual transactions or just indicative prices based on their own valuation techniques.
- The number of sources from which prices have been obtained.
- The quality of the sources used by the consensus pricing service.
- Whether participants include leading market participants

58   Typically consensus prices are only available to subscribers who have submitted their own prices to the service. Accordingly not all entities will have direct access to consensus prices. Because a subscriber generally cannot know how the prices submitted were estimated, other sources of evidence in addition to information from consensus pricing services may be needed for management to support their valuation. In particular, this may be the case if the sources are providing indicative prices based on their own valuation techniques and management is unable to obtain an understanding of how these sources calculated their prices.

Brokers providing broker quotes

59   As brokers provide quotes only as an incidental service for their clients, quotes they provide differ in many respects from prices obtained in pricing services. Brokers may be unwilling to provide information about the process used to develop their quote, but may have access to information on transactions about which a pricing service may not be aware. Broker quotes may be executable or indicative. Indicative quotes are a broker's best estimate of fair value, whereas an executable quote shows that the broker is willing to transact at this price. Executable quotes are strong evidence of fair value. Indicative quotes are less so because of the lack of transparency into the methods used by the broker to establish the quote. In addition the rigor of controls over the brokers' quote often will differ depending on whether the broker also holds the same security in its own portfolio. Broker quotes are often used for securities with level 3 inputs and sometimes may be the only external information available.

Further considerations relating to third-party pricing sources

Understanding how the pricing sources calculated a price enables management to **60** determine whether such information is suitable for use in its valuation, including as an input to a valuation technique and in what level of inputs the security should be categorized for disclosure purposes. For example, third-party pricing sources may value financial instruments using proprietary models, and it is important that management understands the methodology, assumptions and data used.

If fair value measurements obtained from third-party pricing sources are not based **61** on the current prices of an active market, it will be necessary for management to evaluate whether the fair value measurements were derived in a manner that is consistent with the applicable financial reporting framework. Management's understanding of the fair value measurement includes:

- How the fair value measurement was determined—for example, whether the fair value measurement was determined by a valuation technique, in order to assess whether it is consistent with the fair value measurement objective;
- Whether the quotes are indicative prices, indicative spread, or binding offers; and
- How frequently the fair value measurement is estimated by the third-party pricing sources—in order to assess whether it reflects market conditions at the measurement date.

Understanding the bases on which third-party pricing sources have determined their quotes in the context of the particular financial instruments held by the entity assists management in evaluating the relevance and reliability of this evidence to support its valuations.

It is possible that there will be disparities between price indicators from different **62** sources. Understanding how the price indicators were derived, and investigating these disparities, assists management in corroborating the evidence used in developing its valuation of financial instruments in order to evaluate whether the valuation is reasonable. Simply taking the average of the quotes provided, without doing further research, may not be appropriate, because one price in the range may be the most representative of fair value and this may not be the average. To evaluate whether its valuations of financial instruments are reasonable, management may:

- Consider whether actual transactions represent forced transactions rather than transactions between willing buyers and willing sellers. This may invalidate the price as a comparison;
- Analyze the expected future cash flows of the instrument. This could be performed as an indicator of the most relevant pricing data;
- Depending on the nature of what is unobservable, extrapolate from observed prices to unobserved ones (for example, there may be observed prices for maturities up to ten years but not longer, but the ten year price curve may be capable of being extrapolated beyond ten years as an indicator). Care is needed to ensure that extrapolation is not carried so far beyond the observable curve that its link to observable prices becomes too tenuous to be reliable;
- Compare prices within a portfolio of financial instruments to each other to make sure that they are consistent among similar financial instruments;
- Use more than one model to corroborate the results from each one, having regard to the data and assumptions used in each; or
- Evaluate movements in the prices for related hedging instruments and collateral.

In coming to its judgment as to its valuation, an entity may also consider other factors that may be specific to the entity's circumstances.

Use of Valuation Experts

63 Management may engage a valuation expert from an investment bank, broker, or other valuation firm to value some or all of its securities. Unlike pricing services and broker quotes, generally the methodology and data used are more readily available to management when they have engaged an expert to perform a valuation on their behalf. Even though management has engaged an expert, management is ultimately responsible for the valuation used.

Issues Related to Financial Liabilities

64 Understanding the effect of credit risk is an important aspect of valuing both financial assets and financial liabilities. This valuation reflects the credit quality and financial strength of both the issuer and any credit support providers. In some financial reporting frameworks, the measurement of a financial liability assumes that it is transferred to a market participant at the measurement date. Where there is not an observable market price for a financial liability, its value is typically measured using the same method as a counterparty would use to measure the value of the corresponding asset, unless there are factors specific to the liability (such as third-party credit enhancement). In particular, the entity's own credit risk to the liability (such as third-party credit enhancement). In particular, the entity's own credit risk to the liability (such as third-party credit enhancement). In particular, the entity's own credit risk[10] can often be difficult to measure.

Presentation and Disclosure about Financial Instruments

65 Most financial reporting frameworks require disclosures in the financial statements to enable users of the financial statements to make meaningful assessments of the effects of the entity's financial instrument activities, including the risks and uncertainties associated with financial instruments.

66 Most frameworks require the disclosure of quantitative and qualitative information (including accounting policies) relating to financial instruments. The accounting requirements for fair value measurements in financial statement presentation and disclosures are extensive in most financial reporting frameworks and encompass more than just valuation of the financial instruments. For example, qualitative disclosures about financial instruments provide important contextual information about the characteristics of the financial instruments and their future cash flows that may help inform investors about the risks to which entities are exposed.

Categories of Disclosures

67 Disclosure requirements include:

(a) Quantitative disclosures that are derived from the amounts included in the financial statements—for example, categories of financial assets and liabilities;

(b) Quantitative disclosures that require significant judgment—for example, sensitivity analysis for each type of market risk to which the entity is exposed; and

(c) Qualitative disclosures—for example, those that describe the entity's governance over financial instruments; objectives; controls, policies and processes for managing each type of risk arising from financial instruments; and the methods used to measure the risks.

---

[10] *Own credit risk is the amount of change in fair value that is not attributable to changes in market conditions.*

The more sensitive the valuation is to movements in a particular variable, the more **68** likely it is that disclosure will be necessary to indicate the uncertainties surrounding the valuation. Certain financial reporting frameworks may also require disclosure of sensitivity analyses, including the effects of changes in assumptions used in the entity's valuation techniques. For example, the additional disclosures required for financial instruments with fair value measurements that are categorized within level 3 inputs of the fair value hierarchy are aimed at informing users of financial statements about the effects of those fair value measurements that use the most subjective inputs.

Some financial reporting frameworks require disclosure of information that enables **69** users of the financial statements to evaluate the nature and extent of the risks arising from financial instruments to which the entity is exposed at the reporting date. This disclosure may be contained in the notes to the financial statements, or in management's discussion and analysis within its annual report cross-referenced from the audited financial statements. The extent of disclosure depends on the extent of the entity's exposure to risks arising from financial instruments. This includes qualitative disclosures about:

- The exposures to risk and how they arise, including the possible effects on an entity's future liquidity and collateral requirements;
- The entity's objectives, policies and processes for managing the risk and the methods used to measure the risk; and
- Any changes in exposures to risk or objectives, policies or processes for managing risk from the previous period.

Section II—Audit Considerations Relating to Financial Instruments

Certain factors may make auditing financial instruments particularly challenging. **70** For example:

- It may be difficult for both management and the auditor to understand the nature of financial instruments and what they are used for, and the risks to which the entity is exposed.
- Market sentiment and liquidity can change quickly, placing pressure on management to manage their exposures effectively.
- Evidence supporting valuation may be difficult to obtain.
- Individual payments associated with certain financial instruments may be significant, which may increase the risk of misappropriation of assets.
- The amounts recorded in the financial statements relating to financial instruments may not be significant, but there may be significant risks and exposures associated with these financial instruments.
- A few employees may exert significant influence on the entity's financial instruments transactions, in particular where their compensation arrangements are tied to revenue from financial instruments, and there may be possible undue reliance on these individuals by others within the entity.

These factors may cause risks and relevant facts to be obscured, which may affect the auditor's assessment of the risks of material misstatement, and latent risks can emerge rapidly, especially in adverse market conditions.

Professional Skepticism[11]

71   Professional skepticism is necessary to the critical assessment of audit evidence and assists the auditor in remaining alert for possible indications of management bias. This includes questioning contradictory audit evidence and the reliability of documents, responses to inquiries and other information obtained from management and those charged with governance. It also includes being alert to conditions that may indicate possible misstatement due to error or fraud and considering the sufficiency and appropriateness of audit evidence obtained in light of the circumstances.

72   Application of professional skepticism is required in all circumstances, and the need for professional skepticism increases with the complexity of financial instruments, for example with regard to:

- Evaluating whether sufficient appropriate audit evidence has been obtained, which can be particularly challenging when models are used or in determining if markets are inactive.
- Evaluating management's judgments, and the potential for management bias, in applying the entity's applicable financial reporting framework, in particular management's choice of valuation techniques, use of assumptions in valuation techniques, and addressing circumstances in which the auditor's judgments and management's judgments differ.
- Drawing conclusions based on the audit evidence obtained, for example assessing the reasonableness of valuations prepared by management's experts and evaluating whether disclosures in the financial statements achieve fair presentation.

Planning Considerations[12]

73   The auditor's focus in planning the audit is particularly on:

- Understanding the accounting and disclosure requirements;
- Understanding the financial instruments to which the entity is exposed, and their purpose and risks;
- Determining whether specialized skills and knowledge are needed in the audit;
- Understanding and evaluating the system of internal control in light of the entity's financial instrument transactions and the information systems that fall within the scope of the audit;
- Understanding the nature, role and activities of the internal audit function;
- Understanding management's process for valuing financial instruments, including whether management has used an expert or a service organization; and
- Assessing and responding to the risk of material misstatement.

Understanding the Accounting and Disclosure Requirements

74   ISA 540 requires the auditor to obtain an understanding of the requirements of the applicable financial reporting framework relevant to accounting estimates, including related disclosures and any regulatory requirements.[13] The requirements of the

---

[11] *ISA 200, paragraph 15*

[12] *ISA 300, Planning an Audit of Financial Statements*, deals with the auditor's responsibility to plan an audit of financial statements.

[13] *ISA 540, paragraph 8(a)*

applicable financial reporting framework regarding financial instruments may themselves be complex and require extensive disclosures. Reading this IAPN is not a substitute for a full understanding of all the requirements of the applicable financial reporting framework. Certain financial reporting frameworks require consideration of areas such as:

- Hedge accounting;
- Accounting for "Day 1" profits or losses;
- Recognition and derecognition of financial instrument transactions;
- Own credit risk; and
- Risk transfer and derecognition, in particular where the entity has been involved in the origination and structuring of complex financial instruments.

Understanding the Financial Instruments

The characteristics of financial instruments may obscure certain elements of risk and **75** exposure. Obtaining an understanding of the instruments in which the entity has invested or to which it is exposed, including the characteristics of the instruments, helps the auditor to identify whether:

- Important aspects of a transaction are missing or inaccurately recorded;
- A valuation appears appropriate;
- The risks inherent in them are fully understood and managed by the entity; and
- The financial instruments are appropriately classified into current and non-current assets and liabilities.

Examples of matters that the auditor may consider when obtaining an understanding **76** of the entity's financial instruments include:

- To which types of financial instruments the entity is exposed.
- The use to which they are put.
- Management's and, where appropriate, those charged with governance's understanding of the financial instruments, their use and the accounting requirements.
- Their exact terms and characteristics so that their implications can be fully understood and, in particular where transactions are linked, the overall impact of the financial instrument transactions.
- How they fit into the entity's overall risk management strategy.

Inquiries of the internal audit function, the risk management function, if such functions exist, and discussions with those charged with governance may inform the auditor's understanding.

In some cases, a contract, including a contract for a non-financial instrument may **77** contain a derivative. Some financial reporting frameworks permit or require such "embedded" derivatives to be separated from the host contract in some circumstances. Understanding management's process for identifying, and accounting for, embedded derivatives will assist the auditor in understanding the risks to which the entity is exposed.

Using Those with Specialized Skills and Knowledge in the Audit[14]

78   A key consideration in audits involving financial instruments, particularly complex financial instruments, is the competence of the auditor. ISA 220[15] requires the engagement partner to be satisfied that the engagement team, and any auditor's experts who are not part of the engagement team, collectively have the appropriate competence and capabilities to perform the audit engagement in accordance with professional standards and applicable legal and regulatory requirements and to enable an auditor's report that is appropriate in the circumstances to be issued. Further, relevant ethical requirementsrequires the engagement partner to be satisfied that the engagement team, and any auditor's experts who are not part of the engagement team, collectively have the appropriate competence and capabilities to perform the audit engagement in accordance with professional standards and applicable legal and regulatory requirements and to enable an auditor's report that is appropriate in the circumstances to be issued. Further, relevant ethical requirements requires the engagement partner to be satisfied that the engagement team, and any auditor's experts who are not part of the engagement team, collectively have the appropriate competence and capabilities to perform the audit engagement in accordance with professional standards and applicable legal and regulatory requirements and to enable an auditor's report that is appropriate in the circumstances to be issued. Further, relevant ethical requirements[16] require the auditor to determine whether acceptance of the engagement would create any threats to compliance with the fundamental principles, including the professional competence and due care. Paragraph 79 below provides examples of the types of matters that may be relevant to the auditor's considerations in the context of financial instruments.

79   Accordingly, auditing financial instruments may require the involvement of one or more experts or specialists, for example, in the areas of:

- Understanding the financial instruments used by the entity and their characteristics, including their level of complexity. Using specialized skills and knowledge may be needed in checking whether all aspects of the financial instrument and related considerations have been captured in the financial statements, and evaluating whether adequate disclosure in accordance with the applicable financial reporting framework has been made where disclosure of risks is required.
- Understanding the applicable financial reporting framework, especially when there are areas known to be subject to differing interpretations, or practice is inconsistent or developing.
- Understanding the legal, regulatory, and tax implications resulting from the financial instruments, including whether the contracts are enforceable by the entity (for example, reviewing the underlying contracts), may require specialized skills and knowledge.
- Assessing the risks inherent in a financial instrument.

---

[14] *When such a person's expertise is in auditing and accounting, regardless of whether the person is from within or external to the firm, this person is considered to be part of the engagement team and is subject to the requirements of ISA 220, Quality Control for an Audit of Financial Statements.* When such a person's expertise is in a field other than accounting or auditing, such person is considered to be an auditor's expert, and the provisions of ISA 620, *Using the Work of an Auditor's Expert*, apply. ISA 620 explains that distinguishing between specialized areas of accounting or auditing, and expertise in another field, will be a matter of professional judgment, but notes the distinction may be made between expertise in methods of accounting for financial instruments (accounting and auditing expertise) and expertise in complex valuation techniques for financial instruments (expertise in a field other than accounting or auditing).

[15] *ISA 220, paragraph 14*

[16] *IESBA Code of Ethics for Professional Accountants* paragraphs 210.1 and 210.6

- The practitioner's responsibilities in the review engagement, as included in the engagement letter or other suitable form of written agreement.
- Significant findings from the review, for example:
  - The practitioner's views about significant qualitative aspects of the entity's accounting practices, including accounting policies, accounting estimates and financial statement disclosures.
  - Significant findings from the performance of procedures, including situations where the practitioner considered performance of additional procedures necessary under this ISRE. The practitioner may need to confirm that those charged with governance have the same understanding of the facts and circumstances relevant to specific transactions or events.
  - Matters arising that may lead to modification of the practitioner's conclusion.
  - Significant difficulties, if any, encountered during the review; for example, unavailability of expected information; unexpected inability to obtain evidence that the practitioner considers necessary for the review; or restrictions imposed on the practitioner by management. In some circumstances, such difficulties may constitute a scope limitation that, if not addressed by management or those charged with governance, may lead to modification of the practitioner's conclusion or to the practitioner's withdrawal from the engagement in certain circumstances.

In some entities, different persons are responsible for the management and the governance of an entity. In these circumstances, management may have the responsibility to communicate matters of governance interest to those charged with governance. Communication by management with those charged with governance of matters that the practitioner is required to communicate does not relieve the practitioner of the responsibility to also communicate them to those charged with governance. However, communication of these matters by management may affect the form or timing of the practitioner's communication with those charged with governance. **A67**

Communication with Third Parties

In some jurisdictions, the practitioner may be required by law or regulation to, for example: **A68**

- Notify a regulatory or enforcement body of certain matters communicated with those charged with governance. For example, in some jurisdictions the practitioner has a duty to report misstatements to authorities where management and those charged with governance fail to take corrective action.
- Submit copies of certain reports prepared for those charged with governance to relevant regulatory or funding bodies or, in some cases, make such reports publicly available.

Unless required by law or regulation to provide a third party with a copy of the practitioner's written communications with those charged with governance, the practitioner may need the prior consent of management or those charged with governance before doing so. **A69**

Performing the Engagement

Materiality in a Review of Financial Statements (Ref: Para. 43)

A70 The practitioner's consideration of materiality is made in the context of the applicable financial reporting framework. Some financial reporting frameworks discuss the concept of materiality in the context of the preparation and presentation of financial statements. Although financial reporting frameworks may discuss materiality in different terms, they generally explain that:

● Misstatements, including omissions, are considered to be material if they, individually or in the aggregate, could reasonably be expected to influence the economic decisions of users taken on the basis of the financial statements;

● Judgments about materiality are made in light of surrounding circumstances, and are affected by the size or nature of a misstatement, or a combination of both; and

● Judgments about matters that are material to users of the financial statements are based on a consideration of the common financial information needs of users as a group. The possible effect of misstatements on specific individual users, whose needs may vary widely, is not considered.

A71 If present in the applicable financial reporting framework, a discussion of the concept of materiality provides a frame of reference for the practitioner in determining materiality for the review. If not present, the above considerations provide the practitioner with a frame of reference.

A72 The practitioner's determination of materiality is a matter of professional judgment, and is affected by the practitioner's perception of the needs of the intended users of the financial statements. In this context, it is reasonable for the practitioner to assume that users:

● Have a reasonable knowledge of business and economic activities and accounting, and a willingness to study the information in the financial statements with reasonable diligence;

● Understand that financial statements are prepared, presented and reviewed to levels of materiality;

● Recognize the uncertainties inherent in the measurement of amounts based on the use of estimates, judgment and the consideration of future events; and

● Make reasonable economic decisions on the basis of the information in the financial statements.

Further, unless the review engagement is undertaken for financial statements that are intended to meet the particular needs of specific users, the possible effect of misstatements on specific users, whose information needs may vary widely, is not ordinarily considered.

A73 The practitioner's judgment about what is material in relation to the financial statements as a whole is the same regardless of the level of assurance obtained by a practitioner as the basis for expressing the conclusion on the financial statements.

Revising Materiality (Ref: Para. 44)

A74 The practitioner's determination of materiality for the financial statements as a whole may need to be revised during the engagement as a result of:

● A change in the circumstances that occurred during the review (for example, a decision to dispose of a major part of the entity's business).

- Assisting the engagement team gather evidence to support management's valuations or to develop a point estimate or range, especially when fair value is determined by a complex model; when markets are inactive and data and assumptions are difficult to obtain; when unobservable inputs are used; or when management has used an expert.
- Evaluating information technology controls, especially in entities with a high volume of financial instruments. In such entities information technology may be highly complex, for example when significant information about those financial instruments is transmitted, processed, maintained or accessed electronically. In addition, it may include relevant services provided by a service organization.

The nature and use of particular types of financial instruments, the complexities **80** associated with accounting requirements, and market conditions may lead to a need for the engagement team to consult[17] with other accounting and audit professionals, from within or outside the firm, with relevant technical accounting or auditing expertise and experience, taking into account factors such as:

- The capabilities and competence of the engagement team, including the experience of the members of the engagement team.
- The attributes of the financial instruments used by the entity.
- The identification of unusual circumstances or risks in the engagement, as well as the need for professional judgment, particularly with respect to materiality and significant risks.
- Market conditions.

Understanding Internal Control

ISA 315 establishes requirements for the auditor to understand the entity and its **81** environment, including its internal control. Obtaining an understanding of the entity and its environment, including the entity's internal control, is a continuous, dynamic process of gathering, updating and analyzing information throughout the audit. The understanding obtained enables the auditor to identify and assess the risks of material misstatement at the financial statement and assertion levels, thereby providing a basis for designing and implementing responses to the assessed risks of material misstatement. The volume and variety of the financial instrument transactions of an entity typically determines the nature and extent of controls that may exist at an entity. An understanding of how financial instruments are monitored and controlled assists the auditor in determining the nature, timing and extent of audit procedures. The Appendix describes controls that may exist in an entity that deals in a high volume of financial instrument transactions.

Understanding the Nature, Role and Activities of the Internal Audit Function

In many large entities, the internal audit function may perform work that enables **82** senior management and those charged with governance to review and evaluate the entity's controls relating to the use of financial instruments. The internal audit function may assist in identifying the risks of material misstatement due to fraud or error. However, the knowledge and skills required of an internal audit function to understand and perform procedures to provide assurance to management or those charged with governance on the entity's use of financial instruments are generally quite different from those needed for other parts of the business. The extent to which

---

[17] *ISA 220, paragraph 18(b), requires the engagement partner to be satisfied that members of the engagement team have undertaken appropriate consultation during the course of the engagement, both within the engagement team and between the engagement team and others at the appropriate level within or outside the firm.*

Factors to Consider in Determining Whether, and to What Extent, to Test the Operating Effectiveness of Controls

91   An expectation that controls are operating effectively may be more common when dealing with a financial institution with well-established controls, and therefore controls testing may be an effective means of obtaining audit evidence. When an entity has a trading function, substantive tests alone may not provide sufficient appropriate audit evidence due to the volume of contracts and the different systems used. Tests of controls, however, will not be sufficient on their own as the auditor is required by ISA 330 to design and perform substantive procedures for each material class of transactions, account balance and disclosure.[22]

92   Entities with a high volume of trading and use of financial instruments may have more sophisticated controls, and an effective risk management function, and therefore the auditor may be more likely to test controls in obtaining evidence about:

- The occurrence, completeness, accuracy, and cutoff of the transactions; and
- The existence, rights and obligations, and completeness of account balances.

93   In those entities with relatively few financial instrument transactions:

- Management and those charged with governance may have only a limited understanding of financial instruments and how they affect the business;
- The entity may only have a few different types of instruments with little or no interaction between them;
- There is unlikely to be a complex control environment (for example, the controls described in the Appendix may not be in place at the entity);
- Management may use pricing information from third-party pricing sources to value their instruments; and
- Controls over the use of pricing information from third-party pricing sources may be less sophisticated.

94   When an entity has relatively few transactions involving financial instruments, it may be relatively easy for the auditor to obtain an understanding of the entity's objectives for using the financial instruments and the characteristics of the instruments. In such circumstances, much of the audit evidence is likely to be substantive in nature, the auditor may perform the majority of the audit work at year-end, and third-party confirmations are likely to provide evidence in relation to the completeness, accuracy, and existence of the transactions.

95   In reaching a decision on the nature, timing and extent of testing of controls, the auditor may consider factors such as:

- The nature, frequency and volume of financial instrument transactions;
- The strength of controls, including whether controls are appropriately designed to respond to the risks associated with an entity's volume of financial instrument transactions and whether there is a governance framework over the entity's financial instrument activities;
- The importance of particular controls to the overall control objectives and processes in place at the entity, including the sophistication of the information systems to support financial instrument transactions;
- The monitoring of controls and identified deficiencies in control procedures;
- The issues the controls are intended to address, for example, controls related to the exercise of judgments compared with controls over supporting data.

[22] *ISA 330, paragraph 18*

Substantive tests are more likely to be effective than relying on controls related to the exercise of judgment;

- The competency of those involved in the control activities, for example whether the entity has adequate capacity, including during periods of stress, and ability to establish and verify valuations for the financial instruments to which it is exposed;
- The frequency of performance of these control activities;
- The level of precision the controls are intended to achieve;
- The evidence of performance of control activities; and
- The timing of key financial instrument transactions, for example, whether they are close to the period end.

Substantive Procedures

Designing substantive procedures includes consideration of: **96**

- The use of analytical procedures[23]—While analytical procedures undertaken by the auditor can be effective as risk assessment procedures to provide the auditor with information about an entity's business, they may be less effective as substantive procedures when performed alone. This is because the complex interplay of the drivers of the valuation often mask any unusual trends that might arise.
- Non-routine transactions—Many financial transactions are negotiated contracts between an entity and its counterparty (often known as "over the counter" or OTC.) To the extent that financial instrument transactions are not routine and outside an entity's normal activities, a substantive audit approach may be the most effective means of achieving the planned audit objectives. In instances where financial instrument transactions are not undertaken routinely, the auditor's responses to assessed risk, including designing and performing audit procedures, have regard to the entity's possible lack of experience in this area.
- Availability of evidence—For example, when the entity uses a third-party pricing source, evidence concerning the relevant financial statement assertions may not be available from the entity.
- Procedures performed in other audit areas—Procedures performed in other financial statement areas may provide evidence about the completeness of financial instrument transactions. These procedures may include tests of subsequent cash receipts and payments, and the search for unrecorded liabilities.
- Selection of items for testing—In some cases, the financial instrument portfolio will comprise instruments with varying complexity and risk. In such cases, judgmental sampling may be useful.

For example, in the case of an asset-backed security, in responding to the risks of **97** material misstatement for such a security, the auditor may consider performing some of the following audit procedures:

- Examining contractual documentation to understand the terms of the security, the underlying collateral and the rights of each class of security holder.
- Inquiring about management's process of estimating cash flows.
- Evaluating the reasonableness of assumptions, such as prepayment rates, default rates and loss severities.

---

[23] *ISA 315, paragraph 6(b), requires the auditor to apply analytical procedures as risk assessment procedures to assist in assessing the risks of material misstatement in order to provide a basis for designing and implementing responses to the assessed risks. ISA 520, Analytical Procedures, paragraph 6, requires the auditor to use analytical procedures in forming an overall conclusion on the financial statements. Analytical procedures may also be applied at other stages of the audit.*

105   These procedures are particularly important for some financial instruments, such as derivatives or guarantees. This is because they may not have a large initial investment, meaning it may be hard to identify their existence. For example, embedded derivatives are often contained in contracts for non-financial instruments which may not be included in confirmation procedures.

Valuation of Financial Instruments

Financial Reporting Requirements

106   Fair presentation financial reporting frameworks often use fair value hierarchies, for example those used in IFRS and U.S. GAAP. This usually means that the volume and detail of the required disclosures increases as the level of measurement uncertainty increases. The distinction between the levels in the hierarchy may require judgment.

107   The auditor may find it useful to obtain an understanding of how the financial instruments relate to the fair value hierarchy. Ordinarily, the risk of material misstatement, and the level of audit procedures to be applied, increases as the level of measurement uncertainty increases. The use of level 3, and some level 2, inputs from the fair value hierarchy may be a useful guide to the level of measurement uncertainty. Level 2 inputs vary from those which are easily obtained to those which are closer to level 3 inputs. The auditor evaluates available evidence and understands both the fair value hierarchy and the risk of management bias in management's categorization of financial instruments in the fair value hierarchy.

108   In accordance with ISA 540,[26] the auditor considers the entity's valuation policies and methodology for data and assumptions used in the valuation methodology. In many cases, the applicable financial reporting framework does not prescribe the valuation methodology. When this is the case, matters that may be relevant to the auditor's understanding of how management values financial instruments include, for example:

- Whether management has a formal valuation policy and, if so, whether the valuation technique used for a financial instrument is appropriately documented in accordance with that policy;
- Which models may give rise to the greatest risk of material misstatement;
- How management considered the complexity of the valuation of the financial instrument when selecting a particular valuation technique;
- Whether there is a greater risk of material misstatement because management has internally developed a model to be used to value financial instruments or is departing from a valuation technique commonly used to value the particular financial instrument;
- Whether management made use of a third-party pricing source;
- Whether those involved in developing and applying the valuation technique have the appropriate skills and expertise to do so, including whether a management's expert has been used; and
- Whether there are indicators of management bias in selecting the valuation technique to be used.

---

[26] *ISA 540, paragraph 8(c)*

Assessing the Risk of Material Misstatement Related to Valuation

When evaluating whether the valuation techniques used by an entity are appropriate in the circumstances, and whether controls over valuation techniques are in place, the factors considered by the auditor may include: **109**

- Whether the valuation techniques are commonly used by other market participants and have been previously demonstrated to provide a reliable estimate of prices obtained from market transactions;
- Whether the valuation techniques operate as intended and there are no flaws in their design, particularly under extreme conditions, and whether they have been objectively validated. Indicators of flaws include inconsistent movements relative to benchmarks;
- Whether the valuation techniques take account of the risks inherent in the financial instrument being valued, including counterparty creditworthiness, and own credit risk in the case of valuation techniques used to measure financial liabilities;
- How the valuation techniques are calibrated to the market, including the sensitivity of the valuation techniques to changes in variables;
- Whether market variables and assumptions are used consistently and whether new conditions justify a change in the valuation techniques, market variables or assumptions used;
- Whether sensitivity analyses indicate that valuations would change significantly with only small or moderate changes in assumptions;
- The organizational structure, such as the existence of an internal department responsible for developing models to value certain instruments, particularly where level 3 inputs are involved. For example, a model development function that is involved in assisting in pricing deals is less objective than one which is functionally and organizationally segregated from the front office; and
- The competence and objectivity of those responsible for the development and application of the valuation techniques, including management's relative experience with particular models that may be newly developed.

The auditor (or auditor's expert) may also independently develop one or more valuation techniques to compare its output with that of the valuation techniques used by management.

Significant Risks

The auditor's risk assessment process may lead the auditor to identify one or more significant risks relating to the valuation of financial instruments, when any of the following circumstances exist: **110**

- High measurement uncertainty related to the valuation of financial instruments (for example, those with unobservable inputs).[27]
- Lack of sufficient evidence to support management's valuation of its financial instruments.
- Lack of management understanding of its financial instruments or expertise necessary to value such instruments properly, including the ability to determine whether valuation adjustments are needed.
- Lack of management understanding of complex requirements in the applicable financial reporting framework relating to measurement and disclosure of

---

[27] *Where the auditor determines that the high estimation uncertainty related to the valuation of complex financial instruments gives rise to a significant risk, ISA 540 requires the auditor to perform substantive procedures and evaluate the adequacy of the disclosure of their estimation uncertainty. See ISA 540, paragraphs 11, 15 and 20.*

financial instruments, and inability of management to make the judgments required to properly apply those requirements.

- The significance of valuation adjustments made to valuation technique outputs when the applicable financial reporting framework requires or permits such adjustments.

111   For accounting estimates that give rise to significant risks, in addition to other substantive procedures performed to meet the requirements of ISA 330, ISA 540[28] requires the auditor to evaluate the following:

(a)   How management has considered alternative assumptions or outcomes, and why it has rejected them, or how management has otherwise addressed measurement uncertainty in making the accounting estimate;

(b)   Whether the significant assumptions used by management are reasonable; and

(c)   Where relevant to the reasonableness of the significant assumptions used by management, or the appropriate application of the applicable financial reporting framework, management's intent to carry out specific courses of action and its ability to do so.

112   As markets become inactive, the change in circumstances may lead to a move from valuation by market price to valuation by model, or may result in a change from one particular model to another. Reacting to changes in market conditions may be difficult if management does not have policies in place prior to their occurrence. Management may also not possess the expertise necessary to develop a model on an urgent basis, or select the valuation technique that may be appropriate in the circumstances. Even where valuation techniques have been consistently used, there is a need for management to examine the continuing appropriateness of the valuation techniques and assumptions used for determining valuation of financial instruments. Further, valuation techniques may have been selected in times where reasonable market information was available, but may not provide reasonable valuations in times of unanticipated stress.

113   The susceptibility to management bias, whether intentional or unintentional, increases with the subjectivity of the valuation and the degree of measurement uncertainty. For example, management may tend to ignore observable marketplace assumptions or data and instead use their own internally-developed model if the model yields more favorable results. Even without fraudulent intent, there may be a natural temptation to bias judgments towards the most favorable end of what may be a wide spectrum, rather than the point in the spectrum that might be considered to be most consistent with the applicable financial reporting framework. Changing the valuation technique from period to period without a clear and appropriate reason for doing so may also be an indicator of management bias. Although some form of management bias is inherent in subjective decisions relating to the valuation of financial instruments, when there is intention to mislead, management bias is fraudulent in nature.

Developing an Audit Approach

114   In testing how management values the financial instrument and in responding to the assessed risks of material misstatement in accordance with ISA 540,[29] the auditor undertakes one or more of the following procedures, taking account of the nature of the accounting estimates:

---

[28] *ISA 540, paragraph 15(a)-(b)*

[29] *ISA 540, paragraphs 12–14*

(a) Test how management made the accounting estimate and the data on which it is based (including valuation techniques used by the entity in its valuations).
(b) Test the operating effectiveness of the controls over how management made the accounting estimate, together with appropriate substantive procedures.
(c) Develop a point estimate or a range to evaluate management's point estimate.
(d) Determine whether events occurring up to the date of the auditor's report provide audit evidence regarding the accounting estimate.

Many auditors find that a combination of testing how management valued the financial instrument, and the data on which it is based, and testing the operating effectiveness of controls, will be an effective and efficient audit approach. While subsequent events may provide some evidence about the valuation of financial instruments, other factors may need to be taken into account to address any changes in market conditions subsequent to the balance sheet date.[30] If the auditor is unable to test how management made the estimate, the auditor may choose to develop a point estimate or range.

As described in Section I, to estimate the fair value of financial instruments management may:

115

- Utilize information from third-party pricing sources;
- Gather data to develop their own estimate using various techniques including models; and
- Engage an expert to develop an estimate.

Management often may use a combination of these approaches. For example, management may have their own pricing process but use third-party pricing sources to corroborate their own values.

Audit Considerations When Management Uses a Third-Party Pricing Source

Management may make use of a third-party pricing source, such as a pricing service or broker, in valuing the entity's financial instruments. Understanding how management uses the information and how the pricing service operates assists the auditor in determining the nature and extent of audit procedures needed.

116

The following matters may be relevant where management uses a third-party pricing source:

117

- *The type of third-party pricing source*—Some third-party pricing sources make more information available about their process. For example, a pricing service often provides information about their methodology, assumptions and data in valuing financial instruments at the asset class level. By contrast, brokers often provide no, or only limited, information about the inputs and assumptions used in developing the quote.
- *The nature of inputs used and the complexity of the valuation technique*—The reliability of prices from third-party pricing sources varies depending on the observability of inputs (and accordingly, the level of inputs in the fair value hierarchy), and the complexity of the methodology for valuing a specific security or asset class. For example, the reliability of a price for an equity investment actively traded in a liquid market is higher than that of a corporate bond traded in a liquid market that has not traded on the measurement date, which, in turn, is more reliable than that of an asset-backed security that is valued using a discounted cash flow model.

---

[30] *Paragraphs A63–A66 of ISA 540 provide examples of some of the factors that may be relevant.*

- *The reputation and experience of the third-party pricing source*—For example, a third-party pricing source may be experienced in a certain type of financial instrument, and be recognized as such, but may not be similarly experienced in other types of financial instruments. The auditor's past experience with the third-party pricing source may also be relevant in this regard.

- *The objectivity of the third-party pricing source*—For example, if a price obtained by management comes from a counterparty such as the broker who sold the financial instrument to the entity, or an entity with a close relationship with the entity being audited, the price may not be reliable.

- *The entity's controls over the use of third-party pricing sources*—The degree to which management has controls in place to assess the reliability of information from third-party pricing sources affects the reliability of the fair value measurement. For example, management may have controls in place to:
  - o   Review and approve the use of the third-party pricing source, including consideration of the reputation, experience and objectivity of the third-party pricing source.
  - o   Determine the completeness, relevance and accuracy of the prices and pricing-related data.

- *The third-party pricing source's controls*—The controls and processes over valuations for the asset classes of interest to the auditor. For example, a third-party pricing source may have strong controls around how prices are developed, including the use of a formalized process for customers, both buy and sell side, to challenge the prices received from the pricing service, when supported by appropriate evidence, which may enable the third-party pricing source to constantly correct prices to more fully reflect the information available to market participants.

118   Possible approaches to gathering evidence regarding information from third-party pricing sources may include the following:

- For level 1 inputs, comparing the information from third-party pricing sources with observable market prices.
- Reviewing disclosures provided by third-party pricing sources about their controls and processes, valuation techniques, inputs and assumptions.
- Testing the controls management has in place to assess the reliability of information from third-party pricing sources.
- Performing procedures at the third-party pricing source to understand and test the controls and processes, valuation techniques, inputs and assumptions used for asset classes or specific financial instruments of interest.
- Evaluating whether the prices obtained from third-party pricing sources are reasonable in relation to prices from other third-party pricing sources, the entity's estimate or the auditor's own estimate.
- Evaluating the reasonableness of valuation techniques, assumptions and inputs.
- Developing a point estimate or a range for some financial instruments priced by the third-party pricing source and evaluating whether the results are within a reasonable range of each other.
- Obtaining a service auditor's report that covers the controls over validation of the prices.[31]

119   Obtaining prices from multiple third-party pricing sources may also provide useful information about measurement uncertainty. A wide range of prices may indicate

---

[31] *Some pricing services may provide reports for users of its data to explain their controls over pricing data, that is, a report prepared in accordance with International Standard on Assurance Engagements (ISAE) 3402, Assurance Reports on Controls at a Service Organization.* Management may request, and the auditor may consider obtaining, such a report to develop an understanding of how the pricing data is prepared and evaluate whether the controls at the pricing service can be relied upon.

higher measurement uncertainty and may suggest that the financial instrument is sensitive to small changes in data and assumptions. A narrow range may indicate lower measurement uncertainty and may suggest less sensitivity to changes in data and assumptions. Although obtaining prices from multiple sources may be useful, when considering financial instruments that have inputs categorized at levels 2 or 3 of the fair value hierarchy, in particular, obtaining prices from multiple sources is unlikely to provide sufficient appropriate audit evidence on its own. This is because:

(a) What appear to be multiple sources of pricing information may be utilizing the same underlying pricing source; and
(b) Understanding the inputs used by the third-party pricing source in determining the price may be necessary in order to categorize the financial instrument in the fair value hierarchy.

In some situations, the auditor may be unable to gain an understanding of the **120** process used to generate the price, including any controls over the process of how reliably the price is determined, or may not have access to the model, including the assumptions and other inputs used. In such cases, the auditor may decide to undertake to develop a point estimate or a range to evaluate management's point estimate in responding to the assessed risk.

Audit Considerations When Management Estimates Fair Values Using a Model

Paragraph 13(b) of ISA 540 requires the auditor, if testing management's process of **121** making the accounting estimate, to evaluate whether the method of measurement used is appropriate in the circumstances and the assumptions used by management are reasonable in light of the measurement objectives of the applicable financial reporting framework.

Whether management has used a third-party pricing source, or is undertaking its **122** own valuation, models are often used to value financial instruments, particularly when using inputs at levels 2 and 3 of the fair value hierarchy. In determining the nature, timing and extent of audit procedures on models, the auditor may consider the methodology, assumptions and data used in the model. When considering more complex financial instruments such as those using level 3 inputs, testing all three may be a useful source of audit evidence. However, when the model is both simple and generally accepted, such as some bond price calculations, audit evidence obtained from focusing on the assumptions and data used in the model may be a more useful source of evidence.

Testing a model can be accomplished by two main approaches: **123**

(a) The auditor can test management's model, by considering the appropriateness of the model used by management, the reasonableness of the assumptions and data used, and the mathematical accuracy; or
(b) The auditor can develop their own estimate, and then compare the auditor's valuation with that of the entity.

Where valuation of financial instruments is based on unobservable inputs (that is, **124** level 3 inputs), matters that the auditor may consider include, for example, how management supports the following:

• The identification and characteristics of marketplace participants relevant to the financial instrument.
• How unobservable inputs are determined on initial recognition.
• Modifications it has made to its own assumptions to reflect its view of assumptions marketplace participants would use.

- Whether it has incorporated the best input information available in the circumstances.
- Where applicable, how its assumptions take account of comparable transactions.
- Sensitivity analysis of models when unobservable inputs are used and whether adjustments have been made to address measurement uncertainty.

125   In addition, the auditor's industry knowledge, knowledge of market trends, understanding of other entities' valuations (having regard to confidentiality) and other relevant price indicators informs the auditor's testing of the valuations and the consideration of whether the valuations appear reasonable overall. If the valuations appear to be consistently overly aggressive or conservative, this may be an indicator of possible management bias.

126   Where there is a lack of observable external evidence, it is particularly important that those charged with governance have been appropriately engaged to understand the subjectivity of management's valuations and the evidence that has been obtained to support these valuations. In such cases, it may be necessary for the auditor to evaluate whether there has been a thorough review and consideration of the issues, including any documentation, at all appropriate management levels within the entity, including with those charged with governance.

127   When markets become inactive or dislocated, or inputs are unobservable, management's valuations may be more judgmental and less verifiable and, as result, may be less reliable. In such circumstances, the auditor may test the model by a combination of testing controls operated by the entity, evaluating the design and operation of the model, testing the assumptions and data used in the model, and comparing its output to a point estimate or range developed by the auditor or to other third-party valuation techniques.[32]

128   It is likely that in testing the inputs used in an entity's valuation methodology,[33] for example, where such inputs are categorized in the fair value hierarchy, the auditor will also be obtaining evidence to support the disclosures required by the applicable financial reporting framework. For example, the auditor's substantive procedures to evaluate whether the inputs used in an entity's valuation technique (that is, level 1, level 2 and level 3 inputs) are appropriate, and tests of an entity's sensitivity analysis, will be relevant to the auditor's evaluation of whether the disclosures achieve fair presentation.

Evaluating Whether the Assumptions Used by Management Are Reasonable

129   An assumption used in a model may be deemed to be significant if a reasonable variation in the assumption would materially affect the measurement of the financial instrument.[34] Management may have considered alternative assumptions or outcomes by performing a sensitivity analysis. The extent of subjectivity associated with assumptions influences the degree of measurement uncertainty and may lead the auditor to conclude there is a significant risk, for example in the case of level 3 inputs.

---

[32] *ISA 540, paragraph 13(d) describes requirements when the auditor develops a range to evaluate management's point estimate. Valuation techniques developed by third parties and used by the auditor may, in some circumstances be considered the work of an auditor's expert and subject to the requirements in ISA 620.*

[33] *See, for example, paragraph 15 of ISA 540 for requirements relative to the auditor's evaluation of management's assumption regarding significant risks.*

[34] *See ISA 540, paragraph A107.*

Audit procedures to test the assumptions used by management, including those used   **130**
as inputs to models, may include evaluating:

- Whether, and if so, how, management has incorporated market inputs into the development of assumptions, as it is generally preferable to seek to maximize the use of relevant observable inputs and minimize unobservable inputs;
- Whether the assumptions are consistent with observable market conditions, and the characteristics of the financial asset or financial liability;
- Whether the sources of market-participant assumptions are relevant and reliable, and how management has selected the assumptions to use when a number of different marketplace assumptions exist; and
- Whether sensitivity analyses indicate that valuations would change significantly with only small or moderate changes in assumptions.

See paragraphs A77 to A83 of ISA 540 for further considerations relative to evaluating the assumptions used by management.

The auditor's consideration of judgments about the future is based on information   **131**
available at the time at which the judgment is made. Subsequent events may result in
outcomes that are inconsistent with judgments that were reasonable at the time they
were made.

In some cases, the discount rate in a present value calculation may be adjusted to   **132**
account for the uncertainties in the valuation, rather than adjusting each assumption.
In such cases, an auditor's procedures may focus on the discount rate, by looking at
an observable trade on a similar security to compare the discount rates used or
developing an independent model to calculate the discount rate and compare with
that used by management.

Audit Considerations When a Management's Expert Is Used by the Entity

As discussed in Section I, management may engage a valuation expert to value some   **133**
or all of their securities. Such experts may be brokers, investment bankers, pricing
services that also provide expert valuation services, or other specialized valuation
firms.

Paragraph 8 of ISA 500 contains requirements for the auditor when evaluating   **134**
evidence from an expert engaged by management. The extent of the auditor's procedures in relation to a management's expert and that expert's work depend on the
significance of the expert's work for the auditor's purposes. Evaluating the appropriateness of management's expert's work assists the auditor in assessing whether the
prices or valuations supplied by a management's expert provide sufficient appropriate audit evidence to support the valuations. Examples of procedures the auditor
may perform include:

- Evaluating the competence, capabilities and objectivity of management's expert for example: their relationship with the entity; their reputation and standing in the market; their experience with the particular types of instruments; and their understanding of the relevant financial reporting framework applicable to the valuations;
- Obtaining an understanding of the work of the management's expert, for example by assessing the appropriateness of the valuation technique(s) used and the key market variables and assumptions used in the valuation technique(s);
- Evaluating the appropriateness of that expert's work as audit evidence. At this point, the focus is on the appropriateness of the expert's work at the level of the individual financial instrument. For a sample of the relevant instruments, it may

be appropriate to develop an estimate independently (see paragraphs 136 to 137 on developing a point estimate or range), using different data and assumptions, then compare that estimate to that of the management's expert; and

- Other procedures may include:
  - o Modeling different assumptions to derive assumptions in another model, then considering the reasonableness of those derived assumptions.
  - o Comparing management's point estimates with the auditor's point estimates to determine if management's estimates are consistently higher or lower.

135   Assumptions may be made or identified by a management's expert to assist management in valuing its financial instruments. Such assumptions, when used by management, become management's assumptions that the auditor needs to consider in the same manner as management's other assumptions.

Developing a Point Estimate or Range

136   An auditor may develop a valuation technique and adjust the inputs and assumptions used in the valuation technique to develop a range for use in evaluating the reasonableness of management's valuation. Paragraphs 106 to 135 of this IAPN may assist the auditor in developing a point estimate or range. In accordance with ISA 540,[35] if the auditor uses assumptions, or methodologies that differ from management's, the auditor shall obtain an understanding of management's assumptions or methodologies sufficient to establish that the auditor's range takes into account relevant variables and to evaluate any significant differences from management's valuation. The auditor may find it useful to use the work of an auditor's expert to evaluate the reasonableness of management's valuation.

137   In some cases, the auditor may conclude that sufficient evidence cannot be obtained from the auditor's attempts to obtain an understanding of management's assumptions or methodology, for example when a third-party pricing source uses internally developed models and software and does not allow access to relevant information. In such cases, the auditor may not be able to obtain sufficient appropriate audit evidence about the valuation if the auditor is unable to perform other procedures to respond to the risks of material misstatement, such as developing a point estimate or a range to evaluate management's point estimate.[36] ISA 705[37] describes the implications of the auditor's inability to obtain sufficient appropriate audit evidence.

Presentation and Disclosure of Financial Instruments

138   Management's responsibilities include the preparation of the financial statements in accordance with the applicable financial reporting framework.[38] Financial reporting frameworks often require disclosures in the financial statements to enable users of the financial statements to make meaningful assessments of the effects of the entity's financial instrument activities, including the risks and uncertainties associated with these financial instruments. The importance of disclosures regarding the basis of

---

[35] *ISA 540, paragraph 13(c)*

[36] *ISA 540, paragraph 13(d)*

[37] *ISA 705, Modifications to the Opinion in the Independent Auditor's Report*

[38] *See paragraphs 4 and A2 of ISA 200.*

measurement increases as the measurement uncertainty of the financial instruments increases and is also affected by the level of the fair value hierarchy.

In representing that the financial statements are in accordance with the applicable **139** financial reporting framework, management implicitly or explicitly makes assertions regarding the presentation and disclosure of the various elements of financial statements and related disclosures. Assertions about presentation and disclosure encompass:

(a) Occurrence and rights and obligations—disclosed events, transactions, and other matters have occurred and pertain to the entity.
(b) Completeness—all disclosures that should have been included in the financial statements have been included.
(c) Classification and understandability—financial information is appropriately presented and described, and disclosures are clearly expressed.
(d) Accuracy and valuation—financial and other information are disclosed fairly and at appropriate amounts.

The auditor's procedures around auditing disclosures are designed in consideration of these assertions.

Procedures Relating to the Presentation and Disclosure of Financial Instruments

In relation to the presentation and disclosures of financial instruments, areas of **140** particular importance include:

* Financial reporting frameworks generally require additional disclosures regarding estimates, and related risks and uncertainties, to supplement and explain assets, liabilities, income, and expenses. The auditor's focus may need to be on the disclosures relating to risks and sensitivity analysis. Information obtained during the auditor's risk assessment procedures and testing of control activities may provide evidence in order for the auditor to conclude about whether the disclosures in the financial statements are in accordance with the requirements of the applicable financial reporting framework, for example about:
  o The entity's objectives and strategies for using financial instruments, including the entity's stated accounting policies;
  o The entity's control framework for managing its risks associated with financial instruments; and
  o The risks and uncertainties associated with the financial instruments.
* Information may come from systems outside traditional financial reporting systems, such as risk systems. Examples of procedures that the auditor may choose to perform in responding to assessed risks relative to disclosures include testing:
  o The process used to derive the disclosed information; and
  o The operating effectiveness of the controls over the data used in the preparation of disclosures.
* In relation to financial instruments having significant risk,[39] even where the disclosures are in accordance with the applicable financial reporting framework, the auditor may conclude that the disclosure of estimation uncertainty is inadequate in light of the circumstances and facts involved and, accordingly, the financial statements may not achieve fair presentation. ISA 705 provides

---

[39] *ISA 540, paragraph 20, requires the auditor to perform further procedures on disclosures relating to accounting estimates that give rise to significant risks to evaluate the adequacy of the disclosure of their estimation uncertainty in the financial statements in the context of the applicable financial reporting framework.*

guidance on the implications for the auditor's opinion when the auditor believes that management's disclosures in the financial statements are inadequate or misleading.

- Auditors may also consider whether the disclosures are complete and understandable, for example, all relevant information may be included in the financial statements (or accompanying reports) but it may be insufficiently drawn together to enable users of the financial statements to obtain an understanding of the position or there may not be enough qualitative disclosure to give context to the amounts recorded in the financial statements. For example, even when an entity has included sensitivity analysis disclosures, the disclosure may not fully describe the risks and uncertainties that may arise because of changes in valuation, possible effects on debt covenants, collateral requirements, and the entity's liquidity. ISA 260[40] contains requirements and guidance about communicating with those charged with governance, including the auditor's views about significant qualitative aspects of the entity's accounting practices, including accounting policies, accounting estimates and financial statement disclosures.

141   Consideration of the appropriateness of presentation, for example on short-term and long-term classification, in substantive testing of financial instruments is relevant to the auditor's evaluation of the presentation and disclosure.

Other Relevant Audit Considerations

Written Representations

142   ISA 540 requires the auditor to obtain written representations from management and, where appropriate, those charged with governance whether they believe significant assumptions used in making accounting estimates are reasonable.[41] ISA 580[42] requires that if, in addition to such required representations, the auditor determines that it is necessary to obtain one or more written representations to support other audit evidence relevant to the financial statements or one or more specific assertions in the financial statements, the auditor shall request such other written representations. Depending on the volume and degree of complexity of financial instrument activities, written representations to support other evidence obtained about financial instruments may also include:

- Management's objectives with respect to financial instruments, for example, whether they are used for hedging, asset/liability management or investment purposes;
- Representations about the appropriateness of presentation of the financial statements, for example the recording of financial instrument transactions as sales or financing transactions;
- Representations about the financial statement disclosures concerning financial instruments, for example that:
  - o   The records reflect all financial instrument transactions; and
  - o   All embedded derivative instruments have been identified;

---

[40] *ISA 260, Communication with Those Charged with Governance*

[41] *ISA 540, paragraph 22.* Paragraph 4 of *ISA 580, Written Representations,* states that written representations from management do not provide sufficient appropriate audit evidence on their own about any of the matters with which they deal. If the auditor is otherwise unable to obtain sufficient appropriate audit evidence, this may constitute a limitation on the scope of the audit that may have implications for the auditor's report (see ISA 705, *Modification to the Opinion in the Independent Auditor's Report*).

[42] *ISA 580, paragraph 13*

- Whether all transactions have been conducted at arm's length and at market value;
- The terms of transactions;
- The appropriateness of the valuations of financial instruments;
- Whether there are any side agreements associated with any financial instruments;
- Whether the entity has entered into any written options;
- Management's intent and ability to carry out certain actions;[43] and
- Whether subsequent events require adjustment to the valuations and disclosures included in the financial statements.

Communication with Those Charged with Governance and Others

Because of the uncertainties associated with the valuation of financial instruments, **143** the potential effects on the financial statements of any significant risks are likely to be of governance interest. The auditor may communicate the nature and consequences of significant assumptions used in fair value measurements, the degree of subjectivity involved in the development of the assumptions, and the relative materiality of the items being measured at fair value to the financial statements as a whole. In addition, the need for appropriate controls over commitments to enter into financial instrument contracts and over the subsequent measurement processes are matters that may give rise to the need for communication with those charged with governance.

ISA 260 deals with the auditor's responsibility to communicate with those charged **144** with governance in an audit of financial statements. With respect to financial instruments, matters to be communicated to those charged with governance may include:

- A lack of management understanding of the nature or extent of the financial instrument activities or the risks associated with such activities;
- Significant deficiencies in the design or operation of the systems of internal control or risk management relating to the entity's financial instrument activities that the auditor has identified during the audit;[44]
- Significant difficulties encountered when obtaining sufficient appropriate audit evidence relating to valuations performed by management or a management's expert, for example, where management is unable to obtain an understanding of the valuation methodology, assumptions and data used by the management's experts, and such information is not made available to the auditor by management' s expert;
- Significant differences in judgments between the auditor and management or a management's expert regarding valuations;
- The potential effects on the entity's financial statements of material risks and exposures required to be disclosed in the financial statements, including the measurement uncertainty associated with financial instruments;
- The auditor's views about the appropriateness of the selection of accounting policies and presentation of financial instrument transactions in the financial statements;

---

[43] *Paragraph A80 of ISA 540 provides examples of procedures that may be appropriate in the circumstances.*

[44] *ISA 265, Communicating Deficiencies in Internal Control to Those Charged with Governance and Management,* establishes requirements and provides guidance on communicating deficiencies in internal control to management, and communicating significant deficiencies in internal control to those charged with governance. It explains that deficiencies in internal control may be identified during the auditor's risk assessment procedures in accordance with ISA 315 or at any other stage of the audit.

- The auditor's views about the qualitative aspects of the entity's accounting practices and financial reporting for financial instruments; or
- A lack of comprehensive and clearly stated policies for the purchase, sale and holding of financial instruments, including operational controls, procedures for designating financial instruments as hedges, and monitoring exposures.

The appropriate timing for communications will vary with the circumstances of the engagement; however, it may be appropriate to communicate significant difficulties encountered during the audit as soon as practicable if those charged with governance are able to assist the auditor to overcome the difficulty, or if it is likely to lead to a modified opinion.

Communications with Regulators and Others

145   In some cases, auditors may be required,[45] or may consider it appropriate, to communicate directly with regulators or prudential supervisors, in addition to those charged with governance, regarding matters relating to financial instruments. Such communication may be useful throughout the audit. For example, in some jurisdictions, banking regulators seek to cooperate with auditors to share information about the operation and application of controls over financial instrument activities, challenges in valuing financial instruments in inactive markets, and compliance with regulations. This coordination may be helpful to the auditor in identifying risks of material misstatement.

---

[45] *For example, ISA 250, Consideration of Laws and Regulations in an Audit of Financial Statements*, requires auditors to determine whether there is a responsibility to report identified or suspected non-compliance with laws and regulations to parties outside the entity. In addition, requirements concerning the auditor's communication to banking supervisors and others may be established in many countries either by law, by supervisory requirement or by formal agreement or protocol.

Appendix

(Ref: Para. A14)

Examples of Controls Relating to Financial Instruments

1. The following provides background information and examples of controls that may exist in an entity that deals in a high volume of financial instrument transactions, whether for trading or investing purposes. The examples are not meant to be exhaustive and entities may establish different control environments and processes depending on their size, the industry in which they operate, and the extent of their financial instrument transactions. Further information on the use of trade confirmations and clearing houses is contained in paragraphs 25–26.
2. As in any control system, it is sometimes necessary to duplicate controls at different control levels (for example, preventative, detective and monitoring) to avoid the risk of material misstatement.

The Entity's Control Environment

Commitment to Competent Use of Financial Instruments

3. The degree of complexity of some financial instrument activities may mean that only a few individuals within the entity fully understand those activities or have the expertise necessary to value the instruments on an ongoing basis. Use of financial instruments without relevant expertise within the entity increases the risk of material misstatement.

Participation by Those Charged with Governance

4. Those charged with governance oversee and concur with management's establishment of the entity's overall risk appetite and provide oversight over the entity's financial instrument activities. An entity's policies for the purchase, sale and holding of financial instruments are aligned with its attitude toward risk and the expertise of those involved in financial instrument activities. In addition, an entity may establish governance structures and control processes aimed at:
    (a) Communicating investment decisions and assessments of all material measurement uncertainty to those charged with governance; and
    (b) Evaluating the entity's overall risk appetite when engaging in financial instrument transactions.

Organizational Structure

5. Financial instrument activities may be run on either a centralized or a decentralized basis. Such activities and related decision making depend heavily on the flow of accurate, reliable, and timely management information. The difficulty of collecting and aggregating such information increases with the number of locations and businesses in which an entity is involved. The risks of material misstatement associated with financial instrument activities may increase with greater decentralization of control activities. This may especially be true where an entity is based in different locations, some perhaps in other countries.

Assignment of Authority and Responsibility

Investment and Valuation Policies

6. Providing direction, through clearly stated policies approved by those charged with governance for the purchase, sale, and holding of financial instruments enables management to establish an effective approach to taking and managing business risks. These policies are most clear when they state the entity's objectives with regard to its risk management activities, and the investment and hedging alternatives available to meet these objectives, and reflect the:
    (a) Level of management's expertise;
    (b) Sophistication of the entity's internal control and monitoring systems;
    (c) Entity's asset/liability structure;
    (d) Entity's capacity to maintain liquidity and absorb losses of capital;
    (e) Types of financial instruments that management believes will meet its objectives; and
    (f) Uses of financial instruments that management believes will meet its objectives, for example, whether derivatives may be used for speculative purposes or only for hedging purposes.
7. Management may design policies aligned with its valuation capabilities and may establish controls to ensure that these policies are adhered to by those employees responsible for the entity's valuation. These may include:
    (a) Processes for the design and validation of methodologies used to produce valuations, including how measurement uncertainty is addressed; and
    (b) Policies regarding maximizing the use of observable inputs and the types of information to be gathered to support valuations of financial instruments.
8. In smaller entities, dealing in financial instruments may be rare and management's knowledge and experience limited. Nevertheless, establishing policies over financial instruments helps an entity to determine its risk appetite and consider whether investing in particular financial instruments achieves a stated objective.

Human Resource Policies and Practices

9. Entities may establish policies requiring key employees, both front office and back office, to take mandatory time off from their duties. This type of control is used as a means of preventing and detecting fraud, in particular if those engaged in trading activities are creating false trades or inaccurately recording transactions.

Use of Service Organizations

10. Entities may also use service organizations (for example asset managers) to initiate the purchase or sale of financial instruments, to maintain records of transactions for the entity or to value financial instruments. Some entities may be dependent on these service organizations to provide the basis of reporting for the financial instruments held. However, if management does not have an understanding about the controls in place at a service organization, the auditor may not be able to obtain sufficient appropriate audit evidence to rely on controls at that service organization. See ISA 402,[46] which establishes requirements for the auditor to obtain sufficient appropriate audit evidence when an entity uses the services of one or more service organizations.

---

[46] *ISA 402, Audit Considerations Relating to an Entity Using a Service Organization*

11. The use of service organizations may strengthen or weaken the control environment for financial instruments. For example, a service organization's personnel may have more experience with financial instruments than the entity's management or may have more robust internal control over financial reporting. The use of the service organization also may allow for greater segregation of duties. On the other hand, the service organization may have a poor control environment.

The Entity's Risk Assessment Process

12. An entity's risk assessment process exists to establish how management identifies business risks that derive from its use of financial instruments, including how management estimates the significance of the risks, assesses the likelihood of their occurrence and decides upon actions to manage them.

13. The entity's risk assessment process forms the basis for how management determines the risks to be managed. Risk assessment processes exist with the objective of ensuring that management:
    (a) Understands the risks inherent in a financial instrument before management enters into it, including the objective of entering into the transaction and its structure (for example, the economics and business purpose of the entity's financial instrument activities);
    (b) Performs adequate due diligence commensurate with the risks associated with particular financial instruments;
    (c) Monitors the entity's outstanding positions to understand how market conditions are affecting the entity's exposures;
    (d) Has procedures in place to reduce or change risk exposure if necessary and for managing reputational risk; and
    (e) Subjects these processes to rigorous supervision and review.

14. The structure implemented to monitor and manage exposure to risks should:
    (a) Be appropriate and consistent with the entity's attitude toward risk as determined by those charged with governance;
    (b) Specify the approval levels for the authorization of different types of financial instruments and transactions that may be entered into and for what purposes. The permitted instruments and approval levels should reflect the expertise of those involved in financial instrument activities, demonstrating management's commitment to competence;
    (c) Set appropriate limits for the maximum allowable exposure to each type of risk (including approved counterparties). Levels of allowable exposure may vary depending on the type of risk, or counterparty;
    (d) Provide for the objective and timely monitoring of the financial risks and control activities;
    (e) Provide for the objective and timely reporting of exposures, risks and the results of financial instrument activities in managing risk; and
    (f) Evaluate management's track record for assessing the risks of particular financial instruments.

15. The types and levels of risks an entity faces are directly related to the types of financial instruments with which it deals, including the complexity of these instruments and the volume of financial instruments transacted.

Risk Management Function

16. Some entities, for example large financial institutions with a high volume of financial instrument transactions, may be required by law or regulation, or may choose, to establish a formal risk management function. This function is separated from those responsible for undertaking and managing financial

instrument transactions. The function is responsible for reporting on and monitoring financial instrument activities, and may include a formal risk committee established by those charged with governance. Examples of key responsibilities in this area may include:

    (a) Implementing the risk management policy set by those charged with governance (including analyses of the risks to which an entity may be exposed);

    (b) Designing risk limit structures and ensuring these risk limits are implemented in practice;

    (c) Developing stress scenarios and subjecting open position portfolios to sensitivity analysis, including reviews of unusual movements in positions; and

    (d) Reviewing and analyzing new financial instrument products.

17. Financial instruments may have the associated risk that a loss might exceed the amount, if any, of the value of the financial instrument recognized on the balance sheet. For example, a sudden fall in the market price of a commodity may force an entity to realize losses to close a forward position in that commodity due to collateral, or margin, requirements. In some cases, the potential losses may be enough to cast significant doubt on the entity's ability to continue as a going concern. The entity may perform sensitivity analyses or value-at-risk analyses to assess the future hypothetical effects on financial instruments subject to market risks. However, value-at-risk analysis does not fully reflect the extent of the risks that may affect the entity; sensitivity and scenario analyses also may be subject to limitations.

18. The volume and sophistication of financial instrument activity and relevant regulatory requirements will influence the entity's consideration whether to establish a formal risk management function and how the function may be structured. In entities that have not established a separate risk management function, for example entities with relatively few financial instruments or financial instruments that are less complex, reporting on and monitoring financial instrument activities may be a component of the accounting or finance function's responsibility or management's overall responsibility, and may include a formal risk committee established by those charged with governance

The Entity's Information Systems

19. The key objective of an entity's information system is that it is capable of capturing and recording all the transactions accurately, settling them, valuing them, and producing information to enable the financial instruments to be risk managed and for controls to be monitored. Difficulties can arise in entities that engage in a high volume of financial instruments, in particular if there is a multiplicity of systems that are poorly integrated and have manual interfaces without adequate controls.

20. Certain financial instruments may require a large number of accounting entries. As the sophistication or level of the financial instrument activities increases, it is necessary for the sophistication of the information system to also increase. Specific issues which can arise with respect to financial instruments include:

    (a) Information systems, in particular for smaller entities, not having the capability or not being appropriately configured to process financial instrument transactions, especially when the entity does not have any prior experience in dealing with financial instruments. This may result in an increased number of manual transactions which may further increase the risk of error;

    (b) The potential diversity of systems required to process more complex transactions, and the need for regular reconciliations between them, in particular when the systems are not interfaced or may be subject to manual intervention;

(c) The potential that more complex transactions, if they are only traded by a small number of individuals, may be valued or risk managed on spreadsheets rather than on main processing systems, and for the physical and logical password security around those spreadsheets to be more easily compromised;

(d) A lack of review of systems exception logs, external confirmations and broker quotes, where available, to validate the entries generated by the systems;

(e) Difficulties in controlling and evaluating the key inputs to systems for valuation of financial instruments, particularly where those systems are maintained by the group of traders known as the front office or a third-party service provider and/or the transactions in question are non-routine or thinly traded;

(f) Failure to evaluate the design and calibration of complex models used to process these transactions initially and on a periodic basis;

(g) The potential that management has not set up a library of models, with controls around access, change and maintenance of individual models, in order to maintain a strong audit trail of the accredited versions of models and in order to prevent unauthorized access or amendments to those models;

(h) The disproportionate investment that may be required in risk management and control systems, where an entity only undertakes a limited number of financial instrument transactions, and the potential for misunderstanding of the output by management if they are not used to these types of transactions;

(i) The potential requirement for third-party systems provision, for example from a service organization, to record, process, account for or risk manage appropriately financial instrument transactions, and the need to reconcile appropriately and challenge the output from those providers; and

(j) Additional security and control considerations relevant to the use of an electronic network when an entity uses electronic commerce for financial instrument transactions.

21. Information systems relevant to financial reporting serve as an important source of information for the quantitative disclosures in the financial statements. However, entities may also develop and maintain non-financial systems used for internal reporting and to generate information included in qualitative disclosures, for example regarding risks and uncertainties or sensitivity analyses.

The Entity's Control Activities

22. Control activities over financial instrument transactions are designed to prevent or detect problems that hinder an entity from achieving its objectives. These objectives may be either operational, financial reporting, or compliance in nature. Control activities over financial instruments are designed relative to the complexity and volume of transactions of financial instruments and will generally include an appropriate authorization process, adequate segregation of duties, and other policies and procedures designed to ensure that the entity's control objectives are met. Process flow charts may assist in identifying an entity's controls and lack of controls. This IAPN focuses on control activities related to completeness, accuracy and existence, valuation, and presentation and disclosure.

Authorization

23. Authorization can affect the financial statement assertions both directly and indirectly. For example, even if a transaction is executed outside an entity's policies, it nonetheless may be recorded and accounted for accurately. However, unauthorized transactions could significantly increase risk to the entity, thereby significantly increasing the risk of material misstatement since they would be undertaken outside the system of internal control. To mitigate this risk, an entity will often establish a clear policy as to what transactions can be traded by whom and adherence to this policy will then be monitored by an entity's back office. Monitoring trading activities of individuals, for example by reviewing unusually high volumes or significant gains or losses incurred, will assist management in ensuring compliance with the entity's policies, including the authorization of new types of transactions, and evaluating whether fraud has occurred.

24. The function of an entity's deal initiation records is to identify clearly the nature and purpose of individual transactions and the rights and obligations arising under each financial instrument contract, including the enforceability of the contracts. In addition to the basic financial information, such as a notional amount, complete and accurate records at a minimum typically include:
    (a) The identity of the dealer;
    (b) The identity of the person recording the transaction (if not the dealer), when the transaction was initiated (including the date and time of the transaction), and how it was recorded in the entity's information systems; and
    (c) The nature and purpose of the transaction, including whether or not it is intended to hedge an underlying commercial exposure.

Segregation of Duties

25. Segregation of duties and the assignment of personnel is an important control activity, particularly when exposed to financial instruments. Financial instrument activities may be segregated into a number of functions, including:
    (a) Executing the transaction (dealing). In entities with a high volume of financial instrument transactions, this may be done by the front office;
    (b) Initiating cash payments and accepting cash receipts (settlements);
    (c) Sending out trade confirmations and reconciling the differences between the entity's records and replies from counterparties, if any;
    (d) Recording of all transactions correctly in the accounting records;
    (e) Monitoring risk limits. In entities with a high volume of financial instrument transactions, this may be performed by the risk management function; and
    (f) Monitoring positions and valuing financial instruments.

26. Many organizations choose to segregate the duties of those investing in financial instruments, those valuing financial instruments, those settling financial instruments and those accounting/recording financial instruments.

27. Where an entity is too small to achieve proper segregation of duties, the role of management and those charged with governance in monitoring financial instrument activities is of particular importance.

28. A feature of some entities' internal control is an independent price verification (IPV) function. This department is responsible for separately verifying the price of some financial instruments, and may use alternative data sources, methodologies and assumptions. The IPV provides an objective look at the pricing that has been developed in another part of the entity.

29. Ordinarily, the middle or back office is responsible for establishing policies on valuation and ensuring adherence to the policy. Entities with a greater use of financial instruments may perform daily valuations of their financial instrument portfolio and examine the contribution to profit or loss of individual financial instrument valuations as a test of the reasonableness of valuations.

Completeness, Accuracy, and Existence

30. Regular reconciliation of the entity's records to external banks' and custodians' records enables the entity to ensure transactions are properly recorded. Appropriate segregation of duties between those transacting the trades and those reconciling them is important, as is a rigorous process for reviewing reconciliations and clearing reconciling items.
31. Controls may also be established that require traders to identify whether a complex financial instrument may have unique features, for example embedded derivatives. In such circumstances, there may be a separate function that evaluates complex financial instrument transactions at their initiation (which may be known as a product control group), working in connection with an accounting policy group to ensure the transaction is accurately recorded. While smaller entities may not have product control groups, an entity may have a process in place relating to the review of complex financial instrument contracts at the point of origination in order to ensure they are accounted for appropriately in accordance with the applicable financial reporting framework.

Monitoring of Controls

32. The entity's ongoing monitoring activities are designed to detect and correct any deficiencies in the effectiveness of controls over transactions for financial instruments and their valuation. It is important that there is adequate supervision and review of financial instrument activity within the entity. This includes:
    (a) All controls being subject to review, for example, the monitoring of operational statistics such as the number of reconciling items or the difference between internal pricing and external pricing sources;
    (b) The need for robust information technology (IT) controls and monitoring and validating their application; and
    (c) The need to ensure that information resulting from different processes and systems is adequately reconciled. For example, there is little benefit in a valuation process if the output from it is not reconciled properly into the general ledger.
33. In larger entities, sophisticated computer information systems generally keep track of financial instrument activities, and are designed to ensure that settlements occur when due. More complex computer systems may generate automatic postings to clearing accounts to monitor cash movements, and controls over processing are put in place with the objective of ensuring that financial instrument activities are correctly reflected in the entity's records. Computer systems may be designed to produce exception reports to alert management to situations where financial instruments have not been used within authorized limits or where transactions undertaken were not within the limits established for the chosen counterparties. However, even a sophisticated computer system may not ensure the completeness of the recording of financial instrument transactions. Accordingly, management frequently puts additional procedures in place to increase the likelihood that all transactions will be recorded.

Part Four

International Standards on Review Engagements (ISREs)

International Standard on
Review Engagements 2400 (Revised)
Engagements to review historical financial statements

(Effective for reviews of financial statements for periods ending on or after December 31, 2013)

Contents

International Standard on Review Engagements (ISRE) 2400 (Revised), *Engagements to Review Historical Financial Statements*, should be read in conjunction with the *Preface to the International Standards on Quality Control, Auditing, Review, Other Assurance, and Related Services Pronouncements.*

Introduction

Scope of this ISRE

This International Standard on Review Engagements (ISRE) deals with: (Ref: Para.   **1**
A1)

(a) The practitioner's responsibilities when engaged to perform a review of historical financial statements, when the practitioner is not the auditor of the entity's financial statements; and
(b) The form and content of the practitioner's report on the financial statements.

This ISRE does not address a review of an entity's financial statements or interim   **2**
financial information performed by a practitioner who is the independent auditor of
the entity's financial statements (Ref: Para. A2)

This ISRE is to be applied, adapted as necessary, to reviews of other historical   **3**
financial information. Limited assurance engagements other than reviews of historical financial information are performed under ISAE 3000.[1]

Relationship with ISQC 1[2]

Quality control systems, policies and procedures are the responsibility of the firm.   **4**
ISQC 1 applies to firms of professional accountants in respect of a firm's engagements to review financial statements.[3] The provisions of this ISRE regarding quality
control at the level of individual review engagements are premised on the basis that
the firm is subject to ISQC 1 or requirements that are at least as demanding. (Ref:
Para. A3–A5)

The Engagement to Review Historical Financial Statements

The review of historical financial statements is a limited assurance engagement, as   **5**
described in the *International Framework for Assurance Engagements* (the Assurance
Framework).[4] (Ref: Para. A6–A7)

In a review of financial statements, the practitioner expresses a conclusion that is   **6**
designed to enhance the degree of confidence of intended users regarding the preparation of an entity's financial statements in accordance with an applicable financial
reporting framework. The practitioner's conclusion is based on the practitioner
obtaining limited assurance. The practitioner's report includes a description of the
nature of a review engagement as context for the readers of the report to be able to
understand the conclusion.

The practitioner performs primarily inquiry and analytical procedures to obtain   **7**
sufficient appropriate evidence as the basis for a conclusion on the financial statements as a whole, expressed in accordance with the requirements of this ISRE.

[1] *International Standard on Assurance Engagements (ISAE) 3000*, Assurance Engagements Other than Audits
or Reviews of Historical Financial Information.

[2] *International Standard on Quality Control (ISQC) 1*, Quality Control for Firms that Perform Audits and
Reviews of Financial Statements, and Other Assurance and Related Services Engagements.

[3] *ISQC 1, paragraph 4.*

[4] *Assurance Framework, paragraphs 7 and 11*

8   If the practitioner becomes aware of a matter that causes the practitioner to believe the financial statements may be materially misstated, the practitioner designs and performs additional procedures, as the practitioner considers necessary in the circumstances, to be able to conclude on the financial statements in accordance with this ISRE.

Authority of this ISRE

9   This ISRE contains the objectives of the practitioner in following the ISRE which provide the context in which the requirements of this ISRE are set, and are intended to assist the practitioner in understanding what needs to be accomplished in a review engagement.

10   The ISRE contains requirements, expressed using "shall," that are designed to enable the practitioner to meet the stated objectives.

11   In addition, this ISRE contains introductory material, definitions, and application and other explanatory material, that provide context relevant to a proper understanding of the ISRE.

12   The application and other explanatory material provides further explanation of the requirements and guidance for carrying them out. While such guidance does not itself impose a requirement, it is relevant to the proper application of the requirements. The application and other explanatory material may also provide background information on matters addressed in this ISRE that assists in the application of the requirements.

Effective Date

13   This ISRE is effective for reviews of financial statements for periods ending on or after December 31, 2013.

Objectives

14   The practitioner's objectives in a review of financial statements under this ISRE are to:

   (a) Obtain limited assurance, primarily by performing inquiry and analytical procedures, about whether the financial statements as a whole are free from material misstatement, thereby enabling the practitioner to express a conclusion on whether anything has come to the practitioner's attention that causes the practitioner to believe the financial statements are not prepared, in all material respects, in accordance with an applicable financial reporting framework; and

   (b) Report on the financial statements as a whole and communicate, as required by this ISRE.

15   In all cases when limited assurance cannot be obtained and a qualified conclusion in the practitioner's report is insufficient in the circumstances, this ISRE requires that the practitioner either disclaim a conclusion in the report issued for the engagement or, where appropriate, withdraw from the engagement if withdrawal is possible under applicable law or regulation. (Ref. Para. A8–A10, A115–A116)

Definitions

The Handbook's Glossary of Terms[5] (the Glossary) includes the terms defined in this 16 ISRE as well as descriptions of other terms used in this ISRE, to assist in consistent application and interpretation. For example, the terms "management" and "those charged with governance" used throughout this ISRE are as defined in the Glossary. (Ref: Para. A11–A12)

For purposes of this ISRE, the following terms have the meanings attributed below: 17

(a) *Analytical procedures*—Evaluations of financial information through analysis of plausible relationships among both financial and non-financial data. Analytical procedures also encompass such investigation as is necessary of identified fluctuations or relationships that are inconsistent with other relevant information or that differ from expected values by a significant amount.

(b) *Engagement risk*—The risk that the practitioner expresses an inappropriate conclusion when the financial statements are materially misstated.

(c) *General purpose financial statements*—Financial statements prepared in accordance with a general purpose framework.

(d) *General purpose framework*—A financial reporting framework designed to meet the common financial needs of a wide range of users. The financial reporting framework may be a fair presentation framework or a compliance framework.

(e) *Inquiry*—Inquiry consists of seeking information of knowledgeable persons from within or outside the entity.

(f) *Limited assurance*—The level of assurance obtained where engagement risk is reduced to a level that is acceptable in the circumstances of the engagement, but where that risk is greater than for a reasonable assurance engagement, as the basis for expressing a conclusion in accordance with this ISRE. The combination of the nature, timing and extent of evidence gathering procedures is at least sufficient for the practitioner to obtain a meaningful level of assurance. To be meaningful, the level of assurance obtained by the practitioner is likely to enhance the intended users' confidence about the financial statements. (Ref: Para. A13)

(g) *Practitioner*—A professional accountant in public practice. The term includes the engagement partner or other members of the engagement team, or, as applicable, the firm. Where this ISRE expressly intends that a requirement or responsibility be fulfilled by the engagement partner, the term "engagement partner" rather than "practitioner" is used. "Engagement partner" and "firm" are to be read as referring to their public sector equivalents where relevant.

(h) *Professional judgment*—The application of relevant training, knowledge and experience, within the context provided by assurance, accounting and ethical standards, in making informed decisions about the courses of action that are appropriate in the circumstances of the review engagement.

(i) *Relevant ethical requirements*—Ethical requirements the engagement team is subject to when undertaking review engagements. These requirements ordinarily comprise Parts A and B of the International Ethics Standards Board for Accountants' *Code of Ethics for Professional Accountants* (IESBA Code), together with national requirements that are more restrictive.

(j) *Special purpose financial statements*—Financial statements prepared in accordance with a special purpose framework.

---

[5] *The Glossary of Terms relating to International Standards issued by the IAASB in the* Handbook of International Quality Control, Auditing, Review, Other Assurance and Related Services Pronouncements *(the* Handbook*), published by IFAC.*

(k) *Special purpose framework*—A financial reporting framework designed to meet the financial information needs of specific users. The financial reporting framework may be a fair presentation framework or a compliance framework.

Requirements

Conduct of a Review Engagement in Accordance with this ISRE

18   The practitioner shall have an understanding of the entire text of this ISRE, including its application and other explanatory material, to understand its objectives and to apply its requirements properly. (Ref: Para. A14)

Complying with Relevant Requirements

19   The practitioner shall comply with each requirement of this ISRE, unless a requirement is not relevant to the review engagement. A requirement is relevant to the review engagement when the circumstances addressed by the requirement exist.

20   The practitioner shall not represent compliance with this ISRE in the practitioner's report unless the practitioner has complied with all the requirements of this ISRE relevant to the review engagement.

Ethical Requirements

21   The practitioner shall comply with relevant ethical requirements, including those pertaining to independence. (Ref: Para. A15–A16)

Professional Skepticism and Professional Judgment

22   The practitioner shall plan and perform the engagement with professional skepticism recognizing that circumstances may exist that cause the financial statements to be materially misstated. (Ref: Para. A17–A20)

23   The practitioner shall exercise professional judgment in conducting a review engagement. (Ref: Para. A21–A25)

Engagement Level Quality Control

24   The engagement partner shall possess competence in assurance skills and techniques, and competence in financial reporting, appropriate to the engagement circumstances. (Ref: Para. A26)

25   The engagement partner shall take responsibility for: (Ref: Para. A27–A30)

(a) The overall quality of each review engagement to which that partner is assigned;

(b) The direction, supervision, planning and performance of the review engagement in compliance with professional standards and applicable legal and regulatory requirements; (Ref: Para. A31)

(c) The practitioner's report being appropriate in the circumstances; and

(d) The engagement being performed in accordance with the firm's quality control policies, including the following:

(i) Being satisfied that appropriate procedures regarding the acceptance and continuance of client relationships and engagements have been followed, and that conclusions reached are appropriate, including considering whether there is information that would lead the engagement partner to conclude that management lacks integrity; (Ref: Para. A32–A33)

(ii) Being satisfied that the engagement team collectively has the appropriate competence and capabilities, including assurance skills and techniques and expertise in financial reporting, to:

   a. Perform the review engagement in accordance with professional standards and applicable legal and regulatory requirements; and

   b. Enable a report that is appropriate in the circumstances to be issued; and

(iii) Taking responsibility for appropriate engagement documentation being maintained.

Relevant Considerations after Engagement Acceptance

If the engagement partner obtains information that would have caused the firm to decline the engagement had that information been available earlier, the engagement partner shall communicate that information promptly to the firm, so that the firm and the engagement partner can take the necessary action.   **26**

Compliance with Relevant Ethical Requirements

Throughout the engagement, the engagement partner shall remain alert, through observation and making inquiries as necessary, for evidence of non-compliance with relevant ethical requirements by members of the engagement team. If matters come to the engagement partner's attention through the firm's system of quality control or otherwise that indicate that members of the engagement team have not complied with relevant ethical requirements, the engagement partner, in consultation with others in the firm, shall determine the appropriate action.   **27**

Monitoring

An effective system of quality control for a firm includes a monitoring process designed to provide the firm with reasonable assurance that the firm's policies and procedures relating to the system of quality control are relevant, adequate and operate effectively. The engagement partner shall consider the results of the firm's monitoring process as evidenced in the latest information circulated by the firm and, if applicable, other network firms and whether deficiencies noted in that information may affect the review engagement.   **28**

Acceptance and Continuance of Client Relationships and Review Engagements

Factors Affecting Acceptance and Continuance of Client Relationships and Review Engagements

Unless required by law or regulation, the practitioner shall not accept a review engagement if: (Ref: Para. A34–A35)   **29**

(a) The practitioner is not satisfied:

   (i) That there is a rational purpose for the engagement; or (Ref: Para. A36)

   (ii) That a review engagement would be appropriate in the circumstances; (Ref: Para. A37)

(b) The practitioner has reason to believe that relevant ethical requirements, including independence, will not be satisfied;

(c) The practitioner's preliminary understanding of the engagement circumstances indicates that information needed to perform the review engagement is likely to be unavailable or unreliable; (Ref: Para. A38)

(d) The practitioner has cause to doubt management's integrity such that it is likely to affect proper performance of the review; or (Ref: Para. A37(b))

(e) Management or those charged with governance impose a limitation on the scope of the practitioner's work in the terms of a proposed review engagement such that the practitioner believes the limitation will result in the practitioner disclaiming a conclusion on the financial statements.

Preconditions for Accepting a Review Engagement

30   Prior to accepting a review engagement, the practitioner shall: (Ref: Para. A39)

(a) Determine whether the financial reporting framework applied in the preparation of the financial statements is acceptable including, in the case of special purpose financial statements, obtaining an understanding of the purpose for which the financial statements are prepared and of the intended users; and (Ref: Para. A40–A46)

(b) Obtain the agreement of management that it acknowledges and understands its responsibilities: (Ref: Para. A47–A50)

(i)   For preparation of the financial statements in accordance with the applicable financial reporting framework, including, where relevant, their fair presentation;

(ii) For such internal control as management determines is necessary to enable the preparation of financial statements that are free from material misstatement, whether due to fraud or error; and

(iii) To provide the practitioner with:

a.   Access to all information of which management is aware that is relevant to the preparation of the financial statements, such as records, documentation and other matters;

b.   Additional information that the practitioner may request from management for the purpose of the review; and

c.   Unrestricted access to persons within the entity from whom the practitioner determines it necessary to obtain evidence.

31   If the practitioner is not satisfied as to any of the matters set out above as preconditions for accepting a review engagement, the practitioner shall discuss the matter with management or those charged with governance. If changes cannot be made to satisfy the practitioner as to those matters, the practitioner shall not accept the proposed engagement unless required by law or regulation to do so. However, an engagement conducted under such circumstances does not comply with this ISRE. Accordingly, the practitioner shall not include any reference within the practitioner's report to the review having been conducted in accordance with this ISRE.

32   If it is discovered after the engagement has been accepted that the practitioner is not satisfied as to any of the above preconditions, the practitioner shall discuss the matter with management or those charged with governance, and shall determine:

(a) Whether the matter can be resolved;

(b) Whether it is appropriate to continue with the engagement; and

(c) Whether and, if so, how to communicate the matter in the practitioner's report.

Additional Considerations When the Wording of the Practitioner's Report Is Prescribed by Law or Regulation

The practitioner's report issued for the review engagement shall refer to this ISRE only if the report complies with the requirements of paragraph 86.   **33**

In some cases, when the review is performed pursuant to applicable law or regulation of a jurisdiction, the relevant law or regulation may prescribe the layout or wording of the practitioner's report in a form or in terms that are significantly different from the requirements of this ISRE. In those circumstances, the practitioner shall evaluate whether users might misunderstand the assurance obtained from the review of the financial statements and, if so, whether additional explanation in the practitioner's report can mitigate possible misunderstanding. (Ref: Para. A51, A142)   **34**

If the practitioner concludes that additional explanation in the practitioner's report cannot mitigate possible misunderstanding, the practitioner shall not accept the review engagement unless required by law or regulation to do so. A review conducted in accordance with such law or regulation does not comply with this ISRE. Accordingly, the practitioner shall not include any reference within the practitioner's report to the review having been conducted in accordance with this ISRE. (Ref: Para. A51, A142)   **35**

Agreeing the Terms of Engagement

The practitioner shall agree the terms of the engagement with management or those charged with governance, as appropriate, prior to performing the engagement.   **36**

The agreed terms of engagement shall be recorded in an engagement letter or other suitable form of written agreement, and shall include: (Ref: Para. A52–A54, A56)   **37**

(a) The intended use and distribution of the financial statements, and any restrictions on use or distribution where applicable;
(b) Identification of the applicable financial reporting framework;
(c) The objective and scope of the review engagement;
(d) The responsibilities of the practitioner;
(e) The responsibilities of management, including those in paragraph 30(b); (Ref: Para. A47–A50, A55)
(f) A statement that the engagement is not an audit, and that the practitioner will not express an audit opinion on the financial statements; and
(g) Reference to the expected form and content of the report to be issued by the practitioner, and a statement that there may be circumstances in which the report may differ from its expected form and content.

Recurring Engagements

On recurring review engagements, the practitioner shall evaluate whether circumstances, including changes in the engagement acceptance considerations, require the terms of engagement to be revised and whether there is a need to remind management or those charged with governance, as appropriate, of the existing terms of engagement. (Ref: Para. A57)   **38**

Acceptance of a Change in the Terms of the Review Engagement

The practitioner shall not agree to a change in the terms of the engagement where there is no reasonable justification for doing so. (Ref: Para. A58–A60)   **39**

40   If, prior to completing the review engagement, the practitioner is requested to change the engagement to an engagement for which no assurance is obtained, the practitioner shall determine whether there is reasonable justification for doing so. (Ref: Para. A61–A62)

41   If the terms of engagement are changed during the course of the engagement, the practitioner and management or those charged with governance, as appropriate, shall agree on and record the new terms of the engagement in an engagement letter or other suitable form of written agreement.

Communication with Management and Those Charged with Governance

42   The practitioner shall communicate with management or those charged with governance, as appropriate, on a timely basis during the course of the review engagement, all matters concerning the review engagement that, in the practitioner's professional judgment, are of sufficient importance to merit the attention of management or those charged with governance, as appropriate. (Ref: Para. A63–A69)

Performing the Engagement

Materiality in a Review of Financial Statements

43   The practitioner shall determine materiality for the financial statements as a whole, and apply this materiality in designing the procedures and in evaluating the results obtained from those procedures. (Ref: Para. A70–A73)

44   The practitioner shall revise materiality for the financial statements as a whole in the event of becoming aware of information during the review that would have caused the practitioner to have determined a different amount initially. (Ref. Para. A74)

The Practitioner's Understanding

45   The practitioner shall obtain an understanding of the entity and its environment, and the applicable financial reporting framework, to identify areas in the financial statements where material misstatements are likely to arise and thereby provide a basis for designing procedures to address those areas. (Ref: Para. A75–A77)

46   The practitioner's understanding shall include the following: (Ref: Para. A78, A87, A89)

(a) Relevant industry, regulatory, and other external factors including the applicable financial reporting framework;

(b) The nature of the entity, including:
   (i)   Its operations;
   (ii) Its ownership and governance structure;
   (iii) The types of investments that the entity is making and plans to make;
   (iv) The way that the entity is structured and how it is financed; and
   (v)   The entity's objectives and strategies;

(c) The entity's accounting systems and accounting records; and

(d) The entity's selection and application of accounting policies.

Designing and Performing Procedures

In obtaining sufficient appropriate evidence as the basis for a conclusion on the **47** financial statements as a whole, the practitioner shall design and perform inquiry and analytical procedures: (Ref: Para. A79–A83, A87, A89)

(a) To address all material items in the financial statements, including disclosures; and

(b) To focus on addressing areas in the financial statements where material misstatements are likely to arise.

The practitioner's inquiries of management and others within the entity, as appro- **48** priate, shall include the following: (Ref: Para. A84–A87)

(a) How management makes the significant accounting estimates required under the applicable financial reporting framework;

(b) The identification of related parties and related party transactions, including the purpose of those transactions;

(c) Whether there are significant, unusual or complex transactions, events or matters that have affected or may affect the entity's financial statements, including:

(i) Significant changes in the entity's business activities or operations;

(ii) Significant changes to the terms of contracts that materially affect the entity's financial statements, including terms of finance and debt contracts or covenants;

(iii) Significant journal entries or other adjustments to the financial statements;

(iv) Significant transactions occurring or recognized near the end of the reporting period;

(v) The status of any uncorrected misstatements identified during previous engagements; and

(vi) Effects or possible implications for the entity of transactions or relationships with related parties;

(d) The existence of any actual, suspected or alleged:

(i) Fraud or illegal acts affecting the entity; and

(ii) Non-compliance with provisions of laws and regulations that are generally recognized to have a direct effect on the determination of material amounts and disclosures in the financial statements, such as tax and pension laws and regulations;

(e) Whether management has identified and addressed events occurring between the date of the financial statements and the date of the practitioner's report that require adjustment of, or disclosure in, the financial statements;

(f) The basis for management's assessment of the entity's ability to continue as a going concern; (Ref: Para. A88)

(g) Whether there are events or conditions that appear to cast doubt on the entity's ability to continue as a going concern;

(h) Material commitments, contractual obligations or contingencies that have affected or may affect the entity's financial statements, including disclosures; and

(i) Material non-monetary transactions or transactions for no consideration in the financial reporting period under consideration.

In designing analytical procedures, the practitioner shall consider whether the data **49** from the entity's accounting system and accounting records are adequate for the purpose of performing the analytical procedures. (Ref: Para. A89–A91)

Procedures to Address Specific Circumstances

Related parties

50   During the review, the practitioner shall remain alert for arrangements or information that may indicate the existence of related party relationships or transactions that management has not previously identified or disclosed to the practitioner.

51   If the practitioner identifies significant transactions outside the entity's normal course of business in the course of performing the review, the practitioner shall inquire of management about:

   (a)   The nature of those transactions;
   (b)   Whether related parties could be involved; and
   (c)   The business rationale (or lack thereof) of those transactions.

Fraud and non-compliance with laws or regulations

52   When there is an indication that fraud or non-compliance with laws or regulations, or suspected fraud or non-compliance with laws or regulations, has occurred in the entity, the practitioner shall:

   (a)   Communicate that matter to the appropriate level of senior management or those charged with governance as appropriate;
   (b)   Request management's assessment of the effect(s), if any, on the financial statements;
   (c)   Consider the effect, if any, of management's assessment of the effects of fraud or non-compliance with laws or regulations communicated to the practitioner on the practitioner's conclusion on the financial statements and on the practitioner's report; and
   (d)   Determine whether there is a responsibility to report the occurrence or suspicion of fraud or illegal acts to a party outside the entity. (Ref: Para. A92)

Going concern

53   A review of financial statements includes consideration of the entity's ability to continue as a going concern. In considering management's assessment of the entity's ability to continue as a going concern, the practitioner shall cover the same period as that used by management to make its assessment as required by the applicable financial reporting framework, or by law or regulation where a longer period is specified.

54   If, during the performance of the review, the practitioner becomes aware of events or conditions that may cast significant doubt about the entity's ability to continue as a going concern, the practitioner shall: (Ref: Para. A93)

   (a)   Inquire of management about plans for future actions affecting the entity's ability to continue as a going concern and about the feasibility of those plans, and also whether management believes the outcome of those plans will improve the situation regarding the entity's ability to continue as a going concern;
   (b)   Evaluate the results of those inquiries, to consider whether management's responses provide a sufficient basis to:
      (i)   Continue to present the financial statements on the going concern basis if the applicable financial reporting framework includes the assumption of an entity's continuance as a going concern; or

    (ii) Conclude whether the financial statements are materially misstated, or are otherwise misleading regarding the entity's ability to continue as a going concern; and

(c) Consider management's responses in light of all relevant information of which the practitioner is aware as a result of the review.

Use of work performed by others

In performing the review, it may be necessary for the practitioner to use work **55** performed by other practitioners, or the work of an individual or organization possessing expertise in a field other than accounting or assurance. If the practitioner uses work performed by another practitioner or an expert in the course of performing the review, the practitioner shall take appropriate steps to be satisfied that the work performed is adequate for the practitioner's purposes. (Ref: Para. A80)

Reconciling the Financial Statements to the Underlying Accounting Records

The practitioner shall obtain evidence that the financial statements agree with, or **56** reconcile to, the entity's underlying accounting records. (Ref: Para. A94)

Additional Procedures When the Practitioner Becomes Aware that the Financial Statements May Be Materially Misstated

If the practitioner becomes aware of a matter(s) that causes the practitioner to **57** believe the financial statements may be materially misstated, the practitioner shall design and perform additional procedures sufficient to enable the practitioner to: (Ref: Para. A95–A99)

(a) Conclude that the matter(s) is not likely to cause the financial statements as a whole to be materially misstated; or

(b) Determine that the matter(s) causes the financial statements as a whole to be materially misstated.

Subsequent Events

If the practitioner becomes aware of events occurring between the date of the **58** financial statements and the date of the practitioner's report that require adjustment of, or disclosure in, the financial statements, the practitioner shall request management to correct those misstatements.

The practitioner has no obligation to perform any procedures regarding the financial **59** statements after the date of the practitioner's report. However, if, after the date of the practitioner's report but before the date the financial statements are issued, a fact becomes known to the practitioner that, had it been known to the practitioner at the date of the practitioner's report, may have caused the practitioner to amend the report, the practitioner shall:

(a) Discuss the matter with management or those charged with governance, as appropriate;

(b) Determine whether the financial statements need amendment; and

(c) If so, inquire how management intends to address the matter in the financial statements.

If management does not amend the financial statements in circumstances where the **60** practitioner believes they need to be amended, and the practitioner's report has already been provided to the entity, the practitioner shall notify management and those charged with governance not to issue the financial statements to third parties before the necessary amendments have been made. If the financial statements are nevertheless subsequently issued without the necessary amendments, the practitioner shall take appropriate action to seek to prevent reliance on the practitioner's report.

Written Representations

61   The practitioner shall request management to provide a written representation that management has fulfilled its responsibilities described in the agreed terms of engagement. The written representation shall include that: (Ref: Para. A100–A102)

(a) Management has fulfilled its responsibility for the preparation of financial statements in accordance with the applicable financial reporting framework, including where relevant their fair presentation, and has provided the practitioner with all relevant information and access to information as agreed in the terms of the engagement; and

(b) All transactions have been recorded and are reflected in the financial statements.

If law or regulation requires management to make written public statements about its responsibilities, and the practitioner determines that such statements provide some or all of the representations required by subparagraphs (a)–(b), the relevant matters covered by such statements need not be included in the written representation.

62   The practitioner shall also request management's written representations that management has disclosed to the practitioner: (Ref: Para. A101)

(a) The identity of the entity's related parties and all the related party relationships and transactions of which management is aware;

(b) Significant facts relating to any frauds or suspected frauds known to management that may have affected the entity;

(c) Known actual or possible non-compliance with laws and regulations for which the effects of non-compliance affect the entity's financial statements;

(d) All information relevant to use of the going concern assumption in the financial statements;

(e) That all events occurring subsequent to the date of the financial statements and for which the applicable financial reporting framework requires adjustment or disclosure, have been adjusted or disclosed;

(f) Material commitments, contractual obligations or contingencies that have affected or may affect the entity's financial statements, including disclosures; and

(g) Material non-monetary transactions or transactions for no consideration undertaken by the entity in the financial reporting period under consideration.

63   If management does not provide one or more of the requested written representations, the practitioner shall: (Ref: Para. A100)

(a) Discuss the matter with management and those charged with governance, as appropriate;

(b) Re-evaluate the integrity of management, and evaluate the effect that this may have on the reliability of representations (oral or written) and evidence in general; and

(c) Take appropriate actions, including determining the possible effect on the conclusion in the practitioner's report in accordance with this ISRE.

The practitioner shall disclaim a conclusion on the financial statements, or withdraw **64**
from the engagement if withdrawal is possible under applicable law or regulation, as
appropriate, if:

(a) The practitioner concludes that there is sufficient doubt about the integrity of
management such that the written representations are not reliable; or
(b) Management does not provide the required representations required by paragraph 61.

Date of and Period(s) Covered by Written Representations

The date of the written representations shall be as near as practicable to, but not **65**
after, the date of the practitioner's report. The written representations shall be for all
financial statements and period(s) referred to in the practitioner's report.

Evaluating Evidence Obtained from the Procedures Performed

The practitioner shall evaluate whether sufficient appropriate evidence has been **66**
obtained from the procedures performed and, if not, the practitioner shall perform
other procedures judged by the practitioner to be necessary in the circumstances to
be able to form a conclusion on the financial statements. (Ref: Para. A103)

If the practitioner is not able to obtain sufficient appropriate evidence to form a **67**
conclusion, the practitioner shall discuss with management and those charged with
governance, as appropriate, the effects such limitations have on the scope of the
review. (Ref: Para. A104–A105)

Evaluating the Effect on the Practitioner's Report

The practitioner shall evaluate the evidence obtained from the procedures performed **68**
to determine the effect on the practitioner's report. (Ref: Para. A103)

Forming the Practitioner's Conclusion on the Financial Statements

Consideration of the Applicable Financial Reporting Framework in Relation to the Financial Statements

In forming the conclusion on the financial statements, the practitioner shall: **69**

(a) Evaluate whether the financial statements adequately refer to or describe the
applicable financial reporting framework; (Ref: Para. A106–A107)
(b) Consider whether, in the context of the requirements of the applicable financial
reporting framework and the results of procedures performed:
   (i) The terminology used in the financial statements, including the title of each
   financial statement, is appropriate;
   (ii) The financial statements adequately disclose the significant accounting
   policies selected and applied;
   (iii) The accounting policies selected and applied are consistent with the
   applicable financial reporting framework and are appropriate;
   (iv) Accounting estimates made by management appear reasonable;
   (v) The information presented in the financial statements appears relevant,
   reliable, comparable, and understandable; and
   (vi) The financial statements provide adequate disclosures to enable the intended users to understand the effects of material transactions and events on

the information conveyed in the financial statements. (Ref: Para. A108–A110)

70   The practitioner shall consider the impact of:

(a)   Uncorrected misstatements identified during the review, and in the previous year's review of the entity's financial statements, on the financial statements as a whole; and

(b)   Qualitative aspects of the entity's accounting practices, including indicators of possible bias in management's judgments. (Ref: Para. A111–A112)

71   If the financial statements are prepared using a fair presentation framework, the practitioner's consideration shall also include: (Ref: Para. A109)

(a)   The overall presentation, structure and content of the financial statements in accordance with the applicable framework; and

(b)   Whether the financial statements, including the related notes, appear to represent the underlying transactions and events in a manner that achieves fair presentation or gives a true and fair view, as appropriate, in the context of the financial statements as a whole.

Form of the Conclusion

72   The practitioner's conclusion on the financial statements, whether unmodified or modified, shall be expressed in the appropriate form in the context of the financial reporting framework applied in the financial statements.

Unmodified Conclusion

73   The practitioner shall express an unmodified conclusion in the practitioner's report on the financial statements as a whole when the practitioner has obtained limited assurance to be able to conclude that nothing has come to the practitioner's attention that causes the practitioner to believe that the financial statements are not prepared, in all material respects, in accordance with the applicable financial reporting framework.

74   When the practitioner expresses an unmodified conclusion, the practitioner shall, unless otherwise required by law or regulation, use one of the following phrases, as appropriate: (Ref: Para. A113–A114)

(a)   "Based on our review, nothing has come to our attention that causes us to believe that the financial statements do not present fairly, in all material respects (or do not give a true and fair view), ... in accordance with the applicable financial reporting framework," (for financial statements prepared using a fair presentation framework); or

(b)   "Based on our review, nothing has come to our attention that causes us to believe that the financial statements are not prepared, in all material respects, in accordance with the applicable financial reporting framework," (for financial statements prepared using a compliance framework).

Modified Conclusion

75   The practitioner shall express a modified conclusion in the practitioner's report on the financial statements as a whole when:

(a) The practitioner determines, based on the procedures performed and the evidence obtained, that the financial statements are materially misstated; or
(b) The practitioner is unable to obtain sufficient appropriate evidence in relation to one or more items in the financial statements that are material in relation to the financial statements as a whole.

When the practitioner modifies the conclusion expressed on the financial statements, **76** the practitioner shall:

(a) Use the heading "Qualified Conclusion," "Adverse Conclusion" or "Disclaimer of Conclusion," as appropriate, for the conclusion paragraph in the practitioner's report; and
(b) Provide a description of the matter giving rise to the modification, under an appropriate heading (for example, "Basis for Qualified Conclusion," "Basis for Adverse Conclusion" or "Basis for Disclaimer of Conclusion," as appropriate), in a separate paragraph in the practitioner's report immediately before the conclusion paragraph (referred to as the basis for conclusion paragraph).

Financial statements are materially misstated

If the practitioner determines that the financial statements are materially misstated, **77** the practitioner shall express:

(a) A qualified conclusion, when the practitioner concludes that the effects of the matter(s) giving rise to the modification are material, but not pervasive to the financial statements; or
(b) An adverse conclusion, when the effects of the matter(s) giving rise to the modification are both material and pervasive to the financial statements.

When the practitioner expresses a qualified conclusion on the financial statements **78** because of a material misstatement, the practitioner shall, unless otherwise required by law or regulation, use one of the following phrases, as appropriate:

(a) "Based on our review, except for the effects of the matter(s) described in the Basis for Qualified Conclusion paragraph, nothing has come to our attention that causes us to believe that the financial statements do not present fairly, in all material respects (or do not give a true and fair view), ... in accordance with the applicable financial reporting framework," (for financial statements prepared using a fair presentation framework); or
(b) "Based on our review, except for the effects of the matter(s) described in the Basis for Qualified Conclusion paragraph, nothing has come to our attention that causes us to believe that the financial statements are not prepared, in all material respects, in accordance with the applicable financial reporting framework," (for financial statements prepared using a compliance framework).

When the practitioner expresses an adverse conclusion on the financial statements, **79** the practitioner shall, unless otherwise required by law or regulation, use one of the following phrases, as appropriate:

(a) "Based on our review, due to the significance of the matter(s) described in the Basis for Adverse Conclusion paragraph, the financial statements do not present fairly, in all material respects (or do not give a true and fair view), ... in accordance with the applicable financial reporting framework," (for financial statements prepared using a fair presentation framework); or
(b) "Based on our review, due to the significance of the matter(s) described in the Basis for Adverse Conclusion paragraph, the financial statements are not prepared, in all material respects, in accordance with the applicable financial

reporting framework," (for financial statements prepared using a compliance framework).

80   In the basis for conclusion paragraph, in relation to material misstatements that give rise to either a qualified conclusion or an adverse conclusion, the practitioner shall:

(a)   Describe and quantify the financial effects of the misstatement if the material misstatement relates to specific amounts in the financial statements (including quantitative disclosures), unless impracticable, in which case the practitioner shall so state;

(b)   Explain how disclosures are misstated if the material misstatement relates to narrative disclosures; or

(c)   Describe the nature of omitted information if the material misstatement relates to the non-disclosure of information required to be disclosed. Unless prohibited by law or regulation, the practitioner shall include the omitted disclosures where practicable to do so.

Inability to obtain sufficient appropriate evidence

81   If the practitioner is unable to form a conclusion on the financial statements due to inability to obtain sufficient appropriate evidence, the practitioner shall:

(a)   Express a qualified conclusion if the practitioner concludes that the possible effects on the financial statements of undetected misstatements, if any, could be material but not pervasive; or

(b)   Disclaim a conclusion if the practitioner concludes that the possible effects on the financial statements of undetected misstatements, if any, could be both material and pervasive.

82   The practitioner shall withdraw from the engagement if the following conditions are present: (Ref: Para. A115–A117)

(a)   Due to a limitation on the scope of the review imposed by management after the practitioner has accepted the engagement, the practitioner is unable to obtain sufficient appropriate evidence to form a conclusion on the financial statements;

(b)   The practitioner has determined that the possible effects on the financial statements of undetected misstatements are material and pervasive; and

(c)   Withdrawal is possible under applicable law or regulation.

83   When the practitioner expresses a qualified conclusion on the financial statements due to inability to obtain sufficient appropriate evidence, the practitioner shall, unless otherwise required by law or regulation, use one of the following phrases, as appropriate:

(a)   "Based on our review, except for the possible effects of the matter(s) described in the Basis for Qualified Conclusion paragraph, nothing has come to our attention that causes us to believe that the financial statements do not present fairly, in all material respects (or do not give a true and fair view), ... in accordance with the applicable financial reporting framework," (for financial statements prepared using a fair presentation framework); or

(b)   "Based on our review, except for the possible effects of the matter(s) described in the Basis for Qualified Conclusion paragraph, nothing has come to our attention that causes us to believe that the financial statements are not prepared, in all material respects, in accordance with the applicable financial reporting framework," (for financial statements prepared using a compliance framework).

When disclaiming a conclusion on the financial statements the practitioner shall state **84** in the conclusion paragraph that:

(a) Due to the significance of the matter(s) described in the Basis for Disclaimer of Conclusion paragraph, the practitioner is unable to obtain sufficient appropriate evidence to form a conclusion on the financial statements; and

(b) Accordingly, the practitioner does not express a conclusion on the financial statements.

In the basis for conclusion paragraph, in relation to either the qualified conclusion **85** due to inability to obtain sufficient appropriate evidence or when the practitioner disclaims a conclusion, the practitioner shall include the reason(s) for the inability to obtain sufficient appropriate evidence.

The Practitioner's Report

The practitioner's report for the review engagement shall be in writing, and shall **86** contain the following elements: (Ref: Para. A118–A121, A142, A144)

(a) A title, which shall clearly indicate that it is the report of an independent practitioner for a review engagement;

(b) The addressee(s), as required by the circumstances of the engagement;

(c) An introductory paragraph that:

(i) Identifies the financial statements reviewed, including identification of the title of each of the statements contained in the set of financial statements and the date and period covered by each financial statement;

(ii) Refers to the summary of significant accounting policies and other explanatory information; and

(iii) States that the financial statements have been reviewed;

(d) A description of the responsibility of management for the preparation of the financial statements, including an explanation that management is responsible for: (Ref: Para. A122–A125)

(i) Their preparation in accordance with the applicable financial reporting framework including, where relevant, their fair presentation;

(ii) Such internal control as management determines is necessary to enable the preparation of financial statements that are free from material misstatement, whether due to fraud or error;

(e) If the financial statements are special purpose financial statements:

(i) A description of the purpose for which the financial statements are prepared and, if necessary, the intended users, or reference to a note in the special purpose financial statements that contains that information; and

(ii) If management has a choice of financial reporting frameworks in the preparation of such financial statements, a reference within the explanation of management's responsibility for the financial statements to management's responsibility for determining that the applicable financial reporting framework is acceptable in the circumstances;

(f) A description of the practitioner's responsibility to express a conclusion on the financial statements including reference to this ISRE and, where relevant, applicable law or regulation; (Ref: Para. A126–127, A143)

(g) A description of a review of financial statements and its limitations, and the following statements: (Ref: Para. A128)

(i) A review engagement under this ISRE is a limited assurance engagement;

(ii) The practitioner performs procedures, primarily consisting of making inquiries of management and others within the entity, as appropriate, and applying analytical procedures, and evaluates the evidence obtained; and

(iii) The procedures performed in a review are substantially less than those performed in an audit conducted in accordance with International Standards on Auditing (ISAs), and, accordingly, the practitioner does not express an audit opinion on the financial statements;

(h) A paragraph under the heading "Conclusion" that contains:

   (i)   The practitioner's conclusion on the financial statements as a whole in accordance with paragraphs 72–85, as appropriate; and

   (ii) A reference to the applicable financial reporting framework used to prepare the financial statements, including identification of the jurisdiction of origin of the financial reporting framework that is not International Financial Reporting Standards or International Financial Reporting Standard for Small and Medium-sized Entities issued by the International Accounting Standards Board, or International Public Sector Accounting Standards issued by the International Public Sector Accounting Standards Board; (Ref: Para. A129–A130)

(i) When the practitioner's conclusion on the financial statements is modified:

   (i)   A paragraph under the appropriate heading that contains the practitioner's modified conclusion in accordance with paragraphs 72 and 75–85, as appropriate; and

   (ii) A paragraph, under an appropriate heading, that provides a description of the matter(s) giving rise to the modification; (Ref: Para. A131)

(j) A reference to the practitioner's obligation under this ISRE to comply with relevant ethical requirements;

(k) The date of the practitioner's report; (Ref: Para. A138–A141)

(l) The practitioner's signature; and (Ref: Para. A132)

(m) The location in the jurisdiction where the practitioner practices.

Emphasis of Matter and Other Matter Paragraphs in the Practitioner's Report

Emphasis of Matter Paragraphs

87   The practitioner may consider it necessary to draw users' attention to a matter presented or disclosed in the financial statements that, in the practitioner's judgment, is of such importance that it is fundamental to users' understanding of the financial statements. In such cases, the practitioner shall include an Emphasis of Matter paragraph in the practitioner's report, provided the practitioner has obtained sufficient appropriate evidence to conclude that the matter is not likely to be materially misstated as presented in the financial statements. Such paragraph shall refer only to information presented or disclosed in the financial statements.

88   The practitioner's report on special purpose financial statements shall include an Emphasis of Matter paragraph alerting users of the practitioner's report that the financial statements are prepared in accordance with a special purpose framework and that, as a result, the financial statements may not be suitable for another purpose. (Ref: Para. A133–A134)

89   The practitioner shall include an Emphasis of Matter paragraph immediately after the paragraph that contains the practitioner's conclusion on the financial statements under the heading "Emphasis of Matter," or other appropriate heading.

Other Matter Paragraphs

90   If the practitioner considers it necessary to communicate a matter other than those that are presented or disclosed in the financial statements that, in the practitioner's judgment, is relevant to users' understanding of the review, the practitioner's responsibilities or the practitioner's report and this is not prohibited by law or regulation, the practitioner shall do so in a paragraph in the practitioner's report with the heading "Other Matter" or other appropriate heading.

Other Reporting Responsibilities

A practitioner may be requested to address other reporting responsibilities in the **91** practitioner's report on the financial statements that are in addition to the practitioner's responsibilities under this ISRE to report on the financial statements. In such situations, those other reporting responsibilities shall be addressed by the practitioner in a separate section in the practitioner's report headed "Report on Other Legal and Regulatory Requirements," or

otherwise as appropriate to the content of the section, following the section of the report headed "Report on the Financial Statements." (Ref: Para. A135–A137)

Date of the Practitioner's Report

The practitioner shall date the report no earlier than the date on which the practi- **92** tioner has obtained sufficient appropriate evidence as the basis for the practitioner's conclusion on the financial statements, including being satisfied that: (Ref: Para. A138–A141)

(a) All the statements that comprise the financial statements under the applicable financial reporting framework, including the related notes where applicable, have been prepared; and

(b) Those with the recognized authority have asserted that they have taken responsibility for those financial statements.

Documentation

The preparation of documentation for the review provides evidence that the review **93** was performed in accordance with this ISRE, and legal and regulatory requirements where relevant, and a sufficient and appropriate record of the basis for the practitioner's report. The practitioner shall document the following aspects of the engagement in a timely manner, sufficient to enable an experienced practitioner, having no previous connection with the engagement, to understand: (Ref: Para. A145)

(a) The nature, timing, and extent of the procedures performed to comply with this ISRE and applicable legal and regulatory requirements;

(b) Results obtained from the procedures, and the practitioner's conclusions formed on the basis of those results; and

(c) Significant matters arising during the engagement, the practitioner's conclusions reached thereon, and significant professional judgments made in reaching those conclusions.

In documenting the nature, timing and extent of procedures performed as required in **94** this ISRE, the practitioner shall record:

(a) Who performed the work and the date such work was completed; and

(b) Who reviewed the work performed for the purpose of quality control for the engagement, and the date and extent of the review.

95   The practitioner shall also document discussions with management, those charged with governance, and others as relevant to the performance of the review of significant matters arising during the engagement, including the nature of those matters.

96   If, in the course of the engagement, the practitioner identified information that is inconsistent with the practitioner's findings regarding significant matters affecting the financial statements, the practitioner shall document how the inconsistency was addressed.

***

Application and Other Explanatory Material

Scope of this ISRE (Ref: Para. 1–2)

A1   In performing a review of financial statements, the practitioner may be required to comply with legal or regulatory requirements, which may differ from the requirements established in this ISRE. While the practitioner may find aspects of this ISRE helpful in these circumstances, it is the responsibility of the practitioner to ensure compliance with all relevant legal, regulatory and professional obligations.

Reviews of Financial Information of Components in the Context of an Audit of the Financial Statements of a Group of Entities

A2   Review engagements in accordance with this ISRE may be requested for component entities by the auditor of the financial statements of a group of entities.[6] Such a review engagement performed in accordance with this ISRE may be accompanied by a request from the group auditor to undertake additional work or procedures as needed in the circumstances of the group audit engagement.

Relationship with ISQC 1 (Ref: Para. 4)

A3   ISQC 1 deals with the firm's responsibilities to establish and maintain its system of quality control for assurance engagements, including review engagements. Those responsibilities are directed at establishing the firm's:

- Quality control system; and
- Related policies designed to achieve the objective of the quality control system and the firm's procedures to implement and monitor compliance with those policies, including policies and procedures that address each of the following elements:
  o   Leadership responsibilities for quality within the firm.
  o   Relevant ethical requirements.
  o   Acceptance and continuance of client relationships and specific engagements.
  o   Human resources.
  o   Engagement performance.
  o   Monitoring.

A4   Under ISQC 1, the firm has an obligation to establish and maintain a system of quality control to provide it with reasonable assurance that:

---

[6] *ISA 600*, Special Considerations—Audits of Group Financial Statements (Including the Work of Component Auditors, *paragraph A52.*

(a) The firm and its personnel comply with professional standards and applicable legal and regulatory requirements; and

(b) Reports issued by the firm or engagement partners are appropriate in the circumstances.[7]

National requirements that deal with the firm's responsibilities to establish and maintain a system of quality control are at least as demanding as ISQC 1 when they address all the elements referred to in paragraph A3, and impose obligations on the firm that achieve the aims of the requirements set out in ISQC 1. **A5**

The Engagement to Review Historical Financial Statements
(Ref: Para. 5–8, 14)

Reviews of financial statements may be performed for a wide range of entities that vary by type or size, or by the level of complexity in their financial reporting. In some jurisdictions, the review of financial statements of certain types of entity may also be the subject of local laws or regulations and related reporting requirements. **A6**

Reviews may be performed in a variety of circumstances. For example, they may be required for entities that are exempt from requirements specified in law or regulation for mandatory audit. Reviews may also be requested on a voluntary basis, such as in connection with financial reporting undertaken for arrangements under the terms of a private contract, or to support funding arrangements. **A7**

Objectives (Ref: Para. 15)

This ISRE requires the practitioner to disclaim a conclusion on the financial statements if: **A8**

(a) The practitioner issues a report, or is required to issue a report for the engagement; and

(b) The practitioner is unable to form a conclusion on the financial statements due to inability to obtain sufficient appropriate evidence, and the practitioner concludes that the possible effects on the financial statements of undetected misstatements, if any, could be both material and pervasive.

The situation of being unable to obtain sufficient appropriate evidence in a review engagement (referred to as a scope limitation) may arise from: **A9**

(a) Circumstances beyond the control of the entity;

(b) Circumstances relating to the nature or timing of the practitioner's work; or

(c) Limitations imposed by management or those charged with governance of the entity.

This ISRE sets out requirements and guidance for the practitioner when the practitioner encounters a scope limitation, either prior to accepting a review engagement, or during the engagement. **A10**

---

[7] *ISQC 1, paragraph 11.*

Definitions (Ref: Para. 16)

Use of the Terms "Management" and "Those Charged with Governance"

A11   The respective responsibilities of management and those charged with governance will differ between jurisdictions, and between entities of various types. These differences affect the way the practitioner applies the requirements of this ISRE in relation to management or those charged with governance Accordingly, the phrase "management and, where appropriate, those charged with governance" used in various places throughout this ISRE is intended to alert the practitioner to the fact that different entity environments may have different management and governance structures and arrangements.

A12   Various responsibilities relating to preparation of financial information and external financial reporting will fall to either management or those charged with governance according to factors such as:

- The resources and structure of the entity; and
- The respective roles of management and those charged with governance within the entity as set out in relevant law or regulation or, if the entity is not regulated, in any formal governance or accountability arrangements established for the entity (for example, as recorded in contracts, a constitution or other type of establishment documents of the entity).

For example, in small entities there is often no separation of the management and governance roles. In larger entities, management is often responsible for execution of the business or activities of the entity and reporting thereon, while those charged with governance oversee management. In some jurisdictions, the responsibility for preparation of financial statements for an entity is the legal responsibility of those charged with governance, and in some other jurisdictions it is a management responsibility.

Limited Assurance – Use of the Term Sufficient Appropriate Evidence (Ref: Para. 17(f))

A13   Sufficient appropriate evidence is required to obtain limited assurance to support the practitioner's conclusion. Evidence is cumulative in nature and is primarily obtained from the procedures performed during the course of the review.

Conduct of a Review Engagement in Accordance with this ISRE (Ref: Para. 18)

A14   This ISRE does not override laws and regulations that govern a review of financial statements. In the event that those laws and regulations differ from the requirements of this ISRE, a review conducted only in accordance with laws and regulations will not automatically comply with this ISRE.

Ethical Requirements (Ref: Para. 21)

A15   Part A of the IESBA Code establishes the fundamental principles of professional ethics practitioners must comply with, and provides a conceptual framework for applying those principles. The fundamental principles are:

(a) Integrity;
(b) Objectivity;

(c) Professional competence and due care;

(d) Confidentiality; and

(e) Professional behavior.

Part B of the IESBA Code illustrates how the conceptual framework is to be applied in specific situations. In complying with the IESBA Code, threats to the practitioner's compliance with relevant ethical requirements are required to be identified and appropriately addressed.

In the case of an engagement to review financial statements, the IESBA Code requires that the practitioner be independent of the entity whose financial statements are reviewed. The IESBA Code describes independence as comprising both independence of mind and

A16

independence in appearance. The practitioner's independence safeguards the practitioner's ability to form a conclusion without being affected by influences that might otherwise compromise that conclusion. Independence enhances the practitioner's ability to act with integrity, to be objective and to maintain an attitude of professional skepticism.

Professional Skepticism and Professional Judgment

Professional Skepticism (Ref: Para. 22)

Professional skepticism is necessary for the critical assessment of evidence in a review. This includes questioning inconsistencies and investigating contradictory evidence, and questioning the reliability of responses to inquiries and other information obtained from management and those charged with governance. It also includes consideration of the sufficiency and appropriateness of evidence obtained in the light of the engagement circumstances.

A17

Professional skepticism includes being alert to, for example:

A18

- Evidence that is inconsistent with other evidence obtained.
- Information that calls into question the reliability of documents and responses to inquiries to be used as evidence.
- Conditions that may indicate possible fraud.
- Any other circumstances that suggest the need for additional procedures.

Maintaining professional skepticism throughout the review is necessary if the practitioner is to reduce the risks of:

A19

- Overlooking unusual circumstances.
- Over-generalizing when drawing conclusions from evidence obtained.
- Using inappropriate assumptions in determining the nature, timing, and extent of the procedures performed in the review, and evaluating the results thereof.

The practitioner cannot be expected to disregard past experience of the honesty and integrity of the entity's management and those charged with governance. Nevertheless, a belief that management and those charged with governance are honest and have integrity does not relieve the practitioner of the need to maintain professional skepticism or allow the practitioner to be satisfied with evidence that is inadequate for the purpose of the review.

A20

Professional Judgment (Ref: Para. 23)

A21   Professional judgment is essential to the proper conduct of a review engagement. This is because interpretation of relevant ethical requirements and the requirements of this ISRE, and the need for informed decisions throughout the performance of a review engagement, require the application of relevant knowledge and experience to the facts and circumstances of the engagement. Professional judgment is necessary, in particular:

- Regarding decisions about materiality, and the nature, timing, and extent of procedures used to meet the requirements of this ISRE, and to gather evidence.
- When evaluating whether the evidence obtained from the procedures performed reduces the engagement risk to a level that is acceptable in the engagement circumstances.
- When considering management's judgments in applying the entity's applicable financial reporting framework.
- When forming the conclusion on the financial statements based on the evidence obtained, including considering the reasonableness of the estimates made by management in preparing the financial statements.

A22   The distinguishing feature of the professional judgment expected of the practitioner is that it is exercised by a practitioner whose training, knowledge and experience, including in the use of assurance skills and techniques, have assisted in developing the necessary competencies to achieve reasonable judgments. Consultation on difficult or contentious matters during the course of the engagement, both within the engagement team and between the engagement team and others at the appropriate level within or outside the firm, assists the practitioner in making informed and reasonable judgments.

A23   The exercise of professional judgment in individual engagements is based on the facts and circumstances that are known by the practitioner throughout the engagement, including:

- Knowledge acquired from engagements carried out with respect to the entity's financial statements in prior periods, where applicable.
- The practitioner's understanding of the entity and its environment, including its accounting system, and of the application of the applicable financial reporting framework in the entity's industry.
- The extent to which the preparation and presentation of the financial statements require the exercise of management judgment.

A24   Professional judgment can be evaluated based on whether the judgment reached reflects a competent application of assurance and accounting principles, and is appropriate in the light of, and consistent with, the facts and circumstances that were known to the practitioner up to the date of the practitioner's report.

A25   Professional judgment needs to be exercised throughout the engagement. It also needs to be appropriately documented in accordance with the requirements of this ISRE. Professional judgment is not to be used as the justification for decisions that are not otherwise supported by the facts and circumstances of the engagement, or the evidence obtained.

Engagement Level Quality Control (Ref: Para. 24–25)

Assurance skills and techniques include: **A26**

- Applying professional skepticism and professional judgment to planning and performing an assurance engagement, including obtaining and evaluating evidence;
- Understanding information systems and the role and limitations of internal control;
- Linking the consideration of materiality and engagement risks to the nature, timing and extent of procedures for the review;
- Applying procedures as appropriate to the review engagement, which may include other types of procedures in addition to inquiry and analytical procedures (such as inspection, re-calculation, re-performance, observation and confirmation);
- Systematic documentation practices; and
- Application of skills and practices relevant for writing reports for assurance engagements.

Within the context of the firm's system of quality control, engagement teams have a **A27**
responsibility to implement quality control procedures applicable to the engagement, and provide the firm with relevant information to enable the functioning of that part of the firm's system of quality control relating to independence.

The actions of the engagement partner and appropriate messages to the other **A28**
members of the engagement team, in the context of the engagement partner taking responsibility for the overall quality on each review engagement, emphasize the fact that quality is essential in performing a review engagement, and the importance to the quality of the review engagement of:

(a) Performing work that complies with professional standards and regulatory and legal requirements.
(b) Complying with the firm's quality control policies and procedures as applicable.
(c) Issuing a report for the engagement that is appropriate in the circumstances.
(d) The engagement team's ability to raise concerns without fear of reprisals.

Unless information provided by the firm or other parties suggests otherwise, the **A29**
engagement team is entitled to rely on the firm's system of quality control. For example, the engagement team may rely on the firm's system of quality control in relation to:

- Competence of personnel through their recruitment and formal training.
- Independence through the accumulation and communication of relevant independence information.
- Maintenance of client relationships through acceptance and continuance systems.
- Adherence to regulatory and legal requirements through the monitoring process.

In considering deficiencies identified in the firm's system of quality control that may affect the review engagement, the engagement partner may consider measures taken by the firm to rectify those deficiencies.

A deficiency in the firm's system of quality control does not necessarily indicate that **A30**
a review engagement was not performed in accordance with professional standards and applicable legal and regulatory requirements, or that the practitioner's report was not appropriate.

Assignment of Engagement Teams (Ref: Para. 25(b))

A31   When considering the appropriate competence and capabilities expected of the engagement team as a whole, the engagement partner may take into consideration such matters as the team's:

- Understanding of, and practical experience with, review engagements of a similar nature and complexity through appropriate training and participation.
- Understanding of professional standards and applicable legal and regulatory requirements.
- Technical expertise, including expertise with relevant information technology and specialized areas of accounting or assurance.
- Knowledge of relevant industries in which the client operates.
- Ability to apply professional judgment.
- Understanding of the firm's quality control policies and procedures.

Acceptance and Continuance of Client Relationships and Review Engagements (Ref: Para. 25(d)(i))

A32   ISQC 1 requires the firm to obtain information as it considers necessary in the circumstances before accepting an engagement with a new client, when deciding whether to continue an existing engagement, and when considering acceptance of a new engagement with an existing client. Information that assists the engagement partner in determining whether acceptance and continuance of client relationships and review engagements are appropriate may include information concerning:

- The integrity of the principal owners, key management and those charged with governance; and
- Significant matters that have arisen during the current or a previous review engagement, and their implications for continuing the relationship.

A33   If the engagement partner has cause to doubt management's integrity to a degree that is likely to affect proper performance of the review, it is not appropriate under this ISRE to accept the engagement, unless required by law or regulation, as doing so may lead to the practitioner being associated with the entity's financial statements in an inappropriate manner.

Acceptance and Continuance of Client Relationships and Review Engagements (Ref: Para. 29)

A34   The practitioner's consideration of engagement continuance, and relevant ethical requirements, including independence, occurs throughout the engagement, as conditions and changes in circumstances occur. Performing initial procedures on engagement continuance and evaluation of relevant ethical requirements (including independence) at the beginning of an engagement informs the practitioner's decisions and actions prior to the performance of other significant activities for the engagement.

Factors Affecting Acceptance and Continuance of Client Relationships and Review Engagements (Ref: Para. 29)

Assurance engagements may only be accepted when the engagement exhibits certain   **A35**
characteristics[8] that are conducive to achieving the practitioner's objectives specified
for the engagement.

Rational Purpose (Ref: Para. 29(a)(i))

It may be unlikely that there is a rational purpose for the engagement if, for example: **A36**

(a) There is a significant limitation on the scope of the practitioner's work;
(b) The practitioner suspects the engaging party intends to associate the practitioner's name with the financial statements in an inappropriate manner; or
(c) The engagement is intended to meet compliance requirements of relevant law or regulation and such law or regulation requires the financial statements to be audited.

Review Engagement Is Appropriate (Ref: Para. 29(a)(ii))

When the practitioner's preliminary understanding of the engagement circumstances   **A37**
indicates that accepting a review engagement would not be appropriate, the practitioner may consider recommending that another type of engagement be undertaken.
Depending on the circumstances, the practitioner may, for example, believe that
performance of an audit engagement would be more appropriate than a review. In
other cases, if the engagement circumstances preclude performance of an assurance
engagement, the practitioner may recommend a compilation engagement, or other
accounting services engagement, as appropriate.

Information Needed to Perform the Review Engagement (Ref: Para. 29(c))

An example of where the practitioner may have cause to doubt that the information   **A38**
needed to perform the review will be available or reliable is where the accounting
records necessary for purposes of performing analytical procedures are suspected to
be substantially inaccurate or incomplete. This consideration is not directed at the
need that sometimes arises in the course of a review engagement to assist management by recommending adjusting entries required to finalize the financial statements
prepared by management.

Preconditions for Accepting a Review Engagement (Ref: Para. 30)

This ISRE also requires the practitioner to ascertain certain matters, upon which it is   **A39**
necessary for the practitioner and the entity's management to agree, and which are
within the control of the entity, prior to the practitioner accepting the engagement.

---

[8] *Assurance Framework, paragraph 17.*

The Applicable Financial Reporting Framework (Ref: Para. 30(a))

A40   A condition for acceptance of an assurance engagement is that the criteria[9] referred to in the definition of an assurance engagement are suitable and available to intended users.[10] For purposes of this ISRE, the applicable financial reporting framework provides the criteria the practitioner uses to review the financial statements including, where relevant, the fair presentation of the financial statements. Some financial reporting frameworks are fair presentation frameworks, while others are compliance frameworks. The requirements of the applicable financial reporting framework determine the form and content of the financial statements, including what constitutes a complete set of financial statements.

Acceptability of the applicable financial reporting framework

A41   Without an acceptable financial reporting framework, management does not have an appropriate basis for the preparation of the financial statements and the practitioner does not have suitable criteria for the review of the financial statements.

A42   The practitioner's determination of the acceptability of the financial reporting framework applied in the financial statements is made in the context of the practitioner's understanding of who the intended users of the financial statements are. The intended users are the person, persons or group of persons for whom the practitioner prepares the report. The practitioner may not be able to identify all those who will read the assurance report, particularly where there is a large number of people who have access to it.

A43   In many cases, in the absence of any indications to the contrary, the practitioner may presume that the applicable financial reporting framework is acceptable (for example, a financial reporting framework that is prescribed by law or regulation in a jurisdiction to be used in the preparation of general purpose financial statements for certain types of entities).

A44   Factors that are relevant to the practitioner's determination of the acceptability of the financial reporting framework to be applied in the preparation of the financial statements include:

- The nature of the entity (for example, whether it is a business enterprise, a public sector entity or a not-for-profit organization).
- The purpose of the financial statements (for example, whether they are prepared to meet the common financial information needs of a wide range of users or the financial information needs of specific users).
- The nature of the financial statements (for example, whether the financial statements are a complete set of financial statements or a single financial statement).
- Whether the applicable financial reporting framework is prescribed in relevant law or regulation.

A45   If the financial reporting framework used to prepare the financial statements is not acceptable in view of the purpose of the financial statements and management will not agree to use of a financial reporting framework that is acceptable in the practitioner's view, the practitioner is required under this ISRE to decline the engagement.

---

[9] *Assurance Framework, paragraph 34.*

[10] *Assurance Framework, paragraph 17(b)(ii).*

Deficiencies in the applicable financial reporting framework that indicate that the **A46** framework is not acceptable may be encountered after the review engagement has been accepted. When use of that financial reporting framework is not prescribed by law or regulation, management may decide to adopt another framework that is acceptable. When management does so, the practitioner is required under this ISRE to agree the new terms of the review engagement with management to reflect the change in the applicable financial reporting framework.

Responsibilities of Management and Those Charged with Governance (Ref: Para. 30(b), 37(e))

The financial statements subject to review are those of the entity, prepared by **A47** management of the entity with oversight from those charged with governance. This ISRE does not impose responsibilities on management and those charged with governance, nor does it override laws and regulations that govern their respective responsibilities. However, a review in accordance with this ISRE is conducted on the premise that management, and those charged with governance as appropriate, have acknowledged certain responsibilities that are fundamental to the conduct of the review. The review of the financial statements does not relieve management and those charged with governance of their responsibilities.

As part of its responsibility for the preparation of the financial statements, man- **A48** agement is required to exercise judgment in making accounting estimates that are reasonable in the circumstances, and to select and apply appropriate accounting policies. These judgments are made in the context of the applicable financial reporting framework.

Because of the significance of the preconditions for undertaking a review of financial **A49** statements, the practitioner is required under this ISRE to obtain the agreement of management that it understands its responsibilities before accepting a review engagement. The practitioner may obtain management's agreement either orally or in writing. However, management's agreement is subsequently recorded within the written terms of the engagement.

If management, and those charged with governance where appropriate, do not or **A50** will not acknowledge their responsibilities in relation to the financial statements, it is not appropriate to accept the engagement unless law or regulation requires the practitioner to do so. In circumstances where the practitioner is required to accept the review engagement, the practitioner may need to explain to management and those charged with governance, where different, the importance of these matters and the implications for the engagement.

Additional Considerations When the Wording of the Practitioner's Report Is Prescribed by Law or Regulation (Ref: Para. 34–35)

This ISRE requires the practitioner to not represent compliance with this ISRE **A51** unless the practitioner has complied with all the requirements of this ISRE that are relevant to the review engagement. Law or regulation may prescribe matters in relation to an engagement that would ordinarily cause the practitioner to decline the engagement were it possible to do so, for example, if:

- The practitioner considers that the financial reporting framework prescribed by law or regulation is not acceptable; or

- The prescribed layout or wording of the practitioner's report is in a form or in terms that are significantly different from the layout or wording required by this ISRE.

Under this ISRE, a review conducted in these situations does not comply with this ISRE and the practitioner cannot represent compliance with this ISRE in the report issued for the engagement. Notwithstanding that the practitioner is not permitted to represent compliance with this ISRE, the practitioner is, however, encouraged to apply this ISRE, including the reporting requirements, to the extent practicable. When appropriate to avoid misunderstanding, the practitioner may consider including a statement in the report that the review is not conducted in accordance with this ISRE.

Agreeing the Terms of Engagement

Engagement Letter or Other Form of Written Agreement (Ref: Para. 37)

A52   It is in the interests of both management and those charged with governance, and the practitioner, that the practitioner sends an engagement letter prior to performing the review engagement, to help avoid misunderstandings with respect to the engagement.

Form and content of the engagement letter

A53   The form and content of the engagement letter may vary for each engagement. In addition to including the matters required by this ISRE, an engagement letter may make reference to, for example:

- Arrangements concerning the involvement of other practitioners and experts in the review engagement.
- Arrangements to be made with the predecessor practitioner, if any, in the case of an initial engagement.
- The fact that a review engagement will not satisfy any statutory or third party requirements for an audit.
- The expectation that management will provide written representations to the practitioner.
- The agreement of management to inform the practitioner of facts that may affect the financial statements of which management may become aware during the period from the date of the practitioner's report to the date the financial statements are issued.
- A request for management to acknowledge receipt of the engagement letter and to agree to the terms of the engagement outlined therein.

Review of components of groups of entities

A54   The auditor of the financial statements of a group of entities may request that a practitioner perform a review of the financial information of a component entity of the group. Depending on the instructions of the group auditor, a review of the financial information of a component may be performed in accordance with this ISRE. The group auditor may also specify additional procedures to supplement the work done for the review performed under this ISRE. Where the practitioner conducting the review is the auditor of the component entity's financial statements, the review is not performed in accordance with this ISRE.

Responsibilities of management prescribed by law or regulation (Ref: Para. 37(e))

If, in the circumstances of the engagement, the practitioner concludes that it is not **A55** necessary to record certain terms of the engagement in an engagement letter, the practitioner is still required to seek the written agreement from management, and those charged with governance where appropriate, required under this ISRE that they acknowledge and understand their responsibilities set out in this ISRE. This written agreement may use the wording of the law or regulation if the law or regulation establishes responsibilities for management that are equivalent in effect to those described in this ISRE.

Illustrative Engagement Letter (Ref: Para. 37)

An illustrative engagement letter for a review engagement is set out in Appendix 1 to **A56** this ISRE.

Recurring Engagements (Ref: Para. 38)

The practitioner may decide not to send a new engagement letter or other written **A57** agreement each period. However, the following factors may indicate that it is appropriate to revise the terms of the review engagement or to remind management and those charged with governance, as appropriate, of the existing terms of the engagement:

- Any indication that management misunderstands the objective and scope of the review.
- Any revised or special terms of the engagement.
- A recent change of senior management of the entity.
- A significant change in ownership of the entity.
- A significant change in nature or size of the entity's business.
- A change in legal or regulatory requirements affecting the entity.
- A change in the applicable financial reporting framework.

Acceptance of a Change in the Terms of the Review Engagement

Request to Change the Terms of the Review Engagement (Ref: Para. 39)

A request from the entity for the practitioner to change the terms of the review **A58** engagement may result from factors including:

- A change in circumstances affecting the need for the service.
- Misunderstanding as to the nature of a review engagement as originally requested.
- A restriction on the scope of the review engagement, whether imposed by management or caused by other circumstances.

A change in circumstances that affects the entity's requirements or a mis- **A59** understanding concerning the nature of the service originally requested may be considered a reasonable basis for requesting a change to the terms of the review engagement.

In contrast, a change may not be considered reasonable if it appears that the change **A60** relates to information that is incorrect, incomplete or otherwise unsatisfactory. An example might be where the practitioner is unable to obtain sufficient appropriate evidence for a material item in the financial statements, and management asks for the engagement to be changed to a related services engagement to avoid the expression of a modified conclusion by the practitioner.

Request to Change the Nature of the Engagement (Ref: Para. 40)

A61   Before agreeing to change a review engagement to another type of engagement or related service, a practitioner who was engaged to perform a review in accordance with this ISRE may need to assess, in addition to the matters referred to in this ISRE, any legal or contractual implications of the change.

A62   If the practitioner concludes that there is reasonable justification to change the review engagement to another type of engagement or related service, the work performed in the review engagement to the date of change may be relevant to the changed engagement; however, the work required to be performed and the report to be issued would be those appropriate to the revised engagement. In order to avoid confusing the reader, the report on the other engagement or related service would not include reference to:

(a)   The original review engagement; or

(b)   Any procedures that may have been performed in the original review engagement, except where the review engagement is changed to an engagement to perform agreed-upon procedures and thus reference to the procedures performed is a normal part of the report.

Communication with Management and Those Charged with Governance (Ref: Para. 42)

A63   In a review engagement, the practitioner's communications with management and those charged with governance take the form of:

(a)   Inquiries the practitioner makes in the course of performing the procedures for the review; and

(b)   Other communications, in the context of having effective two-way communication to understand matters arising and to develop a constructive working relationship for the engagement.

A64   The appropriate timing for communications will vary with the circumstances of the engagement. Relevant factors include the significance and nature of the matter, and any action expected to be taken by management or those charged with governance. For example, it may be appropriate to communicate a significant difficulty encountered during the review as soon as practicable if management or those charged with governance are able to assist the practitioner to overcome the difficulty.

A65   Law or regulation may restrict the practitioner's communication of certain matters with those charged with governance. For example, law or regulation may specifically prohibit a communication, or other action, that might prejudice an investigation by an appropriate authority into an actual, or suspected, illegal act. In some circumstances, potential conflicts between the practitioner's obligations of confidentiality and obligations to communicate may be complex. In such cases, the practitioner may consider obtaining legal advice.

Communicating Matters Concerning the Review

A66   Matters to be communicated to management or those charged with governance, as appropriate, under this ISRE may include:

- New information, or a change in the practitioner's understanding of the entity and its environment as a result of performing procedures for the review in accordance with this ISRE (for example, if during the review it appears as though actual financial results are likely to be substantially different from the anticipated period-end financial results that were used initially to determine materiality for the financial statements as a whole).

The Practitioner's Understanding (Ref: Para. 45–46)

The practitioner uses professional judgment to determine the extent of the understanding of the entity and its environment required to perform the review of the entity's financial statements in accordance with this ISRE. The practitioner's primary consideration is whether the understanding obtained is sufficient to meet the practitioner's objectives for the engagement. The breadth and depth of the overall understanding that the practitioner obtains is less than that possessed by management.   **A75**

Obtaining an understanding of the entity and its environment is a continual dynamic process of gathering, updating and analyzing information throughout the review engagement. The practitioner's understanding is obtained and applied on an iterative basis throughout performance of the engagement, and is updated as changes in conditions and circumstances occur. Initial procedures for engagement acceptance and continuance at the time of commencement of a review engagement are based on the practitioner's preliminary understanding of the entity and of the engagement circumstances. In a continuing client relationship, the practitioner's understanding includes knowledge obtained from prior engagements performed by the practitioner in relation to the entity's financial statements and other financial information.   **A76**

The understanding establishes a frame of reference within which the practitioner plans and performs the review engagement, and exercises professional judgment throughout the engagement. Specifically, the understanding needs to be sufficient for the practitioner to be able to identify areas in the financial statements where material misstatements are likely to arise, to inform the practitioner's approach to designing and performing procedures to address those areas.   **A77**

In obtaining an understanding of the entity and its environment, and of the applicable financial reporting framework, the practitioner may also consider: **A78**

- Whether the entity is a component of a group of entities, or an associated entity of another entity.
- The complexity of the financial reporting framework.
- The entity's financial reporting obligations or requirements, and whether those obligations or requirements exist under applicable law or regulation or in the context of voluntary financial reporting arrangements established under formalized governance or accountability arrangements, for example, under contractual arrangements with third parties.
- Relevant provisions of laws and regulations that are generally recognized to have a direct effect on the determination of material amounts and disclosures in the financial statements, such as tax and pension laws and regulations.
- The level of development of the entity's management and governance structure regarding management and oversight of the entity's accounting records and financial reporting systems that underpin preparation of the financial statements. Smaller entities often have fewer employees, which may influence how management exercises oversight. For example, segregation of duties may not be practicable. However, in a small owner-managed entity, the owner-manager may be able to exercise more effective oversight than in a larger entity. This

oversight may compensate for the generally more limited opportunities for segregation of duties.

- The "tone at the top" and the entity's control environment through which the entity addresses risks relating to financial reporting and compliance with the entity's financial reporting obligations.
- The level of development and complexity of the entity's financial accounting and reporting systems and related controls through which the entity's accounting records and related information are maintained.
- The entity's procedures for recording, classifying and summarizing transactions, accumulating information for inclusion in the financial statements and related disclosures.
- The types of matters that required accounting adjustments in the entity's financial statements in prior periods.

Designing and Performing Procedures (Ref: Para. 47, 55)

A79   The planned nature, timing and extent of the procedures the practitioner considers are needed to obtain sufficient appropriate evidence as the basis for a conclusion on the financial statements as a whole are influenced by:

(a) The requirements of this ISRE; and
(b) Requirements established under applicable law or regulation, including additional reporting requirements contained in applicable laws or regulations.

A80   When the practitioner is engaged to review the financial statements of a group of entities, the planned nature, timing and extent of the procedures for the review are directed at achieving the practitioner's objectives for the review engagement stated in this ISRE, but in the context of the group financial statements.

A81   The requirements of this ISRE relating to designing and performing inquiry and analytical procedures, and procedures addressing specific circumstances, are designed to enable the practitioner to achieve the objectives specified in this ISRE. The circumstances of review engagements vary widely and, accordingly, there may be circumstances where the practitioner may consider it effective or efficient to design and perform other procedures. For example, if in the course of obtaining an understanding of the entity, the practitioner becomes aware of a significant contract the practitioner may choose to read the contract.

A82   The fact that the practitioner may deem it necessary to perform other procedures does not alter the practitioner's objective of obtaining limited assurance in relation to the financial statements as a whole.

Significant or Unusual Transactions

A83   The practitioner may consider, reviewing the accounting records with a view to identifying significant or unusual transactions that may require specific attention in the review.

Inquiry (Ref: Para. 46–48)

A84   In a review, inquiry includes seeking information of management and other persons within the entity, as the practitioner considers appropriate in the engagement circumstances. The practitioner may also extend inquiries to obtain non-financial data if appropriate. Evaluating the responses provided by management is integral to the inquiry process.

Depending on the engagement circumstances, inquiries may also include inquiries about:

- Actions taken at meetings of owners, those charged with governance and committees thereof, and proceedings at other meetings, if any, that affect the information and disclosures contained in the financial statements.
- Communications the entity has received, or expects to receive or obtain, from regulatory agencies.
- Matters arising in the course of applying other procedures. When performing further inquiries in relation to identified inconsistencies, the practitioner considers the reasonableness and consistency of management's responses in light of the results obtained from other procedures, and the practitioner's knowledge and understanding of the entity and the industry in which it operates.

A85

Evidence obtained through inquiry is often the principal source of evidence about management intent. However, information available to support management's intent may be limited. In that case, understanding management's past history of carrying out its stated intentions, management's stated reasons for choosing a particular course of action, and management's ability to pursue a specific course of action may provide relevant information to corroborate the evidence obtained through inquiry. Application of professional skepticism in evaluating responses provided by management is important to enable the practitioner to evaluate whether there are any matter(s) that would cause the practitioner to believe the financial statements may be materially misstated.

A86

Performing inquiry procedures assists the practitioner also in obtaining or updating the practitioner's understanding of the entity and its environment, to be able to identify areas where material misstatements are likely to arise in the financial statements.

A87

Inquiry about the entity's ability to continue as a going concern (Ref: Para. 48(f))

Often in smaller entities, management may not have prepared an assessment of the entity's ability to continue as a going concern, but instead may rely on knowledge of the business and anticipated future prospects. In these circumstances, it may be appropriate to discuss the medium and long-term prospects and financing of the entity with management, including consideration of whether management's contentions are not inconsistent with the practitioner's understanding of the entity.

A88

Analytical Procedures (Ref: Para. 46–47, 49)

In a review of financial statements, performing analytical procedures assists the practitioner in:

A89

- Obtaining or updating the practitioner's understanding of the entity and its environment, including to be able to identify areas where material misstatements are likely to arise in the financial statements.
- Identifying inconsistencies or variances from expected trends, values or norms in the financial statements such as the level of congruence of the financial statements with key data, including key performance indicators.
-    with key data, including key performance indicators.
-       ng corroborative evidence in relation to other inquiry or analytical
-       es already performed.
-          additional procedures when the practitioner becomes aware of
-          at cause the practitioner to believe that the financial statements may
-          y misstated. An example of such an additional procedure is a
-          nalysis of monthly revenue and cost figures across profit centers,

branches or other components of the entity, to provide evidence about financial information contained in line items or disclosures contained in the financial statements.

A90   Various methods may be used to perform analytical procedures. These methods range from performing simple comparisons to performing complex analysis using statistical techniques. The practitioner may, for example, apply analytical procedures to evaluate the financial information underlying the financial statements through analysis of plausible relationships among both financial and non-financial data, and assessment of results for consistency with expected values with a view to identifying relationships and individual items that appear unusual, or that vary from expected trends or values. The practitioner would compare recorded amounts, or ratios developed from recorded amounts, to expectations developed by the practitioner from information obtained from relevant sources. Examples of sources of information the practitioner often uses to develop expectations, depending on the engagement circumstances, include:

- Financial information for comparable prior period(s), taking known changes into account.
- Information about expected operating and financial results, such as budgets or forecasts including extrapolations from interim or annual data.
- Relationships among elements of financial information within the period.
- Information regarding the industry in which the entity operates, such as gross margin information, or comparison of the entity's ratio of sales to accounts receivable with industry averages or with other entities of comparable size in the same industry.
- Relationships of financial information with relevant non-financial information, such as payroll costs to number of employees.

A91   The practitioner's consideration of whether data to be used for analytical procedures are satisfactory for the intended purpose(s) of those procedures is based on the practitioner's understanding of the entity and its environment, and is influenced by the nature and source of the data, and by the circumstances in which the data are obtained. The following considerations may be relevant:

- Source of the information available. For example, information may be more reliable when it is obtained from independent sources outside the entity;
- Comparability of the information available. For example, broad industry data may need to be supplemented or be adjusted to be comparable to data of an entity that produces and sells specialized products;
- Nature and relevance of the information available; for example, whether the entity's budgets are established as results to be expected rather than as goals to be achieved; and
- The knowledge and expertise involved in the preparation of the information, and related controls that are designed to ensure its completeness, accuracy and validity.

Such controls may include, for example, controls over the preparation, review and maintenance of budgetary information.

Procedures to Address Specific Circumstances

Fraud and non-compliance with laws or regulations (Ref: Para. 52(d))

A92   Under this ISRE, if the practitioner has identified or suspects fraud or illegal acts practitioner is required to determine whether there is a responsibility to re occurrence or suspicion to a party outside the entity. Although the practitioner's professional duty to maintain the confidentiality of client information may preclude such reporting, the practitioner's legal responsibilities may override the duty of confidentiality in some circumstances.

Events or conditions that may cast doubt regarding use of the going concern assumption in the financial statements (Ref: Para. 54)

The list of factors below gives examples of events or conditions that, individually or **A93** collectively, may cast significant doubt about the going concern assumption. The list is not all-inclusive, and the existence of one or more of the items does not always signify that uncertainty exists about whether the entity can continue as a going concern.

Financial

- Net liability or net current liability position
- Fixed-term borrowings approaching maturity without realistic prospects of renewal or repayment, or excessive reliance on short-term borrowings to finance long-term assets
- Indications of withdrawal of financial support by creditors
- Negative operating cash flows indicated by historical or prospective financial statements
- Adverse key financial ratios
- Substantial operating losses or significant deterioration in the value of assets used to generate cash flows
- Arrears or discontinuance of dividends
- Inability to pay creditors on due dates
- Inability to comply with the terms of loan agreements
- Change from credit to cash-on-delivery transactions with suppliers
- Inability to obtain financing for essential new product development or other essential investments

Operating

- Management intentions to liquidate the entity or to cease operations
- Loss of key management without replacement
- Loss of a major market, key customer(s), franchise, license, or principal supplier(s)
- Labor difficulties
- Shortages of important supplies
- Emergence of a highly successful competitor

Other

- Non-compliance with capital or other statutory requirements
- Pending legal or regulatory proceedings against the entity that may, if successful, result in claims that the entity is unlikely to be able to satisfy
- Changes in law or regulation or government policy expected to adversely affect the entity
- Uninsured or underinsured catastrophes when they occur

The significance of such events or conditions often can be mitigated by other factors. For example, the effect of an entity being unable to make its normal debt repayments may be counter-balanced by management's plans to maintain adequate cash flows by alternative means, such as by disposing of assets, rescheduling loan repayments, or obtaining additional capital. Similarly, the loss of a principal supplier may be mitigated by the availability of a suitable alternative source of supply.

Reconciling the Financial Statements to the Underlying Accounting Records (Ref: Para. 56)

A94   The practitioner ordinarily obtains evidence that the financial statements agree with, or reconcile to, the underlying accounting records by tracing the financial statement amounts and balances to the relevant accounting records such as the general ledger, or to a summary record or schedule that reflects the agreement or reconciliation of the financial statement amounts with the underlying accounting records (such as a trial balance).

Performing Additional Procedures (Ref: Para. 57)

A95   Additional procedures are required under this ISRE if the practitioner becomes aware of a matter that causes the practitioner to believe the financial statements may be materially misstated.

A96   The practitioner's response in undertaking additional procedures with respect to an item the practitioner has cause to believe may be materially misstated in the financial statements will vary, depending on the circumstances, and is a matter for the practitioner's professional judgment.

A97   The practitioner's judgment about the nature, timing and extent of additional procedures that are needed to obtain evidence to either conclude that a material misstatement is not likely, or determine that a material misstatement exists, is guided by:

●   Information obtained from the practitioner's evaluation of the results of the procedures already performed;
●   The practitioner's updated understanding of the entity and its environment obtained throughout the course of the engagement; and
●   The practitioner's view on the persuasiveness of evidence needed to address the matter that causes the practitioner to believe that the financial statements may be materially misstated.

A98   Additional procedures focus on obtaining sufficient appropriate evidence to enable the practitioner to form a conclusion on matters that the practitioner believes may cause the financial statements to be materially misstated. The procedures may be:

●   Additional inquiry or analytical procedures, for example, being performed in greater detail or being focused on the affected items (i.e. amounts or disclosures concerning the affected accounts or transactions as reflected in the financial statements); or
●   Other types of procedures, for example, substantive test of details or external confirmations.

A99   The following example illustrates the practitioner's evaluation of the need to perform additional procedures, and the practitioner's response when the practitioner believes additional procedures are necessary.

●   In the course of performing the inquiry and analytical procedures for the review, the practitioner's analysis of accounts receivable shows a material amount of past due accounts receivable, for which there is no allowance for bad or doubtful debts.

- This causes the practitioner to believe that the accounts receivable balance in the financial statements may be materially misstated. The practitioner then inquires of management whether there are uncollectible accounts receivable that would need to be shown as being impaired.
- Depending on management's response, the practitioner's evaluation of the response may:
  - (a) Enable the practitioner to conclude that the accounts receivable balance is not likely to be materially misstated. In that case, no further procedures are required.
  - (b) Enable the practitioner to determine that the matter causes the financial statements to be materially misstated. No further procedures are required, and the practitioner would form the conclusion that the financial statements as a whole are materially misstated.
  - (c) Lead the practitioner to continue to believe that the accounts receivable balance is likely to be materially misstated, while not providing sufficient appropriate evidence for the practitioner to determine that they are in fact misstated. In that case, the practitioner is required to perform additional procedures, for example, requesting from management an analysis of amounts received for those accounts after the balance sheet date to identify uncollectible accounts receivable. The evaluation of the results of the additional procedures may enable the practitioner to get to (a) or (b) above. If not, the practitioner is required to:
    - (i) Continue performing additional procedures until the practitioner reaches either (a) or (b) above; or
    - (ii) If the practitioner is not able to either conclude that the matter is not likely to cause the financial statements as a whole to be materially misstated, or to determine that the matter does cause the financial statements as a whole to be materially misstated, then a scope limitation exists and the practitioner is not able to form an unmodified conclusion on the financial statements.

Written Representations (Ref: Para. 61–63)

Written representations are an important source of evidence in a review engagement. **A100** If management modifies or does not provide the requested written representations, it may alert the practitioner to the possibility that one or more significant issues may exist. Further, a request for written, rather than oral, representations in many cases may prompt management to consider such matters more rigorously, thereby enhancing the quality of the representations.

In addition to the written representations required under this ISRE, the practitioner **A101** may consider it necessary to request other written representations about the financial statements. These may be needed, for example, to complete the practitioner's evidence with respect to certain items or disclosures reflected in the financial statements where the practitioner considers such representations to be important in forming a conclusion on the financial statements on either a modified or unmodified basis.

In some cases, management may include in the written representations qualifying **A102** language to the effect that representations are made to the best of management's knowledge and belief. It is reasonable for the practitioner to accept such wording if the practitioner is satisfied that the representations are being made by those with appropriate responsibilities and knowledge of the matters included in the representations.

Evaluating Evidence Obtained from the Procedures Performed (Ref: Para. 66–68)

A103   In some circumstances, the practitioner may not have obtained the evidence that the practitioner had expected to obtain through the design of primarily inquiry and analytical procedures and procedures addressing specific circumstances. In these circumstances, the practitioner considers that the evidence obtained from the procedures performed is not sufficient and appropriate to be able to form a conclusion on the financial statements. The practitioner may:

● Extend the work performed; or
● Perform other procedures judged by the practitioner to be necessary in the circumstances.

Where neither of these is practicable in the circumstances, the practitioner will not be able to obtain sufficient appropriate evidence to be able to form a conclusion and is required by this ISRE to determine the effect on the practitioner's report, or on the practitioner's ability to complete the engagement, for example, if a member of management is unavailable at the time of the review to respond to the practitioner's inquiries on significant matters. This situation may arise even though the practitioner has not become aware of a matter(s) that causes the practitioner to believe the financial statements may be materially misstated, as addressed in paragraph 57.

Scope Limitations

A104   Inability to perform a specific procedure does not constitute a limitation on the scope of the review if the practitioner is able to obtain sufficient appropriate evidence by performing other procedures.

A105   Limitations on the scope of the review imposed by management may have other implications for the review, such as for the practitioner's consideration of areas where the financial statements are likely to be materially misstated, and engagement continuance.

Forming the Practitioner's Conclusion on the Financial Statements

Description of the Applicable Financial Reporting Framework (Ref: Para. 69(a))

A106   The description of the applicable financial reporting framework in the financial statements is important because it advises users of the financial statements of the framework on which the financial statements are based. If the financial statements are special purpose financial statements, they may be prepared under a special purpose financial reporting framework that is available only to the engaging party and the practitioner. Description of the special purpose financial reporting framework used is important as the special purpose financial statements may not be appropriate for any use other than the intended use identified for the special purpose financial statements.

A107   A description of the applicable financial reporting framework that contains imprecise qualifying or limiting language (for example, "the financial statements are in substantial compliance with International Financial Reporting Standards") is not an adequate description of that framework as it may mislead users of the financial statements.

Disclosure of Effects of Material Transactions and Events on Information Conveyed in the Financial Statements (Ref: Para. 69(b)(vi), 71)

The practitioner is required under this ISRE to evaluate whether the financial statements provide adequate disclosures to enable the intended users to understand the effect of material transactions and events on the entity's financial position, financial performance and cash flows. **A108**

In the case of financial statements prepared in accordance with the requirements of a fair presentation framework, management may need to include additional disclosures in the financial statements beyond those specifically required by the applicable financial reporting framework or, in extremely rare circumstances, to depart from a requirement in the framework, in order to achieve the fair presentation of the financial statements. **A109**

Considerations When a Compliance Framework Is Used

It will be extremely rare for the practitioner to consider financial statements prepared in accordance with a compliance framework to be misleading if, in accordance with this ISRE, the practitioner has determined at the time of engagement acceptance that the framework is acceptable. **A110**

Qualitative Aspects of the Entity's Accounting Practices (Ref: Para. 70(b))

In considering the qualitative aspects of the entity's accounting practices, the practitioner may become aware of possible bias in management's judgments. The practitioner may conclude that the cumulative effect of a lack of neutrality, together with the effect of apparent uncorrected misstatements, causes the financial statements as a whole to be materially misstated. Indicators of a lack of neutrality that may affect the practitioner's evaluation of whether the financial statements as a whole may be materially misstated include the following: **A111**

- The selective correction of apparent misstatements brought to management's attention during the review (for example, correcting misstatements with the effect of increasing reported earnings, but not correcting misstatements that have the effect of decreasing reported earnings).
- Possible management bias in the making of accounting estimates.

Indicators of possible management bias do not necessarily mean there are misstatements for purposes of drawing conclusions on the reasonableness of individual accounting estimates. They may, however, affect the practitioner's consideration of whether the financial statements as a whole may be materially misstated. **A112**

Form of the Conclusion (Ref: Para. 74)

Description of the Information the Financial Statements Present

In the case of financial statements prepared in accordance with a fair presentation framework, the practitioner's conclusion states that nothing has come to the practitioner's attention that causes the practitioner to believe that the financial statements do not present fairly, in all material respects, ... (or do not give a true and fair view of ...) in accordance with [the applicable fair presentation framework]. In the case of many general purpose frameworks, for example, the financial statements are required to fairly present (or give a true and fair view of) the financial position of the entity as **A113** at the end of a period, and the entity's financial performance and cash flows for that period.

"Present fairly, in all material respects" or "gives a true and fair view"

A114   Whether the phrase "present fairly, in all material respects," or the phrase "gives a true and fair view" is used in any particular jurisdiction is determined by the law or regulation governing the review of financial statements in that jurisdiction, or by generally accepted practice in that jurisdiction. Where law or regulation requires the use of different wording, this does not affect the requirement in this ISRE for the practitioner to evaluate the fair presentation of financial statements prepared in accordance with a fair presentation framework.

Inability to Form a Conclusion Due to a Management-Imposed Limitation on the Scope of the Review after Engagement Acceptance (Ref: Para. 15, 82)

A115   The practicality of withdrawing from the engagement may depend on the stage of completion of the engagement at the time that management imposes the scope limitation. If the practitioner has substantially completed the review, the practitioner may decide to complete the review to the extent possible, disclaim a conclusion and explain the scope limitation in the paragraph in the report that describes the basis for disclaiming a conclusion.

A116   In certain circumstances, withdrawal from the engagement may not be possible if the practitioner is required by law or regulation to continue the engagement. For example, this may be the case for a practitioner appointed to review the financial statements of a public sector entity. It may also be the case in jurisdictions where the practitioner is appointed to review the financial statements covering a specific period, or appointed for a specific period,

and is prohibited from withdrawing before the completion of the review of those financial statements or before the end of that period, respectively. The practitioner may also consider it necessary to include an Other Matter paragraph in the practitioner's report to explain why it is not possible for the practitioner to withdraw from the engagement.

Communication with Regulators or the Entity's Owners

A117   When the practitioner concludes that withdrawal from the engagement is necessary because of a scope limitation, there may be a professional, legal or regulatory requirement for the practitioner to communicate matters relating to the withdrawal from the engagement to regulators or the entity's owners.

The Practitioner's Report (Ref: Para. 86–92)

A118   The written report encompasses reports issued in hard copy format and those using an electronic medium.

Elements of the Practitioner's Report (Ref: Para. 86)

A119   A title indicating the report is the report of an independent practitioner, for example, "Independent Practitioner's Review Report," affirms that the practitioner has met all of the relevant ethical requirements regarding independence and, therefore, distinguishes the independent practitioner's report from reports issued by others.

Law or regulation may specify to whom the practitioner's report is to be addressed in that particular jurisdiction. The practitioner's report is normally addressed to those for whom the report is prepared, often either to the shareholders or to those charged with governance of the entity whose financial statements are being reviewed. **A120**

When the practitioner is aware that the financial statements that have been reviewed will be included in a document that contains other information, such as a financial report, the practitioner may consider, if the form of presentation allows, identifying the page numbers on which the financial statements that have been reviewed are presented. This helps users to identify the financial statements to which the practitioner's report relates. **A121**

Management's Responsibility for the Financial Statements (Ref: Para. 86(d))

The requirement of this ISRE that the practitioner must obtain management's agreement that it acknowledges and understands its responsibilities, both in relation to the preparation of the financial statements and in relation to the review engagement, is fundamental to performing the review and reporting on the engagement. The description of management's responsibilities in the practitioner's report provides context for readers of the practitioner's report about management's responsibilities, as they relate to the review engagement performed. **A122**

The practitioner's report need not refer specifically to "management" but instead may use the term that is appropriate in the context of the legal framework in the particular jurisdiction. In some jurisdictions, the appropriate reference is to those charged with governance of the entity. **A123**

There may be circumstances when it is appropriate for the practitioner to add to the description of management's responsibilities as described in this ISRE to reflect additional responsibilities that are relevant to the preparation of the financial statements in the context of a jurisdiction, or due to the type of entity. **A124**

In some jurisdictions, law or regulation prescribing management's responsibilities may specifically refer to a responsibility for the adequacy of the accounting books and records, or accounting system. As books, records and systems are an integral part of internal control, this ISRE does not use these descriptions or make any specific reference to them. **A125**

The Practitioner's Responsibility (Ref: Para. 86(f))

The practitioner's report states that the practitioner's responsibility is to express a conclusion on the financial statements based on the review performed, in order to contrast the practitioner's responsibility with management's responsibility for preparation of the financial statements. **A126**

Reference to standards (Ref: Para. 86(f))

The reference to the standards used by the practitioner for the review conveys to the users of the practitioner's report that the review has been conducted in accordance with established standards. **A127**

Communication of the Nature of a Review of Financial Statements (Ref: Para. 86(g))

A128   The description of the nature of a review engagement in the practitioner's report explains the scope and limitations of the engagement undertaken for the benefit of the readers of the report. This explanation clarifies, for avoidance of doubt, that the review is not an audit and that accordingly, the practitioner does not express an audit opinion on the financial statements.

Description of the Applicable Financial Reporting Framework and How It May Affect the Practitioner's Conclusion (Ref: Para. 86(i)(ii))

A129   The identification of the applicable financial reporting framework in the practitioner's conclusion is intended to advise users of the practitioner's report of the context in which that conclusion is expressed. It is not intended to limit the evaluation required in paragraph 30(a). The applicable financial reporting framework is identified in such terms as:

"... in accordance with International Financial Reporting Standards;" or

"... in accordance with accounting principles generally accepted in Jurisdiction X ..."

A130   When the applicable financial reporting framework encompasses financial reporting standards and legal or regulatory requirements, the framework is identified in such terms as "... in accordance with International Financial Reporting Standards and the requirements of Jurisdiction X Corporations Act."

Basis for Modification Paragraph When the Conclusion Is Modified (Ref: Para. 85(h)(ii))

A131   An adverse conclusion or a disclaimer of conclusion relating to a specific matter described in the basis for modification paragraph does not justify the omission of a description of other identified matters that would have otherwise required a modification of the practitioner's conclusion. In such cases, the disclosure of such other matters of which the practitioner is aware may be relevant to users of the financial statements.

Signature of the Practitioner (Ref: Para. 86(l))

A132   The practitioner's signature is either in the name of the practitioner's firm, the personal name of the individual practitioner, or both, as appropriate for the particular jurisdiction. In addition to the practitioner's signature, in certain jurisdictions, the practitioner may be required to make a declaration in the practitioner's report about professional designations or recognition by the appropriate licensing authority in that jurisdiction.

Alerting Readers that the Financial Statements Are Prepared in Accordance with a Special Purpose Framework (Ref: Para. 88)

A133   The special purpose financial statements may be used for purposes other than those for which they were intended. For example, a regulator may require certain entities to place the special purpose financial statements on public record. For avoidance of misunderstanding, it is important that the practitioner alert users of the practitioner's report that the financial statements are prepared in accordance with a special purpose framework and, therefore, may not be suitable for another purpose.

Restriction on Distribution or Use

In addition to the alert to the reader of the practitioner's report that is required by   **A134**
this ISRE when the financial statements are prepared using a special purpose framework, the practitioner may consider it appropriate to indicate that the
practitioner's report is intended solely for the specific users. Depending on the law or
regulation of the particular jurisdiction, this may be achieved by restricting the
distribution or use of the practitioner's report. In these circumstances, the paragraph
containing the alert about the use of a special purpose framework may be expanded
to include these other matters, and the heading modified accordingly.

Other Reporting Responsibilities (Ref: Para. 91)

In some jurisdictions, the practitioner may have additional responsibilities to report   **A135**
on other matters that are supplementary to the practitioner's responsibility under
this ISRE. For example, the practitioner may be asked to report certain matters if
they come to the practitioner's attention during the course of the review of the
financial statements. Alternatively, the practitioner may be asked to perform and
report on additional specified procedures, or to express a conclusion on specific
matters, such as the adequacy of accounting books and records. Standards on
engagements to review financial statements in the specific jurisdiction may provide
guidance on the practitioner's responsibilities with respect to specific additional
reporting responsibilities in that jurisdiction.

In some cases, the relevant law or regulation may require or permit the practitioner   **A136**
to report on these other responsibilities within the practitioner's report on the
financial statements. In other cases, the practitioner may be required or permitted to
report on them in a separate report.

These other reporting responsibilities are addressed in a separate section of the   **A137**
practitioner's report, to clearly distinguish them from the practitioner's responsibility
under this ISRE to report on the financial statements. Where relevant, this section
may contain sub-heading(s) that describe(s) the content of the other reporting
responsibility paragraph(s). In some jurisdictions, the additional reporting responsibilities may be addressed in a report that is separate from the practitioner's report
provided for the review of the financial statements.

Date of the Practitioner's Report (Ref: Para. 86(k), 92)

The date of the practitioner's report informs the user of the practitioner's report that   **A138**
the practitioner has considered the effect of events and transactions of which the
practitioner became aware and that occurred up to that date.

The practitioner's conclusion is provided on the financial statements and the   **A139**
financial statements are the responsibility of management. The practitioner is not in
a position to conclude that sufficient appropriate evidence has been obtained until
the practitioner is satisfied that all the statements that comprise the financial statements, including the related notes, have been prepared and management has
accepted responsibility for them.

In some jurisdictions, law or regulation identifies the individuals or bodies (for   **A140**
example, the directors) that are responsible for concluding that all the statements
that comprise the financial statements, including the related notes, have been prepared, and specifies the necessary approval process. In such cases, evidence is
obtained of that approval before dating the report on the financial statements. In

other jurisdictions, however, the approval process is not prescribed in law or regulation. In such cases, the procedures the entity follows in preparing and finalizing its financial statements in view of its management and governance structures are considered in order to identify the individuals or body with the authority to conclude that all the statements that comprise the financial statements, including the related notes, have been prepared. In some cases, law or regulation may identify the point in the financial statement reporting process at which the review is expected to be complete.

A141   In some jurisdictions, final approval of the financial statements by shareholders is required before the financial statements are issued publicly. In these jurisdictions, final approval by shareholders is not necessary for the practitioner to conclude on the financial statements. The date of approval of the financial statements for purposes of this ISRE is the earlier date on which those with the recognized authority determine that all the statements that comprise the financial statements, including the related notes, have been prepared and that those with the recognized authority have asserted that they have taken responsibility for them.

Practitioner's Report Prescribed by Law or Regulation (Ref: Para. 34–35, 86)

A142   Consistency in the practitioner's report, when the review has been conducted in accordance with this ISRE, promotes credibility in the global marketplace by making more readily identifiable those reviews of financial statements that have been conducted in accordance with globally recognized standards. The practitioner's report may refer to this ISRE when the differences between the legal or regulatory requirements and this ISRE relate only to the layout or wording of the practitioner's report and, at a minimum, the report complies with the requirements of paragraph 86 of this ISRE. Accordingly, in such circumstances the practitioner is considered to have complied with the requirements of this ISRE, even when the layout and wording used in the practitioner's report are specified by legal or regulatory reporting requirements. Where specific requirements in a particular jurisdiction do not conflict with this ISRE, adoption of the layout and wording used in this ISRE assists users of the practitioner's report to more readily recognize the practitioner's report as a report on a review of financial statements conducted in accordance with this ISRE. Circumstances where law or regulation prescribes the layout or wording of the practitioner's report in terms that are significantly different from the requirements of this ISRE are addressed in the requirements of this ISRE concerning acceptance of review engagements and continuance of client relationships.

Practitioner's Report for Reviews Conducted in Accordance with Both Relevant Standards of a Specific Jurisdiction and this ISRE (Ref: Para. 86(f))

A143   When, in addition to complying with the requirements of this ISRE, the practitioner also complies with relevant national standards, the report may refer to the review having been performed in accordance with both this ISRE and relevant national standards for engagements to review financial statements. However, a reference to both this ISRE and relevant national standards is not appropriate if there is a conflict between the requirements of this ISRE and those in the relevant national standards that would lead the practitioner to form a different conclusion or not to include an Emphasis of Matter paragraph that, in the particular circumstances, would be required by this ISRE. In such a case, the practitioner's report refers only to the relevant standards (either this ISRE or the relevant national standards) in accordance with which the practitioner's report has been prepared.

Illustrative Review Reports (Ref: Para. 86)

Appendix 2 to this ISRE contains illustrations of practitioners' reports for a review **A144** of financial statements incorporating the reporting requirements of this ISRE.

Documentation

Timeliness of Engagement Documentation (Ref: Para. 93)

ISQC 1 requires the firm to establish time limits that reflect the need to complete the **A145** assembly of final engagement files on a timely basis.

Appendix 1 (Ref: Para. A56)

Illustrative Engagement Letter for an Engagement to Review Historical Financial Statements

The following is an example of an engagement letter for a review of general purpose financial statements (prepared in accordance with International Financial Reporting Standards (IFRSs)), which illustrates the relevant requirements and guidance contained in this ISRE. This letter is not authoritative but is intended only to be a guide that may be used in conjunction with the considerations outlined in this ISRE. It will need to be varied according to individual requirements and circumstances. It is drafted to refer to the review of financial statements for a single reporting period and would require adaptation if intended or expected to apply to recurring reviews. It may be appropriate to seek legal advice that any proposed letter is suitable.

***

To the appropriate representative of management or those charged with governance of ABC Company:[11]

[*The objective and scope of the review*]

You[12] have requested that we review the general purpose financial statements of ABC Company, which comprise the statement of financial position as at December 31, 20X1, and the statement of comprehensive income, statement of changes in equity and cash flow statement for the year then ended, and a summary of significant accounting policies and other explanatory information. We are pleased to confirm our acceptance and our understanding of this review engagement by means of this letter.

Our review will be conducted with the objective of expressing our conclusion on the financial statements. Our conclusion, if unmodified, will be in the form "Based on our review, nothing has come to our attention that causes us to believe that these financial statements do not present fairly, in all material respects, (*or do not give a true and fair view of*) the financial position of the company as at [date] and (*of*) its

---

[11] *The addressees and references in the letter would be those that are appropriate in the circumstances of the engagement, including the relevant jurisdiction. It is important to refer to the appropriate persons—see paragraph 36 of this ISRE.*

[12] *Throughout this letter, references to "you," "we," "us," "management," "those charged with governance" and "practitioner" would be used or amended as appropriate in the circumstances.*

financial performance and cash flows for the year then ended in accordance with International Financial Reporting Standards (IFRSs)."

[*The practitioner's responsibilities*]

We will conduct our review in accordance with International Standard on Review Engagements (ISRE) 2400 (Revised), *Engagements to Review Historical Financial Statements*. ISRE 2400 (Revised) requires us to conclude whether anything has come to our attention that causes us to believe that the financial statements, taken as a whole, are not prepared in all material respects in accordance with the applicable financial reporting framework. ISRE 2400 also requires us to comply with relevant ethical requirements.

A review of financial statements in accordance with ISRE 2400 (Revised) is a limited assurance engagement. We will perform procedures, primarily consisting of making inquiries of management and others within the entity, as appropriate, and applying analytical procedures, and evaluate the evidence obtained. We will also perform additional procedures if we become aware of matters that cause us to believe the financial statements as a whole may be materially misstated. These procedures are performed to enable us to express our conclusion on the financial statements in accordance with ISRE 2400 (Revised). The procedures selected will depend on what we consider necessary applying our professional judgment, based on our under-standing of ABC Company and its environment, and our understanding of IFRSs and its application in the industry context.

A review is not an audit of the financial statements, therefore:

(a) There is a commensurate higher risk than there would be in an audit, that any material misstatements that exist in the financial statements reviewed may not be revealed by the review, even though the review is properly performed in accordance with ISRE 2400 (Revised).

(b) In expressing our conclusion from the review of the financial statements, our report on the financial statements will expressly disclaim any audit opinion on the financial statements.

[*The responsibilities of management and identification of the applicable financial reporting framework (for purposes of this example, it is assumed that the practitioner has not determined that the law or regulation prescribes those responsibilities in appropriate terms; the descriptions in paragraph 30(b) of this ISRE are therefore used).*]

Our review will be conducted on the basis that [management and, where appropriate, those charged with governance][13] acknowledge and understand that they have the responsibility:

(a) For preparation and fair presentation of the financial statements in accordance with IFRSs;[14]

(b) For such internal control as management determines is necessary to enable the preparation of financial statements that are free from material misstatement, whether due to fraud or error; and

(c) To provide us with:

---

[13] *Use terminology as appropriate in the circumstances.*

[14] *Or, if appropriate, "For the preparation of financial statements that give a true and fair view in accordance with IFRSs".*

(i)   Access to all information of which management is aware that is relevant to the preparation and fair presentation of the financial statements, such as records, documentation and other matters;

(ii)   Additional information that we may request from management for the purpose of the review; and

(iii)   Unrestricted access to persons within ABC Company from whom we determine it necessary to obtain evidence.

As part of our review, we will request from [management and, where appropriate, those charged with governance], written confirmation concerning representations made to us in connection with the review.

We look forward to full cooperation from your staff during our review.

[*Other relevant information*]

[*Insert other information, such as fee arrangements, billings and other specific terms, as appropriate.*]

[*Reporting*]

[*Insert appropriate reference to the expected form and content of the practitioner's report.*]

The form and content of our report may need to be amended in the light of our findings obtained from the review.

Please sign and return the attached copy of this letter to indicate your acknowledgement of, and agreement with, the arrangements for our review of the financial statements including our respective responsibilities.

XYZ & Co.

Acknowledged and agreed on behalf of ABC Company by

(signed)

....

Name and Title

Date

Appendix 2 (Ref: Para. A144)

Illustrative Practitioners' Review Reports

Review Reports on General Purpose Financial Statements
Illustrative Review Reports with Unmodified Conclusions

- Illustration 1:   A practitioner's report on financial statements prepared in accordance with a fair presentation framework designed to meet the common financial information needs of a wide range of users (for example, the International Financial Reporting Standard for Small and Medium-sized Entities).

Illustrative Review Reports with Modified Conclusions

- Illustration 2:   A practitioner's report containing a qualified conclusion due to an apparent material misstatement of the financial statements. Financial statements prepared in accordance with a compliance framework designed to meet the common information needs of a wide range of users. (Financial statements prepared using a compliance framework)
- Illustration 3:   A practitioner's report containing a qualified conclusion due to the practitioner's inability to obtain sufficient appropriate evidence. (Financial statements prepared using a fair presentation framework—IFRSs)
- Illustration 4:   A practitioner's report containing an adverse conclusion due to material misstatement of the financial statements. (Financial statements prepared using a fair presentation framework—IFRSs)
- Illustration 5:   A practitioner's report containing a disclaimer of conclusion due to the practitioner's inability to obtain sufficient appropriate evidence about multiple elements of the financial statements—resulting in inability to complete the review. (Financial statements prepared using a fair presentation framework—IFRSs)

Review Reports on Special Purpose Financial Statements

- Illustration 6:   A practitioner's report on financial statements prepared in accordance with the financial reporting provisions of a contract (for purposes of this illustration, a compliance framework).
- Illustration 7:   A practitioner's report on a single financial statement prepared in accordance with the cash receipts and disbursements basis of accounting (for purposes of this illustration, a fair presentation framework).

Illustration 1

Circumstances include the following:

- Review of a complete set of financial statements.

- The financial statements are prepared for a general purpose by management of the entity in accordance with the International Financial Reporting Standard for Small and Medium-sized Entities.

- The terms of the review engagement reflect the description of management's responsibility for the financial statements in paragraph 30(b) of this ISRE.

- In addition to the review of the financial statements, the practitioner has other reporting responsibilities under local law.

INDEPENDENT PRACTITIONER'S REVIEW REPORT

[Appropriate Addressee]

Report on the Financial Statements[15]

We have reviewed the accompanying financial statements of ABC Company, which comprise the statement of financial position as at December 31, 20X1, and the statement of comprehensive income, statement of changes in equity and statement of cash flows for the year then ended, and a summary of significant accounting policies and other explanatory information.

Management's[16] Responsibility for the Financial Statements

Management is responsible for the preparation and fair presentation of these financial statements in accordance with the International Financial Reporting Standard for Small and Medium-sized Entities,[17] and for such internal control as management determines is necessary to enable the preparation of financial statements that are free from material misstatement, whether due to fraud or error.

Practitioner's Responsibility

Our responsibility is to express a conclusion on the accompanying financial statements. We conducted our review in accordance with International Standard on Review Engagements (ISRE) 2400 (Revised), *Engagements to Review Historical Financial Statements*. ISRE 2400 (Revised) requires us to conclude whether anything has come to our attention that causes us to believe that the financial statements, taken as a whole, are not prepared in all material respects in accordance with the applicable financial reporting framework. This Standard also requires us to comply with relevant ethical requirements.

---

[15] *The sub-title "Report on the Financial Statements" is unnecessary in circumstances when the second sub-title "Report on Other Legal and Regulatory Requirements" is not applicable.*

[16] *Or other term that is appropriate in the context of the legal framework in the particular jurisdiction.*

[17] *Where management's responsibility is to prepare financial statements that give a true and fair view, this may read: "Management is responsible for the preparation of financial statements that give a true and fair view in accordance with the International Financial Reporting Standard for Small and Medium-sized Entities, and for such ...".*

A review of financial statements in accordance with ISRE 2400 (Revised) is a limited assurance engagement. The practitioner performs procedures, primarily consisting of making inquiries of management and others within the entity, as appropriate, and applying analytical procedures, and evaluates the evidence obtained.

The procedures performed in a review are substantially less than those performed in an audit conducted in accordance with International Standards on Auditing. Accordingly, we do not express an audit opinion on these financial statements.

Conclusion

Based on our review, nothing has come to our attention that causes us to believe that these financial statements do not present fairly, in all material respects, (or *do not give a true and fair view of*) the financial position of ABC Company as at December 31, 20X1, and (*of*) its financial performance and cash flows for the year then ended, in accordance with the International Financial Reporting Standard for Small and Medium-sized Entities.

Report on Other Legal and Regulatory Requirements

[Form and content of this section of the practitioner's report will vary depending on the nature of the practitioner's other reporting responsibilities.]

[Practitioner's signature]

[Date of the practitioner's report]

[Practitioner's address]

Illustration 2

Circumstances include the following:

● Review of a complete set of financial statements required by law or regulation.

● The financial statements are prepared for a general purpose by management of the entity in accordance with the Financial Reporting Framework (XYZ Law) of Jurisdiction X (that is, a financial reporting framework, encompassing law or regulation, designed to meet the common financial information needs of a wide range of users, but which is not a fair presentation framework).

● The terms of the review engagement reflect the description of management's responsibility for the financial statements in paragraph 30(b) of this ISRE.

● Based on the review, inventories are misstated. The misstatement is material but not pervasive to the financial statements.

● In addition to the review of the financial statements, the practitioner has other reporting responsibilities under local law.

INDEPENDENT PRACTITIONER'S REVIEW REPORT

[Appropriate Addressee]

Report on the Financial Statements[18]

We have reviewed the accompanying financial statements of ABC Company, which comprise the statement of financial position as at December 31, 20X1, and the statement of comprehensive income, statement of changes in equity and statement of cash flows for the year then ended, and a summary of significant accounting policies and other explanatory information.

Management's[19] Responsibility for the Financial Statements

Management is responsible for the preparation of these financial statements in accordance with XYZ Law of Jurisdiction X, and for such internal control as management determines is necessary to enable the preparation of financial statements that are free from material misstatement, whether due to fraud or error.

Practitioner's Responsibility

Our responsibility is to express a conclusion on the accompanying financial statements. We conducted our review in accordance with International Standard on Review Engagements (ISRE) 2400 (Revised), *Engagements to Review Historical Financial Statements*. ISRE 2400 (Revised) requires us to conclude whether anything has come to our attention that causes us to believe that the financial statements, taken as a whole, are not prepared in all material respects in accordance with the applicable financial reporting framework. This Standard also requires us to comply with relevant ethical requirements.

---

[18] *The sub-title "Report on the Financial Statements" is unnecessary in circumstances when the second sub-title "Report on Other Legal and Regulatory Requirements" is not applicable.*

[19] *Or other term that is appropriate in the context of the legal framework in the particular jurisdiction.*

A review of financial statements in accordance with ISRE 2400 (Revised) is a limited assurance engagement. The practitioner performs procedures, primarily consisting of making inquiries of management and others within the entity, as appropriate, and applying analytical procedures, and evaluates the evidence obtained.

The procedures performed in a review are substantially less than those performed in an audit conducted in accordance with International Standards on Auditing. Accordingly, we do not express an audit opinion on these financial statements.

Basis for Qualified Conclusion

The company's inventories are carried in the statement of financial position at xxx. Management has not stated the inventories at the lower of cost and net realizable value but has stated them solely at cost, which constitutes a departure from the requirements of the Financial Reporting Framework (XYZ Law) of Jurisdiction X. The company's records indicate that, had management stated the inventories at the lower of cost and net realizable value, an amount of xxx would have been required to write the inventories down to their net realizable value. Accordingly, cost of sales would have been increased by xxx, and income tax, net income and shareholders' equity would have been reduced by xxx, xxx and xxx, respectively.

Qualified Conclusion

Based on our review, except for the effects of the matter described in the Basis for Qualified Conclusion paragraph, nothing has come to our attention that causes us to believe that the financial statements of ABC Company are not prepared, in all material respects, in accordance with the Financial Reporting Framework (XYZ Law) of Jurisdiction X.

Report on Other Legal and Regulatory Requirements

[Form and content of this section of the practitioner's report will vary depending on the nature of the practitioner's other reporting responsibilities.]

[Practitioner's signature]

[Date of the practitioner's report]

[Practitioner's address]

Illustration 3

Circumstances include the following:

- Review of a complete set of general purpose financial statements prepared by management of the entity in accordance with [a financial reporting framework designed to achieve fair presentation other than International Financial Reporting Standards].

- The terms of the review engagement reflect the description of management's responsibility for the financial statements in paragraph 30(b) of this ISRE.

- The practitioner was unable to obtain sufficient appropriate evidence regarding an investment in a foreign affiliate. The possible effects of the inability to obtain sufficient appropriate evidence are deemed to be material but not pervasive to the financial statements.

- The practitioner does not have other reporting responsibilities under local law in addition to the review of the consolidated financial statements.

INDEPENDENT PRACTITIONER'S REVIEW REPORT

[Appropriate Addressee]

We have reviewed the accompanying financial statements of ABC Company, which comprise the statement of financial position as at December 31, 20X1, and the statement of comprehensive income, statement of changes in equity and statement of cash flows for the year then ended, and a summary of significant accounting policies and other explanatory information.

Management's[20] Responsibility for the Financial Statements

Management is responsible for the preparation and fair presentation of these financial statements in accordance with [name of applicable financial reporting framework, including a reference to the jurisdiction or country of origin of the financial reporting framework when the financial reporting framework used is not International Financial Reporting Standards],[21] and for such internal control as management determines is necessary to enable the preparation of financial statements that are free from material misstatement, whether due to fraud or error.

Practitioner's Responsibility

Our responsibility is to express a conclusion on the accompanying financial statements. We conducted our review in accordance with International Standard on Review Engagements (ISRE) 2400 (Revised), *Engagements to Review Historical Financial Statements*. ISRE 2400 (Revised) requires us to conclude whether anything has come to our attention that causes us to believe that the financial statements, taken as a whole, are not prepared in all material respects in accordance with the

---

[20] *Or other term that is appropriate in the context of the legal framework in the particular jurisdiction.*

[21] *Where management's responsibility is to prepare financial statements that give a true and fair view, this may read: "Management is responsible for the preparation of financial statements that give a true and fair view in accordance with [name of applicable financial reporting framework, including a reference to the jurisdiction or country of origin of the financial reporting framework when the financial reporting framework used is not International Financial Reporting Standards], and for such ...".*

applicable financial reporting framework. This Standard also requires us to comply with relevant ethical requirements.

A review of financial statements in accordance with ISRE 2400 (Revised) is a limited assurance engagement. The practitioner performs procedures, primarily consisting of making inquiries of management and others within the entity, as appropriate, and applying analytical procedures, and evaluates the evidence obtained.

The procedures performed in a review are substantially less than those performed in an audit conducted in accordance with International Standards on Auditing. Accordingly, we do not express an audit opinion on these financial statements.

Basis for Qualified Conclusion

ABC Company's investment in XYZ Company, a foreign associate acquired during the year and accounted for by the equity method, is carried at xxx on the statement of financial position as at December 31, 20X1, and ABC's share of XYZ's net income of xxx is included in ABC's income for the year then ended. We were unable to obtain access to the relevant financial information of XYZ concerning the carrying amount of ABC's investment in XYZ as at December 31, 20X1 and ABC's share of XYZ's net income for the year. Consequently, we were unable to perform the procedures we considered necessary.

Qualified Conclusion

Based on our review, except for the possible effects of the matter described in the Basis for Qualified Conclusion paragraph, nothing has come to our attention that causes us to believe that the accompanying financial statements do not present fairly, in all material respects, (or *do not give a true and fair view of*) the financial position of ABC Company as at December 31, 20X1, and (*of*) its financial performance and cash flows for the year then ended in accordance with [name of applicable financial reporting framework, including a reference to the jurisdiction or country of origin of the financial reporting framework when the financial reporting framework used is not International Financial Reporting Standards].

[Practitioner's signature]

[Date of the practitioner's report]

[Practitioner's address]

Illustration 4

Circumstances include the following:

- Review of consolidated general purpose financial statements prepared by management of the parent in accordance with International Financial Reporting Standards.

- The terms of the review engagement reflect the description of management's responsibility for the financial statements in paragraph 30(b) of this ISRE.

- The financial statements are materially misstated due to the non-consolidation of a subsidiary. The material misstatement is deemed to be pervasive to the financial statements. The effects of the misstatement on the financial statements have not been determined because it was not practicable to do so.

- The practitioner does not have other reporting responsibilities under local law in addition to the review of the consolidated financial statements.

INDEPENDENT PRACTITIONER'S REVIEW REPORT

[Appropriate Addressee]

Report on the Consolidated Financial Statements[22]

We have reviewed the accompanying consolidated financial statements of ABC Company, which comprise the consolidated statement of financial position as at December 31, 20X1, and the consolidated statement of comprehensive income, statement of changes in equity and statement of cash flows for the year then ended, and a summary of significant accounting policies and other explanatory information.

Management's[23] Responsibility for the Financial Statements

Management is responsible for the preparation and fair presentation of these consolidated financial statements in accordance with International Financial Reporting Standards,[24] and for such internal control as management determines is necessary to enable the preparation of consolidated financial statements that are free from material misstatement, whether due to fraud or error.

Practitioner's Responsibility

Our responsibility is to express a conclusion on the accompanying consolidated financial statements. We conducted our review in accordance with International Standard on Review Engagements (ISRE) 2400 (Revised), *Engagements to Review Historical Financial Statements*. ISRE 2400 (Revised) requires us to conclude whether anything has come to our attention that causes us to believe that the consolidated financial statements, taken as a whole, are not prepared in all material

---

[22] *The sub-title "Report on the Consolidated Financial Statements" is unnecessary in circumstances when the second sub-title "Report on Other Legal and Regulatory Requirements" is not applicable.*

[23] *Or other term that is appropriate in the context of the legal framework in the particular jurisdiction.*

[24] *Where management's responsibility is to prepare financial statements that give a true and fair view, this may read: "Management is responsible for the preparation of financial statements that give a true and fair view in accordance with International Financial Reporting Standards, and for such ...".*

respects in accordance with the applicable financial reporting framework. This Standard also requires us to comply with relevant ethical requirements.

A review of consolidated financial statements in accordance with ISRE 2400 (Revised) is a limited assurance engagement. The practitioner performs procedures, primarily consisting of making inquiries of management and others within the entity, as appropriate, and applying analytical procedures, and evaluates the evidence obtained.

The procedures performed in a review are substantially less than those performed in an audit conducted in accordance with International Standards on Auditing. Accordingly, we do not express an audit opinion on these consolidated financial statements.

Basis for Adverse Conclusion

As explained in Note X, the company has not consolidated the financial statements of subsidiary XYZ Company it acquired during 20X1 because it has not yet been able to ascertain the fair values of certain of the subsidiary's material assets and liabilities at the acquisition date. This investment is therefore accounted for on a cost basis. Under International Financial Reporting Standards, the subsidiary should have been consolidated because it is controlled by the company. Had XYZ been consolidated, many elements in the accompanying financial statements would have been materially affected.

Adverse Conclusion

Based on our review, due to the significance of the matter discussed in the Basis for Adverse Conclusion paragraph, the consolidated financial statements do not present fairly (or *do not give a true and fair view of*) the financial position of ABC Company and its subsidiaries as at December 31, 20X1, and (*of*) their financial performance and cash flows for the year then ended in accordance with International Financial Reporting Standards.

Report on Other Legal and Regulatory Requirements

[Form and content of this section of the practitioner's report will vary depending on the nature of the practitioner's other reporting responsibilities.]

[Practitioner's signature]

[Date of the practitioner's report]

[Practitioner's address]

Illustration 5

Circumstances include the following:

- Review of a complete set of general purpose financial statements prepared by management of the entity in accordance with International Financial Reporting Standards.

- The terms of the review engagement reflect the description of management's responsibility for the financial statements in paragraph 30(b) of this ISRE.

- The practitioner was unable to form a conclusion on the financial statements, due to inability to obtain sufficient appropriate evidence about multiple elements of the financial statements, and the practitioner believes the effect is material and pervasive to the financial statements. Specifically, the practitioner was unable to obtain evidence about the entity's physical inventory and accounts receivable.

INDEPENDENT PRACTITIONER'S REVIEW REPORT

[Appropriate Addressee]

We were engaged to review the accompanying financial statements of ABC Company, which comprise the statement of financial position as at December 31, 20X1, and the statement of comprehensive income, statement of changes in equity and statement of cash flows for the year then ended, and a summary of significant accounting policies and other explanatory information.

Management's[25] Responsibility for the Financial Statements

Management is responsible for the preparation and fair presentation of these financial statements in accordance with International Financial Reporting Standards,[26] and for such internal control as management determines is necessary to enable the preparation of financial statements that are free from material misstatement, whether due to fraud or error.

Practitioner's Responsibility

Our responsibility is to express a conclusion on the accompanying financial statements. Because of the matter(s) described in the Basis for Disclaimer of Conclusion paragraph, however, we were not able to obtain sufficient appropriate evidence as a basis for expressing a conclusion on the financial statements.

Basis for Disclaimer of Conclusion

Management did not conduct a count of physical inventory on hand at the end of the year. We were unable to perform the procedures we considered necessary concerning the inventory quantities held at December 31, 20X1, which are stated at xxx in the statement of financial position at December 31, 20X1.

---

[25] *Or other term that is appropriate in the context of the legal framework in the particular jurisdiction.*

[26] *Where management's responsibility is to prepare financial statements that give a true and fair view, this may read: "Management is responsible for the preparation of financial statements that give a true and fair view in accordance with International Financial Reporting Standards, and for such ...".*

In addition, the introduction of a new computerized accounts receivable system in September 20X1 resulted in numerous errors in accounts receivable and inventory. As of the date of our report, management was still in the process of rectifying the system deficiencies and correcting the errors. As a result of these matters, we were unable to determine whether any adjustments might have been found necessary in respect of recorded or unrecorded inventories and accounts receivable, and the elements making up the statement of comprehensive income, statement of changes in equity and statement of cash flows.

Disclaimer of Conclusion

Due to the significance of the matters described in the Basis for Disclaimer of Conclusion paragraph, we were unable to obtain sufficient appropriate evidence to form a conclusion on the accompanying financial statements. Accordingly, we do not express a conclusion on these financial statements.

[Practitioner's signature]

[Date of the practitioner's report]

[Practitioner's address]

Illustration 6

Circumstances include the following:

- The financial statements have been prepared by management of the entity in accordance with the financial reporting provisions of a contract (that is, a special purpose framework), to comply with the provisions of the contract. Management does not have a choice of financial reporting frameworks.

- The applicable financial reporting framework is a compliance framework.

- The terms of the review engagement reflect the description of management's responsibility for the financial statements in paragraph 30(b) of this ISRE.

- Distribution or use of the practitioner's report is restricted.

INDEPENDENT PRACTITIONER'S REVIEW REPORT

[Appropriate Addressee]

We have reviewed the accompanying financial statements of ABC Company, which comprise the balance sheet as at December 31, 20X1, and the income statement, statement of changes in equity and cash flow statement for the year then ended, and a summary of significant accounting policies and other explanatory information. The financial statements have been prepared by management of ABC Company based on the financial reporting provisions of Section Z of the contract dated January 1, 20X1 between ABC Company and DEF Company ("the contract").

Management's[27] Responsibility for the Financial Statements

Management is responsible for the preparation of these financial statements in accordance with the financial reporting provisions of Section Z of the contract, and for such internal control as management determines is necessary to enable the preparation of financial statements that are free from material misstatement, whether due to fraud or error.

Practitioner's Responsibility

Our responsibility is to express a conclusion on the accompanying financial statements. We conducted our review in accordance with International Standard on Review Engagements (ISRE) 2400 (Revised), *Engagements to Review Historical Financial Statements*. ISRE 2400 (Revised) requires us to conclude whether anything has come to our attention that causes us to believe that the financial statements, taken as a whole, are not prepared in all material respects in accordance with the applicable financial reporting framework. This Standard also requires us to comply with relevant ethical requirements.

A review of financial statements in accordance with ISRE 2400 (Revised) is a limited assurance engagement. The practitioner performs procedures, primarily consisting of making inquiries of management and others within the entity, as appropriate, and applying analytical procedures, and evaluates the evidence obtained.

---

[27] *Or other term that is appropriate in the context of the legal framework in the particular jurisdiction.*

The procedures performed in a review are substantially less than those performed in an audit conducted in accordance with International Standards on Auditing. Accordingly, we do not express an audit opinion on these financial statements.

Conclusion

Based on our review, nothing has come to our attention that causes us to believe that these financial statements are not prepared, in all material respects, in accordance with the financial reporting provisions of Section Z of the contract.

Basis of Accounting, and Restriction on Distribution and Use

Without modifying our conclusion, we draw attention to Note X to the financial statements, which describes the basis of accounting. The financial statements are prepared to assist ABC Company to comply with the financial reporting provisions of the contract referred to above. As a result, the financial statements may not be suitable for another purpose. Our report is intended solely for ABC Company and DEF Company and should not be distributed to or used by parties other than ABC Company or DEF Company.

[Practitioner's signature]

[Date of the practitioner's report]

[Practitioner's address]

Illustration 7

Circumstances include the following:

- Review of a statement of cash receipts and disbursements

- The financial statement has been prepared by management of the entity in accordance with the cash receipts and disbursements basis of accounting to respond to a request for cash flow information received from a creditor. The basis of accounting applied to prepare the financial statement has been agreed between the entity and the creditor.

- The applicable financial reporting framework is a fair presentation framework designed to meet the financial information needs of specific users.

- The practitioner has determined that it is appropriate to use the phrase "presents fairly, in all material respects," in the practitioner's conclusion.

- The terms of the review engagement reflect the description of management's responsibility for the financial statement in paragraph 30(b) of this ISRE.

- Distribution or use of the practitioner's report is not restricted.

INDEPENDENT PRACTITIONER'S REVIEW REPORT

[Appropriate Addressee]

We have reviewed the accompanying statement of cash receipts and disbursements of ABC Company for the year ended December 31, 20X1, and a summary of significant accounting policies and other explanatory information (together "the financial statement"). The financial statement has been prepared by management of ABC Company using the cash receipts and disbursements basis of accounting described in Note X.

Management's[28] Responsibility for the Financial Statement

Management is responsible for the preparation and fair presentation of this financial statement in accordance with the cash receipts and disbursements basis of accounting described in Note X, and for such internal control as management determines is necessary to enable the preparation of the financial statement that is free from material misstatement, whether due to fraud or error.

Practitioner's Responsibility

Our responsibility is to express a conclusion on the accompanying financial statement. We conducted our review in accordance with International Standard on Review Engagements (ISRE) 2400 (Revised), *Engagements to Review Historical Financial Statements*. ISRE 2400 (Revised) requires us to conclude whether anything has come to our attention that causes us to believe that the financial statement is not prepared in all material respects in accordance with the applicable financial reporting framework. This Standard also requires us to comply with relevant ethical requirements.

A review of financial statements in accordance with ISRE 2400 (Revised) is a limited assurance engagement. The practitioner performs procedures, primarily consisting of

---

[28] *Or other term that is appropriate in the context of the legal framework in the particular jurisdiction.*

making inquiries of management and others within the entity, as appropriate, and applying analytical procedures, and evaluates the evidence obtained.

The procedures performed in a review are substantially less than those performed in an audit conducted in accordance with International Standards on Auditing. Accordingly, we do not express an audit opinion on this financial statement.

Conclusion

Based on our review, nothing has come to our attention that causes us to believe that the financial statement does not present fairly, in all material respects, (or *does not give a true and fair view of)* the cash receipts and disbursements of ABC Company for the year ended December 31, 20X1 in accordance with the cash receipts and disbursements basis of accounting described in Note X.

Basis of Accounting

Without modifying our conclusion, we draw attention to Note X to the financial statement, which describes the basis of accounting. The financial statement is prepared to provide information to XYZ Creditor. As a result, the financial statement may not be suitable for another purpose.

[Practitioner's signature]

[Date of the practitioner's report]

[Practitioner's address]

International Standard on Review Engagements 2410

Review of interim financial information performed by the independent auditor of the entity

*(Effective for reviews of interim financial information for periods
beginning on or after December 15, 2006.
Earlier adoption is permissible.)**

Contents

---

* *ISRE 2410 gave rise to a conforming amendment to ISA 210, "Terms of Audit Engagements" that is effective for audits of financial statements for periods beginning on or after December 15, 2006. It also gave rise to conforming amendments to ISRE 2400, "Engagement to Review Financial Statements" that are effective for reviews of financial statements for periods beginning on or after December 15, 2006. These amendments have been incorporated in the text of ISA 210 and ISRE 2400.*
Paragraph 3a and footnote 4 were inserted in this ISRE in December 2007 to clarify the application of the ISRE.

Appendix 5: Examples of Review Reports with a Qualified Conclusion for a Departure from the Applicable Financial Reporting Framework

Appendix 6: Examples of Review Reports with a Qualified Conclusion for a Limitation on Scope Not Imposed by Management

Appendix 7: Examples of Review Reports with an Adverse Conclusion for a Departure from the Applicable Financial Reporting Framework

International Standard on Review Engagements (ISRE) 2410, "Review of Interim Financial Information Performed by the Independent Auditor of the Entity" should be read in the context of the "Preface to the International Standards on Quality Control, Auditing, Review, Other Assurance and Related Services," which sets out the application and authority of ISREs.

Introduction

The purpose of this International Standard on Review Engagements (ISRE) is to establish standards and provide guidance on the auditor's professional responsibilities when the auditor undertakes an engagement to review interim financial information of an audit client, and on the form and content of the report. The term "auditor" is used throughout this ISRE, not because the auditor is performing an audit function but because the scope of this ISRE is limited to a review of interim financial information performed by the independent auditor of the financial statements of the entity. **1**

For purposes of this ISRE, interim financial information is financial information that is prepared and presented in accordance with an applicable financial reporting framework[1] and comprises either a complete or a condensed set of financial statements for a period that is shorter than the entity's financial year. **2**

The auditor who is engaged to perform a review of interim financial information should perform the review in accordance with this ISRE. Through performing the audit of the annual financial statements, the auditor obtains an understanding of the entity and its environment, including its internal control. When the auditor is engaged to review the interim financial information, this understanding is updated through inquiries made in the course of the review, and assists the auditor in focusing the inquiries to be made and the analytical and other review procedures to be applied. A practitioner who is engaged to perform a review of interim financial information, and who is not the auditor of the entity, performs the review in accordance with ISRE 2400, "Engagements to Review Financial Statements." As the practitioner does not ordinarily have the same understanding of the entity and its environment, including its internal control, as the auditor of the entity, the practitioner needs to carry out different inquiries and procedures to meet the objective of the review. **3**

This ISRE is directed towards a review of interim financial information by an entity's auditor. However, it is to be applied, adapted as necessary in the circumstances, when an entity's auditor undertakes an engagement to review historical financial information other than interim financial information of an audit client. **3a**

General Principles of a Review of Interim Financial Information

The auditor should comply with the ethical requirements relevant to the audit of the annual financial statements of the entity. These ethical requirements govern the auditor's professional responsibilities in the following areas: independence, integrity, objectivity, professional competence and due care, confidentiality, professional behavior, and technical standards. **4**

The auditor should implement quality control procedures that are applicable to the individual engagement. The elements of quality control that are relevant to an individual engagement include leadership responsibilities for quality on the engagement, ethical requirements, acceptance and continuance of client relationships and specific engagements, assignment of engagement teams, engagement performance, and monitoring. **5**

---

[1] *For example, International Financial Reporting Standards as issued by the International Accounting Standards Board.*

6   **The auditor should plan and perform the review with an attitude of professional skepticism, recognizing that circumstances may exist that cause the interim financial information to require a material adjustment for it to be prepared, in all material respects, in accordance with the applicable financial reporting framework.** An attitude of professional skepticism means that the auditor makes a critical assessment, with a questioning mind, of the validity of evidence obtained and is alert to evidence that contradicts or brings into question the reliability of documents or representations by management of the entity.

Objective of an Engagement to Review Interim Financial Information

7   The objective of an engagement to review interim financial information is to enable the auditor to express a conclusion whether, on the basis of the review, anything has come to the auditor's attention that causes the auditor to believe that the interim financial information is not prepared, in all material respects, in accordance with an applicable financial reporting framework. The auditor makes inquiries, and performs analytical and other review procedures in order to reduce to a moderate level the risk of expressing an inappropriate conclusion when the interim financial information is materially misstated.

8   The objective of a review of interim financial information differs significantly from that of an audit conducted in accordance with International Standards on Auditing (ISAs). A review of interim financial information does not provide a basis for expressing an opinion whether the financial information gives a true and fair view, or is presented fairly, in all material respects, in accordance with an applicable financial reporting framework.

9   A review, in contrast to an audit, is not designed to obtain reasonable assurance that the interim financial information is free from material misstatement. A review consists of making inquiries, primarily of persons responsible for financial and accounting matters, and applying analytical and other review procedures. A review may bring significant matters affecting the interim financial information to the auditor's attention, but it does not provide all of the evidence that would be required in an audit.

Agreeing the Terms of the Engagement

10   **The auditor and the client should agree on the terms of the engagement.**

11   The agreed terms of the engagement are ordinarily recorded in an engagement letter. Such a communication helps to avoid misunderstandings regarding the nature of the engagement and, in particular, the objective and scope of the review, management's responsibilities, the extent of the auditor's responsibilities, the assurance obtained, and the nature and form of the report. The communication ordinarily covers the following matters:

- The objective of a review of interim financial information.
- The scope of the review.
- Management's responsibility for the interim financial information.
- Management's responsibility for establishing and maintaining effective internal control relevant to the preparation of interim financial information.
- Management's responsibility for making all financial records and related information available to the auditor.

- Management's agreement to provide written representations to the auditor to confirm representations made orally during the review, as well as representations that are implicit in the entity's records.
- The anticipated form and content of the report to be issued, including the identity of the addressee of the report.
- Management's agreement that where any document containing interim financial information indicates that the interim financial information has been reviewed by the entity's auditor, the review report will also be included in the document.

An illustrative engagement letter is set out in Appendix 1 to this ISRE. The terms of engagement to review interim financial information can also be combined with the terms of engagement to audit the annual financial statements.

Procedures for a Review of Interim Financial Information

Understanding the Entity and its Environment, Including its Internal Control

The auditor should have an understanding of the entity and its environment, including its internal control, as it relates to the preparation of both annual and interim financial information, sufficient to plan and conduct the engagement so as to be able to: **12**

(a) **Identify the types of potential material misstatement and consider the likelihood of their occurrence; and**
(b) **Select the inquiries, analytical and other review procedures that will provide the auditor with a basis for reporting whether anything has come to the auditor's attention that causes the auditor to believe that the interim financial information is not prepared, in all material respects, in accordance with the applicable financial reporting framework.**

As required by ISA 315, "Understanding the Entity and its Environment and   **13** Assessing the Risks of Material Misstatement," the auditor who has audited the entity's financial statements for one or more annual periods has obtained an understanding of the entity and its environment, including its internal control, as it relates to the preparation of annual financial information that was sufficient to conduct the audit. In planning a review of interim financial information, the auditor updates this understanding. The auditor also obtains a sufficient understanding of internal control as it relates to the preparation of interim financial information as it may differ from internal control as it relates to annual financial information.

The auditor uses the understanding of the entity and its environment, including its   **14** internal control, to determine the inquiries to be made and the analytical and other review procedures to be applied, and to identify the particular events, transactions or assertions to which inquiries may be directed or analytical or other review procedures applied.

The procedures performed by the auditor to update the understanding of the entity   **15** and its environment, including its internal control, ordinarily include the following:

- Reading the documentation, to the extent necessary, of the preceding year's audit and reviews of prior interim period(s) of the current year and corresponding interim period(s) of the prior year, to enable the auditor to identify matters that may affect the current-period interim financial information.
- Considering any significant risks, including the risk of management override of controls, that were identified in the audit of the prior year's financial statements.

- Reading the most recent annual and comparable prior period interim financial information.
- Considering materiality with reference to the applicable financial reporting framework as it relates to interim financial information to assist in determining the nature and extent of the procedures to be performed and evaluating the effect of misstatements.
- Considering the nature of any corrected material misstatements and any identified uncorrected immaterial misstatements in the prior year's financial statements.
- Considering significant financial accounting and reporting matters that may be of continuing significance such as material weaknesses in internal control.
- Considering the results of any audit procedures performed with respect to the current year's financial statements.
- Considering the results of any internal audit performed and the subsequent actions taken by management.
- Inquiring of management about the results of management's assessment of the risk that the interim financial information may be materially misstated as a result of fraud.
- Inquiring of management about the effect of changes in the entity's business activities.
- Inquiring of management about any significant changes in internal control and the potential effect of any such changes on the preparation of interim financial information.
- Inquiring of management of the process by which the interim financial information has been prepared and the reliability of the underlying accounting records to which the interim financial information is agreed or reconciled.

16   The auditor determines the nature of the review procedures, if any, to be performed for components and, where applicable, communicates these matters to other auditors involved in the review. Factors to be considered include the materiality of, and risk of misstatement in, the interim financial information of components, and the auditor's understanding of the extent to which internal control over the preparation of such information is centralized or decentralized.

17   **In order to plan and conduct a review of interim financial information, a recently appointed auditor, who has not yet performed an audit of the annual financial statements in accordance with ISAs, should obtain an understanding of the entity and its environment, including its internal control, as it relates to the preparation of both annual and interim financial information.**

18   This understanding enables the auditor to focus the inquiries made, and the analytical and other review procedures applied in performing a review of interim financial information in accordance with this ISRE. As part of obtaining this understanding, the auditor ordinarily makes inquiries of the predecessor auditor and, where practicable, reviews the predecessor auditor's documentation for the preceding annual audit, and for any prior interim periods in the current year that have been reviewed by the predecessor auditor. In doing so, the auditor considers the nature of any corrected misstatements, and any uncorrected misstatements aggregated by the predecessor auditor, any significant risks, including the risk of management override of controls, and significant accounting and any reporting matters that may be of continuing significance, such as material weaknesses in internal control.

Inquiries, Analytical and Other Review Procedures

The auditor should make inquiries, primarily of persons responsible for financial and accounting matters, and perform analytical and other review procedures to enable the auditor to conclude whether, on the basis of the procedures performed, anything has come to the auditor's attention that causes the auditor to believe that the interim financial information is not prepared, in all material respects, in accordance with the applicable financial reporting framework. 19

A review ordinarily does not require tests of the accounting records through   20
inspection, observation or confirmation. Procedures for performing a review of interim financial information are ordinarily limited to making inquiries, primarily of persons responsible for financial and accounting matters, and applying analytical and other review procedures, rather than corroborating information obtained concerning significant accounting matters relating to the interim financial information. The auditor's understanding of the entity and its environment, including its internal control, the results of the risk assessments relating to the preceding audit and the auditor's consideration of materiality as it relates to the interim financial information, affects the nature and extent of the inquiries made, and analytical and other review procedures applied.

The auditor ordinarily performs the following procedures: 21

- Reading the minutes of the meetings of shareholders, those charged with governance, and other appropriate committees to identify matters that may affect the interim financial information, and inquiring about matters dealt with at meetings for which minutes are not available that may affect the interim financial information.
- Considering the effect, if any, of matters giving rise to a modification of the audit or review report, accounting adjustments or unadjusted misstatements, at the time of the previous audit or reviews.
- Communicating, where appropriate, with other auditors who are performing a review of the interim financial information of the reporting entity's significant components.
- Inquiring of members of management responsible for financial and accounting matters, and others as appropriate about the following:
  - Whether the interim financial information has been prepared and presented in accordance with the applicable financial reporting framework.
  - Whether there have been any changes in accounting principles or in the methods of applying them.
  - Whether any new transactions have necessitated the application of a new accounting principle.
  - Whether the interim financial information contains any known uncorrected misstatements.
  - Unusual or complex situations that may have affected the interim financial information, such as a business combination or disposal of a segment of the business.
  - Significant assumptions that are relevant to the fair value measurement or disclosures and management's intention and ability to carry out specific courses of action on behalf of the entity.
  - Whether related party transactions have been appropriately accounted for and disclosed in the interim financial information.
  - Significant changes in commitments and contractual obligations.
  - Significant changes in contingent liabilities including litigation or claims.
  - Compliance with debt covenants.

- o Matters about which questions have arisen in the course of applying the review procedures.
- o Significant transactions occurring in the last several days of the interim period or the first several days of the next interim period.
- o Knowledge of any fraud or suspected fraud affecting the entity involving:
  - – Management;
  - – Employees who have significant roles in internal control; or
  - – Others where the fraud could have a material effect on the interim financial information.
- o Knowledge of any allegations of fraud, or suspected fraud, affecting the entity's interim financial information communicated by employees, former employees, analysts, regulators, or others.
- o Knowledge of any actual or possible noncompliance with laws and regulations that could have a material effect on the interim financial information.

- Applying analytical procedures to the interim financial information designed to identify relationships and individual items that appear to be unusual and that may reflect a material misstatement in the interim financial information. Analytical procedures may include ratio analysis and statistical techniques such as trend analysis or regression analysis and may be performed manually or with the use of computer-assisted techniques. Appendix 2 to this ISRE contains examples of analytical procedures the auditor may consider when performing a review of interim financial information.
- Reading the interim financial information, and considering whether anything has come to the auditor's attention that causes the auditor to believe that the interim financial information is not prepared, in all material respects, in accordance with the applicable financial reporting framework.

22 The auditor may perform many of the review procedures before or simultaneously with the entity's preparation of the interim financial information. For example, it may be practicable to update the understanding of the entity and its environment, including its internal control, and begin reading applicable minutes before the end of the interim period. Performing some of the review procedures earlier in the interim period also permits early identification and consideration of significant accounting matters affecting the interim financial information.

23 The auditor performing the review of interim financial information is also engaged to perform an audit of the annual financial statements of the entity. For convenience and efficiency, the auditor may decide to perform certain audit procedures concurrently with the review of interim financial information. For example, information gained from reading the minutes of meetings of the board of directors in connection with the review of the interim financial information also may be used for the annual audit. The auditor may also decide to perform, at the time of the interim review, auditing procedures that would need to be performed for the purpose of the audit of the annual financial statements, for example, performing audit procedures on significant or unusual transactions that occurred during the period, such as business combinations, restructurings, or significant revenue transactions.

24 A review of interim financial information ordinarily does not require corroborating the inquiries about litigation or claims. It is, therefore, ordinarily not necessary to send an inquiry letter to the entity's lawyer. Direct communication with the entity's lawyer with respect to litigation or claims may, however, be appropriate if a matter comes to the auditor's attention that causes the auditor to question whether the interim financial information is not prepared, in all material respects, in accordance with the applicable financial reporting framework, and the auditor believes the entity's lawyer may have pertinent information.

The auditor should obtain evidence that the interim financial information agrees or 25
reconciles with the underlying accounting records. The auditor may obtain evidence
that the interim financial information agrees or reconciles with the underlying
accounting records by tracing the interim financial information to:

(a) The accounting records, such as the general ledger, or a consolidating schedule
that agrees or reconciles with the accounting records; and
(b) Other supporting data in the entity's records as necessary.

The auditor should inquire whether management has identified all events up to the date 26
of the review report that may require adjustment to or disclosure in the interim financial
information. It is not necessary for the auditor to perform other procedures to
identify events occurring after the date of the review report.

The auditor should inquire whether management has changed its assessment of the 27
entity's ability to continue as a going concern. When, as a result of this inquiry or other
review procedures, the auditor becomes aware of events or conditions that may cast
significant doubt on the entity's ability to continue as a going concern, the auditor
should:

(a) **Inquire of management as to its plans for future actions based on its going concern**
assessment, the feasibility of these plans, and whether management believes that
the outcome of these plans will improve the situation; and
(b) **Consider the adequacy of the disclosure about such matters in the interim financial**
information.

Events or conditions which may cast significant doubt on the entity's ability to 28
continue as a going concern may have existed at the date of the annual financial
statements or may be identified as a result of inquiries of management or in the
course of performing other review procedures. When such events or conditions come
to the auditor's attention, the auditor inquires of management as to its plans for
future action, such as its plans to liquidate assets, borrow money or restructure debt,
reduce or delay expenditures, or increase capital. The auditor also inquires as to the
feasibility of management's plans and whether management believes that the outcome of these plans will improve the situation. However, it is not ordinarily
necessary for the auditor to corroborate the feasibility of management's plans and
whether the outcome of these plans will improve the situation.

When a matter comes to the auditor's attention that leads the auditor to question 29
whether a material adjustment should be made for the interim financial information to
be prepared, in all material respects, in accordance with the applicable financial
reporting framework, the auditor should make additional inquiries or perform other
procedures to enable the auditor to express a conclusion in the review report. For
example, if the auditor's review procedures lead the auditor to question whether a
significant sales transaction is recorded in accordance with the applicable financial
reporting framework, the auditor performs additional procedures sufficient to
resolve the auditor's questions, such as discussing the terms of the transaction with
senior marketing and accounting personnel, or reading the sales contract.

Evaluation of Misstatements

The auditor should evaluate, individually and in the aggregate, whether uncorrected 30
misstatements that have come to the auditor's attention are material to the interim
financial information.

31   A review of interim financial information, in contrast to an audit engagement, is not designed to obtain reasonable assurance that the interim financial information is free from material misstatement. However, misstatements which come to the auditor's attention, including inadequate disclosures, are evaluated individually and in the aggregate to determine whether a material adjustment is required to be made to the interim financial information for it to be prepared, in all material respects, in accordance with the applicable financial reporting framework.

32   The auditor exercises professional judgment in evaluating the materiality of any misstatements that the entity has not corrected. The auditor considers matters such as the nature, cause and amount of the misstatements, whether the misstatements originated in the preceding year or interim period of the current year, and the potential effect of the misstatements on future interim or annual periods.

33   The auditor may designate an amount below which misstatements need not be aggregated, because the auditor expects that the aggregation of such amounts clearly would not have a material effect on the interim financial information. In so doing, the auditor considers the fact that the determination of materiality involves quantitative as well as qualitative considerations, and that misstatements of a relatively small amount could nevertheless have a material effect on the interim financial information.

Management Representations

34   **The auditor should obtain written representation from management that:**

   (a) **It acknowledges its responsibility for the design and implementation of internal control to prevent and detect fraud and error;**
   (b) **The interim financial information is prepared and presented in accordance with the applicable financial reporting framework;**
   (c) **It believes the effect of those uncorrected misstatements aggregated by the auditor during the review are immaterial, both individually and in the aggregate, to the interim financial information taken as a whole. A summary of such items is included in or attached to the written representations;**
   (d) **It has disclosed to the auditor all significant facts relating to any frauds or suspected frauds known to management that may have affected the entity;**
   (e) **It has disclosed to the auditor the results of its assessment of the risks that the interim financial information may be materially misstated as a result of fraud;[2]**
   (f) **It has disclosed to the auditor all known actual or possible noncompliance with laws and regulations whose effects are to be considered when preparing the interim financial information; and**
   (g) **It has disclosed to the auditor all significant events that have occurred subsequent to the balance sheet date and through to the date of the review report that may require adjustment to or disclosure in the interim financial information.**

35   The auditor obtains additional representations as are appropriate related to matters specific to the entity's business or industry. An illustrative management representation letter is set out in Appendix 3 to this ISRE.

---

[2] *Paragraph 35 of ISA 240, "The Auditor's Responsibility to Consider Fraud in an Audit of Financial Statements" explains that the nature, extent and frequency of such an assessment vary from entity to entity and that management may make a detailed assessment on an annual basis or as part of continuous monitoring. Accordingly, this representation, insofar as it relates to the interim financial information, is tailored to the entity's specific circumstances.*

Auditor's Responsibility for Accompanying Information

The auditor should read the other information that accompanies the interim financial   36
information to consider whether any such information is materially inconsistent with the
interim financial information. If the auditor identifies a material inconsistency, the
auditor considers whether the interim financial information or the other information
needs to be amended. If an amendment is necessary in the interim financial information and management refuses to make the amendment, the auditor considers the
implications for the review report. If an amendment is necessary in the other
information and management refuses to make the amendment, the auditor considers
including in the review report an additional paragraph describing the material
inconsistency, or taking other actions, such as withholding the issuance of the review
report or withdrawing from the engagement. For example, management may present
alternative measures of earnings that more positively portray financial performance
than the interim financial information, and such alternative measures are given
excessive prominence, are not clearly defined, or not clearly reconciled to the interim
financial information such that they are confusing and potentially misleading.

If a matter comes to the auditor's attention that causes the auditor to believe that the   37
other information appears to include a material misstatement of fact, the auditor should
discuss the matter with the entity's management. While reading the other information
for the purpose of identifying material inconsistencies, an apparent material misstatement of fact may come to the auditor's attention (i.e., information, not related
to matters appearing in the interim financial information, that is incorrectly stated or
presented). When discussing the matter with the entity's management, the auditor
considers the validity of the other information and management's responses to the
auditor's inquiries, whether valid differences of judgment or opinion exist and
whether to request management to consult with a qualified third party to resolve the
apparent misstatement of fact. If an amendment is necessary to correct a material
misstatement of fact and management refuses to make the amendment, the auditor
considers taking further action as appropriate, such as notifying those charged with
governance and obtaining legal advice.

Communication

When, as a result of performing the review of interim financial information, a matter   38
comes to the auditor's attention that causes the auditor to believe that it is necessary to
make a material adjustment to the interim financial information for it to be prepared, in
all material respects, in accordance with the applicable financial reporting framework,
the auditor should communicate this matter as soon as practicable to the appropriate
level of management.

When, in the auditor's judgment, management does not respond appropriately within a   39
reasonable period of time, the auditor should inform those charged with governance.
The communication is made as soon as practicable, either orally or in writing. The
auditor's decision whether to communicate orally or in writing is affected by factors
such as the nature, sensitivity and significance of the matter to be communicated and
the timing of such communications. If the information is communicated orally, the
auditor documents the communication.

When, in the auditor's judgment, those charged with governance do not respond   40
appropriately within a reasonable period of time, the auditor should consider:

(a) **Whether to modify the report; or**
(b) **The possibility of withdrawing from the engagement; and**

(c)   The possibility of resigning from the appointment to audit the annual financial statements.

41   When, as a result of performing the review of interim financial information, a matter comes to the auditor's attention that causes the auditor to believe in the existence of fraud or noncompliance by the entity with laws and regulations the auditor should communicate the matter as soon as practicable to the appropriate level of management. The determination of which level of management is the appropriate one is affected by the likelihood of collusion or the involvement of a member of management. The auditor also considers the need to report such matters to those charged with governance and considers the implication for the review.

42   The auditor should communicate relevant matters of governance interest arising from the review of interim financial information to those charged with governance. As a result of performing the review of the interim financial information, the auditor may become aware of matters that in the opinion of the auditor are both important and relevant to those charged with governance in overseeing the financial reporting and disclosure process. The auditor communicates such matters to those charged with governance.

Reporting the Nature, Extent and Results of the Review of Interim Financial Information

43   The auditor should issue a written report that contains the following:

(a)   An appropriate title.

(b)   An addressee, as required by the circumstances of the engagement.

(c)   Identification of the interim financial information reviewed, including identification of the title of each of the statements contained in the complete or condensed set of financial statements and the date and period covered by the interim financial information.

(d)   If the interim financial information comprises a complete set of general purpose financial statements prepared in accordance with a financial reporting framework designed to achieve fair presentation, a statement that management is responsible for the preparation and fair presentation of the interim financial information in accordance with the applicable financial reporting framework.

(e)   In other circumstances, a statement that management is responsible for the preparation and presentation of the interim financial information in accordance with the applicable financial reporting framework.

(f)   A statement that the auditor is responsible for expressing a conclusion on the interim financial information based on the review.

(g)   A statement that the review of the interim financial information was conducted in accordance with International Standard on Review Engagements (ISRE) 2410, "Review of Interim Financial Information Performed by the Independent Auditor of the Entity," and a statement that that such a review consists of making inquiries, primarily of persons responsible for financial and accounting matters, and applying analytical and other review procedures.

(h)   A statement that a review is substantially less in scope than an audit conducted in accordance with International Standards on Auditing and consequently does not enable the auditor to obtain assurance that the auditor would become aware of all significant matters that might be identified in an audit and that accordingly no audit opinion is expressed.

(i)   If the interim financial information comprises a complete set of general purpose financial statements prepared in accordance with a financial reporting framework designed to achieve fair presentation, a conclusion as to whether anything has come to the auditor's attention that causes the auditor to believe that the interim financial information does not give a true and fair view, or does not present fairly, in all material respects, in accordance with the applicable financial reporting framework (including a reference to the jurisdiction or country of origin of the financial reporting framework when the financial reporting framework used is not International Financial Reporting Standards).

(j) In other circumstances, a conclusion as to whether anything has come to the auditor's attention that causes the auditor to believe that the interim financial information is not prepared, in all material respects, in accordance with the applicable financial reporting framework (including a reference to the jurisdiction or country of origin of the financial reporting framework when the financial reporting framework used is not International Financial Reporting Standards).

(k) The date of the report.

(l) The location in the country or jurisdiction where the auditor practices.

(m) The auditor's signature.

Illustrative review reports are set out in Appendix 4 to this ISRE.

In some jurisdictions, law or regulation governing the review of interim financial information may prescribe wording for the auditor's conclusion that is different from the wording described in paragraph 43(i) or (j). Although the auditor may be obliged to use the prescribed wording, the auditor's responsibilities as described in this ISRE for coming to the conclusion remain the same. **44**

Departure from the Applicable Financial Reporting Framework

The auditor should express a qualified or adverse conclusion when a matter has come to the auditor's attention that causes the auditor to believe that a material adjustment should be made to the interim financial information for it to be prepared, in all material respects, in accordance with the applicable financial reporting framework. **45**

If matters have come to the auditor's attention that cause the auditor to believe that the interim financial information is or may be materially affected by a departure from the applicable financial reporting framework, and management does not correct the interim financial information, the auditor modifies the review report. The modification describes the nature of the departure and, if practicable, states the effects on the interim financial information. If the information that the auditor believes is necessary for adequate disclosure is not included in the interim financial information, the auditor modifies the review report and, if practicable, includes the necessary information in the review report. The modification to the review report is ordinarily accomplished by adding an explanatory paragraph to the review report, and qualifying the conclusion. Illustrative review reports with a qualified conclusion are set out in Appendix 5 to this ISRE. **46**

When the effect of the departure is so material and pervasive to the interim financial information that the auditor concludes a qualified conclusion is not adequate to disclose the misleading or incomplete nature of the interim financial information, the auditor expresses an adverse conclusion. Illustrative review reports with an adverse conclusion are set out in Appendix 7 to this ISRE. **47**

Limitation on Scope

A limitation on scope ordinarily prevents the auditor from completing the review. **48**

49   **When the auditor is unable to complete the review, the auditor should communicate, in writing, to the appropriate level of management and to those charged with governance the reason why the review cannot be completed, and consider whether it is appropriate to issue a report.**

Limitation on Scope Imposed by Management

50   The auditor does not accept an engagement to review the interim financial information if the auditor's preliminary knowledge of the engagement circumstances indicates that the auditor would be unable to complete the review because there will be a limitation on the scope of the auditor's review imposed by management of the entity.

51   If, after accepting the engagement, management imposes a limitation on the scope of the review, the auditor requests the removal of that limitation. If management refuses to do so, the auditor is unable to complete the review and express a conclusion. In such cases, the auditor communicates, in writing, to the appropriate level of management and those charged with governance the reason why the review cannot be completed. Nevertheless, if a matter comes to the auditor's attention that causes the auditor to believe that a material adjustment to the interim financial information is necessary for it to be prepared, in all material respects, in accordance with the applicable financial reporting framework, the auditor communicates such matters in accordance with the guidance in paragraphs 38-40.

52   The auditor also considers the legal and regulatory responsibilities, including whether there is a requirement for the auditor to issue a report. If there is such a requirement, the auditor disclaims a conclusion, and provides in the review report the reason why the review cannot be completed. However, if a matter comes to the auditor's attention that causes the auditor to believe that a material adjustment to the interim financial information is necessary for it to be prepared, in all material respects, in accordance with the applicable financial reporting framework, the auditor also communicates such a matter in the report.

Other Limitations on Scope

53   A limitation on scope may occur due to circumstances other than a limitation on scope imposed by management. In such circumstances, the auditor is ordinarily unable to complete the review and express a conclusion and is guided by paragraphs 51-52. There may be, however, some rare circumstances where the limitation on the scope of the auditor's work is clearly confined to one or more specific matters that, while material, are not in the auditor's judgment pervasive to the interim financial information. In such circumstances, the auditor modifies the review report by indicating that, except for the matter which is described in an explanatory paragraph to the review report, the review was conducted in accordance with this ISRE, and by qualifying the conclusion. Illustrative review reports with a qualified conclusion are set out in Appendix 6 to this ISRE.

54   The auditor may have expressed a qualified opinion on the audit of the latest annual financial statements because of a limitation on the scope of that audit. The auditor considers whether that limitation on scope still exists and, if so, the implications for the review report.

Going Concern and Significant Uncertainties

In certain circumstances, an emphasis of matter paragraph may be added to a review **55** report, without affecting the auditor's conclusion, to highlight a matter that is included in a note to the interim financial information that more extensively discusses the matter. The paragraph would preferably be included after the conclusion paragraph and ordinarily refers to the fact that the conclusion is not qualified in this respect.

If adequate disclosure is made in the interim financial information, the auditor should **56** **add an emphasis of matter paragraph to the review report to highlight a material uncertainty relating to an event or condition that may cast significant doubt on the entity's ability to continue as a going concern.**

The auditor may have modified a prior audit or review report by adding an emphasis **57** of matter paragraph to highlight a material uncertainty relating to an event or condition that may cast significant doubt on the entity's ability to continue as a going concern. If the material uncertainty still exists and adequate disclosure is made in the interim financial information, the auditor modifies the review report on the current interim financial information by adding a paragraph to highlight the continued material uncertainty.

If, as a result of inquiries or other review procedures, a material uncertainty relating **58** to an event or condition comes to the auditor's attention that may cast significant doubt on the entity's ability to continue as a going concern, and adequate disclosure is made in the interim financial information the auditor modifies the review report by adding an emphasis of matter paragraph.

If a material uncertainty that casts significant doubt about the entity's ability to con- **59** **tinue as a going concern is not adequately disclosed in the interim financial information, the auditor should express a qualified or adverse conclusion, as appropriate. The report should include specific reference to the fact that there is such a material uncertainty.**

The auditor should consider modifying the review report by adding a paragraph to **60** **highlight a significant uncertainty (other than a going concern problem) that came to the auditor's attention, the resolution of which is dependent upon future events and which may affect the interim financial information.**

Other Considerations

The terms of the engagement include management's agreement that where any **61** document containing interim financial information indicates that such information has been reviewed by the entity's auditor, the review report will also be included in the document. If management has not included the review report in the document, the auditor considers seeking legal advice to assist in determining the appropriate course of action in the circumstances.

If the auditor has issued a modified review report and management issues the interim **62** financial information without including the modified review report in the document containing the interim financial information, the auditor considers seeking legal advice to assist in determining the appropriate course of action in the circumstances, and the possibility of resigning from the appointment to audit the annual financial statements.

63   Interim financial information consisting of a condensed set of financial statements does not necessarily include all the information that would be included in a complete set of financial statements, but may rather present an explanation of the events and changes that are significant to an understanding of the changes in the financial position and performance of the entity since the annual reporting date. This is because it is presumed that the users of the interim financial information will have access to the latest audited financial statements, such as is the case with listed entities. In other circumstances, the auditor discusses with management the need for such interim financial information to include a statement that it is to be read in conjunction with the latest audited financial statements. In the absence of such a statement, the auditor considers whether, without a reference to the latest audited financial statements, the interim financial information is misleading in the circumstances, and the implications for the review report.

Documentation

64   **The auditor should prepare review documentation that is sufficient and appropriate to provide a basis for the auditor's conclusion and to provide evidence that the review was performed in accordance with this ISRE and applicable legal and regulatory requirements.** The documentation enables an experienced auditor having no previous connection with the engagement to understand the nature, timing and extent of the inquiries made, and analytical and other review procedures applied, information obtained, and any significant matters considered during the performance of the review, including the disposition of such matters.

Effective Date

65   This ISRE is effective for reviews of interim financial information for periods beginning on or after December 15, 2006. Earlier adoption of the ISRE is permissible.

Public Sector Perspective

1.   *Paragraph 10 requires that the auditor and the client agree on the terms of engagement. Paragraph 11 explains that an engagement letter helps to avoid misunderstandings regarding the nature of the engagement and, in particular, the objective and scope of the review, management's responsibilities, the extent of the auditor's responsibilities, the assurance obtained, and the nature and form of the report. Law or regulation governing review engagements in the public sector ordinarily mandates the appointment of the auditor. Consequently, engagement letters may not be a widespread practice in the public sector. Nevertheless, an engagement letter setting out the matters referred to in paragraph 11 may be useful to both the public sector auditor and the client. Public sector auditors, therefore, consider agreeing with the client the terms of a review engagement by way of an engagement letter.*

2.   *In the public sector, the auditor's statutory audit obligation may extend to other work, such as a review of interim financial information. Where this is the case, the public sector auditor cannot avoid such an obligation and, consequently, may not be in a position not to accept (see paragraph 50) or to withdraw from a review engagement (see paragraphs 36 and 40(b)). The public sector auditor also may not be in the position to resign from the appointment to audit the annual financial statements (see paragraphs 40(c)) and 62).*

3.   *Paragraph 41 discusses the auditor's responsibility when a matter comes to the auditor's attention that causes the auditor to believe in the existence of fraud or noncompliance by the entity with laws and regulations. In the public sector, the auditor may be subject to statutory or other regulatory requirements to report such a matter to regulatory or other public authorities.*

Appendix 1

Example of an Engagement Letter for a Review of Interim Financial Information

The following letter is to be used as a guide in conjunction with the consideration outlined in paragraph 10 of this ISRE and will need to be adapted according to individual requirements and circumstances.

To the Board of Directors (or the appropriate representative of senior management)

We are providing this letter to confirm our understanding of the terms and objectives of our engagement to review the entity's interim balance sheet as at June 30, 20X1 and the related statements of income, changes in equity and cash flows for the six-month period then ended.

Our review will be conducted in accordance with International Standard on Review Engagements 2410, "Review of Interim Financial Information Performed by the Independent Auditor of the Entity" issued by the International Auditing and Assurance Standards Board with the objective of providing us with a basis for reporting whether anything has come to our attention that causes us to believe that the interim financial information is not prepared, in all material respects, in accordance with the [indicate applicable financial reporting framework, including a reference to the jurisdiction or country of origin of the financial reporting when the financial reporting framework used is not International Financial Reporting Standards]. Such a review consists of making inquiries, primarily of persons responsible for financial and accounting matters, and applying analytical and other review procedures and does not, ordinarily, require corroboration of the information obtained. The scope of a review of interim financial information is substantially less than the scope of an audit conducted in accordance with International Standards on Auditing whose objective is the expression of an opinion regarding the financial statements and, accordingly, we shall express no such opinion.

We expect to report on the interim financial information as follows:

[Include text of sample report.]

Responsibility for the interim financial information, including adequate disclosure, is that of management of the entity. This includes designing, implementing and maintaining internal control relevant to the preparation and presentation of interim financial information that is free from material misstatement, whether due to fraud or error; selecting and applying appropriate accounting policies; and making accounting estimates that are reasonable in the circumstances. As part of our review, we will request written representations from management concerning assertions made in connection with the review. We will also request that where any document containing interim financial information indicates that the interim financial information has been reviewed, our report will also be included in the document.

A review of interim financial information does not provide assurance that we will become aware of all significant matters that might be identified in an audit. Further, our engagement cannot be relied upon to disclose whether fraud or errors, or illegal acts exist. However, we will inform you of any material matters that come to our attention.

We look forward to full cooperation with your staff and we trust that they will make available to us whatever records, documentation and other information are requested in connection with our review.

[Insert additional information here regarding fee arrangements and billings, as appropriate.]

This letter will be effective for future years unless it is terminated, amended or superseded (if applicable).

Please sign and return the attached copy of this letter to indicate that it is in accordance with your understanding of the arrangements for our review of the financial statements.

Acknowledged on behalf of ABC Entity by

(signed)

Name and Title

Date

Appendix 2

Analytical Procedures the Auditor May Consider When Performing a Review of Interim Financial Information

Examples of analytical procedures the auditor may consider when performing a review of interim financial information include the following:

- Comparing the interim financial information with the interim financial information of the immediately preceding interim period, with the interim financial information of the corresponding interim period of the preceding financial year, with the interim financial information that was expected by management for the current period, and with the most recent audited annual financial statements.
- Comparing current interim financial information with anticipated results, such as budgets or forecasts (for example, comparing tax balances and the relationship between the provision for income taxes to pretax income in the current interim financial information with corresponding information in (a) budgets, using expected rates, and (b) financial information for prior periods).
- Comparing current interim financial information with relevant non-financial information.
- Comparing the recorded amounts, or ratios developed from recorded amounts, to expectations developed by the auditor. The auditor develops such

expectations by identifying and applying relationships that are reasonably expected to exist based on the auditor's understanding of the entity and of the industry in which the entity operates.

- Comparing ratios and indicators for the current interim period with those of entities in the same industry.
- Comparing relationships among elements in the current interim financial information with corresponding relationships in the interim financial information of prior periods, for example, expense by type as a percentage of sales, assets by type as a percentage of total assets, and percentage of change in sales to percentage of change in receivables.
- Comparing disaggregated data. The following are examples of how data may be disaggregated:
  - By period, for example, revenue or expense items disaggregated into quarterly, monthly, or weekly amounts.
  - By product line or source of revenue.
  - By location, for example, by component.
  - By attributes of the transaction, for example, revenue generated by designers, architects, or craftsmen.
  - By several attributes of the transaction, for example, sales by product and month.

Appendix 3

Example of a Management Representation Letter

The following letter is not intended to be a standard letter. Representations by management will vary from entity to entity and from one interim period to the next.

(Entity Letterhead)

(To Auditor)   (Date)

Opening paragraphs if interim financial information comprises condensed financial statements:

This representation letter is provided in connection with your review of the condensed balance sheet of ABC Entity as of March 31, 20X1 and the related condensed statements of income, changes in equity and cash flows for the three-month period then ended for the purposes of expressing a conclusion whether anything has come to your attention that causes you to believe that the interim financial information is not prepared, in all material respects, in accordance with [indicate applicable financial reporting framework, including a reference to the jurisdiction or country of origin of the financial reporting framework when the financial reporting framework used is not International Financial Reporting Standards].

We acknowledge our responsibility for the preparation and presentation of the interim financial information in accordance with [indicate applicable financial reporting framework].

Opening paragraphs if interim financial information comprises a complete set of general purpose financial statements prepared in accordance with a financial reporting framework designed to achieve fair presentation:

This representation letter is provided in connection with your review of the balance sheet of ABC Entity as of March 31, 20X1 and the related statements of income, changes in equity and cash flows for the three-month period then ended and a summary of the significant accounting policies and other explanatory notes for the purposes of expressing a conclusion whether anything has come to your attention that causes you to believe that the interim financial information does not give a true and fair view of *(or "does not present fairly, in all material respects,")* the financial position of ABC Entity as at March 31, 20X1, and of its financial performance and its cash flows in accordance with [indicate applicable financial reporting framework, including a reference to the jurisdiction or country of origin of the financial reporting framework when the financial reporting framework used is not International Financial Reporting Standards].

We acknowledge our responsibility for the fair presentation of the interim financial information in accordance with [indicate applicable financial reporting framework].

We confirm, to the best of our knowledge and belief, the following representations:

- The interim financial information referred to above has been prepared and presented in accordance with [indicate applicable financial reporting framework].
- We have made available to you all books of account and supporting documentation, and all minutes of meetings of shareholders and the board of directors (namely those held on [insert applicable dates]).
- There are no material transactions that have not been properly recorded in the accounting records underlying the interim financial information.
- There has been no known actual or possible noncompliance with laws and regulations that could have a material effect on the interim financial information in the event of noncompliance.
- We acknowledge responsibility for the design and implementation of internal control to prevent and detect fraud and error.
- We have disclosed to you all significant facts relating to any known frauds or suspected frauds that may have affected the entity.
- We have disclosed to you the results of our assessment of the risk that the interim financial information may be materially misstated as the result of fraud.
- We believe the effects of uncorrected misstatements summarized in the accompanying schedule are immaterial, both individually and in the aggregate, to the interim financial information taken as a whole.
- We confirm the completeness of the information provided to you regarding the identification of related parties.
- The following have been properly recorded and, when appropriate, adequately disclosed in the interim financial information:
  - Related party transactions, including sales, purchases, loans, transfers, leasing arrangements and guarantees, and amounts receivable from or payable to related parties;
  - Guarantees, whether written or oral, under which the entity is contingently liable; and
  - Agreements and options to buy back assets previously sold.
- The presentation and disclosure of the fair value measurements of assets and liabilities are in accordance with [indicate applicable financial reporting framework]. The assumptions used reflect our intent and ability to carry specific courses of action on behalf of the entity, where relevant to the fair value measurements or disclosure.
- We have no plans or intentions that may materially affect the carrying value or classification of assets and liabilities reflected in the interim financial information.

- We have no plans to abandon lines of product or other plans or intentions that will result in any excess or obsolete inventory, and no inventory is stated at an amount in excess of realizable value.
- The entity has satisfactory title to all assets and there are no liens or encumbrances on the entity's assets.
- We have recorded or disclosed, as appropriate, all liabilities, both actual and contingent.
- [Add any additional representations related to new accounting standards that are being implemented for the first time and consider any additional representations required by a new International Standard on Auditing that are relevant to interim financial information.]

To the best of our knowledge and belief, no events have occurred subsequent to the balance sheet date and through the date of this letter that may require adjustment to or disclosure in the aforementioned interim financial information.

_____

(Senior Executive Officer)

_____

(Senior Financial Officer)

Appendix 4

Examples of Review Reports on Interim Financial Information

Complete Set of General Purpose Financial Statements Prepared in Accordance with a Financial Reporting Framework Designed to Achieve Fair Presentation (see paragraph 43(i))

Report on Review of Interim Financial Information

(Appropriate addressee)

Introduction

We have reviewed the accompanying balance sheet of ABC Entity as of March 31, 20X1 and the related statements of income, changes in equity and cash flows for the three-month period then ended, and a summary of significant accounting policies and other explanatory notes.[3] Management is responsible for the preparation and fair presentation of this interim financial information in accordance with [indicate applicable financial reporting framework]. Our responsibility is to express a conclusion on this interim financial information based on our review.

---

[3] *The auditor may wish to specify the regulatory authority or equivalent with whom the interim financial information is filed.*

Scope of Review

We conducted our review in accordance with International Standard on Review Engagements 2410, "Review of Interim Financial Information Performed by the Independent Auditor of the Entity."[4] A review of interim financial information consists of making inquiries, primarily of persons responsible for financial and accounting matters, and applying analytical and other review procedures. A review is substantially less in scope than an audit conducted in accordance with International Standards on Auditing and consequently does not enable us to obtain assurance that we would become aware of all significant matters that might be identified in an audit. Accordingly, we do not express an audit opinion.

Conclusion

Based on our review, nothing has come to our attention that causes us to believe that the accompanying interim financial information does not give a true and fair view of *(or "does not present fairly, in all material respects,")* the financial position of the entity as at March 31, 20X1, and of its financial performance and its cash flows for the three-month period then ended in accordance with [applicable financial reporting framework, including a reference to the jurisdiction or country of origin of the financial reporting framework when the financial reporting framework used is not International Financial Reporting Standards].

AUDITOR

Date

Address

Other Interim Financial Information (see paragraph 43(j))

Report on Review of Interim Financial Information

(Appropriate addressee)

Introduction

We have reviewed the accompanying [condensed] balance sheet of ABC Entity as of March 31, 20X1 and the related [condensed] statements of income, changes in equity and cash flows for the three-month period then ended.[5] Management is responsible for the preparation and presentation of this interim financial information in accordance with [indicate applicable financial reporting framework]. Our responsibility is to express a conclusion on this interim financial information based on our review.

---

[4] *In the case of a review of historical financial information other than interim financial information, this sentence should read as follows: "We conducted our review in accordance with International Standard on Review Engagements 2410, which applies to a review of historical financial information performed by the independent auditor of the entity." The remainder of the report should be adapted as necessary in the circumstances.*

[5] *See footnote 3.*

Scope of Review

We conducted our review in accordance with International Standard on Review Engagements 2410, "Review of Interim Financial Information Performed by the Independent Auditor of the Entity."[6] A review of interim financial information consists of making inquiries, primarily of persons responsible for financial and accounting matters, and applying analytical and other review procedures. A review is substantially less in scope than an audit conducted in accordance with International Standards on Auditing and consequently does not enable us to obtain assurance that we would become aware of all significant matters that might be identified in an audit. Accordingly, we do not express an audit opinion.

Conclusion

Based on our review, nothing has come to our attention that causes us to believe that the accompanying interim financial information is not prepared, in all material respects, in accordance with [applicable financial reporting framework, including a reference to the jurisdiction or country of origin of the financial reporting framework when the financial reporting framework used is not International Financial Reporting Standards].

AUDITOR

Date

Address

Appendix 5

Examples of Review Reports with a Qualified Conclusion for a Departure from the Applicable Financial Reporting Framework

Complete Set of General Purpose Financial Statements Prepared in Accordance with a Financial Reporting Framework Designed to Achieve Fair Presentation (see paragraph 43(i))

Report on Review of Interim Financial Information

(Appropriate addressee)

Introduction

We have reviewed the accompanying balance sheet of ABC Entity as of March 31, 20X1 and the related statements of income, changes in equity and cash flows for the three-month period then ended, and a summary of significant accounting policies and other explanatory notes.[7] Management is responsible for the preparation and fair presentation of this interim financial information in accordance with [indicate applicable financial reporting framework]. Our responsibility is to express a conclusion on this interim financial information based on our review.

---

[6] *See footnote 4.*

[7] *See footnote 3.*

Scope of Review

We conducted our review in accordance with International Standard on Review Engagements 2410, "Review of Interim Financial Information Performed by the Independent Auditor of the Entity."[8] A review of interim financial information consists of making inquiries, primarily of persons responsible for financial and accounting matters, and applying analytical and other review procedures. A review is substantially less in scope than an audit conducted in accordance with International Standards on Auditing and consequently does not enable us to obtain assurance that we would become aware of all significant matters that might be identified in an audit. Accordingly, we do not express an audit opinion.

Basis for Qualified Conclusion

Based on information provided to us by management, ABC Entity has excluded from property and long-term debt certain lease obligations that we believe should be capitalized to conform with [indicate applicable financial reporting framework]. This information indicates that if these lease obligations were capitalized at March 31, 20X1, property would be increased by $_____, long-term debt by $_____, and net income and earnings per share would be increased (decreased) by $_____, $_____, $_____, and $_____, respectively for the three-month period then ended.

Qualified Conclusion

Based on our review, with the exception of the matter described in the preceding paragraph, nothing has come to our attention that causes us to believe that the accompanying interim financial information does not give a true and fair view of *(or "does not present fairly, in all material respects,")* the financial position of the entity as at March 31, 20X1, and of its financial performance and its cash flows for the three-month period then ended in accordance with [indicate applicable financial reporting framework, including the reference to the jurisdiction or country of origin of the financial reporting framework when the financial reporting framework used is not International Financial Reporting Standards].

AUDITOR

Date

Address

Other Interim Financial Information (see paragraph 43(j))

Report on Review of Interim Financial Information

(Appropriate addressee)

Introduction

We have reviewed the accompanying [condensed] balance sheet of ABC Entity as of March 31, 20X1 and the related [condensed] statements of income, changes in equity

[8] *See footnote 4.*

and cash flows for the three-month period then ended.[9] Management is responsible for the preparation and presentation of this interim financial information in accordance with [indicate applicable financial reporting framework]. Our responsibility is to express a conclusion on this interim financial information based on our review.

Scope of Review

We conducted our review in accordance with International Standard on Review Engagements 2410, "Review of Interim Financial Information Performed by the Independent Auditor of the Entity."[10] A review of interim financial information consists of making inquiries, primarily of persons responsible for financial and accounting matters, and applying analytical and other review procedures. A review is substantially less in scope than an audit conducted in accordance with International Standards on Auditing and consequently does not enable us to obtain assurance that we would become aware of all significant matters that might be identified in an audit. Accordingly, we do not express an audit opinion.

Basis for Qualified Conclusion

Based on information provided to us by management, ABC Entity has excluded from property and long-term debt certain lease obligations that we believe should be capitalized to conform with [indicate applicable financial reporting framework]. This information indicates that if these lease obligations were capitalized at March 31, 20X1, property would be increased by $_____, long-term debt by $_____, and net income and earnings per share would be increased (decreased) by $_____, $_____, $_____, and $_____, respectively for the three-month period then ended.

Qualified Conclusion

Based on our review, with the exception of the matter described in the preceding paragraph, nothing has come to our attention that causes us to believe that the accompanying interim financial information is not prepared, in all material respects, in accordance with [indicate applicable financial reporting framework, including a reference to the jurisdiction or country of origin of the financial reporting framework when the financial reporting framework used is not International Financial Reporting Standards].

AUDITOR

Date

Address

---

[9] *See footnote 3.*

[10] *See footnote 4.*

Appendix 6

Examples of Review Reports with a Qualified Conclusion for a Limitation on Scope Not Imposed By Management

Complete Set of General Purpose Financial Statements Prepared in Accordance with a Financial Reporting Framework Designed to Achieve Fair Presentation (see paragraph 43(i))

Report on Review of Interim Financial Information

(Appropriate addressee)

Introduction

We have reviewed the accompanying balance sheet of ABC Entity as of March 31, 20X1 and the related statements of income, changes in equity and cash flows for the three-month period then ended, and a summary of significant accounting policies and other explanatory notes.[11] Management is responsible for the preparation and fair presentation of this interim financial information in accordance with [indicate applicable financial reporting framework]. Our responsibility is to express a conclusion on this interim financial information based on our review.

Scope of Review

Except as explained in the following paragraph, we conducted our review in accordance with International Standard on Review Engagements 2410, "Review of Interim Financial Information Performed by the Independent Auditor of the Entity."[12] A review of interim financial information consists of making inquiries, primarily of persons responsible for financial and accounting matters, and applying analytical and other review procedures. A review is substantially less in scope than an audit conducted in accordance with International Standards on Auditing and consequently does not enable us to obtain assurance that we would become aware of all significant matters that might be identified in an audit. Accordingly, we do not express an audit opinion.

Basis for Qualified Conclusion

As a result of a fire in a branch office on (date) that destroyed its accounts receivable records, we were unable to complete our review of accounts receivable totaling $_____ included in the interim financial information. The entity is in the process of reconstructing these records and is uncertain as to whether these records will support the amount shown above and the related allowance for uncollectible accounts. Had we been able to complete our review of accounts receivable, matters might have come to our attention indicating that adjustments might be necessary to the interim financial information.

---

[11] *See footnote 3.*

[12] *See footnote 4.*

Qualified Conclusion

Except for the adjustments to the interim financial information that we might have become aware of had it not been for the situation described above, based on our review, nothing has come to our attention that causes us to believe that the accompanying interim financial information does not give a true and fair view of *(or "does not present fairly, in all material respects,")* the financial position of the entity as at March 31, 20X1, and of its financial performance and its cash flows for the three-month period then ended in accordance with [indicate applicable financial reporting framework, including a reference to the jurisdiction or country of origin of the financial reporting framework when the financial reporting framework used is not International Financial Reporting Standards].

AUDITOR

Date

Address

Other Interim Financial Information (see paragraph 43(j))

Report on Review of Interim Financial Information

(Appropriate addressee)

Introduction

We have reviewed the accompanying [condensed] balance sheet of ABC Entity as of March 31, 20X1 and the related [condensed] statements of income, changes in equity and cash flows for the three-month period then ended.[13] Management is responsible for the preparation and presentation of this interim financial information in accordance with [indicate applicable financial reporting framework]. Our responsibility is to express a conclusion on this interim financial information based on our review.

Scope of Review

Except as explained in the following paragraph, we conducted our review in accordance with International Standards on Review Engagements 2410, "Review of Interim Financial Information Performed by the Auditor of the Entity."[14] A review of interim financial information consists of making inquiries, primarily of persons responsible for financial and accounting matters, and applying analytical and other review procedures. A review is substantially less in scope than an audit conducted in accordance with International Standards on Auditing and consequently does not enable us to obtain assurance that we would become aware of all significant matters that might be identified in an audit. Accordingly, we do not express an audit opinion.

Basis for Qualified Conclusion

As a result of a fire in a branch office on (date) that destroyed its accounts receivable records, we were unable to complete our review of accounts receivable totaling $_____ included in the interim financial information. The entity is in the process

---

[13] *See footnote 3.*

[14] *See footnote 4.*

of reconstructing these records and is uncertain as to whether these records will support the amount shown above and the related allowance for uncollectible accounts. Had we been able to complete our review of accounts receivable, matters might have come to our attention indicating that adjustments might be necessary to the interim financial information.

Qualified Conclusion

Except for the adjustments to the interim financial information that we might have become aware of had it not been for the situation described above, based on our review, nothing has come to our attention that causes us to believe that the accompanying interim financial information is not prepared, in all material respects, in accordance with [indicate applicable financial reporting framework, including a reference to the jurisdiction or country of origin of the financial reporting framework when the financial reporting framework used is not International Financial Reporting Standards].

AUDITOR

Date

Address

Appendix 7

Examples of Review Reports with an Adverse Conclusion for a Departure from the Applicable Financial Reporting Framework

Complete Set of General Purpose Financial Statements Prepared in Accordance with a Financial Reporting Framework Designed to Achieve Fair Presentation (see paragraph 43(i))

Report on Review of Interim Financial Information

(Appropriate addressee)

Introduction

We have reviewed the accompanying balance sheet of ABC Entity as of March 31, 20X1 and the related statements of income, changes in equity and cash flows for the three-month period then ended, and a summary of significant accounting policies and other explanatory notes.[15] Management is responsible for the preparation and fair presentation of this interim financial information in accordance with [indicate applicable financial reporting framework]. Our responsibility is to express a conclusion on this interim financial information based on our review.

Scope of Review

We conducted our review in accordance with International Standard on Review Engagements 2410, "Review of Interim Financial Information Performed by the

---

[15] *See footnote 3.*

Auditor of the Entity."[16] A review of interim financial information consists of making inquiries, primarily of persons responsible for financial and accounting matters, and applying analytical and other review procedures. A review is substantially less in scope than an audit conducted in accordance with International Standards on Auditing and consequently does not enable us to obtain assurance that we would become aware of all significant matters that might be identified in an audit. Accordingly, we do not express an audit opinion.

Basis for Adverse Conclusion

Commencing this period, management of the entity ceased to consolidate the financial statements of its subsidiary companies since management considers consolidation to be inappropriate because of the existence of new substantial non-controlling interests. This is not in accordance with [indicate applicable financial reporting framework, including a reference to the jurisdiction or country of origin of the financial reporting framework when the financial reporting framework used is not International Financial Reporting Standards]. Had consolidated financial statements been prepared, virtually every account in the interim financial information would have been materially different.

Adverse Conclusion

Our review indicates that, because the entity's investment in subsidiary companies is not accounted for on a consolidated basis, as described in the preceding paragraph, this interim financial information does not give a true and fair view of *(or "does not present fairly, in all material respects,")* the financial position of the entity as at March 31, 20X1, and of its financial performance and its cash flows for the three-month period then ended in accordance with [indicate applicable financial reporting framework, including a reference to the jurisdiction or country of origin of the financial reporting framework when the financial reporting framework used is not International Financial Reporting Standards].

AUDITOR

Date

Address

Other Interim Financial Information (see paragraph 43(j))

Report on Review of Interim Financial Information

(Appropriate addressee)

Introduction

We have reviewed the accompanying [condensed] balance sheet of ABC Entity as of March 31, 20X1 and the related [condensed] statements of income, changes in equity and cash flows for the three-month period then ended.[17] Management is responsible for the preparation and presentation of this interim financial information in

[16] *See footnote 4.*

[17] *See footnote 3.*

accordance with [indicate applicable financial reporting framework]. Our responsibility is to express a conclusion on this interim financial information based on our review.

Scope of Review

We conducted our review in accordance with International Standard on Review Engagements 2410, "Review of Interim Financial Information Performed by the Independence Auditor of the Entity."[18] A review of interim financial information consists of making inquiries, primarily of persons responsible for financial and accounting matters, and applying analytical and other review procedures. A review is substantially less in scope than an audit conducted in accordance with International Standards on Auditing and consequently does not enable us to obtain assurance that we would become aware of all significant matters that might be identified in an audit. Accordingly, we do not express an audit opinion.

Basis for Adverse Conclusion

Commencing this period, management of the entity ceased to consolidate the financial statements of its subsidiary companies since management considers consolidation to be inappropriate because of the existence of new substantial non-controlling interests. This is not in accordance with [indicate applicable financial reporting framework, including the reference to the jurisdiction or country of origin of the financial reporting framework when the financial reporting framework used is not International Financial Reporting Standards]. Had consolidated financial statements been prepared, virtually every account in the interim financial information would have been materially different.

Adverse Conclusion

Our review indicates that, because the entity's investment in subsidiary companies is not accounted for on a consolidated basis, as described in the preceding paragraph, this interim financial information is not prepared, in all material respects, in accordance with [indicate applicable financial reporting framework, including a reference to the jurisdiction or country of origin of the financial reporting framework when the financial reporting framework used is not International Financial Reporting Standards].

AUDITOR

Date

Address

---

[18] *See footnote 4.*

Part Five

International Standards on Assurance Engagements (ISAEs)

International Standard on Assurance Engagements 3000

Assurance engagements other than audits or reviews of historical financial information

(Effective for assurance reports dated on or after January 1, 2005)

Contents

International Standard on Assurance Engagements (ISAE) 3000, "Assurance Engagements Other than Audits or Reviews of Historical Financial Information" should be read in the context of the "Preface to the International Standards on Quality Control, Auditing, Review, Other Assurance and Related Services," which sets out the application and authority of ISAEs.

Introduction

1   The purpose of this International Standard on Assurance Engagements (ISAE) is to establish basic principles and essential procedures for, and to provide guidance to, professional accountants in public practice (for purposes of this ISAE referred to as "practitioners") for the performance of assurance engagements other than audits or reviews of historical financial information covered by International Standards on Auditing (ISAs) or International Standards on Review Engagements (ISREs).

2   This ISAE uses the terms "reasonable assurance engagement" and "limited assurance engagement" to distinguish between the two types of assurance engagement a practitioner is permitted to perform. The objective of a reasonable assurance engagement is a reduction in assurance engagement risk to an acceptably low level in the circumstances of the engagement[1] as the basis for a positive form of expression of the practitioner's conclusion. The objective of a limited assurance engagement is a reduction in assurance engagement risk to a level that is acceptable in the circumstances of the engagement, but where that risk is greater than for a reasonable assurance engagement, as the basis for a negative form of expression of the practitioner's conclusion.

Relationship with the Framework, Other ISAEs, ISAs and ISREs

3   **The practitioner should comply with this ISAE and other relevant ISAEs when performing an assurance engagement other than an audit or review of historical financial information covered by ISAs or ISREs.** This ISAE is to be read in the context of the "International Framework for Assurance Engagements" (the Framework), which defines and describes the elements and objectives of an assurance engagement, and identifies those engagements to which ISAEs apply. This ISAE has been written for general application to assurance engagements other than audits or reviews of historical financial information covered by ISAs or ISREs. Other ISAEs may relate to topics that apply to all subject matters or be subject matter specific. Although ISAs and ISREs do not apply to engagements covered by ISAEs, they may nevertheless provide guidance to practitioners.

Ethical Requirements

4   **The practitioner should comply with the requirements of Parts A and B of the IFAC *Code of Ethics for Professional Accountants* (the Code).**

5   The Code provides a framework of principles that members of assurance teams, firms and network firms use to identify threats to independence,[2] evaluate the

---

[1] *Engagement circumstances include the terms of the engagement, including whether it is a reasonable assurance engagement or a limited assurance engagement, the characteristics of the subject matter, the criteria to be used, the needs of the intended users, relevant characteristics of the responsible party and its environment, and other matters, for example events, transactions, conditions and practices, that may have a significant effect on the engagement.*

[2] *If a professional accountant not in public practice, for example an internal auditor, applies ISAEs, and (a) the Framework or ISAEs are referred to in the professional accountant's report; and (b) the professional accountant or other members of the assurance team and, when applicable, the professional accountant's employer, are not independent of the entity in respect of which the assurance engagement is being performed, the lack of independence and the nature of the relationship(s) with the assurance client are prominently disclosed in the professional accountant's report. Also, that report does not include the word "independent" in its title, and the purpose and users of the report are restricted.*

significance of those threats and, if the threats are other than clearly insignificant, identify and apply safeguards to eliminate the threats or reduce them to an acceptable level, such that independence of mind and independence in appearance are not compromised.

Quality Control

The practitioner should implement quality control procedures that are applicable to the individual engagement. Under International Standard on Quality Control (ISQC) 1, "Quality Control for Firms that Perform Audits and Reviews of Historical Financial Information, and Other Assurance and Related Services Engagements,"[3] a firm of professional accountants has an obligation to establish a system of quality control designed to provide it with reasonable assurance that the firm and its personnel comply with professional standards and regulatory and legal requirements, and that the assurance reports issued by the firm or engagement partners are appropriate in the circumstances. In addition, elements of quality control that are relevant to an individual engagement include leadership responsibilities for quality on the engagement, ethical requirements, acceptance and continuance of client relationships and specific engagements, assignment of engagement teams, engagement performance, and monitoring.

6

Engagement Acceptance and Continuance

The practitioner should accept (or continue where applicable) an assurance engagement only if the subject matter is the responsibility of a party other than the intended users or the practitioner. As indicated in paragraph 27 of the Framework, the responsible party can be one of the intended users, but not the only one. Acknowledgement by the responsible party provides evidence that the appropriate relationship exists, and also establishes a basis for a common understanding of the responsibility of each party. A written acknowledgement is the most appropriate form of documenting the responsible party's understanding. In the absence of an acknowledgement of responsibility, the practitioner considers:

7

(a) Whether it is appropriate to accept the engagement. Accepting it may be appropriate when, for example, other sources, such as legislation or a contract, indicate responsibility; and

(b) If the engagement is accepted, whether to disclose these circumstances in the assurance report.

The practitioner should accept (or continue where applicable) an assurance engagement only if, on the basis of a preliminary knowledge of the engagement circumstances, nothing comes to the attention of the practitioner to indicate that the requirements of the Code or of the ISAEs will not be satisfied. The practitioner considers the matters in paragraph 17 of the Framework and does not accept the engagement unless it exhibits all the characteristics required in that paragraph. Also, if the party engaging the practitioner (the "engaging party") is not the responsible party, the practitioner considers the effect of this on access to records, documentation and other information the practitioner may require to complete the engagement.

8

[3] *ISQC 1, "Quality Control for Firms that Perform Audits and Reviews of Historical Financial Information, and Other Assurance and Related Services Engagements" was issued in February 2004. Systems of quality control in compliance with ISQC 1 are required to be established by June 15, 2005.*

9   **The practitioner should accept (or continue where applicable) an assurance engagement only if the practitioner is satisfied that those persons who are to perform the engagement collectively possess the necessary professional competencies.** A practitioner may be requested to perform assurance engagements on a wide range of subject matters. Some subject matters may require specialized skills and knowledge beyond those ordinarily possessed by an individual practitioner (see paragraphs 26-32).

Agreeing on the Terms of the Engagement

10   **The practitioner should agree on the terms of the engagement with the engaging party.** To avoid misunderstandings, the agreed terms are recorded in an engagement letter or other suitable form of contract. If the engaging party is not the responsible party, the nature and content of an engagement letter or contract may vary. The existence of a legislative mandate may satisfy the requirement to agree on the terms of the engagement. Even in those situations an engagement letter may be useful for both the practitioner and engaging party.

11   **A practitioner should consider the appropriateness of a request, made before the completion of an assurance engagement, to change the engagement to a non-assurance engagement or from a reasonable assurance engagement to a limited assurance engagement, and should not agree to a change without reasonable justification.** A change in circumstances that affects the intended users' requirements, or a misunderstanding concerning the nature of the engagement, ordinarily will justify a request for a change in the engagement. If such a change is made, the practitioner does not disregard evidence that was obtained prior to the change.

Planning and Performing the Engagement

12   **The practitioner should plan the engagement so that it will be performed effectively.** Planning involves developing an overall strategy for the scope, emphasis, timing and conduct of the engagement, and an engagement plan, consisting of a detailed approach for the nature, timing and extent of evidence-gathering procedures to be performed and the reasons for selecting them. Adequate planning helps to devote appropriate attention to important areas of the engagement, identify potential problems on a timely basis and properly organize and manage the engagement in order for it to be performed in an effective and efficient manner. Adequate planning also assists the practitioner to properly assign work to engagement team members, and facilitates their direction and supervision and the review of their work. Further, it assists, where applicable, the coordination of work done by other practitioners and experts. The nature and extent of planning activities will vary with the engagement circumstances, for example the size and complexity of the entity and the practitioner's previous experience with it. Examples of the main matters to be considered include:

- The terms of the engagement.
- The characteristics of the subject matter and the identified criteria.
- The engagement process and possible sources of evidence.
- The practitioner's understanding of the entity and its environment, including the risks that the subject matter information may be materially misstated.
- Identification of intended users and their needs, and consideration of materiality and the components of assurance engagement risk.
- Personnel and expertise requirements, including the nature and extent of experts' involvement.

Planning is not a discrete phase, but rather a continual and iterative process   **13**
throughout the engagement. As a result of unexpected events, changes in conditions,
or the evidence obtained from the results of evidence-gathering procedures, the
practitioner may need to revise the overall strategy and engagement plan, and
thereby the resulting planned nature, timing and extent of further procedures.

The practitioner should plan and perform an engagement with an attitude of profes-   **14**
sional skepticism recognizing that circumstances may exist that cause the subject
matter information to be materially misstated. An attitude of professional skepticism
means the practitioner makes a critical assessment, with a questioning mind, of the
validity of evidence obtained and is alert to evidence that contradicts or brings into
question the reliability of documents or representations by the responsible party.

The practitioner should obtain an understanding of the subject matter and other   **15**
engagement circumstances, sufficient to identify and assess the risks of the subject
matter information being materially misstated, and sufficient to design and perform
further evidence-gathering procedures.

Obtaining an understanding of the subject matter and other engagement circum-   **16**
stances is an essential part of planning and performing an assurance engagement.
That understanding provides the practitioner with a frame of reference for exercising
professional judgment throughout the engagement, for example when:

- Considering the characteristics of the subject matter;
- Assessing the suitability of criteria;
- Identifying where special consideration may be necessary, for example factors
  indicative of fraud, and the need for specialized skills or the work of an expert;
- Establishing and evaluating the continued appropriateness of quantitative
  materiality levels (where appropriate), and considering qualitative materiality
  factors;
- Developing expectations for use when performing analytical procedures;
- Designing and performing further evidence-gathering procedures to reduce
  assurance engagement risk to an appropriate level; and
- Evaluating evidence, including the reasonableness of the responsible party's oral
  and written representations.

The practitioner uses professional judgment to determine the extent of the under-   **17**
standing required of the subject matter and other engagement circumstances. The
practitioner considers whether the understanding is sufficient to assess the risks that
the subject matter information may be materially misstated. The practitioner ordinarily has a lesser depth of understanding than the responsible party.

Assessing the Appropriateness of the Subject Matter

The practitioner should assess the appropriateness of the subject matter. An appro-   **18**
priate subject matter has the characteristics listed in paragraph 33 of the Framework.
The practitioner also identifies those characteristics of the subject matter that are
particularly relevant to the intended users, which are to be described in the assurance
report. As indicated in paragraph 17 of the Framework, a practitioner does not
accept an assurance engagement unless the practitioner's preliminary knowledge of
the engagement circumstances indicates that the subject matter is appropriate. After
accepting the engagement, however, if the practitioner concludes that the subject
matter is not appropriate, the practitioner expresses a qualified or adverse conclusion
or a disclaimer of conclusion. In some cases the practitioner considers withdrawing
from the engagement.

Assessing the Suitability of the Criteria

19   **The practitioner should assess the suitability of the criteria to evaluate or measure the subject matter.** Suitable criteria have the characteristics listed in paragraph 36 of the Framework. As indicated in paragraph 17 of the Framework, a practitioner does not accept an assurance engagement unless the practitioner's preliminary knowledge of the engagement circumstances indicates that the criteria to be used are suitable. After accepting the engagement, however, if the practitioner concludes that the criteria are not suitable, the practitioner expresses a qualified or adverse conclusion or a disclaimer of conclusion. In some cases the practitioner considers withdrawing from the engagement.

20   Paragraph 37 of the Framework indicates that criteria can either be established or specifically developed. Ordinarily, established criteria are suitable when they are relevant to the needs of the intended users. When established criteria exist for a subject matter, specific users may agree to other criteria for their specific purposes. For example, various frameworks can be used as established criteria for evaluating the effectiveness of internal control. Specific users may, however, develop a more detailed set of criteria that meet their specific needs in relation to, for example, prudential supervision. In such cases, the assurance report:

   (a)   Notes, when it is relevant to the circumstances of the engagement, that the criteria are not embodied in laws or regulations, or issued by authorized or recognized bodies of experts that follow a transparent due process; and

   (b)   States that it is only for the use of the specific users and for their purposes.

21   For some subject matters, it is likely that no established criteria exist. In those cases, criteria are specifically developed. The practitioner considers whether specifically developed criteria result in an assurance report that is misleading to the intended users. The practitioner attempts to have the intended users or the engaging party acknowledge that specifically developed criteria are suitable for the intended users' purposes. The practitioner considers how the absence of such an acknowledgement affects what is to be done to assess the suitability of the identified criteria, and the information provided about the criteria in the assurance report.

Materiality and Assurance Engagement Risk

22   **The practitioner should consider materiality and assurance engagement risk when planning and performing an assurance engagement.**

23   The practitioner considers materiality when determining the nature, timing and extent of evidence-gathering procedures, and when evaluating whether the subject matter information is free of misstatement. Considering materiality requires the practitioner to understand and assess what factors might influence the decisions of the intended users. For example, when the identified criteria allow for variations in the presentation of the subject matter information, the practitioner considers how the adopted presentation might influence the decisions of the intended users. Materiality is considered in the context of quantitative and qualitative factors, such as relative magnitude, the nature and extent of the effect of these factors on the evaluation or measurement of the subject matter, and the interests of the intended users. The assessment of materiality and the relative importance of quantitative and qualitative factors in a particular engagement are matters for the practitioner's judgment.

24   **The practitioner should reduce assurance engagement risk to an acceptably low level in the circumstances of the engagement.** In a reasonable assurance engagement, the practitioner reduces assurance engagement risk to an acceptably low level in the

circumstances of the engagement to obtain reasonable assurance as the basis for a positive form of expression of the practitioner's conclusion. The level of assurance engagement risk is higher in a limited assurance engagement than in a reasonable assurance engagement because of the different nature, timing or extent of evidence-gathering procedures. However, in a limited assurance engagement, the combination of the nature, timing, and extent of evidence-gathering procedures is at least sufficient for the practitioner to obtain a meaningful level of assurance as the basis for a negative form of expression. To be meaningful, the level of assurance obtained is likely to enhance the intended users' confidence about the subject matter information to a degree that is clearly more than inconsequential.

Paragraph 49 of the Framework indicates that, in general, assurance engagement risk   25
comprises inherent risk, control risk and detection risk. The degree to which the practitioner considers each of these components is affected by the engagement circumstances, in particular the nature of the subject matter and whether a reasonable assurance or a limited assurance engagement is being performed.

Using the Work of an Expert

**When the work of an expert is used in the collection and evaluation of evidence, the   26
practitioner and the expert should, on a combined basis, possess adequate skill and
knowledge regarding the subject matter and the criteria for the practitioner to determine that sufficient appropriate evidence has been obtained.**

The subject matter and related criteria of some assurance engagements may include   27
aspects requiring specialized knowledge and skills in the collection and evaluation of
evidence. In these situations, the practitioner may decide to use the work of persons
from other professional disciplines, referred to as experts, who have the required
knowledge and skills. This ISAE does not provide guidance with respect to using the
work of an expert for engagements where there is joint responsibility and reporting
by a practitioner and one or more experts.

Due care is a required professional quality for all individuals, including experts,   28
involved in an assurance engagement. Persons involved in assurance engagements
will have different responsibilities assigned to them. The extent of proficiency
required in performing those engagements will vary with the nature of their
responsibilities. While experts do not require the same proficiency as the practitioner
in performing all aspects of an assurance engagement, the practitioner determines
that the experts have a sufficient understanding of the ISAEs to enable them to relate
the work assigned to them to the engagement objective.

The practitioner adopts quality control procedures that address the responsibility of   29
each person performing the assurance engagement, including the work of any experts
who are not professional accountants, to ensure compliance with this ISAE and
other relevant ISAEs in the context of their responsibilities.

**The practitioner should be involved in the engagement and understand the work for   30
which an expert is used, to an extent that is sufficient to enable the practitioner to
accept responsibility for the conclusion on the subject matter information.** The practitioner considers the extent to which it is reasonable to use the work of an expert in
forming the practitioner's conclusion.

The practitioner is not expected to possess the same specialized knowledge and skills   31
as the expert. The practitioner has however, sufficient skill and knowledge to:

(a) Define the objectives of the assigned work and how this work relates to the objective of the engagement;

(b) Consider the reasonableness of the assumptions, methods and source data used by the expert; and

(c) Consider the reasonableness of the expert's findings in relation to the engagement circumstances and the practitioner's conclusion.

32 **The practitioner should obtain sufficient appropriate evidence that the expert's work is adequate for the purposes of the assurance engagement.** In assessing the sufficiency and appropriateness of the evidence provided by the expert, the practitioner evaluates:

(a) The professional competence, including experience, and objectivity of the expert;

(b) The reasonableness of the assumptions, methods and source data used by the expert; and

(c) The reasonableness and significance of the expert's findings in relation to the circumstances of the engagement and the practitioner's conclusion.

Obtaining Evidence

33 **The practitioner should obtain sufficient appropriate evidence on which to base the conclusion.** Sufficiency is the measure of the quantity of evidence. Appropriateness is the measure of the quality of evidence; that is, its relevance and its reliability. The practitioner considers the relationship between the cost of obtaining evidence and the usefulness of the information obtained. However, the matter of difficulty or expense involved is not in itself a valid basis for omitting an evidence-gathering procedure for which there is no alternative. The practitioner uses professional judgment and exercises professional skepticism in evaluating the quantity and quality of evidence, and thus its sufficiency and appropriateness, to support the assurance report.

34 An assurance engagement rarely involves the authentication of documentation, nor is the practitioner trained as or expected to be an expert in such authentication. However, the practitioner considers the reliability of the information to be used as evidence, for example photocopies, facsimiles, filmed, digitized or other electronic documents, including consideration of controls over their preparation and maintenance where relevant.

35 Sufficient appropriate evidence in a reasonable assurance engagement is obtained as part of an iterative, systematic engagement process involving:

(a) Obtaining an understanding of the subject matter and other engagement circumstances which, depending on the subject matter, includes obtaining an understanding of internal control;

(b) Based on that understanding, assessing the risks that the subject matter information may be materially misstated;

(c) Responding to assessed risks, including developing overall responses, and determining the nature, timing and extent of further procedures;

(d) Performing further procedures clearly linked to the identified risks, using a combination of inspection, observation, confirmation, re-calculation, re-performance, analytical procedures and inquiry. Such further procedures involve substantive procedures, including obtaining corroborating information from sources independent of the entity, and depending on the nature of the subject matter, tests of the operating effectiveness of controls; and

(e) Evaluating the sufficiency and appropriateness of evidence.

"Reasonable assurance" is less than absolute assurance. Reducing assurance 36
engagement risk to zero is very rarely attainable or cost beneficial as a result of
factors such as the following:

- The use of selective testing.
- The inherent limitations of internal control.
- The fact that much of the evidence available to the practitioner is persuasive
  rather than conclusive.
- The use of judgment in gathering and evaluating evidence and forming con-
  clusions based on that evidence.
- In some cases, the characteristics of the subject matter.

Both reasonable assurance and limited assurance engagements require the applica- 37
tion of assurance skills and techniques and the gathering of sufficient appropriate
evidence as part of an iterative, systematic engagement process that includes
obtaining an understanding of the subject matter and other engagement circumstances. The nature, timing and extent of procedures for gathering sufficient
appropriate evidence in a limited assurance engagement are, however, deliberately
limited relative to a reasonable assurance engagement. For some subject matters,
there may be specific ISAEs to provide guidance on procedures for gathering sufficient appropriate evidence for a limited assurance engagement. In the absence of a
specific ISAE, the procedures for gathering sufficient appropriate evidence will vary
with the circumstances of the engagement, in particular: the subject matter, and the
needs of the intended users and the engaging party, including relevant time and cost
constraints. For both reasonable assurance and limited assurance engagements, if the
practitioner becomes aware of a matter that leads the practitioner to question
whether a material modification should be made to the subject matter information,
the practitioner pursues the matter by performing other procedures sufficient to
enable the practitioner to report.

Representations by the Responsible Party

The practitioner should obtain representations from the responsible party, as appro- 38
priate. Written confirmation of oral representations reduces the possibility of
misunderstandings between the practitioner and the responsible party. In particular,
the practitioner requests from the responsible party a written representation that
evaluates or measures the subject matter against the identified criteria, whether or
not it is to be made available as an assertion to the intended users. Having no written
representation may result in a qualified conclusion or a disclaimer of conclusion on
the basis of a limitation on the scope of the engagement. The practitioner may also
include a restriction on the use of the assurance report.

During an assurance engagement, the responsible party may make representations to 39
the practitioner, either unsolicited or in response to specific inquiries. When such
representations relate to matters that are material to the subject matter's evaluation
or measurement, the practitioner:

(a) Evaluates their reasonableness and consistency with other evidence obtained,
    including other representations;
(b) Considers whether those making the representations can be expected to be well
    informed on the particular matters; and
(c) Obtains corroborative evidence in the case of a reasonable assurance engage-
    ment. The practitioner may also seek corroborative evidence in the case of a
    limited assurance engagement.

40 Representations by the responsible party cannot replace other evidence the practitioner could reasonably expect to be available. An inability to obtain sufficient appropriate evidence regarding a matter that has, or may have, a material effect on the evaluation or measurement of the subject matter, when such evidence would ordinarily be available, constitutes a limitation on the scope of the engagement, even if a representation from the responsible party has been received on the matter.

Considering Subsequent Events

41 **The practitioner should consider the effect on the subject matter information and on the assurance report of events up to the date of the assurance report.** The extent of consideration of subsequent events depends on the potential for such events to affect the subject matter information and to affect the appropriateness of the practitioner's conclusion. Consideration of subsequent events in some assurance engagements may not be relevant because of the nature of the subject matter. For example, when the engagement requires a conclusion about the accuracy of a statistical return at a point in time, events occurring between that point in time and the date of the assurance report, may not affect the conclusion, or require disclosure in the return or the assurance report.

Documentation

42 **The practitioner should document matters that are significant in providing evidence that supports the assurance report and that the engagement was performed in accordance with ISAEs.**

43 Documentation includes a record of the practitioner's reasoning on all significant matters that require the exercise of judgment, and related conclusions. The existence of difficult questions of principle or judgment, calls for the documentation to include the relevant facts that were known by the practitioner at the time the conclusion was reached.

44 It is neither necessary nor practical to document every matter the practitioner considers. In applying professional judgment to assessing the extent of documentation to be prepared and retained, the practitioner may consider what is necessary to provide an understanding of the work performed and the basis of the principal decisions taken (but not the detailed aspects of the engagement) to another practitioner who has no previous experience with the engagement. That other practitioner may only be able to obtain an understanding of detailed aspects of the engagement by discussing them with the practitioner who prepared the documentation.

Preparing the Assurance Report

45 **The practitioner should conclude whether sufficient appropriate evidence has been obtained to support the conclusion expressed in the assurance report.** In developing the conclusion, the practitioner considers all relevant evidence obtained, regardless of whether it appears to corroborate or to contradict the subject matter information.

46 **The assurance report should be in writing and should contain a clear expression of the practitioner's conclusion about the subject matter information.**

Oral and other forms of expressing conclusions can be misunderstood without the   **47**
support of a written report. For this reason, the practitioner does not report orally or
by use of symbols without also providing a definitive written assurance report that is
readily available whenever the oral report is provided or the symbol is used. For
example, a symbol could be hyperlinked to a written assurance report on the
Internet.

This ISAE does not require a standardized format for reporting on all assurance   **48**
engagements. Instead it identifies in paragraph 49 the basic elements the assurance
report is to include. Assurance reports are tailored to the specific engagement circumstances. The practitioner chooses a "short form" or "long form" style of
reporting to facilitate effective communication to the intended users. "Short-form"
reports ordinarily include only the basic elements. "Long-form" reports often
describe in detail the terms of the engagement, the criteria being used, findings
relating to particular aspects of the engagement and, in some cases, recommendations, as well as the basic elements. Any findings and recommendations are clearly
separated from the practitioner's conclusion on the subject matter information, and
the wording used in presenting them makes it clear they are not intended to affect the
practitioner's conclusion. The practitioner may use headings, paragraph numbers,
typographical devices, for example the bolding of text, and other mechanisms to
enhance the clarity and readability of the assurance report.

Assurance Report Content

The assurance report should include the following basic elements: **49**

(a) **A title that clearly indicates the report is an independent assurance report:**[4] an
    appropriate title helps to identify the nature of the assurance report, and to
    distinguish it from reports issued by others, such as those who do not have to
    comply with the same ethical requirements as the practitioner.
(b) **An addressee:** an addressee identifies the party or parties to whom the assurance
    report is directed. Whenever practical, the assurance report is addressed to all
    the intended users, but in some cases there may be other intended users.
(c) **An identification and description of the subject matter information and, when
    appropriate, the subject matter:** this includes for example:
    - The point in time or period of time to which the evaluation or measurement
      of the subject matter relates;
    - Where applicable, the name of the entity or component of the entity to
      which the subject matter relates; and
    - An explanation of those characteristics of the subject matter or the subject
      matter information of which the intended users should be aware, and how
      such characteristics may influence the precision of the evaluation or mea-
      surement of the subject matter against the identified criteria, or the
      persuasiveness of available evidence. For example:
        o The degree to which the subject matter information is qualitative
          versus quantitative, objective versus subjective, or historical versus
          prospective.
        o Changes in the subject matter or other engagement circumstances that
          affect the comparability of the subject matter information from one
          period to the next.
    When the practitioner's conclusion is worded in terms of the responsible party's
    assertion, that assertion is appended to the assurance report, reproduced in the
    assurance report or referenced therein to a source that is available to the
    intended users.

---

[4] See footnote 2.

(d) **Identification of the criteria:** the assurance report identifies the criteria against which the subject matter was evaluated or measured so the intended users can understand the basis for the practitioner's conclusion. The assurance report may include the criteria, or refer to them if they are contained in an assertion prepared by the responsible party that is available to the intended users or if they are otherwise available from a readily accessible source. The practitioner considers whether it is relevant to the circumstances, to disclose:

- The source of the criteria, and whether or not the criteria are embodied in laws or regulations, or issued by authorized or recognized bodies of experts that follow a transparent due process, that is, whether they are established criteria in the context of the subject matter (and if they are not, a description of why they are considered suitable);
- Measurement methods used when the criteria allow for choice between a number of methods;
- Any significant interpretations made in applying the criteria in the engagement circumstances; and
- Whether there have been any changes in the measurement methods used.

(e) **Where appropriate, a description of any significant, inherent limitation associated with the evaluation or measurement of the subject matter against the criteria:** while in some cases, inherent limitations can be expected to be well understood by readers of an assurance report, in other cases it may be appropriate to make explicit reference in the assurance report. For example, in an assurance report related to the effectiveness of internal control, it may be appropriate to note that the historic evaluation of effectiveness is not relevant to future periods due to the risk that internal control may become inadequate because of changes in conditions, or that the degree of compliance with policies or procedures may deteriorate.

(f) **When the criteria used to evaluate or measure the subject matter are available only to specific intended users, or are relevant only to a specific purpose, a statement restricting the use of the assurance report to those intended users or that purpose:** in addition, whenever the assurance report is intended only for specific intended users or a specific purpose, the practitioner considers stating this fact in the assurance report.[5] This provides a caution to readers that the assurance report is restricted to specific users or for specific purposes.

(g) **A statement to identify the responsible party and to describe the responsible party's and the practitioner's responsibilities:** this informs the intended users that the responsible party is responsible for the subject matter in the case of a direct reporting engagement, or the subject matter information in the case of an assertion-based engagement,[6] and that the practitioner's role is to independently express a conclusion about the subject matter information.

(h) **A statement that the engagement was performed in accordance with ISAEs:** where there is a subject matter specific ISAE, that ISAE may require that the assurance report refer specifically to it.

(i) **A summary of the work performed:** the summary will help the intended users understand the nature of the assurance conveyed by the assurance report. ISA

---

[5] *While an assurance report may be restricted whenever it is intended only for specified intended users or for a specific purpose, the absence of a restriction regarding a particular reader or purpose does not itself indicate that a legal responsibility is owed by the practitioner in relation to that reader or for that purpose. Whether a legal responsibility is owed will depend on the legal circumstances of each case and the relevant jurisdiction.*

[6] *Refer to paragraph 10 of the Framework for an explanation of the distinction between a direct engagement and an assertion-based engagement.*

700, "The Auditor's Report on Financial Statements"[7] and ISRE 2400, "Engagements to Review Financial Statements" provide a guide to the appropriate type of summary.

Where no specific ISAE provides guidance on evidence-gathering procedures for a particular subject matter, the summary might include a more detailed description of the work performed.

Because in a limited assurance engagement an appreciation of the nature, timing, and extent of evidence-gathering procedures performed is essential to understanding the assurance conveyed by a conclusion expressed in the negative form, the summary of the work performed:

(i)   Is ordinarily more detailed than for a reasonable assurance engagement and identifies the limitations on the nature, timing, and extent of evidence-gathering procedures. It may be appropriate to indicate procedures that were not performed that would ordinarily be performed in a reasonable assurance engagement; and

(ii) States that the evidence-gathering procedures are more limited than for a reasonable assurance engagement, and that therefore less assurance is obtained than in a reasonable assurance engagement.

(j)   **The practitioner's conclusion:** where the subject matter information is made up of a number of aspects, separate conclusions may be provided on each aspect. While not all such conclusions need to relate to the same level of evidence-gathering procedures, each conclusion is expressed in the form that is appropriate to either a reasonable-assurance or a limited assurance engagement.

Where appropriate, the conclusion should inform the intended users of the context in which the practitioner's conclusion is to be read: the practitioner's conclusion may, for example, include wording such as: "This conclusion has been formed on the basis of, and is subject to the inherent limitations outlined elsewhere in this independent assurance report." This would be appropriate, for example, when the report includes an explanation of particular characteristics of the subject matter of which the intended users should be aware.

In a reasonable assurance engagement, the conclusion should be expressed in the positive form: for example: "In our opinion internal control is effective, in all material respects, based on *XYZ criteria*" or "In our opinion *the responsible party's* assertion that internal control is effective, in all material respects, based on *XYZ criteria*, is fairly stated."

In a limited assurance engagement, the conclusion should be expressed in the negative form: for example: "Based on our work described in this report, nothing has come to our attention that causes us to believe that internal control is not effective, in all material respects, based on *XYZ criteria*" or "Based on our work described in this report, nothing has come to our attention that causes us to believe that *the responsible party's* assertion that internal control is effective, in all material respects, based on *XYZ criteria*, is not fairly stated."

Where the practitioner expresses a conclusion that is other than unqualified, the assurance report should contain a clear description of all the reasons: (also see paragraphs 51-53).

(k)   **The assurance report date:** this informs the intended users that the practitioner has considered the effect on the subject matter information and on the assurance report of events that occurred up to that date.

(l)   **The name of the firm or the practitioner, and a specific location, which ordinarily is the city where the practitioner maintains the office that has responsibility for the engagement:** this informs the intended users of the individual or firm assuming responsibility for the engagement.

---

[7] *ISA 700, "The Auditor's Report on Financial Statements" was withdrawn in December 2006 when ISA 700, "The Independent Auditor's Report on a Complete Set of General Purpose Financial Statements" became effective.*

50   The practitioner may expand the assurance report to include other information and explanations that are not intended to affect the practitioner's conclusion. Examples include: details of the qualifications and experience of the practitioner and others involved with the engagement, disclosure of materiality levels, findings relating to particular aspects of the engagement, and recommendations. Whether to include any such information depends on its significance to the needs of the intended users. Additional information is clearly separated from the practitioner's conclusion and worded in such a manner so as not to affect that conclusion.

Qualified Conclusions, Adverse Conclusions and Disclaimers of Conclusion

51   **The practitioner should not express an unqualified conclusion when the following circumstances exist and, in the practitioner's judgment, the effect of the matter is or may be material:**

   (a)   **There is a limitation on the scope of the practitioner's work, that is, circumstances prevent, or the responsible party or the engaging party imposes a restriction that prevents, the practitioner from obtaining evidence required to reduce assurance engagement risk to the appropriate level. The practitioner should express a qualified conclusion or a disclaimer of conclusion;**

   (b)   **In those cases where:**

      (i)   **The practitioner's conclusion is worded in terms of the responsible party's assertion, and that assertion is not fairly stated, in all material respects; or**

      (ii) **The practitioner's conclusion is worded directly in terms of the subject matter and the criteria, and the subject matter information is materially misstated,[8] the practitioner should express a qualified or adverse conclusion; or**

   (c)   **When it is discovered, after the engagement has been accepted, that the criteria are unsuitable or the subject matter is not appropriate for an assurance engagement. The practitioner should express:**

      (i)   **A qualified conclusion or adverse conclusion when the unsuitable criteria or inappropriate subject matter is likely to mislead the intended users; or**

      (ii) **A qualified conclusion or a disclaimer of conclusion in other cases.**

52   **The practitioner should express a qualified conclusion when the effect of a matter is not so material or pervasive as to require an adverse conclusion or a disclaimer of conclusion. A qualified conclusion is expressed as being "except for" the effects of the matter to which the qualification relates.**

53   In those cases where the practitioner's unqualified conclusion would be worded in terms of the responsible party's assertion, and that assertion has identified and properly described that the subject matter information is materially misstated, the practitioner either:

   (a)   Expresses a qualified or adverse conclusion worded directly in terms of the subject matter and the criteria; or

   (b)   If specifically required by the terms of the engagement to word the conclusion in terms of the responsible party's assertion, expresses an unqualified conclusion but emphasizes the matter by specifically referring to it in the assurance report.

---

[8] *In those direct reporting engagements where the subject matter information is presented only in the practitioner's conclusion, and the practitioner concludes that the subject matter does not, in all material respects, conform with the criteria, for example: "In our opinion, except for [...],* internal control is effective, in all material respects, based on *XYZ criteria," such a conclusion would also be considered to be qualified (or adverse as appropriate).*

Other Reporting Responsibilities

**The practitioner should consider other reporting responsibilities, including the appro-   54
priateness of communicating relevant matters of governance interest arising from the
assurance engagement with those charged with governance.**

In this ISAE, "governance" describes the role of persons entrusted with the super-   55
vision, control and direction of a responsible party.[9] Those charged with governance
ordinarily are accountable for ensuring that an entity achieves its objectives and for
reporting to interested parties. If the engaging party is different from the responsible
party it may not be appropriate to communicate directly with the responsible party
or those charged with governance over the responsible party.

In this ISAE, "relevant matters of governance interest" are those that arise from the   56
assurance engagement and, in the practitioner's opinion, are both important and
relevant to those charged with governance. Relevant matters of governance interest
include only those matters that have come to the attention of the practitioner while
performing the assurance engagement. If the terms of the engagement do not specifically require it, the practitioner is not required to design procedures for the
specific purpose of identifying matters of governance interest.

Effective Date

This ISAE is effective for assurance engagements where the assurance report is dated   57
on or after January 1, 2005. Earlier application is permissible.

Public Sector Perspective

1.   *This ISAE is applicable to all professional accountants in the public sector who are
     independent of the entity for which they perform assurance engagements. Where
     professional accountants in the public sector are not independent of the entity for
     which they perform an assurance engagement, this ISAE should be applied with
     particular reference to the guidance in footnotes 2 and 4.*

---

[9] *In many countries, principles of governance have been developed as a point of reference for establishing good
governance behavior. Such principles often focus on publicly traded companies; they may however, also serve to
improve governance in other forms of entities. There is no single model of good governance. Governance
structures and practices vary from country to country.*

International Standard on Assurance Engagements 3400

(Previously ISA 810)

The examination of prospective financial information

(This Standard is effective)

Contents

> International Standard on Assurance Engagements (ISAE) 3400, "The Examination of Prospective Financial Information" should be read in the context of the "Preface to the International Standards on Quality Control, Auditing, Review, Other Assurance and Related Services," which sets out the application and authority of ISAEs.

Introduction

The purpose of this International Standard on Assurance Engagements (ISAE) is to   **1**
establish standards and provide guidance on engagements to examine and report on
prospective financial information including examination procedures for best-estimate
and hypothetical assumptions. This ISAE does not apply to the examination of
prospective financial information expressed in general or narrative terms, such as
that found in management's discussion and analysis in an entity's annual report,
though many of the procedures outlined herein may be suitable for such an
examination.

In an engagement to examine prospective financial information, the auditor should   **2**
obtain sufficient appropriate evidence as to whether:

(a) **Management's best-estimate assumptions on which the prospective financial**
    information is based are not unreasonable and, in the case of hypothetical
    assumptions, such assumptions are consistent with the purpose of the information;
(b) **The prospective financial information is properly prepared on the basis of the**
    assumptions;
(c) **The prospective financial information is properly presented and all material**
    assumptions are adequately disclosed, including a clear indication as to whether
    they are best-estimate assumptions or hypothetical assumptions; and
(d) **The prospective financial information is prepared on a consistent basis with his-**
    torical financial statements, using appropriate accounting principles.

"Prospective financial information" means financial information based on assump-   **3**
tions about events that may occur in the future and possible actions by an entity. It is
highly subjective in nature and its preparation requires the exercise of considerable
judgment. Prospective financial information can be in the form of a forecast, a
projection or a combination of both, for example, a one year forecast plus a five year
projection.

A "forecast" means prospective financial information prepared on the basis of   **4**
assumptions as to future events which management expects to take place and the
actions management expects to take as of the date the information is prepared (best-
estimate assumptions).

A "projection" means prospective financial information prepared on the basis of: **5**

(a) Hypothetical assumptions about future events and management actions which
    are not necessarily expected to take place, such as when some entities are in a
    start-up phase or are considering a major change in the nature of operations; or
(b) A mixture of best-estimate and hypothetical assumptions.

Such information illustrates the possible consequences as of the date the information
is prepared if the events and actions were to occur (a "what-if" scenario).

Prospective financial information can include financial statements or one or more   **6**
elements of financial statements and may be prepared:

(a) As an internal management tool, for example, to assist in evaluating a possible
    capital investment; or
(b) For distribution to third parties in, for example:
    • A prospectus to provide potential investors with information about future
      expectations.
    • An annual report to provide information to shareholders, regulatory bodies
      and other interested parties.

- A document for the information of lenders which may include, for example, cash flow forecasts.

7   Management is responsible for the preparation and presentation of the prospective financial information, including the identification and disclosure of the assumptions on which it is based. The auditor may be asked to examine and report on the prospective financial information to enhance its credibility whether it is intended for use by third parties or for internal purposes.

The Auditor's Assurance Regarding Prospective Financial Information

8   Prospective financial information relates to events and actions that have not yet occurred and may not occur. While evidence may be available to support the assumptions on which the prospective financial information is based, such evidence is itself generally future oriented and, therefore, speculative in nature, as distinct from the evidence ordinarily available in the audit of historical financial information. The auditor is, therefore, not in a position to express an opinion as to whether the results shown in the prospective financial information will be achieved.

9   Further, given the types of evidence available in assessing the assumptions on which the prospective financial information is based, it may be difficult for the auditor to obtain a level of satisfaction sufficient to provide a positive expression of opinion that the assumptions are free of material misstatement. Consequently, in this ISAE, when reporting on the reasonableness of management's assumptions the auditor provides only a moderate level of assurance. However, when in the auditor's judgment an appropriate level of satisfaction has been obtained, the auditor is not precluded from expressing positive assurance regarding the assumptions.

Acceptance of Engagement

10   Before accepting an engagement to examine prospective financial information, the auditor would consider, amongst other things:

- The intended use of the information;
- Whether the information will be for general or limited distribution;
- The nature of the assumptions, that is, whether they are best-estimate or hypothetical assumptions;
- The elements to be included in the information; and
- The period covered by the information.

11   **The auditor should not accept, or should withdraw from, an engagement when the assumptions are clearly unrealistic or when the auditor believes that the prospective financial information will be inappropriate for its intended use.**

12   **The auditor and the client should agree on the terms of the engagement.** It is in the interests of both entity and auditor that the auditor sends an engagement letter to help in avoiding misunderstandings regarding the engagement. An engagement letter would address the matters in paragraph 10 and set out management's responsibilities for the assumptions and for providing the auditor with all relevant information and source data used in developing the assumptions.

Knowledge of the Business

The auditor should obtain a sufficient level of knowledge of the business to be able to 13
evaluate whether all significant assumptions required for the preparation of the prospective financial information have been identified. The auditor would also need to
become familiar with the entity's process for preparing prospective financial information, for example, by considering the following:

- The internal controls over the system used to prepare prospective financial
  information and the expertise and experience of those persons preparing the
  prospective financial information.
- The nature of the documentation prepared by the entity supporting management's assumptions.
- The extent to which statistical, mathematical and computer-assisted techniques
  are used.
- The methods used to develop and apply assumptions.
- The accuracy of prospective financial information prepared in prior periods and
  the reasons for significant variances.

The auditor should consider the extent to which reliance on the entity's historical 14
financial information is justified. The auditor requires a knowledge of the entity's
historical financial information to assess whether the prospective financial information has been prepared on a basis consistent with the historical financial
information and to provide a historical yardstick for considering management's
assumptions. The auditor will need to establish, for example, whether relevant historical information was audited or reviewed and whether acceptable accounting
principles were used in its preparation.

If the audit or review report on prior period historical financial information was 15
other than unmodified or if the entity is in a start-up phase, the auditor would
consider the surrounding facts and the effect on the examination of the prospective
financial information.

Period Covered

The auditor should consider the period of time covered by the prospective financial 16
information. Since assumptions become more speculative as the length of the period
covered increases, as that period lengthens, the ability of management to make best-
estimate assumptions decreases. The period would not extend beyond the time for
which management has a reasonable basis for the assumptions. The following are
some of the factors that are relevant to the auditor's consideration of the period of
time covered by the prospective financial information:

- Operating cycle, for example, in the case of a major construction project the
  time required to complete the project may dictate the period covered.
- The degree of reliability of assumptions, for example, if the entity is introducing
  a new product the prospective period covered could be short and broken into
  small segments, such as weeks or months. Alternatively, if the entity's sole
  business is owning a property under long-term lease, a relatively long prospective period might be reasonable.
- The needs of users, for example, prospective financial information may be
  prepared in connection with an application for a loan for the period of time
  required to generate sufficient funds for repayment. Alternatively, the information may be prepared for investors in connection with the sale of debentures
  to illustrate the intended use of the proceeds in the subsequent period.

Examination Procedures

17   **When determining the nature, timing and extent of examination procedures, the auditor's considerations should include:**

(a)   **The likelihood of material misstatement;**

(b)   **The knowledge obtained during any previous engagements;**

(c)   **Management's competence regarding the preparation of prospective financial information;**

(d)   **The extent to which the prospective financial information is affected by the management's judgment; and**

(e)   **The adequacy and reliability of the underlying data.**

18   The auditor would assess the source and reliability of the evidence supporting management's best-estimate assumptions. Sufficient appropriate evidence supporting such assumptions would be obtained from internal and external sources including consideration of the assumptions in the light of historical information and an evaluation of whether they are based on plans that are within the entity's capacity.

19   The auditor would consider whether, when hypothetical assumptions are used, all significant implications of such assumptions have been taken into consideration. For example, if sales are assumed to grow beyond the entity's current plant capacity, the prospective financial information will need to include the necessary investment in the additional plant capacity or the costs of alternative means of meeting the anticipated sales, such as subcontracting production.

20   Although evidence supporting hypothetical assumptions need not be obtained, the auditor would need to be satisfied that they are consistent with the purpose of the prospective financial information and that there is no reason to believe they are clearly unrealistic.

21   The auditor will need to be satisfied that the prospective financial information is properly prepared from management's assumptions by, for example, making clerical checks such as recomputation and reviewing internal consistency, that is, the actions management intends to take are compatible with each other and there are no inconsistencies in the determination of the amounts that are based on common variables such as interest rates.

22   The auditor would focus on the extent to which those areas that are particularly sensitive to variation will have a material effect on the results shown in the prospective financial information. This will influence the extent to which the auditor will seek appropriate evidence. It will also influence the auditor's evaluation of the appropriateness and adequacy of disclosure.

23   When engaged to examine one or more elements of prospective financial information, such as an individual financial statement, it is important that the auditor consider the interrelationship of other components in the financial statements.

24   When any elapsed portion of the current period is included in the prospective financial information, the auditor would consider the extent to which procedures need to be applied to the historical information. Procedures will vary depending on the circumstances, for example, how much of the prospective period has elapsed.

25   **The auditor should obtain written representations from management regarding the intended use of the prospective financial information, the completeness of significant**

management assumptions and management's acceptance of its responsibility for the
prospective financial information.

Presentation and Disclosure

When assessing the presentation and disclosure of the prospective financial infor- **26**
mation, in addition to the specific requirements of any relevant statutes, regulations
or professional standards, the auditor will need to consider whether:

(a) The presentation of prospective financial information is informative and not
misleading;

(b) The accounting policies are clearly disclosed in the notes to the prospective
financial information;

(c) The assumptions are adequately disclosed in the notes to the prospective
financial information. It needs to be clear whether assumptions represent
management's best-estimates or are hypothetical and, when assumptions are
made in areas that are material and are subject to a high degree of uncertainty,
this uncertainty and the resulting sensitivity of results needs to be adequately
disclosed;

(d) The date as of which the prospective financial information was prepared is
disclosed. Management needs to confirm that the assumptions are appropriate
as of this date, even though the underlying information may have been accumulated over a period of time;

(e) The basis of establishing points in a range is clearly indicated and the range is
not selected in a biased or misleading manner when results shown in the prospective financial information are expressed in terms of a range; and

(f) Any change in accounting policy since the most recent historical financial
statements is disclosed, along with the reason for the change and its effect on the
prospective financial information.

Report on Examination of Prospective Financial Information

The report by an auditor on an examination of prospective financial information should **27**
contain the following:

(a) **Title;**

(b) **Addressee;**

(c) **Identification of the prospective financial information;**

(d) **A reference to the ISAE or relevant national standards or practices applicable to
the examination of prospective financial information;**

(e) **A statement that management is responsible for the prospective financial information including the assumptions on which it is based;**

(f) **When applicable, a reference to the purpose and/or restricted distribution of the
prospective financial information;**

(g) **A statement of negative assurance as to whether the assumptions provide a reasonable basis for the prospective financial information;**

(h) **An opinion as to whether the prospective financial information is properly prepared
on the basis of the assumptions and is presented in accordance with the relevant
financial reporting framework;**

(i) **Appropriate caveats concerning the achievability of the results indicated by the
prospective financial information;**

(j) **Date of the report which should be the date procedures have been completed;**

(k) **Auditor's address; and**

(l) **Signature.**

28   Such a report would:

- State whether, based on the examination of the evidence supporting the assumptions, anything has come to the auditor's attention which causes the auditor to believe that the assumptions do not provide a reasonable basis for the prospective financial information.
- Express an opinion as to whether the prospective financial information is properly prepared on the basis of the assumptions and is presented in accordance with the relevant financial reporting framework.
- State that:
    - Actual results are likely to be different from the prospective financial information since anticipated events frequently do not occur as expected and the variation could be material. Likewise, when the prospective financial information is expressed as a range, it would be stated that there can be no assurance that actual results will fall within the range; and
    - In the case of a projection, the prospective financial information has been prepared for (state purpose), using a set of assumptions that include hypothetical assumptions about future events and management's actions that are not necessarily expected to occur. Consequently, readers are cautioned that the prospective financial information is not used for purposes other than that described.

29   The following is an example of an extract from an unmodified report on a forecast:

We have examined the forecast[1] in accordance with the International Standard on Assurance Engagements applicable to the examination of prospective financial information. Management is responsible for the forecast including the assumptions set out in Note X on which it is based.

Based on our examination of the evidence supporting the assumptions, nothing has come to our attention which causes us to believe that these assumptions do not provide a reasonable basis for the forecast. Further, in our opinion the forecast is properly prepared on the basis of the assumptions and is presented in accordance with ....[2]

Actual results are likely to be different from the forecast since anticipated events frequently do not occur as expected and the variation may be material.

30   The following is an example of an extract from an unmodified report on a projection:

We have examined the projection[3] in accordance with the International Standard on Assurance Engagements applicable to the examination of prospective financial information. Management is responsible for the projection including the assumptions set out in Note X on which it is based.

This projection has been prepared for (describe purpose). As the entity is in a start-up phase the projection has been prepared using a set of assumptions that include hypothetical assumptions about future events and management's actions that are not necessarily expected to occur. Consequently, readers are cautioned that this projection may not be appropriate for purposes other than that described above.

[1] *Include name of the entity, the period covered by the forecast and provide suitable identification, such as by reference to page numbers or by identifying the individual statements.*

[2] *Indicate the relevant financial reporting framework.*

[3] *Include name of the entity, the period covered by the projection and provide suitable identification, such as by reference to page numbers or by identifying the individual statements.*

Based on our examination of the evidence supporting the assumptions, nothing has come to our attention which causes us to believe that these assumptions do not provide a reasonable basis for the projection, assuming that (state or refer to the hypothetical assumptions). Further, in our opinion the projection is properly prepared on the basis of the assumptions and is presented in accordance with ....[4]

Even if the events anticipated under the hypothetical assumptions described above occur, actual results are still likely to be different from the projection since other anticipated events frequently do not occur as expected and the variation may be material.

When the auditor believes that the presentation and disclosure of the prospective financial information is not adequate, the auditor should express a qualified or adverse opinion in the report on the prospective financial information, or withdraw from the engagement as appropriate. An example would be where financial information fails to disclose adequately the consequences of any assumptions which are highly sensitive.   31

When the auditor believes that one or more significant assumptions do not provide a reasonable basis for the prospective financial information prepared on the basis of best-estimate assumptions or that one or more significant assumptions do not provide a reasonable basis for the prospective financial information given the hypothetical assumptions, the auditor should either express an adverse opinion in the report on the prospective financial information, or withdraw from the engagement.   32

When the examination is affected by conditions that preclude application of one or more procedures considered necessary in the circumstances, the auditor should either withdraw from the engagement or disclaim the opinion and describe the scope limitation in the report on the prospective financial information.   33

International Standard on Assurance Engagements (ISAE) 3402

Assurance reports on controls at a service organization

(Effective for service auditors' assurance reports covering periods ending on or after June 15, 2011)

Contents

International Standard on Assurance Engagements (ISAE) 3402, "Assurance Reports on Controls at a Service Organization" should be read in conjunction with the "Preface to the International Standards on Quality Control, Auditing, Review, Other Assurance, and Related Services."

Introduction

Scope of this ISAE

1   This International Standard on Assurance Engagements (ISAE) deals with assurance engagements undertaken by a professional accountant in public practice[1] to provide a report for use by user entities and their auditors on the controls at a service organization that provides a service to user entities that is likely to be relevant to user entities' internal control as it relates to financial reporting. It complements ISA 402,[2] in that reports prepared in accordance with this ISAE are capable of providing appropriate evidence under ISA 402. (Ref: Para. A1)

2   The "International Framework for Assurance Engagements" (the Assurance Framework) states that an assurance engagement may be a "reasonable assurance" engagement or a "limited assurance" engagement; that an assurance engagement may be either an "assertion-based" engagement or a "direct reporting" engagement; and, that the assurance conclusion for an assertion-based engagement can be worded either in terms of the responsible party's assertion or directly in terms of the subject matter and the criteria.[3] This ISAE only deals with assertion-based engagements that convey reasonable assurance, with the assurance conclusion worded directly in terms of the subject matter and the criteria.[4]

3   This ISAE applies only when the service organization is responsible for, or otherwise able to make an assertion about, the suitable design of controls. This ISAE does not deal with assurance engagements:

(a)   To report only on whether controls at a service organization operated as described, or

(b)   To report on controls at a service organization other than those related to a service that is likely to be relevant to user entities' internal control as it relates to financial reporting (for example, controls that affect user entities' production or quality control).

This ISAE, however, provides some guidance for such engagements carried out under ISAE 3000.[5] (Ref: Para. A2)

4   In addition to issuing an assurance report on controls, a service auditor may also be engaged to provide reports such as the following, which are not dealt with in this ISAE:

(a)   A report on a user entity's transactions or balances maintained by a service organization; or

(b)   An agreed-upon procedures report on controls at a service organization.

---

[1] *The* Code of Ethics for Professional Accountants *(IESBA Code), issued by the International Ethics Standards Board for Accountants, defines a professional accountant as "an individual who is a member of an IFAC member body," and a professional accountant in public practice as "a professional accountant, irrespective of functional classification (for example, audit, tax or consulting) in a firm that provides professional services. This term is also used to refer to a firm of professional accountants in public practice."*

[2] *ISA 402, "Audit Considerations Relating to an Entity Using a Service Organization."*

[3] *Assurance Framework, paragraphs 10, 11 and 57.*

[4] *Paragraphs 13 and 52(k) of this ISAE.*

[5] *ISAE 3000, "Assurance Engagements Other than Audits or Reviews of Historical Financial Information."*

Relationship with Other Professional Pronouncements

The performance of assurance engagements other than audits or reviews of historical   **5**
financial information requires the service auditor to comply with ISAE 3000. ISAE
3000 includes requirements in relation to such topics as engagement acceptance,
planning, evidence, and documentation that apply to all assurance engagements,
including engagements in accordance with this ISAE. This ISAE expands on how
ISAE 3000 is to be applied in a reasonable assurance engagement to report on
controls at a service organization. The Assurance Framework, which defines and
describes the elements and objectives of an assurance engagement, provides the
context for understanding this ISAE and ISAE 3000.

Compliance with ISAE 3000 requires, among other things, that the service auditor   **6**
comply with the International Ethics Standards Board for Accountants' *Code of
Ethics for Professional Accountants* (IESBA Code), and implement quality control
procedures that are applicable to the individual engagement.[6]

Effective Date

This ISAE is effective for service auditors' assurance reports covering periods ending   **7**
on or after June 15, 2011.

Objectives

The objectives of the service auditor are: **8**

(a) To obtain reasonable assurance about whether, in all material respects, based on
   suitable criteria:
   (i)   The service organization's description of its system fairly presents the
         system as designed and implemented throughout the specified period (or in
         the case of a type 1 report, as at a specified date);
   (ii) The controls related to the control objectives stated in the service organi-
         zation's description of its system were suitably designed throughout the
         specified period (or in the case of a type 1 report, as at a specified date);
   (iii) Where included in the scope of the engagement, the controls operated
         effectively to provide reasonable assurance that the control objectives sta-
         ted in the service organization's description of its system were achieved
         throughout the specified period.
(b) To report on the matters in (a) above in accordance with the service auditor's
   findings.

Definitions

For purposes of this ISAE, the following terms have the meanings attributed below: **9**

(a) Carve-out method – Method of dealing with the services provided by a subservice organization, whereby the service organization's description of its system
   includes the nature of the services provided by a subservice organization, but
   that subservice organization's relevant control objectives and related controls
   are excluded from the service organization's description of its system and from
   the scope of the service auditor's engagement. The service organization's
   description of its system and the scope of the service auditor's engagement

---

[6] *ISAE 3000, paragraphs 4 and 6.*

include controls at the service organization to monitor the effectiveness of controls at the subservice organization, which may include the service organization's review of an assurance report on controls at the subservice organization.

(b) Complementary user entity controls – Controls that the service organization assumes, in the design of its service, will be implemented by user entities, and which, if necessary to achieve control objectives stated in the service organization's description of its system, are identified in that description.

(c) Control objective – The aim or purpose of a particular aspect of controls. Control objectives relate to risks that controls seek to mitigate.

(d) Controls at the service organization – Controls over the achievement of a control objective that is covered by the service auditor's assurance report. (Ref: Para. A3)

(e) Controls at a subservice organization – Controls at a subservice organization to provide reasonable assurance about the achievement of a control objective.

(f) Criteria – Benchmarks used to evaluate or measure a subject matter including, where relevant, benchmarks for presentation and disclosure.

(g) Inclusive method – Method of dealing with the services provided by a subservice organization, whereby the service organization's description of its system includes the nature of the services provided by a subservice organization, and that subservice organization's relevant control objectives and related controls are included in the service organization's description of its system and in the scope of the service auditor's engagement. (Ref: Para. A4)

(h) Internal audit function – An appraisal activity established or provided as a service to the service organization. Its functions include, amongst other things, examining, evaluating and monitoring the adequacy and effectiveness of internal control.

(i) Internal auditors – Those individuals who perform the activities of the internal audit function. Internal auditors may belong to an internal audit department or equivalent function.

(j) Report on the description and design of controls at a service organization (referred to in this ISAE as a "type 1 report") – A report that comprises:

   (i)   The service organization's description of its system;

   (ii) A written assertion by the service organization that, in all material respects, and based on suitable criteria:

      a. The description fairly presents the service organization's system as designed and implemented as at the specified date;

      b. The controls related to the control objectives stated in the service organization's description of its system were suitably designed as at the specified date; and

   (iii) A service auditor's assurance report that conveys reasonable assurance about the matters in (ii)a.–b. above.

(k) Report on the description, design and operating effectiveness of controls at a service organization (referred to in this ISAE as a "type 2 report") – A report that comprises:

   (i)   The service organization's description of its system;

   (ii) A written assertion by the service organization that, in all material respects, and based on suitable criteria:

      a. The description fairly presents the service organization's system as designed and implemented throughout the specified period;

      b. The controls related to the control objectives stated in the service organization's description of its system were suitably designed throughout the specified period; and

      c. The controls related to the control objectives stated in the service organization's description of its system operated effectively throughout the specified period; and

(iii) A service auditor's assurance report that:
    a.   Conveys reasonable assurance about the matters in (ii)a.–c. above; and
    b.   Includes a description of the tests of controls and the results thereof.
(l)   Service auditor – A professional accountant in public practice who, at the request of the service organization, provides an assurance report on controls at a service organization.
(m) Service organization – A third-party organization (or segment of a third-party organization) that provides services to user entities that are likely to be relevant to user entities' internal control as it relates to financial reporting.
(n) Service organization's system (or the system) – The policies and procedures designed and implemented by the service organization to provide user entities with the services covered by the service auditor's assurance report. The service organization's description of its system includes identification of: the services covered; the period, or in the case of a type 1 report, the date, to which the description relates; control objectives; and related controls.
(o) Service organization's assertion – The written assertion about the matters referred to in paragraph 9(k)(ii) (or paragraph 9(j)(ii) in the case of a type 1 report).
(p) Subservice organization – A service organization used by another service organization to perform some of the services provided to user entities that are likely to be relevant to user entities' internal control as it relates to financial reporting.
(q) Test of controls – A procedure designed to evaluate the operating effectiveness of controls in achieving the control objectives stated in the service organization's description of its system.
(r)   User auditor – An auditor who audits and reports on the financial statements of a user entity.[7]
(s)   User entity – An entity that uses a service organization.

Requirements

ISAE 3000

The service auditor shall not represent compliance with this ISAE unless the service auditor has complied with the requirements of this ISAE and ISAE 3000.   **10**

Ethical Requirements

The service auditor shall comply with relevant ethical requirements, including those pertaining to independence, relating to assurance engagements. (Ref: Para. A5)   **11**

Management and Those Charged with Governance

Where this ISAE requires the service auditor to inquire of, request representations from, communicate with, or otherwise interact with the service organization, the service auditor shall determine the appropriate person(s) within the service organization's management or governance structure with whom to interact. This shall include consideration of which person(s) have the appropriate responsibilities for and knowledge of the matters concerned. (Ref: Para. A6)   **12**

---

[7] *In the case of a subservice organization, the service auditor of a service organization that uses the services of the subservice organization is also a user auditor.*

Acceptance and Continuance

13 Before agreeing to accept, or continue, an engagement the service auditor shall:

(a) Determine whether:

  (i) The service auditor has the capabilities and competence to perform the engagement; (Ref: Para. A7)

  (ii) The criteria to be applied by the service organization to prepare the description of its system will be suitable and available to user entities and their auditors; and

  (iii) The scope of the engagement and the service organization's description of its system will not be so limited that they are unlikely to be useful to user entities and their auditors.

(b) Obtain the agreement of the service organization that it acknowledges and understands its responsibility:

  (i) For the preparation of the description of its system, and accompanying service organization's assertion, including the completeness, accuracy and method of presentation of that description and assertion; (Ref: Para. A8)

  (ii) To have a reasonable basis for the service organization's assertion accompanying the description of its system; (Ref: Para. A9)

  (ii) For stating in the service organization's assertion the criteria it used to prepare the description of its system;

  (iii) For stating in the description of its system:

    a. The control objectives; and

    b. Where they are specified by law or regulation, or another party (for example, a user group or a professional body), the party who specified them;

  (iv) For identifying the risks that threaten achievement of the control objectives stated in the description of its system, and designing and implementing controls to provide reasonable assurance that those risks will not prevent achievement of the control objectives stated in the description of its system, and therefore that the stated control objectives will be achieved; and (Ref: Para. A10)

  (v) To provide the service auditor with:

    a. Access to all information, such as records, documentation and other matters, including service level agreements, of which the service organization is aware that is relevant to the description of the service organization's system and the accompanying service organization's assertion;

    b. Additional information that the service auditor may request from the service organization for the purpose of the assurance engagement; and

    c. Unrestricted access to persons within the service organization from whom the service auditor determines it necessary to obtain evidence.

Acceptance of a Change in the Terms of the Engagement

14 If the service organization requests a change in the scope of the engagement before the completion of the engagement, the service auditor shall be satisfied that there is a reasonable justification for the change. (Ref: Para. A11–A12)

Assessing the Suitability of the Criteria

15 As required by ISAE 3000, the service auditor shall assess whether the service organization has used suitable criteria in preparing the description of its system, in

evaluating whether controls are suitably designed, and, in the case of a type 2 report, in evaluating whether controls are operating effectively.[8]

In assessing the suitability of the criteria to evaluate the service organization's description of its system, the service auditor shall determine if the criteria encompass, at a minimum: **16**

(a) Whether the description presents how the service organization's system was designed and implemented, including, as appropriate:
 (i) The types of services provided, including, as appropriate, classes of transactions processed;
 (ii) The procedures, within both information technology and manual systems, by which services are provided, including, as appropriate, procedures by which transactions are initiated, recorded, processed, corrected as necessary, and transferred to the reports and other information prepared for user entities;
 (iii) The related records and supporting information, including, as appropriate, accounting records, supporting information and specific accounts that are used to initiate, record, process and report transactions; this includes the correction of incorrect information and how information is transferred to the reports and other information prepared for user entities;
 (iv) How the service organization's system deals with significant events and conditions, other than transactions;
 (v) The process used to prepare reports and other information for user entities;
 (vi) The specified control objectives and controls designed to achieve those objectives;
 (vii) Complementary user entity controls contemplated in the design of the controls; and
 (viii) Other aspects of the service organization's control environment, risk assessment process, information system (including the related business processes) and communication, control activities and monitoring controls that are relevant to the services provided.
(b) In the case of a type 2 report, whether the description includes relevant details of changes to the service organization's system during the period covered by the description.
(c) Whether the description omits or distorts information relevant to the scope of the service organization's system being described, while acknowledging that the description is prepared to meet the common needs of a broad range of user entities and their auditors and may not, therefore, include every aspect of the service organization's system that each individual user entity and its auditor may consider important in its particular environment.

In assessing the suitability of the criteria to evaluate the design of controls, the service auditor shall determine if the criteria encompass, at a minimum, whether: **17**

(a) The service organization has identified the risks that threaten achievement of the control objectives stated in the description of its system; and
(b) The controls identified in that description would, if operated as described, provide reasonable assurance that those risks do not prevent the stated control objectives from being achieved.

In assessing the suitability of the criteria to evaluate the operating effectiveness of controls in providing reasonable assurance that the stated control objectives identified in the description will be achieved, the service auditor shall determine if the criteria encompass, at a minimum, whether the controls were consistently applied as   **18**

[8] *ISAE 3000, paragraph 19.*

designed throughout the specified period. This includes whether manual controls were applied by individuals who have the appropriate competence and authority. (Ref: Para. A13–A15)

Materiality

19   When planning and performing the engagement, the service auditor shall consider materiality with respect to the fair presentation of the description, the suitability of the design of controls and, in the case of a type 2 report, the operating effectiveness of controls. (Ref: Para. A16–A18)

Obtaining an Understanding of the Service Organization's System

20   The service auditor shall obtain an understanding of the service organization's system, including controls that are included in the scope of the engagement. (Ref: Para. A19–A20)

Obtaining Evidence Regarding the Description

21   The service auditor shall obtain and read the service organization's description of its system, and shall evaluate whether those aspects of the description included in the scope of the engagement are fairly presented, including whether: (Ref: Para. A21–A22)

  (a) Control objectives stated in the service organization's description of its system are reasonable in the circumstances; (Ref: Para. A23)
  (b) Controls identified in that description were implemented;
  (c) Complementary user entity controls, if any, are adequately described; and
  (d) Services performed by a subservice organization, if any, are adequately described, including whether the inclusive method or the carve-out method has been used in relation to them.

22   The service auditor shall determine, through other procedures in combination with inquiries, whether the service organization's system has been implemented. Those other procedures shall include observation, and inspection of records and other documentation, of the manner in which the service organization's system operates and controls are applied. (Ref: Para. A24)

Obtaining Evidence Regarding Design of Controls

23   The service auditor shall determine which of the controls at the service organization are necessary to achieve the control objectives stated in the service organization's description of its system, and shall assess whether those controls were suitably designed. This determination shall include: (Ref: Para. A25–A27)

  (a) Identifying the risks that threaten the achievement of the control objectives stated in the service organization's description of its system; and
  (b) Evaluating the linkage of controls identified in the service organization's description of its system with those risks.

Obtaining Evidence Regarding Operating Effectiveness of Controls

24   When providing a type 2 report, the service auditor shall test those controls that the service auditor has determined are necessary to achieve the control objectives stated

in the service organization's description of its system, and assess their operating effectiveness throughout the period. Evidence obtained in prior engagements about the satisfactory operation of controls in prior periods does not provide a basis for a reduction in testing, even if it is supplemented with evidence obtained during the current period. (Ref: Para. A28–A32)

When designing and performing tests of controls, the service auditor shall: **25**

(a) Perform other procedures in combination with inquiry to obtain evidence about:
   (i) How the control was applied;
   (ii) The consistency with which the control was applied; and
   (iii) By whom or by what means the control was applied;
(b) Determine whether controls to be tested depend upon other controls (indirect controls) and, if so, whether it is necessary to obtain evidence supporting the operating effectiveness of those indirect controls; and (Ref: Para. A33–A34)
(c) Determine means of selecting items for testing that are effective in meeting the objectives of the procedure. (Ref: Para. A35–A36)

When determining the extent of tests of controls, the service auditor shall consider   **26** matters including the characteristics of the population to be tested, which includes the nature of controls, the frequency of their application (for example, monthly, daily, a number of times per day), and the expected rate of deviation.

Sampling

When the service auditor uses sampling, the service auditor shall: (Ref: Para. A35–   **27** A36)

(a) Consider the purpose of the procedure and the characteristics of the population from which the sample will be drawn when designing the sample;
(b) Determine a sample size sufficient to reduce sampling risk to an appropriately low level;
(c) Select items for the sample in such a way that each sampling unit in the population has a chance of selection;
(d) If a designed procedure is not applicable to a selected item, perform the procedure on a replacement item; and
(e) If unable to apply the designed procedures, or suitable alternative procedures, to a selected item, treat that item as a deviation.

Nature and Cause of Deviations

The service auditor shall investigate the nature and cause of any deviations identified   **28** and shall determine whether:

(a) Identified deviations are within the expected rate of deviation and are acceptable; therefore, the testing that has been performed provides an appropriate basis for concluding that the control is operating effectively throughout the specified period;
(b) Additional testing of the control or of other controls is necessary to reach a conclusion on whether the controls relative to a particular control objective are operating effectively throughout the specified period; or (Ref: Para. A25)
(c) The testing that has been performed provides an appropriate basis for concluding that the control did not operate effectively throughout the specified period.

29   In the extremely rare circumstances when the service auditor considers a deviation discovered in a sample to be an anomaly and no other controls have been identified that allow the service auditor to conclude that the relevant control objective is operating effectively throughout the specified period, the service auditor shall obtain a high degree of certainty that such deviation is not representative of the population. The service auditor shall obtain this degree of certainty by performing additional procedures to obtain sufficient appropriate evidence that the deviation does not affect the remainder of the population.

The Work of an Internal Audit Function[9]

Obtaining an Understanding of the Internal Audit Function

30   If the service organization has an internal audit function, the service auditor shall obtain an understanding of the nature of the responsibilities of the internal audit function and of the activities performed in order to determine whether the internal audit function is likely to be relevant to the engagement. (Ref: Para. A37)

Determining Whether and to What Extent to Use the Work of the Internal Auditors

31   The service auditor shall determine:

(a)   Whether the work of the internal auditors is likely to be adequate for purposes of the engagement; and

(b)   If so, the planned effect of the work of the internal auditors on the nature, timing or extent of the service auditor's procedures.

32   In determining whether the work of the internal auditors is likely to be adequate for purposes of the engagement, the service auditor shall evaluate:

(a)   The objectivity of the internal audit function;

(b)   The technical competence of the internal auditors;

(c)   Whether the work of the internal auditors is likely to be carried out with due professional care; and

(d)   Whether there is likely to be effective communication between the internal auditors and the service auditor.

33   In determining the planned effect of the work of the internal auditors on the nature, timing or extent of the service auditor's procedures, the service auditor shall consider: (Ref: Para. A38)

(a)   The nature and scope of specific work performed, or to be performed, by the internal auditors;

(b)   The significance of that work to the service auditor's conclusions; and

(c)   The degree of subjectivity involved in the evaluation of the evidence gathered in support of those conclusions.

Using the Work of the Internal Audit Function

34   In order for the service auditor to use specific work of the internal auditors, the service auditor shall evaluate and perform procedures on that work to determine its adequacy for the service auditor's purposes. (Ref: Para. A39)

[9] *This ISAE does not deal with instances when individual internal auditors provide direct assistance to the service auditor in carrying out audit procedures.*

To determine the adequacy of specific work performed by the internal auditors for **35** the service auditor's purposes, the service auditor shall evaluate whether:

(a) The work was performed by internal auditors having adequate technical training and proficiency;
(b) The work was properly supervised, reviewed and documented;
(c) Adequate evidence has been obtained to enable the internal auditors to draw reasonable conclusions;
(d) Conclusions reached are appropriate in the circumstances and any reports prepared by the internal auditors are consistent with the results of the work performed; and
(e) Exceptions relevant to the engagement or unusual matters disclosed by the internal auditors are properly resolved.

Effect on the Service Auditor's Assurance Report

If the work of the internal audit function has been used, the service auditor shall **36** make no reference to that work in the section of the service auditor's assurance report that contains the service auditor's opinion. (Ref: Para. A40)

In the case of a type 2 report, if the work of the internal audit function has been used **37** in performing tests of controls, that part of the service auditor's assurance report that describes the service auditor's tests of controls and the results thereof shall include a description of the internal auditor's work and of the service auditor's procedures with respect to that work. (Ref: Para. A41)

Written Representations

The service auditor shall request the service organization to provide written repre- **38** sentations: (Ref: Para. A42)

(a) That reaffirm the assertion accompanying the description of the system;
(b) That it has provided the service auditor with all relevant information and access agreed to;[10] and
(c) That it has disclosed to the service auditor any of the following of which it is aware:
 (i) Non-compliance with laws and regulations, fraud, or uncorrected deviations attributable to the service organization that may affect one or more user entities;
 (ii) Design deficiencies in controls;
 (iii) Instances where controls have not operated as described; and
 (iv) Any events subsequent to the period covered by the service organization's description of its system up to the date of the service auditor's assurance report that could have a significant effect on the service auditor's assurance report.

The written representations shall be in the form of a representation letter addressed **39** to the service auditor. The date of the written representations shall be as near as practicable to, but not after, the date of the service auditor's assurance report.

If, having discussed the matter with the service auditor, the service organization does **40** not provide one or more of the written representations requested in accordance with paragraph 38(a) and (b) of this ISAE, the service auditor shall disclaim an opinion. (Ref: Para. A43)

---

[10] *Paragraph 13(b)(v) of this ISAE.*

Other Information

41   The service auditor shall read the other information, if any, included in a document containing the service organization's description of its system and the service auditor's assurance report, to identify material inconsistencies, if any, with that description. While reading the other information for the purpose of identifying material inconsistencies, the service auditor may become aware of an apparent misstatement of fact in that other information.

42   If the service auditor becomes aware of a material inconsistency or an apparent misstatement of fact in the other information, the service auditor shall discuss the matter with the service organization. If the service auditor concludes that there is a material inconsistency or a misstatement of fact in the other information that the service organization refuses to correct, the service auditor shall take further appropriate action. (Ref: Para. A44–A45)

Subsequent Events

43   The service auditor shall inquire whether the service organization is aware of any events subsequent to the period covered by the service organization's description of its system up to the date of the service auditor's assurance report that could have a significant effect on the service auditor's assurance report. If the service auditor is aware of such an event, and information about that event is not disclosed by the service organization, the service auditor shall disclose it in the service auditor's assurance report.

44   The service auditor has no obligation to perform any procedures regarding the description of the service organization's system, or the suitability of design or operating effectiveness of controls, after the date of the service auditor's assurance report.

Documentation

45   The service auditor shall prepare documentation that is sufficient to enable an experienced service auditor, having no previous connection with the engagement, to understand:

(a)   The nature, timing, and extent of the procedures performed to comply with this ISAE and applicable legal and regulatory requirements;

(b)   The results of the procedures performed, and the evidence obtained; and

(c)   Significant matters arising during the engagement, and the conclusions reached thereon and significant professional judgments made in reaching those conclusions.

46   In documenting the nature, timing and extent of procedures performed, the service auditor shall record:

(a)   The identifying characteristics of the specific items or matters being tested;

(b)   Who performed the work and the date such work was completed; and

(c)   Who reviewed the work performed and the date and extent of such review.

47   If the service auditor uses specific work of the internal auditors, the service auditor shall document the conclusions reached regarding the evaluation of the adequacy of the work of the internal auditors, and the procedures performed by the service auditor on that work.

The service auditor shall document discussions of significant matters with the service **48** organization and others including the nature of the significant matters discussed and when and with whom the discussions took place.

If the service auditor has identified information that is inconsistent with the service **49** auditor's final conclusion regarding a significant matter, the service auditor shall document how the service auditor addressed the inconsistency.

The service auditor shall assemble the documentation in an engagement file and **50** complete the administrative process of assembling the final engagement file on a timely basis after the date of the service auditor's assurance report.[11]

After the assembly of the final engagement file has been completed, the service **51** auditor shall not delete or discard documentation before the end of its retention period. (Ref: Para. A46)

If the service auditor finds it necessary to modify existing engagement documentation **52** or add new documentation after the assembly of the final engagement file has been completed and that documentation does not affect the service auditor's report, the service auditor shall, regardless of the nature of the modifications or additions, document:

(a) The specific reasons for making them; and
(b) When and by whom they were made and reviewed.

Preparing the Service Auditor's Assurance Report

Content of the Service Auditor's Assurance Report

The service auditor's assurance report shall include the following basic elements: **53** (Ref: Para. A47)

(a) A title that clearly indicates the report is an independent service auditor's assurance report.
(b) An addressee.
(c) Identification of:
   (i) The service organization's description of its system, and the service organization's assertion, which includes the matters described in paragraph 9(k)(ii) for a type 2 report, or paragraph 9(j)(ii) for a type 1 report.
   (ii) Those parts of the service organization's description of its system, if any, that are not covered by the service auditor's opinion.
   (iii) If the description refers to the need for complementary user entity controls, a statement that the service auditor has not evaluated the suitability of design or operating effectiveness of complementary user entity controls, and that the control objectives stated in the service organization's description of its system can be achieved only if complementary user entity controls are suitably designed or operating effectively, along with the controls at the service organization.
   (iv) If services are performed by a subservice organization, the nature of activities performed by the subservice organization as described in the service organization's description of its system and whether the inclusive method or the carve-out method has been used in relation to them. Where the carve-out method has been used, a statement that the service organization's description of its system excludes the control objectives and related

[11] *International Standard on Quality Control (ISQC) 1, paragraphs A54–A55, provide further guidance.*

controls at relevant subservice organizations, and that the service auditor's procedures do not extend to controls at the subservice organization. Where the inclusive method has been used, a statement that the service organization's description of its system includes control objectives and related controls at the subservice organization, and that the service auditor's procedures extended to controls at the subservice organization.

(d) Identification of the criteria, and the party specifying the control objectives.

(e) A statement that the report and, in the case of a type 2 report, the description of tests of controls are intended only for user entities and their auditors, who have a sufficient understanding to consider it, along with other information including information about controls operated by user entities themselves, when assessing the risks of material misstatements of user entities' financial statements. (Ref: Para. A48)

(f) A statement that the service organization is responsible for:

   (i)   Preparing the description of its system, and the accompanying assertion, including the completeness, accuracy and method of presentation of that description and that assertion;

   (ii) Providing the services covered by the service organization's description of its system;

   (iii) Stating the control objectives (where not identified by law or regulation, or another party, for example, a user group or a professional body); and

   (iv) Designing and implementing controls to achieve the control objectives stated in the service organization's description of its system.

(g) A statement that the service auditor's responsibility is to express an opinion on the service organization's description, on the design of controls related to the control objectives stated in that description and, in the case of a type 2 report, on the operating effectiveness of those controls, based on the service auditor's procedures.

(h) A statement that the engagement was performed in accordance with ISAE 3402, "Assurance Reports on Controls at a Service Organization," which requires that the service auditor comply with ethical requirements and plan and perform procedures to obtain reasonable assurance about whether, in all material respects, the service organization's description of its system is fairly presented and the controls are suitably designed and, in the case of a type 2 report, are operating effectively.

(i) A summary of the service auditor's procedures to obtain reasonable assurance and a statement of the service auditor's belief that the evidence obtained is sufficient and appropriate to provide a basis for the service auditor's opinion, and, in the case of a type 1 report, a statement that the service auditor has not performed any procedures regarding the operating effectiveness of controls and therefore no opinion is expressed thereon.

(j) A statement of the limitations of controls and, in the case of a type 2 report, of the risk of projecting to future periods any evaluation of the operating effectiveness of controls.

(k) The service auditor's opinion, expressed in the positive form, on whether, in all material respects, based on suitable criteria:

   (i)   In the case of a type 2 report:

      a.   The description fairly presents the service organization's system that had been designed and implemented throughout the specified period;

      b.   The controls related to the control objectives stated in the service organization's description of its system were suitably designed throughout the specified period; and

      c.   The controls tested, which were those necessary to provide reasonable assurance that the control objectives stated in the description were achieved, operated effectively throughout the specified period.

   (ii) In the case of a type 1 report:

      a.   The description fairly presents the service organization's system that had been designed and implemented as at the specified date; and

      b.   The controls related to the control objectives stated in the service organization's description of its system were suitably designed as at the specified date.

(l)   The date of the service auditor's assurance report, which shall be no earlier than the date on which the service auditor has obtained sufficient appropriate evidence on which to base the opinion.

(m) The name of the service auditor, and the location in the jurisdiction where the service auditor practices.

54   In the case of a type 2 report, the service auditor's assurance report shall include a separate section after the opinion, or an attachment, that describes the tests of controls that were performed and the results of those tests. In describing the tests of controls, the service auditor shall clearly state which controls were tested, identify whether the items tested represent all or a selection of the items in the population, and indicate the nature of the tests in sufficient detail to enable user auditors to determine the effect of such tests on their risk assessments. If deviations have been identified, the service auditor shall include the extent of testing performed that led to identification of the deviations (including the sample size where sampling has been used), and the number and nature of the deviations noted. The service auditor shall report deviations even if, on the basis of tests performed, the service auditor has concluded that the related control objective was achieved. (Ref: Para. A18 and A49)

Modified Opinions

55   If the service auditor concludes that: (Ref: Para. A50–A52)

(a)   The service organization's description does not fairly present, in all material respects, the system as designed and implemented;

(b)   The controls related to the control objectives stated in the description were not suitably designed, in all material respects;

(c)   In the case of a type 2 report, the controls tested, which were those necessary to provide reasonable assurance that the control objectives stated in the service organization's description of its system were achieved, did not operate effectively, in all material respects; or

(d)   The service auditor is unable to obtain sufficient appropriate evidence,

the service auditor's opinion shall be modified, and the service auditor's assurance report shall contain a clear description of all the reasons for the modification.

Other Communication Responsibilities

56   If the service auditor becomes aware of non-compliance with laws and regulations, fraud, or uncorrected errors attributable to the service organization that are not clearly trivial and may affect one or more user entities, the service auditor shall determine whether the matter has been communicated appropriately to affected user entities. If the matter has not been so communicated and the service organization is unwilling to do so, the service auditor shall take appropriate action. (Ref: Para. A53)

***

Application and Other Explanatory Material

Scope of this ISAE (Ref: Para. 1, 3)

A1   Internal control is a process designed to provide reasonable assurance regarding the achievement of objectives related to the reliability of financial reporting, effectiveness and efficiency of operations and compliance with applicable laws and regulations. Controls related to a service organization's operations and compliance objectives may be relevant to a user entity's internal control as it relates to financial reporting. Such controls may pertain to assertions about presentation and disclosure relating to account balances, classes of transactions or disclosures, or may pertain to evidence that the user auditor evaluates or uses in applying auditing procedures. For example, a payroll processing service organization's controls related to the timely remittance of payroll deductions to government authorities may be relevant to a user entity as late remittances could incur interest and penalties that would result in a liability for the user entity. Similarly, a service organization's controls over the acceptability of investment transactions from a regulatory perspective may be considered relevant to a user entity's presentation and disclosure of transactions and account balances in its financial statements. The determination of whether controls at a service organization related to operations and compliance are likely to be relevant to user entities' internal control as it relates to financial reporting is a matter of professional judgment, having regard to the control objectives set by the service organization and the suitability of the criteria.

A2   The service organization may not be able to assert that the system is suitably designed when, for example, the service organization is operating a system that has been designed by a user entity or is stipulated in a contract between a user entity and the service organization. Because of the inextricable link between the suitable design of controls and their operating effectiveness, the absence of an assertion with respect to the suitability of design will likely preclude the service auditor from concluding that the controls provide reasonable assurance that the control objectives have been met and thus from opining on the operating effectiveness of controls. As an alternative, the practitioner may choose to accept an agreed-upon procedures engagement to perform tests of controls, or an assurance engagement under ISAE 3000 to conclude on whether, based on tests of controls, the controls have operated as described.

Definitions (Ref: Para. 9(d), 9(g))

A3   The definition of "controls at the service organization" includes aspects of user entities' information systems maintained by the service organization, and may also include aspects of one or more of the other components of internal control at a service organization. For example, it may include aspects of a service organization's control environment, monitoring, and control activities when they relate to the services provided. It does not, however, include controls at a service organization that are not related to the achievement of the control objectives stated in the service organization's description of its system, for example, controls related to the preparation of the service organization's own financial statements.

A4   When the inclusive method is used, the requirements in this ISAE also apply to the services provided by the subservice organization, including obtaining agreement regarding the matters in paragraph 13(b)(i)–(v) as applied to the subservice organization rather than the service organization. Performing procedures at the subservice organization entails coordination and communication between the service organization, the subservice organization, and the service auditor. The inclusive method generally is feasible only if the service organization and the subservice organization are related, or if the contract between the service organization and the subservice organization provides for its use.

Ethical Requirements (Ref: Para. 11)

The service auditor is subject to relevant independence requirements, which ordi-   **A5**
narily comprise Parts A and B of the IESBA Code together with national requirements that are more restrictive. In performing an engagement in accordance with this ISAE, the IESBA Code does not require the service auditor to be independent from each user entity.

Management and Those Charged with Governance (Ref: Para. 12)

Management and governance structures vary by jurisdiction and by entity, reflecting   **A6**
influences such as different cultural and legal backgrounds, and size and ownership characteristics. Such diversity means that it is not possible for this ISAE to specify for all engagements the person(s) with whom the service auditor is to interact regarding particular matters. For example, the service organization may be a segment of a third-party organization and not a separate legal entity. In such cases, identifying the appropriate management personnel or those charged with governance from whom to request written representations may require the exercise of professional judgment.

Acceptance and Continuance

Capabilities and Competence to Perform the Engagement (Ref: Para. 13(a)(i))

Relevant capabilities and competence to perform the engagement include matters   **A7**
such as the following:

- Knowledge of the relevant industry;
- An understanding of information technology and systems;
- Experience in evaluating risks as they relate to the suitable design of controls; and
- Experience in the design and execution of tests of controls and the evaluation of the results.

Service Organization's Assertion (Ref: Para. 13(b)(i))

Refusal, by a service organization, to provide a written assertion, subsequent to an   **A8**
agreement by the service auditor to accept, or continue, an engagement, represents a scope limitation that causes the service auditor to withdraw from the engagement. If law or regulation does not allow the service auditor to withdraw from the engagement, the service auditor disclaims an opinion.

Reasonable Basis for Service Organization's Assertion (Ref: Para. 13(b)(ii))

In the case of a type 2 report, the service organization's assertion includes a state-   **A9**
ment that the controls related to the control objectives stated in the service organization's description of its system operated effectively throughout the specified period. This assertion may be based on the service organization's monitoring activities. Monitoring of controls is a process to assess the effectiveness of controls over time. It involves assessing the effectiveness of controls on a timely basis,

identifying and reporting deficiencies to appropriate individuals within the service organization, and taking necessary corrective actions. The service organization accomplishes monitoring of controls through ongoing activities, separate evaluations, or a combination of both. The greater the degree and effectiveness of ongoing monitoring activities, the less need for separate evaluations. Ongoing monitoring activities are often built into the normal recurring activities of a service organization and include regular management and supervisory activities. Internal auditors or personnel performing similar functions may contribute to the monitoring of a service organization's activities. Monitoring activities may also include using information communicated by external parties, such as customer complaints and regulator comments, which may indicate problems or highlight areas in need of improvement. The fact that the service auditor will report on the operating effectiveness of controls is not a substitute for the service organization's own processes to provide a reasonable basis for its assertion.

Identification of Risks (Ref: Para. 13(b)(iv))

A10   As noted in paragraph 9(c), control objectives relate to risks that controls seek to mitigate. For example, the risk that a transaction is recorded at the wrong amount or in the wrong period can be expressed as a control objective that transactions are recorded at the correct amount and in the correct period. The service organization is responsible for identifying the risks that threaten achievement of the control objectives stated in the description of its system. The service organization may have a formal or informal process for identifying relevant risks. A formal process may include estimating the significance of identified risks, assessing the likelihood of their occurrence, and deciding about actions to address them. However, since control objectives relate to risks that controls seek to mitigate, thoughtful identification of control objectives when designing and implementing the service organization's system may itself comprise an informal process for identifying relevant risks.

Acceptance of a Change in the Terms of the Engagement (Ref: Para. 14)

A11   A request to change the scope of the engagement may not have a reasonable justification when, for example, the request is made to exclude certain control objectives from the scope of the engagement because of the likelihood that the service auditor's opinion would be modified; or the service organization will not provide the service auditor with a written assertion and the request is made to perform the engagement under ISAE 3000.

A12   A request to change the scope of the engagement may have a reasonable justification when, for example, the request is made to exclude from the engagement a subservice organization when the service organization cannot arrange for access by the service auditor, and the method used for dealing with the services provided by that subservice organization is changed from the inclusive method to the carve-out method.

Assessing the Suitability of the Criteria (Ref: Para. 15–18)

A13   Criteria need to be available to the intended users to allow them to understand the basis for the service organization's assertion about the fair presentation of its description of the system, the suitability of the design of controls and, in the case of a type 2 report, the operating effectiveness of the controls related to the control objectives.

ISAE 3000 requires the service auditor, among other things, to assess the suitability   **A14**
of criteria, and the appropriateness of the subject matter.[12] The subject matter is the
underlying condition of interest to intended users of an assurance report. The following table identifies the subject matter and minimum criteria for each of the
opinions in type 2 and type 1 reports.

	Subject matter	Criteria	Comment
Opinion about the fair presentation of the description of the service organization's system (type 1 and type 2 reports)	The service organization's system that is likely to be relevant to user entities' internal control as it relates to financial reporting and is covered by the service auditor's assurance report.	The description is fairly presented if it: (a) presents how the service organization's system was designed and implemented including, as appropriate, the matters identified in paragraph 16(a)(i)–(viii); (b) in the case of a type 2 report, includes relevant details of changes to the service organization's system during the period covered by the description; and (c) does not omit or distort information relevant to the scope of the service organization's system being described, while acknowledging that the description is prepared to meet the common needs of a broad range of user entities and may not, therefore, include every aspect of the service organization's system that each individual user entity may consider important in its own particular environment.	The specific wording of the criteria for this opinion may need to be tailored to be consistent with criteria established by, for example, law or regulation, user groups, or a professional body. Examples of criteria for this opinion are provided in the illustrative service organization's assertion in Appendix 1. Paragraphs A21–A24 offer further guidance on determining whether these criteria are met. (In terms of the requirements of ISAE 3000, the subject matter information[13] for this opinion is the service organization's description of its system and the service organization's assertion that the description is fairly presented.)

[12] *ISAE 3000, paragraphs 18–19.*

[13] *The "subject matter information" is the outcome of the evaluation or measurement of the subject matter that results from applying the criteria to the subject matter.*

	Subject matter	Criteria	Comment	
Opinion about suitability of design, and operating effectiveness (type 2 reports)	The suitability of the design and operating effectiveness of those controls that are necessary to achieve the control objectives stated in the service organization's description of its system.	The controls are suitably designed and operating effectively if: (a) the service organization has identified the risks that threaten achievement of the control objectives stated in the description of its system; (b) the controls identified in that description would, if operated as described, provide reasonable assurance that those risks do not prevent the stated control objectives from being achieved; and (c) the controls were consistently applied as designed throughout the specified period. This includes whether manual controls were applied by individuals who have the appropriate competence and authority.	When the criteria for this opinion are met, controls will have provided reasonable assurance that the related control objectives were achieved throughout the specified period. (In terms of the requirements of ISAE 3000, the subject matter information for this opinion is the service organization's assertion that controls are suitably designed and that they are operating effectively.)	The control objectives, which are stated in the service organization's description of its system, are part of the criteria for these opinions. The stated control objectives will differ from engagement to engagement. If, as part of forming the opinion on the description, the service auditor concludes the stated control objectives are not fairly presented then those control objectives would not be suitable as part of the criteria for forming an opinion on either the design or operating effectiveness of controls.
Opinion about suitability of design (type 1 reports)	The suitability of the design of those controls that are necessary to achieve the control objectives stated in the service organization's description of its system.	The controls are suitably designed if: (a) the service organization has identified the risks that threaten achievement of the control objectives stated in the description of its system; and (b) the controls identified in that description would, if operated as described, provide reasonable assurance that those risks do not prevent the stated control objectives from being achieved.	Meeting these criteria does not, of itself, provide any assurance that the related control objectives were achieved because no assurance has been obtained about the operation of controls. (In terms of the requirements of ISAE 3000, the subject matter information for this opinion is the service organization's assertion that controls are suitably designed.)	

Paragraph 16(a) identifies a number of elements that are included in the service **A15**
organization's description of its system as appropriate. These elements may not be
appropriate if the system being described is not a system that processes transactions,
for example, if the system relates to general controls over the hosting of an IT
application but not the controls embedded in the application itself.

Materiality (Ref: Para. 19, 54)

In an engagement to report on controls at a service organization, the concept of **A16**
materiality relates to the system being reported on, not the financial statements of
user entities. The service auditor plans and performs procedures to determine whether the service organization's description of its system is fairly presented in all
material respects, whether controls at the service organization are suitably designed
in all material respects and, in the case of a type 2 report, whether controls at the
service organization are operating effectively in all material respects. The concept of
materiality takes into account that the service auditor's assurance report provides
information about the service organization's system to meet the common information needs of a broad range of user entities and their auditors who have an
understanding of the manner in which that system has been used.

Materiality with respect to the fair presentation of the service organization's **A17**
description of its system, and with respect to the design of controls, includes primarily the consideration of qualitative factors, for example: whether the description
includes the significant aspects of processing significant transactions; whether the
description omits or distorts relevant information; and the ability of controls, as
designed, to provide reasonable assurance that control objectives would be achieved.
Materiality with respect to the service auditor's opinion on the operating effectiveness of controls includes the consideration of both quantitative and qualitative
factors, for example, the tolerable rate and observed rate of deviation (a quantitative
matter), and the nature and cause of any observed deviation (a qualitative matter).

The concept of materiality is not applied when disclosing, in the description of the **A18**
tests of controls, the results of those tests where deviations have been identified. This
is because, in the particular circumstances of a specific user entity or user auditor, a
deviation may have significance beyond whether or not, in the opinion of the service
auditor, it prevents a control from operating effectively. For example, the control to
which the deviation relates may be particularly significant in preventing a certain
type of error that may be material in the particular circumstances of a user entity's
financial statements.

Obtaining an Understanding of the Service Organization's System
(Ref: Para. 20)

Obtaining an understanding of the service organization's system, including controls, **A19**
included in the scope of the engagement, assists the service auditor in:

- Identifying the boundaries of that system, and how it interfaces with other
  systems.
- Assessing whether the service organization's description fairly presents the
  system that has been designed and implemented.
- Determining which controls are necessary to achieve the control objectives
  stated in the service organization's description of its system.
- Assessing whether controls were suitably designed.
- Assessing, in the case of a type 2 report, whether controls were operating
  effectively.

A20   The service auditor's procedures to obtain this understanding may include:

- Inquiring of those within the service organization who, in the service auditor's judgment, may have relevant information.
- Observing operations and inspecting documents, reports, printed and electronic records of transaction processing.
- Inspecting a selection of agreements between the service organization and user entities to identify their common terms.
- Reperforming control procedures.

Obtaining Evidence Regarding the Description (Ref: Para. 21–22)

A21   Considering the following questions may assist the service auditor in determining whether those aspects of the description included in the scope of the engagement are fairly presented in all material respects:

- Does the description address the major aspects of the service provided (within the scope of the engagement) that could reasonably be expected to be relevant to the common needs of a broad range of user auditors in planning their audits of user entities' financial statements?
- Is the description prepared at a level of detail that could reasonably be expected to provide a broad range of user auditors with sufficient information to obtain an understanding of internal control in accordance with ISA 315?[14] The description need not address every aspect of the service organization's processing or the services provided to user entities, and need not be so detailed as to potentially allow a reader to compromise security or other controls at the service organization.
- Is the description prepared in a manner that does not omit or distort information that may affect the common needs of a broad range of user auditors' decisions, for example, does the description contain any significant omissions or inaccuracies in processing of which the service auditor is aware?
- Where some of the control objectives stated in the service organization's description of its system have been excluded from the scope of the engagement, does the description clearly identify the excluded objectives?
- Have the controls identified in the description been implemented?
- Are complementary user entity controls, if any, described adequately? In most cases, the description of control objectives is worded such that the control objectives are capable of being achieved through effective operation of controls implemented by the service organization alone. In some cases, however, the control objectives stated in the service organization's description of its system cannot be achieved by the service organization alone because their achievement requires particular controls to be implemented by user entities. This may be the case where, for example, the control objectives are specified by a regulatory authority. When the description does include complementary user entity controls, the description separately identifies those controls along with the specific control objectives that cannot be achieved by the service organization alone.
- If the inclusive method has been used, does the description separately identify controls at the service organization and controls at the subservice organization? If the carve-out method is used, does the description identify the functions that are performed by the subservice organization? When the carve-out method is used, the description need not describe the detailed processing or controls at the subservice organization.

---

[14] *ISA 315, "Identifying and Assessing Risks of Material Misstatement through Understanding the Entity and Its Environment."*

The service auditor's procedures to evaluate the fair presentation of the description   **A22**
may include:

- Considering the nature of user entities and how the services provided by the service organization are likely to affect them, for example, whether user entities are from a particular industry and whether they are regulated by government agencies.
- Reading standard contracts, or standard terms of contracts, (if applicable) with user entities to gain an understanding of the service organization's contractual obligations.
- Observing procedures performed by service organization personnel.
- Reviewing the service organization's policy and procedure manuals and other systems documentation, for example, flowcharts and narratives.

Paragraph 21(a) requires the service auditor to evaluate whether the control objec-   **A23**
tives stated in the service organization's description of its system are reasonable in
the circumstances. Considering the following questions may assist the service auditor
in this evaluation:

- Have the stated control objectives been designated by the service organization or by outside parties such as a regulatory authority, a user group, or a professional body that follows a transparent due process?
- Where the stated control objectives have been specified by the service organization, do they relate to the types of assertions commonly embodied in the broad range of user entities' financial statements to which controls at the service organization could reasonably be expected to relate? Although the service auditor ordinarily will not be able to determine how controls at a service organization specifically relate to the assertions embodied in individual user entities' financial statements, the service auditor's understanding of the nature of the service organization's system, including controls, and services being provided is used to identify the types of assertions to which those controls are likely to relate.
- Where the stated control objectives have been specified by the service organization, are they complete? A complete set of control objectives can provide a broad range of user auditors with a framework to assess the effect of controls at the service organization on the assertions commonly embodied in user entities' financial statements.

The service auditor's procedures to determine whether the service organization's   **A24**
system has been implemented may be similar to, and performed in conjunction with,
procedures to obtain an understanding of that system. They may also include tracing
items through the service organization's system and, in the case of a type 2 report,
specific inquiries about changes in controls that were implemented during the period.
Changes that are significant to user entities or their auditors are included in the
description of the service organization's system.

Obtaining Evidence Regarding Design of Controls (Ref: Para. 23, 28(b))

From the viewpoint of a *user entity* or a *user auditor*, a control is suitably designed if,   **A25**
individually or in combination with other controls, it would, when complied with
satisfactorily, provide reasonable assurance that material misstatements are prevented, or detected and corrected. A *service organization* or a *service auditor*,
however, is not aware of the circumstances at individual user entities that would
determine whether or not a misstatement resulting from a control deviation is
material to those user entities. Therefore, from the viewpoint of a service auditor, a
control is suitably designed if, individually or in combination with other controls, it

would, when complied with satisfactorily, provide reasonable assurance that control objectives stated in the service organization's description of its system are achieved.

A26   A service auditor may consider using flowcharts, questionnaires, or decision tables to facilitate understanding the design of the controls.

A27   Controls may consist of a number of activities directed at the achievement of a control objective. Consequently, if the service auditor evaluates certain activities as being ineffective in achieving a particular control objective, the existence of other activities may allow the service auditor to conclude that controls related to the control objective are suitably designed.

Obtaining Evidence Regarding Operating Effectiveness of Controls

Assessing Operating Effectiveness (Ref: Para. 24)

A28   From the viewpoint of a *user entity* or a *user auditor*, a control is operating effectively if, individually or in combination with other controls, it provides reasonable assurance that material misstatements, whether due to fraud or error, are prevented, or detected and corrected. A *service organization* or a *service auditor*, however, is not aware of the circumstances at individual user entities that would determine whether a misstatement resulting from a control deviation had occurred and, if so, whether it is material. Therefore, from the viewpoint of a service auditor, a control is operating effectively if, individually or in combination with other controls, it provides reasonable assurance that control objectives stated in the service organization's description of its system are achieved. Similarly, a service organization or a service auditor is not in a position to determine whether any observed control deviation would result in a material misstatement from the viewpoint of an individual user entity.

A29   Obtaining an understanding of controls sufficient to opine on the suitability of their design is not sufficient evidence regarding their operating effectiveness, unless there is some automation that provides for the consistent operation of the controls as they were designed and implemented. For example, obtaining information about the implementation of a manual control at a point in time does not provide evidence about operation of the control at other times. However, because of the inherent consistency of IT processing, performing procedures to determine the design of an automated control, and whether it has been implemented, may serve as evidence of that control's operating effectiveness, depending on the service auditor's assessment and testing of other controls, such as those over program changes.

A30   To be useful to user auditors, a type 2 report ordinarily covers a minimum period of six months. If the period is less than six months, the service auditor may consider it appropriate to describe the reasons for the shorter period in the service auditor's assurance report. Circumstances that may result in a report covering a period of less than six months include when (a) the service auditor is engaged close to the date by which the report on controls is to be issued; (b) the service organization (or a particular system or application) has been in operation for less than six months; or (c) significant changes have been made to the controls and it is not practicable either to wait six months before issuing a report or to issue a report covering the system both before and after the changes.

A31   Certain control procedures may not leave evidence of their operation that can be tested at a later date and, accordingly, the service auditor may find it necessary to test the operating effectiveness of such control procedures at various times throughout the reporting period.

The service auditor provides an opinion on the operating effectiveness of controls **A32** throughout each period, therefore, sufficient appropriate evidence about the operation of controls during the current period is required for the service auditor to express that opinion. Knowledge of deviations observed in prior engagements may, however, lead the service auditor to increase the extent of testing during the current period.

Testing of Indirect Controls (Ref: Para. 25(b))

In some circumstances, it may be necessary to obtain evidence supporting the **A33** effective operation of indirect controls. For example, when the service auditor decides to test the effectiveness of a review of exception reports detailing sales in excess of authorized credit limits, the review and related follow up is the control that is directly of relevance to the service auditor. Controls over the accuracy of the information in the reports (for example, the general IT controls) are described as "indirect" controls.

Because of the inherent consistency of IT processing, evidence about the imple- **A34** mentation of an automated application control, when considered in combination with evidence about the operating effectiveness of the service organization's general controls (in particular, change controls), may also provide substantial evidence about its operating effectiveness.

Means of Selecting Items for Testing (Ref: Para. 25(c), 27)

The means of selecting items for testing available to the service auditor are: **A35**

(a) Selecting all items (100% examination). This may be appropriate for testing controls that are applied infrequently, for example, quarterly, or when evidence regarding application of the control makes 100% examination efficient;

(b) Selecting specific items. This may be appropriate where 100% examination would not be efficient and sampling would not be effective, such as testing controls that are not applied sufficiently frequently to render a large population for sampling, for example, controls that are applied monthly or weekly; and

(c) Sampling. This may be appropriate for testing controls that are applied frequently in a uniform manner and which leave documentary evidence of their application.

While selective examination of specific items will often be an efficient means of **A36** obtaining evidence, it does not constitute sampling. The results of procedures applied to items selected in this way cannot be projected to the entire population; accordingly, selective examination of specific items does not provide evidence concerning the remainder of the population. Sampling, on the other hand, is designed to enable conclusions to be drawn about an entire population on the basis of testing a sample drawn from it.

The Work of an Internal Audit Function

Obtaining an Understanding of the Internal Audit Function (Ref: Para. 30)

An internal audit function may be responsible for providing analyses, evaluations, **A37** assurances, recommendations, and other information to management and those charged with governance. An internal audit function at a service organization may perform activities related to the service organization's own system of internal control, or activities related to the services and systems, including controls, that the service organization is providing to user entities.

Determining Whether and to What Extent to Use the Work of the Internal Auditors (Ref: Para. 33)

A38   In determining the planned effect of the work of the internal auditors on the nature, timing or extent of the service auditor's procedures, the following factors may suggest the need for different or less extensive procedures than would otherwise be the case:

- The nature and scope of specific work performed, or to be performed, by the internal auditors is quite limited.
- The work of the internal auditors relates to controls that are less significant to the service auditor's conclusions.
- The work performed, or to be performed, by the internal auditors does not require subjective or complex judgments.

Using the Work of the Internal Audit Function (Ref: Para. 34)

A39   The nature, timing and extent of the service auditor's procedures on specific work of the internal auditors will depend on the service auditor's assessment of the significance of that work to the service auditor's conclusions (for example, the significance of the risks that the controls tested seek to mitigate), the evaluation of the internal audit function and the evaluation of the specific work of the internal auditors Such procedures may include:

- Examination of items already examined by the internal auditors;
- Examination of other similar items; and
- Observation of procedures performed by the internal auditors.

Effect on the Service Auditor's Assurance Report (Ref: Para. 36–37)

A40   Irrespective of the degree of autonomy and objectivity of the internal audit function, such function is not independent of the service organization as is required of the service auditor when performing the engagement. The service auditor has sole responsibility for the opinion expressed in the service auditor's assurance report, and that responsibility is not reduced by the service auditor's use of the work of the internal auditors.

A41   The service auditor's description of work performed by the internal audit function may be presented in a number of ways, for example:

- By including introductory material to the description of tests of controls indicating that certain work of the internal audit function was used in performing tests of controls.
- Attribution of individual tests to internal audit.

Written Representations (Ref: Para. 38, 40)

A42   The written representations required by paragraph 38 are separate from, and in addition to, the service organization's assertion, as defined at paragraph 9(o).

If the service organization does not provide the written representations requested in accordance with paragraph 38(c) of this ISAE, it may be appropriate for the service auditor's opinion to be modified in accordance with paragraph 55(d) of this ISAE.   **A43**

Other Information (Ref: Para. 42)

The IESBA Code requires that a service auditor not be associated with information where the service auditor believes that the information: **A44**

(a)   Contains a materially false or misleading statement;
(b)   Contains statements or information furnished recklessly; or
(c)   Omits or obscures information required to be included where such omission or obscurity would be misleading.[15]

If other information included in a document containing the service organization's description of its system and the service auditor's assurance report contains future-oriented information such as recovery or contingency plans, or plans for modifications to the system that will address deviations identified in the service auditor's assurance report, or claims of a promotional nature that cannot be reasonably substantiated, the service auditor may request that information be removed or restated.

If the service organization refuses to remove or restate the other information, further actions that may be appropriate include, for example: **A45**

●   Requesting the service organization to consult with its legal counsel as to the appropriate course of action.
●   Describing the material inconsistency or material misstatement of fact in the assurance report.
●   Withholding the assurance report until the matter is resolved.
●   Withdrawing from the engagement.

Documentation (Ref: Para. 51)

ISQC 1 (or national requirements that are at least as demanding) requires firms to establish policies and procedures for the timely completion of the assembly of engagement files.[16] An appropriate time limit within which to complete the assembly of the final engagement file is ordinarily not more than 60 days after the date of the service auditor's report.[17]   **A46**

Preparing the Service Auditor's Assurance Report

Content of the Service Auditor's Assurance Report (Ref: Para. 53)

Illustrative examples of service auditors' assurance reports and related service organizations' assertions are contained in Appendices 1 and 2.   **A47**

---

[15] *IESBA Code, paragraph 110.2.*

[16] *ISQC 1, paragraph 45.*

[17] *ISQC 1, paragraph A54.*

Intended Users and Purposes of the Service Auditor's Assurance Report (Ref: Para. 53(e))

A48   The criteria used for engagements to report on controls at a service organization are relevant only for the purposes of providing information about the service organization's system, including controls, to those who have an understanding of how the system has been used for financial reporting by user entities. Accordingly this is stated in the service auditor's assurance report. In addition, the service auditor may consider it appropriate to include wording that specifically restricts distribution of the assurance report other than to intended users, its use by others, or its use for other purposes.

Description of the Tests of Controls (Ref: Para. 54)

A49   In describing the nature of the tests of controls for a type 2 report, it assists readers of the service auditor's assurance report if the service auditor includes:

- The results of all tests where deviations have been identified, even if other controls have been identified that allow the service auditor to conclude that the relevant control objective has been achieved or the control tested has subsequently been removed from the service organization's description of its system.
- Information about causative factors for identified deviations, to the extent the service auditor has identified such factors.

Modified Opinions (Ref: Para. 55)

A50   Illustrative examples of elements of modified service auditor's assurance reports are contained in Appendix 3.

A51   Even if the service auditor has expressed an adverse opinion or disclaimed an opinion, it may be appropriate to describe in the basis for modification paragraph the reasons for any other matters of which the service auditor is aware that would have required a modification to the opinion, and the effects thereof.

A52   When expressing a disclaimer of opinion because of a scope limitation, it is not ordinarily appropriate to identify the procedures that were performed nor include statements describing the characteristics of a service auditor's engagement; to do so might overshadow the disclaimer of opinion.

Other Communication Responsibilities (Ref: Para. 56)

A53   Appropriate actions to respond to the circumstances identified in paragraph 56 may include:

- Obtaining legal advice about the consequences of different courses of action.
- Communicating with those charged with governance of the service organization.
- Communicating with third parties (for example, a regulator) when required to do so.
- Modifying the service auditor's opinion, or adding an Other Matter paragraph.
- Withdrawing from the engagement.

Appendix 1

Example Service Organization's Assertions

The following examples of service organization's assertions are for guidance only and are not intended to be exhaustive or applicable to all situations.

Example 1: Type 2 Service Organization's Assertion

Assertion by the Service Organization

The accompanying description has been prepared for customers who have used *[the type or name of]* system and their auditors who have a sufficient understanding to consider the description, along with other information including information about controls operated by customers themselves, when assessing the risks of material misstatements of customers' financial statements. *[Entity's name]* confirms that:

(a) The accompanying description at pages *[bb–cc]* fairly presents *[the type or name of]* system for processing customers' transactions throughout the period *[date]* to *[date]*. The criteria used in making this assertion were that the accompanying description:

   (i) Presents how the system was designed and implemented, including:

- The types of services provided, including, as appropriate, classes of transactions processed.
- The procedures, within both information technology and manual systems, by which those transactions were initiated, recorded, processed, corrected as necessary, and transferred to the reports prepared for customers.
- The related accounting records, supporting information and specific accounts that were used to initiate, record, process and report transactions; this includes the correction of incorrect information and how information was transferred to the reports prepared for customers.
- How the system dealt with significant events and conditions, other than transactions.
- The process used to prepare reports for customers.
- Relevant control objectives and controls designed to achieve those objectives.
- Controls that we assumed, in the design of the system, would be implemented by user entities, and which, if necessary to achieve control objectives stated in the accompanying description, are identified in the description along with the specific control objectives that cannot be achieved by ourselves alone.
- Other aspects of our control environment, risk assessment process, information system (including the related business processes) and communication, control activities and monitoring controls that were relevant to processing and reporting customers' transactions.

   (ii) Includes relevant details of changes to the service organization's system during the period *[date]* to *[date]*.

   (iii) Does not omit or distort information relevant to the scope of the system being described, while acknowledging that the description is prepared to meet the common needs of a broad range of customers and their auditors and may not, therefore, include every aspect of the system that each individual customer may consider important in its own particular environment.

(b) The controls related to the control objectives stated in the accompanying description were suitably designed and operated effectively throughout the period *[date]* to *[date]*. The criteria used in making this assertion were that:

   (i)   The risks that threatened achievement of the control objectives stated in the description were identified;

   (ii) The identified controls would, if operated as described, provide reasonable assurance that those risks did not prevent the stated control objectives from being achieved; and

   (iii) The controls were consistently applied as designed, including that manual controls were applied by individuals who have the appropriate competence and authority, throughout the period *[date]* to *[date]*.

Example 2: Type 1 Service Organization's Assertion

The accompanying description has been prepared for customers who have used *[the type or name of]* system and their auditors who have a sufficient understanding to consider the description, along with other information including information about controls operated by customers themselves, when obtaining an understanding of customers' information systems relevant to financial reporting. *[Entity's name]* confirms that:

(a) The accompanying description at pages *[bb–cc]* fairly presents *[the type or name of]* system for processing customers' transactions as at *[date]*. The criteria used in making this assertion were that the accompanying description:

   (i)   Presents how the system was designed and implemented, including:

   • The types of services provided, including, as appropriate, classes of transactions processed.

   • The procedures, within both information technology and manual systems, by which those transactions were initiated, recorded, processed, corrected as necessary, and transferred to the reports prepared for customers.

   • The related accounting records, supporting information and specific accounts that were used to initiate, record, process and report transactions; this includes the correction of incorrect information and how information is transferred to the reports prepared customers.

   • How the system dealt with significant events and conditions, other than transactions.

   • The process used to prepare reports for customers.

   • Relevant control objectives and controls designed to achieve those objectives.

   • Controls that we assumed, in the design of the system, would be implemented by user entities, and which, if necessary to achieve control objectives stated in the accompanying description, are identified in the description along with the specific control objectives that cannot be achieved by ourselves alone.

   • Other aspects of our control environment, risk assessment process, information system (including the related business processes) and communication, control activities and monitoring controls that were relevant to processing and reporting customers' transactions.

   (ii) Does not omit or distort information relevant to the scope of the system being described, while acknowledging that the description is prepared to meet the common needs of a broad range of customers and their auditors and may not, therefore, include every aspect of the system that each individual customer may consider important in its own particular environment.

(b) The controls related to the control objectives stated in the accompanying description were suitably designed as at *[date]*. The criteria used in making this assertion were that:
  (i) The risks that threatened achievement of the control objectives stated in the description were identified; and
  (ii) The identified controls would, if operated as described, provide reasonable assurance that those risks did not prevent the stated control objectives from being achieved.

Appendix 2 (Ref. Para. A47)

Illustrations of Service Auditor's Assurance Reports

The following illustrations of reports are for guidance only and are not intended to be exhaustive or applicable to all situations.

Illustration 1: Type 2 Service Auditor's Assurance Report

Independent Service Auditor's Assurance Report on the Description of Controls, their Design and Operating Effectiveness

To: XYZ Service Organization

Scope

We have been engaged to report on XYZ Service Organization's description at pages *[bb–cc]* of its *[type or name of]* system for processing customers' transactions throughout the period *[date]* to *[date]* (the description), and on the design and operation of controls related to the control objectives stated in the description.[18]

XYZ Service Organization's Responsibilities

XYZ Service Organization is responsible for: preparing the description and accompanying assertion at page *[aa]*, including the completeness, accuracy and method of presentation of the description and assertion; providing the services covered by the description; stating the control objectives; and designing, implementing and effectively operating controls to achieve the stated control objectives.

Service Auditor's Responsibilities

Our responsibility is to express an opinion on XYZ Service Organization's description and on the design and operation of controls related to the control objectives stated in that description, based on our procedures. We conducted our engagement in accordance with International Standard on Assurance Engagements 3402, "Assurance Reports on Controls at a Service Organization," issued by the International Auditing and Assurance Standards Board. That standard requires that we comply with ethical requirements and plan and perform our procedures to obtain reasonable assurance about whether, in all material respects, the description is fairly presented and the controls are suitably designed and operating effectively.

---

[18] *If some elements of the description are not included in the scope of the engagement, this is made clear in the assurance report.*

An assurance engagement to report on the description, design and operating effectiveness of controls at a service organization involves performing procedures to obtain evidence about the disclosures in the service organization's description of its system, and the design and operating effectiveness of controls. The procedures selected depend on the service auditor's judgment, including the assessment of the risks that the description is not fairly presented, and that controls are not suitably designed or operating effectively. Our procedures included testing the operating effectiveness of those controls that we consider necessary to provide reasonable assurance that the control objectives stated in the description were achieved. An assurance engagement of this type also includes evaluating the overall presentation of the description, the suitability of the objectives stated therein, and the suitability of the criteria specified by the service organization and described at page *[aa]*.

We believe that the evidence we have obtained is sufficient and appropriate to provide a basis for our opinion.

Limitations of Controls at a Service Organization

XYZ Service Organization's description is prepared to meet the common needs of a broad range of customers and their auditors and may not, therefore, include every aspect of the system that each individual customer may consider important in its own particular environment. Also, because of their nature, controls at a service organization may not prevent or detect all errors or omissions in processing or reporting transactions. Also, the projection of any evaluation of effectiveness to future periods is subject to the risk that controls at a service organization may become inadequate or fail.

Opinion

Our opinion has been formed on the basis of the matters outlined in this report. The criteria we used in forming our opinion are those described at page *[aa]*. In our opinion, in all material respects:

(a) The description fairly presents the *[the type or name of]* system as designed and implemented throughout the period from *[date]* to *[date]*;

(b) The controls related to the control objectives stated in the description were suitably designed throughout the period from *[date]* to *[date]*; and

(c) The controls tested, which were those necessary to provide reasonable assurance that the control objectives stated in the description were achieved, operated effectively throughout the period from *[date]* to *[date]*.

Description of Tests of Controls

The specific controls tested and the nature, timing and results of those tests are listed on pages *[yy–zz]*.

Intended Users and Purpose

This report and the description of tests of controls on pages *[yy–zz]* are intended only for customers who have used XYZ Service Organization's *[type or name of]* system, and their auditors, who have a sufficient understanding to consider it, along with other information including information about controls operated by customers themselves, when assessing the risks of material misstatements of customers' financial statements.

[Service auditor's signature]

[Date of the service auditor's assurance report]

[Service auditor's address]

Illustration 2: Type 1 Service Auditor's Assurance Report

Independent Service Auditor's Assurance Report on the Description of Controls and their Design

To: XYZ Service Organization

Scope

We have been engaged to report on XYZ Service Organization's description at pages *[bb–cc]* of its *[type or name of]* system for processing customers' transactions as at *[date]* (the description), and on the design of controls related to the control objectives stated in the description.[19]

We did not perform any procedures regarding the operating effectiveness of controls included in the description and, accordingly, do not express an opinion thereon.

XYZ Service Organization's Responsibilities

XYZ Service Organization is responsible for: preparing the description and accompanying assertion at page *[aa]*, including the completeness, accuracy and method of presentation of the description and the assertion; providing the services covered by the description; stating the control objectives; and designing, implementing and effectively operating controls to achieve the stated control objectives.

Service Auditor's Responsibilities

Our responsibility is to express an opinion on XYZ Service Organization's description and on the design of controls related to the control objectives stated in that description, based on our procedures. We conducted our engagement in accordance with International Standard on Assurance Engagements 3402, "Assurance Reports on Controls at a Service Organization," issued by the International Auditing and Assurance Standards Board. That standard requires that we comply with ethical requirements and plan and perform our procedures to obtain reasonable assurance about whether, in all material respects, the description is fairly presented and the controls are suitably designed in all material respects.

An assurance engagement to report on the description and design of controls at a service organization involves performing procedures to obtain evidence about the disclosures in the service organization's description of its system, and the design of controls. The procedures selected depend on the service auditor's judgment, including the assessment that the description is not fairly presented, and that controls are not suitably designed. An assurance engagement of this type also includes evaluating the overall presentation of the description, the suitability of the control objectives stated therein, and the suitability of the criteria specified by the service organization and described at page *[aa]*.

---

[19] *If some elements of the description are not included in the scope of the engagement, this is made clear in the assurance report.*

As noted above, we did not perform any procedures regarding the operating effectiveness of controls included in the description and, accordingly, do not express an opinion thereon.

We believe that the evidence we have obtained is sufficient and appropriate to provide a basis for our opinion.

Limitations of Controls at a Service Organization

XYZ Service Organization's description is prepared to meet the common needs of a broad range of customers and their auditors and may not, therefore, include every aspect of the system that each individual customer may consider important in its own particular environment. Also, because of their nature, controls at a service organization may not prevent or detect all errors or omissions in processing or reporting transactions.

Opinion

Our opinion has been formed on the basis of the matters outlined in this report. The criteria we used in forming our opinion are those described at page *[aa]*. In our opinion, in all material respects:

(a) The description fairly presents the *[the type or name of]* system as designed and implemented as at *[date]*; and

(b) The controls related to the control objectives stated in the description were suitably designed as at *[date]*.

Intended Users and Purpose

This report is intended only for customers who have used XYZ Service Organization's *[type or name of]* system, and their auditors, who have a sufficient understanding to consider it, along with other information including information about controls operated by customers themselves, when obtaining an understanding of customers' information systems relevant to financial reporting.

[Service auditor's signature]

[Date of the service auditor's assurance report]

[Service auditor's address]

Appendix 3   (Ref. Para. A50)

Illustrations of Modified Service Auditor's Assurance Reports

The following illustrations of modified reports are for guidance only and are not intended to be exhaustive or applicable to all situations. They are based on the illustrations of reports in Appendix 2.

Illustration 1: Qualified opinion – the service organization's description of the system is not fairly presented in all material respects

...

Service Auditor's Responsibilities

...

We believe that the evidence we have obtained is sufficient and appropriate to provide a basis for our qualified opinion.

Basis for Qualified Opinion

The accompanying description states at page *[mn]* that XYZ Service Organization uses operator identification numbers and passwords to prevent unauthorized access to the system. Based on our procedures, which included inquiries of staff personnel and observation of activities, we have determined that operator identification numbers and passwords are employed in Applications A and B but not in Applications C and D.

Qualified Opinion

Our opinion has been formed on the basis of the matters outlined in this report. The criteria we used in forming our opinion were those described in XYZ Service Organization's assertion at page *[aa]*. In our opinion, except for the matter described in the Basis for Qualified Opinion paragraph:

(a) ...

Illustration 2: Qualified opinion – the controls are not suitably designed to provide reasonable assurance that the control objectives stated in the service organization's description of its system will be achieved if the controls operate effectively

...

Service Auditor's Responsibilities

...

We believe that the evidence we have obtained is sufficient and appropriate to provide a basis for our qualified opinion.

Basis for Qualified Opinion

As discussed at page *[mn]* of the accompanying description, from time to time XYZ Service Organization makes changes in application programs to correct deficiencies or to enhance capabilities. The procedures followed in determining whether to make changes, in designing the changes and in implementing them, do not include review and approval by authorized individuals who are independent from those involved in making the changes. There are also no specified requirements to test such changes or provide test results to an authorized reviewer prior to implementing the changes.

Qualified Opinion

Our opinion has been formed on the basis of the matters outlined in this report. The criteria we used in forming our opinion were those described in XYZ Service

Organization's assertion at page *[aa]*. In our opinion, except for the matter described in the Basis for Qualified Opinion paragraph:

(a) ...

Illustration 3: Qualified opinion – the controls did not operate effectively throughout the specified period (type 2 report only)

...

Service Auditor's Responsibilities

...

We believe that the evidence we have obtained is sufficient and appropriate to provide a basis for our qualified opinion.

Basis for Qualified Opinion

XYZ Service Organization states in its description that it has automated controls in place to reconcile loan payments received with the output generated. However, as noted at page *[mn]* of the description, this control was not operating effectively during the period from *dd/mm/yyyy* to *dd/mm/yyyy* due to a programming error. This resulted in the non-achievement of the control objective "Controls provide reasonable assurance that loan payments received are properly recorded" during the period from *dd/mm/yyyy* to *dd/mm/yyyy*. XYZ implemented a change to the program performing the calculation as of *[date]*, and our tests indicate that it was operating effectively during the period from *dd/mm/yyyy* to *dd/mm/yyyy*.

Qualified Opinion

Our opinion has been formed on the basis of the matters outlined in this report. The criteria we used in forming our opinion were those described in XYZ Service Organization's assertion at page *[aa]*. In our opinion, except for the matter described in the Basis for Qualified Opinion paragraph:

...

Example 4: Qualified opinion – the service auditor is unable to obtain sufficient appropriate evidence

...

Service Auditor's Responsibilities

...

We believe that the evidence we have obtained is sufficient and appropriate to provide a basis for our qualified opinion.

Basis for Qualified Opinion

XYZ Service Organization states in its description that it has automated controls in place to reconcile loan payments received with the output generated. However, electronic records of the performance of this reconciliation for the period from *dd/mm/yyyy* to *dd/mm/yyyy* were deleted as a result of a computer processing error, and we were therefore unable to test the operation of this control for that period. Consequently, we were unable to determine whether the control objective "Controls provide reasonable assurance that loan payments received are properly recorded" operated effectively during the period from *dd/mm/yyyy* to *dd/mm/yyyy*.

Qualified Opinion

Our opinion has been formed on the basis of the matters outlined in this report. The criteria we used in forming our opinion were those described in XYZ Service Organization's assertion at page *[aa]*. In our opinion, except for the matter described in the Basis for Qualified Opinion paragraph:

(a) ...

13-21.]

International Standard on Assurance Engagements 3410

Assurance engagements on greenhouse gas statements

(Effective for assurance reports covering periods ending on or after September 30, 2013)

Contents

International Standard on Assurance Engagements (ISAE) 3410, *Assurance Engagements on Greenhouse Gas Statements*, should be read in conjunction with the *Preface to the International Standards on Quality Control, Auditing, Review, Other Assurance and Related Services Pronouncements.*

Introduction

1   Given the link between greenhouse gas (GHG) emissions and climate change, many entities are quantifying their GHG emissions for internal management purposes, and many are also preparing a GHG statement:

(a) As part of a regulatory disclosure regime;

(b) As part of an emissions trading scheme; or

(c) To inform investors and others on a voluntary basis. Voluntary disclosures may be, for example, published as a stand-alone document; included as part of a broader sustainability report or in an entity's annual report; or made to support inclusion in a "carbon register."

Scope of this ISAE

2   This International Standard on Assurance Engagements (ISAE) deals with assurance engagements to report on an entity's GHG statement.

3   The practitioner's conclusion in an assurance engagement may cover information in addition to a GHG statement, for example, when the practitioner is engaged to report on a sustainability report of which a GHG statement is only one part. In such cases: (Ref: Para. A1–A2)

(a) This ISAE applies to assurance procedures performed with respect to the GHG statement other than when the GHG statement is a relatively minor part of the overall information subject to assurance; and

(b) ISAE 3000[1] (or another ISAE dealing with a specific subject matter) applies to assurance procedures performed with respect to the remainder of the information covered by the practitioner's conclusion.

4   This ISAE does not deal with, or provide specific guidance for, assurance engagements to report on the following:

(a) Statements of emissions other than GHG emissions, for example, nitrogen oxides (NOx) and sulfur dioxide (SO_2). This ISAE may nonetheless provide guidance for such engagements;[2]

(b) Other GHG-related information, such as product lifecycle "footprints," hypothetical "baseline" information, and key performance indicators based on emissions data; or (Ref: Para. A3)

(c) Instruments, processes or mechanisms, such as offset projects, used by other entities as emissions deductions. However, where an entity's GHG statement includes emissions deductions that are subject to assurance, the requirements of this ISAE apply in relation to those emissions deductions as appropriate (see paragraph 76(f)).

Assertion-Based and Direct Reporting Engagements

5   The *International Framework for Assurance Engagements* (the Assurance Framework) notes that an assurance engagement may be either an assertion-based

---

[1] *ISAE 3000*, Assurance Engagements Other than Audits or Reviews of Historical Financial Information. *ISAE 3000 is currently being revised by the IAASB. There may be conforming amendments to this ISAE as a result of changes to ISAE 3000.*

[2] *NOx (i.e., NO and NO_2, which differ from the GHG nitrous oxide, N_2O) and SO_2 are associated with "acid rain" rather than climate change.*

engagement or a direct reporting engagement. This ISAE deals only with assertion-based engagements.[3]

Procedures for Reasonable Assurance and Limited Assurance Engagements

The Assurance Framework notes that an assurance engagement may be either a   **6**
reasonable assurance engagement or a limited assurance engagement.[4] This ISAE
deals with both reasonable and limited assurance engagements.

In both reasonable assurance and limited assurance engagements on a GHG state-   **7**
ment, the practitioner chooses a combination of assurance procedures, which can
include: inspection; observation; confirmation; recalculation; reperformance; analytical procedures; and inquiry. Determining the assurance procedures to be performed
on a particular engagement is a matter of professional judgment. Because GHG
statements cover a wide range of circumstances, the nature, timing and extent of
procedures are likely to vary considerably from engagement to engagement.

Unless otherwise stated, each requirement of this ISAE applies to both reasonable   **8**
and limited assurance engagements. Because the level of assurance obtained in a
limited assurance engagement is lower than in a reasonable assurance engagement,
the procedures the practitioner will perform in a limited assurance engagement will
vary in nature from, and are less in extent than for, a reasonable assurance
engagement.[5] Requirements that apply to only one or the other type of engagement
have been presented in a columnar format with the letter "L" (limited assurance) or
"R" (reasonable assurance) after the paragraph number. Although some procedures
are required only for reasonable assurance engagements, they may nonetheless be
appropriate in some limited assurance engagements (see also paragraph A90, which
outlines the primary differences between the practitioner's further procedures for a
reasonable assurance engagement and a limited assurance engagement on a GHG
statement). (Ref: Para. A4, A90)

Relationship with ISAE 3000, Other Professional Pronouncements, and Other Requirements

The performance of assurance engagements other than audits or reviews of historical   **9**
financial information requires the practitioner to comply with ISAE 3000. ISAE 3000
includes requirements in relation to such topics as engagement acceptance, planning,
evidence, and documentation that apply to all assurance engagements, including
engagements in accordance with this ISAE. This ISAE expands on how ISAE 3000 is
to be applied in an assurance engagement to report on an entity's GHG statement.
The Assurance Framework, which defines and describes the elements and objectives
of an assurance engagement, provides context for understanding this ISAE and
ISAE 3000. (Ref: Para. A17)

Compliance with ISAE 3000 requires, among other things, that the practitioner   **10**
comply with the independence and other requirements of the *Code of Ethics for
Professional Accountants* issued by the International Ethics Standards Board for

---

[3] *Assurance Framework, paragraph 10.*

[4] *Assurance Framework, paragraph 11.*

[5] *Assurance Framework, paragraph 53, and ISAE 3000, paragraph 37.*

Accountants (IESBA Code) and implement quality control procedures that are applicable to the individual engagement.[6] (Ref: Para. A5–A6)

11   Where the engagement is subject to local laws or regulations or the provisions of an emissions trading scheme, this ISAE does not override those laws, regulations or provisions. In the event that local laws or regulations or the provisions of an emissions trading scheme differ from this ISAE, an engagement conducted in accordance with local laws or regulations or the provisions of a particular scheme will not automatically comply with this ISAE. The practitioner is entitled to represent compliance with this ISAE in addition to compliance with local laws or regulations or the provisions of the emissions trading scheme only when all applicable requirements of this ISAE have been met. (Ref: Para. A7)

Effective Date

12   This ISAE is effective for assurance reports covering periods ending on or after September 30, 2013.

Objectives

13   The objectives of the practitioner are:

(a) To obtain reasonable or limited assurance, as appropriate, about whether the GHG statement is free from material misstatement, whether due to fraud or error, thereby enabling the practitioner to express a conclusion conveying that level of assurance;

(b) To report, in accordance with the practitioner's findings, about whether:

(i)   In the case of a reasonable assurance engagement, the GHG statement is prepared, in all material respects, in accordance with the applicable criteria; or

(ii) In the case of a limited assurance engagement, anything has come to the practitioner's attention that causes the practitioner to believe, on the basis of the procedures performed and evidence obtained, that the GHG statement is not prepared, in all material respects, in accordance with the applicable criteria; and

(c) To communicate as otherwise required by this ISAE, in accordance with the practitioner's findings.

Definitions

14   For purposes of this ISAE, the following terms have the meanings attributed below:[7]

(a) Applicable criteria – The criteria used by the entity to quantify and report its emissions in the GHG statement.

(b) Assertions – Representations by the entity, explicit or otherwise, that are embodied in the GHG statement, as used by the practitioner to consider the different types of potential misstatements that may occur.

(c) Base year – A specific year or an average over multiple years against which an entity's emissions are compared over time.

---

[6] *ISAE 3000, paragraphs 4 and 6.*

[7] *The definitions in ISAE 3000 also apply to this ISAE.*

(d) Cap and trade – A system that sets overall emissions limits, allocates emissions allowances to participants, and allows them to trade allowances and emission credits with each other.

(e) Comparative information – The amounts and disclosures included in the GHG statement in respect of one or more prior periods.

(f) Emissions – The GHGs that, during the relevant period, have been emitted to the atmosphere or would have been emitted to the atmosphere had they not been captured and channeled to a sink. Emissions can be categorized as:
- Direct emissions (also known as Scope 1 emissions), which are emissions from sources that are owned or controlled by the entity. (Ref: Para. A8)
- Indirect emissions, which are emissions that are a consequence of the activities of the entity, but which occur at sources that are owned or controlled by another entity. Indirect emissions can be further categorized as:
  - Scope 2 emissions, which are emissions associated with energy that is transferred to and consumed by the entity. (Ref: Para. A9)
  - Scope 3 emissions, which are all other indirect emissions. (Ref: Para. A10) (g) Emissions deduction – Any item included in the entity's GHG statement that is deducted from the total reported emissions, but which is not a removal; it commonly includes purchased offsets, but can also include a variety of other instruments or mechanisms such as performance credits and allowances that are recognized by a regulatory or other scheme of which the entity is a part. (Ref: Para. A11–A12)

(h) Emissions factor – A mathematical factor or ratio for converting the measure of an activity (for example, liters of fuel consumed, kilometers travelled, the number of animals in husbandry, or tonnes of product produced) into an estimate of the quantity of GHGs associated with that activity.

(i) Emissions trading scheme – A market-based approach used to control greenhouse gases by providing economic incentives for achieving reductions in the emissions of such gases.

(j) Entity – The legal entity, economic entity, or the identifiable portion of a legal or economic entity (for example, a single factory or other form of facility, such as a land fill site), or combination of legal or other entities or portions of those entities (for example, a joint venture) to which the emissions in the GHG statement relate.

(k) Fraud – An intentional act by one or more individuals among management, those charged with governance, employees, or third parties, involving the use of deception to obtain an unjust or illegal advantage.

(l) Further procedures – Procedures performed in response to assessed risks of material misstatement, including tests of controls (if any), tests of details and analytical procedures.

(m) GHG statement – A statement setting out constituent elements and quantifying an entity's GHG emissions for a period (sometimes known as an emissions inventory) and, where applicable, comparative information and explanatory notes including a summary of significant quantification and reporting policies. An entity's GHG statement may also include a categorized listing of removals or emissions deductions. Where the engagement does not cover the entire GHG statement, the term "GHG statement" is to be read as that portion that is covered by the engagement. The GHG statement is the "subject matter information" of the engagement.[8]

(n) Greenhouse gases (GHGs) – Carbon dioxide (CO_2) and any other gases required by the applicable criteria to be included in the GHG statement, such as: methane; nitrous oxide; sulfur hexafluoride; hydrofluorocarbons;

[8] *Assurance Framework, paragraph 8.*

perfluorocarbons; and chlorofluorocarbons. Gases other than carbon dioxide are often expressed in terms of carbon dioxide equivalents (CO_2-e).

(o) Organizational boundary – The boundary that determines which operations to include in the entity's GHG statement.

(p) Performance materiality – The amount or amounts set by the practitioner at less than materiality for the GHG statement to reduce to an appropriately low level the probability that the aggregate of uncorrected and undetected misstatements exceeds materiality for the GHG statement. If applicable, performance materiality also refers to the amount or amounts set by the practitioner at less than the materiality level or levels for particular types of emissions or disclosures.

(q) Purchased offset – An emissions deduction in which the entity pays for the lowering of another entity's emissions (emissions reductions) or the increasing of another entity's removals (removal enhancements), compared to a hypothetical baseline. (Ref: Para. A13)

(r) Quantification – The process of determining the quantity of GHGs that relate to the entity, either directly or indirectly, as emitted (or removed) by particular sources (or sinks).

(s) Removal – The GHGs that the entity has, during the period, removed from the atmosphere, or that would have been emitted to the atmosphere had they not been captured and channeled to a sink. (Ref: Para. A14)

(t) Significant facility – A facility that is of individual significance due to the size of its emissions relative to the aggregate emissions included in the GHG statement or its specific nature or circumstances which give rise to particular risks of material misstatement. (Ref: Para. A15–A16)

(u) Sink – A physical unit or process that removes GHGs from the atmosphere.

(v) Source – A physical unit or process that releases GHGs into the atmosphere.

(w) Type of emission – A grouping of emissions based on, for example, source of emission, type of gas, region, or facility.

Requirements

ISAE 3000

15   The practitioner shall not represent compliance with this ISAE unless the practitioner has complied with the requirements of both this ISAE and ISAE 3000. (Ref: Para. A5–A6, A17, A21–A22, A37, A127)

Acceptance and Continuance of the Engagement

Skills, Knowledge and Experience

16   The engagement partner shall:

(a) Have sufficient assurance skills, knowledge and experience, and sufficient competence in the quantification and reporting of emissions, to accept responsibility for the assurance conclusion; and

(b) Be satisfied that the engagement team and any practitioner's external experts collectively possess the necessary professional competencies, including in the quantification and reporting of emissions and in assurance, to perform the assurance engagement in accordance with this ISAE. (Ref: Para. A18–A19)

Preconditions for the Engagement

In order to establish whether the preconditions for the engagement are present: **17**

(a) The engagement partner shall determine that both the GHG statement and the engagement have sufficient scope to be useful to intended users, considering, in particular: (Ref: Para. A20)

   (i)   If the GHG statement is to exclude significant emissions that have been, or could readily be, quantified, whether such exclusions are reasonable in the circumstances;

   (ii) If the engagement is to exclude assurance with respect to significant emissions that are reported by the entity, whether such exclusions are reasonable in the circumstances; and

   (iii) If the engagement is to include assurance with respect to emissions deductions, whether the nature of the assurance the practitioner will obtain with respect to the deductions and the intended content of the assurance report with respect to them are clear, reasonable in the circumstances, and understood by the engaging party. (Ref: Para. A11-A12)

(b) When assessing the suitability of the applicable criteria, as required by ISAE 3000,[9] the practitioner shall determine whether the criteria encompass at a minimum: (Ref: Para. A23–A26)

   (i)   The method for determining the entity's organizational boundary; (Ref: Para. A27–A28)

   (ii) The GHGs to be accounted for;

   (iii) Acceptable quantification methods, including methods for making adjustments to the base year (if applicable); and

   (iv) Adequate disclosures such that intended users can understand the significant judgments made in preparing the GHG statement. (Ref: Para. A29–A34)

(c) The practitioner shall obtain the agreement of the entity that it acknowledges and understands its responsibility:

   (i)   For designing, implementing and maintaining such internal control as the entity determines is necessary to enable the preparation of a GHG statement that is free from material misstatement, whether due to fraud or error;

   (ii) For the preparation of its GHG statement in accordance with the applicable criteria; and (Ref: Para. A35)

   (iii) For referring to or describing in its GHG statement the applicable criteria it has used and, when it is not readily apparent from the engagement circumstances, who developed them. (Ref: Para. A36)

Agreement on Engagement Terms

The agreed terms of the engagement required by ISAE 3000[10] shall include: (Ref: **18**
Para. A37)

(a) The objective and scope of the engagement;

(b) The responsibilities of the practitioner;

(c) The responsibilities of the entity, including those described in paragraph 17(c);

(d) Identification of the applicable criteria for the preparation of the GHG statement;

---

[9] *ISAE 3000, paragraph 19.*

[10] *ISAE 3000, paragraph 10.*

(e) Reference to the expected form and content of any reports to be issued by the practitioner and a statement that there may be circumstances in which a report may differ from its expected form and content; and

(f) An acknowledgement that the entity agrees to provide written representations at the conclusion of the engagement.

Planning

19   When planning the engagement as required by ISAE 3000,[11] the practitioner shall: (Ref: Para. A38–A41)

(a) Identify the characteristics of the engagement that define its scope;

(b) Ascertain the reporting objectives of the engagement to plan the timing of the engagement and the nature of the communications required;

(c) Consider the factors that, in the practitioner's professional judgment, are significant in directing the engagement team's efforts;

(d) Consider the results of engagement acceptance or continuance procedures and, where applicable, whether knowledge gained on other engagements performed by the engagement partner for the entity is relevant;

(e) Ascertain the nature, timing and extent of resources necessary to perform the engagement, including the involvement of experts and of other practitioners; and (Ref: Para. A42– A43)

(f) Determine the impact of the entity's internal audit function, if any, on the engagement.

Materiality in Planning and Performing the Engagement

Determining Materiality and Performance Materiality When Planning the Engagement

20   When establishing the overall engagement strategy, the practitioner shall determine materiality for the GHG statement. (Ref: Para. A44–A50)

21   The practitioner shall determine performance materiality for purposes of assessing the risks of material misstatement and determining the nature, timing and extent of further procedures.

Revision as the Engagement Progresses

22   The practitioner shall revise materiality for the GHG statement in the event of becoming aware of information during the engagement that would have caused the practitioner to have determined a different amount initially. (Ref: Para. A51)

Understanding the Entity and Its Environment, Including the Entity's Internal Control, and Identifying and Assessing Risks of Material Misstatement

Obtaining an Understanding of the Entity and Its Environment

23   The practitioner shall obtain an understanding of the following: (Ref: Para. A52–A53)

(a) Relevant industry, regulatory, and other external factors including the applicable criteria.

---

[11] *ISAE 3000, paragraph 12.*

(b) The nature of the entity, including:
 (i) The nature of the operations included in the entity's organizational boundary, including: (Ref: Para. A27–A28)
   a. The sources and completeness of emissions and, if any, sinks and emissions deductions;
   b. The contribution of each to the entity's overall emissions; and
   c. The uncertainties associated with the quantities reported in the GHG statement. (Ref: Para. A54–A59)
 (ii) Changes from the prior period in the nature or extent of operations, including whether there have been any mergers, acquisitions, or sales of emissions sources, or outsourcing of functions with significant emissions; and
 (iii) The frequency and nature of interruptions to operations. (Ref: Para. A60)
(c) The entity's selection and application of quantification methods and reporting policies, including the reasons for changes thereto and the potential for double-counting of emissions in the GHG statement.
(d) The requirements of the applicable criteria relevant to estimates, including related disclosures.
(e) The entity's climate change objective and strategy, if any, and associated economic, regulatory, physical and reputational risks. (Ref: Para. A61)
(f) The oversight of, and responsibility for, emissions information within the entity.
(g) Whether the entity has an internal audit function and, if so, its activities and main findings with respect to emissions.

Procedures to Obtain an Understanding and to Identify and Assess Risks of Material Misstatement

The procedures to obtain an understanding of the entity and its environment and to identify and assess risks of material misstatement shall include the following: (Ref: Para. A52–A53, A62)   **24**

(a) Inquiries of those within the entity who, in the practitioner's judgment, have information that is likely to assist in identifying and assessing risks of material misstatement due to fraud or error.
(b) Analytical procedures. (Ref: Para. A63–A65)
(c) Observation and inspection. (Ref: Para. A66–A68)

Obtaining an Understanding of the Entity's Internal Control

Limited Assurance	Reasonable Assurance
25L. For internal control relevant to emissions quantification and reporting, as the basis for identifying and assessing the risks of material misstatement, the practitioner shall obtain an understanding, through inquiries, about: (Ref: Para. A52–A53, A69–A70) (a) The control environment; (b) The information system, including the related business processes, and communication of	25R. The practitioner shall obtain an understanding of the following components of the entity's internal control relevant to emissions quantification and reporting as the basis for identifying and assessing risks of material misstatement: (Ref: Para. A52–A53, A70) (a) The control environment; (b) The information system, including the related business processes, and communication of

Limited Assurance	Reasonable Assurance
emissions reporting roles and responsibilities and significant matters relating to emissions reporting; and (c) The results of the entity's risk assessment process.	emissions reporting roles and responsibilities and significant matters relating to emissions reporting; (c) The entity's risk assessment process; (d) Control activities relevant to the engagement, being those the practitioner judges it necessary to understand in order to assess the risks of material misstatement at the assertion level and design further procedures responsive to assessed risks. An assurance engagement does not require an understanding of all the control activities related to each significant type of emission and disclosure in the GHG statement or to every assertion relevant to them; and (Ref: Para. A71–A72) (e) Monitoring of controls.
	26R. When obtaining the understanding required by paragraph 25R, the practitioner shall evaluate the design of controls and determine whether they have been implemented by performing procedures in addition to inquiry of the entity's personnel. (Ref: Para. A52–A53)

Other Procedures to Obtain an Understanding and to Identify and Assess Risks of Material Misstatement

27 If the engagement partner has performed other engagements for the entity, the engagement partner shall consider whether information obtained is relevant to identifying and assessing risks of material misstatement. (Ref: Para. A73)

28 The practitioner shall make inquiries of management, and others within the entity as appropriate, to determine whether they have knowledge of any actual, suspected or alleged fraud or non-compliance with laws and regulations affecting the GHG statement. (Ref: Para. A84–A86)

29 The engagement partner and other key members of the engagement team, and any key practitioner's external experts, shall discuss the susceptibility of the entity's GHG statement to material misstatement whether due to fraud or error, and the

application of the applicable criteria to the entity's facts and circumstances. The engagement partner shall determine which matters are to be communicated to members of the engagement team, and to any practitioner's external experts not involved in the discussion.

The practitioner shall evaluate whether the entity's quantification methods and **30** reporting policies, including the determination of the entity's organizational boundary, are appropriate for its operations, and are consistent with the applicable criteria and quantification and reporting policies used in the relevant industry and in prior periods.

Performing Procedures on Location at the Entity's Facilities

The practitioner shall determine whether it is necessary in the circumstances of the **31** engagement to perform procedures on location at significant facilities. (Ref: Para. A15–A16, A74–A77)

Internal Audit

Where the entity has an internal audit function that is relevant to the engagement, **32** the practitioner shall: (Ref: Para. A78)

(a) Determine whether, and what extent, to use specific work of the internal audit function; and
(b) If using the specific work of the internal audit function, determine whether that work is adequate for the purposes of the engagement.

Identifying and Assessing Risks of Material Misstatement

Limited Assurance	Reasonable Assurance
33L. The practitioner shall identify and assess risks of material misstatement:	33R. The practitioner shall identify and assess risks of material misstatement:
(a) At the GHG statement level; and (Ref: Para. A79–A80)	(a) At the GHG statement level; and (Ref: Para. A79–A80)
(b) For material types of emissions and disclosures, (Ref: Para. A81)	(b) At the assertion level for material types of emissions and disclosures, (Ref: Para. A81–A82)
as the basis for designing and performing procedures whose nature, timing and extent:	as the basis for designing and performing procedures whose nature, timing and extent: (Ref: Para. A83)
(c) Are responsive to assessed risks of material misstatement; and	(c) Are responsive to assessed risks of material misstatement; and
(d) Allow the practitioner to obtain limited assurance about whether the GHG statement is prepared, in all material respects, in accordance with the applicable criteria.	(d) Allow the practitioner to obtain reasonable assurance about whether the GHG statement is prepared, in all material respects, in accordance with the applicable criteria.

Causes of Risks of Material Misstatement

34   When performing the procedures required by paragraphs 33L or 33R, the practitioner shall consider at least the following factors: (Ref: Para. A84–A89)

(a) The likelihood of intentional misstatement in the GHG statement; (Ref: Para. A84–A86)

(b) The likelihood of non-compliance with the provisions of those laws and regulations generally recognized to have a direct effect on the content of the GHG statement; (Ref: Para. A87)

(c) The likelihood of omission of a potentially significant emission; (Ref: Para. A88(a))

(d) Significant economic or regulatory changes; (Ref: Para. A88(b))

(e) The nature of operations; (Ref: Para. A88(c))

(f) The nature of quantification methods; (Ref: Para. A88(d))

(g) The degree of complexity in determining the organizational boundary and whether related parties are involved; (Ref: Para. A27–A28)

(h) Whether there are significant emissions that are outside the normal course of business for the entity, or that otherwise appear to be unusual; (Ref: Para. A88(e))

(i) The degree of subjectivity in the quantification of emissions; (Ref: Para. A88(e))

(j) Whether Scope 3 emissions are included in the GHG statement; and (Ref: Para. A88(f))

(k) How the entity makes significant estimates and the data on which they are based. (Ref: Para. A88(g))

Overall Responses to Assessed Risks of Material Misstatement and Further Procedures

35   The practitioner shall design and implement overall responses to address the assessed risks of material misstatement at the GHG statement level. (Ref: Para. A90–A93)

36   The practitioner shall design and perform further procedures whose nature, timing and extent are responsive to the assessed risks of material misstatement, having regard to the level of assurance, reasonable or limited, as appropriate. (Ref: Para. A90)

Limited Assurance	Reasonable Assurance
37L. In designing and performing the further procedures in accordance with paragraph 36, the practitioner shall: (Ref: Para. A90, A94)	37R. In designing and performing the further procedures in accordance with paragraph 36, the practitioner shall: (Ref: Para. A90, A94)
(a) Consider the reasons for the assessment given to the risks of material misstatement for material types of emissions and disclosures; and (Ref: Para. A95)	(a) Consider the reasons for the assessment given to the risks of material misstatement at the assertion level for material types of emissions and disclosures, including: (Ref: Para. A95)
(b) Obtain more persuasive evidence the higher the practitioner's assessment of risk. (Ref: Para. A97)	(i) The likelihood of material misstatement due to the particular

Limited Assurance	Reasonable Assurance
	characteristics of the relevant type of emission or disclosure (that is, the inherent risk); and
	(ii) Whether the practitioner intends to rely on the operating effectiveness of controls in determining the nature, timing and extent of other procedures; and (Ref: Para. A96)
	(b) Obtain more persuasive evidence the higher the practitioner's assessment of risk. (Ref: Para. A97)
	Tests of Controls
	38R. The practitioner shall design and perform tests of controls to obtain sufficient appropriate evidence as to the operating effectiveness of relevant controls if: (Ref: Para. A90(a))
	(a) The practitioner intends to rely on the operating effectiveness of controls in determining the nature, timing and extent of other procedures; or (Ref: Para. A96)
	(b) Procedures other than tests of controls cannot alone provide sufficient appropriate evidence at the assertion level. (Ref: Para. A98)
	39R. If deviations from controls upon which the practitioner intends to rely are detected, the practitioner shall make specific inquiries to understand these matters and their potential consequences, and shall determine whether: (Ref: Para. A90)
	(a) The tests of controls that have been performed provide an appropriate basis for reliance on the controls;

Limited Assurance	Reasonable Assurance
	(b) Additional tests of controls are necessary; or
	(c) The potential risks of material misstatement need to be addressed using other procedures.
	Procedures Other than Tests of Controls
	40R. Irrespective of the assessed risks of material misstatement, the practitioner shall design and perform tests of details or analytical procedures in addition to tests of controls, if any, for each material type of emission and disclosure. (Ref: Para. A90, A94)
	41R. The practitioner shall consider whether external confirmation procedures are to be performed. (Ref: Para.A90, A99)
Analytical Procedures Performed in Response to Assessed Risks of Material Misstatement	*Analytical Procedures Performed in Response to Assessed Risks of Material Misstatement*
42L. If designing and performing analytical procedures, the practitioner shall: (Ref: Para. A90(c), A100–A102)	42R. If designing and performing analytical procedures, the practitioner shall: (Ref: Para. A90(c), A100–A102)
(a) Determine the suitability of particular analytical procedures, taking account of the assessed risks of material misstatement and tests of details, if any;	(a) Determine the suitability of particular analytical procedures for given assertions, taking account of the assessed risks of material misstatement and tests of details, if any, for these assertions;
(b) Evaluate the reliability of data from which the practitioner's expectation of recorded quantities or ratios is developed, taking account of the source, comparability, and nature and relevance of information available, and controls over preparation; and	(b) Evaluate the reliability of data from which the practitioner's expectation of recorded quantities or ratios is developed, taking account of the source, comparability, and nature and relevance of information available, and controls over preparation; and
(c) Develop an expectation with respect to recorded quantities or ratios.	(c) Develop an expectation of recorded quantities or ratios which is sufficiently precise
43L. If analytical procedures identify fluctuations or relationships that are inconsistent with other	

Limited Assurance	Reasonable Assurance
relevant information or that differ significantly from expected quantities or ratios, the practitioner shall make inquiries of the entity about such differences. The practitioner shall consider the responses to these inquiries to determine whether other procedures are necessary in the circumstances. (Ref: Para. A90(c))	to identify possible material misstatements. 43R. If analytical procedures identify fluctuations or relationships that are inconsistent with other relevant information or that differ significantly from expected quantities or ratios, the practitioner shall investigate such differences by: (Ref: Para. A90(c)) (a) Inquiring of the entity and obtaining additional evidence relevant to the entity's responses; and (b) Performing other procedures as necessary in the circumstances.

Procedures Regarding Estimates
 	
44L. Based on the assessed risks of material misstatement, the practitioner shall: (Ref: Para. A103–A104)
 	
(a) Evaluate whether:
 	
  (i) The entity has appropriately applied the requirements of the applicable criteria relevant to estimates; and
 	
  (ii) The methods for making estimates are appropriate and have been applied consistently, and whether changes, if any, in reported estimates or in the method for making them from the prior period are appropriate in the circumstances; and
 	
(b) Consider whether other procedures are necessary in the circumstances.
	Procedures Regarding Estimates
	
	44R. Based on the assessed risks of material misstatement, the practitioner shall evaluate whether: (Ref: Para. A103)
	
	(a) The entity has appropriately applied the requirements of the applicable criteria relevant to estimates; and
	
	(b) The methods for making estimates are appropriate and have been applied consistently, and whether changes, if any, in reported estimates or in the method for making them from the prior period are appropriate in the circumstances.
	
	45R. In responding to an assessed risk of material misstatement, the practitioner shall undertake one or more of the following, taking account of the nature of estimates: (Ref: Para. A103)
	
	(a) Test how the entity made the estimate and the data on which it is based. In doing so, the practitioner shall evaluate whether:
	
	  (i) The method of quantification used is

Limited Assurance	Reasonable Assurance
	appropriate in the circumstances; and
	(ii) The assumptions used by the entity are reasonable.
	(b) Test the operating effectiveness of the controls over how the entity made the estimate, together with other appropriate procedures.
	(c) Develop a point estimate or a range to evaluate the entity's estimate. For this purpose:
	(i) If the practitioner uses assumptions or methods that differ from the entity's, the practitioner shall obtain an understanding of the entity's assumptions or methods sufficient to establish that the practitioner's point estimate or range takes into account relevant variables and to evaluate any significant differences from the entity's point estimate.
	(ii) If the practitioner concludes that it is appropriate to use a range, the practitioner shall narrow the range, based on evidence available, until all outcomes within the range are considered reasonable.

Sampling

46   If sampling is used, the practitioner shall, when designing the sample, consider the purpose of the procedure and the characteristics of the population from which the sample will be drawn. (Ref: Para. A90(b), A105)

Fraud, Laws and Regulations

The practitioner shall respond appropriately to fraud or suspected fraud and non-compliance or suspected non-compliance with laws and regulations identified during the engagement. (Ref: Para. A106–A107)   **47**

Limited Assurance	Reasonable Assurance
Procedures Regarding the GHG Statement Aggregation Process	*Procedures Regarding the GHG Statement Aggregation Process*
48L. The practitioner's procedures shall include the following procedures related to the GHG statement aggregation process: (Ref: Para. A108)	48R. The practitioner's procedures shall include the following procedures related to the GHG statement aggregation process: (Ref: Para. A108)
(a) Agreeing or reconciling the GHG statement with the underlying records; and	(a) Agreeing or reconciling the GHG statement with the underlying records; and
(b) Obtaining, through inquiry of the entity, an understanding of material adjustments made during the course of preparing the GHG statement and considering whether other procedures are necessary in the circumstances.	(b) Examining material adjustments made during the course of preparing the GHG statement.
Determining Whether Additional Procedures Are Necessary in a Limited Assurance Engagement	*Revision of Risk Assessment in a Reasonable Assurance Engagement*
49L. If the practitioner becomes aware of a matter(s) that causes the practitioner to believe the GHG statement may be materially misstated, the practitioner shall design and perform additional procedures sufficient to enable the practitioner to: (Ref: Para. A109–A110)	49R. The practitioner's assessment of the risks of material misstatement at the assertion level may change during the course of the engagement as additional evidence is obtained. In circumstances where the practitioner obtains evidence from performing further procedures, or if new information is obtained, either of which is inconsistent with the evidence on which the practitioner originally based the assessment, the practitioner shall revise the assessment and modify the planned procedures accordingly. (Ref: Para. A109)
(a) Conclude that the matter(s) is not likely to cause the GHG statement to be materially misstated; or	
(b) Determine that the matter(s) causes the GHG statement to be materially misstated. (Ref: Para. A111)	

Accumulation of Identified Misstatements

50   The practitioner shall accumulate misstatements identified during the engagement, other than those that are clearly trivial. (Ref: Para. A112)

Consideration of Identified Misstatements as the Engagement Progresses

51   The practitioner shall determine whether the overall engagement strategy and engagement plan need to be revised if:

(a)   The nature of identified misstatements and the circumstances of their occurrence indicate that other misstatements may exist that, when aggregated with misstatements accumulated during the engagement, could be material; or

(b)   The aggregate of misstatements accumulated during the engagement approaches materiality determined in accordance with paragraphs 20–22 of this ISAE.

52   If, at the practitioner's request, the entity has examined a type of emission or disclosure and corrected misstatements that were detected, the practitioner shall perform procedures with respect to the work performed by the entity to determine whether material misstatements remain.

Communication and Correction of Misstatements

53   The practitioner shall communicate on a timely basis all misstatements accumulated during the engagement with the appropriate level within the entity and shall request the entity to correct those misstatements.

54   If the entity refuses to correct some or all of the misstatements communicated by the practitioner, the practitioner shall obtain an understanding of the entity's reasons for not making the corrections and shall take that understanding into account when forming the practitioner's conclusion.

Evaluating the Effect of Uncorrected Misstatements

55   Prior to evaluating the effect of uncorrected misstatements, the practitioner shall reassess materiality determined in accordance with paragraphs 20–22 of this ISAE to confirm whether it remains appropriate in the context of the entity's actual emissions.

56   The practitioner shall determine whether uncorrected misstatements are material, individually or in the aggregate. In making this determination, the practitioner shall consider the size and nature of the misstatements, and the particular circumstances of their occurrence, in relation to particular types of emissions or disclosures and the GHG statement (see paragraph 72).

Using the Work of Other Practitioners

57   When the practitioner intends using the work of other practitioners, the practitioner shall:

(a)   Communicate clearly with those other practitioners about the scope and timing of their work and their findings; and (Ref: Para. A113–A114)

(b)   Evaluate the sufficiency and appropriateness of evidence obtained and the process for including related information in the GHG statement. (Ref: Para. A115)

Written Representations

The practitioner shall request written representations from a person(s) within the **58**
entity with appropriate responsibilities for, and knowledge of, the matters concerned:
(Ref: Para. A116)

(a) That they have fulfilled their responsibility for the preparation of the GHG
    statement, including comparative information where appropriate, in accordance
    with the applicable criteria, as set out in the terms of the engagement;
(b) That they have provided the practitioner with all relevant information and
    access as agreed in the terms of the engagement and reflected all relevant matters
    in the GHG statement;
(c) Whether they believe the effects of uncorrected misstatements are immaterial,
    individually and in the aggregate, to the GHG statement. A summary of such
    items shall be included in, or attached to, the written representation;
(d) Whether they believe that significant assumptions used in making estimates are
    reasonable;
(e) That they have communicated to the practitioner all deficiencies in internal
    control relevant to the engagement that are not clearly trivial of which they are
    aware; and
(f) Whether they have disclosed to the practitioner their knowledge of actual,
    suspected or alleged fraud or non-compliance with laws and regulations where
    the fraud or non-compliance could have a material effect on the GHG
    statement.

The date of the written representations shall be as near as practicable to, but not **59**
after, the date of the assurance report.

The practitioner shall disclaim a conclusion on the GHG statement or withdraw **60**
from the engagement, where withdrawal is possible under applicable laws or regulations, if:

(a) The practitioner concludes that there is sufficient doubt about the integrity of
    the person(s) providing the written representations required by paragraphs 58(a)
    and (b) that written representations in these regards are not reliable; or
(b) The entity does not provide the written representations required by paragraphs
    58(a) and (b).

Subsequent Events

The practitioner shall: (Ref: Para. A117) **61**

(a) Consider whether events occurring between the date of the GHG statement and
    the date of the assurance report require adjustment of, or disclosure in, the
    GHG statement, and evaluate the sufficiency and appropriateness of evidence
    obtained about whether such events are appropriately reflected in that GHG
    statement in accordance with the applicable criteria; and
(b) Respond appropriately to facts that become known to the practitioner after the
    date of the assurance report, that, had they been known to the practitioner at
    that date, may have caused the practitioner to amend the assurance report.

Comparative Information

When comparative information is presented with the current emissions information **62**
and some or all of that comparative information is covered by the practitioner's

conclusion, the practitioner's procedures with respect to the comparative information shall include evaluating whether: (Ref: Para. A118–A121)

(a) The comparative information agrees with the amounts and other disclosures presented in the prior period or, when appropriate, has been properly restated and that restatement has been adequately disclosed; and (Ref Para. A121)

(b) The quantification policies reflected in the comparative information are consistent with those applied in the current period or, if there have been changes, whether they have been properly applied and adequately disclosed.

63 Irrespective of whether the practitioner's conclusion covers the comparative information, if the practitioner becomes aware that there may be a material misstatement in the comparative information presented the practitioner shall:

(a) Discuss the matter with those person(s) within the entity with appropriate responsibilities for, and knowledge of, the matters concerned and perform procedures appropriate in the circumstances; and (Ref: Para. A122–A123)

(b) Consider the effect on the assurance report. If the comparative information presented contains a material misstatement, and the comparative information has not been restated:

    (i) Where the practitioner's conclusion covers the comparative information, the practitioner shall express a qualified conclusion or an adverse conclusion in the assurance report; or

    (ii) Where the practitioner's conclusion does not cover the comparative information, the practitioner shall include an Other Matter paragraph in the assurance report describing the circumstances affecting the comparative information.

Other Information

64 The practitioner shall read other information included in documents containing the GHG statement and the assurance report thereon and, if, in the practitioner's judgment, that other information could undermine the credibility of the GHG statement and the assurance report, shall discuss the matter with the entity and take further action as appropriate. (Ref: Para. A124–A126)

Documentation

65 In documenting the nature, timing and extent of procedures performed, the practitioner shall record: (Ref: Para. A127)

(a) The identifying characteristics of the specific items or matters tested;

(b) Who performed the engagement work and the date such work was completed; and

(c) Who reviewed the engagement work performed and the date and extent of such review.

66 The practitioner shall document discussions of significant matters with the entity and others, including the nature of the significant matters discussed, and when and with whom the discussions took place. (Ref: Para. A127)

Quality Control

The practitioner shall include in the engagement documentation: 67

(a) Issues identified with respect to compliance with relevant ethical requirements and how they were resolved;
(b) Conclusions on compliance with independence requirements that apply to the engagement, and any relevant discussions with the firm that support these conclusions;
(c) Conclusions reached regarding the acceptance and continuance of client relationships and assurance engagements; and
(d) The nature and scope of, and conclusions resulting from, consultations undertaken during the course of the engagement.

Matters Arising after the Date of the Assurance Report

If, in exceptional circumstances, the practitioner performs new or additional pro-   68
cedures or draws new conclusions after the date of the assurance report, the practitioner shall document: (Ref: Para. A128)

(a) The circumstances encountered;
(b) The new or additional procedures performed, evidence obtained, and conclusions reached, and their effect on the assurance report; and
(c) When and by whom the resulting changes to engagement documentation were made and reviewed.

Assembly of the Final Engagement File

The practitioner shall assemble the engagement documentation in an engagement file   69
and complete the administrative process of assembling the final engagement file on a timely basis after the date of the assurance report. After the assembly of the final engagement file has been completed, the practitioner shall not delete or discard engagement documentation of any nature before the end of its retention period. (Ref: Para. A129)

In circumstances other than those envisaged in paragraph 68 where the practitioner   70
finds it necessary to modify existing engagement documentation or add new engagement documentation after the assembly of the final engagement file has been completed, the practitioner shall, regardless of the nature of the modifications or additions, document:

(a) The specific reasons for making them; and
(b) When and by whom they were made and reviewed.

Engagement Quality Control Review

For those engagements, if any, for which a quality control review is required by laws   71
or regulations or for which the firm has determined that an engagement quality control review is required, the engagement quality control reviewer shall perform an objective evaluation of the significant judgments made by the engagement team, and the conclusions reached in formulating the assurance report. This evaluation shall involve: (Ref: Para. A130)

(a) Discussion of significant matters with the engagement partner, including the engagement team's professional competencies with respect to the quantification and reporting of emissions and assurance;

(b) Review of the GHG statement and the proposed assurance report;

(c) Review of selected engagement documentation relating to the significant judgments the engagement team made and the conclusions it reached; and

(d) Evaluation of the conclusions reached in formulating the assurance report and consideration of whether the proposed assurance report is appropriate.

Forming the Assurance Conclusion

72   The practitioner shall conclude as to whether the practitioner has obtained reasonable or limited assurance, as appropriate, about the GHG statement. That conclusion shall take into account the requirements of paragraphs 56 and 73–75 of this ISAE.

Limited Assurance	Reasonable Assurance
73L. The practitioner shall evaluate whether anything has come to the practitioner's attention that causes the practitioner to believe that the GHG statement is not prepared, in all material respects, in accordance with the applicable criteria.	73R. The practitioner shall evaluate whether the GHG statement is prepared, in all material respects, in accordance with the applicable criteria.

74   This evaluation shall include consideration of the qualitative aspects of the entity's quantification methods and reporting practices, including indicators of possible bias in judgments and decisions in the making of estimates and in preparing the GHG statement,[12] and whether, in view of the applicable criteria:

(a) The quantification methods and reporting policies selected and applied are consistent with the applicable criteria and are appropriate;

(b) Estimates made in preparing the GHG statement are reasonable;

(c) The information presented in the GHG statement is relevant, reliable, complete, comparable and understandable;

(d) The GHG statement provides adequate disclosure of the applicable criteria, and other matters, including uncertainties, such that intended users can understand the significant judgments made in its preparation; and (Ref: Para. A29, A131–A133)

(e) The terminology used in the GHG statement is appropriate.

75   The evaluation required by paragraph 73 shall also include consideration of:

(a) The overall presentation, structure and content of the GHG statement; and

(b) When appropriate in the context of the criteria, the wording of the assurance conclusion, or other engagement circumstances, whether the GHG statement represents the underlying emissions in a manner that achieves fair presentation.

---

[12] *Indicators of possible bias do not themselves constitute misstatements for the purposes of drawing conclusions on the reasonableness of individual estimates.*

Assurance Report Content

The assurance report shall include the following basic elements: (Ref: Para. A134) **76**

(a) A title that clearly indicates the report is an independent limited assurance or reasonable assurance report.

(b) The addressee of the assurance report.

(c) Identification of the GHG statement, including the period(s) it covers, and, if any information in that statement is not covered by the practitioner's conclusion, clear identification of the information subject to assurance as well as the excluded information, together with a statement that the practitioner has not performed any procedures with respect to the excluded information and, therefore, that no conclusion on it is expressed. (Ref: Para. A120, A135)

(d) A description of the entity's responsibilities. (Ref: Para. A35)

(e) A statement that GHG quantification is subject to inherent uncertainty. (Ref: Para. A54–A59)

(f) If the GHG statement includes emissions deductions that are covered by the practitioner's conclusion, identification of those emissions deductions, and a statement of the practitioner's responsibility with respect to them. (Ref: Para. A136–A139)

(g) Identification of the applicable criteria;
  (i) Identification of how those criteria can be accessed;
  (ii) If those criteria are available only to specific intended users, or are relevant only to a specific purpose, a statement restricting the use of the assurance report to those intended users or that purpose; and (Ref: Para. A140–A141)
  (iii) If established criteria need to be supplemented by disclosures in the explanatory notes to the GHG statement for those criteria to be suitable, identification of the relevant note(s). (Ref: Para. A131)

(h) A description of the practitioner's responsibility, including:
  (i) A statement that the engagement was performed in accordance with ISAE 3410, *Assurance Engagements on Greenhouse Gas Statements*; and
  (ii) A summary of the practitioner's procedures. In the case of a limited assurance engagement, this shall include a statement that the procedures performed in a limited assurance engagement vary in nature from, and are less in extent than for, a reasonable assurance engagement. As a result, the level of assurance obtained in a limited assurance engagement is substantially lower than the assurance that would have been obtained had a reasonable assurance engagement been performed. (Ref: Para. A142–A144)

(i) The practitioner's conclusion, expressed in the positive form in the case of a reasonable assurance engagement or in the negative form in the case of a limited assurance engagement, about whether the GHG statement is prepared, in all material respects, in accordance with the applicable criteria.

(j) If the practitioner expresses a conclusion that is modified, a clear description of all the reasons therefore.

(k) The practitioner's signature. (Ref: Para. A145)

(l) The date of the assurance report.

(m) The location in the jurisdiction where the practitioner practices.

Emphasis of Matter Paragraphs and Other Matter Paragraphs

If the practitioner considers it necessary to: (Ref: Para. A146–A152) **77**

(a) Draw intended users' attention to a matter presented or disclosed in the GHG statement that, in the practitioner's judgment, is of such importance that it is fundamental to intended users' understanding of the GHG statement (an Emphasis of Matter paragraph); or

(b) Communicate a matter other than those that are presented or disclosed in the GHG statement that, in the practitioner's judgment, is relevant to intended users' understanding of the engagement, the practitioner's responsibilities or the assurance report (an Other Matter paragraph),

and this is not prohibited by laws or regulations, the practitioner shall do so in a paragraph in the assurance report, with an appropriate heading, that clearly indicates the practitioner's conclusion is not modified in respect of the matter.

Other Communication Requirements

78   The practitioner shall communicate to those person(s) with oversight responsibilities for the GHG statement the following matters that come to the practitioner's attention during the course of the engagement, and shall determine whether there is a responsibility to report them to another party within or outside the entity:

(a) Deficiencies in internal control that, in the practitioner's professional judgment, are of sufficient importance to merit attention;

(b) Identified or suspected fraud; and

(c) Matters involving non-compliance with laws and regulations, other than when the matters are clearly trivial. (Ref: Para. A87)

***

Application and Other Explanatory Material

Introduction

Assurance Engagements Covering Information in Addition to the GHG Statement (Ref: Para. 3)

A1   In some cases, the practitioner may perform an assurance engagement on a report that includes GHG information, but that GHG information does not comprise a GHG statement as defined in paragraph 14(m). In such cases, this ISAE may provide guidance for such an engagement.

A2   Where a GHG statement is a relatively minor part of the overall information that is covered by the practitioner's conclusion, the extent to which this ISAE is relevant is a matter for the practitioner's professional judgment in the circumstances of the engagement.

Key Performance Indicators Based on GHG Data (Ref: Para. 4(b))

A3   An example of a key performance indicator based on GHG data is the weighted average of emissions per kilometer of vehicles manufactured by an entity during a period, which is required to be calculated and disclosed by laws or regulations in some jurisdictions.

Procedures for Reasonable Assurance and Limited Assurance Engagements (Ref: Para. 8)

A4   Some procedures that are required only for reasonable assurance engagements may nonetheless be appropriate in some limited assurance engagements. For example, although obtaining an understanding of control activities is not required for limited assurance engagements, in some cases, such as when information is recorded, processed, or reported only in electronic form, the practitioner may nonetheless decide that testing controls, and therefore obtaining an understanding of relevant control activities, is necessary for a limited assurance engagement (see also paragraph A90).

Independence (Ref: Para. 10, 15)

The IESBA Code adopts a threats and safeguards approach to independence. **A5** Compliance with the fundamental principles may potentially be threatened by a broad range of circumstances. Many threats fall into the following categories:

- Self-interest, for example, undue dependence on total fees from the entity.
- Self-review, for example, performing another service for the entity that directly affects the GHG statement, such as involvement in the quantification of the entity's emissions.
- Advocacy, for example, acting as an advocate on behalf of the entity with respect to the interpretation of the applicable criteria.
- Familiarity, for example, a member of the engagement team having a long association, or close or immediate family relationship, with an employee of the entity who is in a position to exert direct and significant influence over the preparation of the GHG statement.
- Intimidation, for example, being pressured to reduce inappropriately the extent of work performed in order to lower fees, or being threatened with withdrawal of the practitioner's registration by a registering authority that is associated with the entity's industry group.

Safeguards created by the profession, laws or regulations, or safeguards in the work **A6** environment, may eliminate or reduce such threats to an acceptable level.

Local Laws and Regulations and the Provisions of an Emissions Trading Scheme (Ref: Para. 11)

Local laws or regulations or the provisions of an emissions trading scheme may: **A7** include requirements in addition to the requirements of this ISAE; require that specific procedures be undertaken on all engagements; or require that procedures be undertaken in a particular way. For example, local laws or regulations or the provisions of an emissions trading scheme may require the practitioner to report in a format that is not in compliance with this ISAE. When the law or regulation prescribes the layout or wording of the assurance report in a form or in terms that are significantly different from this ISAE, and the practitioner concludes that additional explanation in the assurance report cannot mitigate possible misunderstanding, the practitioner may consider including a statement in the report that the engagement is not conducted in accordance with this ISAE.

Definitions

Emissions (Ref: Para. 14(f), Appendix 1)

Scope 1 emissions may include stationary combustion (from fuel burned in the **A8** entity's stationary equipment, such as boilers, incinerators, engines, and flares), mobile combustion (from fuel burned in the entity's transport devices, such as trucks, trains, airplanes and boats), process emissions (from physical or chemical processes, such as cement manufacturing, petrochemical processing, and aluminum smelting), and fugitive emissions (intentional and unintentional releases, such as equipment leaks from joints and seals and emissions from wastewater treatment, pits, and cooling towers).

A9   Almost all entities purchase energy in a form such as electricity, heat or steam; therefore, almost all entities have Scope 2 emissions. Scope 2 emissions are indirect because the emissions associated with, for example, electricity that the entity purchases occur at the power station, which is outside the entity's organizational boundary.

A10   Scope 3 emissions may include emissions associated with, for example: employee business travel; outsourced activities; consumption of fossil fuel or electricity required to use the entity's products; extraction and production of materials purchased as inputs to the entity's processes; and transportation of purchased fuels. Scope 3 emissions are further discussed in paragraphs A31–A34.

Emissions Deductions (Ref: Para. 14(g), 17(a)(iii), Appendix 1)

A11   In some cases, emissions deductions include jurisdiction-specific credits and allowances for which there is no established link between the quantity of emissions allowed by the criteria to be deducted, and any lowering of emissions that may occur as a result of money paid or other action taken by the entity in order for it to claim the emissions deduction.

A12   Where an entity's GHG statement includes emissions deductions that are within the scope of the engagement, the requirements of this ISAE apply in relation to emissions deductions as appropriate (see also paragraphs A136-A139).

Purchased Offset (Ref: Para. 14(q), Appendix 1)

A13   When the entity purchases an offset from another entity, that other entity may spend the money it receives from the sale on emissions reduction projects (such as replacing energy generation using fossil fuels with renewable energy sources, or implementing energy efficiency measures), or on removing emissions from the atmosphere (for example, by planting and maintaining trees that would otherwise not have been planted or maintained), or the money may be compensation for not undertaking an action that would otherwise be undertaken (such as deforestation or forest degradation). In some jurisdictions, offsets can only be purchased if the emissions reduction or removal enhancement has already occurred.

Removal (Ref: Para. 14(s), Appendix 1)

A14   Removal may be achieved by storing GHGs in geological sinks (for example, underground) or biological sinks (for example, trees). Where the GHG statement includes the removal of GHGs that the entity would have otherwise emitted to the atmosphere, they are commonly reported in the GHG statement on a gross basis, that is, both the source and the sink are quantified in the GHG statement. Where removals are covered by the practitioner's conclusion, the requirements of this ISAE apply in relation to those removals as appropriate.

Significant Facility (Ref: Para. 14(t), 31)

A15   As the individual contribution of a facility to the aggregate emissions reported in the GHG statement increases, the risks of material misstatement to the GHG statement ordinarily increase. The practitioner may apply a percentage to a chosen benchmark as an aid to identify facilities that are of individual significance due to the size of their emissions relative to the aggregate emissions included in the GHG statement. Identifying a benchmark and determining a percentage to be applied to it involve the exercise of professional judgment. For example, the practitioner may consider that facilities exceeding 15% of total production volume are significant facilities. A higher or lower percentage may, however, be determined to be appropriate in the circumstances in the practitioner's professional judgment. This may be the case when, for example: there is a small number of facilities, none of which is less than 15% of total production volume, but in the practitioner's professional judgment not all the facilities are significant; or when there are a number of facilities that are marginally below 15% of total production volume which in the practitioner's professional judgment are significant.

The practitioner may also identify a facility as significant due to its specific nature or circumstances which give rise to particular risks of material misstatement. For example, a facility could be using different data gathering processes or quantification techniques from other facilities, require the use of particularly complex or specialized calculations, or involve particularly complex or specialized chemical or physical processes.   **A16**

ISAE 3000 (Ref: Para. 9, 15)

ISAE 3000 includes a number of requirements that apply to all assurance engagements, including engagements in accordance with this ISAE. In some cases, this ISAE may include additional requirements or application material in relation to those topics.   **A17**

Acceptance and Continuance of the Engagement

Competency (Ref: Para. 16(b))

GHG competencies may include: **A18**

- General understanding of climate science, including the scientific processes that relate GHGs to climate change.
- Understanding who the intended users of the information in the entity's GHG statement are, and how they are likely to use that information (see paragraph A47).
- Understanding emissions trading schemes and related market mechanisms, when relevant.
- Knowledge of applicable laws and regulations, if any, that affect how the entity should report its emissions, and may also, for example, impose a limit on the entity's emissions.
- GHG quantification and measurement methodologies, including the associated scientific and estimation uncertainties, and alternative methodologies available.
- Knowledge of the applicable criteria, including, for example:
  o Identifying appropriate emissions factors.
  o Identifying those aspects of the criteria that call for significant or sensitive estimates to be made, or for the application of considerable judgment.
  o Methods used for determining organizational boundaries, i.e., the entities whose emissions are to be included in the GHG statement.
  o Which emissions deductions are permitted to be included in the entity's GHG statement.

A19   The complexity of assurance engagements with respect to a GHG statement varies. In some cases, the engagement may be relatively straightforward, for instance, when an entity has no Scope 1 emissions and is reporting only Scope 2 emissions using an emissions factor specified in regulation, applied to electricity consumption at a single location. In this case, the engagement may focus largely on the system used to record and process electricity consumption figures identified on invoices, and arithmetical application of the specified emissions factor. When, however, the engagement is relatively complex, it is likely to require specialist competence in the quantification and reporting of emissions. Particular areas of expertise that may be relevant in such cases include:

Information systems expertise

- Understanding how emissions information is generated, including how data is initiated, recorded, processed, corrected as necessary, collated and reported in a GHG statement.

Scientific and engineering expertise

- Mapping the flow of materials through a production process, and the accompanying processes that create emissions, including identifying the relevant points at which source data is gathered. This may be particularly important in considering whether the entity's identification of emissions sources is complete.
- Analyzing chemical and physical relationships between inputs, processes and outputs, and relationships between emissions and other variables. The capacity to understand and analyze these relationships will often be important in designing analytical procedures.
- Identifying the effect of uncertainty on the GHG statement.
- Knowledge of the quality control policies and procedures implemented at testing laboratories, whether internal or external.
- Experience with specific industries and related emissions creation and removal processes. Procedures for Scope 1 emissions quantification vary greatly depending on the industries and processes involved, for example, the nature of electrolytic processes in aluminum production; combustion processes in the production of electricity using fossil fuels; and chemical processes in cement production are all different.
- The operation of physical sensors and other quantification methods, and the selection of appropriate emissions factors.

Scope of the GHG Statement and the Engagement (Ref: Para. 17(a))

A20   Examples of circumstances where the reasons for excluding known emissions sources from the GHG statement, or excluding disclosed emissions sources from the engagement, may not be reasonable in the circumstances include where:

- The entity has significant Scope 1 emissions but only includes Scope 2 emissions in the GHG statement.
- The entity is a part of a larger legal entity that has significant emissions that are not being reported on because of the way the organizational boundary has been determined when this is likely to mislead intended users.
- The emissions that the practitioner is reporting on are only a small proportion of the total emissions included in the GHG statement.

Assessing the Appropriateness of the Subject Matter (Ref: Para. 15)

ISAE 3000 requires the practitioner to assess the appropriateness of the subject   A21
matter.[13] In the case of a GHG statement, the entity's emissions (and removals and
emissions deductions if applicable) are the subject matter of the engagement. That
subject matter will be appropriate if, among other things, the entity's emissions are
capable of consistent quantification using suitable criteria.[14]

GHG sources may be quantified by: A22

(a) Direct measurement (or direct monitoring) of GHG concentration and flow
    rates using continuous emissions monitoring or periodic sampling; or
(b) Measuring a surrogate activity, such as fuel consumption, and calculating
    emissions using, for example, mass balance equations,[15] entity-specific emissions
    factors, or average emissions factors for a region, source, industry or process.

Assessing the Suitability of the Criteria

Specifically Developed and Established Criteria (Ref: Para. 17(b))

Suitable criteria exhibit the following characteristics: relevance, completeness,   A23
reliability, neutrality, and understandability. Criteria may be "specifically developed" or they may be "established," that is, embodied in laws or regulations, or
issued by authorized or recognized bodies of experts that follow a transparent due
process.[16] Although criteria established by a regulator can be presumed to be relevant
when that regulator is the intended user, some established criteria may be developed
for a special purpose and be unsuitable for application in other circumstances. For
example, criteria developed by a regulator that include emissions factors for a particular region may render misleading information if used for emissions in another
region; or criteria that are designed to report only on particular regulatory aspects of
emissions may be unsuitable for reporting to intended users other than the regulator
that established the criteria.

Specifically developed criteria may be appropriate when, for example, the entity has   A24
very specialized machinery or is aggregating emissions information from different
jurisdictions where the established criteria used in those jurisdictions differ. Special
care may be necessary when assessing the neutrality and other characteristics of
specifically developed criteria, particularly if they are not substantially based on
established criteria generally used in the entity's industry or region, or are inconsistent with such criteria.

The applicable criteria may comprise established criteria supplemented by dis-   A25
closures, in the explanatory notes to the GHG statement, of specific boundaries,
methods, assumptions, emissions factors, etc. In some cases, established criteria may
not be suitable, even when supplemented by disclosures in the explanatory notes to
the GHG statement, for example, when they do not encompass the matters noted in
paragraph 17(b).

---

[13] *ISAE 3000, paragraph 18.*

[14] *Assurance Framework, paragraphs 34-38, and ISAE 3000, paragraphs 19–21.*

[15] *That is, equating the amount of a substance entering and exiting a defined boundary, for example, the amount
of carbon in a hydrocarbon-based fuel entering a combustion device equals the amount of carbon exiting the
device in the form of carbon dioxide.*

[16] *Assurance Framework, paragraphs 36–37.*

A26 It should be noted that the suitability of the applicable criteria is not affected by the level of assurance, that is, if they are not suitable for a reasonable assurance engagement, they are also not suitable for a limited assurance engagement, and vice versa.

Operations Included in the Entity's Organizational Boundary (Ref: Para. 17(b)(i), 23(b)(i), 34(g))

A27 Determining which operations owned or controlled by the entity to include in the entity's GHG statement is known as determining the entity's organizational boundary. In some cases, laws and regulations define the boundaries of the entity for reporting GHG emissions for regulatory purposes. In other cases, the applicable criteria may allow a choice between different methods for determining the entity's organizational boundary, for example, the criteria may allow a choice between an approach that aligns the entity's GHG statement with its financial statements and another approach that treats, for example, joint ventures or associates differently. Determining the entity's organizational boundary may require the analysis of complex organizational structures such as joint ventures, partnerships, and trusts, and complex or unusual contractual relationships. For example, a facility may be owned by one party, operated by another, and process materials solely for another party.

A28 Determining the entity's organizational boundary is different from what some criteria describe as determining the entity's "operational boundary." The operational boundary relates to which categories of Scope 1, 2 and 3 emissions will be included in the GHG statement, and is determined after setting the organizational boundary.

Adequate Disclosures (Ref: Para. 17(b)(iv), 74(d))

A29 In regulatory disclosure regimes, disclosures specified in the relevant laws or regulations are adequate for reporting to the regulator. Disclosure in the GHG statement of such matters as the following may be necessary in voluntary reporting situations for intended users to understand the significant judgments made in preparing the GHG statement:

(a) Which operations are included in the entity's organizational boundary, and the method used for determining that boundary if the applicable criteria allow a choice between different methods (see paragraphs A27–A28);

(b) Significant quantification methods and reporting policies selected, including:

  (i) The method used to determine which Scope 1 and Scope 2 emissions have been included in the GHG statement (see paragraph A30);

  (ii) Any significant interpretations made in applying the applicable criteria in the entity's circumstances, including data sources and, when choices between different methods are allowed, or entity-specific methods are used, disclosure of the method used and the rationale for doing so; and

  (iii) How the entity determines whether previously reported emissions should be restated.

(c) The categorization of emissions in the GHG statement. As noted in paragraph A14, where the GHG statement includes the removal of GHGs that the entity would have otherwise emitted to the atmosphere, both emissions and removals are commonly reported in the GHG statement on a gross basis, that is, both the source and the sink are quantified in the GHG statement;

(d) A statement regarding the uncertainties relevant to the entity's quantification of its emissions, including: their causes; how they have been addressed; their effects on the GHG statement; and, where the GHG statement includes Scope 3 emissions, an explanation of: (see paragraphs A31–A34)

(i) The nature of Scope 3 emissions, including that it is not practicable for an entity to include all Scope 3 emissions in its GHG statement; and

(ii) The basis for selecting those Scope 3 emissions sources that have been included; and

(e) Changes, if any, in the matters mentioned in this paragraph or in other matters that materially affect the comparability of the GHG statement with a prior period(s) or base year.

Scope 1 and Scope 2 Emissions

Criteria commonly call for all material Scope 1, Scope 2, or both Scope 1 and Scope 2 emissions to be included in the GHG statement. Where some Scope 1 or Scope 2 emissions have been excluded, it is important that the explanatory notes to the GHG statement disclose the basis for determining which emissions are included and which are excluded, particularly if those that are included are not likely to be the largest for which the entity is responsible. **A30**

Scope 3 Emissions

While some criteria require the reporting of specific Scope 3 emissions, more commonly the inclusion of Scope 3 emissions is optional because it would be impracticable for nearly any entity to attempt to quantify the full extent of its indirect emissions as this includes all sources both up and down the entity's supply chain. For some entities, reporting particular categories of Scope 3 emissions provides important information for intended users, for example, where an entity's Scope 3 emissions are considerably larger than its Scope 1 and Scope 2 emissions, as may be the case with many service sector entities. In these cases, the practitioner may consider it inappropriate to undertake an assurance engagement if significant Scope 3 emissions are not included in the GHG statement. **A31**

Where some Scope 3 emissions sources have been included in the GHG statement, it is important that the basis for selecting which sources to include is reasonable, particularly if those included are not likely to be the largest sources for which the entity is responsible. **A32**

In some cases, the source data used to quantify Scope 3 emissions may be maintained by the entity. For example, the entity may keep detailed records as the basis for quantifying emissions associated with employee air travel. In some other cases, the source data used to quantify Scope 3 emissions may be maintained in a well-controlled and accessible source outside the entity. Where this is not the case, however, it may be unlikely that the practitioner will be able to obtain sufficient appropriate evidence with respect to such Scope 3 emissions. In such cases, it may be appropriate to exclude those Scope 3 emissions sources from the engagement. **A33**

It may also be appropriate to exclude Scope 3 emissions from the engagement where the quantification methods in use are heavily dependent on estimation and lead to a high degree of uncertainty in reported emissions. For example, various quantification methods for estimating the emissions associated with air travel can give widely varying quantifications even when **A34**

identical source data is used. If such Scope 3 emissions sources are included in the engagement, it is important that the quantification methods used are selected objectively and that they are fully described along with the uncertainties associated with their use.

The Entity's Responsibility for the Preparation of the GHG Statement (Ref: Para. 17(c)(ii), 76(d))

A35   As noted in paragraph A70, for some engagements concerns about the condition and reliability of an entity's records may cause the practitioner to conclude that it is unlikely that sufficient appropriate evidence will be available to support an unmodified conclusion on the GHG statement. This may occur when the entity has little experience with the preparation of GHG statements. In such circumstances, it may be more appropriate for the quantification and reporting of emissions to be subject to an agreed-upon procedures engagement or a consulting engagement in preparation for an assurance engagement in a later period.

Who Developed the Criteria (Ref: Para. 17(c)(iii))

A36   When the GHG statement has been prepared for a regulatory disclosure regime or emissions trading scheme where the applicable criteria and form of reporting are prescribed, it is likely to be apparent from the engagement circumstances that it is the regulator or body in charge of the scheme that developed the criteria. In voluntary reporting situations, however, it may not be clear who developed the criteria unless it is stated in the explanatory notes to the GHG statement.

Changing the Terms of the Engagement (Ref: Para. 15, 18)

A37   ISAE 3000 requires that the practitioner not agree to a change in the terms of the engagement where there is no reasonable justification for doing so.[17] A request to change the scope of the engagement may not have a reasonable justification when, for example, the request is made to exclude certain emissions sources from the scope of the engagement because of the likelihood that the practitioner's conclusion would be modified.

Planning (Ref: Para. 19)

A38   When establishing the overall engagement strategy, it may be relevant to consider the emphasis given to different aspects of the design and implementation of the GHG information system. For example, in some cases the entity may have been particularly conscious of the need for adequate internal control to ensure the reliability of reported information, while in other cases the entity may have focused more on accurately determining the scientific, operational or technical characteristics of the information to be gathered.

A39   Smaller engagements or more straightforward engagements (see paragraph A19) may be conducted by a very small engagement team. With a smaller team, coordination of, and communication between, team members is easier. Establishing the overall engagement strategy for a smaller engagement, or for a more straightforward engagement, need not be a complex or time-consuming exercise. For example, a brief memorandum, based on discussions with the entity, may serve as the documented engagement strategy if it covers the matters noted in paragraph 19.

---

[17] *ISAE 3000, paragraph 11.*

The practitioner may decide to discuss elements of planning with the entity when **A40** determining the scope of the engagement or to facilitate the conduct and management of the engagement (for example, to coordinate some of the planned procedures with the work of the entity's personnel). Although these discussions often occur, the overall engagement strategy and the engagement plan remain the practitioner's responsibility. When discussing matters included in the overall engagement strategy or engagement plan, care is required in order not to compromise the effectiveness of the engagement. For example, discussing the nature and timing of detailed procedures with the entity may compromise the effectiveness of the engagement by making the procedures too predictable.

The performance of an assurance engagement is an iterative process. As the prac- **A41** titioner performs planned procedures, the evidence obtained may cause the practitioner to modify the nature, timing or extent of other planned procedures. In some cases, information may come to the practitioner's attention that differs significantly from that expected at an earlier stage of the engagement. For example, systematic errors discovered when performing procedures on location at selected facilities may indicate that it is necessary to visit additional facilities.

Planning to Use the Work of Experts or of Other Practitioners (Ref: Para. 19(e))

The engagement may be performed by a multidisciplinary team that includes one or **A42** more experts, particularly on relatively complex engagements when specialist competence in the quantification and reporting of emissions is likely to be required (see paragraph A19). ISAE 3000 contains a number of requirements with respect to using the work of an expert that may need to be considered at the planning stage when ascertaining the nature, timing and extent of resources necessary to perform the engagement.[18]

The work of another practitioner may be used in relation to, for example, a factory **A43** or other form of facility at a remote location; a subsidiary, division or branch in a foreign jurisdiction; or a joint venture or associate. Relevant considerations when the engagement team plans to request another practitioner to perform work on information to be included in the GHG statement may include:

- Whether the other practitioner understands and complies with the ethical requirements that are relevant to the engagement and, in particular, is independent.
- The other practitioner's professional competence.
- The extent of the engagement team's involvement in the work of the other practitioner.
- Whether the other practitioner operates in a regulatory environment that actively oversees that practitioner.

Materiality in Planning and Performing the Engagement

Determining Materiality When Planning the Engagement (Ref: Para. 20–21)

The criteria may discuss the concept of materiality in the context of the preparation **A44** and presentation of the GHG statement. Although criteria may discuss materiality in different terms, the concept of materiality generally includes that:

[18] *ISAE 3000, paragraphs 26–32.*

- Misstatements, including omissions, are considered to be material if they, individually or in the aggregate, could reasonably be expected to influence relevant decisions of users taken on the basis of the GHG statement;
- Judgments about materiality are made in light of surrounding circumstances, and are affected by the size or nature of a misstatement, or a combination of both; and
- Judgments about matters that are material to intended users of the GHG statement are based on a consideration of the common information needs of intended users as a group. The possible effect of misstatements on specific individual users, whose needs may vary widely, is not considered.

A45 Such a discussion, if present in the applicable criteria, provides a frame of reference to the practitioner in determining materiality for the engagement. If the applicable criteria do not include a discussion of the concept of materiality, the characteristics referred to above provide the practitioner with such a frame of reference.

A46 The practitioner's determination of materiality is a matter of professional judgment, and is affected by the practitioner's perception of the common information needs of intended users as a group. In this context, it is reasonable for the practitioner to assume that intended users:

(a) Have a reasonable knowledge of GHG related activities, and a willingness to study the information in the GHG statement with reasonable diligence;

(b) Understand that the GHG statement is prepared and assured to levels of materiality, and have an understanding of any materiality concepts included in the applicable criteria;

(c) Understand that the quantification of emissions involves uncertainties (see paragraphs A54–A59); and

(d) Make reasonable decisions on the basis of the information in the GHG statement.

A47 Intended users and their information needs may include, for example:

- Investors and other stakeholders such as suppliers, customers, employees, and the broader community in the case of voluntary disclosures. Their information needs may relate to decisions to buy or sell equity in the entity; lend to, trade with, or be employed by the entity; or make representations to the entity or others, for example, politicians.
- Market participants in the case of an emissions trading scheme, whose information needs may relate to decisions to trade negotiable instruments (such as permits, credits or allowances) created by the scheme, or impose fines or other penalties on the basis of excess emissions.
- Regulators and policy makers in the case of a regulatory disclosure regime. Their information needs may relate to monitoring compliance with the disclosure regime, and a broad range of government policy decisions related to climate change mitigation and adaptation, usually based on aggregated information.
- Management and those charged with governance of the entity who use information about emissions for strategic and operational decisions, such as choosing between alternative technologies and investment and divestment decisions, perhaps in anticipation of a regulatory disclosure regime or entering an emissions trading scheme.

The practitioner may not be able to identify all those who will read the assurance report, particularly where there are a large number of people who have access to it. In such cases, particularly where possible readers are likely to have a broad range of interests with respect to emissions, intended users may be limited to major stakeholders with significant and common interests. Intended users may be identified in different ways, for example, by agreement between the practitioner and the engaging party, or by laws or regulations.

Judgments about materiality are made in light of surrounding circumstances, and are **A48** affected by both quantitative and qualitative factors. It should be noted, however, that decisions regarding materiality are not affected by the level of assurance, that is, materiality for a reasonable assurance engagement is the same as for a limited assurance engagement.

A percentage is often applied to a chosen benchmark as a starting point in deter- **A49** mining materiality. Factors that may affect the identification of an appropriate benchmark and percentage include:

- The elements included in the GHG statement (for example, Scope 1, Scope 2 and Scope 3 emissions, emissions deductions, and removals). A benchmark that may be appropriate, depending on the circumstances, is gross reported emissions, that is, the aggregate of reported Scope 1, Scope 2 and Scope 3 emissions before subtracting any emissions deductions or removals. Materiality relates to the emissions covered by the practitioner's conclusion. Therefore, when the practitioner's conclusion does not cover the entire GHG statement, materiality is set in relation to only that portion of the GHG statement that is covered by the practitioner's conclusion as if it were the GHG statement.
- The quantity of a particular type of emission or the nature of a particular disclosure. In some cases, there are particular types of emissions or disclosures for which misstatements of lesser or greater amounts than materiality for the GHG statement in its entirety are acceptable. For example, the practitioner may consider it appropriate to set a lower or greater materiality for emissions from a particular jurisdiction, or for a particular gas, scope or facility.
- How the GHG statement presents relevant information, for example, whether it includes a comparison of emissions with a prior period(s), a base year, or a "cap," in which case determining materiality in relation to the comparative information may be a relevant consideration. Where a "cap" is relevant, materiality may be set in relation to the entity's allocation of the cap if it is lower than reported emissions.
- The relative volatility of emissions. For example, if emissions vary significantly from period to period, it may be appropriate to set materiality relative to the lower end of the fluctuation range even if the current period is higher.
- The requirements of the applicable criteria. In some cases, the applicable criteria may set a threshold for accuracy and may refer to this as materiality. For example, the criteria may state an expectation that emissions are measured using a stipulated percentage as the "materiality threshold." Where this is the case, the threshold set by the criteria provides a frame of reference to the practitioner in determining materiality for the engagement.

Qualitative factors may include: **A50**

- The sources of emissions.
- The types of gases involved.
- The context in which the information in the GHG statement will be used (for example, whether the information is for use in an emissions trading scheme, is for submission to a regulator, or is for inclusion in a widely distributed sustainability report); and the types of decisions that intended users are likely to make.
- Whether there are one or more types of emissions or disclosures on which the attention of the intended users tends to be focused, for example, gases that, as well as contributing to climate change, are ozone depleting.

- The nature of the entity, its climate change strategies and progress toward related objectives.
- The industry and the economic and regulatory environment in which the entity operates.

Revision as the Engagement Progresses (Ref: Para. 22)

A51   Materiality may need to be revised as a result of a change in circumstances during the engagement (for example, the disposal of a major part of the entity's business), new information, or a change in the practitioner's understanding of the entity and its operations as a result of performing procedures. For example, it may become apparent during the engagement that actual emissions are likely to be substantially different from those used initially to determine materiality. If during the engagement the practitioner concludes that a lower materiality for the GHG statement (and, if applicable, materiality level or levels for particular types of emissions or disclosures) than that initially determined is appropriate, it may be necessary to revise performance materiality, and the nature, timing and extent of the further procedures.

Understanding the Entity and Its Environment, Including the Entity's Internal Control, and Identifying and Assessing Risks of Material Misstatement (Ref: Para. 23–26)

A52   The practitioner uses professional judgment to determine the extent of the understanding and the nature, timing and extent of procedures to identify and assess risks of material misstatement that are required to obtain reasonable or limited assurance, as appropriate. The practitioner's primary consideration is whether the understanding that has been obtained and the identification and assessment of risks are sufficient to meet the objective stated in this ISAE. The depth of the understanding that is required by the practitioner is less than that possessed by management in managing the entity, and both the depth of the understanding and the nature, timing and extent of procedures to identify and assess risks of material misstatement are less for a limited assurance engagement than for a reasonable assurance engagement.

A53   Obtaining an understanding and identifying and assessing risks of material misstatement is an iterative process. Procedures to obtain an understanding of the entity and its environment and to identify and assess risks of material misstatement by themselves do not provide sufficient appropriate evidence on which to base the assurance conclusion.

Uncertainty (Ref: Para: 23(b)(i)c, 76(e))

A54   The GHG quantification process can rarely be 100% accurate due to:

(a) *Scientific uncertainty*: This arises because of incomplete scientific knowledge about the measurement of GHGs. For example, the rate of GHG sequestration in biological sinks, and the "global warming potential" values used to combine emissions of different gases and report them as carbon dioxide equivalents, are subject to incomplete scientific knowledge. The degree to which scientific uncertainty affects the quantification of reported emissions is beyond the control of the entity. However, the potential for scientific uncertainty to result in unreasonable variations in reported emissions can be negated by the use of criteria that stipulate particular scientific assumptions to be used in preparing the GHG statement, or particular factors that embody those assumptions; and

(b) *Estimation (or measurement) uncertainty*: This results from the measurement and calculation processes used to quantify emissions within the bounds of existing scientific knowledge. Estimation uncertainty may relate to the data on which an estimate is based (for example, it may relate to uncertainty inherent in measurement instruments used), or the method, including where applicable the model, used in making the estimate (sometimes known as parameter and model uncertainty, respectively). The degree of estimation uncertainty is often controllable by the entity. Reducing the degree of estimation uncertainty may involve greater cost.

The fact that quantifying an entity's emissions is subject to uncertainty does not mean that an entity's emissions are inappropriate as a subject matter. For example, the applicable criteria may require Scope 2 emissions from electricity to be calculated by applying a prescribed emissions factor to the number of kilowatt hours consumed. The prescribed emissions factor will be based on assumptions and models that may not hold true in all circumstances. However, as long as the assumptions and models are reasonable in the circumstances and adequately disclosed, information in the GHG statement will ordinarily be capable of being assured.   **A55**

The situation in paragraph A55 can be contrasted with quantification in accordance with criteria that use models and assumptions based on an entity's individual circumstances. Using entity-specific models and assumptions will likely result in more accurate quantification than using, for example, average emissions factors for an industry; it will also likely introduce additional risks of material misstatement with respect to how the entity-specific models and assumptions were arrived at. As noted in paragraph A55, as long as the assumptions and models are reasonable in the circumstances and adequately disclosed, information in the GHG statement will ordinarily be capable of being assured.   **A56**

In some cases, however, the practitioner may decide that it is inappropriate to undertake an assurance engagement if the impact of uncertainty on information in the GHG statement is very high. This may be the case when, for example, a significant proportion of the entity's reported emissions are from fugitive sources (see paragraph A8) that are not monitored and estimation methods are not sufficiently sophisticated, or when a significant proportion of the entity's reported removals are attributable to biological sinks. It should be noted that decisions whether to undertake an assurance engagement in such circumstances are not affected by the level of assurance, that is, if it is not appropriate for a reasonable assurance engagement, it is also not appropriate for a limited assurance engagement, and vice versa.   **A57**

A discussion in the explanatory notes to the GHG statement of the nature, causes, and effects of the uncertainties that affect the entity's GHG statement alerts intended users to the uncertainties associated with the quantification of emissions. This may be particularly important where the intended users did not determine the criteria to be used. For example, a GHG statement may be available to a broad range of intended users even though the criteria used were developed for a particular regulatory purpose.   **A58**

Because uncertainty is a significant characteristic of all GHG statements, paragraph 76(e) requires it to be mentioned in the assurance report regardless of what, if any, disclosures are included in the explanatory notes to the GHG statement.[19]   **A59**

---

[19] *See also ISAE 3000, paragraph 49(e).*

The Entity and Its Environment

Interruptions to Operations (Ref: Para. 23(b)(iii))

A60   Interruptions may include incidents such as shut downs, which may occur unexpectedly, or may be planned, for example, as part of a maintenance schedule. In some cases, the nature of operations may be intermittent, for example, when a facility is only used at peak periods.

Climate Change Objectives and Strategies (Ref: Para. 23(e))

A61   Consideration of the entity's climate change strategy, if any, and associated economic, regulatory, physical and reputational risks, may assist the practitioner to identify risks of material misstatement. For example, if the entity has made commitments to become carbon neutral, this may provide an incentive to understate emissions so the target will appear to be achieved within a declared timeframe. Conversely, if the entity is expecting to be subject to a regulated emissions trading scheme in the future, this may provide an incentive to overstate emissions in the meantime to increase the opportunity for it to receive a larger allowance at the outset of the scheme.

Procedures to Obtain an Understanding and to Identify and Assess Risks of Material Misstatement (Ref: Para. 24)

A62   Although the practitioner is required to perform all the procedures in paragraph 24 in the course of obtaining the required understanding of the entity, the practitioner is not required to perform all of them for each aspect of that understanding.

Analytical Procedures for Obtaining an Understanding of the Entity and Its Environment and Identifying and Assessing Risks of Material Misstatement (Ref: Para. 24(b))

A63   Analytical procedures performed to obtain an understanding of the entity and its environment and to identify and assess risks of material misstatement may identify aspects of the entity of which the practitioner was unaware and may assist in assessing the risks of material misstatement in order to provide a basis for designing and implementing responses to the assessed risks. Analytical procedures may include, for example, comparing GHG emissions from various facilities with production figures for those facilities.

A64   Analytical procedures may help identify the existence of unusual events, and amounts, ratios, and trends that might indicate matters that have implications for the engagement. Unusual or unexpected relationships that are identified may assist the practitioner in identifying risks of material misstatement.

A65   However, when such analytical procedures use data aggregated at a high level (which may be the situation with analytical procedures performed to obtain an understanding of the entity and its environment and to identify and assess risks of material misstatement), the results of those analytical procedures only provide a broad initial indication about whether a material misstatement may exist. Accordingly, in such cases, consideration of other evidence that has been gathered when identifying the risks of material misstatement together with the results of such analytical procedures may assist the practitioner in understanding and evaluating the results of the analytical procedures.

Observation and Inspection (Ref: Para. 24(c))

Observation consists of looking at a process or procedure being performed by others, for example, the practitioner's observation of monitoring devices being calibrated by the entity's personnel, or of the performance of control activities. Observation provides evidence about the performance of a process or procedure, but is limited to the point in time at which the observation takes place, and by the fact that the act of being observed may affect how the process or procedure is performed.   **A66**

Inspection involves: **A67**

(a) Examining records or documents, whether internal or external, in paper form, electronic form, or other media, for example, calibration records of a monitoring device. Inspection of records and documents provides evidence of varying degrees of reliability, depending on their nature and source and, in the case of internal records and documents, on the effectiveness of the controls over their production; or
(b) A physical examination of, for example, a calibrating device.

Observation and inspection may support inquiries of management and others, and may also provide information about the entity and its environment. Examples of such procedures include observation or inspection of the following: **A68**

● The entity's operations. Observing processes and equipment, including monitoring equipment, at facilities may be particularly relevant where significant Scope 1 emissions are included in the GHG statement.
● Documents (such as emissions mitigation plans and strategies), records (such as calibration records and results from testing laboratories), and manuals detailing information collection procedures and internal controls.
● Reports prepared for management or those charged with governance, such as internal or external reports with respect to the entity's environmental management systems.
● Reports prepared by management (such as quarterly management reports) and those charged with governance (such as minutes of board of directors' meetings).

Obtaining an Understanding of the Entity's Internal Control (Ref: Para. 25L–26R)

In a limited assurance engagement, the practitioner is not required to obtain an understanding of all of the components of the entity's internal control relevant to emissions quantification and reporting as is required in a reasonable assurance engagement. In addition, the practitioner is not required to evaluate the design of controls and determine whether they have been implemented. Therefore, in a limited assurance engagement, while it may often be appropriate to inquire of the entity about control activities and monitoring of controls relevant to the quantification and reporting of emissions, it will often not be necessary to obtain a detailed understanding of these components of the entity's internal control.   **A69**

The practitioner's understanding of relevant components of internal control may raise doubts about whether sufficient appropriate evidence is available for the practitioner to complete the engagement. For example (see also paragraphs A71–A72, A92–A93, and A96):   **A70**

● Concerns about the integrity of those preparing the GHG statement may be so serious as to cause the practitioner to conclude that the risk of management misrepresentation in the GHG statement is such that an engagement cannot be conducted.

- Concerns about the condition and reliability of an entity's records may cause the practitioner to conclude that it is unlikely that sufficient appropriate evidence will be available to support an unmodified conclusion on the GHG statement.

Control Activities Relevant to the Engagement (Ref: Para. 25R(d))

A71 The practitioner's judgment about whether particular control activities are relevant to the engagement may be affected by the level of sophistication, documentation and formality of the entity's information system, including the related business processes, relevant to reporting emissions. As reporting of emissions evolves, it can be expected that so too will the level of sophistication, documentation and formality of information systems and related control activities relevant to the quantification and reporting of emissions.

A72 In the case of very small entities or immature information systems, particular control activities are likely to be more rudimentary, less well-documented, and may only exist informally. When this is the case, it is less likely the practitioner will judge it necessary to understand particular control activities in order to assess the risks of material misstatement and design further procedures responsive to assessed risks. In some regulated schemes, on the other hand, the information system and control activities may be required to be formally documented and their design approved by the regulator. Even in some of these cases, however, not all relevant data flows and associated controls may be documented. For example, it may be more likely that control activities with respect to source data collection from continuous monitoring are sophisticated, well-documented, and more formal than control activities with respect to subsequent data processing and reporting (see also paragraphs A70, A92–A93, and A96).

Other Engagements Performed for the Entity (Ref: Para. 27)

A73 Information obtained from other engagements performed for the entity may relate to, for example, aspects of the entity's control environment.

Performing Procedures on Location at the Entity's Facilities (Ref: Para. 31)

A74 Performing observation and inspection, as well as other procedures, on location at a facility (often referred to as a "site visit") may be important in building on the understanding of the entity that the practitioner develops by performing procedures at head office. Because the practitioner's understanding of the entity and identification and assessment of risks of material misstatement can be expected to be more comprehensive for a reasonable assurance engagement than for a limited assurance engagement, the number of facilities at which procedures are performed on location in the case of a reasonable assurance engagement will ordinarily be greater than in the case of a limited assurance engagement.

A75 Performing procedures on location at a facility (or having another practitioner perform such procedures on behalf of the practitioner) may be done as part of planning, when performing procedures to identify and assess risks of material misstatement, or when responding to assessed risks of material misstatement. Performing procedures at significant facilities is often particularly important for an engagement being undertaken for the first time when considering the completeness of Scope 1 sources and of sinks included in the GHG statement, and when establishing whether the entity's data collection and processing systems, and its estimation techniques, are appropriate relative to the underlying physical processes and related uncertainties.

As noted in paragraph A74, performing procedures on location at a facility may be **A76** important in building on the understanding of the entity that the practitioner develops by performing procedures at head office. For many reasonable assurance engagements, the practitioner will also judge it necessary to perform procedures on location at each significant facility to respond to assessed risks of material misstatement, particularly when the entity has significant facilities with Scope 1 emissions. For a limited assurance engagement where the entity has a number of significant facilities with Scope 1 emissions, a meaningful level of assurance may not be able to be obtained without the practitioner having performed procedures at a selection of significant facilities. Where the entity has significant facilities with Scope 1 emissions and the practitioner determines that effective and efficient procedures cannot be performed on location at the facility by the practitioner (or another practitioner on their behalf), alternative procedures may include one or more of the following:

- Reviewing source documents, energy flow diagrams, and material flow diagrams.
- Analyzing questionnaire responses from facility management.
- Inspecting satellite imagery of the facility.

To obtain adequate coverage of total emissions, particularly in a reasonable assur- **A77** ance engagement, the practitioner may decide that it is appropriate to perform procedures on location at a selection of facilities that are not significant facilities. Factors that may be relevant to such a decision include:

- The nature of emissions at different facilities. For example, it is more likely that a practitioner may choose to visit a facility with Scope 1 emissions than a facility with only Scope 2 emissions. In the latter case, the examination of energy invoices at head office is more likely to be a primary source of evidence.
- The number and size of facilities, and their contribution to overall emissions.
- Whether facilities use different processes, or processes using different technologies. Where this is the case, it may be appropriate to perform procedures on location at a selection of facilities using different processes or technologies.
- The methods used at different facilities to gather emissions information.
- The experience of relevant staff at different facilities.
- Varying the selection of facilities over time.

Internal Audit (Ref: Para. 32)

The entity's internal audit function is likely to be relevant to the engagement if the **A78** nature of the internal audit function's responsibilities and activities are related to the quantification and reporting of emissions and the practitioner expects to use the work of the internal audit function to modify the nature or timing, or reduce the extent, of procedures to be performed.

Risks of Material Misstatement at the GHG Statement Level (Ref: Para. 33L(a)–33R(a))

Risks of material misstatement at the GHG statement level refer to risks that relate **A79** pervasively to the GHG statement as a whole. Risks of this nature are not necessarily risks identifiable with a specific type of emission or disclosure level. Rather, they represent circumstances that may increase the risks of material misstatement more generally, for example, through management override of internal control. Risks of material misstatement at the GHG statement level may be especially relevant to the practitioner's consideration of the risks of material misstatement arising from fraud.

A80   Risks at the GHG statement level may derive in particular from a deficient control environment. For example, deficiencies such as management's lack of competence may have a pervasive effect on the GHG statement and may require an overall response by the practitioner. Other risks of material misstatement at the GHG statement level may include, for example:

- Inadequate, poorly controlled or poorly documented mechanisms for collecting data, quantifying emissions and preparing GHG statements.
- Lack of staff competence in collecting data, quantifying emissions and preparing GHG statements.
- Lack of management involvement in quantifying emissions and preparing GHG statements.
- Failure to identify accurately all sources of GHGs.
- Risk of fraud, for example, in connection with emissions trading markets.
- Presenting information covering prior periods that is not prepared on a consistent basis, for example, because of changed boundaries or changes in measurement methodologies.
- Misleading presentation of information in the GHG statement, for example, unduly highlighting particularly favorable data or trends.
- Inconsistent quantification methods and reporting policies, including different methods for determining the organizational boundary, at different facilities.
- Errors in unit conversion when consolidating information from facilities.
- Inadequate disclosure of scientific uncertainties and key assumptions in relation to estimates.

The Use of Assertions (Ref: Para. 33L(b)–33R(b))

A81   Assertions are used by the practitioner in a reasonable assurance engagement, and may be used in a limited assurance engagement, to consider the different types of potential misstatements that may occur.

A82   In representing that the GHG statement is in accordance with the applicable criteria, the entity implicitly or explicitly makes assertions regarding the quantification, presentation and disclosure of emissions. Assertions fall into the following categories and may take the following forms:

(a) Assertions about the quantification of emissions for the period subject to assurance:
  (i) Occurrence—emissions that have been recorded have occurred and pertain to the entity.
  (ii) Completeness—all emissions that should have been recorded have been recorded (see paragraphs A30–A34 for a discussion of completeness with respect to various Scopes).
  (iii) Accuracy—the quantification of emissions has been recorded appropriately.
  (iv) Cutoff—emissions have been recorded in the correct reporting period.
  (v) Classification—emissions have been recorded as the proper type.
(b) Assertions about presentation and disclosure:
  (i) Occurrence and responsibility—disclosed emissions and other matters have occurred and pertain to the entity.
  (ii) Completeness—all disclosures that should have been included in the GHG statement have been included.

(iii) Classification and understandability—emissions information is appropriately presented and described, and disclosures are clearly expressed.

(iv) Accuracy and quantification—emissions quantification and related information included in the GHG statement are appropriately disclosed.

(v) Consistency—quantification policies are consistent with those applied in the prior period, or changes are justified and have been properly applied and adequately disclosed; and comparative information, if any, is as reported in the prior period or has been appropriately restated.

Reliance on Internal Control (Ref: Para. 33R)

If the practitioner's assessment of risks of material misstatement at the assertion level   **A83**
includes an expectation that the controls are operating effectively (that is, the practitioner intends to rely on the operating effectiveness of controls in determining the nature, timing and extent of other procedures), the practitioner is required by paragraph 38R to design and perform tests of the operating effectiveness of those controls.

Causes of Risks of Material Misstatement (Ref: Para. 34)

Fraud (Ref: Para. 28, 34(a))

Misstatements in the GHG statement can arise from either fraud or error. The   **A84**
distinguishing factor between fraud and error is whether the underlying action that results in the misstatement of the GHG statement is intentional or unintentional.

Incentives for intentional misstatement of the GHG statement may arise if, for   **A85**
example, those who are directly involved with, or have the opportunity to influence, the emissions reporting process have a significant portion of their compensation contingent upon achieving aggressive GHG targets. As noted in paragraph A61, other incentives to either under or overstate emissions may result from the entity's climate change strategy, if any, and associated economic, regulatory, physical and reputational risks.

Although fraud is a broad legal concept, for the purposes of this ISAE, the practi-   **A86**
tioner is concerned with fraud that causes a material misstatement in the GHG statement. Although the practitioner may suspect or, in rare cases, identify the occurrence of fraud, the practitioner does not make legal determinations of whether fraud has actually occurred.

Non-Compliance with Laws and Regulations (Ref: Para. 34(b), 78(c))

This ISAE distinguishes the practitioner's responsibilities in relation to compliance   **A87**
with two different categories of laws and regulations as follows:

(a) The provisions of those laws and regulations generally recognized to have a direct effect on the determination of material amounts and disclosures in the GHG statement in that they determine the reported quantities and disclosures in an entity's GHG statement. Paragraph 34(b) requires the practitioner to consider the likelihood of material misstatement due to non-compliance with the provisions of such laws and regulations when performing the procedures required by paragraphs 33L or 33R; and

(b) Other laws and regulations that do not have a direct effect on the determination of the quantities and disclosures in the GHG statement, but compliance with which may be fundamental to the operating aspects of the business, to an entity's ability to continue its business, or to avoid material penalties (for example, compliance with the terms of an operating license, or compliance with environmental regulations). Maintaining professional skepticism throughout the engagement, as required by ISAE 3000,[20] is important in the context of remaining alert to the possibility that procedures applied for the purpose of forming a conclusion on the GHG statement may bring instances of identified or suspected non-compliance with such laws and regulations to the practitioner's attention.

Other Causes of Risks of Material Misstatement (Ref: Para. 34)

A88   Examples of factors referred to in paragraph 34(c)–(k) include:

(a) Omission of one or more emissions sources is more likely for sources that are less obvious and may be overlooked, such as fugitive emissions.

(b) Significant economic or regulatory changes may include, for example, increases in renewable energy targets or significant price changes for allowances under an emissions trading scheme, which may lead to, for example, increased risk of misclassification of sources at an electricity generator.

(c) The nature of the entity's operations may be complex (for example, it may involve multiple and disparate facilities and processes), discontinuous (for example, peak load electricity generation), or result in few or weak relationships between the entity's emissions and other measurable activity levels (for example, a cobalt nickel plant). In such cases, the opportunity for meaningful analytical procedures may be significantly reduced.

Changes in operations or boundaries (for example, introduction of new processes, or the sale, acquisition or outsourcing of emissions sources or removal sinks) may also introduce risks of material misstatement (for example, through unfamiliarity with quantification or reporting procedures). Also, double counting of an emissions source or removals sink may occur due to inadequate coordination in the identification of sources and sinks at a complex installation.

(d) Selection of an inappropriate quantification method (for example, calculating Scope 1 emissions using an emissions factor when using a more accurate direct measurement method is available and would be more appropriate). Selecting an appropriate quantification method is particularly important when the method has been changed. This is because intended users are often interested in emissions trends over time, or relative to a base year. Some criteria may require that quantification methods are only changed when a more accurate method is to be used. Other factors related to the nature of quantification methods include:

- Incorrect application of a quantification method, such as not calibrating meters or not reading them sufficiently frequently, or use of an emissions factor that is inappropriate in the circumstances. For example, an emissions factor may be predicated on an assumption of continuous use and may not be appropriate to use after a shut down.

- Complexity in quantification methods, which will likely involve higher risk of material misstatement, for example: extensive or complex mathematical manipulation of source data (such as the use of complex mathematical models); extensive use of state conversion factors (such as those to convert measures of liquid to measures of gas); or extensive use of unit conversion factors (such as those to convert imperial measures to metric measures).

- Changes in quantification methods or input variables (for example, if the quantification method used is based on the carbon content of biomass, and the composition of the biomass used changes during the period).

[20] *ISAE 3000, paragraph 14.*

(e) Significant non-routine emissions or judgmental matters are a source of greater risk of material misstatement relative to routine, non-complex emissions that are subject to systematic quantification and reporting. Non-routine emissions are those that are unusual, in size or nature, and that therefore occur infrequently (for example, one-off events such as a plant malfunction or major leak). Judgmental matters may include the development of subjective estimates. Risks of material misstatement may be greater because of matters such as:

- Greater management intervention to specify the quantification methods or reporting treatment.
- Greater manual intervention for data collection and processing.
- Complex calculations or quantification methods and reporting principles.
- The nature of non-routine emissions, which may make it difficult for the entity to implement effective controls over the risks.
- Quantification methods and reporting principles for estimates may be subject to differing interpretation.
- Required judgments may be subjective or complex.

(f) The inclusion of Scope 3 emissions where the source data used in quantification are not maintained by the entity, or where quantification methods commonly in use are imprecise or lead to large variations in reported emissions (see paragraphs A31–A34).

(g) Matters that the practitioner may consider in obtaining an understanding of how the entity makes significant estimates and the data on which they are based include, for example:

- An understanding of the data on which estimates are based;
- The method, including where applicable the model, used in making estimates;
- Relevant aspects of the control environment and information system;
- Whether the entity has used an expert;
- The assumptions underlying estimates;
- Whether there has been or ought to have been a change from the prior period in the methods for making estimates and, if so, why; and
- Whether and, if so, how the entity has assessed the effect of estimation uncertainty on the GHG statement, including:
  - o Whether and, if so, how the entity has considered alternative assumptions or outcomes by, for example, performing a sensitivity analysis to determine the effect of changes in the assumptions on an estimate;
  - o How the entity determines the estimate when analysis indicates a number of outcome scenarios; and
  - o Whether the entity monitors the outcome of estimates made in the prior period, and whether it has appropriately responded to the outcome of that monitoring procedure.

Examples of other factors that may lead to risks of material misstatement include: **A89**

- Human error in the quantification of emissions, which may be more likely to occur if personnel are unfamiliar with, or not well-trained regarding, emissions processes or data recording.
- Undue reliance on a poorly designed information system, which may have few effective controls, for example, the use of spreadsheets without adequate controls.
- Manual adjustment of otherwise automatically recorded activity levels, for example, manual input may be required if a flare meter becomes overloaded.
- Significant external developments such as heightened public scrutiny of a particular facility.

Overall Responses to Assessed Risks of Material Misstatement and Further Procedures

Limited and Reasonable Assurance Engagements (Ref: Para. 8, 35–41R, 42L–43R, 46)

A90   Because the level of assurance obtained in a limited assurance engagement is lower than in a reasonable assurance engagement, the procedures the practitioner will perform in a limited assurance engagement will vary in nature from, and are less in extent than for, a reasonable assurance engagement. The primary differences between the practitioner's overall responses to address the assessed risks of material misstatement and further procedures for a reasonable assurance engagement and a limited assurance engagement on a GHG statement are as follows:

(a)   *The emphasis placed on the nature of various procedures*: The emphasis placed on the nature of various procedures as a source of evidence will likely differ, depending on the engagement circumstances. For example:

- The practitioner may judge it to be appropriate in the circumstances of a particular limited assurance engagement to place relatively greater emphasis on inquiries of the entity's personnel and analytical procedures, and relatively less emphasis, if any, on tests of controls and obtaining evidence from external sources than would be the case for a reasonable assurance engagement.
- Where the entity uses continuous measuring equipment to quantify emissions flows, the practitioner may decide in a limited assurance engagement to respond to an assessed risk of material misstatement by inquiring about the frequency with which the equipment is calibrated. In the same circumstances for a reasonable assurance engagement, the practitioner may decide to examine the entity's records of the equipment's calibration or independently test its calibration.
- Where the entity burns coal, the practitioner may decide in a reasonable assurance engagement to independently analyze the characteristics of the coal, but in a limited assurance engagement the practitioner may decide that reviewing the entity's records of laboratory test results is an adequate response to an assessed risk of material misstatement.

(b)   *The extent of further procedures*: The extent of further procedures performed in a limited assurance engagement is less than in a reasonable assurance engagement. This may involve:

- Reducing the number of items to be examined, for example, reducing sample sizes for tests of details;
- Performing fewer procedures (for example, performing only analytical procedures in circumstances when, in a reasonable assurance engagement, both analytical procedures and tests of detail would be performed); or
- Performing procedures on location at fewer facilities.

(c)   *The nature of analytical procedures*: In a reasonable assurance engagement, analytical procedures performed in response to assessed risks of material misstatement involve developing expectations of quantities or ratios that are sufficiently precise to identify material misstatements. In a limited assurance engagement, on the other hand, analytical procedures are often designed to support expectations regarding the direction of trends, relationships and ratios rather than to identify misstatements with the level of precision expected in a reasonable assurance engagement.[21]

Further, when significant fluctuations, relationships or differences are identified, appropriate evidence in a limited assurance engagement may often be obtained

---

[21] *This may not always be the case; for example, in some circumstances the practitioner may develop a precise expectation based on fixed physical or chemical relationships even in a limited assurance engagement.*

by making inquiries of the entity and considering responses received in the light of known engagement circumstances, without obtaining additional evidence as is required by paragraph 43R(a) in the case of a reasonable assurance engagement.

In addition, when undertaking analytical procedures in a limited assurance engagement the practitioner may, for example:

- Use data that is more highly aggregated, for example, data at a regional level rather than at a facility level, or monthly data rather than weekly data.
- Use data that has not been subjected to separate procedures to test its reliability to the same extent as it would be for a reasonable assurance engagement.

Overall Responses to Assessed Risks of Material Misstatement (Ref: Para. 35)

Overall responses to address the assessed risks of material misstatement at the GHG statement level may include: **A91**

- Emphasizing to the assurance personnel the need to maintain professional skepticism.
- Assigning more experienced staff or those with special skills or using experts.
- Providing more supervision.
- Incorporating additional elements of unpredictability in the selection of further procedures to be performed.
- Making general changes to the nature, timing, or extent of procedures, for example: performing procedures at the period end instead of at an interim date; or modifying the nature of procedures to obtain more persuasive evidence.

The assessment of the risks of material misstatement at the GHG statement level, and thereby the practitioner's overall responses, is affected by the practitioner's understanding of the control environment. An effective control environment may allow the practitioner to have more confidence in internal control and the reliability of evidence generated internally within the entity and thus, for example, allow the practitioner to conduct some procedures at an interim date rather than at the period end. Deficiencies in the control environment, however, have the opposite effect. For example, the practitioner may respond to an ineffective control environment by: **A92**

- Conducting more procedures as of the period end rather than at an interim date.
- Obtaining more extensive evidence from procedures other than tests of controls.
- Increasing sample sizes and the extent of procedures, such as the number of facilities at which procedures are performed.

Such considerations, therefore, have a significant bearing on the practitioner's general approach, for example, the relative emphasis on tests of controls versus other procedures (see also paragraphs A70–A72, and A96).   **A93**

Examples of Further Procedures (Ref: Para. 37L–37R, 40R)

Further procedures may include, for example: **A94**

- Testing the operating effectiveness of controls over the collection and recording of activity data, such as kilowatt hours of electricity purchased.
- Agreeing emissions factors to appropriate sources (for example, government publications), and considering their applicability in the circumstances.
- Reviewing joint venture agreements and other contracts relevant to determining the entity's organizational boundary.

- Reconciling recorded data to, for example, odometers on vehicles owned by the entity.
- Reperforming calculations (for example, mass balance and energy balance calculations), and reconciling differences noted.
- Taking readings from continuous monitoring equipment.
- Observing or reperforming physical measurements, such as dipping oil tanks.
- Analyzing the soundness and appropriateness of unique measurement or quantification techniques, particularly complex methods that may involve, for example, recycle or feedback loops.
- Sampling and independently analyzing the characteristics of materials such as coal, or observing the entity's sampling techniques and reviewing records of laboratory test results.
- Checking the accuracy of calculations and the suitability of calculation methods used (for example, the conversion and aggregation of input measurements).
- Agreeing recorded data back to source documents, such as production records, fuel usage records, and invoices for purchased energy.

Factors that May Influence Assessed Risks of Material Misstatement (Ref: Para. 37L(a)–37R(a))

A95 Factors that may influence the assessed risks of material misstatement include:

- Inherent limitations on the capabilities of measurement instruments and the frequency of their calibration.
- The number, nature, geographical spread, and ownership characteristics of facilities from which data is collected.
- The number and nature of the various gases and emissions sources included in the GHG statement.
- Whether processes to which emissions relate are continuous or intermittent, and the risk of disruption to such processes.
- The complexity of methods for activity measurement and for calculating emissions, for example, some processes require unique measurement and calculation methods.
- The risk of unidentified fugitive emissions.
- The extent to which the quantity of emissions correlates with readily available input data.
- Whether personnel who perform data collection are trained in relevant methods, and the frequency of turnover of such personnel.
- The nature and level of automation used in data capture and manipulation.
- The quality control policies and procedures implemented at testing laboratories, whether internal or external.
- The complexity of criteria and of quantification and reporting policies, including how the organizational boundary is determined.

Operating Effectiveness of Controls (Ref: Para. 37R(a)(ii), 38R(a))

A96 In the case of very small entities or immature information systems, there may not be many control activities that could be identified by the practitioner, or the extent to which their existence or operation have been documented by the entity may be limited. In such cases, it may be more efficient for the practitioner to perform further procedures that are primarily other than tests of controls. In some rare cases, however, the absence of control activities or of other components of control may make it impossible to obtain sufficient appropriate evidence (see also paragraphsA70–A72, and A92–A93).

Persuasiveness of Evidence (Ref: Para. 37L(b)–37R(b))

To obtain more persuasive evidence because of a higher assessment of risk of material misstatement, the practitioner may increase the quantity of the evidence, or obtain evidence that is more relevant or reliable, for example, by obtaining corroborating evidence from a number of independent sources.

A97

Risks for Which Tests of Controls Are Necessary to Provide Sufficient Appropriate Evidence (Ref: 38R(b))

The quantification of emissions may include processes that are highly automated with little or no manual intervention, for example, where relevant information is recorded, processed, or reported only in electronic form such as in a continuous monitoring system, or when the processing of activity data is integrated with an information technology-based operational or financial reporting system. In such cases:

A98

- Evidence may be available only in electronic form, and its sufficiency and appropriateness dependent on the effectiveness of controls over its accuracy and completeness.
- The potential for improper initiation or alteration of information to occur and not be detected may be greater if appropriate controls are not operating effectively.

Confirmation Procedures (Ref: Para. 41R)

External confirmation procedures may provide relevant evidence about such information as:

A99

- Activity data collected by a third party, such as data about: employee air travel collated by a travel agent; the inflow of energy to a facility metered by a supplier; or kilometers travelled by entity-owned vehicles recorded by an external fleet manager.
- Industry benchmark data used in calculating emissions factors.
- The terms of agreements, contracts, or transactions between the entity and other parties, or information about whether other parties are, or are not, including particular emissions in their GHG statement, when considering the entity's organizational boundary.
- The results of laboratory analysis of samples (for example, the calorific value of input samples).

Analytical Procedures Performed in Response to Assessed Risks of Material Misstatement (Ref: Para. 42L–42R)

In many cases, the fixed nature of physical or chemical relationships between particular emissions and other measurable phenomena allows for the design of powerful analytical procedures (for example, the relationship between fuel consumption and carbon dioxide and nitrous oxide emissions).

A100

Similarly, a reasonably predictable relationship may exist between emissions and financial or operational information (for example, the relationship between Scope 2 emissions from electricity and the general ledger balance for electricity purchases or hours of operation). Other analytical procedures may involve comparisons of information about the entity's emissions with external data such as industry averages; or the analysis of trends during the period to identify anomalies for further

A101

investigation, and trends across periods for consistency with other circumstances such as the acquisition or disposal of facilities.

A102 Analytical procedures may be particularly effective when disaggregated data is readily available, or when the practitioner has reason to consider the data to be used is reliable, such as when it is extracted from a well-controlled source. In some cases, data to be used may be captured by the financial reporting information system, or may be entered in another information system in parallel with the entry of related financial data, and some common input controls applied. For example, the quantity of fuel purchased as recorded on suppliers' invoices may be input under the same conditions that relevant invoices are entered into an accounts payable system. In some cases, data to be used may be an integral input to operational decisions and therefore subject to increased scrutiny by operational personnel, or subject to separate external audit procedures (for example, as part of a joint venture agreement or oversight by a regulator).

Procedures Regarding Estimates (Ref: Para. 44L–45R)

A103 In some cases, it may be appropriate for the practitioner to evaluate how the entity has considered alternative assumptions or outcomes, and why it has rejected them.

A104 In some limited assurance engagements, it may be appropriate for the practitioner to undertake one or more of the procedures identified in paragraph 45R.

Sampling (Ref: Para. 46)

A105 Sampling involves:

(a) Determining a sample size sufficient to reduce sampling risk to an acceptably low level. Because the acceptable level of assurance engagement risk is lower for a reasonable assurance engagement than for a limited assurance engagement, so too may be the level of sampling risk that is acceptable in the case of tests of details. Therefore, when sampling is used for tests of details in a reasonable assurance engagement, the sample size may be larger than when used in similar circumstances in a limited assurance engagement.

(b) Selecting items for the sample in such a way that each sampling unit in the population has a chance of selection, and performing procedures, appropriate to the purpose, on each item selected. If the practitioner is unable to apply the designed procedures, or suitable alternative procedures, to a selected item, that item is treated as a deviation from the prescribed control, in the case of tests of controls, or a misstatement, in the case of tests of details.

(c) Investigating the nature and cause of deviations or misstatements identified, and evaluating their possible effect on the purpose of the procedure and on other areas of the engagement.

(d) Evaluating:

(i) The results of the sample, including, for tests of details, projecting misstatements found in the sample to the population; and

(ii) Whether the use of sampling has provided an appropriate basis for conclusions about the population that has been tested.

Fraud, Laws and Regulations (Ref: Para. 47)

A106 In responding to fraud or suspected fraud identified during the engagement, it may be appropriate for the practitioner to, for example:

- Discuss the matter with the entity.
- Request the entity to consult with an appropriately qualified third party, such as the entity's legal counsel or a regulator.
- Consider the implications of the matter in relation to other aspects of the engagement, including the practitioner's risk assessment and the reliability of written representations from the entity.
- Obtain legal advice about the consequences of different courses of action.
- Communicate with third parties (for example, a regulator).
- Withhold the assurance report.
- Withdraw from the engagement.

The actions noted in the paragraph A106 may be appropriate in responding to non-compliance or suspected non-compliance with laws and regulations identified during the engagement. It may also be appropriate to describe the matter in an Other Matter paragraph in the assurance report in accordance with paragraph 77 of this ISAE, unless the practitioner: **A107**

(a) Concludes that the non-compliance has a material effect on the GHG statement and has not been adequately reflected in the GHG statement; or
(b) Is precluded by the entity from obtaining sufficient appropriate evidence to evaluate whether non-compliance that may be material to the GHG statement has, or is likely to have, occurred, in which case paragraph 51 of ISAE 3000 applies.

Procedures Regarding the GHG Statement Aggregation Process (Ref: Para. 48L–48R)

As noted in paragraph A71, as reporting of emissions evolves, it can be expected that so too will the level of sophistication, documentation and formality of information systems relevant to the quantification and reporting of emissions. In immature information systems, the aggregation process may be very informal. In more sophisticated systems, the aggregation process may be more systematic and formally documented. The nature, and also the extent, of the practitioner's procedures with respect to adjustments and the manner in which the practitioner agrees or reconciles the GHG statement with the underlying records depends on the nature and complexity of the entity's quantifications and reporting process and the related risks of material misstatement.   **A108**

Additional Procedures (Ref: Para. 49L–49R)

An assurance engagement is an iterative process, and information may come to the practitioner's attention that differs significantly from that on which the determination of planned procedures was based. As the practitioner performs planned procedures, the evidence obtained may cause the practitioner to perform additional procedures. Such procedures may include asking the entity to examine the matter(s) identified by the practitioner, and to make adjustments to the GHG statement if appropriate.   **A109**

Determining Whether Additional Procedures Are Necessary in a Limited Assurance Engagement (Ref: Para. 49L, 49L(b))

The practitioner may become aware of a matter(s) that causes the practitioner to believe the GHG statement may be materially misstated. For example, when performing site visits, the practitioner may identify a potential source of emissions which does not appear to be included in the GHG statement. In such cases, the practitioner makes further inquiries as to whether the potential source has been incorporated into   **A110** the GHG statement. The extent of additional procedures performed, in accordance with paragraph 49L, will be a matter of professional judgment. The greater the likelihood of material misstatement the more persuasive the evidence the practitioner obtains.

A111   If, in the case of a limited assurance engagement, a matter(s) comes to the practitioner's attention that causes the practitioner to believe the GHG statement may be materially misstated, the practitioner is required by paragraph 49L to design and perform additional procedures. If having done so, however, the practitioner is not able to obtain sufficient appropriate evidence to either conclude that the matter(s) is not likely to cause the GHG statement to be materially misstated or determine that it does cause the GHG statement to be materially misstated, a scope limitation exists.

Accumulation of Identified Misstatements (Ref: Para. 50)

A112   The practitioner may designate an amount below which misstatements would be clearly trivial and would not need to be accumulated because the practitioner expects that the accumulation of such amounts clearly would not have a material effect on the GHG statement. "Clearly trivial" is not another expression for "not material." Matters that are clearly trivial will be of a wholly different (smaller) order of magnitude than materiality determined in accordance with this ISAE, and will be matters that are clearly inconsequential, whether taken individually or in the aggregate and whether judged by any criteria of size, nature or circumstances. When there is any uncertainty about whether one or more items are clearly trivial, the matter is considered not to be clearly trivial.

Using the Work of Other Practitioners

Communication to Other Practitioners (Ref: Para. 57(a))

A113   Relevant matters that the engagement team may communicate to other practitioners in respect of the work to be performed, the use to be made of that work, and the form and content of the other practitioner's communication with the engagement team may include:

- A request that the other practitioner, knowing the context in which the engagement team will use the work of the other practitioner, confirms that the other practitioner will cooperate with the engagement team.
- Performance materiality for the work of the other practitioner, which may be lower than performance materiality for the GHG statement (and, if applicable, the materiality level or levels for particular types of emissions or disclosures) and the threshold above which misstatements cannot be regarded as clearly trivial to the GHG statement.
- Identified risks of material misstatement of the GHG statement that are relevant to the work of the other practitioner; and a request that the other practitioner communicate on a timely basis any other risks identified during the engagement that may be material to the GHG statement, and the other practitioner's responses to such risks.

Communication from Other Practitioners (Ref: Para. 57(a))

A114   Relevant matters that the engagement team may request the other practitioner to communicate include:

- Whether the other practitioner has complied with ethical requirements that are relevant to the group engagement, including independence and professional competence.
- Whether the other practitioner has complied with the group engagement team's requirements.
- Information on instances of non-compliance with laws or regulations that could give rise to a material misstatement of the GHG statement.
- A list of uncorrected misstatements identified by the other practitioner during the engagement that are not clearly trivial.
- Indicators of possible bias in the preparation of relevant information.
- Description of any identified significant deficiencies in internal control identified by the other practitioner during the engagement.
- Other significant matters that the other practitioner has communicated or expects to communicate to the entity, including fraud or suspected fraud.
- Any other matters that may be relevant to the GHG statement, or that the other practitioner wishes to draw to the attention of the engagement team, including exceptions noted in any written representations that the other practitioner requested from the entity.
- The other practitioner's overall findings, conclusion or opinion.

Evidence (Ref: Para. 57(b))

Relevant considerations when obtaining evidence regarding the work of the other practitioner may include: **A115**

- Discussions with the other practitioner regarding business activities relevant to that other practitioner's work that are significant to the GHG statement.
- Discussions with the other practitioner regarding the susceptibility of relevant information to material misstatement.
- Reviewing the other practitioner's documentation of identified risks of material misstatement, responses to those risks, and conclusions.

Such documentation may take the form of a memorandum that reflects the other practitioner's conclusion with regard to the identified risks.

Written Representations (Ref: Para. 58)

In addition to the written representations required by paragraph 58, the practitioner may consider it necessary to request other written representations. The person(s) from whom the practitioner requests written representations will ordinarily be a member of senior management or those charged with governance. However, because management and governance structures vary by jurisdiction and by entity, reflecting influences such as different cultural and legal backgrounds, and size and ownership characteristics, it is not possible for this ISAE to specify for all engagements the appropriate person(s) from whom to request written representations. For example, the entity may be a facility that is not a separate legal entity in its own right. In such cases, identifying the appropriate management personnel or those charged with governance from whom to request written representations may require the exercise of professional judgment. **A116**

Subsequent Events (Ref: Para. 61)

Subsequent events may include, for example, the publication of revised emissions factors by a body such as a government agency, changes to relevant legislation or regulations, improved scientific knowledge, significant structural changes in the **A117** entity, the availability of more accurate quantification methods, or the discovery of a significant error.

Comparative Information (Ref: Para. 62–63, 76(c))

A118   Law or regulation, or the terms of the engagement, may specify the requirements in respect of presentation, reporting and assurance of the comparative information in a GHG statement. A key difference between financial statements and a GHG statement is that the amounts presented in a GHG statement measures emissions for a discrete period and are not based on cumulative amounts over time. As a result, the comparative information presented does not affect current year information unless emissions have been recorded in the wrong period and therefore the amounts may be based on the incorrect starting period for measurement.

A119   Where a GHG statement includes references to percentage reductions in emissions, or a similar comparison of period on period information, it is important that the practitioner consider the appropriateness of the comparisons. These may be inappropriate due to:

(a)   Significant changes in operations from the prior period;

(b)   Significant changes in conversion factors; or

(c)   Inconsistency of sources or methods of measurement.

A120   When comparative information is presented with the current emissions information but some or all of that comparative information is not covered by the practitioner's conclusion, it is important that the status of such information is clearly identified in both the GHG statement and the assurance report.

Restatements (Ref: Para. 62(a))

A121   The GHG quantities reported in a prior period may need to be restated in accordance with laws or regulations or the applicable criteria because of, for example, improved scientific knowledge, significant structural changes in the entity, the availability of more accurate quantification methods, or the discovery of a significant error.

Performing Procedures on Comparative Information (Ref: Para 63(a))

A122   In a limited assurance engagement that includes assurance on comparative information, if the practitioner becomes aware that there may be a material misstatement in the comparative information presented, the procedures to be performed are to be in accordance with the requirements of paragraph 49L. In the case of a reasonable assurance engagement, the procedures to be performed are to be sufficient to form an opinion on the comparative information.

A123   If the engagement does not include assurance on comparative information, the requirement to perform procedures in the circumstances addressed by paragraph 63(a) is to satisfy the practitioner's ethical obligation to not knowingly be associated with materially false or misleading information.

Other Information (Ref: Para. 64)

A124   A GHG statement may be published with other information that is not covered by the practitioner's conclusion, for example, a GHG statement may be included as part of an entity's annual report or sustainability report, or included with other climate change-specific information such as:

- A strategic analysis, including a statement about the impact climate change has on the entity's strategic objectives.
- An explanation and qualitative assessment of current and anticipated significant risks and opportunities associated with climate change.
- Disclosures about the entity's actions, including its long-term and short-term plan to address climate change-related risks, opportunities and impacts.
- Disclosures about future outlook, including trends and factors related to climate change that are likely to affect the entity's strategy or the timescale over which achievement of the strategy is planned.
- A description of governance processes and the entity's resources that have been assigned to the identification, management and oversight of climate change-related issues.

In some cases, the entity may publish emissions information that is calculated on a different basis from that used in preparing the GHG statement, for example, the other information may be prepared on a "like-for-like" basis whereby emissions are recalculated to omit the effect of non-recurring events, such as the commissioning of a new plant or the closing down of a facility. The practitioner may seek to have such information removed if the methods used to prepare it would be disallowed by the criteria used to prepare the GHG statement. The practitioner may also seek to have removed any narrative information that is inconsistent with the quantitative data included in the GHG statement or cannot be substantiated (for example, speculative projections or claims about future action). **A125**

Further actions that may be appropriate when other information could undermine the credibility of the GHG statement and the assurance report include, for example: **A126**

- Requesting the entity to consult with a qualified third party, such as the entity's legal counsel.
- Obtaining legal advice about the consequences of different courses of action.
- Communicating with third parties, for example, a regulator.
- Withholding the assurance report.
- Withdrawing from the engagement, where withdrawal is possible under applicable laws or regulations.
- Describing the matter in the assurance report.

Documentation

Documentation of the Procedures Performed and Evidence Obtained (Ref: Para. 15, 65–66)

ISAE 3000 requires the practitioner to document matters that are significant in providing evidence that supports the assurance report and that the engagement was performed in accordance with ISAEs.[22] The following are examples of matters that may be appropriate to include in the engagement documentation: **A127**

- Fraud: The risks of material misstatement and the nature, timing and extent of procedures with respect to fraud; and communications about fraud made to the entity, regulators and others.
- Laws and Regulations: Identified or suspected non-compliance with laws and regulations and the results of discussion with the entity and other parties outside the entity.

---

[22] *ISAE 3000, paragraph 42.*

- Planning: The overall engagement strategy, the engagement plan, and any significant changes made during the engagement, and the reasons for such changes.
- Materiality: The following amounts and the factors considered in their determination: materiality for the GHG statement; if applicable, the materiality level or levels for particular types of emissions or disclosures; performance materiality; and any revision of materiality as the engagement progresses.
- Risks of Material Misstatement: the discussion required by paragraph 29, and the significant decisions reached, key elements of the understanding obtained regarding each of the aspects of the entity and its environment specified in paragraph 23, and the risks of material misstatement for which in the practitioner's professional judgment further procedures were required.
- Further Procedures: the nature, timing and extent of the further procedures performed, the linkage of those further procedures with the risks of material misstatement, and the results of the procedures.
- Evaluation of Misstatements: The amount below which misstatements would be regarded as clearly trivial, misstatements accumulated during the engagement and whether they have been corrected, and the practitioner's conclusion as to whether uncorrected misstatements are material, individually or in the aggregate, and the basis for that conclusion.

Matters Arising after the Date of the Assurance Report (Ref: Para. 68)

A128   Examples of exceptional circumstances include facts which become known to the practitioner after the date of the assurance report but which existed at that date and which, if known at that date, might have caused the GHG statement to be amended or the practitioner to modify the conclusion in the assurance report, for example, the discovery of a significant uncorrected error. The resulting changes to the engagement documentation are reviewed in accordance with the firm's policies and procedures with respect to review responsibilities as required by ISQC 1, with the engagement partner taking final responsibility for the changes.[23]

Assembly of the Final Engagement File (Ref: Para. 69)

A129   ISQC 1 (or national requirements that are at least as demanding) requires firms to establish policies and procedures for the timely completion of the assembly of engagement files.[24] An appropriate time limit within which to complete the assembly of the final engagement file is ordinarily not more than 60 days after the date of the assurance report.[25]

Engagement Quality Control Review (Ref: Para. 71)

A130   Other matters that may be considered in an engagement quality control review include:

- The engagement team's evaluation of the firm's independence in relation to the engagement.

---

[23] *ISQC 1, Quality Control for Firms that Perform Audits and Reviews of Financial Statements, and Other Assurance and Related Services Engagements*, paragraphs 32–33.

[24] *ISQC 1, paragraph 45.*

[25] *ISQC 1, paragraph A54.*

- Whether appropriate consultation has taken place on matters involving differences of opinion or other difficult or contentious matters, and the conclusions arising from those consultations.
- Whether engagement documentation selected for review reflects the work performed in relation to the significant judgments and supports the conclusions reached.

Forming the Assurance Conclusion

Description of the Applicable Criteria (Ref: Para. 74(d), 76(g)(iv))

The preparation of the GHG statement by the entity requires the inclusion of an **A131** adequate description of the applicable criteria in the explanatory notes to the GHG statement. That description advises intended users of the framework on which the GHG statement is based, and is particularly important when there are significant differences between various criteria regarding how particular matters are treated in a GHG statement, for example: which emissions deductions are included, if any; how they have been quantified and what they represent; and the basis for selecting which Scope 3 emissions are included, and how they have been quantified.

A description that the GHG statement is prepared in accordance with particular **A132** criteria is appropriate only if the GHG statement complies with all the requirements of those criteria that are effective during the period covered by the GHG statement.

A description of the applicable criteria that contains imprecise qualifying or limiting **A133** language (for example, "the GHG statement is in substantial compliance with the requirements of XYZ") is not an adequate description as it may mislead users of the GHG statement.

Assurance Report Content

Illustrative Assurance Reports (Ref: Para. 76)

Appendix 2 contains illustrations of assurance reports on GHG statements incor- **A134** porating the elements set forth in paragraph 76.

Information Not Covered by the Practitioner's Conclusion (Ref: Para. 76(c))

To avoid misunderstanding and undue reliance on information that has not been **A135** subject to assurance, where the GHG statement includes information, such as comparatives, that is not covered by the practitioner's conclusion, that information is ordinarily identified as such in the GHG statement and in the practitioner's assurance report.

Emissions Deductions (Ref: Para. 76(f))

The wording of the statement to be included in the assurance report when the GHG **A136** statement includes emissions deductions may vary considerably depending on the circumstances.

The availability of relevant and reliable information in relation to offsets and other **A137** emissions deductions varies greatly and, therefore, so does the evidence available to practitioners to support entities' claimed emissions deductions.

A138 Because of the varied nature of emissions deductions and the often reduced number and nature of procedures that can be applied to emissions deductions by the practitioner, this ISAE requires identification in the assurance report of those emissions deductions, if any, that are covered by the practitioner's conclusion, and a statement of the practitioner's responsibility with respect to them.

A139 A statement of the practitioner's responsibility with respect to emissions deductions may be worded as follows when the emissions deductions are comprised of offsets: "The GHG statement includes a deduction from ABC's emissions for the year of yyy tonnes of CO_{2-e} relating to offsets. We have performed procedures as to whether these offsets were acquired during the year, and whether the description of them in the GHG statement is a reasonable summary of the relevant contracts and related documentation. We have not, however, performed any procedures regarding the external providers of these offsets, and express no opinion about whether the offsets have resulted, or will result, in a reduction of yyy tonnes of CO_{2-e}."

Use of the Assurance Report (Ref: Para. 76(g)(iii))

A140 As well as identifying the addressee of the assurance report, the practitioner may consider it appropriate to include wording in the body of the assurance report that specifies the purpose for which, or the intended users for whom, the report was prepared. For example, when the GHG statement will be lodged on the public record, it may be appropriate for the explanatory notes to the GHG statement and the assurance report to include a statement that the report is intended for users who have a reasonable knowledge of GHG related activities, and who have studied the information in the GHG statement with reasonable diligence and understand that the GHG statement is prepared and assured to appropriate levels of materiality.

A141 In addition, the practitioner may consider it appropriate to include wording that specifically restricts distribution of the assurance report other than to intended users, its use by others, or its use for other purposes.

Summary of the Practitioner's Procedures (Ref: Para. 76(h)(ii))

A142 The assurance report in a reasonable assurance engagement normally follows a standard wording and only briefly describes procedures performed. This is because, in a reasonable assurance engagement, describing in any level of detail the specific procedures performed would not assist users to understand that, in all cases where an unmodified report is issued, sufficient appropriate evidence has been obtained to enable the practitioner to express an opinion.

A143 In a limited assurance engagement, an appreciation of the nature, timing and extent of procedures performed is essential for the intended users to understand the conclusion expressed in a limited assurance report. The description of the practitioner's procedures in a limited assurance engagement is therefore ordinarily more detailed than in a reasonable assurance engagement. It also may be appropriate to include a description of procedures that were not performed that would ordinarily be performed in a reasonable assurance engagement. However, a complete identification of all such procedures may not be possible because the practitioner's required understanding and assessment of risks of material misstatement are less than in a reasonable assurance engagement.

Factors to consider in making that determination and the level of detail to be provided include:

- Circumstances specific to the entity (e.g., the differing nature of the entity's activities compared to those typical in the sector).
- Specific engagement circumstances affecting the nature and extent of the procedures performed.
- The intended users' expectations of the level of detail to be provided in the report, based on market practice, or applicable laws or regulations.

In describing the procedures performed in the limited assurance report, it is **A144** important that they are written in an objective way but are not summarized to the extent that they are ambiguous, nor written in a way that is overstated or embellished or that implies that reasonable assurance has been obtained. It is also important that the description of the procedures not give the impression that an agreed-upon procedures engagement has been undertaken, and in most cases will not detail the entire work plan.

The Practitioner's Signature (Ref: Para. 76(k))

The practitioner's signature is either in the name of the practitioner's firm, the **A145** personal name of the practitioner, or both, as appropriate for the particular jurisdiction. In addition to the practitioner's signature, in certain jurisdictions, the practitioner may be required to declare in the assurance report the practitioner's professional designation or the fact that the practitioner or firm, as appropriate, has been recognized by the appropriate licensing authority in that jurisdiction.

Emphasis of Matter Paragraphs and Other Matter Paragraphs (Ref: Para. 77)

A widespread use of Emphasis of Matter or Other Matter paragraphs diminishes the **A146** effectiveness of the practitioner's communication of such matters.

An Emphasis of Matter paragraph may be appropriate when, for example, different **A147** criteria have been used or the criteria have been revised, updated or interpreted differently than in prior periods and this has had a fundamental effect on reported emissions, or a system breakdown for part of the period being accounted for means that extrapolation was used to estimate emissions for that time and this has been stated in the GHG statement.

An Other Matter paragraph may be appropriate when, for example, the scope of the **A148** engagement has changed significantly from the prior period and this has not been stated in the GHG statement.

The content of an Emphasis of Matter paragraph includes a clear reference to the **A149** matter being emphasized and to where relevant disclosures that fully describe the matter can be found in the GHG statement. It also indicates that the practitioner's conclusion is not modified in respect of the matter emphasized. (See also paragraph A125)

The content of an Other Matter paragraph reflects clearly that such other matter is **A150** not required to be presented and disclosed in the GHG statement. Paragraph 77 limits the use of an Other Matter paragraph to matters relevant to users' understanding of the engagement, the practitioner's responsibilities or the assurance report, that the practitioner considers it necessary to communicate in the assurance report. (See also paragraph A124)

Including the practitioner's recommendations on matters such as improvements to **A151** the entity's information system in the assurance report may imply that those matters have not been appropriately dealt with in preparing the GHG statement. Such recommendations may be communicated, for example, in a management letter or in discussion with those charged with governance. Considerations relevant to deciding whether to include recommendations in the assurance report include whether their nature is relevant to the information needs of intended users, and whether they are worded appropriately to ensure they will not be misunderstood as a qualification of the practitioner's conclusion on the GHG statement.

A152   An Other Matter paragraph does not include information that the practitioner is prohibited from providing by laws, regulations or other professional standards, for example, ethical standards relating to confidentiality of information. An Other Matter paragraph also does not include information that is required to be provided by management.

Appendix 1   (Ref: Para. A8–A14)

Emissions, Removals and Emissions Deductions

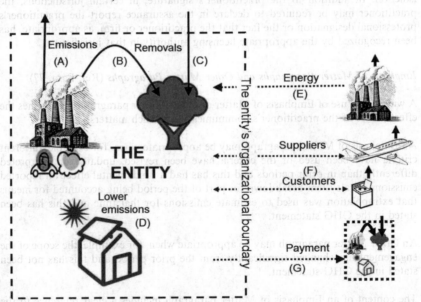

A = Direct, or Scope 1, emissions (see paragraph A8).

B = Removals (emissions that are generated within the entity's boundary but captured and stored within that boundary rather than released into the atmosphere. They are commonly accounted for on a gross basis, that is, as a Scope 1 emission and a removal) (see paragraph A14).

C = Removals (GHGs the entity has removed from the atmosphere) (see paragraph A14).

D = Actions the entity takes to lower its emissions. Such actions might reduce Scope 1 emissions (for example, using more fuel efficient vehicles), Scope 2 emissions (for example, installing solar panels to reduce the quantity of purchased electricity), or Scope 3 emissions (for example, reducing business travel or selling products that require less energy to use). The entity might discuss such actions in the explanatory notes to the GHG statement, but they only affect the quantification of emissions on the face of the entity's GHG statement to the extent that reported emissions are lower than they would otherwise be or they constitute an emissions deduction in accordance with the applicable criteria (see paragraph A11).

E = Scope 2 emissions (see paragraph A9).

F = Scope 3 emissions (see paragraph A10).

G = Emissions deductions, including purchased offsets (see paragraphs A11–A13).

Appendix 2

(Ref: Para. A134)

Illustrations of Assurance Reports on GHG Statements

Illustration 1:

Circumstances include the following:

- **Reasonable assurance engagement.**
- **The entity's GHG statement contains no Scope 3 emissions.**
- **The entity's GHG statement contains no emissions deductions.**
- **The GHG statement contains no comparative information.**

The following illustrative report is for guidance only and is not intended to be exhaustive or applicable to all situations.

INDEPENDENT PRACTITIONER'S REASONABLE ASSURANCE REPORT ON ABC'S GREENHOUSE GAS (GHG) STATEMENT

[Appropriate Addressee]

Report on GHG Statement (*this heading is not needed if this is the only section*)

We have undertaken a reasonable assurance engagement of the accompanying GHG statement of ABC for the year ended December 31, 20X1, comprising the Emissions Inventory and the Explanatory Notes on pages xx–yy. [This engagement was conducted by a multidisciplinary team including assurance practitioners, engineers and environmental scientists.][26]

ABC's Responsibility for the GHG Statement

ABC is responsible for the preparation of the GHG statement in accordance with [*applicable criteria*[27]], applied as explained in Note 1 to the GHG statement. This responsibility includes the design, implementation and maintenance of internal control relevant to the preparation of a GHG statement that is free from material misstatement, whether due to fraud or error.

---

[26] *The sentence should be deleted if it is not applicable to the engagement (for example, if the engagement was to report only on Scope 2 emissions and no other experts were used).*

[27] [*Applicable criteria*] are available for free download from www.######.org.

[As discussed in Note 1 to the GHG statement,][28] GHG quantification is subject to inherent uncertainty because of incomplete scientific knowledge used to determine emissions factors and the values needed to combine emissions of different gases.

Our Independence and Quality Control

We have complied with the *Code of Ethics for Professional Accountants* issued by the International Ethics Standards Board for Accountants, which includes independence and other requirements founded on fundamental principles of integrity, objectivity, professional competence and due care, confidentiality and professional behavior.

In accordance with International Standard on Quality Control 1,[29] *[name of firm]* maintains a comprehensive system of quality control including documented policies and procedures regarding compliance with ethical requirements, professional standards and applicable legal and regulatory requirements.

Our Responsibility

Our responsibility is to express an opinion on the GHG statement based on the evidence we have obtained. We conducted our reasonable assurance engagement in accordance with International Standard on Assurance Engagements 3410, *Assurance Engagements on Greenhouse Gas Statements* ("ISAE 3410"), issued by the International Auditing and Assurance Standards Board. That standard requires that we plan and perform this engagement to obtain reasonable assurance about whether the GHG statement is free from material misstatement.

A reasonable assurance engagement in accordance with ISAE 3410 involves performing procedures to obtain evidence about the quantification of emissions and related information in the GHG statement. The nature, timing and extent of procedures selected depend on the practitioner's judgment, including the assessment of the risks of material misstatement, whether due to fraud or error, in the GHG statement. In making those risk assessments, we considered internal control relevant to ABC's preparation of the GHG statement. A reasonable assurance engagement also includes:

- Assessing the suitability in the circumstances of ABC's use of *[applicable criteria]*, applied as explained in Note 1 to the GHG statement, as the basis for preparing the GHG statement;
- Evaluating the appropriateness of quantification methods and reporting policies used, and the reasonableness of estimates made by ABC; and
- Evaluating the overall presentation of the GHG statement.

We believe that the evidence we have obtained is sufficient and appropriate to provide a basis for our opinion.

Opinion

In our opinion, the GHG statement for the year ended December 31, 20X1 is prepared, in all material respects, in accordance with the *[applicable criteria]* applied as explained in Note 1 to the GHG statement.

[28] *Where there is no discussion of the inherent uncertainty in Note 1 to the GHG statement, this should be deleted.*

[29] ISQC 1, Quality Control for Firms that Perform Audits and Reviews of Financial Statements, and Other Assurance and Related Services Engagements.

Report on Other Legal and Regulatory Requirements *(applicable for some engagements only)*

[Form and content of this section of the assurance report will vary depending on the nature of the practitioner's other reporting responsibilities.]

[Practitioner's signature]

[Date of the assurance report]

[Practitioner's address]

Illustration 2:

Circumstances include the following:

- Limited assurance engagement.

- The entity's GHG statement contains no Scope 3 emissions.

- The entity's GHG statement contains no emissions deductions.

- The GHG statement contains no comparative information

The following illustrative report is for guidance only and is not intended to be exhaustive or applicable to all situations.

INDEPENDENT PRACTITIONER'S LIMITED ASSURANCE REPORT ON ABC'S GREENHOUSE GAS (GHG) STATEMENT

[Appropriate Addressee]

Report on GHG Statement (*this heading is not needed if this is the only section*)

We have undertaken a limited assurance engagement of the accompanying GHG statement of ABC for the year ended December 31, 20X1, comprising the Emissions Inventory [and the Explanatory Notes on pages xx–yy]. [This engagement was conducted by a multidisciplinary team including assurance practitioners, engineers and environmental scientists.][30]

ABC's Responsibility for the GHG Statement

ABC is responsible for the preparation of the GHG statement in accordance with [*applicable criteria*[31]], applied as explained in Note 1 to the GHG statement. This responsibility includes the design, implementation and maintenance of internal control relevant to the preparation of a GHG statement that is free from material misstatement, whether due to fraud or error.

[As discussed in Note 1 to the GHG statement,][32] GHG quantification is subject to inherent uncertainty because of incomplete scientific knowledge used to determine emissions factors and the values needed to combine emissions of different gases.

Our Independence and Quality Control

We have complied with the *Code of Ethics for Professional Accountants* issued by the International Ethics Standards Board for Accountants, which includes independence and other requirements founded on fundamental principles of integrity, objectivity, professional competence and due care, confidentiality and professional behavior.

---

[30] *The sentence should be deleted if it is not applicable to the engagement (for example, if the engagement was to report only on Scope 2 emissions and no other experts were used).*

[31] [*Applicable criteria*] are available for free download from www.######.org.

[32] *Where there is no discussion of the inherent uncertainty in Note 1 to the GHG statement, this should be deleted.*

In accordance with International Standard on Quality Control 1,[33] [*name of firm*] maintains a comprehensive system of quality control including documented policies and procedures regarding compliance with ethical requirements, professional standards and applicable legal and regulatory requirements.

Our Responsibility

Our responsibility is to express a limited assurance conclusion on the GHG statement based on the procedures we have performed and the evidence we have obtained. We conducted our limited assurance engagement in accordance with International Standard on Assurance Engagements 3410, *Assurance Engagements on Greenhouse Gas Statements* ("ISAE 3410"), issued by the International Auditing and Assurance Standards Board. That standard requires that we plan and perform this engagement to obtain limited assurance about whether the GHG statement is free from material misstatement.

A limited assurance engagement undertaken in accordance with ISAE 3410 involves assessing the suitability in the circumstances of ABC's use of [applicable criteria] as the basis for the preparation of the GHG statement, assessing the risks of material misstatement of the GHG statement whether due to fraud or error, responding to the assessed risks as necessary in the circumstances, and evaluating the overall presentation of the GHG statement. A limited assurance engagement is substantially less in scope than a reasonable assurance engagement in relation to both the risk assessment procedures, including an understanding of internal control, and the procedures performed in response to the assessed risks.

The procedures we performed were based on our professional judgment and included inquiries, observation of processes performed, inspection of documents, analytical procedures, evaluating the appropriateness of quantification methods and reporting policies, and agreeing or reconciling with underlying records.

> *[[The practitioner may insert a summary of the nature and extent of procedures performed that, in the practitioner's judgment, provides additional information that may be relevant to the users' understanding of the basis for the practitioner's conclusion.[34] The following section has been provided as guidance, and the example procedures are not an exhaustive list of either the type, or extent, of the procedures which may be important for the users' understanding of the work done.]*[35]

Given the circumstances of the engagement, in performing the procedures listed above we:

- Through inquiries, obtained an understanding of ABC's control environment and information systems relevant to emissions quantification and reporting, but did not evaluate the design of particular control activities, obtain evidence about their implementation or test their operating effectiveness.
- Evaluated whether ABC's methods for developing estimates are appropriate and had been consistently applied. However, our procedures did not include

---

[33] *ISQC 1*, Quality Control for Firms that Perform Audits and Reviews of Financial Statements, and Other Assurance and Related Services Engagements.

[34] *The procedures are to be summarized but not to the extent that they are ambiguous, nor described in a way that is overstated or embellished or that implies that reasonable assurance has been obtained. It is important that the description of the procedures does not give the impression that an agreed-upon procedures engagement has been undertaken, and in most cases will not detail the entire work plan.*

[35] *In the final report, this explanatory paragraph will be deleted.*

testing the data on which the estimates are based or separately developing our own estimates against which to evaluate ABC's estimates.

- Undertook site visits [at three sites] to assess the completeness of the emissions sources, data collection methods, source data and relevant assumptions applicable to the sites. The sites selected for testing were chosen taking into consideration their emissions in relation to total emissions, emissions sources, and sites selected in prior periods. Our procedures [did/did not] include testing information systems to collect and aggregate facility data, or the controls at these sites.][36]

The procedures performed in a limited assurance engagement vary in nature from, and are less in extent than for, a reasonable assurance engagement. As a result, the level of assurance obtained in a limited assurance engagement is substantially lower than the assurance that would have been obtained had we performed a reasonable assurance engagement. Accordingly, we do not express a reasonable assurance opinion about whether ABC's GHG statement has been prepared, in all material respects, in accordance with the [*applicable criteria*] applied as explained in Note 1 to the GHG statement.

Limited Assurance Conclusion

Based on the procedures we have performed and the evidence we have obtained, nothing has come to our attention that causes us to believe that ABC's GHG statement for the year ended December 31, 20X1 is not prepared, in all material respects, in accordance with the [*applicable criteria*] applied as explained in Note 1 to the GHG statement.

Report on Other Legal and Regulatory Requirements *(applicable for some engagements only)*

[Form and content of this section of the assurance report will vary depending on the nature of the practitioner's other reporting responsibilities.]

[Practitioner's signature]

[Date of the assurance report]

[Practitioner's address]

---

[36] *This section should be deleted if the practitioner concludes that the expanded information on the procedures performed is not needed in the circumstances of the engagement.*

Part Six

International Standards on Related Services (ISRSs)

International Standard on
Related Services 4400

(Previously ISA 920)

Engagements to perform agreed-upon procedures regarding financial information

(This Standard is effective)

Contents

International Standard on Related Services (ISRS) 4400, "Engagements to Perform Agreed-upon Procedures Regarding Financial Information" should be read in the context of the "Preface to the International Standards on Quality Control, Auditing, Review, Other Assurance and Related Services," which sets out the application and authority of ISRSs.

Introduction

1   The purpose of this International Standard on Related Services (ISRS) is to establish standards and provide guidance on the auditor's[1] professional responsibilities when an engagement to perform agreed-upon procedures regarding financial information is undertaken and on the form and content of the report that the auditor issues in connection with such an engagement.

2   This ISRS is directed toward engagements regarding financial information. However, it may provide useful guidance for engagements regarding non-financial information, provided the auditor has adequate knowledge of the subject matter in question and reasonable criteria exist on which to base findings. Guidance in the International Standards on Auditing (ISAs) may be useful to the auditor in applying this ISRS.

3   An engagement to perform agreed-upon procedures may involve the auditor in performing certain procedures concerning individual items of financial data (for example, accounts payable, accounts receivable, purchases from related parties and sales and profits of a segment of an entity), a financial statement (for example, a balance sheet) or even a complete set of financial statements.

Objective of an Agreed-Upon Procedures Engagement

4   **The objective of an agreed-upon procedures engagement is for the auditor to carry out procedures of an audit nature to which the auditor and the entity and any appropriate third parties have agreed and to report on factual findings.**

5   As the auditor simply provides a report of the factual findings of agreed-upon procedures, no assurance is expressed. Instead, users of the report assess for themselves the procedures and findings reported by the auditor and draw their own conclusions from the auditor's work.

6   The report is restricted to those parties that have agreed to the procedures to be performed since others, unaware of the reasons for the procedures, may misinterpret the results.

General Principles of an Agreed-Upon Procedures Engagement

7   **The auditor should comply with the *Code of Ethics for Professional Accountants* issued by the International Federation of Accountants.** Ethical principles governing the auditor's professional responsibilities for this type of engagement are:

   (a) Integrity;
   (b) Objectivity;
   (c) Professional competence and due care;
   (d) Confidentiality;
   (e) Professional behavior; and
   (f) Technical standards.

---

[1] *The term "auditor" is used throughout the pronouncements of the International Auditing and Assurance Standards Board when describing both audit, review, other assurance and related services that may be performed. Such reference is not intended to imply that a person performing review, other assurance or related services need be the auditor of the entity's financial statements.*

Independence is not a requirement for agreed-upon procedures engagements; however, the terms or objectives of an engagement or national standards may require the auditor to comply with the independence requirements of IFAC's *Code of Ethics for Professional Accountants*. Where the auditor is not independent, a statement to that effect would be made in the report of factual findings.

**The auditor should conduct an agreed-upon procedures engagement in accordance with   8
this ISRS and the terms of the engagement.**

Defining the Terms of the Engagement

**The auditor should ensure with representatives of the entity and, ordinarily, other   9
specified parties who will receive copies of the report of factual findings, that there is a
clear understanding regarding the agreed procedures and the conditions of the
engagement.** Matters to be agreed include the following:

- Nature of the engagement including the fact that the procedures performed will not constitute an audit or a review and that accordingly no assurance will be expressed.
- Stated purpose for the engagement.
- Identification of the financial information to which the agreed-upon procedures will be applied.
- Nature, timing and extent of the specific procedures to be applied.
- Anticipated form of the report of factual findings.
- Limitations on distribution of the report of factual findings. When such limitation would be in conflict with the legal requirements, if any, the auditor would not accept the engagement.

In certain circumstances, for example, when the procedures have been agreed to   10
between the regulator, industry representatives and representatives of the accounting profession, the auditor may not be able to discuss the procedures with all the parties who will receive the report. In such cases, the auditor may consider, for example, discussing the procedures to be applied with appropriate representatives of the parties involved, reviewing relevant correspondence from such parties or sending them a draft of the type of report that will be issued.

It is in the interests of both the client and the auditor that the auditor sends an   11
engagement letter documenting the key terms of the appointment. An engagement letter confirms the auditor's acceptance of the appointment and helps avoid misunderstanding regarding such matters as the objectives and scope of the engagement, the extent of the auditor's responsibilities and the form of reports to be issued.

Matters that would be included in the engagement letter include the following: 12

- A listing of the procedures to be performed as agreed upon between the parties.
- A statement that the distribution of the report of factual findings would be restricted to the specified parties who have agreed to the procedures to be performed.

In addition, the auditor may consider attaching to the engagement letter a draft of the type of report of factual findings that will be issued. An example of an engagement letter appears in Appendix 1 to this ISRS.

Planning

13 The auditor should plan the work so that an effective engagement will be performed.

Documentation

14 The auditor should document matters which are important in providing evidence to support the report of factual findings, and evidence that the engagement was carried out in accordance with this ISRS and the terms of the engagement.

Procedures and Evidence

15 The auditor should carry out the procedures agreed upon and use the evidence obtained as the basis for the report of factual findings.

16 The procedures applied in an engagement to perform agreed-upon procedures may include the following:

- Inquiry and analysis.
- Recomputation, comparison and other clerical accuracy checks.
- Observation.
- Inspection.
- Obtaining confirmations.

Appendix 2 to this ISRS is an example report which contains an illustrative list of procedures which may be used as one part of a typical agreed-upon procedures engagement.

Reporting

17 The report on an agreed-upon procedures engagement needs to describe the purpose and the agreed-upon procedures of the engagement in sufficient detail to enable the reader to understand the nature and the extent of the work performed.

18 The report of factual findings should contain:

(a) Title;
(b) Addressee (ordinarily the client who engaged the auditor to perform the agreed-upon procedures);
(c) Identification of specific financial or non-financial information to which the agreed-upon procedures have been applied;
(d) A statement that the procedures performed were those agreed upon with the recipient;
(e) A statement that the engagement was performed in accordance with the International Standard on Related Services applicable to agreed-upon procedures engagements, or with relevant national standards or practices;
(f) When relevant a statement that the auditor is not independent of the entity;
(g) Identification of the purpose for which the agreed-upon procedures were performed;
(h) A listing of the specific procedures performed;
(i) A description of the auditor's factual findings including sufficient details of errors and exceptions found;

(j) Statement that the procedures performed do not constitute either an audit or a review and, as such, no assurance is expressed;

(k) A statement that had the auditor performed additional procedures, an audit or a review, other matters might have come to light that would have been reported;

(l) A statement that the report is restricted to those parties that have agreed to the procedures to be performed;

(m) A statement (when applicable) that the report relates only to the elements, accounts, items or financial and non-financial information specified and that it does not extend to the entity's financial statements taken as a whole;

(n) Date of the report;

(o) Auditor's address; and

(p) Auditor's signature.

Appendix 2 to this ISRS contains an example of a report of factual findings issued in connection with an engagement to perform agreed-upon procedures regarding financial information.

Public Sector Perspective

1. *The report in a public sector engagement may not be restricted only to those parties that have agreed to the procedures to be performed, but made available also to a wider range of entities or people (for example, a parliamentary investigation about a specific public entity or governmental department).*

2. *It also has to be noted that public sector mandates vary significantly and caution has to be taken to distinguish engagements that are truly "agreed-upon procedures" from engagements that are expected to be audits of financial information, such as performance reports.*

Appendix 1

Example of an Engagement Letter for an Agreed-Upon Procedures Engagement

The following letter is for use as a guide in conjunction with paragraph 9 of this ISRS and is not intended to be a standard letter. The engagement letter will need to be varied according to individual requirements and circumstances.

To the Board of Directors or other appropriate representatives of the client who engaged the auditor

This letter is to confirm our understanding of the terms and objectives of our engagement and the nature and limitations of the services that we will provide. Our engagement will be conducted in accordance with the International Standard on Related Services (or refer to relevant national standards or practices) applicable to agreed-upon procedures engagements and we will indicate so in our report.

We have agreed to perform the following procedures and report to you the factual findings resulting from our work:

(Describe the nature, timing and extent of the procedures to be performed, including specific reference, where applicable, to the identity of documents and records to be read, individuals to be contacted and parties from whom confirmations will be obtained.)

The procedures that we will perform are solely to assist you in (state purpose). Our report is not to be used for any other purpose and is solely for your information.

The procedures that we will perform will not constitute an audit or a review made in accordance with International Standards on Auditing or International Standards on Review Engagements (or refer to relevant national standards or practices) and, consequently, no assurance will be expressed.

We look forward to full cooperation with your staff and we trust that they will make available to us whatever records, documentation and other information requested in connection with our engagement.

Our fees, which will be billed as work progresses, are based on the time required by the individuals assigned to the engagement plus out-of-pocket expenses. Individual hourly rates vary according to the degree of responsibility involved and the experience and skill required.

Please sign and return the attached copy of this letter to indicate that it is in accordance with your understanding of the terms of the engagement including the specific procedures which we have agreed will be performed.

XYZ & Co

Acknowledged on behalf of ABC Company by

(signed)

Name and Title

Date

Appendix 2

Example of a Report of Factual Findings in Connection with Accounts Payable

REPORT OF FACTUAL FINDINGS

To (those who engaged the auditor)

We have performed the procedures agreed with you and enumerated below with respect to the accounts payable of ABC Company as at (date), set forth in the accompanying schedules (not shown in this example). Our engagement was undertaken in accordance with the International Standard on Related Services (or refer to relevant national standards or practices) applicable to agreed-upon procedures engagements. The procedures were performed solely to assist you in evaluating the validity of the accounts payable and are summarized as follows:

1. We obtained and checked the addition of the trial balance of accounts payable as at (date) prepared by ABC Company, and we compared the total to the balance in the related general ledger account.

2.   We compared the attached list (not shown in this example) of major suppliers and the amounts owing at (date) to the related names and amounts in the trial balance.

3.   We obtained suppliers' statements or requested suppliers to confirm balances owing at (date).

4.   We compared such statements or confirmations to the amounts referred to in 2. For amounts which did not agree, we obtained reconciliations from ABC Company. For reconciliations obtained, we identified and listed outstanding invoices, credit notes and outstanding checks, each of which was greater than xxx. We located and examined such invoices and credit notes subsequently received and checks subsequently paid and we ascertained that they should in fact have been listed as outstanding on the reconciliations.

We report our findings below:

(a)   With respect to item 1 we found the addition to be correct and the total amount to be in agreement.

(b)   With respect to item 2 we found the amounts compared to be in agreement.

(c)   With respect to item 3 we found there were suppliers' statements for all such suppliers.

(d)   With respect to item 4 we found the amounts agreed, or with respect to amounts which did not agree, we found ABC Company had prepared reconciliations and that the credit notes, invoices and outstanding checks over xxx were appropriately listed as reconciling items with the following exceptions:
      (Detail the exceptions)

Because the above procedures do not constitute either an audit or a review made in accordance with International Standards on Auditing or International Standards on Review Engagements (or relevant national standards or practices), we do not express any assurance on the accounts payable as of (date).

Had we performed additional procedures or had we performed an audit or review of the financial statements in accordance with International Standards on Auditing or International Standards on Review Engagements (or relevant national standards or practices), other matters might have come to our attention that would have been reported to you.

Our report is solely for the purpose set forth in the first paragraph of this report and for your information and is not to be used for any other purpose or to be distributed to any other parties. This report relates only to the accounts and items specified above and does not extend to any financial statements of ABC Company, taken as a whole.

AUDITOR

Date
Address

International Standard on Related Services 4410 (Revised)

Compilation Engagements

Basis for Conclusions

This Basis for Conclusions has been prepared by staff of the International Auditing and Assurance Standards Board (IAASB). It relates to, but does not form part of, International Standard on Related Services (ISRS) 4410 (Revised), *Compilation Engagements*, which was approved by the IAASB in December 2011, with the affirmative votes of 18 out of the 18 IAASB members.[1]

Background

1   The IAASB commenced the project to revise the extant ISRS 4410[2] in March 2009. This project was part of IAASB's strategic focus to explore standards for a range of services that are capable of meeting the unique needs of small- and medium-sized entities (SMEs), and the users of their financial information. In taking this initiative, the IAASB recognized the market demand for services, other than the financial statement audit, relevant to enhancing the credibility of the financial information of SMEs. This demand has been particularly apparent in jurisdictions where recent changes to law and regulation have resulted in a significant proportion of corporate entities no longer being required to have their financial statements subject to audit.

2   In undertaking the revision of extant ISRS 4410, the IAASB acknowledged the importance of compilation engagements for SMEs, both within jurisdictions where compilation engagements are already commonplace and those where use of these engagements is relatively new. It also was recognized that, in some jurisdictions, there may be existing types of services performed by professional accountants that, in some respects, are similar to the compilation engagement as described in the international standards, but that also differ in key areas.

3   An important consideration of the project has therefore been to make clear the key distinguishing features of a compilation engagement performed in accordance with ISRS 4410 (Revised), and the value of the engagement in enhancing the usefulness of an entity's financial information. Through the revision of this standard, the IAASB aims to help practitioners performing compilation engagements around the world converge to the use of a globally accepted benchmark for such engagements.

4   In October 2010, the IAASB exposed proposed revised ISRS 4410 (ED-4410). The comment period closed on March 31, 2011, with 49 comment letters from various respondents, including regulators and oversight authorities, national standard setters, IFAC member bodies and other professional bodies, firms and individuals. This Basis for Conclusions explains the more significant issues raised by respondents to the ED, and how the IAASB has addressed them.

---

[1] *See minutes of the December 5–9, 2011 IAASB meeting at www.ifac.org/auditing-assurance/meetings/los-angeles-california under the heading "Minutes."*

[2] *ISRS 4410*, Engagements to Compile Financial Statements.

The IAASB has discussed this project with its Consultative Advisory Group (CAG)   5
on six separate occasions.

Use and Applicability of the Standard

ED-4410 proposed that the standard be applicable when the practitioner is engaged   6
to compile historical financial information *and* provide a report for the engagement
in accordance with ISRS 4410. Accordingly, when a practitioner is engaged only to
compile financial information without providing a report in accordance with ISRS
4410 (Revised), the practitioner does not assert compliance with ISRS 4410
(Revised).

The majority of respondents to ED-4410 who expressly commented on this issue   7
agreed with this proposed scope. Several respondents, however, disagreed. Among
the respondents who disagreed, some were of the view that reporting should be
addressed only within the requirements of the standard, and should not be specified
as a part of the scope of the ISRS. The concern noted was that this formulation of
the scope of the standard could enable practitioners to opt out of using the ISRS by
merely agreeing to undertake an engagement to compile financial information
without providing the required report.

IAASB Decisions

The IAASB reaffirmed its view that ISRS 4410 (Revised) should address compilation   8
engagements that involve the issuance of a report on the engagement in accordance
with the ISRS, and that the matter of reporting should be explicitly acknowledged in
the scope of the standard. (See paragraph 1 of ISRS 4410 (Revised).)

The IAASB recognized that there are types of services performed by professional   9
accountants that, in some respects, are similar to the compilation engagement as
described in the international standards, but that also differ in some areas. One such
area is the need to report to users of the information on the nature of the engagement
performed. The IAASB believes that by specifying reporting as part of the scope of
the engagement, practitioners and others will be better able to determine whether
ISRS 4410 (Revised) applies in the circumstances. The IAASB is of the view that a
practitioner that performs an engagement in accordance with ISRS 4410 (Revised)
needs to communicate in a written report the nature of the practitioner's involvement
with the entity's financial information, and therefore the practitioner's association
with the compiled financial information.

The IAASB acknowledged that it cannot mandate application of the ISRS across all   10
types of compilation engagements. Mandatory application of the ISRS, however,
may be specified in jurisdictions for engagements where practitioners undertake
services relevant to the preparation and presentation of an entity's financial information. If mandatory application is not specified, by law, regulation, professional
standards or otherwise, the practitioner may nevertheless conclude that applying the
ISRS is appropriate in the circumstances. In finalizing ISRS 4410 (Revised), the
IAASB concluded that it is important to state, within the introductory section of the
ISRS, factors that indicate that it may be appropriate to apply the ISRS, including
reporting in accordance with the standard. These factors include whether:

- The financial information is required under provisions of applicable law or
  regulation, and whether it is required to be publicly filed.

- External parties other than the intended users of the compiled financial information are likely to associate the practitioner with the financial information, and there is a risk that the level of the practitioner's involvement with the information may be misunderstood, for example:
  - o   If the financial information is intended for use by parties other than management or those charged with governance, or may be provided to, or obtained by, parties who are not the intended users of the information; and
  - o   If the practitioner's name is identified with the financial information.

(See paragraph 3 of ISRS 4410 (Revised).)

Use of Technical Terms in ISRS 4410 (Revised)

The "Applicable Financial Reporting Framework"

11   ED-4410 focused the compilation engagement performed under ISRS 4410 (Revised) on assisting management with the preparation and presentation of financial information in accordance with an applicable financial reporting framework. In undertaking such engagements the practitioner contributes expertise in accounting and financial reporting, and in particular the practitioner's knowledge and understanding of the application of financial reporting frameworks for different financial reporting purposes.

12   A few respondents expressed the view that the term "applicable financial reporting framework" as used in ED-4410 could be interpreted as implying use of established financial reporting frameworks only, to the exclusion of other types of financial reporting frameworks. This was notwithstanding that ED-4410 also contained guidance explaining that the term is intended to encompass the full range of possible frameworks that can be used for financial reporting purposes (i.e., in the context of financial information prepared for either general or special purposes). Some respondents raised concerns that the intended meaning of the term was not sufficiently explained in ED-4410, and that the standard could be further enhanced through clearer guidance, including in relation to the particular circumstance where financial information is prepared for a special purpose.

IAASB Decisions

13   The IAASB reaffirmed its decision to use the term "applicable financial reporting framework" throughout the requirements and guidance of ISRS 4410 (Revised). The term is intended to be read in its most generic sense, recognizing that there is a wide variety of frameworks that can potentially be used, ranging from established financial reporting frameworks to frameworks developed on a customized basis to address the specific financial reporting needs of particular entities or types of entities. The term is defined in the IAASB's *Glossary of Terms* and is commonly understood by professional accountants using IAASB standards. The IAASB believes that introducing new terminology specific to ISRS 4410 would introduce unnecessary complexity in the standard.

14   However, the IAASB recognized that smaller entities typically use financial reporting frameworks that are less formal and that are often customized to their particular business reporting needs. These needs often reflect a variety of reporting situations for different types of users.(See paragraph 10 of ISRS 4410 (Revised).)

To make this clear, the IAASB agreed to amend ED-4410 to include in the standard, **15** where appropriate, a reference to the alternative term "basis of accounting" , as a way to facilitate practitioners' understanding and interpretation of the requirements and guidance in ISRS 4410 (Revised). (See paragraph A16 and Appendix 2, Illustrative Reports 3–5, of ISRS 4410 (Revised).)

The Terms "Material Misstatement" and "Materially Misstated"

ED-4410 used the terms "material misstatement" and "materially misstated" in the **16** requirements and guidance of the proposed standard for purposes of explaining the practitioner's responsibilities and required actions in the engagement. These requirements and guidance were focused on enabling the practitioner to comply with relevant ethical requirements, particularly in relation to the ethical principle of integrity, as explained in the International Ethics Standards Board for Accountants' *Code of Ethics for Professional Accountants* (the IESBA Code).

Some respondents expressed the view that use of this term would blur the distinction **17** between a compilation engagement and an assurance engagement, because it would imply responsibilities for the practitioner, and associated work effort, that would not be applicable to a compilation engagement.

Several respondents also requested that ISRS 4410 include application guidance to **18** guide practitioners on forming an assessment of materiality as relevant to performing the compilation engagement.

IAASB Decisions

The IAASB reaffirmed its decision to use the terms "material misstatement" and **19** "materially misstated" within the requirements and guidance of ISRS 4410 (Revised), including in relation to the practitioner's compliance with relevant ethical obligations.

The IAASB took the view that, as "misstatement" is a term that practitioners are **20** already very familiar with, ISRS 4410 (Revised) could be further enhanced by explaining the term's particular relevance in a compilation engagement, that is, in the context of the practitioner's ethical obligations under the IESBA Code, for example in respect of being knowingly associated with information that is materially false or misleading.

Therefore, to further enhance the clarity and understandability of the standard for **21** practitioners, the IAASB decided to include a definition of the term "misstatement" within ISRS 4410 (Revised), aligned with the definition in the *Glossary of Terms* but adapted to the context of a compilation engagement. (See paragraph 17(e) of ISRS 4410 (Revised).)

In addition, the IAASB decided to include explanations about the concept of **22** materiality within ISRS 4410 (Revised), to guide the practitioner's consideration of the need to take further action(s) in relation to the compiled financial information, for example, requesting management to amend the compiled financial information if necessary. (See paragraph 34 of ISRS 4410 (Revised).)

Practitioner's Responsibilities—The Applicable Financial Reporting Framework

23   ED-4410 was premised on the condition that the management of an entity is responsible for adopting a financial reporting framework for the preparation and presentation of the entity's financial information that is acceptable in view of the intended use of the financial information, and the needs of the intended users (as reflected also in the definition of the term "applicable financial reporting framework").

24   Further, ED-4410 recognized that, given the practitioner's expertise and in view of the practitioner's ethical obligations described above, the practitioner may provide assistance to management with identification of a financial reporting framework that is acceptable, including in the case where it becomes apparent to the practitioner in the course of performing the compilation engagement that the framework adopted by management is not acceptable in the context described above.

25   Several respondents believed that the requirements and guidance of ED-4410 regarding the practitioner's responsibilities for assisting management in these areas were unclear, and could be more simply stated in the ISRS. These respondents also pointed to the risk that these requirements could be seen as implying greater responsibility on the practitioner than is intended for a compilation engagement.

26   Several respondents also expressed a general concern that the requirements and guidance need to be as clear as possible that the practitioner's responsibilities in performing the compilation engagement are always framed in the context of assisting management with the preparation and presentation of an entity's financial information.

IAASB Decisions

27   The IAASB agreed that ISRS 4410 (Revised) could be enhanced by simplifying the requirements and guidance in respect of the practitioner's responsibilities. The IAASB determined that, to enhance the clarity and understandability of the standard, the context for the requirements should be clearly linked to achieving the practitioner's objectives for the engagement, including complying with relevant ethical requirements.

28   The IAASB accordingly included clearer explanations about the nature of the engagement in the introductory section of the standard, as context for the statement of the practitioner's objectives in a compilation engagement and the requirements of the ISRS designed to achieve those objectives. (See paragraphs 5 and 7 of ISRS 4410 (Revised)).

29   The IAASB also determined that a high-level explanation about the use of financial reporting frameworks in different financial reporting contexts, as part of management's responsibility for preparing the entity's financial information, would enhance understanding of the practitioner' responsibilities in a compilation engagement. Accordingly, the IAASB amended ED-4410 by moving such explanations from the application material into the introductory section of the standard. (See paragraph 10 of ISRS 4410 (Revised)).

30   To address the concern that there could be misunderstanding regarding the practitioner's responsibilities where the practitioner provides assistance to management with the identification of an acceptable financial reporting framework, the IAASB

determined that the guidance for practitioners on proposing changes to the applicable financial reporting framework in the course of a compilation engagement should be deleted. The IAASB believes the practitioner's responsibility to comply with relevant ethical requirements would adequately guide the practitioner in that circumstance. (See paragraph 21 of ISRS 4410 (Revised).)

Practitioner's Responsibilities—Intentional Departures from the Applicable Financial Reporting Framework

ED-4410 included a requirement for the practitioner to withdraw from the compilation engagement if the compiled financial information contained departures from the applicable financial framework that the practitioner believed rendered the compiled information materially misstated or misleading, and management did not agree to amend the compiled financial information. This requirement was expressly supported by the majority of the respondents. **31**

However several respondents disagreed with the requirement. A few of these respondents believed the practitioner should be required to disclose intentional departures from the applicable financial reporting framework described in the compiled financial information, for the benefit of readers of the practitioner's report. Some other respondents were of the view that the practitioner should be permitted to include disclosure of such departures when the practitioner experiences a disagreement with management on the preparation and presentation of the compiled financial information in accordance with the applicable financial reporting framework and management refuses to amend the compiled financial information, as would be the case in an assurance engagement where qualification is possible. **32**

In contrast, some respondents who agreed with the requirement in ED-4410 expressly disagreed that the practitioner's report can be used for the purpose of disclosing such departures, or otherwise to draw them to the attention of readers of the report. These respondents cautioned against the risk that such disclosures by the practitioner could be misunderstood by readers, and be taken as a form of expression of an opinion or conclusion on the compiled financial information. Respondents were also concerned that the ISRS should not include provisions that could lead to the development of an expectations gap among users with respect to financial information compiled by practitioners under ISRS 4410 (Revised). **33**

IAASB Decisions

The IAASB reaffirmed its view that the practitioner, on becoming aware of circumstances that suggest that the compiled financial information is materially misstated or otherwise misleading (including in respect of disclosure of the applicable financial reporting framework actually applied to prepare and present the compiled financial information), should be required to request appropriate amendments to the compiled financial information, or withdraw from the engagement if management refuses to amend the information. (See paragraphs 35-36 of ISRS 4410 (Revised).) **34**

As to respondents who believed the practitioner's report could be used to make disclosures concerning the compiled financial information itself, the IAASB determined that ISRS 4410 (Revised) could be further strengthened in respect of communicating the purpose of the practitioner's report in a compilation engagement. Accordingly, to provide further context for the reporting requirements of the standard, the IAASB amended ED-4410 to expressly state that the practitioner's report is **35** not a vehicle to express an opinion or conclusion on the financial information in any form. (See paragraph 39 of ISRS 4410 (Revised).)

36 [Moved from below, redrafted] In view of the practice sometimes followed of using an established financial reporting framework with certain modifications, the IAASB determined that it is important to direct the practitioner's attention to the adequate disclosure of the applicable financial reporting framework in the compiled financial information. This would include situations where management elects to use an established framework with modifications, or when there are intentional departures from an established framework that are not disclosed within the compiled financial information itself. Accordingly, the IAASB has amended ED-4410 to emphasize that the description of the applicable financial reporting framework actually applied should be adequately referred to or described in the compiled financial information itself, and should not be otherwise misleading to the intended users of the financial information. (See paragraph 34 of ISRS 4410 (Revised)).

37 Further, the IAASB has clarified the requirements of the standard regarding actions the practitioner is required to take, and related considerations, if the practitioner becomes aware of material misstatements in the compiled financial information., This includes misstatements arising from intentional departures from the applicable financial reporting framework that are not adequately disclosed in the compiled financial information itself, on a transparent basis, for the benefit of users of the information. (See paragraph 34 of ISRS 4410 (Revised).)

Work Effort in Relation to Significant Judgments

38 ED-4410 proposed requiring the practitioner to discuss and agree with management significant judgments necessary to compile the financial information including, where applicable, the basis for significant accounting estimates and use of the going concern assumption.

39 Some respondents identified this requirement as an example of a type of procedure that could be misconstrued as one that is performed to gather evidence for the purpose of expressing an opinion or conclusion on the compiled financial information. These respondents expressed the concern that the requirement could be read as implying that the practitioner has obtained a level of understanding and assurance beyond that which is required for purposes of the compilation engagement. They pointed out the need to amend this requirement to avoid blurring the distinction between a compilation engagement and an assurance engagement.

40 In contrast, a respondent emphasized the importance of the practitioner devoting appropriate attention to significant judgments, particularly if the practitioner assists management in developing significant judgments required under the applicable financial reporting framework. It was argued that this would be particularly important as, in the case of many smaller entities, management may not be sufficiently knowledgeable about accounting or financial reporting matters to be able to make the necessary judgments without the practitioner's assistance and expertise.

41 Some respondents also pointed to the wider risk that, in assisting management, the practitioner may be perceived as having implicitly taken responsibility for judgments that are the responsibility of management. Some of these respondents suggested that, in order to address this, ED-4410 should require the practitioner to obtain management's acknowledgement of its responsibility for the final version of the compiled financial information.

IAASB Decisions

The IAASB reaffirmed its view that ISRS 4410 (Revised) should direct the practi-   42
tioner to devote appropriate attention to discussion with management, or those
charged with governance as appropriate, regarding significant judgments required to
compile the financial information in accordance with the applicable financial
reporting framework. However, the IAASB concluded that this requirement should
focus on the situation where the practitioner has provided assistance to management
in relation to making those judgments, in the course of compiling the financial
information. Doing so helps to focus the practitioner's work effort appropriately in
line with the practitioner's role in a compilation engagement, that is, to provide
assistance to management as opposed to gathering evidence for the purpose of
expressing an opinion or conclusion. (See paragraph 30 of ISRS 4410 (Revised).)

Further, in relation to respondents' comments on the risk that the practitioner could   43
be perceived as having taken responsibility for judgments that are management's
responsibility, the IAASB amended ED-4410 by explaining that when the compilation engagement involves assisting management in key areas affecting the
preparation and presentation of the entity's financial information, such assistance is
always provided on the basis that management understands, and accepts responsibility for, the significant judgments reflected in the compiled financial information.
(See paragraph A22 of ISRS 4410 (Revised).)

The IAASB also accepted respondents' suggestion that the standard could be further   44
enhanced by requiring the practitioner to obtain an acknowledgement from management or those charged with governance, as appropriate, that they have taken
responsibility for the final version of the compiled financial information including the
significant judgments reflected therein. The IAASB believes that requirement would
serve not only to emphasize management's responsibility for the compiled financial
information as finalized, including significant judgments reflected therein, but would
also clarify the completion of the compilation engagement by the practitioner. (See
paragraph 37 of ISRS 4410 (Revised).)

The Practitioner's Report—Illustrative Reports

ED-4410 proposed requirements addressing the elements of the practitioner's report,   45
and included several illustrative reports. The IAASB's objective in establishing these
reporting requirements was, among other things, to clearly distinguish the compilation engagement performed under ISRS 4410 (Revised) from an assurance
engagement, as a matter of public interest.

Broadly, the majority of respondents who commented on the proposed reporting   46
requirements and illustrative reports were of the view that these were clear and
appropriate. Many respondents, however, felt that the illustrative reports could
better distinguish the compilation engagement from other reporting engagements,
citing concerns in the following areas:

- The general appearance of the practitioner's report because of some similarities
  with an assurance report.
- The description of the engagement, including limitations.
- With respect to the circumstances when the compiled financial information is
  prepared for a special purpose, the use of an "alert to reader" sub-title in the
  practitioner's report. However it was noted that this alert could potentially be
  viewed by readers of the report as the practitioner expressing a form of opinion
  or conclusion on the compiled financial information.

IAASB Decisions

47   The IAASB determined that the primary consideration is a clear expression of the purpose of the practitioner's report in a compilation engagement. The IAASB concluded that ISRS 4410 (Revised) could be further strengthened in this regard. Accordingly, the IAASB introduced material within the requirements in the ISRS explaining that an important purpose of the practitioner's report is to clearly communicate the nature of the compilation engagement and the practitioner's role and responsibilities in the engagement. Importantly, the IAASB also clarified that the practitioner's report is not a vehicle to express an opinion or conclusion on the financial information in any form. (See paragraph 39 of ISRS 4410 (Revised).)

48   The IAASB agreed with respondents' view that the description of the compilation engagement could be further enhanced, in order to better explain the nature of the engagement for readers of the report. Accordingly, the IAASB modified the illustrative report to include a paragraph that more concisely describes the practitioner's involvement and also more clearly highlights the value contributed by the practitioner – an essential feature to distinguish the compilation engagement from other types of engagements, including assurance engagements. The illustrative practitioner's report now states that the practitioner has applied the practitioner's expertise in accounting and financial reporting to assist management in the preparation and presentation of the compiled financial information, and has complied with relevant ethical requirements, including principles of integrity, objectivity, professional competence and due care.

49   Similarly, the IAASB has included in a single paragraph in the illustrative practitioner's report the statements that address the limitations of the engagement. Further, it has redrafted the required statements by the practitioner to reduce the use of technical wording that may not be fully understood by the reader of the practitioner's report. This paragraph now states that since a compilation engagement is not an assurance engagement, the practitioner is not required to verify the accuracy or completeness of the information that management has provided to the practitioner to compile the financial information and, accordingly, the practitioner does not express an audit opinion or a review conclusion on whether the financial information is prepared in accordance with [the applicable financial reporting framework].

50   The IAASB agreed that while the purpose of the practitioner's report in a compilation engagement is different from that of a report issued in an assurance engagement, the visual appearance of the practitioner's report in a compilation engagement unavoidably bears a resemblance to the report issued for an assurance engagement. This is because there are some required reporting elements that are common to both types of engagements. Nevertheless, the IAASB agreed to amend the reporting requirements of ISRS 4410 (Revised), and the related guidance, to remove the impression that the practitioner is required to:

 • Apply a specific sequencing in the report when presenting the required reporting elements, or
 • Use headings to structure the content of the report (as is done in an assurance report, where the clear identification of the practitioner's opinion or conclusion is a key consideration in the presentation of the report).

Quality Control in a Compilation Engagement

ED-4410 included requirements pertaining to engagement level quality control on the explicit premise that a firm providing compilation engagements under the standard is required to apply ISQC 1[3] or requirements that are at least as demanding. **51**

Many respondents to ED-4410 supported this premise and noted that it would not create implementation difficulties at a national level. Many respondents, however, disagreed with the inclusion of this premise. Several of the respondents who disagreed cited perceived implementation difficulties surrounding ISQC 1 for firms undertaking compilation engagements. It was noted in particular that the premise will not hold in all cases, since ISQC 1 has not been adopted in all jurisdictions for the purpose of related services engagements, including compilation engagements. A few of these respondents believed that ISRS 4410 (Revised) should instead include, as requirements, all the engagement level quality controls that are considered necessary to achieve quality in individual compilation engagements, without reference to ISQC 1. **52**

Several respondents further noted there may be difficulty in complying with ISQC 1 because some requirements of ISQC 1 are perceived as being too onerous for smaller firms, or would require further interpretation for application to compilation engagements. These respondents suggested that development of implementation guidance that will assist smaller firms undertaking compilation engagements in applying ISQC 1 would be helpful. **53**

IAASB Decision

The IAASB concluded that reference to ISQC 1, or requirements that are at least as demanding, should be retained as the premise underlying the provisions of ISRS 4410 (Revised) regarding quality control at the level of individual compilation engagements. (See paragraph 4 of ISRS 4410 (Revised)). **54**

The IAASB determined that it would not be in the public interest to exclude compilation engagements, or other related services, from relevant requirements directed at quality control at the firm level, nor to limit the application of ISQC 1 thereto. Firm-level quality control positively influences engagement level quality control, and it would therefore be inappropriate to exclude consideration of the former. The IAASB also noted that the premise is also sufficiently flexible to accommodate jurisdictions that have not adopted ISQC 1. **55**

The IAASB considered, but did not support, the option of adding all quality control provisions within the standard itself. To do so would add considerably to the length of the ISRS while disproportionately affecting the overall balance of the requirements and guidance. This was seen as an outcome contrary to respondents' general support for the development of an engagement standard for compilation engagements that is as concise and streamlined as possible. **56**

The IAASB believed that if implementation of ISQC 1 by smaller firms needs to be further addressed, it is preferable to address this through other appropriate means. In this regard, the IAASB agreed to explore, as part of its *Strategy and Work Program, 2012-2014*, the development of implementation support materials aimed at promoting the proportionate implementation of ISQC 1 by smaller firms. It is **57**

---

[3] *ISQC 1*, Quality Control for Firms that Perform Audits and Reviews of Financial Statements, and Other Assurance and Related Services Engagements.

envisioned that such material would include guidance relevant to firms undertaking compilation engagements.

Relevant Ethical Requirements—Independence in a Compilation Engagement

58   ED-4410 proposed requiring the practitioner to comply with relevant ethical requirements as they relate to compilation engagements, and for the practitioner's report to include a description of the practitioner's responsibilities in compiling the financial information, including that the engagement was performed in accordance with relevant ethical requirements.

59   Several respondents to ED-4410 commented on the importance of the practitioner's communications with users of the compiled information in the area of independence, through the practitioner's report. Some of these respondents noted that ED-4410 did not include the requirements and guidance in extant ISRS 4410 stating that independence is not a requirement for a compilation engagement, and which require that, when relevant, if the practitioner is not independent, a statement to that effect be made in the practitioner's report.[4] These respondents believed that this material should be retained in ISRS 4410 (Revised), because information about the practitioner's independence is considered important for the users of the compiled financial information.

IAASB Decisions

60   The IAASB concluded that ISRS 4410 (Revised) should continue to require the practitioner to comply with relevant ethical requirements, and for the practitioner's report to describe the practitioner's responsibilities in compiling the financial information, including that the engagement was performed in accordance with relevant ethical requirements.

61   The IAASB also reaffirmed its view that it is not appropriate to retain the requirement in extant ISRS 4410 pertaining to a statement in the practitioner's report regarding independence. The IAASB is of the view that the practitioner implementing ISRS 4410 (Revised) would need to be guided as to the meaning of independence in the context of a compilation engagement in order to be able to comply with such a reporting requirement. The IAASB notes that the IESBA Code is silent with respect to the concept of independence in relation to a compilation engagement, as are some national standards. In light of this, the IAASB questioned how meaningful a reporting requirement would be in an international context.

62   Nevertheless, the IAASB included application material within ISRS 4410 to draw practitioners' attention to the fact that national ethical codes or laws or regulations may specify requirements or disclosure rules pertaining to independence (see paragraph A21 of ISRS 4410 (Revised)). The IAASB recognizes that in adopting ISRS 4410 (Revised) at national-level, the authorized national standard-setting body of a jurisdiction may elect to include further requirements or application material aimed at addressing this area if that is viewed as important in the national context.

---

[4] *Extant ISRS 4410, paragraph 5 read with paragraph 18(d).*

Part Seven

IFAC Statements

International Standard on Quality Control 1

Quality control for firms that perform audits and reviews of financial statements, and other assurance and related services engagements

*(Effective as of December 15, 2009)**

Contents

* Conforming amendments to this ISQC as a result of ISA 610 (Revised 2013), Using the Work of Internal Auditors, will be effective for audits of financial statements for periods ending on or after December 15, 2014.

International Standard on Quality Control (ISQC) 1, *Quality Control for Firms that Perform Audits and Reviews of Financial Statements, and Other Assurance and Related Services Engagements,* should be read in conjunction with ISA 200, *Overall Objectives of the Independent Auditor and the Conduct of an Audit in Accordance with International Standards on Auditing.*

Introduction

Scope of this ISQC

This International Standard on Quality Control (ISQC) deals with a firm's respon-   1
sibilities for its system of quality control for audits and reviews of financial
statements, and other assurance and related services engagements. This ISQC is to be
read in conjunction with relevant ethical requirements.

Other pronouncements of the International Auditing and Assurance Standards   2
Board (IAASB) set out additional standards and guidance on the responsibilities of
firm personnel regarding quality control procedures for specific types of engagements. ISA 220,[1] for example, deals with quality control procedures for audits of
financial statements.

A system of quality control consists of policies designed to achieve the objective set   3
out in paragraph 11 and the procedures necessary to implement and monitor compliance with those policies.

Authority of this ISQC

This ISQC applies to all firms of professional accountants in respect of audits and   4
reviews of financial statements, and other assurance and related services engagements. The nature and extent of the policies and procedures developed by an
individual firm to comply with this ISQC will depend on various factors such as the
size and operating characteristics of the firm, and whether it is part of a network.

This ISQC contains the objective of the firm in following the ISQC, and require-   5
ments designed to enable the firm to meet that stated objective. In addition, it
contains related guidance in the form of application and other explanatory material,
as discussed further in paragraph 8, and introductory material that provides context
relevant to a proper understanding of the ISQC, and definitions.

The objective provides the context in which the requirements of this ISQC are set,   6
and is intended to assist the firm in:

- Understanding what needs to be accomplished; and
- Deciding whether more needs to be done to achieve the objective.

The requirements of this ISQC are expressed using "shall."   7

Where necessary, the application and other explanatory material provides further   8
explanation of the requirements and guidance for carrying them out. In particular, it
may:

- Explain more precisely what a requirement means or is intended to cover; and
- Include examples of policies and procedures that may be appropriate in the
  circumstances.

While such guidance does not in itself impose a requirement, it is relevant to the
proper application of the requirements. The application and other explanatory
material may also provide background information on matters addressed in this
ISQC. Where appropriate, additional considerations specific to public sector audit
organizations or smaller firms are included within the application and other

---

[1] *ISA 220*, Quality Control for an Audit of Financial Statements.

explanatory material. These additional considerations assist in the application of the requirements in this ISQC. They do not, however, limit or reduce the responsibility of the firm to apply and comply with the requirements in this ISQC.

9   This ISQC includes, under the heading "Definitions," a description of the meanings attributed to certain terms for purposes of this ISQC. These are provided to assist in the consistent application and interpretation of this ISQC, and are not intended to override definitions that may be established for other purposes, whether in law, regulation or otherwise. The Glossary of Terms relating to International Standards issued by the IAASB in the *Handbook of International Quality Control, Auditing, Review, Other Assurance, and Related Services Pronouncements* published by IFAC includes the terms defined in this ISQC. It also includes descriptions of other terms found in this ISQC to assist in common and consistent interpretation and translation.

Effective Date

10   Systems of quality control in compliance with this ISQC are required to be established by December 15, 2009.

Objective

11   The objective of the firm is to establish and maintain a system of quality control to provide it with reasonable assurance that:

(a)   The firm and its personnel comply with professional standards and applicable legal and regulatory requirements; and

(b)   Reports issued by the firm or engagement partners are appropriate in the circumstances.

Definitions

12   In this ISQC, the following terms have the meanings attributed below:

(a)   Date of report – The date selected by the practitioner to date the report.

(b)   Engagement documentation – The record of work performed, results obtained, and conclusions the practitioner reached (terms such as "working papers" or "workpapers" are sometimes used).

(c)   Engagement partner[2] – The partner or other person in the firm who is responsible for the engagement and its performance, and for the report that is issued on behalf of the firm, and who, where required, has the appropriate authority from a professional, legal or regulatory body.

(d)   Engagement quality control review – A process designed to provide an objective evaluation, on or before the date of the report, of the significant judgments the engagement team made and the conclusions it reached in formulating the report. The engagement quality control review process is for audits of financial statements of listed entities, and those other engagements, if any, for which the firm has determined an engagement quality control review is required.

(e)   Engagement quality control reviewer – A partner, other person in the firm, suitably qualified external person, or a team made up of such individuals, none of whom is part of the engagement team, with sufficient and appropriate

---

[2] *"Engagement partner," "partner," and "firm" should be read as referring to their public sector equivalents where relevant.*

experience and authority to objectively evaluate the significant judgments the engagement team made and the conclusions it reached in formulating the report.

(f)   Engagement team – All partners and staff performing the engagement, and any individuals engaged by the firm or a network firm who perform procedures on the engagement. This excludes external experts engaged by the firm or a network firm.

(g)   Firm – A sole practitioner, partnership or corporation or other entity of professional accountants.

(h)   Inspection – In relation to completed engagements, procedures designed to provide evidence of compliance by engagement teams with the firm's quality control policies and procedures.

(i)   Listed entity – An entity whose shares, stock or debt are quoted or listed on a recognized stock exchange, or are marketed under the regulations of a recognized stock exchange or other equivalent body.

(j)   Monitoring – A process comprising an ongoing consideration and evaluation of the firm's system of quality control, including a periodic inspection of a selection of completed engagements, designed to provide the firm with reasonable assurance that its system of quality control is operating effectively.

(k)   Network firm – A firm or entity that belongs to a network.

(l)   Network – A larger structure:
   (i)   That is aimed at cooperation, and
   (ii) That is clearly aimed at profit or cost-sharing or shares common ownership, control or management, common quality control policies and procedures, common business strategy, the use of a common brand name, or a significant part of professional resources.

(m)   Partner – Any individual with authority to bind the firm with respect to the performance of a professional services engagement.

(n)   Personnel – Partners and staff.

(o)   Professional standards – IAASB Engagement Standards, as defined in the IAASB's *Preface to the International Standards on Quality Control, Auditing, Review, Other Assurance and Related Services,* and relevant ethical requirements.

(p)   Reasonable assurance – In the context of this ISQC, a high, but not absolute, level of assurance.

(q)   Relevant ethical requirements – Ethical requirements to which the engagement team and engagement quality control reviewer are subject, which ordinarily comprise Parts A and B of the International Ethics Standards Board for Accountants' *Code of Ethics for Professional Accountants* (IESBA Code) together with national requirements that are more restrictive.

(r)   Staff – Professionals, other than partners, including any experts the firm employs.

(s)   Suitably qualified external person – An individual outside the firm with the competence and capabilities to act as an engagement partner, for example, a partner of another firm, or an employee (with appropriate experience) of either a professional accountancy body whose members may perform audits and reviews of historical financial information, or other assurance or related services engagements, or of an organization that provides relevant quality control services.

Requirements

Applying, and Complying with, Relevant Requirements

13   Personnel within the firm responsible for establishing and maintaining the firm's system of quality control shall have an understanding of the entire text of this ISQC, including its application and other explanatory material, to understand its objective and to apply its requirements properly.

14   The firm shall comply with each requirement of this ISQC unless, in the circumstances of the firm, the requirement is not relevant to the services provided in respect of audits and reviews of financial statements, and other assurance and related services engagements. (Ref: Para. A1)

15   The requirements are designed to enable the firm to achieve the objective stated in this ISQC. The proper application of the requirements is therefore expected to provide a sufficient basis for the achievement of the objective. However, because circumstances vary widely and all such circumstances cannot be anticipated, the firm shall consider whether there are particular matters or circumstances that require the firm to establish policies and procedures in addition to those required by this ISQC to meet the stated objective.

Elements of a System of Quality Control

16   The firm shall establish and maintain a system of quality control that includes policies and procedures that address each of the following elements:

   (a)   Leadership responsibilities for quality within the firm.
   (b)   Relevant ethical requirements.
   (c)   Acceptance and continuance of client relationships and specific engagements.
   (d)   Human resources.
   (e)   Engagement performance.
   (f)   Monitoring.

17   The firm shall document its policies and procedures and communicate them to the firm's personnel. (Ref: Para. A2–A3)

Leadership Responsibilities for Quality within the Firm

18   The firm shall establish policies and procedures designed to promote an internal culture recognizing that quality is essential in performing engagements. Such policies and procedures shall require the firm's chief executive officer (or equivalent) or, if appropriate, the firm's managing board of partners (or equivalent) to assume ultimate responsibility for the firm's system of quality control. (Ref: Para. A4–A5)

19   The firm shall establish policies and procedures such that any person or persons assigned operational responsibility for the firm's system of quality control by the firm's chief executive officer or managing board of partners has sufficient and appropriate experience and ability, and the necessary authority, to assume that responsibility. (Ref: Para. A6)

Relevant Ethical Requirements

The firm shall establish policies and procedures designed to provide it with reason- **20** able assurance that the firm and its personnel comply with relevant ethical requirements. (Ref: Para. A7–A10)

Independence

The firm shall establish policies and procedures designed to provide it with reason- **21** able assurance that the firm, its personnel and, where applicable, others subject to independence requirements (including network firm personnel) maintain indepen- dence where required by relevant ethical requirements. Such policies and procedures shall enable the firm to: (Ref: Para. A10)

(a) Communicate its independence requirements to its personnel and, where applicable, others subject to them; and
(b) Identify and evaluate circumstances and relationships that create threats to independence, and to take appropriate action to eliminate those threats or reduce them to an acceptable level by applying safeguards, or, if considered appropriate, to withdraw from the engagement, where withdrawal is possible under applicable law or regulation.

Such policies and procedures shall require: (Ref: Para. A10) **22**
(a) Engagement partners to provide the firm with relevant information about client engagements, including the scope of services, to enable the firm to evaluate the overall impact, if any, on independence requirements;
(b) Personnel to promptly notify the firm of circumstances and relationships that create a threat to independence so that appropriate action can be taken; and
(c) The accumulation and communication of relevant information to appropriate personnel so that:
　(i) The firm and its personnel can readily determine whether they satisfy independence requirements;
　(ii) The firm can maintain and update its records relating to independence; and
　(iii) The firm can take appropriate action regarding identified threats to inde- pendence that are not at an acceptable level.

The firm shall establish policies and procedures designed to provide it with reason- **23** able assurance that it is notified of breaches of independence requirements, and to enable it to take appropriate actions to resolve such situations. The policies and procedures shall include requirements for: (Ref: Para. A10)

(a) Personnel to promptly notify the firm of independence breaches of which they become aware;
(b) The firm to promptly communicate identified breaches of these policies and procedures to:
　(i) The engagement partner who, with the firm, needs to address the breach; and
　(ii) Other relevant personnel in the firm and, where appropriate, the network, and those subject to the independence requirements who need to take appropriate action; and
(c) Prompt communication to the firm, if necessary, by the engagement partner and the other individuals referred to in subparagraph 23(b)(ii) of the actions taken to resolve the matter, so that the firm can determine whether it should take further action.

24   At least annually, the firm shall obtain written confirmation of compliance with its policies and procedures on independence from all firm personnel required to be independent by relevant ethical requirements. (Ref: Para. A10–A11)

25   The firm shall establish policies and procedures: (Ref: Para. A10)

(a) Setting out criteria for determining the need for safeguards to reduce the familiarity threat to an acceptable level when using the same senior personnel on an assurance engagement over a long period of time; and

(b) Requiring, for audits of financial statements of listed entities, the rotation of the engagement partner and the individuals responsible for engagement quality control review, and, where applicable, others subject to rotation requirements, after a specified period in compliance with relevant ethical requirements. (Ref: Para. A12–A17)

Acceptance and Continuance of Client Relationships and Specific Engagements

26   The firm shall establish policies and procedures for the acceptance and continuance of client relationships and specific engagements, designed to provide the firm with reasonable assurance that it will only undertake or continue relationships and engagements where the firm:

(a) Is competent to perform the engagement and has the capabilities, including time and resources, to do so; (Ref: Para. A18, A23)

(b) Can comply with relevant ethical requirements; and

(c) Has considered the integrity of the client, and does not have information that would lead it to conclude that the client lacks integrity. (Ref: Para. A19–A20, A23)

27   Such policies and procedures shall require:

(a) The firm to obtain such information as it considers necessary in the circumstances before accepting an engagement with a new client, when deciding whether to continue an existing engagement, and when considering acceptance of a new engagement with an existing client. (Ref: Para. A21, A23)

(b) If a potential conflict of interest is identified in accepting an engagement from a new or an existing client, the firm to determine whether it is appropriate to accept the engagement.

(c) If issues have been identified, and the firm decides to accept or continue the client relationship or a specific engagement, the firm to document how the issues were resolved.

28   The firm shall establish policies and procedures on continuing an engagement and the client relationship, addressing the circumstances where the firm obtains information that would have caused it to decline the engagement had that information been available earlier. Such policies and procedures shall include consideration of:

(a) The professional and legal responsibilities that apply to the circumstances, including whether there is a requirement for the firm to report to the person or persons who made the appointment or, in some cases, to regulatory authorities; and

(b) The possibility of withdrawing from the engagement or from both the engagement and the client relationship. (Ref: Para. A22–A23)

Human Resources

The firm shall establish policies and procedures designed to provide it with reason- **29**
able assurance that it has sufficient personnel with the competence, capabilities, and
commitment to ethical principles necessary to:

(a) Perform engagements in accordance with professional standards and applicable
     legal and regulatory requirements; and
(b) Enable the firm or engagement partners to issue reports that are appropriate in
     the circumstances. (Ref: Para. A24–A29)

Assignment of Engagement Teams

The firm shall assign responsibility for each engagement to an engagement partner **30**
and shall establish policies and procedures requiring that:

(a) The identity and role of the engagement partner are communicated to key
     members of client management and those charged with governance;
(b) The engagement partner has the appropriate competence, capabilities, and
     authority to perform the role; and
(c) The responsibilities of the engagement partner are clearly defined and com-
     municated to that partner. (Ref: Para. A30)

The firm shall also establish policies and procedures to assign appropriate personnel **31**
with the necessary competence, and capabilities to:

(a) Perform engagements in accordance with professional standards and applicable
     legal and regulatory requirements; and
(b) Enable the firm or engagement partners to issue reports that are appropriate in
     the circumstances. (Ref: Para. A31)

Engagement Performance

The firm shall establish policies and procedures designed to provide it with reason- **32**
able assurance that engagements are performed in accordance with professional
standards and applicable legal and regulatory requirements, and that the firm or the
engagement partner issue reports that are appropriate in the circumstances. Such
policies and procedures shall include:

(a) Matters relevant to promoting consistency in the quality of engagement per-
     formance; (Ref: Para. A32–A33)
(b) Supervision responsibilities; and (Ref: Para. A34)
(c) Review responsibilities. (Ref: Para. A35)

The firm's review responsibility policies and procedures shall be determined on the **33**
basis that work of less experienced team members is reviewed by more experienced
engagement team members.

Consultation

The firm shall establish policies and procedures designed to provide it with reason- **34**
able assurance that:

(a) Appropriate consultation takes place on difficult or contentious matters;
(b) Sufficient resources are available to enable appropriate consultation to take
     place;

(c) The nature and scope of, and conclusions resulting from, such consultations are documented and are agreed by both the individual seeking consultation and the individual consulted; and

(d) Conclusions resulting from consultations are implemented. (Ref: Para. A36–A40)

Engagement Quality Control Review

35 The firm shall establish policies and procedures requiring, for appropriate engagements, an engagement quality control review that provides an objective evaluation of the significant judgments made by the engagement team and the conclusions reached in formulating the report. Such policies and procedures shall:

(a) Require an engagement quality control review for all audits of financial statements of listed entities;

(b) Set out criteria against which all other audits and reviews of historical financial information and other assurance and related services engagements shall be evaluated to determine whether an engagement quality control review should be performed; and (Ref: Para. A41)

(c) Require an engagement quality control review for all engagements, if any, meeting the criteria established in compliance with subparagraph 35(b).

36 The firm shall establish policies and procedures setting out the nature, timing and extent of an engagement quality control review. Such policies and procedures shall require that the engagement report not be dated until the completion of the engagement quality control review. (Ref: Para. A42–A43)

37 The firm shall establish policies and procedures to require the engagement quality control review to include:

(a) Discussion of significant matters with the engagement partner;

(b) Review of the financial statements or other subject matter information and the proposed report;

(c) Review of selected engagement documentation relating to significant judgments the engagement team made and the conclusions it reached; and

(d) Evaluation of the conclusions reached in formulating the report and consideration of whether the proposed report is appropriate. (Ref: Para. A44)

38 For audits of financial statements of listed entities, the firm shall establish policies and procedures to require the engagement quality control review to also include consideration of the following:

(a) The engagement team's evaluation of the firm's independence in relation to the specific engagement;

(b) Whether appropriate consultation has taken place on matters involving differences of opinion or other difficult or contentious matters, and the conclusions arising from those consultations; and

(c) Whether documentation selected for review reflects the work performed in relation to the significant judgments and supports the conclusions reached. (Ref: Para. A45–A46)

Criteria for the Eligibility of Engagement Quality Control Reviewers

39 The firm shall establish policies and procedures to address the appointment of engagement quality control reviewers and establish their eligibility through:

(a) The technical qualifications required to perform the role, including the necessary experience and authority; and (Ref: Para. A47)
(b) The degree to which an engagement quality control reviewer can be consulted on the engagement without compromising the reviewer's objectivity. (Ref: Para. A48)

The firm shall establish policies and procedures designed to maintain the objectivity **40** of the engagement quality control reviewer. (Ref: Para. A49–A51)

The firm's policies and procedures shall provide for the replacement of the engage- **41** ment quality control reviewer where the reviewer's ability to perform an objective review may be impaired.

Documentation of the Engagement Quality Control Review

The firm shall establish policies and procedures on documentation of the engagement **42** quality control review which require documentation that:
(a) The procedures required by the firm's policies on engagement quality control review have been performed;
(b) The engagement quality control review has been completed on or before the date of the report; and
(c) The reviewer is not aware of any unresolved matters that would cause the reviewer to believe that the significant judgments the engagement team made and the conclusions it reached were not appropriate.

Differences of Opinion

The firm shall establish policies and procedures for dealing with and resolving dif- **43** ferences of opinion within the engagement team, with those consulted and, where applicable, between the engagement partner and the engagement quality control reviewer. (Ref: Para. A52–A53)

Such policies and procedures shall require that: **44**

(a) Conclusions reached be documented and implemented; and
(b) The report not be dated until the matter is resolved.

Engagement Documentation

Completion of the assembly of final engagement files

The firm shall establish policies and procedures for engagement teams to complete **45** the assembly of final engagement files on a timely basis after the engagement reports have been finalized. (Ref: Para. A54–A55)

Confidentiality, safe custody, integrity, accessibility and retrievability of engagement documentation

The firm shall establish policies and procedures designed to maintain the con- **46** fidentiality, safe custody, integrity, accessibility and retrievability of engagement documentation. (Ref: Para. A56–A59)

Retention of engagement documentation

47   The firm shall establish policies and procedures for the retention of engagement documentation for a period sufficient to meet the needs of the firm or as required by law or regulation. (Ref: Para. A60–A63)

Monitoring

Monitoring the firm's quality control policies and procedures

48   The firm shall establish a monitoring process designed to provide it with reasonable assurance that the policies and procedures relating to the system of quality control are relevant, adequate, and operating effectively. This process shall:

(a)   Include an ongoing consideration and evaluation of the firm's system of quality control including, on a cyclical basis, inspection of at least one completed engagement for each engagement partner;

(b)   Require responsibility for the monitoring process to be assigned to a partner or partners or other persons with sufficient and appropriate experience and authority in the firm to assume that responsibility; and

(c)   Require that those performing the engagement or the engagement quality control review are not involved in inspecting the engagement. (Ref: Para. A64–A68)

Evaluating, Communicating and Remedying Identified Deficiencies

49   The firm shall evaluate the effect of deficiencies noted as a result of the monitoring process and determine whether they are either:

(a)   Instances that do not necessarily indicate that the firm's system of quality control is insufficient to provide it with reasonable assurance that it complies with professional standards and applicable legal and regulatory requirements, and that the reports issued by the firm or engagement partners are appropriate in the circumstances; or

(b)   Systemic, repetitive or other significant deficiencies that require prompt corrective action.

50   The firm shall communicate to relevant engagement partners and other appropriate personnel deficiencies noted as a result of the monitoring process and recommendations for appropriate remedial action. (Ref: Para. A69)

51   Recommendations for appropriate remedial actions for deficiencies noted shall include one or more of the following:

(a)   Taking appropriate remedial action in relation to an individual engagement or member of personnel;

(b)   The communication of the findings to those responsible for training and professional development;

(c)   Changes to the quality control policies and procedures; and

(d)   Disciplinary action against those who fail to comply with the policies and procedures of the firm, especially those who do so repeatedly.

52   The firm shall establish policies and procedures to address cases where the results of the monitoring procedures indicate that a report may be inappropriate or that procedures were omitted during the performance of the engagement. Such policies and procedures shall require the firm to determine what further action is appropriate to comply with relevant professional standards and applicable legal and regulatory requirements and to consider whether to obtain legal advice.

The firm shall communicate at least annually the results of the monitoring of its system of quality control to engagement partners and other appropriate individuals within the firm, including the firm's chief executive officer or, if appropriate, its managing board of partners. This communication shall be sufficient to enable the firm and these individuals to take prompt and appropriate action where necessary in accordance with their defined roles and responsibilities. Information communicated shall include the following:　　**53**

(a) A description of the monitoring procedures performed.
(b) The conclusions drawn from the monitoring procedures.
(c) Where relevant, a description of systemic, repetitive or other significant deficiencies and of the actions taken to resolve or amend those deficiencies.

Some firms operate as part of a network and, for consistency, may implement some of their monitoring procedures on a network basis. Where firms within a network operate under common monitoring policies and procedures designed to comply with this ISQC, and these firms place reliance on such a monitoring system, the firm's policies and procedures shall require that:　　**54**

(a) At least annually, the network communicate the overall scope, extent and results of the monitoring process to appropriate individuals within the network firms; and
(b) The network communicate promptly any identified deficiencies in the system of quality control to appropriate individuals within the relevant network firm or firms so that the necessary action can be taken,

in order that engagement partners in the network firms can rely on the results of the monitoring process implemented within the network, unless the firms or the network advise otherwise.

Complaints and Allegations

The firm shall establish policies and procedures designed to provide it with reasonable assurance that it deals appropriately with:　　**55**

(a) Complaints and allegations that the work performed by the firm fails to comply with professional standards and applicable legal and regulatory requirements; and
(b) Allegations of non-compliance with the firm's system of quality control.

As part of this process, the firm shall establish clearly defined channels for firm personnel to raise any concerns in a manner that enables them to come forward without fear of reprisals. (Ref: Para. A70)

If during the investigations into complaints and allegations, deficiencies in the design or operation of the firm's quality control policies and procedures or non-compliance with the firm's system of quality control by an individual or individuals are identified, the firm shall take appropriate actions as set out in paragraph 51. (Ref: Para. A71–A72)　　**56**

Documentation of the System of Quality Control

57   The firm shall establish policies and procedures requiring appropriate documentation to provide evidence of the operation of each element of its system of quality control. (Ref: Para. A73–A75)

58   The firm shall establish policies and procedures that require retention of documentation for a period of time sufficient to permit those performing monitoring procedures to evaluate the firm's compliance with its system of quality control, or for a longer period if required by law or regulation.

59   The firm shall establish policies and procedures requiring documentation of complaints and allegations and the responses to them.

***

Application and Other Explanatory Material

Applying, and Complying with, Relevant Requirements

Considerations Specific to Smaller Firms (Ref: Para. 14)

A1   This ISQC does not call for compliance with requirements that are not relevant, for example, in the circumstances of a sole practitioner with no staff. Requirements in this ISQC such as those for policies and procedures for the assignment of appropriate personnel to the engagement team (see paragraph 31), for review responsibilities (see paragraph 33), and for the annual communication of the results of monitoring to engagement partners within the firm (see paragraph 53) are not relevant in the absence of staff.

Elements of a System of Quality Control (Ref: Para. 17)

A2   In general, communication of quality control policies and procedures to firm personnel includes a description of the quality control policies and procedures and the objectives they are designed to achieve, and the message that each individual has a personal responsibility for quality and is expected to comply with these policies and procedures. Encouraging firm personnel to communicate their views or concerns on quality control matters recognizes the importance of obtaining feedback on the firm's system of quality control.

Considerations Specific to Smaller Firms

A3   Documentation and communication of policies and procedures for smaller firms may be less formal and extensive than for larger firms.

Leadership Responsibilities for Quality within the Firm

Promoting an Internal Culture of Quality (Ref: Para. 18)

A4   The firm's leadership and the examples it sets significantly influence the internal culture of the firm. The promotion of a quality-oriented internal culture depends on clear, consistent and frequent actions and messages from all levels of the firm's management that emphasize the firm's quality control policies and procedures, and the requirement to:

(a) perform work that complies with professional standards and applicable legal and regulatory requirements; and
(b) issue reports that are appropriate in the circumstances.

Such actions and messages encourage a culture that recognizes and rewards high quality work. These actions and messages may be communicated by, but are not limited to, training seminars, meetings, formal or informal dialogue, mission statements, newsletters, or briefing memoranda. They may be incorporated in the firm's internal documentation and training materials, and in partner and staff appraisal procedures such that they will support and reinforce the firm's view on the importance of quality and how, practically, it is to be achieved.

Of particular importance in promoting an internal culture based on quality is the need for the firm's leadership to recognize that the firm's business strategy is subject to the overriding requirement for the firm to achieve quality in all the engagements that the firm performs. Promoting such an internal culture includes: **A5**

(a) Establishment of policies and procedures that address performance evaluation, compensation, and promotion (including incentive systems) with regard to its personnel, in order to demonstrate the firm's overriding commitment to quality;
(b) Assignment of management responsibilities so that commercial considerations do not override the quality of work performed; and
(c) Provision of sufficient resources for the development, documentation and support of its quality control policies and procedures.

Assigning Operational Responsibility for the Firm's System of Quality Control (Ref: Para. 19)

Sufficient and appropriate experience and ability enables the person or persons responsible for the firm's system of quality control to identify and understand quality control issues and to develop appropriate policies and procedures. Necessary authority enables the person or persons to implement those policies and procedures. **A6**

Relevant Ethical Requirements

Compliance with Relevant Ethical Requirements (Ref: Para. 20)

The IESBA Code establishes the fundamental principles of professional ethics, which include: **A7**

(a) Integrity;
(b) Objectivity;
(c) Professional competence and due care;
(d) Confidentiality; and
(e) Professional behavior.

Part B of the IESBA Code illustrates how the conceptual framework is to be applied in specific situations. It provides examples of safeguards that may be appropriate to address threats to compliance with the fundamental principles and also provides examples of situations where safeguards are not available to address the threats. **A8**

The fundamental principles are reinforced in particular by: **A9**

- The leadership of the firm;

- Education and training;
- Monitoring; and
- A process for dealing with non-compliance.

Definition of "Firm," "Network" and "Network Firm" (Ref: Para. 20–25)

A10   The definitions of "firm," network" or "network firm" in relevant ethical requirements may differ from those set out in this ISQC. For example, the IESBA Code
defines the "firm" as:

(a) A sole practitioner, partnership or corporation of professional accountants;
(b) An entity that controls such parties through ownership, management or other
means; and
(c) An entity controlled by such parties through ownership, management or other
means.

The IESBA Code also provides guidance in relation to the terms "network" and
"network firm."

In complying with the requirements in paragraphs 20–25, the definitions used in the
relevant ethical requirements apply in so far as is necessary to interpret those ethical
requirements.

Written Confirmation (Ref: Para. 24)

A11   Written confirmation may be in paper or electronic form. By obtaining confirmation
and taking appropriate action on information indicating non-compliance, the firm
demonstrates the importance that it attaches to independence and makes the issue
current for, and visible to, its personnel.

Familiarity Threat (Ref: Para. 25)

A12   The IESBA Code discusses the familiarity threat that may be created by using the
same senior personnel on an assurance engagement over a long period of time and
the safeguards that might be appropriate to address such threats.

A13   Determining appropriate criteria to address familiarity threat may include matters
such as:

- The nature of the engagement, including the extent to which it involves a matter
of public interest; and
- The length of service of the senior personnel on the engagement.

Examples of safeguards include rotating the senior personnel or requiring an
engagement quality control review.

A14   The IESBA Code recognizes that the familiarity threat is particularly relevant in the
context of financial statement audits of listed entities. For these audits, the IESBA
Code requires the rotation of the key audit partner[3] after a pre-defined period,
normally no more than seven years, and provides related standards and guidance.
National requirements may establish shorter rotation periods.

---

[3] *As defined in the IESBA Code.*

Considerations specific to public sector audit organizations

Statutory measures may provide safeguards for the independence of public sector auditors. However, threats to independence may still exist regardless of any statutory measures designed to protect it. Therefore, in establishing the policies and procedures required by paragraphs 20–25, the public sector auditor may have regard to the public sector mandate and address any threats to independence in that context.   **A15**

Listed entities as referred to in paragraphs 25 and A14 are not common in the public sector. However, there may be other public sector entities that are significant due to size, complexity or public interest aspects, and which consequently have a wide range of stakeholders. Therefore, there may be instances when a firm determines, based on its quality control policies and procedures, that a public sector entity is significant for the purposes of expanded quality control procedures.   **A16**

In the public sector, legislation may establish the appointments and terms of office of the auditor with engagement partner responsibility. As a result, it may not be possible to comply strictly with the engagement partner rotation requirements envisaged for listed entities. Nonetheless, for public sector entities considered significant, as noted in paragraph A16, it may be in the public interest for public sector audit organizations to establish policies and procedures to promote compliance with the spirit of rotation of engagement partner responsibility.   **A17**

Acceptance and Continuance of Client Relationships and Specific Engagements

Competence, Capabilities, and Resources (Ref: Para. 26(a))

Consideration of whether the firm has the competence, capabilities, and resources to undertake a new engagement from a new or an existing client involves reviewing the specific requirements of the engagement and the existing partner and staff profiles at all relevant levels, and including whether: **A18**

- Firm personnel have knowledge of relevant industries or subject matters;
- Firm personnel have experience with relevant regulatory or reporting requirements, or the ability to gain the necessary skills and knowledge effectively;
- The firm has sufficient personnel with the necessary competence and capabilities;
- Experts are available, if needed;
- Individuals meeting the criteria and eligibility requirements to perform engagement quality control review are available, where applicable; and
- The firm is able to complete the engagement within the reporting deadline.

Integrity of Client (Ref: Para. 26(c))

With regard to the integrity of a client, matters to consider include, for example: **A19**

- The identity and business reputation of the client's principal owners, key management, and those charged with its governance.
- The nature of the client's operations, including its business practices.
- Information concerning the attitude of the client's principal owners, key management and those charged with its governance towards such matters as aggressive interpretation of accounting standards and the internal control environment.
- Whether the client is aggressively concerned with maintaining the firm's fees as low as possible.

- Indications of an inappropriate limitation in the scope of work.
- Indications that the client might be involved in money laundering or other criminal activities.
- The reasons for the proposed appointment of the firm and non-reappointment of the previous firm.
- The identity and business reputation of related parties.

The extent of knowledge a firm will have regarding the integrity of a client will generally grow within the context of an ongoing relationship with that client.

A20   Sources of information on such matters obtained by the firm may include the following:

- Communications with existing or previous providers of professional accountancy services to the client in accordance with relevant ethical requirements, and discussions with other third parties.
- Inquiry of other firm personnel or third parties such as bankers, legal counsel and industry peers.
- Background searches of relevant databases.

Continuance of Client Relationship (Ref: Para. 27(a))

A21   Deciding whether to continue a client relationship includes consideration of significant matters that have arisen during the current or previous engagements, and their implications for continuing the relationship. For example, a client may have started to expand its business operations into an area where the firm does not possess the necessary expertise.

Withdrawal (Ref: Para. 28)

A22   Policies and procedures on withdrawal from an engagement or from both the engagement and the client relationship address issues that include the following:

- Discussing with the appropriate level of the client's management and those charged with its governance the appropriate action that the firm might take based on the relevant facts and circumstances.
- If the firm determines that it is appropriate to withdraw, discussing with the appropriate level of the client's management and those charged with its governance withdrawal from the engagement or from both the engagement and the client relationship, and the reasons for the withdrawal.
- Considering whether there is a professional, legal or regulatory requirement for the firm to remain in place, or for the firm to report the withdrawal from the engagement, or from both the engagement and the client relationship, together with the reasons for the withdrawal, to regulatory authorities.
- Documenting significant matters, consultations, conclusions and the basis for the conclusions.

Considerations Specific to Public Sector Audit Organizations (Ref: Para. 26–28)

A23   In the public sector, auditors may be appointed in accordance with statutory procedures. Accordingly, certain of the requirements and considerations regarding the acceptance and continuance of client relationships and specific engagements as set out paragraphs 26–28 and A18–A22 may not be relevant. Nonetheless, establishing policies and procedures as described may provide valuable information to public sector auditors in performing risk assessments and in carrying out reporting responsibilities.

Human Resources (Ref: Para. 29)

Personnel issues relevant to the firm's policies and procedures related to human resources include, for example: **A24**

- Recruitment.
- Performance evaluation.
- Capabilities, including time to perform assignments.
- Competence.
- Career development.
- Promotion.
- Compensation.
- The estimation of personnel needs.

Effective recruitment processes and procedures help the firm select individuals of integrity who have the capacity to develop the competence and capabilities necessary to perform the firm's work and possess the appropriate characteristics to enable them to perform competently.

Competence can be developed through a variety of methods, including the following: **A25**

- Professional education.
- Continuing professional development, including training.
- Work experience.
- Coaching by more experienced staff, for example, other members of the engagement team.
- Independence education for personnel who are required to be independent.

The continuing competence of the firm's personnel depends to a significant extent on an appropriate level of continuing professional development so that personnel maintain their knowledge and capabilities. Effective policies and procedures emphasize the need for continuing training for all levels of firm personnel, and provide the necessary training resources and assistance to enable personnel to develop and maintain the required competence and capabilities. **A26**

The firm may use a suitably qualified external person, for example, when internal technical and training resources are unavailable. **A27**

Performance evaluation, compensation and promotion procedures give due recognition and reward to the development and maintenance of competence and commitment to ethical principles. Steps a firm may take in developing and maintaining competence and commitment to ethical principles include: **A28**

- Making personnel aware of the firm's expectations regarding performance and ethical principles;
- Providing personnel with evaluation of, and counseling on, performance, progress and career development; and
- Helping personnel understand that advancement to positions of greater responsibility depends, among other things, upon performance quality and adherence to ethical principles, and that failure to comply with the firm's policies and procedures may result in disciplinary action.

Considerations Specific to Smaller Firms

A29   The size and circumstances of the firm will influence the structure of the firm's performance evaluation process. Smaller firms, in particular, may employ less formal methods of evaluating the performance of their personnel.

Assignment of Engagement Teams

Engagement Partners (Ref: Para. 30)

A30   Policies and procedures may include systems to monitor the workload and availability of engagement partners so as to enable these individuals to have sufficient time to adequately discharge their responsibilities.

Engagement Teams (Ref: Para. 31)

A31   The firm's assignment of engagement teams and the determination of the level of supervision required, include for example, consideration of the engagement team's:

- Understanding of, and practical experience with, engagements of a similar nature and complexity through appropriate training and participation;
- Understanding of professional standards and applicable legal and regulatory requirements;
- Technical knowledge and expertise, including knowledge of relevant information technology;
- Knowledge of relevant industries in which the clients operate;
- Ability to apply professional judgment; and
- Understanding of the firm's quality control policies and procedures.

Engagement Performance

Consistency in the Quality of Engagement Performance (Ref: Para. 32(a))

A32   The firm promotes consistency in the quality of engagement performance through its policies and procedures. This is often accomplished through written or electronic manuals, software tools or other forms of standardized documentation, and industry or subject matter-specific guidance materials. Matters addressed may include:

- How engagement teams are briefed on the engagement to obtain an understanding of the objectives of their work.
- Processes for complying with applicable engagement standards.
- Processes of engagement supervision, staff training and coaching.
- Methods of reviewing the work performed, the significant judgments made and the form of report being issued.
- Appropriate documentation of the work performed and of the timing and extent of the review.
- Processes to keep all policies and procedures current.

A33   Appropriate teamwork and training assist less experienced members of the engagement team to clearly understand the objectives of the assigned work.

Supervision (Ref: Para. 32(b))

A34   Engagement supervision includes the following:

- Tracking the progress of the engagement;
- Considering the competence and capabilities of individual members of the engagement team, whether they have sufficient time to carry out their work, whether they understand their instructions and whether the work is being carried out in accordance with the planned approach to the engagement;
- Addressing significant matters arising during the engagement, considering their significance and modifying the planned approach appropriately; and
- Identifying matters for consultation or consideration by more experienced engagement team members during the engagement.

Review (Ref: Para. 32(c))

A review consits of consideration of whether: **A35**

- The work has been performed in accordance with professional standards and applicable legal and regulatory requirements;
- Significant matters have been raised for further consideration;
- Appropriate consultations have taken place and the resulting conclusions have been documented and implemented;
- There is a need to revise the nature, timing and extent of work performed;
- The work performed supports the conclusions reached and is appropriately documented;
- The evidence obtained is sufficient and appropriate to support the report; and
- The objectives of the engagement procedures have been achieved.

Consultation (Ref: Para. 34)

Consultation includes discussion at the appropriate professional level, with indivi- **A36**
duals within or outside the firm who have specialized expertise.

Consultation uses appropriate research resources as well as the collective experience   **A37**
and technical expertise of the firm. Consultation helps to promote quality and improves the application of professional judgment. Appropriate recognition of consultation in the firm's policies and procedures helps to promote a culture in which consultation is recognized as a strength and encourages personnel to consult on difficult or contentious matters.

Effective consultation on significant technical, ethical and other matters within the   **A38**
firm or, where applicable, outside the firm can be achieved when those consulted:

- Are given all the relevant facts that will enable them to provide informed advice; and
- Have appropriate knowledge, seniority and experience,

and when conclusions resulting from consultations are appropriately documented and implemented.

Documentation of consultations with other professionals that involve difficult or   **A39**
contentious matters that is sufficiently complete and detailed contributes to an understanding of:

- The issue on which consultation was sought; and
- The results of the consultation, including any decisions taken, the basis for those decisions and how they were implemented.

Considerations Specific to Smaller Firms

A40   A firm needing to consult externally, for example, a firm without appropriate internal resources, may take advantage of advisory services provided by:

- Other firms;
- Professional and regulatory bodies; or
- Commercial organizations that provide relevant quality control services.

Before contracting for such services, consideration of the competence and capabilities of the external provider helps the firm to determine whether the external provider is suitably qualified for that purpose.

Engagement Quality Control Review

Criteria for an Engagement Quality Control Review (Ref: Para. 35(b))

A41   Criteria for determining which engagements, other than audits of financial statements of listed entities, are to be subject to an engagement quality control review may include, for example:

- The nature of the engagement, including the extent to which it involves a matter of public interest.
- The identification of unusual circumstances or risks in an engagement or class of engagements.
- Whether laws or regulations require an engagement quality control review.

Nature, Timing and Extent of the Engagement Quality Control Review (Ref: Para. 36–37)

A42   The engagement report is not dated until the completion of the engagement quality control review. However, documentation of the engagement quality control review may be completed after the date of the report.

A43   Conducting the engagement quality control review in a timely manner at appropriate stages during the engagement allows significant matters to be promptly resolved to the engagement quality control reviewer's satisfaction on or before the date of the report.

A44   The extent of the engagement quality control review may depend, among other things, on the complexity of the engagement, whether the entity is a listed entity, and the risk that the report might not be appropriate in the circumstances. The performance of an engagement quality control review does not reduce the responsibilities of the engagement partner.

Engagement Quality Control Review of a Listed Entity (Ref: Para. 38)

A45   Other matters relevant to evaluating the significant judgments made by the engagement team that may be considered in an engagement quality control review of an audit of financial statements of a listed entity include:

- Significant risks identified during the engagement and the responses to those risks.
- Judgments made, particularly with respect to materiality and significant risks.
- The significance and disposition of corrected and uncorrected misstatements identified during the engagement.

- The matters to be communicated to management and those charged with governance and, where applicable, other parties such as regulatory bodies.

These other matters, depending on the circumstances, may also be applicable for engagement quality control reviews for audits of the financial statements of other entities as well as reviews of financial statements and other assurance and related services engagements.

Considerations specific to public sector audit organizations

Although not referred to as listed entities, as described in paragraph A16, certain public sector entities may be of sufficient significance to warrant performance of an engagement quality control review.   **A46**

Criteria for the Eligibility of Engagement Quality Control Reviewers

Sufficient and Appropriate Technical Expertise, Experience and Authority (Ref: Para. 39(a))

What constitutes sufficient and appropriate technical expertise, experience and authority depends on the circumstances of the engagement. For example, the engagement quality control reviewer for an audit of the financial statements of a listed entity is likely to be an individual with sufficient and appropriate experience and authority to act as an audit engagement partner on audits of financial statements of listed entities.   **A47**

Consultation with the Engagement Quality Control Reviewer (Ref: Para. 39(b))

The engagement partner may consult the engagement quality control reviewer during the engagement, for example, to establish that a judgment made by the engagement partner will be acceptable to the engagement quality control reviewer. Such consultation avoids identification of differences of opinion at a late stage of the engagement and need not compromise the engagement quality control reviewer's eligibility to perform the role. Where the nature and extent of the consultations become significant the reviewer's objectivity may be compromised unless care is taken by both the engagement team and the reviewer to maintain the reviewer's objectivity. Where this is not possible, another individual within the firm or a suitably qualified external person may be appointed to take on the role of either the engagement quality control reviewer or the person to be consulted on the engagement.   **A48**

Objectivity of the Engagement Quality Control Reviewer (Ref: Para. 40)

The firm is required to establish policies and procedures designed to maintain objectivity of the engagement quality control reviewer. Accordingly, such policies and procedures provide that the engagement quality control reviewer: **A49**

- Where practicable, is not selected by the engagement partner;
- Does not otherwise participate in the engagement during the period of review;
- Does not make decisions for the engagement team; and
- Is not subject to other considerations that would threaten the reviewer's objectivity.

Considerations specific to smaller firms

A50   It may not be practicable, in the case of firms with few partners, for the engagement partner not to be involved in selecting the engagement quality control reviewer. Suitably qualified external persons may be contracted where sole practitioners or small firms identify engagements requiring engagement quality control reviews. Alternatively, some sole practitioners or small firms may wish to use other firms to facilitate engagement quality control reviews. Where the firm contracts suitably qualified external persons, the requirements in paragraphs 39–41 and guidance in paragraphs A47–A48 apply.

Considerations specific to public sector audit organizations

A51   In the public sector, a statutorily appointed auditor (for example, an Auditor General, or other suitably qualified person appointed on behalf of the Auditor General) may act in a role equivalent to that of engagement partner with overall responsibility for public sector audits. In such circumstances, where applicable, the selection of the engagement quality control reviewer includes consideration of the need for independence from the audited entity and the ability of the engagement quality control reviewer to provide an objective evaluation.

Differences of Opinion (Ref: Para. 43)

A52   Effective procedures encourage identification of differences of opinion at an early stage, provide clear guidelines as to the successive steps to be taken thereafter, and require documentation regarding the resolution of the differences and the implementation of the conclusions reached.

A53   Procedures to resolve such differences may include consulting with another practitioner or firm, or a professional or regulatory body.

Engagement Documentation

Completion of the Assembly of Final Engagement Files (Ref: Para. 45)

A54   Law or regulation may prescribe the time limits by which the assembly of final engagement files for specific types of engagement is to be completed. Where no such time limits are prescribed in law or regulation, paragraph 45 requires the firm to establish time limits that reflect the need to complete the assembly of final engagement files on a timely basis. In the case of an audit, for example, such a time limit would ordinarily not be more than 60 days after the date of the auditor's report.

A55   Where two or more different reports are issued in respect of the same subject matter information of an entity, the firm's policies and procedures relating to time limits for the assembly of final engagement files address each report as if it were for a separate engagement. This may, for example, be the case when the firm issues an auditor's report on a component's financial information for group consolidation purposes and, at a subsequent date, an auditor's report on the same financial information for statutory purposes.

Confidentiality, Safe Custody, Integrity, Accessibility and Retrievability of
Engagement Documentation (Ref: Para. 46)

Relevant ethical requirements establish an obligation for the firm's personnel to **A56**
observe at all times the confidentiality of information contained in engagement
documentation, unless specific client authority has been given to disclose information, or there is a legal or professional duty to do so. Specific laws or regulations may
impose additional obligations on the firm's personnel to maintain client confidentiality, particularly where data of a personal nature are concerned.

Whether engagement documentation is in paper, electronic or other media, the **A57**
integrity, accessibility or retrievability of the underlying data may be compromised if
the documentation could be altered, added to or deleted without the firm's knowledge, or if it could be permanently lost or damaged. Accordingly, controls that the
firm designs and implements to avoid unauthorized alteration or loss of engagement
documentation may include those that:

- Enable the determination of when and by whom engagement documentation
  was created, changed or reviewed;
- Protect the integrity of the information at all stages of the engagement, especially when the information is shared within the engagement team or
  transmitted to other parties via the Internet;
- Prevent unauthorized changes to the engagement documentation; and
- Allow access to the engagement documentation by the engagement team and
  other authorized parties as necessary to properly discharge their responsibilities.

Controls that the firm designs and implements to maintain the confidentiality, safe **A58**
custody, integrity, accessibility and retrievability of engagement documentation may
include the following:

- The use of a password among engagement team members to restrict access to
  electronic engagement documentation to authorized users.
- Appropriate back-up routines for electronic engagement documentation at
  appropriate stages during the engagement.
- Procedures for properly distributing engagement documentation to the team
  members at the start of the engagement, processing it during engagement, and
  collating it at the end of engagement.
- Procedures for restricting access to, and enabling proper distribution and confidential storage of, hardcopy engagement documentation.

For practical reasons, original paper documentation may be electronically scanned **A59**
for inclusion in engagement files. In such cases, the firm's procedures designed to
maintain the integrity, accessibility, and retrievability of the documentation may
include requiring the engagement teams to:

- Generate scanned copies that reflect the entire content of the original paper
  documentation, including manual signatures, cross-references and annotations;
- Integrate the scanned copies into the engagement files, including indexing and
  signing off on the scanned copies as necessary; and
- Enable the scanned copies to be retrieved and printed as necessary.

There may be legal, regulatory or other reasons for a firm to retain original paper
documentation that has been scanned.

Retention of Engagement Documentation (Ref: Para. 47)

A60   The needs of the firm for retention of engagement documentation, and the period of such retention, will vary with the nature of the engagement and the firm's circumstances, for example, whether the engagement documentation is needed to provide a record of matters of continuing significance to future engagements. The retention period may also depend on other factors, such as whether local law or regulation prescribes specific retention periods for certain types of engagements, or whether there are generally accepted retention periods in the jurisdiction in the absence of specific legal or regulatory requirements.

A61   In the specific case of audit engagements, the retention period would ordinarily be no shorter than five years from the date of the auditor's report, or, if later, the date of the group auditor's report.

A62   Procedures that the firm adopts for retention of engagement documentation include those that enable the requirements of paragraph 47 to be met during the retention period, for example to:

- Enable the retrieval of, and access to, the engagement documentation during the retention period, particularly in the case of electronic documentation since the underlying technology may be upgraded or changed over time;
- Provide, where necessary, a record of changes made to engagement documentation after the engagement files have been completed; and
- Enable authorized external parties to access and review specific engagement documentation for quality control or other purposes.

Ownership of engagement documentation

A63   Unless otherwise specified by law or regulation, engagement documentation is the property of the firm. The firm may, at its discretion, make portions of, or extracts from, engagement documentation available to clients, provided such disclosure does not undermine the validity of the work performed, or, in the case of assurance engagements, the independence of the firm or its personnel.

Monitoring

Monitoring the Firm's Quality Control Policies and Procedures (Ref: Para. 48)

A64   The purpose of monitoring compliance with quality control policies and procedures is to provide an evaluation of:

- Adherence to professional standards and applicable legal and regulatory requirements;
- Whether the system of quality control has been appropriately designed and effectively implemented; and
- Whether the firm's quality control policies and procedures have been appropriately applied, so that reports that are issued by the firm or engagement partners are appropriate in the circumstances.

A65   Ongoing consideration and evaluation of the system of quality control include matters such as the following:

- Analysis of:

- o New developments in professional standards and applicable legal and regulatory requirements, and how they are reflected in the firm's policies and procedures where appropriate;
- o Written confirmation of compliance with policies and procedures on independence;
- o Continuing professional development, including training; and
- o Decisions related to acceptance and continuance of client relationships and specific engagements.
- Determination of corrective actions to be taken and improvements to be made in the system, including the provision of feedback into the firm's policies and procedures relating to education and training.
- Communication to appropriate firm personnel of weaknesses identified in the system, in the level of understanding of the system, or compliance with it.
- Follow-up by appropriate firm personnel so that necessary modifications are promptly made to the quality control policies and procedures.

Inspection cycle policies and procedures may, for example, specify a cycle that spans three years. The manner in which the inspection cycle is organized, including the timing of selection of individual engagements, depends on many factors, such as the following: **A66**

- The size of the firm.
- The number and geographic location of offices.
- The results of previous monitoring procedures.
- The degree of authority both personnel and offices have (for example, whether individual offices are authorized to conduct their own inspections or whether only the head office may conduct them).
- The nature and complexity of the firm's practice and organization.
- The risks associated with the firm's clients and specific engagements.

The inspection process includes the selection of individual engagements, some of which may be selected without prior notification to the engagement team. In determining the scope of the inspections, the firm may take into account the scope or conclusions of an independent external inspection program. However, an independent external inspection program does not act as a substitute for the firm's own internal monitoring program.   **A67**

Considerations Specific to Smaller Firms

In the case of small firms, monitoring procedures may need to be performed by individuals who are responsible for design and implementation of the firm's quality control policies and procedures, or who may be involved in performing the engagement quality control review. A firm with a limited number of persons may choose to use a suitably qualified external person or another firm to carry out engagement inspections and other monitoring procedures. Alternatively, the firm may establish arrangements to share resources with other appropriate organizations to facilitate monitoring activities.   **A68**

Communicating Deficiencies (Ref: Para. 50)

The reporting of identified deficiencies to individuals other than the relevant engagement partners need not include an identification of the specific engagements concerned, although there may be cases where such identification may be necessary for the proper discharge of the responsibilities of the individuals other than the engagement partners.   **A69**

Complaints and Allegations

Source of Complaints and Allegations (Ref: Para. 55)

A70   Complaints and allegations (which do not include those that are clearly frivolous) may originate from within or outside the firm. They may be made by firm personnel, clients or other third parties. They may be received by engagement team members or other firm personnel.

Investigation Policies and Procedures (Ref: Para. 56)

A71   Policies and procedures established for the investigation of complaints and allegations may include for example, that the partner supervising the investigation:

*   Has sufficient and appropriate experience;
*   Has authority within the firm; and
*   Is otherwise not involved in the engagement.

The partner supervising the investigation may involve legal counsel as necessary.

Considerations specific to smaller firms

A72   It may not be practicable, in the case of firms with few partners, for the partner supervising the investigation not to be involved in the engagement. These small firms and sole practitioners may use the services of a suitably qualified external person or another firm to carry out the investigation into complaints and allegations.

Documentation of the System of Quality Control (Ref: Para. 57)

A73   The form and content of documentation evidencing the operation of each of the elements of the system of quality control is a matter of judgment and depends on a number of factors, including the following:

*   The size of the firm and the number of offices.
*   The nature and complexity of the firm's practice and organization.

For example, large firms may use electronic databases to document matters such as independence confirmations, performance evaluations and the results of monitoring inspections.

A74   Appropriate documentation relating to monitoring includes, for example:

*   Monitoring procedures, including the procedure for selecting completed engagements to be inspected.
*   A record of the evaluation of:
    o   Adherence to professional standards and applicable legal and regulatory requirements;
    o   Whether the system of quality control has been appropriately designed and effectively implemented; and
    o   Whether the firm's quality control policies and procedures have been appropriately applied, so that reports that are issued by the firm or engagement partners are appropriate in the circumstances.
*   Identification of the deficiencies noted, an evaluation of their effect, and the basis for determining whether and what further action is necessary.

Considerations Specific to Smaller Firms

Smaller firms may use more informal methods in the documentation of their systems   **A75**
of quality control such as manual notes, checklists and forms.

Part Eight

Other Guidance

Bulletin 2010/2 (Revised)
Compendium of illustrative auditor's reports on United Kingdom private sector financial statements for periods ended on or after 15 December 2010

(revised and updated March 2012)

Contents

CLEAN AUDITOR'S OPINIONS

COMPANIES (excluding charitable companies)

Appendix 2   Group and parent company financial statements reported on in a single auditor's report

5.   *Non-publicly traded group preparing financial statements under UK GAAP*
6.   *Non-publicly traded group preparing financial statements under IFRSs as adopted by the European Union (may apply to a group admitted to trading on AIM)*
7.   *Publicly traded standard listed group – Parent company financial statement prepared under UK GAAP and Corporate Governance Statement not included in directors' report*
8.   *Publicly traded premium listed group – Parent company financial statements prepared under IFRSs as adopted by the European Union*

Appendix 3   Group financial statements reported on separately from the parent company financial statements

9.   *Publicly traded premium listed group – Auditor's report on group financial statements prepared under IFRSs as adopted by the European Union*

Appendix 4   Parent company financial statements reported on separately from the group financial statements

10. *Publicly traded group – Auditor's report on parent company financial statements prepared under UK GAAP*
11. *Publicly traded group – Auditor's report on parent company financial statements prepared under IFRSs as adopted by the European Union*

EMPHASIS OF MATTER PARAGRAPHS

Appendix 5

12. *Emphasis of matter – Material uncertainty that may cast significant doubt about the company's ability to continue as a going concern*
13. *Emphasis of matter – Uncertain outcome of a lawsuit*

PARTNERSHIPS

Appendix 6

14. *Limited Liability Partnership preparing financial statements under UK GAAP*
15. *Limited Liability Partnership preparing financial statements under IFRSs as adopted by the EU*
16. *Qualifying Partnership preparing financial statements under UK GAAP*

REGULATED ENTITIES OTHER THAN CHARITIES

Appendix 7   Insurers

17. *Publicly traded insurer with a standard listing preparing financial statements under UK GAAP and having equalisation provisions*
18. *Lloyd's syndicate – annual financial statements*
19. *Lloyd's syndicate – underwriting year accounts – closed year of account*
20. *Lloyd's syndicate – underwriting year accounts – run-off year of account*
21. *Non directive friendly society with no subsidiary companies, preparing financial statements under UK GAAP*
22. *Directive friendly society group preparing financial statements under UK GAAP*

Appendix 8   Banking institutions that are not companies

23. *Building society preparing financial statements under UK GAAP*
24. *Building society preparing financial statements under IFRSs as adopted by the European Union*

Introduction

1   This Bulletin is a compendium of illustrative auditor's reports applicable to United Kingdom private sector financial statements for periods ended on or after 23 March 2011[1]. The auditor's reports support and illustrate the requirements of ISAs (UK and Ireland) 700 "The auditor's report on financial statements", 705 "Modifications to the opinion in the independent auditor's report" and 706 "Emphasis of matter paragraphs and other matter paragraphs in the independent auditor's report"[2]. They also support the requirements of the law and regulations applicable to the particular type of entity to which the illustration applies.

Description of the "scope of the audit"

2   Paragraph 16 of ISA (UK and Ireland) 700 requires:

The auditor's report shall either:

(a)   **Cross refer to a "Statement of the Scope of an Audit" that is maintained on the APB's website; or**

(b)   **Cross refer to a " Statement of the Scope of an Audit" that is included elsewhere within the Annual Report; or**

(c)   **Include the following description of the scope of an audit.**

"An audit involves obtaining evidence about the amounts and disclosures in the financial statements sufficient to give reasonable assurance that the financial statements are free from material misstatement, whether caused by fraud or error. This includes an assessment of: whether the accounting policies are appropriate to the *[describe nature of entity]* circumstances and have been consistently applied and adequately disclosed; the reasonableness of significant accounting estimates made by *[describe those charged with governance]*; and the overall presentation of the financial statements. In addition, we read all the financial and non-financial information in the *[describe the annual report]* to identify material inconsistencies with the audited financial statements. If we become aware of any apparent material misstatements or inconsistencies we consider the implications for our report."[3]

3   In the illustrative auditor's reports in this Bulletin these alternatives are shown by means of two text boxes. The alternative shown by the first text box is the wording that is used when the auditor's report cross refers to a Statement of the Scope of an Audit maintained on the APB's website, or included elsewhere within the Annual Report. The alternative shown by the second text box is the wording that must be used if the description of the Scope of an Audit is included within the auditor's report.

4   With effect for financial statements ended on or after 15 December 2010 the Statement of the Scope of an Audit maintained on the APB website has been revised such

---

[1] *The APB publishes a bulletin of illustrative auditor's reports applicable to the UK public sector and a bulletin of illustrative auditor's reports applicable to the private sector in the Republic of Ireland.*

[2] *The relevant versions of ISAs (UK and Ireland) 700, 705 and 706 are those published in the APB's Compendium of Auditing Standards 2010 and subsequent revisions thereto.*

[3] ~~At the time of writing the APB is consulting on a proposal to revise this wording through the inclusion of an additional paragraph. If, following consultation, the change is made it will be effective for auditor's reports for periods ending on or after 23 March 2011.~~

that a single statement can be used with respect to the auditor's reports of all private sector entities. It can be found on the APB's website at www.frc.org.uk/apb/scope/private.cfm.

Classifications of companies

Company law and the Listing Rules classify companies in a number of different ways and these various classifications affect the content of the auditor's report applicable to a particular company.   5

Publicly traded and non-publicly traded

The primary classification distinguishes between: 6

(a) "publicly traded companies" – defined as "those whose securities are admitted to trading on a regulated market in any Member State in the European Union"; and

(b) "non-publicly traded companies" – defined as "those who do not have any securities that are admitted to trading on a regulated market in any Member State in the European Union" (EU).

Under Article 4 of the IAS Regulation[4], publicly traded companies governed by the law of a Member State are <u>required</u> to prepare their consolidated accounts on the basis of accounting standards issued by the International Accounting Standards Board (IASB) that are adopted by the EU[5]. In CA 2006 such accounts are referred to as "IAS accounts" whereas in the auditor's reports in this Bulletin this framework is referred to as "IFRSs as adopted by the European Union"[6].   7

Article 4 does not apply to a publicly traded company that is not required to prepare consolidated accounts.   8

In the UK (as permitted under Article 5 of the IAS Regulation) the use of IAS accounts has been extended so that: 9

● Publicly traded companies are <u>permitted</u> to use IAS in their individual accounts (this is discussed further in paragraphs 21 to 25 of this Bulletin);

● Non publicly traded companies are <u>permitted </u> to use IAS in both their individual and consolidated accounts; and

● Building societies[7], limited liability partnerships, and certain banking, insurance undertakings and partnerships (to which Part 15 of CA 2006 applies), are <u>permitted</u> to use IAS.

---

[4] *Regulation (EC) No. 1606/2002 of the European Parliament and of the Council of 19 July 2002 on the application of international accounting standards.*

[5] *This requirement has been effected into UK law by virtue of section 403(1) of CA 2006*

[6] *For companies that apply the requirements of applicable UK law and United Kingdom Accounting Standards the financial reporting framework is described as UK Generally Accepted Accounting Practice (UK GAAP).*

[7] *Building societies which prepare consolidated accounts and have securities admitted to trading on a regulated market are required by Article 4 of the IAS Regulation to prepare IAS accounts.*

10   In the UK, CA 2006 does not permit charities to use IAS[8]. In addition charities do not fall within the ambit of Article 4 of the IAS Regulation as non-profit making bodies are specifically excluded.

11   For the purposes of the auditor's report a further implication of being a publicly traded company is that such companies are required to include a Corporate Governance Statement in their annual report. The requirements relating to the content of the Corporate Governance Statement are set out in section 7.2 of the Disclosure and Transparency Rules of the Financial Services Authority (FSA).

12   If the Corporate Governance Statement is not included in the directors' report the Companies Act 2006 (CA 2006) imposes specific reporting responsibilities on the auditor with respect to the Statement. Guidance on the auditor's responsibilities with respect to the Corporate Governance Statement is set out more fully in Bulletin 2009/4. Example 7 illustrates how the auditor is required to report in this circumstance.

Companies subject to the small companies regime

13   Under section 381 of CA 2006, the small companies' regime for accounts applies to a company for a financial year in relation to which the company qualifies as small and is not excluded from the regime. An auditor's report applicable to a company to which the small companies' regime applies is illustrated in example 1.

Quoted companies

14   CA 2006 also classifies companies as being either quoted or unquoted. For the purposes of the auditor's report the implication of being a quoted company is that the company has to prepare a directors' remuneration report and the auditor has to report on certain aspects of it. The definition of "quoted company" for the purposes of the Directors' Remuneration Report is set out in sections 385(1) and 385(2) of CA 2006.

15   The definition of a quoted company differs from that of a publicly traded company. A publicly traded company may not necessarily meet the definition of a quoted company and a non-publicly traded company may be a quoted company. However, for the purposes of the illustrative examples in this Bulletin it is assumed that non-publicly traded companies are not quoted companies and that publicly traded companies are quoted companies. Guidance on the auditor's responsibilities with respect to the Directors' Remuneration Report is set out in Bulletin 2002/2. Examples 3, 4, 7, 8, 10 and 11 illustrate the reporting requirements in respect of the Directors' Remuneration Report.

Listed companies

16   A company that is listed on the Official List maintained by the United Kingdom Listing Authority (UKLA) will either have a Premium or a Standard Listing for each listed security. For the purposes of the auditor's report having a Standard Listing does not give rise to additional requirements over that of a non-traded company with respect to the content of the auditor's report. However, Standard Listed companies are required to meet the requirements for a corporate governance statement as described in paragraph 11 above. As discussed in paragraph 12 there are implications

---

[8] *See sections 395(2) and 403(3) of CA 2006.*

be deleted when the shaded text is included (i.e. the struck out text is included in the auditor's report when the company excludes the profit and loss account from the parent company financial statements). Charitable company groups can also take advantage of the section 408 exemption. In examples 31 and 34 the alternatives are illustrated by the use of square brackets.

Opinion in respect of an additional financial reporting framework

The financial statements of some companies may comply with two financial **29** reporting frameworks (for example IFRSs as adopted by the European Union and IFRSs as issued by the IASB) and those charged with governance may engage the auditor to express an opinion in respect of both frameworks.

ISA (UK and Ireland) 700 (Revised) requires that the second opinion should be **30** clearly separated from the first opinion on the financial statements by use of an appropriate heading. This is illustrated in examples 4, 6, 7, 9 8 and 24[13].

Emphasis of matter paragraphs

An emphasis of matter paragraph refers to a matter that is appropriately presented **31** or disclosed in the financial statements that, in the auditor's judgment, is of such importance that it is fundamental to a user's understanding of the financial statements. When the auditor includes an emphasis of matter paragraph ISA (UK and Ireland) 706 requires the auditor to indicate in its report that the auditor's opinion is not modified in respect of the matter emphasized.

Example of emphasis of matter paragraphs are set out in Appendix 5. These **32** examples have been drafted in the context of auditor's reports on the financial statements of a company. However, the examples can be tailored for use in the auditor's reports of all entities.

Other matter paragraphs

An other matter paragraph refers to a matter other than those presented or disclosed **33** in the financial statement that, in the auditor's judgment, is relevant to a user's understanding of the audit, the auditor's responsibilities or the auditor's report.

Examples 9, 10 and 11 illustrate how an other matter paragraph is included in the **34** auditor's report.

Regulated entities

Further APB guidance with respect to the auditor's reports on the financial state- **35** ments of regulated entities is set out in the following Practice Notes:

---

[13] *The wording used in these examples is illustrative to reflect the requirement of the Securities and Exchange Commission of the USA whose Final Rule "Acceptance From Foreign Private Issuers of Financial Statements Prepared in Accordance With International Financial Reporting Standards Without Reconciliation to US GAAP (4 January 2008) states "...the independent auditor must opine in its report on whether those financial statements comply with IFRS as issued by the IASB. ...the auditor's report can include this language in addition to any opinion relating to compliance with standards required by the home country".*

PN No.	Title	Appendices in this Bulletin
11	The Audit of Charities in the United Kingdom	10, 11 and 12
14	The Audit of Registered Social Landlords in the United Kingdom	9 (example 28)
15	The Audit of Occupational Pension Schemes in the United Kingdom	9 (example 27)
19	The Audit of Banks and Building Societies in the United Kingdom	8 (examples 23 and 24)
20	The Audit of Insurers in the United Kingdom	7 (examples 17 to 20)
24	The Audit of Friendly Societies in the United Kingdom	7 (examples 21 and 22)
27	The Audit of Credit Unions in the United Kingdom	8 (examples 25 and 26)

36   These Practice Notes also contain illustrative examples of auditor's reports that arise from the requirements of regulations and which, therefore, are not required to follow the reporting requirements of ISAs (UK and Ireland).

Modifying the auditor's opinion on the financial statements

37   An auditor's opinion on financial statements is considered to be modified in the following situations.

(a) Qualified opinion arising from either a disagreement or a scope limitation (Illustrative
examples set out in Appendix 13);

(b) Adverse opinion (Illustrative examples set out in Appendix 14); and

(c) Disclaimer of opinion (Illustrative examples set out in Appendix 15).

Modifying the auditor's opinion on the directors' report

38   Section 496 of CA 2006 requires the auditor to state in its report on the company's annual accounts whether in its opinion the information given in the directors' report for the financial year for which the accounts are prepared is consistent with those accounts. The example report in Appendix 16 illustrates a modified opinion on the consistency of the directors' report with the annual accounts.

Illustrative directors' responsibilities statement

39   Example 47 in Appendix 17 is an illustrative example of a Directors' Responsibilities Statement for a non-publicly traded company preparing its parent company financial statements under UK GAAP. Illustrative examples of Directors' Responsibilities Statements for publicly traded companies are not provided as the directors' responsibilities will vary dependent on the rules of the market on which a company's securities are admitted to trading.

Appendix 1 – Company does not prepare group financial statements

1. Non-publicly traded company preparing financial statements under the FRSSE
2. Non-publicly traded company preparing financial statements under UK GAAP
3. Publicly traded standard listed company preparing financial statements under UK
   GAAP
4. Publicly traded premium listed company preparing financial statements under
   IFRSs as adopted by the European Union

Example 1 – Non-publicly traded company preparing financial statements under the FRSSE

- *Company qualifies as a small company.*
- *Company does not prepare group financial statements.*

INDEPENDENT AUDITOR'S REPORT TO THE MEMBERS OF XYZ LIMITED

We have audited the financial statements of (name of company) for the year ended ... which comprise [specify the titles of the primary statements such as the Profit and Loss Account, the Balance Sheet, the Cash Flow Statement, the Statement of Total Recognised Gains and Losses, the Reconciliation of Movements in Shareholders' Funds] and the related notes[14]. The financial reporting framework that has been applied in their preparation is applicable law and the Financial Reporting Standard for Smaller Entities [(Effective April 2008)][15] (United Kingdom Generally Accepted Accounting Practice applicable to Smaller Entities).

Respective responsibilities of directors and auditor

As explained more fully in the Directors' Responsibilities Statement [set out [on page ...]], the directors are responsible for the preparation of the financial statements and for being satisfied that they give a true and fair view. Our responsibility is to audit and express an opinion on the financial statements in accordance with applicable law and International Standards on Auditing (UK and Ireland). Those standards require us to comply with the Auditing Practices Board's [(APB's)] Ethical Standards for Auditors[, including "APB Ethical Standard – Provisions Available for Small Entities (Revised)", in the circumstances set out in note [x] to the financial statements][16].

Scope of the audit of the financial statements

Either:

A description of the scope of an audit of financial statements is [provided on the APB's website at www.frc.org.uk/apb/scope/private.cfm] / [set out [on page ...] of the Annual Report].

Or:

An audit involves obtaining evidence about the amounts and disclosures in the financial statements sufficient to give reasonable assurance that the financial statements are free from material misstatement, whether caused by fraud or error.

[14] *Auditor's reports of entities that do not publish their financial statements on a website or publish them using 'PDF' format may refer to the financial statements by reference to page numbers.*

[15] *Specify the version of The Financial Reporting Standard for Smaller Entities.*

[16] *Delete the words in square brackets if the relief and exemptions provided by ES PASE are not utilised. Paragraph 22 of ES PASE requires disclosure in the auditor's report where the audit firm has taken advantage of an exemption provided by ES PASE. The Appendix to ES PASE provides illustrative disclosures of relevant circumstances where the audit firm has taken advantage of an exemption provided by ES PASE.*

This includes an assessment of: whether the accounting policies are appropriate to the company's circumstances and have been consistently applied and adequately disclosed; the reasonableness of significant accounting estimates made by the directors; and the overall presentation of the financial statements. In addition, we read all the financial and non-financial information in the *[describe the annual report]* to identify material inconsistencies with the audited financial statements. If we become aware of any apparent material misstatements or inconsistencies we consider the implications for our report.

Opinion on financial statements

In our opinion the financial statements:

- give a true and fair view of the state of the company's affairs as at .... and of its profit [loss] for the year then ended[17];
- have been properly prepared in accordance with United Kingdom Generally Accepted Accounting Practice applicable to Smaller Entities; and
- have been prepared in accordance with the requirements of the Companies Act 2006.

Opinion on other matter prescribed by the Companies Act 2006

In our opinion the information given in the Directors' Report for the financial year for which the financial statements are prepared is consistent with the financial statements.[17]

Matters on which we are required to report by exception

We have nothing to report in respect of the following matters where the Companies Act 2006 requires us to report to you if, in our opinion:

- adequate accounting records have not been kept, or returns adequate for our audit have not been received from branches not visited by us; or
- the financial statements are not in agreement with the accounting records and returns; or
- certain disclosures of directors' remuneration specified by law are not made; or
- we have not received all the information and explanations we require for our audit; or
- the directors were not entitled to [prepare the financial statements in accordance with the small companies regime] [and] [take advantage of the small companies' exemption in preparing the directors' report].

[Signature]	*Address*
John Smith *(Senior statutory auditor)*	*Date*
for and on behalf of ABC LLP, Statutory Auditor	

---

[17] *Guidance for auditors when a company takes advantage of the option in section 444(1) of CA 2006 not to file the profit and loss account or the directors' report is set out in paragraph 12 of APB Bulletin 2008/4 "The Special Auditor's Report on Abbreviated Accounts in the United Kingdom".*

Example 2 – Non-publicly traded company preparing financial statements under UK GAAP

- Company is not a quoted company.
- Company either does not qualify as a small company or qualifies as a small company but chooses not to prepare its financial statements in accordance with the FRSSE.
- Company does not prepare group financial statements.

INDEPENDENT AUDITOR'S REPORT TO THE MEMBERS OF XYZ LIMITED/PLC

We have audited the financial statements of (name of company) for the year ended ... which comprise [specify the titles of the primary statements such as the Profit and Loss Account, the Balance Sheet, the Cash Flow Statement, the Statement of Total Recognised Gains and Losses, the Reconciliation of Movements in Shareholders' Funds] and the related notes[18]. The financial reporting framework that has been applied in their preparation is applicable law and United Kingdom Accounting Standards (United Kingdom Generally Accepted Accounting Practice).

Respective responsibilities of directors and auditor

As explained more fully in the Directors' Responsibilities Statement [set out [on page ...]], the directors are responsible for the preparation of the financial statements and for being satisfied that they give a true and fair view. Our responsibility is to audit and express an opinion on the financial statements in accordance with applicable law and International Standards on Auditing (UK and Ireland). Those standards require us to comply with the Auditing Practices Board's [(APB's)] Ethical Standards for Auditors.

Scope of the audit of the financial statements

Either:

A description of the scope of an audit of financial statements is [provided on the APB's website at www.frc.org.uk/apb/scope/private.cfm] / [set out [on page ...] of the Annual Report].

Or:

An audit involves obtaining evidence about the amounts and disclosures in the financial statements sufficient to give reasonable assurance that the financial statements are free from material misstatement, whether caused by fraud or error. This includes an assessment of: whether the accounting policies are appropriate to the company's circumstances and have been consistently applied and adequately disclosed; the reasonableness of significant accounting estimates made by the directors; and the overall presentation of the financial statements. In addition, we read all the financial and non-financial information in the *[describe the annual report]* to identify material inconsistencies with the audited financial statements.

---

[18] *Auditor's reports of entities that do not publish their financial statements on a website or publish them using 'PDF' format may refer to the financial statements by reference to page numbers.*

> If we become aware of any apparent material misstatements or inconsistencies we consider the implications for our report.

Opinion on financial statements

In our opinion the financial statements:

- give a true and fair view of the state of the company's affairs as at .... and of its profit [loss] for the year then ended;
- have been properly prepared in accordance with United Kingdom Generally Accepted Accounting Practice; and
- have been prepared in accordance with the requirements of the Companies Act 2006.

Opinion on other matter prescribed by the Companies Act 2006

In our opinion the information given in the Directors' Report for the financial year for which the financial statements are prepared is consistent with the financial statements.

Matters on which we are required to report by exception

We have nothing to report in respect of the following matters where the Companies Act 2006 requires us to report to you if, in our opinion:

- adequate accounting records have not been kept, or returns adequate for our audit have not been received from branches not visited by us; or
- the financial statements are not in agreement with the accounting records and returns; or
- certain disclosures of directors' remuneration specified by law are not made; or
- we have not received all the information and explanations we require for our audit.

[Signature]   Address
John Smith (Senior statutory auditor)   Date
for and on behalf of ABC LLP, Statutory Auditor

Example 3 – Publicly traded standard listed company preparing financial statements under UK GAAP

- Company is a quoted company and has a standard listing.
- Company does not prepare group financial statements.
- Corporate governance statement incorporated into the directors' report, either directly or by incorporation by reference as explained in APB Bulletin 2009/4 (see example 7 for an illustration of an auditor's report where the corporate governance statement is not incorporated into the directors' report).

INDEPENDENT AUDITOR'S REPORT TO THE MEMBERS OF XYZ PLC

We have audited the financial statements of (name of company) for the year ended ... which comprise [specify the titles of the primary statements such as the Profit and Loss Account, the Balance Sheet, the Cash Flow Statement, the Statement of Total Recognised Gains and Losses, the Reconciliation of Movements in Shareholders' Funds] and the related notes[19]. The financial reporting framework that has been applied in their preparation is applicable law and United Kingdom Accounting Standards (United Kingdom Generally Accepted Accounting Practice).

Respective responsibilities of directors and auditor

As explained more fully in the Directors' Responsibilities Statement [set out [on page ...]], the directors are responsible for the preparation of the financial statements and for being satisfied that they give a true and fair view. Our responsibility is to audit and express an opinion on the financial statements in accordance with applicable law and International Standards on Auditing (UK and Ireland). Those standards require us to comply with the Auditing Practices Board's [(APB's)] Ethical Standards for Auditors.

Scope of the audit of the financial statements

Either:

A description of the scope of an audit of financial statements is [provided on the APB's website at www.frc.org.uk/apb/scope/private.cfm] / [set out [on page ...] of the Annual Report].

Or:

An audit involves obtaining evidence about the amounts and disclosures in the financial statements sufficient to give reasonable assurance that the financial statements are free from material misstatement, whether caused by fraud or error. This includes an assessment of: whether the accounting policies are appropriate to the company's circumstances and have been consistently applied and adequately disclosed; the reasonableness of significant accounting estimates made by the directors; and the overall presentation of the financial statements. In addition, we read all the financial and non-financial information in the *[describe the annual*

---

[19] *Auditor's reports of entities that do not publish their financial statements on a website or publish them using 'PDF' format may refer to the financial statements by reference to page numbers.*

report] to identify material inconsistencies with the audited financial statements. If we become aware of any apparent material misstatements or inconsistencies we consider the implications for our report.

Opinion on financial statements

In our opinion the financial statements:

- give a true and fair view of the state of the company's affairs as at .... and of its profit [loss] for the year then ended;
- have been properly prepared in accordance with United Kingdom Generally Accepted Accounting Practice; and
- have been prepared in accordance with the requirements of the Companies Act 2006.

Opinion on other matters prescribed by the Companies Act 2006

In our opinion:

- the part of the Directors' Remuneration Report to be audited has been properly prepared in accordance with the Companies Act 2006[20]; and
- the information given in the Directors' Report for the financial year for which the financial statements are prepared is consistent with the financial statements.

Matters on which we are required to report by exception

We have nothing to report in respect of the following matters where the Companies Act 2006 requires us to report to you if, in our opinion:

- adequate accounting records have not been kept, or returns adequate for our audit have not been received from branches not visited by us; or
- the financial statements and the part of the Directors' Remuneration Report to be audited are not in agreement with the accounting records and returns; or
- certain disclosures of directors' remuneration specified by law are not made; or
- we have not received all the information and explanations we require for our audit.

[Signature]   *Address*
John Smith *(Senior statutory auditor)*   *Date*
for and on behalf of ABC LLP, Statutory Auditor

---

[20] *Part 3 of Schedule 8 to the Large and Medium-sized Companies and Groups (Accounts and Reports) Regulations 2008 (SI 2008 No. 410) sets out the information in the Directors' Remuneration Report that is subject to audit. Companies should describe clearly within the Directors' Remuneration Report which disclosures have been audited.*

Example 4 – Publicly traded premium listed company preparing financial statements under IFRSs as adopted by the European Union

- Company is a quoted company and has a premium listing.
- Company does not prepare group financial statements.
- Corporate governance statement incorporated into the directors' report, either directly or by incorporation by reference as explained in APB Bulletin 2009/4 (see example 7 for an illustration of an auditor's report where the corporate governance statement is not incorporated into the directors' report).

INDEPENDENT AUDITOR'S REPORT TO THE MEMBERS OF XYZ PLC

We have audited the financial statements of (name of company) for the year ended ... which comprise [specify the titles of the primary statements such as the Statement of Financial Position, the Statement of Comprehensive Income, the Statement of Cash Flows, the Statement of Changes in Equity[21]] and the related notes[22]. The financial reporting framework that has been applied in their preparation is applicable law and International Financial Reporting Standards (IFRSs) as adopted by the European Union.

Respective responsibilities of directors and auditor

As explained more fully in the Directors' Responsibilities Statement [set out [on page ...]], the directors are responsible for the preparation of the financial statements and for being satisfied that they give a true and fair view. Our responsibility is to audit and express an opinion on the financial statements in accordance with applicable law and International Standards on Auditing (UK and Ireland). Those standards require us to comply with the Auditing Practices Board's [(APB's)] Ethical Standards for Auditors.

Scope of the audit of the financial statements

Either:

> A description of the scope of an audit of financial statements is [provided on the APB's website at www.frc.org.uk/apb/scope/private.cfm] / [set out [on page ...] of the Annual Report].

Or:

> An audit involves obtaining evidence about the amounts and disclosures in the financial statements sufficient to give reasonable assurance that the financial statements are free from material misstatement, whether caused by fraud or error. This includes an assessment of: whether the accounting policies are appropriate to the company's circumstances and have been consistently applied and adequately disclosed; the reasonableness of significant accounting estimates made by

---

[21] *The names used for the primary statements in the auditor's report should reflect the precise titles used by the company for them.*

[22] *Auditor's reports of entities that do not publish their financial statements on a website or publish them using 'PDF' format may refer to the financial statements by reference to page numbers.*

the directors; and the overall presentation of the financial statements. In addition, we read all the financial and non-financial information in the *[describe the annual report]* to identify material inconsistencies with the audited financial statements. If we become aware of any apparent material misstatements or inconsistencies we consider the implications for our report.

Opinion on financial statements

In our opinion the financial statements:

- give a true and fair view of the state of the company's affairs as at .... and of its profit [loss] for the year then ended;
- have been properly prepared in accordance with IFRSs as adopted by the European Union; and
- have been prepared in accordance with the requirements of the Companies Act 2006.

[Separate opinion in relation to IFRSs as issued by the IASB

As explained in note [x] to the financial statements, the company in addition to applying IFRSs as adopted by the European Union, has also applied IFRSs as issued by the International Accounting Standards Board (IASB).

In our opinion the financial statements comply with IFRSs as issued by the IASB.][23]

Opinion on other matters prescribed by the Companies Act 2006

In our opinion:

- the part of the Directors' Remuneration Report to be audited has been properly prepared in accordance with the Companies Act 2006[24]; and
- the information given in the Directors' Report for the financial year for which the financial statements are prepared is consistent with the financial statements.

Matters on which we are required to report by exception

We have nothing to report in respect of the following:

Under the Companies Act 2006 we are required to report to you if, in our opinion:

- adequate accounting records have not been kept, or returns adequate for our audit have not been received from branches not visited by us; or
- the financial statements and the part of the Directors' Remuneration Report to be audited are not in agreement with the accounting records and returns; or
- certain disclosures of directors' remuneration specified by law are not made; or
- we have not received all the information and explanations we require for our audit.

---

[23] *See footnote 12*

[24] *Part 3 of Schedule 8 to the Large and Medium-sized Companies and Groups (Accounts and Reports) Regulations 2008 (SI 2008 No. 410) sets out the information in the Directors' Remuneration Report that is subject to audit. Companies should describe clearly within the Directors' Remuneration Report which disclosures have been audited.*

Under the Listing Rules we are required to review:

- the directors' statement, [set out [on page...]], in relation to going concern;
- the part of the Corporate Governance Statement relating to the company's compliance with the nine provisions of the [June 2008 Combined Code] [UK Corporate Governance Code[25]] specified for our review; and
- certain elements of the report to the shareholders by the Board on directors' remuneration[26].

[Signature]   *Address*
John Smith (Senior statutory auditor)   *Date*
for and on behalf of ABC LLP, Statutory Auditor

---

[25] *The UK Corporate Governance Code was issued in May 2010 and applies to financial years beginning on or after 29 June 2010*

[26] *The report on directors' remuneration should clearly identify those elements that have been audited.*

Appendix 2 – Group and parent company financial statements reported on in a single auditor's report

5. Non-publicly traded group preparing financial statements under UK GAAP
6. Non-publicly traded group preparing financial statements under IFRSs as adopted by
   the European Union (applicable to a company admitted to trading on AIM)
7. Publicly traded standard listed group – Parent company financial statement prepared under UK GAAP and corporate governance statement not incorporated into directors' report
8. Publicly traded premium listed group – Parent company financial statements prepared under IFRSs as adopted by the European Union

Example 5 – Non-publicly traded group preparing financial statements under UK GAAP

- Company is not a quoted company.
- Section 408 exemption taken for parent company's own profit and loss account.
- Company does prepare group financial statements.

INDEPENDENT AUDITOR'S REPORT TO THE MEMBERS OF XYZ LIMITED/PLC

We have audited the financial statements of (name of company) for the year ended ... which comprise [specify the titles of the primary statements such as the Group Profit and Loss Account, the Group and Parent Company Balance Sheets, the Group Cash Flow Statement, the Group Statement of Total Recognised Gains and Losses, the Group and Parent Company Reconciliation of Movements in Shareholders' Funds] and the related notes[27]. The financial reporting framework that has been applied in their preparation is applicable law and United Kingdom Accounting Standards (United Kingdom Generally Accepted Accounting Practice).

Respective responsibilities of directors and auditor

As explained more fully in the Directors' Responsibilities Statement [set out [on pages ...]], the directors are responsible for the preparation of the financial statements and for being satisfied that they give a true and fair view. Our responsibility is to audit and express an opinion on the financial statements in accordance with applicable law and International Standards on Auditing (UK and Ireland). Those standards require us to comply with the Auditing Practices Board's [(APB's)] Ethical Standards for Auditors.

Scope of the audit of the financial statements

Either:

> A description of the scope of an audit of financial statements is [provided on the APB's website at www.frc.org.uk/apb/scope/private.cfm] / [set out [on page ...] of the Annual Report].

Or:

> An audit involves obtaining evidence about the amounts and disclosures in the financial statements sufficient to give reasonable assurance that the financial statements are free from material misstatement, whether caused by fraud or error. This includes an assessment of: whether the accounting policies are appropriate to the group's and the parent company's circumstances and have been consistently applied and adequately disclosed; the reasonableness of significant accounting estimates made by the directors; and the overall presentation of the financial statements. In addition, we read all the financial and non-financial information in the *[describe the annual report]* to identify material inconsistencies

---

[27] *Auditor's reports of entities that do not publish their financial statements on a website or publish them using 'PDF' format may refer to the financial statements by reference to page numbers.*

with the audited financial statements. If we become aware of any apparent material misstatements or inconsistencies we consider the implications for our report.

Opinion on financial statements

In our opinion the financial statements:

- give a true and fair view of the state of the group's and of the parent company's affairs as at .... and of the group's profit [loss] for the year then ended;
- have been properly prepared in accordance with United Kingdom Generally Accepted Accounting Practice; and
- have been prepared in accordance with the requirements of the Companies Act 2006.

Opinion on other matter prescribed by the Companies Act 2006

In our opinion the information given in the Directors' Report for the financial year for which the financial statements are prepared is consistent with the financial statements.

Matters on which we are required to report by exception

We have nothing to report in respect of the following matters where the Companies Act 2006 requires us to report to you if, in our opinion:

- adequate accounting records have not been kept by the parent company, or returns adequate for our audit have not been received from branches not visited by us; or
- the parent company financial statements are not in agreement with the accounting records and returns; or
- certain disclosures of directors' remuneration specified by law are not made; or
- we have not received all the information and explanations we require for our audit.

[Signature]   Address
John Smith (Senior statutory auditor)   Date
for and on behalf of ABC LLP, Statutory Auditor

Example 6 – Non-publicly traded group preparing financial statements under IFRSs as adopted by the European Union

- *Company is not a quoted company.*
- *Shaded text to be included and struck through text omitted, where section 408 exemption not taken in respect of parent company's own profit and loss account.*
- *Company does prepare group financial statements.*

INDEPENDENT AUDITOR'S REPORT TO THE MEMBERS OF XYZ LIMITED/PLC

We have audited the financial statements of (name of company) for the year ended ... which comprise [specify the titles of the primary statements such as the Group and Parent Company Statements of Financial Position, the Group and Parent Company Statements of Comprehensive Income, the Group and Parent Company Statements of Cash Flow, the Group and Parent Company Statements of Changes in Equity] and the related notes[28]. The financial reporting framework that has been applied in their preparation is applicable law and International Financial Reporting Standards (IFRSs) as adopted by the European Union and, as regards the parent company financial statements, as applied in accordance with the provisions of the Companies Act 2006.

Respective responsibilities of directors and auditor

As explained more fully in the Directors' Responsibilities Statement [set out [on pages ...]], the directors are responsible for the preparation of the financial statements and for being satisfied that they give a true and fair view. Our responsibility is to audit and express an opinion on the financial statements in accordance with applicable law and International Standards on Auditing (UK and Ireland). Those standards require us to comply with the Auditing Practices Board's [(APB's)] Ethical Standards for Auditors.

Scope of the audit of the financial statements

Either:

> A description of the scope of an audit of financial statements is [provided on the APB's website at www.frc.org.uk/apb/scope/private.cfm] / [set out [on page ...] of the Annual Report].

Or:

> An audit involves obtaining evidence about the amounts and disclosures in the financial statements sufficient to give reasonable assurance that the financial statements are free from material misstatement, whether caused by fraud or error. This includes an assessment of: whether the accounting policies are appropriate to the group's and the parent company's circumstances and have been consistently applied and adequately disclosed; the reasonableness of significant

---

[28] *Auditor's reports of entities that do not publish their financial statements on a website or publish them using 'PDF' format may refer to the financial statements by reference to page numbers.*

accounting estimates made by the directors; and the overall presentation of the financial statements. In addition, we read all the financial and non-financial information in the *[describe the annual report]* to identify material inconsistencies with the audited financial statements. If we become aware of any apparent material misstatements or inconsistencies we consider the implications for our report.

Opinion on financial statements

In our opinion:

- the financial statements give a true and fair view of the state of the group's and of the parent company's affairs as at .... and of the group's and the parent company's profit [loss] for the year then ended;
- the group financial statements have been properly prepared in accordance with IFRSs as adopted by the European Union; and
- the parent company financial statements have been properly prepared in accordance with IFRSs as adopted by the European Union and as applied in accordance with the provisions of the Companies Act 2006; and
- the financial statements have been prepared in accordance with the requirements of the Companies Act 2006.

[Separate opinion in relation to IFRSs as issued by the IASB

As explained in Note X to the financial statements, the group in addition to applying IFRSs as adopted by the European Union, has also applied IFRSs as issued by the International Accounting Standards Board (IASB).

In our opinion the financial statements comply with IFRSs as issued by the IASB.][29]

Opinion on other matter prescribed by the Companies Act 2006

In our opinion the information given in the Directors' Report for the financial year for which the financial statements are prepared is consistent with the financial statements.

Matters on which we are required to report by exception

We have nothing to report in respect of the following matters where the Companies Act 2006 requires us to report to you if, in our opinion:

- adequate accounting records have not been kept by the parent company, or returns adequate for our audit have not been received from branches not visited by us; or
- the parent company financial statements are not in agreement with the accounting records and returns; or
- certain disclosures of directors' remuneration specified by law are not made; or
- we have not received all the information and explanations we require for our audit.

[Signature]   *Address*
John Smith *(Senior statutory auditor)*   *Date*
for and on behalf of ABC LLP, Statutory Auditor

---

[29] *See footnote 12*

Example 7 – Publicly traded standard listed group – Parent company financial statements prepared under UK GAAP and corporate governance statement not incorporated into directors' report

- Company is a quoted company and has a standard listing.
- Shaded text to be included only where section 408 exemption *not* taken in respect of parent company's own profit and loss account.
- Company does prepare group financial statements.
- Corporate governance statement not incorporated into the directors' report, either directly or by incorporation by reference as explained in APB Bulletin 2009/4 (the underlined text is included in the auditor's report as a consequence of the statement not being incorporated into the directors' report).

INDEPENDENT AUDITOR'S REPORT TO THE MEMBERS OF XYZ PLC

We have audited the financial statements of (name of company) for the year ended ... which comprise [specify the titles of the primary statements such as the Group Statement of Financial Position and Parent Company Balance Sheet, the Group Statement of Comprehensive Income, the Parent Company Profit and Loss Account, the Group Statement of Cash Flows, the Group Statement of Changes in Equity, the Parent Company Statement of Total Recognised Gains and Losses, the Parent Company Reconciliation of Movements in Shareholders' Funds] and the related notes[30]. The financial reporting framework that has been applied in the preparation of the group financial statements is applicable law and International Financial Reporting Standards (IFRSs) as adopted by the European Union. The financial reporting framework that has been applied in the preparation of the parent company financial statements is applicable law and United Kingdom Accounting Standards (United Kingdom Generally Accepted Accounting Practice).

Respective responsibilities of directors and auditor

As explained more fully in the Directors' Responsibilities Statement [set out [on page ...]], the directors are responsible for the preparation of the financial statements and for being satisfied that they give a true and fair view. Our responsibility is to audit and express an opinion on the financial statements in accordance with applicable law and International Standards on Auditing (UK and Ireland). Those standards require us to comply with the Auditing Practices Board's [(APB's)] Ethical Standards for Auditors.

Scope of the audit of the financial statements

Either:

> A description of the scope of an audit of financial statements is [provided on the APB's website at www.frc.org.uk/apb/scope/private.cfm] / [set out [on page ...] of the Annual Report].

---

[30] *Auditor's reports of entities that do not publish their financial statements on a website or publish them using 'PDF' format may refer to the financial statements by reference to page numbers.*

Or:

> An audit involves obtaining evidence about the amounts and disclosures in the financial statements sufficient to give reasonable assurance that the financial statements are free from material misstatement, whether caused by fraud or error. This includes an assessment of: whether the accounting policies are appropriate to the group's and the parent company's circumstances and have been consistently applied and adequately disclosed; the reasonableness of significant accounting estimates made by the directors; and the overall presentation of the financial statements. In addition, we read all the financial and non-financial information in the *[describe the annual report]* to identify material inconsistencies with the audited financial statements. If we become aware of any apparent material misstatements or inconsistencies we consider the implications for our report.

Opinion on financial statements

In our opinion:

- the financial statements give a true and fair view of the state of the group's and of the parent company's affairs as at .... and of the group's and the parent company's profit [loss] for the year then ended;
- the group financial statements have been properly prepared in accordance with IFRSs as adopted by the European Union;
- the parent company financial statements have been properly prepared in accordance with United Kingdom Generally Accepted Accounting Practice; and
- the financial statements have been prepared in accordance with the requirements of the Companies Act 2006; and, as regards the group financial statements, Article 4 of the IAS Regulation.

[Separate opinion in relation to IFRSs as issued by the IASB

As explained in note [x] to the group financial statements, the group in addition to complying with its legal obligation to apply IFRSs as adopted by the European Union, has also applied IFRSs as issued by the International Accounting Standards Board (IASB).

In our opinion the group financial statements comply with IFRSs as issued by the IASB.][31]

Opinion on other matters prescribed by the Companies Act 2006

In our opinion:

- the part of the Directors' Remuneration Report to be audited has been properly prepared in accordance with the Companies Act 2006[32];

---

[31] *See footnote 12*

[32] *Part 3 of Schedule 8 to the Large and Medium-sized Companies and Groups (Accounts and Reports) Regulations 2008 (SI 2008 No. 410) sets out the information in the Directors' Remuneration Report that is subject to audit. Companies should describe clearly within the Directors' Remuneration Report which disclosures have been audited.*

- the information given in the Directors' Report for the financial year for which the financial statements are prepared is consistent with the financial statements:
- the information given in the Corporate Governance Statement set out [on pages] [in *describe document*] [at *include web-address*] with respect to internal control and risk management systems in relation to financial reporting processes and about share capital structures is consistent with the financial statements.

Matters on which we are required to report by exception

We have nothing to report in respect of the following matters where the Companies Act 2006 requires us to report to you if, in our opinion:

- adequate accounting records have not been kept by the parent company, or returns adequate for our audit have not been received from branches not visited by us; or
- the parent company financial statements and the part of the Directors' Remuneration Report to be audited are not in agreement with the accounting records and returns; or
- certain disclosures of directors' remuneration specified by law are not made; or
- we have not received all the information and explanations we require for our audit; or
- a Corporate Governance Statement has not been prepared by the company.

[Signature]   *Address*
John Smith (Senior statutory auditor)   *Date*
for and on behalf of ABC LLP, Statutory Auditor

Example 8 – Publicly traded premium listed group – Parent company financial statements prepared under IFRSs as adopted by the European Union

- Company is a quoted company and has a premium listing.
- Shaded text to be included, and struck through text omitted, where section 408 exemption <u>not</u> taken in respect of parent company's own profit and loss account.
- Company does prepare group financial statements.
- Corporate governance statement incorporated into the directors' report

INDEPENDENT AUDITOR'S REPORT TO THE MEMBERS OF XYZ PLC

We have audited the financial statements of (name of company) for the year ended ... which comprise [specify the titles of the primary statements such as, the Group and Parent Company Statements of Financial Position, the Group and Parent Company Statements of Comprehensive Income, the Group and Parent Company Statements of Cash Flow, the Group and Parent Company Statements of Changes in Equity][33] and the related notes[34]. The financial reporting framework that has been applied in their preparation is applicable law and International Financial Reporting Standards (IFRSs) as adopted by the European Union ~~and, as regards the parent company financial statements, as applied in accordance with the provisions of the Companies Act 2006.~~

Respective responsibilities of directors and auditor

As explained more fully in the Directors' Responsibilities Statement [set out [on page ...]], the directors are responsible for the preparation of the financial statements and for being satisfied that they give a true and fair view. Our responsibility is to audit and express an opinion on the financial statements in accordance with applicable law and International Standards on Auditing (UK and Ireland). Those standards require us to comply with the Auditing Practices Board's [(APB's)] Ethical Standards for Auditors.

Scope of the audit of the financial statements

Either:

A description of the scope of an audit of financial statements is [provided on the APB's website at www.frc.org.uk/apb/scope/private.cfm] / [set out [on page ...] of the Annual Report].

Or:

An audit involves obtaining evidence about the amounts and disclosures in the financial statements sufficient to give reasonable assurance that the financial

---

[33] *The names used for the primary statements in the auditor's report should reflect the precise titles used by the company for them.*

[34] *Auditor's reports of entities that do not publish their financial statements on a website or publish them using 'PDF' format may refer to the financial statements by reference to page numbers.*

statements are free from material misstatement, whether caused by fraud or error. This includes an assessment of: whether the accounting policies are appropriate to the group's and the parent company's circumstances and have been consistently applied and adequately disclosed; the reasonableness of significant accounting estimates made by the directors; and the overall presentation of the financial statements. In addition, we read all the financial and non-financial information in the *[describe the annual report]* to identify material inconsistencies with the audited financial statements. If we become aware of any apparent material misstatements or inconsistencies we consider the implications for our report.

Opinion on financial statements

In our opinion:

- the financial statements give a true and fair view of the state of the group's and of the parent company's affairs as at .... and of the group's and the parent company's profit [loss] for the year then ended;
- the ~~group~~ financial statements have been properly prepared in accordance with IFRSs as adopted by the European Union; and
- ~~the parent company financial statements have been properly prepared in accordance with IFRSs as adopted by the European Union and as applied in accordance with the provisions of the Companies Act 2006; and~~
- the financial statements have been prepared in accordance with the requirements of the Companies Act 2006 and, as regards the group financial statements, Article 4 of the IAS Regulation.

[Separate opinion in relation to IFRSs as issued by the IASB

As explained in note [x] to the group financial statements, the group in addition to complying with its legal obligation to apply IFRSs as adopted by the European Union, has also applied IFRSs as issued by the International Accounting Standards Board (IASB).

In our opinion the group financial statements comply with IFRSs as issued by the IASB.][35]

Opinion on other matters prescribed by the Companies Act 2006

In our opinion:

- the part of the Directors' Remuneration Report to be audited has been properly prepared in accordance with the Companies Act 2006[36]; and
- the information given in the Directors' Report for the financial year for which the financial statements are prepared is consistent with the financial statements.

[35] *See footnote 12*

[36] *Part 3 of Schedule 8 to the Large and Medium-sized Companies and Groups (Accounts and Reports) Regulations 2008 (SI 2008 No. 410) sets out the information in the Directors' Remuneration Report that is subject to audit. Companies should describe clearly within the Directors' Remuneration Report which disclosures have been audited.*

Matters on which we are required to report by exception

We have nothing to report in respect of the following:

Under the Companies Act 2006 we are required to report to you if, in our opinion:

- adequate accounting records have not been kept by the parent company, or returns adequate for our audit have not been received from branches not visited by us; or
- the parent company financial statements and the part of the Directors' Remuneration Report to be audited are not in agreement with the accounting records and returns; or
- certain disclosures of directors' remuneration specified by law are not made; or
- we have not received all the information and explanations we require for our audit.

Under the Listing Rules we are required to review:

- the directors' statement, [set out [on page...]], in relation to going concern;
- the part of the Corporate Governance Statement relating to the company's compliance with the nine provisions of the [June 2008 Combined Code] [UK Corporate Governance Code[37]] specified for our review; and
- certain elements of the report to shareholders by the Board on directors' remuneration[38].

[Signature]   *Address*
John Smith (Senior statutory auditor)   *Date*
for and on behalf of ABC LLP, Statutory Auditor

---

[37] *The UK Corporate Governance Code was issued in May 2010 and applies to financial years beginning on or after 29 June 2010*

[38] *The report on directors' remuneration should clearly identify those elements that have been audited.*

Appendix 3 – Group financial statements reported on separately from the parent company financial statements

9. Publicly traded premium listed group – Auditor's report on group financial statements prepared under IFRSs as adopted by the European Union

Example 9 – Publicly traded premium listed group – Auditor's report on group financial statements prepared under IFRSs as adopted by the European Union

- *Company is a quoted company and has a premium listing.*
- *Corporate governance statement reported on in the auditor's report on the group financial statements and incorporated into the directors' report, either directly or by incorporation by reference as explained in APB Bulletin 2009/4 (see example 7 for an illustration of an auditor's report where the corporate governance statement is not incorporated into the directors' report).*
- *Directors' Remuneration Report reported on in the auditor's report on the parent company financial statements.*
- *Company does prepare group financial statements.*

INDEPENDENT AUDITOR'S REPORT TO THE MEMBERS OF XYZ PLC

We have audited the group financial statements of (name of company) for the year ended ... which comprise [specify the titles of the primary statements such as the Group Statement of Financial Position, the Group Statement of Comprehensive Income, the Group Statement of Cash Flows, the Group Statement of Changes in Equity][39] and the related notes[40]. The financial reporting framework that has been applied in their preparation is applicable law and International Financial Reporting Standards (IFRSs) as adopted by the European Union.

Respective responsibilities of directors and auditor

As explained more fully in the Directors' Responsibilities Statement [set out [on page ...]], the directors are responsible for the preparation of the group financial statements and for being satisfied that they give a true and fair view. Our responsibility is to audit and express an opinion on the group financial statements in accordance with applicable law and International Standards on Auditing (UK and Ireland). Those standards require us to comply with the Auditing Practices Board's [(APB's)] Ethical Standards for Auditors.

Scope of the audit of the financial statements

Either:

> A description of the scope of an audit of financial statements is [provided on the APB's website at www.frc.org.uk/apb/scope/private.cfm] / [set out [on page ...] of the Annual Report].

---

[39] *The names used for the primary statements in the auditor's report should reflect the precise titles used by the company for them.*

[40] *Auditor's reports of entities that do not publish their financial statements on a website or publish them using 'PDF' format may refer to the financial statements by reference to page numbers.*

Or:

> An audit involves obtaining evidence about the amounts and disclosures in the financial statements sufficient to give reasonable assurance that the financial statements are free from material misstatement, whether caused by fraud or error. This includes an assessment of: whether the accounting policies are appropriate to the group's circumstances and have been consistently applied and adequately disclosed; the reasonableness of significant accounting estimates made by the directors; and the overall presentation of the financial statements. In addition, we read all the financial and non-financial information in the *[describe the annual report]* to identify material inconsistencies with the audited financial statements. If we become aware of any apparent material misstatements or inconsistencies we consider the implications for our report.

Opinion on financial statements

In our opinion the group financial statements:

- give a true and fair view of the state of the group's affairs as at .... and of its profit [loss] for the year then ended;
- have been properly prepared in accordance with IFRSs as adopted by the European Union; and
- have been prepared in accordance with the requirements of the Companies Act 2006 and Article 4 of the IAS Regulation.

[Separate opinion in relation to IFRSs as issued by the IASB

As explained in note [x] to the group financial statements, the group in addition to complying with its legal obligation to apply IFRSs as adopted by the European Union, has also applied IFRSs as issued by the International Accounting Standards Board (IASB).

In our opinion the group financial statements comply with IFRSs as issued by the IASB.][41]

Opinion on other matter prescribed by the Companies Act 2006

In our opinion the information given in the Directors' Report for the financial year for which the group financial statements are prepared is consistent with the group financial statements.

Matters on which we are required to report by exception

We have nothing to report in respect of the following:

Under the Companies Act 2006 we are required to report to you if, in our opinion:

- certain disclosures of directors' remuneration specified by law are not made; or
- we have not received all the information and explanations we require for our audit.

[41] *See footnote 12*

Under the Listing Rules we are required to review:

- the directors' statement, [set out [on page...]], in relation to going concern; and
- the part of the Corporate Governance Statement relating to the company's compliance with the nine provisions of the [June 2008 Combined Code] [UK Corporate Governance Code[42]] specified for our review;
- certain elements of the report to shareholders by the Board on directors' remuneration[43].

Other matter

We have reported separately on the parent company financial statements of (name of company) for the year ended ... and on the information in the Directors' Remuneration Report that is described as having been audited. [That report includes an emphasis of matter] [The opinion in that report is (qualified)/(an adverse opinion)/(a disclaimer of opinion)].

[Signature]   *Address*
John Smith (Senior statutory auditor)   *Date*
for and on behalf of ABC LLP, Statutory Auditor

---

[42] *The UK Corporate Governance Code was issued in May 2010 and applies to financial years beginning on or after 29 June 2010*

[43] *The report on directors' remuneration should clearly identify those elements that have been audited.*

Appendix 4 – Parent company financial statements reported on separately from the group financial statements

10. Publicly traded group – Auditor's report on parent company financial statements prepared under UK GAAP
11. Publicly traded group – Auditor's report on parent company financial statements prepared under IFRSs as adopted by the European Union

Example 10 – Publicly traded group – Auditor's report on parent company financial statements prepared under UK GAAP

- *Company is a quoted company and could be either standard or premium listed.*
- *Shaded text to be included only where section 408 exemption <u>not</u> taken in respect of parent company's own profit and loss account.*
- *Corporate Governance Statement incorporated into the directors' report. For premium listed companies the review requirements under the Listing Rules are reported on in the auditor's report on the group financial statements.*
- *Directors' Remuneration Report reported on in the auditor's report on the parent company financial statements*
- *Company does prepare group financial statements.*

INDEPENDENT AUDITOR'S REPORT TO THE MEMBERS OF XYZ PLC

We have audited the parent company financial statements of (name of company) for the year ended ... which comprise [specify the titles of the primary statements such as the Parent Company Balance Sheet, the Parent Company Profit and Loss Account, the Parent Company Statement of Total Recognised Gains and Losses, the Parent Company Reconciliation of Movements in Shareholders' Funds] and the related notes[44]. The financial reporting framework that has been applied in their preparation is applicable law and United Kingdom Accounting Standards (United Kingdom Generally Accepted Accounting Practice).

Respective responsibilities of directors and auditor

As explained more fully in the Directors' Responsibilities Statement [set out [on page ...]], the directors are responsible for the preparation of the parent company financial statements and for being satisfied that they give a true and fair view. Our responsibility is to audit and express an opinion on the parent company financial statements in accordance with applicable law and International Standards on Auditing (UK and Ireland). Those standards require us to comply with the Auditing Practices Board's [(APB's)] Ethical Standards for Auditors.

Scope of the audit of the financial statements

Either:

> A description of the scope of an audit of financial statements is [provided on the APB's website at www.frc.org.uk/apb/scope/private.cfm] / [set out [on page ...] of the Annual Report].

---

[44] *Auditor's reports of entities that do not publish their financial statements on a website or publish them using 'PDF' format may refer to the financial statements by reference to page numbers.*

Or:

An audit involves obtaining evidence about the amounts and disclosures in the financial statements sufficient to give reasonable assurance that the financial statements are free from material misstatement, whether caused by fraud or error. This includes an assessment of: whether the accounting policies are appropriate to the parent company's circumstances and have been consistently applied and adequately disclosed; the reasonableness of significant accounting estimates made by the directors; and the overall presentation of the financial statements. In addition, we read all the financial and non-financial information in the *[describe the annual report]* to identify material inconsistencies with the audited financial statements. If we become aware of any apparent material misstatements or inconsistencies we consider the implications for our report.

Opinion on financial statements

In our opinion the parent company financial statements:

- give a true and fair view of the state of the company's affairs as at .... and of its profit [loss] for the year then ended;
- have been properly prepared in accordance with United Kingdom Generally Accepted Accounting Practice; and
- have been prepared in accordance with the requirements of the Companies Act 2006.

Opinion on other matters prescribed by the Companies Act 2006

In our opinion:

- the part of the Directors' Remuneration Report to be audited has been properly prepared in accordance with the Companies Act 2006[45]; and
- the information given in the Directors' Report for the financial year for which the financial statements are prepared is consistent with the parent company financial statements.

Matters on which we are required to report by exception

We have nothing to report in respect of the following matters where the Companies Act 2006 requires us to report to you if, in our opinion:

- adequate accounting records have not been kept by the parent company, or returns adequate for our audit have not been received from branches not visited by us; or
- the parent company financial statements and the part of the Directors' Remuneration Report to be audited are not in agreement with the accounting records and returns; or
- certain disclosures of directors' remuneration specified by law are not made; or
- we have not received all the information and explanations we require for our audit.

---

[45] *Part 3 of Schedule 8 to the Large and Medium-sized Companies and Groups (Accounts and Reports) Regulations 2008 (SI 2008 No. 410) sets out the information in the Directors' Remuneration Report that is subject to audit. Companies should describe clearly within the Directors' Remuneration Report which disclosures have been audited.*

Other matter

We have reported separately on the group financial statements of (name of company) for the year ended .... [That report includes an emphasis of matter] [The opinion in that report is (qualified)/(an adverse opinion)/(a disclaimer of opinion)].

[Signature]   *Address*
John Smith (Senior statutory auditor)   *Date*
for and on behalf of ABC LLP, Statutory Auditor

Example 11 – Publicly traded group – Auditor's report on parent company financial statements prepared under IFRSs as adopted by the European Union

- Company is a quoted company and could be either standard or premium listed.
- Shaded text to be included, and struck through text omitted, where section 408 exemption not taken in respect of parent company's own profit and loss account.
- Corporate Governance Statement incorporated into the directors' statement. For premium listed companies the review requirements under the Listing Rules are reported on in the auditor's report on the group financial statements.
- Directors' Remuneration Report reported on in the auditor's report on the parent company financial statements.
- Company does prepare group financial statements.

INDEPENDENT AUDITOR'S REPORT TO THE MEMBERS OF XYZ PLC

We have audited the parent company financial statements of (name of company) for the year ended ... which comprise [specify the titles of the primary statements such as the Statement of Financial Position, the Statement of Comprehensive Income, the Statement of Cash Flow, the Statement of Changes in Equity]⁴⁶ and the related notes⁴⁷. The financial reporting framework that has been applied in their preparation is applicable law and International Financial Reporting Standards (IFRSs) as adopted by the European Union and as applied in accordance with the provisions of the Companies Act 2006.

Respective responsibilities of directors and auditor

As explained more fully in the Directors' Responsibilities Statement [set out [on page ...]], the directors are responsible for the preparation of the parent company financial statements and for being satisfied that they give a true and fair view. Our responsibility is to audit and express an opinion on the parent company financial statements in accordance with applicable law and International Standards on Auditing (UK and Ireland). Those standards require us to comply with the Auditing Practices Board's [(APB's)] Ethical Standards for Auditors.

Scope of the audit of the financial statements

Either:

> A description of the scope of an audit of financial statements is [provided on the APB's website at www.frc.org.uk/apb/scope/private.cfm] / [set out [on page ...] of the Annual Report].

---

⁴⁶ *The names used for the primary statements in the auditor's report should reflect the precise titles used by the company for them.*

⁴⁷ *Auditor's reports of entities that do not publish their financial statements on a website or publish them using 'PDF' format may refer to the financial statements by reference to page numbers.*

Or:

An audit involves obtaining evidence about the amounts and disclosures in the financial statements sufficient to give reasonable assurance that the financial statements are free from material misstatement, whether caused by fraud or error. This includes an assessment of: whether the accounting policies are appropriate to the parent company's circumstances and have been consistently applied and adequately disclosed; the reasonableness of significant accounting estimates made by the directors; and the overall presentation of the financial statements. In addition, we read all the financial and non-financial information in the *[describe the annual report]* to identify material inconsistencies with the audited financial statements. If we become aware of any apparent material misstatements or inconsistencies we consider the implications for our report.

Opinion on financial statements

In our opinion the parent company financial statements:

*   give a true and fair view of the state of the company's affairs as at .... and of its profit [loss] for the year then ended;
*   have been properly prepared in accordance with IFRSs as adopted by the European Union ~~and as applied in accordance with the provisions of the Companies Act 2006~~; and
*   have been prepared in accordance with the requirements of the Companies Act 2006.

Opinion on other matters prescribed by the Companies Act 2006

In our opinion:

*   the part of the Directors' Remuneration Report to be audited has been properly prepared in accordance with the Companies Act 2006[48]; and
*   the information given in the Directors' Report for the financial year for which the financial statements are prepared is consistent with the parent company financial statements.

Matters on which we are required to report by exception

We have nothing to report in respect of the following matters where the Companies Act 2006 requires us to report to you if, in our opinion:

*   adequate accounting records have not been kept by the parent company, or returns adequate for our audit have not been received from branches not visited by us; or
*   the parent company financial statements and the part of the Directors' Remuneration Report to be audited are not in agreement with the accounting records and returns; or
*   certain disclosures of directors' remuneration specified by law are not made; or

---

[48] *Part 3 of Schedule 8 to the Large and Medium-sized Companies and Groups (Accounts and Reports) Regulations 2008 (SI 2008 No. 410) sets out the information in the Directors' Remuneration Report that is subject to audit. Companies should describe clearly within the Directors' Remuneration Report which disclosures have been audited.*

- we have not received all the information and explanations we require for our audit.

Other matter

We have reported separately on the group financial statements of (name of company) for the year ended .... [That report includes an emphasis of matter] [The opinion in that report is (qualified)/(an adverse opinion)/(a disclaimer of opinion).]

[Signature]   Address
John Smith (Senior statutory auditor)   Date
for and on behalf of ABC LLP, Statutory Auditor

Appendix 5 – Emphasis of matter paragraphs

12. Emphasis of matter: Material uncertainty that may cast significant doubt about the company's ability to continue as a going concern
13. Emphasis of matter: Uncertain outcome of a lawsuit

Example 12 – Emphasis of matter: Material uncertainty that may cast significant doubt about the company's ability to continue as a going concern

- *UK non-publicly traded company prepares UK GAAP financial statements (Example 2).*
- *The company incurred a net loss of £X during the year ended 31 December 20X1 and, as of that date, the company's current liabilities exceeded its total assets by £Y and it had net current liabilities of £Z.*
- *These conditions, along with other matters set forth in the notes to the financial statements, indicate the existence of a material uncertainty, which may cast significant doubt about the Company's ability to continue as a going concern.*
- *The company makes relevant disclosures in the financial statements including those referred to in paragraphs 18 and 19 of ISA (UK and Ireland) 570 "Going Concern".*
- *The auditor issues an unmodified opinion with an emphasis of matter paragraph describing the situation giving rise to the emphasis of matter and its possible effects on the financial statements, including (where practicable) quantification.*

Extract from auditor's report

...

Opinion on financial statements

In our opinion the financial statements:

- give a true and fair view of the state of the company's affairs as at 31 December 20X1 and of its loss for the year then ended;
- have been properly prepared in accordance with United Kingdom Generally Accepted Accounting Practice; and
- have been prepared in accordance with the requirements of the Companies Act 2006.

Emphasis of matter – Going concern

In forming our opinion on the financial statements, which is not modified, we have considered the adequacy of the disclosure made in note [x] to the financial statements concerning the company's ability to continue as a going concern. The company incurred a net loss of £X during the year ended 31 December 201X and, at that date, the company's current liabilities exceeded its total assets by £Y and it had net current liabilities of £Z. These conditions, along with the other matters explained in note [x] to the financial statements, indicate the existence of a material uncertainty which may cast significant doubt about the company's ability to continue as a going concern. The financial statements do not include the adjustments that would result if the company was unable to continue as a going concern.

Opinion on other matter prescribed by the Companies Act 2006

...

Example 13 – Emphasis of matter: Uncertain outcome of a lawsuit

- *UK non-publicly traded company prepares UK GAAP financial statements (Example 2).*
- *A lawsuit alleges that the company has infringed certain patent rights and claims royalties and punitive damages. The company has filed a counter action, and preliminary hearings and discovery proceedings on both actions are in progress.*
- *The ultimate outcome of the matter cannot presently be determined, and no provision for any liability that may result has been made in the financial statements.*
- *The company makes relevant disclosures in the financial statements.*
- *The auditor issues an unmodified opinion with an emphasis of matter paragraph describing the situation giving rise to the emphasis of matter and its possible effects on the financial statements, including that the effect on the financial statements of the resolution of the uncertainty cannot be quantified.*

Extract from auditor's report

...

Opinion on financial statements

In our opinion the financial statements:

- give a true and fair view of the state of the company's affairs as at ... and of its profit [loss] for the year then ended;
- have been properly prepared in accordance with United Kingdom Generally Accepted Accounting Practice; and
- have been prepared in accordance with the requirements of the Companies Act 2006.

Emphasis of matter – uncertain outcome of a lawsuit

In forming our opinion on the financial statements, which is not modified, we have considered the adequacy of the disclosures made in note [x] to the financial statements concerning the uncertain outcome of a lawsuit, alleging infringement of certain patent rights and claiming royalties and punitive damages, where the company is the defendant. The company has filed a counter action, and preliminary hearings and discovery proceedings on both actions are in progress. The ultimate outcome of the matter cannot presently be determined, and no provision for any liability that may result has been made in the financial statements.

Opinion on other matter prescribed by the Companies Act 2006

...

Appendix 6 – Partnerships

Example 14 – Limited liability partnership[49] preparing financial statements under UK GAAP

- The limited liability partnership does not prepare group financial statements.

INDEPENDENT AUDITOR'S REPORT TO THE MEMBERS OF XYZ LLP

We have audited the financial statements of (name of limited liability partnership) for the year ended ... which comprise [specify the titles of the primary statements such as the Balance Sheet, the Profit and Loss Account, the Cash Flow Statement, the Statement of Total Recognised Gains and Losses] and the related notes[50]. The financial reporting framework that has been applied in their preparation is applicable law and United Kingdom Accounting Standards (United Kingdom Generally Accepted Accounting Practice).

Respective responsibilities of members and auditor

As explained more fully in the Members' Responsibilities Statement [set out [on page ...]], the members are responsible for the preparation of the financial statements and for being satisfied that they give a true and fair view. Our responsibility is to audit and express an opinion on the financial statements in accordance with applicable law and International Standards on Auditing (UK and Ireland). Those standards require us to comply with the Auditing Practices Board's [(APB's)] Ethical Standards for Auditors.

Scope of the audit of the financial statements

Either:

> A description of the scope of an audit of financial statements is [provided on the APB's website at www.frc.org.uk/apb/scope/private.cfm] / [set out [on page ...] of the Annual Report].

Or:

> An audit involves obtaining evidence about the amounts and disclosures in the financial statements sufficient to give reasonable assurance that the financial statements are free from material misstatement, whether caused by fraud or error. This includes an assessment of: whether the accounting policies are appropriate to the limited liability partnership's circumstances and have been consistently applied and adequately disclosed; the reasonableness of significant accounting estimates made by the designated members; and the overall presentation of the financial statements. In addition, we read all the financial and non-financial information in the *[describe the annual report]* to identify material inconsistencies

---

[49] *Regulations relevant to audit reports of limited liability partnerships are set out in Statutory Instrument 2008 No. 1911 "The Limited Liability Partnerships (Accounts and Audit) (Application of Companies act 2006) Regulations 2008".*

[50] *Auditor's reports of entities that do not publish their financial statements on a website or publish them using 'PDF' format may refer to the financial statements by reference to page numbers.*

with the audited financial statements. If we become aware of any apparent material misstatements or inconsistencies we consider the implications for our report.

Opinion on financial statements

In our opinion the financial statements:

- give a true and fair view of the state of the limited liability partnership's affairs as at ... and of its profit [loss] for the year then ended;
- have been properly prepared in accordance with United Kingdom Generally Accepted Accounting Practice; and
- have been prepared in accordance with the requirements of the Companies Act 2006 as applied to limited liability partnerships by the Limited Liability Partnerships (Accounts and Audit) (Application of Companies Act 2006) Regulations 2008.

Matters on which we are required to report by exception

We have nothing to report in respect of the following matters where the Companies Act 2006 as applied to limited liability partnerships requires us to report to you if, in our opinion:

- adequate accounting records have not been kept, or returns adequate for our audit have not been received from branches not visited by us; or
- the financial statements are not in agreement with the accounting records and returns; or
- we have not received all the information and explanations we require for our audit[; or
- the members were not entitled to prepare financial statements in accordance with the small limited liability partnerships' regime][51].

[Signature]   *Address*
John Smith (Senior statutory auditor)   *Date*
for and on behalf of ABC LLP, Statutory Auditor

---

[51] *This bullet point is only required where the LLP has prepared the financial statements in accordance with the small LLP's regime.*

Example 15 – Limited liability partnership[52] preparing financial statements under IFRSs as adopted by the EU

- The limited liability partnership does not prepare group financial statements.

INDEPENDENT AUDITOR'S REPORT TO THE MEMBERS OF XYZ LLP

We have audited the financial statements of (name of limited liability partnership) for the year ended ... which comprise [specify the titles of the primary statements such as the Statement of Financial Position, the Statement of Comprehensive Income, the Statement of Cash Flows, the Statement of Changes in Equity] and the related notes[53]. The financial reporting framework that has been applied in their preparation is applicable law and International Financial Reporting Standards (IFRSs) as adopted by the European Union.

Respective responsibilities of members and auditor

As explained more fully in the Members' Responsibilities Statement [set out [on page ...]], the members are responsible for the preparation of the financial statements and for being satisfied that they give a true and fair view. Our responsibility is to audit and express an opinion on the financial statements in accordance with applicable law and International Standards on Auditing (UK and Ireland). Those standards require us to comply with the Auditing Practices Board's [(APB's)] Ethical Standards for Auditors.

Scope of the audit of the financial statements

Either:

> A description of the scope of an audit of financial statements is [provided on the APB's website at www.frc.org.uk/apb/scope/private.cfm] / [set out [on page ...] of the Annual Report].

Or:

> An audit involves obtaining evidence about the amounts and disclosures in the financial statements sufficient to give reasonable assurance that the financial statements are free from material misstatement, whether caused by fraud or error. This includes an assessment of: whether the accounting policies are appropriate to the limited liability partnership's circumstances and have been consistently applied and adequately disclosed; the reasonableness of significant accounting estimates made by the designated members; and the overall presentation of the financial statements. In addition, we read all the financial and non-financial information in the *[describe the annual report]* to identify material inconsistencies

---

[52] *Regulations relevant to audit reports of limited liability partnerships are set out in Statutory Instrument 2008 No. 1911 "The Limited Liability Partnerships (Accounts and Audit) (Application of Companies act 2006) Regulations 2008".*

[53] *Auditor's reports of entities that do not publish their financial statements on a website or publish them using 'PDF' format may refer to the financial statements by reference to page numbers.*

with the audited financial statements. If we become aware of any apparent material misstatements or inconsistencies we consider the implications for our report.

Opinion on financial statements

In our opinion the financial statements:

- give a true and fair view of the state of the limited liability partnership's affairs as at .... and of its profit [loss] for the year then ended;
- have been properly prepared in accordance with IFRSs as adopted by the European Union; and
- have been prepared in accordance with the requirements of the Companies Act 2006 as applied to limited liability partnerships by the Limited Liability Partnerships (Accounts and Audit) (Application of Companies Act 2006) Regulations 2008.

Matters on which we are required to report by exception

We have nothing to report in respect of the following matters where the Companies Act 2006 as applied to limited liability partnerships requires us to report to you if, in our opinion:

- adequate accounting records have not been kept, or returns adequate for our audit have not been received from branches not visited by us; or
- the financial statements are not in agreement with the accounting records and returns; or
- we have not received all the information and explanations we require for our audit[; or
- the members were not entitled to prepare financial statements in accordance with the small limited liability partnerships' regime]⁵⁴.

[Signature]   *Address*
John Smith (Senior statutory auditor)   *Date*
for and on behalf of ABC LLP, Statutory Auditor

---

⁵⁴ *This bullet point is only required where the LLP has prepared the financial statements in accordance with the small LLP's regime.*

Example 16 – Qualifying partnership[55] preparing financial statements under UK GAAP

INDEPENDENT AUDITOR'S REPORT TO THE MEMBERS OF XYZ PARTNERSHIP

We have audited the financial statements of (name of qualifying partnership) for the year ended ... which comprise [specify the titles of the primary statements such as the Profit and Loss Account, the Balance Sheet, the Cash Flow Statement, the Statement of Total Recognised Gains and Losses, the Reconciliation of Movements in Members' Funds] and the related notes[56]. The financial reporting framework that has been applied in their preparation is applicable law and United Kingdom Accounting Standards (United Kingdom Generally Accepted Accounting Practice).

Respective responsibilities of members and auditor

As explained more fully in the Members' Responsibilities Statement [set out [on page ...]], the members are responsible for the preparation of the financial statements and for being satisfied that they give a true and fair view. Our responsibility is to audit and express an opinion on the financial statements in accordance with applicable law and International Standards on Auditing (UK and Ireland). Those standards require us to comply with the Auditing Practices Board's [(APB's)] Ethical Standards for Auditors.

Scope of the audit of the financial statements

Either:

A description of the scope of an audit of financial statements is [provided on the APB's website at www.frc.org.uk/apb/scope/private.cfm] / [set out [on page ...] of the Annual Report].

Or:

An audit involves obtaining evidence about the amounts and disclosures in the financial statements sufficient to give reasonable assurance that the financial statements are free from material misstatement, whether caused by fraud or error. This includes an assessment of: whether the accounting policies are appropriate to the qualifying partnership's circumstances and have been consistently applied and adequately disclosed; the reasonableness of significant accounting estimates made by the members; and the overall presentation of the financial statements. In addition, we read all the financial and non-financial information in the *[describe the annual report]* to identify material inconsistencies with the audited financial statements. If we become aware of any apparent material misstatements or inconsistencies we consider the implications for our report.

---

[55] *Regulations relevant to auditor's reports of qualifying partnerships are set out in Statutory Instrument 2008 No. 569 "The Partnerships (Accounts) Regulations 2008".*

[56] *Auditor's reports of entities that do not publish their financial statements on a website or publish them using 'PDF' format may refer to the financial statements by reference to page numbers.*

Opinion on financial statements

In our opinion the financial statements:

- give a true and fair view of the state of the qualifying partnership's affairs as at .... and of its profit [loss] for the year then ended;
- have been properly prepared in accordance with United Kingdom Generally Accepted Accounting Practice; and
- have been prepared in accordance with the requirements of the Companies Act 2006 as applied to qualifying partnerships by The Partnerships (Accounts) Regulations 2008.

Matters on which we are required to report by exception

We have nothing to report in respect of the following matters where the Companies Act 2006 as applied to qualifying partnerships requires us to report to you if, in our opinion:

- adequate accounting records have not been kept, or returns adequate for our audit have not been received from branches not visited by us; or
- the financial statements are not in agreement with the accounting records and returns; or
- certain disclosures of members' remuneration specified by law are not made; or
- we have not received all the information and explanations we require for our audit.

[Signature]   Address
John Smith (Senior statutory auditor)   Date
for and on behalf of ABC LLP, Statutory Auditor

Appendix 7 – Insurers

17. Publicly traded insurer with a standard listing preparing financial statements under UK GAAP and having equalisation provisions
18. Lloyd's syndicate – annual financial statements
19. Lloyd's syndicate – underwriting year accounts – closed year of account
20. Lloyd's syndicate – underwriting year accounts – run off year of account
21. Non-directive friendly society with no subsidiaries preparing financial statements under UK GAAP
22. Directive friendly society group preparing financial statements under UK GAAP

Example 17 – Publicly traded insurer with a standard listing preparing financial statements under UK GAAP and having equalisation provisions

- *Insurer is a quoted company and has a standard listing.*
- *Insurer does not prepare group financial statements*
- *Corporate governance statement incorporated into the directors' report.*

INDEPENDENT AUDITOR'S REPORT TO THE MEMBERS OF XYZ PLC

We have audited the financial statements of (name of insurer) for the year ended ... which comprise [specify the titles of the primary statements such as the Profit and Loss Account, the Balance Sheet, the Cash Flow Statement, the Statement of Total Recognised Gains and Losses, the Reconciliation of Movements in Shareholders' Funds] and the related notes[57]. The financial reporting framework that has been applied in their preparation is applicable law and United Kingdom Accounting Standards (United Kingdom Generally Accepted Accounting Practice), having regard to the statutory requirement for insurance companies to maintain equalisation provisions. The nature of equalisation provisions, the amounts set aside at ..., and the effect of the movement in those provisions during the year on shareholders' funds, the balance on the general business technical account and profit before tax, are disclosed in note x.

Respective responsibilities of directors and auditor

As explained more fully in the Directors' Responsibilities Statement [set out [on page ...]], the directors are responsible for the preparation of the financial statements and for being satisfied that they give a true and fair view. Our responsibility is to audit and express an opinion on the financial statements in accordance with applicable law and International Standards on Auditing (UK and Ireland). Those standards require us to comply with the Auditing Practices Board's [(APB's)] Ethical Standards for Auditors.

Scope of the audit of the financial statements

Either:

> A description of the scope of an audit of financial statements is [provided on the APB's website at www.frc.org.uk/apb/scope/private.cfm] / [set out [on page ...] of the Annual Report].

Or:

> An audit involves obtaining evidence about the amounts and disclosures in the financial statements sufficient to give reasonable assurance that the financial statements are free from material misstatement, whether caused by fraud or error. This includes an assessment of: whether the accounting policies are appropriate to the insurer's circumstances and have been consistently applied and adequately

---

[57] *Auditor's reports of entities that do not publish their financial statements on a website or publish them using 'PDF' format may refer to the financial statements by reference to page numbers.*

disclosed; the reasonableness of significant accounting estimates made by the directors; and the overall presentation of the financial statements. In addition, we read all the financial and non-financial information in the *[describe the annual report]* to identify material inconsistencies with the audited financial statements. If we become aware of any apparent material misstatements or inconsistencies we consider the implications for our report.

Opinion on financial statements

In our opinion the financial statements:

- give a true and fair view of the state of the company's affairs as at .... and of its profit [loss] for the year then ended;
- have been properly prepared in accordance with United Kingdom Generally Accepted Accounting Practice; and
- have been prepared in accordance with the requirements of the Companies Act 2006.

Opinion on other matters prescribed by the Companies Act 2006

In our opinion:

- the part of the Directors' Remuneration Report to be audited has been properly prepared in accordance with the Companies Act 2006[58]; and
- the information given in the Directors' Report for the financial year for which the financial statements are prepared is consistent with the financial statements.

Matters on which we are required to report by exception

We have nothing to report in respect of the following matters where the Companies Act 2006 requires us to report to you if, in our opinion:

- adequate accounting records have not been kept, or returns adequate for our audit have not been received from branches not visited by us; or
- the financial statements and the part of the Directors' Remuneration Report to be audited are not in agreement with the accounting records and returns; or
- certain disclosures of directors' remuneration specified by law are not made; or
- we have not received all the information and explanations we require for our audit.

[Signature]   *Address*
John Smith *(Senior statutory auditor)*   *Date*
for and on behalf of ABC LLP, Statutory Auditor

---

[58] *Part 3 of Schedule 8 to the Large and Medium-sized Companies and Groups (Accounts and Reports) Regulations 2008 (SI 2008 No. 410) sets out the information in the Directors' Remuneration Report that is subject to audit. Companies should describe clearly within the Directors' Remuneration Report which disclosures have been audited.*

Example 18 – Lloyd's syndicate annual financial statements

INDEPENDENT AUDITOR'S REPORT TO THE MEMBERS OF SYNDICATE XYZ

We have audited the syndicate annual financial statements for the year ended ... which comprise [specify the titles of the primary financial statements such as the Profit and Loss Account, the Balance Sheet, the Cash Flow Statement, the Statement of Total Recognised Gains and Losses][59], [the Statement of Accounting Policies][60] and the related notes 1 to X[61]. The financial reporting framework that has been applied in their preparation is applicable law and United Kingdom Accounting Standards (United Kingdom Generally Accepted Accounting Practice).

Respective responsibilities of the managing agent and the auditor

As explained more fully in the Statement of Managing Agent's Responsibilities [set out [on page ...]], the managing agent is responsible for the preparation of syndicate annual financial statements which give a true and fair view. Our responsibility is to audit and express an opinion on the syndicate annual financial statements in accordance with applicable law and International Standards on Auditing (UK and Ireland). Those standards require us to comply with the Auditing Practices Board's [(APB's)] Ethical Standards for Auditors.

Scope of the audit of the syndicate annual financial statements

Either:

A description of the scope of an audit of financial statements is [provided on the APB's website at www.frc.org.uk/apb/scope/private.cfm] / [set out [on page ...] of the Annual Report].

Or:

An audit involves obtaining evidence about the amounts and disclosures in the annual financial statements sufficient to give reasonable assurance that the annual financial statements are free from material misstatement, whether caused by fraud or error. This includes an assessment of: whether the accounting policies are appropriate to the syndicate's circumstances and have been consistently applied and adequately disclosed; the reasonableness of significant accounting estimates made by the managing agent; and the overall presentation of the annual financial statements. In addition, we read all the financial and non-financial information in the *[describe the annual report]* to identify material inconsistencies with the audited financial statements. If we become aware of any apparent

---

[59] *The terms used to describe the primary financial statements should be the same as those used by the managing agent.*

[60] *Reference is only made to the Statement of Accounting Polices where the accounting policies are not included within the numbered notes to the financial statements.*

[61] *Auditor's reports of syndicates that do not publish their financial statements on a website or publish them using "PDF" format may refer to the financial statements by reference to page numbers.*

material misstatements or inconsistencies we consider the implications for our report.

Opinion on syndicate annual financial statements

In our opinion the annual financial statements:

- give a true and fair view of the syndicate's affairs as at ... and of its profit [loss] for the year then ended;
- have been properly prepared in accordance with United Kingdom Generally Accepted Accounting Practice; and
- have been prepared in accordance with the requirements of The Insurance Accounts Directive (Lloyd's Syndicate and Aggregate Accounts) Regulations 2008.

Opinion on other matter prescribed by The Insurance Accounts Directive (Lloyd's Syndicate and Aggregate Accounts) Regulations 2008

In our opinion the information given in the Managing Agent's Report for the financial year in which the annual financial statements are prepared is consistent with the annual financial statements.

Matters on which we are required to report by exception

We have nothing to report in respect of the following matters where The Insurance Accounts Directive (Lloyds's Syndicate and Aggregate Accounts) Regulations 2008 requires us to report to you, if in our opinion:

- the managing agent in respect of the syndicate has not kept adequate accounting records; or
- the syndicate annual financial statements are not in agreement with the accounting records; or
- we have not received all the information and explanations we require for our audit.

[Signature]   *Address*
John Smith (Senior statutory auditor)   *Date*
for and on behalf of ABC LLP, Statutory Auditor

Example 19 – Lloyd's syndicate underwriting year accounts – closed year of account

INDEPENDENT AUDITOR'S REPORT TO THE MEMBERS OF SYNDICATE XYZ – 20XX CLOSED YEAR OF ACCOUNT

We have audited the syndicate underwriting year accounts for the 20XX year of account of syndicate [XYZ] for the three years ended ...... which comprise [specify the titles of the primary financial statements such as the Profit and Loss Account, the Balance Sheet, the Cash Flow Statement, the Statement of Total Recognised Gains and Losses][62], [the Statement of Accounting Policies][63], the related notes 1 to X[64] and the Statement of Managing Agent's Responsibilities. The financial reporting framework that has been applied in their preparation is applicable law and United Kingdom Accounting Standards (United Kingdom Generally Accepted Accounting Practice).

Respective responsibilities of the managing agent and the auditor

As explained more fully in the Statement of Managing Agent's Responsibilities [set out [on page ...]], the managing agent is responsible for the preparation of the syndicate underwriting year accounts, under the Insurance Accounts Directive (Lloyd's Syndicate and Aggregate Accounts) Regulations 2008 and in accordance with the Lloyd's Syndicate Accounting Byelaw (no. 8 of 2005), which give a true and fair view. Our responsibility is to audit and express an opinion on the syndicate underwriting year accounts in accordance with applicable legal and regulatory requirements and International Standards on Auditing (UK and Ireland). Those standards require us to comply with the Auditing Practices Board's [(APB's)] Ethical Standards for Auditors.

Scope of the audit of the syndicate underwriting year accounts

Either:

A description of the scope of an audit of financial statements is [provided on the APB's website at www.frc.org.uk/apb/scope/private.cfm] / [set out [on page ...] of the Annual Report].

Or:

An audit involves obtaining evidence about the amounts and disclosures in the syndicate underwriting year accounts sufficient to give reasonable assurance that the syndicate underwriting year accounts are free from material misstatement, whether caused by fraud or error. This includes an assessment of: whether the

---

[62] *The terms used to describe the primary financial statements should be the same as those used by the managing agent.*

[63] *Reference is only made to the Statement of Accounting Polices where the accounting policies are not included within the numbered notes to the financial statements.*

[64] *Auditor's reports of syndicates that do not publish their financial statements on a website or publish them using "PDF" format may refer to the financial statements by reference to page numbers.*

accounting policies are appropriate to the syndicate's circumstances and have been consistently applied and adequately disclosed; the reasonableness of significant accounting estimates made by the managing agent; and the overall presentation of the syndicate underwriting year accounts. In addition, we read all the financial and non-financial information in the *[describe the annual report]* to identify material inconsistencies with the audited financial statements. If we become aware of any apparent material misstatements or inconsistencies we consider the implications for our report.

Opinion on syndicate underwriting year accounts

In our opinion the syndicate underwriting year accounts:

- give a true and fair view of the profit [loss] for the 201X closed year of account;
- have been properly prepared in accordance with United Kingdom Generally Accepted Accounting Practice; and
- have been prepared in accordance with the requirements of the Insurance Accounts Directive (Lloyd's Syndicate and Aggregate Accounts) Regulations 2008 and have been properly prepared in accordance with the Lloyd's Syndicate Accounting Byelaw (no. 8 of 2005).

Matters on which we are required to report by exception

We have nothing to report in respect of the following matters where the Lloyd's Syndicate Accounting Byelaw (no. 8 of 2005) requires us to report to you if, in our opinion:

- the managing agent in respect of the syndicate has not kept proper accounting records; or
- the syndicate underwriting year accounts are not in agreement with the accounting records.

[Signature]   *Address*
John Smith (Senior statutory auditor)   *Date*
for and on behalf of ABC LLP, Statutory Auditor

Example 20 – Lloyd's syndicate underwriting year accounts – run-off year of account

INDEPENDENT AUDITOR'S REPORT TO THE MEMBERS OF SYNDICATE XYZ

We have audited the syndicate underwriting year accounts for the 20XX run-off year of account for the xx years ended ......, which comprise [specify the titles of the primary financial statements such as the Profit and Loss Account, the Balance Sheet, the Cash Flow Statement the Statement of Total Recognised Gains and Losses][65], [the statement of accounting policies][66], the related notes 1 to X[67] and the Statement of Managing Agent's Responsibilities. The financial reporting framework that has been applied in their preparation is applicable law, the Lloyd's Syndicate Accounting Byelaw (no. 8 of 2005) and applicable United Kingdom Accounting Standards.

Respective responsibilities of the managing agent and the auditor

As explained more fully in the Statement of Managing Agent's Responsibilities [set out [on page ...]], the managing agent is responsible for the preparation of the syndicate underwriting year accounts in accordance with the financial reporting framework described above. Our responsibility is to audit and express an opinion on the syndicate underwriting year accounts in accordance with applicable legal and regulatory requirements and International Standards on Auditing (UK and Ireland). Those standards require us to comply with the Auditing Practices Board's [(APB's)] Ethical Standards for Auditors.

Scope of the audit of the syndicate underwriting year accounts

Either:

> A description of the scope of an audit of financial statements is [provided on the APB's website at www.frc.org.uk/apb/scope/private.cfm] / [set out [on page ...] of the Annual Report.

Or:

> An audit involves obtaining evidence about the amounts and disclosures in the syndicate underwriting year accounts sufficient to give reasonable assurance that the syndicate underwriting year accounts are free from material misstatement, whether caused by fraud or error. This includes an assessment of: whether the accounting policies are appropriate to the syndicate's circumstances and have been consistently applied and adequately disclosed; the reasonableness of significant accounting estimates made by the managing agent; and the overall

---

[65] *The terms used to describe the primary financial statements should be the same as those used by the managing agent.*

[66] *Reference is only made to the Statement of Accounting Policies where the accounting policies are not included within the numbered notes to the financial statements.*

[67] *Auditor's reports of syndicates that do not publish their financial statements on a website or publish them using "PDF" format may refer to the financial statements by reference to page numbers.*

presentation of the syndicate underwriting year accounts. In addition, we read all the financial and non-financial information in the *[describe the annual report]* to identify material inconsistencies with the audited financial statements. If we become aware of any apparent material misstatements or inconsistencies we consider the implications for our report.

Opinion on syndicate underwriting year accounts

In our opinion the syndicate underwriting year accounts for the ... run-off year of account have been properly prepared in accordance with the Lloyd's Syndicate Accounting Byelaw (no. 8 of 2005).

Matters on which we are required to report by exception

We have nothing to report in respect of the following matters where the Lloyd's Syndicate Accounting Byelaw (no. 8 of 2005) requires us to report to you if, in our opinion:

- the managing agent in respect of the syndicate has not kept proper accounting records; or
- the syndicate underwriting year accounts are not in agreement with the accounting records.

[Signature]   *Address*
John Smith (Senior statutory auditor)   *Date*
for and on behalf of ABC LLP, Statutory Auditor

Example 21 – Non directive friendly society with no subsidiary companies, preparing financial statements under UK GAAP

INDEPENDENT AUDITOR'S REPORT TO THE MEMBERS OF XYZ FRIENDLY SOCIETY

We have audited the financial statements of (name of friendly society) for the year ended ... which comprise [specify the titles of the primary statements such as the Income and Expenditure Account, the Balance Sheet] and the related notes[68]. The financial reporting framework that has been applied in their preparation is applicable law and United Kingdom Accounting Standards (United Kingdom Generally Accepted Accounting Practice).

Respective responsibilities of the Committee of Management and auditor

As explained more fully in the Committee of Management's Responsibilities Statement [set out [on page ...]], the Committee of Management is responsible for preparing financial statements which give a true and fair view. Our responsibility is to audit and express an opinion on the financial statements in accordance with applicable law and International Standards on Auditing (UK and Ireland). Those standards require us to comply with the Auditing Practices Boards [(APB's)] Ethical Standards for Auditors.

Scope of the audit of the financial statements

Either:

> A description of the scope of an audit of financial statements is [provided on the APB's website at www.frc.org.uk/apb/scope/private.cfm] / [set out [on page] of the Annual Report]

Or:

> An audit involves obtaining evidence about the amounts and disclosures in the financial statements sufficient to give reasonable assurance that the financial statements are free from material misstatement, whether caused by fraud or error. This includes an assessment of: whether the accounting policies are appropriate to the company's circumstances and have been consistently applied and adequately disclosed; the reasonableness of significant accounting estimates made by the Committee of Management; and the overall presentation of the financial statements. In addition, we read all the financial and non-financial information in the *[describe the annual report]* to identify material inconsistencies with the audited financial statements. If we become aware of any apparent material misstatements or inconsistencies we consider the implications for our report.

---

[68] *Auditor's reports of societies that do not publish their financial statements on a website or publish them using 'PDF' format may refer to the financial statements by reference to page numbers.*

Opinion on financial statements

In our opinion the financial statements:

- give a true and fair view, in accordance with UK Generally Accepted Accounting Practice, of the state of the society's affairs as at ... and of its income and expenditure for the year then ended; and
- have been properly prepared in accordance with the Friendly Societies Act 1992.

Opinion on other matters prescribed by the Friendly Societies Act 1992

In our opinion the Report of the Committee of Management has been prepared in accordance with the Friendly Societies Act 1992 and the regulations made under it, and the information given therein is consistent with the financial statements for the financial year.

Matters on which we are required to report by exception

We have nothing to report in respect of the following matters where the Friendly Societies Act 1992 requires us to report to you if, in our opinion:

- proper accounting records have not been kept; or
- the financial statements are not in agreement with the accounting records; or
- we have not received all the information and explanations and access to documents that we require for our audit.

In accordance with our instructions from the Society we review whether the Corporate Governance Statement reflects the Society's compliance with those provisions of the Annotated UK Corporate Governance Code specified for our review by the Association of Financial Mutuals.

Statutory Auditor   *Address*
Date

Example 22 – Directive friendly society group preparing financial statements under UK GAAP

INDEPENDENT AUDITOR'S REPORT TO THE MEMBERS OF XYZ FRIENDLY SOCIETY

We have audited the financial statements of (name of friendly society) for the year ended ... which comprise (specify the titles of the primary statements such as the Group and Society Income and Expenditure Accounts, the Group and Society Balance Sheets) and the related notes[69]. The financial reporting framework that has been applied in their preparation is applicable law and United Kingdom Accounting Standards (United Kingdom Generally Accepted Accounting Practice)[, having regard to the statutory requirement to maintain equalisation provisions. The nature of equalisation provisions, the amounts set aside at ..., and the effect of the movement in those provisions during the year on the fund for future appropriations, the balance on the general business technical account and on excess of income over expenditure before tax are disclosed in note x[70]].

Respective responsibilities of the Committee of Management and auditor

As explained more fully in the Committee of Management's Responsibilities Statement [set out [on page ...]], the Committee of Management is responsible for preparing financial statements which give a true and fair view. Our responsibility is to audit and express an opinion on the financial statements in accordance with applicable law and International Standards on Auditing (UK and Ireland). Those standards require us to comply with the Auditing Practices Boards [(APB's)] Ethical Standards for Auditors.

Scope of the audit of the financial statements

Either:

> A description of the scope of an audit of financial statements is [provided on the APB's website at www.frc.org.uk/apb/scope/private.cfm] / [set out [on page] of the Annual Report]

Or:

> An audit involves obtaining evidence about the amounts and disclosures in the financial statements sufficient to give reasonable assurance that the financial statements are free from material misstatement, whether caused by fraud or error. This includes an assessment of: whether the accounting policies are appropriate to the company's circumstances and have been consistently applied and adequately disclosed; the reasonableness of significant accounting estimates made by the Committee of Management; and the overall presentation of the financial

---

[69] *Auditor's reports of societies that do not publish their financial statements on a website or publish them using 'PDF' format may refer to the financial statements by reference to page numbers.*

[70] *The wording in square brackets is only included where the society has one or more general insurance subsidiaries that prepare financial statements in accordance with UK GAAP and which are required to provide statutory equalisation provisions.*

statements. In addition, we read all the financial and non-financial information in the *[describe the annual report]* to identify material inconsistencies with the audited financial statements. If we become aware of any apparent material misstatements or inconsistencies we consider the implications for our report.

Opinion on financial statements

In our opinion the financial statements:

- give a true and fair view, in accordance with UK Generally Accepted Accounting Practice, of the state of the society's and the group's affairs as at ... and of the income and expenditure of the society and the group for the year then ended; and
- have been properly prepared in accordance with the Friendly Societies Act 1992.

Opinion on other matters prescribed by the Friendly Societies Act 1992

In our opinion the Report of the Committee of Management has been prepared in accordance with the Friendly Societies Act 1992 and the regulations made under it, and the information given therein is consistent with the financial statements for the financial year.

Matters on which we are required to report by exception

We have nothing to report in respect of the following matters where the Friendly Societies Act 1992 requires us to report to you if, in our opinion:

- proper accounting records have not been kept; or
- the financial statements are not in agreement with the accounting records; or
- we have not received all the information and explanations and access to documents that we require for our audit.

In accordance with our instructions from the Society we review whether the Corporate Governance Statement reflects the Society's compliance with those provisions of the Annotated UK Corporate Governance Code specified for our review by the Association of Financial Mutuals.

[Signature]   *Address*
John Smith (Senior statutory auditor)   *Date*
For and on behalf of ABC LLP, Statutory Auditor

Appendix 8 – Banking institutions that are not companies

23. Building society preparing financial statements under UK GAAP
24. Building society preparing financial statements under IFRSs as adopted by the European Union
25. Credit union in Great Britain
26. Credit Union in Northern Ireland

Example 23 – Building society preparing financial statements under UK GAAP

- Group and Society financial statements reported on in a single auditor's report

INDEPENDENT AUDITOR'S REPORT TO THE MEMBERS OF XYZ BUILDING SOCIETY

We have audited the [Group and Society] financial statements of (name of Building Society) for the year ended ... which comprise [specify the titles of the primary statements such as the [Group and Society] Profit and Loss Account[s], [Group and Society] Balance Sheet[s], the Group Cash Flow Statement, the Group Statement of Total Recognised Gains and Losses and the [Group and Society] Statement[s] of Movements in Member's Interests] [, the Accounting Policies[71]] and the related notes[72]. The financial reporting framework that has been applied in their preparation is applicable law and United Kingdom Accounting Standards (United Kingdom Generally Accepted Accounting Practice).

Respective responsibilities of directors and auditor

As explained more fully in the Directors' Responsibilities Statement [set out [on pages..]], the directors are responsible for the preparation of financial statements which give a true and fair view. Our responsibility is to audit and express an opinion on the financial statements in accordance with applicable law and International Standards on Auditing (UK and Ireland). Those standards require us to comply with the Auditing Practices Board's [(APB's)] Ethical Standards for Auditors.

Scope of the audit of the financial statements

Either:

> A description of the scope of an audit of financial statements is [provided on the APB's website at www.frc.org.uk/apb/scope/private.cfm] / [set out [on page] of the Annual Report].

Or:

> An audit involves obtaining evidence about the amounts and disclosures in the financial statements sufficient to give reasonable assurance that the financial statements are free from material misstatement, whether caused by fraud or error. This includes an assessment of: whether the accounting policies are appropriate to the [Group's and] Society's circumstances and have been consistently applied and adequately disclosed; the reasonableness of significant accounting estimates made by the directors; and the overall presentation of the financial statements. In addition, we read all the financial and non-financial information in the *[describe the annual report]* to identify material inconsistencies with the audited financial

---

[71] *Include if the accounting policies are presented in a separate statement and not as a note to the financial statements.*

[72] *Auditor's reports of building societies that do not publish their financial statements on a website or publish them using "PDF" format may refer to the financial statements by reference to page numbers.*

statements. If we become aware of any apparent material misstatements or inconsistencies we consider the implications for our report.

Opinion on financial statements

In our opinion the financial statements:

- give a true and fair view, in accordance with United Kingdom Generally Accepted Accounting Practice, of the state of the [Group's and the] Society's affairs as at ... and of [the Group's and] the Society's income and expenditure for the year then ended; and
- have been prepared in accordance with the requirements of the Building Societies Act 1986.

Opinion on other matters prescribed by the Building Societies Act 1986

In our opinion:

- the Annual Business Statement and the Directors' Report have been prepared in accordance with the requirements of the Building Societies Act 1986;
- the information given in the Directors' Report for the financial year for which the financial statements are prepared is consistent with the accounting records and the financial statements; and
- the information given in the Annual Business Statement (other than the information upon which we are not required to report) gives a true representation of the matters in respect of which it is given.

Matters on which we are required to report by exception

We have nothing to report in respect of the following matters where the Building Societies Act 1986 requires us to report to you if, in our opinion:

- proper accounting records have not been kept by the Society; or
- the [Society] financial statements are not in agreement with the accounting records; or
- we have not received all the information and explanations and access to documents we require for our audit.

[Signature]   *Address*
John Smith (Senior Statutory Auditor)   *Date*
for and on behalf of ABC LLP, Statutory Auditor

Example 24 – Building society preparing financial statements under IFRSs as adopted by the European Union

● Group and Society financial statements are both prepared under IFRSs as adopted by the EU and reported on in a single auditor's report

INDEPENDENT AUDITOR'S REPORT TO THE MEMBERS OF XYZ BUILDING SOCIETY

We have audited the [Group and Society] financial statements of (name of Building Society) for the year ended ... which comprise [specify the titles of the primary statements such as the [Group and Society] Income Statement[s], [Group and Society] Statement[s] of Comprehensive Income, [Group and Society] Balance Sheet[s] and the [Group and Society] Statement[s] of Movements in Member's Interests and the [Group and Society] Cash Flow Statement[s]], [the Accounting Policies[73]] and the related notes[74]. The financial reporting framework that has been applied in their preparation is applicable law and International Financial Reporting Standards (IFRSs) as adopted by the European Union.

Respective responsibilities of directors and auditor

As explained more fully in the Directors' Responsibilities Statement [set out [on pages..]], the directors are responsible for the preparation of the financial statements which give a true and fair view. Our responsibility is to audit and express an opinion on the financial statements in accordance with applicable law and International Standards on Auditing (UK and Ireland). Those standards require us to comply with the Auditing Practices Board's [(APB's)] Ethical Standards for Auditors.

Scope of the audit of the financial statements

Either:

A description of the scope of an audit of financial statements is [provided on the APB's website at www.frc.org.uk/apb/scope/private.cfm] / [set out [on page] of the Annual Report].

Or:

An audit involves obtaining evidence about the amounts and disclosures in the financial statements sufficient to give reasonable assurance that the financial statements are free from material misstatement, whether caused by fraud or error. This includes an assessment of: whether the accounting policies are appropriate to the [Group's and] Society's circumstances and have been consistently applied and adequately disclosed; the reasonableness of significant accounting estimates made by the directors; and the overall presentation of the financial statements. In addition, we read all the financial and non-financial information in the *[describe*

---

[73] *Include if the accounting policies are presented in a separate statement and not as a note to the financial statements.*

[74] *Auditor's reports of entities that do not publish their financial statements on a website or publish them using "PDF" format may refer to the financial statements by reference to page numbers.*

> *the annual report]* to identify material inconsistencies with the audited financial statements. If we become aware of any apparent material misstatements or inconsistencies we consider the implications for our report.

Opinion on financial statements

In our opinion the financial statements:

- give a true and fair view, in accordance with IFRSs as adopted by the European Union, of the state of the [Group's and the] Society's affairs as at ... and of [the Group's and] the Society's income and expenditure for the year then ended; and
- have been prepared in accordance with the requirements of the Building Societies Act 1986 [and, as regards the group financial statements, Article 4 of the IAS Regulation].

[Separate opinion in relation to IFRSs as issued by the IASB

As explained in note [x] to the group financial statements, the group in addition to complying with its legal obligation to apply IFRSs as adopted by the European Union, has also applied IFRSs as issued by the International Accounting Standards Board (IASB).

In our opinion the group financial statements comply with IFRSs as issued by the IASB.][75]

Opinion on other matters prescribed by the Building Societies Act 1986

In our opinion:

- the Annual Business Statement and the Directors' Report have been prepared in accordance with the requirements of the Building Societies Act 1986;
- the information given in the Directors' Report for the financial year for which the financial statements are prepared is consistent with the accounting records and the financial statements; and
- the information given in the Annual Business Statement (other than the information upon which we are not required to report) gives a true representation of the matters in respect of which it is given.

Matters on which we are required to report by exception

We have nothing to report in respect of the following matters where the Building Societies Act 1986 requires us to report to you if, in our opinion:

- proper accounting records have not been kept by the Society; or
- the [Society] financial statements are not in agreement with the accounting records; or
- we have not received all the information and explanations and access to documents we require for our audit.

[Signature]   Address
John Smith *(Senior Statutory Auditor)*   Date
for and on behalf of ABC LLP, Statutory Auditor

---

[75] *See footnote 12.*

Example 25 – Credit Union in Great Britain

INDEPENDENT AUDITOR'S REPORT TO THE MEMBERS OF XYZ CREDIT UNION

We have audited the financial statements of (name of credit union) for the year ended ... which comprise [specify the titles of the primary statements such as the income and expenditure account, appropriation account, the statement of general reserve, the balance sheet] and the related notes[76]. The financial reporting framework that has been applied in their preparation is applicable law and United Kingdom Accounting Standards (United Kingdom Generally Accepted Accounting Practice).

Respective responsibilities of directors and auditor

As explained more fully in the Directors' Responsibilities Statement [set out [on page ...]] the directors are responsible for the preparation of financial statements which give a true and fair view. Our responsibility is to audit and express an opinion on the financial statements in accordance with applicable law and International Standards on Auditing (UK and Ireland). Those standards require us to comply with the Auditing Practices Board's [(APB's)] Ethical Standards for Auditors.

Scope of the audit of the financial statements

Either:

A description of the scope of an audit of financial statements is [provided on the APB's website at www.frc.org.uk/apb/scope/private.cfm] / [set out [on page ...] of the Annual Report].

Or:

An audit involves obtaining evidence about the amounts and disclosures in the financial statements sufficient to give reasonable assurance that the financial statements are free from material misstatement, whether caused by fraud or error. This includes an assessment of: whether the accounting policies are appropriate to the credit union's circumstances and have been consistently applied and adequately disclosed; the reasonableness of significant accounting estimates made by the directors; and the overall presentation of the financial statements. In addition, we read all the financial and non-financial information in the *[describe the annual report]* to identify material inconsistencies with the audited financial statements. If we become aware of any apparent material misstatements or inconsistencies we consider the implications for our report.

---

[76] *Auditor's reports of credit unions that do not publish their financial statements on a website or publish them using "pdf" format may refer to the financial statements by reference to page numbers.*

Opinion on financial statements

In our opinion the financial statements:

- give a true and fair view of the state of the credit union's affairs as at .... and of its income and expenditure for the year then ended;and
- have been properly prepared in accordance with United Kingdom Generally Accepted Accounting Practice, and with the Industrial and Provident Societies Acts 1965 to 2002 and the Credit Unions Act 1979.

Matters on which we are required to report by exception

We have nothing to report in respect of the following matters where the Friendly and Industrial and Provident Societies Acts 1965 to 2002 require us to report to you if, in our opinion:

- proper books of account have not been kept by the credit union in accordance with the requirements of the legislation,
- a satisfactory system of control over transactions has not been maintained by the credit union in accordance with the requirements of the legislation,
- the revenue account or the other accounts (if any) to which our report relates, and the balance sheet are not in agreement with the books of account of the credit union.
- we have not obtained all the information and explanations necessary for the purposes of our audit.

Statutory Auditor   *Address*
Date

Example 26 – Credit Union in Northern Ireland

INDEPENDENT AUDITOR'S REPORT TO THE MEMBERS OF XYZ CREDIT UNION LIMITED

We have audited the financial statements of (name of Credit union) for the year ended ... which comprise [specify the titles of the primary statements such as the income and expenditure account, appropriation account, the statement of general reserve, the balance sheet] and the related notes[77]. The financial reporting framework that has been applied in their preparation is applicable law and United Kingdom Accounting Standards (United Kingdom Generally Accepted Accounting Practice).

Respective responsibilities of directors and auditor

As explained more fully in the Directors' Responsibilities Statement [set out [on page ...]] the directors are responsible for the preparation of financial statements which give a true and fair view. Our responsibility is to audit and express an opinion on the financial statements in accordance with applicable law and International Standards on Auditing (UK and Ireland). Those standards require us to comply with the Auditing Practices Board's [(APB's)] Ethical Standards for Auditors.

Scope of the audit of the financial statements

Either:

A description of the scope of an audit of financial statements is [provided on the APB's website at www.frc.org.uk/apb/scope/private.cfm] / [set out [on page ...]] of the Annual Report].

Or:

An audit involves obtaining evidence about the amounts and disclosures in the financial statements sufficient to give reasonable assurance that the financial statements are free from material misstatement, whether caused by fraud or error. This includes an assessment of: whether the accounting policies are appropriate to the credit union's circumstances and have been consistently applied and adequately disclosed; the reasonableness of significant accounting estimates made by the directors; and the overall presentation of the financial statements. In addition, we read all the financial and non-financial information in the *[describe the annual report]* to identify material inconsistencies with the audited financial statements. If we become aware of any apparent material misstatements or inconsistencies we consider the implications for our report.

---

[77] *Auditor's reports of credit unions that do not publish their financial statements on a website or publish them using "pdf" format may refer to the financial statements by reference to page numbers.*

Opinion on financial statements

In our opinion the financial statements:

- give a true and fair view of the state of the credit union's affairs as at ... and of its income and expenditure for the year then ended; and
- have been properly prepared in accordance with United Kingdom Generally Accepted Accounting Practice, and with the Credit Unions (Northern Ireland) Order 1985.

Matters on which we are required to report by exception

We have nothing to report in respect of the following matters where the Credit Unions (Northern Ireland) Order 1985 requires us to report to you if, in our opinion:

- proper books of account have not been kept by the credit union in accordance with the requirements of the legislation,
- a satisfactory system of control over transactions has not been maintained by the credit union in accordance with the requirements of the legislation,
- the revenue account or the other accounts (if any) to which our report relates, and the balance sheet are not in agreement with the books of account of the credit union.
- we have not obtained all the information and explanations necessary for the purposes of our audit.

Statutory Auditor   *Address*
Date

Appendix 9 – Other regulated entities

27. Occupational pension scheme
28. Housing Association registered in England that is an industrial and provident society

Example 27 – Occupational pension scheme

INDEPENDENT AUDITOR'S REPORT TO THE TRUSTEES OF THE XYZ PENSION SCHEME

We have audited the financial statements of (name of pension scheme for the year ended .... which comprise the fund account, the net assets statement and the related notes[78]. The financial reporting framework that has been applied in their preparation is applicable law and United Kingdom Accounting Standards (United Kingdom Generally Accepted Accounting Practice).

Respective responsibilities of trustees and auditor

As explained more fully in the Trustees' Responsibilities Statement [set out [on page ...]], the scheme's trustees are responsible for the preparation of financial statements which give a true and fair view. Our responsibility is to audit and express an opinion on the financial statements in accordance with applicable law and International Standards on Auditing (UK and Ireland). Those standards require us to comply with the Auditing Practices Board's [(APB's)] Ethical Standards for Auditors.

Scope of the audit of the financial statements

Either:

> A description of the scope of an audit of financial statements is [provided on the APB's website at www.frc.org.uk/apb/scope/private.cfm] / [set out [on page ...] of the Trustees' Annual Report].

Or:

> An audit involves obtaining evidence about the amounts and disclosures in the financial statements sufficient to give reasonable assurance that the financial statements are free from material misstatement, whether caused by fraud or error. This includes an assessment of: whether the accounting policies are appropriate to the scheme's circumstances and have been consistently applied and adequately disclosed; the reasonableness of significant accounting estimates made by the trustees; and the overall presentation of the financial statements. In addition, we read all the financial and non-financial information in the *[describe the annual report]* to identify material inconsistencies with the audited financial statements. If we become aware of any apparent material misstatements or inconsistencies we consider the implications for our report.

---

[78] *Auditor's reports of schemes that do not publish their financial statements on a website or publish them using "PDF" format may refer to the financial statements by reference to page numbers.*

Opinion on financial statements

In our opinion the financial statements:

- show a true and fair view of the financial transactions of the scheme during the year ended ..., and of the amount and disposition at that date of its assets and liabilities, other than the liabilities to pay pensions and benefits after the end of the year;
- have been properly prepared in accordance with United Kingdom Generally Accepted Accounting Practice; and
- contain the information specified in Regulation 3 of, and the Schedule to, the Occupational Pension Schemes (Requirement to obtain Audited Accounts and a Statement from the Auditor) Regulations 1996, made under the Pensions Act 1995.

Statutory Auditor   *Address*
Date

Example 28 – Housing Association registered in England that is an Industrial and Provident Society

INDEPENDENT AUDITOR'S REPORT TO THE MEMBERS OF XYZ HOUSING ASSOCIATION

We have audited the financial statements of [name of housing association] for the year ended ... which comprise (state the primary financial statements such as the Income and Expenditure Account, the Balance Sheet, the Cash Flow Statement, the Statement of Total Recognised Gains and Losses)[79] and the related notes. The financial reporting framework that has been applied in their preparation is applicable law and United Kingdom Accounting Standards (United Kingdom Generally Accepted Accounting Practice).

Respective responsibilities of the board and the auditor

As explained more fully in the Statement of Board's Responsibilities [set out [on page]], the board is responsible for the preparation of financial statements which give a true and fair view. Our responsibility is to audit and express an opinion on the financial statements in accordance with applicable law and International Standards on Auditing (UK and Ireland). Those standards require us to comply with the Auditing Practices Board's [(APB's)] Ethical Standards for Auditors.

Scope of the audit of the financial statements

Either:

> A description of the scope of an audit of financial statements is [provided on the APB's website at www.frc.org.uk/apb/scope/private.cfm] / [set out [on page ...] of the Annual Report].

Or:

> An audit involves obtaining evidence about the amounts and disclosures in the financial statements sufficient to give reasonable assurance that the financial statements are free from material misstatement, whether caused by fraud or error. This includes an assessment of: whether the accounting policies are appropriate to the association's circumstances and have been consistently applied and adequately disclosed; the reasonableness of significant accounting estimates made by the board; and the overall presentation of the financial statements. In addition, we read all the financial and non-financial information in the *[describe the annual report]* to identify material inconsistencies with the audited financial statements. If we become aware of any apparent material misstatements or inconsistencies we consider the implications for our report.

---

[79] *Auditors' reports on Housing Associations that do not publish their financial statements on a website or publish them using 'PDF' format may refer to the financial statements by reference to page numbers.*

Opinion on financial statements

In our opinion the financial statements:

- give a true and fair view of the state of the association's affairs as at ... and of its income and expenditure for the year then ended; and
- have been properly prepared in accordance with the Industrial and Provident Societies Acts, 1965 to 2002, the Housing and Regeneration Act 2008[80] and The Accounting Requirements for Registered Social Landlords General Determination 2006.

Matters on which we are required to report by exception

We have nothing to report in respect of the following matters where the Industrial and Provident Societies Acts, 1965 to 2002 require us to report to you if, in our opinion:

- a satisfactory system of control over transactions has not been maintained; or
- the association has not kept proper accounting records; or
- the financial statements are not in agreement with the books of account; or
- we have not received all the information and explanations we need for our audit.

Statutory Auditor   *Address*
Date

---

[80] *For periods ending before 1 April 2010 the Housing Act 1996 is the relevant legislation that should be referred to.*

Appendix 10 – Charitable companies registered in England & Wales

29. Charitable company audited under the Charities Act 2011
30. Charitable company audited under the Companies Act 2006
31. Charitable company group whose consolidated financial statements are prepared and audited under both the Companies Act 2006 and the Charities Act 2011

Example 29 – Charitable company audited under the Charities Act 2011

INDEPENDENT AUDITOR'S REPORT TO THE TRUSTEES OF XYZ CHARITABLE COMPANY [LIMITED]

We have audited the financial statements of (name of charitable company) for the year ended ... which comprise [specify the titles of the primary statements such as the Statement of Financial Activities, the Summary Income and Expenditure Account, the Balance Sheet, the Cash Flow Statement] and the related notes[81]. The financial reporting framework that has been applied in their preparation is applicable law and United Kingdom Accounting Standards (United Kingdom Generally Accepted Accounting Practice).

Respective responsibilities of trustees and auditor

As explained more fully in the Trustees' Responsibilities Statement [set out [on page...]], the trustees (who are also the directors of the charitable company for the purposes of company law) are responsible for the preparation of the financial statements and for being satisfied that they give a true and fair view.

The trustees have elected for the financial statements to be audited in accordance with the Charities Act 2011 rather than the Companies Act 2006. Accordingly we have been appointed as auditor under section 144[82] of the Charities Act 2011 and report in accordance with regulations made under section 154 of that Act.

Our responsibility is to audit and express an opinion on the financial statements in accordance with applicable law and International Standards on Auditing (UK and Ireland). Those standards require us to comply with the Auditing Practices Board's [(APB's)] Ethical Standards for Auditors.

Scope of the audit of the financial statements

Either:

> A description of the scope of an audit of financial statements is [provided on the APB's website at www.frc.org.uk/apb/scope/private.cfm] / [set out [on page ...] of the Trustees' Annual Report].

Or:

> An audit involves obtaining evidence about the amounts and disclosures in the financial statements sufficient to give reasonable assurance that the financial statements are free from material misstatement, whether caused by fraud or error. This includes an assessment of: whether the accounting policies are appropriate to the charitable company's circumstances and have been consistently applied

---

[81] *Auditor's reports of entities that do not publish their financial statements on a website or publish them using "PDF" format may refer to the financial statements by reference to page numbers.*

[82] *If a charity which is below the thresholds where a charity audit is required decides to have its accounts audited, the auditor is appointed under section 145 of the Charities Act 2011.*

and adequately disclosed; the reasonableness of significant accounting estimates made by the trustees; and the overall presentation of the financial statements. In addition, we read all the financial and non-financial information in the *[describe the annual report]* to identify material inconsistencies with the audited financial statements. If we become aware of any apparent material misstatements or inconsistencies we consider the implications for our report.

Opinion on financial statements

In our opinion the financial statements:

- give a true and fair view of the state of the charitable company's affairs as at ..., and of its incoming resources and application of resources, including its income and expenditure, for the year then ended;
- have been properly prepared in accordance with United Kingdom Generally Accepted Accounting Practice; and
- have been prepared in accordance with the requirements of the Companies Act 2006.

Matters on which we are required to report by exception

We have nothing to report in respect of the following matters where the Charities Act 2011 requires us to report to you if, in our opinion:

- the information given in the Trustees' Annual Report is inconsistent in any material respect with the financial statements; or
- the charitable company has not kept adequate accounting records; or
- the financial statements are not in agreement with the accounting records and returns; or
- we have not received all the information and explanations we require for our audit.

Statutory Auditor   *Address*
Date
ABC LLP is eligible to act as an auditor in terms of section 1212 of the Companies Act 2006

Example 30 – Charitable company audited under the Companies Act 2006

INDEPENDENT AUDITOR'S REPORT TO THE MEMBERS OF XYZ CHARITABLE COMPANY [LIMITED]

We have audited the financial statements of (name of charitable company) for the year ended ... which comprise [specify the titles of the primary statements such as the Statement of Financial Activities, the Summary Income and Expenditure Account, the Balance Sheet, the Cash Flow Statement] and the related notes[83]. The financial reporting framework that has been applied in their preparation is applicable law and United Kingdom Accounting Standards (United Kingdom Generally Accepted Accounting Practice).

Respective responsibilities of trustees and auditor

As explained more fully in the Trustees' Responsibilities Statement [set out [on page...]], the trustees (who are also the directors of the charitable company for the purposes of company law) are responsible for the preparation of the financial statements and for being satisfied that they give a true and fair view.

Our responsibility is to audit and express an opinion on the financial statements in accordance with applicable law and International Standards on Auditing (UK and Ireland). Those standards require us to comply with the Auditing Practices Board's [(APB's)] Ethical Standards for Auditors.

Scope of the audit of the financial statements

Either:

A description of the scope of an audit of financial statements is [provided on the APB's website at www.frc.org.uk/apb/scope/private.cfm] / [set out [on page ...] of the Trustees' Annual Report].

Or:

An audit involves obtaining evidence about the amounts and disclosures in the financial statements sufficient to give reasonable assurance that the financial statements are free from material misstatement, whether caused by fraud or error. This includes an assessment of: whether the accounting policies are appropriate to the charitable company's circumstances and have been consistently applied and adequately disclosed; the reasonableness of significant accounting estimates made by the trustees; and the overall presentation of the financial statements. In addition, we read all the financial and non-financial information in the *[describe the annual report]* to identify material inconsistencies with the audited financial statements. If we become aware of any apparent material misstatements or inconsistencies we consider the implications for our report.

---

[83] *Auditor's reports of entities that do not publish their financial statements on a website or publish them using "PDF" format may refer to the financial statements by reference to page numbers.*

Opinion on financial statements

In our opinion the financial statements:

- give a true and fair view of the state of the charitable company's affairs as at ... and of its incoming resources and application of resources, including its income and expenditure, for the year then ended;
- have been properly prepared in accordance with United Kingdom Generally Accepted Accounting Practice; and
- have been prepared in accordance with the requirements of the Companies Act 2006.

Opinion on other matter prescribed by the Companies Act 2006

In our opinion the information given in the Trustees' Annual Report for the financial year for which the financial statements are prepared is consistent with the financial statements.

Matters on which we are required to report by exception

We have nothing to report in respect of the following matters where the Companies Act 2006 requires us to report to you if, in our opinion:

- adequate accounting records have not been kept or returns adequate for our audit have not been received from branches not visited by us; or
- the financial statements are not in agreement with the accounting records and returns; or
- certain disclosures of trustees' remuneration specified by law are not made; or
- we have not received all the information and explanations we require for our audit. [or
- the trustees were not entitled to prepare the financial statements in accordance with the small companies regime [and] [take advantage of the small companies exemption in preparing the directors' report]].[84]

[Signature]   *Address*
John Smith *(Senior statutory auditor)*   Date
for and on behalf of ABC LLP, Statutory Auditor

---

[84] *Only applicable if a charitable company, below the small companies threshold, has chosen to prepare its financial statements and Trustees' Annual Report (including the requirements of the directors' report) in accordance with the small companies regime.*

Example 31 – Charitable company group whose consolidated financial statements are prepared and audited under both the Companies Act 2006 and the Charities Act 2011

INDEPENDENT AUDITOR'S REPORT TO THE MEMBERS AND TRUSTEES OF XYZ CHARITABLE COMPANY [LIMITED]

We have audited the financial statements of (name of charitable company) for the year ended which comprise [specify the titles of the primary statements such as the Group [and Parent Charitable Company] Statement of Financial Activities, the Group [and Parent Charitable Company] Summary Income and Expenditure Account, the Group and Parent Charitable Company Balance Sheets, the Group [and Parent Charitable Company] Cash Flow Statement] and the related notes[85]. The financial reporting framework that has been applied in their preparation is applicable law and United Kingdom Accounting Standards (United Kingdom Generally Accepted Accounting Practice).

Respective responsibilities of trustees and auditor

As explained more fully in the Trustees' Responsibilities Statement [set out [on page...]], the trustees (who are also the directors of the charitable company for the purposes of company law) are responsible for the preparation of the financial statements and for being satisfied that they give a true and fair view.

We have been appointed auditor under the Companies Act 2006 and section 151 of the Charities Act 2011 and report in accordance with those Acts. Our responsibility is to audit and express an opinion on the financial statements in accordance with applicable law and International Standards on Auditing (UK and Ireland). Those standards require us to comply with the Auditing Practices Board's [(APB's)] Ethical Standards for Auditors.

Scope of the audit of the financial statements

Either:

A description of the scope of an audit of financial statements is [provided on the APB's website at www.frc.org.uk/apb/scope/private.cfm] / [set out [on page ...] of the Trustees' Annual Report].

Or:

An audit involves obtaining evidence about the amounts and disclosures in the financial statements sufficient to give reasonable assurance that the financial statements are free from material misstatement, whether caused by fraud or error. This includes an assessment of: whether the accounting policies are appropriate to the charitable company's circumstances and have been consistently applied and adequately disclosed; the reasonableness of significant accounting estimates made by the trustees; and the overall presentation of the financial statements. In addition, we read all the financial and non-financial information in the *[describe*

---

[85] *Auditor's reports of entities that do not publish their financial statements on a website or publish them using "PDF" format may refer to the financial statements by reference to page numbers.*

the annual report] to identify material inconsistencies with the audited financial statements. If we become aware of any apparent material misstatements or inconsistencies we consider the implications for our report.

Opinion on financial statements

In our opinion the financial statements:

- give a true and fair view of the state of the group's and the parent charitable company's affairs as at ..., and of the group's incoming resources and application of resources, including its income and expenditure, for the year then ended;
- have been properly prepared in accordance with United Kingdom Generally Accepted Accounting Practice; and
- have been prepared in accordance with the requirements of the Companies Act 2006 and the Charities Act 2011.

Opinion on other matter prescribed by the Companies Act 2006

In our opinion the information given in the Trustees' Annual Report for the financial year for which the financial statements are prepared is consistent with the financial statements.

Matters on which we are required to report by exception

We have nothing to report in respect of the following matters where the Companies Act 2006 and the Charities Act 2011 requires us to report to you if, in our opinion:

- the parent charitable company has not kept adequate and sufficient accounting records, or returns adequate for our audit have not been received from branches not visited by us; or
- the parent charitable company financial statements are not in agreement with the accounting records and returns; or
- certain disclosures of trustees' remuneration specified by law are not made; or
- we have not received all the information and explanations we require for our audit. [or
- the trustees were not entitled to prepare the financial statements in accordance with the small companies regime [and] [take advantage of the small companies exemption in preparing the directors' report]].[86]

[Signature]   *Address*
John Smith *(Senior statutory auditor)*   *Date*
for and on behalf of ABC LLP, Statutory Auditor
ABC LLP is eligible to act as an auditor in terms of section 1212 of the Companies Act 2006.

---

[86] *Only applicable if a charitable company, below the small companies threshold, has chosen to prepare its financial statements and Trustees' Annual Report (including the requirements of the directors' report) in accordance with the small companies regime.*

Appendix 11 – Charitable companies registered either in Scotland or in both Scotland and England & Wales

32. Charitable company where an election has been made for audit exemption under the Companies Act 2006
33. Charitable company audited under the Charities and Trustee Investment (Scotland) Act 2005 and the Companies Act 2006
34. Large charitable company group whose consolidated financial statements are required to be prepared and audited under the Companies Act 2006

Example 32 – Charitable company where an election has been made for audit exemption under the Companies Act 2006

INDEPENDENT AUDITOR'S REPORT TO THE TRUSTEES OF XYZ CHARITABLE COMPANY [LIMITED]

We have audited the financial statements of (name of charitable company) for the year ended ... which comprise [specify the titles of the primary statements such as the Statement of Financial Activities, the Summary Income and Expenditure Account, the Balance Sheet, the Cash Flow Statement] and the related notes[87]. The financial reporting framework that has been applied in their preparation is applicable law and United Kingdom Accounting Standards (United Kingdom Generally Accepted Accounting Practice).

Respective responsibilities of trustees and auditor

As explained more fully in the Trustees' Responsibilities Statement [set out [on page ...]], the trustees (who are also the directors of the charitable company for the purposes of company law) are responsible for the preparation of the financial statements and for being satisfied that they give a true and fair view

The trustees have elected for the financial statements to be audited in accordance with the Charities and Trustee Investment (Scotland) Act 2005 [and the Charities Act 2011][88] rather than also with the Companies Act 2006. Accordingly we have been appointed as auditor under section 44(1)(c) of the Charities and Trustee Investment (Scotland) Act 2005 [and under section 144 of the Charities Act 2011][89] and report in accordance with [that] [those] Act[s].

Our responsibility is to audit and express an opinion on the financial statements in accordance with applicable law and International Standards on Auditing (UK and Ireland). Those standards require us o comply with the Auditing Practices Board's [(APB's)] Ethical Standards for Auditors.

Scope of the audit of the financial statements

Either:

> A description of the scope of an audit of financial statements is [provided on the APB's website at www.frc.org.uk/apb/scope/private.cfm] / [set out [on page ...] of the Trustees' Annual Report].

---

[87] *Auditor's reports of entities that do not publish their financial statements on a website or publish them using "PDF" format may refer to the financial statements by reference to page numbers.*

[88] *This should only be included for cross border charitable companies registered in Scotland and England and Wales*

[89] *This should only be included for cross border charitable companies registered in Scotland and England and Wales*

Or:

> An audit involves obtaining evidence about the amounts and disclosures in the financial statements sufficient to give reasonable assurance that the financial statements are free from material misstatement, whether caused by fraud or error. This includes an assessment of: whether the accounting policies are appropriate to the charitable company's circumstances and have been consistently applied and adequately disclosed; the reasonableness of significant accounting estimates made by the trustees; and the overall presentation of the financial statements. In addition, we read all the financial and non-financial information in the *[describe the annual report]* to identify material inconsistencies with the audited financial statements. If we become aware of any apparent material misstatements or inconsistencies we consider the implications for our report.

Opinion on financial statements

In our opinion the financial statements:

- give a true and fair view of the state of the charitable company's affairs as at ... and of its incoming resources and application of resources, including its income and expenditure, for the year then ended;
- have been properly prepared in accordance with United Kingdom Generally Accepted Accounting Practice; and
- have been prepared in accordance with the requirements of the Companies Act 2006, the Charities and Trustee Investment (Scotland) Act 2005 and regulation 8 of the Charities Accounts (Scotland) Regulations 2006 (as amended).

Matters on which we are required to report by exception

We have nothing to report in respect of the following matters where the Charities Accounts (Scotland) Regulations 2006 (as amended) [and the Charities Act 2011][90] requires us to report to you if, in our opinion:

- the information given in the Trustees' Annual Report is inconsistent in any material respect with the financial statements; or
- the charitable company has not kept proper and adequate accounting records; or
- the financial statements are not in agreement with the accounting records and returns; or
- we have not received all the information and explanations we require for our audit.

Statutory Auditor   *Address*
Date
ABC LLP is eligible to act as an auditor in terms of section 1212 of the Companies Act 2006

---

[90] *This is only included in respect of cross border charities registered in both Scotland and in England and Wales*

Example 33 – Charitable company audited under the Charities and Trustee Investment (Scotland) Act 2005 and the Companies Act 2006

INDEPENDENT AUDITOR'S REPORT TO THE TRUSTEES AND MEMBERS OF XYZ CHARITABLE COMPANY [LIMITED]

We have audited the financial statements of (name of charitable company) for the year ended ... which comprise [specify the titles of the primary statements such as the Statement of Financial Activities, the Summary Income and Expenditure Account, the Balance Sheet, the Cash Flow Statement] and the related notes[91]. The financial reporting framework that has been applied in their preparation is applicable law and United Kingdom Accounting Standards (United Kingdom Generally Accepted Accounting Practice).

Respective responsibilities of trustees and auditor

As explained more fully in the Trustees' Responsibilities Statement [set out [on page...]], the trustees (who are also the directors of the charitable company for the purposes of company law) are responsible for the preparation of the financial statements and for being satisfied that they give a true and fair view.

We have been appointed as auditor under section 44(1)(c) of the Charities and Trustee Investment (Scotland) Act 2005 and under the Companies Act 2006 and report in accordance with regulations made under those Acts.

Our responsibility is to audit and express an opinion on the financial statements in accordance with applicable law and International Standards on Auditing (UK and Ireland). Those standards require us to comply with the Auditing Practices Board's [(APB's)] Ethical Standards for Auditors.

Scope of the audit of the financial statements

Either:

> A description of the scope of an audit of financial statements is [provided on the APB's website at www.frc.org.uk/apb/scope/private.cfm] / [set out [on page ...] of the Trustees' Annual Report].

Or:

> An audit involves obtaining evidence about the amounts and disclosures in the financial statements sufficient to give reasonable assurance that the financial statements are free from material misstatement, whether caused by fraud or error. This includes an assessment of: whether the accounting policies are appropriate to the charitable company's circumstances and have been consistently applied and adequately disclosed; the reasonableness of significant accounting estimates made by the trustees; and the overall presentation of the financial statements. In addition, we read all the financial and non-financial information in the *[describe*

---

[91] *Auditor's reports of entities that do not publish their financial statements on a website or publish them using "PDF" format may refer to the financial statements by reference to page numbers.*

the annual report] to identify material inconsistencies with the audited financial statements. If we become aware of any apparent material misstatements or inconsistencies we consider the implications for our report.

Opinion on financial statements

In our opinion the financial statements:

- give a true and fair view of the state of the charitable company's affairs as at ... and of its incoming resources and application of resources, including its income and expenditure, for the year then ended;
- have been properly prepared in accordance with United Kingdom Generally Accepted Accounting Practice; and
- have been prepared in accordance with the requirements of the Companies Act 2006, the Charities and Trustee Investment (Scotland) Act 2005 and regulation 8 of the Charities Accounts (Scotland) Regulations 2006 (as amended).

Opinion on other matter prescribed by the Companies Act 2006

In our opinion the information given in the Trustees' Annual Report for the financial year for which the financial statements are prepared is consistent with the financial statements.

Matters on which we are required to report by exception

We have nothing to report in respect of the following matters where the Companies Act 2006 and the Charities Accounts (Scotland) Regulations 2006 (as amended) requires us to report to you if, in our opinion:

- the charitable company has not kept proper and adequate accounting records or returns adequate for our audit have not been received from branches not visited by us; or
- the financial statements are not in agreement with the accounting records and returns; or
- certain disclosures of trustees' remuneration specified by law are not made; or
- we have not received all the information and explanations we require for our audit [or
- the trustees were not entitled to prepare the financial statements in accordance with the small companies regime [and] [take advantage of the small companies exemption in preparing the directors' report]].[92]

[Signature]   *Address*
John Smith *(Senior statutory auditor)*   *Date*
for and on behalf of ABC LLP, Statutory Auditor
ABC LLP is eligible to act as an auditor in terms of section 1212 of the Companies Act 2006

---

[92] *Only applicable if a charitable company, below the small companies threshold, has chosen to prepare its financial statements and Trustees' Annual Report (including the requirements of the directors' report) in accordance with the small companies regime.*

Example 34 – Large charitable company group whose consolidated financial statements are required to be prepared and audited under the Companies Act 2006

INDEPENDENT AUDITOR'S REPORT TO THE MEMBERS AND TRUSTEES OF XYZ CHARITABLE COMPANY (LIMITED)

We have audited the financial statements of (name of charitable company) for the year ended ... which comprise [specify the titles of the primary statements such as the Group [and Parent] Charitable Company Statements of Financial Activities, the Group [and Parent] Charitable Company Summary Income and Expenditure Accounts, the Group and Parent Charitable Company Balance Sheets, the Group [and Parent] Charitable Company Cash Flow Statements] and the related notes[93]. The financial reporting framework that has been applied in their preparation is applicable law and United Kingdom Accounting Standards (United Kingdom Generally Accepted Accounting Practice).

Respective responsibilities of trustees and auditor

As explained more fully in the Trustees' Responsibilities Statement [set out [on page ...]], the trustees (who are also the directors of the charitable company for the purposes of company law) are responsible for the preparation of the financial statements and for being satisfied that they give a true and fair view.

We have been appointed as auditor under section 44(1)(c) of the Charities and Trustee Investment (Scotland) Act 2005 and under the Companies Act 2006 and report in accordance with regulations made under those Acts.

Our responsibility is to audit and express an opinion on the financial statements in accordance with applicable law and International Standards on Auditing (UK and Ireland). Those standards require us to comply with the Auditing Practices Board's [(APB's)] Ethical Standards for Auditors.

Scope of the audit of the financial statements

Either:

A description of the scope of an audit of financial statements is [provided on the APB's website at www.frc.org.uk/apb/scope/private.cfm] / [set out [on page ...] of the Trustees' Annual Report].

Or:

An audit involves obtaining evidence about the amounts and disclosures in the financial statements sufficient to give reasonable assurance that the financial statements are free from material misstatement, whether caused by fraud or error. This includes an assessment of: whether the accounting policies are appropriate to the group's and the parent charitable company's circumstances and have been consistently applied and adequately disclosed; the reasonableness of significant

[93] *Auditor's reports of entities that do not publish their financial statements on a website or publish them using "PDF" format may refer to the financial statements by reference to page numbers.*

accounting estimates made by the trustees; and the overall presentation of the financial statements. In addition, we read all the financial and non-financial information in the *[describe the annual report]* to identify material inconsistencies with the audited financial statements. If we become aware of any apparent material misstatements or inconsistencies we consider the implications for our report.

Opinion on financial statements

In our opinion the financial statements:

- give a true and fair view of the state of the group's and the parent charitable company's affairs as at ... and of the group's [and the parent] charitable company's incoming resources and application of resources, including [its] [the group's and the parent] income and expenditure, for the year then ended;
- have been properly prepared in accordance with United Kingdom Generally Accepted Accounting Practice; and
- have been prepared in accordance with the requirements of the Companies Act 2006, the Charities and Trustee Investment (Scotland) Act 2005 and regulations 6 and 8 of the Charities Accounts (Scotland) Regulations 2006 (as amended).

Opinion on other matter prescribed by the Companies Act 2006

In our opinion the information given in the Trustees' Annual Report for the financial year for which the financial statements are prepared is consistent with the financial statements.

Matters on which we are required to report by exception

We have nothing to report in respect of the following matters where the Companies Act 2006 and the Charities Accounts (Scotland) Regulations 2006 (as amended) requires us to report to you if, in our opinion:

- the parent charitable company has not kept proper and adequate accounting records or returns adequate for our audit have not been received from branches not visited by us; or
- the parent charitable company's financial statements are not in agreement with the accounting records or returns; or
- certain disclosures of trustees' remuneration specified by law are not made; or
- we have not received all the information and explanations we require for our audit.

[Signature]   *Address*
John Smith (Senior statutory auditor)   *Date*
for and on behalf of ABC LLP, Statutory Auditor
ABC LLP is eligible to act as an auditor in terms of section 1212 of the Companies Act 2006

Appendix 12 – Non-company charities

35. Charity registered in England & Wales
36. Charity registered in Scotland

Example 35 – Charity registered in England & Wales

INDEPENDENT AUDITOR'S REPORT TO THE TRUSTEES OF XYZ CHARITY

We have audited the financial statements of (name of charity) for the year ended ... which comprise [specify the titles of the primary statements such as the Statement of Financial Activities, the Balance Sheet, the Cash Flow Statement] and the related notes[94]. The financial reporting framework that has been applied in their preparation is applicable law and United Kingdom Accounting Standards (United Kingdom Generally Accepted Accounting Practice).

Respective responsibilities of trustees and auditor

As explained more fully in the Trustees' Responsibilities Statement [set out [on page ...]], the trustees are responsible for the preparation of financial statements which give a true and fair view.

We have been appointed as auditor under section 144[95] of the Charities Act 2011 and report in accordance with regulations made under section 154 of that Act. Our responsibility is to audit and express an opinion on the financial statements in accordance with applicable law and International Standards on Auditing (UK and Ireland). Those standards require us to comply with the Auditing Practices Board's [(APB's)] Ethical Standards for Auditors.

Scope of the audit of the financial statements

Either:

> A description of the scope of an audit of financial statements is [provided on the APB's website at www.frc.org.uk/apb/scope/private.cfm] / [set out [on page ...] of the Trustees' Annual Report].

Or:

> An audit involves obtaining evidence about the amounts and disclosures in the financial statements sufficient to give reasonable assurance that the financial statements are free from material misstatement, whether caused by fraud or error. This includes an assessment of: whether the accounting policies are appropriate to the charity's circumstances and have been consistently applied and adequately disclosed; the reasonableness of significant accounting estimates made by the trustees; and the overall presentation of the financial statements. In addition, we read all the financial and non-financial information in the *[describe the annual report]* to identify material inconsistencies with the audited financial statements. If we become aware of any apparent material misstatements or inconsistencies we consider the implications for our report.

---

[94] *Auditor's reports of entities that do not publish their financial statements on a website or publish them using "PDF" format may refer to the financial statements by reference to page numbers.*

[95] *If a charity which is below the thresholds where a charity audit is required decides to have its accounts audited, the auditor is appointed under section 145 of the Charities Act 2011.*

Opinion on financial statements

In our opinion the financial statements:

- give a true and fair view of the state of the charity's affairs as at ..., and of its incoming resources and application of resources, for the year then ended;
- have been properly prepared in accordance with United Kingdom Generally Accepted Accounting Practice; and
- have been prepared in accordance with the requirements of the Charities Act 2011.

Matters on which we are required to report by exception

We have nothing to report in respect of the following matters where the Charities Act 2011 requires us to report to you if, in our opinion:

- the information given in the Trustees' Annual Report is inconsistent in any material respect with the financial statements; or
- sufficient accounting records have not been kept; or
- the financial statements are not in agreement with the accounting records and returns; or
- we have not received all the information and explanations we require for our audit.

Statutory Auditor   *Address*
Date
ABC LLP is eligible to act as an auditor in terms of section 1212 of the Companies Act 2006

Example 36 – Charity registered in Scotland

INDEPENDENT AUDITOR'S REPORT TO THE TRUSTEES OF XYZ CHARITY

We have audited the financial statements of (name of charity) for the year ended ... which comprise [specify the titles of the primary statements such as the Statement of Financial Activities, the Balance Sheet, the Cash Flow Statement] and the related notes[96]. The financial reporting framework that has been applied in their preparation is applicable law and United Kingdom Accounting Standards (United Kingdom Generally Accepted Accounting Practice).

Respective responsibilities of trustees and auditor

As explained more fully in the Trustees' Responsibilities Statement [set out [on page ...]], the trustees are responsible for the preparation of financial statements which give a true and fair view.

We have been appointed as auditor under section 44(1)(c) of the Charities and Trustee Investment (Scotland) Act 2005 and report in accordance with regulations made under that Act. Our responsibility is to audit and express an opinion on the financial statements in accordance with applicable law and International Standards on Auditing (UK and Ireland). Those standards require us to comply with the Auditing Practices Board's [(APB's)] Ethical Standards for Auditors.

Scope of the audit of the financial statements

Either:

> A description of the scope of an audit of financial statements is [provided on the APB's website at www.frc.org.uk/apb/scope/private.cfm] / [set out [on page ...] of the Trustees' Annual Report].

Or:

> An audit involves obtaining evidence about the amounts and disclosures in the financial statements sufficient to give reasonable assurance that the financial statements are free from material misstatement, whether caused by fraud or error. This includes an assessment of: whether the accounting policies are appropriate to the charity's circumstances and have been consistently applied and adequately disclosed; the reasonableness of significant accounting estimates made by the trustees; and the overall presentation of the financial statements. In addition, we read all the financial and non-financial information in the *[describe the annual report]* to identify material inconsistencies with the audited financial statements. If we become aware of any apparent material misstatements or inconsistencies we consider the implications for our report.

---

[96] *Auditor's reports of entities that do not publish their financial statements on a website or publish them using "PDF" format may refer to the financial statements by reference to page numbers.*

Opinion on financial statements

In our opinion the financial statements:

- give a true and fair view of the state of the charity's affairs as at ... and of its incoming resources and application of resources, for the year then ended;
- have been properly prepared in accordance with United Kingdom Generally Accepted Accounting Practice; and
- have been prepared in accordance with the requirements of the Charities and Trustee Investment (Scotland) Act 2005 and regulation 8 of the Charities Accounts (Scotland) Regulations 2006 (as amended).

Matters on which we are required to report by exception

We have nothing to report in respect of the following matters where the Charity Accounts (Scotland) Regulations 2006 (as amended) requires us to report to you if, in our opinion:

- the information given in the Trustees' Annual Report is inconsistent in any material respect with the financial statements; or
- proper accounting records have not been kept; or
- the financial statements are not in agreement with the accounting records and returns; or
- we have not received all the information and explanations we require for our audit.

Statutory Auditor   *Address*
Date
ABC LLP is eligible to act as an auditor in terms of section 1212 of the Companies Act 2006

Appendix 13 – Qualified opinion on financial statements

37. Disagreement – Inappropriate accounting treatment of debtors
38. Disagreement – Non-disclosure of a going concern problem
39. Disagreement – Non-disclosure of information required to be disclosed
40. Scope Limitation – Auditor not appointed at the time of the stocktaking
41. Scope Limitation – Directors did not prepare cash flow forecasts sufficiently far
    into the future to be able to assess the going concern status of the company

Example 37 – Qualified opinion: Disagreement – Inappropriate accounting treatment of debtors

- *UK non-publicly traded company prepares UK GAAP financial statements (Example 2).*
- *The debtors shown on the balance sheet include an amount of £Y due from a company which has ceased trading. XYZ Limited has no security for this debt.*
- *The auditor's opinion is that the company is unlikely to receive any payment and full provision of £Y should have been made.*
- *The auditor believes that the effect of the disagreement is material but not pervasive to the financial statements and accordingly issues a qualified opinion – except for disagreement about the accounting treatment of debtors.*

EXTRACT FROM AUDITOR'S REPORT

...

Basis for qualified opinion on financial statements

Included in the debtors shown on the balance sheet is an amount of £Y due from a company which has ceased trading. XYZ Limited has no security for this debt. In our opinion the company is unlikely to receive any payment and full provision of £Y should have been made. Accordingly, debtors should be reduced by £Y, the deferred tax liability should be reduced by £X and profit for the year and retained earnings should be reduced by £Z.

Qualified opinion on financial statements

In our opinion, except for the effects of the matter described in the Basis for Qualified Opinion paragraph, the financial statements:

- give a true and fair view of the state of the company's affairs as at ... and of its profit [loss] for the year then ended;
- have been properly prepared in accordance with United Kingdom Generally Accepted Accounting Practice; and
- have been prepared in accordance with the requirements of the Companies Act 2006.

Opinion on other matter prescribed by the Companies Act 2006

In our opinion the information given in the Directors' Report for the financial year for which the financial statements are prepared is consistent with the financial statements.

Matters on which we are required to report by exception[97]

We have nothing to report in respect of the following matters where the Companies Act 2006 requires us to report to you if, in our opinion:

- adequate accounting records have not been kept, or returns adequate for our audit have not been received from branches not visited by us; or

---

[97] *The auditor needs to consider whether the circumstances leading to the disagreement about the accounting treatment affect the matters on which the auditor is required to report by exception.*

- the financial statements are not in agreement with the accounting records and returns; or
- certain disclosures of directors' remuneration specified by law are not made; or
- we have not received all the information and explanations we require for our audit.

Example 38 – Qualified opinion: Disagreement – Non-disclosure of a going concern problem

- *UK non-publicly traded company prepares UK GAAP financial statements (Example 2).*
- *The company's year-end is 31 December 20X1 and neither the financial statements nor the directors' report disclose that the Company's financing arrangements expire and amounts outstanding are payable on 19 July 20X2 and that the Company has been unable to re-negotiate or obtain replacement financing. The directors continue to talk to potential alternative providers of finance.*
- *This situation indicates the existence of a material uncertainty which may cast significant doubt on the company's ability to continue as a going concern and therefore it may be unable to realise its assets and discharge its liabilities in the normal course of business.*
- *The auditor concludes that there is a significant level of concern about going concern and disagrees with the failure to disclose this information in the financial statements. The auditor believes that the lack of disclosure although material is not pervasive to the financial statements and accordingly issues a qualified opinion describing the disagreement.*

EXTRACT FROM AUDITOR'S REPORT

...

Basis for qualified opinion on financial statements

The company's financing arrangements expire and amounts outstanding are payable on 19 July 20X2. While the directors continue to investigate alternative sources of finance, the company has so far been unable to re-negotiate or obtain replacement financing. This situation indicates the existence of a material uncertainty which may cast significant doubt on the company's ability to continue as a going concern and therefore it may be unable to realise its assets and discharge its liabilities in the normal course of business. The financial statements (and notes thereto) do not disclose this fact.

Qualified opinion on financial statements

In our opinion, except for the effects of the matter described in the Basis for Qualified Opinion paragraph, the financial statements:

- give a true and fair view of the state of the company's affairs as at 31 December 20X1 and of its profit [loss] for the year then ended;
- have been properly prepared in accordance with United Kingdom Generally Accepted Accounting Practice; and
- have been prepared in accordance with the requirements of the Companies Act 2006.

Opinion on other matter prescribed by the Companies Act 2006

...

Example 39 – Qualified opinion: Disagreement – Non-disclosure of information required to be disclosed

- *UK non-publicly traded company prepares UK GAAP financial statements (Example 2).*
- *The company has not disclosed that one of its bankers has a fixed and floating charge over all of the company's assets as security for a long term loan. Such disclosure is required by paragraph 61 of Part 2 to Schedule 1 of The Large and Medium-sized Companies and Groups (Accounts and Reports) Regulations 2008.*

EXTRACT FROM AUDITOR'S REPORT

...

Basis for qualified opinion on financial statements

The notes to the financial statements do not disclose that one of the company's bankers has a fixed and floating charge over all of the company's assets as security for a bank loan of £5 million which is included in creditors: amounts falling due after more than one year. Such disclosure is required by the Companies Act 2006

Qualified opinion on financial statements

In our opinion, except for the effects of the matter described in the Basis for Qualified Opinion paragraph, the financial statements:

- give a true and fair view of the state of the company's affairs as at 31 December 20X1 and of its profit [loss] for the year then ended;
- have been properly prepared in accordance with United Kingdom Generally Accepted Accounting Practice; and
- have been prepared in accordance with the requirements of the Companies Act 2006.

Opinion on other matter prescribed by the Companies Act 2006

...

Example 40 – Qualified opinion: Limitation on scope – Auditor not appointed at the time of the stocktaking

- UK non-publicly traded company prepares UK GAAP financial statements *(Example 2)*.
- The evidence available to the auditor was limited because they did not observe the counting of the physical stock as at 31 December 20X1, since that date was prior to the time the auditor was initially engaged as auditor for the company. Owing to the nature of the company's records, the auditor was unable to satisfy itself as to stock quantities using other audit procedures.
- The limitation in audit scope causes the auditor to issue a qualified opinion "except for" any adjustments that might have been found to be necessary had it been able to obtain sufficient evidence concerning stock.
- The limitation of scope was determined by the auditor to be material but not pervasive to the financial statements.

EXTRACT FROM AUDITOR'S REPORT

Basis for qualified opinion on financial statements

With respect to stock having a carrying amount of £X the audit evidence available to us was limited because we did not observe the counting of the physical stock as at 31 December 20X1, since that date was prior to our appointment as auditor of the company. Owing to the nature of the company's records, we were unable to obtain sufficient appropriate audit evidence regarding the stock quantities by using other audit procedures.

Qualified opinion on financial statements

In our opinion, except for the possible effects of the matters described in the Basis for Qualified Opinion paragraph, the financial statements:

- give a true and fair view of the state of the company's affairs as at 31 December 20X1 and of its profit [loss]for the year then ended;
- have been properly prepared in accordance with United Kingdom Generally Accepted Accounting Practice; and
- have been prepared in accordance with the requirements of the Companies Act 2006.

Opinion on other matter prescribed by the Companies Act 2006

In our opinion the information given in the Directors' Report for the financial year for which the financial statements are prepared is consistent with the financial statements.

Matters on which we are required to report by exception

In respect solely of the limitation on our work relating to stock, described above:

- we have not obtained all the information and explanations that we considered necessary for the purpose of our audit; and

- we were unable to determine whether adequate accounting records had been kept.

We have nothing to report in respect of the following matters where the Companies Act 2006 requires us to report to you if, in our opinion:

- returns adequate for our audit have not been received from branches not visited by us; or
- the financial statements are not in agreement with the accounting records and returns; or
- certain disclosures of directors' remuneration specified by law are not made.

[Signature]   *Address*
John Smith (Senior statutory auditor)   *Date*
for and on behalf of ABC LLP, Statutory Auditor

Example 41 – Qualified opinion: Limitation of scope – Directors did not prepare cash flow forecasts sufficiently far into the future to be able to assess the going concern status of the company

- *UK non-publicly traded company prepares UK GAAP financial statements (Example 2).*
- *The evidence available to the auditor was limited because the company had prepared cash flow forecasts and other information needed for the assessment of the appropriateness of the going concern basis of preparation of the financial statements only for a period of nine months from the date of approval of the financial statements and there were no sufficient alternative procedures that the auditor could perform.*
- *Although this fact is disclosed in the financial statements had the information been available the auditor might have formed a different opinion. The auditor considers that the directors have not taken adequate steps to satisfy themselves that it is appropriate for them to adopt the going concern basis.*
- *The auditor does not consider that the future period to which the directors have paid particular attention in assessing going concern is reasonable in the company's circumstances. The auditor considers that the particular circumstances of the company and the nature of the company's business require that such information be prepared, and reviewed by the directors and auditor for a period of at least twelve months from the date of approval of the financial statements.*
- *The auditor considers that the possible effect of the limitation of scope is material but not pervasive.*
- *The auditor issues a qualified opinion referring to the adjustments that might have been found to be necessary had they obtained sufficient evidence concerning the appropriateness of the going concern basis of preparation of the financial statements.*

EXTRACT FROM AUDITOR'S REPORT

...

Basis for qualified opinion on financial statements

The audit evidence available to us was limited because the directors of the company have prepared cash flow forecasts and other information needed for the assessment of the appropriateness of the going concern basis of preparation of the financial statements for a period of only nine months from the date of approval of these financial statements. We consider that the directors have not taken adequate steps to satisfy themselves that it is appropriate for them to adopt the going concern basis because the circumstances of the company and the nature of the business require that such information be prepared, and reviewed by the directors and ourselves, for a period of at least twelve months from the date of approval of the financial statements. Had this information been available to us we might have formed a different opinion on the financial statements.

Qualified opinion on financial statements

In our opinion, except for the possible effects of the matter described in the Basis for Qualified Opinion paragraph, the financial statements:

- give a true and fair view of the state of the company's affairs as at ... and of its profit [loss] for the year then ended;

- have been properly prepared in accordance with United Kingdom Generally Accepted Accounting Practice; and
- have been prepared in accordance with the requirements of the Companies Act 2006.

Opinion on other matter prescribed by the Companies Act 2006

In our opinion the information given in the Directors' Report for the financial year for which the financial statements are prepared is consistent with the financial statements.

Matters on which we are required to report by exception

In respect solely of the limitation on our work relating to the assessment of the appropriateness of the going concern basis of preparation of the financial statements, described above, we have not obtained all the information and explanations that we considered necessary for the purpose of our audit.

We have nothing to report in respect of the following matters where the Companies Act 2006 requires us to report to you if, in our opinion:

- adequate accounting records have not been kept, or returns adequate for our audit have not been received from branches not visited by us; or
- the financial statements are not in agreement with the accounting records and returns; or
- certain disclosures of directors' remuneration specified by law are not made.

[Signature]   *Address*
John Smith (Senior statutory auditor)   *Date*
for and on behalf of ABC LLP, Statutory Auditor

Appendix 14 – Adverse opinion on financial statements

42. Adverse opinion: No provision made for losses expected to arise on long term contracts
43. Adverse opinion: Significant level of concern about going concern status that is not disclosed in the financial statements

Example 42 – Adverse opinion: No provision made for losses expected to arise on long-term contracts

- *UK non-publicly traded company prepares UK GAAP financial statements (Example 2).*
- *No provision has been made for losses expected to arise on certain long-term contracts currently in progress, as the directors consider that such losses should be off-set against amounts recoverable on other long-term contracts.*
- *In the auditor's opinion, provision should be made for foreseeable losses on individual contracts as required by SSAP 9.*
- *In the auditor's view, the financial effect of this disagreement in accounting treatment is both material and pervasive to the financial statements such that an "except for" qualification of the auditor's opinion would not be sufficient to disclose the misleading nature of the financial statements.*
- *The auditor issues an adverse opinion due to the failure to provide for the losses and quantifies the impact on the profit for the year, the contract work in progress and the deferred tax liability at the year end.*
- *The auditor considers that notwithstanding its adverse opinion on the financial statements that adequate accounting records had been kept by the company and that it had received all the information and explanations it required for the audit.*

EXTRACT FROM AUDITOR'S REPORT

...

Basis for adverse opinion on financial statements

As more fully explained in note [x] to the financial statements no provision has been made for losses expected to arise on certain long-term contracts currently in progress, as the directors consider that such losses should be off-set against amounts recoverable on other long-term contracts. In our opinion, provision should be made for foreseeable losses on individual contracts as required by Statement of Standard Accounting Practice 9: *Stocks and long-term contracts*. If losses had been so recognised the effect would have been to reduce the carrying amount of contract work in progress by £X, the deferred tax liability by £Y and the profit for the year and retained earnings at 31 December 20X1 by £Z.

Adverse opinion on financial statements

In our opinion, because of the significance of the matter described in the Basis for Adverse Opinion paragraph, the financial statements:

- do not give a true and fair view of the state of the company's affairs as at 31 December 20X1 and of its profit [loss] for the year then ended; and
- have not been properly prepared in accordance with United Kingdom Generally Accepted Accounting Practice.

In all other respects, in our opinion the financial statements have been prepared in accordance with the requirements of the Companies Act 2006.

Opinion on other matter prescribed by the Companies Act 2006

Notwithstanding our adverse opinion on the financial statements, in our opinion the information given in the Directors' Report for the financial year for which the financial statements are prepared is consistent with the financial statements.

Matters on which we are required to report by exception[98]

We have nothing to report in respect of the following matters where the Companies Act 2006 requires us to report to you if, in our opinion:

- adequate accounting records have not been kept, or returns adequate for our audit have not been received from branches not visited by us; or
- the financial statements are not in agreement with the accounting records and returns; or
- certain disclosures of directors' remuneration specified by law are not made; or
- we have not received all the information and explanations we require for our audit.

[Signature]   Address

John Smith *(Senior statutory auditor)*   Date

for and on behalf of ABC LLP, Statutory Auditor

---

[98] *The auditor needs to consider whether the circumstances leading to the adverse opinion on the financial statements affect the matters on which the auditor is required to report by exception.*

Example 43 – Adverse opinion: Significant level of concern about going concern status that is not disclosed in the financial statements

- *UK non-publicly traded company prepares UK GAAP financial statements (Example 2).*
- *Although there is a significant level of concern about the company's ability to continue as a going concern the financial statements and notes do not disclose this fact and the directors have prepared the financial statements on the going concern basis.*
- *The auditor considers that the financial statements should disclose that there is a material uncertainty, which may cast significant doubt on the company's ability to continue as a going concern.*
- *As the effect of this disagreement is both material and pervasive to the amounts included within the financial statements the auditor concludes that a qualification of the opinion is not adequate to disclose the misleading and incomplete nature of the financial statements.*
- *The auditor issues an adverse audit opinion stating that, because the material uncertainty regarding going concern is not disclosed, the financial statements do not give a true and fair view.*

EXTRACT FROM AUDITOR'S REPORT

...

Basis for adverse opinion on financial statements

As explained in note [x] to the financial statements the company's financing arrangements expired and the amount outstanding was payable on [a past date]. The company has been unable to re-negotiate or obtain replacement financing and the directors of the company are considering whether the company should enter insolvency proceedings [but are continuing to investigate alternative sources of finance]. These events indicate a material uncertainty which may cast significant doubt on the company's ability to continue as a going concern and, therefore, it may be unable to realise its assets and discharge its liabilities in the normal course of business. The financial statements (and notes thereto) do not disclose this fact and have been prepared on the going concern basis.

Adverse opinion on financial statements

In our opinion, because of the significance of the matter described in the Basis for Adverse Opinion paragraph:

- the financial statements do not give a true and fair view of the state of the company's affairs as at ... and of its profit [loss] for the year then ended; and
- have not been properly prepared in accordance with United Kingdom Generally Accepted Accounting Practice.

In all other respects, in our opinion the financial statements have been prepared in accordance with the requirements of the Companies Act 2006.

Opinion on other matter prescribed by the Companies Act 2006

Notwithstanding our adverse opinion on the financial statements, in our opinion the information given in the Directors' Report for the financial year for which the financial statements are prepared is consistent with the financial statements.

Matters on which we are required to report by exception

We have nothing to report in respect of the following matters where the Companies Act 2006 requires us to report to you if, in our opinion:

- adequate accounting records have not been kept, or returns adequate for our audit have not been received from branches not visited by us; or
- the financial statements are not in agreement with the accounting records and returns; or
- certain disclosures of directors' remuneration specified by law are not made; or
- we have not received all the information and explanations we require for our audit.

[Signature]   *Address*
John Smith (Senior statutory auditor)   *Date*
for and on behalf of ABC LLP, Statutory Auditor

Appendix 15 – Disclaimer of opinion on financial statements

44. Disclaimer of opinion: Auditor unable to attend stocktaking and confirm trade debtors
45. Disclaimer of opinion: Multiple uncertainties

Example 44 – Disclaimer of opinion: Auditor unable to attend stocktaking and confirm trade debtors

- *UK non-publicly traded company prepares UK GAAP financial statements (Example 2).*
- *The evidence available to the auditor was limited because the auditor was not able to observe all physical stock and confirm trade debtors due to limitations placed on the scope of the auditor's work by the directors of the company.*
- *The limitation in scope is considered by the auditor to be both material and pervasive so that it is unable to form an opinion on the financial statements.*
- *As a result, the auditor issues a modified opinion disclaiming an opinion on the financial statements.*

INDEPENDENT AUDITOR'S REPORT TO THE MEMBERS OF XYZ LIMITED

We were engaged to audit the financial statements of (name of entity) for the year ended ... which comprise [specify the titles of the primary statements such as the Profit and Loss Account, the Balance Sheet, the Cash Flow Statement, the Statement of Total Recognised Gains and Losses, the Reconciliation of Movements in Shareholders' Funds] and the related notes[99]. The financial reporting framework that has been applied in their preparation is applicable law and United Kingdom Accounting Standards (United Kingdom Generally Accepted Accounting Practice).

Respective responsibilities of directors and auditor

As explained more fully in the Directors' Responsibilities Statement [set out [on page ...]], the directors are responsible for the preparation of the financial statements and for being satisfied that they give a true and fair view. Our responsibility is to audit and express an opinion on the financial statements in accordance with applicable law and International Standards on Auditing (UK and Ireland). Those standards require us to comply with the Auditing Practices Board's [(APB's)] Ethical Standards for Auditors. Because of the matter described in the Basis for Disclaimer of Opinion paragraph, however, we were not able to obtain sufficient appropriate audit evidence to provide a basis for an audit opinion.

Scope of the audit of the financial statements

Either:

> A description of the scope of an audit of financial statements is [provided on the APB's website at www.frc.org.uk/apb/scope/private.cfm] / [set out [on page ...] of the Annual Report].

Or:

> An audit involves obtaining evidence about the amounts and disclosures in the financial statements sufficient to give reasonable assurance that the financial statements are free from material misstatement, whether caused by fraud or error.

---

[99] *Auditor's reports of entities that do not publish their financial statements on a website or publish them using 'PDF' format may refer to the financial statements by reference to page numbers.*

This includes an assessment of: whether the accounting policies are appropriate to the company's circumstances and have been consistently applied and adequately disclosed; the reasonableness of significant accounting estimates made by the directors; and the overall presentation of the financial statements. In addition, we read all the financial and non-financial information in the *[describe the annual report]* to identify material inconsistencies with the audited financial statements. If we become aware of any apparent material misstatements or inconsistencies we consider the implications for our report.

Basis for disclaimer of opinion on financial statements

The audit evidence available to us was limited because we were unable to observe the counting of physical stock having a carrying amount of £X and send confirmation letters to trade debtors having a carrying amount of £Y due to limitations placed on the scope of our work by the directors of the company. As a result of this we have been unable to obtain sufficient appropriate audit evidence concerning both stock and trade debtors.

Disclaimer of opinion on financial statements

Because of the significance of the matter described in the Basis for Disclaimer of Opinion on Financial Statements paragraph, we have not been able to obtain sufficient appropriate audit evidence to provide a basis for an audit opinion. Accordingly we do not express an opinion on the financial statements.

Opinion on other matter prescribed by the Companies Act 2006

Notwithstanding our disclaimer of an opinion on the financial statements, in our opinion the information given in the Directors' Report for the financial year for which the financial statements are prepared is consistent with the financial statements.

Matters on which we are required to report by exception

Arising from the limitation of our work referred to above:

- we have not obtained all the information and explanations that we considered necessary for the purpose of our audit; and
- we were unable to determine whether adequate accounting records have been kept.

We have nothing to report in respect of the following matters where the Companies Act 2006 requires us to report to you if, in our opinion:

- returns adequate for our audit have not been received from branches not visited by us; or
- the financial statements are not in agreement with the accounting records and returns; or
- certain disclosures of directors' remuneration specified by law are not made.

[Signature]   *Address*
John Smith *(Senior statutory auditor)*   *Date*
for and on behalf of ABC LLP, Statutory Auditor

Example 45 – Disclaimer of opinion: Multiple uncertainties

- *As discussed in ISA (UK and Ireland) 705 paragraph 10 the auditor disclaims an opinion when, in extremely rare circumstances involving multiple uncertainties, the auditor concludes that, notwithstanding having obtained sufficient appropriate audit evidence regarding each of the individual uncertainties, it is not possible to form an opinion on the financial statements due to the potential interaction of the uncertainties and their possible cumulative effect on the financial statements.*
- *This example does not include a description of the multiple uncertainties that might lead to a disclaimer of opinion because circumstances will vary and auditors will have to use their judgment when deciding whether it is an extreme case involving multiple uncertainties that are significant to the financial statements. Often, if the matters constituting the multiple uncertainties were considered individually the auditor may be able to issue an unqualified auditor's opinion with an emphasis of matter paragraph describing the situation giving rise to the emphasis of matter and its possible effects on the financial statements, including (where practicable) quantification but the audit opinion would be unmodified.*

INDEPENDENT AUDITOR'S REPORT TO THE MEMBERS OF XYZ LIMITED

We were engaged to audit the financial statements of (name of entity) for the year ended ... which comprise [specify the titles of the primary statements such as the Profit and Loss Account, the Balance Sheet, the Cash Flow Statement, the Statement of Total Recognised Gains and Losses, the Reconciliation of Movements in Share-holders' Funds] and the related notes[100]. The financial reporting framework that has been applied in their preparation is applicable law and United Kingdom Accounting Standards (United Kingdom Generally Accepted Accounting Practice).

Respective responsibilities of directors and auditor

As explained more fully in the Directors' Responsibilities Statement [set out [on page ...]], the directors are responsible for the preparation of the financial statements and for being satisfied that they give a true and fair view. Our responsibility is to audit and express an opinion on the financial statements in accordance with applicable law and International Standards on Auditing (UK and Ireland). Those standards require us to comply with the Auditing Practices Board's [(APB's)] Ethical Standards for Auditors. Because of the matters described in the Basis for Disclaimer of Opinion paragraph, however, we were not able to obtain sufficient appropriate audit evidence to provide a basis for an audit opinion.

Scope of the audit of the financial statements

Either:

> A description of the scope of an audit of financial statements is [provided on the APB's website at www.frc.org.uk/apb/scope/private.cfm] / [set out [on page ...] of the Annual Report].

---

[100] *Auditor's reports of entities that do not publish their financial statements on a website or publish them using 'PDF' format may refer to the financial statements by reference to page numbers.*

Or:

An audit involves obtaining evidence about the amounts and disclosures in the financial statements sufficient to give reasonable assurance that the financial statements are free from material misstatement, whether caused by fraud or error. This includes an assessment of: whether the accounting policies are appropriate to the company's circumstances and have been consistently applied and adequately disclosed; the reasonableness of significant accounting estimates made by the directors; and the overall presentation of the financial statements. In addition, we read all the financial and non-financial information in the *[describe the annual report]* to identify material inconsistencies with the audited financial statements. If we become aware of any apparent material misstatements or inconsistencies we consider the implications for our report.

Basis for disclaimer of opinion on financial statements

In seeking to form an opinion on the financial statements we considered the implications of the significant uncertainties disclosed in the financial statements concerning the following matters:

- [Describe uncertainty 1]
- [Describe uncertainty 2]

There is potential for the uncertainties to interact with one another such that we have been unable to obtain sufficient appropriate audit evidence regarding the possible effect of the uncertainties taken together.

Disclaimer of opinion on financial statements

Because of the significance of the possible impact of the uncertainties, described in the Basis for Disclaimer of Opinion on Financial Statements paragraph, to the financial statements, we have not been able to obtain sufficient appropriate audit evidence to provide a basis for an audit opinion. Accordingly we do not express an opinion on the financial statements.

Opinion on other matter prescribed by the Companies Act 2006

Notwithstanding our disclaimer of an opinion on the financial statements, in our opinion the information given in the Directors' Report for the financial year for which the financial statements are prepared is consistent with the financial statements.

Matters on which we are required to report by exception[101]

We have nothing to report in respect of the following matters where the Companies Act 2006 requires us to report to you if, in our opinion:

- adequate accounting records have not been kept, or returns adequate for our audit have not been received from branches not visited by us; or

---

[101] *The auditor needs to consider whether the circumstances leading to the disclaimer of opinion on the financial statements affects the matters on which the auditor is required to report by exception.*

- the financial statements are not in agreement with the accounting records and returns; or
- certain disclosures of directors' remuneration specified by law are not made; or
- we have not received all the information and explanations we require for our audit.

[Signature]	*Address*
John Smith (Senior statutory auditor)	*Date*
for and on behalf of ABC LLP, Statutory Auditor	

Appendix 16 – Modified opinion on other requirements of the Companies Act 2006

46. Qualified opinion on the consistency of the financial statements with the directors' report

Example 46 – Qualified opinion on the consistency of the financial statements with the directors' report

- *UK non-publicly traded company prepares UK GAAP financial statements (Example 2).*
- *Auditor gives an unqualified opinion on the financial statements.*
- *There is an unresolved inconsistency between the directors' report and the financial statements.*

EXTRACT FROM AUDITOR'S REPORT

...

Opinion on financial statements

In our opinion the financial statements:

- give a true and fair view of the state of the company's affairs as at .... and of its profit [loss] for the year then ended;
- have been properly prepared in accordance with United Kingdom Generally Accepted Accounting Practice; and
- have been prepared in accordance with the requirements of the Companies Act 2006.

Qualified opinion on other matter prescribed by the Companies Act 2006

In our opinion, the information given in the seventh paragraph of the Business Review in the Directors' Report is not consistent with the financial statements. That paragraph states without amplification that "the company's trading for the period resulted in a 10% increase in profit over the previous period's profit". The profit and loss account, however, shows that the company's profit for the period includes a profit of £Z which did not arise from trading but arose from the disposal of assets of a discontinued operation. Without this profit on the disposal of assets the company would have reported a profit for the year of £Y, representing a reduction in profit of 25% over the previous period's profit on a like for like basis. Except for this matter, in our opinion the information given in the Directors' Report is consistent with the financial statements.

Matters on which we are required to report by exception

We have nothing to report in respect of the following matters where the Companies Act 2006 requires us to report to you if, in our opinion:

- adequate accounting records have not been kept, or returns adequate for our audit have not been received from branches not visited by us; or
- the financial statements are not in agreement with the accounting records and returns; or
- certain disclosures of directors' remuneration specified by law are not made; or
- we have not received all the information and explanations we require for our audit.

[Signature]   *Address*
John Smith (Senior statutory auditor)   *Date*
for and on behalf of ABC LLP, Statutory Auditor

Appendix 17 – Directors' Responsibilities Statement

47. Directors' Responsibilities Statement for a non-publicly traded company preparing financial statements under UK GAAP

Example 47 – Directors' Responsibilities Statement for a non-publicly traded company preparing financial statements under UK GAAP

DIRECTORS' RESPONSIBILITIES STATEMENT

The directors are responsible for preparing the Directors' Report and the financial statements in accordance with applicable law and regulations.

Company law requires the directors to prepare financial statements for each financial year. Under that law the directors have elected to prepare the financial statements in accordance with United Kingdom Generally Accepted Accounting Practice (United Kingdom Accounting Standards and applicable law). Under company law the directors must not approve the financial statements unless they are satisfied that they give a true and fair view of the state of affairs of the company and the profit or loss of the company for that period.

In preparing these financial statements, the directors are required to:

- select suitable accounting policies and then apply them consistently;
- make judgments and accounting estimates that are reasonable and prudent;[102]
- state whether applicable UK Accounting Standards have been followed, subject to any material departures disclosed and explained in the financial statements;[103]
- prepare the financial statements on the going concern basis unless it is inappropriate to presume that the company will continue in business[104].

The directors are responsible for keeping adequate accounting records that are sufficient to show and explain the company's transactions and disclose with reasonable accuracy at any time the financial position of the company and enable them to ensure that the financial statements comply with the Companies Act 2006. They are also responsible for safeguarding the assets of the company and hence for taking reasonable steps for the prevention and detection of fraud and other irregularities.

---

[102] *Paragraph 13 of Part II of Schedule 2 to each of the "The Small Companies and Groups (Accounts and Reports) Regulations 2008" (SI 2008 No. 409) and "The Large and Medium-sized Companies and Groups (Accounts and Reports) Regulations 2008" (SI 2008 No. 410) require that the amount of any item must be determined on a prudent basis.*

[103] *This bullet does not apply to companies subject to the small companies regime and medium-sized companies as defined by CA 2006.*

[104] *Included where no separate statement on going concern is made by the directors.*

Briefing Paper

Professional scepticism – Establishing a common understanding and reaffirming its central role in delivering audit quality

Contents

Section 1 – Introduction

This paper sets out the APB's considered views on the nature of auditor scepticism and its role in the audit. Given the significance of scepticism to the quality of individual audits, and to the value of audit more generally, we believe that this document is an important point of reference on this topic and one which we hope all auditors will consider with great care.

It is written in an unusual format for an APB document, being much more discursive than is customary and drawing analogies from a diverse group of areas. This is because we believe that what is meant by scepticism needs to be more broadly understood and that drawing these analogies will assist in broadening that understanding. We are also keen to stimulate and provide input to an international debate on the issue of scepticism and believe that this broader and more discursive approach will provide a valuable input to that debate.

This document builds on the APB Discussion Paper published in August 2010 'Auditor Scepticism: Raising the Bar' and the subsequent Feedback Paper published in March 2011, which summarised the comments received and outlined the actions that the APB, and other parts of the FRC, intended to take in light of the responses received.

The Feedback Paper noted the following[1]:

- Responses suggested a wide range of views about what the initial mindset should be and raised concerns for the APB that there is a lack of consensus about the nature of professional scepticism and its role in the conduct of an audit.
- The APB did not accept that the auditor's role is limited to ensuring that management have appropriate evidence to support its assertions if this means accepting the evidence management present without subjecting it to robust challenge and comparison to alternative sources of evidence.
- The APB questioned whether a 'neutral mindset', or indeed just an 'inquiring mind', is appropriate for an auditor. The auditor's mindset is applied during audit planning to assess the risk of misstatement of the financial statements and such risk assessments determine the nature and extent of audit evidence to be obtained. It is also applied in assessing the validity of accounting estimates that are subject both to significant uncertainties and to considerable management judgment.

The first of the areas in which the APB proposed to undertake further work was ensuring that there is a consistent understanding of the nature of professional scepticism and its role in the conduct of an audit.

Section 2 considers the philosophical origins of scepticism in ancient Greece and how it later influenced scepticism in the scientific method that began to flourish in the 17th Century. The relationship between scepticism and the disposition to believe or disbelieve is explored as well as the influences of evidence and behaviours on that disposition.

Section 3 seeks to provide insight into the mind-set required to develop the audit strategy and plan and to evaluate the audit evidence obtained, by demonstrating how another learning – science – has developed a sceptical approach that now commands respect.

---

[1] See 'Auditor scepticism: Raising the bar: Feedback Statement' – March 2011 http://www.frc.org.uk/apb/publications/pub2343.html.

Section 4 seeks to provide further insight into the mindset of the auditor by considering the nature of the agency relationships, and the resultant need for assurance, that gave rise to early auditing traditions in manorial households from the 14th Century.

Section 5 sets out the APB's conclusions from the foregoing analysis as to what a sceptical audit looks like. It suggests that professional scepticism is the cornerstone of audit quality – it defines the quality of each audit judgment and through these the overall effectiveness of the audit in meeting the needs of shareholders and other stakeholders.

Section 6 sets out the APB's views about the conditions that are necessary for auditors to demonstrate the appropriate degree of professional scepticism. It highlights the APB's expectations of individual auditors, engagement teams, audit firms and of the supporting role that can be played by audit committees, management and others.

Finally, Section 7 sets out how the APB proposes to take these matters forward.

Section 2 – Exploring the roots of scepticism and identifying lessons for its role in the conduct of an audit

Scepticism is derived from the Greek word "σκέψις" (skepsis), meaning[2]: *examination, inquiry into, hesitation or doubt, especially of the Sceptics or Pyrrhone philosophers.* Greek philosophical Scepticism was a school of thought from the 5th Century BC that doubted the certainty of knowledge. From this developed the philosophical viewpoint that it is not possible to gain certain knowledge (truth) about the natural world.

Scepticism in Greek philosophy

Beyond understanding the etymological basis for the modern term "scepticism", what more can we learn from early Greek philosophical scepticism?

- First, the essence of scepticism is doubt and that doubt stimulates informed challenge and inquiry. The sceptics' doubts arose from the many conflicting views that persisted about fundamental issues. Their doubt stimulated them to challenge conventional wisdom and to inquire after a better understanding of the nature of knowledge.
- Second, in the face of doubt they would suspend their judgment about the truth.
- Third, in its extreme forms scepticism is not pragmatic as it may lead to the conclusion that no judgments about the truth can be made[3].

The disposition to believe or disbelieve and its conditioning influences

Today, scepticism commonly means 'doubt as to the truth of some assertion or supposed fact'[4]. Doubt is unbelief, whose antonyms include belief and trust[5]. Neither doubt nor trust need be absolute. Each has expression in different degrees. Uncertainty lies between them and absolute trust (belief) and absolute distrust (disbelief) are at their extremes. Doubt, trust and uncertainty are passive concepts – states of mind. They describe an individual's disposition to believe or disbelieve an assertion.

The actual level of doubt or trust in the state of mind conditions the individual's response. When the levels of both trust and doubt are low, there is uncertainty which either may result in a passive response – the indefinite suspension of judgment – or may stimulate an active inquiry to pursue the truth or falseness of the assertion. The results of that inquiry will further condition the state of mind and the process may be repeated. Only if and when a state of mind of trust or doubt is sufficiently high will the active response – acceptance or rejection of belief in the assertion – ensue.

---

[2] *Liddell & Scott Greek-English Lexicon.*

[3] *Bertrand Russell, in his 1958 book: "The Will to Doubt" illustrates such "heroic" scepticism by retelling the following: "A story is told of Pyrrho, the founder of Pyrrhonism (which was the old name for scepticism). He maintained that we never know enough to be sure that one course of action is wiser than another. In his youth, when he was taking his constitutional one afternoon, he saw his teacher in philosophy (from whom he had imbibed his principles) with his head stuck in a ditch, unable to get out. After contemplating him for some time, he walked on, maintaining that there was no sufficient ground for thinking he would do any good by pulling the man out. Others, less sceptical, effected a rescue, and blamed Pyrrho for his heartlessness. But his teacher, true to his principles, praised him for his consistency.*

[4] *The Shorter Oxford English Dictionary.*

[5] *See Roget's Thesaurus of synonyms and antonyms: categories 484 (Belief) and 485 (Unbelief; Doubt).*

The disposition to believe or disbelieve an assertion may be conditioned by many influences. These include not only the results of inquiry but also potentially the biases of the individual (whether conscious or sub-conscious) and the individual's perceptions and assessments of their self-interest. These other conditioning influences must be filtered out if objective truth is to be attained.

In the context of audit judgments, it may be helpful to understand the implications of the behavioural rules ('heuristics') underlying human decision-making and judgment processes. A number of heuristics have been proposed to help explain these processes, especially in the face of complex problems or incomplete information. It is also thought that they may, in some circumstances, introduce systematic errors or biases into these processes.

One illustration of these ideas may be found in a recent academic paper[6], which shows that people are less likely to adjust their beliefs in response to evidence that contradicts their optimistic beliefs than to evidence that contradicts their pessimistic beliefs.

What is needed to counteract this is a mechanism to encourage a structured consideration of the alternative point of view. One example of such a mechanism being applied in a financial services context is 'reverse stress testing'. In this form of stress testing, the directors consider what it would take to make the entity fail and then assess the evidence as to the likelihood of those circumstances arising.

Evidence based theories of knowledge and scientific scepticism

Later Sceptics were more pragmatic, arguing that there were ways of approaching (even if not quite attaining) the absolute truth. The Empirical school of thought proposed that the only or primary source of knowledge is experience gained through the senses. It therefore emphasised the role of empirical (observed) evidence in inducing knowledge rather than deducing knowledge from innate ideas and traditions.

Empiricism was highly influential in the development of science and the scientific method in the 17th Century. Scientific scepticism doubts the veracity of assertions that are not supported by empirical evidence that is reproducible and therefore seeks to exclude other influences from the scientific search for truth.

Evidence, trust and agency in the audit process

An audit is an evidence-based process to assess and report on the truth and fairness of the financial statements prepared by the directors to whom capital resources are entrusted by the shareholders. The audit is entrusted to another agent of the shareholders – the auditor.

This description refers to two features of an audit which are relevant to scepticism – the evidence-based nature of the audit and the entrustment and agency relationships

[6] *See:* How unrealistic optimism is maintained in the face of reality, *by Sharot, Korn and Dolan, in Nature Neuroscience, Nov 2011. This and earlier research considering the impact of new evidence on existing beliefs is discussed in a recent Research Paper from Societe Generale:* In defence of the doom merchants: when hearing isn't listening, *Jan 2012 at: http://www.frc.org.uk/images/uploaded/documents/Societe%20Generale%20 Research%20Paper%20January%202012.pdf. The Paper suggests that people have a natural tendency to take note of the evidence which backs their own theories and to ignore evidence which contradicts them. If anything, this tendency is exacerbated when they are exhorted to try harder.*

inherent in the audit. The role of scepticism in relation to each of these is explored further below. The evidence-based nature of the process suggests some parallels with, and is explored in the context of, the scientific method and scientific scepticism in Section 3. In Section 4, lessons about the expression of professional scepticism are also identified by considering the nature of the entrustment and agency relationships and the need for assurance that gave rise to the tradition of auditing servants in the manorial estates of the fourteenth century in the origins of the modern audit in the UK.

Section 3 – Scientific scepticism and the scientific method

The scientific method seeks to understand the causes and effects of natural processes by:

- *Empirical observation* of their behaviours in different conditions;
- Postulating how they work (*constructing theories* of cause and effect that are consistent with the observations) – an approach that relies on inductive logic.
- Predicting effects that would necessarily follow from the truth of a theory in specific conditions (*constructing hypotheses*) – an approach that relies on deductive logic.
- *Testing* those hypotheses by considering not only what evidence would support them but also what evidence would falsify them – accordingly, experiments are designed and performed to find such evidence.
- Each step of the process is *transparent and repeatable,* subject to the critical review of other scientists and capable of being challenged and retested by them.
- In the development of scientific knowledge in a new area, there may be several competing theories, each of which has survived hypothesis testing. The advancement of a theory to the status of accepted scientific knowledge requires a *'critical experiment'*, one capable of providing evidence that will prove the superiority of one theory over all the other competing theories.

This process can disprove a postulated theory but cannot absolutely prove it. If testing falsifies a hypothesis, then theories are reassessed in light of the new observations and if necessary new ones are postulated. A theory that survives rigorous testing remains plausible, for the time being. Scientific knowledge is therefore dynamic and constantly subject to challenge.

Prior to the development of the scientific method, knowledge of the natural world was largely based on accepted ancient wisdom (axiomatic truths) and advanced by developing consequential "knowledge" by logical deduction (the deductive method). A critical development in the evolution of the scientific method was the acceptance that there are no axiomatic truths that can be observed and that there is a continuing need to question and challenge all matters that may appear to be so.

Robert Boyle is widely recognised as the father of modern chemistry and an early proponent of the scientific method. His treatise on the new approach is aptly called 'The Sceptical Chymist'[7].

Scepticism in the scientific method can be described as a <u>systematic form of continual informed questioning</u> that requires the scientist:

- To <u>critically appraise</u> existing theories, actively looking for alternative plausible mechanisms of cause and effect that are consistent with their rigorous assessment of the empirical (observed) evidence;
- To undertake experiments that are repeatable and transparent, to look for <u>evidence that contradicts rather than supports</u> the validity of any given theory; and
- To <u>suspend judgment</u> about the validity of any given theory (ie to defer making an active decision to believe or disbelieve it) until it has both survived destructive testing and has been subjected to critical experiments the evidence from which makes it possible to conclude that one theory is superior to all other current plausible theories.

---

[7] *Robert Boyle, 1661: The Sceptical Chymist: or Chymico-Physical Doubts & Paradoxes Touching the Spagyrist's Principles Commonly call'd Hypostatical As they are wont to be Propos'd and Defended by the Generality of Alchemists.*

There are many parallels between the scientific method and the audit and, whilst this analogy should, of course, not be taken too far, at a certain level there is much to learn from a consideration of the nature of scientific scepticism and the role it plays in the conduct of the scientific method. Scientific scepticism is the backbone of the scientific method, influencing every judgment in the process of learning and ultimately supporting the whole body of scientific knowledge.

However, the subject matters of scientific and audit inquiry are different in nature. The subject matter of Science is knowledge of the natural world, which experience shows to ordinarily behave in a systematic way. The subject matter of auditing is the outputs from the business performance and reporting systems of the entity, which though usually intended to operate systematically often do not as they are subject to the vagaries of external influences, as well as human error and fraud.

In science, the potential variables are identified and can be controlled and varied individually under laboratory conditions. In the audit, they cannot and the outputs of the business performance and reporting systems of the entity must be observed in real world (multivariate) conditions.

Notwithstanding these limitations to the analogy between the audit and the scientific method, elements of the scientific method suggest critical audit activities which will underpin appropriate scepticism in the audit:

- Empirical observation *suggests* developing a good understanding of the business of the audited entity and of the environment;
- Constructing falsifiable hypotheses *suggests* actively considering that material misstatements may exist and designing audit tests to identify them, rather than only considering how well the evidence obtained by management supports their conclusion that there are none; and
- Transparency and repeatability *suggest* the importance of documentation in underpinning transparency and repeatability of the audit work to internal reviewers and to external inspectors.

The comparison says less about how far the auditor should go in pursuing these activities:

- When should the active search for risks of material misstatement stop?
- How far should the auditor's understanding be pursued?
- How much testing and stress testing should the auditor undertake?
- When is the evidence sufficient?

The scientific analogy suggests there is no absolute level to which such matters should be pursued. Scientific scepticism is pursued up to the point where other similarly objective scientists would want to go before they accept or reject a hypothesis. In the scientific field, acceptance of a hypothesis only occurs when the level of trust in that hypothesis is approaching virtual certainty. This may not be the most appropriate point to which professional scepticism should be pursued in the audit. This is considered further in the next section in the context of the historical origins of the modern audit in the UK.

Section 4 – The origins of the modern audit

The origins of the modern audit can be seen in the tradition of auditing household servants in manorial estates that developed from the fourteenth century[8]. The auditor was the most trusted servant in the household and all other servants were required to account to the auditor for the resources entrusted to them.

In its simplest form, an account was required from each household servant of all money and other assets entrusted to them – they were "charged" with the assets when placed in their care and "discharged" when the auditor had heard and accepted their account.

When free incorporation joint stock companies were established in the Joint Stock Companies Act of 1844, there were default provisions for auditors to be appointed, that built on these traditions. Under the default provisions, at least one of the auditors should be appointed by the shareholders, their fees should be paid by the company but set by a government agency (the Commissioners of the Treasury) as they saw fit, and their report should be made publicly available. The auditor was neither required to be a shareholder nor a professional accountant but often was a shareholder and frequently employed professional accountants to assist them.

The Joint Stock Companies Act of 1856 enhanced the earlier default provisions to specifically allow the auditor to employ accountants to assist them at the company's expense and to prohibit the auditor from being a director or an officer of the company and from having any interest in any transaction of the company other than as a shareholder. The absolute requirement that companies should have an audit (initially just for joint stock banks but later extended to all companies) as opposed to optional default provisions, originated in the 1879 Companies Act following the collapse of the City Bank of Glasgow. In time, the practice of appointing share-holders as auditors fell away and public accountants were employed to undertake the role directly.

Looking back, it would seem that, in its origin, the audit was essentially a check, carried out on behalf of a principal by their trusted associate or agent, on the fidelity of other agents to whom the principal's resources were entrusted. The trust that existed between principal and auditor was a critical ingredient, if not the critical ingredient of the audit. The importance of professional skills only came later. The whole rationale for the audit was that the principal could not assume, and therefore sought assurance about, the fidelity of those to whom their assets were entrusted.

This may suggest how far the auditor should pursue professional scepticism in the audit. The strong bond of trust between the principal and the auditor and the principal's need for assurance about the fidelity of those to whom they had entrusted their assets would have determined the mindset of the auditor. That would have guided the appropriate degree of scepticism in the auditor when holding a hearing to question those entrusted with the principal's assets and to assess whether they had given a proper account of their handling of those assets. They would have asked the questions they would expect their principal to ask, they would have challenged where they would expect their principal to challenge and they would have pursued matters until they were satisfied that the evidence would satisfy their principal.

[8] *See* Be careful what you wish for: How accountants and Congress created the problem of auditor independence, *2004, Sean M. O'Connor at: http://www.bc.edu/dam/files/schools/law/lawreviews/journals/bclawr/45_4/01_FMS.htm.*

This is perhaps a fair lens through which to understand the necessary degree of scepticism in the modern audit. What would the shareholders (and other stakeholders) expect the auditor to ask, what matters would they expect them to challenge and what evidence would they need to satisfy those challenges?

Whilst fidelity may have been the issue in the 19th Century and much of the 20th Century (and remains an issue in the 21st Century), the development and increased complexity of business activity, and the increased size and reach of such businesses, combined with the arrival of the technological age mean that there are many other areas in relation to which shareholders (and other users) seek information and reassurance. For example, misalignment of their personal interests may simply lead to misalignment of risk taking appetite between the directors and shareholders.

This suggests that whilst the sceptical mindset is a constant, the degree of action taken by a sceptical auditor (by way of inquiry, challenge and testing) is responsive both to the expectations of shareholders (and other stakeholders) and to what emerges as the audit proceeds. This is the 'sliding scale' that was referred to in *Auditor Scepticism: Raising the Bar*.

Because of the need to consider their expectations, the perspective of shareholders and other stakeholders (as users) is embedded in the auditing standards in relation to materiality, and scepticism should embed that perspective in the making of all audit judgments. Against this background, the APB believes that when undertaking a modern audit the following factors accentuate the need for the auditor to be especially vigilant and aware of his or her responsibilities for the exercise of professional scepticism:

- There is potential for auditors not to be sceptical or thought not to be sceptical because they are engaged and paid by the company in a way that is relatively detached from shareholders. In addition, they have little, if any, direct contact with shareholders throughout the audit process; as a result, shareholders have no way of observing, and thereby gaining trust in, the audit process. This emphasises the need for strong governance generally and, in particular, the importance of the responsibility that audit committees have in both assessing and communicating to investors whether the auditors have executed a high quality, sceptical audit;
- Auditors necessarily have strong working relationships with management and audit committees, which may lead them to develop trust that may lead to either a lack of, or reduced, scepticism; and
- The audit firms' business models encourage a culture of building strong relationships with audited entities. This introduces the moral hazard of the auditor putting his or her interests ahead of those of shareholders and could lead the audit firm and the auditor to develop trust or self-interest motivations that may compromise either their objectivity or willingness to challenge management to the extent required.

It is perhaps not surprising that auditors often refer to the audited entity as the 'client', given the strength of these relationships and the all but formal appointment of the auditor by the directors and not by the shareholders. However, trust in management may compromise the auditor's exercise of scepticism because that trust may colour his/her judgement as to when and where a sceptical approach is required. It is important to lean against unjustified trust developing, just as it is important to address threats to the auditor's objectivity that may arise from the provision of non-audit services – it is interesting to note in this context that the auditor originally was not permitted to have any interest in any transaction with the company.

The factors described above are widely recognised to pose challenges to the reality and perception of auditors' professional integrity (including their objectivity and independence). The need to address these challenges gives rise to a variety of responses that seek to lean against them, including the responsibilities, liabilities and disclosures relating to the audit and the auditor established in the law and professional standards, including the Ethical Standards. This is also one of the principal reasons for the need for the application and demonstration of appropriate professional scepticism in the audit.

Despite the increasing role of audit committees as independent non-executive directors in monitoring and challenging the entity's financial information and controls (in effect as the representatives of the shareholders), there is also a risk that audit committees' views may be seen too readily by the auditor as a surrogate for those of the shareholders. Just addressing the concerns of the audit committee does not necessarily amount to meeting the expectations of shareholders (and other stakeholders).

For all of these reasons, the rigorous assessment of when, and the degree to which, professional scepticism is required is fundamental to an effective audit.

Section 5 – Conclusions about professional scepticism in the audit

In the growth and development of a living thing, the expression of its DNA in the formation of its cells defines its essence and its effectiveness in meeting the challenges of its environment. In the words of Richard Dawkins[9]:

DNA neither cares nor knows. DNA just is. And we dance to its music.

In the same way, the expression of professional scepticism by the audit team defines the essence of the particular audit. It defines the quality of each audit judgment and, through these, the overall effectiveness of the audit in addressing the challenges it faces in meeting the needs of shareholders (and other stakeholders) who rely on it. The reality and perception of the expression of professional scepticism define and underpin the confidence that others place in the audit and in turn the confidence they place in the audited financial statements.

The preceding analysis suggests that the appropriate application of professional scepticism in the audit requires a mindset which rigorously questions and challenges management's assertions with a degree of doubt that reflects the expectations of shareholders (and other stakeholders) for whose benefit it is performed. All judgments made in the course of the audit should be founded on the perspective of the shareholders (and other stakeholders). That mindset demands the sort of hard evidence – to back each audit judgment and, ultimately, the board's assertion that the financial statements give a true and fair view – that would be convincing and persuasive to shareholders (and other stakeholders), given the auditor's risk assessment.

The analysis suggests that in an appropriately sceptical audit:

- The auditor's risk assessment process should involve a <u>critical appraisal</u> of management's assertions, <u>actively looking for risks</u> of material misstatement. These may arise due to fraud or error and may reflect weaknesses in the design or the operation of management's system for controlling and reporting the entity's financial position and performance (such that relevant matters are not identified, or are not adequately controlled or reported, or that the design has not been implemented and operated effectively[10]).
- The auditor develops a high degree of knowledge of the audited entity's business and the environment in which it operates, sufficient to enable it to make its risk assessment through its own fresh and independent eyes rather than through the eyes of management.
- This enables the auditor to make informed challenge of consensus views and to consider the possible incidence of low probability high impact events. The alternative would give rise to the risk of what is known in science as "hypothesis bias" which is an example of "group-think". The challenges in acquiring sufficient knowledge and experience should not be underestimated, especially in relation to complex business models. The traditional pyramid structure of the audit team may not always be appropriate and different models may need to be explored, such as including experienced business people on the team.
- The auditor designs audit procedures to <u>consider actively if there is any evidence that would contradict</u> management assertions not only to consider the extent to which management has identified evidence that is consistent with them. The

---

[9] *Richard Dawkins: River Out of Eden: A Darwinian View of Life (1995), 133.*

[10] *This is not to suggest that the auditor must always test the operating effectiveness of the financial reporting system, rather than taking a substantive approach and testing the outputs from that system.*

opposite of a sceptical audit might be one in which the auditor merely ratio-
nalises and documents management's assertions.
- The auditor has strong skills in making evidence-based judgments and suspends
  judgment about whether the financial statements do or do not give a true and
  fair view until satisfied that:
  o There has been sufficient inquiry and challenge;
  o Sufficient testing of management's assertions has been undertaken;
  o The quality of the resulting evidence obtained has been critically appraised
    and judged by the auditor to be sufficiently persuasive; and
  o Where there are plausible alternative treatments of an item in the financial
    statements (such as different valuation bases), an assessment has been made
    as to whether one is superior and whether sufficient disclosure of the
    alternatives has been given, in order to give a true and fair view.
- The auditor approaches and documents audit judgments and audit review
  processes in a manner that facilitates challenge and demonstrates the rigour of
  that challenge.

The auditor's documentation of audit judgments is conclusive rather than conclusionary and therefore always sets out not only the auditor's conclusion but also their
rationale for the conclusion, relating it to the nature of the challenges raised in the
underlying work and reviews, the strength of the evidence obtained and the perspective of shareholders (and other stakeholders). The auditor needs strong skills in
logical argument to do this effectively.

Section 6 – Fostering conditions necessary for auditors to demonstrate the appropriate degree of professional scepticism

The application of an appropriate degree of professional scepticism is a crucial skill for auditors. Unless auditors are prepared to challenge management's assertions they will not be able to confirm with confidence that a company's financial statements present a true and fair view.

The APB believes that in order to demonstrate the value of the audit, the auditor should perform a sceptical audit, evidence the exercise of appropriate scepticism in the audit documentation and convince audit committees and ultimately the shareholders (and other stakeholders) that it has done so.

The challenge for firms is to identify, develop and retain people with the necessary skills and to deploy them appropriately. It also involves nurturing the conditions that allow professional scepticism to flourish.

The prospects for a sceptical audit are likely to be enhanced if the environment in which the auditor operates also recognises and supports the important role that scepticism plays in the audit.

The APB considers that the conditions necessary for auditors to demonstrate the appropriate degree of professional scepticism are likely to include the following.

Individual auditors

- Develop a good understanding of the entity and its business.
- Have a questioning mind and are willing to challenge management assertions.
- Assess critically the information and explanations obtained in the course of their work and corroborate them.
- Seek to understand management motivations for possible misstatement of the financial statements.
- Investigate the nature and cause of deviations or misstatements identified and avoid jumping to conclusions without appropriate audit evidence.
- Are alert for evidence that is inconsistent with other evidence obtained or calls into question the reliability of documents and responses to inquiries.
- Have the confidence to challenge management and the persistence to follow things through to a conclusion – even if predisposed to agree with management's assertion, the auditor should actively consider the alternative views and challenge management to demonstrate that they are not more appropriate.

Engagement teams

- Have good business knowledge and experience.
- Actively consider in what circumstances management numbers may be misstated, whether due to fraud or error, and the possible sources of misstatement, notwithstanding existing knowledge and relationships.
- Develop a good understanding of the entity and its business in order to provide a basis for identifying unusual events or transactions and share information on a regular basis.
- Partners and managers are actively involved in assessing risk and planning the audit procedures to be performed – they think about the changes that are taking place in the entity and its environment and plan audit tests that are responsive to them.

- Partners and managers actively lead and participate in audit team planning meetings to discuss the susceptibility of the entity's financial statements to material misstatement including through fraud and the misuse of related parties.
- Partners and managers are accessible to other staff during the audit and encourage them to consult with them on a timely basis.
- Engagement teams document their key audit judgments and conclusions, especially those reported to the audit committee, in a way that clearly demonstrates that they have exercised an appropriate degree of challenge to management and professional scepticism. In particular, the reasons why the audit team concurs with management's assertions are clearly articulated in a way that, where appropriate, discusses the appropriateness of reasonably credible alternative views and the reasons why they have not been adopted.
- Partners and managers bring additional scepticism to the audit through taking the steps necessary to carry out, face to face where appropriate, a diligent challenge and review of the audit work performed, and the adequacy of the documentation prepared, by other members of the engagement team.

Audit firms

- The culture within the firm emphasises the importance of:
  - understanding and pursuing the perspective of the shareholders (and other stakeholders) of the audited entity in making audit judgments;
  - coaching less experienced staff to foster appropriate scepticism;
  - sharing experiences about difficult audit judgments within the firm;
  - consultation with others about difficult audit judgments; and
  - supporting audit partners when they need to take and communicate difficult audit judgements.
- Scepticism is embedded in the firm's training and competency frameworks used for evaluating and rewarding partner and staff performance.
- The firm requires rigorous engagement quality control reviews that challenge engagement teams' judgments and conclusions.
- Firm methodologies and review processes emphasise the importance of, and provide practical support for auditors in:
  - developing a thorough understanding of the entity's business and its environment, sufficient to enable the auditor to carry out a robust risk assessment through their own fresh eyes;
  - identifying issues early in the planning cycle to allow adequate time for them to be investigated and resolved;
  - rigorously taking such steps as are appropriate to the scale and complexity of the financial reporting systems, to identify unusual transactions;
  - changing risk assessments, materiality and the audit plan in response to audit findings;
  - documenting audit judgments in a conclusive rather than a conclusionary manner and therefore setting out not only the conclusion but also the rationale for the conclusion, relating it to the nature of the challenges
  - raised in the underlying work and reviews, the strength of the evidence obtained and the perspective of shareholders (and other stakeholders);
  - raising matters with the Audit Committee (or those charged with governance) in relation to which the auditor believes the perspective of shareholders (and other stakeholders) about the treatment or disclosure of the matter in the financial statements or related narrative reports could well be different from that adopted by the entity; and
  - ensuring that the disclosures relating to such matters are carefully assessed to ensure that those of relevance to shareholders (and other stakeholders)

are sufficient and appropriate in the circumstances, having regard to the auditor's consideration of the true and fair view[11].

The role of Audit Committees and management

Whilst it is the responsibility of the auditor to ensure that an appropriate degree of professional scepticism is applied in an audit, the Audit Committee and management can have a significant influencing role.

The Audit Committee's role includes overseeing the integrity of financial reporting and the related processes (including internal financial controls, the independence and objectivity of the external auditor and the effectiveness of the audit process). In this role, the APB believes that Audit Committees should seek to foster appropriate professional scepticism in the external audit, for example, through:

- Promoting the development of a culture within the entity which elicits a constructive response from management and staff to auditor challenge;
- Challenging whether the auditor has developed an adequate understanding of the business and its environment and provided an appropriately informed fresh perspective in making its risk assessment;
- Ensuring that, where management and auditor have resolved either contentious issues or issues that involve significant judgment, these are brought to the audit committee's attention; and
- Seeking to understand in relation to issues brought to their attention (including issues where management and auditor agree the position) whether or not an appropriate degree of challenge was exercised by the auditor – for example, by demanding an explanation of the auditor's rationale for particular conclusions, what alternatives were considered and why the specific judgment was considered to be the most appropriate of the alternatives.

The APB believes that this is consistent with the FRC's *Effective Company Stewardship* proposals[12], under which it is proposed that Audit Committees should produce fuller reports for the Board, in particular setting out their advice on the integrity of the Annual Report and explaining how they discharged their responsibilities for this and other aspects of their remit (such as their oversight of the external audit process and appointment of external auditors). Taken together with the proposal for Boards to discuss these matters in the Annual Report, the effect should be to ensure that the Annual Report demonstrates that the audit addressed those matters of most interest to shareholders and other stakeholders with appropriate challenge and scepticism.

---

[11] *See the FRC document:* True and Fair – July 2011 *at: http://www.frc.org.uk/images/uploaded/documents/ Paper%20True%20and%20Fair1.pdf.*

[12] *See http://www.frc.org.uk/about/effcompsteward.cfm.*

Section 7 – Taking these matters forward

The main purpose of this document is to explain the APB's views on professional scepticism and to encourage auditors to apply its principles in executing high quality sceptical audits and in documenting and demonstrating that they have done so. The APB has also considered the definition of professional scepticism and the extent and manner in which it has been dealt with in the ISAs (UK & I) and in ISQC 1 (UK &I), in light of the conclusions drawn in this Paper.

Although these standards contain many elements[13] that support the understanding of professional scepticism developed in this Paper, it is also possible for an auditor to follow the 'letter' of the standards without conducting a truly sceptical audit. The APB acknowledges that these standards may well need to be improved further to reflect better some of the conclusions reflected in this Paper and to be clearer about the performance, documentation and communication of professional scepticism.

Accordingly, whilst it has concluded that in taking these matters forward, the immediate emphasis should be on encouraging auditors and others to deliver a step change in behaviours that will achieve consistency in the manner in which professional scepticism is exercised in the conduct of their audits, it also intends to seek to influence the IAASB to enhance the auditing standards in due course.

The APB therefore proposes to:

- Stimulate debate and acceptance by stakeholders of the conclusions set out in this Paper about the nature and role of professional scepticism in the audit;
- Encourage the auditing profession and the audit firms to consider the implications of these conclusions for their business models and culture and for their approach to audits and to implement such changes as are necessary to respond to the challenges they identify – including the need to reflect the perspective of shareholders (and other stakeholders) in exercising their professional judgment;
- Promote these conclusions with Audit Committee members and management to encourage them to recognise and act on the important contribution that they can make to support the appropriate exercise of professional scepticism;
- Promote with those preparing the financial statements and Annual Report the benefits of open communication and consideration of the key judgments involved in doing so and in responding to the challenges raised in the audit; and
- Promote the conclusions set out in this Paper internationally, with a view to identifying ways in which the International Standards on Auditing might be developed to better reflect these conclusions, as part of the post Clarity ISA implementation review.

---

[13] See IAASB Staff Questions and Answers on "Professional Skepticism in an audit of Financial Statements" at: http://www.ifac.org/sites/default/files/publications/files/IAASB%20Professional%20Skepticism%20QandA-final. pdf.

Part Nine

IESBA and ICAEW Codes of Ethics

Handbook of the Code of Ethics for Professional Accountants

Contents

Preface

The International Ethics Standards Board for Accountants (IESBA) develops and issues, under its own authority, the *Code of Ethics for Professional Accountants* (the Code) for use by professional accountants around the world.

A member body of IFAC or firm shall not apply less stringent standards than those stated in this Code. However, if a member body or firm is prohibited from complying with certain parts of this Code by law or regulation, they shall comply with all other parts of this Code.

Some jurisdictions may have requirements and guidance that differ from those contained in this Code. Professional accountants in those jurisdictions need to be aware of those differences and comply with the more stringent requirements and guidance unless prohibited by law or regulation.

Part A—General application of the IESBA Code

Section 100 Introduction and Fundamental Principles
Section 110 Integrity
Section 120 Objectivity
Section 130 Professional Competence and Due Care
Section 140 Confidentiality
Section 150 Professional Behavior

Section 100

Introduction and Fundamental Principles

100.1   A distinguishing mark of the accountancy profession is its acceptance of the responsibility to act in the public interest. Therefore, a professional accountant's responsibility is not exclusively to satisfy the needs of an individual client or employer. In acting in the public interest, a professional accountant shall observe and comply with this Code. If a professional accountant is prohibited from complying with certain parts of this Code by law or regulation, the professional accountant shall comply with all other parts of this Code.

100.2   This Code contains three parts. Part A establishes the fundamental principles of professional ethics for professional accountants and provides a conceptual framework that professional accountants shall apply to:

(a) Identify threats to compliance with the fundamental principles;
(b) Evaluate the significance of the threats identified; and
(c) Apply safeguards, when necessary, to eliminate the threats or reduce them to an acceptable level. Safeguards are necessary when the professional accountant determines that the threats are not at a level at which a reasonable and informed third party would be likely to conclude, weighing all the specific facts and circumstances available to the professional accountant at that time, that compliance with the fundamental principles is not compromised.

A professional accountant shall use professional judgment in applying this conceptual framework.

100.3   Parts B and C describe how the conceptual framework applies in certain situations. They provide examples of safeguards that may be appropriate to address threats to compliance with the fundamental principles. They also describe situations where safeguards are not available to address the threats, and consequently, the circumstance or relationship creating the threats shall be avoided. Part B applies to professional accountants in public practice. Part C applies to professional accountants in business. Professional accountants in public practice may also find Part C relevant to their particular circumstances.

100.4   The use of the word "shall" in this Code imposes a requirement on the professional accountant or firm to comply with the specific provision in which "shall" has been used. Compliance is required unless an exception is permitted by this Code.

Fundamental Principles

100.5   A professional accountant shall comply with the following fundamental principles:

(a) Integrity – to be straightforward and honest in all professional and business relationships.
(b) Objectivity – to not allow bias, conflict of interest or undue influence of others to override professional or business judgments.
(c) Professional Competence and Due Care – to maintain professional knowledge and skill at the level required to ensure that a client or employer receives competent professional services based on current developments in practice, legislation and techniques and act diligently and in accordance with applicable technical and professional standards.
(d) Confidentiality – to respect the confidentiality of information acquired as a result of professional and business relationships and, therefore, not disclose any

such information to third parties without proper and specific authority, unless there is a legal or professional right or duty to disclose, nor use the information for the personal advantage of the professional accountant or third parties.

(e) Professional Behavior – to comply with relevant laws and regulations and avoid any action that discredits the profession.

Each of these fundamental principles is discussed in more detail in Sections 110–150.

Conceptual Framework Approach

The circumstances in which professional accountants operate may create specific threats to compliance with the fundamental principles. It is impossible to define every situation that creates threats to compliance with the fundamental principles and specify the appropriate action. In addition, the nature of engagements and work assignments may differ and, consequently, different threats may be created, requiring the application of different safeguards. Therefore, this Code establishes a conceptual framework that requires a professional accountant to identify, evaluate, and address threats to compliance with the fundamental principles. The conceptual framework approach assists professional accountants in complying with the ethical requirements of this Code and meeting their responsibility to act in the public interest. It accommodates many variations in circumstances that create threats to compliance with the fundamental principles and can deter a professional accountant from concluding that a situation is permitted if it is not specifically prohibited. **100.6**

When a professional accountant identifies threats to compliance with the fundamental principles and, based on an evaluation of those threats, determines that they are not at an acceptable level, the professional accountant shall determine whether appropriate safeguards are available and can be applied to eliminate the threats or reduce them to an acceptable level. In making that determination, the professional accountant shall exercise professional judgment and take into account whether a reasonable and informed third party, weighing all the specific facts and circumstances available to the professional accountant at the time, would be likely to conclude that the threats would be eliminated or reduced to an acceptable level by the application of the safeguards, such that compliance with the fundamental principles is not compromised. **100.7**

A professional accountant shall evaluate any threats to compliance with the fundamental principles when the professional accountant knows, or could reasonably be expected to know, of circumstances or relationships that may compromise compliance with the fundamental principles. **100.8**

A professional accountant shall take qualitative as well as quantitative factors into account when evaluating the significance of a threat. When applying the conceptual framework, a professional accountant may encounter situations in which threats cannot be eliminated or reduced to an acceptable level, either because the threat is too significant or because appropriate safeguards are not available or cannot be applied. In such situations, the professional accountant shall decline or discontinue the specific professional service involved or, when necessary, resign from the engagement (in the case of a professional accountant in public practice) or the employing organization (in the case of a professional accountant in business). **100.9**

A professional accountant may inadvertently violate a provision of this Code. Depending on the nature and significance of the matter, such an inadvertent violation may be deemed not to compromise compliance with the fundamental principles **100.10** provided, once the violation is discovered, the violation is corrected promptly and any necessary safeguards are applied.

100.11   When a professional accountant encounters unusual circumstances in which the application of a specific requirement of the Code would result in a disproportionate outcome or an outcome that may not be in the public interest, it is recommended that the professional accountant consult with a member body or the relevant regulator.

Threats and Safeguards

100.12   Threats may be created by a broad range of relationships and circumstances. When a relationship or circumstance creates a threat, such a threat could compromise, or could be perceived to compromise, a professional accountant's compliance with the fundamental principles. A circumstance or relationship may create more than one threat, and a threat may affect compliance with more than one fundamental principle. Threats fall into one or more of the following categories:

(a)   Self-interest threat – the threat that a financial or other interest will inappropriately influence the professional accountant's judgment or behavior;

(b)   Self-review threat – the threat that a professional accountant will not appropriately evaluate the results of a previous judgment made or service performed by the professional accountant, or by another individual within the professional accountant's firm or employing organization, on which the accountant will rely when forming a judgment as part of providing a current service;

(c)   Advocacy threat – the threat that a professional accountant will promote a client's or employer's position to the point that the professional accountant's objectivity is compromised;

(d)   Familiarity threat – the threat that due to a long or close relationship with a client or employer, a professional accountant will be too sympathetic to their interests or too accepting of their work; and

(e)   Intimidation threat – the threat that a professional accountant will be deterred from acting objectively because of actual or perceived pressures, including attempts to exercise undue influence over the professional accountant.

Parts B and C of this Code explain how these categories of threats may be created for professional accountants in public practice and professional accountants in business, respectively. Professional accountants in public practice may also find Part C relevant to their particular circumstances.

100.13   Safeguards are actions or other measures that may eliminate threats or reduce them to an acceptable level. They fall into two broad categories:

(a)   Safeguards created by the profession, legislation or regulation; and

(b)   Safeguards in the work environment.

100.14   Safeguards created by the profession, legislation or regulation include:

- Educational, training and experience requirements for entry into the profession.
- Continuing professional development requirements.
- Corporate governance regulations.
- Professional standards.
- Professional or regulatory monitoring and disciplinary procedures.
- External review by a legally empowered third party of the reports, returns, communications or information produced by a professional accountant.

Parts B and C of this Code discuss safeguards in the work environment for pro- **100.15** fessional accountants in public practice and professional accountants in business, respectively.

Certain safeguards may increase the likelihood of identifying or deterring unethical **100.16** behavior. Such safeguards, which may be created by the accounting profession, legislation, regulation, or an employing organization, include:

- Effective, well-publicized complaint systems operated by the employing orga- nization, the profession or a regulator, which enable colleagues, employers and members of the public to draw attention to unprofessional or unethical behavior.
- An explicitly stated duty to report breaches of ethical requirements.

Ethical Conflict Resolution

A professional accountant may be required to resolve a conflict in complying with **100.17** the fundamental principles.

When initiating either a formal or informal conflict resolution process, the following **100.18** factors, either individually or together with other factors, may be relevant to the resolution process:

(a) Relevant facts;
(b) Ethical issues involved;
(c) Fundamental principles related to the matter in question;
(d) Established internal procedures; and
(e) Alternative courses of action.

Having considered the relevant factors, a professional accountant shall determine the appropriate course of action, weighing the consequences of each possible course of action. If the matter remains unresolved, the professional accountant may wish to consult with other appropriate persons within the firm or employing organization for help in obtaining resolution.

Where a matter involves a conflict with, or within, an organization, a professional **100.19** accountant shall determine whether to consult with those charged with governance of the organization, such as the board of directors or the audit committee.

It may be in the best interests of the professional accountant to document the sub- **100.20** stance of the issue, the details of any discussions held, and the decisions made concerning that issue.

If a significant conflict cannot be resolved, a professional accountant may consider **100.21** obtaining professional advice from the relevant professional body or from legal advisors. The professional accountant generally can obtain guidance on ethical issues without breaching the fundamental principle of confidentiality if the matter is dis- cussed with the relevant professional body on an anonymous basis or with a legal advisor under the protection of legal privilege. Instances in which the professional accountant may consider obtaining legal advice vary. For example, a professional accountant may have encountered a fraud, the reporting of which could breach the professional accountant's responsibility to respect confidentiality. The professional accountant may consider obtaining legal advice in that instance to determine whe- ther there is a requirement to report.

100.22   If, after exhausting all relevant possibilities, the ethical conflict remains unresolved, a professional accountant shall, where possible, refuse to remain associated with the matter creating the conflict. The professional accountant shall determine whether, in the circumstances, it is appropriate to withdraw from the engagement team or specific assignment, or to resign altogether from the engagement, the firm or the employing organization.

Section 110

Integrity

The principle of integrity imposes an obligation on all professional accountants to be straightforward and honest in all professional and business relationships. Integrity also implies fair dealing and truthfulness. **110.1**

A professional accountant shall not knowingly be associated with reports, returns, communications or other information where the professional accountant believes that the information: **110.2**

(a) Contains a materially false or misleading statement;
(b) Contains statements or information furnished recklessly; or
(c) Omits or obscures information required to be included where such omission or obscurity would be misleading.

When a professional accountant becomes aware that the accountant has been associated with such information, the accountant shall take steps to be disassociated from that information.

A professional accountant will be deemed not to be in breach of paragraph 110.2 if the professional accountant provides a modified report in respect of a matter contained in paragraph 110.2. **110.3**

Section 120

Objectivity

120.1   The principle of objectivity imposes an obligation on all professional accountants not to compromise their professional or business judgment because of bias, conflict of interest or the undue influence of others.

120.2   A professional accountant may be exposed to situations that may impair objectivity. It is impracticable to define and prescribe all such situations. A professional accountant shall not perform a professional service if a circumstance or relationship biases or unduly influences the accountant's professional judgment with respect to that service.

Section 130

Professional Competence and Due Care

The principle of professional competence and due care imposes the following obligations on all professional accountants: **130.1**

(a) To maintain professional knowledge and skill at the level required to ensure that clients or employers receive competent professional service; and
(b) To act diligently in accordance with applicable technical and professional standards when providing professional services.

Competent professional service requires the exercise of sound judgment in applying professional knowledge and skill in the performance of such service. Professional competence may be divided into two separate phases: **130.2**

(a) Attainment of professional competence; and
(b) Maintenance of professional competence.

The maintenance of professional competence requires a continuing awareness and an understanding of relevant technical, professional and business developments. Continuing professional development enables a professional accountant to develop and maintain the capabilities to perform competently within the professional environment. **130.3**

Diligence encompasses the responsibility to act in accordance with the requirements of an assignment, carefully, thoroughly and on a timely basis. **130.4**

A professional accountant shall take reasonable steps to ensure that those working under the professional accountant's authority in a professional capacity have appropriate training and supervision. **130.5**

Where appropriate, a professional accountant shall make clients, employers or other users of the accountant's professional services aware of the limitations inherent in the services. **130.6**

Section 140

Confidentiality

140.1   The principle of confidentiality imposes an obligation on all professional accountants to refrain from:

(a)   Disclosing outside the firm or employing organization confidential information acquired as a result of professional and business relationships without proper and specific authority or unless there is a legal or professional right or duty to disclose; and

(b)   Using confidential information acquired as a result of professional and business relationships to their personal advantage or the advantage of third parties.

140.2   A professional accountant shall maintain confidentiality, including in a social environment, being alert to the possibility of inadvertent disclosure, particularly to a close business associate or a close or immediate family member.

140.3   A professional accountant shall maintain confidentiality of information disclosed by a prospective client or employer.

140.4   A professional accountant shall maintain confidentiality of information within the firm or employing organization.

140.5   A professional accountant shall take reasonable steps to ensure that staff under the professional accountant's control and persons from whom advice and assistance is obtained respect the professional accountant's duty of confidentiality.

140.6   The need to comply with the principle of confidentiality continues even after the end of relationships between a professional accountant and a client or employer. When a professional accountant changes employment or acquires a new client, the professional accountant is entitled to use prior experience. The professional accountant shall not, however, use or disclose any confidential information either acquired or received as a result of a professional or business relationship.

140.7   The following are circumstances where professional accountants are or may be required to disclose confidential information or when such disclosure may be appropriate:

(a)   Disclosure is permitted by law and is authorized by the client or the employer;

(b)   Disclosure is required by law, for example:

(i)   Production of documents or other provision of evidence in the course of legal proceedings; or

(ii)   Disclosure to the appropriate public authorities of infringements of the law that come to light; and

(c)   There is a professional duty or right to disclose, when not prohibited by law:

(i)   To comply with the quality review of a member body or professional body;

(ii)   To respond to an inquiry or investigation by a member body or regulatory body;

(iii)   To protect the professional interests of a professional accountant in legal proceedings; or

(iv)   To comply with technical standards and ethics requirements.

140.8   In deciding whether to disclose confidential information, relevant factors to consider include:

- Whether the interests of all parties, including third parties whose interests may be affected, could be harmed if the client or employer consents to the disclosure of information by the professional accountant.
- Whether all the relevant information is known and substantiated, to the extent it is practicable; when the situation involves unsubstantiated facts, incomplete information or unsubstantiated conclusions, professional judgment shall be used in determining the type of disclosure to be made, if any.
- The type of communication that is expected and to whom it is addressed.
- Whether the parties to whom the communication is addressed are appropriate recipients.

Section 150

Professional Behavior

150.1   The principle of professional behavior imposes an obligation on all professional accountants to comply with relevant laws and regulations and avoid any action that the professional accountant knows or should know may discredit the profession. This includes actions that a reasonable and informed third party, weighing all the specific facts and circumstances available to the professional accountant at that time, would be likely to conclude adversely affects the good reputation of the profession.

150.2   In marketing and promoting themselves and their work, professional accountants shall not bring the profession into disrepute. Professional accountants shall be honest and truthful and not:

(a) Make exaggerated claims for the services they are able to offer, the qualifications they possess, or experience they have gained; or

(b) Make disparaging references or unsubstantiated comparisons to the work of others.

Part B—Professional accountants in public practice

Section 200

Introduction

200.1   This Part of the Code describes how the conceptual framework contained in Part A applies in certain situations to professional accountants in public practice. This Part does not describe all of the circumstances and relationships that could be encountered by a professional accountant in public practice that create or may create threats to compliance with the fundamental principles. Therefore, the professional accountant in public practice is encouraged to be alert for such circumstances and relationships.

200.2   A professional accountant in public practice shall not knowingly engage in any business, occupation, or activity that impairs or might impair integrity, objectivity or the good reputation of the profession and as a result would be incompatible with the fundamental principles.

Threats and Safeguards

200.3   Compliance with the fundamental principles may potentially be threatened by a broad range of circumstances and relationships. The nature and significance of the threats may differ depending on whether they arise in relation to the provision of services to an audit client and whether the audit client is a public interest entity, to an assurance client that is not an audit client, or to a non-assurance client.

Threats fall into one or more of the following categories:

(a)   Self-interest;
(b)   Self-review;
(c)   Advocacy;
(d)   Familiarity; and
(e)   Intimidation.

These threats are discussed further in Part A of this Code.

200.4   Examples of circumstances that create self-interest threats for a professional accountant in public practice include:

- A member of the assurance team having a direct financial interest in the assurance client.
- A firm having undue dependence on total fees from a client.
- A member of the assurance team having a significant close business relationship with an assurance client.
- A firm being concerned about the possibility of losing a significant client.
- A member of the audit team entering into employment negotiations with the audit client.
- A firm entering into a contingent fee arrangement relating to an assurance engagement.
- A professional accountant discovering a significant error when evaluating the results of a previous professional service performed by a member of the professional accountant's firm.

200.5   Examples of circumstances that create self-review threats for a professional accountant in public practice include:

- A firm issuing an assurance report on the effectiveness of the operation of financial systems after designing or implementing the systems.
- A firm having prepared the original data used to generate records that are the subject matter of the assurance engagement.
- A member of the assurance team being, or having recently been, a director or officer of the client.
- A member of the assurance team being, or having recently been, employed by the client in a position to exert significant influence over the subject matter of the engagement.
- The firm performing a service for an assurance client that directly affects the subject matter information of the assurance engagement.

Examples of circumstances that create advocacy threats for a professional accountant in public practice include: **200.6**

- The firm promoting shares in an audit client.
- A professional accountant acting as an advocate on behalf of an audit client in litigation or disputes with third parties.

Examples of circumstances that create familiarity threats for a professional accountant in public practice include: **200.7**

- A member of the engagement team having a close or immediate family member who is a director or officer of the client.
- A member of the engagement team having a close or immediate family member who is an employee of the client who is in a position to exert significant influence over the subject matter of the engagement.
- A director or officer of the client or an employee in a position to exert significant influence over the subject matter of the engagement having recently served as the engagement partner.
- A professional accountant accepting gifts or preferential treatment from a client, unless the value is trivial or inconsequential.
- Senior personnel having a long association with the assurance client.

Examples of circumstances that create intimidation threats for a professional accountant in public practice include: **200.8**

- A firm being threatened with dismissal from a client engagement.
- An audit client indicating that it will not award a planned non-assurance contract to the firm if the firm continues to disagree with the client's accounting treatment for a particular transaction.
- A firm being threatened with litigation by the client.
- A firm being pressured to reduce inappropriately the extent of work performed in order to reduce fees.
- A professional accountant feeling pressured to agree with the judgment of a client employee because the employee has more expertise on the matter in question.
- A professional accountant being informed by a partner of the firm that a planned promotion will not occur unless the accountant agrees with an audit client's inappropriate accounting treatment.

Safeguards that may eliminate or reduce threats to an acceptable level fall into two broad categories: **200.9**

(a) Safeguards created by the profession, legislation or regulation; and
(b) Safeguards in the work environment.

Examples of safeguards created by the profession, legislation or regulation are described in paragraph 100.14 of Part A of this Code.

200.10   A professional accountant in public practice shall exercise judgment to determine how best to deal with threats that are not at an acceptable level, whether by applying safeguards to eliminate the threat or reduce it to an acceptable level or by terminating or declining the relevant engagement. In exercising this judgment, a professional accountant in public practice shall consider whether a reasonable and informed third party, weighing all the specific facts and circumstances available to the professional accountant at that time, would be likely to conclude that the threats would be eliminated or reduced to an acceptable level by the application of safeguards, such that compliance with the fundamental principles is not compromised. This consideration will be affected by matters such as the significance of the threat, the nature of the engagement and the structure of the firm.

200.11   In the work environment, the relevant safeguards will vary depending on the circumstances. Work environment safeguards comprise firm-wide safeguards and engagement-specific safeguards.

200.12   Examples of firm-wide safeguards in the work environment include:

- Leadership of the firm that stresses the importance of compliance with the fundamental principles.
- Leadership of the firm that establishes the expectation that members of an assurance team will act in the public interest.
- Policies and procedures to implement and monitor quality control of engagements.
- Documented policies regarding the need to identify threats to compliance with the fundamental principles, evaluate the significance of those threats, and apply safeguards to eliminate or reduce the threats to an acceptable level or, when appropriate safeguards are not available or cannot be applied, terminate or decline the relevant engagement.
- Documented internal policies and procedures requiring compliance with the fundamental principles.
- Policies and procedures that will enable the identification of interests or relationships between the firm or members of engagement teams and clients.
- Policies and procedures to monitor and, if necessary, manage the reliance on revenue received from a single client.
- Using different partners and engagement teams with separate reporting lines for the provision of non-assurance services to an assurance client.
- Policies and procedures to prohibit individuals who are not members of an engagement team from inappropriately influencing the outcome of the engagement.
- Timely communication of a firm's policies and procedures, including any changes to them, to all partners and professional staff, and appropriate training and education on such policies and procedures.
- Designating a member of senior management to be responsible for overseeing the adequate functioning of the firm's quality control system.
- Advising partners and professional staff of assurance clients and related entities from which independence is required.
- A disciplinary mechanism to promote compliance with policies and procedures.
- Published policies and procedures to encourage and empower staff to communicate to senior levels within the firm any issue relating to compliance with the fundamental principles that concerns them.

200.13   Examples of engagement-specific safeguards in the work environment include:

- Having a professional accountant who was not involved with the non-assurance service review the non-assurance work performed or otherwise advise as necessary.
- Having a professional accountant who was not a member of the assurance team review the assurance work performed or otherwise advise as necessary.
- Consulting an independent third party, such as a committee of independent directors, a professional regulatory body or another professional accountant.
- Discussing ethical issues with those charged with governance of the client.
- Disclosing to those charged with governance of the client the nature of services provided and extent of fees charged.
- Involving another firm to perform or re-perform part of the engagement.
- Rotating senior assurance team personnel.

Depending on the nature of the engagement, a professional accountant in public practice may also be able to rely on safeguards that the client has implemented. However it is not possible to rely solely on such safeguards to reduce threats to an acceptable level. **200.14**

Examples of safeguards within the client's systems and procedures include: **200.15**

- The client requires persons other than management to ratify or approve the appointment of a firm to perform an engagement.
- The client has competent employees with experience and seniority to make managerial decisions.
- The client has implemented internal procedures that ensure objective choices in commissioning non-assurance engagements.
- The client has a corporate governance structure that provides appropriate oversight and communications regarding the firm's services.

Section 210

Professional Appointment

Client Acceptance

210.1   Before accepting a new client relationship, a professional accountant in public practice shall determine whether acceptance would create any threats to compliance with the fundamental principles. Potential threats to integrity or professional behavior may be created from, for example, questionable issues associated with the client (its owners, management or activities).

210.2   Client issues that, if known, could threaten compliance with the fundamental principles include, for example, client involvement in illegal activities (such as money laundering), dishonesty or questionable financial reporting practices.

210.3   A professional accountant in public practice shall evaluate the significance of any threats and apply safeguards when necessary to eliminate them or reduce them to an acceptable level.

Examples of such safeguards include:

- Obtaining knowledge and understanding of the client, its owners, managers and those responsible for its governance and business activities; or
- Securing the client's commitment to improve corporate governance practices or internal controls.

210.4   Where it is not possible to reduce the threats to an acceptable level, the professional accountant in public practice shall decline to enter into the client relationship.

210.5   It is recommended that a professional accountant in public practice periodically review acceptance decisions for recurring client engagements.

Engagement Acceptance

210.6   The fundamental principle of professional competence and due care imposes an obligation on a professional accountant in public practice to provide only those services that the professional accountant in public practice is competent to perform. Before accepting a specific client engagement, a professional accountant in public practice shall determine whether acceptance would create any threats to compliance with the fundamental principles. For example, a self-interest threat to professional competence and due care is created if the engagement team does not possess, or cannot acquire, the competencies necessary to properly carry out the engagement.

210.7   A professional accountant in public practice shall evaluate the significance of threats and apply safeguards, when necessary, to eliminate them or reduce them to an acceptable level. Examples of such safeguards include:

- Acquiring an appropriate understanding of the nature of the client's business, the complexity of its operations, the specific requirements of the engagement and the purpose, nature and scope of the work to be performed;
- Acquiring knowledge of relevant industries or subject matters;
- Possessing or obtaining experience with relevant regulatory or reporting requirements;
- Assigning sufficient staff with the necessary competencies;
- Using experts where necessary;

- Agreeing on a realistic time frame for the performance of the engagement; or
- Complying with quality control policies and procedures designed to provide reasonable assurance that specific engagements are accepted only when they can be performed competently.

When a professional accountant in public practice intends to rely on the advice or work of an expert, the professional accountant in public practice shall determine whether such reliance is warranted. Factors to consider include: reputation, expertise, resources available and applicable professional and ethical standards. Such information may be gained from prior association with the expert or from consulting others.   **210.8**

Changes in a Professional Appointment

A professional accountant in public practice who is asked to replace another professional accountant in public practice, or who is considering tendering for an engagement currently held by another professional accountant in public practice, shall determine whether there are any reasons, professional or otherwise, for not accepting the engagement, such as circumstances that create threats to compliance with the fundamental principles that cannot be eliminated or reduced to an acceptable level by the application of safeguards. For example, there may be a threat to professional competence and due care if a professional accountant in public practice accepts the engagement before knowing all the pertinent facts.   **210.9**

A professional accountant in public practice shall evaluate the significance of any threats. Depending on the nature of the engagement, this may require direct communication with the existing accountant to establish the facts and circumstances regarding the proposed change so that the professional accountant in public practice can decide whether it would be appropriate to accept the engagement. For example, the apparent reasons for the change in appointment may not fully reflect the facts and may indicate disagreements with the existing accountant that may influence the decision to accept the appointment.   **210.10**

Safeguards shall be applied when necessary to eliminate any threats or reduce them to an acceptable level. Examples of such safeguards include: **210.11**

- When replying to requests to submit tenders, stating in the tender that, before accepting the engagement, contact with the existing accountant will be requested so that inquiries may be made as to whether there are any professional or other reasons why the appointment should not be accepted;
- Asking the existing accountant to provide known information on any facts or circumstances that, in the existing accountant's opinion, the proposed accountant needs to be aware of before deciding whether to accept the engagement; or
- Obtaining necessary information from other sources.

When the threats cannot be eliminated or reduced to an acceptable level through the application of safeguards, a professional accountant in public practice shall, unless there is satisfaction as to necessary facts by other means, decline the engagement.

A professional accountant in public practice may be asked to undertake work that is complementary or additional to the work of the existing accountant. Such circumstances may create threats to professional competence and due care resulting from, for example, a lack of or incomplete information. The significance of any threats shall be evaluated and safeguards applied when necessary to eliminate the threat or reduce it to an acceptable level. An example of such a safeguard is notifying the existing accountant of the proposed work, which would give the existing accountant   **210.12** the opportunity to provide any relevant information needed for the proper conduct of the work.

210.13 An existing accountant is bound by confidentiality. Whether that professional accountant is permitted or required to discuss the affairs of a client with a proposed accountant will depend on the nature of the engagement and on:

(a) Whether the client's permission to do so has been obtained; or

(b) The legal or ethical requirements relating to such communications and disclosure, which may vary by jurisdiction.

Circumstances where the professional accountant is or may be required to disclose confidential information or where such disclosure may otherwise be appropriate are set out in Section 140 of Part A of this Code.

210.14 A professional accountant in public practice will generally need to obtain the client's permission, preferably in writing, to initiate discussion with an existing accountant. Once that permission is obtained, the existing accountant shall comply with relevant legal and other regulations governing such requests. Where the existing accountant provides information, it shall be provided honestly and unambiguously. If the proposed accountant is unable to communicate with the existing accountant, the proposed accountant shall take reasonable steps to obtain information about any possible threats by other means, such as through inquiries of third parties or background investigations of senior management or those charged with governance of the client.

Section 220

Conflicts of Interest

A professional accountant in public practice shall take reasonable steps to identify **220.1** circumstances that could pose a conflict of interest. Such circumstances may create threats to compliance with the fundamental principles. For example, a threat to objectivity may be created when a professional accountant in public practice competes directly with a client or has a joint venture or similar arrangement with a major competitor of a client. A threat to objectivity or confidentiality may also be created when a professional accountant in public practice performs services for clients whose interests are in conflict or the clients are in dispute with each other in relation to the matter or transaction in question.

A professional accountant in public practice shall evaluate the significance of any **220.2** threats and apply safeguards when necessary to eliminate the threats or reduce them to an acceptable level. Before accepting or continuing a client relationship or specific engagement, the professional accountant in public practice shall evaluate the significance of any threats created by business interests or relationships with the client or a third party.

Depending upon the circumstances giving rise to the conflict, application of one of **220.3** the following safeguards is generally necessary:

(a) Notifying the client of the firm's business interest or activities that may represent a conflict of interest and obtaining their consent to act in such circumstances; or
(b) Notifying all known relevant parties that the professional accountant in public practice is acting for two or more parties in respect of a matter where their respective interests are in conflict and obtaining their consent to so act; or
(c) Notifying the client that the professional accountant in public practice does not act exclusively for any one client in the provision of proposed services (for example, in a particular market sector or with respect to a specific service) and obtaining their consent to so act.

The professional accountant shall also determine whether to apply one or more of **220.4** the following additional safeguards:

(a) The use of separate engagement teams;
(b) Procedures to prevent access to information (for example, strict physical separation of such teams, confidential and secure data filing);
(c) Clear guidelines for members of the engagement team on issues of security and confidentiality;
(d) The use of confidentiality agreements signed by employees and partners of the firm; and
(e) Regular review of the application of safeguards by a senior individual not involved with relevant client engagements.

Where a conflict of interest creates a threat to one or more of the fundamental **220.5** principles, including objectivity, confidentiality, or professional behavior, that cannot be eliminated or reduced to an acceptable level through the application of safeguards, the professional accountant in public practice shall not accept a specific engagement or shall resign from one or more conflicting engagements.

Where a professional accountant in public practice has requested consent from a **220.6** client to act for another party (which may or may not be an existing client) in respect of a matter where the respective interests are in conflict and that consent has been refused by the client, the professional accountant in public practice shall not continue to act for one of the parties in the matter giving rise to the conflict of interest.

Section 230

Second Opinions

Situations where a professional accountant in public practice is asked to provide a **230.1** second opinion on the application of accounting, auditing, reporting or other standards or principles to specific circumstances or transactions by or on behalf of a company or an entity that is not an existing client may create threats to compliance with the fundamental principles. For example, there may be a threat to professional competence and due care in circumstances where the second opinion is not based on the same set of facts that were made available to the existing accountant or is based on inadequate evidence. The existence and significance of any threat will depend on the circumstances of the request and all the other available facts and assumptions relevant to the expression of a professional judgment.

When asked to provide such an opinion, a professional accountant in public practice **230.2** shall evaluate the significance of any threats and apply safeguards when necessary to eliminate them or reduce them to an acceptable level. Examples of such safeguards include seeking client permission to contact the existing accountant, describing the limitations surrounding any opinion in communications with the client and providing the existing accountant with a copy of the opinion.

If the company or entity seeking the opinion will not permit communication with the **230.3** existing accountant, a professional accountant in public practice shall determine whether, taking all the circumstances into account, it is appropriate to provide the opinion sought.

Section 240

Fees and Other Types of Remuneration

240.1   When entering into negotiations regarding professional services, a professional accountant in public practice may quote whatever fee is deemed appropriate. The fact that one professional accountant in public practice may quote a fee lower than another is not in itself unethical. Nevertheless, there may be threats to compliance with the fundamental principles arising from the level of fees quoted. For example, a self-interest threat to professional competence and due care is created if the fee quoted is so low that it may be difficult to perform the engagement in accordance with applicable technical and professional standards for that price.

240.2   The existence and significance of any threats created will depend on factors such as the level of fee quoted and the services to which it applies. The significance of any threat shall be evaluated and safeguards applied when necessary to eliminate the threat or reduce it to an acceptable level. Examples of such safeguards include:

- Making the client aware of the terms of the engagement and, in particular, the basis on which fees are charged and which services are covered by the quoted fee; or
- Assigning appropriate time and qualified staff to the task.

240.3   Contingent fees are widely used for certain types of non-assurance engagements.[1] They may, however, create threats to compliance with the fundamental principles in certain circumstances. They may create a self-interest threat to objectivity. The existence and significance of such threats will depend on factors including:

- The nature of the engagement.
- The range of possible fee amounts.
- The basis for determining the fee.
- Whether the outcome or result of the transaction is to be reviewed by an independent third party.

240.4   The significance of any such threats shall be evaluated and safeguards applied when necessary to eliminate or reduce them to an acceptable level. Examples of such safeguards include:

- An advance written agreement with the client as to the basis of remuneration;
- Disclosure to intended users of the work performed by the professional accountant in public practice and the basis of remuneration;
- Quality control policies and procedures; or
- Review by an independent third party of the work performed by the professional accountant in public practice.

240.5   In certain circumstances, a professional accountant in public practice may receive a referral fee or commission relating to a client. For example, where the professional accountant in public practice does not provide the specific service required, a fee may be received for referring a continuing client to another professional accountant in public practice or other expert. A professional accountant in public practice may receive a commission from a third party (for example, a software vendor) in connection with the sale of goods or services to a client. Accepting such a referral fee or commission creates a self-interest threat to objectivity and professional competence and due care.

---

[1] *Contingent fees for non-assurance services provided to audit clients and other assurance clients are discussed in Sections 290 and 291 of this Code.*

A professional accountant in public practice may also pay a referral fee to obtain a client, for example, where the client continues as a client of another professional accountant in public practice but requires specialist services not offered by the existing accountant. The payment of such a referral fee also creates a self-interest threat to objectivity and professional competence and due care.

240.6

The significance of the threat shall be evaluated and safeguards applied when necessary to eliminate the threat or reduce it to an acceptable level. Examples of such safeguards include:

240.7

- Disclosing to the client any arrangements to pay a referral fee to another professional accountant for the work referred;
- Disclosing to the client any arrangements to receive a referral fee for referring the client to another professional accountant in public practice; or
- Obtaining advance agreement from the client for commission arrangements in connection with the sale by a third party of goods or services to the client.

A professional accountant in public practice may purchase all or part of another firm on the basis that payments will be made to individuals formerly owning the firm or to their heirs or estates. Such payments are not regarded as commissions or referral fees for the purpose of paragraphs 240.5–240.7 above.

240.8

Section 250

Marketing Professional Services

250.1   When a professional accountant in public practice solicits new work through advertising or other forms of marketing, there may be a threat to compliance with the fundamental principles. For example, a self-interest threat to compliance with the principle of professional behavior is created if services, achievements, or products are marketed in a way that is inconsistent with that principle.

250.2   A professional accountant in public practice shall not bring the profession into disrepute when marketing professional services. The professional accountant in public practice shall be honest and truthful, and not:

(a)   Make exaggerated claims for services offered, qualifications possessed, or experience gained; or

(b)   Make disparaging references or unsubstantiated comparisons to the work of another.

If the professional accountant in public practice is in doubt about whether a proposed form of advertising or marketing is appropriate, the professional accountant in public practice shall consider consulting with the relevant professional body.

Section 260

Gifts and Hospitality

A professional accountant in public practice, or an immediate or close family member, may be offered gifts and hospitality from a client. Such an offer may create threats to compliance with the fundamental principles. For example, a self-interest or familiarity threat to objectivity may be created if a gift from a client is accepted; an intimidation threat to objectivity may result from the possibility of such offers being made public. **260.1**

The existence and significance of any threat will depend on the nature, value, and intent of the offer. Where gifts or hospitality are offered that a reasonable and informed third party, weighing all the specific facts and circumstances, would consider trivial and inconsequential, a professional accountant in public practice may conclude that the offer is made in the normal course of business without the specific intent to influence decision making or to obtain information. In such cases, the professional accountant in public practice may generally conclude that any threat to compliance with the fundamental principles is at an acceptable level. **260.2**

A professional accountant in public practice shall evaluate the significance of any threats and apply safeguards when necessary to eliminate the threats or reduce them to an acceptable level. When the threats cannot be eliminated or reduced to an acceptable level through the application of safeguards, a professional accountant in public practice shall not accept such an offer. **260.3**

Section 270

Custody of Client Assets

270.1   A professional accountant in public practice shall not assume custody of client monies or other assets unless permitted to do so by law and, if so, in compliance with any additional legal duties imposed on a professional accountant in public practice holding such assets.

270.2   The holding of client assets creates threats to compliance with the fundamental principles; for example, there is a self-interest threat to professional behavior and may be a self-interest threat to objectivity arising from holding client assets. A professional accountant in public practice entrusted with money (or other assets) belonging to others shall therefore:

(a)   Keep such assets separately from personal or firm assets;

(b)   Use such assets only for the purpose for which they are intended;

(c)   At all times be ready to account for those assets and any income, dividends, or gains generated, to any persons entitled to such accounting; and

(d)   Comply with all relevant laws and regulations relevant to the holding of and accounting for such assets.

270.3   As part of client and engagement acceptance procedures for services that may involve the holding of client assets, a professional accountant in public practice shall make appropriate inquiries about the source of such assets and consider legal and regulatory obligations. For example, if the assets were derived from illegal activities, such as money laundering, a threat to compliance with the fundamental principles would be created. In such situations, the professional accountant may consider seeking legal advice.

Section 280

Objectivity—All Services

A professional accountant in public practice shall determine when providing any professional service whether there are threats to compliance with the fundamental principle of objectivity resulting from having interests in, or relationships with, a client or its directors, officers or employees. For example, a familiarity threat to objectivity may be created from a family or close personal or business relationship. **280.1**

A professional accountant in public practice who provides an assurance service shall be independent of the assurance client. Independence of mind and in appearance is necessary to enable the professional accountant in public practice to express a conclusion, and be seen to express a conclusion, without bias, conflict of interest, or undue influence of others. Sections 290 and 291 provide specific guidance on independence requirements for professional accountants in public practice when performing assurance engagements. **280.2**

The existence of threats to objectivity when providing any professional service will depend upon the particular circumstances of the engagement and the nature of the work that the professional accountant in public practice is performing. **280.3**

A professional accountant in public practice shall evaluate the significance of any threats and apply safeguards when necessary to eliminate them or reduce them to an acceptable level. Examples of such safeguards include: **280.4**

- Withdrawing from the engagement team;
- Supervisory procedures;
- Terminating the financial or business relationship giving rise to the threat;
- Discussing the issue with higher levels of management within the firm; or
- Discussing the issue with those charged with governance of the client.

If safeguards cannot eliminate or reduce the threat to an acceptable level, the professional accountant shall decline or terminate the relevant engagement.

Section 290

Independence—audit and review engagements

Contents

Structure of Section

This section addresses the independence requirements for audit engagements and review engagements, which are assurance engagements in which a professional accountant in public practice expresses a conclusion on financial statements. Such engagements comprise audit and review engagements to report on a complete set of financial statements and a single financial statement. Independence requirements for assurance engagements that are not audit or review engagements are addressed in Section 291. **290.1**

In certain circumstances involving audit engagements where the audit report includes a restriction on use and distribution and provided certain conditions are met, the independence requirements in this section may be modified as provided in paragraphs 290.500 to 290.514. The modifications are not permitted in the case of an audit of financial statements required by law or regulation. **290.2**

In this section, the term(s): **290.3**

(a) "Audit," "audit team," "audit engagement," "audit client" and "audit report" includes review, review team, review engagement, review client and review report; and
(b) "Firm" includes network firm, except where otherwise stated.

A Conceptual Framework Approach to Independence

In the case of audit engagements, it is in the public interest and, therefore, required by this Code, that members of audit teams, firms and network firms shall be independent of audit clients. **290.4**

The objective of this section is to assist firms and members of audit teams in applying the conceptual framework approach described below to achieving and maintaining independence. **290.5**

Independence comprises: **290.6**

(a) Independence of Mind
    The state of mind that permits the expression of a conclusion without being affected by influences that compromise professional judgment, thereby allowing an individual to act with integrity and exercise objectivity and professional skepticism.
(b) Independence in Appearance
    The avoidance of facts and circumstances that are so significant that a reasonable and informed third party would be likely to conclude, weighing all the specific facts and circumstances, that a firm's, or a member of the audit team's, integrity, objectivity or professional skepticism has been compromised.

The conceptual framework approach shall be applied by professional accountants to: **290.7**

(a) Identify threats to independence;
(b) Evaluate the significance of the threats identified; and
(c) Apply safeguards, when necessary, to eliminate the threats or reduce them to an acceptable level.

When the professional accountant determines that appropriate safeguards are not available or cannot be applied to eliminate the threats or reduce them to an acceptable level, the professional accountant shall eliminate the circumstance or relationship creating the threats or decline or terminate the audit engagement.

A professional accountant shall use professional judgment in applying this conceptual framework.

290.8   Many different circumstances, or combinations of circumstances, may be relevant in assessing threats to independence. It is impossible to define every situation that creates threats to independence and to specify the appropriate action. Therefore, this Code establishes a conceptual framework that requires firms and members of audit teams to identify, evaluate, and address threats to independence. The conceptual framework approach assists professional accountants in practice in complying with the ethical requirements in this Code. It accommodates many variations in circumstances that create threats to independence and can deter a professional accountant from concluding that a situation is permitted if it is not specifically prohibited.

290.9   Paragraphs 290.100 and onwards describe how the conceptual framework approach to independence is to be applied. These paragraphs do not address all the circumstances and relationships that create or may create threats to independence.

290.10   In deciding whether to accept or continue an engagement, or whether a particular individual may be a member of the audit team, a firm shall identify and evaluate threats to independence. If the threats are not at an acceptable level, and the decision is whether to accept an engagement or include a particular individual on the audit team, the firm shall determine whether safeguards are available to eliminate the threats or reduce them to an acceptable level. If the decision is whether to continue an engagement, the firm shall determine whether any existing safeguards will continue to be effective to eliminate the threats or reduce them to an acceptable level or whether other safeguards will need to be applied or whether the engagement needs to be terminated. Whenever new information about a threat to independence comes to the attention of the firm during the engagement, the firm shall evaluate the significance of the threat in accordance with the conceptual framework approach.

290.11   Throughout this section, reference is made to the significance of threats to independence. In evaluating the significance of a threat, qualitative as well as quantitative factors shall be taken into account.

290.12   This section does not, in most cases, prescribe the specific responsibility of individuals within the firm for actions related to independence because responsibility may differ depending on the size, structure and organization of a firm. The firm is required by *International Standards on Quality Control* (ISQCs) to establish policies and procedures designed to provide it with reasonable assurance that independence is maintained when required by relevant ethical requirements. In addition, *International Standards on Auditing* (ISAs) require the engagement partner to form a conclusion on compliance with the independence requirements that apply to the engagement.

Networks and Network Firms

290.13   If a firm is deemed to be a network firm, the firm shall be independent of the audit clients of the other firms within the network (unless otherwise stated in this Code). The independence requirements in this section that apply to a network firm apply to any entity, such as a consulting practice or professional law practice, that meets the definition of a network firm irrespective of whether the entity itself meets the definition of a firm.

To enhance their ability to provide professional services, firms frequently form larger structures with other firms and entities. Whether these larger structures create a network depends on the particular facts and circumstances and does not depend on whether the firms and entities are legally separate and distinct. For example, a larger structure may be aimed only at facilitating the referral of work, which in itself does not meet the criteria necessary to constitute a network. Alternatively, a larger structure might be such that it is aimed at co-operation and the firms share a common brand name, a common system of quality control, or significant professional resources and consequently is deemed to be a network.   **290.14**

The judgment as to whether the larger structure is a network shall be made in light of whether a reasonable and informed third party would be likely to conclude, weighing all the specific facts and circumstances, that the entities are associated in such a way that a network exists. This judgment shall be applied consistently throughout the network.   **290.15**

Where the larger structure is aimed at co-operation and it is clearly aimed at profit or cost sharing among the entities within the structure, it is deemed to be a network. However, the sharing of immaterial costs does not in itself create a network. In addition, if the sharing of costs is limited only to those costs related to the development of audit methodologies, manuals, or training courses, this would not in itself create a network. Further, an association between a firm and an otherwise unrelated entity to jointly provide a service or develop a product does not in itself create a network.   **290.16**

Where the larger structure is aimed at cooperation and the entities within the structure share common ownership, control or management, it is deemed to be a network. This could be achieved by contract or other means.   **290.17**

Where the larger structure is aimed at co-operation and the entities within the structure share common quality control policies and procedures, it is deemed to be a network. For this purpose, common quality control policies and procedures are those designed, implemented and monitored across the larger structure.   **290.18**

Where the larger structure is aimed at co-operation and the entities within the structure share a common business strategy, it is deemed to be a network. Sharing a common business strategy involves an agreement by the entities to achieve common strategic objectives. An entity is not deemed to be a network firm merely because it co-operates with another entity solely to respond jointly to a request for a proposal for the provision of a professional service.   **290.19**

Where the larger structure is aimed at co-operation and the entities within the structure share the use of a common brand name, it is deemed to be a network. A common brand name includes common initials or a common name. A firm is deemed to be using a common brand name if it includes, for example, the common brand name as part of, or along with, its firm name, when a partner of the firm signs an audit report.   **290.20**

Even though a firm does not belong to a network and does not use a common brand name as part of its firm name, it may give the appearance that it belongs to a network if it makes reference in its stationery or promotional materials to being a member of an association of firms. Accordingly, if care is not taken in how a firm describes such memberships, a perception may be created that the firm belongs to a network.   **290.21**

290.22   If a firm sells a component of its practice, the sales agreement sometimes provides that, for a limited period of time, the component may continue to use the name of the firm, or an element of the name, even though it is no longer connected to the firm. In such circumstances, while the two entities may be practicing under a common name, the facts are such that they do not belong to a larger structure aimed at co-operation and are, therefore, not network firms. Those entities shall determine how to disclose that they are not network firms when presenting themselves to outside parties.

290.23   Where the larger structure is aimed at co-operation and the entities within the structure share a significant part of professional resources, it is deemed to be a network. Professional resources include:

- Common systems that enable firms to exchange information such as client data, billing and time records;
- Partners and staff;
- Technical departments that consult on technical or industry specific issues, transactions or events for assurance engagements;
- Audit methodology or audit manuals; and
- Training courses and facilities.

290.24   The determination of whether the professional resources shared are significant, and therefore the firms are network firms, shall be made based on the relevant facts and circumstances. Where the shared resources are limited to common audit methodology or audit manuals, with no exchange of personnel or client or market information, it is unlikely that the shared resources would be significant. The same applies to a common training endeavor. Where, however, the shared resources involve the exchange of people or information, such as where staff are drawn from a shared pool, or a common technical department is created within the larger structure to provide participating firms with technical advice that the firms are required to follow, a reasonable and informed third party is more likely to conclude that the shared resources are significant.

Public Interest Entities

290.25   Section 290 contains additional provisions that reflect the extent of public interest in certain entities. For the purpose of this section, public interest entities are:

(a)   All listed entities; and
(b)   Any entity:
    (i)   Defined by regulation or legislation as a public interest entity; or
    (ii)   For which the audit is required by regulation or legislation to be conducted in compliance with the same independence requirements that apply to the audit of listed entities. Such regulation may be promulgated by any relevant regulator, including an audit regulator.

290.26   Firms and member bodies are encouraged to determine whether to treat additional entities, or certain categories of entities, as public interest entities because they have a large number and wide range of stakeholders. Factors to be considered include:

- The nature of the business, such as the holding of assets in a fiduciary capacity for a large number of stakeholders. Examples may include financial institutions, such as banks and insurance companies, and pension funds;
- Size; and
- Number of employees.

Related Entities

In the case of an audit client that is a listed entity, references to an audit client in this **290.27** section include related entities of the client (unless otherwise stated). For all other audit clients, references to an audit client in this section include related entities over which the client has direct or indirect control. When the audit team knows or has reason to believe that a relationship or circumstance involving another related entity of the client is relevant to the evaluation of the firm's independence from the client, the audit team shall include that related entity when identifying and evaluating threats to independence and applying appropriate safeguards.

Those Charged with Governance

Even when not required by the Code, applicable auditing standards, law or reg- **290.28** ulation, regular communication is encouraged between the firm and those charged with governance of the audit client regarding relationships and other matters that might, in the firm's opinion, reasonably bear on independence. Such communication enables those charged with governance to:

(a) Consider the firm's judgments in identifying and evaluating threats to independence,
(b) Consider the appropriateness of safeguards applied to eliminate them or reduce them to an acceptable level, and
(c) Take appropriate action.

Such an approach can be particularly helpful with respect to intimidation and familiarity threats.

Documentation

Documentation provides evidence of the professional accountant's judgments in **290.29** forming conclusions regarding compliance with independence requirements. The absence of documentation is not a determinant of whether a firm considered a particular matter nor whether it is independent.

The professional accountant shall document conclusions regarding compliance with independence requirements, and the substance of any relevant discussions that support those conclusions. Accordingly:

(a) When safeguards are required to reduce a threat to an acceptable level, the professional accountant shall document the nature of the threat and the safeguards in place or applied that reduce the threat to an acceptable level; and
(b) When a threat required significant analysis to determine whether safeguards were necessary and the professional accountant concluded that they were not because the threat was already at an acceptable level, the professional accountant shall document the nature of the threat and the rationale for the conclusion.

Engagement Period

Independence from the audit client is required both during the engagement period **290.30** and the period covered by the financial statements. The engagement period starts when the audit team begins to perform audit services. The engagement period ends when the audit report is issued. When the engagement is of a recurring nature, it ends at the later of the notification by either party that the professional relationship has terminated or the issuance of the final audit report.

290.31   When an entity becomes an audit client during or after the period covered by the financial statements on which the firm will express an opinion, the firm shall determine whether any threats to independence are created by:

(a) Financial or business relationships with the audit client during or after the period covered by the financial statements but before accepting the audit engagement; or

(b) Previous services provided to the audit client.

290.32   If a non-assurance service was provided to the audit client during or after the period covered by the financial statements but before the audit team begins to perform audit services and the service would not be permitted during the period of the audit engagement, the firm shall evaluate any threat to independence created by the service. If a threat is not at an acceptable level, the audit engagement shall only be accepted if safeguards are applied to eliminate any threats or reduce them to an acceptable level. Examples of such safeguards include:

• Not including personnel who provided the non-assurance service as members of the audit team;

• Having a professional accountant review the audit and non-assurance work as appropriate; or

• Engaging another firm to evaluate the results of the non-assurance service or having another firm re-perform the non-assurance service to the extent necessary to enable it to take responsibility for the service.

Mergers and Acquisitions

290.33   When, as a result of a merger or acquisition, an entity becomes a related entity of an audit client, the firm shall identify and evaluate previous and current interests and relationships with the related entity that, taking into account available safeguards, could affect its independence and therefore its ability to continue the audit engagement after the effective date of the merger or acquisition.

290.34   The firm shall take steps necessary to terminate, by the effective date of the merger or acquisition, any current interests or relationships that are not permitted under this Code. However, if such a current interest or relationship cannot reasonably be terminated by the effective date of the merger or acquisition, for example, because the related entity is unable by the effective date to effect an orderly transition to another service provider of a non-assurance service provided by the firm, the firm shall evaluate the threat that is created by such interest or relationship. The more significant the threat, the more likely the firm's objectivity will be compromised and it will be unable to continue as auditor. The significance of the threat will depend upon factors such as:

• The nature and significance of the interest or relationship;

• The nature and significance of the related entity relationship (for example, whether the related entity is a subsidiary or parent); and

• The length of time until the interest or relationship can reasonably be terminated.

The firm shall discuss with those charged with governance the reasons why the interest or relationship cannot reasonably be terminated by the effective date of the merger or acquisition and the evaluation of the significance of the threat.

If those charged with governance request the firm to continue as auditor, the firm shall do so only if: **290.35**

(a) The interest or relationship will be terminated as soon as reasonably possible and in all cases within six months of the effective date of the merger or acquisition;
(b) Any individual who has such an interest or relationship, including one that has arisen through performing a non-assurance service that would not be permitted under this section, will not be a member of the engagement team for the audit or the individual responsible for the engagement quality control review; and
(c) Appropriate transitional measures will be applied, as necessary, and discussed with those charged with governance. Examples of transitional measures include:
   • Having a professional accountant review the audit or non-assurance work as appropriate;
   • Having a professional accountant, who is not a member of the firm expressing the opinion on the financial statements, perform a review that is equivalent to an engagement quality control review; or
   • Engaging another firm to evaluate the results of the non-assurance service or having another firm re-perform the non-assurance service to the extent necessary to enable it to take responsibility for the service.

The firm may have completed a significant amount of work on the audit prior to the effective date of the merger or acquisition and may be able to complete the remaining audit procedures within a short period of time. In such circumstances, if those charged with governance request the firm to complete the audit while continuing with an interest or relationship identified in paragraph 290.33, the firm shall do so only if it: **290.36**

(a) Has evaluated the significance of the threat created by such interest or relationship and discussed the evaluation with those charged with governance;
(b) Complies with the requirements of paragraph 290.35(b)–(c); and
(c) Ceases to be the auditor no later than the issuance of the audit report.

When addressing previous and current interests and relationships covered by paragraphs 290.33 to 290.36, the firm shall determine whether, even if all the requirements could be met, the interests and relationships create threats that would remain so significant that objectivity would be compromised and, if so, the firm shall cease to be the auditor.   **290.37**

The professional accountant shall document any interests or relationships covered by paragraphs 290.34 and 36 that will not be terminated by the effective date of the merger or acquisition and the reasons why they will not be terminated, the transitional measures applied, the results of the discussion with those charged with governance, and the rationale as to why the previous and current interests and relationships do not create threats that would remain so significant that objectivity would be compromised.   **290.38**

Other Considerations

There may be occasions when there is an inadvertent violation of this section. If such an inadvertent violation occurs, it generally will be deemed not to compromise independence provided the firm has appropriate quality control policies and procedures in place, equivalent to those required by ISQCs, to maintain independence and, once discovered, the violation is corrected promptly and any necessary safeguards   **290.39** are applied to eliminate any threat or reduce it to an acceptable level. The firm shall determine whether to discuss the matter with those charged with governance.

Paragraphs 290.40 to 290.99 are intentionally left blank.

Application of the Conceptual Framework Approach to Independence

290.100   Paragraphs 290.102 to 290.231 describe specific circumstances and relationships that create or may create threats to independence. The paragraphs describe the potential threats and the types of safeguards that may be appropriate to eliminate the threats or reduce them to an acceptable level and identify certain situations where no safeguards could reduce the threats to an acceptable level. The paragraphs do not describe all of the circumstances and relationships that create or may create a threat to independence. The firm and the members of the audit team shall evaluate the implications of similar, but different, circumstances and relationships and determine whether safeguards, including the safeguards in paragraphs 200.12 to 200.15, can be applied when necessary to eliminate the threats to independence or reduce them to an acceptable level.

290.101   Paragraphs 290.102 to 290.126 contain references to the materiality of a financial interest, loan, or guarantee, or the significance of a business relationship. For the purpose of determining whether such an interest is material to an individual, the combined net worth of the individual and the individual's immediate family members may be taken into account.

Financial Interests

290.102   Holding a financial interest in an audit client may create a self-interest threat. The existence and significance of any threat created depends on:

(a)   The role of the person holding the financial interest,
(b)   Whether the financial interest is direct or indirect, and
(c)   The materiality of the financial interest.

290.103   Financial interests may be held through an intermediary (for example, a collective investment vehicle, estate or trust). The determination of whether such financial interests are direct or indirect will depend upon whether the beneficial owner has control over the investment vehicle or the ability to influence its investment decisions. When control over the investment vehicle or the ability to influence investment decisions exists, this Code defines that financial interest to be a direct financial interest. Conversely, when the beneficial owner of the financial interest has no control over the investment vehicle or ability to influence its investment decisions, this Code defines that financial interest to be an indirect financial interest.

290.104   If a member of the audit team, a member of that individual's immediate family, or a firm has a direct financial interest or a material indirect financial interest in the audit client, the self-interest threat created would be so significant that no safeguards could reduce the threat to an acceptable level. Therefore, none of the following shall have a direct financial interest or a material indirect financial interest in the client: a member of the audit team; a member of that individual's immediate family; or the firm.

290.105   When a member of the audit team has a close family member who the audit team member knows has a direct financial interest or a material indirect financial interest in the audit client, a self-interest threat is created. The significance of the threat will depend on factors such as:

- The nature of the relationship between the member of the audit team and the close family member; and
- The materiality of the financial interest to the close family member.

The significance of the threat shall be evaluated and safeguards applied when necessary to eliminate the threat or reduce it to an acceptable level. Examples of such safeguards include:

- The close family member disposing, as soon as practicable, of all of the financial interest or disposing of a sufficient portion of an indirect financial interest so that the remaining interest is no longer material;
- Having a professional accountant review the work of the member of the audit team; or
- Removing the individual from the audit team.

If a member of the audit team, a member of that individual's immediate family, or a firm has a direct or material indirect financial interest in an entity that has a controlling interest in the audit client, and the client is material to the entity, the self-interest threat created would be so significant that no safeguards could reduce the threat to an acceptable level. Therefore, none of the following shall have such a financial interest: a member of the audit team; a member of that individual's immediate family; and the firm.   290.106

The holding by a firm's retirement benefit plan of a direct or material indirect financial interest in an audit client creates a self-interest threat. The significance of the threat shall be evaluated and safeguards applied when necessary to eliminate the threat or reduce it to an acceptable level.   290.107

If other partners in the office in which the engagement partner practices in connection with the audit engagement, or their immediate family members, hold a direct financial interest or a material indirect financial interest in that audit client, the self-interest threat created would be so significant that no safeguards could reduce the threat to an acceptable level. Therefore, neither such partners nor their immediate family members shall hold any such financial interests in such an audit client.   290.108

The office in which the engagement partner practices in connection with the audit engagement is not necessarily the office to which that partner is assigned. Accordingly, when the engagement partner is located in a different office from that of the other members of the audit team, professional judgment shall be used to determine in which office the partner practices in connection with that engagement.   290.109

If other partners and managerial employees who provide non-audit services to the audit client, except those whose involvement is minimal, or their immediate family members, hold a direct financial interest or a material indirect financial interest in the audit client, the self-interest threat created would be so significant that no safeguards could reduce the threat to an acceptable level. Accordingly, neither such personnel nor their immediate family members shall hold any such financial interests in such an audit client.   290.110

Despite paragraphs 290.108 and 290.110, the holding of a financial interest in an audit client by an immediate family member of: 290.111

(a) A partner located in the office in which the engagement partner practices in connection with the audit engagement; or

(b) A partner or managerial employee who provides non-audit services to the audit client

is deemed not to compromise independence if the financial interest is received as a result of the immediate family member's employment rights (for example, through pension or share option plans) and, when necessary, safeguards are applied to eliminate any threat to independence or reduce it to an acceptable level.

However, when the immediate family member has or obtains the right to dispose of the financial interest or, in the case of a stock option, the right to exercise the option, the financial interest shall be disposed of or forfeited as soon as practicable.

290.112   A self-interest threat may be created if the firm or a member of the audit team, or a member of that individual's immediate family, has a financial interest in an entity and an audit client also has a financial interest in that entity. However, independence is deemed not to be compromised if these interests are immaterial and the audit client cannot exercise significant influence over the entity. If such interest is material to any party, and the audit client can exercise significant influence over the other entity, no safeguards could reduce the threat to an acceptable level. Accordingly, the firm shall not have such an interest and any individual with such an interest shall, before becoming a member of the audit team, either:

(a) Dispose of the interest; or
(b) Dispose of a sufficient amount of the interest so that the remaining interest is no longer material.

290.113   A self-interest, familiarity or intimidation threat may be created if a member of the audit team, or a member of that individual's immediate family, or the firm, has a financial interest in an entity when a director, officer or controlling owner of the audit client is also known to have a financial interest in that entity. The existence and significance of any threat will depend upon factors such as:

- The role of the professional on the audit team;
- Whether ownership of the entity is closely or widely held;
- Whether the interest gives the investor the ability to control or significantly influence the entity; and
- The materiality of the financial interest.

The significance of any threat shall be evaluated and safeguards applied when necessary to eliminate the threat or reduce it to an acceptable level. Examples of such safeguards include:

- Removing the member of the audit team with the financial interest from the audit team; or
- Having a professional accountant review the work of the member of the audit team.

290.114   The holding by a firm, or a member of the audit team, or a member of that individual's immediate family, of a direct financial interest or a material indirect financial interest in the audit client as a trustee creates a self-interest threat. Similarly, a self-interest threat is created when:

(a) A partner in the office in which the engagement partner practices in connection with the audit;
(b) Other partners and managerial employees who provide non-assurance services to the audit client, except those whose involvement is minimal; or
(c) Their immediate family members, hold a direct financial interest or a material indirect financial interest in the audit client as trustee.

Such an interest shall not be held unless:

(a) Neither the trustee, nor an immediate family member of the trustee, nor the firm are beneficiaries of the trust;
(b) The interest in the audit client held by the trust is not material to the trust;
(c) The trust is not able to exercise significant influence over the audit client; and
(d) The trustee, an immediate family member of the trustee, or the firm cannot significantly influence any investment decision involving a financial interest in the audit client.

Members of the audit team shall determine whether a self-interest threat is created by any known financial interests in the audit client held by other individuals including: **290.115**

(a) Partners and professional employees of the firm, other than those referred to above, or their immediate family members; and
(b) Individuals with a close personal relationship with a member of the audit team.

Whether these interests create a self-interest threat will depend on factors such as:

- The firm's organizational, operating and reporting structure; and
- The nature of the relationship between the individual and the member of the audit team.

The significance of any threat shall be evaluated and safeguards applied when necessary to eliminate the threat or reduce it to an acceptable level. Examples of such safeguards include:

- Removing the member of the audit team with the personal relationship from the audit team;
- Excluding the member of the audit team from any significant decision-making concerning the audit engagement; or
- Having a professional accountant review the work of the member of the audit team.

If a firm or a partner or employee of the firm, or a member of that individual's immediate family, receives a direct financial interest or a material indirect financial interest in an audit client, for example, by way of an inheritance, gift or as a result of a merger and such interest would not be permitted to be held under this section, then: **290.116**

(a) If the interest is received by the firm, the financial interest shall be disposed of immediately, or a sufficient amount of an indirect financial interest shall be disposed of so that the remaining interest is no longer material;
(b) If the interest is received by a member of the audit team, or a member of that individual's immediate family, the individual who received the financial interest shall immediately dispose of the financial interest, or dispose of a sufficient amount of an indirect financial interest so that the remaining interest is no longer material; or
(c) If the interest is received by an individual who is not a member of the audit team, or by an immediate family member of the individual, the financial interest shall be disposed of as soon as possible, or a sufficient amount of an indirect financial interest shall be disposed of so that the remaining interest is no longer material. Pending the disposal of the financial interest, a determination shall be made as to whether any safeguards are necessary.

When an inadvertent violation of this section as it relates to a financial interest in an audit client occurs, it is deemed not to compromise independence if: **290.117**

(a)   The firm has established policies and procedures that require prompt notification to the firm of any breaches resulting from the purchase, inheritance or other acquisition of a financial interest in the audit client;

(b)   The actions in paragraph 290.116 (a)–(c) are taken as applicable; and

(c)   The firm applies other safeguards when necessary to reduce any remaining threat to an acceptable level. Examples of such safeguards include:

- Having a professional accountant review the work of the member of the audit team; or
- Excluding the individual from any significant decision-making concerning the audit engagement.

The firm shall determine whether to discuss the matter with those charged with governance.

Loans and Guarantees

290.118   A loan, or a guarantee of a loan, to a member of the audit team, or a member of that individual's immediate family, or the firm from an audit client that is a bank or a similar institution may create a threat to independence. If the loan or guarantee is not made under normal lending procedures, terms and conditions, a self-interest threat would be created that would be so significant that no safeguards could reduce the threat to an acceptable level. Accordingly, neither a member of the audit team, a member of that individual's immediate family, nor a firm shall accept such a loan or guarantee.

290.119   If a loan to a firm from an audit client that is a bank or similar institution is made under normal lending procedures, terms and conditions and it is material to the audit client or firm receiving the loan, it may be possible to apply safeguards to reduce the self-interest threat to an acceptable level. An example of such a safeguard is having the work reviewed by a professional accountant from a network firm that is neither involved with the audit nor received the loan.

290.120   A loan, or a guarantee of a loan, from an audit client that is a bank or a similar institution to a member of the audit team, or a member of that individual's immediate family, does not create a threat to independence if the loan or guarantee is made under normal lending procedures, terms and conditions. Examples of such loans include home mortgages, bank overdrafts, car loans and credit card balances.

290.121   If the firm or a member of the audit team, or a member of that individual's immediate family, accepts a loan from, or has a borrowing guaranteed by, an audit client that is not a bank or similar institution, the self-interest threat created would be so significant that no safeguards could reduce the threat to an acceptable level, unless the loan or guarantee is immaterial to both (a) the firm or the member of the audit team and the immediate family member, and (b) the client.

290.122   Similarly, if the firm or a member of the audit team, or a member of that individual's immediate family, makes or guarantees a loan to an audit client, the self-interest threat created would be so significant that no safeguards could reduce the threat to an acceptable level, unless the loan or guarantee is immaterial to both (a) the firm or the member of the audit team and the immediate family member, and (b) the client.

290.123   If a firm or a member of the audit team, or a member of that individual's immediate family, has deposits or a brokerage account with an audit client that is a bank, broker or similar institution, a threat to independence is not created if the deposit or account is held under normal commercial terms.

Business Relationships

A close business relationship between a firm, or a member of the audit team, or a   **290.124**
member of that individual's immediate family, and the audit client or its management, arises from a commercial relationship or common financial interest and may create self-interest or intimidation threats. Examples of such relationships include:

- Having a financial interest in a joint venture with either the client or a controlling owner, director, officer or other individual who performs senior managerial activities for that client.
- Arrangements to combine one or more services or products of the firm with one or more services or products of the client and to market the package with reference to both parties.
- Distribution or marketing arrangements under which the firm distributes or markets the client's products or services, or the client distributes or markets the firm's products or services.

Unless any financial interest is immaterial and the business relationship is insignificant to the firm and the client or its management, the threat created would be so significant that no safeguards could reduce the threat to an acceptable level. Therefore, unless the financial interest is immaterial and the business relationship is insignificant, the business relationship shall not be entered into, or it shall be reduced to an insignificant level or terminated.

In the case of a member of the audit team, unless any such financial interest is immaterial and the relationship is insignificant to that member, the individual shall be removed from the audit team.

If the business relationship is between an immediate family member of a member of the audit team and the audit client or its management, the significance of any threat shall be evaluated and safeguards applied when necessary to eliminate the threat or reduce it to an acceptable level.

A business relationship involving the holding of an interest by the firm, or a member   **290.125**
of the audit team, or a member of that individual's immediate family, in a closely-held entity when the audit client or a director or officer of the client, or any group thereof, also holds an interest in that entity does not create threats to independence if:

(a) The business relationship is insignificant to the firm, the member of the audit team and the immediate family member, and the client;
(b) The financial interest is immaterial to the investor or group of investors; and
(c) The financial interest does not give the investor, or group of investors, the ability to control the closely-held entity.

The purchase of goods and services from an audit client by the firm, or a member of   **290.126**
the audit team, or a member of that individual's immediate family, does not generally create a threat to independence if the transaction is in the normal course of business and at arm's length. However, such transactions may be of such a nature or magnitude that they create a self-interest threat. The significance of any threat shall be evaluated and safeguards applied when necessary to eliminate the threat or reduce it to an acceptable level. Examples of such safeguards include:

- Eliminating or reducing the magnitude of the transaction; or
- Removing the individual from the audit team.

Family and Personal Relationships

290.127   Family and personal relationships between a member of the audit team and a director or officer or certain employees (depending on their role) of the audit client may create self-interest, familiarity or intimidation threats. The existence and significance of any threats will depend on a number of factors, including the individual's responsibilities on the audit team, the role of the family member or other individual within the client and the closeness of the relationship.

290.128   When an immediate family member of a member of the audit team is:

(a)   a director or officer of the audit client; or
(b)   an employee in a position to exert significant influence over the preparation of the client's accounting records or the financial statements on which the firm will express an opinion,

or was in such a position during any period covered by the engagement or the financial statements, the threats to independence can only be reduced to an acceptable level by removing the individual from the audit team. The closeness of the relationship is such that no other safeguards could reduce the threat to an acceptable level. Accordingly, no individual who has such a relationship shall be a member of the audit team.

290.129   Threats to independence are created when an immediate family member of a member of the audit team is an employee in a position to exert significant influence over the client's financial position, financial performance or cash flows. The significance of the threats will depend on factors such as:

- The position held by the immediate family member; and
- The role of the professional on the audit team.

The significance of the threat shall be evaluated and safeguards applied when necessary to eliminate the threat or reduce it to an acceptable level. Examples of such safeguards include:

- Removing the individual from the audit team; or
- Structuring the responsibilities of the audit team so that the professional does not deal with matters that are within the responsibility of the immediate family member.

290.130   Threats to independence are created when a close family member of a member of the audit team is:

(a)   A director or officer of the audit client; or
(b)   An employee in a position to exert significant influence over the preparation of the client's accounting records or the financial statements on which the firm will express an opinion.

The significance of the threats will depend on factors such as:

- The nature of the relationship between the member of the audit team and the close family member;
- The position held by the close family member; and
- The role of the professional on the audit team.

The significance of the threat shall be evaluated and safeguards applied when necessary to eliminate the threat or reduce it to an acceptable level. Examples of such safeguards include:

- Removing the individual from the audit team; or
- Structuring the responsibilities of the audit team so that the professional does not deal with matters that are within the responsibility of the close family member.

Threats to independence are created when a member of the audit team has a close relationship with a person who is not an immediate or close family member, but who is a director or officer or an employee in a position to exert significant influence over the preparation of the client's accounting records or the financial statements on which the firm will express an opinion. A member of the audit team who has such a relationship shall consult in accordance with firm policies and procedures. The significance of the threats will depend on factors such as: **290.131**

- The nature of the relationship between the individual and the member of the audit team;
- The position the individual holds with the client; and
- The role of the professional on the audit team.

The significance of the threats shall be evaluated and safeguards applied when necessary to eliminate the threats or reduce them to an acceptable level. Examples of such safeguards include:

- Removing the professional from the audit team; or
- Structuring the responsibilities of the audit team so that the professional does not deal with matters that are within the responsibility of the individual with whom the professional has a close relationship.

Self-interest, familiarity or intimidation threats may be created by a personal or family relationship between (a) a partner or employee of the firm who is not a member of the audit team and (b) a director or officer of the audit client or an employee in a position to exert significant influence over the preparation of the client's accounting records or the financial statements on which the firm will express an opinion. Partners and employees of the firm who are aware of such relationships shall consult in accordance with firm policies and procedures. The existence and significance of any threat will depend on factors such as: **290.132**

- The nature of the relationship between the partner or employee of the firm and the director or officer or employee of the client;
- The interaction of the partner or employee of the firm with the audit team;
- The position of the partner or employee within the firm; and
- The position the individual holds with the client.

The significance of any threat shall be evaluated and safeguards applied when necessary to eliminate the threat or reduce it to an acceptable level. Examples of such safeguards include:

- Structuring the partner's or employee's responsibilities to reduce any potential influence over the audit engagement; or
- Having a professional accountant review the relevant audit work performed.

When an inadvertent violation of this section as it relates to family and personal relationships occurs, it is deemed not to compromise independence if: **290.133**

(a) The firm has established policies and procedures that require prompt notification to the firm of any breaches resulting from changes in the employment status of their immediate or close family members or other personal relationships that create threats to independence;

(b)   The inadvertent violation relates to an immediate family member of a member of the audit team becoming a director or officer of the audit client or being in a position to exert significant influence over the preparation of the client's accounting records or the financial statements on which the firm will express an opinion, and the relevant professional is removed from the audit team; and

(c)   The firm applies other safeguards when necessary to reduce any remaining threat to an acceptable level. Examples of such safeguards include:

(i)   Having a professional accountant review the work of the member of the audit team; or

(ii)   Excluding the relevant professional from any significant decision-making concerning the engagement.

The firm shall determine whether to discuss the matter with those charged with governance.

Employment with an Audit Client

290.134   Familiarity or intimidation threats may be created if a director or officer of the audit client, or an employee in a position to exert significant influence over the preparation of the client's accounting records or the financial statements on which the firm will express an opinion, has been a member of the audit team or partner of the firm.

290.135   If a former member of the audit team or partner of the firm has joined the audit client in such a position and a significant connection remains between the firm and the individual, the threat would be so significant that no safeguards could reduce the threat to an acceptable level. Therefore, independence would be deemed to be compromised if a former member of the audit team or partner joins the audit client as a director or officer, or as an employee in a position to exert significant influence over the preparation of the client's accounting records or the financial statements on which the firm will express an opinion, unless:

(a)   The individual is not entitled to any benefits or payments from the firm, unless made in accordance with fixed pre-determined arrangements, and any amount owed to the individual is not material to the firm; and

(b)   The individual does not continue to participate or appear to participate in the firm's business or professional activities.

290.136   If a former member of the audit team or partner of the firm has joined the audit client in such a position, and no significant connection remains between the firm and the individual, the existence and significance of any familiarity or intimidation threats will depend on factors such as:

•   The position the individual has taken at the client;

•   Any involvement the individual will have with the audit team;

•   The length of time since the individual was a member of the audit team or partner of the firm; and

•   The former position of the individual within the audit team or firm, for example, whether the individual was responsible for maintaining regular contact with the client's management or those charged with governance.

The significance of any threats created shall be evaluated and safeguards applied when necessary to eliminate the threats or reduce them to an acceptable level. Examples of such safeguards include:

- Modifying the audit plan;
- Assigning individuals to the audit team who have sufficient experience in relation to the individual who has joined the client; or
- Having a professional accountant review the work of the former member of the audit team.

If a former partner of the firm has previously joined an entity in such a position and the entity subsequently becomes an audit client of the firm, the significance of any threat to independence shall be evaluated and safeguards applied when necessary to eliminate the threat or reduce it to an acceptable level.

290.137

A self-interest threat is created when a member of the audit team participates in the audit engagement while knowing that the member of the audit team will, or may, join the client some time in the future. Firm policies and procedures shall require members of an audit team to notify the firm when entering employment negotiations with the client. On receiving such notification, the significance of the threat shall be evaluated and safeguards applied when necessary to eliminate the threat or reduce it to an acceptable level. Examples of such safeguards include:

290.138

- Removing the individual from the audit team; or
- A review of any significant judgments made by that individual while on the team.

Audit Clients that are Public Interest Entities

Familiarity or intimidation threats are created when a key audit partner joins the audit client that is a public interest entity as:

290.139

(a) A director or officer of the entity; or
(b) An employee in a position to exert significant influence over the preparation of the client's accounting records or the financial statements on which the firm will express an opinion.

Independence would be deemed to be compromised unless, subsequent to the partner ceasing to be a key audit partner, the public interest entity had issued audited financial statements covering a period of not less than twelve months and the partner was not a member of the audit team with respect to the audit of those financial statements.

An intimidation threat is created when the individual who was the firm's Senior or Managing Partner (Chief Executive or equivalent) joins an audit client that is a public interest entity as:

290.140

(a) An employee in a position to exert significant influence over the preparation of the entity's accounting records or its financial statements; or
(b) A director or officer of the entity.

Independence would be deemed to be compromised unless twelve months have passed since the individual was the Senior or Managing Partner (Chief Executive or equivalent) of the firm.

Independence is deemed not to be compromised if, as a result of a business combination, a former key audit partner or the individual who was the firm's former Senior or Managing Partner is in a position as described in paragraphs 290.139 and 290.140, and:

290.141

(a) The position was not taken in contemplation of the business combination;

(b) Any benefits or payments due to the former partner from the firm have been settled in full, unless made in accordance with fixed predetermined arrangements and any amount owed to the partner is not material to the firm;

(c) The former partner does not continue to participate or appear to participate in the firm's business or professional activities; and

(d) The position held by the former partner with the audit client is discussed with those charged with governance.

Temporary Staff Assignments

290.142   The lending of staff by a firm to an audit client may create a self-review threat. Such assistance may be given, but only for a short period of time and the firm's personnel shall not be involved in:

(a) Providing non-assurance services that would not be permitted under this section; or

(b) Assuming management responsibilities.

In all circumstances, the audit client shall be responsible for directing and supervising the activities of the loaned staff.

The significance of any threat shall be evaluated and safeguards applied when necessary to eliminate the threat or reduce it to an acceptable level. Examples of such safeguards include:

- Conducting an additional review of the work performed by the loaned staff;
- Not giving the loaned staff audit responsibility for any function or activity that the staff performed during the temporary staff assignment; or
- Not including the loaned staff as a member of the audit team.

Recent Service with an Audit Client

290.143 Self-interest, self-review or familiarity threats may be created if a member of the audit team has recently served as a director, officer, or employee of the audit client. This would be the case when, for example, a member of the audit team has to evaluate elements of the financial statements for which the member of the audit team had prepared the accounting records while with the client.

290.144   If, during the period covered by the audit report, a member of the audit team had served as a director or officer of the audit client, or was an employee in a position to exert significant influence over the preparation of the client's accounting records or the financial statements on which the firm will express an opinion, the threat created would be so significant that no safeguards could reduce the threat to an acceptable level. Consequently, such individuals shall not be assigned to the audit team.

290.145   Self-interest, self-review or familiarity threats may be created if, before the period covered by the audit report, a member of the audit team had served as a director or officer of the audit client, or was an employee in a position to exert significant influence over the preparation of the client's accounting records or financial statements on which the firm will express an opinion. For example, such threats would be created if a decision made or work performed by the individual in the prior period, while employed by the client, is to be evaluated in the current period as part of the current audit engagement. The existence and significance of any threats will depend on factors such as:

- The position the individual held with the client;
- The length of time since the individual left the client; and
- The role of the professional on the audit team.

The significance of any threat shall be evaluated and safeguards applied when necessary to reduce the threat to an acceptable level. An example of such a safeguard is conducting a review of the work performed by the individual as a member of the audit team.

Serving as a Director or Officer of an Audit Client

If a partner or employee of the firm serves as a director or officer of an audit client, the self-review and self-interest threats created would be so significant that no safeguards could reduce the threats to an acceptable level. Accordingly, no partner or employee shall serve as a director or officer of an audit client.   **290.146**

The position of Company Secretary has different implications in different jurisdictions. Duties may range from administrative duties, such as personnel management and the maintenance of company records and registers, to duties as diverse as ensuring that the company complies with regulations or providing advice on corporate governance matters. Generally, this position is seen to imply a close association with the entity.   **290.147**

If a partner or employee of the firm serves as Company Secretary for an audit client, self-review and advocacy threats are created that would generally be so significant that no safeguards could reduce the threats to an acceptable level. Despite paragraph 290.146, when this practice is specifically permitted under local law, professional rules or practice, and provided management makes all relevant decisions, the duties and activities shall be limited to those of a routine and administrative nature, such as preparing minutes and maintaining statutory returns. In those circumstances, the significance of any threats shall be evaluated and safeguards applied when necessary to eliminate the threats or reduce them to an acceptable level.   **290.148**

Performing routine administrative services to support a company secretarial function or providing advice in relation to company secretarial administration matters does not generally create threats to independence, as long as client management makes all relevant decisions.   **290.149**

Long Association of Senior Personnel (Including PartnerRotation) with an Audit Client

General Provisions

Familiarity and self-interest threats are created by using the same senior personnel on an audit engagement over a long period of time. The significance of the threats will depend on factors such as: **290.150**

- How long the individual has been a member of the audit team;
- The role of the individual on the audit team;
- The structure of the firm;
- The nature of the audit engagement;
- Whether the client's management team has changed; and

- Whether the nature or complexity of the client's accounting and reporting issues has changed.

The significance of the threats shall be evaluated and safeguards applied when necessary to eliminate the threats or reduce them to an acceptable level. Examples of such safeguards include:

- Rotating the senior personnel off the audit team;
- Having a professional accountant who was not a member of the audit team review the work of the senior personnel; or
- Regular independent internal or external quality reviews of the engagement.

Audit Clients that are Public Interest Entities

290.151   In respect of an audit of a public interest entity, an individual shall not be a key audit partner for more than seven years. After such time, the individual shall not be a member of the engagement team or be a key audit partner for the client for two years. During that period, the individual shall not participate in the audit of the entity, provide quality control for the engagement, consult with the engagement team or the client regarding technical or industry-specific issues, transactions or events or otherwise directly influence the outcome of the engagement.

290.152   Despite paragraph 290.151, key audit partners whose continuity is especially important to audit quality may, in rare cases due to unforeseen circumstances outside the firm's control, be permitted an additional year on the audit team as long as the threat to independence can be eliminated or reduced to an acceptable level by applying safeguards. For example, a key audit partner may remain on the audit team for up to one additional year in circumstances where, due to unforeseen events, a required rotation was not possible, as might be the case due to serious illness of the intended engagement partner.

290.153   The long association of other partners with an audit client that is a public interest entity creates familiarity and self-interest threats. The significance of the threats will depend on factors such as:

- How long any such partner has been associated with the audit client;
- The role, if any, of the individual on the audit team; and
- The nature, frequency and extent of the individual's interactions with the client's management or those charged with governance.

The significance of the threats shall be evaluated and safeguards applied when necessary to eliminate the threats or reduce them to an acceptable level. Examples of such safeguards include:

- Rotating the partner off the audit team or otherwise ending the partner's association with the audit client; or
- Regular independent internal or external quality reviews of the engagement.

290.154   When an audit client becomes a public interest entity, the length of time the individual has served the audit client as a key audit partner before the client becomes a public interest entity shall be taken into account in determining the timing of the rotation. If the individual has served the audit client as a key audit partner for five years or less when the client becomes a public interest entity, the number of years the individual may continue to serve the client in that capacity before rotating off the engagement is seven years less the number of years already served. If the individual has served the audit client as a key audit partner for six or more years when the client becomes a public interest entity, the partner may continue to serve in that capacity for a maximum of two additional years before rotating off the engagement.

When a firm has only a few people with the necessary knowledge and experience to serve as a key audit partner on the audit of a public interest entity, rotation of key audit partners may not be an available safeguard. If an independent regulator in the relevant jurisdiction has provided an exemption from partner rotation in such circumstances, an individual may remain a key audit partner for more than seven years, in accordance with such regulation, provided that the independent regulator has specified alternative safeguards which are applied, such as a regular independent external review.

290.155

Provision of Non-assurance Services to an Audit Client

Firms have traditionally provided to their audit clients a range of non-assurance services that are consistent with their skills and expertise. Providing non-assurance services may, however, create threats to the independence of the firm or members of the audit team. The threats created are most often self-review, self-interest and advocacy threats.

290.156

New developments in business, the evolution of financial markets and changes in information technology make it impossible to draw up an all-inclusive list of non-assurance services that might be provided to an audit client. When specific guidance on a particular non-assurance service is not included in this section, the conceptual framework shall be applied when evaluating the particular circumstances.

290.157

Before the firm accepts an engagement to provide a non-assurance service to an audit client, a determination shall be made as to whether providing such a service would create a threat to independence. In evaluating the significance of any threat created by a particular non-assurance service, consideration shall be given to any threat that the audit team has reason to believe is created by providing other related non-assurance services. If a threat is created that cannot be reduced to an acceptable level by the application of safeguards, the non-assurance service shall not be provided.

290.158

Providing certain non-assurance services to an audit client may create a threat to independence so significant that no safeguards could reduce the threat to an acceptable level. However, the inadvertent provision of such a service to a related entity, division or in respect of a discrete financial statement item of such a client will be deemed not to compromise independence if any threats have been reduced to an acceptable level by arrangements for that related entity, division or discrete financial statement item to be audited by another firm or when another firm re-performs the non-assurance service to the extent necessary to enable it to take responsibility for that service.

290.159

A firm may provide non-assurance services that would otherwise be restricted under this section to the following related entities of the audit client:

290.160

(a) An entity, which is not an audit client, that has direct or indirect control over the audit client;

(b) An entity, which is not an audit client, with a direct financial interest in the client if that entity has significant influence over the client and the interest in the client is material to such entity; or

(c) An entity, which is not an audit client, that is under common control with the audit client, if it is reasonable to conclude that (a) the services do not create a self-review threat because the results of the services will not be subject to audit procedures and (b) any threats that are created by the provision of such services are eliminated or reduced to an acceptable level by the application of safeguards.

290.161   A non-assurance service provided to an audit client does not compromise the firm's independence when the client becomes a public interest entity if:

(a) The previous non-assurance service complies with the provisions of this section that relate to audit clients that are not public interest entities;

(b) Services that are not permitted under this section for audit clients that are public interest entities are terminated before or as soon as practicable after the client becomes a public interest entity; and

(c) The firm applies safeguards when necessary to eliminate or reduce to an acceptable level any threats to independence arising from the service.

Management Responsibilities

290.162   Management of an entity performs many activities in managing the entity in the best interests of stakeholders of the entity. It is not possible to specify every activity that is a management responsibility. However, management responsibilities involve leading and directing an entity, including making significant decisions regarding the acquisition, deployment and control of human, financial, physical and intangible resources.

290.163   Whether an activity is a management responsibility depends on the circumstances and requires the exercise of judgment. Examples of activities that would generally be considered a management responsibility include:

- Setting policies and strategic direction;
- Directing and taking responsibility for the actions of the entity's employees;
- Authorizing transactions;
- Deciding which recommendations of the firm or other third parties to implement;
- Taking responsibility for the preparation and fair presentation of the financial statements in accordance with the applicable financial reporting framework; and
- Taking responsibility for designing, implementing and maintaining internal control.

290.164   Activities that are routine and administrative, or involve matters that are insignificant, generally are deemed not to be a management responsibility. For example, executing an insignificant transaction that has been authorized by management or monitoring the dates for filing statutory returns and advising an audit client of those dates is deemed not to be a management responsibility. Further, providing advice and recommendations to assist management in discharging its responsibilities is not assuming a management responsibility.

290.165   If a firm were to assume a management responsibility for an audit client, the threats created would be so significant that no safeguards could reduce the threats to an acceptable level. For example, deciding which recommendations of the firm to implement will create self-review and self-interest threats. Further, assuming a management responsibility creates a familiarity threat because the firm becomes too closely aligned with the views and interests of management. Therefore, the firm shall not assume a management responsibility for an audit client.

To avoid the risk of assuming a management responsibility when providing non-assurance services to an audit client, the firm shall be satisfied that a member of management is responsible for making the significant judgments and decisions that are the proper responsibility of management, evaluating the results of the service and accepting responsibility for the actions to be taken arising from the results of the service. This reduces the risk of the firm inadvertently making any significant judgments or decisions on behalf of management. The risk is further reduced when the firm gives the client the opportunity to make judgments and decisions based on an objective and transparent analysis and presentation of the issues.

290.166

Preparing Accounting Records and Financial Statements

General Provisions

Management is responsible for the preparation and fair presentation of the financial statements in accordance with the applicable financial reporting framework. These responsibilities include:

290.167

- Originating or changing journal entries, or determining the account classifications of transactions; and
- Preparing or changing source documents or originating data, in electronic or other form, evidencing the occurrence of a transaction (for example, purchase orders, payroll time records, and customer orders).

Providing an audit client with accounting and bookkeeping services, such as preparing accounting records or financial statements, creates a self-review threat when the firm subsequently audits the financial statements.

290.168

The audit process, however, necessitates dialogue between the firm and management of the audit client, which may involve:

290.169

- The application of accounting standards or policies and financial statement disclosure requirements;
- The appropriateness of financial and accounting control and the methods used in determining the stated amounts of assets and liabilities; or
- Proposing adjusting journal entries;

These activities are considered to be a normal part of the audit process and do not, generally, create threats to independence.

Similarly, the clientmay request technical assistance from the firm on matters such as resolving account reconciliation problems or analyzing and accumulating information for regulatory reporting. In addition, the client may request technical advice on accounting issues such as the conversion of existing financial statements from one financial reporting framework to another (for example, to comply with group accounting policies or to transition to a different financial reporting framework such as International Financial Reporting Standards). Such services do not, generally, create threats to independence provided the firm does not assume a management responsibility for the client.

290.170

Audit clients that are not public interest entities

The firm may provide services related to the preparation of accounting records and financial statements to an audit client that is not a public interest entity where the services are of a routine or mechanical nature, so long as any self-review threat created is reduced to an acceptable level. Examples of such services include:

290.171

- Providing payroll services based on client-originated data;
- Recording transactions for which the client has determined or approved the appropriate account classification;
- Posting transactions coded by the client to the general ledger;
- Posting client-approved entries to the trial balance; and
- Preparing financial statements based on information in the trial balance.

In all cases, the significance of any threat created shall be evaluated and safeguards applied when necessary to eliminate the threat or reduce it to an acceptable level. Examples of such safeguards include:

- Arranging for such services to be performed by an individual who is not a member of the audit team; or
- If such services are performed by a member of the audit team, using a partner or senior staff member with appropriate expertise who is not a member of the audit team to review the work performed.

Audit clients that are public interest entities

290.172   Except in emergency situations, a firm shall not provide to an audit client that is a public interest entity accounting and bookkeeping services, including payroll services, or prepare financial statements on which the firm will express an opinion or financial information which forms the basis of the financial statements.

290.173   Despite paragraph 290.172, a firm may provide accounting and bookkeeping services, including payroll services and the preparation of financial statements or other financial information, of a routine or mechanical nature for divisions or related entities of an audit client that is a public interest entity if the personnel providing the services are not members of the audit team and:

(a)   The divisions or related entities for which the service is provided are collectively immaterial to the financial statements on which the firm will express an opinion; or

(b)   The services relate to matters that are collectively immaterial to the financial statements of the division or related entity.

Emergency Situations

290.174   Accounting and bookkeeping services, which would otherwise not be permitted under this section, may be provided to audit clients in emergency or other unusual situations, when it is impractical for the audit client to make other arrangements. This may be the case when (a) only the firm has the resources and necessary knowledge of the client's systems and procedures to assist the client in the timely preparation of its accounting records and financial statements, and (b) a restriction on the firm's ability to provide the services would result in significant difficulties for the client (for example, as might result from a failure to meet regulatory reporting requirements). In such situations, the following conditions shall be met:

(a)   Those who provide the services are not members of the audit team;

(b)   The services are provided for only a short period of time and are not expected to recur; and

(c)   The situation is discussed with those charged with governance.

Valuation Services

General Provisions

A valuation comprises the making of assumptions with regard to future develop-   **290.175**
ments, the application of appropriate methodologies and techniques, and the
combination of both to compute a certain value, or range of values, for an asset, a
liability or for a business as a whole.

Performing valuation services for an audit client may create a self-review threat. The   **290.176**
existence and significance of any threat will depend on factors such as:

- Whether the valuation will have a material effect on the financial statements.
- The extent of the client's involvement in determining and approving the
  valuation methodology and other significant matters of judgment.
- The availability of established methodologies and professional guidelines.
- For valuations involving standard or established methodologies, the degree of
  subjectivity inherent in the item.
- The reliability and extent of the underlying data.
- The degree of dependence on future events of a nature that could create sig-
  nificant volatility inherent in the amounts involved.
- The extent and clarity of the disclosures in the financial statements.

The significance of any threat created shall be evaluated and safeguards applied when
necessary to eliminate the threat or reduce it to an acceptable level. Examples of such
safeguards include:

- Having a professional who was not involved in providing the valuation service
  review the audit or valuation work performed; or
- Making arrangements so that personnel providing such services do not participate in the audit engagement.

Certain valuations do not involve a significant degree of subjectivity. This is likely   **290.177**
the case where the underlying assumptions are either established by law or regulation, or are widely accepted and when the techniques and methodologies to be used
are based on generally accepted standards or prescribed by law or regulation. In such
circumstances, the results of a valuation performed by two or more parties are not
likely to be materially different.

If a firm is requested to perform a valuation to assist an audit client with its tax   **290.178**
reporting obligations or for tax planning purposes and the results of the valuation
will not have a direct effect on the financial statements, the provisions included in
paragraph 290.191 apply.

Audit clients that are not public interest entities

In the case of an audit client that is not a public interest entity, if the valuation   **290.179**
service has a material effect on the financial statements on which the firm will express
an opinion and the valuation involves a significant degree of subjectivity, no safeguards could reduce the self-review threat to an acceptable level. Accordingly a firm
shall not provide such a valuation service to an audit client.

Audit clients that are public interest entities

290.180   A firm shall not provide valuation services to an audit client that is a public interest entity if the valuations would have a material effect, separately or in the aggregate, on the financial statements on which the firm will express an opinion.

Taxation Services

290.181   Taxation services comprise a broad range of services, including:

- Tax return preparation;
- Tax calculations for the purpose of preparing the accounting entries;
- Tax planning and other tax advisory services; and
- Assistance in the resolution of tax disputes.

While taxation services provided by a firm to an audit client are addressed separately under each of these broad headings; in practice, these activities are often interrelated.

290.182   Performing certain tax services creates self-review and advocacy threats. The existence and significance of any threats will depend on factors such as:

- The system by which the tax authorities assess and administer the tax in question and the role of the firm in that process;
- The complexity of the relevant tax regime and the degree of judgment necessary in applying it;
- The particular characteristics of the engagement; and
- The level of tax expertise of the client's employees.

Tax Return Preparation

290.183   Tax return preparation services involve assisting clients with their tax reporting obligations by drafting and completing information, including the amount of tax due (usually on standardized forms) required to be submitted to the applicable tax authorities. Such services also include advising on the tax return treatment of past transactions and responding on behalf of the audit client to the tax authorities' requests for additional information and analysis (including providing explanations of and technical support for the approach being taken). Tax return preparation services are generally based on historical information and principally involve analysis and presentation of such historical information under existing tax law, including precedents and established practice. Further, the tax returns are subject to whatever review or approval process the tax authority deems appropriate. Accordingly, providing such services does not generally create a threat to independence if management takes responsibility for the returns including any significant judgments made.

Tax Calculations for the Purpose of Preparing Accounting Entries

Audit clients that are not public interest entities

290.184   Preparing calculations of current and deferred tax liabilities (or assets) for an audit client for the purpose of preparing accounting entries that will be subsequently audited by the firm creates a self-review threat. The significance of the threat will depend on:

(a) The complexity of the relevant tax law and regulation and the degree of judgment necessary in applying them;

(b) The level of tax expertise of the client's personnel; and
(c) The materiality of the amounts to the financial statements.

Safeguards shall be applied when necessary to eliminate the threat or reduce it to an acceptable level. Examples of such safeguards include:

- Using professionals who are not members of the audit team to perform the service;
- If the service is performed by a member of the audit team, using a partner or senior staff member with appropriate expertise who is not a member of the audit team to review the tax calculations; or
- Obtaining advice on the service from an external tax professional.

Audit clients that are public interest entities

Except in emergency situations, in the case of an audit client that is a public interest entity, a firm shall not prepare tax calculations of current and deferred tax liabilities (or assets) for the purpose of preparing accounting entries that are material to the financial statements on which the firm will express an opinion. **290.185**

The preparation of calculations of current and deferred tax liabilities (or assets) for an audit client for the purpose of the preparation of accounting entries, which would otherwise not be permitted under this section, may be provided to audit clients in emergency or other unusual situations when it is impractical for the audit client to make other arrangements. This may be the case when (a) only the firm has the resources and necessary knowledge of the client's business to assist the client in the timely preparation of its calculations of current and deferred tax liabilities (or assets), and (b) a restriction on the firm's ability to provide the services would result in significant difficulties for the client (for example, as might result from a failure to meet regulatory reporting requirements). In such situations, the following conditions shall be met: **290.186**

(a) Those who provide the services are not members of the audit team;
(b) The services are provided for only a short period of time and are not expected to recur; and
(c) The situation is discussed with those charged with governance.

Tax Planning and Other Tax Advisory Services

Tax planning or other tax advisory services comprise a broad range of services, such as advising the client how to structure its affairs in a tax efficient manner or advising on the application of a new tax law or regulation. **290.187**

A self-review threat may be created where the advice will affect matters to be reflected in the financial statements. The existence and significance of any threat will depend on factors such as: **290.188**

- The degree of subjectivity involved in determining the appropriate treatment for the tax advice in the financial statements;
- The extent to which the outcome of the tax advice will have a material effect on the financial statements;
- Whether the effectiveness of the tax advice depends on the accounting treatment or presentation in the financial statements and there is doubt as to the appropriateness of the accounting treatment or presentation under the relevant financial reporting framework;
- The level of tax expertise of the client's employees;

- The extent to which the advice is supported by tax law or regulation, other precedent or established practice; and
- Whether the tax treatment is supported by a private ruling or has otherwise been cleared by the tax authority before the preparation of the financial statements.

For example, providing tax planning and other tax advisory services where the advice is clearly supported by tax authority or other precedent, by established practice or has a basis in tax law that is likely to prevail does not generally create a threat to independence.

290.189   The significance of any threat shall be evaluated and safeguards applied when necessary to eliminate the threat or reduce it to an acceptable level. Examples of such safeguards include:

- Using professionals who are not members of the audit team to perform the service;
- Having a tax professional, who was not involved in providing the tax service, advise the audit team on the service and review the financial statement treatment;
- Obtaining advice on the service from an external tax professional; or
- Obtaining pre-clearance or advice from the tax authorities.

290.190   Where the effectiveness of the tax advice depends on a particular accounting treatment or presentation in the financial statements and:

(a) The audit team has reasonable doubt as to the appropriateness of the related accounting treatment or presentation under the relevant financial reporting framework; and

(b) The outcome or consequences of the tax advice will have a material effect on the financial statements on which the firm will express an opinion;

The self-review threat would be so significant that no safeguards could reduce the threat to an acceptable level. Accordingly, a firm shall not provide such tax advice to an audit client.

290.191   In providing tax services to an audit client, a firm may be requested to perform a valuation to assist the client with its tax reporting obligations or for tax planning purposes. Where the result of the valuation will have a direct effect on the financial statements, the provisions included in paragraphs 290.175 to 290.180 relating to valuation services are applicable. Where the valuation is performed for tax purposes only and the result of the valuation will not have a direct effect on the financial statements (that is, the financial statements are only affected through accounting entries related to tax), this would not generally create threats to independence if such effect on the financial statements is immaterial or if the valuation is subject to external review by a tax authority or similar regulatory authority. If the valuation is not subject to such an external review and the effect is material to the financial statements, the existence and significance of any threat created will depend upon factors such as:

- The extent to which the valuation methodology is supported by tax law or regulation, other precedent or established practice and the degree of subjectivity inherent in the valuation.
- The reliability and extent of the underlying data.

The significance of any threat created shall be evaluated and safeguards applied when necessary to eliminate the threat or reduce it to an acceptable level. Examples of such safeguards include:

- Using professionals who are not members of the audit team to perform the service;
- Having a professional review the audit work or the result of the tax service; or
- Obtaining pre-clearance or advice from the tax authorities.

Assistance in the Resolution of Tax Disputes

An advocacy or self-review threat may be created when the firm represents an audit   290.192
client in the resolution of a tax dispute once the tax authorities have notified the
client that they have rejected the client's arguments on a particular issue and either
the tax authority or the client is referring the matter for determination in a formal
proceeding, for example before a tribunal or court. The existence and significance of
any threat will depend on factors such as:

- Whether the firm has provided the advice which is the subject of the tax dispute;
- The extent to which the outcome of the dispute will have a material effect on the financial statements on which the firm will express an opinion;
- The extent to which the matter is supported by tax law or regulation, other precedent, or established practice;
- Whether the proceedings are conducted in public; and
- The role management plays in the resolution of the dispute.

The significance of any threat created shall be evaluated and safeguards applied when
necessary to eliminate the threat or reduce it to an acceptable level. Examples of such
safeguards include:

- Using professionals who are not members of the audit team to perform the service;
- Having a tax professional, who was not involved in providing the tax service, advise the audit team on the services and review the financial statement treatment; or
- Obtaining advice on the service from an external tax professional.

Where the taxation services involve acting as an advocate for an audit client before a   290.193
public tribunal or court in the resolution of a tax matter and the amounts involved
are material to the financial statements on which the firm will express an opinion, the
advocacy threat created would be so significant that no safeguards could eliminate or
reduce the threat to an acceptable level. Therefore, the firm shall not perform this
type of service for an audit client. What constitutes a "public tribunal or court" shall
be determined according to how tax proceedings are heard in the particular
jurisdiction.

The firm is not, however, precluded from having a continuing advisory role (for   290.194
example, responding to specific requests for information, providing factual accounts
or testimony about the work performed or assisting the client in analyzing the tax
issues) for the audit client in relation to the matter that is being heard before a public
tribunal or court.

Internal Audit Services

General Provisions

The scope and objectives of internal audit activities vary widely and depend on the   290.195
size and structure of the entity and the requirements of management and those
charged with governance. Internal audit activities may include:

- Monitoring of internal control – reviewing controls, monitoring their operation and recommending improvements thereto;
- Examination of financial and operating information – reviewing the means used to identify, measure, classify and report financial and operating information, and specific inquiry into individual items including detailed testing of transactions, balances and procedures;
- Review of the economy, efficiency and effectiveness of operating activities including non-financial activities of an entity; and
- Review of compliance with laws, regulations and other external requirements, and with management policies and directives and other internal requirements.

290.196 Internal audit services involve assisting the audit client in the performance of its internal audit activities. The provision of internal audit services to an audit client creates a self-review threat to independence if the firm uses the internal audit work in the course of a subsequent external audit. Performing a significant part of the client's internal audit activities increases the possibility that firm personnel providing internal audit services will assume a management responsibility. If the firm's personnel assume a management responsibility when providing internal audit services to an audit client, the threat created would be so significant that no safeguards could reduce the threat to an acceptable level. Accordingly, a firm's personnel shall not assume a management responsibility when providing internal audit services to an audit client.

290.197 Examples of internal audit services that involve assuming management responsibilities include:

(a) Setting internal audit policies or the strategic direction of internal audit activities;

(b) Directing and taking responsibility for the actions of the entity's internal audit employees;

(c) Deciding which recommendations resulting from internal audit activities shall be implemented;

(d) Reporting the results of the internal audit activities to those charged with governance on behalf of management;

(e) Performing procedures that form part of the internal control, such as reviewing and approving changes to employee data access privileges;

(f) Taking responsibility for designing, implementing and maintaining internal control; and

(g) Performing outsourced internal audit services, comprising all or a substantial portion of the internal audit function, where the firm is responsible for determining the scope of the internal audit work and may have responsibility for one or more of the matters noted in (a)–(f).

290.198 To avoid assuming a management responsibility, the firm shall only provide internal audit services to an audit client if it is satisfied that:

(a) The client designates an appropriate and competent resource, preferably within senior management, to be responsible at all times for internal audit activities and to acknowledge responsibility for designing, implementing, and maintaining internal control;

(b) The client's management or those charged with governance reviews, assesses and approves the scope, risk and frequency of the internal audit services;

(c) The client's management evaluates the adequacy of the internal audit services and the findings resulting from their performance;

(d) The client's management evaluates and determines which recommendations resulting from internal audit services to implement and manages the implementation process; and

(e) The client's management reports to those charged with governance the significant findings and recommendations resulting from the internal audit services.

When a firm uses the work of an internal audit function, ISAs require the performance of procedures to evaluate the adequacy of that work. When a firm accepts an engagement to provide internal audit services to an audit client, and the results of those services will be used in conducting the external audit, a self-review threat is created because of the possibility that the audit team will use the results of the internal audit service without appropriately evaluating those results or exercising the same level of professional skepticism as would be exercised when the internal audit work is performed by individuals who are not members of the firm. The significance of the threat will depend on factors such as:

290.199

- The materiality of the related financial statement amounts;
- The risk of misstatement of the assertions related to those financial statement amounts; and
- The degree of reliance that will be placed on the internal audit service.

The significance of the threat shall be evaluated and safeguards applied when necessary to eliminate the threat or reduce it to an acceptable level. An example of such a safeguard is using professionals who are not members of the audit team to perform the internal audit service.

Audit clients that are public interest entities

In the case of an audit client that is a public interest entity, a firm shall not provide internal audit services that relate to:

290.200

(a) A significant part of the internal controls over financial reporting;
(b) Financial accounting systems that generate information that is, separately or in the aggregate, significant to the client's accounting records or financial statements on which the firm will express an opinion; or
(c) Amounts or disclosures that are, separately or in the aggregate, material to the financial statements on which the firm will express an opinion.

IT Systems Services

General Provisions

Services related to information technology (IT) systems include the design or implementation of hardware or software systems. The systems may aggregate source data, form part of the internal control over financial reporting or generate information that affects the accounting records or financial statements, or the systems may be unrelated to the audit client's accounting records, the internal control over financial reporting or financial statements. Providing systems services may create a self-review threat depending on the nature of the services and the IT systems.

290.201

The following IT systems services are deemed not to create a threat to independence as long as the firm's personnel do not assume a management responsibility:

290.202

(a) Design or implementation of IT systems that are unrelated to internal control over financial reporting;
(b) Design or implementation of IT systems that do not generate information forming a significant part of the accounting records or financial statements;

(c) Implementation of "off-the-shelf" accounting or financial information reporting software that was not developed by the firm if the customization required to meet the client's needs is not significant; and

(d) Evaluating and making recommendations with respect to a system designed, implemented or operated by another service provider or the client.

Audit clients that are not public interest entities

290.203 Providing services to an audit client that is not a public interest entity involving the design or implementation of IT systems that (a) form a significant part of the internal control over financial reporting or (b) generate information that is significant to the client's accounting records or financial statements on which the firm will express an opinion creates a self-review threat.

290.204 The self-review threat is too significant to permit such services unless appropriate safeguards are put in place ensuring that:

(a) The client acknowledges its responsibility for establishing and monitoring a system of internal controls;

(b) The client assigns the responsibility to make all management decisions with respect to the design and implementation of the hardware or software system to a competent employee, preferably within senior management;

(c) The client makes all management decisions with respect to the design and implementation process;

(d) The client evaluates the adequacy and results of the design and implementation of the system; and

(e) The client is responsible for operating the system (hardware or software) and for the data it uses or generates.

290.205 Depending on the degree of reliance that will be placed on the particular IT systems as part of the audit, a determination shall be made as to whether to provide such non-assurance services only with personnel who are not members of the audit team and who have different reporting lines within the firm. The significance of any remaining threat shall be evaluated and safeguards applied when necessary to eliminate the threat or reduce it to an acceptable level. An example of such a safeguard is having a professional accountant review the audit or non-assurance work.

Audit clients that are public interest entities

290.206 In the case of an audit client that is a public interest entity, a firm shall not provide services involving the design or implementation of IT systems that

(a) form a significant part of the internal control over financial reporting or

(b) generate information that is significant to the client's accounting records or financial statements on which the firm will express an opinion.

Litigation Support Services

290.207 Litigation support services may include activities such as acting as an expert witness, calculating estimated damages or other amounts that might become receivable or payable as the result of litigation or other legal dispute, and assistance with document management and retrieval. These services may create a self-review or advocacy threat.

If the firm provides a litigation support service to an audit client and the service involves estimating damages or other amounts that affect the financial statements on which the firm will express an opinion, the valuation service provisions included in paragraphs 290.175 to 290.180 shall be followed. In the case of other litigation support services, the significance of any threat created shall be evaluated and safeguards applied when necessary to eliminate the threat or reduce it to an acceptable level. **290.208**

Legal Services

For the purpose of this section, legal services are defined as any services for which the person providing the services must either be admitted to practice law before the courts of the jurisdiction in which such services are to be provided or have the required legal training to practice law. Such legal services may include, depending on the jurisdiction, a wide and diversified range of areas including both corporate and commercial services to clients, such as contract support, litigation, mergers and acquisition legal advice and support and assistance to clients' internal legal departments. Providing legal services to an entity that is an audit client may create both self-review and advocacy threats. **290.209**

Legal services that support an audit client in executing a transaction (for example, contract support, legal advice, legal due diligence and restructuring) may create self-review threats. The existence and significance of any threat will depend on factors such as: **290.210**

- The nature of the service;
- Whether the service is provided by a member of the audit team; and
- The materiality of any matter in relation to the client's financial statements.

The significance of any threat created shall be evaluated and safeguards applied when necessary to eliminate the threat or reduce it to an acceptable level. Examples of such safeguards include:

- Using professionals who are not members of the audit team to perform the service; or
- Having a professional who was not involved in providing the legal services provide advice to the audit team on the service and review any financial statement treatment.

Acting in an advocacy role for an audit client in resolving a dispute or litigation when the amounts involved are material to the financial statements on which the firm will express an opinion would create advocacy and self-review threats so significant that no safeguards could reduce the threat to an acceptable level. Therefore, the firm shall not perform this type of service for an audit client. **290.211**

When a firm is asked to act in an advocacy role for an audit client in resolving a dispute or litigation when the amounts involved are not material to the financial statements on which the firm will express an opinion, the firm shall evaluate the significance of any advocacy and self-review threats created and apply safeguards when necessary to eliminate the threat or reduce it to an acceptable level. Examples of such safeguards include: **290.212**

- Using professionals who are not members of the audit team to perform the service; or
- Having a professional who was not involved in providing the legal services advise the audit team on the service and review any financial statement treatment.

290.213   The appointment of a partner or an employee of the firm as General Counsel for legal affairs of an audit client would create self-review and advocacy threats that are so significant that no safeguards could reduce the threats to an acceptable level. The position of General Counsel is generally a senior management position with broad responsibility for the legal affairs of a company, and consequently, no member of the firm shall accept such an appointment for an audit client.

Recruiting Services

General Provisions

290.214   Providing recruiting services to an audit client may create self-interest, familiarity or intimidation threats. The existence and significance of any threat will depend on factors such as:

- The nature of the requested assistance; and
- The role of the person to be recruited.

The significance of any threat created shall be evaluated and safeguards applied when necessary to eliminate the threat or reduce it to an acceptable level. In all cases, the firm shall not assume management responsibilities, including acting as a negotiator on the client's behalf, and the hiring decision shall be left to the client.

The firm may generally provide such services as reviewing the professional qualifications of a number of applicants and providing advice on their suitability for the post. In addition, the firm may interview candidates and advise on a candidate's competence for financial accounting, administrative or control positions.

Audit clients that are public interest entities

290.215   A firm shall not provide the following recruiting services to an audit client that is a public interest entity with respect to a director or officer of the entity or senior management in a position to exert significant influence over the preparation of the client's accounting records or the financial statements on which the firm will express an opinion:

- Searching for or seeking out candidates for such positions; and
- Undertaking reference checks of prospective candidates for such positions.

Corporate Finance Services

290.216   Providing corporate finance services such as:

- Assisting an audit client in developing corporate strategies;
- Identifying possible targets for the audit client to acquire;
- Advising on disposal transactions;
- Assisting finance raising transactions; and
- Providing structuring advice,

may create advocacy and self-review threats. The significance of any threat shall be evaluated and safeguards applied when necessary to eliminate the threat or reduce it to an acceptable level. Examples of such safeguards include:

- Using professionals who are not members of the audit team to provide the services; or

- Having a professional who was not involved in providing the corporate finance service advise the audit team on the service and review the accounting treatment and any financial statement treatment.

Providing a corporate finance service, for example advice on the structuring of a corporate finance transaction or on financing arrangements that will directly affect amounts that will be reported in the financial statements on which the firm will provide an opinion may create a self-review threat. The existence and significance of any threat will depend on factors such as: 290.217

- The degree of subjectivity involved in determining the appropriate treatment for the outcome or consequences of the corporate finance advice in the financial statements;
- The extent to which the outcome of the corporate finance advice will directly affect amounts recorded in the financial statements and the extent to which the amounts are material to the financial statements; and
- Whether the effectiveness of the corporate finance advice depends on a particular accounting treatment or presentation in the financial statements and there is doubt as to the appropriateness of the related accounting treatment or presentation under the relevant financial reporting framework.

The significance of any threat shall be evaluated and safeguards applied when necessary to eliminate the threat or reduce it to an acceptable level. Examples of such safeguards include:

- Using professionals who are not members of the audit team to perform the service; or
- Having a professional who was not involved in providing the corporate finance service to the client advise the audit team on the service and review the accounting treatment and any financial statement treatment.

Where the effectiveness of corporate finance advice depends on a particular accounting treatment or presentation in the financial statements and: 290.218

(a) The audit team has reasonable doubt as to the appropriateness of the related accounting treatment or presentation under the relevant financial reporting framework; and

(b) The outcome or consequences of the corporate finance advice will have a material effect on the financial statements on which the firm will express an opinion.

The self-review threat would be so significant that no safeguards could reduce the threat to an acceptable level, in which case the corporate finance advice shall not be provided.

Providing corporate finance services involving promoting, dealing in, or underwriting an audit client's shares would create an advocacy or self-review threat that is so significant that no safeguards could reduce the threat to an acceptable level. Accordingly, a firm shall not provide such services to an audit client.   290.219

Fees

Fees—Relative Size

When the total fees from an audit client represent a large proportion of the total fees of the firm expressing the audit opinion, the dependence on that client and concern   290.220

about losing the client creates a self-interest or intimidation threat. The significance of the threat will depend on factors such as:

- The operating structure of the firm;
- Whether the firm is well established or new; and
- The significance of the client qualitatively and/or quantitatively to the firm.

The significance of the threat shall be evaluated and safeguards applied when necessary to eliminate the threat or reduce it to an acceptable level. Examples of such safeguards include:

- Reducing the dependency on the client;
- External quality control reviews; or
- Consulting a third party, such as a professional regulatory body or a professional accountant, on key audit judgments.

290.221   A self-interest or intimidation threat is also created when the fees generated from an audit client represent a large proportion of the revenue from an individual partner's clients or a large proportion of the revenue of an individual office of the firm. The significance of the threat will depend upon factors such as:

- The significance of the client qualitatively and/or quantitatively to the partner or office; and
- The extent to which the remuneration of the partner, or the partners in the office, is dependent upon the fees generated from the client.

The significance of the threat shall be evaluated and safeguards applied when necessary to eliminate the threat or reduce it to an acceptable level. Examples of such safeguards include:

- Reducing the dependency on the audit client;
- Having a professional accountant review the work or otherwise advise as necessary; or
- Regular independent internal or external quality reviews of the engagement.

Audit Clients that are Public Interest Entities

290.222   Where an audit client is a public interest entity and, for two consecutive years, the total fees from the client and its related entities (subject to the considerations in paragraph 290.27) represent more than 15% of the total fees received by the firm expressing the opinion on the financial statements of the client, the firm shall disclose to those charged with governance of the audit client the fact that the total of such fees represents more than 15% of the total fees received by the firm, and discuss which of the safeguards below it will apply to reduce the threat to an acceptable level, and apply the selected safeguard:

- Prior to the issuance of the audit opinion on the second year's financial statements, a professional accountant, who is not a member of the firm expressing the opinion on the financial statements, performs an engagement quality control review of that engagement or a professional regulatory body performs a review of that engagement that is equivalent to an engagement quality control review ("a pre-issuance review"); or
- After the audit opinion on the second year's financial statements has been issued, and before the issuance of the audit opinion on the third year's financial statements, a professional accountant, who is not a member of the firm expressing the opinion on the financial statements, or a professional regulatory body performs a review of the second year's audit that is equivalent to an engagement quality control review ("a post-issuance review").

When the total fees significantly exceed 15%, the firm shall determine whether the significance of the threat is such that a post-issuance review would not reduce the threat to an acceptable level and, therefore, a preissuance review is required. In such circumstances a pre-issuance review shall be performed.

Thereafter, when the fees continue to exceed 15% each year, the disclosure to and discussion with those charged with governance shall occur and one of the above safeguards shall be applied. If the fees significantly exceed 15%, the firm shall determine whether the significance of the threat is such that a post-issuance review would not reduce the threat to an acceptable level and, therefore, a pre-issuance review is required. In such circumstances a pre-issuance review shall be performed.

Fees—Overdue

A self-interest threat may be created if fees due from an audit client remain unpaid for a long time, especially if a significant part is not paid before the issue of the audit report for the following year. Generally the firm is expected to require payment of such fees before such audit report is issued. If fees remain unpaid after the report has been issued, the existence and significance of any threat shall be evaluated and safeguards applied when necessary to eliminate the threat or reduce it to an acceptable level. An example of such a safeguard is having an additional professional accountant who did not take part in the audit engagement provide advice or review the work performed. The firm shall determine whether the overdue fees might be regarded as being equivalent to a loan to the client and whether, because of the significance of the overdue fees, it is appropriate for the firm to be reappointed or continue the audit engagement.

290.223

Contingent Fees

Contingent fees are fees calculated on a predetermined basis relating to the outcome of a transaction or the result of the services performed by the firm. For the purposes of this section, a fee is not regarded as being contingent if established by a court or other public authority.

290.224

A contingent fee charged directly or indirectly, for example through an intermediary, by a firm in respect of an audit engagement creates a self-interest threat that is so significant that no safeguards could reduce the threat to an acceptable level. Accordingly, a firm shall not enter into any such fee arrangement.

290.225

A contingent fee charged directly or indirectly, for example through an intermediary, by a firm in respect of a non-assurance service provided to an audit client may also create a self-interest threat. The threat created would be so significant that no safeguards could reduce the threat to an acceptable level if:

290.226

(a) The fee is charged by the firm expressing the opinion on the financial statements and the fee is material or expected to be material to that firm;

(b) The fee is charged by a network firm that participates in a significant part of the audit and the fee is material or expected to be material to that firm; or

(c) The outcome of the non-assurance service, and therefore the amount of the fee, is dependent on a future or contemporary judgment related to the audit of a material amount in the financial statements.

Accordingly, such arrangements shall not be accepted.

290.227   For other contingent fee arrangements charged by a firm for a non-assurance service to an audit client, the existence and significance of any threats will depend on factors such as:

- The range of possible fee amounts;
- Whether an appropriate authority determines the outcome of the matter upon which the contingent fee will be determined;
- The nature of the service; and
- The effect of the event or transaction on the financial statements.

The significance of any threats shall be evaluated and safeguards applied when necessary to eliminate the threats or reduce them to an acceptable level. Examples of such safeguards include:

- Having a professional accountant review the relevant audit work or otherwise advise as necessary; or
- Using professionals who are not members of the audit team to perform the non-assurance service.

Compensation and Evaluation Policies

290.228   A self-interest threat is created when a member of the audit team is evaluated on or compensated for selling non-assurance services to that audit client. The significance of the threat will depend on:

- The proportion of the individual's compensation or performance evaluation that is based on the sale of such services;
- The role of the individual on the audit team; and
- Whether promotion decisions are influenced by the sale of such services.

The significance of the threat shall be evaluated and, if the threat is not at an acceptable level, the firm shall either revise the compensation plan or evaluation process for that individual or apply safeguards to eliminate the threat or reduce it to an acceptable level. Examples of such safeguards include:

- Removing such members from the audit team; or
- Having a professional accountant review the work of the member of the audit team.

290.229   A key audit partner shall not be evaluated on or compensated based on that partner's success in selling non-assurance services to the partner's audit client. This is not intended to prohibit normal profit-sharing arrangements between partners of a firm.

Gifts and Hospitality

290.230   Accepting gifts or hospitality from an audit client may create self-interest and familiarity threats. If a firm or a member of the audit team accepts gifts or hospitality, unless the value is trivial and inconsequential, the threats created would be so significant that no safeguards could reduce the threats to an acceptable level. Consequently, a firm or a member of the audit team shall not accept such gifts or hospitality.

Actual or Threatened Litigation

When litigation takes place, or appears likely, between the firm or a member of the   **290.231**
audit team and the audit client, self-interest and intimidation threats are created. The
relationship between client management and the members of the audit team must be
characterized by complete candor and full disclosure regarding all aspects of a client's business operations. When the firm and the client's management are placed in
adversarial positions by actual or threatened litigation, affecting management's
willingness to make complete disclosures, self-interest and intimidation threats are
created. The significance of the threats created will depend on such factors as:

- The materiality of the litigation; and
- Whether the litigation relates to a prior audit engagement.

The significance of the threats shall be evaluated and safeguards applied when
necessary to eliminate the threats or reduce them to an acceptable level. Examples of
such safeguards include:

- If the litigation involves a member of the audit team, removing that individual
  from the audit team; or
- Having a professional review the work performed.

If such safeguards do not reduce the threats to an acceptable level, the only
appropriate action is to withdraw from, or decline, the audit engagement.

Paragraphs 290.232 to 290.499 are intentionally left blank.

Reports that Include a Restriction on Use and Distribution

Introduction

The independence requirements in Section 290 apply to all audit engagements.   **290.500**
However, in certain circumstances involving audit engagements where the report
includes a restriction on use and distribution, and provided the conditions described
in paragraphs 290.501 to 290.502 are met, the independence requirements in this
section may be modified as provided in paragraphs 290.505 to 290.514. These
paragraphs are only applicable to an audit engagement on special purpose financial
statements (a) that is intended to provide a conclusion in positive or negative form
that the financial statements are prepared in all material respects, in accordance with
the applicable financial reporting framework, including, in the case of a fair presentation framework, that the financial statements give a true and fair view or are
presented fairly, in all material respects, in accordance with the applicable financial
reporting framework, and (b) where the audit report includes a restriction on use and
distribution. The modifications are not permitted in the case of an audit of financial
statements required by law or regulation.

The modifications to the requirements of Section 290 are permitted if the intended   **290.501**
users of the report (a) are knowledgeable as to the purpose and limitations of the
report, and (b) explicitly agree to the application of the modified independence
requirements. Knowledge as to the purpose and limitations of the report may be
obtained by the intended users through their participation, either directly or indirectly through their representative who has the authority to act for the intended users,
in establishing the nature and scope of the engagement. Such participation enhances
the ability of the firm to communicate with intended users about independence
matters, including the circumstances that are relevant to the evaluation of the threats

to independence and the applicable safeguards necessary to eliminate the threats or reduce them to an acceptable level, and to obtain their agreement to the modified independence requirements that are to be applied.

290.502   The firm shall communicate (for example, in an engagement letter) with the intended users regarding the independence requirements that are to be applied with respect to the provision of the audit engagement. Where the intended users are a class of users (for example, lenders in a syndicated loan arrangement) who are not specifically identifiable by name at the time the engagement terms are established, such users shall subsequently be made aware of the independence requirements agreed to by the representative (for example, by the representative making the firm's engagement letter available to all users).

290.503   If the firm also issues an audit report that does not include a restriction on use and distribution for the same client, the provisions of paragraphs 290.500 to 290.514 do not change the requirement to apply the provisions of paragraphs 290.1 to 290.232 to that audit engagement.

290.504   The modifications to the requirements of Section 290 that are permitted in the circumstances set out above are described in paragraphs 290.505 to 290.514. Compliance in all other respects with the provisions of Section 290 is required.

Public Interest Entities

290.505   When the conditions set out in paragraphs 290.500 to 290.502 are met, it is not necessary to apply the additional requirements in paragraphs 290.100 to 290.232 that apply to audit engagements for public interest entities.

Related Entities

290.506   When the conditions set out in paragraphs 290.500 to 290.502 are met, references to audit client do not include its related entities. However, when the audit team knows or has reason to believe that a relationship or circumstance involving a related entity of the client is relevant to the evaluation of the firm's independence of the client, the audit team shall include that related entity when identifying and evaluating threats to independence and applying appropriate safeguards.

Networks and Network Firms

290.507   When the conditions set out in paragraphs 290.500 to 290.502 are met, reference to the firm does not include network firms. However, when the firm knows or has reason to believe that threats are created by any interests and relationships of a network firm, they shall be included in the evaluation of threats to independence.

Financial Interests, Loans and Guarantees, Close Business Relationships and Family and Personal Relationships

290.508   When the conditions set out in paragraphs 290.500 to 290.502 are met, the relevant provisions set out in paragraphs 290.102 to 290.145 apply only to the members of the engagement team, their immediate family members and close family members.

290.509   In addition, a determination shall be made as to whether threats to independence are created by interests and relationships, as described in paragraphs 290.102 to 290.145, between the audit client and the following members of the audit team:

(a) Those who provide consultation regarding technical or industry specific issues, transactions or events; and

(b) Those who provide quality control for the engagement, including those who perform the engagement quality control review.

An evaluation shall be made of the significance of any threats that the engagement team has reason to believe are created by interests and relationships between the audit client and others within the firm who can directly influence the outcome of the audit engagement, including those who recommend the compensation of, or who provide direct supervisory, management or other oversight of the audit engagement partner in connection with the performance of the audit engagement (including those at all successively senior levels above the engagement partner through to the individual who is the firm's Senior or Managing Partner (Chief Executive or equivalent)).

An evaluation shall also be made of the significance of any threats that the engagement team has reason to believe are created by financial interests in the audit client held by individuals, as described in paragraphs 290.108 to 290.111 and paragraphs 290.113 to 290.115. **290.510**

Where a threat to independence is not at an acceptable level, safeguards shall be applied to eliminate the threat or reduce it to an acceptable level. **290.511**

In applying the provisions set out in paragraphs 290.106 and 290.115 to interests of the firm, if the firm has a material financial interest, whether direct or indirect, in the audit client, the self-interest threat created would be so significant that no safeguards could reduce the threat to an acceptable level. Accordingly, the firm shall not have such a financial interest. **290.512**

Employment with an Audit Client

An evaluation shall be made of the significance of any threats from any employment relationships as described in paragraphs 290.134 to 290.138. Where a threat exists that is not at an acceptable level, safeguards shall be applied to eliminate the threat or reduce it to an acceptable level. Examples of safeguards that might be appropriate include those set out in paragraph 290.136. **290.513**

Provision of Non-Assurance Services

If the firm conducts an engagement to issue a restricted use and distribution report for an audit client and provides a non-assurance service to the audit client, the provisions of paragraphs 290.156 to 290.232 shall be complied with, subject to paragraphs 290.504 to 290.507. **290.514**

Section 291
Independence—Other assurance engagements

Contents

Structure of Section

This section addresses independence requirements for assurance engagements that are not audit or review engagements. Independence requirements for audit and review engagements are addressed in Section 290. If the assurance client is also an audit or review client, the requirements in Section 290 also apply to the firm, network firms and members of the audit or review team. In certain circumstances involving assurance engagements where the assurance report includes a restriction on use and distribution and provided certain conditions are met, the independence requirements in this section may be modified as provided in paragraphs 291.21 to 291.27.   **291.1**

Assurance engagements are designed to enhance intended users' degree of confidence about the outcome of the evaluation or measurement of a subject matter against criteria. The International Framework for Assurance Engagements (the Assurance Framework) issued by the International Auditing and Assurance Standards Board describes the elements and objectives of an assurance engagement and identifies engagements to which International Standards on Assurance Engagements (ISAEs) apply. For a description of the elements and objectives of an assurance engagement, refer to the Assurance Framework.   **291.2**

Compliance with the fundamental principle of objectivity requires being independent of assurance clients. In the case of assurance engagements, it is in the public interest and, therefore, required by this Code of Ethics, that members of assurance teams and firms be independent of assurance clients and that any threats that the firm has reason to believe are created by a network firm's interests and relationships be evaluated. In addition, when the assurance team knows or has reason to believe that a relationship or circumstance involving a related entity of the assurance client is relevant to the evaluation of the firm's independence from the client, the assurance team shall include that related entity when identifying and evaluating threats to independence and applying appropriate safeguards.   **291.3**

A Conceptual Framework Approach to Independence

The objective of this section is to assist firms and members of assurance teams in applying the conceptual framework approach described below to achieving and maintaining independence.   **291.4**

Independence comprises: **291.5**

(a) Independence of Mind
    The state of mind that permits the expression of a conclusion without being affected by influences that compromise professional judgment, thereby allowing an individual to act with integrity and exercise objectivity and professional skepticism.
(b) Independence in Appearance
    The avoidance of facts and circumstances that are so significant that a reasonable and informed third party would be likely to conclude, weighing all the specific facts and circumstances, that a firm's, or a member of the assurance team's, integrity, objectivity or professional skepticism has been compromised.

The conceptual framework approach shall be applied by professional accountants to: **291.6**

(a) Identify threats to independence;
(b) Evaluate the significance of the threats identified; and

(c) Apply safeguards when necessary to eliminate the threats or reduce them to an acceptable level.

When the professional accountant determines that appropriate safeguards are not available or cannot be applied to eliminate the threats or reduce them to an acceptable level, the professional accountant shall eliminate the circumstance or relationship creating the threats or decline or terminate the assurance engagement.

A professional accountant shall use professional judgment in applying this conceptual framework.

291.7 Many different circumstances, or combinations of circumstances, may be relevant in assessing threats to independence. It is impossible to define every situation that creates threats to independence and to specify the appropriate action. Therefore, this Code establishes a conceptual framework that requires firms and members of assurance teams to identify, evaluate, and address threats to independence. The conceptual framework approach assists professional accountants in public practice in complying with the ethical requirements in this Code. It accommodates many variations in circumstances that create threats to independence and can deter a professional accountant from concluding that a situation is permitted if it is not specifically prohibited.

291.8 Paragraphs 291.100 and onwards describe how the conceptual framework approach to independence is to be applied. These paragraphs do not address all the circumstances and relationships that create or may create threats to independence.

291.9 In deciding whether to accept or continue an engagement, or whether a particular individual may be a member of the assurance team, a firm shall identify and evaluate any threats to independence. If the threats are not at an acceptable level, and the decision is whether to accept an engagement or include a particular individual on the assurance team, the firm shall determine whether safeguards are available to eliminate the threats or reduce them to an acceptable level. If the decision is whether to continue an engagement, the firm shall determine whether any existing safeguards will continue to be effective to eliminate the threats or reduce them to an acceptable level or whether other safeguards will need to be applied or whether the engagement needs to be terminated. Whenever new information about a threat comes to the attention of the firm during the engagement, the firm shall evaluate the significance of the threat in accordance with the conceptual framework approach.

291.10 Throughout this section, reference is made to the significance of threats to independence. In evaluating the significance of a threat, qualitative as well as quantitative factors shall be taken into account.

291.11 This section does not, in most cases, prescribe the specific responsibility of individuals within the firm for actions related to independence because responsibility may differ depending on the size, structure and organization of a firm. The firm is required by ISQCs to establish policies and procedures designed to provide it with reasonable assurance that independence is maintained when required by relevant ethical standards.

Assurance Engagements

291.12 As further explained in the Assurance Framework, in an assurance engagement the professional accountant in public practice expresses a conclusion designed to enhance the degree of confidence of the intended users (other than the responsible party) about the outcome of the evaluation or measurement of a subject matter against criteria.

The outcome of the evaluation or measurement of a subject matter is the information **291.13** that results from applying the criteria to the subject matter. The term "subject matter information" is used to mean the outcome of the evaluation or measurement of a subject matter. For example, the Framework states that an assertion about the effectiveness of internal control (subject matter information) results from applying a framework for evaluating the effectiveness of internal control, such as COSO[2] or CoCo[3] (criteria), to internal control, a process (subject matter).

Assurance engagements may be assertion-based or direct reporting. In either case, **291.14** they involve three separate parties: a professional accountant in public practice, a responsible party and intended users.

In an assertion-based assurance engagement, the evaluation or measurement of the **291.15** subject matter is performed by the responsible party, and the subject matter information is in the form of an assertion by the responsible party that is made available to the intended users.

In a direct reporting assurance engagement, the professional accountant in public **291.16** practice either directly performs the evaluation or measurement of the subject matter, or obtains a representation from the responsible party that has performed the evaluation or measurement that is not available to the intended users. The subject matter information is provided to the intended users in the assurance report.

Assertion-Based Assurance Engagements

In an assertion-based assurance engagement, the members of the assurance team and **291.17** the firm shall be independent of the assurance client (the party responsible for the subject matter information, and which may be responsible for the subject matter). Such independence requirements prohibit certain relationships between members of the assurance team and (a) directors or officers, and (b) individuals at the client in a position to exert significant influence over the subject matter information. Also, a determination shall be made as to whether threats to independence are created by relationships with individuals at the client in a position to exert significant influence over the subject matter of the engagement. An evaluation shall be made of the significance of any threats that the firm has reason to believe are created by network firm[4] interests and relationships.

In the majority of assertion-based assurance engagements, the responsible party is **291.18** responsible for both the subject matter information and the subject matter. However, in some engagements, the responsible party may not be responsible for the subject matter. For example, when a professional accountant in public practice is engaged to perform an assurance engagement regarding a report that an environmental consultant has prepared about a company's sustainability practices for distribution to

---

[2] *"Internal Control—Integrated Framework" The Committee of Sponsoring Organizations of the Treadway Commission.*

[3] *"Guidance on Assessing Control—The CoCo Principles" Criteria of Control Board, The Canadian Institute of Chartered Accountants.*

[4] *See paragraphs 290.13 to 290.24 for guidance on what constitutes a network firm.*

intended users, the environmental consultant is the responsible party for the subject matter information but the company is responsible for the subject matter (the sustainability practices).

291.19   In assertion-based assurance engagements where the responsible party is responsible for the subject matter information but not the subject matter, the members of the assurance team and the firm shall be independent of the party responsible for the subject matter information (the assurance client). In addition, an evaluation shall be made of any threats the firm has reason to believe are created by interests and relationships between a member of the assurance team, the firm, a network firm and the party responsible for the subject matter.

Direct Reporting Assurance Engagements

291.20   In a direct reporting assurance engagement, the members of the assurance team and the firm shall be independent of the assurance client (the party responsible for the subject matter). An evaluation shall also be made of any threats the firm has reason to believe are created by network firm interests and relationships.

Reports that Include a Restriction on Use and Distribution

291.21   In certain circumstances where the assurance report includes a restriction on use and distribution, and provided the conditions in this paragraph and in paragraph 291.22 are met, the independence requirements in this section may be modified. The modifications to the requirements of Section 291 are permitted if the intended users of the report (a) are knowledgeable as to the purpose, subject matter information and limitations of the report and (b) explicitly agree to the application of the modified independence requirements. Knowledge as to the purpose, subject matter information, and limitations of the report may be obtained by the intended users through their participation, either directly or indirectly through their representative who has the authority to act for the intended users, in establishing the nature and scope of the engagement. Such participation enhances the ability of the firm to communicate with intended users about independence matters, including the circumstances that are relevant to the evaluation of the threats to independence and the applicable safeguards necessary to eliminate the threats or reduce them to an acceptable level, and to obtain their agreement to the modified independence requirements that are to be applied.

291.22   The firm shall communicate (for example, in an engagement letter) with the intended users regarding the independence requirements that are to be applied with respect to the provision of the assurance engagement. Where the intended users are a class of users (for example, lenders in a syndicated loan arrangement) who are not specifically identifiable by name at the time the engagement terms are established, such users shall subsequently be made aware of the independence requirements agreed to by the representative (for example, by the representative making the firm's engagement letter available to all users).

291.23   If the firm also issues an assurance report that does not include a restriction on use and distribution for the same client, the provisions of paragraphs 291.25 to 291.27 do not change the requirement to apply the provisions of paragraphs 291.1 to 291.159 to that assurance engagement. If the firm also issues an audit report, whether or not it includes a restriction on use and distribution, for the same client, the provisions of Section 290 shall apply to that audit engagement.

The modifications to the requirements of Section 291 that are permitted in the circumstances set out above are described in paragraphs 291.25 to 291.27. Compliance in all other respects with the provisions of Section 291 is required. **291.24**

When the conditions set out in paragraphs 291.21 and 291.22 are met, the relevant provisions set out in paragraphs 291.104 to 291.134 apply to all members of the engagement team, and their immediate and close family members. In addition, a determination shall be made as to whether threats to independence are created by interests and relationships between the assurance client and the following other members of the assurance team: **291.25**

(a) Those who provide consultation regarding technical or industry specific issues, transactions or events; and
(b) Those who provide quality control for the engagement, including those who perform the engagement quality control review.

An evaluation shall also be made, by reference to the provisions set out in paragraphs 291.104 to 291.134, of any threats that the engagement team has reason to believe are created by interests and relationships between the assurance client and others within the firm who can directly influence the outcome of the assurance engagement, including those who recommend the compensation, or who provide direct supervisory, management or other oversight, of the assurance engagement partner in connection with the performance of the assurance engagement.

Even though the conditions set out in paragraphs 291.21 to 291.22 are met, if the firm had a material financial interest, whether direct or indirect, in the assurance client, the self-interest threat created would be so significant that no safeguards could reduce the threat to an acceptable level. Accordingly, the firm shall not have such a financial interest. In addition, the firm shall comply with the other applicable provisions of this section described in paragraphs 291.113 to 291.159. **291.26**

An evaluation shall also be made of any threats that the firm has reason to believe are created by network firm interests and relationships. **291.27**

Multiple Responsible Parties

In some assurance engagements, whether assertion-based or direct reporting, there might be several responsible parties. In determining whether it is necessary to apply the provisions in this section to each responsible party in such engagements, the firm may take into account whether an interest or relationship between the firm, or a member of the assurance team, and a particular responsible party would create a threat to independence that is not trivial and inconsequential in the context of the subject matter information. This will take into account factors such as: **291.28**

- The materiality of the subject matter information (or of the subject matter) for which the particular responsible party is responsible; and
- The degree of public interest associated with the engagement.

If the firm determines that the threat to independence created by any such interest or relationship with a particular responsible party would be trivial and inconsequential, it may not be necessary to apply all of the provisions of this section to that responsible party.

Documentation

291.29   Documentation provides evidence of the professional accountant's judgments in forming conclusions regarding compliance with independence requirements. The absence of documentation is not a determinant of whether a firm considered a particular matter nor whether it is independent.

The professional accountant shall document conclusions regarding compliance with independence requirements, and the substance of any relevant discussions that support those conclusions. Accordingly:

(a)   When safeguards are required to reduce a threat to an acceptable level, the professional accountant shall document the nature of the threat and the safeguards in place or applied that reduce the threat to an acceptable level; and

(b)   When a threat required significant analysis to determine whether safeguards were necessary and the professional accountant concluded that they were not because the threat was already at an acceptable level, the professional accountant shall document the nature of the threat and the rationale for the conclusion.

Engagement Period

291.30   Independence from the assurance client is required both during the engagement period and the period covered by the subject matter information. The engagement period starts when the assurance team begins to perform assurance services with respect to the particular engagement. The engagement period ends when the assurance report is issued. When the engagement is of a recurring nature, it ends at the later of the notification by either party that the professional relationship has terminated or the issuance of the final assurance report.

291.31   When an entity becomes an assurance client during or after the period covered by the subject matter information on which the firm will express a conclusion, the firm shall determine whether any threats to independence are created by:

(a)   Financial or business relationships with the assurance client during or after the period covered by the subject matter information but before accepting the assurance engagement; or

(b)   Previous services provided to the assurance client.

291.32   If a non-assurance service was provided to the assurance client during or after the period covered by the subject matter information but before the assurance team begins to perform assurance services and the service would not be permitted during the period of the assurance engagement, the firm shall evaluate any threat to independence created by the service. If any threat is not at an acceptable level, the assurance engagement shall only be accepted if safeguards are applied to eliminate any threats or reduce them to an acceptable level. Examples of such safeguards include:

● Not including personnel who provided the non-assurance service as members of the assurance team;

● Having a professional accountant review the assurance and non-assurance work as appropriate; or

● Engaging another firm to evaluate the results of the non-assurance service or having another firm re-perform the non-assurance service to the extent necessary to enable it to take responsibility for the service.

However, if the non-assurance service has not been completed and it is not practical to complete or terminate the service before the commencement of professional services in connection with the assurance engagement, the firm shall only accept the assurance engagement if it is satisfied:

(a) The non-assurance service will be completed within a short period of time; or
(b) The client has arrangements in place to transition the service to another provider within a short period of time.

During the service period, safeguards shall be applied when necessary. In addition, the matter shall be discussed with those charged with governance.

Other Considerations

There may be occasions when there is an inadvertent violation of this section. If such an inadvertent violation occurs, it generally will be deemed not to compromise independence provided the firm has appropriate quality control policies and procedures in place equivalent to those required by ISQCs to maintain independence and, once discovered, the violation is corrected promptly and any necessary safeguards are applied to eliminate any threat or reduce it to an acceptable level. The firm shall determine whether to discuss the matter with those charged with governance. **291.33**

Paragraphs 291.34 to 291.99 are intentionally left blank.

Application of the Conceptual Framework Approach toIndependence

Paragraphs 291.104 to 291.159 describe specific circumstances and relationships that create or may create threats to independence. The paragraphs describe the potential threats and the types of safeguards that may be appropriate to eliminate the threats or reduce them to an acceptable level and identify certain situations where no safeguards could reduce the threats to an acceptable level. The paragraphs do not describe all of the circumstances and relationships that create or may create a threat to independence. The firm and the members of the assurance team shall evaluate the implications of similar, but different, circumstances and relationships and determine whether safeguards, including the safeguards in paragraphs 200.11 to 200.14 can be applied when necessary to eliminate the threats to independence or reduce them to an acceptable level. **291.100**

The paragraphs demonstrate how the conceptual framework approach applies to assurance engagements and are to be read in conjunction with paragraph 291.28 which explains that, in the majority of assurance engagements, there is one responsible party and that responsible party is the assurance client. However, in some assurance engagements there are two or more responsible parties. In such circumstances, an evaluation shall be made of any threats the firm has reason to believe are created by interests and relationships between a member of the assurance team, the firm, a network firm and the party responsible for the subject matter. For assurance reports that include a restriction on use and distribution, the paragraphs are to be read in the context of paragraphs 291.21 to 291.27. **291.101**

Interpretation 2005–01 provides further guidance on applying the independence requirements contained in this section to assurance engagements. **291.102**

291.103   Paragraphs 291.104 to 291.120 contain references to the materiality of a financial interest, loan, or guarantee, or the significance of a business relationship. For the purpose of determining whether such an interest is material to an individual, the combined net worth of the individual and the individual's immediate family members may be taken into account.

Financial Interests

291.104   Holding a financial interest in an assurance client may create a self-interest threat. The existence and significance of any threat created depends on:

(a)   The role of the person holding the financial interest,
(b)   Whether the financial interest is direct or indirect, and
(c)   The materiality of the financial interest.

291.105   Financial interests may be held through an intermediary (for example, a collective investment vehicle, estate or trust). The determination of whether such financial interests are direct or indirect will depend upon whether the beneficial owner has control over the investment vehicle or the ability to influence its investment decisions. When control over the investment vehicle or the ability to influence investment decisions exists, this Code defines that financial interest to be a direct financial interest. Conversely, when the beneficial owner of the financial interest has no control over the investment vehicle or ability to influence its investment decisions, this Code defines that financial interest to be an indirect financial interest.

291.106   If a member of the assurance team, a member of that individual's immediate family, or a firm has a direct financial interest or a material indirect financial interest in the assurance client, the self-interest threat created would be so significant that no safeguards could reduce the threat to an acceptable level. Therefore, none of the following shall have a direct financial interest or a material indirect financial interest in the client: a member of the assurance team; a member of that individual's immediate family member; or the firm.

291.107   When a member of the assurance team has a close family member who the assurance team member knows has a direct financial interest or a material indirect financial interest in the assurance client, a self-interest threat is created. The significance of the threat will depend on factors such as

●   The nature of the relationship between the member of the assurance team and the close family member; and
●   The materiality of the financial interest to the close family member.

The significance of the threat shall be evaluated and safeguards applied when necessary to eliminate the threat or reduce it to an acceptable level. Examples of such safeguards include:

●   The close family member disposing, as soon as practicable, of all of the financial interest or disposing of a sufficient portion of an indirect financial interest so that the remaining interest is no longer material;
●   Having a professional accountant review the work of the member of the assurance team; or
●   Removing the individual from the assurance team.

291.108   If a member of the assurance team, a member of that individual's immediate family, or a firm has a direct or material indirect financial interest in an entity that has a controlling interest in the assurance client, and the client is material to the entity, the self-interest threat created would be so significant that no safeguards could reduce the threat to an acceptable level. Therefore, none of the following shall have such a financial interest: a member of the assurance team; a member of that individual's immediate family; and the firm.

The holding by a firm or a member of the assurance team, or a member of that **291.109** individual's immediate family, of a direct financial interest or a material indirect financial interest in the assurance client as a trustee creates a self-interest threat. Such an interest shall not be held unless:

(a)   Neither the trustee, nor an immediate family member of the trustee, nor the firm are beneficiaries of the trust;
(b)   The interest in the assurance client held by the trust is not material to the trust;
(c)   The trust is not able to exercise significant influence over the assurance client; and
(d)   The trustee, an immediate family member of the trustee, or the firm cannot significantly influence any investment decision involving a financial interest in the assurance client.

Members of the assurance team shall determine **291.110** whether a self-interest threat is created by any known financial interests in the assurance client held by other individuals including:

● Partners and professional employees of the firm, other than those referred to above, or their immediate family members; and
● Individuals with a close personal relationship with a member of the assurance team.

Whether these interests create a self-interest threat will depend on factors such as:

● The firm's organizational, operating and reporting structure; and
● The nature of the relationship between the individual and the member of the assurance team.

The significance of any threat shall be evaluated and safeguards applied when necessary to eliminate the threat or reduce it to an acceptable level. Examples of such safeguards include:

● Removing the member of the assurance team with the personal relationship from the assurance team;
● Excluding the member of the assurance team from any significant decision-making concerning the assurance engagement; or
● Having a professional accountant review the work of the member of the assurance team.

If a firm, a member of the assurance team, or an immediate family member of the **291.111** individual, receives a direct financial interest or a material indirect financial interest in an assurance client, for example, by way of an inheritance, gift or as a result of a merger, and such interest would not be permitted to be held under this section, then:

(a)   If the interest is received by the firm, the financial interest shall be disposed of immediately, or a sufficient amount of an indirect financial interest shall be disposed of so that the remaining interest is no longer material, or
(b)   If the interest is received by a member of the assurance team, or a member of that individual's immediate family, the individual who received the financial interest shall immediately dispose of the financial interest, or dispose of a sufficient amount of an indirect financial interest so that the remaining interest is no longer material.

291.112   When an inadvertent violation of this section as it relates to a financial interest in an assurance client occurs, it is deemed not to compromise independence if:

(a)   The firm has established policies and procedures that require prompt notification to the firm of any breaches resulting from the purchase, inheritance or other acquisition of a financial interest in the assurance client;

(b)   The actions taken in paragraph 291.111(a)–(b) are taken as applicable; and

(c)   The firm applies other safeguards when necessary to reduce any remaining threat to an acceptable level. Examples of such safeguards include:

- Having a professional accountant review the work of the member of the assurance team; or
- Excluding the individual from any significant decision-making concerning the assurance engagement.

The firm shall determine whether to discuss the matter with those charged with governance.

Loans and Guarantees

291.113   A loan, or a guarantee of a loan, to a member of the assurance team, or a member of that individual's immediate family, or the firm from an assurance client that is a bank or a similar institution, may create a threat to independence. If the loan or guarantee is not made under normal lending procedures, terms and conditions, a self-interest threat would be created that would be so significant that no safeguards could reduce the threat to an acceptable level. Accordingly, neither a member of the assurance team, a member of that individual's immediate family, nor a firm shall accept such a loan or guarantee.

291.114   If a loan to a firm from an assurance client that is a bank or similar institution is made under normal lending procedures, terms and conditions and it is material to the assurance client or firm receiving the loan, it may be possible to apply safeguards to reduce the self-interest threat to an acceptable level. An example of such a safeguard is having the work reviewed by a professional accountant from a network firm that is neither involved with the assurance engagement nor received the loan.

291.115   A loan, or a guarantee of a loan, from an assurance client that is a bank or a similar institution to a member of the assurance team, or a member of that individual's immediate family, does not create a threat to independence if the loan or guarantee is made under normal lending procedures, terms and conditions. Examples of such loans include home mortgages, bank overdrafts, car loans and credit card balances.

291.116   If the firm or a member of the assurance team, or a member of that individual's immediate family, accepts a loan from, or has a borrowing guaranteed by, an assurance client that is not a bank or similar institution, the self-interest threat created would be so significant that no safeguards could reduce the threat to an acceptable level, unless the loan or guarantee is immaterial to both the firm, or the member of the assurance team and the immediate family member, and the client.

291.117   Similarly, if the firm, or a member of the assurance team, or a member of that individual's immediate family, makes or guarantees a loan to an assurance client, the self-interest threat created would be so significant that no safeguards could reduce the threat to an acceptable level, unless the loan or guarantee is immaterial to both the firm, or the member of the assurance team and the immediate family member, and the client.

If a firm or a member of the assurance team, or a member of that individual's **291.118** immediate family, has deposits or a brokerage account with an assurance client that is a bank, broker, or similar institution, a threat to independence is not created if the deposit or account is held under normal commercial terms.

Business Relationships

A close business relationship between a firm, or a member of the assurance team, or a **291.119** member of that individual's immediate family, and the assurance client or its management arises from a commercial relationship or common financial interest and may create self-interest or intimidation threats. Examples of such relationships include:

- Having a financial interest in a joint venture with either the client or a controlling owner, director or officer or other individual who performs senior managerial activities for that client.
- Arrangements to combine one or more services or products of the firm with one or more services or products of the client and to market the package with reference to both parties.
- Distribution or marketing arrangements under which the firm distributes or markets the client's products or services, or the client distributes or markets the firm's products or services.

Unless any financial interest is immaterial and the business relationship is insignificant to the firm and the client or its management, the threat created would be so significant that no safeguards could reduce the threat to an acceptable level. Therefore, unless the financial interest is immaterial and the business relationship is insignificant, the business relationship shall not be entered into, or shall be reduced to an insignificant level or terminated.

In the case of a member of the assurance team, unless any such financial interest is immaterial and the relationship is insignificant to that member, the individual shall be removed from the assurance team.

If the business relationship is between an immediate family member of a member of the assurance team and the assurance client or its management, the significance of any threat shall be evaluated and safeguards applied when necessary to eliminate the threat or reduce it to an acceptable level.

The purchase of goods and services from an assurance client by the firm, or a **291.120** member of the assurance team, or a member of that individual's immediate family, does not generally create a threat to independence if the transaction is in the normal course of business and at arm's length. However, such transactions may be of such a nature or magnitude that they create a self-interest threat. The significance of any threat shall be evaluated and safeguards applied when necessary to eliminate the threat or reduce it to an acceptable level. Examples of such safeguards include:

- Eliminating or reducing the magnitude of the transaction; or
- Removing the individual from the assurance team.

Family and Personal Relationships

Family and personal relationships between a member of the assurance team and a **291.121** director or officer or certain employees (depending on their role) of the assurance client, may create self-interest, familiarity or intimidation threats. The existence and significance of any threats will depend on a number of factors, including the individual's responsibilities on the assurance team, the role of the family member or other individual within the client, and the closeness of the relationship.

291.122   When an immediate family member of a member of the assurance team is:

(a) A director or officer of the assurance client, or

(b) An employee in a position to exert significant influence over the subject matter information of the assurance engagement,

or was in such a position during any period covered by the engagement or the subject matter information, the threats to independence can only be reduced to an acceptable level by removing the individual from the assurance team. The closeness of the relationship is such that no other safeguards could reduce the threat to an acceptable level. Accordingly, no individual who has such a relationship shall be a member of the assurance team.

291.123   Threats to independence are created when an immediate family member of a member of the assurance team is an employee in a position to exert significant influence over the subject matter of the engagement. The significance of the threats will depend on factors such as:

- The position held by the immediate family member; and
- The role of the professional on the assurance team.

The significance of the threat shall be evaluated and safeguards applied when necessary to eliminate the threat or reduce it to an acceptable level. Examples of such safeguards include:

- Removing the individual from the assurance team; or
- Structuring the responsibilities of the assurance team so that the professional does not deal with matters that are within the responsibility of the immediate family member.

291.124   Threats to independence are created when a close family member of a member of the assurance team is:

- A director or officer of the assurance client; or
- An employee in a position to exert significant influence over the subject matter information of the assurance engagement.

The significance of the threats will depend on factors such as:

- The nature of the relationship between the member of the assurance team and the close family member;
- The position held by the close family member; and
- The role of the professional on the assurance team.

The significance of the threat shall be evaluated and safeguards applied when necessary to eliminate the threat or reduce it to an acceptable level. Examples of such safeguards include:

- Removing the individual from the assurance team; or
- Structuring the responsibilities of the assurance team so that the professional does not deal with matters that are within the responsibility of the close family member.

291.125   Threats to independence are created when a member of the assurance team has a close relationship with a person who is not an immediate or close family member, but who is a director or officer or an employee in a position to exert significant influence over the subject matter information of the assurance engagement. A member of the assurance team who has such a relationship shall consult in accordance with firm policies and procedures. The significance of the threats will depend on factors such as:

- The nature of the relationship between the individual and the member of the assurance team;
- The position the individual holds with the client; and
- The role of the professional on the assurance team.

The significance of the threats shall be evaluated and safeguards applied when necessary to eliminate the threats or reduce them to an acceptable level. Examples of such safeguards include:

- Removing the professional from the assurance team; or
- Structuring the responsibilities of the assurance team so that the professional does not deal with matters that are within the responsibility of the individual with whom the professional has a close relationship.

Self-interest, familiarity or intimidation threats may be created by a personal or family relationship between (a) a partner or employee of the firm who is not a member of the assurance team and (b) a director or officer of the assurance client or an employee in a position to exert significant influence over the subject matter information of the assurance engagement. The existence and significance of any threat will depend on factors such as: **291.126**

- The nature of the relationship between the partner or employee of the firm and the director or officer or employee of the client;
- The interaction of the partner or employee of the firm with the assurance team;
- The position of the partner or employee within the firm; and
- The role of the individual within the client.

The significance of any threat shall be evaluated and safeguards applied when necessary to eliminate the threat or reduce it to an acceptable level. Examples of such safeguards include:

- Structuring the partner's or employee's responsibilities to reduce any potential influence over the assurance engagement; or
- Having a professional accountant review the relevant assurance work performed.

When an inadvertent violation of this section as it relates to family and personal relationships occurs, it is deemed not to compromise independence if: **291.127**

(a) The firm has established policies and procedures that require prompt notification to the firm of any breaches resulting from changes in the employment status of their immediate or close family members or other personal relationships that create threats to independence;

(b) The inadvertent violation relates to an immediate family member of a member of the assurance team becoming a director or officer of the assurance client or being in a position to exert significant influence over the subject matter information of the assurance engagement, and the relevant professional is removed from the assurance team; and

(c) The firm applies other safeguards when necessary to reduce any remaining threat to an acceptable level. Examples of such safeguards include:

- Having a professional accountant review the work of the member of the assurance team; or

- Excluding the relevant professional from any significant decision-making concerning the engagement.

The firm shall determine whether to discuss the matter with those charged with governance.

Employment with an Assurance Client

291.128   Familiarity or intimidation threats may be created if a director or officer of the assurance client, or an employee who is in a position to exert significant influence over the subject matter information of the assurance engagement, has been a member of the assurance team or partner of the firm.

291.129   If a former member of the assurance team or partner of the firm has joined the assurance client in such a position, the existence and significance of any familiarity or intimidation threats will depend on factors such as:

- The position the individual has taken at the client;
- Any involvement the individual will have with the assurance team;
- The length of time since the individual was a member of the assurance team or partner of the firm; and
- The former position of the individual within the assurance team or firm, for example, whether the individual was responsible for maintaining regular contact with the client's management or those charged with governance.

In all cases the individual shall not continue to participate in the firm's business or professional activities.

The significance of any threats created shall be evaluated and safeguards applied when necessary to eliminate the threats or reduce them to an acceptable level. Examples of such safeguards include:

- Making arrangements such that the individual is not entitled to any benefits or payments from the firm, unless made in accordance with fixed pre-determined arrangements.
- Making arrangements such that any amount owed to the individual is not material to the firm;
- Modifying the plan for the assurance engagement;
- Assigning individuals to the assurance team who have sufficient experience in relation to the individual who has joined the client; or
- Having a professional accountant review the work of the former member of the assurance team.

291.130   If a former partner of the firm has previously joined an entity in such a position and the entity subsequently becomes an assurance client of the firm, the significance of any threats to independence shall be evaluated and safeguards applied when necessary, to eliminate the threat or reduce it to an acceptable level.

291.131   A self-interest threat is created when a member of the assurance team participates in the assurance engagement while knowing that the member of the assurance team will, or may, join the client some time in the future. Firm policies and procedures shall require members of an assurance team to notify the firm when entering employment negotiations with the client. On receiving such notification, the significance of the threat shall be evaluated and safeguards applied when necessary to eliminate the threat or reduce it to an acceptable level. Examples of such safeguards include:

- Removing the individual from the assurance team; or
- A review of any significant judgments made by that individual while on the team.

Recent Service with an Assurance Client

Self-interest, self-review or familiarity threats may be created if a member of the assurance team has recently served as a director, officer, or employee of the assurance client. This would be the case when, for example, a member of the assurance team has to evaluate elements of the subject matter information the member of the assurance team had prepared while with the client.

291.132

If, during the period covered by the assurance report, a member of the assurance team had served as director or officer of the assurance client, or was an employee in a position to exert significant influence over the subject matter information of the assurance engagement, the threat created would be so significant that no safeguards could reduce the threat to an acceptable level. Consequently, such individuals shall not be assigned to the assurance team.

291.133

Self-interest, self-review or familiarity threats may be created if, before the period covered by the assurance report, a member of the assurance team had served as director or officer of the assurance client, or was an employee in a position to exert significant influence over the subject matter information of the assurance engagement. For example, such threats would be created if a decision made or work performed by the individual in the prior period, while employed by the client, is to be evaluated in the current period as part of the current assurance engagement. The existence and significance of any threats will depend on factors such as:

291.134

- The position the individual held with the client;
- The length of time since the individual left the client; and
- The role of the professional on the assurance team.

The significance of any threat shall be evaluated and safeguards applied when necessary to reduce the threat to an acceptable level. An example of such a safeguard is conducting a review of the work performed by the individual as part of the assurance team.

Serving as a Director or Officer of an Assurance Client

If a partner or employee of the firm serves a director or officer of an assurance client, the self-review and self-interest threats would be so significant that no safeguards could reduce the threats to an acceptable level. Accordingly, no partner or employee shall serve as a director or officer of an assurance client.

291.135

The position of Company Secretary has different implications in different jurisdictions. Duties may range from administrative duties, such as personnel management and the maintenance of company records and registers, to duties as diverse as ensuring that the company complies with regulation or providing advice on corporate governance matters. Generally, this position is seen to imply a close association with the entity.

291.136

291.137   If a partner or employee of the firm serves as Company Secretary for an assurance client, self-review and advocacy threats are created that would generally be so significant that no safeguards could reduce the threats to an acceptable level. Despite paragraph 291.135, when this practice is specifically permitted under local law, professional rules or practice, and provided management makes all relevant decisions, the duties and activities shall be limited to those of a routine and administrative nature, such as preparing minutes and maintaining statutory returns. In those circumstances, the significance of any threats shall be evaluated and safeguards applied when necessary to eliminate the threats or reduce them to an acceptable level.

291.138   Performing routine administrative services to support a company secretarial function or providing advice in relation to company secretarial administration matters does not generally create threats to independence, as long as client management makes all relevant decisions.

Long Association of Senior Personnel with an Assurance Client

291.139   Familiarity and self-interest threats are created by using the same senior personnel on an assurance engagement over a long period of time. The significance of the threats will depend on factors such as:

- How long the individual has been a member of the assurance team;
- The role of the individual on the assurance team;
- The structure of the firm;
- The nature of the assurance engagement;
- Whether the client's management team has changed; and
- Whether the nature or complexity of the subject matter information has changed.

The significance of the threats shall be evaluated and safeguards applied when necessary to eliminate the threats or reduce them to an acceptable level. Examples of such safeguards include:

- Rotating the senior personnel off the assurance team;
- Having a professional accountant who was not a member of the assurance team review the work of the senior personnel; or
- Regular independent internal or external quality reviews of the engagement.

Provision of Non-assurance Services to an Assurance Client

291.140   Firms have traditionally provided to their assurance clients a range of non-assurance services that are consistent with their skills and expertise. Providing non-assurance services may, however, create threats to the independence of the firm or members of the assurance team. The threats created are most often self-review, self-interest and advocacy threats.

291.141   When specific guidance on a particular non-assurance service is not included in this section, the conceptual framework shall be applied when evaluating the particular circumstances.

291.142   Before the firm accepts an engagement to provide a non-assurance service to an assurance client, a determination shall be made as to whether providing such a service would create a threat to independence. In evaluating the significance of any threat created by a particular non-assurance service, consideration shall be given to any threat that the assurance team has reason to believe is created by providing other related non-assurance services. If a threat is created that cannot be reduced to an acceptable level by the application of safeguards the non-assurance service shall not be provided.

Management Responsibilities

Management of an entity performs many activities in managing the entity in the best interests of stakeholders of the entity. It is not possible to specify every activity that is a management responsibility. However, management responsibilities involve leading and directing an entity, including making significant decisions regarding the acquisition, deployment and control of human, financial, physical and intangible resources. **291.143**

Whether an activity is a management responsibility depends on the circumstances and requires the exercise of judgment. Examples of activities that would generally be considered a management responsibility include: **291.144**

- Setting policies and strategic direction;
- Directing and taking responsibility for the actions of the entity's employees;
- Authorizing transactions;
- Deciding which recommendations of the firm or other third parties to implement; and
- Taking responsibility for designing, implementing and maintaining internal control.

Activities that are routine and administrative, or involve matters that are insignificant, generally are deemed not to be a management responsibility. **291.145**

For example, executing an insignificant transaction that has been authorized by management or monitoring the dates for filing statutory returns and advising an assurance client of those dates is deemed not to be a management responsibility. Further, providing advice and recommendations to assist management in discharging its responsibilities is not assuming a management responsibility.

Assuming a management responsibility for an assurance client may create threats to independence. If a firm were to assume a management responsibility as part of the assurance service, the threats created would be so significant that no safeguards could reduce the threats to an acceptable level. Accordingly, in providing assurance services to an assurance client, a firm shall not assume a management responsibility as part of the assurance service. If the firm assumes a management responsibility as part of any other services provided to the assurance client, it shall ensure that the responsibility is not related to the subject matter and subject matter information of an assurance engagement provided by the firm. **291.146**

To avoid the risk of assuming a management responsibility related to the subject matter or subject matter information of the assurance engagement, the firm shall be satisfied that a member of management is responsible for making the significant judgments and decisions that are the proper responsibility of management, evaluating the results of the service and accepting responsibility for the actions to be taken arising from the results of the service. This reduces the risk of the firm inadvertently making any significant judgments or decisions on behalf of management. This risk is further reduced when the firm gives the client the opportunity to make judgments and decisions based on an objective and transparent analysis and presentation of the issues. **291.147**

Other Considerations

291.148   Threats to independence may be created when a firm provides a non-assurance service related to the subject matter information of an assurance engagement. In such cases, an evaluation of the significance of the firm's involvement with the subject matter information of the engagement shall be made, and a determination shall be made of whether any self-review threats that are not at an acceptable level can be reduced to an acceptable level by the application of safeguards.

291.149   A self-review threat may be created if the firm is involved in the preparation of subject matter information which is subsequently the subject matter information of an assurance engagement. For example, a self-review threat would be created if the firm developed and prepared prospective financial information and subsequently provided assurance on this information. Consequently, the firm shall evaluate the significance of any self-review threat created by the provision of such services and apply safeguards when necessary to eliminate the threat or reduce it to an acceptable level.

291.150   When a firm performs a valuation that forms part of the subject matter information of an assurance engagement, the firm shall evaluate the significance of any self-review threat and apply safeguards when necessary to eliminate the threat or reduce it to an acceptable level.

Fees

Fees—Relative Size

291.151   When the total fees from an assurance client represent a large proportion of the total fees of the firm expressing the conclusion, the dependence on that client and concern about losing the client creates a self-interest or intimidation threat. The significance of the threat will depend on factors such as:

- The operating structure of the firm;
- Whether the firm is well established or new; and
- The significance of the client qualitatively and/or quantitatively to the firm.

The significance of the threat shall be evaluated and safeguards applied when necessary to eliminate the threat or reduce it to an acceptable level. Examples of such safeguards include:

- Reducing the dependency on the client;
- External quality control reviews; or
- Consulting a third party, such as a professional regulatory body or a professional accountant, on key assurance judgments.

291.152   A self-interest or intimidation threat is also created when the fees generated from an assurance client represent a large proportion of the revenue from an individual partner's clients. The significance of the threat shall be evaluated and safeguards applied when necessary to eliminate the threat or reduce it to an acceptable level. An example of such a safeguard is having an additional professional accountant who was not a member of the assurance team review the work or otherwise advise as necessary.

Fees—Overdue

A self-interest threat may be created if fees due from an assurance client remain unpaid for a long time, especially if a significant part is not paid before the issue of the assurance report, if any, for the following period. Generally the firm is expected to require payment of such fees before any such report is issued. If fees remain unpaid after the report has been issued, the existence and significance of any threat shall be evaluated and safeguards applied when necessary to eliminate the threat or reduce it to an acceptable level. An example of such a safeguard is having another professional accountant who did not take part in the assurance engagement provide advice or review the work performed. The firm shall determine whether the overdue fees might be regarded as being equivalent to a loan to the client and whether, because of the significance of the overdue fees, it is appropriate for the firm to be re-appointed or continue the assurance engagement.   **291.153**

Contingent Fees

Contingent fees are fees calculated on a predetermined basis relating to the outcome of a transaction or the result of the services performed by the firm. For the purposes of this section, fees are not regarded as being contingent if established by a court or other public authority.   **291.154**

A contingent fee charged directly or indirectly, for example through an intermediary, by a firm in respect of an assurance engagement creates a self-interest threat that is so significant that no safeguards could reduce the threat to an acceptable level. Accordingly, a firm shall not enter into any such fee arrangement.   **291.155**

A contingent fee charged directly or indirectly, for example through an intermediary, by a firm in respect of a non-assurance service provided to an assurance client may also create a self-interest threat. If the outcome of the non-assurance service, and therefore, the amount of the fee, is dependent on a future or contemporary judgment related to a matter that is material to the subject matter information of the assurance engagement, no safeguards could reduce the threat to an acceptable level. Accordingly, such arrangements shall not be accepted.   **291.156**

For other contingent fee arrangements charged by a firm for a non-assurance service to an assurance client, the existence and significance of any threats will depend on factors such as: **291.157**

- The range of possible fee amounts;
- Whether an appropriate authority determines the outcome of the matter upon which the contingent fee will be determined;
- The nature of the service; and
- The effect of the event or transaction on the subject matter information.

The significance of any threats shall be evaluated and safeguards applied when necessary to eliminate the threats or reduce them to an acceptable level. Examples of such safeguards include:

- Having a professional accountant review the relevant assurance work or otherwise advise as necessary; or
- Using professionals who are not members of the assurance team to perform the non-assurance service.

Gifts and Hospitality

291.158 Accepting gifts or hospitality from an assurance client may create self-interest and familiarity threats. If a firm or a member of the assurance team accepts gifts or hospitality, unless the value is trivial and inconsequential, the threats created would be so significant that no safeguards could reduce the threats to an acceptable level. Consequently, a firm or a member of the assurance team shall not accept such gifts or hospitality.

Actual or Threatened Litigation

291.159 When litigation takes place, or appears likely, between the firm or a member of the assurance team and the assurance client, self-interest and intimidation threats are created. The relationship between client management and the members of the assurance team must be characterized by complete candor and full disclosure regarding all aspects of a client's business operations. When the firm and the client's management are placed in adversarial positions by actual or threatened litigation, affecting management's willingness to make complete disclosures self-interest and intimidation threats are created. The significance of the threats created will depend on such factors as:

- The materiality of the litigation; and
- Whether the litigation relates to a prior assurance engagement.

The significance of the threats shall be evaluated and safeguards applied when necessary to eliminate the threats or reduce them to an acceptable level. Examples of such safeguards include:

- If the litigation involves a member of the assurance team, removing that individual from the assurance team; or
- Having a professional review the work performed.

If such safeguards do not reduce the threats to an acceptable level, the only appropriate action is to withdraw from, or decline, the assurance engagement.

Interpretation 2005–01 (Revised July 2009 to conform to changes resulting from the IESBA's project to improve the clarity of the Code)

Application of Section 291 to Assurance Engagements that are Not Financial Statement Audit Engagements

This interpretation provides guidance on the application of the independence requirements contained in Section 291 to assurance engagements that are not financial statement audit engagements.

This interpretation focuses on the application issues that are particular to assurance engagements that are not financial statement audit engagements. There are other matters noted in Section 291 that are relevant in the consideration of independence requirements for all assurance engagements. For example, paragraph 291.3 states that an evaluation shall be made of any threats the firm has reason to believe are created by a network firm's interests and relationships. It also states that when the assurance team has reason to believe that a related entity of such an assurance client is relevant to the evaluation of the firm's independence of the client, the assurance team shall include the related entity when evaluating threats to independence and when necessary applying safeguards. These matters are not specifically addressed in this interpretation.

As explained in the International Framework for Assurance Engagements issued by the International Auditing and Assurance Standards Board, in an assurance engagement, the professional accountant in public practice expresses a conclusion designed to enhance the degree of confidence of the intended users other than the responsible party about the outcome of the evaluation or measurement of a subject matter against criteria.

Assertion-Based Assurance Engagements

In an assertion-based assurance engagement, the evaluation or measurement of the subject matter is performed by the responsible party, and the subject matter information is in the form of an assertion by the responsible party that is made available to the intended users.

In an assertion-based assurance engagement independence is required from the responsible party, which is responsible for the subject matter information and may be responsible for the subject matter.

In those assertion-based assurance engagements where the responsible party is responsible for the subject matter information but not the subject matter, independence is required from the responsible party. In addition, an evaluation shall be made of any threats the firm has reason to believe are created by interests and relationships between a member of the assurance team, the firm, a network firm and the party responsible for the subject matter.

Direct Reporting Assurance Engagements

In a direct reporting assurance engagement, the professional accountant in public practice either directly performs the evaluation or measurement of the subject matter, or obtains a representation from the responsible party that has performed the evaluation or measurement that is not available to the intended users. The subject matter information is provided to the intended users in the assurance report.

In a direct reporting assurance engagement independence is required from the responsible party, which is responsible for the subject matter.

Multiple Responsible Parties

In both assertion-based assurance engagements and direct reporting assurance engagements there may be several responsible parties. For example, a public accountant in public practice may be asked to provide assurance on the monthly circulation statistics of a number of independently owned newspapers. The assignment could be an assertion based assurance engagement where each newspaper measures its circulation and the statistics are presented in an assertion that is available to the intended users. Alternatively, the assignment could be a direct reporting assurance engagement, where there is no assertion and there may or may not be a written representation from the newspapers.

In such engagements, when determining whether it is necessary to apply the provisions in Section 291 to each responsible party, the firm may take into account whether an interest or relationship between the firm, or a member of the assurance team, and a particular responsible party would create a threat to independence that is not trivial and inconsequential in the context of the subject matter information. This will take into account:

(a) The materiality of the subject matter information (or the subject matter) for which the particular responsible party is responsible; and
(b) The degree of public interest that is associated with the engagement.

If the firm determines that the threat to independence created by any such relationships with a particular responsible party would be trivial and inconsequential it may not be necessary to apply all of the provisions of this section to that responsible party.

Example

The following example has been developed to demonstrate the application of Section 291. It is assumed that the client is not also a financial statement audit client of the firm, or a network firm.

A firm is engaged to provide assurance on the total proven oil reserves of 10 independent companies. Each company has conducted geographical and engineering surveys to determine their reserves (subject matter). There are established criteria to determine when a reserve may be considered to be proven which the professional accountant in public practice determines to be suitable criteria for the engagement. The proven reserves for each company as at December 31, 20X0 were as follows:

	Proven oil reserves thousands of barrels
Company 1	5,200
Company 2	725
Company 3	3,260
Company 4	15,000
Company 5	6,700
Company 6	39,126
Company 7	345
Company 8	175
Company 9	24,135
Company 10	9,635
Total	**104,301**

The engagement could be structured in differing ways:

Assertion-Based Engagements

A1 Each company measures its reserves and provides an assertion to the firm and to intended users.

A2 An entity other than the companies measures the reserves and provides an assertion to the firm and to intended users.

Direct Reporting Engagements

D1 Each company measures the reserves and provides the firm with a written representation that measures its reserves against the established criteria for measuring proven reserves. The representation is not available to the intended users.

D2 The firm directly measures the reserves of some of the companies.

Application of Approach

A1 Each company measures its reserves and provides an assertion to the firm and to intended users.

There are several responsible parties in this engagement (Companies 1–10). When determining whether it is necessary to apply the independence provisions to all of the companies, the firm may take into account whether an interest or relationship with a particular company would create a threat to independence that is not at an acceptable level. This will take into account factors such as:

- The materiality of the company's proven reserves in relation to the total reserves to be reported on; and
- The degree of public interest associated with the engagement (paragraph 291.28).

For example Company 8 accounts for 0.17% of the total reserves, therefore a business relationship or interest with Company 8 would create less of a threat than a similar relationship with Company 6, which accounts for approximately 37.5% of the reserves.

Having determined those companies to which the independence requirements apply, the assurance team and the firm are required to be independent of those responsible parties that would be considered to be the assurance client (paragraph 291.28).

A2 An entity other than the companies measures the reserves and provides an assertion to the firm and to intended users.

The firm shall be independent of the entity that measures the reserves and provides an assertion to the firm and to intended users (paragraph 291.19). That entity is not responsible for the subject matter and so an evaluation shall be made of any threats the firm has reason to believe are created by interests/relationships with the party responsible for the subject matter (paragraph 291.19). There are several parties responsible for the subject matter in this engagement (Companies 1–10). As discussed in example A1 above, the firm may take into account whether an interest or relationship with a particular company would create a threat to independence that is not at an acceptable level.

D1 Each company provides the firm with a representation that measures its reserves against the established criteria for measuring proven reserves. The representation is not available to the intended users.

There are several responsible parties in this engagement (Companies 1–10). When determining whether it is necessary to apply the independence provisions to all of the companies, the firm may take into account whether an interest or relationship with a particular company would create a threat to independence that is not at an acceptable level. This will take into account factors such as:

- The materiality of the company's proven reserves in relation to the total reserves to be reported on; and

- The degree of public interest associated with the engagement (paragraph 291.28).

For example, Company 8 accounts for 0.17% of the reserves, therefore a business relationship or interest with Company 8 would create less of a threat than a similar relationship with Company 6 that accounts for approximately 37.5% of the reserves.

Having determined those companies to which the independence requirements apply, the assurance team and the firm shall be independent of those responsible parties that would be considered to be the assurance client (paragraph 291.28).

D2 The firm directly measures the reserves of some of the companies.

The application is the same as in example D1.

Part C—Professional accountants in business

Section 300

Introduction

300.1   This Part of the Code describes how the conceptual framework contained in Part A applies in certain situations to professional accountants in business. This Part does not describe all of the circumstances and relationships that could be encountered by a professional accountant in business that create or may create threats to compliance with the fundamental principles. Therefore, the professional accountant in business is encouraged to be alert for such circumstances and relationships.

300.2   Investors, creditors, employers and other sectors of the business community, as well as governments and the public at large, all may rely on the work of professional accountants in business. Professional accountants in business may be solely or jointly responsible for the preparation and reporting of financial and other information, which both their employing organizations and third parties may rely on. They may also be responsible for providing effective financial management and competent advice on a variety of business-related matters.

300.3   A professional accountant in business may be a salaried employee, a partner, director (whether executive or non-executive), an owner manager, a volunteer or another working for one or more employing organization. The legal form of the relationship with the employing organization, if any, has no bearing on the ethical responsibilities incumbent on the professional accountant in business.

300.4   A professional accountant in business has a responsibility to further the legitimate aims of the accountant's employing organization. This Code does not seek to hinder a professional accountant in business from properly fulfilling that responsibility, but addresses circumstances in which compliance with the fundamental principles may be compromised.

300.5   A professional accountant in business may hold a senior position within an organization. The more senior the position, the greater will be the ability and opportunity to influence events, practices and attitudes. A professional accountant in business is expected, therefore, to encourage an ethics-based culture in an employing organization that emphasizes the importance that senior management places on ethical behavior.

300.6   A professional accountant in business shall not knowingly engage in any business, occupation, or activity that impairs or might impair integrity, objectivity or the good reputation of the profession and as a result would be incompatible with the fundamental principles.

300.7   Compliance with the fundamental principles may potentially be threatened by a broad range of circumstances and relationships. Threats fall into one or more of the following categories:

(a)   Self-interest;
(b)   Self-review;
(c)   Advocacy;
(d)   Familiarity; and
(e)   Intimidation.

These threats are discussed further in Part A of this Code.

Examples of circumstances that may create self-interest threats for a professional accountant in business include: **300.8**

- Holding a financial interest in, or receiving a loan or guarantee from the employing organization.
- Participating in incentive compensation arrangements offered by the employing organization.
- Inappropriate personal use of corporate assets.
- Concern over employment security.
- Commercial pressure from outside the employing organization.

An example of a circumstance that creates a self-review threat for a professional accountant in business is determining the appropriate accounting treatment for a business combination after performing the feasibility study that supported the acquisition decision.   **300.9**

When furthering the legitimate goals and objectives of their employing organizations, professional accountants in business may promote the organization's position, provided any statements made are neither false nor misleading. Such actions generally would not create an advocacy threat.   **300.10**

Examples of circumstances that may create familiarity threats for a professional accountant in business include: **300.11**

- Being responsible for the employing organization's financial reporting when an immediate or close family member employed by the entity makes decisions that affect the entity's financial reporting.
- Long association with business contacts influencing business decisions.
- Accepting a gift or preferential treatment, unless the value is trivial and inconsequential.

Examples of circumstances that may create intimidation threats for a professional accountant in business include: **300.12**

- Threat of dismissal or replacement of the professional accountant in business or a close or immediate family member over a disagreement about the application of an accounting principle or the way in which financial information is to be reported.
- A dominant personality attempting to influence the decision making process, for example with regard to the awarding of contracts or the application of an accounting principle.

Safeguards that may eliminate or reduce threats to an acceptable level fall into two broad categories: **300.13**

(a) Safeguards created by the profession, legislation or regulation; and
(b) Safeguards in the work environment.

Examples of safeguards created by the profession, legislation or regulation are detailed in paragraph 100.14 of Part A of this Code.

Safeguards in the work environment include: **300.14**

- The employing organization's systems of corporate oversight or other oversight structures.
- The employing organization's ethics and conduct programs.
- Recruitment procedures in the employing organization emphasizing the importance of employing high caliber competent staff.

- Strong internal controls.
- Appropriate disciplinary processes.
- Leadership that stresses the importance of ethical behavior and the expectation that employees will act in an ethical manner.
- Policies and procedures to implement and monitor the quality of employee performance.
- Timely communication of the employing organization's policies and procedures, including any changes to them, to all employees and appropriate training and education on such policies and procedures.
- Policies and procedures to empower and encourage employees to communicate to senior levels within the employing organization any ethical issues that concern them without fear of retribution.
- Consultation with another appropriate professional accountant.

300.15 In circumstances where a professional accountant in business believes that unethical behavior or actions by others will continue to occur within the employing organization, the professional accountant in business may consider obtaining legal advice. In those extreme situations where all available safeguards have been exhausted and it is not possible to reduce the threat to an acceptable level, a professional accountant in business may conclude that it is appropriate to resign from the employing organization.

Section 310

Potential Conflicts

A professional accountant in business shall comply with the fundamental principles. **310.1** There may be times, however, when a professional accountant's responsibilities to an employing organization and professional obligations to comply with the fundamental principles are in conflict. A professional accountant in business is expected to support the legitimate and ethical objectives established by the employer and the rules and procedures drawn up in support of those objectives. Nevertheless, where a relationship or circumstance creates a threat to compliance with the fundamental principles, a professional accountant in business shall apply the conceptual framework approach described in Section 100 to determine a response to the threat.

As a consequence of responsibilities to an employing organization, a professional **310.2** accountant in business may be under pressure to act or behave in ways that could create threats to compliance with the fundamental principles. Such pressure may be explicit or implicit; it may come from a supervisor, manager, director or another individual within the employing organization. A professional accountant in business may face pressure to:

- Act contrary to law or regulation.
- Act contrary to technical or professional standards.
- Facilitate unethical or illegal earnings management strategies.
- Lie to others, or otherwise intentionally mislead (including misleading by remaining silent) others, in particular:
  o The auditors of the employing organization; or
  o Regulators.
- Issue, or otherwise be associated with, a financial or non-financial report that materially misrepresents the facts, including statements in connection with, for example:
  o The financial statements;
  o Tax compliance;
  o Legal compliance; or
  o Reports required by securities regulators.

The significance of any threats arising from such pressures, such as intimidation **310.3** threats, shall be evaluated and safeguards applied when necessary to eliminate them or reduce them to an acceptable level. Examples of such safeguards include:

- Obtaining advice, where appropriate, from within the employing organization, an independent professional advisor or a relevant professional body.
- Using a formal dispute resolution process within the employing organization.
- Seeking legal advice.

Section 320

Preparation and Reporting of Information

320.1 Professional accountants in business are often involved in the preparation and reporting of information that may either be made public or used by others inside or outside the employing organization. Such information may include financial or management information, for example, forecasts and budgets, financial statements, management's discussion and analysis, and the management letter of representation provided to the auditors during the audit of the entity's financial statements. A professional accountant in business shall prepare or present such information fairly, honestly and in accordance with relevant professional standards so that the information will be understood in its context.

320.2 A professional accountant in business who has responsibility for the preparation or approval of the general purpose financial statements of an employing organization shall be satisfied that those financial statements are presented in accordance with the applicable financial reporting standards.

320.3 A professional accountant in business shall take reasonable steps to maintain information for which the professional accountant in business is responsible in a manner that:

(a) Describes clearly the true nature of business transactions, assets, or liabilities;
(b) Classifies and records information in a timely and proper manner; and
(c) Represents the facts accurately and completely in all material respects.

320.4 Threats to compliance with the fundamental principles, for example, self-interest or intimidation threats to objectivity or professional competence and due care, are created where a professional accountant in business is pressured (either externally or by the possibility of personal gain) to become associated with misleading information or to become associated with misleading information through the actions of others.

320.5 The significance of such threats will depend on factors such as the source of the pressure and the degree to which the information is, or may be, misleading. The significance of the threats shall be evaluated and safeguards applied when necessary to eliminate them or reduce them to an acceptable level. Such safeguards include consultation with superiors within the employing organization, the audit committee or those charged with governance of the organization, or with a relevant professional body.

320.6 Where it is not possible to reduce the threat to an acceptable level, a professional accountant in business shall refuse to be or remain associated with information the professional accountant determines is misleading. A professional accountant in business may have been unknowingly associated with misleading information. Upon becoming aware of this, the professional accountant in business shall take steps to be disassociated from that information. In determining whether there is a requirement to report, the professional accountant in business may consider obtaining legal advice. In addition, the professional accountant may consider whether to resign.

Section 330

Acting with Sufficient Expertise

The fundamental principle of professional competence and due care requires that a **330.1** professional accountant in business only undertake significant tasks for which the professional accountant in business has, or can obtain, sufficient specific training or experience. A professional accountant in business shall not intentionally mislead an employer as to the level of expertise or experience possessed, nor shall a professional accountant in business fail to seek appropriate expert advice and assistance when required.

Circumstances that create a threat to a professional accountant in business per- **330.2** forming duties with the appropriate degree of professional competence and due care include having:

- Insufficient time for properly performing or completing the relevant duties.
- Incomplete, restricted or otherwise inadequate information for performing the duties properly.
- Insufficient experience, training and/or education.
- Inadequate resources for the proper performance of the duties.

The significance of the threat will depend on factors such as the extent to which the **330.3** professional accountant in business is working with others, relative seniority in the business, and the level of supervision and review applied to the work. The significance of the threat shall be evaluated and safeguards applied when necessary to eliminate the threat or reduce it to an acceptable level. Examples of such safeguards include:

- Obtaining additional advice or training.
- Ensuring that there is adequate time available for performing the relevant duties.
- Obtaining assistance from someone with the necessary expertise.
- Consulting, where appropriate, with:
  - Superiors within the employing organization;
  - Independent experts; or
  - A relevant professional body.

When threats cannot be eliminated or reduced to an acceptable level, professional **330.4** accountants in business shall determine whether to refuse to perform the duties in question. If the professional accountant in business determines that refusal is appropriate, the reasons for doing so shall be clearly communicated.

Section 340

Financial Interests

340.1   Professional accountants in business may have financial interests, or may know of financial interests of immediate or close family members, that, in certain circumstances, may create threats to compliance with the fundamental principles. For example, self-interest threats to objectivity or confidentiality may be created through the existence of the motive and opportunity to manipulate price sensitive information in order to gain financially. Examples of circumstances that may create self-interest threats include situations where the professional accountant in business or an immediate or close family member:

- Holds a direct or indirect financial interest in the employing organization and the value of that financial interest could be directly affected by decisions made by the professional accountant in business;
- Is eligible for a profit related bonus and the value of that bonus could be directly affected by decisions made by the professional accountant in business;
- Holds, directly or indirectly, share options in the employing organization, the value of which could be directly affected by decisions made by the professional accountant in business;
- Holds, directly or indirectly, share options in the employing organization which are, or will soon be, eligible for conversion; or
- May qualify for share options in the employing organization or performance related bonuses if certain targets are achieved.

340.2   The significance of any threat shall be evaluated and safeguards applied when necessary to eliminate the threat or reduce it to an acceptable level. In evaluating the significance of any threat, and, when necessary, determining the appropriate safeguards to be applied to eliminate the threat or reduce it to an acceptable level, a professional accountant in business shall evaluate the nature of the financial interest. This includes evaluating the significance of the financial interest and determining whether it is direct or indirect. What constitutes a significant or valuable stake in an organization will vary from individual to individual, depending on personal circumstances. Examples of such safeguards include:

- Policies and procedures for a committee independent of management to determine the level or form of remuneration of senior management.
- Disclosure of all relevant interests, and of any plans to trade in relevant shares to those charged with the governance of the employing organization, in accordance with any internal policies.
- Consultation, where appropriate, with superiors within the employing organization.
- Consultation, where appropriate, with those charged with the governance of the employing organization or relevant professional bodies.
- Internal and external audit procedures.
- Up-to-date education on ethical issues and on the legal restrictions and other regulations around potential insider trading.

340.3   A professional accountant in business shall neither manipulate information nor use confidential information for personal gain.

Section 350

Inducements

Receiving Offers

A professional accountant in business or an immediate or close family member may be offered an inducement. Inducements may take various forms, including gifts, hospitality, preferential treatment, and inappropriate appeals to friendship or loyalty.

350.1

Offers of inducements may create threats to compliance with the fundamental principles. When a professional accountant in business or an immediate or close family member is offered an inducement, the situation shall be evaluated. Self-interest threats to objectivity or confidentiality are created when an inducement is made in an attempt to unduly influence actions or decisions, encourage illegal or dishonest behavior, or obtain confidential information. Intimidation threats to objectivity or confidentiality are created if such an inducement is accepted and it is followed by threats to make that offer public and damage the reputation of either the professional accountant in business or an immediate or close family member.

350.2

The existence and significance of any threats will depend on the nature, value and intent behind the offer. If a reasonable and informed third party, weighing all the specific facts and circumstances, would consider the inducement insignificant and not intended to encourage unethical behavior, then a professional accountant in business may conclude that the offer is made in the normal course of business and may generally conclude that there is no significant threat to compliance with the fundamental principles.

350.3

The significance of any threats shall be evaluated and safeguards applied when necessary to eliminate them or reduce them to an acceptable level. When the threats cannot be eliminated or reduced to an acceptable level through the application of safeguards, a professional accountant in business shall not accept the inducement. As the real or apparent threats to compliance with the fundamental principles do not merely arise from acceptance of an inducement but, sometimes, merely from the fact of the offer having been made, additional safeguards shall be adopted. A professional accountant in business shall evaluate any threats created by such offers and determine whether to take one or more of the following actions:

350.4

(a) Informing higher levels of management or those charged with governance of the employing organization immediately when such offers have been made;

(b) Informing third parties of the offer – for example, a professional body or the employer of the individual who made the offer; a professional accountant in business may however, consider seeking legal advice before taking such a step; and

(c) Advising immediate or close family members of relevant threats and safeguards where they are potentially in positions that might result in offers of inducements, for example, as a result of their employment situation; and

(d) Informing higher levels of management or those charged with governance of the employing organization where immediate or close family members are employed by competitors or potential suppliers of that organization.

Making Offers

350.5   A professional accountant in business may be in a situation where the professional accountant in business is expected, or is under other pressure, to offer inducements to influence the judgment or decision-making process of an individual or organization, or obtain confidential information.

350.6   Such pressure may come from within the employing organization, for example, from a colleague or superior. It may also come from an external individual or organization suggesting actions or business decisions that would be advantageous to the employing organization, possibly influencing the professional accountant in business improperly.

350.7   A professional accountant in business shall not offer an inducement to improperly influence professional judgment of a third party.

350.8   Where the pressure to offer an unethical inducement comes from within the employing organization, the professional accountant shall follow the principles and guidance regarding ethical conflict resolution set out in Part A of this Code.

Definitions

In this *Code of Ethics for Professional Accountants*, the following expressions have the following meanings assigned to them:

Acceptable level A level at which a reasonable and informed third party would be likely to conclude, weighing all the specific facts and circumstances available to the professional accountant at that time, that compliance with the fundamental principles is not compromised.

Advertising The communication to the public of information as to the services or skills provided by professional accountants in public practice with a view to procuring professional business.

Assurance client The responsible party that is the person (or persons) who:

(a) In a direct reporting engagement, is responsible for the subject matter; or

(b) In an assertion-based engagement, is responsible for the subject matter information and may be responsible for the subject matter.

Assurance An engagement in which a professional accountant in public engagement practice expresses a conclusion designed to enhance the degree of confidence of the intended users other than the responsible party about the outcome of the evaluation or measurement of a subject matter against criteria.

(For guidance on assurance engagements see the International Framework for Assurance Engagements issued by the International Auditing and Assurance Standards Board which describes the elements and objectives of an assurance engagement and identifies engagements to which International Standards on Auditing (ISAs), International Standards on Review Engagements (ISREs) and International Standards on Assurance Engagements (ISAEs) apply.)

Assurance team (a) All members of the engagement team for the assurance engagement;

(b) All others within a firm who can directly influence the outcome of the assurance engagement, including:

(i) Those who recommend the compensation of, or who provide direct supervisory, management or other oversight of the assurance engagement partner in connection with the performance of the assurance engagement;

(ii) Those who provide consultation regarding technical or industry specific issues, transactions or events for the assurance engagement; and

(iii) Those who provide quality control for the assurance engagement, including those who perform the engagement quality control review for the assurance engagement.

Audit client	An entity in respect of which a firm conducts an audit engagement. When the client is a listed entity, audit client will always include its related entities. When the audit client is not a listed entity, audit client includes those related entities over which the client has direct or indirect control.
Audit engagement	A reasonable assurance engagement in which a professional accountant in public practice expresses an opinion whether financial statements are prepared, in all material respects (or give a true and fair view or are presented fairly, in all material respects,), in accordance with an applicable financial reporting framework, such as an engagement conducted in accordance with International Standards on Auditing. This includes a Statutory Audit, which is an audit required by legislation or other regulation.
Audit team	(a) All members of the engagement team for the audit engagement;

(b) All others within a firm who can directly influence the outcome of the audit engagement, including:

    (i) Those who recommend the compensation of, or who provide direct supervisory, management or other oversight of the engagement partner in connection with the performance of the audit engagement including those at all successively senior levels above the engagement partner through to the individual who is the firm's Senior or Managing Partner (Chief Executive or equivalent);

    (ii) Those who provide consultation regarding technical or industry-specific issues, transactions or events for the engagement; and

    (iii) Those who provide quality control for the engagement, including those who perform the engagement quality control review for the engagement; and

(c) All those within a network firm who can directly influence the outcome of the audit engagement.

Close family	A parent, child or sibling who is not an immediate family member.
Contingent fee	A fee calculated on a predetermined basis relating to the outcome of a transaction or the result of the services performed by the firm. A fee that is established by a court or other public authority is not a contingent fee.
Direct financial interest	A financial interest:

(a) Owned directly by and under the control of an individual or entity (including those managed on a discretionary basis by others); or

(b) Beneficially owned through a collective investment vehicle, estate, trust or other intermediary over which the individual or entity has control, or the ability to influence investment decisions.

Director or officer	Those charged with the governance of an entity, or acting in an equivalent capacity, regardless of their title, which may vary from jurisdiction to jurisdiction.

Engagement partner	The partner or other person in the firm who is responsible for the engagement and its performance, and for the report that is issued on behalf of the firm, and who, where required, has the appropriate authority from a professional, legal or regulatory body.
Engagement quality control review	A process designed to provide an objective evaluation, on or before the report is issued, of the significant judgments the engagement team made and the conclusions it reached in formulating the report.
Engagement team	All partners and staff performing the engagement, and any individuals engaged by the firm or a network firm who perform assurance procedures on the engagement. This excludes external experts engaged by the firm or a network firm.
Existing accountant	A professional accountant in public practice currently holding an audit appointment or carrying out accounting, taxation, consulting or similar professional services for a client.
External expert	An individual (who is not a partner or a member of the professional staff, including temporary staff, of the firm or a network firm) or organization possessing skills, knowledge and experience in a field other than accounting or auditing, whose work in that field is used to assist the professional accountant in obtaining sufficient appropriate evidence.
Financial interest	An interest in an equity or other security, debenture, loan or other debt instrument of an entity, including rights and obligations to acquire such an interest and derivatives directly related to such interest.
Financial statements	A structured representation of historical financial information, including related notes, intended to communicate an entity's economic resources or obligations at a point in time or the changes therein for a period of time in accordance with a financial reporting framework. The related notes ordinarily comprise a summary of significant accounting policies and other explanatory information. The term can relate to a complete set of financial statements, but it can also refer to a single financial statement, for example, a balance sheet, or a statement of revenues and expenses, and related explanatory notes.
Financial statements on which the firm will express an opinion	In the case of a single entity, the financial statements of that entity. In the case of consolidated financial statements, also referred to as group financial statements, the consolidated financial statements.
Firm	(a) A sole practitioner, partnership or corporation of professional accountants; (b) An entity that controls such parties, through ownership, management or other means; and (c) An entity controlled by such parties, through ownership, management or other means.

Historical financial information	Information expressed in financial terms in relation to a particular entity, derived primarily from that entity's accounting system, about economic events occurring in past time periods or about economic conditions or circumstances at points in time in the past.
Immediate family	A spouse (or equivalent) or dependent.
Independence	Independence is: (a) Independence of mind – the state of mind that permits the expression of a conclusion without being affected by influences that compromise professional judgment, thereby allowing an individual to act with integrity, and exercise objectivity and professional skepticism. (b) Independence in appearance – the avoidance of facts and circumstances that are so significant that a reasonable and informed third party would be likely to conclude, weighing all the specific facts and circumstances, that a firm's, or a member of the audit or assurance team's, integrity, objectivity or professional skepticism has been compromised.
Indirect financial interest	A financial interest beneficially owned through a collective investment vehicle, estate, trust or other intermediary over which the individual or entity has no control or ability to influence investment decisions.
Key audit partner	The engagement partner, the individual responsible for the engagement quality control review, and other audit partners, if any, on the engagement team who make key decisions or judgments on significant matters with respect to the audit of the financial statements on which the firm will express an opinion. Depending upon the circumstances and the role of the individuals on the audit, "other audit partners" may include, for example, audit partners responsible for significant subsidiaries or divisions.
Listed entity	An entity whose shares, stock or debt are quoted or listed on a recognized stock exchange, or are marketed under the regulations of a recognized stock exchange or other equivalent body.
Network	A larger structure: (a) That is aimed at co-operation; and (b) That is clearly aimed at profit or cost sharing or shares common ownership, control or management, common quality control policies and procedures, common business strategy, the use of a common brand-name, or a significant part of professional resources.
Network firm	A firm or entity that belongs to a network.
Office	A distinct sub-group, whether organized on geographical or practice lines
Professional accountant	An individual who is a member of an IFAC member body.

Professional accountant in business	A professional accountant employed or engaged in an executive or non-executive capacity in such areas as commerce, industry, service, the public sector, education, the not for profit sector, regulatory bodies or professional bodies, or a professional accountant contracted by such entities.
Professional accountant in public practice	A professional accountant, irrespective of functional classification (for example, audit, tax or consulting) in a firm that provides professional services. This term is also used to refer to a firm of professional accountants in public practice.
Professional services	Services requiring accountancy or related skills performed by a professional accountant including accounting, auditing, taxation, management consulting and financial management services.

Public interest entity

    (a) A listed entity; and

    (b) An entity:

        (i) Defined by regulation or legislation as a public interest entity; or

        (ii) For which the audit is required by regulation or legislation to be conducted in compliance with the same independence requirements that apply to the audit of listed entities. Such regulation may be promulgated by any relevant regulator, including an audit regulator.

Related entity

An entity that has any of the following relationships with the client:

    (a) An entity that has direct or indirect control over the client if the client is material to such entity;

    (b) An entity with a direct financial interest in the client if that entity has significant influence over the client and the interest in the client is material to such entity;

    (c) An entity over which the client has direct or indirect control;

    (d) An entity in which the client, or an entity related to the client under (c) above, has a direct financial interest that gives it significant influence over such entity and the interest is material to the client and its related entity in (c); and

    (e) An entity which is under common control with the client (a "sister entity") if the sister entity and the client are both material to the entity that controls both the client and sister entity.

Review client

An entity in respect of which a firm conducts a review engagement.

Review engagement	An assurance engagement, conducted in accordance with International Standards on Review Engagements or equivalent, in which a professional accountant in public practice expresses a conclusion on whether, on the basis of the procedures which do not provide all the evidence that would be required in an audit, anything has come to the accountant's attention that causes the accountant to believe that the financial statements are not prepared, in all material respects, in accordance with an applicable financial reporting framework.

Review team

(a) All members of the engagement team for the review engagement; and

(b) All others within a firm who can directly influence the outcome of the review engagement, including:

    (i) Those who recommend the compensation of, or who provide direct supervisory, management or other oversight of the engagement partner in connection with the performance of the review engagement including those at all successively senior levels above the engagement partner through to the individual who is the firm's Senior or Managing Partner (Chief Executive or equivalent);

    (ii) Those who provide consultation regarding technical or industry specific issues, transactions or events for the engagement; and

    (iii) Those who provide quality control for the engagement, including those who perform the engagement quality control review for the engagement; and

(c) All those within a network firm who can directly influence the outcome of the review engagement.

Special purpose financial statements	Financial statements prepared in accordance with a financial reporting framework designed to meet the financial information needs of specified users.
Those charged with governance	The persons with responsibility for overseeing the strategic direction of the entity and obligations related to the accountability of the entity. This includes overseeing the financial reporting process.

Effective Date

This Code is effective on January 1, 2011; early adoption is permitted. The Code is subject to the following transitional provisions:

Public Interest Entities

1 Section 290 of the Code contains additional independence provisions when the audit or review client is a public interest entity. The additional provisions that are applicable because of the new definition of a public interest entity or the guidance in paragraph 290.26 are effective on January 1, 2012. For partner rotation requirements, the transitional provisions contained in paragraphs 2 and 3 below apply.

Partner Rotation

For a partner who is subject to the rotation provisions in paragraph 290.151 because **2** the partner meets the definition of the new term "key audit partner," and the partner is neither the engagement partner nor the individual responsible for the engagement quality control review, the rotation provisions are effective for the audits or reviews of financial statements for years beginning on or after December 15, 2011. For example, in the case of an audit client with a calendar year-end, a key audit partner, who is neither the engagement partner nor the individual responsible for the engagement quality control review, who had served as a key audit partner for seven or more years (that is, the audits of 2003–2010), would be required to rotate after serving for one more year as a key audit partner (that is, after completing the 2011 audit).

For an engagement partner or an individual responsible for the engagement quality **3** control review who immediately prior to assuming either of these roles served in another key audit partner role for the client, and who, at the beginning of the first fiscal year beginning on or after December 15, 2010, had served as the engagement partner or individual responsible for the engagement quality control review for six or fewer years, the rotation provisions are effective for the audits or reviews of financial statements for years beginning on or after December 15, 2011. For example, in the case of an audit client with a calendar year-end, a partner who had served the client in another key audit partner role for four years (that is, the audits of 2002–2005) and subsequently as the engagement partner for five years (that is, the audits of 2006–2010) would be required to rotate after serving for one more year as the engagement partner (that is, after completing the 2011 audit).

Non-assurance Services

Paragraphs 290.156–290.219 address the provision of non-assurance services to an **4** audit or review client. If, at the effective date of the Code, services are being provided to an audit or review client and the services were permissible under the June 2005 Code (revised July 2006) but are either prohibited or subject to restrictions under the revised Code, the firm may continue providing such services only if they were contracted for and commenced prior to January 1, 2011, and are completed before July 1, 2011.

Fees—Relative Size

Paragraph 290.222 provides that, in respect of an audit or review client that is a **5** public interest entity, when the total fees from that client and its related entities (subject to the considerations in paragraph 290.27) for two consecutive years represent more than 15% of the total fees of the firm expressing the opinion on the financial statements, a pre-or post-issuance review (as described in paragraph 290.222) of the second year's audit shall be performed. This requirement is effective for audits or reviews of financial statements covering years that begin on or after December 15, 2010. For example, in the case of an audit client with a calendar year end, if the total fees from the client exceeded the 15% threshold for 2011 and 2012, the pre-or post-issuance review would be applied with respect to the audit of the 2012 financial statements.

Compensation and Evaluation Policies

6   Paragraph 290.229 provides that a key audit partner shall not be evaluated or compensated based on that partner's success in selling non-assurance services to the partner's audit client. This requirement is effective on January 1, 2012. A key audit partner may, however, receive compensation after January 1, 2012 based on an evaluation made prior to January 1, 2012 of that partner's success in selling non-assurance services to the audit client.

ICAEW Code of Ethics

Contents

Effective from 1 January 2011. Where guidance relates to projects or engagements commencing prior to that date, previous guidance may be applied up to completion of the project or engagement. Transitional arrangements are available in respect of Independence – Audit and Review Engagements (section 290).

Approach, scope and authority

- **Introduction**
- **Approach**
- **Scope**
- **Authority**
- **Relationship with other ethical requirements**
- **Sources of guidance**

Introduction

1.1   One of the principal objects of the Royal Charter is to maintain a high standard of efficiency and professional conduct by member firms where relevant. These are referred to in the remainder of this Code as professional accountants.

1.2   Professional accountants have a responsibility to take into consideration the public interest (considered in more detail in paragraph 100.1) and to maintain the reputation of the accountancy profession. Personal self-interest must not prevail over those duties. This Code helps professional accountants to meet these obligations by providing them with ethical guidance. Failure to follow this Code may lead to a professional accountant becoming liable to disciplinary action as outlined in the Disciplinary Bye-laws 4, 5, 6 and 6A.

Approach

1.3   Guidance is given in the form of fundamental principles and illustrations of how they are to be applied in specific situations. These are available at www.icaew.com/ethics. The fundamental principles are drawn from the duties owed by professional accountants, whether in practice or not, and from the requirements of the Royal Charter. They are framed in broad and general terms and constitute basic requirements of professional behaviour. The illustrations provide guidance on what is expected of professional accountants in relation to particular situations that commonly arise either in practice or in business. The value of this principles-based approach is that it avoids excessive legalism by not having to anticipate every contingency, whilst at the same time being helpful in giving examples of problem situations. In some instances, prohibitions or mandatory actions arise from the analysis of threats: these are considered further in paragraph 100.12.

Scope

1.4   Professional accountants shall follow the guidance contained in the fundamental principles in all of their professional and business activities whether carried out with or without reward and in other circumstances where to fail to do so would bring discredit to the profession. This Code also includes a number of specific requirements, which are shown by use of the word 'shall'. This means that a professional accountant shall follow the requirements, including prohibitions or mandatory actions, where circumstances are the same as, or analogous to, those addressed by those requirements. Failure to follow such guidance may be justified in those rare circumstances where to follow a precise prohibition or mandated action would result in failure to adhere to the fundamental principles.

For convenience, the illustrations in this Code are grouped into parts applicable principally to professional accountants working in public practice, business and insolvency respectively, but professional accountants may find any of them of use in relevant circumstances. **1.5**

Professional accountants shall be guided not merely by the terms but also by the spirit of this Code and the fact that particular conduct does not appear among a list of examples does not prevent it amounting to misconduct. **1.6**

Professional accountants shall ensure that work for which they are responsible, which is undertaken by others on their behalf, is carried out in accordance with the requirements of this Code. **1.7**

Member firms are reminded that this Code applies to their employees, whether members or not, and that they are responsible for applying this requirement. **1.8**

Certain areas of work are reserved by statute to professional accountants who are in practice, whether or not with other persons, namely investment business, insolvency and audit. In these areas professional accountants may be subject to rules laid down by laws and regulation, breach of which can give rise to disciplinary proceedings against the professional accountant. **1.9**

If the advice in this Code conflicts with laws and regulations, professional accountants are bound to follow the laws and regulations. **1.10**

Professional accountants working overseas shall comply with this Code unless to do so would breach local laws and regulations. **1.11**

Authority

In determining whether or not a complaint is proved, the Investigation and Disciplinary Committees may have regard to any code of practice, ethical or technical, and to any regulations affecting professional accountants, laid down or approved by the ICAEW's Council. **1.12**

Paragraph 100.2 notes that safeguards are required to be put into place to eliminate or reduce the threats to an acceptable level. In the event of a complaint, the Investigation and Disciplinary Committees will consider the matter, including whether a reasonable and informed third party would conclude, weighing all the specific facts and circumstances available to the professional accountant at that time, that compliance with the fundamental principles is compromised. **1.13**

Relationship with other ethical requirements

Except as noted below, this Code has been derived from the International Ethics Standards Board of Accountants (IESBA) Code of Ethics issued in July 2009 by the International Federation of Accountants. Accordingly, compliance with the remainder of this Code will ensure compliance with the principles of the IESBA **1.14**

Code. Paragraph numbering in the rest of this Code replicates that used in the IESBA Code of Ethics, except in respect of:

- Sections 221, 241 and Part D which have no direct equivalent in the IESBA Code of Ethics;
- Text framed in grey in parts A, B and C is where ICAEW's Council considers additional discussion and/or requirements to be useful or necessary.
- The fact that wording is or is not framed in grey does not indicate any difference in the degree of importance that should be attached to it.
- A direct link has been retained to paragraph numbering in the IESBA Code of Ethics. However, as a result of the additional discussion and requirements noted above, and deletion of material that is not applicable to the professional accountants of the ICAEW, the paragraph referencing in this Code is not necessarily consecutive.

1.15 In accordance with UK legislation, ICAEW has adopted, as regards auditor audit engagements in accordance with ISAs (UK and Ireland), professional accountants shall comply with the requirements of the APB's Ethical Standards for Auditors, including Provisions Available for Small Entities (ES-PASE). For other audit and assurance engagements ICAEW's Code may apply (see 1.17 below).

1.16 The APB has stated, in ISA (UK and Ireland) 200, that it is not aware of any significant instances where the relevant parts of IESBA Code of Ethics are more restrictive than the APB's Ethical Standards.

1.17 The independence requirements to be adopted for different types of assurance engagement, are set out below:

Type of assurance engagement	Independence requirements to be followed
Audit engagements in accordance with ISAs (UK and Ireland)	APB's Ethical Standards for Auditors
Audit engagements performed in accordance with other standards	Section 290 of this Code or if more convenient to apply, the independence requirements of the APB's Ethical Standards for Auditors.
Review engagements (see appendix to section 290)	Section 290 of this Code or if more convenient to apply, the independence requirements of the APB's Ethical Standards for Auditors.
Other types of assurance engagements	Section 291 of this Code.

1.18 Note that the Statements of Investment Circular Reporting Standards (SIRS), issued by the APB require compliance with the APB's Ethical Standard for Reporting Accountants (ESRA). Accordingly, any professional accountant in public practice issuing a report that states that the work has been carried out in accordance with the SIRS will need to comply with the independence requirements of the ESRA.

Sources of guidance

1.19 Professional accountants who are in doubt as to their ethical position may seek advice from the following sources, available to all members of ICAEW:

- ICAEW's Technical Advisory Services by email: ethics@icaew.com or phone +44 (0)1908 248250. This service is confidential and the advisors are free from the duty to report professional misconduct within ICAEW. Further information on the Technical Advisory Services can be found at www.icaew.com/ethicsadvice, along with helpsheets and answers to a number of frequently asked questions.
- The Support Members Scheme. This is wider in scope than the Technical Advisory Services. The Support Members Scheme is run by volunteer members of the ICAEW from a wide range of backgrounds. It is a confidential, free service exempt from the duty to report misconduct and provides advice and help to members in difficulties. A member can contact the Support Members Scheme by phone on +44 (0) 800 917 3526.

Seeking advice from the Technical Advisory Services does not discharge a professional accountant's duty to report misconduct, including their own misconduct (see 'The duty to report misconduct'). **1.20**

A professional accountant is encouraged to consider taking legal advice to resolve issues arising from the application of laws and regulations to particular situations relating to confidentiality, disclosure, privilege, self-incrimination and other areas. **1.21**

Additional information on ethics, including case studies is available at www.icaew.com/ethics. These case studies provide practical guidance for resolving ethical dilemmas on topics such as conflicts of interest, confidentiality and questionable accounting and business practices. **1.22**

Code of Ethics A

Effective from 1st January 2011. This section establishes the fundamental principles of professional ethics for professional accountants and provides a conceptual framework that professional accountants can follow.

Except as noted below, this Code has been derived from the International Ethics Standards Board of Accountants' (IESBA) Code of Ethics issued in July 2009 by the International Federation of Accountants. Accordingly, compliance with the remainder of this Code will ensure compliance with the principles of the IESBA Code. Paragraph numbering in the rest of this Code replicates that used in the IESBA Code of Ethics, except in respect of Sections 221, 241 and Part D which have no direct equivalent in the IESBA Code of Ethics.

Wording replicates the IESBA Code of Ethics.

Text framed in grey is where ICAEW's Council considers additional discussion and/ or requirements to be useful or necessary.

The fact that wording is or is not framed in grey does not indicate any difference in the degree of importance that should be attached to it.

- **100 Introduction and fundamental principles**
  - o   Fundamental principles
  - o   Conceptual framework approach
  - o   Threats and safeguards
  - o   Ethical conflict resolution
- **110 Integrity**
- **120 Objectivity**
- **130 Professional competence and due care**
- **140 Confidentiality**
  - o   The principle of confidentiality
  - o   Disclosure of confidential information
- **150 Professional behaviour**
- **Appendix**

100 Introduction and fundamental principles

100.1   A distinguishing mark of the accountancy profession is its acceptance of the responsibility to act in the public interest.

Acting in the public interest involves having regard to the legitimate interests of clients, government, financial institutions, employers, employees, investors, the business and financial community and others who rely upon the objectivity and integrity of the accounting profession to support the propriety and orderly functioning of commerce. This reliance imposes a public interest responsibility on the profession. Professional accountants shall take into consideration the public interest and reasonable and informed public perception in deciding whether to accept or continue with an engagement or appointment, bearing in mind that the level of the public interest will be greater in larger entities and entities which are in the public eye.

Therefore, a professional accountant's responsibility is not exclusively to satisfy the needs of an individual client or employer. In acting in the public interest, a professional accountant shall observe and comply with this Code. If a professional accountant is prohibited from complying with certain parts of this Code by law or regulation, the professional accountant shall comply with all other parts of this Code.

This Code contains four parts. Part A establishes the fundamental principles of professional ethics for professional accountants and provides a conceptual framework that professional accountants shall apply to: **100.2**

- Identify threats to compliance with the fundamental principles;
- Evaluate the significance of the threats identified; and
- Apply safeguards, when necessary, to eliminate the threats or reduce them to an acceptable level. Safeguards are necessary when the professional accountant determines that the threats are not at a level at which a reasonable and informed third party would be likely to conclude, weighing all the specific facts and circumstances available to the professional accountant at that time, that compliance with the fundamental principles is not compromised.

A professional accountant shall use professional judgment in applying this conceptual framework.

Where a professional accountant decides to accept or continue an engagement, appointment, task or employment in a situation where a significant threat to the fundamental principles has been identified, the professional accountant is expected to be able to demonstrate that the availability and effectiveness of safeguards has been considered and that it was reasonable to conclude that those safeguards will adequately preserve their compliance with the fundamental principles. It may be useful to document the reasoning and other evidence which supports the evaluation of threats and safeguards to such an extent that it enables a reasonable and informed third party to conclude that the decisions are acceptable.

Parts B and C describe how the conceptual framework applies in certain situations. They provide examples of safeguards that may be appropriate to address threats to compliance with the fundamental principles. They also describe situations where safeguards are not available to address the threats, and consequently, the circumstance or relationship creating the threats shall be avoided. Part B applies to professional accountants in public practice. Part C applies to professional accountants in business. Professional accountants in public practice may also find Part C relevant to their particular circumstances. **100.3**

Part D deals with professional accountants undertaking insolvency work.

The use of the word "shall" in this Code imposes a requirement on the professional accountant or firm to comply with the specific provision in which "shall" has been used. Compliance is required unless an exception is permitted by this Code. (See Code of Ethics 1.4) **100.4**

Fundamental principles

A professional accountant shall comply with the following fundamental principles: **100.5**

- **Integrity** – to be straightforward and honest in all professional and business relationships.
- **Objectivity** – to not allow bias, conflict of interest or undue influence of others to override professional or business judgments.
- **Professional competence and due care** – to maintain professional knowledge and skill at the level required to ensure that a client or employer receives competent

professional services based on current developments in practice, legislation and techniques and act diligently and in accordance with applicable technical and professional standards.

- **Confidentiality** – to respect the confidentiality of information acquired as a result of professional and business relationships and, therefore, not disclose any such information to third parties without proper and specific authority, unless there is a legal or professional right or duty to disclose, nor use the information for the personal advantage of the professional accountant or third parties.
- **Professional behaviour** – to comply with relevant laws and regulations and avoid any action that discredits the profession.

Each of these fundamental principles is discussed in more detail in sections 110-150.

Conceptual framework approach

100.6   The circumstances in which professional accountants operate may create specific threats to compliance with the fundamental principles. It is impossible to define every situation that creates threats to compliance with the fundamental principles and specify the appropriate action. In addition, the nature of engagements and work assignments may differ and, consequently, different threats may be created, requiring the application of different safeguards. Therefore, this Code establishes a conceptual framework that requires a professional accountant to identify, evaluate, and address threats to compliance with the fundamental principles. The conceptual framework approach assists professional accountants in complying with the ethical requirements of this Code and meeting their responsibility to act in the public interest. It accommodates many variations in circumstances that create threats to compliance with the fundamental principles and can deter a professional accountant from concluding that a situation is permitted if it is not specifically prohibited.

100.7   When a professional accountant identifies threats to compliance with the fundamental principles and, based on an evaluation of those threats, determines that they are not at an acceptable level, the professional accountant shall determine whether appropriate safeguards are available and can be applied to eliminate the threats or reduce them to an acceptable level. In making that determination, the professional accountant shall exercise professional judgment and take into account whether a reasonable and informed third party, weighing all the specific facts and circumstances available to the professional accountant at the time, would be likely to conclude that the threats would be eliminated or reduced to an acceptable level by the application of the safeguards, such that compliance with the fundamental principles is not compromised.

100.8   A professional accountant shall evaluate any threats to compliance with the fundamental principles when the professional accountant knows, or could reasonably be expected to know, of circumstances or relationships that may compromise compliance with the fundamental principles.

100.9   A professional accountant shall take qualitative as well as quantitative factors into account when evaluating the significance of a threat. When applying the conceptual framework, a professional accountant may encounter situations in which threats cannot be eliminated or reduced to an acceptable level, either because the threat is too significant or because appropriate safeguards are not available or cannot be applied. In such situations, the professional accountant shall decline or discontinue the specific professional service involved or, when necessary, resign from the engagement (in the case of a professional accountant in public practice) or the employing organisation (in the case of a professional accountant in business).

A professional accountant may inadvertently violate a provision of this Code. **100.10** Depending on the nature and significance of the matter, such an inadvertent violation may be deemed not to compromise compliance with the fundamental principles provided, once the violation is discovered, the violation is corrected promptly and any necessary safeguards are applied.

When a professional accountant encounters unusual circumstances in which the **100.11** application of a specific requirement of the Code would result in a disproportionate outcome or an outcome that may not be in the public interest, it is recommended that the professional accountant consult with ICAEW (see Sources of Guidance in section 1 of this Code) or the relevant regulator.

Threats may be created by a broad range of relationships and circumstances. When a **100.12** relationship or circumstance creates a threat, such a threat could compromise, or could be perceived to compromise, a professional accountant's compliance with the fundamental principles. A circumstance or relationship may create more than one threat, and a threat may affect compliance with more than one fundamental principle. Threats fall into one or more of the following categories:

- Self-interest threat – the threat that a financial or other interest will inappropriately influence the professional accountant's judgment or behaviour;
- Self-review threat – the threat that a professional accountant will not appropriately evaluate the results of a previous judgment made or service performed by the professional accountant, or by another individual within the professional accountant's firm or employing organisation, on which the accountant will rely when forming a judgment as part of providing a current service;
- Advocacy threat – the threat that a professional accountant will promote a client's or employer's position to the point that the professional accountant's objectivity is compromised;
- Familiarity threat – the threat that due to a long or close relationship with a client or employer, a professional accountant will be too sympathetic to their interests or too accepting of their work; and
- Intimidation threat – the threat that a professional accountant will be deterred from acting objectively because of actual or perceived pressures, including attempts to exercise undue influence over the professional accountant.

Parts B and C of this Code explain how these categories of threats may be created for professional accountants in public practice and professional accountants in business, respectively. Professional accountants in public practice may also find Part C relevant to their particular circumstances.

Code of Ethics Part D deals with professional accountants undertaking insolvency work.

Professional accountants shall note that each of the categories of threat discussed above may arise in relation to the professional accountant's own person or in relation to connected persons such as members of their family or partners or persons who are close to the professional accountants for some other reason, for instance by reason of a past or present association, obligation or indebtedness.

Threats and safeguards

Safeguards are actions or other measures that may eliminate threats or reduce them **100.13** to an acceptable level. They fall into two broad categories:

- Safeguards created by the profession, legislation or regulation; and

- Safeguards in the work environment.

100.14   Safeguards created by the profession, legislation or regulation include:

- Educational, training and experience requirements for entry into the profession.
- Continuing professional development requirements.
- Corporate governance regulations.
- Professional standards.
- Professional or regulatory monitoring and disciplinary procedures.
- External review by a legally empowered third party of the reports, returns, communications or information produced by a professional accountant.

100.15   Parts B and C of this Code discuss safeguards in the work environment for professional accountants in public practice and professional accountants in business, respectively.

100.16   Certain safeguards may increase the likelihood of identifying or deterring unethical behaviour. Such safeguards, which may be created by the accounting profession, legislation, regulation, or an employing organisation, include:

- Effective, well-publicised complaint systems operated by the employing organisation, the profession or a regulator, which enable colleagues, employers and members of the public to draw attention to unprofessional or unethical behaviour.
- An explicitly stated duty to report breaches of ethical requirements.

Ethical conflict resolution

100.17   A professional accountant may be required to resolve a conflict in complying with the fundamental principles.

100.18   When initiating either a formal or informal conflict resolution process, the following factors, either individually or together with other factors, may be relevant to the resolution process:

- Relevant facts;
- Relevant parties;
- Ethical issues involved;
- Fundamental principles related to the matter in question;
- Established internal procedures; and
- Alternative courses of action.

Having considered the relevant factors, a professional accountant shall determine the appropriate course of action, weighing the consequences of each possible course of action. If the matter remains unresolved, the professional accountant may wish to consult with other appropriate persons within the firm or employing organisation for help in obtaining resolution.

It will generally be preferable for the ethical conflict to be resolved within the employing organisation before consulting individuals outside the employing organisation.

100.19   Where a matter involves a conflict with, or within, an organisation, a professional accountant shall determine whether to consult with those charged with governance of the organisation, such as the board of directors or the audit committee.

It may be in the best interests of the professional accountant to document the sub- **100.20**
stance of the issue, the details of any discussions held, and the decisions made
concerning that issue.

If a significant conflict cannot be resolved, a professional accountant may consider **100.21**
obtaining professional advice from ICAEW or from legal advisors. The professional
accountant generally can obtain guidance on ethical issues without breaching the
fundamental principle of confidentiality if the matter is discussed with ICAEW's
ethics helpline or with a legal advisor under the protection of legal privilege.
Instances in which the professional accountant may consider obtaining legal advice
vary. For example, a professional accountant may have encountered a fraud, the
reporting of which could breach the professional accountant's responsibility to
respect confidentiality. The professional accountant may consider obtaining legal
advice in that instance to determine whether there is a requirement to report.

Further information on sources of guidance is available in section 1.

If, after exhausting all relevant possibilities, the ethical conflict remains unresolved, a **100.22**
professional accountant shall, where possible, refuse to remain associated with the
matter creating the conflict. The professional accountant shall determine whether, in
the circumstances, it is appropriate to withdraw from the engagement team or specific assignment, or to resign altogether from the engagement, the firm or the
employing organisation.

More detailed guidance on the ethical conflict resolution process is available in the
Appendix to Part A.

110 Integrity

The principle of integrity imposes an obligation on all professional accountants to be **110.1**
straightforward and honest in all professional and business relationships. Integrity
also implies fair dealing and truthfulness.

It follows that a professional accountant's advice and work must be uncorrupted by
self-interest and not be influenced by the interests of other parties.

A professional accountant shall not knowingly be associated with reports, returns, **110.2**
communications or other information where the professional accountant believes
that the information:

- Contains a materially false or misleading statement;
- Contains statements or information furnished recklessly; or
- Omits or obscures information required to be included where such omission or
  obscurity would be misleading.

When a professional accountant becomes aware that the accountant has been
associated with such information, the accountant shall take steps to be disassociated
from that information.

A professional accountant will be deemed not to be in breach of paragraph 110.2 if **110.3**
the professional accountant provides a modified report in respect of a matter contained in paragraph 110.2.

Further discussion on integrity, which is not part of the Code requirements, is
available at www.icaew.com/ethics.

120 Objectivity

120.1   The principle of objectivity imposes an obligation on all professional accountants not to compromise their professional or business judgment because of bias, conflict of interest or the undue influence of others.

Objectivity is the state of mind which has regard to all considerations relevant to the task in hand but no other.

120.2   A professional accountant may be exposed to situations that may impair objectivity. It is impracticable to define and prescribe all such situations. A professional accountant shall not perform a professional service if a circumstance or relationship biases or unduly influences the accountant's professional judgment with respect to that service.

130 Professional competence and due care

130.1   The principle of professional competence and due care imposes the following obligations on all professional accountants:

- To maintain professional knowledge and skill at the level required to ensure that clients or employers receive competent professional service; and
- To act diligently in accordance with applicable technical and professional standards when providing professional services.

130.2   Competent professional service requires the exercise of sound judgment in applying professional knowledge and skill in the performance of such service. Professional competence may be divided into two separate phases:

- Attainment of professional competence; and
- Maintenance of professional competence.

130.3   The maintenance of professional competence requires a continuing awareness and an understanding of relevant technical, professional and business developments. Continuing professional development enables a professional accountant to develop and maintain the capabilities to perform competently within the professional environment.

Further guidance on continuing professional development is available at www.icaew. com/cpd and in the Regulations relating to learning and professional development which are available at www.icaew.com/regulations.

130.4   Diligence encompasses the responsibility to act in accordance with the requirements of an assignment, carefully, thoroughly and on a timely basis.

130.5   A professional accountant shall take reasonable steps to ensure that those working under the professional accountant's authority in a professional capacity have appropriate training and supervision.

130.6   Where appropriate, a professional accountant shall make clients, employers or other users of the accountant's professional services aware of the limitations inherent in the services.

140 Confidentiality

The principle of confidentiality

The principle of confidentiality is not only to keep information confidential, but also to take all reasonable steps to preserve confidentiality. Whether information is confidential or not will depend on its nature. A safe and proper approach for professional accountants to adopt is to assume that all unpublished information about a client's or employer's affairs, however gained, is confidential. Some clients or employers may regard the mere fact of their relationship with a professional accountant as being confidential. **140.0**

The principle of confidentiality imposes an obligation on all professional accountants to refrain from: **140.1**

- Disclosing outside the firm or employing organisation confidential information acquired as a result of professional and business relationships without proper and specific authority or unless there is a legal or professional right or duty to disclose; and
- Using confidential information acquired as a result of professional and business relationships to their personal advantage or the advantage of third parties.

Professional accountants in public practice must not disclose confidential information to a client even though the information is relevant to an engagement for, or would be beneficial to, that client.

Where professional accountants in public practice have confidential information which affects an assurance report, or other report which requires a professional accountant to state their opinion, the professional accountant cannot provide an opinion which they already know, from whatever source, to be untrue. If the professional accountant in public practice is to continue the engagement, the professional accountant must resolve this disparity. In order to do so, the professional accountant is entitled to apply normal procedures and to make such enquiries in order to enable the professional accountant to obtain that same information but from another source. Under no circumstances, however, shall there be any disclosure of confidential information outside the firm.

A professional accountant shall maintain confidentiality, including in a social environment, being alert to the possibility of inadvertent disclosure, particularly to a close business associate or a close or immediate family member. **140.2**

A professional accountant shall maintain confidentiality of information disclosed by a prospective client or employer. **140.3**

This requirement extends not only to clients, past and present, but also to third parties from or about whom information has been received in confidence. The principle of confidentiality clearly does not prevent an employee from using the skills acquired while working with a former employer in undertaking a new role with a different organisation. Professional accountants shall neither use nor appear to use special knowledge which could only have been acquired with access to confidential information. It is a matter of judgement as to the dividing line which separates experience gained from special knowledge acquired.

A professional accountant shall maintain confidentiality of information within the firm or employing organisation. **140.4**

140.5   A professional accountant shall take reasonable steps to ensure that staff under the professional accountant's control and persons from whom advice and assistance is obtained respect the professional accountant's duty of confidentiality.

Member firms shall ensure that all who work on their behalf are trained in, and understand:

- The importance of confidentiality;
- The importance of identifying any conflicts of interest and confidentiality issues between clients, or between themselves or the firm and a client, in relation to a current or prospective engagement; and
- The procedures the firm has in place for the recognition and consideration of possible conflicts of interest and confidentiality issues.

140.6   The need to comply with the principle of confidentiality continues even after the end of relationships between a professional accountant and a client or employer. When a professional accountant changes employment or acquires a new client, the professional accountant is entitled to use prior experience. The professional accountant shall not, however, use or disclose any confidential information either acquired or received as a result of a professional or business relationship.

140.6a   Detailed guidance on conflicts of interest, including situations where such conflicts may result in threats (or perceived threats) to preservation of confidentiality, are included in section 220.

Disclosure of confidential information

140.7   The following are circumstances where professional accountants are or may be required to disclose confidential information or when such disclosure may be appropriate:

- Disclosure is permitted by law and is authorised by the client or the employer;
- Disclosure is required by law, for example:
  o   Production of documents or other provision of evidence in the course of legal proceedings; or
  o   Disclosure to the appropriate public authorities of infringements of the law that come to light; and
  Where required by law or regulations to disclose confidential information, for example as a result of anti-money laundering or anti-terrorist legislation, or in connection with legal proceedings involving either themselves or their employing organisation, professional accountants shall always disclose that information in compliance with relevant legal requirements. Professional accountants shall take care when communicating relevant facts to others relating to known or suspected money laundering or terrorist activities. Under the UK Money Laundering Regulations 2007, the Terrorism Act 2000 and the Terrorism Act 2006, it is a criminal offence to 'tip off' a money launderer or terrorist. For further discussion, please refer to the money laundering legislation and guidance available at www.icaew.com/moneylaundering.
- There is a professional duty or right to disclose, when not prohibited by law:
  o   To comply with the quality review of ICAEW or professional regulator or professional body;
  o   To respond to an inquiry or investigation by ICAEW a regulatory body or regulatory body;
  o   To protect the professional interests of a professional accountant in legal proceedings; or
  o   To comply with technical standards and ethics requirements.

A professional accountant may disclose confidential information to third parties, when not obliged to do so by law or regulations, if the disclosure can be justified in the public interest and is not contrary to laws and regulations. Before making such disclosure, professional accountants are encouraged to obtain legal or professional advice regarding their duties and obligations in the context of their professional and business relationships, and possible protection under the UK Public Interest Disclosure Act 1998. Further guidance on disclosure in the public interest is available in Professional conduct and disclosure in relation to defaults or unlawful acts.

Confidentiality and privilege is a complex area. For example, information which is confidential may not be privileged and, therefore, may be admissible in court proceedings. Privilege is a difficult area, quite distinct from confidentiality, and it is recommended that further advice be taken if a professional accountant is in doubt as to the action to be taken.

Guidance on money laundering reporting requirements in privileged circumstances is included in Technical Release 02/06, available at www.icaew.com/technical.

In deciding whether to disclose confidential information, relevant factors to consider include: **140.8**

- Whether the interests of all parties, including third parties whose interests may be affected, could be harmed if the client or employer consents to the disclosure of information by the professional accountant;
- Whether all the relevant information is known and substantiated, to the extent it is practicable; when the situation involves unsubstantiated facts, incomplete information or unsubstantiated conclusions, professional judgment shall be used in determining the type of disclosure to be made, if any;
- The type of communication that is expected and to whom it is addressed; and
- Whether the parties to whom the communication is addressed are appropriate recipients.
- Whether or not the information is privileged, either under Legal Professional Privilege or in Privileged Circumstances under section 330 of the UK Proceeds of Crime Act 2002 (see Technical Release 02/06); and
- The legal and regulatory obligations and the possible implications of disclosure for the professional accountant.

The paragraphs above deal with professional accountants' treatment of confidential information belonging to a client or employer. There is another context in which professional accountants will be given or may obtain information which they must handle sensitively. Professional accountants may be approached in confidence with information about alleged illegal or improper actions on the part of employees or management of the business for which the informant works or with which the informant has some other relationship. Professional accountants may receive that information because of being trusted by the informant, or may receive it in connection with work their firm is carrying out for the informant's employer. Whatever the circumstances in which the information comes to professional accountants, the professional accountants shall: **140.9**

- Advise informants to pass the information to their employer through the medium of the employer's own internal procedures (if they exist);
- Use their best endeavours to protect the identity of the informant, taking care not to mislead the informant as to the extent to which this can be done, and shall only cause the employer to be made aware of the informant's identity where this cannot be avoided; and
- Take care in determining the quality of the information and how best to use it, if at all.

140.10 For a more detailed explanation of the operation of the provisions of the UK Public Interest Disclosure Act 1998, professional accountants are referred to ICAEW Technical Releases 16/99 'Receipt of Information in Confidence by Auditors' and 17/99 'Public Interest Disclosure Act 1998' (www.icaew.com/technicalreleases).

150 Professional behaviour

150.1 The principle of professional behaviour imposes an obligation on all professional accountants to comply with relevant laws and regulations and avoid any action that the professional accountant knows or should know may discredit the profession. This includes actions that a reasonable and informed third party, weighing all the specific facts and circumstances available to the professional accountant at that time, would be likely to conclude adversely affects the good reputation of the profession.

Professional accountants shall conduct themselves with courtesy and consideration towards all with whom they come into contact when performing their work.

150.2 In marketing and promoting themselves and their work, professional accountants shall not bring the profession into disrepute. Professional accountants shall be honest and truthful and not:

- Make exaggerated claims for the services they are able to offer, the qualifications they possess, or experience they have gained; or
- Make disparaging references or unsubstantiated comparisons to the work of others.

Appendix to Part A – further guidance on ethical conflict resolution

Further guidance on the matters discussed in paragraph 100.18:

(a) Relevant facts

Seek to establish the known facts of the situation and any limitations. It may not be possible to obtain all relevant facts but the professional accountant may be able to obtain more background information to address the limitations by:

- Referring to the organisation's policy, procedures, code of conduct and previous history;
- Discussing the matter with parties internal and external to the organisation. For example trusted managers and colleagues.

(b) Relevant parties

Consider affected parties ranging from individuals, organisations to society. The parties to be considered include, but are not limited to, employees, employers, shareholders, consumers/clients, investors, government and the community at large.

(c) Ethical issues involved

Analyse the professional, organisational and personal ethical issues of the matter.

(d) Fundamental principles related to the matter in question

Refer to the guidance contained in this Code in order to establish which fundamental principles are affected by the situation.

(e) Established internal procedures

Refer to the employing organisation's internal procedures and also consider which parties ought to be involved in the ethical conflict resolution process, in what role and at what stage. For example, the professional accountant needs to consider when it would be appropriate to refer to external sources for help, such as ICAEW (see paragraphs 1.19 to 1.22 of this Code for sources of advice and guidance).

Professional accountants may find it useful to discuss the ethical conflict issue within the organisation with the following parties:

- Immediate superior;
- The next level of management;
- A corporate governance body, for example, the audit committee;
- Other departments in the organisation which include, but are not limited to, legal, audit and human resources departments.

(f) Alternative courses of action

In considering courses of action, the professional accountant is encouraged to consider the following:

When evaluating the suggested course of action, a professional accountant is expected to test the adequacy of the suggested course of action by considering the following:

- The organisation's policies, procedures and guidelines;
- Applicable laws and regulations;
- Universal values and principles adopted by society;
- Long term and short term consequences;
- Symbolic consequences;
- Private and public consequences.

When evaluating the suggested course of action, a professional accountant is expected to test the adequacy of the suggested course of action by considering the following:

- Have all consequences associated with the course of action been discussed and evaluated?
- Is there any reason why the suggested course of action will not stand the test of time?
- Would a similar course of action be undertaken in a similar situation?
- Would the suggested course of action stand scrutiny from peers, family and friends?

Code of Ethics B

Effective from 1st January 2011. This part of the Code describes how the conceptual framework contained in General Application applies in certain situations to professional accountants in public practice.

Except as noted below, this Code has been derived from the International Ethics Standards Board of Accountants' (IESBA) Code of Ethics issued in July 2009 by the International Federation of Accountants. Accordingly, compliance with the remainder of this Code will ensure compliance with the principles of the IESBA Code. Paragraph numbering in the rest of this Code replicates that used in the IESBA Code of Ethics, except in respect of Sections 221, 241 and Part D which have no direct equivalent in the IESBA Code of Ethics.

Wording replicates the IESBA Code of Ethics.

Text framed in grey is where ICAEW's Council considers additional discussion and/ or requirements to be useful or necessary.

The fact that wording is or is not framed in grey does not indicate any difference in the degree of importance that should be attached to it.

- **200 Introduction**
  - o   Fundamental principles
  - o   Threats and safeguards
- **210 Professional appointment**
  - o   Client acceptance
  - o   Engagement acceptance
  - o   Changes in a professional appointment
  - o   Transfer of records
- **Section 210 Appendix – Changes in professional appointment procedures**
  - o   Prospective accountants
  - o   Existing accountants
  - o   Further information
- **220 Conflicts of interest**
- **221 Corporate finance advice**
  - o   Introduction
  - o   Categories of corporate finance activity
  - o   General principles applicable to all professional accountants
  - o   General corporate cinance advice applicable to professional accountants in public practice
  - o   Takeovers and mergers
  - o   Underwriting and marketing of shares
  - o   Sponsors, nominated advisers and corporate advisers
  - o   Appendix 1 to Section 221 – Corporate finance advice
  - o   Appendix 2 to Section 221 – Corporate finance advice
  - o   Appendix 3 to Section 221 – Corporate Finance Advice
- **230 Second opinions**

200 Introduction

200.1   This Part of the Code describes how the conceptual framework contained in Part A applies in certain situations to professional accountants in public practice. This Part does not describe all of the circumstances and relationships that could be encountered by a professional accountant in public practice that create or may create threats to compliance with the fundamental principles. Therefore, the professional accountant in public practice is encouraged to be alert for such circumstances and relationships.

A professional accountant in public practice shall not knowingly engage in any business, occupation, or activity that impairs or might impair integrity, objectivity or the good reputation of the profession and as a result would be incompatible with the fundamental principles. **200.2**

Fundamental principles

A professional accountant shall comply with the following fundamental principles: **200.2a**

- **Integrity** – to be straightforward and honest in all professional and business relationships
- **Objectivity** – to not allow bias, conflict of interest or undue influence of others to override professional or business judgments.
- **Professional Competence and Due Care** – to maintain professional knowledge and skill at the level required to ensure that a client or employer receives competent professional services based on current developments in practice, legislation and techniques and act diligently and in accordance with applicable technical and professional standards.
- **Confidentiality** – to respect the confidentiality of information acquired as a result of professional and business relationships and, therefore, not disclose any such information to third parties without proper and specific authority, unless there is a legal or professional right or duty to disclose, nor use the information for the personal advantage of the professional accountant or third parties.
- **Professional** – to comply with relevant laws and regulations and avoid any action that discredits the profession.

Threats and safeguards

Compliance with the fundamental principles may potentially be threatened by a broad range of circumstances and relationships. The nature and significance of the threats may differ depending on whether they arise in relation to the provision of services to an audit client and whether the audit client is a public interest entity, to an assurance client that is not an audit client, or to a non-assurance client. Threats fall into one or more of the following categories: **200.3**

- Self-interest;
- Self-review;
- Advocacy;
- Familiarity; and;
- Intimidation.

These threats are discussed further in Part A of this Code.

The paragraphs below set out examples of the circumstances that may result in threat and the types of safeguards that may be applicable, depending on the particular circumstances. They are not an exhaustive list nor do they imply that such circumstances will always create a significant threat. Regard should be had to the specific requirements in sections 210 to 291, when the circumstances are the same as, or analogous to, those addressed by them.

200.4   Examples of circumstances that create self-interest threats for a professional accountant in public practice include:

- A member of the assurance team having a direct financial interest in the assurance client.
- A firm having undue dependence on total fees from a client.
- A member of the assurance team having a significant close business relationship with an assurance client.
- A firm being concerned about the possibility of losing a significant client.
- A member of the audit team entering into employment negotiations with the audit client.
- A firm entering into a contingent fee arrangement relating to an assurance engagement.
- A professional accountant discovering a significant error when evaluating the results of a previous professional service performed by a member of the professional accountant's firm.

200.5   Examples of circumstances that create self-review threats for a professional accountant in public practice include:

- A firm issuing an assurance report on the effectiveness of the operation of financial systems after designing or implementing the systems.
- A firm having prepared the original data used to generate records that are the subject matter of the assurance engagement.
- A member of the assurance team being, or having recently been, a director or officer of the client.
- A member of the assurance team being, or having recently been, employed by the client in a position to exert significant influence over the subject matter of the engagement.
- The firm performing a service for an assurance client that directly affects the subject matter information of the assurance engagement.

200.6   Examples of circumstances that create advocacy threats for a professional accountant in public practice include:

- The firm promoting shares in an audit client.
- A professional accountant acting as an advocate on behalf of an audit client in litigation or disputes with third parties.

200.7   Examples of circumstances that create familiarity threats for a professional accountant in public practice include:

- A member of the engagement team having a close or immediate family member who is a director or officer of the client.
- A member of the engagement team having a close or immediate family member who is an employee of the client who is in a position to exert significant influence over the subject matter of the engagement.
- A director or officer of the client or an employee in a position to exert significant influence over the subject matter of the engagement having recently served as the engagement partner.
- A professional accountant accepting gifts or preferential treatment from a client, unless the value is trivial or inconsequential.
- Senior personnel having a long association with the assurance client.

200.8   Examples of circumstances that create intimidation threats for a professional accountant in public practice include:

- A firm being threatened with dismissal from a client engagement.

- An audit client indicating that it will not award a planned non-assurance contract to the firm if the firm continues to disagree with the client's accounting treatment for a particular transaction.
- A firm being threatened with litigation by the client.
- A firm being pressured to reduce inappropriately the extent of work performed in order to reduce fees.
- A professional accountant feeling pressured to agree with the judgment of a client employee because the employee has more expertise on the matter in question.
- A professional accountant being informed by a partner of the firm that a planned promotion will not occur unless the accountant agrees with an audit client's inappropriate accounting treatment.

Safeguards that may eliminate or reduce threats to an acceptable level fall into two broad categories:

200.9

- Safeguards created by the profession, legislation or regulation; and
- Safeguards in the work environment.

Examples of safeguards created by the profession, legislation or regulation are described in paragraph 100.14 of Part A of this Code.

A professional accountant in public practice shall exercise judgment to determine how best to deal with threats that are not at an acceptable level, whether by applying safeguards to eliminate the threat or reduce it to an acceptable level or by terminating or declining the relevant engagement. In exercising this judgment, a professional accountant in public practice shall consider whether a reasonable and informed third party, weighing all the specific facts and circumstances available to the professional accountant at that time, would be likely to conclude that the threats would be eliminated or reduced to an acceptable level by the application of safeguards, such that compliance with the fundamental principles is not compromised. This consideration will be affected by matters such as the significance of the threat, the nature of the engagement and the structure of the firm.

200.10

In the work environment, the relevant safeguards will vary depending on the circumstances. Work environment safeguards comprise firm-wide safeguards and engagement-specific safeguards.

200.11

Examples of firm-wide safeguards in the work environment include:

200.12

- Leadership of the firm that stresses the importance of compliance with the fundamental principles.
- Leadership of the firm that establishes the expectation that members of an assurance team will act in the public interest.
- Policies and procedures to implement and monitor quality control of engagements.
- Documented policies regarding the need to identify threats to compliance with the fundamental principles, evaluate the significance of those threats, and apply safeguards to eliminate or reduce the threats to an acceptable level or, when appropriate safeguards are not available or cannot be applied, terminate or decline the relevant engagement.
- Documented internal policies and procedures requiring compliance with the fundamental principles.
- Policies and procedures that will enable the identification of interests or relationships between the firm or members of engagement teams and clients.
- Policies and procedures to monitor and, if necessary, manage the reliance on revenue received from a single client.

- Using different partners and engagement teams with separate reporting lines for the provision of non-assurance services to an assurance client.
- Policies and procedures to prohibit individuals who are not members of an engagement team from inappropriately influencing the outcome of the engagement.
- Timely communication of a firm's policies and procedures, including any changes to them, to all partners and professional staff, and appropriate training and education on such policies and procedures.
- Designating a member of senior management to be responsible for overseeing the adequate functioning of the firm's quality control system.
- Advising partners and professional staff of assurance clients and related entities from which independence is required.
- A disciplinary mechanism to promote compliance with policies and procedures.
- Published policies and procedures to encourage and empower staff to communicate to senior levels within the firm any issue relating to compliance with the fundamental principles that concerns them.

200.13   Examples of engagement-specific safeguards in the work environment include:

- Having a professional accountant who was not involved with the non-assurance service review the non-assurance work performed or otherwise advise as necessary.
- Having a professional accountant who was not a member of the assurance team review the assurance work performed or otherwise advise as necessary.
- Consulting an independent third party, such as a committee of independent directors, a professional regulatory body or another professional accountant.
- Discussing ethical issues with those charged with governance of the client.
- Disclosing to those charged with governance of the client the nature of services provided and extent of fees charged.
- Involving another firm to perform or re-perform part of the engagement.
- Rotating senior assurance team personnel.

200.14   Depending on the nature of the engagement, a professional accountant in public practice may also be able to rely on safeguards that the client has implemented. However it is not possible to rely solely on such safeguards to reduce threats to an acceptable level.

200.15   Examples of safeguards within the client's systems and procedures include:

- The client requires persons other than management to ratify or approve the appointment of a firm to perform an engagement.
- The client has competent employees with experience and seniority to make managerial decisions.
- The client has implemented internal procedures that ensure objective choices in commissioning non-assurance engagements.
- The client has a corporate governance structure that provides appropriate oversight and communications regarding the firm's services.

200.16   Professional accountants who are in doubt as to their ethical position may seek advice from the ICAEW's Technical Advisory Services by email: ethics@icaew.com or phone +44 (0)1908 248 250. Further information on guidance is available in section 1, paragraphs 1.19 to 1.22.

210 Professional Appointment

Clients have the right to choose their accountants, whether as auditors or profes-   **210.0**
sional advisers, and to change their accountants if they so desire. Professional
accountants have the right to choose for whom they act.

Client Acceptance

Before accepting a new client relationship, a professional accountant in public   **210.1**
practice shall determine whether acceptance would create any threats to compliance
with the fundamental principles. Potential threats to integrity or professional
behaviour may be created from, for example, questionable issues associated with the
client (its owners, management or activities).

Client issues that, if known, could threaten compliance with the fundamental prin-   **210.2**
ciples include, for example, client involvement in illegal activities (such as money
laundering), dishonesty or questionable financial reporting practices.

Further information relating to money laundering legislation and guidance is
included in paragraph 210.13.

A professional accountant in public practice shall evaluate the significance of any   **210.3**
threats and apply safeguards when necessary to eliminate them or reduce them to an
acceptable level. Examples of such safeguards include:

- Obtaining knowledge and understanding of the client, its owners, managers and
  those responsible for its governance and business activities; or
- Securing the client's commitment to improve corporate governance practices or
  internal controls.

Where it is not possible to reduce the threats to an acceptable level, the professional   **210.4**
accountant in public practice shall decline to enter into the client relationship.

It is recommended that a professional accountant in public practice periodically   **210.5**
review acceptance decisions for recurring client engagements.

Engagement Acceptance

The fundamental principle of professional competence and due care imposes an   **210.6**
obligation on a professional accountant in public practice to provide only those
services that the professional accountant in public practice is competent to perform.
Before accepting a specific client engagement, a professional accountant in public
practice shall determine whether acceptance would create any threats to compliance
with the fundamental principles. For example, a self-interest threat to professional
competence and due care is created if the engagement team does not possess, or
cannot acquire, the competencies necessary to properly carry out the engagement.

A professional accountant in public practice shall evaluate the significance of threats   **210.7**
and apply safeguards, when necessary, to eliminate them or reduce them to an
acceptable level. Examples of such safeguards include:

- Acquiring an appropriate understanding of the nature of the client's business,
  the complexity of its operations, the specific requirements of the engagement
  and the purpose, nature and scope of the work to be performed.
- Acquiring knowledge of relevant industries or subject matters.

- Possessing or obtaining experience with relevant regulatory or reporting requirements.
- Assigning sufficient staff with the necessary competencies.
- Using experts where necessary.
- Agreeing on a realistic time frame for the performance of the engagement.
- Complying with quality control policies and procedures designed to provide reasonable assurance that specific engagements are accepted only when they can be performed competently.

210.8   When a professional accountant in public practice intends to rely on the advice or work of an expert, the professional accountant in public practice shall determine whether such reliance is warranted. Factors to consider include: reputation, expertise, resources available and applicable professional and ethical standards. Such information may be gained from prior association with the expert or from consulting others.

Changes in a Professional appointment

210.9   A professional accountant in public practice who is asked to replace another professional accountant in public practice, or who is considering tendering for an engagement currently held by another professional accountant in public practice, shall determine whether there are any reasons, professional or otherwise, for not accepting the engagement, such as circumstances that create threats to compliance with the fundamental principles that cannot be eliminated or reduced to an acceptable level by the application of safeguards. For example, there may be a threat to professional competence and due care if a professional accountant in public practice accepts the engagement before knowing all the pertinent facts.

Upon being asked to accept an appointment, professional accountants shall undertake the same procedures with all accountants, irrespective of whether the accountant works in public practice or not

210.10   A professional accountant in public practice shall evaluate the significance of any threats. Depending on the nature of the engagement, this may require direct communication with the existing accountant to establish the facts and circumstances regarding the proposed change so that the professional accountant in public practice can decide whether it would be appropriate to accept the engagement. For example, the apparent reasons for the change in appointment may not fully reflect the facts and may indicate disagreements with the existing accountant that may influence the decision to accept the appointment.

Having been asked to accept an appointment, the professional accountant in public practice shall at least seek to contact the existing accountant. The appropriate procedures are considered further in the Appendix to this Section.

210.11   Safeguards shall be applied when necessary to eliminate any threats or reduce them to an acceptable level. Examples of such safeguards include:

- When replying to requests to submit tenders, stating in the tender that, before accepting the engagement, contact with the existing accountant will be requested so that inquiries may be made as to whether there are any professional or other reasons why the appointment shall not be accepted;
- Asking the existing accountant to provide known information on any facts or circumstances that, in the existing accountant's opinion, the proposed accountant needs to be aware of before deciding whether to accept the engagement; or
- Obtaining necessary information from other sources.

When the threats cannot be eliminated or reduced to an acceptable level through the application of safeguards, a professional accountant in public practice shall, unless there is satisfaction as to necessary facts by other means, decline the engagement.

Counsel has advised that as far as UK law is concerned, an existing accountant who communicates to a prospective accountant matters damaging to the client or to any individuals concerned with the client's business will have a strong measure of protection were any action for defamation to be brought against the existing accountant in that the communication will be protected by qualified privilege. This means that the existing accountant shall not be liable to pay damages for defamatory statements even if they turn out to be untrue, provided that they are made without malice. There is little likelihood of an existing accountant being held to have acted maliciously provided that:

- Only what is sincerely believed to be true is stated; and
- Reckless imputations are not made against a client or connected individuals for which there can be no reason to believe they are true.

A professional accountant in public practice may be asked to undertake work that is complementary or additional to the work of the existing accountant. Such circumstances may create threats to professional competence and due care resulting from, for example, a lack of or incomplete information. The significance of any threats shall be evaluated and safeguards applied when necessary to eliminate the threat or reduce it to an acceptable level. An example of such a safeguard is notifying the existing accountant of the proposed work, which would give the existing accountant the opportunity to provide any relevant information needed for the proper conduct of the work. **210.12**

In circumstances where the professional accountant is asked to undertake work which is relevant to the work of the existing accountant, the professional accountant shall notify the existing accountant of the proposed work, unless the client provides acceptable reasons why the existing accountant cannot be informed. The professional accountant ought to be aware of the risks of undertaking such work without the advantage of communicating with the other accountant. Further guidance on providing second opinions is available in section 230 of this Code.

An existing accountant is bound by confidentiality. Whether that professional accountant is permitted or required to discuss the affairs of a client with a proposed accountant will depend on the nature of the engagement and on: **210.13**

- Whether the client's permission to do so has been obtained; or
- The legal or ethical requirements relating to such communications and disclosure, which may vary by jurisdiction.

Circumstances where the professional accountant is or may be required to disclose confidential information or where such disclosure may otherwise be appropriate are set out in section 140 of Part A of this Code.

However, care must be taken when communicating all relevant facts to a professional accountant in situations where the existing accountant knows or suspects that their client is involved in money laundering or a terrorist activity. Under the UK Money Laundering regulations 2007, the Terrorism Act 2000 and the Terrorism Act 2006, it is a criminal offence to 'tip off' a money launderer or terrorist. Accordingly:

- The prospective accountant shall not specifically enquire whether the existing accountant has reported suspicions of money laundering or terrorism. Such questions place the existing accountant in a difficult position and are likely not to be answered. In addition, the prospective accountant shall not ask the existing accountant whether client identification or 'knowing your client' procedures have been carried out under anti-money laundering legislation. The prospective accountant has responsibility for obtaining information for client identification and 'knowing your client' and this cannot be delegated to the existing accountant.

- Disclosure of money laundering or terrorist suspicion reporting by the existing accountant to the potential successor shall be avoided because this information may be discussed with the client or former client.

For further discussion, please refer to the money laundering legislation and guidance and the ICAEW's Ethics Advisory helpsheet on 'changes in professional appointments'.

210.14 A professional accountant in public practice will generally need to obtain the client's permission, preferably in writing, to initiate discussion with an existing accountant. Once that permission is obtained, the existing accountant shall comply with relevant legal and other regulations governing such requests. Where the existing accountant provides information, it shall be provided honestly and unambiguously. If the proposed accountant is unable to communicate with the existing accountant, the proposed accountant shall take reasonable steps to obtain information about any possible threats by other means, such as through inquiries of third parties or background investigations of senior management or those charged with governance of the client.

If the client fails or refuses to grant the existing accountant permission to discuss the client's affairs with the proposed successor, the existing accountant shall report this fact to the prospective accountant who shall consider carefully the reason for such failure or refusal when determining whether or not to accept nomination/appointment.

210.15 Guidance on appropriate procedures to be adopted by professional accountants relating to changes in professional appointments is included as an Appendix to this Section.

Transfer of Records

210.16 An existing accountant shall deal promptly with any reasonable request for the transfer of records and may have the right of particular lien if there are unpaid fees (see section 240 of this Code and 'Documents and records: ownership, lien and right of access' at (icaew.com/regulations). The courts have held that no lien can exist over books or documents of a registered company which, either by statute or by articles of association of the company, have to be available for public inspection (see 'Documents and records: ownership, lien and rights of access' at (icaew.com/regulations). It may be necessary for professional accountants to obtain legal advice prior to the exercise of a lien.

If the existing accountant has fees outstanding from a client they are entitled to mention this to the potential successor. However, if this is as a result of genuine reservations by the client, this may not be a reason to withhold cooperation with a successor. It may be useful to consider the section on fee disputes in 'Duty on firms to investigate complaints – guidance on how to handle or avoid them' at (icaew.com/regulations).

The prospective accountant often asks the existing accountant for information as to the client's affairs. If the client is unable to provide the information and lack thereof might prejudice the client's interests, such information shall be promptly given. In such circumstances, no charge shall normally be made unless there is good reason to the contrary. An example of such a reason would be that a significant amount of work is involved. Where a charge is made, the arrangements shall comply with section 240 of this Code.

210.17

Attention is drawn to Chapter 3 of the Audit regulations and Guidance relating to access to all relevant information held by the existing accountant in respect of the last audit report and Technical Release AAF 01/08 Access to Information by Successor Auditors.

210.18

Appendix to Section 210 – Changes in Professional Appointments Procedures

Prospective Accountants

In the majority of cases, the appropriate procedures for any professional accountant who is invited to act in succession to another, whether the changeover is at the insistence of the client or of the existing accountant, is to:

1

- Explain to the prospective client that there is a professional duty to communicate with the existing accountant; and
- Request the client (i) to confirm the proposed change in accountant to the existing accountant and (ii) to authorise the existing accountant to co-operate with the prospective accountant; and
- Write to the existing accountant regarding the prospective involvement with the client and request disclosure of any issue or circumstance which might be relevant to the successor's decision to accept or decline the appointment (making oral enquiry if no written reply is forthcoming).

When these procedural steps have been taken, the prospective accountant shall consider, in light of the information received from the existing accountant, or any other factors, including conclusions reached following discussion with the client, whether:

2

- To accept the engagement, or
- Accept it only after having addressed any factors arising from the information received from the existing accountant (this may include imposing conditions on acceptance), or
- Decline it.

The prospective accountant shall ordinarily treat in confidence any information provided by the existing accountant, unless it is needed to be disclosed to perform the role required (such as making investigations into matters which need the perspective of the client's officers or senior employees).

3

In circumstances where the enquiries referred to above are not answered, the prospective accountant shall write to the existing accountant by recorded delivery service stating an intention to accept the engagement in the absence of a reply within a specific and reasonable period. The prospective accountant is entitled to assume that the existing accountant's silence implies there was no adverse comment to be made, although this does not obviate the requirement in 210.9 to consider all appropriate circumstances.

4

5   A professional accountant who is nominated as a joint auditor shall communicate with all existing auditors and be guided by similar principles to those set out in relation to nomination as an auditor. Where it is proposed that a joint audit appointment becomes a sole appointment, the surviving auditor shall communicate formally with the other joint auditor as though for a new appointment.

6   A professional accountant invited to accept nomination on the death of a sole practitioner shall endeavour to obtain such information as may be needed from the latter's alternate (where appropriate), the administrators of the estate, or other source.

7   If the prospective accountant accepts the engagement, the prospective accountant shall comply with the relevant legal and regulatory requirements as indicated in paragraph 13.

Existing accountants

8   The appropriate procedure for any professional accountant who receives any communication in terms of the above paragraphs, whether or not the professional accountant is still in office, is to:

- Answer promptly any communication from the potential successor about the client's affairs; and
- Confirm whether there are any matters about those affairs which the prospective accountant ought to know, explaining them meaningfully, or confirm there are no such matters.

9   If the existing accountant has made one or more suspicious activity reports relating to money laundering or terrorism, the existing accountant shall not disclose that fact to the prospective accountant, or make other disclosures that could amount to tipping off. However, the existing accountant's legal and professional obligations remain. In order to meet these obligations, the existing accountant can undertake one or more of the following actions:

- Contact the relevant investigating authority, for example, the Serious Organised Crime Agency (SOCA), to ascertain if appropriate wording can be agreed in a communication;
- Include a factual reference to the irregularities; (further discussion is included in the ICAEW's Ethics Advisory Services Helpsheet on Changes in Professional Appointments);
- Consider seeking legal advice.

Guidance on money laundering reporting requirements in privileged circumstances is included in Technical Release 02/06.

10   The above actions are also relevant when the existing accountant is preparing the required statement of circumstances in accordance with Section 519 of the UK Companies Act 2006, or other similar statutory provisions, of matters connected with ceasing to hold office which, the auditor believes, shall be brought to the notice of the professional accountants, shareholders or creditors of the client or under the relevant professional and other regulatory bodies. Further guidance can be found in Chapter 3 of the 2008 Audit regulations and Guidance.

11   It is best practice for the prospective accountant and the existing accountant to record in writing such discussions as are referred to in the paragraphs above.

Where the professional accountant decides to accept nomination/appointment **12** having been given notice of any matters which are the subject of contention between the existing accountant and the client, the professional accountant shall be prepared, if requested to do so, to demonstrate to the professional and regulatory investigating authorities that proper consideration has been given to those matters and the relevant legal, regulatory and ethical requirements have been met.

Further Information

Professional accountants' attention is drawn to additional guidance as follows: **13**

- Chapter 3 of the 2008 Audit regulations and Guidance, in particular technical standards relating to changes in professional appointments and access to relevant information relating to the signed audit report.
- ISQC (UK & Ireland) – quality control for firms that perform audits and reviews of historical financial information, and other assurance and related services engagements (frc.org.uk/apb/publications).
- Statement of Auditing Standards frc.org.uk/apb/publications:
- ISA 240 (UK and Ireland) – The auditor's responsibility to consider fraud in an audit of financial statements;
- ISA 250 (UK and Ireland) – Consideration of laws and regulations in an audit of financial statements;
- ISA 510 (UK and Ireland) Initial engagements – opening balances and continuing engagements – opening balances.
- Practice Note 12 (Revised) 'Money laundering' frc.org.uk/apb/publications.
- Anti-money laundering for the Accountancy Sector at icaew.com/regulations.
- Technical Release 02/06 – 'Guidance on changes to the money laundering reporting requirements: the exemption from reporting knowledge or suspicion of money laundering formed in privileged circumstances' (icaew.com/technical).
- Practice Helpsheet – Changes in a professional appointment (icaew.com/ethicsadvice).

220 Conflicts of Interest

A professional accountant in public practice shall take reasonable steps to identify **220.1** circumstances that could pose a conflict of interest. Such circumstances may create threats to compliance with the fundamental principles. For example, a threat to objectivity may be created when a professional accountant in public practice competes directly with a client or has a joint venture or similar arrangement with a major competitor of a client. A threat to objectivity or confidentiality may also be created when a professional accountant in public practice performs services for clients whose interests are in conflict or the clients are in dispute with each other in relation to the matter or transaction in question.

Subject to the specific provisions, there is, however, nothing improper in a professional accountant in public practice having two clients whose interests are in conflict.

A professional accountant in public practice shall evaluate the significance of any **220.2** threats and apply safeguards when necessary to eliminate the threats or reduce them to an acceptable level. Before accepting or continuing a client relationship or specific engagement, the professional accountant in public practice shall evaluate the significance of any threats created by business interests or relationships with the client or a third party.

A test is whether a reasonable and informed observer would perceive that the objectivity of professional accountants or their firms is likely to be impaired. The professional accountants or their firms shall be able to satisfy themselves and the client that any conflict can be managed with available safeguards. Attention is also drawn to the ethical conflict resolution process in Part A.

220.3   Depending upon the circumstances giving rise to the conflict, application of one of the following safeguards is generally necessary:

- Notifying the client of the firm's business interest or activities that may represent a conflict of interest and obtaining their consent to act in such circumstances; or
- Notifying all known relevant parties that the professional accountant in public practice is acting for two or more parties in respect of a matter where their respective interests are in conflict and obtaining their consent to so act; or
- Notifying the client that the professional accountant in public practice does not act exclusively for any one client in the provision of proposed services (for example, in a particular market sector or with respect to a specific service) and obtaining their consent to so act.

Professional accountants' attention is drawn to section 240 Fees and other types of remuneration and section 241 Agencies and referrals which provide additional guidance on the ethical and legal considerations relating to these areas, including fiduciary relationships and accounting for commission and other benefits.

220.4   The professional accountant shall also determine whether to apply one or more of the following additional safeguards:

- The use of separate engagement teams;
- Procedures to prevent access to information (e.g., strict physical separation of such teams, confidential and secure data filing);
- Clear guidelines for members of the engagement team on issues of security and confidentiality;
- The use of confidentiality agreements signed by employees and partners of the firm; and
- regular review of the application of safeguards by a senior individual not involved with relevant client engagements.

220.4a   Where a conflict of interest arises, the preservation of confidentiality, and the perception thereof will be of paramount importance. Therefore firms shall deploy safeguards, which generally will take the form of information barriers. These information barriers may include the following features:

- Ensuring that there is, and continues to be, no overlap between the teams servicing the relevant clients and that each has separate internal reporting lines;
- Physically separating, and restricting access to, departments providing different professional services, or creating such divisions within departments if necessary, so that confidential information about one client is not accessible by anyone providing services to another client where their interests conflict;
- Setting strict and carefully defined procedures for dealing with any apparent need to disseminate information beyond a barrier and for maintaining proper records where this occurs.

The professional accountant shall ensure that the adequacy and effectiveness of the barriers are closely and independently monitored and that appropriate disciplinary sanctions are applied for breaches of them. The overall arrangements shall regularly be reviewed by a designated senior partner.

Professional accountants shall note that it has been suggested by the courts that in some circumstances information barriers must be constructed as part of the organisational structure of the firm to be effective, rather than on an ad hoc basis.

If client service issues render it impracticable to put in place such safeguards or **220.4b** suitable alternatives, it is important that relevant parties, who have conflicts of interest which may result in threats to preservation of confidentiality, are made aware of and agree to the professional accountant continuing to act for them.

Where a conflict of interest creates a threat to one or more of the fundamental **220.5** principles, including objectivity, confidentiality, or professional behaviour, that cannot be eliminated or reduced to an acceptable level through the application of safeguards, the professional accountant in public practice shall not accept a specific engagement or shall resign from one or more conflicting engagements.

Where a professional accountant in public practice has requested consent from a **220.6** client to act for another party (which may or may not be an existing client) in respect of a matter where the respective interests are in conflict and that consent has been refused by the client, the professional accountant in public practice shall not continue to act for one of the parties in the matter giving rise to the conflict of interest.

Professional accountants' attention is drawn to section 221, Corporate Finance Advice, section 290, Independence Audit and review engagements, section 400, Code of Ethics for Insolvency Practitioners, for guidance on issues arising from certain corporate finance activities, reporting assignments, and insolvency appointments.

221 Corporate Finance Advice

(Updated as regards to changes in legislation as at 1 April 2010)

Introduction

The nature of corporate finance activities is wide ranging. Therefore, the threats to a **221.0** professional accountant's objectivity, integrity and independence will depend on the nature of the corporate finance activities being provided and the particular circumstances and relationships involved.

Categories of Corporate Finance Activity

Categories of activity covered by this section are as follows: **221.1**

* general corporate finance advice;
* acting as adviser in relation to takeovers and mergers;
* underwriting and marketing or placing securities on behalf of a client; and
* acting as sponsor, nominated adviser or corporate adviser under the Listing Rules, the AIM Rules and the PLUS Rules respectively.

Professional accountants shall note that the guidance given in relation to general **221.2** corporate finance advice is applicable to all categories of activity.

General Principles applicable to all Professional accountants

Statutory and other regulatory requirements

221.3   Professional accountants must be aware of and comply with legislative and regulatory measures and professional guidance governing corporate finance assignments. As a guide, a list of legislative and regulatory measures current at 1 April 2010 is given in Appendix 1 to this section but professional accountants shall ensure that they are aware of the most up-to-date legislative and regulatory requirements.

221.4   Professional accountants are required to comply with the City Code on Takeovers and Mergers ('the City Code') (see Appendix 2 to this Section) in respect of all relevant takeover transactions involving companies governed by the City Code and shall treat the general principles of the City Code as best practice guidance in respect of other takeover transactions.

221.5   Professional accountants proposing to provide corporate finance advice to a client or his employer shall at the outset draw attention to the legislative and regulatory responsibilities which will apply to the client or his employer. The professional accountant shall make clear to the client or his employer that, where necessary, legal advice shall be taken. The professional accountant shall also draw attention to his own responsibilities outlined in this Code and if appropriate, the Auditing Practices Board's Ethical Standards for Auditors and the Auditing Practices Board's Ethical Standards for Reporting Accountants.

Acquisition searches

221.6   It may be appropriate for a professional accountant to conduct an acquisition search which could identify another client or his employer as a target provided the search is based solely on information which is not confidential to that client.

Interests of Shareholders and Owners

221.7   Professional accountants shall remain aware when giving advice that they shall have regard to the interests of all shareholders and owners unless they are specifically acting for a single or defined group thereof. This is particularly so when advising on a proposal which is stated to be agreed by directors and/or majority shareholders or owners.

Preparation of documents

221.8   Any document shall be prepared in accordance with normal professional standards of integrity and objectivity and with a proper degree of care. All statements or observations therein must be capable, taken individually or as a whole, of being justified on an objective examination of the available facts.

221.9   In order to differentiate the roles and responsibilities of the various advisers, professional accountants shall ensure that these roles and responsibilities are clearly described in all public documents and circulars and that each adviser is named.

221.10   Professional accountants intending to comment on published audited accounts shall act in accordance with paragraphs 221.20-22 below.

Overseas transactions

This section has been drafted with regard to the situation in the UK and the Republic of Ireland. Professional accountants shall apply the spirit of the guidance, subject to local legislation and regulation, to overseas transactions of a similar nature.

221.11

General corporate finance advice applicable to professional accountants in public practice

The nature of corporate finance activities is so wide ranging that all the threats to the fundamental principles identified in section 100 and section 200, can arise when professional accountants in public practice provide corporate finance advice to both assurance clients and non-assurance clients: the self-interest threat, the self-review threat, the advocacy threat, the familiarity threat and the intimidation threat.

221.12

When advising a non-assurance client there can be no objection to a professional accountant in public practice accepting an engagement which is designed primarily with a view to advancing that client's case, though the professional accountant in public practice shall be aware that the self-interest threat could arise. Where a non-assurance client has received advice over a period of time on a series of related or unrelated transactions it is likely that, additionally, the familiarity threat may exist. But where a professional accountant in public practice advises an assurance client which is subject to a takeover bid or where a professional accountant in public practice acts as sponsor nominated adviser or corporate adviser to an assurance client involved in the issue of securities, the self-interest threat will become more acute and the advocacy threat will arise.

Some corporate finance activities such as marketing or underwriting of securities contain so strong an element of advocacy as to be incompatible with the objectivity required for the reporting roles of an auditor or reporting accountant. Even where the activities of an auditor or reporting accountant are restricted to ensuring their clients' compliance with the Listing Roles, the AIM Roles or the PLUS Roles it is likely that a self-review threat could arise.

It may be in the best interests of a company for corporate finance advice to be provided by its auditor and there is nothing improper in the professional accountant in public practice supporting an assurance client in this way.

221.13

A professional accountant in public practice's objectivity may be seriously threatened if their role involves undertaking the management responsibilities of an assurance client. Co-ordination tasks, such as initiating and organising meetings, issuing timetables and reporting progress, are unlikely to threaten reporting objectivity. When involved in negotiations on behalf of an assurance client, the professional accountant in public practice shall ensure that he does not assume the role of taking decisions for a client which would prejudice reporting objectivity. Accordingly, the professional accountant in public practice shall ensure that the client takes foll responsibility for the final decisions arising from any such negotiations.

221.14

Conflict of Interest

Professional accountants in public practice shall be aware of the danger of a conflict of interest arising. All reasonable steps shall be taken to ascertain whether a conflict of interest exists or is likely to arise in the future between a professional accountant

221.15

in public practice and his clients, both with regard to new clients and to the changing circumstances of existing clients, and including any implications arising from the possession of confidential information.

221.16 The attention of professional accountants in public practice is directed to section 220, 'Conflicts of interest' and to the safeguards indicated in paragraphs 220.3 and 220.4 of that section. Where there appears to be a conflict of interest between clients but after careful consideration the professional accountant in public practice believes that either the conflict is not material or is unlikely seriously to prejudice the interests of any of those clients and that its safeguards are sufficient, the professional accountant in public practice may accept or continue the engagement. Unless client confidentiality considerations dictate otherwise it would be advisable, if appropriate, to seek the clients' consent. Considerations that lead to a conclusion to accept or continue the engagement shall be explicitly recorded.

221.17 Where a professional accountant in public practice acts or continues to act for two or more clients having obtained consent, if appropriate, in accordance with the previous paragraphs, safeguards will need to be implemented to manage any conflict which arises. The safeguards may include:

- the use of different partners and teams for different clients, each having separate internal reporting lines;
- all necessary steps being taken to prevent the leakage of confidential information between different teams and sections within the firm;
- regular review of the situation by a senior partner or compliance officer not personally involved with either client; and
- advising the clients to seek additional independent advice, where it is appropriate.

Any decision on the part of a sole practitioner shall take account of the fact that the safeguards at (a) to (c) of the above paragraph will not be available to him or her. Similar considerations apply to small firms where the number of partners is insufficient to spread the work as indicated above.

221.18 Where a conflict of interest is so fundamental that it cannot be managed effectively by the implementation of appropriate safeguards and is likely seriously to prejudice the interests of a client, the engagement shall not be accepted or continued even if all relevant clients consent to the engagement.

221.19 Where a professional accountant in public practice is required for any reason to disengage from an existing client, the professional accountant in public practice shall do so as speedily as practicable having regard to the interest of the client.

Documents for client and public use

221.20 In the case of a document prepared solely for the client and its professional advisers, it shall be a condition of the engagement that the document shall not be disclosed to any third party without the firm's prior written consent.

221.21 A professional accountant in public practice is, in the absence of any indication to the contrary, entitled to assume that a company's published financial information that has been reported on by a professional accountant in public practice has been prepared properly and in accordance with all relevant Accounting Standards. If a professional accountant in public practice is commenting in a public document on such financial information and where scope for alternative accounting treatment exists, and the accuracy of the comment or observation is dependent on an assumption as to the actual accounting treatment chosen, that assumption must be stated, together with any other assumptions material to the commentary. Where the professional accountant in public practice is not in possession of sufficient information to warrant a clear opinion this shall be declared in the document.

A professional accountant in public practice must take responsibility for anything **221.22** published under his name, provided he consented to such publication, and the published document shall make clear the client for whom the professional accountant in public practice is acting. To prevent misleading or out-of-context quotations, it shall be a condition of the engagement that, if anything less than the foll document is to be published, the text and its context shall be expressly agreed with the professional accountant in public practice.

Takeovers and Mergers

City code transactions

Professional accountants in public practice are reminded that, if in doubt as to the **221.23** propriety of any aspect of a City Code transaction with which they are involved, they shall consult the Panel on Takeovers and Mergers ('the Takeover Panel'). (See Appendix 2 of this section).

Where a professional accountant in public practice finds itself acting as auditor or **221.24** reporting accountant for two or more parties involved in a transaction subject to the City Code, a perceived conflict of interest may arise. In such circumstances (subject to paragraph 221.26 below) a professional accountant in public practice may act for more than one party, including both offeror and offeree companies as auditor, as reporting accountants, and in the provision of incidental advice consistent with these roles but must implement adequate safeguards (see paragraph 221.17 above).

Lead advisers in city code transactions

For the purposes of this Section, a 'lead adviser' is the professional accountant in **221.25** public practice primarily responsible for advising on, organising and presenting an offer or the response to an offer. This definition would include an 'independent financial adviser' required under Role 3 of the City Code.

In no circumstances shall a professional accountant in public practice be a lead **221.26** adviser to more than one party involved in a transaction subject to the City Code. Where a professional accountant in public practice finds itself acting in an auditor or reporting accountant role for any party involved in a transaction subject to the City Code, the professional accountant in public practice shall not act as lead adviser for any party involved, save in the circumstances set out below in paragraphs 221.27-221.29.

A professional accountant in public practice who is auditor to a target company may **221.27** be requested to act as lead adviser to a bidder on an offer subject to the City Code. Where the bid is hostile, it is likely that the professional accountant in public practice's objectivity will be perceived to be prejudiced by its possession of material confidential information on the target and it will not therefore be able to advise on the offer. However, if the bid is agreed, the professional accountant in public practice may be able to act or continue to act as lead adviser to the bidder with the agreement of the target and subject to the prior approval of the Takeover Panel. The professional accountant in public practice shall obtain confirmation from its clients that their interests would not be prejudiced if the professional accountant in public practice were to act or continue to act in both capacities.

221.28 Where a professional accountant in public practice is acting as lead adviser to a company which is involved in a bid subject to the City Code, conflicts of interest for the professional accountant in public practice may arise due to an existing relationship with a second or subsequent bidder. Providing that the relationship with the second or subsequent bidder is confined to that of auditor or reporting accountant, and subject to the prior approval of the Takeover Panel, the professional accountant in public practice may continue to act as lead adviser, providing that it is satisfied that the implementation of safeguards (see paragraph 221.27 above) provides the necessary level of protection to each of the clients involved.

221.29 Where a professional accountant in public practice is requested to act as lead adviser to a target company in relation to a bid which is subject to the City Code from a company which is an existing assurance client, they may act as lead adviser to the target company only with the prior approval of the Takeover Panel.

The ethical guidance for professional accountants in public practice seeking to act for more than one party in a takeover transaction subject to the City Code is summarised in Appendix 3 to this section. Appendix 3 has been prepared only as a useful reference and is not intended to form part of this section.

Transactions not subject to the city code

221.30 Where a takeover is not subject to the City Code, and there is no substantial public interest involved, a professional accountant in public practice may, subject to the implementation of appropriate safeguards (see paragraphs 221.16 and 221.17 above), provide financial advice to both sides or to competing bidders. However, the professional accountant in public practice shall not act as lead adviser to both the target and a bidder in respect of such a transaction. The professional accountant in public practice shall be alive to the possibility of conflicts of interest arising in relation to minority interests and shall ensure that any such conflicts are addressed. Where appropriate, the advisory client and minority interests shall be advised as to the desirability of the minority interests appointing a wholly independent adviser.

Underwriting and marketing of shares

221.31 A professional accountant in public practice who is an auditor or reporting accountant shall not deal in, underwrite or promote shares for their client (see also APB's Ethical Standard 5 and APB's Ethical Standard for Reporting Accountants) .Involvement of this kind would give rise to an advocacy threat, self-review threat and self-interest threat such that the professional accountant in public practice's objectivity and independence would be threatened.

221.32 It may be appropriate:

- for an auditor or reporting accountant otherwise to assist a client in raising capital; or
- for an auditor or reporting accountant otherwise to provide independent advice to a client, or its professional advisers, in connection with the issue or sale of shares or securities to the public; or
- for an auditor or reporting accountant otherwise to provide advice as sponsor, as an AIM nominated adviser or as a PLUS corporate adviser to a company as set out below.

In these situations the professional accountant in public practice shall adopt steps similar to those described in paragraph 220.3 and 220.4 of section 220 and, additionally, set up procedures to review and identify any potential conflicts of interest which could compromise the professional accountant in public practice's objectivity.

Sponsors, nominated advisers and corporate advisers

The attention of professional accountants in public practice is drawn to:

221.33

- the UK Listing Authority's Listing Rules when a firm accepts the responsibilities of a sponsor;
- the London Stock Exchange's Alternative Investment Market ('AIM') Roles and, AIM Rules for Nominated Advisers (which include the Eligibility Criteria for Nominated Advisers.) AIM's requirement is that for AIM companies to maintain their trading facility they shall have a nominated adviser at all times. In this context professional accountants in public practice shall have in place procedures to enable them to identify whether any conflicts exist or are likely to arise in the future before acting as a nominated adviser. Professional accountants in public practice shall note the policy of the London Stock Exchange that it will not normally allow a nominated adviser to be the reporting accountant to the issuer unless appropriate safeguards are in place as set out in paragraph 221.17 above. Furthermore, professional accountants in public practice shall note that the London Stock Exchange does not permit a nominated adviser to act for any other party to a transaction or takeover other than its AIM client company. In cases of doubt, professional accountants in public practice shall consult the London Stock Exchange.
- the PLUS Rules and in particular the PLUS Corporate Advisers Handbook when acting as a Corporate Adviser defined by the PLUS Rules. PLUS's requirement is that for PLUS companies to maintain their trading facility they shall have a corporate adviser at all times. In this context professional accountants in public practice shall have in place procedures to enable them to identify whether any conflicts exist or are likely to arise in the future before acting as a corporate adviser. Professional accountants in public practice shall note that PLUS does not permit a corporate adviser to act for any other party to a transaction or takeover other than its PLUS client company. In cases of doubt, professional accountants in public practice shall consult PLUS.

Considerable care needs to be taken if a professional accountant in public practice is also to act as sponsor, nominated adviser or corporate adviser to an assurance client. A threat to the objectivity of the auditor or reporting accountant can arise as the duties of a sponsor, nominated adviser or corporate adviser are different from those of an auditor or reporting accountant and are owed to a different party. Although it is quite possible that no conflict will arise between the two roles, professional accountants in public practice need to recognise the possibility of conflicts arising, particularly if the role of sponsor, nominated adviser or corporate adviser is to include any advocacy of the directors' views or if the transaction is to involve any issue of securities. To comply with the requirements of paragraph 221.31 above, where there is an issue of securities associated with such a transaction, a separate broker shall be appointed to take responsibility for any underwriting or marketing of the company's shares.

221.34

Appendix 1 to Section 221 – Corporate finance advice

Information on statutory and other regulatory and professional requirements

For the assistance of professional accountants a list of the relevant legislative and regulatory measures and professional guidance is set out below. This reflects the position as at **1 April 2010**. Professional accountants shall be aware that this list may be subject to variation in the future and when undertaking corporate finance assignments professional accountants shall ensure they are aware of the current status of the list.

1   The Financial Services and Markets Act 2000, the Companies Act 1985 as amended, the Companies Act 2006, Part V of the Criminal Justice Act 1993 and, where applicable, the requirements of the Financial Services Authority's Handbook (fsa.-gov.uk/Pages/handbook) or the ICAEW's Designated Professional Body Handbook (icaew.com/dpb).

2   The City Code on Takeovers and Mergers (the 'City Code').

3   The Financial Services Authority Handbook which includes:

- the Listing Rules;
- the Prospectus Rules;
- the Disclosure and Transparency Rules; and
- the London Stock Exchange's AIM Rules and AIM Rules for Nominated Advisers (which include the Eligibility Criteria for Nominated Advisers)

4   The PLUS Market Corporate Adviser Handbook.

5   The Admission and Disclosure Standards of the London Stock Exchange.

6   The Auditing Practices Board's Ethical Standards, in particular ES 5 Non-Audit Services Provided to Audit clients and the Ethical Standard for Reporting Accountants (frc.org.uk/apb/publications).

And in the Republic of Ireland:

7   Investment Intermediaries Act, 1995 as amended by the Investor Compensation Act, 1998 and the Insurance Act, 2000 ('IIA'), and where applicable the requirements of the Central Bank of Ireland's Role Book or the ICAEW's Investment Business regulations and Guidance.

8   Irish Takeover Panel Act, 1997.

9   The Listing Rules of the Irish Stock Exchange: the IEX Roles.

10   Code of Conduct issued by the Central Bank of Ireland under Section 37 of the IIA, as amended by S. 30 of the Insurance Act 2000.

11   European Communities (Takeover Bids (Directive 2004/25/EC) regulations 2006 (RoI).

12   Investment Funds, Companies and Miscellaneous Provisions Act, 2005 (RoI).

13   Market Abuse (Directive 2003/6/EC) regulations 2005 (RoI).

14   Prospectus (Directive 2003/71/EC) regulations 2005.

Appendix 2 to Section 221 – Corporate finance advice

A professional accountant in public practice who provides takeover services for clients is required to comply with the City Code and with all rulings made and guidance issued under it by the Panel on Takeovers and Mergers ('the Takeover Panel'). **1**

Accordingly a professional accountant in public practice proposing to provide takeover services to a client shall at the outset: **2**

- explain that these responsibilities will apply; and
- include in the terms of the engagement recognition of the professional accountant in public practice's obligation to comply with the City Code including any steps which the professional accountant in public practice may be obliged to take in performing those responsibilities. A specimen clause for the engagement letter is set out in paragraph 3 below.

Specimen clause for engagement letters

The client agrees and acknowledges that where the services provided by the professional accountant in public practice relate to a transaction within the scope of the City Code, the client and the professional accountant in public practice will comply with the provisions of the City Code and will observe the terms of the Guidance Note published by the Institutes of Chartered Accountants relevant to such services or transactions. In particular, the client acknowledges that: **3**

- if the client or its advisers or agents fail to comply with the City Code then the professional accountant in public practice may withdraw from acting for the client; and
- the professional accountant in public practice is obliged to supply to the Takeover Panel any information, books, documents or other records concerning the services or transaction which the Takeover Panel may require.

Scope of takeover services

Takeover services' means any professional services provided by a professional accountant in public practice to a client in connection with a transaction to which the City Code applies. **4**

The kinds of activities most commonly relevant for this purpose include: **5**

- acting as financial adviser to one of the parties (for example, as 'Role 3 adviser' to the offeree company);
- reporting on profit forecasts and/or valuations for the purposes of takeover documents;
- conducting acquisition searches for clients, and introducing clients to other parties with a view to effecting transactions;
- advising in relation to acquisitions and disposals of securities of companies which are subject to City Code.
- acting as a reporting accountant where both the City Code and the Listing Rules or Take Over Roles apply.

Whilst the City Code does not define precisely the range of activities and transactions within its scope, paragraph 3 of the Introduction to the City Code describes the companies and transactions which are subject to the City Code. In practice, those engaged in providing takeover services rarely experience difficulty in determining **6** whether the City Code is or may be relevant to the activities proposed to be undertaken for any particular client. In cases of any doubt the Takeover Panel shall be consulted.

Special responsibilities

7   A professional accountant in public practice who has provided or is providing takeover services to a client shall:

- supply to the Takeover Panel any information, books, documents or other records concerning the relevant transaction or arrangement which the Takeover Panel may properly require and which are in the possession or under the control of the professional accountant in public practice; and
- otherwise render all such assistance as the professional accountant in public practice is reasonably able to give to the Takeover Panel, provided that in each case the relevant information, books, documents or other records were acquired by the professional accountant in public practice in the course of providing the relevant takeover services.

8   Except with the consent of the Takeover Panel, a professional accountant in public practice shall not provide or continue to provide any takeover services to any person if the Takeover Panel has stated that it considers that such a person is not likely to comply with the standards of conduct for the time being expected in the United Kingdom concerning the practices of those involved in takeovers, mergers or substantial acquisitions of shares and the Takeover Panel has not subsequently indicated a change in this view. A person to whom this paragraph applies will normally have been named in a statement published by the Takeover Panel, inter alia, for the purposes of Role 4.3.1 of the Financial Services Authority's Handbook on Market Conduct.

9   If professional accountants in public practice have included in the engagement letter agreed with the client a provision as outlined in paragraph 3 above, they will be able to discharge their responsibilities under paragraph 7 and/or 8 above, without any breach of confidentiality or duty to the client. While professional accountants in public practice shall include such a provision, it is recognised that, on occasion, compliance with such responsibilities may still involve a breach of confidentiality to a third party or a breach of some other duty owed to the client. In such circumstances this Appendix is not applicable.

The Financial Services and Markets Act 2000

10   The provision of corporate finance services may require authorisation by the Financial Services Authority or a licence under the Designated Professional Body arrangements. However, this Guidance Note applies to all professional accountants in public practice whether authorised/licensed or not.

Appendix 3 to Section 221 – Corporate Finance Advice

Guidance for firms seeking to act for more than one party in a takeover subject to the City Code

This table is intended for illustrative purposes only and shall be read in conjunction with section 221, Corporate Finance Advice.

	Bid Situation	Target	Bidder	Subsequent Bidder	Comments
A	Agreed – relationship with one bidder	Ass	Ass	–	Permitted – see paragraph 221.24
B		Adv	Ass	–	Permitted by agreement with the Takeover Panel – see paragraph 221.29
C		Ass	Adv	–	Permitted with conditions – see paragraph 221.27
D		Adv	Adv		Prohibited – see paragraph 221.26
E	Hostile one bidder	Ass	Ass	–	Permitted with conditions – see paragraph 221.24
F		Adv	Ass		Permitted by agreement with the Takeover Panel – see paragraph 221.29
G		Ass	Adv		Prohibited – see paragraph 221.26 and 221.27
H		Adv	Adv		Prohibited – see paragraph 221.26
I	Subsequent bidder emerges	Ass	Ass	Ass	Permitted – see paragraph 221.24
J		Ass		Ass	Permitted see paragraph 221.24
K		Adv		Ass	Permitted – see paragraph 221.28
L		Ass		Adv	Prohibited – see paragraph 221.26

M		Adv		Adv	Prohibited – see paragraph 221.26
N	Acting for rival bidders		Ass	Ass	Permitted – see paragraph 221.24
O			Adv	Ass	Permitted – see paragraph 221.28
P			Ass	Adv	Prohibited – see paragraph 221.26
Q			Adv	Adv	Prohibited – see paragraph 221.26

In all of the above cases where professional accountants in public practice may be permitted to act for more than one party, the professional accountants in public practice must consider the potential threats and put in place the appropriate safeguards as set out in paragraph 221.33. Furthermore, where stated, permission for the professional accountant in public practice to act for more than one party shall be obtained from the Takeover Panel.

Key

Adv   Professional accountant in public practice acts as lead adviser (see paragraph 221.17)

Ass   Professional accountant in public practice acts as auditor or reporting accountant.

As regards the application of this guidance to non-audit assurance engagements, professional accountant in public practice's attention is drawn to the explanatory note contained in the Definitions to Parts A, B and C.

Notes

1.   This matrix does not address a reverse takeover situation, where the offeror is required by the City Code to appoint advisers.
2.   The matrix does not cover the takeover of private companies, except those which are subject to the City Code. Private companies are subject to the general requirements of this Code.

230 Second Opinions

230.0   Opinions expressed informally by a professional accountant may be acted on, and professional accountants shall bear in mind the potential consequences of those opinions. Oral opinions shall as a matter of good practice, because of legal implications, be confirmed in writing as soon as practicable after giving the opinion. If a professional accountant is asked for a 'general opinion' (one relative to a hypothetical situation not related to specific entities or circumstances), whether written or oral, the professional accountant shall ensure that the recipient of the opinion understands that it has been given in the context of that particular hypothetical situation only.

Situations where a professional accountant in public practice is asked to provide a 230.1 second opinion on the application of accounting, auditing, reporting or other standards or principles to specific circumstances or transactions by or on behalf of a company or an entity that is not an existing client may create threats to compliance with the fundamental principles. For example, there may be a threat to professional competence and due care in circumstances where the second opinion is not based on the same set of facts that were made available to the existing accountant or is based on inadequate evidence. The existence and significance of any threat will depend on the circumstances of the request and all the other available facts and assumptions relevant to the expression of a professional judgment.

This section does not apply to expert evidence assignments, opinions pursuant to litigation and opinions provided to other firms and their clients jointly.

When asked to provide such an opinion, a professional accountant in public practice 230.2 shall evaluate the significance of any threats and apply safeguards when necessary to eliminate them or reduce them to an acceptable level. Examples of such safeguards include seeking client permission to contact the existing accountant, describing the limitations surrounding any opinion in communications with the client and providing the existing accountant with a copy of the opinion.

Professional accountant providing a second opinion will normally need to seek contact with the existing accountant (particularly if the existing accountant is engaged as auditor) and the client in order to:

• Ascertain the circumstances in which the consultation has been made; and
• Be apprised of all the facts relevant to the issue at the time the opinion is given.

If the company or entity seeking the opinion will not permit communication with the 230.3 existing accountant, a professional accountant in public practice shall determine whether, taking all the circumstances into account, it is appropriate to provide the opinion sought.

If the client will not allow the opinion-giver to carry out any of the steps referred to above, the opinion-giver must normally decline to act (particularly if the existing accountant is engaged as auditor).

240 Fees and other types of remuneration

ICAEW does not set charge-out rates or otherwise prescribe the basis for calculating 240.0 fees, nor does it ordinarily investigate complaints relating solely to the quantum of fees charged. However, professional accountants in public practice have certain professional responsibilities in relation to fees as set out in the following paragraphs.

When entering into negotiations regarding professional services, a professional 240.1 accountant in public practice may quote whatever fee is deemed appropriate. The fact that one professional accountant in public practice may quote a fee lower than another is not in itself unethical. Nevertheless, there may be threats to compliance with the fundamental principles arising from the level of fees quoted. For example, a self-interest threat to professional competence and due care is created if the fee quoted is so low that it may be difficult to perform the engagement in accordance with applicable technical and professional standards for that price.

240.2   The existence and significance of any threats created will depend on factors such as the level of fee quoted and the services to which it applies. The significance of any threat shall be evaluated and safeguards applied when necessary to eliminate the threat or reduce it to an acceptable level. Examples of such safeguards include:

- Making the client aware of the terms of the engagement and, in particular, the basis on which fees are charged and which services are covered by the quoted fee.
- Assigning appropriate time and qualified staff to the task.

240.2a   The basis on which fees will be calculated shall be discussed and explained at the earliest opportunity together with, where practicable, the estimated initial fee. Fees shall be determined by reference to:

- The seniority and professional expertise of the persons necessarily engaged on the work;
- The time expended by each;
- The degree of risk and responsibility which the work entails;
- The nature of the client's business, the complexity of its operation and the work to be performed;
- The priority and importance of the work to the client;
- Expenses properly incurred.

240.2b   The arrangements agreed shall be confirmed in writing prior to the commencement of any engagement, normally in an engagement letter, including a confirmation of any estimate, quotation or other indication, and where the basis of future fees will differ from that of initial fees, the basis on which such fees will be rendered. Where there is no engagement letter the professional accountant in public practice shall confirm the initial discussion in writing to the client as soon as practicable.

240.2c   In the case of assurance work, and in particular audit work, professional accountants in public practice who obtain work having quoted levels of fees which they have reason to believe are significantly lower than existing fees or, for example, those quoted by other tendering firms, shall be aware that their objectivity and the quality of their work may appear to be threatened by self-interest in securing the client. Such professional accountants in public practice shall ensure that their work complies with relevant standards, guidelines and regulations and, in particular, quality control procedures.

240.2d   In the event of a complaint being made to ICAEW where fees were a feature in obtaining or retaining the work, professional accountants in public practice shall demonstrate that:

- The work done was in accordance with relevant standards; and
- The client was not misled as to the basis on which fees for the current and/or subsequent years are to be determined.

240.3   Contingent fees are widely used for certain types of non-assurance engagements.[1] They may, however, create threats to compliance with the fundamental principles in certain circumstances. They may create a self-interest threat to objectivity. The existence and significance of such threats will depend on factors including:

- The nature of the engagement.
- The range of possible fee amounts.
- The basis for determining the fee.
- Whether the outcome or result of the transaction is to be reviewed by an independent third party.

The significance of any such threats shall be evaluated and safeguards applied when necessary to eliminate or reduce them to an acceptable level. Examples of such safeguards include: **240.4**

- An advance written agreement with the client as to the basis of remuneration.
- Disclosure to intended users of the work performed by the professional accountant in public practice and the basis of remuneration.
- Quality control policies and procedures.
- Review by an independent third party of the work performed by the professional accountant in public practice.

In some formal appointments under insolvency legislation, in particular bankruptcies, liquidations and administrations, the remuneration of the professional accountant in public practice may, by statute, be based on a percentage of: **240.4a**

- Realisations or the value of the property with which the professional accountant in public practice has to deal; and/or
- Distributions.

Consequently, it may not be possible to base the fee on the principle in paragraph 240.4 above.

In some circumstances, such as advising on a management buy-in or buy-out, the raising of venture capital, acquisition searches or sales mandates, where no professional opinion is given, it may not be appropriate to charge fees save on a contingent fee basis: to require otherwise might deprive potential clients of professional assistance, for example where the capacity of the client to pay is dependent upon the success or failure of the venture. **240.4b**

Due diligence assignments, particularly those performed in relation to a prospective transaction, typically involve a high level of risk and responsibility. A higher fee may be charged for such work in respect of a completed transaction than for the same transaction if it is not completed, for whatever reason, provided that the difference reflects any additional risk and responsibility. **240.4c**

Fee information and disputes

A professional accountant in public practice shall furnish, either in the fee account or subsequently on request, and without further charge, such details as are reasonable to enable the client to understand the basis on which the fee account has been prepared. **240.4d**

Where fees rendered without prior agreement exceed, by more than a reasonable amount, a quotation or estimate or indication of fees given by a professional accountant in public practice, the professional accountant in public practice shall be prepared to provide the client with a full and detailed explanation of the excess and to take steps to resolve speedily any dispute which arises. **240.4e**

A professional accountant in public practice whose fees have not been paid may be entitled to retain certain books and papers of a client by exercising a lien and may refuse to pass on information to the client or the successor accountant until those fees are paid (but see section 210, 'Professional appointment'). However, a professional accountant in public practice who so acts shall be prepared to take reasonable and prompt steps to resolve any dispute relating to the amount of that fee. In respect of any fee dispute, a professional accountant in public practice shall be aware of the fee arbitration services offered by the Institute. **240.4f**

240.4g   Overdue fees may give rise to a perceived or real self-interest threat (see section 280). Similar considerations apply to work-in-progress for a client if billing is unduly deferred.

Referrals and commissions

240.5   In certain circumstances, a professional accountant in public practice may receive a referral fee or commission relating to a client. For example, where the professional accountant in public practice does not provide the specific service required, a fee may be received for referring a continuing client to another professional accountant in public practice or other expert. A professional accountant in public practice may receive a commission from a third party (e.g., a software vendor) in connection with the sale of goods or services to a client. Accepting such a referral fee or commission creates a self-interest threat to objectivity and professional competence and due care.

240.6.   A professional accountant in public practice may also pay a referral fee to obtain a client, for example, where the client continues as a client of another professional accountant in public practice but requires specialist services not offered by the existing accountant. The payment of such a referral fee also creates a self-interest threat to objectivity and professional competence and due care.

240.7   The significance of the threat shall be evaluated and safeguards applied when necessary to eliminate the threat or reduce it to an acceptable level. Examples of such safeguards include:

- Disclosing to the client any arrangements to pay a referral fee to another professional accountant for the work referred.
- Disclosing to the client any arrangements to receive a referral fee for referring the client to another professional accountant in public practice.
- Obtaining advance agreement from the client for commission arrangements in connection with the sale by a third party of goods or services to the client.

Remuneration of employees would not normally be included within the scope of the payments addressed above.

240.7a   A fiduciary relationship between a professional accountant in public practice and his or her client will arise where the accountant acts as the client's agent; and/or where the accountant gives professional advice to the client so as to give rise to a relationship which the law would regard as one of 'trust and confidence'. Where a fiduciary relationship exists at the time between a professional accountant in public practice and a client, the professional accountant in public practice is legally bound to account to the client for any commission, fee or other benefit received from a third party at any time. ICAEW is advised that the effect is that a professional accountant in public practice will require the informed consent of the client if the professional accountant in public practice is to retain the commission, fee or other benefit or any part of it. If professional accountants in public practice are in doubt as to whether the circumstances give rise to a fiduciary relationship, they are recommended to seek appropriate legal advice.

240.7b   Under the general law, professional accountants must adopt one of the following courses in respect of commission receivable[2] :

- Account to the client for the commission or other benefit. This could be effected:
  - By payment of the whole commission or benefit to the client, or
  - By deducting the amount received from the fees otherwise chargeable to the client and by showing such deduction on the face of the bill.

- Obtain the client's advance consent to each receipt of commission
  This involves obtaining consent before the commission is received and the firm must disclose, in advance, the actual amount of the commission (or its basis of calculation) and the terms and timing of its payment.
- Obtain the client's advance general consent to the member's retaining commission.
  This could be by way of the engagement letter, or by a supplementary agreement, containing explicit wording permitting such retention, such as the following:
  'In some circumstances, commissions or other benefits may become payable to us [or to one of our associates] in respect of transactions we [or such associates] arrange for you, in which case you will be notified in writing of the amount and terms of payment. [The fees that would otherwise be payable by you as described above will [or will not] be abated by such amounts.] You consent to such commission or other benefits being retained by us [or, as the case may be, by our associates,] without our, [or their,] being liable to account to you for any such amounts.'
  Note:
  - o Before the client agrees to any such provision, examples must be given of likely commissions that may be received and the likely amounts, and it shall be emphasised that these are only examples and may not cover all receipts in the future. If, in the future, abnormally large commissions are received which were not envisaged when the engagement letter was signed, it would be advisable to obtain specific consent to the retention of those commissions in order to meet any assertion that retention of such commission was not authorised by the engagement letter.
  - o Any further provision which indicated likely levels of commission, and then continued 'Commissions of less than £X will be retained by us, and commissions of more than £X will be divided equally between yourselves and ourselves' might be effective. Members are advised, however, to consult with their lawyers before including such a provision.
  - o Where an existing client of the member is to sign a new engagement letter containing such a provision as is referred to above, the firm shall explain that, in the absence of the signed engagement letter, the firm could retain the commission only if the client gave full and informed consent on each occasion after receiving full disclosure of the amount involved, whereas, once the letter is signed, the firm can keep the commission.
- Obtain the client's subsequent consent
  If the member does not obtain the client's consent in one of the ways referred to in paragraph 240.7b above, the commission may still be able to be retained if the client subsequently expressly consents to such retention (on the basis of foll disclosure of the amount, terms and timing of payment).

Alternatively professional accountants will be able to retain the commission if the client (with knowledge of all relevant facts) impliedly consents by acquiescing in such retention, for instance by deciding to proceed with the transaction having been notified both of the fact that the firm will receive commission and of the foll details of that commission. **240.7c**

Even where a fiduciary relationship does not exist, where a professional accountant in public practice becomes aware that any commission, fee or other benefit may be received (directly or indirectly), there shall be disclosed to the client in writing: **240.7d**

- That commission or benefit will result or is likely to result, and
- When the fact is known, that such commission or benefit will be received, and

- As early as possible, the amount and terms of the benefit to the professional accountant in public practice.

240.7e   As regards payments of referral fees, professional accountants in public practice have a responsibility to ascertain that a referral manner is in accordance with this Code because professional accountants in public practice must not do, or be seen to do, through others what they may not do themselves. To this end, professional accountants in public practice shall consider whether there are any indications that the work or client has been initially procured in an unprofessional manner. In addition, where needed to complete a referred engagement properly, professional accountants in public practice shall:

- Satisfy themselves as to the competence and professional standards of staff within their firm whose work on the engagement it would be their duty to review; and
- Ensure their right of direct access to the client and, in appropriate circumstances, render their own fee account to the client.

240.7f   In the case of insolvency work, Insolvency Practitioners shall have regard to Part D of this Code.

240.7g   Where an invitation to conduct a statutory audit comes other than directly from the client, the professional accountant in public practice shall first ensure that the audit appointment has properly been made in accordance with statute. It shall be made clear to all interested parties on all relevant documents that the professional accountant in public practice is acting as principal, with all that that function implies. In those circumstances, professional accountants in public practice shall deal directly with the client and shall render their own fee account in addition to complying with the other requirements above.

240.8   A professional accountant in public practice may purchase all or part of another firm on the basis that payments will be made to individuals formerly owning the firm or to their heirs or estates. Such payments are not regarded as commissions or referral fees for the purpose of paragraphs 240.5-240.7 above.

Attention is drawn to additional requirements in respect of agency and referral arrangements, in section 241.

241 Agencies and referrals

241.1   When referring or receiving referred work or when establishing agency arrangements, which are in effect permanent arrangements for making referrals, professional accountants in public practice are required to assess threats to compliance with the fundamental principles and to apply safeguards. A referral covers a formal request made in the course of a professional relationship for advice on the selection of a potential professional adviser and may also cover an informal request, regardless of whether there is an existing relationship.

Attention is drawn to additional requirements in respect of referral fee arrangements, in section 240.

Duty of care

In making a referral, a duty of care may arise. The extent of a duty of care varies **241.2** according to the circumstances, including whether the exchange or provision of information was solicited or not. A greater duty of care will arise for matters which are reasonably expected to be within a professional accountant in public practice's knowledge or where a fee is charged. A professional accountant in public practice needs to look at this from the client's or enquirer's point of view and what their expectations would be of what a professional accountant in public practice would be expected to know:

- Where a referral fee is received, or where the service referred is in a professional or finance-related sphere, the client (or enquirer) can reasonably presume knowledge by the professional accountant in public practice. Any limitation of knowledge would clearly need to be explained.
- Where the enquiry relates to a service outside the normal sphere of expertise of an accountant and no referral fee is contemplated, then it is reasonable to presume that the enquiry is being made in a personal capacity, unless circumstances suggest otherwise. It is still advisable to express any limitations of knowledge and to clarify, in case of doubt, that any opinion is based on personal experience rather than in a professional capacity.

When making a referral, disclosure of relevant knowledge limitations shall be con- **241.3** sidered. Professional accountants in public practice shall consider whether it would be in their interest for such knowledge limitations to be disclosed in writing, according to the circumstances. Factors that a professional accountant in public practice shall consider when making such a decision include:

- The nature of the professional relationship with the enquirer (an existing client, someone who could reasonably be considered to be making the enquiry as a prospective client or a casual enquiry).
- The context in which the enquiry is made. Is it professional or personal, casual or formal?
- The nature of the personal relationship. Does the enquirer know the professional accountant in public practice is a Chartered Accountant and are they consulting them as a respected professional?
- The scope of enquiry and whether a referral fee is contemplated, as considered in section 240.
- The enquirer's expectations.

A referral arises typically, when the professional accountant in public practice does **241.4** not have the expertise and/or resource in house to undertake the potential engagement. It follows that the professional accountant in public practice will not necessarily know enough to be able to completely assess whether the third party is the optimum choice or not. This is an inevitable limitation in most referrals, and what the referral is based on will vary. However, the professional accountant in public practice shall consider the fitness for purpose of the third party to address the client's needs.

In making that consideration, the professional accountant in public practice: **241.5**

- Can take account of the professional or regulatory status of the prospective referee;
- Is not normally expected to have to make additional enquiries about the prospective referee and can make the assessment based on what is already known.

241.6   A referral shall not normally be made to a third party even with a disclaimer, when, taking into account known factors, the professional accountant in public practice knows of a better alternative. If the client or enquirer insists on being referred to a particular third party and the professional accountant in public practice believes there is a better alternative, the reference may be made but the client or enquirer shall be made aware of the professional accountant in public practice's concerns. Where the referral relates to an end product or service, rather than an intermediary, and the professional accountant in public practice knows there are other alternatives but does not know if they are better, this shall be explained.

241.7   If there is a relationship with the third party, for example a family connection or an automatic referral arrangement, there are clear self-interest or familiarity threats and the connection shall be disclosed. This is particularly important where a professional accountant in public practice is considering recommending the products of another supplier with which there is an agency, and/or a principal or employee of the professional accountant in public practice's firm is a principal or officer of the other supplier. If in substance there is a one-to-one relationship between the professional accountant in public practice and the third party (for example, the professional accountant in public practice is the only accountant in the area and the third party is the only solicitor), which implies automatic referral, this shall also be disclosed.

241.8   In summary, professional accountants in public practice shall:

- Consider any factors they are aware of that would indicate the proposed third party is not fit for purpose in terms of the potential engagement. The professional accountant in public practice shall take into account what a reasonable person might expect a Chartered Accountant to know;
- Make clients (or enquirers), that are proposed to be referred, aware of limitations in knowledge;
- Disclose any referral arrangement;
- Ensure that any contractual arrangement does not override the needs of an individual client.

Establishing Agencies

241.9   The guidance which follows is intended to assist professional accountants in public practice in their arrangements with other suppliers of services and products.

241.10   This section addresses agreements that in effect provide for permanent arrangements for referrals. The issues are considered to be similar to those above for referrals in general except that an agency contract will usually bind the agent in terms of whom it can refer to for particular types of work. When professional accountants in public practice are considering the establishment of an agency, the terms of the agency contract (actual or implied) shall not require exclusive referral of all clients regardless of suitability. For example, professional accountants in public practice shall not be party to an agency by which they are constrained to channel all funds received by it for investment into a single bank/building society. Such a clause would make important safeguards inoperable.

241.11   Before accepting appointment as auditor of another entity of which they are an agent, professional accountants in public practice shall consider whether the agency constitutes a material business relationship. See section 290, 'Independence – audit and review engagements.'

241.12   Professional accountants in public practice shall not, because of the self-interest threat, enter into any financial arrangements with another supplier either personally or through their firm which would prejudice the objectivity of themselves or their firm.

Before accepting or continuing an agency with another supplier, professional accountants in public practice shall satisfy themselves that their ability to discharge their professional obligations to their clients is not compromised. **241.13**

A professional accountant in public practice shall not in any circumstances conduct its practice in such a manner as to give the impression that the professional accountant is a principal rather than an agent. This would include considering signs on premises and any other outward signs or literature used. This would relate in particular to agencies with entities such as banks and building societies, where confusion as to status can arise (see also 'The names and letterheads of practising firms' at (icaew.com/regulations). **241.14**

Firms in the Republic of Ireland must be authorised under the Investment Intermediaries Act, 1995 to hold an agency with a building society and that arrangement shall relate solely to deposit taking and not for example relate to products of a particular insurance company or unit trust organisation for which the building society is an appointed representative. Firms holding building society agencies must ensure that their agency agreement contains no obligation which would cause, or would be perceived to cause, them to breach the provisions of either the Act or the Institute of Chartered Accountants in Ireland's Investment Business regulations and Guidance. Firms cannot hold agencies with banks. **241.15**

Investment business agencies and introductions

When considering referrals of investment business ('introductions') or the establishment of investment business agencies, professional accountants in public practice shall apply the general principles and requirements set out in the previous Sections. However, they will also need to consider: **241.16**

- Whether the introduction or agency is permitted by regulation; and
- Whether the status of the third party investment business provider is compatible with the requirement to give objective advice.

Regulated activities under the Financial Services and Markets Act 2000 (United Kingdom)

In order to make a decision about whether an introduction is a regulated activity, the professional accountant in public practice must look at how the introduction is made and also what type of investment the client is considering (such as life assurance and pensions, unit trusts, shares, mortgages or general insurance). A regulated introduction can only be made under the terms of the Act by a firm which is licensed by ICAEW as a Designated Professional Body ('DPB') (a licensed firm) or a firm which is authorised by the Financial Services Authority ('authorised'). Unauthorised / unlicensed firms are restricted in that they can only make introductions for general financial advice where no specific type of investment is referred to, or for a restricted range of investments, such as shares and unit trusts. Such introductions can only be made to those authorised firms who can give independent advice. However, unauthorised / unlicensed firms can provide information to a client about a third party provided no recommendation is made. **241.17**

Further guidance on the difference between a regulated introduction and the provision of information in respect of insurance business, and the regulatory **241.18** consequences thereof, is set out in Schedule 6 to Part 3 of the DPB Handbook, available at icaew.com/dpb.

241.19 Having established that an introduction can be made in compliance with regulatory requirements, professional accountants in public practice shall bear in mind the need to provide their clients with objective advice, in compliance with these ethical standards.

241.20 Professional accountants in public practice can become appointed representatives of another authorised firm. When selecting which authorised firm to become an appointed representative of, professional accountants in public practice shall again bear in mind the need to provide their clients with objective advice.

Regulated Activities under the Investment Intermediaries Act, 1995 (Republic of Ireland)

241.21 Professional accountants in public practice may only make an introduction or refer clients to another authorised firm if they are themselves authorised to conduct investment business under the Investment Intermediaries Act 1995 and where required hold an appropriate letter of appointment.

241.22 Professional accountants in public practice when selecting an authorised firm shall bear in mind the need to provide their clients with objective advice.

Status of investment business providers

241.23 Authorised firms can fall into the following categories:

Type of firm	What the firm can recommend	Can there generally be introductions to this type of firm?
Independent	Recommend products from the whole market and offer clients the ability to pay by fee. Only these firms can describe themselves as independent financial advisers. The client may be able to elect for the adviser to be paid by commission	Yes (241.24 below)
Whole of market (UK only)	Recommend products from the whole market but do not offer clients the ability to pay by fee. The firm is remunerated by commission.	Yes (241.25 below)
Multi-tied (Multi-agency in RoI)	Recommend the products of more than one product provider with whom the firm has agreements, but recommends on less than the whole market.	Depends on scope of choice (241.26 below)
Tied	Recommend the products of one product provider.	No (241.27 below)

An introduction to an independent firm would be likely to meet the requirement to give objective advice but professional accountants in public practice are reminded of the general requirements above. **241.24**

Professional accountants in public practice may also regard 'whole of market' authorised firms as equivalent to independent firms as the method by which the authorised firm is remunerated (which is the difference between independent and whole of market) is not relevant for the purposes of compliance with this statement. **241.25**

Professional accountants in public practice may in some situations be able to introduce to multi-tied firms and still comply with the ethical requirements (however, see paragraphs 241.16-241.18 above as to whether the introduction can only be made by a DPB licensed firm or an FSA authorised firm, if it is a 'regulated' activity). Clearly the principal threat is that clients might not be offered the most appropriate choice. The professional accountant in public practice will need to assess the client's requirements and whether the multi-tied firm places business with the product providers who account for a large majority of the relevant market or offer the sector of the market which is most suitable for the client's needs. However, members must ensure that in making such an assessment, they are not effectively making their own recommendation unless they are able to do so under the terms of a licence or authorisation. The professional accountant in public practice may decide that this does not restrict the client's access to the range of product providers to an extent where there is any potential detriment. The professional accountant in public practice shall make the client aware of restrictions in the range of investments offered by the firm to which the client is being referred. **241.26**

An introduction to a tied firm restricts the client's ability to obtain independent advice and would therefore not be objective. **241.27**

Similar considerations to those noted above apply to whether a professional accountant in public practice shall become an appointed representative under the Financial Services and Markets Act 2000. Thus, for example, a professional firm cannot become an appointed representative for regulated investment business, of a tied firm as the agency agreement would probably oblige the firm to make referrals to the principal in all circumstances and the firm would be unable to provide objective advice. **241.28**

250 Marketing Professional services

When a professional accountant in public practice solicits new work through advertising or other forms of marketing, there may be a threat to compliance with the fundamental principles. For example, a self-interest threat to compliance with the principle of professional behaviour is created if services, achievements, or products are marketed in a way that is inconsistent with that principle. **250.1.**

A professional accountant in public practice shall not bring the profession into disrepute when marketing professional services. The professional accountant in public practice shall be honest and truthful and not: **250.2**

- Make exaggerated claims for services offered, qualifications possessed, or experience gained; or
- Make disparaging references or unsubstantiated comparisons to the work of another.

In particular, where professional accountants in public practice seek to make comparisons of their promotional material between their practices or services and those of others, great care will be required. In particular, they shall ensure that such comparisons:

● Are objective and not misleading,
● Relate to the same services,
● Are factual and verifiable, and
● Do not discredit or denigrate the practice or services of others.

particular care is needed in unclear or subjective claims of size or quality. For example, it is impossible to know whether a claim to be 'the largest firm' in an area is a reference to the number of partners or staff, the number of offices or the amount of fee income. A claim to be 'the best firm' is unlikely to be able to be substantiated.

If the professional accountant in public practice is in doubt about whether a proposed form of advertising or marketing is appropriate, the professional accountant in public practice shall consider consulting with ICAEW.

250.3   A professional accountant in public practice shall ensure that all advertisements, including letterheads, invoices and other practice documents, comply with the law and conform with the requirements of the relevant Advertising Standards Authority (for example, the British Code of Advertising) notably, as to legality, decency, clarity, honesty and truthfulness.

250.4   If reference is made in promotional material to fees, the basis on which the fees are calculated, or to hourly or other charging rates, the greatest care shall be taken to ensure that such reference does not mislead as to the precise range of services and the time commitment that the reference is intended to cover. Professional accountants in public practice are unlikely to be able to comply with the requirements of 250.2 if making a comparison in such material between their fees and the fees of another accounting practice, whether members or not. A professional accountant in public practice may offer a free consultation at which fees are discussed.

250.5   Professional accountants in public practice shall never promote or seek to promote their services, or the services of other professional accountants in public practice, in such a way, or to such an extent, as to amount to harassment of a potential client.

It shall be noted that special roles apply in relation to the conduct of Insolvency Practice and licensed practitioners shall have regard to the relevant legislation and to Part D. Similarly professional accountants in public practice whose firm is registered for the conduct of investment business shall have recourse to the relevant Investment Business regulations.

250.6   Further guidance on marketing professional services is available to members in a helpsheet from the Ethics Advisory Services (icaew.com/ethicsadvice). See also sections 210, 'Professional appointment' and 230, 'Second opinions'.

260 Gifts and hospitality

260.1   A professional accountant in public practice, or an immediate or close family member, may be offered gifts and hospitality from a client. Such an offer may create threats to compliance with the fundamental principles. For example, a self-interest or familiarity threat to objectivity may be created if a gift from a client is accepted; an intimidation threat to objectivity may result from the possibility of such offers being made public.

The existence and significance of any threat will depend on the nature, value, and intent of the offer. Where gifts or hospitality are offered that a reasonable and informed third party, weighing all the specific facts and circumstances, would consider trivial and inconsequential, a professional accountant in public practice may conclude that the offer is made in the normal course of business without the specific intent to influence decision making or to obtain information. In such cases, the professional accountant in public practice may generally conclude that any threat to compliance with the fundamental principles is at an acceptable level.

260.2

A professional accountant in public practice shall evaluate the significance of any threats and apply safeguards when necessary to eliminate the threats or reduce them to an acceptable level. When the threats cannot be eliminated or reduced to an acceptable level through the application of safeguards, a professional accountant in public practice shall not accept such an offer.

260.3

Further guidance on dealing with gifts and hospitality in an assurance engagement is available in paragraph 290.230.

260.4

270 Custody of client assets

A professional accountant in public practice shall not assume custody of client monies or other assets unless permitted to do so by law and, if so, in compliance with any additional legal duties imposed on a professional accountant in public practice holding such assets.

270.1

The holding of client assets creates threats to compliance with the fundamental principles; for example, there is a self-interest threat to professional behaviour and may be a self interest threat to objectivity arising from holding client assets. A professional accountant in public practice entrusted with money (or other assets) belonging to others shall therefore:

270.2

- Keep such assets separately from personal or firm assets;
- Use such assets only for the purpose for which they are intended;
- At all times be ready to account for those assets and any income, dividends, or gains generated, to any persons entitled to such accounting; and
- Comply with all relevant laws and regulations relevant to the holding of and accounting for such assets.

regulations on the procedures required to be adopted by professional accountants holding client monies are available at 'Clients' money regulations'. For firms licensed by ICAEW under the Designated Professional Bodies arrangements, additional requirements are included in Chapter 4 of the Designated Professional Bodies Handbook.

As part of client and engagement acceptance procedures for services that may involve the holding of client assets, a professional accountant in public practice shall make appropriate inquiries about the source of such assets and consider legal and regulatory obligations. For example, if the assets were derived from illegal activities, such as money laundering, a threat to compliance with the fundamental principles would be created. In such situations, the professional accountant may consider seeking legal advice.

270.3

Further guidance on money laundering regulation and legislation is available in 'Anti-money laundering guidance for the accountancy sector'.

See also 'Document and records: ownership, lien and rights of access'.

280 Objectivity – all services

280.1 A professional accountant in public practice shall determine when providing any professional service whether there are threats to compliance with the fundamental principle of objectivity resulting from having interests in, or relationships with, a client or its directors, officers or employees. For example, a familiarity threat to objectivity may be created from a family or close personal or business relationship.

280.2 A professional accountant in public practice who provides an assurance service shall be independent of the assurance client. Independence of mind and in appearance is necessary to enable the professional accountant in public practice to express a conclusion, and be seen to express a conclusion, without bias, conflict of interest, or undue influence of others. Sections 290 and 291 provide specific guidance on independence requirements for professional accountants in public practice when performing assurance engagements.

280.3 The existence of threats to objectivity when providing any professional service will depend upon the particular circumstances of the engagement and the nature of the work that the professional accountant in public practice is performing.

280.4 A professional accountant in public practice shall evaluate the significance of any threats and apply safeguards when necessary to eliminate them or reduce them to an acceptable level. Examples of such safeguards include:

- Withdrawing from the engagement team.
- Supervisory procedures.
- Terminating the financial or business relationship giving rise to the threat.
- Discussing the issue with higher levels of management within the firm.
- Discussing the issue with those charged with governance of the client.

If safeguards cannot eliminate or reduce the threat to an acceptable level, the professional accountant shall decline or terminate the relevant engagement.

290 Independence – audit and review engagements

Introduction

290.0a In accordance with UK legislation, ICAEW has adopted, as regards auditor independence requirements, the Ethical Standards for Auditors, issued by the Auditing Practices Board ('APB'). Therefore, when conducting audit engagements in accordance with ISAs (UK and Ireland), professional accountants shall comply with the requirements of the APB's Ethical Standards for Auditors, including Provisions Available for Small Entities (ES-PASE). For other audit and assurance engagements ICAEW's Code may apply (see 290.0c below).

290.0b The APB has stated, in ISA (UK and Ireland) 200, that it is not aware of any significant instances where the relevant parts of the IESBA Code of Ethics are more restrictive than the APB's Ethical Standards.

The independence requirements to be adopted for different types of assurance engagement, are set out below:

290.0c

Type of assurance engagement	Independence requirements to be followed
Audit engagements in accordance with ISAs (UK and Ireland)	The APB's Ethical Standards for Auditors
Audit engagements performed in accordance with other standards	Section 290 of this Code or if more convenient to apply, the independence requirements of the APB's Ethical Standards for Auditors.
Review engagements (see appendix to section 290)	Section 290 of this Code or if more convenient to apply, the independence requirements of the APB's Ethical Standards for Auditors.
Other types of assurance engagements	Section 291 of this Code.

Note that the Statements of Investment Circular Reporting Standards (SIRS), issued by the APB require compliance with the APB's Ethical Standard for Reporting Accountants (ESRA). Accordingly, any professional accountant in public practice issuing a report that states that the work has been carried out in accordance with the SIRS will need to comply with the independence requirements of the ESRA.

290.0d

Structure of section

This section addresses the independence requirements for audit engagements and review engagements, which are assurance engagements in which a professional accountant in public practice expresses a conclusion on financial statements. Such engagements comprise audit and review engagements to report on a complete set of financial statements and a single financial statement. Independence requirements for assurance engagements that are not audit or review engagements are addressed in section 291.

290.1

In certain circumstances involving audit engagements where the audit report includes a restriction on use and distribution and provided certain conditions are met, the independence requirements in this section may be modified as provided in paragraphs 290.500 to 290.514. The modifications are not permitted in the case of an audit of financial statements required by law or regulation.

290.2

In this section, the term(s):

290.3

- "Audit," "audit team," "audit engagement," "audit client" and "audit report" includes review, review team, review engagement, review client and review report; and
- "Firm" includes network firm, except where otherwise stated.

A conceptual framework approach to independence

In the case of audit engagements, it is in the public interest and, therefore, required by this Code of Ethics, that members of audit teams, firms and network firms shall be independent of audit clients.

290.4

290.5 The objective of this section is to assist firms and members of audit teams in applying the conceptual framework approach described below to achieving and maintaining independence.

290.6 Independence comprises:

- independence of Mind

  The state of mind that permits the expression of a conclusion without being affected by influences that compromise professional judgment, thereby allowing an individual to act with integrity and exercise objectivity and professional scepticism.

- independence in Appearance

  The avoidance of facts and circumstances that are so significant that a reasonable and informed third party would be likely to conclude, weighing all the specific facts and circumstances, that a firm's, or a member of the audit team's, integrity, objectivity or professional scepticism has been compromised.

290.7 The conceptual framework approach shall be applied by professional accountants to:

- Identify threats to independence;
- Evaluate the significance of the threats identified; and
- Apply safeguards, when necessary, to eliminate the threats or reduce them to an acceptable level.

When the professional accountant determines that appropriate safeguards are not available or cannot be applied to eliminate the threats or reduce them to an acceptable level, the professional accountant shall eliminate the circumstance or relationship creating the threats or decline or terminate the audit engagement.

A professional accountant shall use professional judgment in applying this conceptual framework.

290.8 Many different circumstances, or combinations of circumstances, may be relevant in assessing threats to independence. It is impossible to define every situation that creates threats to independence and to specify the appropriate action. Therefore, this Code establishes a conceptual framework that requires firms and members of audit teams to identify, evaluate, and address threats to independence. The conceptual framework approach assists professional accountants in practice in complying with the ethical requirements in this Code. It accommodates many variations in circumstances that create threats to independence and can deter a professional accountant from concluding that a situation is permitted if it is not specifically prohibited.

290.9 Paragraphs 290.100 and onwards describe how the conceptual framework approach to independence is to be applied. These paragraphs do not address all the circumstances and relationships that create or may create threats to independence.

290.10 In deciding whether to accept or continue an engagement, or whether a particular individual may be a member of the audit team, a firm shall identify and evaluate threats to independence. If the threats are not at an acceptable level, and the decision is whether to accept an engagement or include a particular individual on the audit team, the firm shall determine whether safeguards are available to eliminate the threats or reduce them to an acceptable level. If the decision is whether to continue an engagement, the firm shall determine whether any existing safeguards will continue to be effective to eliminate the threats or reduce them to an acceptable level or whether other safeguards will need to be applied or whether the engagement needs to be terminated. Whenever new information about a threat to independence comes to the attention of the firm during the engagement, the firm shall evaluate the significance of the threat in accordance with the conceptual framework approach.

Throughout this section, reference is made to the significance of threats to independence. In evaluating the significance of a threat, qualitative as well as quantitative factors shall be taken into account.

290.11

This section does not, in most cases, prescribe the specific responsibility of individuals within the firm for actions related to independence because responsibility may differ depending on the size, structure and organisation of a firm. The firm is required by International Standards on Quality Control to establish policies and procedures designed to provide it with reasonable assurance that independence is maintained when required by relevant ethical requirements. In addition, International Standards on Auditing require the engagement partner to form a conclusion on compliance with the independence requirements that apply to the engagement.

290.12

Networks and network firms

If a firm is deemed to be a network firm, the firm shall be independent of the audit clients of the other firms within the network (unless otherwise stated in this Code). The independence requirements in this section that apply to a network firm apply to any entity, such as a consulting practice or professional law practice, that meets the definition of a network firm irrespective of whether the entity itself meets the definition of a firm.

290.13

To enhance their ability to provide professional services, firms frequently form larger structures with other firms and entities. Whether these larger structures create a network depends on the particular facts and circumstances and does not depend on whether the firms and entities are legally separate and distinct. For example, a larger structure may be aimed only at facilitating the referral of work, which in itself does not meet the criteria necessary to constitute a network. Alternatively, a larger structure might be such that it is aimed at co-operation and the firms share a common brand name, a common system of quality control, or significant professional resources and consequently is deemed to be a network.

290.14

The judgment as to whether the larger structure is a network shall be made in light of whether a reasonable and informed third party would be likely to conclude, weighing all the specific facts and circumstances, that the entities are associated in such a way that a network exists. This judgment shall be applied consistently throughout the network.

290.15

Where the larger structure is aimed at co-operation and it is clearly aimed at profit or cost sharing among the entities within the structure, it is deemed to be a network. However, the sharing of immaterial costs does not in itself create a network. In addition, if the sharing of costs is limited only to those costs related to the development of audit methodologies, manuals, or training courses, this would not in itself create a network. Further, an association between a firm and an otherwise unrelated entity to jointly provide a service or develop a product does not in itself create a network.

290.16

Where the larger structure is aimed at cooperation and the entities within the structure share common ownership, control or management, it is deemed to be a network. This could be achieved by contract or other means.

290.17

290.18   Where the larger structure is aimed at co-operation and the entities within the structure share common quality control policies and procedures, it is deemed to be a network. For this purpose, common quality control policies and procedures are those designed, implemented and monitored across the larger structure.

290.19   Where the larger structure is aimed at co-operation and the entities within the structure share a common business strategy, it is deemed to be a network. Sharing a common business strategy involves an agreement by the entities to achieve common strategic objectives. An entity is not deemed to be a network firm merely because it co-operates with another entity solely to respond jointly to a request for a proposal for the provision of a professional service.

290.20   Where the larger structure is aimed at co-operation and the entities within the structure share the use of a common brand name, it is deemed to be a network. A common brand name includes common initials or a common name. A firm is deemed to be using a common brand name if it includes, for example, the common brand name as part of, or along with, its firm name, when a partner of the firm signs an audit report.

290.21   Even though a firm does not belong to a network and does not use a common brand name as part of its firm name, it may give the appearance that it belongs to a network if it makes reference in its stationery or promotional materials to being a member of an association of firms. Accordingly, if care is not taken in how a firm describes such memberships, a perception may be created that the firm belongs to a network.

290.22   If a firm sells a component of its practice, the sales agreement sometimes provides that, for a limited period of time, the component may continue to use the name of the firm, or an element of the name, even though it is no longer connected to the firm. In such circumstances, while the two entities may be practising under a common name, the facts are such that they do not belong to a larger structure aimed at co-operation and are, therefore, not network firms. Those entities shall determine how to disclose that they are not network firms when presenting themselves to outside parties.

290.23   Where the larger structure is aimed at co-operation and the entities within the structure share a significant part of professional resources, it is deemed to be a network. Professional resources include:

- Common systems that enable firms to exchange information such as client data, billing and time records;
- Partners and staff;
- Technical departments that consult on technical or industry specific issues, transactions or events for assurance engagements;
- Audit methodology or audit manuals; and
- Training courses and facilities.

290.24   The determination of whether the professional resources shared are significant, and therefore the firms are network firms, shall be made based on the relevant facts and circumstances. Where the shared resources are limited to common audit methodology or audit manuals, with no exchange of personnel or client or market information, it is unlikely that the shared resources would be significant. The same applies to a common training endeavour. Where, however, the shared resources involve the exchange of people or information, such as where staff are drawn from a shared pool, or a common technical department is created within the larger structure to provide participating firms with technical advice that the firms are required to follow, a reasonable and informed third party is more likely to conclude that the shared resources are significant.

Public interest entities

Section 290 contains additional provisions that reflect the extent of public interest in certain entities. For the purpose of this section, public interest entities are: **290.25**

- All listed entities; and
- Any entity:
  - Defined by regulation or legislation as a public interest entity or
  - For which the audit is required by regulation or legislation to be conducted in compliance with the same independence requirements that apply to the audit of listed entities. Such regulation may be promulgated by any relevant regulator, including an audit regulator.

Firms are encouraged to determine whether to treat additional entities, or certain categories of entities, as public interest entities because they have a large number and wide range of stakeholders. Factors to be considered include: **290.26**

- The nature of the business, such as the holding of assets in a fiduciary capacity for a large number of stakeholders. Examples may include financial institutions, such as banks and insurance companies, and pension funds;
- Size; and
- Number of employees.

Related Entities

In the case of an audit client that is a listed entity, references to an audit client in this section include related entities of the client (unless otherwise stated). For all other audit clients, references to an audit client in this section include related entities over which the client has direct or indirect control. When the audit team knows or has reason to believe that a relationship or circumstance involving another related entity of the client is relevant to the evaluation of the firm's independence from the client, the audit team shall include that related entity when identifying and evaluating threats to independence and applying appropriate safeguards. **290.27**

Those charged with governance

Even when not required by the Code, applicable auditing standards, law or regulation, regular communication is encouraged between the firm and those charged with governance of the audit client regarding relationships and other matters that might, in the firm's opinion, reasonably bear on independence. Such communication enables those charged with governance to: **290.28**

- consider the firm's judgments in identifying and evaluating threats to independence,
- consider the appropriateness of safeguards applied to eliminate them or reduce them to an acceptable level, and
- take appropriate action. Such an approach can be particularly helpful with respect to intimidation and familiarity threats.

Documentation

Documentation provides evidence of the professional accountant's judgments in forming conclusions regarding compliance with independence requirements. The absence of documentation is not a determinant of whether a firm considered a particular matter nor whether it is independent. The professional accountant shall document conclusions regarding compliance with independence requirements, and **290.29** the substance of any relevant discussions that support those conclusions. Accordingly:

- When safeguards are required to reduce a threat to an acceptable level, the professional accountant shall document the nature of the threat and the safeguards in place or applied that reduce the threat to an acceptable level; and
- When a threat required significant analysis to determine whether safeguards were necessary and the professional accountant concluded that they were not because the threat was already at an acceptable level, the professional accountant shall document the nature of the threat and the rationale for the conclusion.

Engagement Period

290.30   Independence from the audit client is required both during the engagement period and the period covered by the financial statements. The engagement period starts when the audit team begins to perform audit services. The engagement period ends when the audit report is issued. When the engagement is of a recurring nature, it ends at the later of the notification by either party that the professional relationship has terminated or the issuance of the final audit report.

290.31   When an entity becomes an audit client during or after the period covered by the financial statements on which the firm will express an opinion, the firm shall determine whether any threats to independence are created by:

- Financial or business relationships with the audit client during or after the period covered by the financial statements but before accepting the audit engagement; or
- Previous services provided to the audit client.

290.32   If a non-assurance service was provided to the audit client during or after the period covered by the financial statements but before the audit team begins to perform audit services and the service would not be permitted during the period of the audit engagement, the firm shall evaluate any threat to independence created by the service. If a threat is not at an acceptable level, the audit engagement shall only be accepted if safeguards are applied to eliminate any threats or reduce them to an acceptable level. Examples of such safeguards include:

- Not including personnel who provided the non-assurance service as members of the audit team;
- Having a professional accountant review the audit and non-assurance work as appropriate; or
- Engaging another firm to evaluate the results of the non-assurance service or having another firm re-perform the non-assurance service to the extent necessary to enable it to take responsibility for the service.

Mergers and Acquisitions

290.33   When, as a result of a merger or acquisition, an entity becomes a related entity of an audit client, the firm shall identify and evaluate previous and current interests and relationships with the related entity that, taking into account available safeguards, could affect its independence and therefore its ability to continue the audit engagement after the effective date of the merger or acquisition.

290.34   The firm shall take steps necessary to terminate, by the effective date of the merger or acquisition, any current interests or relationships that are not permitted under this Code. However, if such a current interest or relationship cannot reasonably be terminated by the effective date of the merger or acquisition, for example, because the related entity is unable by the effective date to effect an orderly transition to another service provider of a non-assurance service provided by the firm, the firm shall evaluate the threat that is created by such interest or relationship. The more significant the threat, the more likely the firm's objectivity will be compromised and it will be unable to continue as auditor. The significance of the threat will depend upon factors such as:

- The nature and significance of the interest or relationship;
- The nature and significance of the related entity relationship (for example, whether the related entity is a subsidiary or parent); and
- The length of time until the interest or relationship can reasonably be terminated.

The firm shall discuss with those charged with governance the reasons why the interest or relationship cannot reasonably be terminated by the effective date of the merger or acquisition and the evaluation of the significance of the threat.

If those charged with governance request the firm to continue as auditor, the firm shall do so only if: **290.35**

- the interest or relationship will be terminated as soon as reasonably possible and in all cases within six months of the effective date of the merger or acquisition;
- any individual who has such an interest or relationship, including one that has arisen through performing a non-assurance service that would not be permitted under this section, will not be a member of the engagement team for the audit or the individual responsible for the engagement quality control review; and
- appropriate transitional measures will be applied, as necessary, and discussed with those charged with governance. Examples of transitional measures include:
  - Having a professional accountant review the audit or non-assurance work as appropriate;
  - Having a professional accountant, who is not a member of the firm expressing the opinion on the financial statements, perform a review that is equivalent to an engagement quality control review; or
  - Engaging another firm to evaluate the results of the non-assurance service or having another firm re-perform the non-assurance service to the extent necessary to enable it to take responsibility for the service.

The firm may have completed a significant amount of work on the audit prior to the effective date of the merger or acquisition and may be able to complete the remaining audit procedures within a short period of time. In such circumstances, if those charged with governance request the firm to complete the audit while continuing with an interest or relationship identified in 290.33, the firm shall do so only if it: **290.36**

- Has evaluated the significance of the threat created by such interest or relationship and discussed the evaluation with those charged with governance;
- Complies with the requirements of paragraph 290.35(b)-(c); and
- Ceases to be the auditor no later than the issuance of the audit report.

When addressing previous and current interests and relationships covered by paragraphs 290.33 to 290.36, the firm shall determine whether, even if all the requirements could be met, the interests and relationships create threats that would remain so significant that objectivity would be compromised and, if so, the firm shall cease to be the auditor.   **290.37**

The professional accountant shall document any interests or relationships covered by paragraphs 290.34 and 36 that will not be terminated by the effective date of the   **290.38** merger or acquisition and the reasons why they will not be terminated, the transitional measures applied, the results of the discussion with those charged with governance, and the rationale as to why the previous and current interests and relationships do not create threats that would remain so significant that objectivity would be compromised.

Other considerations

290.39   There may be occasions when there is an inadvertent violation of this section. If such an inadvertent violation occurs, it generally will be deemed not to compromise independence provided the firm has appropriate quality control policies and procedures in place, equivalent to those required by International Standards on Quality Control, to maintain independence and, once discovered, the violation is corrected promptly and any necessary safeguards are applied to eliminate any threat or reduce it to an acceptable level. The firm shall determine whether to discuss the matter with those charged with governance.

Paragraphs 290.40 to 290.99 are intentionally left blank.

Application of the conceptual framework approach to independence

290.100   Paragraphs 290.102 to 290.231 describe specific circumstances and relationships that create or may create threats to independence. The paragraphs describe the potential threats and the types of safeguards that may be appropriate to eliminate the threats or reduce them to an acceptable level and identify certain situations where no safeguards could reduce the threats to an acceptable level. The paragraphs do not describe all of the circumstances and relationships that create or may create a threat to independence. The firm and the members of the audit team shall evaluate the implications of similar, but different, circumstances and relationships and determine whether safeguards, including the safeguards in paragraphs 200.12 to 200.15, can be applied when necessary to eliminate the threats to independence or reduce them to an acceptable level.

290.101   Paragraphs 290.102 to 290.126 contain references to the materiality of a financial interest, loan, or guarantee, or the significance of a business relationship. For the purpose of determining whether such an interest is material to an individual, the combined net worth of the individual and the individual's immediate family members may be taken into account.

Financial interests

290.102   Holding a financial interest in an audit client may create a self-interest threat. The existence and significance of any threat created depends on:

- the role of the person holding the financial interest,
- whether the financial interest is direct or indirect, and
- the materiality of the financial interest.

290.103   Financial interests may be held through an intermediary (e.g. a collective investment vehicle, estate or trust). The determination of whether such financial interests are direct or indirect will depend upon whether the beneficial owner has control over the investment vehicle or the ability to influence its investment decisions. When control over the investment vehicle or the ability to influence investment decisions exists, this Code defines that financial interest to be a direct financial interest. Conversely, when the beneficial owner of the financial interest has no control over the investment vehicle or ability to influence its investment decisions, this Code defines that financial interest to be an indirect financial interest.

290.104 If a member of the audit team, a member of that individual's immediate family or a firm has a direct financial interest or a material indirect financial interest in the audit client, the self-interest threat created would be so significant that no safeguards could reduce the threat to an acceptable level. Therefore, none of the following shall have a direct financial interest or a material indirect financial interest in the client: a member of the audit team; a member of that individual's immediate family; or the firm.

290.105 When a member of the audit team has a close family member who the audit team member knows has a direct financial interest or a material indirect financial interest in the audit client, a self-interest threat is created. The significance of the threat will depend on factors such as:

- The nature of the relationship between the member of the audit team and the close family member; and
- The materiality of the financial interest to the close family member.

The significance of the threat shall be evaluated and safeguards applied when necessary to eliminate the threat or reduce it to an acceptable level. Examples of such safeguards include:

- The close family member disposing, as soon as practicable, of all of the financial interest or disposing of a sufficient portion of an indirect financial interest so that the remaining interest is no longer material;
- Having a professional accountant review the work of the member of the audit team; or
- Removing the individual from the audit team.

290.106 If a member of the audit team, a member of that individual's immediate family, or a firm has a direct or material indirect financial interest in an entity that has a controlling interest in the audit client, and the client is material to the entity, the self-interest threat created would be so significant that no safeguards could reduce the threat to an acceptable level. Therefore, none of the following shall have such a financial interest: a member of the audit team; a member of that individual's immediate family; and the firm.

290.107 The holding by a firm's retirement benefit plan of a direct or material indirect financial interest in an audit client creates a self-interest threat. The significance of the threat shall be evaluated and safeguards applied when necessary to eliminate the threat or reduce it to an acceptable level.

290.108 If other partners in the office in which the engagement partner practices in connection with the audit engagement, or their immediate family members, hold a direct financial interest or a material indirect financial interest in that audit client, the self-interest threat created would be so significant that no safeguards could reduce the threat to an acceptable level. Therefore, neither such partners nor their immediate family members shall hold any such financial interests in such an audit client.

290.109 The office in which the engagement partner practices in connection with the audit engagement is not necessarily the office to which that partner is assigned. Accordingly, when the engagement partner is located in a different office from that of the other members of the audit team, professional judgment shall be used to determine in which office the partner practices in connection with that engagement.

290.110   If other partners and managerial employees who provide non-audit services to the audit client, except those whose involvement is minimal, or their immediate family members, hold a direct financial interest or a material indirect financial interest in the audit client, the self-interest threat created would be so significant that no safeguards could reduce the threat to an acceptable level. Accordingly, neither such personnel nor their immediate family members shall hold any such financial interests in such an audit client.

290.111   Despite paragraphs 290.108 and 290.110, the holding of a financial interest in an audit client by an immediate family member of :

- a partner located in the office in which the engagement partner practices in connection with the audit engagement, or
- a partner or managerial employee who provides non-audit services to the audit client, is deemed not to compromise independence if the financial interest is received as a result of the immediate family member's employment rights (e.g., through pension or share option plans) and, when necessary, safeguards are applied to eliminate any threat to independence or reduce it to an acceptable level.

However, when the immediate family member has or obtains the right to dispose of the financial interest or, in the case of a stock option, the right to exercise the option, the financial interest shall be disposed of or forfeited as soon as practicable.

290.112   A self-interest threat may be created if the firm or a member of the audit team, or a member of that individual's immediate family, has a financial interest in an entity and an audit client also has a financial interest in that entity. However, independence is deemed not to be compromised if these interests are immaterial and the audit client cannot exercise significant influence over the entity. If such interest is material to any party, and the audit client can exercise significant influence over the other entity, no safeguards could reduce the threat to an acceptable level. Accordingly, the firm shall not have such an interest and any individual with such an interest shall, before becoming a member of the audit team, either:

- Dispose of the interest; or
- Dispose of a sufficient amount of the interest so that the remaining interest is no longer material.

290.113   A self-interest, familiarity or intimidation threat may be created if a member of the audit team, or a member of that individual's immediate family, or the firm, has a financial interest in an entity when a director, officer or controlling owner of the audit client is also known to have a financial interest in that entity. The existence and significance of any threat will depend upon factors such as:

- The role of the professional on the audit team;
- Whether ownership of the entity is closely or widely held;
- Whether the interest gives the investor the ability to control or significantly influence the entity; and
- The materiality of the financial interest.

The significance of any threat shall be evaluated and safeguards applied when necessary to eliminate the threat or reduce it to an acceptable level. Examples of such safeguards include:

- Removing the member of the audit team with the financial interest from the audit team; or
- Having a professional accountant review the work of the member of the audit team.

The holding by a firm, or a member of the audit team, or a member of that individual's immediate family, of a direct financial interest or a material indirect financial interest in the audit client as a trustee creates a self-interest threat. Similarly, a self-interest threat is created when: **290.114**

- a partner in the office in which the engagement partner practices in connection with the audit,
- other partners and managerial employees who provide non-assurance services to the audit client, except those whose involvement is minimal, or
- their immediate family members, hold a direct financial interest or a material indirect financial interest in the audit client as trustee.

Such an interest shall not be held unless:

- Neither the trustee, nor an immediate family member of the trustee, nor the firm are beneficiaries of the trust;
- The interest in the audit client held by the trust is not material to the trust;
- The trust is not able to exercise significant influence over the audit client; and
- The trustee, an immediate family member of the trustee, or the firm cannot significantly influence any investment decision involving a financial interest in the audit client.

Members of the audit team shall determine whether a self-interest threat is created by any known financial interests in the audit client held by other individuals including: **290.115**

- Partners and professional employees of the firm, other than those referred to above, or their immediate family members; and
- Individuals with a close personal relationship with a member of the audit team.

Whether these interests create a self-interest threat will depend on factors such as:

- The firm's organisational, operating and reporting structure; and
- The nature of the relationship between the individual and the member of the audit team.

The significance of any threat shall be evaluated and safeguards applied when necessary to eliminate the threat or reduce it to an acceptable level. Examples of such safeguards include:

- Removing the member of the audit team with the personal relationship from the audit team;
- Excluding the member of the audit team from any significant decision-making concerning the audit engagement; or
- Having a professional accountant review the work of the member of the audit team.

If a firm or a partner or employee of the firm, or a member of that individual's immediate family, receives a direct financial interest or a material indirect financial interest in an audit client, for example, by way of an inheritance, gift or as a result of a merger and such interest would not be permitted to be held under this section, then: **290.116**

- If the interest is received by the firm, the financial interest shall be disposed of immediately, or a sufficient amount of an indirect financial interest shall be disposed of so that the remaining interest is no longer material;
- If the interest is received by a member of the audit team, or a member of that individual's immediate family, the individual who received the financial interest shall immediately dispose of the financial interest, or dispose of a sufficient amount of an indirect financial interest so that the remaining interest is no longer material; or

- If the interest is received by an individual who is not a member of the audit team, or by an immediate family member of the individual, the financial interest shall be disposed of as soon as possible, or a sufficient amount of an indirect financial interest shall be disposed of so that the remaining interest is no longer material. Pending the disposal of the financial interest, a determination shall be made as to whether any safeguards are necessary.

290.117   When an inadvertent violation of this section as it relates to a financial interest in an audit client occurs, it is deemed not to compromise independence if:

- The firm has established policies and procedures that require prompt notification to the firm of any breaches resulting from the purchase, inheritance or other acquisition of a financial interest in the audit client;
- The actions in paragraph 290.116 (a)-(c) are taken as applicable; and
- The firm applies other safeguards when necessary to reduce any remaining threat to an acceptable level. Examples of such safeguards include:
  o   Having a professional accountant review the work of the member of the audit team; or
  o   Excluding the individual from any significant decision-making concerning the audit engagement.
- The firm shall determine whether to discuss the matter with those charged with governance.

Loans and Guarantees

290.118   A loan or a guarantee of a loan, to a member of the audit team, or a member of that individual's immediate family, or the firm from an audit client that is a bank or a similar institution may create a threat to independence. If the loan or guarantee is not made under normal lending procedures, terms and conditions, a self-interest threat would be created that would be so significant that no safeguards could reduce the threat to an acceptable level. Accordingly, neither a member of the audit team, a member of that individual's immediate family, nor a firm shall accept such a loan or guarantee.

290.119   If a loan to a firm from an audit client that is a bank or similar institution is made under normal lending procedures, terms and conditions and it is material to the audit client or firm receiving the loan, it may be possible to apply safeguards to reduce the self-interest threat to an acceptable level. An example of such a safeguard is having the work reviewed by a professional accountant from a network firm that is neither involved with the audit nor received the loan.

290.120   A loan, or a guarantee of a loan, from an audit client that is a bank or a similar institution to a member of the audit team, or a member of that individual's immediate family, does not create a threat to independence if the loan or guarantee is made under normal lending procedures, terms and conditions. Examples of such loans include home mortgages, bank overdrafts, car loans and credit card balances.

290.121   If the firm or a member of the audit team, or a member of that individual's immediate family, accepts a loan from, or has a borrowing guaranteed by, an audit client that is not a bank or similar institution, the self-interest threat created would be so significant that no safeguards could reduce the threat to an acceptable level, unless the loan or guarantee is immaterial to both (a) the firm or the member of the audit team and the immediate family member, and (b) the client.

290.122   Similarly, if the firm or a member of the audit team, or a member of that individual's immediate family, makes or guarantees a loan to an audit client, the self-interest threat created would be so significant that no safeguards could reduce the threat to an acceptable level, unless the loan or guarantee is immaterial to both (a) the firm or the member of the audit team and the immediate family member, and (b) the client.

If a firm or a member of the audit team, or a member of that individual's immediate family, has deposits or a brokerage account with an audit client that is a bank, broker or similar institution, a threat to independence is not created if the deposit or account is held under normal commercial terms. **290.123**

Business relationships

A close business relationship between a firm, or a member of the audit team, or a member of that individual's immediate family, and the audit client or its management, arises from a commercial relationship or common financial interest and may create self-interest or intimidation threats. Examples of such relationships include: **290.124**

- Having a financial interest in a joint venture with either the client or a controlling owner, director, officer or other individual who performs senior managerial activities for that client.
- Arrangements to combine one or more services or products of the firm with one or more services or products of the client and to market the package with reference to both parties.
- Distribution or marketing arrangements under which the firm distributes or markets the client's products or services, or the client distributes or markets the firm's products or services.

Unless any financial interest is immaterial and the business relationship is insignificant to the firm and the client or its management, the threat created would be so significant that no safeguards could reduce the threat to an acceptable level. Therefore, unless the financial interest is immaterial and the business relationship is insignificant, the business relationship shall not be entered into, or it shall be reduced to an insignificant level or terminated.

In the case of a member of the audit team, unless any such financial interest is immaterial and the relationship is insignificant to that member, the individual shall be removed from the audit team.

If the business relationship is between an immediate family member of a member of the audit team and the audit client or its management, the significance of any threat shall be evaluated and safeguards applied when necessary to eliminate the threat or reduce it to an acceptable level.

A business relationship involving the holding of an interest by the firm, or a member of the audit team, or a member of that individual's immediate family, in a closely-held entity when the audit client or a director or officer of the client, or any group thereof, also holds an interest in that entity does not create threats to independence if: **290.125**

- The business relationship is insignificant to the firm, the member of the audit team and the immediate family member, and the client;
- The financial interest is immaterial to the investor or group of investors; and
- The financial interest does not give the investor, or group of investors, the ability to control the closely-held entity.

The purchase of goods and services from an audit client by the firm, or a member of the audit team, or a member of that individual's immediate family, does not **290.126** generally create a threat to independence if the transaction is in the normal course of business and at arm's length. However, such transactions may be of such a nature or magnitude that they create a self-interest threat. The significance of any threat shall be evaluated and safeguards applied when necessary to eliminate the threat or reduce it to an acceptable level. Examples of such safeguards include:

- Eliminating or reducing the magnitude of the transaction; or
- Removing the individual from the audit team.

Family and Personal Relationships

290.127   Family and personal relationships between a member of the audit team and a director or officer or certain employees (depending on their role) of the audit client may create self-interest, familiarity or intimidation threats. The existence and significance of any threats will depend on a number of factors, including the individual's responsibilities on the audit team, the role of the family member or other individual within the client and the closeness of the relationship.

290.128   When an immediate family member of a member of the audit team is:

- A director or officer of the audit client; or
- An employee in a position to exert significant influence over the preparation of the client's accounting records or the financial statements on which the firm will express an opinion,

or was in such a position during any period covered by the engagement or the financial statements, the threats to independence can only be reduced to an acceptable level by removing the individual from the audit team. The closeness of the relationship is such that no other safeguards could reduce the threat to an acceptable level. Accordingly, no individual who has such a relationship shall be a member of the audit team.

290.129   Threats to independence are created when an immediate family member of a member of the audit team is an employee in a position to exert significant influence over the client's financial position, financial performance or cash flows. The significance of the threats will depend on factors such as:

- The position held by the immediate family member; and
- The role of the professional on the audit team.

The significance of the threat shall be evaluated and safeguards applied when necessary to eliminate the threat or reduce it to an acceptable level. Examples of such safeguards include:

- Removing the individual from the audit team; or
- Structuring the responsibilities of the audit team so that the professional does not deal with matters that are within the responsibility of the immediate family member.

290.130   Threats to independence are created when a close family member of a member of the audit team is:

- A director or officer of the audit client; or
- An employee in a position to exert significant influence over the preparation of the client's accounting records or the financial statements on which the firm will express an opinion.

The significance of the threats will depend on factors such as:

- The nature of the relationship between the member of the audit team and the close family member;
- The position held by the close family member; and
- The role of the professional on the audit team.

The significance of the threat shall be evaluated and safeguards applied when necessary to eliminate the threat or reduce it to an acceptable level. Examples of such safeguards include:

- Removing the individual from the audit team; or
- Structuring the responsibilities of the audit team so that the professional does not deal with matters that are within the responsibility of the close family member.

Threats to independence are created when a member of the audit team has a close relationship with a person who is not an immediate or close family member, but who is a director or officer or an employee in a position to exert significant influence over the preparation of the client's accounting records or the financial statements on which the firm will express an opinion. A member of the audit team who has such a relationship shall consult in accordance with firm policies and procedures. The significance of the threats will depend on factors such as: **290.131**

- The nature of the relationship between the individual and the member of the audit team;
- The position the individual holds with the client; and
- The role of the professional on the audit team.

The significance of the threats shall be evaluated and safeguards applied when necessary to eliminate the threats or reduce them to an acceptable level. Examples of such safeguards include:

- Removing the professional from the audit team; or
- Structuring the responsibilities of the audit team so that the professional does not deal with matters that are within the responsibility of the individual with whom the professional has a close relationship.

Self-interest, familiarity or intimidation threats may be created by a personal or family relationship between (a) a partner or employee of the firm who is not a member of the audit team and (b) a director or officer of the audit client or an employee in a position to exert significant influence over the preparation of the client's accounting records or the financial statements on which the firm will express an opinion. Partners and employees of the firm who are aware of such relationships shall consult in accordance with firm policies and procedures. The existence and significance of any threat will depend on factors such as: **290.132**

- The nature of the relationship between the partner or employee of the firm and the director or officer or employee of the client;
- The interaction of the partner or employee of the firm with the audit team;
- The position of the partner or employee within the firm; and
- The position the individual holds with the client.

The significance of any threat shall be evaluated and safeguards applied when necessary to eliminate the threat or reduce it to an acceptable level. Examples of such safeguards include:

- Structuring the partner's or employee's responsibilities to reduce any potential influence over the audit engagement; or
- Having a professional accountant review the relevant audit work performed.

290.133   When an inadvertent violation of this section as it relates to family and personal relationships occurs, it is deemed not to compromise independence if:

- The firm has established policies and procedures that require prompt notification to the firm of any breaches resulting from changes in the employment status of their immediate or close family members or other personal relationships that create threats to independence;
- The inadvertent violation relates to an immediate family member of a member of the audit team becoming a director or officer of the audit client or being in a position to exert significant influence over the preparation of the client's accounting records or the financial statements on which the firm will express an opinion, and the relevant professional is removed from the audit team; and
- The firm applies other safeguards when necessary to reduce any remaining threat to an acceptable level. Examples of such safeguards include:
  - Having a professional accountant review the work of the member of the audit team; or
  - Excluding the relevant professional from any significant decision-making concerning the engagement.

The firm shall determine whether to discuss the matter with those charged with governance.

Employment with an audit client

290.134   Familiarity or intimidation threats may be created if a director or officer of the audit client, or an employee in a position to exert significant influence over the preparation of the client's accounting records or the financial statements on which the firm will express an opinion, has been a member of the audit team or partner of the firm.

290.135   If a former member of the audit team or partner of the firm has joined the audit client in such a position and a significant connection remains between the firm and the individual, the threat would be so significant that no safeguards could reduce the threat to an acceptable level. Therefore, independence would be deemed to be compromised if a former member of the audit team or partner joins the audit client as a director or officer, or as an employee in a position to exert significant influence over the preparation of the client's accounting records or the financial statements on which the firm will express an opinion, unless:

- The individual is not entitled to any benefits or payments from the firm, unless made in accordance with fixed pre-determined arrangements, and any amount owed to the individual is not material to the firm; and
- The individual does not continue to participate or appear to participate in the firm's business or professional activities.

290.136   If a former member of the audit team or partner of the firm has joined the audit client in such a position, and no significant connection remains between the firm and the individual, the existence and significance of any familiarity or intimidation threats will depend on factors such as:

- The position the individual has taken at the client;
- Any involvement the individual will have with the audit team;
- The length of time since the individual was a member of the audit team or partner of the firm; and
- The former position of the individual within the audit team or firm, for example, whether the individual was responsible for maintaining regular contact with the client's management or those charged with governance.

The significance of any threats created shall be evaluated and safeguards applied when necessary to eliminate the threats or reduce them to an acceptable level. Examples of such safeguards include:

- Modifying the audit plan;
- Assigning individuals to the audit team who have sufficient experience in relation to the individual who has joined the client; or
- Having a professional accountant review the work of the former member of the audit team.

If a former partner of the firm has previously joined an entity in such a position and the entity subsequently becomes an audit client of the firm, the significance of any threat to independence shall be evaluated and safeguards applied when necessary to eliminate the threat or reduce it to an acceptable level. **290.137**

A self-interest threat is created when a member of the audit team participates in the audit engagement while knowing that the member of the audit team will, or may, join the client some time in the future. Firm policies and procedures shall require members of an audit team to notify the firm when entering employment negotiations with the client. On receiving such notification, the significance of the threat shall be evaluated and safeguards applied when necessary to eliminate the threat or reduce it to an acceptable level. Examples of such safeguards include: **290.138**

- Removing the individual from the audit team; or
- A review of any significant judgments made by that individual while on the team.

Audit clients that are public interest entities

Familiarity or intimidation threats are created when a key audit partner joins the audit client that is a public interest entity as: **290.139**

- A director or officer of the entity; or
- An employee in a position to exert significant influence over the preparation of the client's accounting records or the financial statements on which the firm will express an opinion.

Independence would be deemed to be compromised unless, subsequent to the partner ceasing to be a key audit partner, the public interest entity had issued audited financial statements covering a period of not less than twelve months and the partner was not a member of the audit team with respect to the audit of those financial statements.

An intimidation threat is created when the individual who was the firm's Senior or Managing Partner (Chief Executive or equivalent) joins an audit client that is a public interest entity as: **290.140**

- an employee in a position to exert significant influence over the preparation of the entity's accounting records or its financial statements; or
- a director or officer of the entity. Independence would be deemed to be compromised unless twelve months have passed since the individual was the Senior or Managing Partner (Chief Executive or equivalent) of the firm.

Independence is deemed not to be compromised if, as a result of a business combination, a former key audit partner or the individual who was the firm's former Senior or Managing Partner is in a position as described in paragraphs 290.139 and 290.140, and: **290.141**

- The position was not taken in contemplation of the business combination;
- Any benefits or payments due to the former partner from the firm have been settled in full, unless made in accordance with fixed pre-determined arrangements and any amount owed to the partner is not material to the firm;
- The former partner does not continue to participate or appear to participate in the firm's business or professional activities; and
- The position held by the former partner with the audit client is discussed with those charged with governance.

Temporary staff assignments

290.142 The lending of staff by a firm to an audit client may create a self-review threat. Such assistance may be given, but only for a short period of time and the firm's personnel shall not be involved in:

- Providing non-assurance services that would not be permitted under this section; or
- Assuming management responsibilities.

In all circumstances, the audit client shall be responsible for directing and supervising the activities of the loaned staff. The significance of any threat shall be evaluated and safeguards applied when necessary to eliminate the threat or reduce it to an acceptable level. Examples of such safeguards include:

- Conducting an additional review of the work performed by the loaned staff;
- Not giving the loaned staff audit responsibility for any function or activity that the staff performed during the temporary staff assignment; or
- Not including the loaned staff as a member of the audit team.

Recent service with an audit client

290.143 Self-interest, self-review or familiarity threats may be created if a member of the audit team has recently served as a director, officer, or employee of the audit client. This would be the case when, for example, a member of the audit team has to evaluate elements of the financial statements for which the member of the audit team had prepared the accounting records while with the client.

290.144 If, during the period covered by the audit report, a member of the audit team had served as a director or officer of the audit client, or was an employee in a position to exert significant influence over the preparation of the client's accounting records or the financial statements on which the firm will express an opinion, the threat created would be so significant that no safeguards could reduce the threat to an acceptable level. Consequently, such individuals shall not be assigned to the audit team.

290.145 Self-interest, self-review or familiarity threats may be created if, before the period covered by the audit report, a member of the audit team had served as a director or officer of the audit client, or was an employee in a position to exert significant influence over the preparation of the client's accounting records or financial statements on which the firm will express an opinion. For example, such threats would be created if a decision made or work performed by the individual in the prior period, while employed by the client, is to be evaluated in the current period as part of the current audit engagement. The existence and significance of any threats will depend on factors such as:

- The position the individual held with the client;
- The length of time since the individual left the client; and

- The role of the professional on the audit team.

The significance of any threat shall be evaluated and safeguards applied when necessary to reduce the threat to an acceptable level. An example of such a safeguard is conducting a review of the work performed by the individual as a member of the audit team.

Serving as a Director or Officer of an audit client

If a partner or employee of the firm serves as a director or officer of an audit client, the self-review and self-interest threats created would be so significant that no safeguards could reduce the threats to an acceptable level. Accordingly, no partner or employee shall serve as a director or officer of an audit client.   **290.146**

The position of Company Secretary has different implications in different jurisdictions. Duties may range from administrative duties, such as personnel management and the maintenance of company records and registers, to duties as diverse as ensuring that the company complies with regulations or providing advice on corporate governance matters. Generally, this position is seen to imply a close association with the entity.   **290.147**

If a partner or employee of the firm serves as Company Secretary for an audit client, self-review and advocacy threats are created that would generally be so significant that no safeguards could reduce the threats to an acceptable level. Despite paragraph 290.146, when this practice is specifically permitted under local law, professional roles or practice, and provided management makes all relevant decisions, the duties and activities shall be limited to those of a routine and administrative nature, such as preparing minutes and maintaining statutory returns. In those circumstances, the significance of any threats shall be evaluated and safeguards applied when necessary to eliminate the threats or reduce them to an acceptable level.   **290.148**

Performing routine administrative services to support a company secretarial function or providing advice in relation to company secretarial administration matters does not generally create threats to independence, as long as client management makes all relevant decisions.   **290.149**

Long association of senior personnel (including partner rotation) with an audit client

General provisions

Familiarity and self-interest threats are created by using the same senior personnel on an audit engagement over a long period of time. The significance of the threats will depend on factors such as: **290.150**

- How long the individual has been a member of the audit team;
- The role of the individual on the audit team;
- The structure of the firm;
- The nature of the audit engagement;
- Whether the client's management team has changed; and
- Whether the nature or complexity of the client's accounting and reporting issues has changed.

The significance of the threats shall be evaluated and safeguards applied when necessary to eliminate the threats or reduce them to an acceptable level. Examples of such safeguards include:

- Rotating the senior personnel off the audit team;
- Having a professional accountant who was not a member of the audit team review the work of the senior personnel; or
- regular independent internal or external quality reviews of the engagement.

Audit clients that are public interest entities

290.151　In respect of an audit of a public interest entity, an individual shall not be a key audit partner for more than seven years. After such time, the individual shall not be a member of the engagement team or be a key audit partner for the client for two years. During that period, the individual shall not participate in the audit of the entity, provide quality control for the engagement, consult with the engagement team or the client regarding technical or industry-specific issues, transactions or events or otherwise directly influence the outcome of the engagement.

290.152　Despite paragraph 290.151, key audit partners whose continuity is especially important to audit quality may, in rare cases due to unforeseen circumstances, outside the firm's control, be permitted an additional year on the audit team as long as the threat to independence can be eliminated or reduced to an acceptable level by applying safeguards. For example, a key audit partner may remain on the audit team for up to one additional year in circumstances where, due to unforeseen events, a required rotation was not possible, as might be the case due to serious illness of the intended engagement partner.

290.153　The long association of other partners with an audit client that is a public interest entity creates familiarity and self-interest threats. The significance of the threats will depend on factors such as:

- How long any such partner has been associated with the audit client;
- The role, if any, of the individual on the audit team; and
- The nature, frequency and extent of the individual's interactions with the client's management or those charged with governance.

The significance of the threats shall be evaluated and safeguards applied when necessary to eliminate the threats or reduce them to an acceptable level. Examples of such safeguards include:

- Rotating the partner off the audit team or otherwise ending the partner's association with the audit client; or
- regular independent internal or external quality reviews of the engagement.

290.154　When an audit client becomes a public interest entity, the length of time the individual has served the audit client as a key audit partner before the client becomes a public interest entity shall be taken into account in determining the timing of the rotation. If the individual has served the audit client as a key audit partner for five years or less when the client becomes a public interest entity, the number of years the individual may continue to serve the client in that capacity before rotating off the engagement is seven years less the number of years already served. If the individual has served the audit client as a key audit partner for six or more years when the client becomes a public interest entity, the partner may continue to serve in that capacity for a maximum of two additional years before rotating off the engagement.

290.155　When a firm has only a few people with the necessary knowledge and experience to serve as a key audit partner on the audit of a public interest entity, rotation of key audit partners may not be an available safeguard. If an independent regulator in the relevant jurisdiction has provided an exemption from partner rotation in such circumstances, an individual may remain a key audit partner for more than seven years, in accordance with such regulation, provided that the independent regulator has specified alternative safeguards which are applied, such as a regular independent external review.

Provision of Non-assurance Services to Audit clients

Firms have traditionally provided to their audit clients a range of non-assurance services that are consistent with their skills and expertise. Providing non-assurance services may, however, create threats to the independence of the firm or members of the audit team. The threats created are most often self-review, self-interest and advocacy threats.

290.156

New developments in business, the evolution of financial markets and changes in information technology make it impossible to draw up an all-inclusive list of non-assurance services that might be provided to an audit client. When specific guidance on a particular non-assurance service is not included in this section, the conceptual framework shall be applied when evaluating the particular circumstances.

290.157

Before the firm accepts an engagement to provide a non-assurance service to an audit client, a determination shall be made as to whether providing such a service would create a threat to independence. In evaluating the significance of any threat created by a particular non-assurance service, consideration shall be given to any threat that the audit team has reason to believe is created by providing other related non-assurance services. If a threat is created that cannot be reduced to an acceptable level by the application of safeguards, the non-assurance service shall not be provided.

290.158

Providing certain non-assurance services to an audit client may create a threat to independence so significant that no safeguards could reduce the threat to an acceptable level. However, the inadvertent provision of such a service to a related entity, division or in respect of a discrete financial statement item of such a client will be deemed not to compromise independence if any threats have been reduced to an acceptable level by arrangements for that related entity, division or discrete financial statement item to be audited by another firm or when another firm re-performs the non-assurance service to the extent necessary to enable it to take responsibility for that service.

290.159

A firm may provide non-assurance services that would otherwise be restricted under this section to the following related entities of the audit client:

290.160

- An entity, which is not an audit client, that has direct or indirect control over the audit client;
- An entity, which is not an audit client, with a direct financial interest in the client if that entity has significant influence over the client and the interest in the client is material to such entity; or
- An entity, which is not an audit client, that is under common control with the audit client.

If it is reasonable to conclude that (a) the services do not create a self-review threat because the results of the services will not be subject to audit procedures and (b) any threats that are created by the provision of such services are eliminated or reduced to an acceptable level by the application of safeguards.

A non-assurance service provided to an audit client does not compromise the firm's independence when the client becomes a public interest entity if:

290.161

- The previous non-assurance service complies with the provisions of this section that relate to audit clients that are not public interest entities;
- Services that are not permitted under this section for audit clients that are public interest entities are terminated before or as soon as practicable after the client becomes a public interest entity; and
- The firm applies safeguards when necessary to eliminate or reduce to an acceptable level any threats to independence arising from the service.

Management responsibilities

290.162   Management of an entity performs many activities in managing the entity in the best interests of stakeholders of the entity. It is not possible to specify every activity that is a management responsibility. However, management responsibilities involve leading and directing an entity, including making significant decisions regarding the acquisition, deployment and control of human, financial, physical and intangible resources.

290.163   Whether an activity is a management responsibility depends on the circumstances and requires the exercise of judgment. Examples of activities that would generally be considered a management responsibility include:

- Setting policies and strategic direction;
- Directing and taking responsibility for the actions of the entity's employees;
- Authorising transactions;
- Deciding which recommendations of the firm or other third parties to implement;
- Taking responsibility for the preparation and fair presentation of the financial statements in accordance with the applicable financial reporting framework; and
- Taking responsibility for designing, implementing and maintaining internal control.

290.164   Activities that are routine and administrative, or involve matters that are insignificant, generally are deemed not to be a management responsibility. For example, executing an insignificant transaction that has been authorised by management or monitoring the dates for filing statutory returns and advising an audit client of those dates is deemed not to be a management responsibility. Further, providing advice and recommendations to assist management in discharging its responsibilities is not assuming a management responsibility.

290.165   If a firm were to assume a management responsibility for an audit client, the threats created would be so significant that no safeguards could reduce the threats to an acceptable level. For example, deciding which recommendations of the firm to implement will create self-review and self-interest threats. Further, assuming a management responsibility creates a familiarity threat because the firm becomes too closely aligned with the views and interests of management. Therefore, the firm shall not assume a management responsibility for an audit client.

290.166   To avoid the risk of assuming a management responsibility when providing non-assurance services to an audit client, the firm shall be satisfied that a member of management is responsible for making the significant judgments and decisions that are the proper responsibility of management, evaluating the results of the service and accepting responsibility for the actions to be taken arising from the results of the service. This reduces the risk of the firm inadvertently making any significant judgments or decisions on behalf of management. The risk is further reduced when the firm gives the client the opportunity to make judgments and decisions based on an objective and transparent analysis and presentation of the issues.

Preparing Accounting Records and Financial statements

General provisions

Management is responsible for the preparation and fair presentation of the financial statements in accordance with the applicable financial reporting framework. These responsibilities include: **290.167**

- Originating or changing journal entries, or determining the account classifications of transactions; and
- Preparing or changing source documents or originating data, in electronic or other form, evidencing the occurrence of a transaction (for example, purchase orders, payroll time records, and customer orders).

Providing an audit client with accounting and bookkeeping services, such as preparing accounting records or financial statements, creates a self-review threat when the firm subsequently audits the financial statements. **290.168**

The audit process, however, necessitates dialogue between the firm and management of the audit client, which may involve: **290.169**

- the application of accounting standards or policies and financial statement disclosure requirements,
- the appropriateness of financial and accounting control and the methods used in determining the stated amounts of assets and liabilities, or
- proposing adjusting journal entries. These activities are considered to be a normal part of the audit process and do not, generally, create threats to independence.

Similarly, the client may request technical assistance from the firm on matters such as resolving account reconciliation problems or analysing and accumulating information for regulatory reporting. In addition, the client may request technical advice on accounting issues such as the conversion of existing financial statements from one financial reporting framework to another (for example, to comply with group accounting policies or to transition to a different financial reporting framework such as International Financial Reporting Standards). Such services do not, generally, create threats to independence provided the firm does not assume a management responsibility for the client. **290.170**

Audit clients that are not public interest entities

The firm may provide services related to the preparation of accounting records and financial statements to an audit client that is not a public interest entity where the services are of a routine or mechanical nature, so long as any self-review threat created is reduced to an acceptable level. Examples of such services include: **290.171**

- Providing payroll services based on client-originated data;
- Recording transactions for which the client has determined or approved the appropriate account classification;
- Posting transactions coded by the client to the general ledger;
- Posting client-approved entries to the trial balance; and
- Preparing financial statements based on information in the trial balance.

In all cases, the significance of any threat created shall be evaluated and safeguards applied when necessary to eliminate the threat or reduce it to an acceptable level. Examples of such safeguards include:

While taxation services provided by a firm to an audit client are addressed separately under each of these broad headings; in practice, these activities are often interrelated.

290.182   Performing certain tax services creates self-review and advocacy threats. The existence and significance of any threats will depend on factors such as (a) the system by which the tax authorities assess and administer the tax in question and the role of the firm in that process, (b) the complexity of the relevant tax regime and the degree of judgment necessary in applying it, (c) the particular characteristics of the engagement, and (d) the level of tax expertise of the client's employees.

Tax return preparation

290.183   Tax return preparation services involve assisting clients with their tax reporting obligations by drafting and completing information, including the amount of tax due (usually on standardised forms) required to be submitted to the applicable tax authorities. Such services also include advising on the tax return treatment of past transactions and responding on behalf of the audit client to the tax authorities' requests for additional information and analysis (including providing explanations of and technical support for the approach being taken). Tax return preparation services are generally based on historical information and principally involve analysis and presentation of such historical information under existing tax law, including precedents and established practice. Further, the tax returns are subject to whatever review or approval process the tax authority deems appropriate. Accordingly, providing such services does not generally create a threat to independence if management takes responsibility for the returns including any significant judgments made.

Tax calculations for the purpose of preparing accounting entries

Audit clients that are not public interest entities

290.184   Preparing calculations of current and deferred tax liabilities (or assets) for an audit client for the purpose of preparing accounting entries that will be subsequently audited by the firm creates a self-review threat. The significance of the threat will depend on (a) the complexity of the relevant tax law and regulation and the degree of judgment necessary in applying them, (b) the level of tax expertise of the client's personnel, and (c) the materiality of the amounts to the financial statements. Safeguards shall be applied when necessary to eliminate the threat or reduce it to an acceptable level. Examples of such safeguards include:

- Using professionals who are not members of the audit team to perform the service;
- If the service is performed by a member of the audit team, using a partner or senior staff member with appropriate expertise who is not a member of the audit team to review the tax calculations; or
- Obtaining advice on the service from an external tax professional.

Audit clients that are public interest entities

290.185   Except in emergency situations, in the case of an audit client that is a public interest entity, a firm shall not prepare tax calculations of current and deferred tax liabilities (or assets) for the purpose of preparing accounting entries that are material to the financial statements on which the firm will express an opinion.

The preparation of calculations of current and deferred tax liabilities (or assets) for an audit client for the purpose of the preparation of accounting entries, which would otherwise not be permitted under this section, may be provided to audit clients in emergency or other unusual situations when it is impractical for the audit client to make other arrangements. This may be the case when (a) only the firm has the resources and necessary knowledge of the client's business to assist the client in the timely preparation of its calculations of current and deferred tax liabilities (or assets), and (b) a restriction on the firm's ability to provide the services would result in significant difficulties for the client (for example, as might result from a failure to meet regulatory reporting requirements). In such situations, the following conditions shall be met:

290.186

- Those who provide the services are not members of the audit team;
- The services are provided for only a short period of time and are not expected to recur; and
- The situation is discussed with those charged with governance.

Tax planning and other tax advisory services

Tax planning or other tax advisory services comprise a broad range of services, such as advising the client how to structure its affairs in a tax efficient manner or advising on the application of a new tax law or regulation.

290.187

A self-review threat may be created where the advice will affect matters to be reflected in the financial statements. The existence and significance of any threat will depend on factors such as:

290.188

- The degree of subjectivity involved in determining the appropriate treatment for the tax advice in the financial statements;
- The extent to which the outcome of the tax advice will have a material effect on the financial statements;
- Whether the effectiveness of the tax advice depends on the accounting treatment or presentation in the financial statements and there is doubt as to the appropriateness of the accounting treatment or presentation under the relevant financial reporting framework;
- The level of tax expertise of the client's employees;
- The extent to which the advice is supported by tax law or regulation, other precedent or established practice; and
- Whether the tax treatment is supported by a private ruling or has otherwise been cleared by the tax authority before the preparation of the financial statements.

For example, providing tax planning and other tax advisory services where the advice is clearly supported by tax authority or other precedent, by established practice or has a basis in tax law that is likely to prevail does not generally create a threat to independence.

The significance of any threat shall be evaluated and safeguards applied when necessary to eliminate the threat or reduce it to an acceptable level. Examples of such safeguards include:

290.189

- Using professionals who are not members of the audit team to perform the service;
- Having a tax professional, who was not involved in providing the tax service, advise the audit team on the service and review the financial statement treatment;
- Obtaining advice on the service from an external tax professional; or
- Obtaining pre-clearance or advice from the tax authorities.

290.190   Where the effectiveness of the tax advice depends on a particular accounting treatment or presentation in the financial statements and:

- The audit team has reasonable doubt as to the appropriateness of the related accounting treatment or presentation under the relevant financial reporting framework; and
- The outcome or consequences of the tax advice will have a material effect on the financial statements on which the firm will express an opinion;

The self-review threat would be so significant that no safeguards could reduce the threat to an acceptable level. Accordingly, a firm shall not provide such tax advice to an audit client.

290.191   In providing tax services to an audit client, a firm may be requested to perform a valuation to assist the client with its tax reporting obligations or for tax planning purposes. Where the result of the valuation will have a direct effect on the financial statements, the provisions included in paragraphs 290.175 to 290.180 relating to valuation services are applicable. Where the valuation is performed for tax purposes only and the result of the valuation will not have a direct effect on the financial statements (i.e. the financial statements are only affected through accounting entries related to tax), this would not generally create threats to independence if such effect on the financial statements is immaterial or if the valuation is subject to external review by a tax authority or similar regulatory authority. If the valuation is not subject to such an external review and the effect is material to the financial statements, the existence and significance of any threat created will depend upon factors such as:

- The extent to which the valuation methodology is supported by tax law or regulation, other precedent or established practice and the degree of subjectivity inherent in the valuation.
- The reliability and extent of the underlying data.

The significance of any threat created shall be evaluated and safeguards applied when necessary to eliminate the threat or reduce it to an acceptable level. Examples of such safeguards include:

- Using professionals who are not members of the audit team to perform the service;
- Having a professional review the audit work or the result of the tax service; or
- Obtaining pre-clearance or advice from the tax authorities.

Assistance in the resolution of tax disputes

290.192   An advocacy or self-review threat may be created when the firm represents an audit client in the resolution of a tax dispute once the tax authorities have notified the client that they have rejected the client's arguments on a particular issue and either the tax authority or the client is referring the matter for determination in a formal proceeding, for example before a tribunal or court. The existence and significance of any threat will depend on factors such as:

- Whether the firm has provided the advice which is the subject of the tax dispute;
- The extent to which the outcome of the dispute will have a material effect on the financial statements on which the firm will express an opinion;
- The extent to which the matter is supported by tax law or regulation, other precedent, or established practice;
- Whether the proceedings are conducted in public; and
- The role management plays in the resolution of the dispute.

The significance of any threat created shall be evaluated and safeguards applied when necessary to eliminate the threat or reduce it to an acceptable level. Examples of such safeguards include:

- Using professionals who are not members of the audit team to perform the service;
- Having a tax professional, who was not involved in providing the tax service, advise the audit team on the services and review the financial statement treatment; or
- Obtaining advice on the service from an external tax professional.

Where the taxation services involve acting as an advocate for an audit client before a public tribunal or court in the resolution of a tax matter and the amounts involved are material to the financial statements on which the firm will express an opinion, the advocacy threat created would be so significant that no safeguards could eliminate or reduce the threat to an acceptable level. Therefore, the firm shall not perform this type of service for an audit client. What constitutes a "public tribunal or court" shall be determined according to how tax proceedings are heard in the particular jurisdiction.   **290.193**

The firm is not, however, precluded from having a continuing advisory role (for example, responding to specific requests for information, providing factual accounts or testimony about the work performed or assisting the client in analysing the tax issues) for the audit client in relation to the matter that is being heard before a public tribunal or court.   **290.194**

Internal audit services

General provisions

The scope and objectives of internal audit activities vary widely and depend on the size and structure of the entity and the requirements of management and those charged with governance. Internal audit activities may include: **290.195**

- Monitoring of internal control-reviewing controls, monitoring their operation and recommending improvements thereto;
- Examination of financial and operating information-reviewing the means used to identify, measure, classify and report financial and operating information, and specific inquiry into individual items including detailed testing of transactions, balances and procedures;
- Review of the economy, efficiency and effectiveness of operating activities including non-financial activities of an entity; and
- Review of compliance with laws, regulations and other external requirements, and with management policies and directives and other internal requirements.

Internal audit services involve assisting the audit client in the performance of its internal audit activities. The provision of internal audit services to an audit client creates a self-review threat to independence if the firm uses the internal audit work in the course of a subsequent external audit. Performing a significant part of the client's internal audit activities increases the possibility that firm personnel providing internal audit services will assume a management responsibility. If the firm's personnel assume a management responsibility when providing internal audit services to an audit client, the threat created would be so significant that no safeguards could reduce the threat to an acceptable level. Accordingly, a firm's personnel shall not assume a management responsibility when providing internal audit services to an audit client.   **290.196**

290.197   Examples of internal audit services that involve assuming management responsibilities include:

- Setting internal audit policies or the strategic direction of internal audit activities;
- Directing and taking responsibility for the actions of the entity's internal audit employees;
- Deciding which recommendations resulting from internal audit activities shall be implemented;
- Reporting the results of the internal audit activities to those charged with governance on behalf of management;
- Performing procedures that form part of the internal control, such as reviewing and approving changes to employee data access privileges;
- Taking responsibility for designing, implementing and maintaining internal control; and
- Performing outsourced internal audit services, comprising all or a substantial portion of the internal audit function, where the firm is responsible for determining the scope of the internal audit work and may have responsibility for one or more of the matters noted in (a)-(f).

290.198   To avoid assuming a management responsibility, the firm shall only provide internal audit services to an audit client if it is satisfied that:

- The client designates an appropriate and competent resource, preferably within senior management, to be responsible at all times for internal audit activities and to acknowledge responsibility for designing, implementing, and maintaining internal control;
- The client's management or those charged with governance reviews, assesses and approves the scope, risk and frequency of the internal audit services;
- The client's management evaluates the adequacy of the internal audit services and the findings resulting from their performance;
- The client's management evaluates and determines which recommendations resulting from internal audit services to implement and manages the implementation process; and
- The client's management reports to those charged with governance the significant findings and recommendations resulting from the internal audit services.

290.199   When a firm uses the work of an internal audit function, International Standards on Auditing require the performance of procedures to evaluate the adequacy of that work. When a firm accepts an engagement to provide internal audit services to an audit client, and the results of those services will be used in conducting the external audit, a self-review threat is created because of the possibility that the audit team will use the results of the internal audit service without appropriately evaluating those results or exercising the same level of professional scepticism as would be exercised when the internal audit work is performed by individuals who are not members of the firm. The significance of the threat will depend on factors such as:

- The materiality of the related financial statement amounts;
- The risk of misstatement of the assertions related to those financial statement amounts; and
- The degree of reliance that will be placed on the internal audit service.

The significance of the threat shall be evaluated and safeguards applied when necessary to eliminate the threat or reduce it to an acceptable level. An example of such a safeguard is using professionals who are not members of the audit team to perform the internal audit service.

Audit clients that are public interest entities

In the case of an audit client that is a public interest entity, a firm shall not provide internal audit services that relate to: **290.200**

- A significant part of the internal controls over financial reporting;
- Financial accounting systems that generate information that is, separately or in the aggregate, significant to the client's accounting records or financial statements on which the firm will express an opinion; or
- Amounts or disclosures that are, separately or in the aggregate, material to the financial statements on which the firm will express an opinion.

IT Systems Services

General Provisions

Services related to information technology ("IT") systems include the design or implementation of hardware or software systems. The systems may aggregate source data, form part of the internal control over financial reporting or generate information that affects the accounting records or financial statements, or the systems may be unrelated to the audit client's accounting records, the internal control over financial reporting or financial statements. Providing systems services may create a self-review threat depending on the nature of the services and the IT systems. **290.201**

The following IT systems services are deemed not to create a threat to independence as long as the firm's personnel do not assume a management responsibility: **290.202**

- Design or implementation of IT systems that are unrelated to internal control over financial reporting;
- Design or implementation of IT systems that do not generate information forming a significant part of the accounting records or financial statements;
- Implementation of "off-the-shelf" accounting or financial information reporting software that was not developed by the firm if the customisation required to meet the client's needs is not significant; and
- Evaluating and making recommendations with respect to a system designed, implemented or operated by another service provider or the client.

Audit clients that are not public interest entities

Providing services to an audit client that is not a public interest entity involving the design or implementation of IT systems that (a) form a significant part of the internal control over financial reporting or (b) generate information that is significant to the client's accounting records or financial statements on which the firm will express an opinion creates a self-review threat. **290.203**

The self-review threat is too significant to permit such services unless appropriate safeguards are put in place ensuring that: **290.204**

- The client acknowledges its responsibility for establishing and monitoring a system of internal controls;
- The client assigns the responsibility to make all management decisions with respect to the design and implementation of the hardware or software system to a competent employee, preferably within senior management;
- The client makes all management decisions with respect to the design and implementation process;

- The client evaluates the adequacy and results of the design and implementation of the system; and
- The client is responsible for operating the system (hardware or software) and for the data it uses or generates.

290.205   Depending on the degree of reliance that will be placed on the particular IT systems as part of the audit, a determination shall be made as to whether to provide such non-assurance services only with personnel who are not members of the audit team and who have different reporting lines within the firm. The significance of any remaining threat shall be evaluated and safeguards applied when necessary to eliminate the threat or reduce it to an acceptable level. An example of such a safeguard is having a professional accountant review the audit or non-assurance work.

Audit clients that are public interest entities

290.206   In the case of an audit client that is a public interest entity, a firm shall not provide services involving the design or implementation of IT systems that (a) form a significant part of the internal control over financial reporting or (b) generate information that is significant to the client's accounting records or financial statements on which the firm will express an opinion.

Litigation Support Services

290.207   Litigation support services may include activities such as acting as an expert witness, calculating estimated damages or other amounts that might become receivable or payable as the result of litigation or other legal dispute, and assistance with document management and retrieval. These services may create a self-review or advocacy threat.

290.208   If the firm provides a litigation support service to an audit client and the service involves estimating damages or other amounts that affect the financial statements on which the firm will express an opinion, the valuation service provisions included in paragraphs 290.175 to 290.180 shall be followed. In the case of other litigation support services, the significance of any threat created shall be evaluated and safeguards applied when necessary to eliminate the threat or reduce it to an acceptable level.

Legal Services

290.209   For the purpose of this section, legal services are defined as any services for which the person providing the services must either be admitted to practice law before the courts of the jurisdiction in which such services are to be provided or have the required legal training to practice law. Such legal services may include, depending on the jurisdiction, a wide and diversified range of areas including both corporate and commercial services to clients, such as contract support, litigation, mergers and acquisition legal advice and support and assistance to clients' internal legal departments. Providing legal services to an entity that is an audit client may create both self-review and advocacy threats.

290.210   Legal services that support an audit client in executing a transaction (e.g., contract support, legal advice, legal due diligence and restructuring) may create self-review threats. The existence and significance of any threat will depend on factors such as:

- The nature of the service;
- Whether the service is provided by a member of the audit team; and

- The materiality of any matter in relation to the client's financial statements.

The significance of any threat created shall be evaluated and safeguards applied when necessary to eliminate the threat or reduce it to an acceptable level. Examples of such safeguards include:

- Using professionals who are not members of the audit team to perform the service; or
- Having a professional who was not involved in providing the legal services provide advice to the audit team on the service and review any financial statement treatment.

Acting in an advocacy role for an audit client in resolving a dispute or litigation when the amounts involved are material to the financial statements on which the firm will express an opinion would create advocacy and self-review threats so significant that no safeguards could reduce the threat to an acceptable level. Therefore, the firm shall not perform this type of service for an audit client. **290.211**

When a firm is asked to act in an advocacy role for an audit client in resolving a dispute or litigation when the amounts involved are not material to the financial statements on which the firm will express an opinion, the firm shall evaluate the significance of any advocacy and self-review threats created and apply safeguards when necessary to eliminate the threat or reduce it to an acceptable level. Examples of such safeguards include: **290.212**

- Using professionals who are not members of the audit team to perform the service; or
- Having a professional who was not involved in providing the legal services advise the audit team on the service and review any financial statement treatment.

The appointment of a partner or an employee of the firm as General Counsel for legal affairs of an audit client would create self-review and advocacy threats that are so significant that no safeguards could reduce the threats to an acceptable level. The position of General Counsel is generally a senior management position with broad responsibility for the legal affairs of a company, and consequently, no member of the firm shall accept such an appointment for an audit client. **290.213**

Recruiting Services

General provisions

Providing recruiting services to an audit client may create self-interest, familiarity or intimidation threats. The existence and significance of any threat will depend on factors such as: **290.214**

- The nature of the requested assistance; and
- The role of the person to be recruited.

The significance of any threat created shall be evaluated and safeguards applied when necessary to eliminate the threat or reduce it to an acceptable level. In all cases, the firm shall not assume management responsibilities, including acting as a negotiator on the client's behalf, and the hiring decision shall be left to the client.

The firm may generally provide such services as reviewing the professional qualifications of a number of applicants and providing advice on their suitability for the post. In addition, the firm may interview candidates and advise on a candidate's competence for financial accounting, administrative or control positions.

Audit clients that are public interest entities

290.215   A firm shall not provide the following recruiting services to an audit client that is a public interest entity with respect to a director or officer of the entity or senior management in a position to exert significant influence over the preparation of the client's accounting records or the financial statements on which the firm will express an opinion:

- Searching for or seeking out candidates for such positions; and
- Undertaking reference checks of prospective candidates for such positions.

Corporate Finance Services

290.216   Providing corporate finance services such as:

- assisting an audit client in developing corporate strategies,
- identifying possible targets for the audit client to acquire,
- advising on disposal transactions,
- assisting finance raising transactions, and
- providing structuring advice

may create advocacy and self-review threats. The significance of any threat shall be evaluated and safeguards applied when necessary to eliminate the threat or reduce it to an acceptable level. Examples of such safeguards include:

- Using professionals who are not members of the audit team to provide the services; or
- Having a professional who was not involved in providing the corporate finance service advise the audit team on the service and review the accounting treatment and any financial statement treatment.

290.217   Providing a corporate finance service, for example advice on the structuring of a corporate finance transaction or on financing arrangements that will directly affect amounts that will be reported in the financial statements on which the firm will provide an opinion may create a self-review threat. The existence and significance of any threat will depend on factors such as:

- The degree of subjectivity involved in determining the appropriate treatment for the outcome or consequences of the corporate finance advice in the financial statements;
- The extent to which the outcome of the corporate finance advice will directly affect amounts recorded in the financial statements and the extent to which the amounts are material to the financial statements; and
- Whether the effectiveness of the corporate finance advice depends on a particular accounting treatment or presentation in the financial statements and there is doubt as to the appropriateness of the related accounting treatment or presentation under the relevant financial reporting framework.

The significance of any threat shall be evaluated and safeguards applied when necessary to eliminate the threat or reduce it to an acceptable level. Examples of such safeguards include:

- Using professionals who are not members of the audit team to perform the service; or

- Having a professional who was not involved in providing the corporate finance service to the client advise the audit team on the service and review the accounting treatment and any financial statement treatment.

Where the effectiveness of corporate finance advice depends on a particular accounting treatment or presentation in the financial statements and: **290.218**

- The audit team has reasonable doubt as to the appropriateness of the related accounting treatment or presentation under the relevant financial reporting framework; and
- The outcome or consequences of the corporate finance advice will have a material effect on the financial statements on which the firm will express an opinion;

The self-review threat would be so significant that no safeguards could reduce the threat to an acceptable level, in which case the corporate finance advice shall not be provided.

Providing corporate finance services involving promoting, dealing in, or under-writing an audit client's shares would create an advocacy or self-review threat that is so significant that no safeguards could reduce the threat to an acceptable level. Accordingly, a firm shall not provide such services to an audit client.   **290.219**

Fees

Fees – relative size

When the total fees from an audit client represent a large proportion of the total fees of the firm expressing the audit opinion, the dependence on that client and concern about losing the client creates a self-interest or intimidation threat. The significance of the threat will depend on factors such as: **290.220**

- The operating structure of the firm;
- Whether the firm is well established or new; and
- The significance of the client qualitatively and/or quantitatively to the firm.

The significance of the threat shall be evaluated and safeguards applied when necessary to eliminate the threat or reduce it to an acceptable level. Examples of such safeguards include:

- Reducing the dependency on the client;
- External quality control reviews; or
- Consulting a third party, such as a professional regulatory body or a profes-sional accountant, on key audit judgments.

A self-interest or intimidation threat is also created when the fees generated from an audit client represent a large proportion of the revenue from an individual partner's clients or a large proportion of the revenue of an individual office of the firm. The significance of the threat will depend upon factors such as: **290.221**

- The significance of the client qualitatively and/or quantitatively to the partner or office; and
- The extent to which the remuneration of the partner, or the partners in the office, is dependent upon the fees generated from the client.

The significance of the threat shall be evaluated and safeguards applied when necessary to eliminate the threat or reduce it to an acceptable level. Examples of such safeguards include:

- Reducing the dependency on the audit client;
- Having a professional accountant review the work or otherwise advise as necessary; or
- regular independent internal or external quality reviews of the engagement.

Audit clients that are public interest entities

290.222 Where an audit client is a public interest entity and, for two consecutive years, the total fees from the client and its related entities (subject to the considerations in paragraph 290.27) represent more than 15% of the total fees received by the firm expressing the opinion on the financial statements of the client, the firm shall disclose to those charged with governance of the audit client the fact that the total of such fees represents more than 15% of the total fees received by the firm, and discuss which of the safeguards below it will apply to reduce the threat to an acceptable level, and apply the selected safeguard:

- Prior to the issuance of the audit opinion on the second year's financial statements, a professional accountant, who is not a member of the firm expressing the opinion on the financial statements, performs an engagement quality control review of that engagement or a professional regulatory body performs a review of that engagement that is equivalent to an engagement quality control review ("a pre-issuance review"); or
- After the audit opinion on the second year's financial statements has been issued, and before the issuance of the audit opinion on the third year's financial statements, a professional accountant, who is not a member of the firm expressing the opinion on the financial statements, or a professional regulatory body performs a review of the second year's audit that is equivalent to an engagement quality control review ("a post-issuance review").

When the total fees significantly exceed 15%, the firm shall determine whether the significance of the threat is such that a post-issuance review would not reduce the threat to an acceptable level and, therefore, a pre-issuance review is required. In such circumstances a pre-issuance review shall be performed.

Thereafter, when the fees continue to exceed 15% each year, the disclosure to and discussion with those charged with governance shall occur and one of the above safeguards shall be applied. If the fees significantly exceed 15%, the firm shall determine whether the significance of the threat is such that a post-issuance review would not reduce the threat to an acceptable level and, therefore, a pre-issuance review is required. In such circumstances a pre-issuance review shall be performed.

Fees – overdue

290.223 A self-interest threat may be created if fees due from an audit client remain unpaid for a long time, especially if a significant part is not paid before the issue of the audit report for the following year. Generally the firm is expected to require payment of such fees before such audit report is issued. If fees remain unpaid after the report has been issued, the existence and significance of any threat shall be evaluated and safeguards applied when necessary to eliminate the threat or reduce it to an acceptable level. An example of such a safeguard is having an additional professional accountant who did not take part in the audit engagement provide advice or review the work performed. The firm shall determine whether the overdue fees might be regarded as being equivalent to a loan to the client and whether, because of the significance of the overdue fees, it is appropriate for the firm to be re-appointed or continue the audit engagement.

Contingent fees

Contingent fees are fees calculated on a predetermined basis relating to the outcome of a transaction or the result of the services performed by the firm. For the purposes of this section, a fee is not regarded as being contingent if established by a court or other public authority.

290.224

A contingent fee charged directly or indirectly, for example through an intermediary, by a firm in respect of an audit engagement creates a self-interest threat that is so significant that no safeguards could reduce the threat to an acceptable level. Accordingly, a firm shall not enter into any such fee arrangement.

290.225

A contingent fee charged directly or indirectly, for example through an intermediary, by a firm in respect of a non-assurance service provided to an audit client may also create a self-interest threat. The threat created would be so significant that no safeguards could reduce the threat to an acceptable level if:

290.226

- The fee is charged by the firm expressing the opinion on the financial statements and the fee is material or expected to be material to that firm;
- The fee is charged by a network firm that participates in a significant part of the audit and the fee is material or expected to be material to that firm; or
- The outcome of the non-assurance service, and therefore the amount of the fee, is dependent on a future or contemporary judgment related to the audit of a material amount in the financial statements.

Accordingly, such arrangements shall not be accepted.

For other contingent fee arrangements charged by a firm for a non-assurance service to an audit client, the existence and significance of any threats will depend on factors such as:

290.227

- The range of possible fee amounts;
- Whether an appropriate authority determines the outcome of the matter upon which the contingent fee will be determined;
- The nature of the service; and
- The effect of the event or transaction on the financial statements.

The significance of any threats shall be evaluated and safeguards applied when necessary to eliminate the threats or reduce them to an acceptable level. Examples of such safeguards include:

- Having a professional accountant review the relevant audit work or otherwise advise as necessary; or
- Using professionals who are not members of the audit team to perform the non-assurance service.

Compensation and evaluation policies

A self-interest threat is created when a member of the audit team is evaluated on or compensated for selling non-assurance services to that audit client. The significance of the threat will depend on:

290.228

- The proportion of the individual's compensation or performance evaluation that is based on the sale of such services;
- The role of the individual on the audit team; and
- Whether promotion decisions are influenced by the sale of such services.

The significance of the threat shall be evaluated and, if the threat is not at an acceptable level, the firm shall either revise the compensation plan or evaluation process for that individual or apply safeguards to eliminate the threat or reduce it to an acceptable level. Examples of such safeguards include:

- Removing such members from the audit team; or
- Having a professional accountant review the work of the member of the audit team.

290.229   A key audit partner shall not be evaluated on or compensated based on that partner's success in selling non-assurance services to the partner's audit client. This is not intended to prohibit normal profit-sharing arrangements between partners of a firm.

Gifts and hospitality

290.230   Accepting gifts or hospitality from an audit client may create self-interest and familiarity threats. If a firm or a member of the audit team accepts gifts or hospitality, unless the value is trivial and inconsequential, the threats created would be so significant that no safeguards could reduce the threats to an acceptable level. Consequently, a firm or a member of the audit team shall not accept such gifts or hospitality.

Actual or threatened litigation

290.231   When litigation takes place, or appears likely, between the firm or a member of the audit team and the audit client, self-interest and intimidation threats are created. The relationship between client management and the members of the audit team must be characterised by complete candour and foll disclosure regarding all aspects of a client's business operations. When the firm and the client's management are placed in adversarial positions by actual or threatened litigation, affecting management's willingness to make complete disclosures, self-interest and intimidation threats are created. The significance of the threats created will depend on such factors as:

- The materiality of the litigation; and
- Whether the litigation relates to a prior audit engagement.

The significance of the threats shall be evaluated and safeguards applied when necessary to eliminate the threats or reduce them to an acceptable level. Examples of such safeguards include:

- If the litigation involves a member of the audit team, removing that individual from the audit team; or
- Having a professional review the work performed.

If such safeguards do not reduce the threats to an acceptable level, the only appropriate action is to withdraw from, or decline, the audit engagement.

Paragraphs 290.232 to 290.499 are intentionally left blank.

Reports that Include a Restriction on Use and Distribution

Introduction

The independence requirements in section 290 apply to all audit engagements. However, in certain circumstances involving audit engagements where the report includes a restriction on use and distribution, and provided the conditions described in 290.501 to 290.502 are met, the independence requirements in this section may be modified as provided in paragraphs 290.505 to 290.514. These paragraphs are only applicable to an audit engagement on special purpose financial statements (a) that is intended to provide a conclusion in positive or negative form that the financial statements are prepared in all material respects, in accordance with the applicable financial reporting framework, including, in the case of a fair presentation frame-work, that the financial statements give a true and fair view or are presented fairly, in all material respects, in accordance with the applicable financial reporting frame-work, and (b) where the audit report includes a restriction on use and distribution. The modifications are not permitted in the case of an audit of financial statements required by law or regulation.

290.500

The modifications to the requirements of section 290 are permitted if the intended users of the report (a) are knowledgeable as to the purpose and limitations of the report, and (b) explicitly agree to the application of the modified independence requirements. Knowledge as to the purpose and limitations of the report may be obtained by the intended users through their participation, either directly or indir-ectly through their representative who has the authority to act for the intended users, in establishing the nature and scope of the engagement. Such participation enhances the ability of the firm to communicate with intended users about independence matters, including the circumstances that are relevant to the evaluation of the threats to independence and the applicable safeguards necessary to eliminate the threats or reduce them to an acceptable level, and to obtain their agreement to the modified independence requirements that are to be applied.

290.501

The firm shall communicate (for example, in an engagement letter) with the intended users regarding the independence requirements that are to be applied with respect to the provision of the audit engagement. Where the intended users are a class of users (for example, lenders in a syndicated loan arrangement) who are not specifically identifiable by name at the time the engagement terms are established, such users shall subsequently be made aware of the independence requirements agreed to by the representative (for example, by the representative making the firm's engagement letter available to all users).

290.502

If the firm also issues an audit report that does not include a restriction on use and distribution for the same client, the provisions of paragraphs 290.500 to 290.514 do not change the requirement to apply the provisions of paragraphs 290.1 to 290.232 to that audit engagement.

290.503

The modifications to the requirements of section 290 that are permitted in the cir-cumstances set out above are described in paragraphs 290.505 to 290.514. Compliance in all other respects with the provisions of section 290 is required.

290.504

Public interest entities

When the conditions set out in paragraphs 290.500 to 290.502 are met, it is not necessary to apply the additional requirements in paragraphs 290.100 to 290.232 that apply to audit engagements for public interest entities.

290.505

Related Entities

290.506   When the conditions set out in paragraphs 290.500 to 290.502 are met, references to audit client do not include its related entities. However, when the audit team knows or has reason to believe that a relationship or circumstance involving a related entity of the client is relevant to the evaluation of the firm's independence of the client, the audit team shall include that related entity when identifying and evaluating threats to independence and applying appropriate safeguards.

Networks and network firms

290.507   When the conditions set out in paragraphs 290.500 to 290.502 are met, reference to the firm does not include network firms. However, when the firm knows or has reason to believe that threats are created by any interests and relationships of a network firm, they shall be included in the evaluation of threats to independence.

Financial interests, loans and guarantees, close business relationships and family and personal relationships

290.508   When the conditions set out in paragraphs 290.500 to 290.502 are met, the relevant provisions set out in paragraphs 290.102 to 290.145 apply only to the members of the engagement team, their immediate family members and close family members.

290.509   In addition, a determination shall be made as to whether threats to independence are created by interests and relationships, as described in paragraphs 290.102 to 290.145, between the audit client and the following members of the audit team:

- Those who provide consultation regarding technical or industry specific issues, transactions or events; and
- Those who provide quality control for the engagement, including those who perform the engagement quality control review.

An evaluation shall be made of the significance of any threats that the engagement team has reason to believe are created by interests and relationships between the audit client and others within the firm who can directly influence the outcome of the audit engagement, including those who recommend the compensation of, or who provide direct supervisory, management or other oversight of the audit engagement partner in connection with the performance of the audit engagement (including those at all successively senior levels above the engagement partner through to the individual who is the firm's Senior or Managing Partner (Chief Executive or equivalent)).

290.510   An evaluation shall also be made of the significance of any threats that the engagement team has reason to believe are created by financial interests in the audit client held by individuals, as described in paragraphs 290.108 to 290.111 and paragraphs 290.113 to 290.115.

290.511   Where a threat to independence is not at an acceptable level, safeguards shall be applied to eliminate the threat or reduce it to an acceptable level.

290.512   In applying the provisions set out in paragraphs 290.106 and 290.115 to interests of the firm, if the firm has a material financial interest, whether direct or indirect, in the audit client, the self-interest threat created would be so significant that no safeguards could reduce the threat to an acceptable level. Accordingly, the firm shall not have such a financial interest.

Employment with an audit client

An evaluation shall be made of the significance of any threats from any employment **290.513**
relationships as described in paragraphs 290.134 to 290.138. Where a threat exists
that is not at an acceptable level, safeguards shall be applied to eliminate the threat
or reduce it to an acceptable level. Examples of safeguards that might be appropriate
include those set out in paragraph 290.136.

Provision of non-assurance services

If the firm conducts an engagement to issue a restricted use and distribution report **290.514**
for an audit client and provides a non-assurance service to the audit client, the
provisions of paragraphs 290.156 to 290.232 shall be complied with, subject to
paragraphs 290.504 to 290.507.

Appendix to Section 290 – nature of assurance engagements

The IESBA and ICAEW Codes include two different sets of requirements to ensure 1
independence is maintained in assurance engagements. If the engagement is an audit
engagement, or a review engagement, the requirements of section 290 apply (or the
APB Ethical Standards – see 290.0c). For other assurance engagements, section 291
applies.

To assist professional accountants in public practice determine which section to 2
apply, set out below are a number of examples of engagements typically undertaken
and an indication of whether they would normally be regarded as audit or review
(thus section 290 or APB) or other assurance (thus section 291).

As individual engagements can vary, even within categories, professional accoun- 3
tants in public practice should consider the examples as indicative rather than
definitive and should have regard to the nature of the conclusion to be given. In
particular they should have regard to the definitions of 'review engagement' and
'financial statements' in the IESBA and ICAEW Codes, which are:

"Review engagement – An assurance engagement, conducted in accordance with
International Standards on Review Engagements or equivalent, in which a professional accountant in public practice expresses a conclusion on whether, on the basis
of the procedures which do not provide all the evidence that would be required in an
audit, anything has come to the accountant's attention that causes the accountant to
believe that the financial statements are not prepared, in all material respects, in
accordance with an applicable financial reporting framework."

"Financial statements – A structured representation of historical financial information, including related notes, intended to communicate an entity's economic
resources or obligations at a point in time or the changes therein for a period of time
in accordance with a financial reporting framework. The related notes ordinarily
comprise a summary of significant accounting policies and other explanatory
information. The term can relate to a complete set of financial statements, but it can
also refer to a single financial statement, for example, a balance sheet, or a statement
of revenues and expenses, and related explanatory notes."

Taken together, the key elements in determining that an assurance engagement is a 4
review engagement are:

- the subject matter: historical financial information, and
- the nature of the report: limited procedures but nothing has come to attention to indicate the information is not prepared in accordance with applicable financial reporting framework.

Examples of engagements that would normally be considered to be audit or review engagements (section 290 or APB)

- Statutory or other audits, or engagements possessing the characteristics of an audit (i.e. involving a 'true and fair' or 'fairly presents' conclusion).
- Review in accordance with ISRE 2410 (UK and Ireland): review of interim financial information performed by independent auditor of the entity, or ISRE 2400: engagements to review financial statements
- Review in accordance with the ICAEW Assurance Service.
- Independent Examination of Charities: again historical financial information and a negative opinion indicating no evidence of non compliance with a specified framework
- Public sector year-end audits
- Special report on the abbreviated accounts of a small company (the report must be prepared by the auditors, who as such, should apply section 290/APB).

Examples of engagements that would normally be considered to be other assurance engagements (section 291)

- Assurance reports on internal controls of service organisations, conducted in accordance with, for example, AAF 01/06.
- Assurance reports on the outsourced provision of information services and information processing services, conducted in accordance with, for example, ITF 01/07.
- Any assurance conducted based on AAF 02/07 A framework for assurance reports on third party operations.
- Any assurance engagements on prospective financial or non-financial information.
- Any other assurance engagements based on ISAE 3000 including narrative information, greenhouse gas and sustainability reports if conducted outside the scope of annual accounts.
- Independent accountant's report on grant claims, conducted in accordance with, for example, AAF 01/10

Note that for all of the above and any other engagements, if the professional accountant in public practice is also the auditor of the entity, section 290/ APB Ethical standards will already have to be followed. No additional compliance with section 291 is necessary in such circumstances.

TRANSITIONAL PROVISIONS

Effective date

This Code is effective on January 1, 2011; early adoption is permitted. This Code is subject to the following transitional provisions:

Public interest entities

1   Section 290 of the Code contains additional independence provisions when the audit or review client is a public interest entity. The additional provisions that are applicable because of the new definition of a public interest entity or the guidance in

paragraph 290.26 are effective on January 1, 2012. For partner rotation requirements, the transitional provisions contained in paragraphs 2 and 3 below apply

Partner rotation

For a partner who is subject to the rotation provisions in paragraph 290.151 because the partner meets the definition of the new term "key audit partner," and the partner is neither the engagement partner nor the individual responsible for the engagement quality control review, the rotation provisions are effective for the audits or reviews of financial statements for years beginning on or after December 15, 2011. For example, in the case of an audit client with a calendar year-end, a key audit partner, who is neither the engagement partner nor the individual responsible for the engagement quality control review, who had served as a key audit partner for seven or more years (i.e., the audits of 2003-2010), would be required to rotate after serving for one more year as a key audit partner (i.e., after completing the 2011 audit).   **2**

For an engagement partner or an individual responsible for the engagement quality control review who immediately prior to assuming either of these roles served in another key audit partner role for the client, and who, at the beginning of the first fiscal year beginning on or after December 15, 2010, had served as the engagement partner or individual responsible for the engagement quality control review for six or fewer years, the rotation provisions are effective for the audits or reviews of financial statements for years beginning on or after December 15, 2011. For example, in the case of an audit client with a calendar year-end, a partner who had served the client in another key audit partner role for four years (i.e., the audits of 2002-2005) and subsequently as the engagement partner for five years (i.e., the audits of 2006-2010) would be required to rotate after serving for one more year as the engagement partner (i.e., after completing the 2011 audit).   **3**

Non-assurance services

Paragraphs 290.156-290.219 address the provision of non-assurance services to an audit or review client. If, at the effective date of the Code, services are being provided to an audit or review client and the services were permissible under the June 2005 Code (revised July 2006) but are either prohibited or subject to restrictions under the revised Code, the firm may continue providing such services only if they were contracted for and commenced prior to January 1, 2011, and are completed before July 1, 2011.   **4**

Fees – relative size

Paragraph 290.222 provides that, in respect of an audit or review client that is a public interest entity, when the total fees from that client and its related entities (subject to the considerations in paragraph 290.27) for two consecutive years represent more than 15% of the total fees of the firm expressing the opinion on the financial statements, a pre- or post-issuance review (as described in paragraph 290.222) of the second year's audit shall be performed. This requirement is effective for audits or reviews of financial statements covering years that begin on or after December 15, 2010. For example, in the case of an audit client with a calendar year end, if the total fees from the client exceeded the 15% threshold for 2011 and 2012, the pre- or post-issuance review would be applied with respect to the audit of the 2012 financial statements.   **5**

Compensation and evaluation policies

6   Paragraph 290.229 provides that a key audit partner shall not be evaluated or compensated based on that partner's success in selling non-assurance services to the partner's audit client. This requirement is effective on January 1, 2012. A key audit partner may, however, receive compensation after January 1, 2012 based on an evaluation made prior to January 1, 2012 of that partner's success in selling non-assurance services to the audit client.

291 Independence – other assurance engagements

Structure of section

291.1   This section addresses independence requirements for assurance engagements that are not audit or review engagements. As indicated in paragraphs 1.14 to 1.17 independence requirements for audit and review engagements are addressed in section 290. If the assurance client is also an audit or review client, the requirements in section 290 also apply to the firm, network firms and members of the audit or review team. In certain circumstances involving assurance engagements where the assurance report includes a restriction on use and distribution and provided certain conditions are met, the independence requirements in this section may be modified as provided in 291.21 to 291.27.

291.2   Assurance engagements are designed to enhance intended users' degree of confidence about the outcome of the evaluation or measurement of a subject matter against criteria. The International Framework for Assurance engagements (the Assurance Framework) issued by the International Auditing and Assurance Standards Board describes the elements and objectives of an assurance engagement and identifies engagements to which International Standards on Assurance engagements (ISAEs) apply. For a description of the elements and objectives of an assurance engagement, refer to the Assurance Framework.

291.3   Compliance with the fundamental principle of objectivity requires being independent of assurance clients. In the case of assurance engagements, it is in the public interest and, therefore, required by this Code of Ethics, that members of assurance teams and firms be independent of assurance clients and that any threats that the firm has reason to believe are created by a network firm's interests and relationships be evaluated. In addition, when the assurance team knows or has reason to believe that a relationship or circumstance involving a related entity of the assurance client is relevant to the evaluation of the firm's independence from the client, the assurance team shall include that related entity when identifying and evaluating threats to independence and applying appropriate safeguards.

A conceptual framework approach to independence

291.4   The objective of this section is to assist firms and members of assurance teams in applying the conceptual framework approach described below to achieving and maintaining independence.

291.5   Independence comprises:

- Independence of Mind
  The state of mind that permits the expression of a conclusion without being affected by influences that compromise professional judgment, thereby allowing

an individual to act with integrity and exercise objectivity and professional scepticism.

- Independence in Appearance
  The avoidance of facts and circumstances that are so significant that a reasonable and informed third party would be likely to conclude, weighing all the specific facts and circumstances, that a firm's, or a member of the assurance team's, integrity, objectivity or professional scepticism has been compromised.

The conceptual framework approach shall be applied by professional accountants to: **291.6**

- Identify threats to independence;
- Evaluate the significance of the threats identified; and
- Apply safeguards when necessary to eliminate the threats or reduce them to an acceptable level.

When the professional accountant determines that appropriate safeguards are not available or cannot be applied to eliminate the threats or reduce them to an acceptable level, the professional accountant shall eliminate the circumstance or relationship creating the threats or decline or terminate the assurance engagement.

A professional accountant shall use professional judgment in applying this conceptual framework.

Many different circumstances, or combinations of circumstances, may be relevant in **291.7**
assessing threats to independence. It is impossible to define every situation that creates threats to independence and to specify the appropriate action. Therefore, this Code establishes a conceptual framework that requires firms and members of assurance teams to identify, evaluate, and address threats to independence. The conceptual framework approach assists professional accountants in public practice in complying with the ethical requirements in this Code. It accommodates many variations in circumstances that create threats to independence and can deter a professional accountant from concluding that a situation is permitted if it is not specifically prohibited.

Paragraphs 291.100 and onwards describe how the conceptual framework approach **291.8**
to independence is to be applied. These paragraphs do not address all the circumstances and relationships that create or may create threats to independence.

In deciding whether to accept or continue an engagement, or whether a particular **291.9**
individual may be a member of the assurance team, a firm shall identify and evaluate any threats to independence. If the threats are not at an acceptable level, and the decision is whether to accept an engagement or include a particular individual on the assurance team, the firm shall determine whether safeguards are available to eliminate the threats or reduce them to an acceptable level. If the decision is whether to continue an engagement, the firm shall determine whether any existing safeguards will continue to be effective to eliminate the threats or reduce them to an acceptable level or whether other safeguards will need to be applied or whether the engagement needs to be terminated. Whenever new information about a threat comes to the attention of the firm during the engagement, the firm shall evaluate the significance of the threat in accordance with the conceptual framework approach.

Throughout this section, reference is made to the significance of threats to inde- **291.10**
pendence. In evaluating the significance of a threat, qualitative as well as quantitative factors shall be taken into account.

291.11   This section does not, in most cases, prescribe the specific responsibility of individuals within the firm for actions related to independence because responsibility may differ depending on the size, structure and organisation of a firm. The firm is required by International Standards on Quality Control to establish policies and procedures designed to provide it with reasonable assurance that independence is maintained when required by relevant ethical standards.

Assurance engagements

291.12   As further explained in the Assurance Framework, in an assurance engagement the professional accountant in public practice expresses a conclusion designed to enhance the degree of confidence of the intended users (other than the responsible party) about the outcome of the evaluation or measurement of a subject matter against criteria.

291.13   The outcome of the evaluation or measurement of a subject matter is the information that results from applying the criteria to the subject matter. The term "subject matter information" is used to mean the outcome of the evaluation or measurement of a subject matter. For example, the Framework states that an assertion about the effectiveness of internal control (subject matter information) results from applying a framework for evaluating the effectiveness of internal control, such as COSO or CoCo (criteria), to internal control, a process (subject matter).

291.14   Assurance engagements may be assertion-based or direct reporting. In either case, they involve three separate parties: a professional accountant in public practice, a responsible party and intended users.

291.15   In an assertion-based assurance engagement, the evaluation or measurement of the subject matter is performed by the responsible party, and the subject matter information is in the form of an assertion by the responsible party that is made available to the intended users.

291.16   In a direct reporting assurance engagement, the professional accountant in public practice either directly performs the evaluation or measurement of the subject matter, or obtains a representation from the responsible party that has performed the evaluation or measurement that is not available to the intended users. The subject matter information is provided to the intended users in the assurance report.

Assertion-based assurance engagements

291.17   In an assertion-based assurance engagement, the members of the assurance team and the firm shall be independent of the assurance client (the party responsible for the subject matter information, and which may be responsible for the subject matter). Such independence requirements prohibit certain relationships between members of the assurance team and (a) directors or officers, and (b) individuals at the client in a position to exert significant influence over the subject matter information. Also, a determination shall be made as to whether threats to independence are created by relationships with individuals at the client in a position to exert significant influence over the subject matter of the engagement. An evaluation shall be made of the significance of any threats that the firm has reason to believe are created by network firm interests and relationships.

291.18   In the majority of assertion-based assurance engagements, the responsible party is responsible for both the subject matter information and the subject matter. However, in some engagements, the responsible party may not be responsible for the subject matter. For example, when a professional accountant in public practice is engaged to perform an assurance engagement regarding a report that an environmental consultant has prepared about a company's sustainability practices for distribution to intended users, the environmental consultant is the responsible party for the subject matter information but the company is responsible for the subject matter (the sustainability practices).

In assertion-based assurance engagements where the responsible party is responsible for the subject matter information but not the subject matter, the members of the assurance team and the firm shall be independent of the party responsible for the subject matter information (the assurance client). In addition, an evaluation shall be made of any threats the firm has reason to believe are created by interests and relationships between a member of the assurance team, the firm, a network firm and the party responsible for the subject matter. **291.19**

Direct reporting assurance engagements

In a direct reporting assurance engagement, the members of the assurance team and the firm shall be independent of the assurance client (the party responsible for the subject matter). An evaluation shall also be made of any threats the firm has reason to believe are created by network firm interests and relationships. **291.20**

Reports that include a restriction on use and distribution

In certain circumstances where the assurance report includes a restriction on use and distribution, and provided the conditions in this paragraph and in 291.22 are met, the independence requirements in this section may be modified. The modifications to the requirements of section 291 are permitted if the intended users of the report (a) are knowledgeable as to the purpose, subject matter information and limitations of the report and (b) explicitly agree to the application of the modified independence requirements. Knowledge as to the purpose, subject matter information, and limitations of the report may be obtained by the intended users through their participation, either directly or indirectly through their representative who has the authority to act for the intended users, in establishing the nature and scope of the engagement. Such participation enhances the ability of the firm to communicate with intended users about independence matters, including the circumstances that are relevant to the evaluation of the threats to independence and the applicable safeguards necessary to eliminate the threats or reduce them to an acceptable level, and to obtain their agreement to the modified independence requirements that are to be applied. **291.21**

The firm shall communicate (for example, in an engagement letter) with the intended users regarding the independence requirements that are to be applied with respect to the provision of the assurance engagement. Where the intended users are a class of users (for example, lenders in a syndicated loan arrangement) who are not specifically identifiable by name at the time the engagement terms are established, such users shall subsequently be made aware of the independence requirements agreed to by the representative (for example, by the representative making the firm's engagement letter available to all users). **291.22**

If the firm also issues an assurance report that does not include a restriction on use and distribution for the same client, the provisions of paragraphs 291.25 to 291.27 do not change the requirement to apply the provisions of paragraphs 291.1 to 291.159 to that assurance engagement. If the firm also issues an audit report, whether or not it **291.23** includes a restriction on use and distribution, for the same client, the provisions of section 290 shall apply to that audit engagement.

291.24   The modifications to the requirements of section 291 that are permitted in the circumstances set out above are described in paragraphs 291.25 to 291.27. Compliance in all other respects with the provisions of section 291 is required.

291.25   When the conditions set out in paragraphs 291.21 and 291.22 are met, the relevant provisions set out in paragraphs 291.104 to 291.134 apply to all members of the engagement team, and their immediate and close family members. In addition, a determination shall be made as to whether threats to independence are created by interests and relationships between the assurance client and the following other members of the assurance team:

- Those who provide consultation regarding technical or industry specific issues, transactions or events; and
- Those who provide quality control for the engagement, including those who perform the engagement quality control review.

An evaluation shall also be made, by reference to the provisions set out in paragraphs 291.104 to 291.134, of any threats that the engagement team has reason to believe are created by interests and relationships between the assurance client and others within the firm who can directly influence the outcome of the assurance engagement, including those who recommend the compensation, or who provide direct supervisory, management or other oversight, of the assurance engagement partner in connection with the performance of the assurance engagement.

291.26   Even though the conditions set out in paragraphs 291.21 to 291.22 are met, if the firm had a material financial interest, whether direct or indirect, in the assurance client, the self-interest threat created would be so significant that no safeguards could reduce the threat to an acceptable level. Accordingly, the firm shall not have such a financial interest. In addition, the firm shall comply with the other applicable provisions of this section described in paragraphs 291.113 to 291.159.

291.27   An evaluation shall also be made of any threats that the firm has reason to believe are created by network firm interests and relationships.

Multiple responsible parties

291.28   In some assurance engagements, whether assertion-based or direct reporting, there might be several responsible parties. In determining whether it is necessary to apply the provisions in this section to each responsible party in such engagements, the firm may take into account whether an interest or relationship between the firm, or a member of the assurance team, and a particular responsible party would create a threat to independence that is not trivial and inconsequential in the context of the subject matter information. This will take into account factors such as:

- The materiality of the subject matter information (or of the subject matter) for which the particular responsible party is responsible; and
- The degree of public interest associated with the engagement.

If the firm determines that the threat to independence created by any such interest or relationship with a particular responsible party would be trivial and inconsequential, it may not be necessary to apply all of the provisions of this section to that responsible party.

Documentation

Documentation provides evidence of the professional accountant's judgments in forming conclusions regarding compliance with independence requirements. The absence of documentation is not a determinant of whether a firm considered a particular matter nor whether it is independent. The professional accountant shall document conclusions regarding compliance with independence requirements, and the substance of any relevant discussions that support those conclusions. Accordingly:

291.29

- When safeguards are required to reduce a threat to an acceptable level, the professional accountant shall document the nature of the threat and the safeguards in place or applied that reduce the threat to an acceptable level; and
- When a threat required significant analysis to determine whether safeguards were necessary and the professional accountant concluded that they were not because the threat was already at an acceptable level, the professional accountant shall document the nature of the threat and the rationale for the conclusion.

Engagement period

Independence from the assurance client is required both during the engagement period and the period covered by the subject matter information. The engagement period starts when the assurance team begins to perform assurance services with respect to the particular engagement. The engagement period ends when the assurance report is issued. When the engagement is of a recurring nature, it ends at the later of the notification by either party that the professional relationship has terminated or the issuance of the final assurance report.

291.30

When an entity becomes an assurance client during or after the period covered by the subject matter information on which the firm will express a conclusion, the firm shall determine whether any threats to independence are created by:

291.31

- Financial or business relationships with the assurance client during or after the period covered by the subject matter information but before accepting the assurance engagement; or
- Previous services provided to the assurance client.

If a non-assurance service was provided to the assurance client during or after the period covered by the subject matter information but before the assurance team begins to perform assurance services and the service would not be permitted during the period of the assurance engagement, the firm shall evaluate any threat to independence created by the service. If any threat is not at an acceptable level, the assurance engagement shall only be accepted if safeguards are applied to eliminate any threats or reduce them to an acceptable level. Examples of such safeguards include:

291.32

- Not including personnel who provided the non-assurance service as members of the assurance team;
- Having a professional accountant review the assurance and non-assurance work as appropriate; or
- Engaging another firm to evaluate the results of the non-assurance service or having another firm re-perform the non-assurance service to the extent necessary to enable it to take responsibility for the service.

However, if the non-assurance service has not been completed and it is not practical to complete or terminate the service before the commencement of professional services in connection with the assurance engagement, the firm shall only accept the assurance engagement if it is satisfied:

- The non-assurance service will be completed within a short period of time; or
- The client has arrangements in place to transition the service to another provider within a short period of time.

During the service period, safeguards shall be applied when necessary. In addition, the matter shall be discussed with those charged with governance.

Other considerations

291.33   There may be occasions when there is an inadvertent violation of this section. If such an inadvertent violation occurs, it generally will be deemed not to compromise independence provided the firm has appropriate quality control policies and procedures in place equivalent to those required by International Standards on Quality Control to maintain independence and, once discovered, the violation is corrected promptly and any necessary safeguards are applied to eliminate any threat or reduce it to an acceptable level. The firm shall determine whether to discuss the matter with those charged with governance.

Paragraphs 291.34 to 291.99 are intentionally left blank.

Application of the conceptual framework approach to independence

291.100   Paragraphs 291.104 to 291.159 describe specific circumstances and relationships that create or may create threats to independence. The paragraphs describe the potential threats and the types of safeguards that may be appropriate to eliminate the threats or reduce them to an acceptable level and identify certain situations where no safeguards could reduce the threats to an acceptable level. The paragraphs do not describe all of the circumstances and relationships that create or may create a threat to independence. The firm and the members of the assurance team shall evaluate the implications of similar, but different, circumstances and relationships and determine whether safeguards, including the safeguards in paragraphs 200.11 to 200.14 can be applied when necessary to eliminate the threats to independence or reduce them to an acceptable level.

291.101   The paragraphs demonstrate how the conceptual framework approach applies to assurance engagements and are to be read in conjunction with paragraph 291.28 which explains that, in the majority of assurance engagements, there is one responsible party and that responsible party is the assurance client. However, in some assurance engagements there are two or more responsible parties. In such circumstances, an evaluation shall be made of any threats the firm has reason to believe are created by interests and relationships between a member of the assurance team, the firm, a network firm and the party responsible for the subject matter. For assurance reports that include a restriction on use and distribution, the paragraphs are to be read in the context of paragraphs 291.21 to 291.27.

291.102   Interpretation 2005-01 provides further guidance on applying the independence requirements contained in this section to assurance engagements.

291.103   Paragraphs 291.104 to 291.120 contain references to the materiality of a financial interest, loan, or guarantee, or the significance of a business relationship. For the purpose of determining whether such an interest is material to an individual, the combined net worth of the individual and the individual's immediate family members may be taken into account.

Financial interests

Holding a financial interest in an assurance client may create a self-interest threat. The existence and significance of any threat created depends on:

291.104

- the role of the person holding the financial interest,
- whether the financial interest is direct or indirect, and
- the materiality of the financial interest.

Financial interests may be held through an intermediary (e.g. a collective investment vehicle, estate or trust). The determination of whether such financial interests are direct or indirect will depend upon whether the beneficial owner has control over the investment vehicle or the ability to influence its investment decisions. When control over the investment vehicle or the ability to influence investment decisions exists, this Code defines that financial interest to be a direct financial interest. Conversely, when the beneficial owner of the financial interest has no control over the investment vehicle or ability to influence its investment decisions, this Code defines that financial interest to be an indirect financial interest.

291.105

If a member of the assurance team, a member of that individual's immediate family or a firm has a direct financial interest or a material indirect financial interest in the assurance client, the self-interest threat created would be so significant that no safeguards could reduce the threat to an acceptable level. Therefore, none of the following shall have a direct financial interest or a material indirect financial interest in the client: a member of the assurance team; a member of that individual's immediate family member; or the firm.

291.106

When a member of the assurance team has a close family member who the assurance team member knows has a direct financial interest or a material indirect financial interest in the assurance client, a self-interest threat is created. The significance of the threat will depend on factors such as

291.107

- The nature of the relationship between the member of the assurance team and the close family member; and
- The materiality of the financial interest to the close family member.

The significance of the threat shall be evaluated and safeguards applied when necessary to eliminate the threat or reduce it to an acceptable level. Examples of such safeguards include:

- The close family member disposing, as soon as practicable, of all of the financial interest or disposing of a sufficient portion of an indirect financial interest so that the remaining interest is no longer material;
- Having a professional accountant review the work of the member of the assurance team; or
- Removing the individual from the assurance team.

If a member of the assurance team, a member of that individual's immediate family, or a firm has a direct or material indirect financial interest in an entity that has a controlling interest in the assurance client, and the client is material to the entity, the self-interest threat created would be so significant that no safeguards could reduce the threat to an acceptable level. Therefore, none of the following shall have such a financial interest: a member of the assurance team; a member of that individual's immediate family; and the firm.

291.108

291.109   The holding by a firm or a member of the assurance team, or a member of that individual's immediate family, of a direct financial interest or a material indirect financial interest in the assurance client as a trustee creates a self-interest threat. Such an interest shall not be held unless:

- Neither the trustee, nor an immediate family member of the trustee, nor the firm are beneficiaries of the trust;
- The interest in the assurance client held by the trust is not material to the trust;
- The trust is not able to exercise significant influence over the assurance client; and
- The trustee, an immediate family member of the trustee, or the firm cannot significantly influence any investment decision involving a financial interest in the assurance client.

291.110   Members of the assurance team shall determine whether a self-interest threat is created by any known financial interests in the assurance client held by other individuals including:

- Partners and professional employees of the firm, other than those referred to above, or their immediate family members; and
- Individuals with a close personal relationship with a member of the assurance team.

Whether these interests create a self-interest threat will depend on factors such as:

- The firm's organisational, operating and reporting structure; and
- The nature of the relationship between the individual and the member of the assurance team.

The significance of any threat shall be evaluated and safeguards applied when necessary to eliminate the threat or reduce it to an acceptable level. Examples of such safeguards include:

- Removing the member of the assurance team with the personal relationship from the assurance team;
- Excluding the member of the assurance team from any significant decision-making concerning the assurance engagement; or
- Having a professional accountant review the work of the member of the assurance team.

291.111   If a firm, a member of the assurance team, or an immediate family member of the individual, receives a direct financial interest or a material indirect financial interest in an assurance client, for example, by way of an inheritance, gift or as a result of a merger, and such interest would not be permitted to be held under this section, then:

- If the interest is received by the firm, the financial interest shall be disposed of immediately, or a sufficient amount of an indirect financial interest shall be disposed of so that the remaining interest is no longer material, or
- If the interest is received by a member of the assurance team, or a member of that individual's immediate family, the individual who received the financial interest shall immediately dispose of the financial interest, or dispose of a sufficient amount of an indirect financial interest so that the remaining interest is no longer material.

291.112   When an inadvertent violation of this section as it relates to a financial interest in an assurance client occurs, it is deemed not to compromise independence if:

- The firm has established policies and procedures that require prompt notification to the firm of any breaches resulting from the purchase, inheritance or other acquisition of a financial interest in the assurance client;
- The actions taken in paragraph 291.111(a) – (b) are taken as applicable; and
- The firm applies other safeguards when necessary to reduce any remaining threat to an acceptable level. Examples of such safeguards include:
  - Having a professional accountant review the work of the member of the assurance team; or
  - Excluding the individual from any significant decision-making concerning the assurance engagement.

The firm shall determine whether to discuss the matter with those charged with governance.

Loans and guarantees

A loan, or a guarantee of a loan, to a member of the assurance team, or a member of that individual's immediate family, or the firm from an assurance client that is a bank or a similar institution, may create a threat to independence. If the loan or guarantee is not made under normal lending procedures, terms and conditions, a self-interest threat would be created that would be so significant that no safeguards could reduce the threat to an acceptable level. Accordingly, neither a member of the assurance team, a member of that individual's immediate family, nor a firm shall accept such a loan or guarantee.   **291.113**

If a loan to a firm from an assurance client that is a bank or similar institution is made under normal lending procedures, terms and conditions and it is material to the assurance client or firm receiving the loan, it may be possible to apply safeguards to reduce the self-interest threat to an acceptable level. An example of such a safeguard is having the work reviewed by a professional accountant from a network firm that is neither involved with the assurance engagement nor received the loan.   **291.114**

A loan, or a guarantee of a loan, from an assurance client that is a bank or a similar institution to a member of the assurance team, or a member of that individual's immediate family, does not create a threat to independence if the loan or guarantee is made under normal lending procedures, terms and conditions. Examples of such loans include home mortgages, bank overdrafts, car loans and credit card balances.   **291.115**

If the firm or a member of the assurance team, or a member of that individual's immediate family, accepts a loan from, or has a borrowing guaranteed by, an assurance client that is not a bank or similar institution, the self-interest threat created would be so significant that no safeguards could reduce the threat to an acceptable level, unless the loan or guarantee is immaterial to both the firm, or the member of the assurance team and the immediate family member, and the client.   **291.116**

Similarly, if the firm, or a member of the assurance team, or a member of that individual's immediate family, makes or guarantees a loan to an assurance client, the self-interest threat created would be so significant that no safeguards could reduce the threat to an acceptable level, unless the loan or guarantee is immaterial to both the firm, or the member of the assurance team and the immediate family member, and the client.   **291.117**

If a firm or a member of the assurance team, or a member of that individual's immediate family, has deposits or a brokerage account with an assurance client that   **291.118** is a bank, broker, or similar institution, a threat to independence is not created if the deposit or account is held under normal commercial terms.

Business relationships

291.119   A close business relationship between a firm, or a member of the assurance team, or a member of that individual's immediate family, and the assurance client or its management arises from a commercial relationship or common financial interest and may create self-interest or intimidation threats. Examples of such relationships include:

- Having a financial interest in a joint venture with either the client or a controlling owner, director or officer or other individual who performs senior managerial activities for that client.
- Arrangements to combine one or more services or products of the firm with one or more services or products of the client and to market the package with reference to both parties.
- Distribution or marketing arrangements under which the firm distributes or markets the client's products or services, or the client distributes or markets the firm's products or services.

Unless any financial interest is immaterial and the business relationship is insignificant to the firm and the client or its management, the threat created would be so significant that no safeguards could reduce the threat to an acceptable level. Therefore, unless the financial interest is immaterial and the business relationship is insignificant, the business relationship shall not be entered into, or shall be reduced to an insignificant level or terminated.

In the case of a member of the assurance team, unless any such financial interest is immaterial and the relationship is insignificant to that member, the individual shall be removed from the assurance team.

If the business relationship is between an immediate family member of a member of the assurance team and the assurance client or its management, the significance of any threat shall be evaluated and safeguards applied when necessary to eliminate the threat or reduce it to an acceptable level.

291.120   The purchase of goods and services from an assurance client by the firm, or a member of the assurance team, or a member of that individual's immediate family, does not generally create a threat to independence if the transaction is in the normal course of business and at arm's length. However, such transactions may be of such a nature or magnitude that they create a self-interest threat. The significance of any threat shall be evaluated and safeguards applied when necessary to eliminate the threat or reduce it to an acceptable level. Examples of such safeguards include:

- Eliminating or reducing the magnitude of the transaction; or
- Removing the individual from the assurance team.

Family and personal relationships

291.121   Family and personal relationships between a member of the assurance team and a director or officer or certain employees (depending on their role) of the assurance client, may create self-interest, familiarity or intimidation threats. The existence and significance of any threats will depend on a number of factors, including the individual's responsibilities on the assurance team, the role of the family member or other individual within the client, and the closeness of the relationship.

When an immediate family member of a member of the assurance team is: **291.122**

- A director or officer of the assurance client, or
- An employee in a position to exert significant influence over the subject matter information of the assurance engagement,

or was in such a position during any period covered by the engagement or the subject matter information, the threats to independence can only be reduced to an acceptable level by removing the individual from the assurance team. The closeness of the relationship is such that no other safeguards could reduce the threat to an acceptable level. Accordingly, no individual who has such a relationship shall be a member of the assurance team.

Threats to independence are created when an immediate family member of a member **291.123**
of the assurance team is an employee in a position to exert significant influence over the subject matter of the engagement. The significance of the threats will depend on factors such as:

- The position held by the immediate family member; and
- The role of the professional on the assurance team.

The significance of the threat shall be evaluated and safeguards applied when necessary to eliminate the threat or reduce it to an acceptable level. Examples of such safeguards include:

- Removing the individual from the assurance team; or
- Structuring the responsibilities of the assurance team so that the professional does not deal with matters that are within the responsibility of the immediate family member.

Threats to independence are created when a close family member of a member of the **291.124**
assurance team is:

- A director or officer of the assurance client; or
- An employee in a position to exert significant influence over the subject matter information of the assurance engagement.

The significance of the threats will depend on factors such as:

- The nature of the relationship between the member of the assurance team and the close family member;
- The position held by the close family member; and
- The role of the professional on the assurance team.

The significance of the threat shall be evaluated and safeguards applied when necessary to eliminate the threat or reduce it to an acceptable level. Examples of such safeguards include:

- Removing the individual from the assurance team; or
- Structuring the responsibilities of the assurance team so that the professional does not deal with matters that are within the responsibility of the close family member.

Threats to independence are created when a member of the assurance team has a **291.125**
close relationship with a person who is not an immediate or close family member, but who is a director or officer or an employee in a position to exert significant influence over the subject matter information of the assurance engagement. A member of the assurance team who has such a relationship shall consult in accordance with firm

policies and procedures. The significance of the threats will depend on factors such as:

- The nature of the relationship between the individual and the member of the assurance team;
- The position the individual holds with the client; and
- The role of the professional on the assurance team.

The significance of the threats shall be evaluated and safeguards applied when necessary to eliminate the threats or reduce them to an acceptable level. Examples of such safeguards include:

- Removing the professional from the assurance team; or
- Structuring the responsibilities of the assurance team so that the professional does not deal with matters that are within the responsibility of the individual with whom the professional has a close relationship.

291.126 Self-interest, familiarity or intimidation threats may be created by a personal or family relationship between (a) a partner or employee of the firm who is not a member of the assurance team and (b) a director or officer of the assurance client or an employee in a position to exert significant influence over the subject matter information of the assurance engagement. The existence and significance of any threat will depend on factors such as:

- The nature of the relationship between the partner or employee of the firm and the director or officer or employee of the client;
- The interaction of the partner or employee of the firm with the assurance team;
- The position of the partner or employee within the firm; and
- The role of the individual within the client.

The significance of any threat shall be evaluated and safeguards applied when necessary to eliminate the threat or reduce it to an acceptable level. Examples of such safeguards include:

- Structuring the partner's or employee's responsibilities to reduce any potential influence over the assurance engagement; or
- Having a professional accountant review the relevant assurance work performed.

291.127 When an inadvertent violation of this section as it relates to family and personal relationships occurs, it is deemed not to compromise independence if:

- The firm has established policies and procedures that require prompt notification to the firm of any breaches resulting from changes in the employment status of their immediate or close family members or other personal relationships that create threats to independence;
- The inadvertent violation relates to an immediate family member of a member of the assurance team becoming a director or officer of the assurance client or being in a position to exert significant influence over the subject matter information of the assurance engagement, and the relevant professional is removed from the assurance team; and
- The firm applies other safeguards when necessary to reduce any remaining threat to an acceptable level. Examples of such safeguards include:
  - Having a professional accountant review the work of the member of the assurance team; or
  - Excluding the relevant professional from any significant decision-making concerning the engagement.

The firm shall determine whether to discuss the matter with those charged with governance.

Employment with assurance clients

Familiarity or intimidation threats may be created if a director or officer of the assurance client, or an employee who is in a position to exert significant influence over the subject matter information of the assurance engagement, has been a member of the assurance team or partner of the firm. **291.128**

If a former member of the assurance team or partner of the firm has joined the assurance client in such a position, the existence and significance of any familiarity or intimidation threats will depend on factors such as: **291.129**

- The position the individual has taken at the client;
- Any involvement the individual will have with the assurance team;
- The length of time since the individual was a member of the assurance team or partner of the firm; and
- The former position of the individual within the assurance team or firm, for example, whether the individual was responsible for maintaining regular contact with the client's management or those charged with governance.

In all cases the individual shall not continue to participate in the firm's business or professional activities. The significance of any threats created shall be evaluated and safeguards applied when necessary to eliminate the threats or reduce them to an acceptable level. Examples of such safeguards include:

- Making arrangements such that the individual is not entitled to any benefits or payments from the firm, unless made in accordance with fixed pre-determined arrangements.
- Making arrangements such that any amount owed to the individual is not material to the firm;
- Modifying the plan for the assurance engagement;
- Assigning individuals to the assurance team who have sufficient experience in relation to the individual who has joined the client; or
- Having a professional accountant review the work of the former member of the assurance team.

If a former partner of the firm has previously joined an entity in such a position and the entity subsequently becomes an assurance client of the firm, the significance of any threats to independence shall be evaluated and safeguards applied when necessary, to eliminate the threat or reduce it to an acceptable level. **291.130**

A self-interest threat is created when a member of the assurance team participates in the assurance engagement while knowing that the member of the assurance team will, or may, join the client some time in the future. Firm policies and procedures shall require members of an assurance team to notify the firm when entering employment negotiations with the client. On receiving such notification, the significance of the threat shall be evaluated and safeguards applied when necessary to eliminate the threat or reduce it to an acceptable level. Examples of such safeguards include: **291.131**

- Removing the individual from the assurance team; or
- A review of any significant judgments made by that individual while on the team.

Recent service with an assurance client

291.132   Self-interest, self-review or familiarity threats may be created if a member of the assurance team has recently served as a director, officer, or employee of the assurance client. This would be the case when, for example, a member of the assurance team has to evaluate elements of the subject matter information the member of the assurance team had prepared while with the client.

291.133   If, during the period covered by the assurance report, a member of the assurance team had served as director or officer of the assurance client, or was an employee in a position to exert significant influence over the subject matter information of the assurance engagement, the threat created would be so significant that no safeguards could reduce the threat to an acceptable level. Consequently, such individuals shall not be assigned to the assurance team.

291.134   Self-interest, self-review or familiarity threats may be created if, before the period covered by the assurance report, a member of the assurance team had served as director or officer of the assurance client, or was an employee in a position to exert significant influence over the subject matter information of the assurance engagement. For example, such threats would be created if a decision made or work performed by the individual in the prior period, while employed by the client, is to be evaluated in the current period as part of the current assurance engagement. The existence and significance of any threats will depend on factors such as:

- The position the individual held with the client;
- The length of time since the individual left the client; and
- The role of the professional on the assurance team.

The significance of any threat shall be evaluated and safeguards applied when necessary to reduce the threat to an acceptable level. An example of such a safeguard is conducting a review of the work performed by the individual as part of the assurance team.

Serving as a Director or Officer of an assurance client

291.135   If a partner or employee of the firm serves a director or officer of an assurance client, the self-review and self-interest threats would be so significant that no safeguards could reduce the threats to an acceptable level. Accordingly, no partner or employee shall serve as a director or officer of an assurance client.

291.136   The position of Company Secretary has different implications in different jurisdictions. Duties may range from administrative duties, such as personnel management and the maintenance of company records and registers, to duties as diverse as ensuring that the company complies with regulation or providing advice on corporate governance matters. Generally, this position is seen to imply a close association with the entity.

291.137   If a partner or employee of the firm serves as Company Secretary for an assurance client, self-review and advocacy threats are created that would generally be so significant that no safeguards could reduce the threats to an acceptable level. Despite paragraph 291.135, when this practice is specifically permitted under local law, professional roles or practice, and provided management makes all relevant decisions, the duties and activities shall be limited to those of a routine and administrative nature, such as preparing minutes and maintaining statutory returns. In those circumstances, the significance of any threats shall be evaluated and safeguards applied when necessary to eliminate the threats or reduce them to an acceptable level.

Performing routine administrative services to support a company secretarial function **291.138** or providing advice in relation to company secretarial administration matters does not generally create threats to independence, as long as client management makes all relevant decisions.

Long association of senior personnel with assurance clients

Familiarity and self-interest threats are created by using the same senior personnel **291.139** on an assurance engagement over a long period of time. The significance of the threats will depend on factors such as:

- How long the individual has been a member of the assurance team;
- The role of the individual on the assurance team;
- The structure of the firm;
- The nature of the assurance engagement;
- Whether the client's management team has changed; and
- Whether the nature or complexity of the subject matter information has changed.

The significance of the threats shall be evaluated and safeguards applied when necessary to eliminate the threats or reduce them to an acceptable level. Examples of such safeguards include:

- Rotating the senior personnel off the assurance team;
- Having a professional accountant who was not a member of the assurance team review the work of the senior personnel; or
- regular independent internal or external quality reviews of the engagement.

Provision of non-assurance services to assurance clients

Firms have traditionally provided to their assurance clients a range of non-assurance **291.140** services that are consistent with their skills and expertise. Providing non-assurance services may, however, create threats to the independence of the firm or members of the assurance team. The threats created are most often self-review, self-interest and advocacy threats.

When specific guidance on a particular non-assurance service is not included in this **291.141** section, the conceptual framework shall be applied when evaluating the particular circumstances.

Before the firm accepts an engagement to provide a non-assurance service to an **291.142** assurance client, a determination shall be made as to whether providing such a service would create a threat to independence. In evaluating the significance of any threat created by a particular non-assurance service, consideration shall be given to any threat that the assurance team has reason to believe is created by providing other related non-assurance services. If a threat is created that cannot be reduced to an acceptable level by the application of safeguards the non-assurance service shall not be provided.

Management responsibilities

291.143   Management of an entity performs many activities in managing the entity in the best interests of stakeholders of the entity. It is not possible to specify every activity that is a management responsibility. However, management responsibilities involve leading and directing an entity, including making significant decisions regarding the acquisition, deployment and control of human, financial, physical and intangible resources.

291.144   Whether an activity is a management responsibility depends on the circumstances and requires the exercise of judgment. Examples of activities that would generally be considered a management responsibility include:

- Setting policies and strategic direction;
- Directing and taking responsibility for the actions of the entity's employees;
- Authorising transactions;
- Deciding which recommendations of the firm or other third parties to implement; and
- Taking responsibility for designing, implementing and maintaining internal control.

291.145   Activities that are routine and administrative, or involve matters that are insignificant, generally are deemed not to be a management responsibility. For example, executing an insignificant transaction that has been authorised by management or monitoring the dates for filing statutory returns and advising an assurance client of those dates is deemed not to be a management responsibility. Further, providing advice and recommendations to assist management in discharging its responsibilities is not assuming a management responsibility.

291.146   Assuming a management responsibility for an assurance client may create threats to independence. If a firm were to assume a management responsibility as part of the assurance service, the threats created would be so significant that no safeguards could reduce the threats to an acceptable level. Accordingly, in providing assurance services to an assurance client, a firm shall not assume a management responsibility as part of the assurance service. If the firm assumes a management responsibility as part of any other services provided to the assurance client, it shall ensure that the responsibility is not related to the subject matter and subject matter information of an assurance engagement provided by the firm.

291.147   To avoid the risk of assuming a management responsibility related to the subject matter or subject matter information of the assurance engagement, the firm shall be satisfied that a member of management is responsible for making the significant judgments and decisions that are the proper responsibility of management, evaluating the results of the service and accepting responsibility for the actions to be taken arising from the results of the service. This reduces the risk of the firm inadvertently making any significant judgments or decisions on behalf of management. This risk is further reduced when the firm gives the client the opportunity to make judgments and decisions based on an objective and transparent analysis and presentation of the issues.

Other considerations

291.148   Threats to independence may be created when a firm provides a non-assurance service related to the subject matter information of an assurance engagement. In such cases, an evaluation of the significance of the firm's involvement with the subject matter information of the engagement shall be made, and a determination shall be made of whether any self-review threats that are not at an acceptable level can be reduced to an acceptable level by the application of safeguards.

A self-review threat may be created if the firm is involved in the preparation of subject matter information which is subsequently the subject matter information of an assurance engagement. For example, a self-review threat would be created if the firm developed and prepared prospective financial information and subsequently provided assurance on this information. Consequently, the firm shall evaluate the significance of any self-review threat created by the provision of such services and apply safeguards when necessary to eliminate the threat or reduce it to an acceptable level. **291.149**

When a firm performs a valuation that forms part of the subject matter information of an assurance engagement, the firm shall evaluate the significance of any self-review threat and apply safeguards when necessary to eliminate the threat or reduce it to an acceptable level. **291.150**

Fees

Fees – relative size

When the total fees from an assurance client represent a large proportion of the total fees of the firm expressing the conclusion, the dependence on that client and concern about losing the client creates a self-interest or intimidation threat. The significance of the threat will depend on factors such as: **291.151**

- The operating structure of the firm;
- Whether the firm is well established or new; and
- The significance of the client qualitatively and/or quantitatively to the firm.

The significance of the threat shall be evaluated and safeguards applied when necessary to eliminate the threat or reduce it to an acceptable level. Examples of such safeguards include:

- Reducing the dependency on the client;
- External quality control reviews; or
- Consulting a third party, such as a professional regulatory body or a professional accountant, on key assurance judgments.

A self-interest or intimidation threat is also created when the fees generated from an assurance client represent a large proportion of the revenue from an individual partner's clients. The significance of the threat shall be evaluated and safeguards applied when necessary to eliminate the threat or reduce it to an acceptable level. An example of such a safeguard is having an additional professional accountant who was not a member of the assurance team review the work or otherwise advise as necessary. **291.152**

Fees – overdue

A self-interest threat may be created if fees due from an assurance client remain unpaid for a long time, especially if a significant part is not paid before the issue of the assurance report, if any, for the following period. Generally the firm is expected to require payment of such fees before any such report is issued. If fees remain unpaid after the report has been issued, the existence and significance of any threat shall be evaluated and safeguards applied when necessary to eliminate the threat or reduce it to an acceptable level. An example of such a safeguard is having another **291.153** professional accountant who did not take part in the assurance engagement provide advice or review the work performed. The firm shall determine whether the overdue fees might be regarded as being equivalent to a loan to the client and whether, because of the significance of the overdue fees, it is appropriate for the firm to be re-appointed or continue the assurance engagement.

Contingent fees

291.154   Contingent fees are fees calculated on a predetermined basis relating to the outcome of a transaction or the result of the services performed by the firm. For the purposes of this section, fees are not regarded as being contingent if established by a court or other public authority.

291.155   A contingent fee charged directly or indirectly, for example through an intermediary, by a firm in respect of an assurance engagement creates a self-interest threat that is so significant that no safeguards could reduce the threat to an acceptable level. Accordingly, a firm shall not enter into any such fee arrangement.

291.156   A contingent fee charged directly or indirectly, for example through an intermediary, by a firm in respect of a non-assurance service provided to an assurance client may also create a self-interest threat. If the outcome of the non-assurance service, and therefore, the amount of the fee, is dependent on a future or contemporary judgment related to a matter that is material to the subject matter information of the assurance engagement, no safeguards could reduce the threat to an acceptable level. Accordingly, such arrangements shall not be accepted.

291.157   For other contingent fee arrangements charged by a firm for a non-assurance service to an assurance client, the existence and significance of any threats will depend on factors such as:

- The range of possible fee amounts;
- Whether an appropriate authority determines the outcome of the matter upon which the contingent fee will be determined;
- The nature of the service; and
- The effect of the event or transaction on the subject matter information.

The significance of any threats shall be evaluated and safeguards applied when necessary to eliminate the threats or reduce them to an acceptable level. Examples of such safeguards include:

- Having a professional accountant review the relevant assurance work or otherwise advise as necessary; or
- Using professionals who are not members of the assurance team to perform the non-assurance service.

Gifts and hospitality

291.158   Accepting gifts or hospitality from an assurance client may create self-interest and familiarity threats. If a firm or a member of the assurance team accepts gifts or hospitality, unless the value is trivial and inconsequential, the threats created would be so significant that no safeguards could reduce the threats to an acceptable level. Consequently, a firm or a member of the assurance team shall not accept such gifts or hospitality.

Actual or threatened litigation

When litigation takes place, or appears likely, between the firm or a member of the **291.159** assurance team and the assurance client, self-interest and intimidation threats are created. The relationship between client management and the members of the assurance team must be characterised by complete candour and full disclosure regarding all aspects of a client's business operations. When the firm and the client's management are placed in adversarial positions by actual or threatened litigation, affecting management's willingness to make complete disclosures self-interest and intimidation threats are created. The significance of the threats created will depend on such factors as:

- The materiality of the litigation; and
- Whether the litigation relates to a prior assurance engagement.

The significance of the threats shall be evaluated and safeguards applied when necessary to eliminate the threats or reduce them to an acceptable level. Examples of such safeguards include:

- If the litigation involves a member of the assurance team, removing that individual from the assurance team; or
- Having a professional review of the work performed.

If such safeguards do not reduce the threats to an acceptable level, the only appropriate action is to withdraw from, or decline, the assurance engagement.

Interpretation 2005-01 (Revised July 2009 to conform to changes resulting from the IESBA's project to improve the clarity of the Code)

Application of section 291 to Assurance engagements that are not Financial statement Audit engagements

This interpretation provides guidance on the application of the independence requirements contained in section 291 to assurance engagements that are not financial statement audit engagements.

This interpretation focuses on the application issues that are particular to assurance engagements that are not financial statement audit engagements. There are other matters noted in section 291 that are relevant in the consideration of independence requirements for all assurance engagements. For example, paragraph 291.3 states that an evaluation shall be made of any threats the firm has reason to believe are created by a network firm's interests and relationships. It also states that when the assurance team has reason to believe that a related entity of such an assurance client is relevant to the evaluation of the firm's independence of the client, the assurance team shall include the related entity when evaluating threats to independence and when necessary applying safeguards. These matters are not specifically addressed in this interpretation.

As explained in the International Framework for Assurance engagements issued by the International Auditing and Assurance Standards Board, in an assurance engagement, the professional accountant in public practice expresses a conclusion designed to enhance the degree of confidence of the intended users other than the responsible party about the outcome of the evaluation or measurement of a subject matter against criteria.

Assertion-Based Assurance engagements

In an assertion-based assurance engagement, the evaluation or measurement of the subject matter is performed by the responsible party, and the subject matter information is in the form of an assertion by the responsible party that is made available to the intended users.

In an assertion-based assurance engagement independence is required from the responsible party, which is responsible for the subject matter information and may be responsible for the subject matter.

In those assertion-based assurance engagements where the responsible party is responsible for the subject matter information but not the subject matter, independence is required from the responsible party. In addition, an evaluation shall be made of any threats the firm has reason to believe are created by interests and relationships between a member of the assurance team, the firm, a network firm and the party responsible for the subject matter.

Direct Reporting Assurance engagements

In a direct reporting assurance engagement, the professional accountant in public practice either directly performs the evaluation or measurement of the subject matter, or obtains a representation from the responsible party that has performed the evaluation or measurement that is not available to the intended users. The subject matter information is provided to the intended users in the assurance report.

In a direct reporting assurance engagement independence is required from the responsible party, which is responsible for the subject matter.

Multiple Responsible Parties

In both assertion-based assurance engagements and direct reporting assurance engagements there may be several responsible parties. For example, a public accountant in public practice may be asked to provide assurance on the monthly circulation statistics of a number of independently owned newspapers. The assignment could be an assertion based assurance engagement where each newspaper measures its circulation and the statistics are presented in an assertion that is available to the intended users. Alternatively, the assignment could be a direct reporting assurance engagement, where there is no assertion and there may or may not be a written representation from the newspapers.

In such engagements, when determining whether it is necessary to apply the provisions in section 291 to each responsible party, the firm may take into account whether an interest or relationship between the firm, or a member of the assurance team, and a particular responsible party would create a threat to independence that is not trivial and inconsequential in the context of the subject matter information. This will take into account:

- The materiality of the subject matter information (or the subject matter) for which the particular responsible party is responsible; and
- The degree of public interest that is associated with the engagement.

If the firm determines that the threat to independence created by any such relationships with a particular responsible party would be trivial and inconsequential it may not be necessary to apply all of the provisions of this section to that responsible party.

Example

The following example has been developed to demonstrate the application of section 291. It is assumed that the client is not also a financial statement audit client of the firm, or a network firm.

A firm is engaged to provide assurance on the total proven oil reserves of 10 independent companies. Each company has conducted geographical and engineering surveys to determine their reserves (subject matter). There are established criteria to determine when a reserve may be considered to be proven which the professional accountant in public practice determines to be suitable criteria for the engagement.

The proven reserves for each company as at December 31, 20X0 were as follows:

	Proven oil reserves thousands of barrels
Company 1	5,200
Company 2	725
Company 3	3,260
Company 4	15,000
Company 5	6,700
Company 6	39,126
Company 7	345
Company 8	175
Company 9	24,135
Company 10	9,635
Total	**104,301**

The engagement could be structured in differing ways:

Assertion-Based Engagements

A1 Each company measures its reserves and provides an assertion to the firm and to intended users.
A2 An entity other than the companies measures the reserves and provides an assertion to the firm and to intended users.

Direct Reporting Engagements

D1 Each company measures the reserves and provides the firm with a written representation that measures its reserves against the established criteria for measuring proven reserves. The representation is not available to the intended users.
D2 The firm directly measures the reserves of some of the companies.

Application of Approach

A1 Each company measures its reserves and provides an assertion to the firm and to intended users.

There are several responsible parties in this engagement (companies 1–10). When determining whether it is necessary to apply the independence provisions to all of the companies, the firm may take into account whether an interest or relationship with a particular company would create a threat to independence that is not at an acceptable level. This will take into account factors such as:

- The materiality of the company's proven reserves in relation to the total reserves to be reported on; and
- The degree of public interest associated with the engagement (paragraph 291.28).

For example Company 8 accounts for 0.17% of the total reserves, therefore a business relationship or interest with Company 8 would create less of a threat than a similar relationship with Company 6, which accounts for approximately 37.5% of the reserves.

Having determined those companies to which the independence requirements apply, the assurance team and the firm are required to be independent of those responsible parties that would be considered to be the assurance client (paragraph 291.28).

A2 An entity other than the companies measures the reserves and provides an assertion to the firm and to intended users.

The firm shall be independent of the entity that measures the reserves and provides an assertion to the firm and to intended users (paragraph 291.19). That entity is not responsible for the subject matter and so an evaluation shall be made of any threats the firm has reason to believe are created by interests/relationships with the party responsible for the subject matter (paragraph 291.19). There are several parties responsible for the subject matter in this engagement (Companies 1–10). As discussed in example A1 above, the firm may take into account whether an interest or relationship with a particular company would create a threat to independence that is not at an acceptable level.

D1 Each company provides the firm with a representation that measures its reserves against the established criteria for measuring proven reserves. The representation is not available to the intended users.

There are several responsible parties in this engagement (Companies 1–10). When determining whether it is necessary to apply the independence provisions to all of the companies, the firm may take into account whether an interest or relationship with a particular company would create a threat to independence that is not at an acceptable level. This will take into account factors such as:

- The materiality of the company's proven reserves in relation to the total reserves to be reported on; and
- The degree of public interest associated with the engagement. (Paragraph 291.28).

For example, Company 8 accounts for 0.17% of the reserves, therefore a business relationship or interest with Company 8 would create less of a threat than a similar relationship with Company 6 that accounts for approximately 37.5% of the reserves.

Having determined those companies to which the independence requirements apply, the assurance team and the firm shall be independent of those responsible parties that would be considered to be the assurance client (paragraph 291.28).

D2 The firm directly measures the reserves of some of the companies.

The application is the same as in example D1.

References

Contingent fees for non-assurance services provided to a audit clients and other assurance clients are discussed in sections 290 and 291 of this Part of the Code.   1

Professional accountants are reminded that where detailed regulatory requirements cover the same issues as this Code, the regulatory requirements prevail where these are more onerous.   2

"Internal Control – Integrated Framework" The Committee of Sponsoring Organisations of the Treadway Commission.   3

"Guidance on Assessing Control – The CoCo Principles" Criteria of Control Board, The Canadian Institute of Chartered Accountants.   4

See paragraphs 290.13 to 290.24 for guidance on what constitutes a network firm.   5

Code of Ethics C

- **Introduction**
- **Potential conflicts**
- **Preparation and reporting of information**
- **Acting with sufficient expertise**
- **Financial interests**
- **Inducements**

Introduction

300.1   This Part of the Code describes how the conceptual framework contained in Part A applies in certain situations to professional accountants in business. This Part does not describe all of the circumstances and relationships that could be encountered by a professional accountant in business that create or may create threats to compliance with the fundamental principles. Therefore, the professional accountant in business is encouraged to be alert for such circumstances and relationships.

Professional accountants in business shall also read Part A which sets out the fundamental principles and conceptual framework that professional accountants are required to adhere to. It may also be helpful for professional accountants in business to refer to other parts of this Code in relevant circumstances: for example, sections 221, 'Corporate finance advice', and 241, 'Agencies and referrals'.

300.2   Investors, creditors, employers and other sectors of the business community, as well as governments and the public at large, all may rely on the work of professional accountants in business. Professional accountants in business may be solely or jointly responsible for the preparation and reporting of financial and other information, which both their employing organisations and third parties may rely on. They may also be responsible for providing effective financial management and competent advice on a variety of business-related matters.

Professional accountants in business are engaged in an executive or non-executive capacity in such areas as commerce, industry, the public and service sectors (including public sector bodies), education, the not for profit sector, regulatory bodies or professional bodies.

300.3   A professional accountant in business may be a salaried employee, a partner, director (whether executive or non-executive), an owner manager, a volunteer or another working for one or more employing organisation. The legal form of the relationship with the employing organisation, if any, has no bearing on the ethical responsibilities incumbent on the professional accountant in business.

Professional accountants are reminded that this Code applies to all their professional and business activities, with and without reward.

300.4   A professional accountant in business has a responsibility to further the legitimate aims of the accountant's employing organisation. This Code does not seek to hinder a professional accountant in business from properly fulfilling that responsibility, but addresses circumstances in which compliance with the fundamental principles may be compromised.

300.5   A professional accountant in business may hold a senior position within an organisation. The more senior the position, the greater will be the ability and opportunity to influence events, practices and attitudes. A professional accountant in business is expected, therefore, to encourage an ethics-based culture in an employing organisation that emphasises the importance that senior management places on ethical behaviour.

A professional accountant in business shall not knowingly engage in any business, occupation, or activity that impairs or might impair integrity, objectivity or the good reputation of the profession and as a result would be incompatible with the fundamental principles. **300.6**

Fundamental principles

A professional accountant shall comply with the following fundamental principles: **300.6a**

- **Integrity** – to be straightforward and honest in all professional and business relationships.
- **Objectivity** - to not allow bias, conflict of interest or undue influence of others to override professional or business judgments
- **Professional Competence and Due Care** - to maintain professional knowledge and skill at the level required to ensure that a client or employer receives competent professional services based on current developments in practice, legislation and techniques and act diligently and in accordance with applicable technical and professional standards.
- **Confidentiality** – to respect the confidentiality of information acquired as a result of professional and business relationships and, therefore, not disclose any such information to third parties without proper and specific authority, unless there is a legal or professional right or duty to disclose, nor use the information for the personal advantage of the professional accountant or third parties.
- **Professional Behaviour** - to comply with relevant laws and regulations and avoid any action that discredits the profession.

Compliance with the fundamental principles may potentially be threatened by a broad range of circumstances and relationships. Threats fall into one or more of the following categories: **300.7**

- self-interest
- self-review
- advocacy
- familiarity
- intimidation.

These threats are discussed further in Part A of this Code.

Examples of circumstances that may create self-interest threats for a professional accountant in business include: **300.8**

- Holding a financial interest in, or receiving a loan or guarantee from the employing organisation.
- Participating in incentive compensation arrangements offered by the employing organisation.
- Inappropriate personal use of corporate assets.
- Concern over employment security.
- Commercial pressure from outside the employing organisation.

An example of a circumstance that creates a self-review threat for a professional accountant in business is determining the appropriate accounting treatment for a **300.9** business combination after performing the feasibility study that supported the acquisition decision.

300.10   When furthering the legitimate goals and objectives of their employing organisations, professional accountants in business may promote the organisation's position, provided any statements made are neither false nor misleading. Such actions generally would not create an advocacy threat.

300.11   Examples of circumstances that may create familiarity threats for a professional accountant in business include:

- Being responsible for the employing organisation's financial reporting when an immediate or close family member employed by the entity makes decisions that affect the entity's financial reporting.
- Long association with business contacts influencing business decisions.
- Accepting a gift or preferential treatment, unless the value is trivial and inconsequential.

300.12   Examples of circumstances that may create intimidation threats for a professional accountant in business include:

- Threat of dismissal or replacement of the professional accountant in business or a close or immediate family member over a disagreement about the application of an accounting principle or the way in which financial information is to be reported.
- A dominant personality attempting to influence the decision making process, for example with regard to the awarding of contracts or the application of an accounting principle.

300.13   Safeguards that may eliminate or reduce threats to an acceptable level fall into two broad categories:

- Safeguards created by the profession, legislation or regulation; and
- Safeguards in the work environment.

Examples of safeguards created by the profession, legislation or regulation are detailed in paragraph 100.14 of Part A of this Code.

300.14   Safeguards in the work environment include:

- The employing organisation's systems of corporate oversight or other oversight structures.
- The employing organisation's ethics and conduct programs.
- Recruitment procedures in the employing organisation emphasizing the importance of employing high calibre competent staff.
- Strong internal controls.
- Appropriate disciplinary processes.
- Leadership that stresses the importance of ethical behaviour and the expectation that employees will act in an ethical manner.
- Policies and procedures to implement and monitor the quality of employee performance.
- Timely communication of the employing organisation's policies and procedures, including any changes to them, to all employees and appropriate training and education on such policies and procedures.
- Policies and procedures to empower and encourage employees to communicate to senior levels within the employing organisation any ethical issues that concern them without fear of retribution.
- Consultation with another appropriate professional accountant.

In circumstances where a professional accountant in business believes that unethical behaviour or actions by others will continue to occur within the employing organisation, the professional accountant in business may consider obtaining legal advice. In those extreme situations where all available safeguards have been exhausted and it is not possible to reduce the threat to an acceptable level, a professional accountant in business may conclude that it is appropriate to disassociate from the task and/or resign from the employing organisation.   **300.15**

To assist professional accountants to determine an appropriate course of action when faced with a situation which could threaten their compliance with the fundamental principles the following sections (preparing and reporting of information; acting with sufficient expertise; financial information; inducements and disclosing confidential information) give examples of specific areas of activity which could give rise to ethical dilemmas and the action which could be taken in response. This is not a comprehensive list of examples but aims to cover the key areas most likely to be encountered by professional accountants. Illustrative case studies of how the guidance might be applied in example situations are available at www.icaew.com/ethics.   **300.16**

Professional accountants who are in doubt as to their ethical position may seek advice from the ICAEW's Technical Advisory Services by email: ethics@icaew.com or phone +44 (0)1908 248 250. Further guidance on sources of advice is available in section 1.   **300.17**

Potential conflicts

A professional accountant in business shall comply with the fundamental principles. There may be times, however, when a professional accountant's responsibilities to an employing organisation and professional obligations to comply with the fundamental principles are in conflict. A professional accountant in business is expected to support the legitimate and ethical objectives established by the employer and the rules and procedures drawn up in support of those objectives. Nevertheless, where a relationship or circumstance creates a threat to compliance with the fundamental principles, a professional accountant in business shall apply the conceptual framework approach described in section 100 to determine a response to the threat.   **310.1**

As a consequence of responsibilities to an employing organisation, a professional accountant in business may be under pressure to act or behave in ways that could create threats to compliance with the fundamental principles. Such pressure may be explicit or implicit; it may come from a supervisor, manager, director or another individual within the employing organisation. A professional accountant in business may face pressure to: **310.2**

- Act contrary to law or regulation.
- Act contrary to technical or professional standards.
- Facilitate unethical or illegal earnings management strategies.
- Lie to others, or otherwise intentionally mislead (including misleading by remaining silent) others, in particular:
  - The auditors of the employing organisation; or
  - Regulators.
- Issue, or otherwise be associated with, a financial or non-financial report that materially misrepresents the facts, including statements in connection with, for example:
  - The financial statements;
  - Tax compliance;

– Legal compliance; or
– Reports required by securities regulators.

310.3   The significance of any threats arising from such pressures, such as intimidation threats, shall be evaluated and safeguards applied when necessary to eliminate them or reduce them to an acceptable level. Examples of such safeguards include:

- Obtaining advice, where appropriate, from within the employing organisation, an independent professional advisor or ICAEW (see section 1 of this Code).
- Using a formal dispute resolution process within the employing organisation.
- Seeking legal advice.

Informal discussions with fellow professional accountants in business or in practice may assist in clarifying the steps needed to be taken.

Preparation and reporting of information

320.1   Professional accountants in business are often involved in the preparation and reporting of information that may either be made public or used by others inside or outside the employing organisation. Such information may include financial or management information, for example, forecasts and budgets, financial statements, management's discussion and analysis, and the management letter of representation provided to the auditors during the audit of the entity's financial statements. A professional accountant in business shall prepare or present such information fairly, honestly and in accordance with relevant professional standards so that the information will be understood in its context.

320.2   A professional accountant in business who has responsibility for the preparation or approval of the general purpose financial statements of an employing organisation shall be satisfied that those financial statements are presented in accordance with the applicable financial reporting standards.

320.3   A professional accountant in business shall take reasonable steps to maintain information for which the professional accountant in business is responsible in a manner that:

- Describes clearly the true nature of business transactions, assets, or liabilities;
- Classifies and records information in a timely and proper manner; and
- Represents the facts accurately and completely in all material respects.

320.4   Threats to compliance with the fundamental principles, for example, self-interest or intimidation threats to objectivity or professional competence and due care, are created where a professional accountant in business is pressured (either externally or by the possibility of personal gain) to become associated with misleading information or to become associated with misleading information through the actions of others.

Accordingly, professional accountants shall not be associated with reports, returns, communications or other information where they believe that the information:

- Contains a materially false or misleading statement;
- Contains statements or information furnished recklessly;
- Omits or obscures information required to be included where such omission or obscurity would be misleading.

320.5   The significance of such threats will depend on factors such as the source of the pressure and the degree to which the information is, or may be, misleading. The significance of the threats shall be evaluated and safeguards applied when necessary to eliminate them or reduce them to an acceptable level. Such safeguards include consultation with superiors within the employing organisation, the audit committee or those charged with governance of the organisation, or with ICAEW.

Where it is not possible to reduce the threat to an acceptable level, a professional accountant in business shall refuse to be or remain associated with information the professional accountant determines is misleading. A professional accountant in business may have been unknowingly associated with misleading information. Upon becoming aware of this, the professional accountant in business shall take steps to be disassociated from that information. In determining whether there is a requirement to report, the professional accountant in business may consider obtaining legal advice. In addition, the professional accountant may consider whether to resign.   **320.6**

Acting with sufficient expertise

The fundamental principle of professional competence and due care requires that a professional accountant in business only undertake significant tasks for which the professional accountant in business has, or can obtain, sufficient specific training or experience. A professional accountant in business shall not intentionally mislead an employer as to the level of expertise or experience possessed, nor shall a professional accountant in business fail to seek appropriate expert advice and assistance when required.   **330.1**

Circumstances that create a threat to a professional accountant in business performing duties with the appropriate degree of professional competence and due care include having: **330.2**

- Insufficient time for properly performing or completing the relevant duties.
- Incomplete, restricted or otherwise inadequate information for performing the duties properly.
- Insufficient experience, training and/or education.
- Inadequate resources for the proper performance of the duties.

The significance of the threat will depend on factors such as the extent to which the professional accountant in business is working with others, relative seniority in the business, and the level of supervision and review applied to the work. The significance of the threat shall be evaluated and safeguards applied when necessary to eliminate the threat or reduce it to an acceptable level. Examples of such safeguards include: **330.3**

- Obtaining additional advice or training.
- Ensuring that there is adequate time available for performing the relevant duties.
- Obtaining assistance from someone with the necessary expertise.
- Consulting, where appropriate, with:
- Superiors within the employing organisation;
- Independent experts; or
- ICAEW

When threats cannot be eliminated or reduced to an acceptable level, professional accountants in business shall determine whether to refuse to perform the duties in question. If the professional accountant in business determines that refusal is appropriate, the reasons for doing so shall be clearly communicated.   **330.4**

Financial interests

340.1   Professional accountants in business may have financial interests, or may know of financial interests of immediate or close family members, that, in certain circumstances, may create threats to compliance with the fundamental principles. For example, self-interest threats to objectivity or confidentiality may be created through the existence of the motive and opportunity to manipulate price sensitive information in order to gain financially. Examples of circumstances that may create self-interest threats include situations where the professional accountant in business or an immediate or close family member:

- Holds a direct or indirect financial interest in the employing organisation and the value of that financial interest could be directly affected by decisions made by the professional accountant in business;
- Is eligible for a profit related bonus and the value of that bonus could be directly affected by decisions made by the professional accountant in business;
- Holds, directly or indirectly, share options in the employing organisation, the value of which could be directly affected by decisions made by the professional accountant in business;
- Holds, directly or indirectly, share options in the employing organisation which are, or will soon be, eligible for conversion; or
- May qualify for share options in the employing organisation or performance related bonuses if certain targets are achieved.

340.2   The significance of any threat shall be evaluated and safeguards applied when necessary to eliminate the threat or reduce it to an acceptable level. In evaluating the significance of any threat, and, when necessary, determining the appropriate safeguards to be applied to eliminate the threat or reduce it to an acceptable level, a professional accountant in business shall evaluate the nature of the financial interest. This includes evaluating the significance of the financial interest and determining whether it is direct or indirect. What constitutes a significant or valuable stake in an organisation will vary from individual to individual, depending on personal circumstances. Examples of such safeguards include:

- Policies and procedures for a committee independent of management to determine the level or form of remuneration of senior management.
- Disclosure of all relevant interests and of any plans to trade in relevant shares to those charged with the governance of the employing organisation, in accordance with any internal policies.
- Consultation, where appropriate, with superiors within the employing organisation.
- Consultation, where appropriate, with those charged with the governance of the employing organisation or relevant professional bodies.
- Internal and external audit procedures.
- Up-to-date education on ethical issues and on the legal restrictions and other regulations around potential insider trading.

340.3   A professional accountant in business shall neither manipulate information nor use confidential information for personal gain.

Inducements

Receiving offers

A professional accountant in business or an immediate or close family member may be offered an inducement. Inducements may take various forms, including gifts, hospitality, preferential treatment, and inappropriate appeals to friendship or loyalty. **350.1**

Offers of inducements may create threats to compliance with the fundamental principles. When a professional accountant in business or an immediate or close family member is offered an inducement, the situation shall be evaluated. Self-interest threats to objectivity or confidentiality are created when an inducement is made in an attempt to unduly influence actions or decisions, encourage illegal or dishonest behaviour, or obtain confidential information. Intimidation threats to objectivity or confidentiality are created if such an inducement is accepted and it is followed by threats to make that offer public and damage the reputation of either the professional accountant in business or an immediate or close family member. **350.2**

The existence and significance of any threats will depend on the nature, value and intent behind the offer. If a reasonable and informed third party, weighing all the specific facts and circumstances, would consider the inducement insignificant and not intended to encourage unethical behaviour, then a professional accountant in business may conclude that the offer is made in the normal course of business and may generally conclude that there is no significant threat to compliance with the fundamental principles. **350.3**

The significance of any threats shall be evaluated and safeguards applied when necessary to eliminate them or reduce them to an acceptable level. When the threats cannot be eliminated or reduced to an acceptable level through the application of safeguards, a professional accountant in business shall not accept the inducement. As the real or apparent threats to compliance with the fundamental principles do not merely arise from acceptance of an inducement but, sometimes, merely from the fact of the offer having been made, additional safeguards shall be adopted. A professional accountant in business shall evaluate any threats created by such offers and determine whether to take one or more of the following actions: **350.4**

- Informing higher levels of management or those charged with governance of the employing organisation immediately when such offers have been made;
- Informing third parties of the offer – for example, ICAEW or the employer of the individual who made the offer; a professional accountant in business may however, consider seeking legal advice before taking such a step; and
- Advising immediate or close family members of relevant threats and safeguards where they are potentially in positions that might result in offers of inducements, for example, as a result of their employment situation; and
- Informing higher levels of management or those charged with governance of the employing organisation where immediate or close family members are employed by competitors or potential suppliers of that organisation.

Making offers

A professional accountant in business may be in a situation where the professional accountant in business is expected, or is under other pressure, to offer inducements to influence the judgment or decision-making process of an individual or organisation, or obtain confidential information. **350.5**

350.6 Such pressure may come from within the employing organisation, for example, from a colleague or superior. It may also come from an external individual or organisation suggesting actions or business decisions that would be advantageous to the employing organisation, possibly influencing the professional accountant in business improperly.

350.7 A professional accountant in business shall not offer an inducement to improperly influence professional judgment of a third party.

350.8 Where the pressure to offer an unethical inducement comes from within the employing organisation, the professional accountant shall follow the principles and guidance regarding ethical conflict resolution set out in Part A of this Code.

Code of Ethics ABC definitions

Acceptable level

A level at which a reasonable and informed third party would be likely to conclude, weighing all the specific facts and circumstances available to the professional accountant at that time, that compliance with the fundamental principles is not compromised.

Advertising

The communication to the public of information as to the services or skills provided by professional accountants in public practice with a view to procuring professional business.

Affiliates

A person granted affiliate status by ICAEW under its regulations.

Assurance client

The responsible party that is the person (or persons) who:

- In a direct reporting engagement, is responsible for the subject matter; or
- In an assertion-based engagement, is responsible for the subject matter information and may be responsible for the subject matter.

Assurance engagement

An engagement in which a professional accountant in public practice expresses a conclusion designed to enhance the degree of confidence of the intended users other than the responsible party about the outcome of the evaluation or measurement of a subject matter against criteria.

(For guidance on assurance engagements see the International Framework for Assurance engagements issued by the International Auditing and Assurance Standards Board which describes the elements and objectives of an assurance engagement and identifies engagements to which International Standards on Auditing (ISAs), International Standards on Review engagements (ISREs) and International

Standards on Assurance engagements (ISAEs) apply.) www.ifac.org/IAASB/Pronouncements.php

Assurance team

- All members of the engagement team for the assurance engagement;
- All others within a firm who can directly influence the outcome of the assurance engagement, including:
  - those who recommend the compensation of, or who provide direct supervisory, management or other oversight of the assurance engagement partner in connection with the performance of the assurance engagement;
  - those who provide consultation regarding technical or industry specific issues, transactions or events for the assurance engagement; and
  - those who provide quality control for the assurance engagement, including those who perform the engagement quality control review for the assurance engagement.

Audit client

An entity in respect of which a firm conducts an audit engagement. When the client is a listed entity, audit client will always include its related entities. When the audit client is not a listed entity, audit client includes those related entities over which the client has direct or indirect control.

Audit committee

Those charged with governance. This may be a separate committee or the full Board.

Audit engagement

A reasonable assurance engagement in which a professional accountant in public practice expresses an opinion whether financial statements are prepared, in all material respects (or give a true and fair view or are presented fairly, in all material respects), in accordance with an applicable financial reporting framework, such as an engagement conducted in accordance with International Standards on Auditing. This includes a Statutory Audit, which is an audit required by legislation or other regulation.

Audit team

- All members of the engagement team for the audit engagement;
- All others within a firm who can directly influence the outcome of the audit engagement, including:
  - Those who recommend the compensation of, or who provide direct supervisory, management or other oversight of the engagement partner in connection with the performance of the audit engagement including those at all successively senior levels above the engagement partner through to the individual who is the firm's Senior or Managing Partner (Chief Executive or equivalent);
  - Those who provide consultation regarding technical or industry-specific issues, transactions or events for the engagement; and

o   Those who provide quality control for the engagement, including those who perform the engagement quality control review for the engagement; and

o   All those within a network firm who can directly influence the outcome of the audit engagement.

Close family

A parent, child or sibling who is not an immediate family member.

Contingent fee

A fee calculated on a predetermined basis relating to the outcome of a transaction or the result of the services performed by the firm. A fee that is established by a court or other public authority is not a contingent fee.

Direct financial interest

A financial interest:

•   Owned directly by and under the control of an individual or entity (including those managed on a discretionary basis by others); or
•   Beneficially owned through a collective investment vehicle, estate, trust or other intermediary over which the individual or entity has control, or the ability to influence investment decisions.

Director or officer

Those charged with the governance of an entity, or acting in an equivalent capacity, regardless of their title, which may vary from jurisdiction to jurisdiction.

Engagement partner

The partner or other person in the firm who is responsible for the engagement and its performance, and for the report that is issued on behalf of the firm, and who, where required, has the appropriate authority from a professional, legal or regulatory body.

Engagement quality control review

A process designed to provide an objective evaluation, on or before the report is issued, of the significant judgments the engagement team made and the conclusions it reached in formulating the report.

Engagement team

All partners and staff performing the engagement, and any individuals engaged by the firm or a network firm who perform assurance procedures on the engagement. This excludes external experts engaged by the firm or a network firm.

Existing accountant

A professional accountant in public practice currently holding an audit appointment or carrying out accounting, taxation, consulting or similar professional services for a client.

External expert

An individual (who is not a partner or a member of the professional staff, including temporary staff, of the firm or a network firm) or organisation possessing skills, knowledge and experience in a field other than accounting or auditing, whose work in that field is used to assist the professional accountant in obtaining sufficient appropriate evidence.

Financial interest

An interest in equity or other security, debenture, loan or other debt instrument of an entity, including rights and obligations to acquire such an interest and derivatives directly related to such interest.

Financial statements

A structured representation of historical financial information, including related notes, intended to communicate an entity's economic resources or obligations at a point in time or the changes therein for a period of time in accordance with a financial reporting framework. The related notes ordinarily comprise a summary of significant accounting policies and other explanatory information. The term can relate to a complete set of financial statements, but it can also refer to a single financial statement, for example, a balance sheet, or a statement of revenues and expenses, and related explanatory notes.

Financial statements on which the firm will express an opinion

In the case of a single entity, the financial statements of that entity. In the case of consolidated financial statements, also referred to as group financial statements, the consolidated financial statements.

Firm

- A member firm;
- An entity that controls a member firm, through ownership, management or other means; and
- An entity controlled by a member firm, through ownership, management or other means.

Historical financial information

Information expressed in financial terms in relation to a particular entity, derived primarily from that entity's accounting system, about economic events occurring in past time periods or about economic conditions or circumstances at points in time in the past.

Immediate family

A spouse (or equivalent) or dependent. Independence

- independence of mind – the state of mind that permits the expression of a conclusion without being affected by influences that compromise professional judgment, thereby allowing an individual to act with integrity, and exercise objectivity and professional scepticism
- independence in appearance – the avoidance of facts and circumstances that are so significant that a reasonable and informed third party would be likely to conclude, weighing all the specific facts and circumstances, that a firm's, or a member of the audit or assurance team's, integrity, objectivity or professional scepticism has been compromised.

Indirect financial interest

A financial interest beneficially owned through a collective investment vehicle, estate, trust or other intermediary over which the individual or entity has no control or ability to influence investment decisions.

Key audit partner

The engagement partner, the individual responsible for the engagement quality control review, and other audit partners, if any, on the engagement team who make key decisions or judgments on significant matters with respect to the audit of the financial statements on which the firm will express an opinion. Depending upon the circumstances and the role of the individuals on the audit, "other audit partners" may include, for example, audit partners responsible for significant subsidiaries or divisions.

Listed entity

An entity whose shares, stock or debt are quoted or listed on a recognised stock exchange, or are marketed under the regulations of a recognised stock exchange or other equivalent body.

Loan

A sum of money lent, whether direct or through a third party, with the intention that it will be repaid with or without interest.

Member

A member of ICAEW, an affiliate, an employee of a member firm or affiliate, or a provisional member.

Member firm

This means, for the purposes of this Code:

- A member engaged in public practice as a sole practitioner, or
- A partnership engaged in public practice of which more than 50 per cent of the right to vote on all, or substantially all, matters of substance at meetings of the partnership is held by members; or

- A limited liability partnership engaged in public practice of which more than 50 per cent of the rights to vote on all, or substantially all, matters of substance at meetings of the partnership is held by members; or
- Any body corporate (other than a limited liability partnership) engaged in public practice of which:
- 50 per cent or more of the directors are members; and
- More than 50 per cent of the nominal value of the voting shares is held by members; and
- More than 50 per cent of the aggregate in nominal value of the voting and non-voting shares is held by members.

Network

A larger structure:

- That is aimed at co-operation; and
- That is clearly aimed at profit or cost sharing or shares common ownership, control or management, common quality control policies and procedures, common business strategy, the use of a common brand-name, or a significant part of professional resources.

Network firm

A firm or entity that belongs to a network.

Office

A distinct sub-group, whether organised on geographical or practice lines.

Officer

Those charged with the governance of an entity, or acting in an equivalent capacity, regardless of their title, which may vary from jurisdiction to jurisdiction.

Partner or principal

References to a partner or principal of a firm include the following:

- A partner/principal;
- A sole-practitioner;
- A director of a corporate firm;
- A member of a limited liability partnership;
- An employee of a corporate firm who is:
  - A responsible individual within the meaning of the Audit Regulations;
  - A licensed insolvency practitioner;
  - Defined as such in circumstances determined by Council

Professional accountant

An individual who is a member of an IFAC member body.

Professional accountant in business

A professional accountant employed or engaged in an executive or non-executive capacity in such areas as commerce, industry, service, the public sector, education, the not for profit sector, regulatory bodies or professional bodies, or a professional accountant contracted by such entities.

A professional accountant in business may be a salaried employee, a partner, director (whether executive or non-executive), an owner manager, a volunteer, or another working for one or more employing organisations. The legal form of the relationship with the employing organisation, if any, has no bearing on the ethical responsibilities incumbent on the professional accountant in business.

Professional accountant in public practice

A professional accountant, irrespective of functional classification (e.g., audit, tax or consulting) in a firm that provides professional services. This term is also used to refer to a firm of professional accountants in public practice.

Professional service

Services requiring accountancy or related skills performed by a professional accountant including accounting, auditing, taxation, management consulting and financial management services.

Provisional member

A person:

- who is training under a training agreement; or has registered their period of approved training
- who has trained under such agreement or period of approved training and is eligible either to sit for the ACA examinations of ICAEW or, having success-fully sat those examinations, to apply for membership;

and for the purposes only of this definition an order under bye-law 22(7) (d) of the Disciplinary Bye-laws (concerning eligibility to sit examinations) shall be disregarded.

Public interest entity

- A listed entity; and
- An entity (a) defined by regulation or legislation as a public interest entity or (b) for which the audit is required by regulation or legislation to be conducted in compliance with the same independence requirements that apply to the audit of listed entities. Such regulation may be promulgated by any relevant regulator, including an audit regulator.

Related entity

An entity that has any of the following relationships with the client:

- An entity that has direct or indirect control over the client if the client is material to such entity;

- An entity with a direct financial interest in the client if that entity has significant influence over the client and the interest in the client is material to such entity;
- An entity over which the client has direct or indirect control;
- An entity in which the client, or an entity related to the client under (c) above, has a direct financial interest that gives it significant influence over such entity and the interest is material to the client and its related entity (c); and
- An entity which is under common control with the client (a "sister entity") if the sister entity and the client are both material to the entity that controls both the client and sister entity.

Review client

An entity in respect of which a firm conducts a review engagement.

Review engagement

An assurance engagement, conducted in accordance with International Standards on Review engagements or equivalent, in which a professional accountant in public practice expresses a conclusion on whether, on the basis of the procedures which do not provide all the evidence that would be required in an audit, anything has come to the accountant's attention that causes the accountant to believe that the financial statements are not prepared, in all material respects, in accordance with an applicable financial reporting framework.

Review team

- All members of the engagement team for the review engagement; and
- All others within a firm who can directly influence the outcome of the review engagement, including:
  - Those who recommend the compensation of, or who provide direct supervisory, management or other oversight of the engagement partner in connection with the performance of the review engagement including those at all successively senior levels above the engagement partner through to the individual who is the firm's Senior or Managing Partner (Chief Executive or equivalent);
  - Those who provide consultation regarding technical or industry specific issues, transactions or events for the engagement; and
  - Those who provide quality control for the engagement, including those who perform the engagement quality control review for the engagement; and
- All those within a network firm who can directly influence the outcome of the review engagement.

Code of Ethics D

- **General application of the code**
  - ○ Practice of insolvency
  - ○ Identification of threats to the fundamental principles
  - ○ Framework of approach
  - ○ Evaluation of threats
  - ○ Possible safeguards
- **Specific application of the code**
  - ○ Insolvency appointments
  - ○ Conflicts of interest
  - ○ Practice mergers
  - ○ Transparency
  - ○ Professional competence and due care
  - ○ Professional and personal relationships
  - ○ Identifying relationships
  - ○ Is the relationship significant to the conduct of the insolvency appointment?
  - ○ Dealing with the assets of an entity
  - ○ Obtaining specialist advice and services
- **Fees and other types of remuneration**
  - ○ Prior to accepting an insolvency appointments
  - ○ After accepting an insolvency appointments
  - ○ Obtaining insolvency appointments
  - ○ Gifts and hospitality
  - ○ Record keeping
- **The application of the framework to specific situations**
  - ○ Introduction to specific situation
  - ○ Examples that do not relate to a previous of existing insolvency appointment
  - ○ Examples that relate to previous or existing insolvency appointments
  - ○ Examples in respect of cases conducted under Scottish law
- **Definitions**

General application of the code

Practice of insolvency

400.1   This Code is intended to assist Insolvency Practitioners meet the obligations expected of them by providing professional and ethical guidance.

400.2   This Code applies to all Insolvency Practitioners. Insolvency Practitioners should take steps to ensure that the Code is applied in all professional work relating to an insolvency appointment, and to any professional work that may lead to such an insolvency appointment. Although an insolvency appointment will be of the Insolvency practitioner personally rather than his practice, he should ensure that the standards set out in this Code are applied to all members of the insolvency team.

400.3   It is this Code, and the spirit that underlies it, that governs the conduct of Insolvency Practitioners. Failure to observe this Code may not, of itself, constitute professional misconduct, but will be taken into account in assessing the conduct of an Insolvency practitioner.

Fundamental principles

An Insolvency practitioner is required to comply with the following fundamental principles: **400.4**

- Integrity
  An Insolvency practitioner should be straightforward and honest in all professional and business relationships.
- Objectivity
  An Insolvency practitioner should not allow bias, conflict of interest or undue influence of others to override professional or business judgements.
- Professional competence and due care
  An Insolvency practitioner has a continuing duty to maintain professional knowledge and skill at the level required to ensure that a client or employer receives competent professional service based on current developments in practice, legislation and techniques. An Insolvency practitioner should act diligently and in accordance with applicable technical and professional standards when providing professional services.
- Confidentiality
  An Insolvency practitioner should respect the confidentiality of information acquired as a result of professional and business relationships and should not disclose any such information to third parties without proper and specific authority unless there is a legal or professional right or duty to disclose. Confidential information acquired as a result of professional and business relationships should not be used for the personal advantage of the Insolvency practitioner or third parties.
- Professional behaviour
  An Insolvency practitioner should comply with relevant laws and regulations and should avoid any action that discredits the profession. Insolvency Practitioners should conduct themselves with courtesy and consideration towards all with whom they come into contact when performing their work.

Framework approach

The framework approach is amethod which Insolvency Practitioners can use to identify actual or potential threats to the fundamental principles and determine whether there are any safeguards that might be available to offset them. The framework approach requires an Insolvency practitioner to: **400.5**

- take reasonable steps to identify any threats to compliance with the fundamental principles;
- evaluate any such threats; and
- respond in an appropriate manner to those threats.

Throughout this Code there are examples of threats and possible safeguards. These examples are illustrative and should not be considered as exhaustive lists of all relevant threats or safeguards. It is impossible to define every situation that creates a threat to compliance with the fundamental principles or to specify the safeguards that may be available. **400.6**

Identification of threats to the fundamental principles

An Insolvency practitioner should take reasonable steps to identify the existence of any threats to compliance with the fundamental principles which arise during the course of his professional work. **400.7**

400.8   An Insolvency practitioner should take particular care to identify the existence of threats which exist prior to or at the time of taking an insolvency appointment or which, at that stage, it may reasonably be expected might arise during the course of such an insolvency appointment. Sections insolvency appointments and professional and personal relationships below contain particular factors an Insolvency practitioner should take into account when deciding whether to accept an insolvency appointment.

400.9   In identifying the existence of any threats, an Insolvency practitioner should have regard to relationships whereby the practice is held out as being part of a national or an international association.

400.10   Many threats fall into one or more of five categories:

- **Self-interest threats:** which may occur as a result of the financial or other interests of a practice or an Insolvency practitioner or of a close or immediate family member of an individual within the practice;
- **Self-review threats:** which may occur when a previous judgement made by an individual within the practice needs to be re-evaluated by the Insolvency practitioner;
- **Advocacy threats:** which may occur when an individual within the practice promotes a position or opinion to the point that subsequent objectivity may be compromised;
- **Familiarity threats:** which may occur when, because of a close relationship, an individual within the practice becomes too sympathetic or antagonistic to the interests of others; and
- **Intimidation threats:** which may occur when an Insolvency practitioner may be deterred from acting objectively by threats, actual or perceived.

400.11   The following paragraphs give examples of the possible threats that an Insolvency practitioner may face.

400.12   Examples of circumstances that may create self-interest threats for an Insolvency practitioner include:

- An individual within the practice having an interest in a creditor or potential creditor with a claim which requires subjective adjudication.
- Concern about the possibility of damaging a business relationship.
- Concerns about potential future employment.

400.13   Examples of circumstances that may create self-review threats include:

- The acceptance of an insolvency appointment in respect of an entity where an individual within the practice has recently been employed by or seconded to that entity.
- An Insolvency practitioner or the practice has carried out professional work of any description, including sequential insolvency appointments, for that entity.

Such self-review threats may diminish over the passage of time.

400.14   Examples of circumstances that may create advocacy threats include:

- Acting in an advisory capacity for a creditor of an entity.
- Acting as an advocate for a client in litigation or dispute with an entity.

400.15   Examples of circumstances that may create familiarity threats include:

- An individual within the practice having a close relationship with any individual having a financial interest in the insolvent entity.
- An individual within the practice having a close relationship with a potential purchaser of an insolvent's assets and/or business.

In this regard a close relationship includes both a close professional relationship and a close personal relationship.

Examples of circumstances that may create intimidation threats include: **400.16**

- The threat of dismissal or replacement being used to:
  - ○ Apply pressure not to follow regulations, this Code, any other applicable code, technical or professional standards.
  - ○ Exert influence over an insolvency appointment where the Insolvency practitioner is an employee rather than a principal of the practice.
- Being threatened with litigation.
- The threat of a complaint being made to the Insolvency practitioner's authorising body.

Evaluation of threats

An Insolvency practitioner should take reasonable steps to evaluate any threats to compliance with the fundamental principles that he has identified. **400.17**

In particular, an Insolvency practitioner should consider what a reasonable and informed third party, having knowledge of all relevant information, including the significance of the threat, would conclude to be acceptable. **400.18**

Possible safeguards

Having identified and evaluated a threat to the fundamental principles an Insolvency practitioner should consider whether there any safeguards that may be available to reduce the threat to an acceptable level. The relevant safeguards will vary depending on the circumstances. Generally safeguards fall into two broad categories. Firstly, safeguards created by the profession, legislation or regulation. Secondly, safeguards in the work environment. In the insolvency context safeguards in the work environment can include safeguards specific to an insolvency appointment. These are considered in section insolvency appointments below. In addition, safeguards can be introduced across the practice. These safeguards seek to create a work environment in which threats are identified and the introduction of appropriate safeguards is encouraged. Some examples include: **400.19**

- Leadership that stresses the importance of compliance with the fundamental principles.
- Policies and procedures to implement and monitor quality control of engagements.
- Documented policies regarding the identification of threats to compliance with the fundamental principles, the evaluation of the significance of these threats and the identification and the application of safeguards to eliminate or reduce the threats, other than those that are trivial, to an acceptable level.
- Documented internal policies and procedures requiring compliance with the fundamental principles.
- Policies and procedures to consider the fundamental principles of this Code before the acceptance of an insolvency appointment.
- Policies and procedures regarding the identification of interests or relationships between individuals within the practice and third parties.

- Policies and procedures to prohibit individuals who are not members of the insolvency team from inappropriately influencing the outcome of an insolvency appointment.
- Timely communication of a practice's policies and procedures, including any changes to them, to all individuals within the practice, and appropriate training and education on such policies and procedures.
- Designating a member of senior management to be responsible for overseeing the adequate functioning of the safeguarding system.
- A disciplinary mechanism to promote compliance with policies and procedures.
- Published policies and procedures to encourage and empower individuals within the practice to communicate to senior levels within the practice and/or the Insolvency practitioner any issue relating to compliance with the fundamental principles that concerns them.

Part 2 Specific application of the code

Insolvency appointments

400.20   The practice of insolvency is principally governed by statute and secondary legislation and in many cases is subject ultimately to the control of the Court. Where circumstances are dealt with by statute or secondary legislation, an Insolvency practitioner must comply with such provisions. An Insolvency practitioner must also comply with any relevant judicial authority relating to his conduct and any directions given by the Court.

400.21   An Insolvency practitioner should act in a manner appropriate to his position as an officer of the Court (where applicable) and in accordance with any quasi-judicial, fiduciary or other duties that he may be under.

400.22   Before agreeing to accept any insolvency appointment (including a joint appointment), an Insolvency practitioner should consider whether acceptance would create any threats to compliance with the fundamental principles. Of particular importance will be any threats to the fundamental principle of objectivity created by conflicts of interest or by any significant professional or personal relationships. These are considered in more detail below.

400.23   In considering whether objectivity or integrity may be threatened, an Insolvency practitioner should identify and evaluate any professional or personal relationship (see section dealing with the assets of an entity below) which may affect compliance with the fundamental principles. The appropriate response to the threats arising from any such relationships should then be considered, together with the introduction of any possible safeguards.

400.24   Generally, it will be inappropriate for an Insolvency practitioner to accept an insolvency appointment where a threat to the fundamental principles exists or may reasonably be expected might arise during the course of the insolvency appointment unless:

- disclosure is made, prior to the insolvency appointment, of the existence of such a threat to the Court or to the creditors on whose behalf the Insolvency practitioner would be appointed to act and no objection is made to the Insolvency practitioner being appointed; and
- safeguards are or will be available to eliminate or reduce that threat to an acceptable level. If the threat is other than trivial, safeguards should be

considered and applied as necessary to reduce them to an acceptable level, where possible.

The following safeguards may be considered:

400.25

- Involving and/or consulting another Insolvency practitioner from within the practice to review the work done.
- Consulting an independent third party, such as a committee of creditors, an authorising body or another Insolvency practitioner.
- Involving another Insolvency practitioner to perform part of the work, which may include another Insolvency practitioner taking a joint appointment where the conflict arises during the course of the insolvency appointment.
- Obtaining legal advice from a solicitor or barrister with appropriate experience and expertise.
- Changing the members of the insolvency team.
- The use of separate Insolvency Practitioners and/or staff.
- Procedures to prevent access to information by the use of information barriers (e.g. strict physical separation of such teams, confidential and secure data filing).
- Clear guidelines for individuals within the practice on issues of security and confidentiality.
- The use of confidentiality agreements signed by individuals within the practice.
- Regular review of the application of safeguards by a senior individual within the practice not involved with the insolvency appointment.
- Terminating the financial or business relationship that gives rise to the threat.
- Seeking directions from the court.

As regards joint appointments, where an Insolvency practitioner is specifically pre-cluded by this Code from accepting an insolvency appointment as an individual, a joint appointment will not be an appropriate safeguard and will not make accepting the insolvency appointment appropriate.

400.26

In deciding whether to take an insolvency appointment in circumstances where a threat to the fundamental principles has been identified, the Insolvency practitioner should consider whether the interests of those on whose behalf he would be appointed to act would best be served by the appointment of another Insolvency practitioner who did not face the same threat and, if so, whether any such appro-priately qualified and experienced other Insolvency practitioner is likely to be available to be appointed.

400.27

An Insolvency practitioner will encounter situations where no safeguards can reduce a threat to an acceptable level. Where this is the case, an Insolvency practitioner should conclude that it is not appropriate to accept an insolvency appointment.

400.28

Following acceptance, any threats should continue to be kept under appropriate review and an Insolvency practitioner should be mindful that other threats may come to light or arise. There may be occasions when the Insolvency practitioner is no longer in compliance with this Code because of changed circumstances or something which has been inadvertently overlooked. This would generally not be an issue provided the Insolvency practitioner has appropriate quality control policies and procedures in place to deal with such matters and, once discovered, the matter is corrected promptly and any necessary safeguards are applied. In deciding whether to continue an insolvency appointment the Insolvency practitioner may take into account the wishes of the creditors, who after full disclosure has been made have the right to retain or replace the Insolvency practitioner.

400.29

400.30   In all cases an Insolvency practitioner will need to exercise his judgment to determine how best to deal with an identified threat. In exercising his judgment, an Insolvency practitioner should consider what a reasonable and informed third party, having knowledge of all relevant information, including the significance of the threat and the safeguards applied, would conclude to be acceptable. This consideration will be affected by matters such as the significance of the threat, the nature of the work and the structure of the practice.

Conflicts of interest

400.31   An Insolvency practitioner should take reasonable steps to identify circumstances that could pose a conflict of interest. Such circumstances may give rise to threats to compliance with the fundamental principles. Examples of where a conflict of interest may arise are where:

- An Insolvency practitioner has to deal with claims between the separate and conflicting interests of entities over whom he is appointed.
- There are a succession of or sequential insolvency appointments (see section on the application of the framework to specific situations).
- A significant relationship has existed with the entity or someone connected with the entity (see also section on professional and personal relationships)

400.32   Some of the safeguards listed at 400.25 may be applied to reduce the threats created by a conflict of interest to an acceptable level. Where a conflict of interest arises, the preservation of confidentiality will be of paramount importance; therefore, the safeguards used should generally include the use of effective information barriers.

Practice mergers

400.33   Where practices merge, they should subsequently be treated as one for the purposes of assessing threats to the fundamental principles. At the time of the merger, existing insolvency appointments should be reviewed and any threats identified. Principals and employees of the merged practice become subject to common ethical constraints in relation to accepting new insolvency appointments to clients of either of the former practices. However, existing insolvency appointments which are rendered in apparent breach of the Code by such a merger need not be determined automatically, provided that a considered review of the situation by the practice discloses no obvious and immediate ethical conflict.

400.34   Where an individual within the practice has, in any former practice, undertaken work upon the affairs of an entity in a capacity that is incompatible with an insolvency appointment of the new practice, the individual should not work or be employed on that assignment.

Transparency

400.35   Both before and during an insolvency appointment an Insolvency practitioner may acquire personal information that is not directly relevant to the insolvency or confidential commercial information relating to the affairs of third parties. The information may be such that others might expect that confidentiality would be maintained.

400.36   Nevertheless an Insolvency practitioner in the role as office holder has a professional duty to report openly to those with an interest in the outcome of the insolvency. An Insolvency practitioner should always report on his acts and dealings as fully as possible given the circumstances of the case, in a way that is transparent and understandable. An Insolvency practitioner should bear in mind the expectations of others and what a reasonable and informed third party would consider appropriate.

Professional competence and due care

Prior to accepting an insolvency appointment the Insolvency practitioner should ensure that he is satisfied that the following matters have been considered:

    400.37

- Obtaining knowledge and understanding of the entity, its owners, managers and those responsible for its governance and business activities.
- Acquiring an appropriate understanding of the nature of the entity's business, the complexity of its operations, the specific requirements of the engagement and the purpose, nature and scope of the work to be performed.
- Acquiring knowledge of relevant industries or subject matters.
- Possessing or obtaining experience with relevant regulatory or reporting requirements.
- Assigning sufficient staff with the necessary competencies.
- Using experts where necessary.
- Complying with quality control policies and procedures designed to provide reasonable assurance that specific engagements are accepted only when they can be performed competently.

The fundamental principle of professional competence and due care requires that an Insolvency practitioner should only accept an insolvency appointment when the Insolvency practitioner has sufficient expertise. For example, a self interest threat to the fundamental principle of professional competence and due care is created if the Insolvency practitioner or the insolvency team does not possess or cannot acquire the competencies necessary to carry out the insolvency appointment. Expertise will include appropriate training, technical knowledge, knowledge of the entity and the business with which the entity is concerned.

    400.38

Maintaining and acquiring professional competence requires a continuing awareness and understanding of relevant technical and professional developments, including:

    400.39

- Developments in insolvency legislation.
- Statements of Insolvency Practice.
- The regulations of their authorising body, including any continuing professional development requirements.
- Guidance issued by their authorising body or the Insolvency Service.
- Technical issues being discussed within the profession.

Professional and personal relationships

The environment in which Insolvency Practitioners work and the relationships formed in their professional and personal lives can lead to threats to the fundamental principle of objectivity.

    400.40

Identifying relationships

In particular, the principle of objectivity may be threatened if any individual within the practice, the close or immediate family of an individual within the practice or the practice itself, has or has had a professional or personal relationship which relates to the insolvency appointment being considered.

    400.41

400.42   Professional or personal relationships may include (but are not restricted to) relationships with:

- the entity
- any director or shadow director or former director or shadow director of the entity
- shareholders of the entity
- any principal or employee of the entity
- business partners of the entity
- companies or entities controlled by the entity
- companies which are under common control;
- creditors (including debenture holders) of the entity
- debtors of the entity
- close or immediate family of the entity (if an individual) or its officers (if a corporate body);
- others with commercial relationships with the practice.

400.43   Safeguards within the practice should include policies and procedures to identify relationships between individuals within the practice and third parties in a way that is proportionate and reasonable in relation to the insolvency appointment being considered.

Is the relationship significant to the conduct of the insolvency appointment?

400.44   Where a professional or personal relationship of the type described in paragraph 400.41 has been identified the Insolvency practitioner should evaluate the impact of the relationship in the context of the insolvency appointment being sought or considered. Issues to consider in evaluating whether a relationship creates a threat to the fundamental principles may include the following:

- The nature of the previous duties undertaken by a practice during an earlier relationship with the entity.
- The impact of the work conducted by the practice on the financial state and/or the financial stability of the entity in respect of which the insolvency appointment is being considered.
- Whether the fee received for the work by the practice is or was significant to the practice itself or is or was substantial.
- How recently any professional work was carried out. It is likely that greater threats will arise (or may be seen to arise) where work has been carried out within the previous three years. However, there may still be instances where, in respect of non-audit work, any threat is at an acceptable level. Conversely, there may be situations whereby the nature of the work carried out was such that a considerably longer period should elapse before any threat can be reduced to an acceptable level.
- Whether the insolvency appointment being considered involves consideration of any work previously undertaken by the practice for that entity.
- The nature of any personal relationship and the proximity of the Insolvency practitioner to the individual with whom the relationship exists and, where appropriate, the proximity of that individual to the entity in relation to which the insolvency appointment relates.
- Whether any reporting obligations will arise in respect of the relevant individual with whom the relationship exists (e.g. an obligation to report on the conduct of directors and shadow directors of a company to which the insolvency appointment relates).
- The nature of any previous duties undertaken by an individual within the practice during any earlier relationship with the entity.

- The extent of the insolvency team's familiarity with the individuals connected with the entity.

Having identified and evaluated a relationship that may create a threat to the fundamental principles, the Insolvency practitioner should consider his response including the introduction of any possible safeguards to reduce the threat to an acceptable level.

400.45

Some of the safeguards which may be considered to reduce the threat created by a professional or personal relationship to an acceptable level are considered in paragraph 400.25. Other safeguards may include:

400.46

- Withdrawing from the insolvency team.
- Terminating (where possible) the financial or business relationship giving rise to the threat.
- Disclosure of the relationship and any financial benefit received by the practice (whether directly or indirectly) to the entity or to those on whose behalf the Insolvency practitioner would be appointed to act.

An Insolvency practitioner may encounter situations in which no or no reasonable safeguards can be introduced to eliminate a threat arising from a professional or personal relationship, or to reduce it to an acceptable level. In such situations, the relationship in question will constitute a significant professional relationship ('Significant Professional Relationship') or a significant personal relationship ('Significant Personal Relationship'). Where this is case the Insolvency practitioner should conclude that it is not appropriate to take the insolvency appointment.

400.47

Consideration should always be given to the perception of others when deciding whether to accept an insolvency appointment. Whilst an Insolvency practitioner may regard a relationship as not being significant to the insolvency appointment, the perception of others may differ and this may in some circumstances be sufficient to make the relationship significant.

400.48

Dealing with the assets of an entity

Actual or perceived threats (for example self interest threats) to the fundamental principles may arise when during an insolvency appointment, an Insolvency practitioner realises assets.

400.49.

Save in circumstances which clearly do not impair the Insolvency Practitioner's objectivity, Insolvency Practitioners appointed to any insolvency appointment in relation to an entity, should not themselves acquire, directly or indirectly, any of the assets of an entity, nor knowingly permit any individual within the practice, or any close or immediate family member of the Insolvency practitioner or of an individual within the practice, directly or indirectly, to do so.

400.50

Where the assets and business of an insolvent company are sold by an Insolvency practitioner shortly after appointment on pre-agreed terms, this could lead to an actual or perceived threat to objectivity. The sale may also be seen as a threat to objectivity by creditors or others not involved in the prior agreement. The threat to objectivity may be eliminated or reduced to an acceptable level by safeguards such as obtaining an independent valuation of the assets or business being sold, or the consideration of other potential purchasers.

400.51

It is also particularly important for an Insolvency practitioner to take care to ensure (where to do so does not conflict with any legal or professional obligation) that his

400.52

decision making processes are transparent, understandable and readily identifiable to all third parties who may be affected by the sale or proposed sale.

Obtaining specialist advice and services

400.53   When an Insolvency practitioner intends to rely on the advice or work of another, the Insolvency practitioner should evaluate whether such reliance is warranted. The Insolvency practitioner should consider factors such as reputation, expertise, resources available and applicable professional and ethical standards. Any payment to the third party should reflect the value of the work undertaken.

400.54   Threats to the fundamental principles (for example familiarity threats and self interest threats) can arise if services are provided by a regular source independent of the practice.

400.55   Safeguards should be introduced to reduce such threats to an acceptable level. These safeguards should ensure that a proper business relationship is maintained between the parties and that such relationships are reviewed periodically to ensure that best value and service is being obtained in relation to each insolvency appointment. Additional safeguards may include clear guidelines and policies within the practice on such relationships. An Insolvency practitioner should also consider disclosure of the existence of such business relationships to the general body of creditors or the creditor's committee if one exists.

400.56   Threats to the fundamental principles can also arise where services are provided from within the practice or by a party with whom the practice, or an individual within the practice, has a business or personal relationship. An Insolvency practitioner should take particular care in such circumstances to ensure that the best value and service is being provided.

Fees and other types of remuneration

Prior to accepting an insolvency appointment

400.57   Where an engagement may lead to an insolvency appointment, an Insolvency practitioner should make any party to the work aware of the terms of the work and, in particular, the basis on which any fees are charged and which services are covered by those fees.

400.58   Where an engagement may lead to an insolvency appointment, Insolvency Practitioners should not accept referral fees or commissions unless they have established safeguards to reduce the threats created by such fees or commissions to an acceptable level.

400.59   Safeguards may include disclosure in advance of any arrangements. If after receiving any such payments, an Insolvency practitioner accepts an insolvency appointment, the amount and source of any fees or commissions received should be disclosed to creditors.

After accepting an insolvency appointment

During an insolvency appointment, accepting referral fees or commissions represents a significant threat to objectivity. Such fees or commissions should not therefore be accepted other than where to do so is for the benefit of the insolvent estate.

400.60

If such fees or commissions are accepted they should only be accepted for the benefit of the estate; not for the benefit of the Insolvency practitioner or the practice.

400.61

Further, where such fees or commissions are accepted an Insolvency practitioner should consider making disclosure to creditors.

400.62

Obtaining insolvency appointments

The special nature of insolvency appointments makes the payment or offer of any commission for or the furnishing of any valuable consideration towards, the introduction of insolvency appointments inappropriate. This does not, however, preclude an arrangement between an Insolvency practitioner and an employee whereby the employee's remuneration is based in whole or in part on introductions obtained for the Insolvency practitioner through the efforts of the employee.

400.63

When an Insolvency practitioner seeks an insolvency appointment or work that may lead to an insolvency appointment through advertising or other forms of marketing, there may be threats to compliance with the fundamental principles.

400.64

When considering whether to accept an insolvency appointment an Insolvency practitioner should satisfy himself that any advertising or other form of marketing pursuant to which the insolvency appointment may have been obtained is or has been:

400.65

- Fair and not misleading.
- Avoids unsubstantiated or disparaging statements.
- Complies with relevant codes of practice and guidance in relation to advertising.

Advertisements and other forms of marketing should be clearly distinguishable as such and be legal, decent, honest and truthful.

400.66

If reference is made in advertisements or other forms of marketing to fees or to the cost of the services to be provided, the basis of calculation and the range of services that the reference is intended to cover should be provided. Care should be taken to ensure that such references do not mislead as to the precise range of services and the time commitment that the reference is intended to cover.

400.67

An Insolvency practitioner should never promote or seek to promote his services, or the services of another Insolvency practitioner, in such a way, or to such an extent as to amount to harassment.

400.68

Where an Insolvency practitioner or the practice advertises for work via a third party, the Insolvency practitioner is responsible for ensuring that the third party follows the above guidance.

400.69

Gifts and hospitality

An Insolvency practitioner, or a close or immediate family member, may be offered gifts and hospitality. In relation to an insolvency appointment, such an offer will give

400.70

rise to threats to compliance with the fundamental principles. For example, self-interest threats may arise if a gift is accepted and intimidation threats may arise from the possibility of such offers being made public.

400.71   The significance of such threats will depend on the nature, value and intent behind the offer. In deciding whether to accept any offer of a gift or hospitality the Insolvency practitioner should have regard to what a reasonable and informed third party having knowledge of all relevant information would consider to be appropriate. Where such a reasonable and informed third party would consider the gift to be made in the normal course of business without the specific intent to influence decision making or obtain information the Insolvency practitioner may generally conclude that there is no significant threat to compliance with the fundamental principles.

400.72   Where appropriate, safeguards should be considered and applied as necessary to eliminate any threats to the fundamental principles or reduce them to an acceptable level. If an Insolvency practitioner encounters a situation in which no or no reasonable safeguards can be introduced to reduce a threat arising from offers of gifts or hospitality to an acceptable level he should conclude that it is not appropriate to accept the offer.

400.73   An Insolvency practitioner should also not offer or provide gifts or hospitality where this would give rise to an unacceptable threat to compliance with the fundamental principles.

Record keeping

400.74   It will always be for the Insolvency practitioner to justify his actions. An Insolvency practitioner will be expected to be able to demonstrate the steps that he took and the conclusions that he reached in identifying, evaluating and responding to any threats, both leading up to and during an insolvency appointment, by reference to written contemporaneous records.

400.75   The records an Insolvency practitioner maintains, in relation to the steps that he took and the conclusions that he reached, should be sufficient to enable a reasonable and informed third party to reach a view on the appropriateness of his actions.

The application of the framework to specific situations

Introduction to specific situations

400.76   The following examples describe specific circumstances and relationships that will create threats to compliance with the fundamental principles. The examples may assist an Insolvency practitioner and the members of the insolvency team to assess the implications of similar, but different, circumstances and relationships.

400.77   The examples are divided into three parts. Part 1 contains examples which do not relate to a previous or existing insolvency appointment. Part 2 contains examples that do relate to a previous or existing insolvency appointment. Part 3 contains some examples under Scottish law. The examples are not intended to be exhaustive.

Part 1 – Examples that do not relate to a previous or existing insolvency appointment

The following situations involve a professional relationship which does not consist of a previous insolvency appointment. **400.78**

Insolvency appointment following audit related work **400.79**

Relationship: The practice or an individual within the practice has previously carried out audit related work within the previous 3 years.

Response: A Significant Professional Relationship will arise: an Insolvency practitioner should conclude that it is not appropriate to take the insolvency appointment.

Where audit related work was carried out more than three years before the proposed date of the appointment of the Insolvency practitioner a threat to compliance with the fundamental principles may still arise. The Insolvency practitioner should evaluate any such threat and consider whether the threat can be eliminated or reduced to an acceptable level by the existence or introduction of safeguards.

This restriction does not apply where the insolvency appointment is in a members' voluntary liquidation; an Insolvency practitioner may normally take an appointment as liquidator. However, the Insolvency practitioner should consider whether there are any other circumstances that give rise to an unacceptable threat to compliance with the fundamental principles. Further, the Insolvency practitioner should satisfy himself that the directors' declaration of solvency is likely to be substantiated by events.

Appointment as Investigating Accountant at the instigation of a creditor **400.80**

Previous relationship: The practice or an individual within the practice was instructed by, or at the instigation of, a creditor or other party having a financial interest in an entity, to investigate, monitor or advise on its affairs.

Response: A Significant Professional Relationship would not normally arise in these circumstances provided that:-

- there has not been a direct involvement by an individual within the practice in the management of the entity; and
- the practice had its principal client relationship with the creditor or other party, rather than with the company or proprietor of the business; and
- the entity was aware of this.

An Insolvency practitioner should however consider all the circumstances before accepting an insolvency appointment, including the effect of any discussions or lack of discussions about the financial affairs of the company with its directors, and whether such circumstances give rise to an unacceptable threat to compliance with the fundamental principles.

Where such an investigation was conducted at the request of, or at the instigation of, a secured creditor who then requests an Insolvency practitioner to accept an insolvency appointment as an administrator or administrative receiver, the Insolvency practitioner should satisfy himself that the company, acting by its board of directors, does not object to him taking such an insolvency appointment. If the secured creditor does not give prior warning of the insolvency appointment to the company or if such warning is given and the company objects but the secured creditor still wishes to appoint the Insolvency practitioner, he should consider whether the circumstances give rise to an unacceptable threat to compliance with the fundamental principles.

Part 2 – Examples relating to previous or existing insolvency appointments

400.81   The following situations involve a prior professional relationship that involves a previous or existing insolvency appointment:-

400.82   *Insolvency appointment following an appointment as Administrative or other Receiver*

Previous appointment: An individual within the practice has been administrative or other receiver.

Proposed appointment: Any insolvency appointment.

Response: An Insolvency practitioner should not accept any insolvency appointment.

This restriction does not, however, apply where the individual within the practice was appointed a receiver by the Court. In such circumstances, the Insolvency practitioner should however consider whether any other circumstances which give rise to an unacceptable threat to compliance with the fundamental principles.

400.83   *Administration or Liquidation following appointment as Supervisor of a Voluntary Arrangement*

Previous appointment: An individual within the practice has been supervisor of a company voluntary arrangement.

Proposed appointment : Administrator or liquidator.

Response: An Insolvency practitioner may normally accept an appointment as administrator or liquidator. However the Insolvency practitioner should consider whether there are any circumstances that give rise to an unacceptable threat to compliance with the fundamental principles.

400.84   *Liquidation following appointment as Administrator*

Previous Appointment: An individual within the practice has been administrator.

Proposed Appointment: Liquidator.

Response: An Insolvency practitioner may normally accept an appointment as liquidator provided he has complied with the relevant legislative requirements. However, the Insolvency practitioner should also consider whether there are any circumstances that give rise to an unacceptable threat to compliance with the fundamental principles.

400.85   *Conversion of Members' Voluntary Liquation into Creditors' Voluntary Liquidation*

Previous appointment: An individual within the practice has been the liquidator of a company in a members' voluntary liquidation.

Proposed appointment: Liquidator in a creditors' voluntary liquidation, where it has been necessary to convene a creditors' meeting.

Response: Where there has been a Significant Professional Relationship, an Insolvency practitioner may continue or accept an appointment (subject to creditors' approval) only if he concludes that the company will eventually be able to pay its debts in full, together with interest.

However, the Insolvency practitioner should consider whether there are any other circumstances that give rise to an unacceptable threat to compliance with the fundamental principles.

Bankruptcy following appointment as Supervisor of an Individual Voluntary Arrangement   **400.86**

Previous appointment: An individual within the practice has been supervisor of an individual voluntary arrangement.

Proposed Appointment: Trustee in bankruptcy.

Response: An Insolvency practitioner may normally accept an appointment as trustee in bankruptcy. However, the Insolvency practitioner should consider whether there are any circumstances that give rise to an unacceptable threat to compliance with the fundamental principles.

Part 3 – *Examples in respect of cases conducted under Scottish Law*

Sequestration following appointment as Trustee under a Trust Deed for creditors   **400.87**

Previous appointment: An individual within the practice has been trustee under a trust deed for creditors.

Proposed appointment: Interim trustee or trustee in sequestration.

Response An Insolvency practitioner may normally accept an appointment as an interim trustee or trustee in sequestration. However, the Insolvency practitioner should consider whether there are any circumstances that give rise to an unacceptable threat to compliance with the fundamental principles.

Sequestration where the Accountant in Bankruptcy is Trustee following appointment as Trustee under a Trust Deed for creditors   **400.88**

Previous appointment: An individual within the practice has been trustee under a trust deed for creditors.

Proposed appointment: Agent for the Accountant in Bankruptcy in sequestration.

Response: An Insolvency practitioner may normally accept an appointment as agent for the Accountant in Bankruptcy. However, the Insolvency practitioner should consider whether there are any circumstances that give rise to an unacceptable threat to compliance with the fundamental principles.

Definitions

Authorising body	A body declared to be a recognised professional body or a competent authority under any legislation governing the administration of insolvency in the United Kingdom.
Close or immediate family	A spouse (or equivalent), dependant, parent, child or sibling.
Entity	Any natural or legal person or any group of such persons, including a partnership.
He/she	In this Code, he is to be read as including she.
Individual within the practice	The Insolvency practitioner, any principals in the practice and any employees within the practice.
Insolvency appointment	A formal appointment: <ul><li>which, under the terms of legislation must be undertaken by an Insolvency Practitioner; or</li><li>as a nominee or supervisor of a voluntary arrangement.</li></ul>
Insolvency Practitioner	An individual who is authorised or recognised to act as an Insolvency Practitioner in the United Kingdom by an authorising body. For the purpose of the application of this Code only, the term Insolvency Practitioner also includes an individual who acts as a nominee or supervisor of a voluntary arrangement.
Insolvency team	Any person under the control or direction of an Insolvency Practitioner.
Practice	The organisation in which the Insolvency practitioner practices.
Principal	In respect of a practice: <ul><li>which is a company: a director;</li><li>which is a partnership: a partner;</li><li>which is a limited liability partnership: a member;</li><li>which is comprised of a sole practitioner: that person;</li></ul> Alternatively any person within the practice who is held out as being a director, partner or member.

Part Ten

FRC Ethical Standards

APB Ethical Standards

ACTIVITIES

APB Ethical Standards for Auditors (ESs) were originally issued in December 2004 and revised versions were issued in April 2008, following a review of their implementation.

In October 2009 the APB issued a consultation paper in response to the Treasury Select Committee's recommendation for the Financial Reporting Council to consult on a prohibition on audit firms conducting non-audit work for the companies that they audit. At the same time the APB also finalised revisions to ES 3 in connection with partner rotation which were effective for audits of financial statements for periods commencing on or after 15 December 2009. Amendments in respect of other matters which were subject to consultation in March 2009 were deferred pending responses to the consultation paper on non-audit services, so as to avoid implementation problems arising from frequent changes to the ESs for relatively detailed matters.

Responses to the October 2009 Consultation Paper indicated that commentators (irrespective of the constituency involved) were overwhelmingly of the view that there should be no outright prohibition and no major change to the conceptual approach taken to the provision of non-audit services by auditors to the entities that they audit. In July 2010 the APB issued a further consultation paper seeking views on:

- Proposals to address the perception that confidence in the audit can be reduced where certain non-audit services are provided by the auditor, especially where there is a high ratio of non-audit fees to audit fees paid to an entity's auditor. These proposals were based on improved transparency and governance and included:
  - guidance on disclosing non-audit services provided to those charged with governance;
  - a requirement for discussions with the audit firm's Ethics Partner in the case of listed companies where there are relatively high levels of non-audit services provided;
  - amendments to the FRC's Guidance on Audit Committees.
- Amendments to the ESs arising from the March 2009 consultation.
- Proposals in relation to restructuring services, contingent fees and conflicts of interest which were identified by respondents to the October 2009 consultation as giving rise to concern.

Revisions to the ESs were published in December 2010 and become effective from 30 April 2011. Revisions that were associated with improved transparency and governance are supported by amendments to the FRC Guidance on Audit Committees that was published at the same time. In addition to resolving issues from the March 2009 consultation, other amendments were made in respect of extended and internal audit services and to clarify the threats and safeguards approach and the Ethics Partner role. In respect of the issues that were subject to an open consultation:

- A new section was added to ES 5 on restructuring services, which addresses the management, advocacy and self-review threats associated with the provision of these services.
- The definition of a contingent fee basis was revised and the current prohibitions were extended to apply to the provision of all non-audit services.

- Guidance was added to ES 1 to recognise that where there are known conflicts arising as a result of relationships with a connected party, an assessment of the associated threats and safeguards will be made.

In 2011 the APB will review the Ethical Standard for Reporting Accountants (ESRA), in order that it continues to provide a standard for investment circular reporting activity which is closely based on the ESs.

APB Ethical Standard 1 (Revised)
Integrity, Objectivity and Independence

(Revised December 2010, updated December 2011)

Contents

Preface

APB Ethical Standards apply in the audit of financial statements. They are read in the context of the Auditing Practices Board's Statement "The Auditing Practices Board – Scope and Authority of Pronouncements (Revised)" which sets out the application and authority of APB Ethical Standards.

The terms used in APB Ethical Standards are explained in the Glossary.

APB Ethical Standards apply to audits of financial statements in both the private and the public sectors. However, auditors in the public sector are subject to more complex ethical requirements than their private sector counterparts. This includes, for example, compliance with legislation such as the Prevention of Corruption Act 1916, concerning gifts and hospitality, and with Cabinet Office guidance.

Introduction

1   The financial statements of an entity may have a number of different users. For example, they may be used by suppliers and customers, joint venture partners, bankers and other suppliers of finance, taxation and regulatory authorities, employees, trades unions and environmental groups. In the case of a listed company, the financial statements are an important source of information to the capital markets. But the primary purpose of the financial statements of an entity is to provide its owners – the shareholders (or those in an equivalent position) – with information on the state of affairs of the entity and its performance and to assist them in assessing the stewardship exercised by the directors (or those in an equivalent position) over the business that has been entrusted to them.

2   The financial statements of an entity are the responsibility of its board of directors and are prepared by them, or by others on their behalf, for the shareholders or, in some circumstances, for other third parties.

3   The primary objective of an audit of the financial statements is for the auditor to provide independent assurance to the shareholders that the directors have prepared the financial statements properly. The auditor issues a report that includes an opinion as to whether or not the financial statements give a true and fair view[1]. Thus the auditor assists the shareholders to exercise their proprietary powers as shareholders in the Annual General Meeting.

4   Public confidence in the operation of the capital markets and in the conduct of public interest entities depends, in part, upon the credibility of the opinions and reports issued by the auditor in connection with the audit of the financial statements. Such credibility depends on beliefs concerning the integrity, objectivity and independence of the auditor and the quality of audit work performed. APB establishes quality control, auditing and ethical standards to provide a framework for audit practice. The Auditors' Code underlies APB's standards and sets out the fundamental principles, which APB expects to guide the conduct of auditors.

5   APB Ethical Standards are concerned with the integrity, objectivity and independence of auditors. Ethical guidance on other matters, together with statements of

---

[1] *In the case of certain bodies in the public sector, the auditor expresses an opinion as to whether the financial statements 'present fairly' the financial position.*

fundamental ethical principles governing the work of all professional accountants, are issued by professional accountancy bodies.

Auditors shall conduct the audit of the financial statements of an entity with integrity, objectivity and independence.   6

Integrity

Integrity is a prerequisite for all those who act in the public interest. It is essential   7
that auditors act, and are seen to act, with integrity, which requires not only honesty but a broad range of related qualities such as fairness, candour, courage, intellectual honesty and confidentiality.

Integrity requires that the auditor is not affected, and is not seen to be affected, by   8
conflicts of interest. Conflicts of interest may arise from personal, financial, business, employment, and other relationships which the audit engagement team, the audit firm or its partners or staff have with the audited entity and its connected parties.[2]

It is important that the directors and management of an audited entity can rely on   9
the auditor to treat the information obtained during an audit as confidential[3], unless they have authorised its disclosure, unless it is already known to third parties or unless the auditor has a legal right or duty to disclose it. Without this, there is a danger that the directors and management will fail to disclose such information to the auditor and that the effectiveness of the audit will thereby be impaired.

Objectivity

Objectivity is a state of mind that excludes bias, prejudice and compromise and that   10
gives fair and impartial consideration to all matters that are relevant to the task in hand, disregarding those that are not. Like integrity, objectivity is a fundamental ethical principle and requires that the auditor's judgment is not affected by conflicts of interest.

The need for auditors to be objective arises from the fact that many of the important   11
issues involved in the preparation of financial statements do not relate to questions of fact but rather to questions of judgment. For example, there are choices to be made by the board of directors in deciding on the accounting policies to be adopted by the entity: the directors have to select the ones that they consider most appropriate and this decision can have a material impact on the financial statements. Furthermore, many items included in the financial statements cannot be measured with absolute precision and certainty. In many cases, estimates have to be made and the directors may have to choose one value from a range of possible outcomes. When exercising discretion in these areas, the directors have regard to the applicable financial

---

[2] *For this purpose an audited entity's connected parties are:*
a. *its affiliates;*
b. *key members of management (including but not limited to directors and those charged with governance) of the audited entity and its significant affiliates; and*
c. *any person or entity with an ability to influence (other than in their capacity as professional advisor), whether directly or indirectly, key members of management and those charged with governance of the audited entity and its significant affiliates in relation to their responsibility for, or approach to, any matter or judgment that is material to the entity's financial statements.*

[3] *The fundamental principle of confidentiality is addressed in the ethical guidance issued by the auditor's professional accountancy body. This principle does not constrain the proper communication between the auditor and shareholders (or equivalent) of the audited entity.*

reporting framework. If the directors, whether deliberately or inadvertently, make a biased judgment or an otherwise inappropriate decision, the financial statements may be misstated or misleading.

12   It is against this background that the auditor is required to express an opinion on the financial statements. The audit involves considering the process followed and the choices made by the directors in preparing the financial statements and concluding whether the result gives a true and fair view. The auditor's objectivity requires that an impartial opinion is expressed in the light of all the available audit evidence and the auditor's professional judgment. Objectivity also requires that the auditor adopts a rigorous and robust approach and is prepared to disagree, where necessary, with the directors' judgments.

Independence

13   Independence is freedom from situations and relationships which make it probable that a reasonable and informed third party would conclude that objectivity either is impaired or could be impaired. Independence is related to and underpins objectivity. However, whereas objectivity is a personal behavioural characteristic concerning the auditor's state of mind, independence relates to the circumstances surrounding the audit, including the financial, employment, business and personal relationships between the auditor and the audited entity and its connected parties. Relationships with parties whose interests may be contrary to the interests of the audited entity (for example, a hostile bidder) may also be relevant to the appearance of the auditor's independence.

14   The need for independence arises because, in most cases, users of the financial statements and other third parties do not have all the information necessary for judging whether the auditor is, in fact, objective. Although the auditor may be satisfied that the auditor's objectivity is not impaired by a particular situation, a third party may reach a different conclusion. For example, if a third party were aware that the auditor had certain financial, employment, business or personal relationships with the audited entity, that individual might reasonably conclude that the auditor could be subject to undue influence from the directors or would not be impartial or unbiased. Public confidence in the auditor's objectivity could therefore suffer as a result of this perception, irrespective of whether there is any actual impairment.

15   Accordingly, in evaluating the likely consequences of such situations and relationships, the test to be applied is not whether the auditor considers that the auditor's objectivity is impaired but whether it is probable that a reasonable and informed third party would conclude that the auditor's objectivity either is impaired or is likely to be impaired. As a result of the influence that the board of directors and management have over the appointment and remuneration of the auditor absolute independence cannot be achieved or maintained. The audit engagement partner considers the application of safeguards where there are threats to auditor independence (both actual and perceived).

Compliance with ethical standards

16   **The audit firm shall establish policies and procedures, appropriately documented and communicated, designed to ensure that, in relation to each audit engagement, the audit firm, and all those who are in a position to influence the conduct and outcome of the audit, act with integrity, objectivity and independence.**

For the purposes of APB Ethical Standards, a person in a position to influence the   **17**
conduct and outcome of the audit is:

(a) any person who is directly involved in the audit ('the engagement team'),
    including:
    (i)   the audit partners, audit managers and audit staff ('the audit team');
    (ii) professional personnel from other disciplines involved in the audit (for
          example, lawyers, actuaries, taxation specialists, IT specialists, treasury
          management specialists);[4]
    (iii) those who provide quality control or direct oversight of the audit;
(b) any person who forms part of the chain of command for the audit within the
    audit firm;
(c) any person within the audit firm who, due to any other circumstances, may be in
    a position to exert such influence.

Compliance with the requirements regarding the auditor's integrity, objectivity and   **18**
independence is a responsibility of both the audit firm and of individual partners and
professional staff. The audit firm establishes policies and procedures, appropriate to
the size and nature of the audit firm, to promote and monitor compliance with those
requirements by any person who is in a position to influence the conduct and outcome of the audit.[5, 6]

The leadership of the audit firm shall take responsibility for establishing a control   **19**
environment within the firm that places adherence to ethical principles and compliance
with APB Ethical Standards above commercial considerations.

The leadership of the audit firm influences the internal culture of the firm by its   **20**
actions and by its example ('the tone at the top'). Achieving a robust control
environment requires that the leadership gives clear, consistent and frequent messages, backed up by appropriate actions, which emphasise the importance of
compliance with APB Ethical Standards.

In order to promote a strong control environment, the audit firm establishes policies   **21**
and procedures that include:

(a) requirements for partners and staff to report where applicable:
    • family and other personal relationships involving an entity audited by the
      firm;
    • financial interests in an entity audited by the firm;
    • decisions to join an audited entity.
(b) monitoring of compliance with the firm's policies and procedures relating to
    integrity, objectivity and independence. Such monitoring procedures include, on
    a test basis, periodic review of the audit engagement partners' documentation of
    the consideration of the auditor's objectivity and independence, addressing, for
    example:

---

[4] *Where external consultants are involved in the audit, ISA (UK and Ireland) 620 'Using the Work of an Auditor's Expert' states that the auditor shall evaluate the objectivity of the expert.*

[5] *Monitoring of compliance with ethical requirements will often be performed as part of a broader quality control process. ISQC (UK & Ireland) 1 'Quality Control for Firms that Perform Audits and Reviews of Financial Statements and other Assurance and Related Services Engagements' establishes requirements in relation to a firm's responsibilities for its system of quality control for audits.*

[6] *In addition, UK legislation provides that each of the Recognised Supervisory Bodies must have adequate rules and practices to ensure that the audit firm has arrangements to prevent any person from being able to exert any influence over the way in which a statutory audit is conducted in circumstances in which that influence would be likely to affect the independence or integrity of the audit.*

- financial interests in audited entities;
- economic dependence on audited entities;
- the performance of non-audit services;
- audit partner rotation;

(c) identification of the audited entities which partners in the chain of command and their immediate family need to be independent from[7];

(d) prompt communication of possible or actual breaches of the firm's policies and procedures to the relevant audit engagement partners;

(e) evaluation by audit engagement partners of the implications of any identified possible or actual breaches of the firm's policies and procedures that are reported to them;

(f) reporting by audit engagement partners of particular circumstances or relationships as required by APB Ethical Standards;

(g) operation of an enforcement mechanism to promote compliance with policies and procedures;

(h) empowerment of staff to communicate to senior levels within the firm any issue of objectivity or independence that concerns them; this includes establishing clear communication channels open to staff, encouraging staff to use these channels and ensuring that staff who use these channels are not subject to disciplinary proceedings as a result.

22 **Save where the circumstances contemplated in paragraph 26 apply, the audit firm shall designate a partner in the firm ('the Ethics Partner') as having responsibility for:**

(a) **the adequacy of the firm's policies and procedures relating to integrity, objectivity and independence, its compliance with APB Ethical Standards, and the effectiveness of its communication to partners and staff on these matters within the firm; and**

(b) **providing related guidance to individual partners with a view to achieving a consistent approach to the application of the APB Ethical Standards.**

23 In this role, the Ethics Partner has particular responsibility for engendering a culture in which the audit firm approaches ethical issues following the principles in the Ethical Standards. The Ethics Partner is an individual possessing seniority, relevant experience, and authority at leadership levels within the audit firm. Where the Ethics Partner undertakes this role together with a role such as Compliance or Risk Management he or she ensures that the responsibilities of the Ethics Partner set out in paragraph 22 above take precedence over the responsibilities of other functions.

24 In the case of audit firms that audit listed companies, the Ethics Partner has direct access to the independent non-executives[8] where such roles are introduced in an audit firm or, alternatively, to the firm's most senior governance body.

25 In assessing the effectiveness of the firm's communication of its policies and procedures relating to integrity, objectivity and independence, Ethics Partners consider whether the ethics are covered properly in induction programmes, professional training and continuing professional development for all partners and staff. Ethics Partners also provide guidance on matters referred to them and on matters which they otherwise become aware of, where a difficult and objective judgment needs to be

---

[7] *Such identification is necessary for those in the chain of command to understand how their firm responsibilities result in connections with different entities audited by the firm. It can be achieved by listing the individual audited entities or by a broader statement regarding categories of audited entity, for example, those of a certain business unit.*

[8] *Independent non-executives appointed in accordance with the Audit Firm Governance Code are not regarded as part of the Chain of Command for the purposes of these Ethical Standards.*

made or a consistent position reached. Ethics Partners are proactive in considering the ethical implications of developments in the business of the audit firm and the environment in which it operates and in providing advice and guidance to partners and staff where appropriate.

In audit firms with three or fewer partners who are 'responsible individuals'[9], it may **26** not be practicable for an Ethics Partner to be designated. In these circumstances all partners will regularly discuss ethical issues amongst themselves, so ensuring that they act in a consistent manner and observe the principles set out in APB Ethical Standards. In the case of a sole practitioner, advice on matters where a difficult and objective judgment needs to be made is obtained through the ethics helpline of the auditor's professional body, or through discussion with a practitioner from another firm. In all cases, it is important that such discussions are documented.

To be able to discharge his or her responsibilities, the Ethics Partner is provided with **27** sufficient staff support and other resources, commensurate with the size of the firm. Alternative arrangements are established to allow for:

- the provision of guidance on those audits where the Ethics Partner is the audit engagement partner; and
- situations where the Ethics Partner is unavailable, for example due to illness or holidays.

Where such support is shared with other functions such as Compliance or Risk Management, the Ethics Partner establishes policies and procedures to ensure that:

- matters delegated to support staff by the Ethics Partner, whether directly or indirectly through the operation of delegation policies established by the Ethics Partner, are clearly identified in internal documentation as relating to the Ethics Partner role and are addressed and supervised in a manner consistent with the Ethics Partner role, avoiding conflicts with other objectives; and
- all matters required to be communicated to, consulted upon with, or approved by the Ethics Partner are communicated to him or her or an authorised delegate personally, on a timely basis.

Whenever a possible or actual breach of an APB Ethical Standard, or of policies and **28** procedures established pursuant to the requirements of an APB Ethical Standard, is identified, the audit engagement partner, in the first instance, and the Ethics Partner, where appropriate, assesses the implications of the breach, determines whether there are safeguards that can be put in place or other actions that can be taken to address any potential adverse consequences and considers whether there is a need to resign from the audit engagement.

An inadvertent violation of this Standard does not necessarily call into question the **29** audit firm's ability to give an audit opinion, provided that:

(a) the audit firm has established policies and procedures that require all partners and staff to report any breach promptly to the audit engagement partner or to the Ethics Partner, as appropriate;
(b) the audit engagement partner or Ethics Partner promptly notifies the relevant partner or member of staff that any matter which has given rise to a breach is to be addressed as soon as possible and ensures that such action is taken;

---

[9] *A 'responsible individual' is a partner or employee of the audit firm who is responsible for audit work and designated as such under the audit regulations of a Recognised Supervisory Body.*

(c) safeguards, where appropriate, are applied, (for example, having another partner review the work done by the relevant partner or member of staff or removing him or her from the engagement team); and

(d) the actions taken and the rationale for them are documented.

Identification and assessment of threats

30   The auditor identifies and assesses the circumstances which could adversely affect the auditor's objectivity ('threats'), including any perceived loss of independence, and applies procedures ('safeguards'), which will either:

(a) eliminate the threat (for example, by eliminating the circumstances, such as removing an individual from the engagement team or disposing of a financial interest in the audited entity); or

(b) reduce the threat to an acceptable level, that is a level at which it is not probable that a reasonable and informed third party would conclude that the auditor's objectivity is impaired or is likely to be impaired (for example, by having the audit work reviewed by another partner or by another audit firm).

When considering safeguards, where the audit engagement partner chooses to reduce rather than to eliminate a threat to objectivity and independence, he or she recognises that this judgment may not be shared by users of the financial statements and that he or she may be required to justify the decision.

Threats to objectivity and independence

31   **The audit firm shall establish policies and procedures to require persons in a position to influence the conduct and outcome of the audit to be constantly alert to circumstances that might reasonably be considered threats to their objectivity or the perceived loss of independence and, where such circumstances are identified, to report them to the audit engagement partner or to the Ethics Partner, as appropriate.**

32   Such policies and procedures require that threats to the auditor's objectivity and independence are communicated to the appropriate person, having regard to the nature of the threats and to the part of the firm and the identity of any person involved. The consideration of all threats on an individual and cumulative[10] basis and the action taken is documented. If the audit engagement partner is personally involved, or is unsure about the action to be taken, the matter is resolved through consultation with the Ethics Partner.

33   **The audit firm shall establish policies and procedures which require that partners and employees of the firm, including those providing non-audit services to an audited entity or its affiliates, do not take decisions that are the responsibility of management of the audited entity.**

34   It is not possible to specify all types of decision that are the responsibility of management, but they typically involve leading and directing the audited entity, including making significant judgments and taking decisions regarding the acquisition, deployment and control of human, financial, physical and intangible resources. Examples of judgments and decisions that are not made by the auditor include:

●   Setting policies and strategic direction;

---

[10] *For this purpose, 'cumulative' means all current relationships and any past completed relationships that may be expected to have a continuing relevance to the auditor's independence and consideration of the threats that might exist.*

- Directing and taking responsibility for the actions of the entity's employees;
- Authorising transactions;
- Deciding which recommendations of the audit firm or other third parties should be implemented;
- Taking responsibility for the preparation and fair presentation of the financial statements in accordance with the applicable financial reporting framework; and
- Taking responsibility for designing, implementing and maintaining internal control.

The principal types of threats to the auditor's objectivity and independence are: **35**

- *self-interest threat*

  A self-interest threat arises when the auditor has financial or other interests which might cause the auditor to be reluctant to take actions that would be adverse to the interests of the audit firm or any individual in a position to influence the conduct or outcome of the audit (for example, where the auditor has an investment in the audited entity, is seeking to provide additional services to the audited entity or needs to recover long-outstanding fees from the audited entity).

- *self-review threat*

  A self-review threat arises when the results of a non-audit service performed by the auditor or by others within the audit firm are reflected in the amounts included or disclosed in the financial statements (for example, where the audit firm has been involved in maintaining the accounting records, or undertaking valuations that are incorporated in the financial statements). In the course of the audit, the auditor may need to re-evaluate the work performed in the non-audit service. As, by virtue of providing the non-audit service, the audit firm is associated with aspects of the preparation of the financial statements, the auditor may be (or may be perceived to be) unable to take an impartial view of relevant aspects of those financial statements.

- *management threat*

  Paragraph 30 prohibits partners and employees of the audit firm from taking decisions on behalf of the management of the audited entity. A management threat can also arise when the audit firm undertakes an engagement to provide non-audit services in relation to which management are required to make judgments and take decisions based on that work (for example, the design, selection and implementation of a financial information technology system). In such work, the audit firm may become closely aligned with the views and interests of management and the auditor's objectivity and independence may be impaired, or may be perceived to be, impaired.

- *advocacy threat*

  An advocacy threat arises when the audit firm undertakes work that involves acting as an advocate for an audited entity and supporting a position taken by management in an adversarial context (for example, by acting as a legal advocate for the audited entity in litigation or a regulatory investigation). In order to act in an advocacy role, the audit firm has to adopt a position closely aligned to that of management. This creates both actual and perceived threats to the auditor's objectivity and independence.

- *familiarity (or trust) threat*

  A familiarity (or trust) threat arises when the auditor is predisposed to accept, or is insufficiently questioning of, the audited entity's point of view (for example, where close personal relationships are developed with the audited entity's personnel through long association with the audited entity).

- *intimidation threat*

  An intimidation threat arises when the auditor's conduct is influenced by fear or threats (for example, where the auditor encounters an aggressive and dominating individual).

These categories may not be entirely distinct: certain circumstances may give rise to more than one type of threat. For example, where an audit firm wishes to retain the fee income from a large audited entity, but encounters an aggressive and dominating individual, there may be a self-interest threat as well as an intimidation threat. Furthermore, relationships with the audited entity's connected parties may give rise to similar threats.

36   Threats to the auditor's objectivity, including a perceived loss of independence, may arise where the audit firm is appointed to a non-audit service engagement for an entity not audited by the firm, but where an audited entity makes this decision. In such cases, even if the entity not audited by the firm pays the fee for the non-audit service engagement, the auditor considers the implication of the threats (especially the self-interest threat) that arise from the appointment.

37   Similarly threats may arise where the auditor has a relationship with any connected party of the audited entity. Where any member of the engagement team is aware of such relationships, an assessment of the threats and available safeguards is made.

38   **The audit firm shall establish policies and procedures to require the audit engagement partner to identify and assess the significance of threats to the auditor's objectivity on an individual and cumulative[10] basis, including any perceived loss of independence:**

       (a)   **when considering whether to accept or retain an audit engagement;[11]**
       (b)   **when planning the audit;**
       (c)   **when forming an opinion on the financial statements;[12]**
       (d)   **when considering whether to accept or retain an engagement to provide non-audit services to an audited entity; and**
       (e)   **when potential threats are reported to him or her.**

39   An initial assessment of the threats to objectivity and independence is required when the audit engagement partner is considering whether to accept or retain an audit engagement. That assessment is reviewed and updated at the planning stage of each audit. At the end of the audit process, when forming an opinion on the financial statements but before issuing the report, the audit engagement partner draws an overall conclusion as to whether all threats to objectivity and independence have been properly addressed on an individual and cumulative basis in accordance with APB Ethical Standards. If, at any time, the auditor is invited to accept an engagement to provide non-audit services, the audit engagement partner considers the impact this may have on the auditor's objectivity and independence.

40   When identifying and assessing threats to the auditor's objectivity and independence, the audit engagement partner takes into account current relationships with the audited entity (including non-audit service engagements and known relationships with connected parties of the audited entity) and with other parties in certain circumstances (see paragraph 41), those that existed prior to the current audit engagement and any known to be in prospect following the current audit engagement. This is because those prior and subsequent relationships may be perceived as

---

[11] *Consideration of whether to accept or retain an audit engagement does not arise with those bodies in the public sector where responsibility for the audit is assigned by legislation.*

[12] *In the case of listed companies, the auditor also assesses whether there is any threat to the auditor's objectivity and independence when discharging responsibilities in relation to preliminary announcements and when reporting on interim results.*

likely to influence the auditor in the performance of the audit or as otherwise impairing the auditor's objectivity and independence.

Threats to the auditor's objectivity, including a perceived loss of independence, may arise where a non-audit service is provided by the audit firm to a third party which is connected (through a relationship) to an audited entity, and the outcome of that service has a material impact on the financial statements of the audited entity. For example, if the audit firm provides actuarial services to the pension scheme of an audited entity, which is in deficit, and the audit firm subsequently gives an opinion on financial statements that include judgments given in connection with that service. **41**

Where the audited entity or a third party calls into question the objectivity and independence of the audit firm in relation to a particular audited entity, the Ethics Partner carries out such investigations as may be appropriate. **42**

Identification and assessment of safeguards

If the audit engagement partner identifies threats to the auditor's objectivity, including any perceived loss of independence, he or she shall identify and assess the effectiveness of the available safeguards and apply such safeguards as are sufficient to eliminate the threats or reduce them to an acceptable level. **43**

The nature and extent of safeguards to be applied depend on the significance of the threats. Where a threat is clearly insignificant, no safeguards are needed. **44**

Other APB Ethical Standards address specific circumstances which can create threats to the auditor's objectivity or loss of independence. They give examples of safeguards that can, in some circumstances, eliminate the threat or reduce it to an acceptable level. In circumstances where this is not possible, the auditor either does not accept or withdraws from the audit engagement as appropriate. **45**

APB Ethical Standards contain certain additional requirements or prohibitions that apply only in the case of listed company audited entities: **46**

- ES 1, paragraphs 51 and 67;
- ES 3, paragraphs 12, 19 and 20;
- ES 4, paragraphs 22, 31 and 35;
- ES 5, paragraphs 28, 77, 84, 99, 110, 117, 153 and 160.

These additional requirements also apply where regulation or legislation requires that the audit of an entity is conducted in accordance with the auditing standards or ethical requirements that are applicable to the audit of listed companies.

The audit firm shall establish policies and procedures which set out the circumstances in which those additional requirements listed in paragraph 46 that apply to listed companies are applied to other audit engagements. **47**

Such policies and procedures take into consideration any additional criteria set by the audit firm, such as the nature of the entity's business, its size, the number of its employees and the range of its stakeholders. For example, a firm may decide to extend the additional requirements to audit engagements of certain regulated financial institutions such as large non-listed banks and insurance companies. **48**

49   **The audit engagement partner shall not accept or shall not continue an audit engagement if he or she concludes that any threats to the auditor's objectivity and independence cannot be reduced to an acceptable level.**

50   Where a reasonable and informed third party would regard ceasing to act as the auditor as detrimental to the shareholders (or equivalent) of the audited entity, then resignation may not be immediate. However, the audit firm discloses full details of the position to those charged with governance of the audited entity, and establishes appropriate safeguards.

Engagement quality control review

51   **In the case of listed companies the engagement quality control reviewer[13] shall:**

   (a)   **consider the audit firm's compliance with APB Ethical Standards in relation to the audit engagement;**

   (b)   **form an independent opinion as to the appropriateness and adequacy of the safeguards applied; and**

   (c)   **consider the adequacy of the documentation of the audit engagement partner's consideration of the auditor's objectivity and independence.**

52   The audit firm's policies and procedures set out whether there are circumstances in which an engagement quality control review is performed for other audit engagements as described in paragraph 47.

53   Where the involvement of an engagement quality control reviewer provides a safeguard to reduce to an acceptable level those threats to independence that have been identified as potentially arising from the provision of non-audit services, his or her review specifically addresses the related threat by ensuring that the work that was performed in the course of the non-audit service engagement has been properly and effectively assessed in the context of the audit of the financial statements.

Overall conclusion

54   **At the end of the audit process, when forming an opinion but before issuing the report on the financial statements, the audit engagement partner shall reach an overall conclusion that any threats to objectivity and independence on an individual and cumulative basis have been properly addressed in accordance with APB Ethical Standards. If the audit engagement partner cannot make such a conclusion, he or she shall not report and the audit firm shall resign as auditor.**

55   In addition to assessing individual threats to auditor objectivity and independence, the audit engagement partner assesses the cumulative impact of all the threats identified on the audit engagement so as to reach a conclusion that the threats identified, when viewed individually and cumulatively, have been reduced to an acceptable level through the application of safeguards.

56   If the audit engagement partner remains unable to conclude that any individual threats to objectivity and independence, or all threats to objectivity and

---

[13] *ISA (UK and Ireland) 220 'Quality Control for an Audit of Financial Statements'*, requires the audit engagement partner to determine that an engagement quality control reviewer has been appointed for all audits of listed entities. The engagement quality control review involves consideration of the engagement team's evaluation of the firm's independence in relation to the audit engagement.

independence viewed on a cumulative basis, have been properly addressed in accordance with APB Ethical Standards, or if there is a disagreement between the audit engagement partner and the engagement quality control reviewer, he or she consults the Ethics Partner.

In concluding on compliance with the requirements for objectivity and indepen- **57**
dence, the audit engagement partner is entitled to rely on the completeness and accuracy of the data developed by the audit firm's systems relating to independence (for example, in relation to the reporting of financial interests by staff), unless informed otherwise by the firm.

Other auditors involved in the audit of group financial statements

The group audit engagement partner shall be satisfied that other auditors (whether a **58**
network firm or another audit firm) involved in the audit of the group financial state-
ments, who are not subject to APB Ethical Standards, are objective and document the
rationale for that conclusion.

The group audit engagement partner obtains appropriate evidence[14] that the other **59**
auditors have a sufficient understanding of and have complied with the current Code of Ethics for Professional Accountants, including the independence requirements[15].

In the case of a listed company, the group audit engagement partner establishes that **60**
the company has communicated its policy[16] on the engagement of the external auditor to supply non-audit services to its affiliates and obtains confirmation that the other auditors will comply with this policy.

Network firms not involved in the audit

The audit firm shall establish that network firms which are not involved in the audit are **61**
required to comply with global policies and procedures that are designed to meet the
requirements of the current IESBA Code[15].

The IESBA Code requires all network firms to be independent of the entities audited **62**
by other network firms[17]. International audit networks commonly meet this requirement through global independence policies and procedures designed to

---

[14] *ISA (UK and Ireland) 600 'Special Considerations – Audits of Group Financial Statements (Including the Work of Component Auditors)'* requires that the group engagement team shall obtain an understanding of whether the component auditor understands and will comply with the ethical requirements that are relevant to the group audit and, in particular, is independent.

[15] *The Code of Ethics for Professional Accountants (the IESBA Code) issued by the International Ethics Standards Board for Accountants establishes a conceptual framework for applying the fundamental principles of professional ethics for professional accountants. Section 290 of the IESBA Code illustrates the application of the conceptual framework to independence requirements for audit engagements and represents the international standard on which national standards should be based. No Member Body of the International Federation of Accountants (IFAC) is allowed to apply less stringent standards than those stated in that section. In addition, members of the IFAC Forum of Firms have agreed to apply ethical standards, which are at least as rigorous as those of the IESBA Code.*

[16] *The UK Corporate Governance Code requires audit committees to develop the company's policy on the engagement of the external auditor to supply non-audit services.*

[17] *Paragraph 290.13 of the IESBA Code, as updated in July 2009.*

comply with the current IESBA Code which are supported by appropriate monitoring and compliance processes within the network.

Communication with those charged with governance

63   **The audit engagement partner shall ensure that those charged with governance of the audited entity are appropriately informed on a timely basis of all significant facts and matters that bear upon the auditor's objectivity and independence.**

64   The audit committee, where one exists, is usually responsible for oversight of the relationship between the auditor and the entity and of the conduct of the audit process. It therefore has a particular interest in being informed about the auditor's ability to express an objective opinion on the financial statements. Where there is no audit committee, this role is undertaken by the board of directors.[18, 19]

65   The aim of these communications is to ensure full and fair disclosure by the auditor to those charged with governance of the audited entity on matters in which they have an interest. These will generally include the key elements of the audit engagement partner's consideration of objectivity and independence, such as:

- the principal threats, if any, to objectivity and independence identified by the auditor, including consideration of all relationships between the audited entity, its affiliates and directors and the audit firm;
- any safeguards adopted and the reasons why they are considered to be effective, including any independent partner review;
- the overall assessment of threats and safeguards;
- information about the general policies and processes within the audit firm for maintaining objectivity and independence.

66   Communications between the auditor and those charged with the governance of the audited entity will be needed at the planning stage and whenever significant judgments are made about threats to objectivity and independence and the appropriateness of safeguards put in place, for example, when accepting an engagement to provide non-audit services.

Additional provisions related to audits of listed companies

67   **In the case of listed companies, the audit engagement partner shall ensure that the audit committee is provided with:**

(a)   **a written disclosure of relationships (including the provision of non-audit services) that bear on the auditor's objectivity and independence, the threats to auditor independence that these create, any safeguards that have been put in place and why they address such threats, together with any other information necessary to enable the auditor's objectivity and independence to be assessed;**

(b)   **details of non-audit services provided and the fees charged in relation thereto;**

(c)   **written confirmation that the auditor is independent;**

(d)   **details of any inconsistencies between APB Ethical Standards and the company's policy for the supply of non-audit services by the audit firm and any apparent breach of that policy.**

---

[18] *Where there is no audit committee, references to communication with the audit committee are to be construed as including communication with the board of directors.*

[19] *Some bodies in the public sector have audit committees but others have different governance models.*

(e) an opportunity to discuss auditor independence issues.

The most appropriate time for these final written confirmations of independence is usually at the conclusion of the audit.   **68**

The auditor of a listed company discloses in writing details of all relationships between the auditor and the audited entity, and its directors and senior management and its affiliates, including all services provided by the audit firm and its network to the audited entity, its directors and senior management and its affiliates, and other services provided to other known connected parties that the auditor considers may reasonably be thought to bear on the auditor's objectivity and independence and the related safeguards that are in place.   **69**

The auditor ensures that the total amount of fees that the auditor and its network firms have charged to the audited entity and its affiliates for the provision of services during the reporting period, analysed into appropriate categories are disclosed. The Appendix contains an illustrative template for the provision of such information to an audit committee[20]. Separately, the auditor provides information on any contingent fee arrangements[21], the amounts of any future services which have been contracted, and details of any written proposal to provide non-audit services that has been submitted.   **70**

The written confirmation that the auditor is independent indicates that the auditor considers that the audit firm complies with APB Ethical Standards and that, in the auditor's professional judgment, the audit firm is independent and its objectivity is not compromised. If it is not possible to make such a confirmation, the communication will include any concerns that the auditor has that the audit firm's objectivity and independence may be compromised (including instances where the group audit engagement partner does not consider an other auditor to be objective) and an explanation of the actions which necessarily follow from this.   **71**

Documentation

The audit engagement partner shall ensure that his or her consideration of the auditor's objectivity and independence is appropriately documented on a timely basis.   **72**

The requirement to document these issues contributes to the clarity and rigour of the audit engagement partner's thinking and the quality of his or her judgments. In addition, such documentation provides evidence that the audit engagement partner's consideration of the auditor's objectivity and independence was properly performed and, for listed companies, provides the basis for review by the engagement quality control reviewer.   **73**

Matters to be documented[22] include all key elements of the process and any significant judgments concerning: **74**

---

[20] *When considering how to present this analysis of fees, the auditor takes account of any applicable legislation.*

[21] *Paragraph 22 of ES 4 requires the audit engagement partner to disclose to the audit committee, in writing, any contingent fee arrangements for non-audit services provided by the auditor or its network firms.*

[22] *The necessary working papers can be combined with those prepared pursuant to paragraph 24 of ISA (UK and Ireland) 220 'Quality Control for an Audit of Financial Statements'*, which requires that: "The auditor shall include in the audit documentation conclusions on compliance with independence requirements that apply to the audit engagement, and any relevant discussions with the firm that support these conclusions."

- threats identified, other than those which are clearly insignificant, and the process used in identifying them;
- safeguards adopted and the reasons why they are considered to be effective;
- review by an engagement quality control reviewer or an independent partner;
- overall assessment of threats, on an individual and cumulative basis, and safeguards; and
- communication with those charged with governance.

Effective date

75   This revised Ethical Standard becomes effective on 30 April 2011.

76   Firms may complete audit engagements relating to periods commencing on or before 31 December 2010 in accordance with existing ethical standards, putting in place any necessary changes in the subsequent engagement period.

Appendix: Illustrative template for communicating information on audit and non-audit services provided to the group

	Current year £m	Prior year £m
Audit of company	X	X
Audit of subsidiaries	X	X
Total audit	X	X
Audit related assurance services[23]	X	X
Other assurance services[24][25]	X	X
Total assurance services	X	X
Tax compliance services (i.e. related to assistance with corporate tax returns)	X	X
Tax advisory services	X	X
Services relating to taxation	X	X
Internal audit services	X	X
Services related to corporate finance transactions not covered above	X	X
Other non-audit services not covered above	X	X
Total other non-audit services	X	X
Total non-audit services	X	X
Total fees	X	X
Occupational pension scheme audits	X	X
Non-audit services in respect of the audited entity provided to a third party[26].	X	X

Disclosure of contingent fee arrangements under paragraph 22 of ES 4 can also be facilitated through the use of a footnote to this template.

Disclosures required under UK company legislation[27] are indicated by those categories in bold type above. Fuller information can be provided by companies if desired.

[23] *This will, and will only, include those services which are identified as audit related services in paragraph 55 of ES 5.*

[24] *This will not include any tax or internal audit services, all of which should be disclosed under those headings.*

[25] *The definition of an assurance engagement is provided in the Glossary of Terms included in APB's Compendium of Standards and Guidance which is published annually. Services provided under such engagements will include assurance engagements such as those which involve reporting on historical financial information which are included in an investment circular in accordance with the Standards for Investment Reporting 2000 (Revised): Investment reporting standards applicable to public reporting engagements on historical financial information.*

[26] *For the purposes of APB Ethical Standards non-audit services include services provided to another entity in respect of the audited entity, for example, where the audit firm provides transaction related services, in respect of an audited entity's financial information, to a prospective acquirer of the audited entity (see paragraph 12 of ES 5).*

[27] *Disclosure requirements in the Republic of Ireland are set out in European Communities (Statutory Audits) (Directive 2006/43/EC) Regulations 2010. An information sheet on this topic "Disclosure of auditors' remuneration" was developed by the Consultative Committee of Accountancy Bodies in Ireland and published by Chartered Accountants Ireland in January 2011: this is available at: http://www.charteredaccountants.ie/ Members/Technical1/Financial-Reporting/Resources/Disclosure-of-Auditor-Remuneration/.*

APB Ethical Standard 2 (Revised)
Financial, business, employment and personal relationships

(Revised December 2010)

Contents

Preface

APB Ethical Standards apply in the audit of financial statements. They are read in the context of the Auditing Practices Board's Statement "The Auditing Practices Board – Scope and Authority of Pronouncements (Revised)" which sets out the application and authority of APB Ethical Standards.

The terms used in APB Ethical Standards are explained in the Glossary.

APB Ethical Standards apply to audits of financial statements in both the private and the public sectors. However, auditors in the public sector are subject to more complex ethical requirements than their private sector counterparts. This includes, for example, compliance with legislation such as the Prevention of Corruption Act 1916, concerning gifts and hospitality, and with Cabinet Office guidance.

Introduction

APB Ethical Standard 1 requires the audit engagement partner to identify and assess   **1** the circumstances which could adversely affect the auditor's objectivity ('threats'), including any perceived loss of independence, and to apply procedures ('safeguards') which will either:

(a) eliminate the threat; or

(b) reduce the threat to an acceptable level (that is, a level at which it is not probable that a reasonable and informed third party would conclude that the auditor's objectivity and independence is impaired or is likely to be impaired).

When considering safeguards, where the audit engagement partner chooses to reduce rather than to eliminate a threat to objectivity and independence, he or she recognises that this judgment may not be shared by users of the financial statements and that he or she may be required to justify the decision.

This Standard provides requirements and guidance on specific circumstances arising   **2** out of financial, business, employment and personal relationships with the audited entity, which may create threats to the auditor's objectivity or perceived loss of independence. It gives examples of safeguards that can, in some circumstances, eliminate the threat or reduce it to an acceptable level. In circumstances where this is not possible, either the relationship in question is not entered into or the auditor either does not accept or withdraws from the audit engagement, as appropriate.

Whenever a possible or actual breach of an APB Ethical Standard is identified, the   **3** audit engagement partner, in the first instance, and the Ethics Partner, where appropriate, assesses the implications of the breach, determines whether there are safeguards that can be put in place or other actions that can be taken to address any potential adverse consequences and considers whether there is a need to resign from the audit engagement.

An inadvertent violation of this Standard does not necessarily call into question the   **4** audit firm's ability to give an audit opinion provided that:

    (a) the audit firm has established policies and procedures that require all partners and staff to report any breach promptly to the audit engagement partner or to the Ethics Partner as appropriate;

    (b) the audit engagement partner or Ethics Partner promptly notifies the partner or member of staff that any matter which has given rise to a breach is to be addressed as soon as possible and ensures that such action is taken;

    (c) safeguards, if appropriate, are applied (for example, having another partner review the work done by the relevant partner or member of staff or by removing him or her from the engagement team); and

    (d) the actions taken and the rationale for them are documented.

FINANCIAL RELATIONSHIPS

General considerations

5   A financial interest is an equity or other security, debenture, loan or other debt instrument of an entity, including rights and obligations to acquire such an interest and derivatives directly related to such an interest.

6   Financial interests may be:

    (a) owned directly, rather than through intermediaries (a 'direct financial interest'); or

    (b) owned through intermediaries, for example, an open ended investment company or a pension scheme (an 'indirect financial interest').

7   **Save where the circumstances contemplated in paragraphs 9, 10, 12, 19 or 21 apply, the audit firm, any partner in the audit firm, a person in a position to influence the conduct and outcome of the audit or an immediate family member of such a person shall not hold:**

    (a) any direct financial interest in an audited entity or an affiliate of an audited entity; or

    (b) any indirect financial interest in an audited entity or an affiliate of an audited entity, where the investment is material to the audit firm or the individual, or to the intermediary; or

    (c) any indirect financial interest in an audited entity or an affiliate of an audited entity, where the person holding it has both:

        (i) the ability to influence the investment decisions of the intermediary; and

        (ii) actual knowledge of the existence of the underlying investment in the audited entity.

8   The threats to the auditor's objectivity and independence, where a direct financial interest or a material indirect financial interest in the audited entity is held by the audit firm or by one of the individuals specified in paragraph 7, are such that no safeguards can eliminate them or reduce them to an acceptable level.

9   Where a person joins the audit firm as a partner, he or she or an immediate family member is not required to dispose of financial interests held where:

    (a) the financial interests were acquired before the new partner joined the audit firm; and

    (b) the individual is not able to influence the affairs of the audited entity; and

    (c) either there is no market for such interests, or the individual does not have the power to sell or direct the sale of the interest; and

    (d) the new partner:

        • is not in a position to influence the conduct and outcome of the audit;

        • does not work in the same part of the firm as the audit engagement partner; and

        • is not involved in the provision of a non-audit service to the audit client.

Such a financial interest is disposed of as soon as possible after the individual becomes able to make a disposal. The audit firm ensures that:

- such financial interests are approved by the Ethics Partner;
- a record is maintained of such individuals, including a description of the circumstances; and
- this information is communicated to the relevant audit engagement partner.

Where an immediate family member of a partner who is not in a position to influence   **10**
the conduct and outcome of the audit holds a financial interest in an audited entity or an affiliate of an audited entity as a consequence of:

- their compensation arrangements (for example, a share option scheme, where the shares have not vested); or
- a decision made, or a transaction undertaken, by an entity with whom that immediate family member has a contractual business or employment arrangement (for example, a partnership agreement);

such financial interests are not generally considered to threaten the auditor's objectivity and independence. However, where such interests are significant or the relevant partner has close working contacts with the engagement team, the Ethics Partner considers whether any safeguards need to be put in place.

For the purposes of paragraph 7, where holdings in an authorised unit or investment   **11**
trust, an open ended investment company or an equivalent investment vehicle which is audited by the audit firm, are held by a partner in the audit firm, who is not in a position to influence the conduct and outcome of the audit, or an immediate family member of such a partner, these are to be treated as indirect financial interests. Such interests can therefore be held as long as:

(a) they are not material to the individual; and
(b) the individual has no influence over the investment decisions of the audited entity.

Where a person in a position to influence the conduct and outcome of the audit or a   **12**
partner in the audit firm, or any of their immediate family members are members or shareholders of an audited entity, as a result of membership requirements, or equivalent, the audit firm ensures that no more than the minimum number of shares necessary to comply with the requirement are held and that this shareholding is not material to either the audited entity or the individual. Disclosure of such shareholdings will be made to those charged with governance of the audited entity, in accordance with APB Ethical Standard 1, paragraph 63.

Where one of the financial interests specified in paragraph 7 is held by: **13**

(a) *the audit firm, a partner in the audit firm or an immediate family member of such a partner:* the entire financial interest is disposed of, a sufficient amount of an indirect financial interest is disposed of so that the remaining interest is no longer material, or the firm does not accept (or withdraws from) the audit engagement;

(b) *a person in a position to influence the conduct and outcome of the audit:* the entire financial interest is disposed of, a sufficient amount of an indirect financial interest is disposed of so that the remaining interest is no longer material, or that person does not retain a position in which they exert such influence on the audit engagement;

(c) *an immediate family member of a person in a position to influence the conduct and outcome of the audit:* the entire financial interest is disposed of, a sufficient amount of an indirect financial interest is disposed of so that the remaining interest is no longer material, or the person in a position to influence the conduct and outcome of the audit does not retain a position in which they exert such influence on the audit engagement.

14   Where one of the financial interests specified in paragraph 7 is acquired unintentionally, as a result of an external event (for example, inheritance, gift, or merger of firms or companies), the disposal of the financial interest is required immediately, or as soon as possible after the relevant person has actual knowledge of, and the right to dispose of, the interest.

15   Where the disposal of a financial interest does not take place immediately, the audit firm adopts safeguards to preserve its objectivity until the financial interest is disposed of. These may include the temporary exclusion of the person in a position to influence the conduct and outcome of the audit from such influence on the audit, or a review of the relevant person's audit work by an audit partner having sufficient experience and authority to fulfill the role who is not involved in the audit engagement.

16   Where the audit firm or one of the individuals specified in paragraph 7 holds an indirect financial interest but does not have both:

(a)   the ability to influence the investment decisions of the intermediary; and
(b)   actual knowledge of the existence of the underlying investment in the audited entity;

there may not be a threat to the auditor's objectivity and independence. For example, where the indirect financial interest takes the form of an investment in a pension fund, the composition of the funds and the size and nature of any underlying investment in the audited entity may be known but there is unlikely to be any influence on investment decisions, as the fund will generally be managed independently on a discretionary basis. In the case of an 'index tracker' fund, the investment in the audited entity is determined by the composition of the relevant index and there may be no threat to objectivity. As long as the person holding the indirect interest is not directly involved in the audit of the intermediary, nor able to influence the individual investment decisions of the intermediary, any threat to the auditor's objectivity and independence may be regarded as insignificant.

17   Where the audit firm or one of the individuals specified in paragraph 7 holds a beneficial interest in a properly operated 'blind' trust, they are (by definition) completely unaware of the identity of the underlying investments. If these include an investment in the audited entity, this means that they are unaware of the existence of an indirect financial interest. In these circumstances, there is no threat to the auditor's objectivity and independence.

18   **Where a person in a position to influence the conduct and outcome of the audit or a partner in the audit firm becomes aware that a close family member holds one of the financial interests specified in paragraph 7, that individual shall report the matter to the audit engagement partner to take appropriate action. If it is a close family member of the audit engagement partner, or if the audit engagement partner is in doubt as to the action to be taken, the audit engagement partner shall resolve the matter through consultation with the Ethics Partner.**

Financial interests held as trustee

19   Where a direct or an indirect financial interest in the audited entity or its affiliates is held in a trustee capacity by a person in a position to influence the conduct and

outcome of the audit, or an immediate family member of such a person, a self-interest threat may be created because either the existence of the trustee interest may influence the conduct of the audit or the trust may influence the actions of the audited entity. Accordingly, such a trustee interest is only held when:

- the relevant person is not an identified potential beneficiary of the trust; and
- the financial interest held by the trust in the audited entity is not material to the trust; and
- the trust is not able to exercise significant influence over the audited entity or an affiliate of the audited entity; and
- the relevant person does not have significant influence over the investment decisions made by the trust, in so far as they relate to the financial interest in the audited entity.

Where it is not clear whether the financial interest held by the trust in the audited entity is material to the trust or whether the trust is able to exercise significant influence over the audited entity, the financial interest is reported to the Ethics Partner, so that a decision can be made as to the steps that need to be taken.   **20**

A direct or an indirect financial interest in the audited entity or its affiliates held in a trustee capacity by the audit firm or by a partner in the audit firm (other than a partner in a position to influence the conduct and outcome of the audit), or an immediate family member of such a person, can only be held when the relevant person is not an identified potential beneficiary of the trust.   **21**

Financial interests held by audit firm pension schemes

Where the pension scheme of an audit firm has a financial interest in an audited entity or its affiliates and the firm has any influence over the trustees' investment decisions (other than indirect strategic and policy decisions), the self-interest threat created is such that no safeguards can eliminate it or reduce it to an acceptable level. In other cases (for example, where the pension scheme invests through a collective investment scheme and the firm's influence is limited to investment policy decisions, such as the allocation between different categories of investment), the Ethics Partner considers the acceptability of the position, having regard to the materiality of the financial interest to the pension scheme.   **22**

Loans and guarantees

Where audit firms, persons in a position to influence the conduct and outcome of the audit or immediate family members of such persons: **23**

(a) accept a loan[1] or a guarantee of their borrowings from an audited entity; or
(b) make a loan to or guarantee the borrowings of an audited entity,

a self-interest threat and an intimidation threat to the auditor's objectivity can be created or there may be a perceived loss of independence. In a number of situations, no safeguards can eliminate this threat or reduce it to an acceptable level.

Audit firms, persons in a position to influence the conduct and outcome of the audit and immediate family members of such persons shall not make a loan to, or guarantee the borrowings of, an audited entity or its affiliates unless this represents a deposit made   **24**

---

[1] *For the purpose of this standard, the term 'loan' does not include ordinary trade credit arrangements or deposits placed for goods or services, unless they are material to either party (see paragraph 29).*

with a bank or similar deposit taking institution in the ordinary course of business and on normal business terms.

25   **Audit firms shall not accept a loan from, or have their borrowings guaranteed by, the audited entity or its affiliates unless:**

    (a) the audited entity is a bank or similar deposit taking institution; and

    (b) the loan or guarantee is made in the ordinary course of business on normal business terms; and

    (c) the loan or guarantee is not material to both the audit firm and the audited entity.

26   **Persons in a position to influence the conduct and outcome of the audit and immediate family members of such persons shall not accept a loan from, or have their borrowings guaranteed by, the audited entity or its affiliates unless:**

    (a) the audited entity is a bank or similar deposit taking institution; and

    (b) the loan or guarantee is made in the ordinary course of business on normal business terms; and

    (c) the loan or guarantee is not material to the audited entity.

27   Loans by an audited entity that is a bank or similar institution to a person in a position to influence the conduct and outcome of the audit, or an immediate family member of such a person (for example, home mortgages, bank overdrafts or car loans), do not create an unacceptable threat to objectivity and independence, provided that normal business terms apply. However, where such loans are in arrears by a significant amount, this creates an intimidation threat that is unacceptable. Where such a situation arises, the person in a position to influence the conduct and outcome of the audit reports the matter to the audit engagement partner or to the Ethics Partner, as appropriate and ceases to have any involvement with the audit. The audit engagement partner or, where appropriate, the Ethics Partner considers whether any audit work is to be reperformed.

Business relationships

28   A business relationship between:

    (a) the audit firm or a person who is in a position to influence the conduct and outcome of the audit, or an immediate family member of such a person; and

    (b) the audited entity or its affiliates, or its management;

involves the two parties having a common commercial interest. Business relationships may create self-interest, advocacy or intimidation threats to the auditor's objectivity and perceived loss of independence. Examples include:

- joint ventures with the audited entity or with a director, officer or other individual who performs a management role for the audited entity;
- arrangements to combine one or more services or products of the audit firm with one or more services or products of the audited entity and to market the package with reference to both parties;
- distribution or marketing arrangements under which the audit firm acts as a distributor or marketer of any of the audited entity's products or services, or the audited entity acts as the distributor or marketer of any of the products or services of the audit firm;
- other commercial transactions, such as the audit firm leasing its office space from the audited entity.

Audit firms, persons in a position to influence the conduct and outcome of the audit and immediate family members of such persons shall not enter into business relationships with an audited entity, its management or its affiliates except where they: 29

- **involve the purchase of goods and services from the audit firm or the audited entity in the ordinary course of business and on an arm's length basis and which are not material to either party; or**
- **are clearly inconsequential to either party.**

Where a business relationship exists, that is not permitted under paragraph 29, and has been entered into by: 30

(a) *the audit firm:* either the relationship is terminated or the firm does not accept (or withdraws from) the audit engagement;
(b) *a person in a position to influence the conduct and outcome of the audit:* either the relationship is terminated or that person does not retain a position in which they exert such influence on the audit engagement;
(c) *an immediate family member of a person in a position to influence the conduct and outcome of the audit:* either the relationship is terminated or the person in a position to influence the conduct and outcome of the audit does not retain such a position.

Where there is an unavoidable delay in the termination of a business relationship, the audit firm adopts safeguards to preserve its objectivity until the relationship is terminated. These may include a review of the relevant person's audit work or a temporary exclusion of the relevant person from influence on conduct and outcome of the audit.

Compliance with paragraph 29 is not intended to prevent an audit firm giving advice in accordance with regulatory requirements[2] to a third party in relation to investment products or services, including those supplied by an audited entity. In such circumstances, the audit firm considers the advocacy and self-interest threats that might be created by the provision of this advice where it gives rise to commission or similar payments by the audited entity to the audit firm and assesses whether any safeguards are required. 31

Where a person in a position to influence the conduct and outcome of the audit becomes aware that a close family member has entered into one of the business relationships specified in paragraph 28, that individual shall report the matter to the audit engagement partner to take appropriate action. If it is a close family member of the audit engagement partner or if the audit engagement partner is in doubt as to the action to be taken, the audit engagement partner shall resolve the matter through consultation with the Ethics Partner. 32

Where there are doubts as to whether a transaction or series of transactions are either in the ordinary course of business and on an arm's length basis or of such materiality that they constitute a threat to the audit firm's objectivity and independence, the audit engagement partner reports the issue: 33

- to the Ethics Partner, so that a decision can be made as to the appropriate action that needs to be taken to ensure that the matter is resolved; and
- to those charged with governance of the audited entity, together with other significant facts and matters that bear upon the auditor's objectivity and independence, to obtain their views on the matter.

---

[2] *Firms providing such services will be authorised either by the Financial Services Authority or by their professional accountancy body acting as a Designated Professional Body.*

34   Where there are doubts about whether a reasonable and informed third party would conclude that a business relationship is clearly inconsequential to either party and would not therefore present a threat to independence, then it is not clearly inconsequential.

35   **An audit firm shall not provide audit services to any entity or person able to influence the affairs of the audit firm or the performance of any audit engagement undertaken by the audit firm.**

36   This prohibition applies to:

   (a)   any entity that owns any significant part of an audit firm, or is an affiliate of such an entity; or
   (b)   any shareholder, director or other person in a position to direct the affairs of such an entity or its affiliate.

   A significant ownership is one that carries the ability to influence materially the policy of an entity.[3]

Employment relationships

MANAGEMENT ROLE WITH AN AUDITED ENTITY

37   **An audit firm shall not admit to the partnership, or employ a person to undertake audit work, if that person is also employed by the audited entity or its affiliates ('dual employment').**

Loan staff assignments

38   **An audit firm shall not enter into an agreement with an audited entity to provide a partner or employee to work for a temporary period as if that individual were an employee of the audited entity or its affiliates (a 'loan staff assignment') unless:**

   (a)   **the agreement is for a short period of time and does not involve staff or partners performing non-audit services that would not be permitted under APB Ethical Standard 5; and**
   (b)   **the audited entity agrees that the individual concerned will not hold a management position, and acknowledges its responsibility for directing and supervising the work to be performed, which will not include such matters as:**
   ●   **making management decisions; or**
   ●   **exercising discretionary authority to commit the audited entity to a particular position or accounting treatment.**

39   Where an audit firm agrees to assist an audited entity by providing loan staff, threats to objectivity and independence may be created. A management threat may arise if the employee undertakes work that involves making judgments and taking decisions that are properly the responsibility of management. Thus, for example, interim management arrangements involving participation in the financial reporting function are not acceptable.

40   A self-review threat may also arise if the individual, during the loan staff assignment, is in a position to influence the preparation of the audited entity's financial

---

[3] *For companies, competition authorities have generally treated a 15% shareholding as sufficient to provide a material ability to influence policy.*

statements and then, on completion of that assignment, is assigned to the engagement team for that entity, with responsibility to report on matters for which he or she was responsible whilst on that loan staff assignment.

Where a partner or employee returns to the firm on completion of a loan staff   **41**
assignment, that individual shall not be given any role on the audit involving any
function or activity that he or she performed or supervised during that assignment.

In considering for how long this restriction is to be observed, the need to realise the   **42**
potential value to the effectiveness of the audit of the increased knowledge of the audited entity's business gained through the assignment has to be weighed against the potential threats to objectivity and independence. Those threats increase with the length of the assignment and with the intended level of responsibility of the individual within the engagement team. As a minimum, this restriction will apply to at least the first audit of the financial statements following the completion of the loan staff assignment.

Partners and engagement team members joining an audited entity

Where a former partner in the audit firm joins the audited entity, the audit firm shall   **43**
take action as quickly as possible – and, in any event, before any further work is done
by the audit firm in connection with the audit – to ensure that no significant connections
remain between the firm and the individual.

Ensuring that no significant connections remain between the firm and the individual   **44**
requires that:

- all capital balances and similar financial interests be fully settled (including retirement benefits) unless these are made in accordance with pre-determined arrangements that cannot be influenced by any remaining connections between the individual and the firm; and
- the individual does not participate or appear to participate in the audit firm's business or professional activities.

Audit firms shall establish policies and procedures that require: **45**

(a) all partners in the audit firm to notify the firm of any situation involving their
     potential employment with any entity audited by the firm; and
(b) senior members of any engagement team to notify the audit firm of any situation
     involving their potential employment with the relevant audited entity; and
(c) other members of any engagement team to notify the audit firm of any situation
     involving their probable employment with the relevant audited entity; and
(d) anyone who has given such notice to be removed from the engagement team; and
(e) a review of the audit work performed by the resigning or former engagement team
     member in the current and, where appropriate, the most recent audit.

Objectivity and independence may be threatened where a director, an officer or an   **46**
employee of the audited entity who is in a position to exert direct and significant influence over the preparation of the financial statements, has recently been a partner in the audit firm or a member of the engagement team. Such circumstances may create self-interest, familiarity and intimidation threats, particularly when significant connections remain between the individual and the audit firm. Similarly, objectivity and independence may be threatened when an individual knows, or has reason to believe, that he or she will or may be joining the audited entity at some time in the future.

47   Where a partner in the audit firm or a member of the engagement team for a particular audited entity has left the audit firm and taken up employment with that entity, the significance of the self-interest, familiarity and intimidation threats is assessed and normally depends on such factors as:

- the position that individual had in the engagement team or firm;
- the position that individual has taken at the audited entity;
- the amount of involvement that individual will have with the engagement team (especially where it includes former colleagues with whom he or she worked);
- the length of time since that individual was a member of the engagement team or employed by the audit firm.

Following the assessment of any such threats, appropriate safeguards are applied where necessary.

48   Any review of audit work is performed by a more senior audit professional. If the individual joining the audited entity is an audit partner, the review is performed by an audit partner who is not involved in the audit engagement. Where, due to its size, the audit firm does not have a partner who was not involved in the audit engagement, it seeks either a review by another audit firm or advice from its professional body.

49   **Where a partner leaves the firm and is appointed as a director (including as a non-executive director) or to a key management position with an audited entity[4], having acted as audit engagement partner (or as an engagement quality control reviewer, key partner involved in the audit or a partner in the chain of command) at any time in the two years prior to this appointment, the firm shall resign as auditor.[5] The firm shall not accept re-appointment as auditor until a two-year period, commencing when the former partner ceased to have an ability to influence the conduct and outcome of the audit, has elapsed or the former partner ceases employment with the former audited entity, whichever is the sooner.**

50   **Where a former member of the engagement team (other than an audit engagement partner, a key partner involved in the audit or a partner in the chain of command) leaves the audit firm and, within two years of ceasing to hold that position, joins the audited entity as a director (including as a non-executive director) or in a key management position, the audit firm shall consider whether the composition of the audit team is appropriate.**

51   In such circumstances, the audit firm evaluates the appropriateness of the composition of the audit team by reference to the factors listed in paragraph 47 and alters or strengthens the audit team to address any threat to the auditor's objectivity and independence that may be identified.

---

[4] *UK legislation provides that each of the Recognised Supervisory Bodies must have adequate rules and practices to ensure that a key audit partner (the individual responsible for the statutory audit and individuals responsible for a parent undertaking or a material subsidiary undertaking) of a firm appointed by a public interest entity as auditor is prohibited from being appointed as a director or other officer of the entity during a period of two years commencing on the date on which his or her work as key audit partner ended.*

[5] *The timing of the audit firm's resignation as auditor is determined in accordance with paragraph 50 of APB Ethical Standard 1. In the case of those public sector bodies where the responsibility for the audit is assigned by legislation, the auditor cannot resign from the audit engagement and considers alternative safeguards that can be put in place.*

Family members employed by an audited entity

Where a person in a position to influence the conduct and outcome of the audit, or a   52
partner in the audit firm, becomes aware that an immediate or close family member is
employed by an audited entity in a position to exercise influence on the accounting
records or financial statements, that individual shall either:

(a) in the case of an immediate family member of a person in a position to influence the
     conduct and outcome of the audit, cease to hold a position in which they exert such
     influence on the audit; or

(b) in the case of a close family member of a person in a position to influence the
     conduct and outcome of the audit, or any family member of a partner in the audit
     firm, report the matter to the audit engagement partner to take appropriate action.
     If it is a close family member of the audit engagement partner or if the audit
     engagement partner is in doubt as to the action to be taken, the audit engagement
     partner shall resolve the matter in consultation with the Ethics Partner.

GOVERNANCE ROLE WITH AN AUDITED ENTITY

Paragraphs 54 to 56 are supplementary to certain statutory or regulatory provisions   53
that prohibit directors of entities from being appointed as their auditor.[6]

The audit firm or a partner or employee of the audit firm shall not accept appointment   54
or perform a role:

(a) as an officer[7] or member of the board of directors of the audited entity;

(b) as a member of any subcommittee of that board; or

(c) in such a position in an entity which holds directly or indirectly more than 20% of
     the voting rights in the audited entity, or in an entity in which the audited entity
     holds directly or indirectly more than 20% of the voting rights.

Where a person in a position to influence the conduct and outcome of the audit becomes   55
aware that an immediate or close family member holds a position described in paragraph 54, the audit firm shall take appropriate steps to ensure that the relevant person
does not retain a position in which they exert influence on the conduct and outcome of
the audit engagement.

Where a partner or employee of the audit firm, not being a member of the engagement   56
team, becomes aware that an immediate or close family member holds a position
described in paragraph 54, that individual shall report that fact to the audit engagement
partner, who shall consider whether the relationship might be regarded by a reasonable
and informed third party as impairing, or being thought to impair, the auditor's
objectivity. If the audit engagement partner concludes that the auditor's objectivity may
be impaired, that individual shall consult with the Ethics Partner to determine whether
appropriate safeguards exist. If no such safeguards exist, the audit firm withdraws from
the audit engagement.

---

[6] *For example, in the case of limited companies and certain other organisations, section 1214 of the Companies
Act 2006 contains detailed provisions. Amongst other things, these state that:*
*'...A person may not act as statutory auditor of an audited person if [he] is (a) an officer or employee of the
audited person, or (b) a partner or employee of such a person, or a partnership of which such a person is a
partner.'*

[7] *As defined in Section 1173 of the Companies Act 2006 as including a director, manager or secretary.*

EMPLOYMENT WITH AUDIT FIRM

57   Objectivity and independence may be threatened where a former director or employee of the audited entity becomes a member of the engagement team. Self-interest, self-review and familiarity threats may be created where a member of the engagement team has to report on, for example, financial statements which he or she prepared, or elements of the financial statements for which he or she had responsibility, while with the audited entity.

58   **Where a former director or a former employee of an audited entity, who was in a position to exert significant influence over the preparation of the financial statements, joins the audit firm, that individual shall not be assigned to a position in which he or she is able to influence the conduct and outcome of the audit for that entity or its affiliates for a period of two years following the date of leaving the audited entity.**

59   In certain circumstances, a longer period of exclusion from the engagement team may be appropriate. For example, threats to objectivity and independence may exist in relation to the audit of the financial statements of any period which are materially affected by the work of that person whilst occupying his or her former position of influence with the audited entity. The significance of these threats depends on factors such as:

- the position the individual held with the audited entity;
- the length of time since the individual left the audited entity;
- the position the individual holds in the engagement team.

Family and other personal relationships

60   A relationship between a person who is in a position to influence the conduct and outcome of the audit and another party does not generally affect the consideration of the auditor's objectivity and independence. However, if it is a family relationship, and if the family member also has a financial, business or employment relationship with the audited entity, then self-interest, familiarity or intimidation threats to the auditor's objectivity and independence may be created. The significance of any such threats depends on such factors as:

- the relevant person's involvement in the audit;
- the nature of the relationship between the relevant person and his or her family member;
- the family member's relationship with the audited entity.

61   A distinction is made between immediate family relationships and close family relationships. Immediate family members comprise an individual's spouse (or equivalent) and dependents, whereas close family members comprise parents, non-dependent children and siblings. While an individual can usually be presumed to be aware of matters concerning his or her immediate family members and to be able to influence their behaviour, it is generally recognised that the same levels of knowledge and influence do not exist in the case of close family members.

62   When considering family relationships, it needs to be acknowledged that, in an increasingly secular, open and inclusive society, the concept of what constitutes a family is evolving and relationships between individuals which have no status formally recognised by law may nevertheless be considered as significant as those which do. It may therefore be appropriate to regard certain other personal relationships,

particularly those that would be considered close personal relationships, as if they are family relationships.

The audit firm shall establish policies and procedures that require: 63

(a) **partners and professional staff to report to the audit firm any immediate family, close family and other personal relationships involving an entity audited by the firm, to which they are a party and which they consider might create a threat to the auditor's objectivity or a perceived loss of independence;**
(b) **the relevant audit engagement partners to be notified promptly of any immediate family, close family and other personal relationships reported by partners and other professional staff.**

The audit engagement partner shall: 64

(a) **assess the threats to the auditor's objectivity and independence arising from immediate family, close family and other personal relationships on the basis of the information reported to the firm by persons in a position to influence the conduct and outcome of the audit;**
(b) **apply appropriate safeguards to eliminate the threat or reduce it to an acceptable level; and**
(c) **where there are unresolved matters or the need for clarification, consult with the Ethics Partner.**

Where such matters are identified or reported, the audit engagement partner or the 65 Ethics Partner assesses the information available and the potential for there to be a threat to the auditor's objectivity and independence, treating any personal relationship as if it were a family relationship.

External consultants involved in the audit

Audit firms may employ external consultants as experts in order to obtain sufficient 66 appropriate audit evidence regarding certain financial statement assertions.[8] There is a risk that an expert's objectivity and independence will be impaired if the expert is related to the entity, for example by being financially dependent upon or having an investment in, the entity.

The audit engagement partner shall be satisfied that any external consultant involved in 67 **the audit will be objective and document the rationale for that conclusion.**

The audit engagement partner obtains information from the external consultant as to 68 the existence of any connections that they have with the audited entity including:

- financial interests;
- business relationships;
- employment (past, present and future);
- family and other personal relationships.

Effective date

This revised Ethical Standard becomes effective on 30 April 2011. 69

---

[8] *ISA (UK and Ireland) 620 'Using the Work of an Auditor's Expert'* requires that the auditor shall evaluate whether the expert has the necessary objectivity.

70   Firms may complete audit engagements relating to periods commencing prior to 31 December 2010 in accordance with existing ethical standards, putting in place any necessary changes in the subsequent engagement period.

71   On appointment as auditor to an entity, an audit firm may continue in a business relationship or a loan staff arrangement which is already contracted at the date of appointment, until the earlier of either:

(i)   the completion of the specific obligations under the contract or the end of the contract term, where this is set out in the contract; or

(ii)   one year after the date of appointment, where obligations or a term are not defined,

provided that the need for additional safeguards is assessed and if considered necessary, those additional safeguards are applied.

APB Ethical Standard 3 (Revised)
Long association with the audit engagement

(Revised October 2009)

Contents

Preface

APB Ethical Standards apply in the audit of financial statements. They are read in the context of the Auditing Practices Board's Statement "The Auditing Practices Board – Scope and Authority of Pronouncements (Revised)" which sets out the application and authority of APB Ethical Standards.

The terms used in APB Ethical Standards are explained in the Glossary.

APB Ethical Standards apply to audits of financial statements in both the private and the public sectors. However, auditors in the public sector are subject to more complex ethical requirements than their private sector counterparts. This includes, for example, compliance with legislation such as the Prevention of Corruption Act 1916, concerning gifts and hospitality, and with Cabinet Office guidance.

Introduction

1 APB Ethical Standard 1 requires the audit engagement partner to identify and assess the circumstances which could adversely affect the auditor's objectivity ('threats'), including any perceived loss of independence, and to apply procedures ('safeguards') which will either:

   (a) eliminate the threat; or
   (b) reduce the threat to an acceptable level (that is, a level at which it is not probable that a reasonable and informed third party would conclude that the auditor's objectivity and independence either is impaired or is likely to be impaired).

   When considering safeguards, where the audit engagement partner chooses to reduce rather than to eliminate a threat to objectivity and independence, he or she recognises that this judgment may not be shared by users of the financial statements and that he or she may be required to justify the decision.

2 This Standard provides requirements and guidance on specific circumstances arising out of long association with the audit engagement, which may create threats to the auditor's objectivity or perceived loss of independence. It gives examples of safeguards that can, in some circumstances, eliminate the threat or reduce it to an acceptable level. In circumstances where this is not possible, the auditor either does not accept or withdraws from the audit engagement, as appropriate.

3 Whenever a possible or actual breach of an APB Ethical Standard is identified, the audit engagement partner, in the first instance, and the Ethics Partner, where appropriate, assesses the implications of the breach, determines whether there are safeguards that can be put in place or other actions that can be taken to address any potential adverse consequences and considers whether there is a need to resign from the audit engagement.

4 An inadvertent violation of this Standard does not necessarily call into question the audit firm's ability to give an audit opinion provided that:

   (a) the audit firm has established policies and procedures that require all partners and staff to report any breach promptly to the audit engagement partner or to the Ethics Partner, as appropriate;
   (b) the audit engagement partner or Ethics Partner ensures that any matter which has given rise to a breach is addressed as soon as possible;

(c) safeguards, if appropriate, are applied (for example, by having another partner review the work done by the relevant partner or member of staff or by removing him or her from the engagement team): and

(d) the actions taken and the rationale for them are documented.

General provisions

The audit firm shall establish policies and procedures to monitor the length of time that 5 **audit engagement partners, key partners involved in the audit and partners and staff in senior positions, including those from other disciplines, serve as members of the engagement team for each audit.**

6 **Where audit engagement partners, key partners involved in the audit, and partners and staff in senior positions have a long association with the audit, the audit firm shall assess the threats to the auditor's objectivity and independence and shall apply safeguards to reduce the threats to an acceptable level. Where appropriate safeguards cannot be applied, the audit firm shall either resign as auditor or not stand for reappointment, as appropriate.[1]**

Where audit engagement partners, key partners involved in the audit, other partners 7 and staff in senior positions have a long association with the audited entity, self-interest, self-review and familiarity threats to the auditor's objectivity may arise. Similarly, such circumstances may result in an actual or perceived loss of independence. The significance of such threats depends upon factors such as:

- the role of the individual in the engagement team;
- the proportion of time that the audited entity contributes to the individual's annual billable hours;
- the length of time that the individual has been associated with that audit engagement.

In order to address such threats, audit firms apply safeguards. Appropriate safe- 8 guards may include:

- removing ('rotating') the partners and the other senior members of the engagement team after a pre-determined number of years;
- involving an additional partner, who is not and has not recently been a member of the engagement team, to review the work done by the partners and the other senior members of the engagement team and to advise as necessary;
- applying independent internal quality reviews to the engagement in question.

Once an audit engagement partner has held this role for a continuous period of ten 9 years, careful consideration is given as to whether a reasonable and informed third party would consider the audit firm's objectivity and independence to be impaired. Where the individual concerned is not rotated after ten years, it is important that:

(a) safeguards other than rotation, such as those noted in paragraph 8, are applied; or

(b) (i) the reasoning as to why the individual continues to participate in the audit engagement without any safeguards is documented; and

(ii) the facts are communicated to those charged with governance of the audited entity in accordance with paragraphs 63 – 71 of APB Ethical Standard 1.

---

[1] *In the case of those public sector bodies where the responsibility for the audit is assigned by legislation, the auditor cannot resign from the audit engagement and considers alternative safeguards that can be put in place.*

10   The audit firm's policies and procedures set out whether there are circumstances in which the audit engagement partners, engagement quality control reviewers and key partners involved in the audit of non-listed entities are subject to accelerated rotation requirements, such as those set out in paragraph 12, as described in paragraph 47 of APB Ethical Standard 1.

11   Any scheme of rotation of partners and other senior members of the engagement team needs to take into account the factors which affect the quality of the audit work, including the experience and continuity of members of the engagement team and the need to ensure appropriate succession planning.

Additional provisions related to audits of listed companies

The audit engagement partner

12   **In the case of listed companies, save where the circumstances contemplated in paragraph 15 and 16 apply, the audit firm shall establish policies and procedures to ensure that:**

(a)   **no one shall act as audit engagement partner for more than five years; and**

(b)   **anyone who has acted as the audit engagement partner for a particular audited entity for a period of five years, shall not subsequently participate in the audit engagement until a further period of five years has elapsed.**

13   The roles that constitute participating in an audit engagement for the purposes of paragraph 12(b), include providing quality control for the engagement, advising or consulting with the engagement team or the client regarding technical or industry specific issues, transactions or events, or otherwise directly influencing the outcome of the audit engagement. This does not include responding to queries in relation to any completed audit engagement. This is not intended to preclude partners whose primary responsibility within a firm is to be consulted on technical or industry specific issues from providing such consultation to the engagement team or client after a period of two years has elapsed from their ceasing to act as audit engagement partner, provided that such consultation is in respect of new issues or new types of transactions or events that were not previously required to be considered by that individual in the course of acting as audit engagement partner.

14   Where an audit engagement partner continues in a non-audit role having been rotated off the engagement team, the new audit engagement partner and the individual concerned ensure that that person, while acting in this new role, does not exert any influence on the audit engagement. Positions in which an individual is responsible for the firm's client relationship with the particular audited entity would not be an acceptable non-audit role.

15   When an audited entity becomes a listed company, the length of time the audit engagement partner has served the audited entity in that capacity is taken into account in calculating the period before the audit engagement partner is rotated off the engagement team. However, where the audit engagement partner has already served for four or more years, that individual may continue to serve as the audit engagement partner for not more than two years after the audited entity becomes a listed company.

16   In circumstances where the audit committee (or equivalent) of the audited entity decide that a degree of flexibility over the timing of rotation is necessary to safeguard the quality of the audit and the audit firm agrees, the audit engagement partner may

continue in this position for an additional period of up to two years, so that no longer than seven years in total is spent in the position of audit engagement partner. An audit committee and the audit firm may consider that such flexibility safeguards the quality of the audit, for example, where:

- substantial change has recently been made or will soon be made to the nature or structure of the audited entity's business; or
- there are unexpected changes in the senior management of the audited entity.

In these circumstances alternative safeguards are applied to reduce any threats to an acceptable level. Such safeguards may include ensuring that an expanded review of the audit work is undertaken by the engagement quality control reviewer or an audit partner, who is not involved in the audit engagement.

Where it has been determined that the audit engagement partner may act for a   **17** further period (not to exceed two years) in the interests of audit quality, this fact and the reasons for it, are to be disclosed to the audited entity's shareholders as early as practicable and in each of the additional years. If the audited entity is not prepared to make such a disclosure, the audit firm does not permit the audit engagement partner to continue in this role.

In the case of joint audit arrangements for listed companies, audit firms will make   **18** arrangements for changes of audit engagement partners over a five-year period so that the familiarity threat is avoided, whilst also taking into consideration factors that affect the quality of the audit work.

Engagement quality control reviewers and key partners involved in the audit

In the case of listed companies, the audit firm shall establish policies and procedures to   **19** **ensure that:**

(a) no one shall act as the engagement quality control reviewer or a key partner involved in the audit for a period longer than seven years;

(b) where an engagement quality control reviewer or a key partner involved in the audit becomes the audit engagement partner, the combined period of service in these positions shall not exceed seven years; and

(c) anyone who has acted:

    (i) as an engagement quality control reviewer for a particular audited entity for a period of seven years, whether continuously or in aggregate, shall not participate in the audit engagement until a further period of five years has elapsed;

    (ii) as a key partner involved in the audit for a particular audited entity for a period of seven years, whether continuously or in aggregate, shall not participate in the audit engagement until a further period of two years has elapsed;

    (iii) in a combination of roles as:
- **the engagement quality control reviewer,**
- **a key partner involved in the audit, or**
- **the audit engagement partner**

    for a particular audited entity for a period of seven years, whether continuously or in aggregate, shall not participate in the audit engagement until a further period of five years has elapsed.

Other partners and staff in senior positions

In the case of listed companies, the audit engagement partner shall review the safe-   **20** **guards put in place to address the threats to the auditor's objectivity and independence arising where partners and staff have been involved in the audit in senior positions for a**

continuous period longer than seven years and shall discuss those situations with the engagement quality control reviewer. Any unresolved problems or issues shall be referred to the Ethics Partner.

21   The significance of the threats arising where partners and staff have been involved in the audit in senior positions for a continuous period longer than seven years will depend on:

- the total period of time that the individual has been involved in the audit;
- changes in the nature of the work and the role performed by the individual during that period; and

the portion of time the individual has spent on the audit and non-audit engagements with the audited entity during that period.

22   Following the assessment of any such threats, appropriate safeguards are applied where necessary. Safeguards that address these threats might include:

- changes in the roles within the engagement team;
- an additional review of the work done by the individual by the audit engagement partner or other partners in the engagement team;
- additional procedures carried out as part of the engagement quality control review.

If such safeguards do not reduce the threats to an acceptable level, the partner or member of staff is removed from the engagement team.

Effective date

23   Revisions to this Ethical Standard become effective for audits of financial statements for periods commencing on or after 15 December 2009. Earlier adoption of the revisions is permitted.

24   Where a partner becomes a key partner involved in the audit as a result of the change in definition introduced with effect from 6 April 2008 the transitional arrangements in the previous version of ES 3 (Revised) continue to apply.

APB Ethical Standard 4 (Revised)
Fees, remuneration and evaluation policies, litigation, gifts and hospitality

(Revised December 2010)

Contents

Preface

APB Ethical Standards apply in the audit of financial statements. They are read in the context of the Auditing Practices Board's Statement "The Auditing Practices Board – Scope and Authority of Pronouncements (Revised)" which sets out the application and authority of APB Ethical Standards.

The terms used in APB Ethical Standards are explained in the Glossary.

APB Ethical Standards apply to audits of financial statements in both the private and the public sectors. However, auditors in the public sector are subject to more complex ethical requirements than their private sector counterparts. This includes, for example, compliance with legislation such as the Prevention of Corruption Act 1916, concerning gifts and hospitality, and with Cabinet Office guidance.

Introduction

1   APB Ethical Standard 1 requires the audit engagement partner to identify and assess the circumstances which could adversely affect the auditor's objectivity ('threats'), including any perceived loss of independence, and to apply procedures ('safeguards') which will either:

(a)   eliminate the threat; or

(b)   reduce the threat to an acceptable level (that is, a level at which it is not probable that a reasonable and informed third party would conclude that the auditor's objectivity and independence either is impaired or is likely to be impaired).

When considering safeguards, where the audit engagement partner chooses to reduce rather than to eliminate a threat to objectivity and independence, he or she recognises that this judgment may not be shared by users of the financial statements and that he or she may be required to justify the decision.

2   This Standard provides requirements and guidance on specific circumstances arising out of fees, economic dependence, litigation, remuneration and evaluation of partners and staff, and gifts and hospitality, which may create threats to the auditor's objectivity or perceived loss of independence. It gives examples of safeguards that can, in some situations, eliminate the threat or reduce it to an acceptable level. In circumstances where this is not possible, either the situation is avoided or the auditor either does not accept or withdraws from the audit engagement, as appropriate.

3   Whenever a possible or actual breach of an APB Ethical Standard is identified, the audit engagement partner, in the first instance, and the Ethics Partner, where appropriate, assesses the implications of the breach, determines whether there are safeguards that can be put in place or other actions that can be taken to address any potential adverse consequences and considers whether there is a need to resign from the audit engagement.

4   An inadvertent violation of this Standard does not necessarily call into question the audit firm's ability to give an audit opinion provided that:

(a)   the audit firm has established policies and procedures that require all partners and staff to report any breach promptly to the audit engagement partner or to the Ethics Partner, as appropriate;

(b)   the audit engagement partner or Ethics Partner ensures that any matter which has given rise to a breach is addressed as soon as possible;

(c) safeguards, if appropriate, are applied (for example, having another partner review the work done by the relevant partner or member of staff or by removing him or her from the engagement team); and

(d) the actions taken and the rationale for them are documented.

Fees

The audit engagement partner shall be satisfied and able to demonstrate that the audit   5
engagement has assigned to it sufficient partners and staff with appropriate time and
skill to perform the audit in accordance with all applicable Auditing and Ethical
Standards, irrespective of the audit fee to be charged.

Paragraph 5 is not intended to prescribe the approach to be taken by audit firms to   6
the setting of audit fees, but rather to emphasise that there are no circumstances
where the amount of the audit fee can justify any lack of appropriate resource or
time taken to perform a proper audit in accordance with applicable Auditing and
Ethical Standards.

The audit engagement partner shall ensure that audit fees are not influenced or   7
determined by the provision of non-audit services to the audited entity.

The audit fee ordinarily reflects the time spent, the skills and experience of the   8
personnel performing the audit in accordance with all the relevant requirements, and
the competitive situation in the audit market. Paragraph 7 is intended to prevent any
relationship between the appropriate cost of the audit and the actual or potential
provision of non-audit services.

Paragraph 7 is not intended to prohibit proper cost savings that can be achieved as a   9
result of providing non-audit services in accordance with APB Ethical Standard 5 to
the audited entity, for example, where information gained through undertaking a
non-audit service is referred to by audit staff when carrying out the audit of the
financial statements.

An audit shall not be undertaken on a contingent fee basis.   10

A contingent fee basis is any arrangement made under which a fee is calculated on a   11
pre-determined basis relating to the outcome or result of a transaction, or other
event, or the result of the work performed. A fee that is established by a court or
other public authority is not a contingent fee.

Contingent fee arrangements in respect of audit engagements create self-interest   12
threats to the auditor's objectivity and independence that are so significant that they
cannot be eliminated or reduced to an acceptable level by the application of any
safeguards.

The audit fee does not depend on whether the auditor's report on the financial   13
statements is qualified or unqualified. The basis for the calculation of the audit fee is
agreed with the audited entity each year before significant audit work is undertaken.
Arrangements under which estimated audit fees are agreed with the audited entity on
terms where the fees may be varied based on the level of audit work required do not
constitute contingent fee arrangements.

Contingent fee arrangements in respect of non-audit services provided by the auditor   14
in respect of an audited entity can create significant self-interest threats to the

auditor's objectivity and independence as the auditor may have, or may appear to have, an interest in the outcome of the non-audit service.

15   The audit firm shall not undertake an engagement to provide non-audit services in respect of an audited entity on a contingent fee basis where:

   (a)   the contingent fee is material to the audit firm, or that part of the firm by reference to which the audit engagement partner's profit share is calculated; or

   (b)   the outcome of those non-audit services (and, therefore, the amount of the fee) is dependent on a future or contemporary audit judgment relating to a material matter in the financial statements of an audited entity.

16   Where non-audit services are provided on a contingent fee basis, there may be a perception that the audit firm's interests are so closely aligned with the audited entity that the auditor's objectivity and independence is threatened. The significance of the self-interest threat is primarily determined by the materiality of the contingent fee to the audit firm or to the part of the firm by reference to which the audit engagement partner's profit share is calculated. Where the contingent fee and the outcome of the non-audit service is dependent on a future or contemporary audit judgment on a material matter included in the financial statements of an audited entity, the self interest threat cannot be eliminated or reduced to an acceptable level by the application of safeguards.

17   Paragraph 15 is not intended to prohibit an audit firm from charging a lower fee where the engagement relates to a transaction or engagement that was either aborted or prematurely terminated for whatever reason and where the rationale for the lower fee is to take account of either the reduced risk and responsibility involved or the fact that less work was undertaken than had been anticipated.

18   For non-audit services provided on a contingent fee basis, other than those prohibited under paragraph 15, the audit engagement partner assesses the significance of the self-interest threat and considers whether there are safeguards that could be applied which would be effective to eliminate the threat or reduce it to an acceptable level. The significance of the self-interest threat will depend on factors such as:

   ● the range of possible fee amounts;
   ● the nature of the non-audit service;
   ● the effect of the outcome of the non-audit service on the financial statements of the audited entity.

19   Examples of safeguards that might be applied to reduce to an acceptable level any self-interest threats arising from the provision of non-audit services on a contingent fee basis (other than those set out in paragraph 15 above) include:

   ● the provision of such non-audit services by partners and staff who have no involvement in the external audit of the financial statements;
   ● review of the audit of the financial statements by an audit partner who is not involved in the audit engagement to ensure that the subject matter of the non-audit service engagement has been properly and effectively addressed in the context of the audit of the financial statements.

20   The audit firm shall establish policies and procedures to ensure that the audit engagement partner and the Ethics Partner are notified where others within the audit firm propose to adopt contingent fee arrangements in relation to the provision of non-audit services to the audited entity or its affiliates.

Contingent fee arrangements in respect of non-audit services provided by the auditor may create a threat to the auditor's objectivity and independence. The circumstances in which such fee arrangements are not permitted for non-audit services are dealt with in paragraph 15 of this standard and paragraph 95 of APB Ethical Standard 5. **21**

In the case of listed companies the audit engagement partner shall disclose to the audit committee, in writing, any contingent fee arrangements for non-audit services provided by the auditor or its network firms. **22**

In the case of a group audit of a listed company, which involves other auditors, the letter of instruction sent by the group audit engagement partner to the other auditors requests disclosure of any contingent fees for non-audit services charged or proposed to be charged by the other auditors. **23**

The actual amount of the audit fee for the previous audit and the arrangements for its payment shall be agreed with the audited entity before the audit firm formally accepts appointment as auditor in respect of the following period. **24**

Ordinarily, any outstanding fees for the previous audit period are paid before the audit firm commences any new audit work. Where they are not, it is important for the audit engagement partner to understand the nature of any disagreement or other issue. **25**

Where fees for professional services from the audited entity are overdue and the amount cannot be regarded as trivial, the audit engagement partner, in consultation with the Ethics Partner, shall consider whether the audit firm can continue as auditor or whether it is necessary to resign. **26**

Where fees due from an audited entity, whether for audit or for non-audit services, remain unpaid for a long time – and, in particular, where a significant part is not paid before the auditor's report on the financial statements for the following year is due to be issued – a self-interest threat to the auditor's objectivity and independence is created because the issue of an unqualified audit report may enhance the audit firm's prospects of securing payment of such overdue fees. **27**

Where the outstanding fees are in dispute and the amount involved is significant, the threats to the auditor's objectivity and independence may be such that no safeguards can eliminate them or reduce them to an acceptable level. The audit engagement partner therefore considers whether the audit firm can continue with the audit engagement. **28**

Where the outstanding fees are unpaid because of exceptional circumstances (including financial distress), the audit engagement partner considers whether the audited entity will be able to resolve its difficulties. In deciding what action to take, the audit engagement partner weighs the threats to the auditor's objectivity and independence, if the audit firm were to remain in office, against the difficulties the audited entity would be likely to face in finding a successor, and therefore the public interest considerations, if the audit firm were to resign. **29**

In any case where the audit firm does not resign from the audit engagement, the audit engagement partner applies appropriate safeguards (such as a review by an audit partner who is not involved in the audit engagement) and notifies the Ethics Partner of the facts concerning the overdue fees. **30**

31   Where it is expected that the total fees for both audit and non-audit services receivable from a listed audited entity and its subsidiaries audited by the audit firm[1] will regularly exceed 10% of the annual fee income of the audit firm[2] or, where profits are not shared on a firm-wide basis, of the part of the firm by reference to which the audit engagement partner's profit share is calculated, the firm shall not act as the auditor of that entity and shall either resign as auditor or not stand for reappointment, as appropriate.[3]

32   Where it is expected that the total fees for both audit and non-audit services receivable from a non-listed audited entity and its subsidiaries audited by the audit firm will regularly exceed 15% of the annual fee income of the audit firm or, where profits are not shared on a firm-wide basis, of the part of the firm by reference to which the audit engagement partner's profit share is calculated, the firm shall not act as the auditor of that entity and shall either resign as auditor or not stand for reappointment, as appropriate.

33   Where it is expected that the total fees for both audit and non-audit services receivable from an audited entity and its subsidiaries that are audited by the audit firm will regularly exceed 10% in the case of listed companies and 15% in the case of non-listed entities of the annual fee income of the part of the firm by reference to which the audit engagement partner's profit share is calculated, it may be possible to assign the engagement to another part of the firm.

34   Paragraphs 31 and 32 are not intended to require the audit firm to resign as auditor or not stand for reappointment as a result of an individual event or engagement, the nature or size of which was unpredictable and where a reasonable and informed third party would regard ceasing to act as detrimental to the shareholders (or equivalent) of the audited entity. However, in such circumstances, the auditor discloses full details of the position to the Ethics Partner and to those charged with governance of the audited entity and discusses with both what, if any, safeguards may be appropriate.

35   Where it is expected that the total fees for both audit and non-audit services receivable from a listed audited entity and its subsidiaries audited by the audit firm will regularly exceed 5% of the annual fee income of the audit firm or the part of the firm by reference to which the audit engagement partner's profit share is calculated, but will not regularly exceed 10%, the audit engagement partner shall disclose that expectation to the Ethics Partner and to those charged with governance of the audited entity and consider whether appropriate safeguards need to be applied to eliminate or reduce to an acceptable level the threat to the auditor's objectivity and independence.

36   It is fundamental to the auditor's objectivity that the auditor be willing and able, if necessary, to disagree with the directors and management, regardless of the consequences to its own position. Where the auditor is, to any significant extent, economically dependent on the audited entity, this may inhibit the auditor's willingness or constrain the auditor's ability to express a qualified opinion on the financial statements, since this could be viewed as likely to lead to the auditor losing the audit engagement and the entity as a client.

---

[1] *Total fees will include those billed by others where the audit firm is entitled to the fees, but will not include fees billed by the audit firm where it is acting as agent for another party.*

[2] *In the case of a sole practitioner, annual fee income of the audit firm includes all earned income received by the individual.*

[3] *Paragraphs 31 to 40 do not apply to the audits of those public sector bodies where the responsibility for the audit is assigned by legislation. In such cases, the auditor cannot resign from the audit engagement, irrespective of considerations of economic dependence.*

An audit firm is deemed to be economically dependent on a listed audited entity if the total fees for audit and all other services from that entity and its subsidiaries which are audited by the audit firm represent 10% of the total fees of the audit firm or the part of the firm by reference to which the audit engagement partner's profit share is calculated. Where such fees are between 5% and 10%, the audit engagement partner and the Ethics Partner consider the significance of the threat and the need for appropriate safeguards. **37**

Such safeguards might include: **38**

- taking steps to reduce the non-audit work to be undertaken and therefore the fees earned from the audited entity;
- applying independent internal quality control reviews.

Where it is expected that the total fees for both audit and non-audit services receivable from a non-listed audited entity and its subsidiaries audited by the audit firm will regularly exceed 10% of the annual fee income of the audit firm or the part of the firm by reference to which the audit engagement partner's profit share is calculated, but will not regularly exceed 15%, the audit engagement partner shall disclose that expectation to the Ethics Partner and to those charged with governance of the audited entity and the firm shall arrange an external independent quality control review of the audit engagement to be undertaken before the auditor's report is finalised. **39**

A quality control review involves discussion with the audit engagement partner, a review of the financial statements and the auditor's report, and consideration of whether the report is appropriate. It also involves a review of selected working papers relating to the significant judgments the engagement team has made and the conclusions they have reached. The extent of the review depends on the complexity of the engagement and the risk that the report might not be appropriate in the circumstances. The review includes considering the following: **40**

- Significant risks identified during the audit and the responses to those risks.
- Judgments made, particularly with respect to materiality and significant risks.
- Whether appropriate consultation has taken place on matters involving differences of opinion or other difficult or contentious matters, and the conclusions arising from those consultations.
- The significance and disposition of corrected and uncorrected misstatements identified during the audit.
- The appropriateness of the report to be issued.

Where the quality control reviewer makes recommendations that the audit engagement partner does not accept and the matter is not resolved to the reviewer's satisfaction, the report is not issued until the matter is resolved by following the audit firm's procedures for dealing with differences of opinion.

A new audit firm seeking to establish itself may find the requirements relating to economic dependence difficult to comply with in the short term. In these circumstances, such firms would: **41**

(a) not undertake any audits of listed companies, where fees from such an audited entity would represent 10% or more of the annual fee income of the firm; and
(b) for a period not exceeding two years, require external independent quality control reviews of those audits of unlisted entities that represent more than 15% of the annual fee income before the audit opinion is issued.

The firm might also develop its practice by accepting work from entities not audited by the firm so as to bring the fees payable by each audited entity below 15%.

42   A self-interest threat may also be created where an audit partner in the engagement team:

- is employed exclusively or principally on that audit engagement; and
- is remunerated on the basis of the performance of part of the firm which is substantially dependent on fees from that audited entity.

43   Where the circumstances described in paragraph 42 arise, the audit firm assesses the significance of the threat and applies safeguards to reduce the threat to an acceptable level. Such safeguards might include:

- reducing the dependence of the office, partner or person in a position to influence the conduct and outcome of the audit by reallocating the work within the practice;
- a review by an audit partner who is not involved with the audit engagement to ensure that the auditor's objectivity and independence is not affected by the self-interest threat.

Remuneration and evaluation policies

44   **The audit firm shall establish policies and procedures to ensure that each of the following is true in relation to each audited entity:**

(a)   **the objectives of the members of the engagement team do not include selling non-audit services to the entity they audit;**

(b)   **the criteria for evaluating the performance or promotion of members of the engagement team do not include success in selling non-audit services to the entity they audit; and**

(c)   **no specific element of the remuneration of a member of the engagement team is based on his or her success in selling non-audit services to the entity they audit.**

This requirement does not apply to those members of the engagement team from specialist practice areas where the nature and extent of their involvement in the audit is clearly insignificant.

45   Where the auditor identifies areas for possible improvement in an audited entity the auditor may provide general business advice, which might include suggested solutions to problems. Before discussing any non-audit service that might be provided by the audit firm or effecting any introductions to colleagues from outside the engagement team, the audit engagement partner considers the threats that such a service would have on the audit engagement, in line with the requirements of APB Ethical Standard 5.

46   The last sentence of paragraph 44 recognises the fact that an engagement team may include personnel from specialist practice areas and that it would be inappropriate to limit the business development activities of such persons where their involvement in the audit is clearly insignificant.

47   The policies and procedures required for compliance with paragraph 44 are not intended to inhibit normal profit-sharing arrangements. However, such policies and procedures are central to an audit firm's ability to demonstrate its objectivity and independence and to rebut any suggestion that an audit that it has undertaken and the opinion that it has given are influenced by the nature and extent of any non-audit services that it has provided to that audited entity. Because it is possible that, despite such policies and procedures, such factors may be taken into account in the evaluation and remuneration of members of an engagement team, the Ethics Partner

pays particular attention to the actual implementation of those policies and procedures and is available for consultation when needed.

Threatened and actual litigation

Where litigation in relation to audit or non-audit services between the audited entity or its affiliates and the audit firm, which is other than insignificant, is already in progress, or where the audit engagement partner considers such litigation to be probable, the audit firm shall either not continue with or not accept the audit engagement.[4] 48

Where litigation (in relation to audit or non-audit services) actually takes place between the audit firm (or any person in a position to influence the conduct and outcome of the audit) and the audited entity, or where litigation is threatened and there is a realistic prospect of such litigation being commenced, self-interest, advocacy and intimidation threats to the auditor's objectivity and independence are created because the audit firm's interest will be the achievement of an outcome to the dispute or litigation that is favourable to itself. In addition, an effective audit process requires complete candour and full disclosure between the audited entity's management and the engagement team: such disputes or litigation may place the two parties in opposing adversarial positions and may affect management's willingness to make complete disclosure of relevant information. Where the auditor can foresee that such a threat may arise, the auditor informs the audit committee of its intention to resign or, where there is no audit committee, the board of directors. 49

The auditor is not required to resign immediately in circumstances where a reasonable and informed third party would not regard it as being in the interests of the shareholders for it to do so. Such circumstances might arise, for example, where: 50

- the litigation was commenced as the audit was about to be completed and shareholder interests would be adversely affected by a delay in the audit of the financial statements;
- on appropriate legal advice, the audit firm deems that the threatened or actual litigation is vexatious or designed solely to bring pressure to bear on the opinion to be expressed by the auditor.

Gifts and hospitality

The audit firm, those in a position to influence the conduct and outcome of the audit and immediate family members of such persons shall not accept gifts from the audited entity, unless the value is clearly insignificant. 51

Those in a position to influence the conduct and outcome of the audit and immediate family members of such persons shall not accept hospitality from the audited entity, unless it is reasonable in terms of its frequency, nature and cost. 52

Where gifts or hospitality are accepted from an audited entity, self-interest and familiarity threats to the auditor's objectivity and independence are created. Familiarity threats also arise where gifts or hospitality are offered to an audited entity. 53

---

[4] *Paragraphs 48 to 50 do not apply to the audits of those public sector bodies where the responsibility for the audit is assigned by legislation. In such cases, the auditor cannot resign from the audit engagement: the auditor reports significant litigation to the relevant legislative authority.*

54   Gifts from the audited entity, unless their value is clearly insignificant, create threats to objectivity and independence which no safeguards can eliminate or reduce.

55   Hospitality is a component of many business relationships and can provide valuable opportunities for developing an understanding of the audited entity's business and for gaining the insight on which an effective and successful working relationship depends. Therefore, the auditor's objectivity and independence is not necessarily impaired as a result of accepting hospitality from the audited entity, provided it is reasonable in terms of its frequency, its nature and its cost.

56   **The audit firm shall establish policies on the nature and value of gifts and hospitality that may be accepted from and offered to audited entities, their directors, officers and employees, and shall issue guidance to assist partners and staff to comply with such policies.**

57   In assessing the acceptability of gifts and hospitality, the test to be applied is not whether the auditor considers that the auditor's objectivity is impaired but whether it is probable that a reasonable and informed third party would conclude that it is or is likely to be impaired.

58   Where there is any doubt as to the acceptability of gifts or hospitality offered by the audited entity, members of the engagement team discuss the position with the audit engagement partner. If there is any doubt as to the acceptability of gifts or hospitality offered to the audit engagement partner, or if the audit engagement partner has any residual doubt about the acceptability of gifts or hospitality to other individuals, the audit engagement partner reports the facts to the Ethics Partner, for further consideration regarding any action to be taken.

59   Where the cumulative amount of gifts or hospitality accepted from the audited entity appears abnormally high, the audit engagement partner reports the facts to both:

   ● the Ethics Partner; and
   ● the audit committee (or, where there is no audit committee, the board of directors),

   together with other significant facts and matters that bear upon the auditor's objectivity and independence.

Effective date

60   This revised Ethical Standard becomes effective on 30 April 2011.

61   Firms may complete audit engagements relating to periods commencing on or before 31 December 2010 in accordance with existing ethical standards, putting in place any necessary changes in the subsequent engagement period.

62   An audit firm may continue to provide non-audit services that would be prohibited under paragraph 15, where these have already been contracted at 31 December 2010, until the earlier of either:

   a.   the completion of the specific task or the end of the contract term, where one is set out in the contract; or
   b.   31 December 2011.

APB Ethical Standard 5 (Revised)
Non-audit services provided to audited entities

(Revised December 2010, updated December 2011)

Contents

Preface

APB Ethical Standards apply in the audit of financial statements. They are read in the context of the Auditing Practices Board's Statement "The Auditing Practices Board – Scope and Authority of Pronouncements (Revised)" which sets out the application and authority of APB Ethical Standards.

The terms used in APB Ethical Standards are explained in the Glossary.

APB Ethical Standards apply to audits of financial statements in both the private and the public sectors. However, auditors in the public sector are subject to more complex ethical requirements than their private sector counterparts. This includes, for example, compliance with legislation such as the Prevention of Corruption Act 1916, concerning gifts and hospitality, and with Cabinet Office guidance.

Introduction

1   APB Ethical Standard 1 requires the audit engagement par~~~~~~~~~
the circumstances which could adve~~~~~~pendence, and to apply procedures ('safeguards')
including any perceived l~~~~~~
which will either:

(a)   eliminate the threat; or
(b)   reduce the threat to an acceptable level (that is, a level at which it is not probable that a reasonable and informed third party would conclude that the auditor's objectivity and independence either is impaired or is likely to be impaired).

When considering safeguards, where the audit engagement partner chooses to reduce rather than to eliminate a threat to objectivity and independence, he or she recognises that this judgment may not be shared by users of the financial statements and that he or she may be required to justify the decision.

2   This Standard provides requirements and guidance on specific circumstances arising from the provision of non-audit services by audit firms to entities audited by them which may create threats to the auditor's objectivity or perceived loss of independence. It gives examples of safeguards that can, in some circumstances, eliminate the threat or reduce it to an acceptable level. In circumstances where this is not possible, either the non-audit service engagement in question is not undertaken or the auditor either does not accept or withdraws from the audit engagement, as appropriate.

3   Whenever a possible or actual breach of an APB Ethical Standard is identified, the audit engagement partner, in the first instance, and the Ethics Partner, where appropriate, assess the implications of the breach, determine whether there are safeguards that can be put in place or other actions that can be taken to address any potential adverse consequences and consider whether there is a need to resign from the audit engagement.

4   An inadvertent violation of this Standard does not necessarily call into question the audit firm's ability to give an audit opinion provided that:

(a)   the audit firm has established policies and procedures that require all partners and staff to report any breach promptly to the audit engagement partner or to the Ethics Partner, as appropriate;

(b) the audit engagement partner promptly notifies the partner or member of staff that any matter which has given rise to a breach is to be addressed as soon as possible and ensures that such action is taken;

(c) safeguards, if appropriate, are applied (for example, by having another partner review the work done by the relevant partner or member of staff or by removing him or her from the engagement team); and

(d) the actions taken and the rationale for them are documented.

General approach to non-audit services

Paragraphs 6 to 53 of this Standard set out the general approach to be adopted by 5 audit firms and auditors in relation to the provision of non-audit services to entities audited by them. This approach is applicable irrespective of the nature of the non-audit services, which may be in question in a given case. (Paragraphs 54 to 168 of this Standard illustrate the application of the general approach to a number of common non-audit services.)

An audit is the term used to describe the work that is undertaken by the auditor to 6 enable him or her to express an independent audit opinion on an entity's financial statements and, where the entity is a parent company, on the group financial statements and/or the separate financial statements of its components[1].

International Standards on Auditing (UK and Ireland) require that the auditor 7 exercise professional judgment and maintain professional scepticism throughout the planning and performance of the audit and, among other things:

- Identify and assess risks of material misstatement, whether due to fraud or error, based on an understanding of the entity and its environment, including the entity's internal control.

- Obtain sufficient appropriate audit evidence about whether material misstatements exist, through designing and implementing appropriate responses to the assessed risks.

- Form an opinion on the financial statements based on conclusions drawn from the audit evidence obtained[2].

Judgments regarding the nature and extent of evidence necessary to support the audit 8 opinion are a matter for the auditor but will include:

- Identifying, evaluating and testing, where appropriate, those internal control systems the effectiveness of which is necessary for the audit of the financial statements and where, if any control weaknesses are identified, extended testing will be required; and

- additional work undertaken to respond to risks identified by management or the audit committee that the auditor considers could impact the auditor's opinion on the financial statements.

Other work undertaken by the engagement team at the request of management or 9 those charged with governance will not be categorised as part of the audit irrespective of whether it forms part of the audit proposal or engagement, unless it is

---

[1] In the public sector the statutory scope of an audit can extend beyond expressing an independent opinion on an entity's financial statements to include reporting on an entity's arrangements to ensure the proper conduct of its financial affairs, manage its performance or use of its resources.

[2] ISA (UK and Ireland) 200 'Overall Objectives of the Independent Auditor and the Conduct of an Audit in Accordance with International Standards on Auditing (UK and Ireland)' paragraph 7.

clear that the predominant rationale for the performance of the work in question is to enable a soundly based audit opinion on the financial statements to be expressed. Therefore, an audit of financial statements does not include work where:

- The objective of that work is not to gather evidence to support the auditor's opinion on the financial statements; or
- The nature and extent of testing is not determined by the external auditor, or in the case of a group, the component auditors, in the context of expressing an opinion on the financial statements; or
- The principal terms and conditions differ from that of the audit.

10   If additional work on financial information[3] and/or financial controls is authorised by those charged with governance, but the objective of that work is not to enable the auditor to provide an audit opinion on the entity's financial statements, it will be considered as an 'audit related service' for the purpose of this Standard provided that it:

- is integrated with the work performed in the audit and performed largely by the existing audit team; and
- is performed on the same principal terms and conditions as the audit.
  As a consequence of these factors, any threats to auditor independence arising from the performance of such additional work are considered to be clearly insignificant.

11   Other additional work that:

- does not relate to financial information and/or financial controls; or
- is not integrated with the work performed in the audit, or is not performed largely by the existing audit team, or
- is not on the same principal terms and conditions as the audit;
  will be regarded as an 'other non-audit service' for the purpose of this Standard.

12   'Non-audit services' comprise any engagement in which an audit firm provides professional services to:

- an audited entity;
- an audited entity's affiliates; or
- another entity in respect of the audited entity[4];

other than the audit of financial statements of the audited entity.

13   There may be circumstances where the audit firm is engaged to provide a non-audit service and where that engagement and its scope are determined by an entity which is not audited by the firm. However, it might be contemplated that an audited entity may gain some benefit from that engagement[5]. In these circumstances, whilst there may be no threat to the audit firm's objectivity and independence at the time of appointment, the audit firm considers how the engagement may be expected to develop, whether there are any threats that the audit firm may be subject to if

---

[3] *This does not include accounting services.*

[4] *For example, where an engagement is undertaken to assist in the preparation of listing particulars for a company acquiring the audited entity.*

[5] *For example, in a vendor due diligence engagement, the engagement is initiated and scoped by the vendor before the purchaser is identified. If an entity audited by the firm undertaking the due diligence engagement is the purchaser, that audited entity may gain the benefit of the report issued by its auditor, it may be a party to the engagement letter and it may pay an element of the fee.*

additional relevant parties which are audited entities are identified, and whether any safeguards need to be put in place.

The audit firm shall establish policies and procedures that require others within the firm, when considering whether to accept a proposed engagement to provide a non-audit service to an audited entity or any of its affiliates, to communicate details of the proposed engagement to the audit engagement partner.   **14**

The audit firm establishes appropriate channels of internal communication to ensure that, in relation to an entity audited by the firm, the audit engagement partner (or their delegate) is informed about any proposed engagement to provide a non-audit service to the audited entity or any of its affiliates and that he or she considers the implications for the auditor's objectivity and independence before the engagement is accepted. Additionally, when addressing services provided to another entity in respect of the audited entity, the procedures address any requirement to preserve client confidentiality.   **15**

In the case of a listed company, the group audit engagement partner establishes that the company has communicated its policy on the engagement of the external auditor to supply non-audit services to its affiliates and obtains confirmation that the auditors of the affiliates will comply with this policy.[6] The group audit engagement partner also requires that relevant information on non-audit services provided by network firms is communicated on a timely basis.   **16**

IDENTIFICATION AND ASSESSMENT OF THREATS AND SAFEGUARDS

Before the audit firm accepts a proposed engagement to provide a non-audit service, the audit engagement partner shall: **17**

(a)   **consider whether it is probable that a reasonable and informed third party would regard the objectives of the proposed engagement as being inconsistent with the objectives of the audit of the financial statements; and**
(b)   **identify and assess the significance of any related threats to the auditor's objectivity, including any perceived loss of independence; and**
(c)   **identify and assess the effectiveness of the available safeguards to eliminate the threats or reduce them to an acceptable level.**

When assessing the significance of threats to the auditor's objectivity and independence, the audit engagement partner considers the following factors: **18**

- The likely relevance and impact of the subject matter on the financial statements;
- The extent to which performance of the proposed engagement will involve the exercise of professional judgment;

---

[6] *The UK Corporate Governance Code requires audit committees to develop the company's policy on the engagement of the external auditor to supply non-audit services.*

- The size of the engagement and the associated fee;
- The basis on which the fee is to be calculated;
- The staff who would be carrying out the non-audit service[7];
- The staff from the audited entity who would be involved in the non-audit service[8].

To ensure that this assessment is made with a proper understanding of the nature of the engagement, it may be necessary to refer to a draft engagement letter in respect of the proposed non-audit services or to discuss the engagement with the partner involved.

19   The assessment of the threats to the auditor's objectivity and independence arising from any particular non-audit engagement is a matter for the audit engagement partner. The audit engagement partner may decide to delegate some information gathering activities to senior personnel on the audit team and may allow such personnel to make decisions in relation to routine non-audit services. If this is the case, the audit engagement partner will:

- provide specific criteria for such decisions that reflect both the requirements of APB Ethical Standards and the audited entity's policy for the purchase of non-audit services; and
- monitor the decisions being made on a regular basis.

20   Where the audit engagement partner is not able to undertake the assessment of the significance of threats in relation to a proposed engagement to provide a non-audit service to an audited entity, for example due to illness or holidays, alternative arrangements are established (for example, by authorising the engagement quality control reviewer to consider the proposed engagement).

21   The objective of the audit of financial statements is to express an opinion on the preparation and presentation of those financial statements. For example, in the case of a limited company, legislation requires the auditor to make a report to the members on all annual accounts laid before the company in general meeting during its tenure of office. The report must include a statement as to whether, in the auditor's opinion, the accounts have been properly prepared in accordance with the requirements of the legislation, and, in particular, whether they give a true and fair view of the state of the affairs and profit or loss for the year.

22   **Where the audit engagement partner considers that it is probable that a reasonable and informed third party would regard the objectives of the proposed non-audit service engagement as being inconsistent with the objectives of the audit of the financial statements, the audit firm shall either:**

   (a)   not undertake the non-audit service engagement; or
   (b)   not accept or withdraw from the audit engagement.

23   The objectives of engagements to provide non-audit services vary and depend on the specific terms of the engagement. In some cases these objectives may be inconsistent with those of the audit, and, in such cases, this may give rise to a threat to the

---

[7] *For example, where those handling the non-audit service engagement are particularly expert so that the audit team (or persons advising it) may have difficulty in reviewing effectively the advice given or the work undertaken by the non-audit service team in the course of conducting a subsequent audit, with the result that the effectiveness of the audit might be compromised.*

[8] *For example, the safeguards necessary to address any self-review threat will require careful consideration where those involved are particularly senior and can be expected to be actively involved in any audit discussion as this may also create an intimidation threat.*

auditor's objectivity and to the appearance of its independence. Audit firms do not undertake non-audit service engagements where the objectives of such engagements are inconsistent with the objectives of the audit, or they do not accept or withdraw from the audit engagement as appropriate.

Similarly, in relation to a possible appointment as auditor to an entity that the audit firm has not audited before, consideration needs to be given to recent, current and potential engagements to provide non-audit services by the audit firm and whether the scope and objectives of those engagements are consistent with the proposed audit engagement. In the case of listed companies, when tendering for a new audit engagement, the audit firm ensures that relevant information on recent non-audit services is drawn to the attention of the audit committee, including: **24**

- when recent non-audit services were provided;
- the materiality of those non-audit services to the proposed audit engagement;
- whether those non-audit services would have been prohibited if the entity had been an audited entity at the time when they were undertaken; and
- the extent to which the outcomes of non-audit services have been audited or reviewed by another audit firm.

Threats to objectivity and independence

The principal types of threats to the auditor's objectivity and independence are: **25**
- self-interest threat;
- self-review threat;
- management threat;
- advocacy threat;
- familiarity (or trust) threat; and
- intimidation threat.

The auditor remains alert to the possibility that any of these threats may occur in connection with non-audit services. However, the threats most commonly associated with non-audit services are self-interest threat, self-review threat, management threat and advocacy threat.

A **self-interest threat** exists when the auditor has financial or other interests which   **26** might cause the auditor to be reluctant to take actions that would be adverse to the interests of the audit firm or any individual in a position to influence the conduct or outcome of the audit. In relation to non-audit services, the main self-interest threat concerns fees and economic dependence and these are addressed in APB Ethical Standard 4.

Where substantial fees are regularly generated from the provision of non-audit   **27** services and the fees for non-audit services are greater than the annual audit fees, the audit engagement partner has regard to the possibility that there may be perceived to be a loss of independence resulting from the expected or actual level of fees for non-audit services. The audit engagement partner determines whether there is any risk that there will be an actual loss of independence and objectivity by the engagement team. In making that assessment, the audit engagement partner considers matters such as whether the engagement or engagements giving rise to the fees for non-audit services were:

- audit related services;
- provided on a contingent fee basis;
- consistent with the engagements undertaken and fees received on a consistent basis in previous years;

- in the case of a group, disproportionate in relation to any individual group entity;
- unusual in size but unlikely to recur; and/or
- of such a size and nature that a reasonable and informed third party would be concerned at the effect that such engagements would have on the objectivity and independence of the engagement team.

Having made that assessment, the audit engagement partner determines whether the threats to independence from the level of fees for non-audit services are at an acceptable level (or can be reduced to an acceptable level by putting in place appropriate safeguards) and appropriately informs those charged with governance of the position on a timely basis in accordance with paragraphs 48 to 50 of this Standard.

28 **In the case of listed companies where the fees for non-audit services for a financial year are expected to be greater than the annual audit fees, the audit engagement partner shall provide details of the circumstances to the Ethics Partner and discuss them with him or her. Where the audit firm provides audit services to a group, the obligation to provide information to the Ethics Partner shall be on a group basis for all services provided by the audit firm and its network firms to all entities in the group.**

29 Discussing the level of fees for non-audit services with the Ethics Partner ensures that appropriate attention is paid to the issue by the audit firm. The audit firm's policies and procedures will set out whether there are circumstances in which the audit engagement partner discusses the level of non-audit fees with the Ethics Partner for non-listed audited entities as described in paragraph 47 of APB Ethical Standard 1.

30 Where fees for non-audit services are calculated on a contingent fee basis, there is a risk that a reasonable and informed third party may regard the audit firm's interests to be so closely aligned with the audited entity that it threatens the auditor's objectivity and independence. Consequently, the audit firm does not accept a non-audit services engagement on a contingent fee basis where:

(a) that contingent fee is material to the audit firm, or that part of the firm by reference to which the audit engagement partner's profit share is calculated; or
(b) the outcome of the service (and, therefore, the amount of the fee) is dependent on a future or contemporary audit judgment relating to a material matter in the financial statements of an audited entity.

31 A **self-review threat** exists when the results of a non-audit service performed by the engagement team or by others within the audit firm are reflected in the amounts included or disclosed in the financial statements.

32 A threat to objectivity and independence arises because, in the course of the audit, the auditor may need to re-evaluate the work performed in the non-audit service. As, by virtue of providing the non-audit service, the audit firm is associated with aspects of the preparation of the financial statements, it may be (or may appear to be) unable to take an impartial view of relevant aspects of those financial statements.

33 In assessing the significance of the self-review threat, the auditor considers the extent to which the non-audit service will:

- involve a significant degree of subjective judgment; and
- have a material effect on the preparation and presentation of the financial statements.

Where a significant degree of judgment relating to the financial statements is 34
involved in a non-audit service engagement, the auditor may be inhibited from
questioning that judgment in the course of the audit. Whether a significant degree of
subjective judgment is involved will depend upon whether the non-audit service
involves the application of well-established principles and procedures, and whether
reliable information is available. If such circumstances do not exist because the non-
audit service is based on concepts, methodologies or assumptions that require
judgment and are not established by the audited entity or by authoritative guidance,
the auditor's objectivity and the appearance of its independence may be adversely
affected. Where the provision of a proposed non-audit service would also have a
material effect on the financial statements, it is unlikely that any safeguard can
eliminate or reduce to an acceptable level the self-review threat.

A **management threat** exists when the audit firm undertakes work that involves 35
making judgments and taking decisions that are properly the responsibility of
management.

Paragraph 33 of APB Ethical Standard 1 prohibits partners and employees of the 36
audit firm from taking decisions on behalf of the management of the audited entity.
A threat to objectivity and independence also arises where the audit firm undertakes
an engagement to provide non-audit services in relation to which management are
required to make judgments and take decisions based on that work. The auditor may
become closely aligned with the views and interests of management and this may
erode the distinction between the audited entity and the audit firm, in turn, impairing
or calling into question the auditor's ability to apply a proper degree of professional
scepticism in auditing the financial statements. The auditor's objectivity and the
appearance of its independence therefore may be, or may be perceived to be,
impaired.

In determining whether a non-audit service does or does not give rise to a man- 37
agement threat, the auditor considers whether there is informed management.
Informed management exists when:

- the auditor is satisfied that a member of management (or senior employee of the
  audited entity) has been designated by the audited entity to receive the results of
  the non-audit service and has been given the authority to make any judgments
  and decisions of the type set out in paragraph 34 of APB Ethical Standard 1 that
  are needed;
- the auditor concludes that that member of management has the capability to
  make independent management judgments and decisions on the basis of the
  information provided; and
- the results of the non-audit service are communicated to the audited entity and,
  where judgments or decisions are to be made they are supported by an objective
  analysis of the issues to consider and the audited entity is given the opportunity
  to decide between reasonable alternatives.

In the absence of such informed management it is unlikely that any other safeguards 38
can eliminate a management threat or reduce it to an acceptable level.

An **advocacy threat** exists when the audit firm undertakes work that involves acting 39
as an advocate for an audited entity and supporting a position taken by management
in an adversarial context.

A threat to objectivity and independence arises because, in order to act in an 40
advocacy role, the audit firm has to adopt a position closely aligned to that of
management. This creates both actual and perceived threats to the auditor's

objectivity and independence. For example, where the audit firm, acting as advocate, has supported a particular contention of management, it may be difficult for the auditor to take an impartial view of this in the context of the audit of the financial statements.

41   Where the provision of a non-audit service would require the auditor to act as an advocate for the audited entity in relation to matters that are material to the financial statements, it is unlikely that any safeguards can eliminate or reduce to an acceptable level the advocacy threat that would exist.

42   Threats to the auditor's objectivity, including a perceived loss of independence, may arise where a non-audit service is provided by the audit firm to a third party which is connected (through a relationship) to an audited entity, and the outcome of that service has a material impact on the financial statements of the audited entity. For example, if the audit firm provides actuarial services to the pension scheme of an audited entity, which is in deficit and the audit firm subsequently gives an opinion on financial statements that include judgments given in connection with that service.

Safeguards

43   Where any threat to the auditor's objectivity and the appearance of its independence is identified, the audit engagement partner assesses the significance of that threat and considers whether there are safeguards that could be applied and which would be effective to eliminate the threat or reduce it to an acceptable level. If such safeguards can be identified and are applied, the non-audit service may be provided. However, where no such safeguards are applied, the only course is for the audit firm either not to undertake the engagement to provide the non-audit service in question or not to accept (or to withdraw from) the audit engagement.

44   When considering what safeguards, if any, would be effective in reducing the threats to independence and objectivity to an acceptable level, the audit engagement partner has regard to the following safeguards which, individually or in combination, may be effective, depending on the circumstances:

(a) The non-audit services are provided by a separate team from the engagement team, and:
- if circumstances require, to address the threat identified, there is effective physical and electronic segregation of the individuals in each team, and of their documentation, at all times during the provision of the audit and non-audit services; and/or
- the team providing the non-audit services avoids taking any action or making any statement that compromises the independence or objectivity of the engagement team, for example, expressing any opinion about the approach that the engagement team might take or the conclusion it might reach when considering the appropriateness of accounting or other audit judgments.

The Ethics Partner establishes policies and procedures to ensure that, where safeguards of this nature are considered appropriate, the arrangements put in place are effective at all times. This will involve the Ethics Partner being satisfied that there are effective arrangements in place for each member of the non-audit services team to acknowledge their responsibilities and for each member of the engagement team to notify him or her of any breach of this requirement that the team member becomes aware. Where notified of a breach, the Ethics Partner considers together with the audit engagement partner the significance of the breach and the implications for the independence and objectivity of the engagement team, including whether any further safeguards are necessary and whether the matter should be reported to those charged with governance of the audited entity;

(b) The Engagement Quality Control Reviewer, or another audit partner of sufficient relevant experience and seniority who is, and is seen to be, an effective challenge to both the audit engagement partner and the partner leading the non-audit services engagement, reviews the work and conclusions of the engagement team in relation to their consideration of the audit judgments, if any, relating to the subject matter of the non-audit service, having regard to the self-review threat identified, and determines and documents his or her conclusions as to whether the work is sufficient and the conclusions of the engagement team are appropriate. Where the review partner has concerns, the audit engagement partner does not sign the audit opinion until those concerns have been subject to full consultation, including escalation through any processes required by the audit firm's policies. Where this safeguard is considered appropriate, the Ethics Partner is satisfied that the review partner undertaking this role is appropriate, that the review partner is aware of the circumstances leading to the conclusion that there is a significant self-review threat and that any concerns raised by the review partner have been satisfactorily resolved before signature of the audit opinion.

Where the audit engagement partner concludes that no appropriate safeguards are available to eliminate or reduce to an acceptable level the threats to the auditor's objectivity, including any perceived loss of independence, related to a proposed engagement to provide a non-audit service to an audited entity, he or she shall inform the others concerned within the audit firm of that conclusion and the firm shall either: **45**

(a) not undertake the non-audit service engagement; or
(b) not accept or withdraw from the audit engagement.

If the audit engagement partner is in doubt as to the appropriate action to be taken, he or she shall resolve the matter through consultation with the Ethics Partner.

An initial assessment of the threats to objectivity and independence and the safeguards to be applied is required when the audit engagement partner is considering the acceptance of an engagement to provide a non-audit service. The assessment of the threats and the safeguards applied is reviewed whenever the scope and objectives of the non-audit service change significantly. If such a review suggests that safeguards cannot reduce the threat to an acceptable level, the audit firm withdraws from the non-audit service engagement, or does not accept or withdraws from the audit engagement as appropriate.   **46**

Where there is doubt as to the appropriate action to be taken, consultation with the Ethics Partner ensures that an objective judgment is made and the firm's position is consistent.   **47**

COMMUNICATION WITH THOSE CHARGED WITH GOVERNANCE

The audit engagement partner shall ensure that those charged with governance of the audited entity are appropriately informed on a timely basis of: **48**

(a) all significant facts and matters that bear upon the auditor's objectivity and independence, related to the provision of non-audit services, including the safeguards put in place; and

(b) **for listed companies, any inconsistencies between APB Ethical Standards and the company's policy for the supply of non-audit services by the audit firm and any apparent breach of that policy.**[6]

49   Transparency is a key element in addressing the issues raised by the provision of non-audit services by audit firms to the entities audited by them. This can be facilitated by timely communication with those charged with governance of the audited entity (see APB Ethical Standard 1, paragraphs 63 to 71). Such communications are addressed to the audit committee, where there is one; in other circumstances, they are addressed to the board of directors (or those in an equivalent position). In the case of listed companies, ensuring that the audit committee is properly informed about the issues associated with the provision of non-audit services will assist them to comply with the provisions of the UK Corporate Governance Code relating to reviewing and monitoring the external auditor's independence and objectivity and to developing a policy on the engagement of the external auditor to supply non-audit services. This will include discussion of any inconsistencies between the company's policy and APB Ethical Standards and ensuring that the policy is communicated to affiliates.

50   Communications with those charged with governance regarding the impact on auditor objectivity of non-audit services are likely to be facilitated if disclosure of such non-audit services distinguishes between audit related services and other non-audit services (as defined in this Standard).

DOCUMENTATION

51   **The audit engagement partner shall ensure that the reasoning for a decision to undertake an engagement to provide non-audit services, and any safeguards adopted, is appropriately documented.**

52   Matters to be documented include any significant judgments concerning:

- threats identified;
- safeguards adopted and the reasons why they are considered to be effective; and
- communication with those charged with governance.

53   In situations where a management threat is identified in connection with the provision of non-audit services, this documentation will include the auditor's assessment of whether there is informed management. The documentation of communications with the audited entity where judgments and decisions are made by management may take a variety of forms, for example an informal meeting note covering the matters discussed.

Application of general principles to specific non-audit services

AUDIT RELATED SERVICES

54   Audit related services are those non-audit services specified in this Standard that are largely carried out by members of the engagement team and where the work involved is closely related to the work performed in the audit and the threats to auditor independence are clearly insignificant and, as a consequence, safeguards need not be applied.

55   Audit related services are:

- Reporting required by law or regulation to be provided by the auditor;

- Reviews of interim financial information;
- Reporting on regulatory returns;
- Reporting to a regulator on client assets:
- Reporting on government grants;
- Reporting on internal financial controls when required by law or regulation;
- Extended audit work that is authorised by those charged with governance performed on financial information[9] and/or financial controls where this work is integrated with the audit work and is performed on the same principal terms and conditions.

56 **The audit engagement partner shall ensure that only those non-audit services listed in paragraph 55 are described as audit related services in communications with those charged with governance of the audited entity.**

There may be other services that the auditor considers are closely related to an audit. 57
However the threats to auditor independence arising from such services are not necessarily clearly insignificant and the auditor considers whether such services give rise to threats to independence and, where appropriate, the need to apply safeguards.

INTERNAL AUDIT SERVICES

The range of 'internal audit services' is wide and they may not be termed as such by 58
the audited entity. For example, the audit firm may be engaged:

- to outsource the audited entity's entire internal audit function; or
- to supplement the audited entity's internal audit function in specific areas (for example, by providing specialised technical services or resources in particular locations); or
- to provide occasional internal audit services to the audited entity on an *ad hoc* basis.

All such engagements would fall within the term 'internal audit services'.

The nature of possible internal audit services is also wide. While the internal audit 59
remit will vary from company to company, it often involves assurance activities designed to assess the design and operating effectiveness of existing or proposed systems or controls and advisory activities where advice is given to an entity on the design and implementation of risk management, control and governance processes.

The nature and extent of the threats to the external auditor's independence when 60
undertaking internal audit services vary depending on the nature of the services provided. The main threats to the auditor's objectivity and independence arising from the provision of internal audit services are the self-review threat and the management threat. Generally these will be lower for activities that are primarily designed to provide assurance to those charged with governance, for example that internal controls are operating effectively, than for advisory activities designed to assist the entity in improving the effectiveness of its risk management, control and governance processes.

Engagements to provide internal audit services – other than those prohibited in 61
paragraph 63 – may be undertaken, provided that the auditor is satisfied that there is informed management and appropriate safeguards are applied to reduce the self-review threat to an acceptable level.

[9] *This does not include accounting services.*

62   Examples of safeguards that may be appropriate when internal audit services are
      provided to an audited entity include ensuring that:

      ● internal audit projects undertaken by the audit firm are performed by partners
        and staff who have no involvement in the external audit of the financial
        statements;
      ● the audit of the financial statements is reviewed by an audit partner who is not
        involved in the audit engagement, to ensure that the internal audit work per-
        formed by the audit firm has been properly and effectively assessed in the
        context of the audit of the financial statements.

63   **The audit firm shall not undertake an engagement to provide internal audit services to**
      an audited entity where it is reasonably foreseeable that:

      (a) for the purposes of the audit of the financial statements, the auditor would place
           significant reliance on the internal audit work performed by the audit firm; or
      (b) for the purposes of the internal audit services, the audit firm would undertake part
           of the role of management.

64   The self-review threat is unacceptably high where substantially all of the internal
      audit activity is outsourced to the audit firm and this is significant to the audited
      entity or the auditor cannot perform the audit of the financial statements without
      placing significant reliance on the work performed for the purposes of the internal
      audit services engagement. In the case of listed companies the provision of internal
      audit services in relation to the following examples is likely to be unacceptable as the
      external audit team is likely to place significant reliance on the work performed by
      the internal audit team in relation to the audited entity's internal financial controls:

      ● a significant part of the internal controls over financial reporting;
      ● financial accounting systems which generate information that is significant to
        the client's accounting records;
      ● amounts or disclosures that are material to the financial statements of the
        audited entity.

65   The management threat is unacceptably high where the audit firm provides internal
      audit services that involve audit firm personnel taking decisions or making judg-
      ments, which are properly the responsibility of management. For example, such
      situations arise where the internal audit function is outsourced to the audit firm and
      this is significant to the audited entity or where the nature of the internal audit work
      involves:

      ● Taking decisions on the scope and nature of the internal audit services to be
        provided to the audited entity;
      ● Designing internal controls or implementing changes thereto;
      ● Taking responsibility for risk management decisions;
      ● Undertaking work to evaluate the cost effectiveness of activities, systems and
        controls;
      ● Undertaking pre-implementation work on non-financial systems.

66   During the course of the audit, the auditor generally evaluates the design and tests
      the operating effectiveness of some of the entity's internal financial controls, and the
      operation of any relevant internal audit function, and provides management with
      observations on matters that have come to the attention of the auditor, including
      comments on weaknesses in the internal control systems and/or the internal audit
      function together with suggestions for addressing them. This work is a by-product of
      the audit service rather than the result of a specific engagement to provide non-audit
      services and therefore does not constitute internal audit services for the purposes of
      this Standard.

In some circumstances, additional work is undertaken to respond to risks identified   **67**
by management or those charged with governance. Where the auditor considers that
such risks could impact their opinion on the financial statements, such work is
considered to be audit work for the purposes of this Standard (see paragraphs 10 and
11).

If extended audit work on financial information and/or financial controls is   **68**
authorised by those charged with governance, it will be considered as an 'audit
related service' provided that it is integrated with the work performed in the audit
and performed largely by the existing audit team, and is performed on the same
principal terms and conditions as the audit.

Additional work will not be considered an audit related service if it: **69**

- does not relate to financial information and/or financial controls; or
- is not authorised by those charged with governance; or
- is not integrated with the work performed in the audit, or is not performed
  largely by the existing audit team; or
- is not on the same principal terms and conditions as the audit.

In such circumstances the threats and the safeguards will be communicated to those
charged with governance. The audit engagement partner reviews the scope and
objectives of the proposed work and assesses the threats to which it gives rise and the
safeguards available. Whether it is appropriate for this work to be undertaken by the
audit firm will depend on the extent to which it gives rise to threats to the auditor's
objectivity and independence.

INFORMATION TECHNOLOGY SERVICES

Design, provision and implementation of information technology (including finan-   **70**
cial information technology) systems by audit firms for entities audited by them
creates threats to the auditor's objectivity and independence. The principal threats
are the self-review threat and the management threat.

Engagements to design, provide or implement information technology systems that   **71**
are not important to any significant part of the accounting system or to the production of the financial statements and do not have significant reliance placed on
them by the auditor, may be undertaken, provided that there is informed management and appropriate safeguards are applied to reduce the self-review threat to an
acceptable level.

Examples of safeguards that may be appropriate when information technology   **72**
services are provided to an audited entity include ensuring that:

- information technology projects undertaken by the audit firm are performed by
  partners and staff who have no involvement in the external audit of the financial
  statements;
- the audit of the financial statements is reviewed by an audit partner who is not
  involved in the audit engagement to ensure that the information technology
  work performed has been properly and effectively assessed in the context of the
  audit of the financial statements.

The audit firm shall not undertake an engagement to design, provide or implement   **73**
information technology systems for an audited entity where:

(a)   the systems concerned would be important to any significant part of the accounting system or to the production of the financial statements and the auditor would place significant reliance upon them as part of the audit of the financial statements; or

(b)   for the purposes of the information technology services, the audit firm would undertake part of the role of management.

74   Where it is reasonably apparent that, having regard to the activities and size of the audited entity and the range and complexity of the proposed system, management lacks the expertise required to take responsibility for the systems concerned, it is unlikely that any safeguards would be sufficient to eliminate these threats or to reduce them to an acceptable level. In particular, formal acceptance by management of the systems designed and installed by the audit firm is unlikely to be an effective safeguard when, in substance, the audit firm has been retained by management as experts and makes important decisions in relation to the design or implementation of systems of internal control and financial reporting.

75   The provision and installation of information technology services associated with a standard 'off the shelf accounting package' (including basic set-up procedures to make the package operate on the audited entity's existing platform and peripherals, setting up the chart of accounts and the entry of standard data such as the audited entity's product names and prices) is unlikely to create a level of threat to the auditor's objectivity and independence that cannot be addressed through applying appropriate safeguards.

VALUATION SERVICES

76   A valuation comprises the making of assumptions with regard to future develop-ments, the application of appropriate methodologies and techniques, and the combination of both to compute a certain value, or range of values, for an asset, a liability or for a business as a whole.

77   **The audit firm shall not undertake an engagement to provide a valuation to:**

(a)   **an audited entity that is a listed company or a significant affiliate of such an entity, where the valuation would have a material effect on the listed company's financial statements, either separately or in aggregate with other valuations provided; or**

(b)   **any other audited entity, where the valuation would both involve a significant degree of subjective judgment and have a material effect on the financial state-ments either separately or in aggregate with other valuations provided.**

78   The main threats to the auditor's objectivity and independence arising from the provision of valuation services are the self-review threat and the management threat. In all cases, the self-review threat is considered too high to allow the provision of valuation services which involve the valuation of amounts with a significant degree of subjectivity and have a material effect on the financial statements.

79   For listed companies, or significant affiliates of such entities, the threats to the auditor's objectivity and independence that would be perceived to be created are too high to allow the audit firm to undertake any valuation that has a material effect on the listed company's financial statements.

80   The audit firm's policies and procedures will set out whether there are circumstances in which valuation services are not undertaken for non-listed audited entities as described in paragraph 47 of APB Ethical Standard 1.

In circumstances where the auditor is designated by legislation or regulation as being **81** required to carry out a valuation the restrictions in paragraph 77 do not apply. In such circumstances, the audit engagement partner applies relevant safeguards.

It is usual for the auditor to provide management with accounting advice in relation **82** to valuation matters that have come to the auditor's attention during the course of the audit. Such matters might typically include:

- comments on valuation assumptions and their appropriateness;
- errors identified in a valuation calculation and suggestions for correcting them;
- advice on accounting policies and any valuation methodologies used in their application.

Advice on such matters does not constitute valuation services for the purpose of this Standard.

Where the auditor is engaged to collect and verify the accuracy of data to be used in a **83** valuation to be performed by others, such engagements do not constitute valuation services under this Standard.

ACTUARIAL VALUATION SERVICES

The audit firm shall not undertake an engagement to provide actuarial valuation ser- **84** **vices to:**

(a) **an audited entity that is a listed company or a significant affiliate of such an entity, unless the firm is satisfied that the valuation has no material effect on the listed company's financial statements, either separately or in aggregate with other valuations provided; or**

(b) **any other audited entity, unless the firm is satisfied that either all significant judgments, including the assumptions, are made by informed management or the valuation has no material effect on the financial statements, either separately or in aggregate with other valuations provided.**

Actuarial valuation services are subject to the same general principles as other **85** valuation services. In all cases, where they involve the audit firm in making a sub-jective judgment and have a material effect on the financial statements, actuarial valuations give rise to an unacceptable level of self-review threat and so may not be performed by audit firms for entities audited by them.

In the case of non-listed companies where all significant judgments concerning the **86** assumptions, methodology and data for the actuarial valuation are made by informed management and the audit firm's role is limited to applying proven methodologies using the given data, for which the management takes responsibility, it may be possible to establish effective safeguards to protect the auditors' objectivity and the appearance of its independence.

For listed companies, or significant affiliates of such entities, the threats to the **87** auditor's objectivity and independence that would be perceived to be created are too high to allow the audit firm to undertake any actuarial valuation unless the firm is satisfied that the valuation has no material effect on the listed company's financial statements.

The audit firm's policies and procedures will set out whether there are circumstances **88** in which actuarial valuation services are not undertaken for non-listed audited entities as described in paragraph 47 of APB Ethical Standard 1.

TAX SERVICES

89   The range of activities encompassed by the term 'tax services' is wide. Three broad categories of tax service can be distinguished. They are where the audit firm:

(a)   provides advice to the audited entity on one or more specific matters at the request of the audited entity; or

(b)   undertakes a substantial proportion of the tax planning or compliance work for the audited entity; or

(c)   promotes tax structures or products to the audited entity, the effectiveness of which is likely to be influenced by the manner in which they are accounted for in the financial statements.

Whilst it is possible to consider tax services under broad headings, such as tax planning or compliance, in practice these services are often interrelated and it is impracticable to analyse services in this way for the purposes of attempting to identify generically the threats to which specific engagements give rise. As a result, audit firms need to identify and assess, on a case-by-case basis, the potential threats to the auditor's objectivity and independence before deciding whether to undertake a proposed engagement to provide tax services to an audited entity.

90   The provision of tax services by audit firms to entities audited by them may give rise to a number of threats to the auditor's objectivity and independence, including the self-interest threat, the management threat, the advocacy threat and, where the work involves a significant degree of subjective judgment and has a material effect on the financial statements, the self-review threat.

91   Where the audit firm provides advice to the audited entity on one or more specific matters at the request of the audited entity, a self-review threat may be created. This self-review threat is more significant where the audit firm undertakes a substantial proportion of the tax planning and compliance work for the audited entity. However, the auditor may be able to undertake such engagements, provided that there is informed management and appropriate safeguards are applied to reduce the self-review threat to an acceptable level.

92   Examples of such safeguards that may be appropriate when tax services are provided to an audited entity include ensuring that:

*   the tax services are provided by partners and staff who have no involvement in the audit of the financial statements;
*   the tax services are reviewed by an independent tax partner, or other senior tax employee;
*   external independent advice is obtained on the tax work;
*   tax computations prepared by the audit team are reviewed by a partner or senior staff member with appropriate expertise who is not a member of the audit team; or
*   an audit partner not involved in the audit engagement reviews whether the tax work has been properly and effectively addressed in the context of the audit of the financial statements.

93   **The audit firm shall not promote tax structures or products or undertake an engagement to provide tax advice to an audited entity where the audit engagement partner has, or ought to have, reasonable doubt as to whether the related accounting treatment involved is based on well established interpretations or is appropriate, having regard to the requirement for the financial statements to give a true and fair view in accordance with the relevant financial reporting framework.**

Where the audit firm promotes tax structures or products or undertakes an engagement to provide tax advice to the audited entity, it may be necessary to adopt an accounting treatment that is not based on well established interpretations or may not be appropriate, in order to achieve the desired result. A self-review threat arises in the course of an audit because the auditor may be unable to form an impartial view of the accounting treatment to be adopted for the purposes of the proposed arrangements. Accordingly, this Standard does not permit the promotion of tax structures or products by audit firms to entities audited by them where, in the view of the audit engagement partner, after such consultation as is appropriate, there is reasonable doubt as to whether the effectiveness of the tax structure or product depends on an accounting treatment that is well established and appropriate.

94

The audit firm shall not undertake an engagement to provide tax services wholly or partly on a contingent fee basis where the outcome of those tax services (and, therefore, the amount of the fee) is dependent on the proposed application of tax law which is uncertain or has not been established.

95

Where tax services, such as advising on corporate structures and structuring transactions to achieve a particular effect, are undertaken on a contingent fee basis, self-interest threats to the auditor's objectivity and independence may arise. The auditor may have, or may appear to have, an interest in the success of the tax services, causing the audit firm to make an audit judgment about which there is reasonable doubt as to its appropriateness. Where the contingent fee is determined by the outcome of the application of tax law which is uncertain or has not been established, the self-interest threat cannot be eliminated or reduced to an acceptable level by the application of any safeguards.

96

The audit firm shall not undertake an engagement to provide tax services to an audited entity where the engagement would involve the audit firm undertaking a management role.

97

When providing tax services to an audited entity, there is a risk that the audit firm undertakes a management role, unless the firm is working with informed management.

98

Where an audited entity is a listed company or a significant affiliate of such an entity, the audit firm shall not undertake an engagement to prepare current or deferred tax calculations that are or may reasonably be expected to be used when preparing accounting entries that are material to the financial statements of the audited entity, save where the circumstances contemplated in paragraph 164 apply.

99

For listed companies or significant affiliates of such entities, the threats to the auditor's objectivity and independence that would be created are too high to allow the audit firm to undertake an engagement to prepare calculations of current or deferred tax liabilities (or assets) for the purpose of preparing accounting entries that are material to the relevant financial statements, together with associated disclosure notes, save where the circumstances contemplated in paragraph 164 apply.

100

Paragraph 99 is not intended to prevent an audit firm preparing tax calculations after the completion of the audit for the purpose of submitting tax returns.

101

For entities other than listed companies or significant affiliates of listed companies, the auditor may undertake an engagement to prepare current or deferred tax calculations for the purpose of preparing accounting entries, provided that:

(a) such services:

102

(i)　do not involve initiating transactions or taking management decisions; and

(ii)　are of a technical, mechanical or an informative nature; and

(b)　appropriate safeguards are applied.

103　The audit firm's policies and procedures will set out whether there are circumstances in which current or deferred tax calculations for the purpose of preparing accounting entries are not prepared for non-listed audited entities as described in paragraph 47 of APB Ethical Standard 1.

104　**The audit firm shall not undertake an engagement to provide tax services to an audited entity where this would involve acting as an advocate for the audited entity, before an appeals tribunal or court[10] in the resolution of an issue:**

(a)　**that is material to the financial statements; or**

(b)　**where the outcome of the tax issue is dependent on a future or contemporary audit judgment.**

105　Where the tax services to be provided by the audit firm include representing the audited entity in any negotiations or proceedings involving the tax authorities, advocacy threats to the auditor's objectivity and independence may arise.

106　The audit firm is not acting as an advocate where the tax services involve the provision of information to the tax authorities (including an explanation of the approach being taken and the arguments being advanced by the audited entity). In such circumstances effective safeguards may exist and the tax authorities will undertake their own review of the issues.

107　Where the tax authorities indicate that they are minded to reject the audited entity's arguments on a particular issue and the matter is likely to be determined by an appeals tribunal or court, the audit firm may become so closely identified with management's arguments that the auditor is inhibited from forming an impartial view of the treatment of the issue in the financial statements. In such circumstances, if the issue is material to the financial statements or is dependent on a future or contemporary audit judgment, the audit firm discusses the matter with the audited entity and makes it clear that it will have to withdraw from that element of the engagement to provide tax services that requires it to act as advocate for the audited entity, or resign from the audit engagement from the time when the matter is formally listed for hearing before the appeals tribunal.

108　The audit firm is not, however, precluded from having a continuing role (for example, responding to specific requests for information) for the audited entity in relation to the appeal. The audit firm assesses the threat associated with any continuing role in accordance with the provisions of paragraphs 109 to 112 of this Standard.

LITIGATION SUPPORT SERVICES

109　Although management and advocacy threats may arise in litigation support services, such as acting as an expert witness, the primary issue is that a self-review threat will arise in all cases where such services involve a subjective estimation of the likely outcome of a matter that is material to the amounts to be included or the disclosures to be made in the financial statements.

---

[10] *The restriction applies to the first level of Tax Court that is independent of the tax authorities and to more authoritative bodies. In the UK this would be the General or Special Commissioners of HM Revenue & Customs or the VAT and Duties Tribunal.*

The audit firm shall not undertake an engagement to provide litigation support services to: 110

(a)   an audited entity that is a listed company or a significant affiliate of such an entity, where this would involve the estimation by the audit firm of the likely outcome of a pending legal matter that could be material to the amounts to be included or the disclosures to be made in the listed company's financial statements, either separately or in aggregate with other estimates and valuations provided; or

(b)   any other audited entity, where this would involve the estimation by the audit firm of the likely outcome of a pending legal matter that could be material to the amounts to be included or the disclosures to be made in the financial statements, either separately or in aggregate with other estimates and valuations provided and there is a significant degree of subjectivity involved.

In the case of non-listed entities, litigation support services that do not involve such subjective estimations are not prohibited, provided that the audit firm has carefully considered the implications of any threats and established appropriate safeguards.   111

The audit firm's policies and procedures will set out whether there are circumstances in which litigation support services are not undertaken for non-listed audited entities as described in paragraph 47 of APB Ethical Standard 1.   112

LEGAL SERVICES

The audit firm shall not undertake an engagement to provide legal services to an audited entity where this would involve acting as the solicitor formally nominated to represent the audited entity in the resolution of a dispute or litigation which is material to the amounts to be included or the disclosures to be made in the financial statements.   113

Although the provision by the auditor of certain types of legal services to its audited entities may create advocacy, self-review and management threats, this Standard does not impose a general prohibition on the provision of legal services. However, in view of the degree of advocacy involved in litigation or other types of dispute resolution procedures and the potential importance of any assessment by the auditor of the merits of the audited entity's position when auditing its financial statements, this Standard prohibits an audit firm from acting as the formally nominated representative for an audited entity in the resolution of a dispute or litigation which is material to the financial statements (either in terms of the amounts recognised or disclosed in the financial statements).   114

RECRUITMENT AND REMUNERATION SERVICES

The audit firm shall not undertake an engagement to provide recruitment services to an audited entity that would involve the firm taking responsibility for the appointment of any director or employee of the audited entity.   115

A management threat arises where audit firm personnel take responsibility for any decision as to who is appointed by the audited entity.   116

For an audited entity that is a listed company, the audit firm shall not undertake an engagement to provide recruitment services in relation to a key management position of the audited entity, or a significant affiliate of such an entity.   117

A familiarity threat arises if the audit firm plays a significant role in relation to the identification and recruitment of senior members of management within the   118 company, as the engagement team may be less likely to be critical of the information or explanations provided by such individuals than might otherwise be the case. Accordingly, for listed companies, and for significant affiliates of such entities, the audit firm does not undertake engagements that involve the recruitment of individuals for key management positions.

119 The audit firm's policies and procedures will set out whether there are circumstances in which recruitment services are not undertaken for non-listed audited entities as described in paragraph 47 of APB Ethical Standard 1.

120 Recruitment services involve a specifically identifiable, and separately remunerated, engagement. Audit firms and engagement teams may contribute to an entity's recruitment process in less formal ways. The prohibition set out in paragraph 117 does not extend to:

- senior members of an audit team interviewing prospective directors or employees of the audited entity and advising on the candidate's technical financial competence; or
- the audit entity using information gathered by the audit firm, including that relating to salary surveys.

121 **The audit firm shall not undertake an engagement to provide advice on the quantum of the remuneration package or the measurement criteria on which the quantum is calculated, for a director or key management position of an audited entity.**

122 The provision of advice on remuneration packages (including bonus arrangements, incentive plans and other benefits) to existing or prospective employees of the audited entity gives rise to familiarity threats. The significance of the familiarity threat is considered too high to allow advice on the overall amounts to be paid or on the quantitative measurement criteria included in remuneration packages for directors and key management positions.

123 For other employees, these threats can be adequately addressed by the application of safeguards, such as the advice being provided by partners and staff who have no involvement in the audit of the financial statements.

124 In cases where all significant judgments concerning the assumptions, methodology and data for the calculation of remuneration packages for directors and key management are made by informed management or a third party and the audit firm's role is limited to applying proven methodologies using the given data, for which the management takes responsibility, it may be possible to establish effective safeguards to protect the auditor's objectivity and independence.

125 Advice on tax, pensions and interpretation of accounting standards relating to remuneration packages for directors and key management can be provided by the audit firm, provided they are not prohibited by the requirements of this Standard relating to tax, actuarial valuations and accounting services. Disclosure of the provision of any such advice would be made to those charged with governance of the audited entity (see APB Ethical Standard 1, paragraphs 63 to 71).

CORPORATE FINANCE SERVICES

126 The range of services encompassed by the term 'corporate finance services' is wide. For example, the audit firm may be engaged:

- to identify possible purchasers for parts of the audited entity's business and provide advisory services in the course of such sales; or
- to identify possible 'targets' for the audited entity to acquire; or
- to advise the audited entity on how to fund its financing requirements; or
- to act as sponsor on admission to listing on the London Stock Exchange, or as Nominated Advisor on the admission of the audited entity on the Alternative Investments Market (AIM); or
- to act as financial adviser to audited entity offerors or offerees in connection with public takeovers.

The potential for the auditor's objectivity and independence to be impaired through **127** the provision of corporate finance services varies considerably depending on the precise nature of the service provided. The main threats to auditor's objectivity and independence arising from the provision of corporate finance services are the self-review, management and advocacy threats. Self-interest threats may also arise, especially in situations where the audit firm is paid on a contingent fee basis.

When providing corporate finance services to an audited entity, there is a risk that **128** the audit firm undertakes a management role, unless the firm is working with informed management. Appropriate safeguards are applied to reduce the self-review threat to an acceptable level.

Examples of safeguards that may be appropriate when corporate finance services are **129** provided to an audited entity include ensuring that:

- the corporate finance advice is provided by partners and staff who have no involvement in the audit of the financial statements;
- any advice provided is reviewed by an independent corporate finance partner within the audit firm;
- external independent advice on the corporate finance work is obtained;
- an audit partner who is not involved in the audit engagement reviews the audit work performed in relation to the subject matter of the corporate finance services provided to ensure that such audit work has been properly and effectively reviewed and assessed in the context of the audit of the financial statements.

Where the audit firm undertakes an engagement to provide corporate finance ser- **130** vices to an audited entity in connection with conducting the sale or purchase of a material part of the audited entity's business, the audit engagement partner informs the audit committee (or equivalent) about the engagement, as set out in paragraphs 63 to 71 of APB Ethical Standard 1.

The audit firm shall not undertake an engagement to provide corporate finance services **131**
in respect of an audited entity where:

(a) **the engagement would involve the audit firm taking responsibility for dealing in, underwriting, or promoting shares; or**
(b) **the audit engagement partner has, or ought to have, reasonable doubt as to whether an accounting treatment that is subject to a contemporary or future audit judgment relating to a material matter in the financial statements of the audited entity, and upon which the success of the related transaction depends:**
  (i) **is based on well established interpretations; or**
  (ii) **is appropriate,**
  having regard to the requirement for the financial statements to give a true and fair view in accordance with the relevant financial reporting framework; or
(c) **the engagement would involve the audit firm undertaking a management role in the audited entity.**

132   An unacceptable advocacy threat arises where, in the course of providing a corporate finance service, the audit firm promotes the interests of the audited entity by taking responsibility for dealing in, underwriting, or promoting shares.

133   Where the audit firm acts as a sponsor under the Listing Rules[11], or as Nominated Adviser on the admission of the audited entity to the AIM, the audit firm is required to confirm that the audited entity has satisfied all applicable conditions for listing and other relevant requirements of the listing (or AIM) rules. Where there is, or there ought to be, reasonable doubt that the audit firm will be able to give that confirmation, it does not enter into such an engagement.

134   A self-review threat arises where the outcome or consequences of the corporate finance service provided by the audit firm may be material to the financial statements of the audited entity, which are, or will be, subject to audit by the same firm. Where the audit firm provides corporate finance services, for example advice to the audited entity on financing arrangements, it may be necessary to adopt an accounting treatment that is not based on well established interpretations or which may not be appropriate, in order to achieve the desired result. A self-review threat is created because the auditor may be unable to form an impartial view of the accounting treatment to be adopted for the purposes of the proposed arrangements. Accordingly, this Standard does not permit the provision of such services by audit firms in respect of entities audited by them where there is or ought to be reasonable doubt as to whether an accounting treatment that is subject to a contemporary or future audit judgment relating to a material matter in the financial statements of the audited entity and on which the success of a transaction depends is well established and appropriate.

135   Advice to audited entities on funding issues and banking arrangements, where there is no reasonable doubt as to the appropriateness of the accounting treatment, is not prohibited provided this does not involve the audit firm in taking decisions or making judgments which are properly the responsibility of management.

136   These restrictions do not apply in circumstances where the auditor is designated by legislation or regulation as being required to carry out a particular service. In such circumstances, the audit engagement partner establishes appropriate safeguards.

TRANSACTION RELATED SERVICES

137   In addition to corporate finance services, there are other non-audit services associated with transactions that an audit firm may undertake for an audited entity. For example:

- investigations into possible acquisitions or disposals ('due diligence' investigations); or
- investigations into the tax affairs of possible acquisitions or disposals; or
- the provision of information to management or sponsors in relation to prospectuses and other investment circulars (for example, long form reports, comfort letters on the adequacy of working capital); or
- agreed upon procedures or reports provided to management in relation to particular transactions (for example, securitisations).

[11] *In the United Kingdom, the UK Listing Authority's publication the 'Listing Rules'. In the Republic of Ireland, the United Kingdom 'Listing Rules' as modified by the 'Notes on the Listing Rules' published by the Irish Stock Exchange.*

When providing transaction related services to an audited entity, there is a risk that the audit firm may face a management threat, unless the firm is working with informed management. Appropriate safeguards are applied to reduce the self-review threat to an acceptable level.   **138**

Examples of safeguards that may be appropriate when transaction related services are provided to an audited entity include ensuring that: **139**

* the transaction related advice is provided by partners and staff who have no involvement in the audit of the financial statements;
* any advice provided is reviewed by an independent transactions partner within the audit firm;
* external independent advice on the transaction related work is obtained;
* an audit partner who is not involved in the audit engagement reviews the audit work performed in relation to the subject matter of the transaction related service provided to ensure that such audit work has been properly and effectively reviewed and assessed in the context of the audit of the financial statements.

The audit firm shall not undertake an engagement to provide transaction related services in respect of an audited entity where: **140**

(a) the audit engagement partner has, or ought to have, reasonable doubt as to whether an accounting treatment that is subject to a contemporary or future audit judgment relating to a material matter in the financial statements of the audited entity, and upon which the success of the related transaction depends;
  (i)   is based on well established interpretations; or
  (ii) is appropriate,
  having regard to the requirement for the financial statements to give a true and fair view in accordance with the relevant financial reporting framework; or
(b) the engagement would involve the audit firm undertaking a management role in the audited entity.

A self-review threat arises where the outcome of the transaction related services undertaken by the audit firm may be material to the financial statements of the audited entity which are, or will be, subject to audit by the same firm. Where the audited entity proposes to undertake a transaction, it may be necessary to adopt an accounting treatment that is not based on well established interpretations or may not be appropriate, in order to achieve the desired result of the transaction (for example, to take assets off the balance sheet). A self-review threat is created if the auditor undertakes transaction related services in connection with such a transaction. Accordingly, this Standard does not permit the provision of services by audit firms in respect of entities audited by them where there is or ought to be reasonable doubt as to whether an accounting treatment, that is subject to a contemporary or future audit judgment relating to a material matter in the financial statements of the audited entity and on which the success of a related transaction depends, is well established and appropriate.   **141**

These restrictions do not apply in circumstances where the auditor is designated by legislation or regulation as being required to carry out a particular service. In such circumstances, the audit engagement partner establishes appropriate safeguards.   **142**

RESTRUCTURING SERVICES

Restructuring services are any non-audit services provided to an audited entity in connection with the entity's development or implementation of a transaction or   **143** package of transactions (a 'restructuring plan') designed to change its equity or debt financing structure, its corporate structure, or its operating structure. There are a variety of possible purposes for developing a restructuring plan, for example to address financial or operating difficulties, to support tax planning, to improve operating efficiency, or to improve the cost of capital. The range of non-audit services that may be regarded as 'Restructuring Services' is extensive, and the nature of those services may encompass many of the other types of non-audit services discussed in this Ethical Standard. Where applicable, the related requirements and guidance covered elsewhere in this standard apply to Restructuring Services.

144   The services that an entity may engage an audit firm to provide may vary considerably and may range from the incidental and routine to advice that is fundamental to the efficacy of the restructuring plan. Consequently, where such services are provided by the entity's auditor, the audit engagement partner evaluates:

- the threats that the services may present to the audit firm's ability to conduct any contemporary or future audit with objectivity and independence; and
- the likelihood that a reasonable and informed third party would conclude that the auditor's objectivity and independence would be compromised.

145   **The audit firm shall not undertake an engagement to provide restructuring services in respect of an audited entity where:**

   (a)   the engagement would involve the audit firm undertaking a management role in or on behalf of the audited entity; or

   (b)   the engagement would require the audit firm to act as an advocate for the audited entity in relation to matters that are material to the financial statements.

146   The potential for the auditor's objectivity and independence to be impaired through the provision of restructuring services varies depending on the nature of the service provided. Two of the main threats to auditor objectivity and independence arising from the provision of restructuring services arise where the auditor undertakes a management or advocacy role:

- An audit firm undertakes a management role if the entity does not have informed management capable of taking responsibility for the decisions to be made.
- To avoid undertaking an advocacy role on behalf of the audited entity, the audit firm takes particular care not to assume (or seen to be assuming) responsibility for the entity's proposals or being regarded as negotiating on behalf of the entity or advocating the appropriateness of the proposals such that its independence is compromised. This is particularly important when the auditor attends meetings with the entity's bank or other interested parties.

If the audit firm undertakes a management role or acts as advocate for the audited entity, the threats to that auditor's objectivity and independence are such that no safeguards can reduce the threat to an acceptable level[12].

147   **The audit firm shall not undertake an engagement to provide restructuring services in respect of an audited entity where that engagement may give rise to a self review threat in the course of a contemporary or future audit unless it is satisfied that such threats can be reduced to an acceptable level by appropriate safeguards and that such safeguards have been put in place.**

---

[12] *'ES – Provisions Available for Small Entities (Revised)' provides exemptions relating to informed management and the advocacy threat for auditors of small entities.*

The provision of restructuring services gives rise to a self review threat where the **148** restructuring services to be provided involve advice or judgments which are likely to be material to a contemporary or future audit judgment.

Examples of restructuring services that the audit firm may be requested to undertake **149** and which may give rise to a self review threat include:

- Providing preliminary general advice on the options and choices available to management or stakeholders of an entity facing urgent financial or other difficulties.
- Undertaking a review of the business of the entity with a view to advising the audited entity on liquidity management or operational restructuring options.
- Advising on the development of forecasts or projections, for presentation to lenders and other stakeholders, including assumptions.
- Advising the audited entity on how to fund its financing requirements, including equity and debt restructuring programmes.
- Participating in the design or implementation of an overall restructuring plan including, for example, participating in the preparation of cash flow and other forecasts and financial models underpinning the overall restructuring plan.

The self review threat arising from the provision of such services is particularly **150** significant where it has potential to impact the auditor's assessment of whether it is appropriate to prepare the entity's financial statements on a going concern basis. Where the audit firm has been involved in aspects of the preparation of a cash flow, a forecast or a financial model, it is probable that a reasonable and informed third party would conclude that the auditor would have a significant self-review threat in considering the going concern assumption.

The self review threat arising from the provision of such services is also particularly **151** significant where the restructuring services are provided in respect of an audited entity and involve developing or implementing a restructuring plan to address the actual or anticipated financial or operational difficulties that threaten the survival of that entity as a going concern (an 'audited entity in distress').

The audit firm puts in place those safeguards that it regards as appropriate to reduce **152** the threats to its objectivity and independence to an acceptable level. If the audit firm concludes that the threats arising from some or all of the restructuring services involved cannot be addressed by putting appropriate safeguards in place, it declines the engagement, or those parts of the engagement affected by those threats that cannot be addressed.

Where an audited entity in distress is a listed company or a significant affiliate of a **153** **listed audited entity, the restructuring services provided by the audit firm shall be limited to providing:**

(a) **preliminary general advice to an entity in distress;**
(b) **assistance with the implementation of elements of an overall restructuring plan, such as the sale of a non-significant component business, provided those elements are not material to the overall restructuring plan;**
(c) **challenging, but in no circumstances developing, the projections and assumptions within a financial model that has been produced by the audited entity;**
(d) **reporting on a restructuring plan, or aspects of it, in connection with the proposed issue of an investment circular; and**
(e) **where specifically permitted by a regulatory body with oversight of the audited entity.**

154   Except to the extent identified in paragraph 153, the significance of the self-review threat is too high to permit the provision of other restructuring services to an audited entity in distress that is a listed company or a significant affiliate of a listed audited entity because there are no safeguards that would be sufficient to reduce the resultant threats to an acceptable level.

155   The audit firm's policies and procedures will set out whether there are circumstances in which restructuring services are not undertaken for non-listed audited entities in distress as described in paragraph 47 of APB Ethical Standard 1.

ACCOUNTING SERVICES

156   In this Standard, the term 'accounting services' is defined as the provision of services that involve the maintenance of accounting records or the preparation of financial statements that are then subject to audit. Advice on the implementation of current and proposed accounting standards is not included in the term 'accounting services'.

157   The range of activities encompassed by the term 'accounting services' is wide. In some cases, the audited entity may ask the audit firm to provide a complete service including maintaining all of the accounting records and the preparation of the financial statements. Other common situations are:

- the audit firm may take over the provision of a specific accounting function on an outsourced basis (for example, payroll);
- the audited entity maintains the accounting records, undertakes basic book-keeping and prepares a year-end trial balance and asks the audit firm to assist with the preparation of the necessary adjustments and the financial statements.

158   The provision of accounting services by the audit firm to the audited entity creates threats to the auditor's objectivity and independence, principally self-review and management threats, the significance of which depends on the nature and extent of the accounting services in question and upon the level of public interest in the audited entity.

159   When providing accounting services to an audited entity, unless the firm is working with informed management, there is a risk that the audit firm undertakes a management role.

160   **The audit firm shall not undertake an engagement to provide accounting services to:**

(a)   **an audited entity that is a listed company or a significant affiliate of such an entity, save where the circumstances contemplated in paragraph 164 apply; or**

(b)   **any other audited entity, where those accounting services would involve the audit firm undertaking part of the role of management.**

161   Even where there is no engagement to provide any accounting services, it is usual for the auditor to provide the management with accounting advice on matters that have come to the auditor's attention during the course of the audit. Such matters might typically include:

- comments on weaknesses in the accounting records and suggestions for addressing them;
- errors identified in the accounting records and in the financial statements and suggestions for correcting them;
- advice on the accounting policies in use and on the application of current and proposed accounting standards.

This advice is a by-product of the audit service rather than the result of any engagement to provide non-audit services. Consequently, as it is part of the audit service, such advice is not regarded as giving rise to any threat to the auditor's objectivity and independence.

For listed companies or significant affiliates of such entities, the threats to the auditor's objectivity and independence that would be created are too high to allow the audit firm to undertake an engagement to provide any accounting services, save where the circumstances contemplated in paragraph 164 apply. **162**

The audit firm's policies and procedures will set out whether there are circumstances in which accounting services are not undertaken for non-listed audited entities as described in paragraph 47 of APB Ethical Standard 1. **163**

In emergency situations, the audit firm may provide a listed audited entity, or a significant affiliate of such a company, with accounting services to assist the company in the timely preparation of its financial statements. This might arise when, due to external and unforeseeable events, the audit firm personnel are the only people with the necessary knowledge of the audited entity's systems and procedures. A situation could be considered an emergency where the audit firm's refusal to provide these services would result in a severe burden for the audited entity (for example, withdrawal of credit lines), or would even threaten its going concern status. In such circumstances, the audit firm ensures that: **164**

(a) any staff involved in the accounting services have no involvement in the audit of the financial statements; and
(b) the engagement would not lead to any audit firm staff or partners taking decisions or making judgments which are properly the responsibility of management.

For entities other than listed companies or significant affiliates of listed companies, the auditor may undertake an engagement to provide accounting services, provided that: **165**

(a) such services:
   (i) do not involve initiating transactions or taking management decisions; and
   (ii) are of a technical, mechanical or an informative nature; and
(b) appropriate safeguards are applied to reduce the self-review threat to an acceptable level.

The maintenance of the accounting records and the preparation of the financial statements are the responsibility of the management of the audited entity. Accordingly, in any engagement to provide the audited entity with accounting services, the audit firm does not initiate any transactions or take any decisions or make any judgments, which are properly the responsibility of the management. These include: **166**

* authorising or approving transactions;
* preparing originating data (including valuation assumptions);
* determining or changing journal entries, or the classifications for accounts or transactions, or other accounting records without management approval.

Examples of accounting services of a technical or mechanical nature or of an informative nature include: **167**

* recording transactions for which management has determined the appropriate account classification, posting coded transactions to the general ledger, posting entries approved by management to the trial balance or providing certain data-processing services (for example, payroll);

- assistance with the preparation of the financial statements where management takes all decisions on issues requiring the exercise of judgment and has prepared the underlying accounting records.

168 Examples of safeguards that may be appropriate when accounting services are provided to an audited entity include:

- accounting services provided by the audit firm are performed by partners and staff who have no involvement in the external audit of the financial statements;
- the accounting services are reviewed by a partner or other senior staff member with appropriate expertise who is not a member of the audit team;
- the audit of the financial statements is reviewed by an audit partner who is not involved in the audit engagement to ensure that the accounting services performed have been properly and effectively assessed in the context of the audit of the financial statements.

Effective date

169 This revised Ethical Standard becomes effective on 30 April 2011.

170 Firms may complete audit engagements relating to periods commencing on or before 31 December 2010 in accordance with existing ethical standards, putting in place any necessary changes in the subsequent engagement period.

171 Where compliance with the requirements of ES 5 would result in a service not being supplied, services contracted before 31 December 2010 may continue to be provided until the earlier of either:

(a) the completion of the specific task or the end of the contract term, where this is set out in the contract; or

(b) 31 December 2011 (or, in the case of services prohibited under paragraph 95, 31 December 2014) as long as the following apply:

- the engagement was permitted by existing ethical standards (including transitional provisions);
- any safeguards required by existing ethical standards continue to be applied; and
- the need for additional safeguards is assessed, including where possible any additional safeguards specified by ES 5, and if considered necessary, those additional safeguards are applied.

172 In the first year of appointment as auditor to an audited entity, an audit firm may continue to provide non-audit services which are already contracted at the date of appointment, until the earlier of either:

(i) the completion of the specific task or the end of the contract term, where this is set out in the contract; or

(ii) one year after the date of appointment, where a task or term is not defined,

provided that the need for additional safeguards is assessed and if considered necessary, those additional safeguards are applied.

APB Ethical Standard
Provisions available for small entities (Revised)

(Revised December 2010)

Contents

Preface

APB Ethical Standards apply in the audit of financial statements. They are read in the context of the Auditing Practices Board's Statement "The Auditing Practices Board – Scope and Authority of Pronouncements (Revised)" which sets out the application and authority of APB Ethical Standards.

The terms used in APB Ethical Standards are explained in the Glossary.

Introduction

1   The APB issues Ethical Standards which set out the standards that auditors are required to comply with in order to discharge their responsibilities in respect of their integrity, objectivity and independence. The Ethical Standards 1 to 5 address such matters as:

- How audit firms set policies and procedures to ensure that, in relation to each audit, the audit firm and all those who are in a position to influence the conduct and outcome of an audit act with integrity, objectivity and independence;
- Financial, business, employment and personal relationships;
- Long association with the audit engagement;
- Fees, remuneration and evaluation policies, litigation, gifts and hospitality;
- Non-audit services provided to audited entities.

These Ethical Standards apply to all audit firms and to all audits and must be read in order to understand the alternative provisions and exemptions contained in this Standard.

2   The APB is aware that a limited number of the requirements in Ethical Standards 1 to 5 are difficult for certain audit firms to comply with, particularly when auditing a small entity. Whilst the APB is clear that those standards are appropriate in the interests of establishing the integrity, objectivity and independence of auditors, it accepts that certain dispensations, as set out in this Standard, are appropriate to facilitate the cost effective audit of the financial statements of Small Entities (as defined below).

3   This Standard provides alternative provisions for auditors of Small Entities to apply in respect of the threats arising from economic dependence and where tax or accounting services are provided and allows the option of taking advantage of exemptions from certain of the requirements in APB Ethical Standards 1 to 5 for a Small Entity audit engagement. Where an audit firm takes advantage of the exemptions within this Standard, it is required to:

(a) take the steps described in this Standard; and

(b) disclose in the audit report the fact that the firm has applied APB Ethical Standard – Provisions Available for Small Entities.

4   (i)   In this Standard, for the UK a 'Small Entity' is:

     (a) any company, which is not a UK listed company or an affiliate thereof, that qualifies as a small company under Section 382 of the Companies Act 2006;

     (b) where group accounts are produced, any group that qualifies as small under Section 383 of the Companies Act 2006;

     (c) any charity with an income of less than the turnover threshold applicable to small companies as identified in Section 382 of the Companies Act 2006;

(d) any pension fund with less than 100 members (including active, deferred and pensioner members)[1];

(e) any firm regulated by the FSA, which is not required to appoint an auditor in accordance with chapter 3 of the FSA Supervision Manual which forms a part of the FSA Handbook[2];

(f) any credit union which is a mutually owned financial co-operative established under the Credit Unions Act 1979 and the Industrial and Provident Societies Act 1965 (or equivalent legislation), which meets the criteria set out in (a) above;

(g) any entity registered under the Industrial and Provident Societies Act 1965, incorporated under the Friendly Societies Act 1992 or registered under the Friendly Societies Act 1974 (or equivalent legislation), which meets the criteria set out in (a) above;

(h) any registered social landlord with less than 250 units; and

(i) any other entity, such as a club, which would be a Small Entity if it were a company.

(ii) In this Standard, for the Republic of Ireland a 'Small Entity' is:

(a) any company, which is not an Irish listed company or an affiliate thereof, that meets two or more of the following requirements in both the current financial year and the preceding financial year:
   - not more than €7.3 million turnover;
   - not more than €3.65 million balance sheet total;
   - not more than 50 employees.

(b) any charity with an income of less than €7.3 million;

(c) any pension fund with less than 1,000 members (including active, deferred and pensioner members)[3]; and

(d) any other entity, such as a club or credit union, which would be a Small Entity if it were a company.

Where an entity falls into more than one of the above categories, it is only regarded as a 'Small Entity' if it meets the criteria of all relevant categories.

Alternative provisions

ECONOMIC DEPENDENCE

When auditing the financial statements of a Small Entity an audit firm is not required to comply with the requirement in APB Ethical Standard 4, paragraph 39 that an external independent quality control review is performed.   5

APB Ethical Standard 4, paragraph 39 provides that, where it is expected that the total fees for both audit and non-audit services receivable from a non-listed audited entity and its subsidiaries audited by the audit firm will regularly exceed 10% of the annual fee income of the audit firm or the part of the firm by reference to which the audit engagement partner's profit share is calculated, but will not regularly exceed 15% the firm shall arrange an external independent quality control review of the   6

---

[1] *In cases where a scheme with more than 100 members has been in wind-up over a number of years, such a scheme does not qualify as a Small Entity, even where the remaining number of members falls below 100.*

[2] *This relates to those firms that are not required to appoint an auditor under rule SUP 3.3.2R of the FSA Supervision Manual.*

[3] *In cases where a scheme with more than 1,000 members has been in wind-up over a number of years, such a scheme does not qualify as a Small Entity, even where the remaining number of members falls below 1,000.*

audit engagement to be undertaken before the auditors' report is finalised. Although an external independent quality control review is not required, nevertheless the audit engagement partner discloses the expectation that fees will amount to between 10% and 15% of the firm's annual fee income to the Ethics Partner and to those charged with governance of the audited entity.

SELF-REVIEW THREAT – NON-AUDIT SERVICES

7   **When undertaking non-audit services for a Small Entity audited entity, the audit firm is not required to apply safeguards to address a self-review threat provided:**

   (a) **the audited entity has 'informed management'; and**
   (b) **the audit firm extends the cyclical inspection of completed engagements that is performed for quality control purposes.**

8   APB Ethical Standard 5 requires that, when an audit firm provides non-audit services to an audited entity, appropriate safeguards are applied in order to reduce any self-review threat to an acceptable level. APB Ethical Standard 5 provides examples of safeguards that may be appropriate when non-audit services are provided to an audited entity (for example in paragraphs 92 for tax services and 168 for accounting services). In the case of an audit of a Small Entity, alternative procedures involve discussions with 'informed management', supplemented by an extension of the firm's cyclical inspection of completed engagements that is performed for quality control purposes.

9   The audit firm extends the number of engagements inspected under the requirements of ISQC (UK and Ireland) 1 *'Quality Control for Firms that Perform Audits and Reviews of Financial Statements, and other Assurance and Related Services Engagements'*[4] to include a random selection of audit engagements where non-audit services have been provided. Particular attention is given to ensuring that there is documentary evidence that 'informed management' has made such judgments and decisions that are needed in relation to the presentation and disclosure of information in the financial statements.

10   Those inspecting the engagements are not involved in performing the engagement. Small audit firms may wish to use a suitably qualified external person or another firm to carry out engagement inspections.

11   In addition to the documentation requirements of ISQC (UK and Ireland) 1, those inspecting the engagements document their evaluation of whether the documentary evidence that 'informed management' made such judgments and decisions that were needed in relation to the presentation and disclosure of information in the financial statements.

Exemptions

MANAGEMENT THREAT – NON-AUDIT SERVICES

12   **When undertaking non-audit services for Small Entity audited entities, the audit firm is not required to adhere to the prohibitions in APB Ethical Standard 5, relating to**

---

[4] *ISQC (UK and Ireland) 1 requires audit firms to establish policies and procedures which include a periodic inspection of a selection of completed engagements. Engagements selected for inspection include at least one engagement for each engagement partner over the inspection cycle, which ordinarily spans no more than three years.*

providing non-audit services that involve the audit firm undertaking part of the role of management, provided that:

(a) it discusses objectivity and independence issues related to the provision of non-audit services with those charged with governance, confirming that management accept responsibility for any decisions taken; and
(b) it discloses the fact that it has applied this Standard in accordance with paragraph 24.

APB Ethical Standard 5, paragraph 38 provides that where an audit firm provides non-audit services to an audited entity where there is no 'informed management', it is unlikely that any other safeguards can eliminate a management threat or reduce it to an acceptable level with the consequence that such non-audit services may not be provided to that audited entity. This is because the absence of a member of management, who has the authority and capability to: **13**

• receive the results of the non-audit services provided by the audit firm; and
• make any judgments and decisions that are needed, on the basis of the information provided,

means that there is an increased management threat since the audit firm will be closer to those decisions and judgments which are properly the responsibility of management and more aligned with the views and interests of management.

An audit firm auditing a Small Entity is exempted from the requirements of APB Ethical Standard 5, paragraphs 63(b) (internal audit services), 73(b) (information technology services), 97 (tax services), 131(c) (corporate finance services), 140(b) (transaction related services), 145(a) (restructuring services) and 160(b) (accounting services) in circumstances when there is no 'informed management' as envisioned by APB Ethical Standard 5, provided it discusses objectivity and independence issues related to the provision of non-audit services with those charged with governance, confirming that management accept responsibility for any decisions taken and discloses the fact that it has applied this Standard in accordance with paragraph 24.   **14**

ADVOCACY THREAT – NON-AUDIT SERVICES

The audit firm of a Small Entity is not required to comply with APB Ethical Standard 5, paragraphs 104 and 145(b) provided that it discloses the fact that it has applied this Standard in accordance with paragraph 24.   **15**

APB Ethical Standard 5, paragraph 104 provides that 'the audit firm shall not undertake an engagement to provide tax services to an audited entity where this would involve acting as an advocate for the audited entity, before an appeals tribunal or court in the resolution of an issue: **16**

(a) that is material to the financial statements; or
(b) where the outcome of the tax issue is dependent on a future or contemporary audit judgment'.

Such circumstances may create an advocacy threat which it is unlikely any safeguards can eliminate or reduce to an acceptable level.

APB Ethical Standard 5, paragraph 145(b) provides that 'the audit firm shall not undertake an engagement to provide restructuring services in respect of an audited entity where the engagement would require the auditor to act as an advocate for the entity in relation to matters that are material to the financial statements'.   **17**

18   Such circumstances may create an advocacy threat which it is unlikely any safeguards can eliminate or reduce to an acceptable level.

19   Where an audit firm auditing a Small Entity takes advantage of the dispensation in paragraph 15, it discloses the fact that it has applied this Standard in accordance with paragraph 24.

PARTNERS JOINING AN AUDITED ENTITY

20   **The audit firm of a Small Entity is not required to comply with APB Ethical Standard 2, paragraph 49 provided that:**

(a)   **it takes appropriate steps to determine that there has been no significant threat to the audit team's integrity, objectivity and independence; and**

(b)   **it discloses the fact that it has applied this Standard in accordance with paragraph 24.**

21   APB Ethical Standard 2, paragraph 49 provides that where a former partner 'is appointed as a director (including as a non-executive director) or to a key management position with an audited entity, having acted as audit engagement partner (or as an engagement quality control reviewer, key partner involved in the audit or a partner in the chain of command) at any time in the two years prior to this appointment, the firm shall resign as auditors. The firm shall not accept re-appointment until a two-year period, commencing when the former partner ceased to have an ability to influence the conduct and outcome of the audit, has elapsed or the former partner ceases employment with the former audited entity, whichever is the sooner'. Such circumstances may create self-interest, familiarity and intimidation threats.

22   An audit firm takes appropriate steps to determine that there has been no significant threat to the audit team's integrity, objectivity and independence as a result of the former partner's employment by an audited entity that is a Small Entity by:

(a)   assessing the significance of the self-interest, familiarity or intimidation threats, having regard to the following factors:

- the position the individual has taken at the audited entity;
- the nature and amount of any involvement the individual will have with the audit team or the audit process;
- the length of time that has passed since the individual was a member of the audit team or firm; and
- the former position of the individual within the audit team or firm, and

(b)   if the threat is other than clearly insignificant, applying alternative procedures such as:

- considering the appropriateness or necessity of modifying the audit plan for the audit engagement;
- assigning an audit team to the subsequent audit engagement that is of sufficient experience in relation to the individual who has joined the audited entity;
- involving an audit partner or senior staff member with appropriate expertise, who was not a member of the audit team, to review the work done or otherwise advise as necessary; or
- undertaking an engagement quality control review of the audit engagement.

23   When an audit firm auditing a Small Entity takes advantage of paragraph 20 it discloses the fact that it has applied this Standard in accordance with paragraph 24 and documents the steps that it has taken to comply with this Standard.

Disclosure requirements

Where the audit firm has taken advantage of an exemption provided in paragraphs 12, 24
15 or 20 of this Standard, the audit engagement partner shall ensure that:

(a) the auditor's report discloses this fact, and

(b) either the financial statements, or the auditor's report, discloses the type of non-audit services provided to the audited entity or the fact that a former audit engagement partner has joined the audited entity.

The fact that an audit firm has taken advantage of an exemption from APB Ethical 25
Standard – Provisions Available for Small Entities is set out in the auditor's report as part of the auditor's responsibilities paragraph. It does not affect the Opinion paragraph. An illustrative example of such disclosure is set out in the Appendix.

The audit engagement partner ensures that within the financial statements reference 26
is made to the type of non-audit services provided to the audited entity or the fact that a former partner has joined the audited entity. An illustration of possible disclosures is set out in the Appendix. Where such a disclosure is not made within the financial statements it is included in the auditor's report.

Effective date

This revised Ethical Standard becomes effective on 30 April 2011.
27

Appendix: Illustrative disclosures

(a) Illustrative disclosure of the fact that the audit firm has taken advantage of an exemption within the auditor's report

Respective responsibilities of directors and auditor

As explained more fully in the Directors' Responsibilities Statement [set out [on page ...]], the directors are responsible for the preparation of the financial statements and for being satisfied that they give a true and fair view. Our responsibility is to audit and express an opinion on the financial statements in accordance with applicable law and International Standards on Auditing (UK and Ireland). Those standards require us to comply with the Auditing Practices Board's (APB's) Ethical Standards for Auditors, including "APB Ethical Standard – Provisions Available for Small Entities (Revised)", in the circumstances set out in note [x] to the financial statements.

Scope of the audit of the financial statements

Either:

> A description of the scope of an audit of financial statements is [provided on the APB's website at ...] / [set out [on page ...] of the Annual Report].

Or:

> An audit involves obtaining evidence about the amounts and disclosures in the financial statements ...

Opinion on financial statements

In our opinion the financial statements:

- give a true and fair view of the state of the company's affairs as at ...and of its profit [loss] for the year then ended; ...

[Date of the auditor's report, *auditor's signature and* address]

(b) Illustrative disclosure of relevant circumstances within the financial statements

Note [x]   In common with many other businesses of our size and nature we use our auditors to prepare and submit returns to the tax authorities and assist with the preparation of the financial statements[5].

Note [x]   In common with many other businesses of our size and nature we use our auditors to provide tax advice and to represent us, as necessary, at tax tribunals[6].

---

[5] *Where exemption in paragraph 12 (Management threat in relation non-audit services) is applied.*

[6] *Where exemption in paragraph 15 (Advocacy threat – tax services) is applied.*

Note [x]   XYZ, a former partner of [audit firm] joined [audited entity] as [a director] on [date][7].

Glossary of Terms

Glossary of terms[1]

This Glossary defines terms used in the ISAs (UK and Ireland), the ISQC (UK and Ireland) and APB Ethical Standards for Auditors. It is based on the IAASB glossary of terms, with supplemental definitions used in the APB standards shown in grey highlighted text.

Separate glossaries are used in connection with the SIRs and the Ethical Standard for Reporting Accountants. These are included in SIR 1000 at Appendix 4 and in the ESRA at Appendix 1.

Access controls—Procedures designed to restrict access to on-line terminal devices, programs and data. Access controls consist of "user authentication" and "user authorization". "User authentication" typically attempts to identify a user through unique logon identifications, passwords, access cards or biometric data. "User authorization" consists of access rules to determine the computer resources each user may access. Specifically, such procedures are designed to prevent or detect:

(a) Unauthorized access to on-line terminal devices, programs and data;
(b) Entry of unauthorized transactions;
(c) Unauthorized changes to data files;
(d) The use of computer programs by unauthorized personnel; and
(e) The use of computer programs that have not been authorized.

Accounting estimate—An approximation of a monetary amount in the absence of a precise means of measurement. This term is used for an amount measured at fair value where there is estimation uncertainty, as well as for other amounts that require estimation. Where ISA (UK and Ireland) 540[2] addresses only accounting estimates involving measurement at fair value, the term "fair value accounting estimates" is used.

Accounting records—The records of initial accounting entries and supporting records, such as checks and records of electronic fund transfers; invoices; contracts; the general and subsidiary ledgers, journal entries and other adjustments to the financial statements that are not reflected in formal journal entries; and records such as work sheets and spreadsheets supporting cost allocations, computations, reconciliations and disclosures.

Accounting services—The provision of services that involve the maintenance of accounting records or the preparation of financial statements that are then subject to audit.

---

[1] *In the case of public sector engagements, the terms in this glossary should be read as referring to their public sector equivalents.*
Where accounting terms have not been defined in the pronouncements of the International Auditing and Assurance Standards Board, reference should be made to the Glossary of Terms published by the International Accounting Standards Board.

[2] *ISA (UK and Ireland) 540, "Auditing Accounting Estimates, Including Fair Value Accounting Estimates, and Related Disclosures".*

Affiliate—An entity that has any of the following relationships with the audited entity:

(a) An entity that has direct or indirect control over the audited entity if the audited entity is material, quantitatively or qualitatively, to such entity;

(b) An entity with a direct financial interest in the audited entity if that entity has significant influence over the audited entity and the interest in the audited entity is material, quantitatively or qualitatively, to such entity;

(c) An entity over which the audited entity has direct or indirect control;

(d) An entity in which the audited entity, or an affiliate of the audited entity under (c) above, has a direct financial interest that gives it significant influence over such entity and the interest is material, quantitatively or qualitatively, to the audited entity and its affiliate in (c); and

(e) An entity which is under common control with the audited entity client (a "sister entity") if the sister entity and the audited entity are both material, quantitatively or qualitatively, to the entity that controls both the audited entity and sister entity.

Factors that may be relevant in determining whether an entity or an interest in an entity is material to another entity include:

- the extent and nature of the relationships between the audited entity and the other entity and the impact these have on the relationships of either entity with the auditor of the audited entity, and

- the extent and nature of the relationship(s) between the auditor of the audited entity and the other entity and the impact that this has on their independence as auditor of the audited entity.

Agreed-upon procedures engagement—An engagement in which an auditor is engaged to carry out those procedures of an audit nature to which the auditor and the entity and any appropriate third parties have agreed and to report on factual findings. The recipients of the report form their own conclusions from the report by the auditor. The report is restricted to those parties that have agreed to the procedures to be performed since others, unaware of the reasons for the procedures may misinterpret the results.

Analytical procedures—Evaluations of financial information through analysis of plausible relationships among both financial and non-financial data. Analytical procedures also encompass such investigation as is necessary of identified fluctuations or relationships that are inconsistent with other relevant information or that differ from expected values by a significant amount.

Annual report—A document issued by an entity, ordinarily on an annual basis, which includes its financial statements together with the auditor's report thereon.

Anomaly—A misstatement or deviation that is demonstrably not representative of misstatements or deviations in a population.

Applicable financial reporting framework—The financial reporting framework adopted by management and, where appropriate, those charged with governance in the preparation of the financial statements that is acceptable in view of the nature of the entity and the objective of the financial statements, or that is required by law or regulation.

The term "fair presentation framework" is used to refer to a financial reporting framework that requires compliance with the requirements of the framework and:

(a) Acknowledges explicitly or implicitly that, to achieve fair presentation of the financial statements, it may be necessary for management to provide disclosures beyond those specifically required by the framework; or

(b) Acknowledges explicitly that it may be necessary for management to depart from a requirement of the framework to achieve fair presentation of the financial statements. Such departures are expected to be necessary only in extremely rare circumstances.

The term "compliance framework" is used to refer to a financial reporting framework that requires compliance with the requirements in (a) or requirements of the framework, but does not acknowledge above.

Application controls in information technology— Manual or automated procedures that typically operate at a business process level. Application controls can be preventative or detective in nature and are designed to ensure the integrity of the accounting records. Accordingly, application controls relate to procedures used to initiate, record, process and report transactions or other financial data.

Appropriateness (of audit evidence)—The measure of the quality of audit evidence; that is, its relevance and its reliability in providing support for the conclusions on which the auditor's opinion is based.

Arm's length transaction—A transaction conducted on such terms and conditions as between a willing buyer and a willing seller who are unrelated and are acting independently of each other and pursuing their own best interests.

Assertions—Representations by management, explicit or otherwise, that are embodied in the financial statements, as used by the auditor to consider the different types of potential misstatements that may occur.

Assess—Analyze identified risks of to conclude on their significance. "Assess", by convention, is used only in relation to risk. (also see *Evaluate*)

Association—(see *Auditor association with financial information*)

Assurance—(see *Reasonable assurance*)

Assurance engagement—An engagement in which a practitioner expresses a conclusion designed to enhance the degree of confidence of the intended users other than the responsible party about the outcome of the evaluation or measurement of a subject matter against criteria. The outcome of the evaluation or measurement of a subject matter is the information that results from applying the criteria (also see *Subject matter information*). Under the "International Framework for Assurance Engagements" there are two types of assurance engagement a practitioner is permitted to perform: a reasonable assurance engagement and a limited assurance engagement.

Reasonable assurance engagement—The objective of a reasonable assurance engagement is a reduction in assurance engagement risk to an acceptably low level in the circumstances of the engagement[3] as the basis for a positive form of expression of the practitioner's conclusion.

Limited assurance engagement—The objective of a limited assurance engagement is a reduction in assurance engagement risk to a level that is accept___ in the circumstances of the engagement, but where that risk is gre___ than for a reasonable assurance engagement, as the basis for a negati___ ___ of expression of the practitioner's conclusion.

Assurance engagement risk—The risk that th___ ___ ___oner expresses an inappropriate conclusion when the subject matter inf___ is materially misstated.

___ of audit procedures performed, relevant audit

Audit documentation—The ___sions the auditor reached (terms such as "working evidence obtained, and ___ are also sometimes used). papers" or "w___pa___

Audit evidence—Information used by the auditor in arriving at the conclusions on which the auditor's opinion is based. Audit evidence includes both information contained in the accounting records underlying the financial statements and other information. (See *Sufficiency of audit evidence* and *Appropriateness of audit evidence*.)

Audit file—One or more folders or other storage media, in physical or electronic form, containing the records that comprise the audit documentation for a specific engagement.

Audit firm—(see *Firm*)

Audit opinion—(see *Modified opinion* and *Unmodified opinion*)

Audit risk—The risk that the auditor expresses an inappropriate audit opinion when the financial statements are materially misstated. Audit risk is a function of the risks of material misstatement and detection risk.

Audit sampling (sampling)—The application of audit procedures to less than 100% of items within a population of audit relevance such that all sampling units have a chance of selection in order to provide the auditor with a reasonable basis on which to draw conclusions about the entire population.

Audit team—For the purposes of APB Ethical Standards this is all audit professionals who, regardless of their legal relationship with the auditor or audit firm, are assigned to a particular audit engagement in order to perform the audit task (e.g. audit partner(s), audit manager(s) and audit staff).

This does not include internal audit personnel who are involved in directly assisting the external auditor in carrying out external audit procedures provided that appropriate quality control arrangements are established as described in ISA (UK and Ireland) 610.

---

[3] *Engagement circumstances include the terms of the engagement, including whether it is a reasonable assurance engagement or a limited assurance engagement, the characteristics of the subject matter, the criteria to be used, the needs of the intended users, relevant characteristics of the responsible party and its environment, and other matters, for example events, transactions, conditions and practices, that may have a significant effect on the engagement.*

Audited entity—The entity whose financial statements are subject to audit by the audit firm.

Auditor—"Auditor" is used to refer to the person or persons conducting the audit, usually the engagement partner or other members of the engagement team, or, as applicable, the firm. Where an ISA (UK and Ireland) expressly intends that a requirement or responsibility be fulfilled by the engagement partner, the term "engagement partner" rather than "auditor" is used. "Engagement partner" and "firm" are to be read as referring to their public sector equivalents where relevant.

Auditor association with financial information—An auditor is associated with financial information when the auditor attaches a report to that information or consents to the use of the auditor's name in a professional connection.

Auditor's expert—An individual or organization possessing expertise in a field other than accounting or auditing, whose work in that field is used by the auditor to assist the auditor in obtaining sufficient appropriate audit evidence. An auditor's expert may be either an auditor's internal expert (who is a partner[4] or staff, including temporary staff, of the auditor's firm or a network firm), or an auditor's external expert.

Auditor's point estimate or auditor's range—The amount, or range of amounts, respectively, derived from audit evidence for use in evaluating management's point estimate.

Auditor's range—(see *Auditor's point estimate*)

Business risk—A risk resulting from significant conditions, events, circumstances, actions or inactions that could adversely affect an entity's ability to achieve its objectives and execute its strategies, or from the setting of inappropriate objectives and strategies.

Chain of command—All persons who have a direct supervisory, management or other oversight responsibility over either any audit partner of the audit team or over the conduct of audit work in the audit firm. This includes all partners, principals and shareholders who may prepare, review or directly influence the performance appraisal of any audit partner of the audit team as a result of that partner's involvement with the audit engagement. It does not include any non-executive individuals on a supervisory or equivalent board.

Close family—A non-dependent parent, child or sibling.

Comparative financial statements—Comparative information where amounts and other disclosures for the prior period are included for comparison with the financial statements of the current period but, if audited, are referred to in the auditor's opinion. The level of information included in those comparative financial statements is comparable with that of the financial statements of the current period.

---

[4] *"Partner" and "firm" should be read as referring to their public sector equivalents where relevant.*

Comparative information—The amounts and disclosures included in the financial statements in respect of one or more prior periods in accordance with the applicable financial reporting framework.

Compilation engagement—An engagement in which accounting expertise, as opposed to auditing expertise, is used to collect, classify and summarize financial information.

Complementary user entity controls—Controls that the service organization assumes, in the design of its service, will be implemented by user entities, and which, if necessary to achieve control objectives, are identified in the description of its system.

Compliance framework—(see *Applicable financial reporting framework* and *General purpose framework*)

Component—An entity or business activity for which group or component management prepares financial information that should be included in the group financial statements.

Component auditor—An auditor who, at the request of the group engagement team, performs work on financial information related to a component for the group audit.

Component management—Management responsible for the preparation of the financial information of a component.

Component materiality—The materiality for a component determined by the group engagement team.

Computer-assisted audit techniques—Applications of auditing procedures using the computer as an audit tool (also known as CAATs).

Connected parties—An audited entity's connected parties are:

a. its affiliates;
b. key members of management (including but not limited to directors and those charged with governance) of the audited entity and its significant affiliates, individually or collectively; and
c. any person or entity with an ability to influence (other than in the capacity of professional advisors), whether directly or indirectly, key members of management or those charged with governance of the audited entity and its significant affiliates, individually or collectively, in relation to their responsibility for or approach to any matter or judgment that is material to the entity's financial statements.

Contingent fee basis—Any arrangement made under which a fee is calculated on a pre-determined basis relating to the outcome or result of a transaction, or other event, or the result of the work performed. A fee that is established by a court or other public authority is not a contingent fee.

Control activities—Those policies and procedures that help ensure that management directives are carried out. Control activities are a component of internal control.

Control environment—Includes the governance and management functions and the attitudes, awareness and actions of those charged with governance and management concerning the entity's internal control and its importance in the entity. The control environment is a component of internal control.

Control risk—(see *Risk of material misstatement*)

Corporate governance—(see *Governance*)

Corresponding figures—Comparative information where amounts and other disclosures for the prior period are included as an integral part of the current period financial statements, and are intended to be read only in relation to the amounts and other disclosures relating to the current period (referred to as "current period figures"). The level of detail presented in the corresponding amounts and disclosures is dictated primarily by its relevance to the current period figures.

Date of approval of the financial statements—The date on which all the statements that comprise the financial statements, including the related notes, have been prepared and those with the recognized authority have asserted that they have taken responsibility for those financial statements.

Date of report (in relation to ISQC (UK and Ireland) 1)—The date selected by the practitioner to date the report.

Date of the auditor's report—The date the auditor dates the report on the financial statements in accordance with ISA (UK and Ireland) 700ISA (UK and Ireland) 700, "The Auditor's Report on Financial Statements"..

Date of the financial statements—The date of the end of the latest period covered by the financial statements.

Date the financial statements are issued—The date that the auditor's report and audited financial statements are made available to third parties.

Deficiency in internal control—This exists when:

(a) A control is designed, implemented or operated in such a way that it is unable to prevent, or detect and correct, misstatements in the financial statements on a timely basis; or

(b) A control necessary to prevent, or detect and correct, misstatements in the financial statements on a timely basis is missing.

Detection risk—The risk that the procedures performed by the auditor to reduce audit risk to an acceptably low level will not detect a misstatement that exists and that could be material, either individually or when aggregated with other misstatements.

Emphasis of Matter paragraph—A paragraph included in the auditor's report that refers to a matter appropriately presented or disclosed in the financial statements that, in the auditor's judgment, is of such importance that it is fundamental to users' understanding of the financial statements.

Engagement documentation—The record of work performed, results obtained, and conclusions the practitioner reached (terms such as "working papers" or "workpapers" are sometimes used).

Engagement letter—Written terms of an engagement in the form of a letter.

Engagement partner[5]—The partner or other person in the firm who is responsible for the engagement and its performance, and for the report that is issued on behalf of the firm, and who, where required, has the appropriate authority from a professional, legal or regulatory body.

Engagement quality control review—A process designed to provide an objective evaluation, on or before the date of the report, of the significant judgments the engagement team made and the conclusions it reached in formulating the report. The engagement quality control review process is for audits of financial statements of listed entities and those other engagements, if any, for which the firm has determined an engagement quality control review is required.

Engagement quality control reviewer—A partner, other person in the firm, suitably qualified external person, or a team made up of such individuals, none of whom is part of the engagement team, with sufficient and appropriate experience and authority to objectively evaluate the significant judgments the engagement team made and the conclusions it reached in formulating the report.

Engagement team—All partners and staff performing the engagement, and any individuals engaged by the firm or a network firm who perform procedures on the engagement. This excludes external experts engaged by the firm or a network firm.[6]

For the purposes of APB Ethical Standards, engagement team comprises all persons who are directly involved in the acceptance and performance of a particular audit. This includes the audit team, professional personnel from other disciplines involved in the audit engagement and those who provide quality control (other than the engagement quality control reviewer) or direct oversight of the audit engagement, but it does not include any auditor's external experts contracted by the firm.

Entity in distress—An entity with actual or anticipated financial or operational difficulties that threaten the survival of that entity as a going concern.

Entity's risk assessment process—A component of internal control that is the entity's process for identifying business risks relevant to financial reporting objectives and deciding about actions to address those risks, and the results thereof.

Error—An unintentional misstatement in financial statements, including the omission of an amount or a disclosure.

Estimation uncertainty—The susceptibility of an accounting estimate and related disclosures to an inherent lack of precision in its measurement.

Ethics Partner—The partner or other person in the audit firm having responsibility for the adequacy of the firm's policies and procedures relating to integrity, objectivity and independence, their compliance with APB Ethical Standards and

---

[5] *"Engagement partner", "partner", and "firm" should be read as referring to their public sector equivalents where relevant.*

[6] *ISA (UK and Ireland) 620, "Using the Work of an Auditor's Expert", paragraph 6(a), defines the term "auditor's expert".*

the effectiveness of their communication to partners and staff within the firm and providing related guidance to individual partners.

Evaluate—Identify and analyze the relevant issues, including performing further procedures as necessary, to come to a specific conclusion on a matter. "Evaluation", by convention, is used only in relation to a range of matters, including evidence, the results of procedures and the effectiveness of management's response to a risk. (also see *Assess*)

Exception—A response that indicates a difference between information requested to be confirmed, or contained in the entity's records, and information provided by the confirming party.

Experienced auditor—An individual (whether internal or external to the firm) who has practical audit experience, and a reasonable understanding of:

(a) Audit processes;
(b) ISAs (UK and Ireland) and applicable legal and regulatory requirements;
(c) The business environment in which the entity operates; and
(d) Auditing and financial reporting issues relevant to the entity's industry.

Expert—(see *Auditor's expert* and *Management's expert*)

Expertise—Skills, knowledge and experience in a particular field.

External confirmation—Audit evidence obtained as a direct written response to the auditor from a third party (the confirming party), in paper form, or by electronic or other medium.

Fair presentation framework—(see *Applicable financial reporting framework* and *General purpose framework*)

Financial interest—An equity or other security, debenture, loan or other debt instrument of an entity, including rights and obligations to acquire such an interest and derivatives directly related to such an interest.

Financial statements—A structured representation of historical financial information, including related notes, intended to communicate an entity's economic resources or obligations at a point in time or the changes therein for a period of time in accordance with a financial reporting framework. The related notes ordinarily comprise a summary of significant accounting policies and other explanatory information. The term "financial statements" ordinarily refers to a complete set of financial statements as determined by the requirements of the applicable financial reporting framework, but it can also refer to a single financial statement.

Firm—A sole practitioner, partnership or corporation or other entity of professional accountants.

For the purpose of APB Ethical Standards, audit firm includes network firms in the UK and Ireland which are controlled by the audit firm or its partners.

Forecast—Prospective financial information prepared on the basis of assumptions as to future events which management expects to take place and the actions management expects to take as of the date the information is prepared (best-estimate assumptions).

Fraud—An intentional act by one or more individuals among management, those charged with governance, employees, or third parties, involving the use of deception to obtain an unjust or illegal advantage.

Fraud risk factors—Events or conditions that indicate an incentive or pressure to commit fraud or provide an opportunity to commit fraud.

Fraudulent financial reporting—Involves intentional misstatements, including omissions of amounts or disclosures in financial statements, to deceive financial statement users.

General IT-controls—Policies and procedures that relate to many applications and support the effective functioning of application controls by helping to ensure the continued proper operation of information systems. General IT-controls commonly include controls over data center and network operations; system software acquisition, change and maintenance; access security; and application system acquisition, development, and maintenance.

General purpose financial statements—Financial statements prepared in accordance with a general purpose framework.

General purpose framework—A financial reporting framework designed to meet the common financial information needs of a wide range of users. The financial reporting framework may be a fair presentation framework or a compliance framework.

The term "fair presentation framework" is used to refer to a financial reporting framework that requires compliance with the requirements of the framework and:

(a) Acknowledges explicitly or implicitly that, to achieve fair presentation of the financial statements, it may be necessary for management to provide disclosures beyond those specifically required by the framework; or

(b) Acknowledges explicitly that it may be necessary for management to depart from a requirement of the framework to achieve fair presentation of the financial statements. Such departures are expected to be necessary only in extremely rare circumstances.

The term "compliance framework" is used to refer to a financial reporting framework that requires compliance with the requirements of the framework, but does not contain the acknowledgements in (a) or (b) above.[7]

Governance—Describes the role of person(s) or organization(s) with responsibility for overseeing the strategic direction of the entity and obligations related to the accountability of the entity.

Group—All the components whose financial information is included in the group financial statements. A group always has more than one component.

Group audit—The audit of group financial statements.

---

[7] *ISA (UK and Ireland) 200, "Overall Objectives of the Independent Auditor and the Conduct of an Audit in Accordance with International Standards on Auditing", paragraph 13(a).*

Group audit opinion—The audit opinion on the group financial statements.

Group engagement partner—The partner or other person in the firm who is responsible for the group audit engagement and its performance, and for the auditor's report on the group financial statements that is issued on behalf of the firm. Where joint auditors conduct the group audit, the joint engagement partners and their engagement teams collectively constitute the group engagement partner and the group engagement team.

Group engagement team—Partners, including the group engagement partner, and staff who establish the overall group audit strategy, communicate with component auditors, perform work on the consolidation process, and evaluate the conclusions drawn from the audit evidence as the basis for forming an opinion on the group financial statements.

Group financial statements—Financial statements that include the financial information of more than one component. The term "group financial statements" also refers to combined financial statements aggregating the financial information prepared by components that have no parent but are under common control.

Group management—Management responsible for the preparation of the group financial statements.

Group-wide controls—Controls designed, implemented and maintained by group management over group financial reporting.

Historical financial information—Information expressed in financial terms in relation to a particular entity, derived primarily from that entity's accounting system, about economic events occurring in past time periods or about economic conditions or circumstances at points in time in the past.

Immediate family—A spouse (or equivalent) or dependent.

Inconsistency—Other information that contradicts information contained in the audited financial statements. A material inconsistency may raise doubt about the audit conclusions drawn from audit evidence previously obtained and, possibly, about the basis for the auditor's opinion on the financial statements.

Independence

APB Ethical Standard 1 defines independence as freedom from situations and relationships which make it probable that a reasonable and informed third party would conclude that objectivity either is impaired or could be impaired. Independence is related to and underpins objectivity. However, whereas objectivity is a personal behavioural characteristic concerning the auditor's state of mind, independence relates to the circumstances surrounding the audit, including the financial, employment, business and personal relationships between the auditor and the audited entity.

Information system relevant to financial reporting—A component of internal control that includes the financial reporting system, and consists of the procedures and records established to initiate, record, process and report entity transactions (as well as events and conditions) and to maintain accountability for the related assets, liabilities and equity.

> *Informed management*—Member of management (or senior employee) of the audited entity who has the authority and capability to make independent management judgments and decisions in relation to non-audit services on the basis of information provided by the audit firm.

Inherent risk—(see *Risk of material misstatement*)

Initial audit engagement—An engagement in which either:

(a) The financial statements for the prior period were not audited; or
(b) The financial statements for the prior period were audited by a predecessor auditor.

Inquiry—Inquiry consists of seeking information of knowledgeable persons, both financial and non-financial, within the entity or outside the entity.

Inspection (as an audit procedure)—Examining records or documents, whether internal or external, in paper form, electronic form, or other media, or a physical examination of an asset.

Inspection (in relation to quality control)—In relation to completed engagements, procedures designed to provide evidence of compliance by engagement teams with the firm's quality control policies and procedures.

Interim financial information or statements—Financial information (which may be less than a complete set of financial statements as defined above) issued at interim dates (usually half-yearly or quarterly) in respect of a financial period.

Internal audit function—An appraisal activity established or provided as a service to the entity. Its functions include, amongst other things, examining, evaluating and monitoring the adequacy and effectiveness of internal control.

Internal auditors—Those individuals who perform the activities of the internal audit function. Internal auditors may belong to an internal audit department or equivalent function.

Internal control—The process designed, implemented and maintained by those charged with governance, management and other personnel to provide reasonable assurance about the achievement of an entity's objectives with regard to reliability of financial reporting, effectiveness and efficiency of operations, and compliance with applicable laws and regulations. The term "controls" refers to any aspects of one or more of the components of internal control.

International Financial Reporting Standards—The International Financial Reporting Standards issued by the International Accounting Standards Board.

Investigate—Inquire into matters arising from other procedures to resolve them.

IT environment—The policies and procedures that the entity implements and the IT infrastructure (hardware, operating systems, etc.) and application software that it uses to support business operations and achieve business strategies.

Key management position—Any position at the audited entity which involves the responsibility for fundamental management decisions at the audited entity (e.g. as a CEO or CFO), including an ability to influence the accounting policies and the preparation of the financial statements of the audited entity. A key management position also arises where there are contractual and factual arrangements which in substance allow an individual to participate in exercising such a management function in a different way (e.g. via a consulting contract).

Key partner involved in the audit—A partner, or other person in the engagement team (other than the audit engagement partner or engagement quality control reviewer) who either:

- is involved at the group level and is responsible for key decisions or judgments on significant matters or risk factors that relate to the audit of that audited entity, or
- is primarily responsible for the audit of a 'significant affiliate or division' (see separate definition) of the audited entity.

Limited assurance engagement—(see *Assurance engagement*)

Listed entity—An entity whose shares, stock or debt are quoted or listed on a recognized stock exchange, or are marketed under the regulations of a recognized stock exchange or other equivalent body.

For the purpose of APB Ethical Standards, listed company includes any company in which the public can trade shares on the open market, such as those listed on the London Stock Exchange (including those admitted to trade on the Alternative Investments Market), PLUS Markets and the Irish Stock Exchange (including those admitted to trade on the Irish Enterprise Exchange).

Management—The person(s) with executive responsibility for the conduct of the entity's operations. For some entities in some jurisdictions, management includes some or all of those charged with governance, for example, executive members of a governance board, or an owner-manager.

In the UK and Ireland, management will not normally include non-executive directors.

Management bias—A lack of neutrality by management in the preparation of information.

Management's expert—An individual or organization possessing expertise in a field other than accounting or auditing, whose work in that field is used by the entity to assist the entity in preparing the financial statements.

Management's point estimate—The amount selected by management for recognition or disclosure in the financial statements as an accounting estimate.

Misappropriation of assets—Involves the theft of an entity's assets and is often perpetrated by employees in relatively small and immaterial amounts. However, it can also involve management who are usually more capable of disguising or concealing misappropriations in ways that are difficult to detect.

Misstatement—A difference between the amount, classification, presentation, or disclosure of a reported financial statement item and the amount, classification, presentation, or disclosure that is required for the item to be in accordance with the applicable financial reporting framework. Misstatements can arise from error or fraud. Where the auditor expresses an opinion on whether the financial statements are presented fairly, in all material respects, or give a true and fair view, misstatements also include those adjustments of amounts, classifications, presentation, or disclosures that, in the auditor's judgment, are necessary for the financial statements to be presented fairly, in all material respects, or to give a true and fair view.

Misstatement of fact—Other information that is unrelated to matters appearing in the audited financial statements that is incorrectly stated or presented. A material misstatement of fact may undermine the credibility of the document containing audited financial statements.

Modified opinion—A qualified opinion, an adverse opinion or a disclaimer of opinion.

Monitoring (in relation to quality control)—A process comprising an ongoing consideration and evaluation of the firm's system of quality control, including a periodic inspection of a selection of completed engagements, designed to provide the firm with reasonable assurance that its system of quality control is operating effectively.

Monitoring of controls—A process to assess the effectiveness of internal control performance over time. It includes assessing the design and operation of controls on a timely basis and taking necessary corrective actions modified for changes in conditions. Monitoring of controls is a component of internal control.

Negative confirmation request—A request that the confirming party respond directly to the auditor only if the confirming party disagrees with the information provided in the request.

Network—A larger structure:

(a) That is aimed at cooperation, and
(b) That is clearly aimed at profit or cost-sharing or shares common ownership, control or management, common quality control policies and procedures, common business strategy, the use of a common brand name, or a significant part of professional resources.

Network firm—A firm or entity that belongs to a network.

For the purpose of APB Ethical Standards, a network firm is any entity which is part of a larger structure that is aimed at co-operation and which is:

(i)   controlled by the audit firm; or
(ii) under common control, ownership or management; or
(iii) part of a larger structure that is clearly aimed at profit or cost sharing; or
(iv) otherwise affiliated or associated with the audit firm through common quality control policies and procedures, common business strategy, the use of a common name or through the sharing of significant common professional resources.

Non-audit services – Any engagement in which an audit firm provides professional services to an audited entity, its affiliates or another entity in respect of the audited entity other than the audit of financial statements.

Non-compliance (in the context of ISA (UK and Ireland) 250[8]—Acts of omission or commission by the entity, either intentional or unintentional, which are contrary to the prevailing laws or regulations. Such acts include transactions entered into by, or in the name of, the entity, or on its behalf, by those charged with governance, management or employees. Non-compliance does not include personal misconduct (unrelated to the business activities of the entity) by those charged with governance, management or employees of the entity.

Non-response—A failure of the confirming party to respond, or fully respond, to a positive confirmation request, or a confirmation request returned undelivered.

Non-sampling risk—The risk that the auditor reaches an erroneous conclusion for any reason not related to sampling risk.

Observation—Consists of looking at a process or procedure being performed by others, for example, the auditor's observation of inventory counting by the entity's personnel, or of the performance of control activities.

Opening balances—Those account balances that exist at the beginning of the period. Opening balances are based upon the closing balances of the prior period and reflect the effects of transactions and events of prior periods and accounting policies applied in the prior period. Opening balances also include matters requiring disclosure that existed at the beginning of the period, such as contingencies and commitments.

Other information—Financial and non-financial information (other than the financial statements and the auditor's report thereon) which is included, either by law, regulation, or custom, in a document containing audited financial statements and the auditor's report thereon.

Other Matter paragraph—A paragraph included in the auditor's report that refers to a matter other than those presented or disclosed in the financial statements that, in the auditor's judgment, is relevant to users' understanding of the audit, the auditor's responsibilities or the auditor's report.

Outcome of an accounting estimate—The actual monetary amount which results from the resolution of the underlying transaction(s), event(s) or condition(s) addressed by the accounting estimate.

Overall audit strategy—Sets the scope, timing and direction of the audit, and guides the development of the more detailed audit plan.

Partner—Any individual with authority to bind the firm with respect to the performance of a professional services engagement.

Performance materiality—The amount or amounts set by the auditor at less than materiality for the financial statements as a whole to reduce to an appropriately low

---

[8] *ISA (UK and Ireland) 250 Section A, "Consideration of Laws and Regulations in an Audit of Financial Statements", and ISA (UK and Ireland) 250 Section B, "The Auditor's Right and Duty to Report to Regulators in the Financial Sector".*

level the probability that the aggregate of uncorrected and undetected misstatements exceeds materiality for the financial statements as a whole. If applicable, performance materiality also refers to the amount or amounts set by the auditor at less than the materiality level or levels for particular classes of transactions, account balances or disclosures.

Person in a position to influence the conduct and outcome of the audit—This is:

(a) Any person who is directly involved in the audit (the engagement team), including:
    (i) the audit partners, audit managers and audit staff (the audit team);
    (ii) professional personnel from other disciplines involved in the audit (for example, lawyers, actuaries, taxation specialists, IT specialists, treasury management specialists);
    (iii) those who provide quality control or direct oversight of the audit;

(b) Any person, who forms part of the chain of command for the audit within the audit firm;

(c) Any person within the audit firm who, due to any other circumstances, may be in a position to exert such influence.

Personnel—Partners and staff.

Pervasive—A term used, in the context of misstatements, to describe the effects on the financial statements of misstatements or the possible effects on the financial statements of misstatements, if any, that are undetected due to an inability to obtain sufficient appropriate audit evidence. Pervasive effects on the financial statements are those that, in the auditor's judgment:

(a) Are not confined to specific elements, accounts or items of the financial statements;

(b) If so confined, represent or could represent a substantial proportion of the financial statements; or

(c) In relation to disclosures, are fundamental to users' understanding of the financial statements.

Population—The entire set of data from which a sample is selected and about which the auditor wishes to draw conclusions.

Positive confirmation request—A request that the confirming party respond directly to the auditor indicating whether the confirming party agrees or disagrees with the information in the request, or providing the requested information.

Practitioner—A professional accountant in public practice.

Preconditions for an audit—The use by management of an acceptable financial reporting framework in the preparation of the financial statements and the agreement of management and, where appropriate, those charged with governance to the premise[9] on which an audit is conducted.

Predecessor auditor—The auditor from a different audit firm, who audited the financial statements of an entity in the prior period and who has been replaced by the current auditor.

---

[9] *ISA (UK and Ireland) 200, paragraph 13.*

Premise, relating to the responsibilities of management and, where appropriate, those charged with governance, on which an audit is conducted—That management and, where appropriate, those charged with governance have acknowledged and understand that they have the following responsibilities that are fundamental to the conduct of an audit in accordance with ISAs (UK and Ireland). That is, responsibility:

(a) For the preparation of the financial statements in accordance with the applicable financial reporting framework, including where relevant their fair presentation;

(b) For such internal control as management and, where appropriate, those charged with governance determine is necessary to enable the preparation of financial statements that are free from material misstatement, whether due to fraud or error; and

(c) To provide the auditor with:

  (i) Access to all information of which management and, where appropriate, those charged with governance are aware that is relevant to the preparation of the financial statements such as records, documentation and other matters;

  (ii) Additional information that the auditor may request from management and, where appropriate, those charged with governance for the purpose of the audit; and

  (iii) Unrestricted access to persons within the entity from whom the auditor determines it necessary to obtain audit evidence.

In the case of a fair presentation framework, (a) above may be restated as "for the preparation and *fair* presentation of the financial statements in accordance with the financial reporting framework", or "for the preparation of financial statements *that give a true and fair view* in accordance with the financial reporting framework".

The "premise, relating to the responsibilities of management and, where appropriate, those charged with governance, on which an audit is conducted" may also be referred to as the "premise".

Professional accountant

For the purpose of the ISAs (UK and Ireland) and APB Ethical Standards, *Professional accountants* are those persons who are members of a professional accountancy body, whether in public practice (including a sole practitioner, partnership or corporate body), industry, commerce, the public sector or education.

Professional accountant in public practice—A professional accountant, irrespective of functional classification (for example, audit, tax or consulting) in a firm that provides professional services. This term is also used to refer to a firm of professional accountants in public practice.

Professional judgment—The application of relevant training, knowledge and experience, within the context provided by auditing, accounting and ethical standards, in making informed decisions about the courses of action that are appropriate in the circumstances of the audit engagement.

Professional skepticism—An attitude that includes a questioning mind, being alert to conditions which may indicate possible misstatement due to error or fraud, and a critical assessment of evidence.

Professional standards—International Standards on Auditing (ISAs) (UK and Ireland) and relevant ethical requirements.

> In the UK and Ireland, professional standards in the context of ISQC (UK and Ireland) 1 are the APB Ethical and Engagement Standards as described in the Statement "The Auditing Practices Board – Scope and Authority of Pronouncements".

Projection—Prospective financial information prepared on the basis of:

(a) Hypothetical assumptions about future events and management actions which are not necessarily expected to take place, such as when some entities are in a startup phase or are considering a major change in the nature of operations; or
(b) A mixture of best-estimate and hypothetical assumptions.

Prospective financial information—Financial information based on assumptions about events that may occur in the future and possible actions by an entity. Prospective financial information can be in the form of a forecast, a projection or a combination of both. (see *Forecast* and *Projection*)

Public sector—National governments, regional (for example, state, provincial, territorial) governments, local (for example, city, town) governments and related governmental entities (for example, agencies, boards, commissions and enterprises).

Reasonable assurance (in the context of assurance engagements, including audit engagements, and quality control)—A high, but not absolute, level of assurance.

Reasonable assurance engagement—(see *Assurance engagement*)

Recalculation—Consists of checking the mathematical accuracy of documents or records.

Related party—A party that is either:

(a) A related party as defined in the applicable financial reporting framework; or
(b) Where the applicable financial reporting framework establishes minimal or no related party requirements:
    (i) A person or other entity that has control or significant influence, directly or indirectly through one or more intermediaries, over the reporting entity;
    (ii) Another entity over which the reporting entity has control or significant influence, directly or indirectly through one or more intermediaries; or
    (iii) Another entity that is under common control with the reporting entity through having:
        a. Common controlling ownership;
        b. Owners who are close family members; or
        c. Common key management.
    However, entities that are under common control by a state (that is, a national, regional or local government) are not considered related unless they engage in significant transactions or share resources to a significant extent with one another.

In the UK and Ireland relevant definitions of "related party" are set out in the applicable financial reporting frameworks (for example, the definitions in International Accounting Standard 24, "Related Party Disclosures", Financial Reporting Standard 8, "Related Party Disclosures" or the Financial Reporting Standard for Smaller Entities).

Related services—Comprise agreed-upon procedures and compilations.

Relevant ethical requirements

In the UK and Ireland the relevant ethical pronouncements with which the auditor complies are the APB's Ethical Standards for Auditors and the ethical pronouncements relating to the work of auditors issued by the auditor's relevant professional body - see the Statement "The Auditing Practices Board – Scope and Authority of Pronouncements".

Reperformance—The auditor's independent execution of procedures or controls that were originally performed as part of the entity's internal controls.

Report on the description and design of controls at a service organization (referred to in ISA (UK and Ireland) 402[10] *as a type 1 report)*—A report that comprises:

(a) A description, prepared by management of the service organization, of the service organization's system, control objectives and related controls that have been designed and implemented as at a specified date; and

(b) A report by the service auditor with the objective of conveying reasonable assurance that includes the service auditor's opinion on the description of the service organization's system, control objectives and related controls and the suitability of the design of the controls to achieve the specified control objectives.

Report on the description, design, and operating effectiveness of controls at a service organization (referred to in ISA (UK and Ireland) 402 as a type 2 report)—A report that comprises:

(a) A description, prepared by management of the service organization, of the service organization's system, control objectives and related controls, their design and implementation as at a specified date or throughout a specified period and, in some cases, their operating effectiveness throughout a specified period; and

(b) A report by the service auditor with the objective of conveying reasonable assurance that includes:

(i) The service auditor's opinion on the description of the service organization's system, control objectives and related controls, the suitability of the design of the controls to achieve the specified control objectives, and the operating effectiveness of the controls; and

(ii) A description of the service auditor's tests of the controls and the results thereof.

Review (in relation to quality control)—Appraising the quality of the work performed and conclusions reached by others.

[10] *ISA (UK and Ireland) 402, "Audit Considerations Relating to an Entity Using a Service Organization".*

Review engagement—The objective of a review engagement is to enable an auditor to state whether, on the basis of procedures which do not provide all the evidence that would be required in an audit, anything has come to the auditor's attention that causes the auditor to believe that the financial statements are not prepared, in all material respects, in accordance with an applicable financial reporting framework.

Review procedures—The procedures deemed necessary to meet the objective of a review engagement, primarily inquiries of entity personnel and analytical procedures applied to financial data.

Risk assessment procedures—The audit procedures performed to obtain an understanding of the entity and its environment, including the entity's internal control, to identify and assess the risks of material misstatement, whether due to fraud or error, at the financial statement and assertion levels.

Risk of material misstatement—The risk that the financial statements are materially misstated prior to audit. This consists of two components, described as follows at the assertion level:

(a) Inherent risk—The susceptibility of an assertion about a class of transaction, account balance or disclosure to a misstatement that could be material, either individually or when aggregated with other misstatements, before consideration of any related controls.

(b) Control risk—The risk that a misstatement that could occur in an assertion about a class of transaction, account balance or disclosure and that could be material, either individually or when aggregated with other misstatements, will not be prevented, or detected and corrected, on a timely basis by the entity's internal control.

Sampling—(see *Audit sampling*)

Sampling risk—The risk that the auditor's conclusion based on a sample may be different from the conclusion if the entire population were subjected to the same audit procedure. Sampling risk can lead to two types of erroneous conclusions:

(a) In the case of a test of controls, that controls are more effective than they actually are, or in the case of a test of details, that a material misstatement does not exist when in fact it does. The auditor is primarily concerned with this type of erroneous conclusion because it affects audit effectiveness and is more likely to lead to an inappropriate audit opinion.

(b) In the case of a test of controls, that controls are less effective than they actually are, or in the case of a test of details, that a material misstatement exists when in fact it does not. This type of erroneous conclusion affects audit efficiency as it would usually lead to additional work to establish that initial conclusions were incorrect.

Sampling unit—The individual items constituting a population.

Scope of a review—The review procedures deemed necessary in the circumstances to achieve the objective of the review.

Service auditor—An auditor who, at the request of the service organization, provides an assurance report on the controls of a service organization.

Service organization—A third-party organization (or segment of a third-party organization) that provides services to user entities that are part of those entities' information systems relevant to financial reporting.

Service organization's system—The policies and procedures designed, implemented and maintained by the service organization to provide user entities with the services covered by the service auditor's report.

Significance—The relative importance of a matter, taken in context. The significance of a matter is judged by the practitioner in the context in which it is being considered. This might include, for example, the reasonable prospect of its changing or influencing the decisions of intended users of the practitioner's report; or, as another example, where the context is a judgment about whether to report a matter to those charged with governance, whether the matter would be regarded as important by them in relation to their duties. Significance can be considered in the context of quantitative and qualitative factors, such as relative magnitude, the nature and effect on the subject matter and the expressed interests of intended users or recipients.

Significant affiliate—For the purposes of the APB Ethical Standards, an affiliate identified by the group audit team (i) that is of individual financial significance to the group, or (ii) that, due to its specific nature or circumstances, is likely to include significant risks of material misstatement of the group financial statements.

Significant component—A component identified by the group engagement team (i) that is of individual financial significance to the group, or (ii) that, due to its specific nature or circumstances, is likely to include significant risks of material misstatement of the group financial statements.

Significant deficiency in internal control—A deficiency or combination of deficiencies in internal control that, in the auditor's professional judgment, is of sufficient importance to merit the attention of those charged with governance.

Significant risk—An identified and assessed risk of material misstatement that, in the auditor's judgment, requires special audit consideration.

Smaller entity—An entity which typically possesses qualitative characteristics such as:

(a) Concentration of ownership and management in a small number of individuals (often a single individual – either a natural person or another enterprise that owns the entity provided the owner exhibits the relevant qualitative characteristics); and
(b) One or more of the following:
  (i) Straightforward or uncomplicated transactions;
  (ii) Simple record-keeping;
  (iii) Few lines of business and few products within business lines;
  (iv) Few internal controls;
  (v) Few levels of management with responsibility for a broad range of controls; or
  (vi) Few personnel, many having a wide range of duties.
  These qualitative characteristics are not exhaustive, they are not exclusive to smaller entities, and smaller entities do not necessarily display all of these characteristics.

In the UK and Ireland, company law provides a lighter reporting regime for companies that are defined, by legislation, as small. A company qualifies as "small" if it meets particular thresholds in respect of turnover, balance sheet total/

gross assets and number of employees and certain other criteria. The thresholds and other criteria are subject to change and reference to the relevant legislation should be made to determine what they are in respect of a particular accounting period.

For the purpose of APB Ethical Standards, a small entity is defined in "APB Ethical Standard – Provisions Available for Small Entities".

Special purpose financial statements—Financial statements prepared in accordance with a special purpose framework.

Special purpose framework—A financial reporting framework designed to meet the financial information needs of specific users. The financial reporting framework may be a fair presentation framework or a compliance framework.[11]

Staff—Professionals, other than partners, including any experts the firm employs.

Statistical sampling—An approach to sampling that has the following characteristics:

(a) Random selection of the sample items; and
(b) The use of probability theory to evaluate sample results, including measurement of sampling risk.

A sampling approach that does not have characteristics (a) and (b) is considered non-statistical sampling.

Stratification—The process of dividing a population into sub-populations, each of which is a group of sampling units which have similar characteristics (often monetary value).

Subsequent events—Events occurring between the date of the financial statements and the date of the auditor's report, and facts that become known to the auditor after the date of the auditor's report.

Subservice organization—A service organization used by another service organization to perform some of the services provided to user entities that are part of those user entities' information systems relevant to financial reporting.

Substantive procedure—An audit procedure designed to detect material misstatements at the assertion level. Substantive procedures comprise:

(a) Tests of details (of classes of transactions, account balances, and disclosures); and
(b) Substantive analytical procedures.

Sufficiency (of audit evidence)—The measure of the quantity of audit evidence. The quantity of the audit evidence needed is affected by the auditor's assessment of the risks of material misstatement and also by the quality of such audit evidence.

Suitably qualified external person—An individual outside the firm with the competence and capabilities to act as an engagement partner, for example a partner of another firm, or an employee (with appropriate experience) of either a professional

---

[11] *ISA (UK and Ireland) 200, paragraph 13(a).*

accountancy body whose members may perform audits and reviews of historical financial information, or other assurance or related services engagements, or of an organization that provides relevant quality control services.

Supplementary information—Information that is presented together with the financial statements that is not required by the applicable financial reporting framework used to prepare the financial statements, normally presented in either supplementary schedules or as additional notes.

Test—The application of procedures to some or all items in a population.

Tests of controls—An audit procedure designed to evaluate the operating effectiveness of controls in preventing, or detecting and correcting, material misstatements at the assertion level.

Those charged with governance—The person(s) or organization(s) (for example, a corporate trustee) with responsibility for overseeing the strategic direction of the entity and obligations related to the accountability of the entity. This includes overseeing the financial reporting process. For some entities in some jurisdictions, those charged with governance may include management personnel, for example, executive members of a governance board of a private or public sector entity, or an owner-manager.[12]

In the UK and Ireland, those charged with governance include the directors (executive and non-executive) of a company and the members of an audit committee where one exists. For other types of entity it usually includes equivalent persons such as the partners, proprietors, committee of management or trustees.

Tolerable misstatement—A monetary amount set by the auditor in respect of which the auditor seeks to obtain an appropriate level of assurance that the monetary amount set by the auditor is not exceeded by the actual misstatement in the population.

Tolerable rate of deviation—A rate of deviation from prescribed internal control procedures set by the auditor in respect of which the auditor seeks to obtain an appropriate level of assurance that the rate of deviation set by the auditor is not exceeded by the actual rate of deviation in the population.

Uncertainty—A matter whose outcome depends on future actions or events not under the direct control of the entity but that may affect the financial statements.

Uncorrected misstatements—Misstatements that the auditor has accumulated during the audit and that have not been corrected.

Unmodified opinion—The opinion expressed by the auditor when the auditor concludes that the financial statements are prepared, in all material respects, in accordance with the applicable financial reporting framework.

User auditor—An auditor who audits and reports on the financial statements of a user entity.

---

[12] *For discussion of the diversity of governance structures, see paragraphs A1-A8 of ISA (UK and Ireland) 260, "Communication with Those Charged with Governance".*

User entity—An entity that uses a service organization and whose financial statements are being audited.

Walk-through test—Involves tracing a few transactions through the financial reporting system.

Written representation—A written statement by management provided to the auditor to confirm certain matters or to support other audit evidence. Written representations in this context do not include financial statements, the assertions therein, or supporting books and records.